# COGNITION

*Second Edition*

# Cognition

## EXPLORING THE SCIENCE OF THE MIND

*Second Edition*

## Daniel Reisberg

**Reed College**

W. W. NORTON & COMPANY

NEW YORK LONDON

Copyright © 2001, 1997 by W. W. Norton & Company, Inc.

The text of this book is composed in Palatino
with the display set in Univers.
Compositon by UG / GGS Information Services, Inc.; makeup by Cathy Lombardi
Manufacturing by Courier
Book design by Joan Greenfield
Editor: Jon Durbin
Associate Managing Editor: Jane Carter
Project Editor: Kate Barry
Copy Editor: Traci Nagle
Manufacturing Director: Roy Tedoff
Editorial Assistants: Rob Whiteside and Aaron Javsicas

Library of Congress Cataloging-in-Publication Data

Reisberg, Daniel.
    Cognition : exploring the science of the mind / Daniel Reisberg—2nd ed.
       p.   cm.
Includes bibliographical references and index.
ISBN 0-393-97622-X
1. Cognitive psychology. I. Title.

BF201 .R45 2001
153—dc21

                                                          00–046293


W. W. Norton & Company, Inc., 500 Fifth Avenue, New York, N. Y. 10110
                    www.wwnorton.com


W. W. Norton & Company Ltd., Castle House, 75/76 Wells Street, London W1T 3QT

4 5 6 7 8 9 0

FOR KURT

# Contents

# *Preface*

I was a college sophomore when I took my first course in cognitive psychology, and I've been excited about this field ever since. Why? First, cognitive psychologists are asking terrific questions. Some of the questions concern broad issues that have intrigued humanity for thousands of years. Why do we think the things we think? Why do we believe the things we believe? What are the limits of human ability? How can we make ourselves better, as individuals, and as a species?

Other questions asked by cognitive psychologists are of a more immediate, personal, concern: How can I help myself to remember more of the material that I'm studying in school? Is there some better way to solve the problems I encounter? Why is it that my roommate can study with the radio on, but I can't?

And sometimes the questions have important consequences for our social institutions: If an eyewitness reports what he saw at a crime, should we trust him? If a newspaper raises questions about a candidate's integrity, how will the voters react?

Of course, we want more than interesting questions. We would like some answers as well, and this is the second reason I find cognitive psychology so exciting: In the last half century, the field has made extraordinary progress on many fronts, providing us, now, with a rich understanding of the nature of memory, the processes of thought, and the content of knowledge. There are, to be sure, many things still to be discovered—that's part of the fun. Even so, we already have something to say about all of the questions just posed, and many more as well. We can speak to the specific questions and to the general, to the theoretical issues and to the practical. Our research has provided data of interest to scholars engaged in a range of intellectual pursuits; we have uncovered principles useful for improving the educational process; and we have made discoveries of considerable importance for the courts. What I've

learned, as a cognitive psychologist, has changed how I think about my own memory; it's changed how I make decisions; it's changed how I draw conclusions when I'm thinking about events in my life.

On top of all this, I'm excited about the intellectual connections that cognitive psychology makes possible. In the modern academic world, intellectual disciplines are becoming more and more sophisticated, with their own methods and their own conceptual framework. As a consequence, these disciplines often become isolated from each other, sometimes working on closely related problems without even realizing it. In contrast, cognitive psychology has, in the last decades, actively sought out contact with neighboring disciplines, and, in this book, we will touch on topics in philosophy, economics, biology, linguistics, politics, computer science, and medicine. These connections bring obvious benefits, since insights and information can be traded back and forth between the domains. In addition, these connections highlight the importance of the material we will be examining, and provide a strong signal that we are working on a project of considerable power and scope.

I have tried, in this text, to convey all this excitement. I've done my best to put in view the questions being asked within my field, the substantial answers we can provide for these questions, and finally, some indications of how cognitive psychology is (and has to be) interwoven with several other intellectual endeavors.

I have also had other goals in writing this text. In my own teaching, I work hard at maintaining a balance among several different elements—the nuts and bolts of how our science proceeds, the data provided by the science, the practical implications of our findings, and the theoretical framework that holds all of these pieces together. I've tried to find the same balance in this text. In particular, I've tried to make certain that the presentation of our science—the procedures we use, the exact nature of our data, and so on—is fully integrated with a presentation of the ideas and theories that derive from cognitive psychology research. These ideas provide the narrative that binds the pieces of the science together, and, indeed, it is these ideas that make the research interesting; it is these ideas that drive our endeavor forward. Therefore, I have tried, within each chapter, and from one chapter to the next, to convey how the various pieces fit together into a coherent package. In short, I have tried to emphasize what the results mean, and what the science is telling us.

I have also aimed at a text that is broad in its coverage and up-to-date in its presentation. Our field changes quickly, and students are entitled to a text that stays close to the current state of the art. Moreover, our theories are often rich and subtle in their treatment of a topic, and students deserve a text that conveys this sophistication. I've therefore tried, overall, to write a book that is deep enough, serious enough, but also clear enough so that by the book's close, students will have a full, rich, and contemporary understanding of cognition.

Perhaps most important, I have tried to write this book with language that is compatible with all these goals. To help students see how the pieces of our field fit together, the prose needs to emphasize the flow of ideas in research. To help students grasp the technical material, the prose needs to be approachable, but to provide real understanding of these issues, the prose needs to be precise. I hope my writing style will achieve these aims—but you, the reader, will need to be the judge of this.

Indeed, in general, others will have to decide whether I've accomplished what I set out to. In fact, I look forward to hearing from my readers—both the students I'm hoping to reach and the colleagues I'm hoping to serve. I would be happy to hear from both constituencies what I have done well in the book, and what I could have done better; what I've covered (but should have omitted) and what I've left out. It is unlikely that I'll be able to respond to every comment, but I do welcome the comments, either via regular mail (through W. W. Norton) or via e-mail (cogtext@reed.edu).

The book's fifteen chapters are designed to cover the major topics within cognitive psychology. The first section of this book lays the foundation. Chapter 1 provides the conceptual and historical background for the subsequent chapters. In addition, this chapter seeks to convey the extraordinary scope of this field and why, therefore, research on cognition is so important. This chapter also highlights the relationship between theory and evidence in this domain, and discusses the logic on which the field of cognitive psychology is built.

Chapter 2 then offers a brief introduction to the study of the brain. Most of cognitive psychology is concerned with the functions that our brains make possible, and not the brain itself. Nonetheless, our understanding of cognition has certainly been enhanced by the study of the brain, and, throughout this book, we will use biological evidence as one means of evaluating our theories. Chapter 2 is designed to make this evidence fully accessible to the reader—by providing a quick survey of the research tools used in studying the brain, an overview of the brain's anatomy, and also an example of how we can use brain evidence as a source of insight into cognitive phenomena.

In the second section of the book, we consider the problems of object recognition, and then the problem of attention. Chapter 3 discusses how we recognize the objects that surround us. This seems a straightforward matter—what could be easier than recognizing a telephone, or a coffee cup, or the letter"Q"? As we will see, however, recognition is surprisingly complex. Chapter 4 considers what it means to "pay attention.' The first half of the chapter is concerned largely with selective attention, in which one seeks to focus on a target while ignoring distractors. The second half of the chapter is concerned with divided attention, in which one seeks to focus on more than one target, or more than one task, at the same time. Here, too, we will see that seemingly simple processes often turn out to be more complicated than one might suppose.

The third section turns to the broad problem of memory. Chapters 5, 6, and 7 start with a discussion of how information is "entered" into long-term storage, but then turn to the complex interdependence between how information is first learned and how that same information is subsequently retrieved. A recurrent theme in this section is that learning that is effective for one sort of task, one sort of use, may be quite *in*effective for other uses. This theme is examined in several contexts, and leads to a discussion of current research on "memory without awareness." These chapters also offer a broad assessment of human memory: How accurate are our memories? How complete? How long-lasting? These issues are pursued both with regard to theoretical treatments of memory, and also the practical consequences of memory research, including the application of this research to the assessment, in the courtroom, of eyewitness testimony.

The book's fourth section is about knowledge. Earlier chapters showed over and over that humans are, in many ways, guided in their thinking and experiences by the broad pattern of things they already know. This invites the questions posed by Chapters 8, 9, 10, and 11: What is knowledge? How is it represented in the mind? Chapter 8 examines the idea that knowledge can be represented via a complex network, and includes a discussion of associative networks in general and connectionist modeling in particular. Chapter 9 turns to the question of how "concepts," the building blocks of our knowledge, are represented in the mind. Chapters 10 and 11 focus on two special types of knowledge. Chapter 10 examines our knowledge about language, with discussion both of "linguistic competence" and "linguistic performance." Chapter 11 considers "visual knowledge" and examines what is known about mental imagery.

The chapters in the fifth section are concerned with the topic of thinking. Chapter 12 examines how each of us draws conclusions from evidence—including cases in which we are trying to be careful and deliberate in our judgments, and also cases of informal judgments of the sort we often make in our everyday lives. Chapter 13 turns to the question of how we reason from our beliefs—how we check on whether our beliefs are correct, and how we draw

conclusions, based on things we already believe. Both of these chapters examine the strategies that guide our thinking, and some of the ways that these strategies can, on occasion, lead to error. The chapters then turn to the pragmatic issue of how these errors can be diminished through education. Chapter 13 also discusses how we make decisions and choices, with a special focus first on "economic" theories of decision-making, and then on some of the seeming "irrationality" in human decision-making. Next, Chapter 14 considers how we solve problems. The first half of the chapter discusses problem-solving strategies of a general sort, useful for all problems; the chapter then turns to more specialized strategies, and with this, the topic of expertise. The chapter concludes with a discussion of the role of creativity and insight within problem solving.

The final chapter in the book does double service. First, it pulls together many of the strands of contemporary research relevant to the topic of consciousness—what consciousness is, and what consciousness is for. In addition, most students will reach this chapter at the end of a full semester's work, a point at which students are well served by a review of the topics already covered, and also a point at which students are ill served by the introduction of much new material. Therefore, this chapter draws most of its themes and evidence from previous chapters, and in that fashion serves as a review for many points that appear earlier in the book. By the same token, Chapter 15 highlights the fact that we are using these materials to approach some of the greatest questions ever asked about the mind, and, in that way, this chapter should help to convey some of the power of the material we have been discussing throughout the book.

Finally, let me turn to the happiest of chores—thanking all of those who have contributed to this book. Let me begin with those who helped with the first edition; happily, I had the benefit of help from many sources. Two colleagues, Bob Crowder (Yale University) and Bob Logie (University of Aberdeen), read through the entire text, and I am deeply grateful for their comments, their insights, and their corrections. In addition, a number of colleagues helped me with specific chapters, and the first edition was much improved for their efforts. Therefore, let me offer sincere thanks to Paul Rozin (University of Pennsylvania) (Chapters 1 and 3), Mike McCloskey (Johns Hopkins University) (Chapters 4, 5, and 6), Hal Pashler (University of California, San Diego) (Chapters 4 and 5), Henry Gleitman (University of Pennsylvania) (Chapters 5, 6, 7, and 15), Peter Graf (University of British Columbia) (Chapter 6), Frank Keil (Cornell University) (Chapters 8, 9, and 11), Enriqueta Canseco-Gonzalez (Reed College) (Chapter 10), Lila Gleitman (University of Pennsylvania) (Chapter 10), and Steve Pinker (MIT) (Chapter 10). Finally, I received a range of useful suggestions from three colleagues who read the almost-finished first edition, and so thanks also go to Rich Carlson (Pennsylvania State University), John Henderson (Michigan Stage University), and Jim Hoffman (University of Delaware).

A number of other colleagues provided enormously helpful reviews for the second edition, and so I'm happy to thank Steve Palmer (University of California, Berkeley) (Chapters 2 and 3), Martin Conway (University of Bristol) (Chapters 2, 3, 4, 5, and 6), Eldar Shafir (Princeton University) (Chapters 12, 13, and 14), Kathleen Eberhard (Notre Dame) (Chapter 2), Henry L. Roediger (Washington University) (Chapter 2), Bill Gehrig (Michigan) (Chapters 2 and 3), and Howard Egeth (Johns Hopkins University) (Chapter 3). In addition, Chapter 2 draws heavily on materials that Alan Fridlund, Henry Gleitman, and I developed for our textbook, *Psychology*, and I want to express my deepest thanks to them—not just for helping me with neuroscience, but for their input, advice, and criticism on a wide range of topics.

Reed College has been generous in its support of this book, and most of the work on the second edition was made possible by a sabbatical funded by Reed. In addition, two colleagues (and, I say happily, two friends) at Reed have had a powerful impact on the book as well. Allen Neuringer has, over the years, forced me to examine assumptions; he's kept me mindful of my history; he has also shown me again and again what truly great teaching is supposed to look like. Dell Rhodes has always provided a model for how a fabulously committed, careful, wonderfully clear instructor can bring students to a fully sophisticated understanding of the state of the art. She has been a constant reminder that one needs to keep one's guard up in scrutinizing arguments and data, and she has also taught me an enormous amount about neuroscience. Together Allen and Dell have made me a better colleague and a better author.

Let me also express thanks to the people at Norton. It was originally Don Fusting who drew me into the textbook world, Cathy Wick who shepherded me through my early projects, and Jon Durbin who accompanied me on this most recent adventure. I'm grateful for all of their efforts and their input. Rob Whiteside has also been a fabulous help in the madness of finishing this book, and I want to thank Traci Nagle and Kate Barry for their clear-headed editing.

Finally, the three people who have contributed the most: Jacob and Solomon are, together, what makes all of this worthwhile. Friderike Heuer is my partner in all of my projects and has certainly received vastly less public acknowledgment than she has earned. She's my most severe but most constructive editor, and in all things, my most important source of support. There aren't words enough to express my gratitude to these three individuals.

Daniel Reisberg
Portland, Oregon

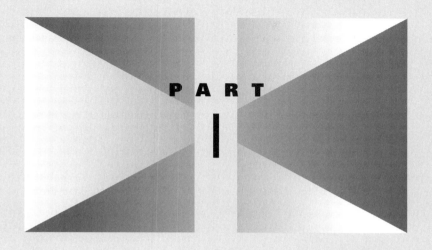

PART

I

# The Foundations
of Cognitive Psychology

What is cognitive psychology? In Chapter 1, we will seek to define this discipline and, with that, we'll offer an early sketch of what this field can teach us—both in terms of theory and in terms of practical applications. We will also provide a brief history, in order to explain why cognitive psychology emerged as a discipline and why it takes the form that it does.

Chapter 2 has a different focus: In the last decade or two, cognitive psychology has formed an increasingly productive partnership with the field of cognitive neuroscience. Investigators in these two fields work together to describe how the mind works, what is involved in various mental processes, and how the brain makes these achievements and processes possible. In this book, our main emphasis will be on psychology, not neuroscience, but we'll make use of neuroscience evidence at various points in our discussion. To do this, though, we first need to provide some background, which is the main purpose of Chapter 2. We'll include a rough map of "what's where" in the brain, but we should be clear from the start about what this means: Each area of the brain performs a specific function, but that doesn't mean that there are large scale "centers" in the brain—a "reading center," for example, or a "memory center." Instead, any mental achievement you can name depends on the coordinated functioning of many different brain regions, with each region contributing its own small bit to the overall achievement. We'll show evidence for this pattern of "cerebral teamwork" at the very beginning of Chapter 2, when we consider a bizarre form of brain damage. This pattern will then remain in view throughout the chapter, and will certainly be visible late in the chapter when we'll zoom in on the visual system as a case study of how one brain system functions.

# The Science of the Mind

This is a book about intellectual functioning. It will take us several pages to spell out just what this means, but some of the questions to be asked are obvious from the start:

There you are, studying for next Wednesday's examination, but for some reason, the material just won't "stick" in your memory. You find yourself wishing, therefore, for a better strategy to use in studying and memorizing. What would that strategy be? Is it possible to have a "better memory"?

While you're studying, your friend is moving around in the room, and you find this terribly distracting. Why can't you just "shut out" your friend's motion? Why don't you have better control over your attention and your ability to concentrate?

An attorney is interviewing a witness to a crime and is amazed by how little the witness remembers. You've been introduced to a woman at a party, but minutes later, you realize (to your embarrassment) that you have forgotten her name. Why do we forget? What sorts of things are we likely to forget, and what sorts of things are we likely to remember?

You pick up the morning newspaper and are horrified to learn how many people have decided to vote for Candidate X. How do people decide whom to vote for? For that matter, how do people decide what college to attend, or which car to buy, or even what to have for dinner? What forces drive our decisions?

Cognitive psychologists know an enormous amount about all these topics and, before we are through, we will have considered evidence pertinent to each of the scenarios just mentioned. In addition, note that in the cases just described, things aren't going as you might have wished: You fail to remember; you are unable to ignore a distraction; the voters make a choice you don't like.

3

But what about the other side of things? What about the great intellectual feats that humans produce—brilliant deductions, or extraordinary feats of memory, or incredibly creative solutions to problems? Before we are done, we will also have a lot to say about how these are possible, and thus how it is that we accomplish the great things we do.

## The Psychology of the Ordinary

It has been said that poetry serves "to make the mysterious familiar and the familiar mysterious." We might debate this claim about poetry, but it is, in any case, a claim surely true of psychology. In this book, we will discover that many phenomena which appear complex at first inspection are actually rather simple when examined closely. We will see that this is true, for example, when we consider how people make judgments about facts they have observed, or evidence they have encountered. As we will see, a few unsophisticated strategies lie at the heart of an extraordinary range of judgments; if we understand these strategies, we understand a great deal. Likewise, our ability to solve problems often seems subtle and mysterious; here, too, we will discover that much of the work is done by means of a few simple strategies. In that sense, then, we will make the mysterious seem familiar.

We will discover also that many apparently simple achievements are, in fact, remarkably complicated. You look at this page, read the words, and know what they mean. You choose to stop reading, and pay attention instead to some sound that is reaching your ears. Or perhaps you choose to think about how you spent last weekend, and you spend a minute remembering. These seem like ordinary accomplishments. You take no pride in reading—all college students can read. Likewise, it's usually no trick to pay attention to this or that; you have been able to control your attention, with only occasional lapses, ever since you were a child. Similarly, the remembering is immediate, effortless; there's no indication of any complexities here.

When closely examined, though, these accomplishments are complex, and amazingly so. We will spend most of Chapter 3 describing the processes needed to recognize the words on a page; in Chapter 10, we'll examine the further steps required when you put these words together into meaningful sentences. In Chapter 4, we'll see that the simple act of "paying attention" involves a mechanism with many parts; attending is possible, therefore, only when all of these "components" are working properly together. In these ways, we will discover that our ordinary achievements are less straightforward than one might guess. The familiar, in other words, is remarkably mysterious.

### THE COMPLEXITY OF COGNITION: AN EXAMPLE

As one way of conveying these points, consider this little story (adopted from Charniak, 1972): "Betsy wanted to bring Jacob a present. She shook her piggy bank. It made no sound. She went to look for her mother."

No one has any trouble understanding this four-sentence tale, but you should reflect for a moment on what makes this possible. The story is comprehensible, indeed, it is *coherent*, only because you provide some important bits of background. For example, in order to understand this story, you need to know these facts:

1. The things one gives as presents are often things bought for the occasion, rather than things already owned. Otherwise, why did Betsy go to her piggy bank at all? (Surely you did not think she intended to give the piggy bank as the present, or its contents!)

2. Money is kept in piggy banks. One often does not keep track of how much money is in the bank, and one cannot simply look into a piggy bank to learn its contents. Without these facts, how could we explain why Betsy shook the bank?

3. Piggy banks are made out of hard material. It's usually coins, not bills, that are kept in piggy

banks. Coins make noise when they contact hard material. Otherwise, why would it be informative that the bank made no sound?

4. Children, not adults, are the ones who keep piggy banks, and children tend not to have credit cards. Otherwise, Betsy could compensate for her lack of cash by pulling an American Express card out of her wallet. If you didn't know this, then you wouldn't understand why she went to see her mother!

This list of relevant facts could easily be expanded, but by now the point is clear: The story makes sense only because of the knowledge you bring to it. Without this knowledge, you would be unable to see why the second sentence of the story is a logical sequel to the first, or why the third sentence conveys any information at all.

This story, therefore, starts to reveal some of the complexities involved in our moment-by-moment intellectual commerce with the world. Anyone, even a child, could understand this brief story. Nonetheless, in order to understand it, you must engage in some (usually unnoticed) activity—dredging information out of your memory, integrating that information with the sentences you are reading, making some inferences, and so on.

Moreover, let's emphasize that these background facts needed to understand this story all involve simple bits of common sense—e.g., the fact that coins are kept in children's piggy banks, or the fact that children don't have credit cards. Surely, you know a vast number of these low-level facts: You know that ceilings are above floors, not below them; you know that it's generally cold in the winter; you know that one usually invites friends to birthday parties, not enemies or total strangers; you know that $2 + 2 = 4$, that red is a color, that there's no royal family in the United States, and on and on and on.

These commonsense facts are all available in your memory, as part of your **generic knowledge**—knowledge about how things work in general. Also in memory is a wide range of **episodic knowledge**—knowledge about specific episodes within your life. You remember how you spent last summer, what you had for breakfast this morning, and a huge number of other episodes as well. It seems, then, that there is actually an enormous quantity of information in your memory: generic knowledge, episodic knowledge, and (as we'll see) more. This vastness of knowledge is impressive, but it also creates a problem: With all this information stored in memory, how do you manage to find just the information you need? Moreover, how do you manage to find the information rapidly—so rapidly, in fact, that you don't even realize you've just pulled information out of memory? (In the Betsy and Jacob story, for example, you probably didn't notice your "contribution" until we pointed it out.)

Many people speak of memory as though it were a "library" or "filing system," not so different in its functioning from an actual library or filing system. As we'll see in later chapters, these comparisons are somewhat misleading, but let's pursue them for a moment. Who serves the role of librarian, or file clerk? When you need some information from memory, you're usually not aware of searching for it; instead, the sought-after information simply "pops" into mind for you. Therefore, it would seem, it is not the conscious self doing the memory search. As Flanagan (1991, p. 176) puts it, then,

> perhaps this is evidence for a secretarial homunculus [literally, "little man"], a sort of mental office manager, who races around performing the boring matches and searches and only passes on information to me when I, as the executive director of the operation, really need it. But if there really is such an office manager in my mind, he or she or it is really quite a bit smarter than I am, and possesses skills that I certainly don't have. It is inconceivable to me that I could figure out a filing and retrieval system, as well as perform the filing and retrieval, for the 100 trillion bits of information which, according to some estimates, are encoded in my brain.

Once again, therefore, there is a puzzle to be figured out. The comprehension of even a simple story requires the integration of that story with prior knowledge. This in turn requires that the knowledge be drawn from memory and, in fact, be drawn rapidly enough so that the process doesn't derail the comprehension of the story itself. But, given how much is in memory, how much there is to be searched through, this knowledge retrieval is far from trivial. What is the filing system? Who runs it? Is the retrieval reliable—does it always succeed, or does it occasionally fail to locate the sought-after information? These are questions we must answer if we're to understand even the simplest bit of our intellectual functioning, such as the comprehension of a four-sentence child's story.

## THE SCOPE OF COGNITIVE PSYCHOLOGY

The processes we've mentioned so far—remembering, comprehending text, making judgments about evidence, solving problems—all fall squarely within the realm of cognitive psychology. In its modern form, cognitive psychology is an enterprise only four or five decades old. Classic, pioneering research was done in the 1950s (e.g., Broadbent, 1958; Bruner, Goodnow & Austin, 1956; Miller, 1956); the first modern textbook was published in 1967 (Neisser, 1967). In these early works, cognitive psychology was often understood as the scientific study of *knowledge*. How is knowledge acquired? How is knowledge retained, so that it's available when needed? How is knowledge used, as a basis for action, or as a basis for generating further knowledge? This first of these questions (how is knowledge acquired?) leads us to be interested in the processes of perception, and how perceived objects are categorized and understood. The second question (how is knowledge retained?) leads to the study of memory—both the formation of memories and the subsequent retrieval of information from memory. The third question (how is knowledge used?) invites the study of decision-making, judgment, and inference.

These topics continue to define the broad outlines of cognitive psychology, and thus the selection of topics covered in this book: Chapter 2 will be concerned with the brain mechanisms that make cognition possible. Chapters 3 and 4 will be largely concerned with our acquisition of new information from the world, obviously an important source of our knowledge. Chapters 5, 6, and 7 will then examine the nature of memory—how memories are created, how memories are retrieved when needed. Chapters 8 and 9 will seek to characterize our knowledge itself: How is the knowledge recorded within our minds, within our memories? Chapter 10 will examine a special type of knowledge—our knowledge about language. Chapter 11 then focuses on visual knowledge and visual imagery, and we'll consider the contrast between these and knowledge that's more verbal in character. The remainder of the book will then be concerned with how our knowledge gets used: In Chapter 12, we will consider how we make judgments or draw conclusions about things we have experienced. In Chapter 13, we will ask what we *do* with our knowledge, once we've got it. What implications do we consider? How do we then make decisions, based on our knowledge, and based on our perceptions of our various options? Then, once we have made a decision and chosen a goal, how do we select a path toward that goal? This will be our focus in Chapter 14. Finally, in Chapter 15 we will gather together some strands that will have run throughout the book, considering in particular just how much of our thought is unconscious. In the process, we will consider what consciousness is for.

## THE WIDE IMPLICATIONS OF COGNITION RESEARCH

This catalogue of topics should convey the considerable breadth of cognitive psychology. Perhaps a better way to convey this breadth, though, is to look "within" these topics, examining what each includes. Consider, for example, the study of memory: When we study memory, what are we studying? Or, to turn this around, what tasks rely on memory? When you are taking an exam, you obviously rely on memory—memory for what you have learned during the term. Likewise, you rely on memory when you are at the supermarket and are trying to remember the cheesecake recipe, so you can buy the ingredients. You rely on memory when you are reminiscing about childhood. But what else draws on memory?

The "Betsy and Jacob" story presented earlier in the chapter should have made clear that we also rely on our memories to supplement materials we read, tales we hear, scenes we examine. Without this use of memory, anyone *telling* the Betsy and Jacob story would need to spell out all the connections, and all the assumptions. That is, the story would have to include all the background facts that we earlier enumerated, background facts that, with memory, are supplied by you. In this case, the story would have to be fifty times longer than it currently is, and the telling of it fifty times slower. The same would be true for every story we hear, every conversation we participate in. In short, without memory, conversation and reading would be impossibly slow. Memory is crucial for each of these activities. Likewise, without memory, you wouldn't be able to *retain* anything you've learned—and so, no memory, no learning; no memory, no ability to benefit in any way from experience.

Here is a different sort of example: In Chapter 6, we will consider various cases of clinical **amnesia**— cases in which someone, because of brain damage, has lost the ability to remember certain materials. These cases are fascinating at many levels, including the fact that they give us key insights into what memory is for: Without memory, what is disrupted?

One well-studied amnesia patient was a gentleman identified as H.M. We'll have much more to say about H.M. in Chapter 6, but let us here make a few observations: H.M.'s memory loss was the unanticipated by-product of brain surgery (surgery intended to control his epilepsy). The memory loss is quite profound: H.M. remembers well events prior to the surgery, but seems unable to recall any event that has occurred subsequent to the surgery. This has, of course, had massive consequences for his life, and some of the consequences are perhaps surprising. For example, H.M. had an uncle of whom he was very fond, and H.M. often asks about his uncle: How is he? What's he doing these days? Unfortunately, the uncle died some time after H.M.'s surgery. H.M. can (and does) learn of this fact, but he cannot remember it. As a result, each time H.M. hears about his uncle's death, he is hearing the news "for the first time"—with all the shock, all the grief. Because of his amnesia, he soon forgets that he has heard this terrible news, and so has no opportunity to "live with" the news, to adjust to it. Hence, his grief cannot subside. Without memory, H.M. cannot come to terms with his uncle's death.

A different glimpse of memory function comes from H.M.'s poignant comments about his state and about "who he is." Each of us has a conception of who we are, of what sort of person we are. That conception is supported by numerous memories: We know whether we're deserving of praise for our good deeds or blame for our transgressions, because we remember our good deeds and our transgressions. We know whether we've kept our promises, or achieved our goals, because, again, we have the relevant memories. None of this is true for amnesics, and H.M. sometimes comments on the fact that, in important ways, he doesn't know who he is. He doesn't know if he should be proud of his accomplishments or ashamed of his crimes; he doesn't know if he's been clever or stupid, honorable or dishonest, industrious or lazy. In a sense, then, it would seem that, without a memory, there is no self. (For broader discussion see Hilts, 1995; Conway & Pleydell-Pearce, 2000.)

What, then, is the scope of cognitive psychology? As we mentioned earlier, this field is sometimes defined as the scientific study of the acquisition, retention, and use of knowledge. This makes it sound like the field is concerned with purely intellectual matters; it makes it sound like the field has a fairly narrow scope. We have just considered some examples, though, that show the opposite to be true: Our self-concept, it seems, depends on our knowledge (and, in particular, on our episodic knowledge). Our emotional adjustments to the world, as we have seen, rely on our memories. Or, to take much more ordinary cases, our ability to understand a story we've read, or a conversation, or, presumably, *any* of our experiences, depends on our supplementing that experience with some knowledge.

In short, cognitive psychology, and a reliance on our knowledge, on our ability to learn, to remember, and to make judgments, is relevant to virtually every waking moment of our lives. Activities that don't, on the surface, appear "intellectual" would nonetheless collapse without the support of our cognitive functioning. This is true whether we're considering our actions, our social lives, our emotions, or almost any other domain. This is the scope of cognitive psychology and, in a real sense, is the scope of this book.

## A Brief History

We have already mentioned that cognitive psychology is a relatively young endeavor—about 40 years old, making it one of psychology's youngest branches. Despite this youth, cognitive psychology has had an enormous impact on the field—so much so that many speak of the "cognitive revolution" within psychology. This (alleged) revolution, taking place across the late 1950s and 1960s, represented a striking change in the style of research and theorizing employed by psychologists. The new styles were intended initially for studying problems we have already met: problems of learning, memory, and so on. But these new styles were soon "exported" to other domains and have provided important insights into these domains. In important ways, then, the "Cognitive Revolution" has changed the intellectual map of our field.

### THE YEARS OF INTROSPECTION

To understand all of this, we need some historical context. In the late nineteenth century, scholars—notably Wilhelm Wundt (1832–1920) and his student, Edward Bradford Titchener (1867–1927)—launched the new enterprise of research psychology, defining their field for the first time as an endeavor separate from philosophy or from biology and physiology.

In those years, psychologists were largely concerned with the study of conscious mental events—our feelings, our thoughts, our perceptions, our recollections. Moreover, there was just one way, they argued, to study these events. They started with the obvious fact that there is no way for you to experience my thoughts, or I yours. The only person who can ex-

perience or observe your thoughts is *you*. They concluded, therefore, that the only way to study thoughts is for each of us to **introspect**, or "look within," to observe and record the content of our own mental lives, and the sequence of our own experiences.

Wundt and Titchener insisted, though, that the introspection cannot be casual. Instead, introspectors had to be meticulously trained—they were given a vocabulary, to describe what they observed; they were trained to be as careful and as complete as possible; and above all, they were trained simply to report on their experiences, with a minimum of interpretation.

This style of research was quite influential for several years, but psychologists soon became disenchanted with it, and it is easy to see why. As one concern, debate soon emerged about *unconscious* thought. If such thought existed, then introspection was necessarily inadequate, since introspection, by its nature, is the study of conscious experiences!

In fact, present-day scholars are convinced that unconscious thought plays a large part in our mental lives. For example, what is your phone number? Now, how did you find this out? One might expect that you used some system or strategy for "looking up" this information in your memory and then bringing this information into awareness. Indeed, we'll see in later chapters that a complex series of steps is required even for this simple bit of remembering. None of these events, however, is part of your conscious experience. Instead, the telephone number simply "comes to you," without any effort, without any noticeable steps or strategies on your part. If we relied on introspection as our means of studying mental events, then we would have no way of examining these processes.

As a different concern, it seems clear that science needs some way of testing its assertions, of confirming or disconfirming its claims. Hand in hand with this, science needs some way of resolving disagreements: If you claim that there are ten planets in our solar system, and I insist that there are nine, we need some way of determining who is right. Otherwise, we have no way of locating the fact of the matter, and so our "science" will become a matter of opinion, not fact.

With introspection, though, this "testability" of claims is often unattainable. Let's imagine that you insist that your headaches are worse than mine. How could we ever test your claims? It might be true that you describe your headaches in extreme terms—you talk about your "unbelievable, agonizing, excruciating" headaches. But that might simply mean that you are inclined toward extravagant descriptions—it might reflect your verbal style, not your headaches. Similarly, it might be true that you need bed rest whenever one of your headaches strikes. Does that mean your headaches are truly intolerable? It might mean instead that you are self-indulgent and rest even in the face of mild pain. Perhaps our headaches are identical, but I'm stoic about mine, whereas you're not.

How, therefore, should we test your claim about your headaches? What we need is some means of directly comparing your headaches to mine, and that would require "transplanting" one of your headaches into my experience, or vice versa. Then one of us could make the appropriate comparison. But there is obviously no way to do this, leaving us, in the end, truly unable to determine if your headache reports are exaggerated or not, distorted or accurate. We're left, in other words, with no access to the objective facts. Our only information about your headaches is what comes to us through the "filter" of your description, and we have no way to know how (or whether) that "filter" is coloring the evidence.

For purposes of science, this is just not good enough. For science, we need objective observations, observations that we can count on. We need observations that aren't dependent on a particular point of view, or a particular descriptive style. It is not enough to consider "the world as one person sees it." Instead, we want to consider the world as it objectively is. In scientific discourse, we usually achieve this objectivity by making sure all the facts are out in plain view, so that you can inspect my evidence, and I yours. In that way, we can be certain that neither of us is distorting, or misreporting, or exaggerating, the facts. And that is precisely what we cannot do with introspection.

## THE YEARS OF BEHAVIORISM

The concerns just raised led many psychologists, particularly those in the United States, to abandon introspection as a research method. One could not do science, they argued, with introspective data. Instead, psychology needed *objective* data. That means we must focus on data that are out in the open, for all to observe.

An organism's behaviors fall into this category: You can watch my actions, and so can anyone else who is appropriately positioned. Therefore, data concerned with behavior will be objective data, and so are grist for the scientific mill. Likewise, stimuli in the world are in this same "objective" category: These are measurable, recordable, physical events. Moreover, you can arrange to record the stimuli I experience day after day after day and also the behaviors I produce each day. This will allow you to record how the pattern of behaviors changes with the passage of time and with the accumulation of experience. Thus, my *learning history* can also be objectively recorded and scientifically studied.

Of course, my beliefs, my wishes, my goals, and my expectations are all things that cannot be directly observed and cannot be objectively recorded. Thus we need to rule out any discussion of these **mentalistic** notions. These can be studied only via introspection (or so the argument goes), and introspection, we have suggested, is worthless as a scientific tool. Hence, a scientific psychology needs to avoid these "invisible" internal processes or events.

It was this perspective that led researchers to the **behaviorist** movement, a movement that dominated psychology in America for roughly the first half of the twentieth century. This movement produced some impressive discoveries—broad principles concerned with how our behavior changes in response to different configurations of stimuli (including stimuli we often call "rewards" and "punishments"). These principles apply to a wide range of behaviors and, as it turns out, to a wide range of organisms. Many of these principles remain in place within contemporary psychology, and provide the base for an important theoretical enterprise, as well as a range of practical applications. (For a description of these principles, see Schwartz & Robbins, 1995.)

However, by the late 1950s, psychologists were convinced that a great deal of our behavior could not be explained in this way. The problem in a nutshell is this: When you respond to some stimulus in the world, your reaction is usually guided by your *understanding* of the stimulus, and not by the stimulus itself. Therefore, if we try to predict your behavior by focusing on the stimulus *per se*, by focusing on the objective situation, then we will regularly make the wrong predictions. In the same way, your choice of a response is generally guided by what the response means—that is, by how you understand the response, and by how you believe others will understand the response. Once again, therefore, if we want to predict your behavior, we need to consider more than the objectively defined response; we also need to consider your *understanding* of the response.

These broad claims spell trouble for the behaviorists' program. The behaviorists, in striving for objectivity, sought to exclude such invisible entities as "beliefs" or "understanding" (not to mention plans, strategies, preferences, perceptions, and the like). Yet, it seems, we may need these mentalistic notions if we're to achieve a scientific understanding of human actions and perhaps an understanding of other creatures, as well. Thus we *can't* study these mentalistic notions within the behaviorists' perspective, but we *must* study these notions if we're going to understand behavior.

The evidence for these assertions is threaded throughout the chapters of this book. Over and over, we will find it necessary to mention people's perceptions and strategies and understanding, as we strive to explain *why* (and *how*) they perform various tasks and accomplish various goals. Indeed, we've already seen an example of this pattern: Imagine that we present the "Betsy and Jacob" story to people and then ask them various questions about the story: Why did Betsy shake her piggy bank? Why did she go to look for her mother? Their responses will surely reflect their understanding of the story, which in turn depends on far more than the physical stimulus—i.e., the 29 syllables of the story itself. If we

wanted to predict their responses, therefore, we would need to refer to the story but also to the persons' knowledge and their understanding of, and contribution to, this stimulus.

Here's a different example that makes the same general point: There you sit in the dining hall. A friend produces this physical stimulus: "Pass the salt, please." You immediately produce a bit of salt-passing behavior. So far, all is fine from the behaviorists' perspective: There was a physical stimulus and an easily defined response. But notice that things would have run off in the same way if your friend had offered a different stimulus. "Could I have the salt?" would have done the trick. Ditto for "Salt, please!" or "Hmm, this sure needs salt!" If your friend is both loquacious and obnoxious, the utterance might have been, "Excuse me, but after briefly contemplating the gustatory qualities of these comestibles, I have discerned that their sensory qualities would be improved by the addition of a number of sodium and chloride ions, delivered in roughly equal proportions and in crystalline form; could you aid me in this endeavor?" You might giggle (or snarl) at your friend, but you would still pass the salt.

Now let's work on the "science of salt-passing behavior." When is this behavior produced? Since we've just observed that the behavior is evoked by all of these stimuli, we would surely want to ask: What do these stimuli have in common? The answer, quite simply, is that they have very little in common at the level of observable, objective data. After all, the actual sounds being produced are rather different in that long utterance about "sodium and chloride ions" and the utterance, "Salt, please!" And, in many circumstances, similar sounds *would not* lead to salt-passing behavior. Imagine that your friend says, "Salt the pass," or "Sass the palt." These *are* similar to "pass the salt," but wouldn't have the same impact. Or imagine that your friend said, "She has only a small part in the play. All she gets to say is, 'Pass the salt, please.'" In this case, exactly the right syllables were uttered, but you wouldn't pass the salt in response.

It seems, then, that our science of salt-passing won't get very far if we insist on talking only about the physical stimulus. Stimuli that are physically different from each other ("Salt, please" and the bit about the ions) have similar effects. Stimuli that are similar to each other ("Pass the salt" and "Sass the palt") have different effects. Physical similarity, therefore, is plainly *not* what unites the various stimuli that evoke salt-passing.

Of course, the stimuli that evoke salt-passing do have something in common with each other, even if the shared attribute isn't physical. What they have in common is that they all *mean* the same thing. These utterances may have different physical forms and different *literal* meanings, but in our culture they're all understood as ways of requesting salt. In order to produce a "science of salt-passing," therefore, or more modestly, to predict your behavior in this situation, we need to consider what these stimuli *mean to you*. This seems an extraordinarily simple point, but it is a point, echoed over and over by countless other examples, that indicates the impossibility of a complete behaviorist psychology.[1]

## THE ROOTS OF THE COGNITIVE REVOLUTION

We seem to be nearing an impasse: If we wish to explain or predict behavior, we need to make reference to the mental world—the world of perceptions, understandings, and intentions. But how to study this world? We could employ introspection, but we've argued that introspective data are (at best) problematic. It would seem, then, that the world of the objective is (for our purposes) inadequate, yet the world of the subjective is unstudiable.

The solution to this impasse is actually one suggested many years ago, perhaps most clearly by the philosopher Immanuel Kant (1724–1804). It is his

method that, in many ways, led to the principal research strategy of cognitive psychology. To use Kant's "transcendental method," one begins with the observable facts. For Kant, these included the fact that humans can and do reason about spatial and temporal relations, and also the fact that we can and do reason about cause and effect. Kant's research strategy was then to work backward from these observations. Given these "effects," what can we figure out about the "causes"? What must the mental world be like in order to make these observations possible? In essence, Kant asked, "How could the observed state of affairs have come about?" (See Flanagan, 1991, for further discussion of this method.)

This method is sometimes called "inference to best explanation," since what one seeks is the best possible explanation of all the available facts. As it turns out, this method is crucial for a great deal of modern science. Physicists, for example, do not observe electrons directly. They instead infer electron activity from the "tracks" electrons leave in cloud chambers, by momentary fluctuations in magnetic fields, and so on. From these *effects* of electrons, physicists figure out what the *causes* must be like, and in this fashion they infer the properties of the electron (or any other particle). Thus physicists, too, are using Kant's research strategy, and "doing science on the invisible." In this way, they are making important discoveries about particles that no one has ever seen, reaching firm conclusions about events they have never observed. Kant's method is a powerful one and, in using it, cognitive psychologists are in good company.

## THE COMPUTER AS METAPHOR

In Kant's method, one starts with observed data and seeks to reconstruct the unseen processes that led to these data. But what form should this reconstruction take? What sort of mechanisms might one propose for our ability to remember, or our ability to solve problems? Should we seek to explain the data in terms of magnetic fields, or biochemistry, or divine intervention? If we seek the "best explanation" for

---

[1]We should mention briefly that the behaviorists themselves quickly realized this point. Hence modern behaviorism has abandoned the radical rejection of mentalistic terms, and, indeed, it's hard to draw a line between modern behaviorism and a field called "animal cognition," a field that often employs mentalistic language! The behaviorism being criticized here is a historically defined behaviorism, and it's this perspective that, in large measure, gave birth to modern cognitive psychology.

the observed data, then in what terms should that explanation be cast?

In the 1950s, a new approach to psychological explanation became available, and it turned out to be immensely fruitful. This new approach was suggested by the rapid developments in electronic information processing, including developments in computer technology. It quickly became clear that computers were capable of tremendously efficient information storage and retrieval ("memory"), as well as performance that seemed to involve decision-making and problem-solving. Psychologists therefore began to explore the possibility that the human mind employed processes and procedures similar to those used in computers, and so psychological data were soon being explained in terms of "buffers" and "gates" and "central processors," all terms borrowed from computer technology. (See, for example, Broadbent, 1958; Miller, Galanter & Pribram, 1960.)

The computer metaphor provided a new language for describing psychological processes, explaining psychological data. Given a particular performance, say, on a memory task, one could hypothesize a series of **information-processing** events that made the performance possible. As we will see, hypotheses framed in these terms led psychologists to predict a host of new observations, and so the hypotheses both organized the available information and also led to many new discoveries.

In essence, then, the computer metaphor allowed us to run the Kantian logic: Given a set of data, one could propose a particular sequence of information-processing events as the hypothesized source of those data. One could then ask whether some other, perhaps simpler, information-processing sequence could also explain the data, or whether some other sequence could explain both these data and some other findings. (Recall that we're seeking the *best* explanation.) More important, one could then *test* these proposed sequences: If such-and-such mechanism lies behind these data, then things should work somewhat differently in this circumstance, or that one. (We'll offer an example of how this works in just a few pages.)

In these ways, the influence of the computer metaphor led to a blossoming of psychological re-search in the 1960s and 1970s, and this provided a major impetus for the development of modern cognitive psychology. It is worth noting, though, that the use of this metaphor does not commit us to claiming that "the mind is just like a computer," or "the mind is nothing more than a complex computer." Instead, we are suggesting only that the mind is *enough* like a computer that we can profitably explain much about the mind by using the language of computer processing. Likewise, the mind seems to be enough like a computer so that the use of such language leads to the discovery of new facts about intellectual performance.

## MULTIPLE LEVELS OF DESCRIPTION

We should be clear, though, about just what is meant by the "language of computer processing." There is, in fact, considerable flexibility here. Consider, for example, a computer designed to play the game of chess: How should we understand this computer's functioning? The answer to this depends on our *purposes* and on just what it is we are seeking to understand. Imagine, for example, that the computer is broken. No matter what you do, it produces no response. No matter what program you try to run, the result is the same—still no response. In this case, you might investigate the machine's hardware: Is it properly connected? Is it receiving electricity?

Imagine, as a different case, that the computer functions reasonably well most of the time. Every so often, however, it produces a sequence of bizarre moves, each of which simply undoes the move before. (The Queen moves one space left, then one space right, then one space left, then right again.) In this case, you might suspect that the problem lies in the computer's software. If the computer is doing *other* tasks perfectly well, you'll probably reason that the problem doesn't lie in the wiring or in some defective component. Instead, somewhere within the chess-playing program, someone has given the computer the wrong instruction. Hence, to fix the "bug," you would probably call a programmer, not an electrician.

Imagine, as yet another case, that you're playing *against* this computer in a chess tournament. For this purpose, you will probably care about the strategies and goals contained within the computer's program. What gambits is the machine likely to try? What traps will it detect, and what traps will it fall into? You probably won't care about the hardware—your response to a "pawn gambit" will be the same whether the computer is built out of silicon chips or out of relays. You also might not care exactly how the computer was programmed. You won't care, for example, what language the computer's instructions are written in. If there are bugs in the program, you want to know about them, but perhaps no bugs have been detected. You won't care how the computer's strategies are labeled, or in which "memory registers" the strategies are listed. This information isn't useful to you in deciding what moves you should make, and what strategies you should try.

Each of these levels of description—at the level of hardware, at the level of the program, or at the level of goals and strategies—is legitimate and often useful. Which level of description you use will depend on your situation. Thus, the "language of computer processing" is, in an important way, opportunistic: You use the language appropriate to your goals.

The same is true within cognitive psychology. In many cases, our understanding of mental function depends on close consideration of neurological or physiological mechanisms. In these cases, we will need to consider the "hardware" of the mind—i.e., the brain. In other cases, we will find it useful to offer a more abstract level of analysis—making reference to beliefs and assumptions and strategies, terms familiar to us all. In still other cases, we will use an intermediate level of analysis to explain the data in terms of "memory buffers" and "response selectors" and the like.

Our choice among these levels of description will be governed, throughout, by the same Kantian logic. For each phenomenon, we will begin with the observable facts, and ask what unseen mechanism makes these facts possible. When an explanation in terms of "hardware" seems the best account of the facts, that is the idiom we will use. When an explanation in terms

of beliefs or strategies seems more economical, more straightforward, then we will shift to that level. In each case, though, we will then seek to test our account by asking what new predictions we can derive from it. In this sense, our enterprise is based on inference, but our inferences must themselves be testable.

## Research in Cognitive Psychology—An Example

Our discussion of research in cognitive psychology has so far been rather abstract, and so it may help at this point to provide a concrete example. We will return to this example in Chapter 5, and there put it into a richer theoretical context. For now, though, our focus is on the method, rather than the theory itself.

As we turn to method, though, let us emphasize that what characterizes cognitive research is not a particular group of experimental procedures or a particular laboratory paradigm. Instead, the research is characterized largely by the *logic* of the methods used and, to a smaller extent, by the types of data that are typically collected. With that proviso in place, let us turn to the example.

### WORKING MEMORY: SOME INITIAL OBSERVATIONS

Many of the sentences in this book—including the present one, which consists of 19 words—are rather long. In many of these sentences, words that must be understood together (such as "sentences . . . are . . . long") are widely separated (note the 12 words interposed between "sentences" and "are"). Yet you have no trouble understanding these sentences.

This simple observation implies a form of memory in use as you read: You must somehow remember the early words in the sentence as you forge ahead. Then, once you have read enough, you can integrate what you have decoded so far. In this section's very first sentence, you needed to remember the first 7 words ("Many of the sentences in this book") while you read the interposed phrase ("including . . . 19 words"). Then you had to bring those first 7 words back into play, to integrate them with the sentence's end ("are rather long").

Psychologists have proposed that the memory relevant to this task is qualitatively different from the memory used for storing, say, your recollection of last summer, or for storing your "mental encyclopedia," in which you store your generic knowledge. These latter examples are drawn from *long-term storage*, a vast repository holding all your knowledge in "dormant" form. In contrast, our example of sentence-reading relies on *short-term storage*, or in the terms we'll use, it relies on *working memory*. Working memory is relatively small in size, but holds information in an easily accessible form. Working memory, in effect, keeps information "at your fingertips," so that it is instantly available when you need it. Thus, having decoded the first part of a sentence, you store its semantic content in working memory, so that it is ready at hand a moment later, when you are all set to integrate this content with the sentence's end.

We'll have much more to say about long-term memory and working memory in Chapter 5. There we'll consider evidence for the claim that these memories are, in fact, qualitatively different from each other; we'll also provide a more refined view of how these memories interact. For now, though, let's consider just a few facts—some basic observations about working memory's size and its function.

First, working memory's capacity is sometimes measured via a "span test." In this test, you read to someone a list of, say, four items, perhaps four letters ("A D G W"). The person has to report these back, immediately, in sequence. If she succeeds, we try it again with five letters ("Q D W U F"). If she can repeat these back correctly, we try six letters, and so on, until we find a list that the person cannot report back accurately. Generally, people start making errors with sequences of 7 or 8 letters. Most people's **letter span**, therefore, is about 7 or 8.

Interestingly enough, when people do make errors in this task, their errors are often systematic. Often people will inadvertently substitute one letter for another with a similar sound. For example, having heard "S" they'll report back "F," or having heard "V" they'll report back "B." The problem is

not in hearing the letters in the first place: We get similar sound-alike confusions if the letters are presented *visually*. Thus, having seen "F" people are likely to report back "S." They are not likely, in this situation, to report back the similar-*looking* "E."

## WORKING MEMORY: A PROPOSAL

Alan Baddeley and Graham Hitch (e.g., 1974) proposed a model to explain the facts we've just described, and a variety of other data as well. Their model starts by stipulating that working memory is not a single entity. Instead, working memory has several separate parts, and so they prefer to speak of a **working-memory system**. At the heart of the system is the **central executive**. This is the part that runs the show and that does the real work.

The executive often calls on a number of low-level "assistants." These assistants are not very sophisticated—they are useful for mere storage of information and not much more. If any work needs to be done on the information—interpretation or analysis—the assistants can't do it; the executive is needed. Nonetheless, these assistants are highly useful: Information that will soon be needed, but isn't needed right now, can be sent off to the them for temporary storage. Therefore, the executive isn't burdened by the mere storage of this information, and is freed up to do other tasks.

In effect, the assistants serve the same function as a piece of scratch paper on your desk. When you're going to need some bit of information soon, you write it down on the scratch paper. Of course, the scratch paper has no mind of its own, and so it can't do anything with the "stored" information; all it does is hold on to the information. But that's helpful enough: With the information stored in this manner, you can cease thinking about it, and so are free to think about something else instead. That is the gain. Then, once you are ready for the stored information, you glance at your notes, and there the information is.

One of working memory's most important assistants is the **articulatory rehearsal loop**. This loop is used for storing verbal materials, or nonverbal materials that can be "translated" into some verbal code.

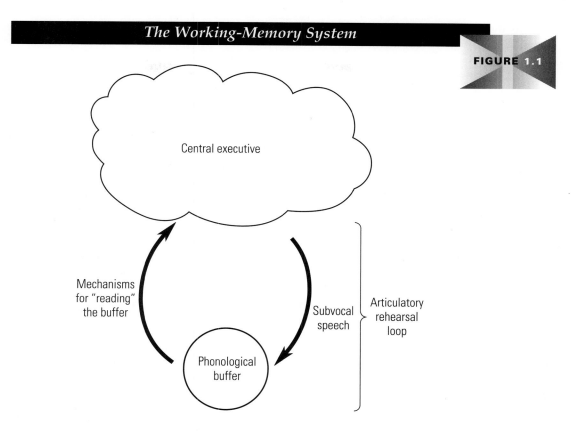

## The Working-Memory System

**FIGURE 1.1**

The central executive controls all functions within working memory, but the executive is supported by a number of low-level assistants. One assistant, the articulatory rehearsal loop, involves two components—subvocal speech (the "inner voice") and a phonological buffer (the "inner ear"). Items are rehearsed by using subvocalization to "load" the buffer. While this is going on, the executive is free to work on other matters. However, the executive is needed to "read" the contents of the buffer before they decay; the executive can then pronounce the items again, launching another cycle through the loop.

To use the loop, the central executive launches the activity of *pronouncing* the to-be-remembered items. The pronunciation isn't out loud; instead, you "talk to yourself"—you go through the motions of speaking but without making a sound. This is referred to as **subvocalization**. Even though it is silent, subvocalization does cause a record of this "speech" to be loaded into a sort of internal echo box, a passive repository that is part of the mental apparatus normally used for hearing. You can think of the "inner voice" loading a record into the "inner ear." More technically, subvocalization creates a record in a **phonological buffer**. Once in that buffer, however, the record begins to fade away. At this point, the executive must intercede: The executive "reads" the contents of the buffer, and launches another cycle. (See Figure 1.1.)

Note, then, that this loop—from executive to sub-vocalization to buffer, and then back to executive—places only an intermittent demand on the executive for the launching of each cycle. Once launched, though, the inner voice can run pretty much on its own, thanks to the fact that speech is enormously well practiced and thus largely automatic. Likewise, the phonological buffer is a passive storage device—information simply arrives there, and starts to decay, with no action needed. Therefore, for most of the duration of the rehearsal cycle, the executive is free to work on other matters, which is the advantage of using this loop.

## EVIDENCE FOR THE WORKING-MEMORY SYSTEM

This proposal neatly handles the observations we've already offered, and leads to many new predictions. For example, notice that the rehearsal loop employs some of the mechanisms of hearing: The "inner ear" is literally part of the auditory system. Consequently, letters that sound alike, when heard, also sound alike in the inner ear. It is no wonder, then, that "sound alike" errors crop up in working memory—these errors are the result of using the loop.

Against this backdrop, imagine that we ask people to take our span test while simultaneously saying "tah-tah-tah" over and over, out loud. This **concurrent articulation task** obviously requires the mechanisms for speech production. Therefore, these mechanisms are not available for other use, including subvocalization. (See Figure 1.2.) You can't subvocalize one sequence while overtly vocalizing something else.

According to the model, how will this matter? First, note that our initial span test measures the *combined capacities* of the central executive and the loop. That is, when people take a span test, they store some of the to-be-remembered items in the loop, and other items via the central executive. (This is an extravagant use of the central executive, which is capable of vastly more than mere storage. It's akin to using a supercomputer to record your shopping list. But mere storage is all that the span task requires.) With concurrent articulation, though, the loop isn't

available for use, and so we are now measuring the capacity of working memory *without* the rehearsal loop. We should predict, therefore, that concurrent articulation, as easy as it is, should cut memory span drastically. This prediction turns out to be correct.

Second, with visually presented items, concurrent articulation should eliminate the sound-alike errors. Roughly put, the relevant sequence of events is this: With visual presentation, items are initially seen, and registered by the central executive. The executive then launches the subvocalization of the to-be-remembered items, using the inner voice, and this loads a record of these items into the inner ear. It is here, in the inner ear, that the sound-alike errors arise. This sequence of events is blocked, however, by concurrent articulation: With the inner voice unavailable, there's no way for these items to reach the inner ear, and so no way for such errors to arise. If errors do occur, they'll be errors of some other sort—perhaps look-alike errors, rather than sound-alike errors. These predictions are, once again, correct: With concurrent articulation, sound-alike errors are largely eliminated.

Third, we can also test people's memory spans using complex visual shapes. People are shown these shapes and then must echo the sequence back by drawing what they have just seen. If we choose shapes that are not easily named, then the shapes cannot be rehearsed via the inner-voice/inner-ear combination. (What would one subvocalize to rehearse these?) With such stimuli, there should be no effect of concurrent articulation: If people aren't using the rehearsal loop, there is no cost attached to denying them use of the loop. This prediction is also correct.

Fourth, let's focus on the overlap between subvocalization and overt speech. We've already appealed to this overlap in explaining the effects of concurrent articulation. But the overlap has other implications as well. In particular, we might expect the inner voice to share certain traits with overt speech, and it does: For example, some words obviously take longer to pronounce than others (e.g., three-syllable words vs. one-syllable words), and we might expect that this would matter for the inner voice: If a word takes

## The Effects of Concurrent Articulation

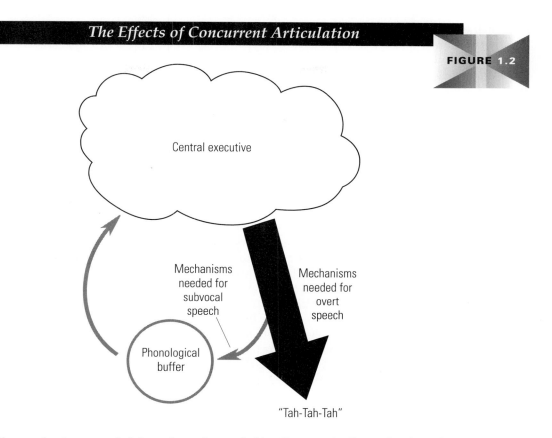

FIGURE 1.2

The mechanisms needed for subvocal speech (the "inner voice") overlap heavily with those needed for actual, overt speech. Therefore, if these mechanisms are in use for actual speech, they are not available for subvocal rehearsal. Hence, many experiments block rehearsal by requiring participants to say "tah-tah-tah" out loud.

more time to vocalize, then it should also take more time to subvocalize, and so it should be more difficult to rehearse. Consistent with this observation, memory span turns out to be smaller for longer words: If we test your span with one-syllable words, we'll estimate your memory's capacity at 8 or 9 items. If we test your span with three-syllable words, our estimate will be closer to 4 or 5. This is often referred to as the **word-length effect**.

Finally, here is a different sort of prediction: We have claimed that the rehearsal loop is required only for storage; this loop (like all of working memory's

assistants) is incapable of any more sophisticated operations. Therefore, these other operations should not be compromised if the loop is unavailable. This turns out to be correct: Concurrent articulation blocks use of the loop, but has no effect on someone's ability to read brief sentences, to do logic problems, and so on. Likewise, we can present people with a string of three or four letters and ask them to remember these while solving a simple problem. After they've solved the problem, they report back the original letters. It turns out that "half filling" working memory in this fashion has virtually no impact on problem-solving;

performance is just as fast and just as accurate under these circumstances as it is without the memory load. That is because this memory load is accommodated within the rehearsal loop, placing no burden on the executive. And it is the executive, not the loop, that is needed for problem-solving, again in accord with the overall model.

### THE NATURE OF THE WORKING-MEMORY EVIDENCE

Let's highlight a few points about the evidence just catalogued. First, the results we have just surveyed, and many other findings as well, fit well with the Baddeley and Hitch conception of a working-memory system. Note, though, that no one has ever seen the "inner voice" or the "inner ear" directly. Instead, we propose that these entities exist because they play a key role in a well-supported account of the data. That is, we infer the existence of these entities because they seem required if we are to explain the evidence. In this sense, we *reconstruct* what the unobserved structures and processes must be.

Second, notice that in supporting our account, we have many forms of data available to us. We can manipulate research participants' activities, as we did with concurrent articulation, and look at how this changes their performance (i.e., the size of the measured memory span). We can also manipulate the stimuli themselves, as we did with the word-length effect, and see how this changes things. We can also look in detail at the nature of the performance, asking not just about the overall level of performance, but also at the specific errors (sound-alike vs. look-alike). We can also measure the speed of participants' performance and ask how this is influenced by various manipulations. We did this, for example, in asking whether problem-solving is compromised by a concurrent memory load. The obvious assumption here is that mental processes are very quick, but nonetheless do take a measurable amount of time. By timing how quickly participants answer various questions, or perform various tasks, we can ask what factors speed up mental processes, and what factors slow them down.

Other sorts of data can also be brought into play. For example, what exactly is the nature of subvocalization? Does it literally involve covert speech and thus movements (perhaps tiny movements) of the tongue, the vocal chords, and so on? One way to find out would be to paralyze these various muscles. Would this disrupt use of the rehearsal loop? As it turns out, we don't have to perform this experiment; nature has performed it for us. Because of specific forms of neurological damage, some individuals have no ability to move these various muscles, and thus are quite unable to speak. These individuals are **anarthric**—i.e., without speech. Data indicate, however, that these individuals show a word-length effect in their data, and also sound-alike confusions, just as ordinary participants do. Apparently, then, actual muscle movements are not needed for subvocalization. Instead, "inner speech" probably relies on the brain areas responsible for *planning* the muscle movements of speech. This is by itself an interesting fact, but for present purposes, note the relevance of yet another type of data—observations from **neuropsychology**, concerned with how various forms of brain dysfunction influence observed performance.

We can pursue similar questions by examining the brain activity of people without any brain damage. Recent developments in **brain-imaging** technology allow us to examine which parts of the brain are more or less active as a research participant works on a task. When a participant is engaged in working-memory rehearsal, considerable brain activity is observed in areas that we know (from other evidence) are crucially involved in the production of spoken language, as well as in areas that play an important role in the perception and understanding of spoken language. These data are drawn from **cognitive neuroscience**—the study of the biological basis for cognitive functioning—and lend further support to the idea that claims about the "inner voice" and "inner ear" are more than casual metaphors.

We might also mention a sort of evidence we have *not* considered, namely, the research participants' own reports on what is going on in these tasks, or on what strategies they are using. As we discussed earlier, introspection is a research tool of uncertain value, and it seems entirely possible that people do not know exactly how they perform a memory span task. They might well have the intuition that they are talking to themselves (i.e., subvocalizing) in this task, but the relation between the inner ear and actual hearing, or the relation between the rehearsal loop and the executive, is not intuitively obvious. Hence participants' testimonials play little role in our account.

Finally, it is crucial to note that we have built our argument with several lines of evidence: Our account had to be compatible with the initial observations, but the account also led us to predict other observations, predictions that, as it turns out, were all correct. This pattern is a common one in research: We start with data, construct an account of those data, then seek further results to confirm, or disconfirm, our account. In addition, it is important that no one line of evidence is by itself decisive. There are probably other ways to explain our initial observations about span, if those effects were all we had to go on. There are also other ways to explain the other individual results we have mentioned, if these likewise were considered in isolation. The key comes in finding an account that will fit with all of the available data. Of course, sometimes the account we began with *doesn't* fit with all the data; in that case, we must revise our theory and start the process all over again. (As it turns out, some investigators think this is the case with the working-memory model we've been discussing; we'll return to this point in Chapter 5.) But when we have done our work well, there will be just one theoretical account that fits with the full data pattern, and this will be our assurance that we have correctly reconstructed what is going on, invisibly and never directly observed, in the mind. At that point, we will conclude that there is no other way to explain the data. This is what tells us we have the theory right.

## WORKING MEMORY IN A BROADER CONTEXT

Having made all of these methodological points, let us round out this section with one final comment: Why should we care about the structure of working mem-

ory? Why is this interesting? The memory-span task itself seems quite unnatural—how often do we need to memorize a set of unrelated numbers or letters? For that matter, how often do we need to work on some problem while simultaneously saying "tah-tah-tah" over and over? In short, what does this task, and this procedure, have to do with things we care about?

The answer to these questions allows us to replay an issue we have already discussed: There is a vast number of circumstances in which we rely on working memory and so, if we understand working memory, we move toward an understanding of this far broader set of problems and issues. For example, bear in mind our initial comments about the role of working memory in reading, or in any other task in which you must store early "products," keeping them ready for integration with later products. One might imagine that many tasks have this character—reading, reasoning, and problem-solving are a few. If you make effective use of working memory, therefore, you will have an advantage in all of these domains. Indeed, some scholars have suggested that "intelligence" in many domains amounts to nothing more than excess capacity in working memory. (See, for example, Kyllonen & Cristal, 1990.)

In a similar vein, the use of articulatory rehearsal seems a simple trick—a trick you use quite spontaneously, a trick in which you take no special pride. But it is a trick you had to learn, and young children, for example, often seem not to know the trick. There is some indication that this can be a problem for these children in learning to read: Without the option of relying on articulatory rehearsal, reading becomes much more difficult. It also appears that the rehearsal loop plays an important role when someone is learning new vocabulary, including vocabulary in a new language (Baddeley, Gathercole & Papagno, 1998; Gathercole et al., 1999). So here, too, is an important function of the working-memory system.

Here is a rather different example: Many individuals seem particularly vulnerable to depression. Sad memories and unhappy ideas spontaneously intrude into their thoughts, poisoning their mood and their subsequent thinking. This sequence of thoughts, it turns out, is recorded (where else?) in working memory, and so it seems possible to defeat these intrusive thoughts by seizing control of working memory and occupying it with other contents. In this way, there is at least some indication that the saddening thoughts, and so the depression, can be avoided. By understanding working memory, we understand how this dynamic might function. (For discussion, see Teasdale et al., 1993.)

These examples can easily be multiplied but, by now, the point should be clear: Working memory and articulatory rehearsal are relevant to a wide range of mental activities, in adults and in children. Understanding working memory, therefore, may give us insight into a broad range of tasks. Similar claims can be made about many other cognitive resources: By understanding what it means to pay attention, we move toward an understanding of all the contexts in which attention plays a role. By understanding how we comprehend text, or how we use our knowledge to supplement our perceptions, we move toward an understanding of all the contexts in which these play a part. And in each case the number of such contexts is vast.

We end this section, therefore, by echoing a comment we have already made: The machinery of cognition is essential to virtually all of our waking activities (and perhaps some of our sleeping activities, as well). We have given a few examples, including some that seem explicitly "intellectual" (reasoning, problem-solving) and some that seem not (depression). The scope of cognitive psychology is broad indeed, and the relevance of our research is wide.

## Chapter Summary

1. Cognitive psychology is concerned with how people remember, pay attention, and think. The importance of all these issues arises in part from the fact that most of what we do, think, and feel is guided by things we already know. One example is the comprehension of a simple story, which turns out to be heavily influenced by the knowledge we supply.

2. Cognitive psychology emerged as a separate discipline in the late 1950s, and its powerful impact on the wider field of psychology has led many to speak of this emergence as the *cognitive revolution*. One predecessor of cognitive psychology was the nineteenth-century movement that emphasized *introspection* as the main research tool for psychology. Psychologists soon became disenchanted with this movement, however, for several reasons. Introspection cannot inform us about unconscious mental events. Even with conscious events, claims rooted in introspection are often untestable, since there is no way for an independent observer to check on the accuracy or completeness of an introspective report.

3. The *behaviorist* movement rejected introspection as a method, and insisted instead that psychology speak only of mechanisms and processes that were objective and out in the open for all to observe. However, evidence suggests that our thinking, behavior, and feelings are often shaped by our perception or understanding of the events we experience. This is problematic for the behaviorists: "Perception" and "understanding" are exactly the sort of mental process that the behaviorists regarded as subjective and not open to scientific study.

4. In order to study mental events, psychologists have turned to a method in which one focuses on observable events, but then asks what (invisible) events must have taken place in order to make these (visible) effects possible. In many cases, this involves hypotheses about *information-processing* events, so that, in general, human mental processes can be described in terms similar to those used to describe computer processes.

5. Research in *working memory* provides an example of how cognitive psychologists use evidence. One theory of working memory proposes that this memory consists of a *central executive* and a small number of *low-level assistants* including the *articulatory rehearsal loop*, which stores material by means of covert speech. Many forms of evidence are used in supporting this account: measures of working memory's holding capacity in various circumstances, the nature of errors people make when using working memory, the speed of performance in working-memory tasks, evidence drawn from the study of people with brain damage, and evidence drawn from brain-imaging technology.

# *The Neural Basis for Cognition*

In Chapter 1, we noted that cognitive psychologists rely on many sorts of evidence—response times, error rates, patterns that are uniform from one person to the next, and patterns that describe how people differ from one another. No one source of data is more important or more useful than the others; all contribute to the broad fabric of evidence that allows us to test our theories.

One form of evidence, however, does need its own treatment, and indeed its own chapter: evidence concerning the brain functioning that makes cognition possible. We will encounter this biologically rooted evidence throughout this book, woven together with other sorts of data as we develop and test our theories. But, first, we need to lay the appropriate foundation—some background information about the brain and about the methods used to study the brain.

## Capgras Syndrome: An Initial Example

The human brain is an extraordinarily complex organ, in which the functioning of the whole is dependent on many interconnected systems. Because of this complexity, the brain's functioning can break down in many different ways, with damage virtually anywhere in the brain producing detectable—and often highly disruptive—symptoms. These symptoms are often tragic for the afflicted persons and their families, but they can also be a rich source of insight into how the brain is organized and how the various systems in the brain function.

Consider, for example, a remarkable disorder known as **Capgras Syndrome** (Capgras & Reboul-Lachaux, 1923). This disorder is rare on its own, but seems to be one of the accompaniments to Alzheimer's Syndrome, and so is sometimes observed among the elderly (Harwood, Barker, Ownby & Duara, 1999). Someone with Capgras Syndrome is still fully able to recognize the people in her world—her husband, her parents, her friends—but she is utterly convinced that these people are not who they appear to be. The real husband, the real son, the afflicted person insists, has been kidnapped (or worse). The person now on the scene, therefore, isn't the genuine article; instead, he or she must be a well-trained, well-disguised impostor.

Imagine what it is like to have this disorder. You turn to someone you know extremely well—perhaps your father—and say, "You look like my father, sound like him, and act like him. But I can tell that you're not my father. *Who are you?*"

Often a person with this syndrome insists that there are slight differences between the impostor and the person he or she has replaced—subtle changes in personality, or tiny changes in appearance. Of course, no one else detects these (non-existent) differences, compounding the bewilderment experienced by the Capgras sufferer. These feelings spiral upward, with the patient developing all sorts of paranoid suspicions about why a loved one has been replaced, and why no one seems to acknowledge this replacement. In the extreme, the Capgras sufferer may be led to desperate steps, in some cases murdering the sup-posed impostor in an attempt to end the charade and relocate the "genuine" character. In one case, a Capgras patient was convinced his father had been replaced by a robot and so decapitated him in order to look for the batteries and microfilm in his head (Blount, 1984).

What is going on here? The answer, according to some researchers, lies in the fact that facial recognition involves two separate systems in the brain, one of which leads to a cognitive appraisal ("I recall what my father looks like, and you closely resemble him") and the other to a more global, somewhat emotional appraisal ("You look wonderfully familiar to me, and also trigger a warm response in me"). The concordance of these two appraisals then leads to the certainty of recognition ("You obviously *are* my father"). In Capgras Syndrome, though, the latter (affective) processing is disrupted, leading to the intellectual identification without the global familiarity response (Ellis & Young, 1990; De Haan et al., 1992; Ramachandran & Blakeslee, 1998); "You resemble my father, but trigger no sense of familiarity, so you must be someone else."

### TESTING CLAIMS ABOUT CAPGRAS SYNDROME

This account fits well with the basic symptoms of Capgras Syndrome, but is it correct? One line of support comes from studies with neurologically undamaged people. These studies confirm that memory for factual knowledge is, in fact, often separable from the warm sense of familiarity, so that we can sometimes have familiarity with no supporting factual memories, and factual memories with no sense of familiarity. Likewise, familiarity and memory for factual knowledge are responsive to different sorts of influences, as we might expect if they depend on different brain systems. (We will have more to say about these issues, and about the sense of familiarity, in Chapter 6.)

These claims, drawn from the way ordinary people behave in various memory tests, lend support to the "two systems" account of Capgras Syndrome. We can find further support for the theory by looking at the brains of people with this syndrome. Is the syndrome reliably produced by damage to particular structures in the brain? If so, which structures are they?

Fifty years ago, questions like these could be answered only through *post mortem* examination of the brain. In the last few decades, however, medical researchers have developed extraordinary **neuroimaging techniques** that allow us to take high-quality, three-dimensional "pictures" of living brains, without in any way disturbing the brains' owners. We will have more to say about neuroimaging later, but first, what do these techniques tell us about Capgras Syndrome?

Neuroimaging data suggest a link between this syndrome and abnormalities in several different brain sites, generally on the right side of the head, and particularly in the *temporal* and *frontal* lobes (e.g., Edelstyn & Oyebode, 1999; also O'Connor et al., 1996; see Figure 2.1). Why should damage here be associated with Capgras Syndrome? One proposal suggests that the key problem in the temporal region is damage to circuits involving the **amygdala**, whereas damage in the frontal area is likely to involve damage to the **right prefrontal cortex**. What function do these structures support when they're not damaged? The amygdala seems in many contexts to serve as an "emotional evaluator," helping an organism to detect threats of various sorts, and presumably helping the organism to detect "lack of threat." It seems plausible, then, that the amygdala is essential for making the judgment of "you look familiar to me, and trigger a warm emotional feeling"—one-half of our two-systems hypothesis.

What about the prefrontal cortex, the area of the frontal lobe that is also damaged in Capgras Syndrome? Here we can rely on neuroimaging to track activity levels in different sites in a living brain. This allows us to answer such questions as, When a person is reading, which brain regions are particularly active? How about when a person is listening to music? And so on. With studies of this sort, we have learned that the prefrontal cortex is particularly active whenever someone is engaged in activities that require what we might call "executive control," or "executive decisions." To see how this might apply to Capgras Syndrome, consider a study done with patients suffering from an entirely different problem, schizophrenia (Silbersweig et al., 1995). Neuroimaging revealed *diminished* activity in the patients' frontal lobes when these patients were experiencing hallucinations. One plausible explanation of this finding is that the diminished activity reflects a decreased ability to distinguish internal events (thoughts) from external ones (voices), or to distinguish imagined events from real ones. (For supporting data, see Glisky et al., 1995.)

How is this relevant to Capgras Syndrome? With damage to the frontal lobe, Capgras patients may be less able to keep track of what is real and what is not; what is plausible and what is not. As a result, a Capgras patient may end up accepting delusions that you or I would find utterly bizarre—delusions, for example, about robots impersonating people, and so on.

Further support for this idea comes from the fact that neuroimaging studies show strong activation in the right prefrontal cortex during tasks that require "strategic memory retrieval"—that is, memory retrieval that is deliberate, effortful, and controlled (Moscovitch, 1994; Schacter, 1996). One plausible interpretation of this finding is that the right prefrontal cortex plays a crucial role in deciding what happened when, in figuring out which elements were part of which episodes. This fits with the fact that damage to the right prefrontal cortex is often associated with a class of memory error called **confabulations**: sincerely offered, detailed, but utterly false recollections. For example, one patient with damage in this brain region recalled confidently that he and his wife had been married for only four months, when in fact they had been married for over 30 years. Remarkably, this same patient correctly remembered that he and his wife had four children, the youngest of whom was 22 (Moscovitch, 1995).

These data fit well with the picture we are building of Capgras Syndrome. The right prefrontal cortex, it seems, plays a central role whenever we need to sort through the episodes of our lives, figuring out what happened in which context and which episodes did not happen at all. Damage here can (in some patients) lead to confabulation, but (if accompanied by other sorts of brain damage) can also contribute to the bizarre beliefs that are one of the symptoms of Capgras Syndrome.

## WHAT DO WE LEARN FROM CAPGRAS SYNDROME?

As we have now seen, several lines of evidence fit together nicely in our account of Capgras Syndrome. Behavioral data, from neurologically intact individuals, support the idea that familiarity and factual memory depend on different brain systems. One of the sites of brain damage in Capgras Syndrome is likely to be the amygdala; this could plausibly be the source of the disruption to familiarity judgments. Another site of the brain damage, the right prefrontal cortex, could make possible the paranoid delusions experienced by the Capgras patient; we can confirm this by means of neuroimaging data in normal people, and also by examining the role of the prefrontal cortex in other patients—patients with schizophrenia, for example, or patients with different sorts of memory problems. Overall, then, many findings support our account, leaving us, it seems, with a reasonably compelling explanation of a truly bizarre syndrome. (For more on this syndrome and further discussion of the evidence pertinent to this account, see Ramachandran & Blakeslee, 1998.)

Note in addition, that this account of Capgras Syndrome actually serves us in several ways. For medical purposes, this account helps us understand why these patients show the symptoms they do, and why this pattern of brain damage leads to this pattern of behaviors. We can hope that this understanding will lead to better forms of therapy for these patients, and perhaps someday, even a cure.

This account of Capgras Syndrome also serves those hoping to understand how the brain functions in ordinary people—that is, people without brain damage. By studying this syndrome (and others), we gain important information about how the brain works when all systems are intact. As an illustration, consider what this syndrome teaches us about how the various parts of the brain must work together for even the simplest achievement. The task of recognizing your father, for example, seems to rely on several

different brain areas: One part of the brain stores the factual memory of what your father looks like. Another part of the brain is responsible for analyzing the visual input and then comparing this input to the factual information provided from memory in order to determine if there's a "match" or not. A third site (involving the amygdala) provides the emotional evaluation of the input (this is apparently one of the sites disrupted in Capgras Syndrome). A fourth site presumably assembles the data from all these other sites, and so registers the fact that the face being inspected does match the factual recollection of your father's face and (in a normal brain) also produces a warm sense of familiarity. Ordinarily, all of these brain areas work together, allowing the recognition of your father's face to go smoothly forward. When the coordination among these areas is disrupted, as it seems to be in Capgras Syndrome, weird symptoms result.

In short, then, the study of Capgras Syndrome can tell us about cases of *brain damage*, and can also tell us about the brain's functioning in the *absence* of damage. In addition, let's be clear that, in this book, our emphasis will not be on the brain itself. Instead, our focus will be on the various capacities that the brain makes possible—our ability to remember, for example, or to reason, or to pay attention. Sometimes, we can make great progress in understanding these capacities without a close consideration of the brain, but in many other cases, information about the brain can move us forward considerably—by suggesting possible mechanisms for a particular function, or confirming mechanisms already hypothesized.

For example, consider the common experience in which a friend has gotten new glasses or changed his hair style. You look at your friend and immediately know that *something* has changed, but you are at a loss to specify *what* has changed. (And often in this situation, you end up offering lame hypotheses, perhaps asking, "Did you just grow that beard?" even though you've seen the beard a thousand times before.) Observations like these can be explained with reference to the separate memory systems we've already described, with one memory system providing a basis for familiarity and the other providing our factual knowledge. If a friend changed his style of glasses, the familiarity system detects the change (because with the new glasses, your friend looks a bit *less* familiar), but the factual knowledge system may not be able to specify what exactly the change was.

We will return to this odd phenomenon in Chapter 6, but, in the meantime, we can welcome the Capgras evidence as a way of testing claims about these two separate memory systems—what jobs they do, and how they (usually) work together. In this fashion, our understanding of cases involving brain damage can be used to evaluate claims about ordinary memory functioning, including cases (like the one just described) in which memory doesn't provide us with all the information we want.

Overall, then, the study of Capgras Syndrome can serve us on many levels—providing us with information of clinical importance, telling us about the brain's ordinary functioning, and also providing evidence pertinent to the study of day-to-day cognition. In addition, our discussion of Capgras serves us in one further way: In considering the source of this bizarre syndrome, we had to refer to different brain areas (the amygdala, for example, and the frontal cortex); we also had to rely on several different research techniques. Thus, we can use this case to illustrate the fact, stated at this chapter's start, that this is clearly a domain in which we need some technical foundations before we can build our theories. Let's start building those foundations.

## The Principal Structures of the Brain

The human brain weighs between 3 and 4 pounds; it's roughly the size of a small melon. Yet this relatively small structure has been estimated to contain 1,000,000,000,000 nerve cells (that's $10^{12}$), each of which is connected to 10,000 or so of the others—for a total of roughly 10 million billion connections. How should we begin our study of this densely packed, incredibly complex organ?

Let's start with the fact that different parts of the brain clearly perform different jobs. We have known this for more than a century, since clinical evidence has long made it clear that the symptoms observed

after brain damage depend heavily on where in the brain the damage occurred. In 1848, a horrible construction accident caused Phineas Gage to suffer damage in the frontmost part of his brain; this damage led to severe intellectual and emotional problems. In 1861, physician Paul Broca noted that damage in a different location, on the left side of the brain, led to a severe disruption of language skills. In 1911, Edouard Claparède reported his observations with patients who suffered from profound memory loss, a loss produced by damage in still another part of the brain.

Clearly, therefore, we will need to understand brain functioning with reference to brain anatomy. Where was the damage that Gage suffered? Where exactly was the damage in Broca's patients, or Claparède's? In this section, we fill in some basics of brain anatomy.

### HINDBRAIN, MIDBRAIN, FOREBRAIN

The human brain is divided into three main structures: the hindbrain, the midbrain, and the forebrain. The **hindbrain** sits directly atop the spinal cord and includes several structures crucial for controlling key life functions. It's here, for example, that the rhythm of heartbeats is controlled, and the rhythm of breathing. The hindbrain also plays an essential role in maintaining the body's overall "tone," both in the musculature (the hindbrain helps maintain posture and balance) and in the rest of the brain (the hindbrain helps regulate the brain's level of alertness and is responsible for initiating sleep and dreaming).

The largest area of the hindbrain is the **cerebellum**. For many years, investigators believed the cerebellum's main role was in the coordination of our bodily movements and balance. Recent studies, however, suggest that the cerebellum also plays an important role in some sorts of learning—in particular, the learning of motor skills, such as how to ride a bicycle or execute a dance step.

The **midbrain** also plays an important role in coordinating our movements, including the skilled, precise movements of our eyes as we explore the visual world. Also located in the midbrain are circuits that play a key role in relaying auditory information from the ears to the areas (in the forebrain) where

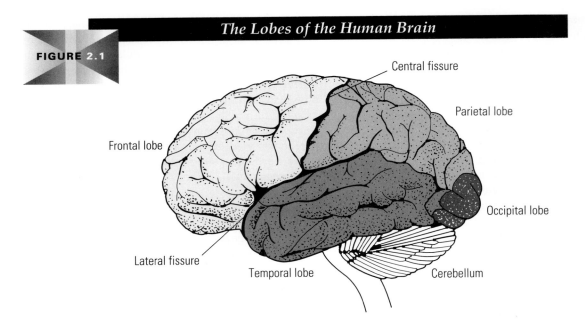

## The Lobes of the Human Brain

**FIGURE 2.1**

Central fissure

Parietal lobe

Frontal lobe

Occipital lobe

Lateral fissure

Temporal lobe

Cerebellum

The four lobes of the forebrain surround (and hide from view) the midbrain and most of the hindbrain. (The cerebellum is the only part of the hindbrain that is visible.) This side-view shows the brain's left cerebral hemisphere (and so, here, the left-hand side of the drawing is the front of the head); the structures on the right side of the brain are similar.

such information is processed and interpreted. Still other structures in the midbrain help to regulate our experience of pain.

For our purposes, though, the most interesting brain region (and also, in humans, the largest region) is the **forebrain**. Pictures of the brain (like the one in Figure 2.1) show very little other than the forebrain, because this structure surrounds (and hides from view) the entire midbrain and most of the hindbrain. Of course, it is only the outer surface of the forebrain that is visible in such pictures; this is the **cortex** (from the Latin word for "tree bark").

The cortex is just a thin covering on the outer surface of the brain; on average, it is a mere 3 mm thick. Nonetheless, there is a great deal of cortical tissue; by some estimates, the cortex comprises 80% of the human brain. This considerable volume is made pos-

sible by the fact that the cortex, thin as it is, consists of a very large sheet of tissue; if stretched out flat, it would cover roughly two square feet. But the cortex isn't stretched flat; instead, it is all crumpled up and jammed into the limited space inside the skull. It's this crumpling that produces the brain's most obvious visual feature—the wrinkles or **convolutions** that cover the brain's outer surface.

Some of the "valleys" in between the wrinkles are actually deep grooves that anatomically divide the brain into different sections. The deepest groove is the *longitudinal fissure*, which separates the left **cerebral hemisphere** from the right. Other fissures divide the cortex in each hemisphere into four lobes (as shown in Figure 2.1). The **frontal lobes** form the front of the brain—right behind the forehead. The *central fissure* divides the frontal lobes on each side of the brain from the **parietal lobes**, the brain's topmost part. The bottom edge of the frontal lobes is marked by the *lateral fissure*, and below this are the **temporal lobes**. Finally, at the very back of the brain, connected to the parietal and temporal lobes, are the **occipital lobes**.

## SUBCORTICAL STRUCTURES

The cortex, as large as it is, is only part of the forebrain. Hidden from view, underneath the cortex, are many other structures. One of these is the **thalamus**, a brain region that acts as a "relay station" for nearly all the sensory information going to the cortex. Directly underneath the thalamus is the **hypothalamus**, a structure that plays a crucial role in the control of motivated behaviors such as eating, drinking, and sexual activity.

Surrounding the thalamus and hypothalamus is another set of interconnected structures that together form the **limbic system** (see Figure 2.2). Included here are the **hippocampus**, the **mammillary bodies**, and the **amygdala**, all located underneath the cortex in the temporal lobe. These structures play a crucial role in learning and memory, and in emotional processing. The patient H.M., whom we discussed in Chapter 1, developed his profound amnesia after surgeons removed his hippocampus and mammillary bodies—a strong confirmation of the role of these structures in the formation of new memories. Damage to the amygdala is, as we have seen, likely to be one of the contributors to Capgras Syndrome. We suggested earlier that this is because the amygdala serves as some sort of emotional evaluator. Without an amygdala, therefore, an individual is unable to experience the warm sense of familiarity that is usually produced by seeing a loved one's face.

Like most parts of the brain, these subcortical structures come in pairs, and so there is a hippocampus on the left side of the brain and another on the

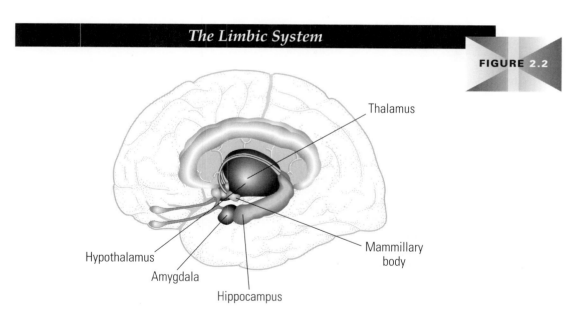

**The Limbic System**

FIGURE 2.2

Thalamus

Hypothalamus

Amygdala

Hippocampus

Mammillary body

In this drawing, we have pretended that the left cerebral hemisphere is transparent, so that we can see through it to the limbic system underneath. This system includes a number of subcortical structures that play a crucial role in learning and memory and in emotional processing.

right, a left-side amygdala and a right one. Of course, the same is true for cortical structures: There is a temporal cortex in the left hemisphere and another in the right, a left occipital cortex and a right one, and so on. In all cases, cortical and subcortical, the two structures in each pair have roughly the same shape, the same position in their respective sides of the brain, and the same pattern of connections to other brain areas. Even so, there are differences between the left-side and right-side structures. Often, there are small contrasts in shape or size. In many other cases, we can document differences in *function*, with the left-hemisphere structure involved in somewhat different tasks, and presumably playing a somewhat different role, from the corresponding right-hemisphere structure.

Let's bear in mind, though, that the two halves of the brain work together; the functioning of one side is closely integrated with that of the other side. This integration is made possible by the **commissures**, thick bundles of fibers that carry information back and forth between the two hemispheres. The largest commissure is the **corpus callosum**; this is the main structure that is severed when doctors perform "split brain surgery" as a remedy for epilepsy.

## EVIDENCE FOR FUNCTIONAL SPECIALIZATION

As we have noted, the specific symptoms that result from brain damage depend heavily on the site of the damage. A **lesion** (a specific area of damage) on the hippocampus produces memory problems but not language disorders; a lesion on the occipital cortex produces problems in vision but spares the other sense modalities. The consequences of brain lesions also depend on *which hemisphere* is damaged: damage to the left side of the frontal lobe (but not the right) is likely to produce a disruption of language use; damage to the right parietal lobe (but not the left) is likely to produce disruption in the ability to recognize faces. These facts obviously suggest that different brain areas perform different functions,

**FIGURE 2.3**

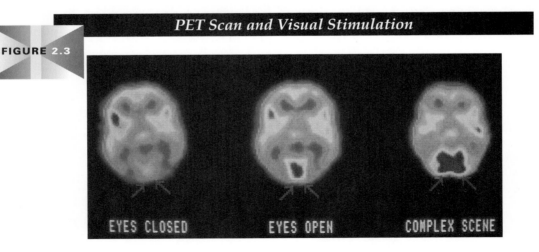

*PET Scan and Visual Stimulation*

EYES CLOSED      EYES OPEN      COMPLEX SCENE

PET scans measure how much glucose (the brain's fuel) is being used at specific locations within the brain; this provides a measurement of that location's activity level at a certain moment in time. In the figure, the brain is viewed from above, with the front of the head at the top of the drawing, and the back at the bottom. As the figure shows, visual processing involves increased activity in the occipital cortex. (Photograph by Dr. John Mazziotta et al./Photo Researchers)

*Magnetic Resonance Imaging*

**FIGURE** 2.4

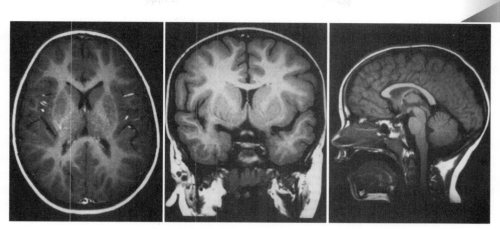

Magnetic resonance imaging produces magnificently detailed pictures of the brain. The left panel shows a 'slice' of the brain viewed from the top of the head (the front of the head is at the top of the image). The middle panel shows a 'slice' of the brain viewed from the front; the separation of the two hemispheres is clearly visible, and so are some of the commissures linking the two brain halves. The right panel shows a 'slice' of the brain viewed from the side; many of the structures in the limbic system (Figure 2.2) are easily seen.

with the pattern of symptoms tied to the specific functions that have been disrupted.

A similar conclusion follows from neuroimaging data. As we mentioned in our discussion of Capgras Syndrome, neuroimaging techniques allow us to take precise three-dimensional pictures of the brain. Several such techniques are available, including computerized axial tomography, or **CT scans** (sometimes called CAT scans), and positron emission tomography, or **PET scans** (see Figure 2.3). CT scans use X-rays to study the brain's *anatomy*. PET scans provide a precise assessment of how blood is flowing through each region of the brain, to study the brain's functioning. (This method rests on the fact that, when a particular brain area is more active, it needs—and receives—a greater blood flow.)

In general, these techniques rely on a bank of detectors surrounding the head—a bank of X-ray detectors for CT scans, a bank of positron detectors for PET scans. A computer then compares the signals received by each of the detectors, and uses this information to pinpoint the source of each signal. In this way, the computer can reconstruct a three-dimensional map (or image) of the brain—a map, in CT scans, that tells us what structures are where, or, in PET scans, that tells us what regions are particularly active or inactive at any point in time.

In recent years, investigators have relied more and more on two newer techniques: **magnetic resonance imaging (MRI;** see Figure 2.4) and **functional magnetic-resonance imaging (fMRI)**. MRI scans start by passing a magnetic field through the brain; this allows investigators, first, to align the spins of the atoms that make up the brain tissue, and then to disrupt this alignment with a further pulse of energy. This causes minute fluctuations in the brain's magnetic field, and these fluctuations are (as in the other forms of scanning) recorded by a bank of detectors arrayed around the person's head, analyzed by a computer, and assembled into a detailed three-dimensional representation of the brain. An fMRI scan uses similar principles, but measures the rapidly changing pattern of blood flow and oxygen use in each region of the brain. In this way, fMRI scans provide an incredibly precise picture of the brain's moment-by-moment activities.

PET and fMRI scans show us that the pattern of activation across the brain depends heavily on what task the person is performing. Thus, for example, the brain sites particularly active during silent reading are different from the brain sites particularly active during problem-solving or when someone is mentally rehearsing a list of to-be-remembered items. Again, this suggests that different brain areas perform different functions and make different contributions to the task under way. If a particular function is crucial for a specific task, then the relevant brain area will be highly activated when that task is being performed; if the particular function plays little or no role in that task, then we will observe low levels of activation in the relevant brain area during the task.

It's clear, therefore, that different portions of the brain perform different functions, but how should we think about these functions? What job does the occipital cortex perform? What work does the temporal lobe do? Answering these questions is referred to as the **localization of function**.

Popular accounts of the brain speak of the "hunger center," the "reading center," and so on, with the suggestion that specific regions of the brain have sole responsibility over this or that complex task. However, these descriptions cast things in too simple a fashion. Recall our discussion of Capgras Syndrome, which suggested that the simple task of recognizing one's father relied on multiple brain areas. It turns out that the same is true for virtually any cognitive task, whether it's remembering last summer's vacation,

making a decision, or forming a visual image. This obviously speaks against the simple-minded notion that this or that brain structure is the "processing center" needed for a single task.

Nonetheless, the fact remains that different brain sites do perform different functions. In the next sections, we'll look at the functions of some of the larger brain structures we have already discussed.

## PRIMARY MOTOR PROJECTION AREAS

The discovery of the **primary motor projection areas** dates back to the 1860s, when investigators began to apply mild electric current to various portions of the cortex in anesthetized animals. This stimulation often led to specific movements, so that current applied to one site caused a movement of the left front leg, while current applied to a different site caused the ears to perk up, and so on. These movements showed a pattern of **contralateral control**, with stimulation to the left hemisphere leading to movements on the right side of the body, and vice versa.

The sites stimulated in these studies are generally in the primary motor projection area, a strip of tissue toward the rear of the frontal lobe (Figure 2.5A). This strip of tissue seems to be the departure point for nerve cells that send their signals to lower parts of the brain and the spinal cord and that carry the directives that ultimately result in muscle movement. The term "projection" is borrowed from geography, because these brain areas seem to form "maps" of the body, with particular positions on the cortex corresponding to particular parts of the body.

Investigators have been able to draw these maps in some detail, and Figure 2.5B shows one representation of the result. In the figure, a drawing of a person has been overlaid on a depiction of the brain, with each part of the little person positioned on top of the area of the brain that controls its movement. As the figure shows, areas of the body that we can move with great precision (fingers and lips, for instance) have a lot of cortical area devoted to them; areas of the body over which we have less control (the shoulder or the back, for instance) receive less cortical coverage.

## The Primary Motor Projection Area

FIGURE 2.5

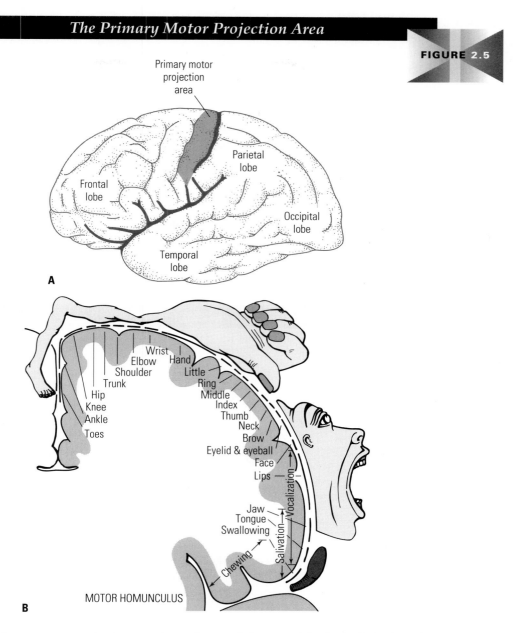

Primary motor projection area

Parietal lobe

Frontal lobe

Occipital lobe

Temporal lobe

**A**

Wrist
Elbow  Hand
Shoulder  Little
Trunk  Ring
Hip  Middle
Knee  Index
Ankle  Thumb
Toes  Neck
Brow
Eyelid & eyeball
Face
Lips

Jaw
Tongue
Swallowing

Chewing

Salivation

Vocalization

MOTOR HOMUNCULUS

**B**

The primary motor projection area, located toward the rear of the frontal lobe (Panel A), sends out the signals that ultimately result in muscle movement. Panel B shows which parts of the body are controlled by different parts of the projection area; clearly, more cortical space is devoted to the body parts that we can move with greatest precision. (After Penfield & Roberts, 1959; Rasmussen and Milner, 1977)

## PRIMARY SENSORY PROJECTION AREAS

The primary *motor* projection areas, then, are the departure point for information *leaving* the cortex and heading toward the muscles. Similarly, the **primary sensory projection areas** are the main points of *arrival* in the cortex for information from the eyes, the ears, and other sensory organs.

Information arriving from the skin senses (your sense of touch, or your sense of temperature) is projected to a region in the parietal lobe, just behind the motor projection area; this is labeled the "somatosensory" area in Figure 2.6. If a patient's brain is stimulated in this region (with electrical current or touch), the patient will typically report a tingling sensation in a specific part of his body. Figure 2.6 also shows the region in the temporal lobes that functions as the primary projection area for hearing. If directly stimulated here, patients hear clicks, buzzes, and hums. An area in the occipital lobes serves as the primary projection area for vision; stimulation here produces the experience of seeing flashes of light or visual patterns.

These sensory projection areas differ from each other in important ways, but they also have certain features in common. First, each of these areas provides a "map" of the sensory environment. In the parietal lobe, each part of the body's surface is represented by its own region on the cortex; areas of the body that are near to each other are typically represented by similarly nearby areas in the brain. In the occipital lobe, different regions of *visual space* each

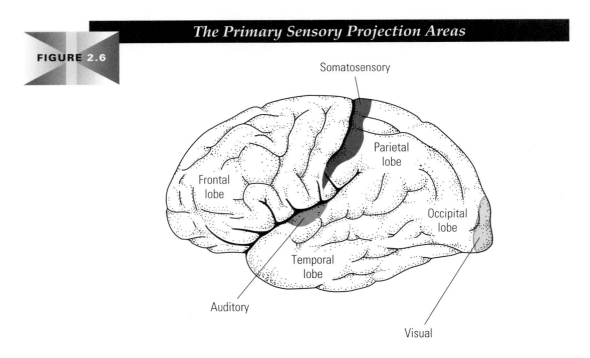

**The Primary Sensory Projection Areas**

**FIGURE 2.6**

Information arriving from the skin senses is projected to a region in the parietal lobe (the somatosensory projection area). Information arriving from the eyes is projected to the occipital lobe; information from the ears to the temporal lobe. (After Cobb, 1941)

## The Sensory Homunculus

**FIGURE** 2.7

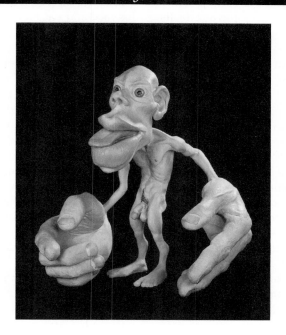

In the somatosensory projection area, a lot of cortical space is devoted to parts of the body that are extremely sensitive to touch (e.g., the lips, tongue, and fingers). Relatively little space is devoted to parts of the body that are less sensitive (e.g., the shoulders or the legs). Here is an artist's rendition of what a person would look like if his actual appearance were proportional to the cortical area allotted to each body part! (Courtesy of the Natural History Museum, London)

have their own cortical representation, and again, adjacent areas of space are usually represented by adjacent brain sites. In the temporal lobe, different *frequencies of sound* each have their own cortical sites, and adjacent brain sites are responsive to adjacent frequencies.

Second, in each of these maps, the assignment of cortical space is governed by function, not by anatomical proportions. In the parietal lobes, parts of the body that are not very discriminating with regard to touch, even if they're physically large, get relatively little cortical area (Figure 2.7). Other, more sensitive, areas of the body (the lips, tongue, and fin-

gers, for example) get far more space. In the occipital lobes, more cortical surface is devoted to the *fovea*, the part of the eyeball that is most sensitive to detail.

Finally, these projection areas all respect the principle of contralateral control: The left parietal lobe receives its main input from the right side of the body, for example; the right temporal lobe receives its main input from the left ear. The same principle applies to the visual projection areas, but here the projection is not contralateral with regard to body parts; instead, it's contralateral with regard to *physical space*. Specifically, the visual projection area in the right cerebral hemisphere receives information from both the left eye and from the right, but the information it receives corresponds to the left half of visual space (that is, all of the things you see toward the left when you are looking straight ahead). The reverse is true for the left cerebral hemisphere—it receives information from both eyes, but only from the right half of visual space.

## ASSOCIATION AREAS

The projection areas described so far—both motor and sensory—make up only a small part of the human cortex—roughly 25%. The remaining cortical areas are traditionally referred to as the **association cortex**, on the idea that this section of the brain performs the task of *associating* simple ideas and sensations in order to form more complex thoughts and behaviors.

This terminology, however, may not be fully appropriate. For one thing, many areas of the association cortex seem to serve as projection areas—*nonprimary motor regions* critical for initiating and coordinating skilled movements, and *nonprimary sensory areas*, which play essential roles in the processing of visual and auditory information.

In addition, the term "association cortex" does nothing to reflect the fact that this large volume of brain tissue can be subdivided further on both functional and anatomical grounds. These subdivisions are perhaps best revealed by the diversity of symptoms that can result if the cortex is damaged in one or another specific location. For example, some lesions in the frontal lobe produce **apraxias**, disturbances in the initiation or organization of voluntary action. Other lesions (generally in the occipital cortex, or in the rearmost part of the parietal lobe) lead to **agnosias**, or disruptions in a person's ability to identify familiar objects. Agnosias usually affect one modality only, so that a patient with visual agnosia, for example, can recognize a fork by touch, but not by looking at it. A patient with auditory agnosia, by contrast, might be unable to identify the source of familiar voices, but might still recognize the face of the person speaking.

Still other lesions (usually in the parietal lobe) produce **neglect syndrome**, in which the individual seems to ignore half of the visual world. A patient afflicted with this syndrome will shave only half of his face and eat food from only half of his plate. If asked to read the word "pigpen," he will read "pen," and so on.

Damage in other areas causes still other symptoms. We mentioned earlier that lesions in the left frontal lobe, usually at sites just above the lateral fissure, can result in disruption to language capacities, a problem referred to as **aphasia**. The specific form of the aphasia depends on where exactly the lesion is located. Damage toward the front of this region, for example, close to the motor projection area, leads to difficulties with the production of speech; damage slightly further back in the brain (close to the auditory projection area) leads to problems in comprehending speech. Damage in nearby areas produces other language problems—problems with vocabulary, for example.

Finally, damage to the frontmost part of the frontal lobe, the **prefrontal area**, causes a variety of different problems; as we mentioned in our discussion of Capgras Syndrome, these generally seem to be problems of planning and the forming and implementing of strategies. Patients with damage here also show problems in inhibiting their own behaviors, probably because they are unable to use rules (whether social rules or self-generated ones) to control their actions; they are also prone to a variety of confusions, such as whether a remembered episode actually happened or was simply imagined.

We will have more to say about many of these diagnostic categories—aphasia, agnosia, neglect, and more—in upcoming chapters. There we'll be able to consider these disorders in the context of other things we know about language, object recognition, attention, and so on, and this will allow us to draw important lessons from these clinical data. Our point for the moment, though, is a more modest one: These various clinical patterns make it clear that the so-called association cortex contains many subregions, each specialized for a particular function, but with all of the subregions working together in virtually all aspects of our daily lives.

# The Visual System

So far, we have taken a fairly coarse view of the brain. We have spoken about large anatomical structures (the various lobes, the hippocampus, etc.) and large-scale *functionally* defined areas, such as the regions in which damage produces aphasia (suggesting that these regions are crucial for language) or regions in which damage produces amnesia (apparently regions crucial for memory).

But it is also useful to take a closer look at the brain, in order to examine the operations that make these larger-scale functions possible. In this section, we'll illustrate this sort of closer look by considering the brain systems that make *vision* possible. We've chosen vision as our example for two reasons: First, it is a modality through which humans acquire a huge amount of information, whether by reading or simply by viewing the objects and events that surround us. If we understand vision, therefore, we understand the processes that bring us much of our knowledge. Second, investigators in this area have made enormous progress, providing us with a rich portrait of how the visual system operates, and so the study of vision provides an impressive illustration of how the close study of the brain can proceed, and what it can teach us.

## THE PHOTORECEPTORS

You look around the world, and you are conscious of the many objects that surround you, each identifiable and each having a particular size, position, color, and texture. What makes all of this possible? The sequence of events begins, of course, with the eye.

Light is produced by many objects in our surroundings—the sun, candles, lamps, and so on—and this light then reflects off of most other objects. It is usually this reflected light—reflected from this book page, or from a friend's face—that launches the processes of vision. Some of this light hits the front surface of the eyeball, passes through the **cornea** and then the **lens**, and then hits the **retina**—the light-sensitive tissue that lines the back of the eyeball (Figure 2.8). The cornea and lens focus the incoming light, just as a camera lens might, so that a sharp image is cast onto the retina. The cornea is fixed in its shape, but the shape of the lens can be adjusted by a band of muscle that surrounds it. When the muscle tightens, the lens bulges somewhat, creating the proper shape for focusing images cast by nearby objects; when the muscle relaxes, the lens returns to a flatter shape, allowing the proper focus of farther-away objects.

On the retina, there are two types of **photoreceptors**, cells that respond directly to the incoming light. These two types—the **rods** and the **cones**—are different in many ways. Rods are sensitive to much lower levels of light, and so play an essential role whenever we're moving around in semidarkness, or whenever we're trying to view a fairly dim stimulus. But the rods are also color blind: They distinguish among different *intensities* of light (and so contribute to our perception of brightness) but provide no means of discriminating one hue from another.

Cones are, overall, less sensitive than rods, and so need more incoming light to operate at all. But cones are sensitive to color differences. More precisely, there are three different types of cones, each having its own pattern of sensitivities to different wavelengths. We perceive color, therefore, by comparing the outputs from these three cone types. Strong firing from only the cones that prefer short wavelengths, for example, accompanied by weak (or no) firing from the other cone types signals *purple*. *Blue* is signaled by equally strong firing from the cones that prefer short wavelengths and those that prefer medium wavelengths, with only modest firing by cones that prefer long wavelengths. And so on.

Cones also have another crucial function: They allow us to discern fine detail. The ability to see detail is referred to as **acuity**, and acuity is much higher for the cones than it is for the rods. This explains why we point our eyes toward a target whenever we wish to perceive it in detail. What we are actually doing is positioning our eyes so that the image of the target falls onto the **fovea**—the very center of the retina. Here cones far outnumber rods, and as a result, this is the region of the retina with the greatest acuity.

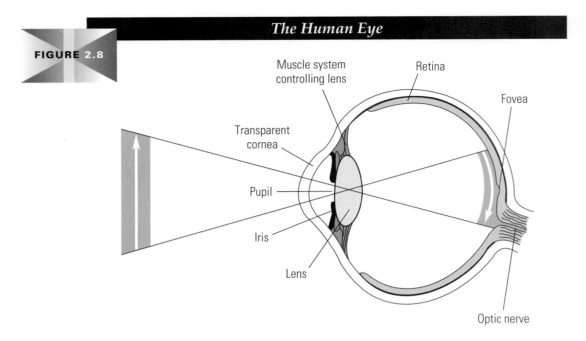

*The Human Eye*

**FIGURE 2.8**

Muscle system
controlling lens

Retina

Fovea

Transparent
cornea

Pupil

Iris

Lens

Optic nerve

Light enters the eye through the pupil and is focused by the cornea and the lens so that a sharp image is projected onto the light-sensitive retina. The fovea is the region of the retina with the greatest sensitivity to detail.

As one moves away from the fovea and into the **visual periphery**, the rods predominate; well out into the periphery, there are no cones at all. This is why we're better able to see very dim lights out of the corner of our eyes. Sailors and astronomers have known this for years; when looking at a barely visible star, they know that it's best not to look directly at the star's location. By looking slightly away from the star, they ensure that the star's image will fall outside of the fovea, onto a region of the retina replete with the more light-sensitive rods.

### THE OPTIC NERVE

Rods and cones do not report directly to the brain. Instead, the photoreceptors directly stimulate *bipolar cells*, which in turn excite *ganglion cells*. The ganglion cells collect information from all over the retina and then gather together to form the bundle of nerve fibers that we call the **optic nerve**. The optic nerve leaves the eyeball and carries information to various sites in the brain. Most of the fibers go first to an important waystation in the thalamus called the **lateral geniculate nucleus**, or LGN; from there, information is transmitted to the primary projection area for vision, in the occipital cortex (Figure 2.9).

Let's be clear, though, that the optic nerve is far more than a mere cable that conducts signals from one site to another. Instead, the cells that link retina to brain are already engaged in the task of analyzing the visual input. One example of this lies in the phenomenon of **lateral inhibition**, a pattern in which cells, when stimulated, inhibit the activity of neighboring

## The Path from Eyeball to Brain

**FIGURE** 2.9

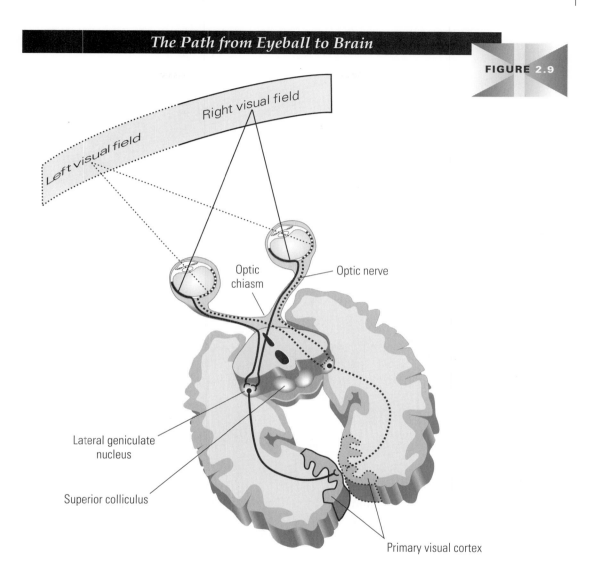

Right visual field

Left visual field

Optic chiasm

Optic nerve

Lateral geniculate nucleus

Superior colliculus

Primary visual cortex

Ganglion cells collect information from all over the retina and then gather together to form the bundle of nerve fibers we call the optic nerve. Most of the fibers pass through the lateral geniculate nucleus and project from there to the primary visual cortex in the occipital lobe. Notice that half of the fibers in the optic nerve cross from one side to the other; as a result, the left cerebral hemisphere receives visual information from the right side of space, and the right hemisphere receives visual information from the left side of space.

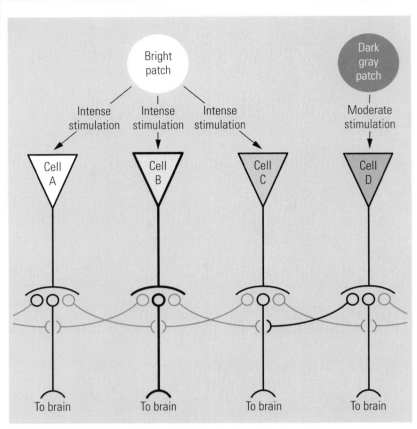

## *Lateral Inhibition and Edge Enhancement*

**FIGURE 2.10**

Cell B is strongly stimulated by the bright patch, but receives lateral inhibition from both of its (strongly activated) neighbors, A and C. As a result, Cell B sends a diminished signal to the brain. Cell C initially receives the same input as B, but ends up sending a stronger signal to the brain. This is because C receives lateral inhibition from only one of its neighbors. (Its other neighbor, Cell D, is only slightly activated, and so is sending out only a small amount of inhibition.) In this fashion, lateral inhibition creates a pattern in which cells receiving input from the *edge* of a surface send out stronger signals. This *edge enhancement* makes it easier for the brain to discern shapes in the incoming visual information.

cells. This form of inhibition can be observed at many levels in the visual system. To see why this is important, consider two cells, each receiving stimulation from a brightly lit area (Figure 2.10). One cell (Cell B in the figure) is receiving its stimulation from the middle of the lit area. It is strongly stimulated, but so are its neighbors, and so all of the cells in this area are inhibiting each other. As a result, the activity level of Cell B is increased by the stimulation but decreased by the lateral inhibition it is receiving. This combination leads to only a moderate level of activity overall.

In contrast, another cell (Cell C in the figure) is receiving its stimulation from the *edge* of the lit area. It is strongly stimulated, and so are its neighbors *on one side*. Therefore this cell will receive inhibition from one side, but not from the other side, and so will be less inhibited than Cell B (which, you'll notice, is receiving inhibition from *all* sides). So, in short, cells B and C initially receive the same input, but C is less inhibited than B and will therefore end up firing more strongly than B.

The pattern of lateral inhibition, then, actually leads to stronger responses from cells detecting the *edge* of a surface (such as Cell C) than from cells detecting the *middle* of a surface (such as Cell B). This will, in effect, lead to an exaggerated response along the surface's edges, making those edges easier to detect. This process, called **edge enhancement**, makes it easier for the visual system to discern the shapes contained within the incoming visual information. And, most important for our discussion here, this is a process that occurs within the cells of the optic nerve. Those cells aren't merely "transmitting" information, they are also starting the *analysis* of that information.

## SINGLE NEURONS AND SINGLE-CELL RECORDING

Part of what we know about the optic nerve, and indeed, part of what we know about the entire brain, comes from a technique called **single-cell recording**. As the name implies, this is a procedure through which investigators can record, microsecond by microsecond, the pattern of electrical changes within a single neuron.

To understand this technique, it will be useful to know a bit more about **neurons**, the cells that do the main work of carrying information back and forth in the nervous system. Neurons come in many shapes and sizes, but they generally have three identifiable regions (see Figure 2.11): The **dendrites** are the part of the neuron that usually detects incoming signals. The **cell body** contains the neuron's nucleus and the metabolic machinery that sustains the cell. Finally, the **axon** is the part of the neuron that transmits a signal to another location. Axons vary in length, but can in some cases be rather long. The axons of the retinal ganglion cells, for example, stretch from the retina to the LGN, a distance of a couple of inches. Other axons in the body are longer; the axons that send command signals from the spinal cord to the legs can be a full meter in length.

The axon often has several branches which terminate on other neurons. They do not touch these other neurons directly; instead, there is a small gap between the adjacent neurons. Communication across this gap is generally done via chemical signals. **Neurotransmitters** are released through the membrane at the end of the axon; these chemicals drift across the gap and stimulate the next neuron. This site—the end of the axon, plus the gap, plus the receiving membrane of the next neuron—is called a **synapse**. The axon's end is therefore called the **presynaptic membrane**; the receiving membrane (typically on the next neuron's dendrites) is the **postsynaptic membrane**.

When the neurotransmitters arrive at the postsynaptic membrane, they cause changes in the membrane that allow certain ions to flow into and out of the postsynaptic cell. If these ionic flows are relatively small, then the postsynaptic cell quickly recovers, and nothing more happens. But if the ionic flows are large enough, this triggers a response from the postsynaptic cell. In formal terms, if the incoming signal reaches the postsynaptic cell's **threshold**, then the cell **fires**—that is, it sends a signal down its axon, which in turn releases neurotransmitters at the next synapse, potentially causing the next cell to fire.

Notice, therefore, that the postsynaptic neuron's initial response can vary in size; the incoming signal can cause a small ionic flow or a large one. The magnitude of this response depends on several factors: How much neurotransmitter did the presynaptic cell release? How sensitive is the postsynaptic cell at this site? Both of these measures can vary from one neuron to the next and also can be altered with experi-

## A Typical Neuron

FIGURE 2.11

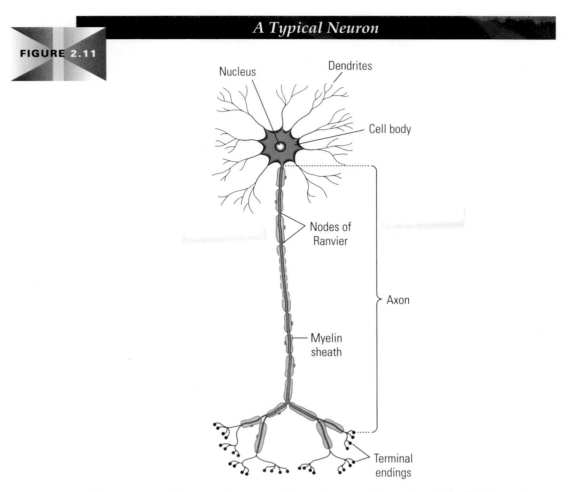

Neurons come in many shapes and sizes, but most have three identifiable regions:
The dendrites are the part of the neuron that usually detects incoming signals. The
cell body contains the metabolic machinery that sustains the cell. The axon is the
part of the neuron that transmits a signal to another location. When the cell fires,
neurotransmitters are released from the terminal endings at the tip of the axon.
(After Katz, 1952)

ence; this alteration is likely to be the neural basis
for much of what we call "learning." In addition, the
presynaptic cell may fire many times in succession;
these inputs can accumulate, and so small ionic
flows may eventually lead to a response in the postsynaptic cell. Likewise, the postsynaptic cell is likely
to be receiving inputs from many other cells; these
inputs, too, can accumulate, leading to a response.

Crucially, though, once these inputs reach the postsynaptic neuron's firing threshold, the signal that is produced does *not* vary in size. Either a signal is sent down the axon or it is not; if the signal is sent, it is always of the same magnitude, a fact referred to as the **all-or-none law**. If the cell is stimulated strongly, it may fire more frequently, or it may keep firing for a longer time, but the size of the signal that is sent along the axon never changes.

When investigators record the activity of a single neuron, therefore, what they are recording is the cell's firing—in particular, its firing rate. This rate can then be examined in conjunction with a scrutiny of the circumstances in order to figure out what event—either in the external world or elsewhere in the nervous system—triggered the firing. In this way, we can figure out roughly what job the neuron does within the broad context of the entire nervous system.

The technique of single-cell recording has been used with enormous success in the study of vision. In a typical study, the animal being studied is first immobilized. Then, electrodes are inserted into a single neuron in the animal's optic nerve or brain. Next a computer screen is placed in front of the animal's eyes, and various patterns are flashed on the computer screen—circles, lines at various angles, or squares of various sizes at various positions. Researchers can then ask, Which patterns cause that neuron to fire? To what visual inputs does that cell respond?

By analogy, we know that a smoke detector is a smoke detector because it "fires" (makes noise) when smoke is on the scene. We know that a motion detector is a motion detector because it "fires" when something moves nearby. But what kind of detector is a given neuron? Is it responsive to *any* light in *any* position within the field of view? In that case, we might call it a "light detector." Or is it perhaps responsive only to certain shapes at certain positions (and therefore is a shape detector)? With this logic, we can map out precisely what it is that the cell responds to; this is referred to as the cell's **receptive field**—that is, the size and shape of the area in the visual world to which that cell responds. With that, we learn what kind of detector the cell is.

## MULTIPLE TYPES OF RECEPTIVE FIELDS

Classic data from single-cell recording come from studies by David Hubel and Torsten Wiesel (1959; 1968), who were awarded the Nobel Prize for their work; many subsequent studies have elaborated and extended their findings. Hubel and Wiesel documented the existence of several types of neurons within the visual system, each of which has a different kind of visual trigger, a different type of receptive field. Some neurons in the visual system seem to function as "dot detectors." These cells fire at their maximum rate when light is presented in a small, roughly circular area, in a specific position within the field of view. Presentations of light just outside of this area cause the cell to fire at *less* than its usual "resting" rate, so the input must be precisely positioned to make this cell fire. Figure 2.12A depicts such a receptive field.

Such cells are often called **center-surround cells**, to mark the fact that light presented to the central region of the receptive field has one influence, whereas light presented to the surrounding ring has the opposite influence. If *both* the center and surround are strongly stimulated, the cell will fire neither more nor less than usual; for this cell, a strong uniform stimulus is equivalent to no stimulus at all. In addition, many "compromises" are possible. Imagine, for example, that we present a stimulus as shown in Figure 2.12B. The entire center of the receptive field is being stimulated, but only a portion of the surround. In this case, the positive signal would outweigh the negative, and so the cell's firing rate would increase.

Other cells fire at their maximum if a stimulus containing an edge of just the right orientation appears within their receptive fields. Some cells prefer vertical edges, some prefer horizontal, some prefer

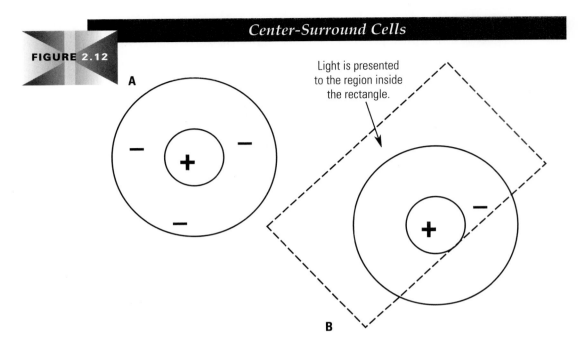

**Center-Surround Cells**

**FIGURE 2.12**

Light is presented to the region inside the rectangle.

Some neurons function as "dot detectors," and have receptive fields with a *center-surround* organization. If light shines onto the central region, the cell increases its firing rate; this is why the center is marked "+". If light shines onto the peripheral region, the cell *decreases* its firing. If both regions are illuminated, the cell will not change its firing rate in either direction. Stimuli presented outside the periphery have no effect on the cell. If we present a stimulus as shown in B, the entire center is stimulated, but only a portion of the surround. Therefore, the positive signal outweighs the negative, and so the cell's firing rate would increase somewhat.

orientations in between. If a cell's preference is, say, for horizontal edges, then nearly horizontal edges will evoke some response from the cell, but the response will be less than that for the cell's favored orientation (see Figure 2.13). Edges sharply different from the cell's preferred orientation (say, a vertical edge for a cell that prefers horizontal) will elicit no response. (In Hubel and Wiesel's original research, these orientation-sensitive cells were referred to as *simple* cells; other cells, with more complicated receptive fields, were referred to as *complex* and *hypercomplex* cells. These terms, however, are rapidly falling out of use.)

Other cells, elsewhere in the visual cortex, fire maximally only if an *angle* of a particular size appears in their receptive fields; others fire maximally in response to corners and notches. Other cells appear to be *movement detectors*, and will fire strongly if a stimulus moves, say, from right to left across the cell's receptive field. Other cells favor left-to-right movement, and so on through the various possible directions of movement.

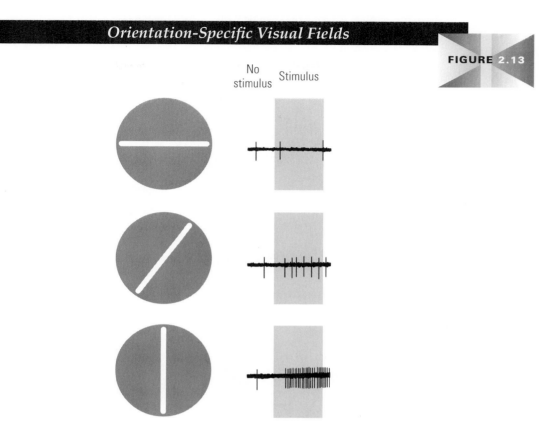

*Orientation-Specific Visual Fields*

**FIGURE 2.13**

Some cells in the visual system fire only when the input contains a line segment at the proper orientation. For example, one cell might fire very little in response to a horizontal line, fire only occasionally in response to a diagonal, and fire at its maximum rate only when a vertical line is present. (After Hubel, 1963)

Each of these cell types is found in a particular location in the brain. Center-surround cells are frequent in the LGN, and also in one of the layers of **Area V1**, the site on the occipital lobe where axons from the LGN first reach the cortex (see Figure 2.14). Other layers of Area V1, however, have different patterns of sensitivity. One layer of tissue in V1 seems highly sensitive to differences in color; cells here will fire only if the input stimulus has the right hue. For these cells, it doesn't matter how the input stimulus is oriented, or whether it is moving or not. A different layer of tissue in V1 contains cells that seem indifferent to the stimulus's color but are highly sensitive to the input's orientation and direction of movement.

**PARALLEL PROCESSING IN THE VISUAL SYSTEM**

This proliferation of cell types suggests that the visual system relies on a "divide and conquer" strategy, with different areas of the brain each specializing in a

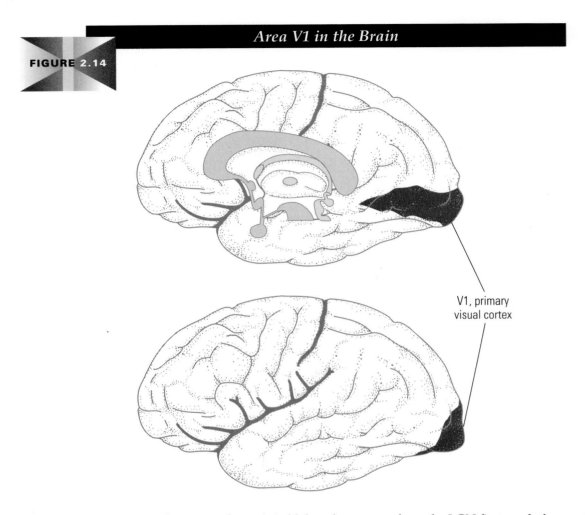

**Area V1 in the Brain**

FIGURE 2.14

V1, primary
visual cortex

Area V1 is the site on the occipital lobe where axons from the LGN first reach the cortex. The top panel shows the brain as if sliced down the middle; the bottom panel shows the brain viewed from the side. As the two panels show, most of Area V1 is located on the cortical surface *between* the two cerebral hemispheres.

particular kind of analysis. This pattern is certainly visible in V1, in which, as we've just seen, different layers of tissue appear to perform different jobs. The pattern becomes all the more evident as we consider other areas in the occipital cortex and other lobes. Figure 2.15, for example, reflects one recent summary of some of the brain areas known (on the basis of single-cell recording) to be involved in vision. Some of these areas (V1, V2, V3, V4, PO, and MT) are in the occipital cortex; other areas are in the parietal cortex; others are in the temporal cortex (we'll have more to say in a moment about these visual areas outside of the occipital cortex). Each area seems to have its own function. Neurons in Area MT, for example, are

## *The Visual Processing Pathways*

**FIGURE** 2.15

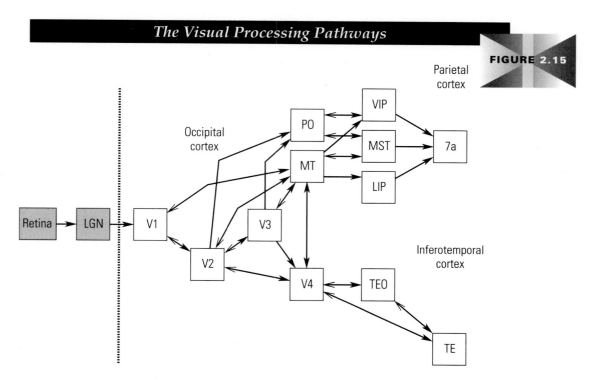

The visual system relies heavily on parallel processing, with different brain areas engaged in their own specific analyses. Information from the LGN is primarily sent to Area V1, but, from there, information is sent along several different pathways. (Adapted from art by Steven Luck)

acutely sensitive to direction and speed of movement. Cells in Area V4 fire most strongly when the input is of a certain color and a certain shape.

This pattern of specialization makes it clear that the visual system relies on **parallel processing**—a system in which many different steps (in this case, many different kinds of analysis) are going on at the same time. (The term "parallel processing" is usually contrasted with "serial processing," in which steps are carried out one at a time—that is, in a *series*.) One advantage of this simultaneous processing is speed: Brain areas trying to discern the shape of the incoming stimulus don't need to wait until the motion analysis or the color analysis is complete. Instead, all of the analyses go forward in parallel, with no waiting time.

Another advantage of parallel processing is the possibility of mutual influence among multiple systems. To see why this is important, consider the fact that sometimes our interpretation of an object's *motion* depends on our understanding of the object's three-dimensional *shape*. This suggests that it might be best if the perception of shape happened first. That way, we could use the results of this processing step as a guide to later analyses. In other cases, though, it turns out that the relationship between shape and motion is reversed: In these cases, our interpretation of an object's three-dimensional *shape* depends on our understanding of its *motion*. To allow for this possibility, it might be best if the perception of motion happened first, so that it could guide the subsequent analysis of shape!

How to deal with these conflicting demands? The visual system has evolved a pattern in which both sorts of analysis go on simultaneously, so that each type of analysis can be enriched and informed by the other. Put differently, neither the shape-analyzing system nor the motion-analyzing system gets priority over the other. Instead, the two systems work concurrently and "negotiate" a solution that satisfies both systems (Van Essen & DeYoe, 1995).

Parallel processing is evident in virtually every aspect of the visual system. Within the optic nerve itself, there are (at least) two different types of cells. *P cells* have smaller receptive fields than do *M cells* and also have a different pattern of responding to a sustained stimulus: P cells continue to fire if a stimulus remains unchanged; M cells fire when the stimulus appears, and then again when it disappears, but not in between. These two types of cells then feed into different areas in the LGN: P cells provide the main input for *parvocellular* cells in the LGN; M cells provide the primary input for *magnocellular* cells in the LGN. (The terms "parvocellular" and "magnocellular" refer to the relative sizes of these cells; *parvo* derives from the Latin word for "small" and *magno* from the Latin word for "large.")

What purpose is served by this specialization? The P cells in the optic nerve and the parvocellular cells in the LGN appear to be specialized for spatial analysis and the detailed analysis of form. The M cells in the optic nerve and the magnocellular cells in the LGN are probably specialized for the detection of motion and the perception of depth.

Evidence for parallel processing continues as we move beyond the occipital cortex. As Figure 2.16 indicates, some of the information is transmitted from the occipital lobe to the cortex of the temporal lobe. This pathway, often called the **"what" system**, plays a major role in the identification of visual objects, telling us whether the object is a cat, an apple, or whatever. A second pathway, which carries information to the parietal cortex, is often called the **"where" system** and seems to perform the function of telling us where an object is located—above or below us, to our right or to our left (Ungerleider & Mishkin, 1982; Ungerleider & Haxby, 1994; for a slightly different conception of the data, see Goodale, 1995; for some complications, see Sereno & Maunsell, 1998).

The contrasting roles of these two systems can be revealed in many ways, including studies of brain damage in monkeys. If the monkeys have suffered damage to the occipital-temporal pathway (the "what" system), they show serious impairment in identifying objects, and so cannot learn a task that requires them always to reach for, say, a cube wherever they see one. If the monkeys have suffered damage to the occipital-parietal pathway (the "where" system), they're impaired in tasks that involve visual location, and so cannot, for example, learn a task that requires them always to reach to the left, no matter whether they're reaching for a cube or a sphere.

Similar observations have been made on humans. Patients with lesions in the occipital-temporal pathway show visual agnosia—an inability to recognize visually presented objects, including such common things as a cup or a pencil. On the other hand, these patients show little disorder in recognizing visual orientation or in reaching. The reverse pattern is observed with patients who have suffered lesions in the occipital-parietal pathway: difficulty in reaching, but no problem in object identification (Newcombe, Ratcliffe & Damasio, 1987; Damasio, Tranel & Damasio, 1989; Farah, 1990; Goodale, 1995).

Other clinical data echo this broad theme of parallel processing among separate systems. In our earlier discussion of the occipital cortex, for example, we noted that there are different brain areas that are critical for the perception of color, motion, and form. If this is right, then someone who has suffered damage in just one of these areas should show problems in the perception of color but not the perception of motion or form, or problems in the perception of motion but not the perception of form or color.

These predictions are correct: Some patients do suffer a specific loss of color vision through damage to

## The "What" and "Where" Pathways

**FIGURE** 2.16

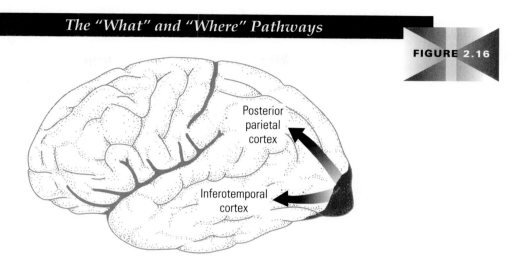

Information from the primary visual cortex (located at the back of the head) is transmitted both to the inferotemporal cortex (the so-called "what" system) and to the posterior parietal cortex (the "where" system).

the central nervous system, even though their perception of form and motion remains normal (Meadows, 1974; Gazzaniga et al., 1998).[1] To them, the entire world is clothed only in "dirty shades of gray." Other patients suffer damage to the motion system and so develop a disorder dubbed "akinetopsia" (Zihl et al., 1983). For such patients, the world is described as a succession of static photographs. They're unable to report the speed or direction of a moving object; as one patient put it, "When I'm looking at the car first, it seems far away. But then when I want to cross the road, suddenly the car is very near." Cases like these provide dramatic confirmation of the separateness of our visual system's various elements, and the ways in which the visual system is vulnerable to very specific forms of damage.

[1]This is different from color blindness, which is usually present from birth and results from abnormalities that are outside of the brain itself—e.g., abnormalities in the photoreceptors. Achromatopsia, in contrast, usually emerges only late in life, specifically as the result of focal brain damage.

### PUTTING THE PIECES BACK TOGETHER

Over and over in this chapter, we have seen that our intellectual achievements depend on an array of different brain areas working together. This was evident in our consideration of Capgras Syndrome, and the same pattern emerged when we zoomed in for a closer look at vision. Here, too, many brain areas must work together: the "what" system and the "where" system, areas specialized for the detection of movement and areas specialized for the identification of simple forms.

We have identified certain advantages that derive from this cerebral division of labor. Parallel processing allows speed. It also ensures that no one area gains mastery over the others; instead, the various systems can work together in a reasonably democratic fashion, each influencing and influenced by the others. It also allows specialization, since each brain area can be "tuned" to perform its own specific function—even if that function is just a tiny portion of the overall task.

At the same time, though, this division-of-labor strategy creates its own problem: If multiple brain areas contribute to an overall task, how is their functioning coordinated? When we see a ballet dancer in a graceful leap, the leap itself is registered by motion-sensitive neurons, while the recognition of the ballet dancer depends on shape-sensitive neurons. How are the pieces put back together? When we reach for a coffee cup, but stop midway because we see that the cup is empty, the reach itself is guided by the "where" system; the fact that the cup is empty is registered by the "what" system. How are these two streams of processing coordinated?

Investigators refer to this broad issue as the **binding problem**—the task of reuniting the various elements of a scene, elements that are initially dealt with by different systems in different parts of the brain. And obviously this problem *is* solved: What we perceive is not an unordered catalogue of sensory elements; instead, we perceive a coherent, integrated perceptual world. Apparently, then, this is a case in which the various pieces of Humpty Dumpty are re-assembled to form an organized whole.

## VISUAL MAPS

Look around you. Your visual system registers whiteness and blueness and brown-ness; it also registers a small cylindrical shape (your coffee cup), a medium-sized rectangle (this book page), and a much larger rectangle (your desk). How do you put these pieces together, so that you see that it's the coffee cup that's blue, and not the book page, the desktop that's brown, and not the cup?

The issue at stake here is, again, the binding problem—how we reunite the various elements within the scene so that the appropriate color gets "glued" onto the appropriate shape, and so on. Investigators are not yet certain how the visual system solves this problem, but we can identify two elements that certainly contribute to the solution. One element is *attention*. If you focus your attention on just the cup (for example), this will narrow the range of information you're receiving. You will still be sensitive to the cup's shape and color, but will be less sensitive to the other shapes and colors in view. This diminishes the possibility of confusion about what elements go with what, moving you toward a solution of the binding problem.

But this still leaves a problem: If the cup's color is being registered by one brain area, and the cup's shape by another, how do you coordinate the two? How do you make certain that you're focusing attention on the right shape to go with this color, or the right motion pattern to go with this shape? The answer, in a nutshell, is *spatial position*. The part of the brain registering the cup's shape is separate from the parts registering its color or its motion; nonetheless, these various brain areas all have something in common: They each keep track of *where* the target is— where the cylindrical shape was located, and where the blueness was; where there was motion detected, and where things were still. Thus, the reassembling of these pieces can be done with reference to spatial position. In essence, you can overlay the map of "which forms are where" on top of the map of "which colors are where" to get the right colors with the right forms, and likewise for the map showing "which motion patterns are where."

Information about spatial position is of course important for its own sake: You have an obvious reason to care whether the tiger is close to you or far away, or whether the bus is on your side of the street or the other. But, in addition, location information can provide the frame of reference needed to solve the binding problem. Given this double function, we shouldn't be surprised that spatial position is a major organizing theme within all the various brain areas concerned with vision, with each area seeming to provide its own map of the visual world.

As we mentioned earlier, these maps are readily detectable in the sensory projection areas. Single-cell recording confirms that adjacent cells within a bit of brain tissue are usually responsive to adjacent positions within the visual field—so that, in fact, the receptive fields really *do* form a map of visual space. If there are multiple brain areas responsible for different aspects of vision, then there must be multiple maps; indeed, more than 30 such maps have been documented (Gazzaniga et al., 1998).

## Chapter Summary

1. The brain is divided into several different structures, but of particular importance for cognitive psychology is the *forebrain*. In the forebrain, each *cerebral hemisphere* is divided into the *frontal lobe, parietal lobe, temporal lobe*, and *occipital lobe*. In understanding these brain areas, one important source of evidence comes from studies of brain damage, allowing us to examine what sorts of symptoms result from *lesions* in specific brain locations. This has allowed a *localization of function*, an effort that is also supported by *neuroimaging* research, which shows that the pattern of activation in the brain depends heavily on the particular task being performed.

2. Different parts of the brain perform different jobs, but, for virtually any mental process, different brain areas must work together in a closely integrated fashion. When this integration is lost (as it is, for example, in *Capgras Syndrome*) bizarre symptoms result.

3. The *primary motor projection areas* are the departure point for nerve cells that initiate muscle movement. The *primary sensory projection areas* are the main points of arrival for information from the eyes, ears, and other sense organs. All of these projection areas show the pattern of *contralateral control*, with tissue in the left hemisphere sending or receiving its main signals from the right side of the body, and vice versa. The projection areas each provide a map of the environment or the relevant body part, but the assignment of space in this map is governed by function, not anatomical proportions.

4. Most of the forebrain's cortex has traditionally been referred to as the *association cortex*, but this area is itself subdivided into specialized regions. This is reflected in the varying consequences of brain damage, with lesions in the occipital lobe leading to *visual agnosia*, damage in the temporal lobes leading to *aphasia*, and so on. Damage to the *prefrontal area* causes many different problems, but these are generally problems in the forming and implementing of strategies.

5. One brain area that has been mapped in considerable detail is the *visual system*. The system takes its main input from the *rods* and *cones* on the retina. Then, information is sent via the *optic nerve* to the brain. Importantly, cells in the optic nerve do much more than transmit information; they also begin the analysis of the visual input. This is reflected in the phenomenon of *lateral inhibition*, which leads to *edge enhancement*.

6. Part of what we know about the brain comes from *single-cell recording*, which can record the electrical activity of an individual *neuron*. In the visual system, this recording has allowed researchers to map the *receptive fields* for many cells, and this has provided evidence for a high degree of specialization among the various parts of the visual system, with some parts specialized for the perception of motion, other parts specialized for the perception of color, and so on. These various areas function in parallel, and this allows great speed; it also allows mutual influence among multiple systems.

7. *Parallel processing* begins in the optic nerve and continues throughout the visual system. For example, the *"what" system* (in the temporal lobe) appears to be specialized for the identification of visual objects; the *"where" system* (in the parietal lobe) seems to tell us where an object is located.

8. The reliance on parallel processing creates a problem of reuniting the various elements of a scene, so that these elements are perceived in an integrated fashion. This is called the *binding problem*. One key in solving this problem, though, lies in the fact that different brain systems are organized in terms of maps, so that spatial position can be used as a framework for reuniting the separately analyzed aspects of the visual scene.

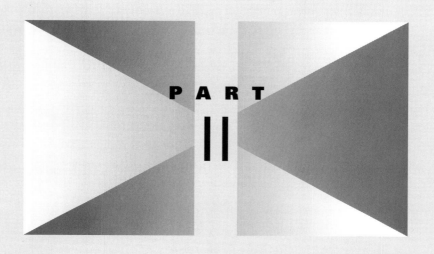

PART

II

# Learning about the World Around Us

In the previous section, we described some of the early steps involved in vision, but it is important to realize that there's still much to be understood about how visual perception proceeds. We begin Chapter 3, therefore, with a discussion of the active nature of perceiving and the various ways in which the perceiver analyzes, organizes, and interprets the visual input. We'll turn next to the broad issue of how we recognize the various objects that surround us in the world, and here we'll discover the ways in which object recognition is influenced by learning and guided by some of the regular patterns that exist in the world. We'll then spend much of the chapter describing the ways in which a mechanism made up of very simple components can accomplish all of this, and that will lead us into a discussion of how complex knowledge and complicated processes can be "distributed" across a mechanism that's not at all complicated. (This notion of "distributed processing" is important in this chapter and in other settings, and we'll return to this idea later in the book.)

Chapter 4 then turns to the study of *attention*. As we'll see, "paying attention" is a complex achievement involving many different elements. Some of the steps needed for attention will be the same no matter what it is a person is paying attention to; some steps will depend on the particular task. In either case, paying attention requires that one commit some "mental resources," and, in the *absence* of those resources, performance—even in very simple tasks—drops off markedly. In addition, these "resources" are available only in limited quantities, and this may set "boundaries" on human performance. Part of what's at stake in this chapter, therefore, is a discussion of what people can or cannot accomplish, and whether there may be ways to escape the apparent limits on attention.

# Recognizing Objects in the World

As we saw in Chapter 2, information about the visual world is picked up by a large array of detectors, with each detector tuned to a particular aspect of the stimulus information. Some detectors specialize in horizontal line segments, others detect vertical lines or diagonals. Still others pick out certain colors or specific patterns of movement. There are also more sophisticated detectors: neurons that fire only when certain angles or notches or corners are in view. For that matter, there are even neurons (in the monkey's brain) that fire only when a monkey's hand is in view (whether the fingers are stretched out or clenched in a fist) or only when another monkey's face is in view!

However, visual perception involves far more than a simple "detection" of the stimulus input's properties. As one consideration, we have already mentioned the fact that the input's various attributes are detected by separate brain systems, and so a further step is required to reunite these various attributes, so that we recognize that it is the squirrel that is brown and moving and the leaves that are green and still, rather than some other combination of these features. But the complexities of perception do not stop there. In this chapter, we'll consider some of the other steps that are involved in perceiving the visual world, and, with that, we'll discuss just how large a role the perceiver plays—not just as a *detector* of incoming information, but as an *interpreter* of that information.

## Visual Perception

We receive information about the world through various sense modalities: We hear the sound of the approaching train, we smell the chocolate cake almost ready to come out of the oven, we feel the tap on our shoulder. There is no question, though, that for humans, vision is the dominant sense. This fact is reflected in how much brain area is devoted to vision compared to that devoted to any of the other senses. It is also reflected in many aspects of our behavior. For example, if visual information conflicts with information received from other senses, we usually place our trust in vision. This is, for example, the main basis for *ventriloquism*, in which we see the dummy's mouth moving, even though, of course, the sounds themselves are coming from the dummy's master. Vision wins out in this contest, and so we experience the illusion that the voice is coming from the dummy.

Vision tells us many things about our world. What is this object now before us? This is a question of *form perception*. Where is the object located—close to us or far, to our left or to our right? This is a question about *depth perception*. Finally, what is the object doing—is it moving, or is it still? This is a question about *motion perception*. In the interest of brevity, we will have little to say in this text about depth and motion perception. (For an overview of depth and motion perception, consider Gleitman, Fridlund & Reisberg, 1999, pgs. 218–225.) But what does form perception involve?

### WHY IS FORM PERCEPTION CRUCIAL?

You open your eyes, and you see around you a world filled with familiar objects—chairs and desks, windows and walls, telephones and pencils. As you read this page, you can see the individual letters printed here. They are letters that you know and can identify. The letters form words, and you can recognize the words—you could say them out loud if requested, and you know what is being said, so that you easily understand these sentences.

How is any of this possible? How do you know that the chairs are chairs, or the telephones are telephones? How do you know that the letter "Q" is a Q and not an R or a Z or, for that matter, a map of Brazil? When you recognize these objects, you are identifying or categorizing the objects in your environment, and the process of doing all this is broadly referred to as **object recognition**.

Virtually all knowledge and all *use* of knowledge depend on object recognition. To see this, think about a physician who might know how to *treat* diabetes, but who doesn't know how to *recognize* a case of diabetes. In this case, the physician's knowledge about treatment becomes useless, because the physician doesn't know when (or with which patients) to use the treatment. Likewise, you know a great deal about telephones, and you use that knowledge in many ways. But you could not do this if you couldn't recognize a telephone when you saw one. Without recognition, one cannot bring one's knowledge to bear on the world.

In a similar fashion, object recognition is also crucial for learning. In virtually all learning, one must combine new information with information learned previously. Otherwise, no accumulation of knowledge would be possible—each learning episode would stand separately, unintegrated with other learning episodes. But for this to happen, one must categorize things properly. Today you learn something about Solomon. Yesterday you learned something about Solomon. If you are to integrate the new knowledge with the old, you need to realize that the person before you today is the same person as the one you met yesterday. Without proper categorization, there is no way to combine and integrate information.

One way to drive all this home is to consider people who cannot recognize objects. A number of different problems—different sorts of lesions in the brain, for example—can create such a disability. In some of these cases, the person's vision seems essentially intact—the person can easily see and recognize colors and simple forms and movement. Even so, the person seems unable to put these pieces together to recognize *objects*. This pattern—intact vision, but an inability to recognize objects—is called **object agnosia** (Farah, 1990). For example, consider the case of "Dr. P.," described in an essay by Oliver Sacks:

"What is this?" I asked, holding up a glove.

"May I examine it?" he asked, and, taking it from me, he proceeded to examine it. "A continuous surface," he announced at last, "infolded in itself. It appears to have"—he hesitated—"five outpouchings, if this is the word."

"Yes," I said cautiously. " . . . Now tell me what it is."

"A container of some sort?"

"Yes," I said, "and what would it contain?"

"It would contain its contents!" said Dr. P., with a laugh. "There are many possibilities. It could be a change purse, for example, for coins of five sizes. It could . . ." (Sacks, 1985, pg. 14).

This agnosic is obviously quite intelligent and he certainly can see, but he has immense difficulties in acquiring knowledge or using what he knows. As Sacks describes, Dr. P. fails to put on his shoe, because he does not recognize it as a shoe. (At one point, Dr. P. is confused about which is his shoe and which is his foot.) At the end of his first meeting with Sacks, Dr. P. "reached out his hand and took hold of his wife's head, tried to lift it off, to put it on. He had apparently mistaken his wife for a hat!" (pg. 11).

Thus, object recognition may not be a glamorous skill, but it does seem to be a crucial one for even our most ordinary commerce with the world. Moreover, it is the essential base for learning and memory. For our purposes, therefore, we will start our inquiry where much of knowledge starts—with the recognition and identification of objects in the world.

## BEYOND THE INFORMATION GIVEN

How does object recognition proceed? The first step lies in organizing and perceiving the simple patterns in front of your eyes. Before you can recognize a bicycle as a bicycle, for example, you need to see that there is a pair of circles in front of you, linked by a group of narrow cylinders. Then you can move on from there—identifying the circles as the wheels, the cylinders as the elements of the bike's frame, etc.

We need to start, therefore, by asking how these simple patterns are perceived—circles and cylinders, cubes and pyramids and the like. In Chapter 2, we saw how this process begins—with the detection of simple visual features. As we've already suggested, though, there is much more to the process than simple detection, and in fact, this is a suggestion with a long history. Early in the 20th century, the **Gestalt psychologists** argued that our perception of the visual world is organized in ways that the stimulus input is not. They argued, therefore, that the organization must be contributed by the perceiver; this is why, they claimed, the perceptual "whole" is often different from the sum of its parts. Some years later, Jerome Bruner voiced similar claims and coined the phrase *"beyond the information given"* to describe some of the ways that our perception of a stimulus differs from (and goes beyond) the stimulus itself (e.g., Bruner, 1973).

Consider the top form shown in Figure 3.1—the **Necker cube**. This drawing is called an "**ambiguous figure**" because there is more than one way to perceive it. As one option, it can be perceived as a cube viewed from above (in which case it is similar to the cube marked "A" in the figure); alternatively, it can be perceived as a cube viewed from below (in which case it is similar to the cube marked "B"). Both perceptions "fit" perfectly well with the information received by your eyes, and so the drawing itself is fully compatible with either of these perceptions. Put differently, the lines on the page are neutral with regard to the shape's configuration in depth.

Your perception of the cube, however, is not neutral. Instead, you perceive the cube as having one configuration or the other—similar either to cube A or to cube B. Your perception, in other words, goes *beyond the information given* by specifying an arrangement in depth.

The same point can be made for many other stimuli. Consider, for example, the vase/profiles figure (panel C in Figure 3.1). This figure can be perceived as "vase and not profiles," but it can equally well be perceived as "profiles and not vase." The drawing by itself, it seems, is fully compatible with either of these perceptions, and so, once again, the drawing is neutral with regard to perceptual organization. In par-

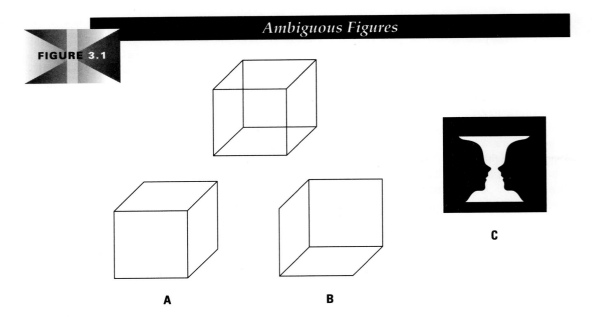

FIGURE 3.1

*Ambiguous Figures*

**A**          **B**

**C**

The Necker cube (top) can be perceived as if viewed from above (in which case it is a transparent version of Cube A) or as if viewed from below (i.e., a transparent version of Cube B). The figure on the right is also ambiguous. It can be perceived either as a white vase against a black background or as two black profiles against a white background.

ticular, it is neutral with regard to **figure/ground organization**—the determination of what is the *figure* (the central object, displayed against a background) and what is the *ground*.

Your perception of this figure, however, is not neutral about this point. Instead, your perception somehow specifies that you are looking at the vase and not at the profiles, *or* that you are looking at the profiles and not at the vase. This specification turns out to have a variety of consequences—for how your eyes move as you examine the figure, for how the dimensions of the figure are understood, for how you will remember the figure, and so on.

## PARSING

Does the pattern shown in Figure 3.2A contain the numeral "4"? Is the pattern in 3.2C contained in Figure 3.2B? In each case, the answer is "yes," although this may not be obvious without some scrutiny of the figures. If we focus just on the geometry of the physical stimuli, the **embedded figures** are present in the larger figures (A and B). Whether the embedded figure is *detected*, though, depends on how the perceiver organizes the stimulus—which parts are perceived as going together, and which are perceived as separate.

To see how this works, let's look again at Figure 3.2B. Is there a parallelogram embedded in this figure? Geometrically there is, but whether the parallelogram is detected depends on how the perceiver **parses** the figure—that is, how the perceiver understands the parts of the figure. If the perceiver parses the whole into two "roman numeral tens" or into two triangles (one right-side-up, one upside-down), then no parallelogram is (perceptually) present. If the perceiver parses the whole into two overlapping parallelograms, then of course the target is visible.

All our examples so far have involved simple drawings on an otherwise blank ground. The real importance of parsing, though, comes into view when we consider more complex scenes, like the one shown in Figure 3.3. In this scene, you easily recognize the banana, the pitcher, and so on, but, to do this, you first have to group the elements of the scene appropriately. For example, you have to unite Portion B (one half of the apple) with Portion E (the other half of the apple), even though they are separated by Portion D (the banana). Portion B must not be united with Portion A (a bunch of grapes), even though they are adjacent and approximately the same color. The bit of the apple hidden from view by the banana must also be somehow filled in, so that you can perceive an intact apple rather than two apple slices.

## THE LOGIC OF PERCEPTION

In several ways, therefore, perceiving involves more than the detection of stimulus elements. Perceiving also requires a parsing of the input into its appropriate components; it requires an organization of the input into figure and ground; it requires an interpretation of the input's three-dimensional configuration. These interpretive steps obviously *depend on* the stimulus input—because the interpretation must be compatible with the information in the stimulus. But these interpretive steps are not *determined by* the input. This is evident in the fact that, often, more than one interpretation is possible—and so the cube in Figure 3.1 can be perceived either as the shape in

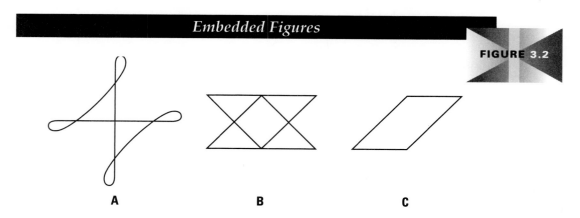

**Embedded Figures**

**FIGURE 3.2**

A                    B                    C

Pattern A contains the numeral "4," but most participants fail to detect the numeral. Likewise, Pattern B *contains* Pattern C, but this isn't obvious until you search for the "hidden" form. Thus, perception of forms depends on how one "dissects" the overall pattern.

**FIGURE 3.3**

*The Importance of Parsing*

To determine what these various objects are, the perceptual system must first decide what goes with what—that portion B and portion E are different bits of the same object (even though they are separated by portion D), that portion B and portion A are different objects (even though they are adjacent and the same color).

3.1A or the one in 3.1B; the right panel in Figure 3.1 can be perceived either as vase or profiles, and so on. Clearly, then, the interpretation is "in the eye of the beholder" and not, strictly speaking, driven by the stimulus itself.

Observations like these make it plain that the perceiver is not a passive receiver of stimulus information. Instead, the perceiver actively interprets and organizes the stimulus pattern, and this in turn has important consequences for object recognition. For example, will the perceiver recognize the vase in Fig-

ure 3.1 or the parallelogram in Figure 3.2B? The answer depends on how the perceiver organizes these forms. Or, as a different example, consider Figure 3.4. Do you recognize the form? Try re-organizing it. Try thinking of the form as a white shape on a black background, rather than the more customary black shape on white. Try thinking of the left side as being the top, rather than the side topmost on the page. Without these steps of reorganization, few people recognize the form. With the reorganization, many recognize the map of Europe (Kanizsa, 1979).

Clearly, therefore, whether we recognize a form as familiar and whether we can identify the form at all depends on how we have organized and interpreted the perceptual information. But how does this interpretation happen? What are the processes through which the interpretation is generated? We do not yet have a full account, although investigators are making impressive progress in understanding how these processes unfold. Some of the progress involves detailing the relevant brain mechanisms, and this work connects well with the materials described in Chapter 2. (Hoffman, 2000, and Palmer, 1999, provide recent reviews.) Other lines of research and other lines of theory focus more on the "logic" of the processes,

rather than the biological steps implementing this logic (e.g., Rock, 1983).

In what sense is perception "logical"? Let's note, first, that the interpretation achieved by the perceptual system—the organization of figure and ground, the parsing, and so on—must fit with *all* the incoming stimulus information. Just like a good scientist, your perceptual apparatus requires a hypothesis that fits with all the data. Second, the perceptual system seems to prefer the *simplest* explanation of the stimulus. Again, just like a good scientist, the perceptual system seems to avoid overly elaborate explanations of the "data," if a simpler explanation will do. Third, the perceptual system also seems to avoid interpre-

## A Hidden Figure

FIGURE 3.4

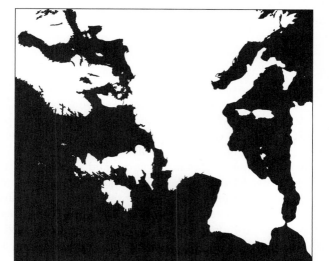

Whether an object is recognized or not depends on the physical stimulus *and also* on how the stimulus is interpreted and organized by the perceiver. In this figure, most people do not recognize the familiar form. If they change their understanding of what is figure, and what is ground, however, this helps. (Try thinking of the form as a white shape on a black background.) Likewise, if they change their understanding of the form's orientation, this helps, too. (Try thinking of the left side as being the form's top.)

*Avoiding Coincidences*

FIGURE 3.5

This form could be perceived as two "V" shapes, one on the top and one on the bottom. Or it could be parsed as two "V" shapes, with one on the left and one on the right. The visual system seems to avoid these interpretations, however, because they involve an element of coincidence: This is what two V's would look like *if* they just happened to be positioned perfectly, touching and aligned, but with no overlap.

tations that involve *coincidences*. As an example, consider Figure 3.5. This form could be parsed as two "V" shapes, one on the top and one on the bottom. Or it could be parsed as two "V" shapes, with one on the left and one on the right. Or the form could be parsed as two lines crossing, and for most people, this is the parsing that seems most natural. This is the way the form appears when first encountered. Why? Because the other interpretations involve coincidence: Yes, two "V" shapes would look like this *if* the V's were in exactly the right positions—just touching, with no overlap. In any other positions, the combined V's would look quite different. Therefore, this overall configuration might be perceived as two "V" shapes that *just happen to be positioned perfectly*. This last clause, however, reveals the role of coincidence in getting the shapes into just the right locations, and it's this coincidence that seems to count against this interpretation of the form.

Let's be clear that we are not proposing that there really is a little scientist inside your brain, generating hypotheses about the input, calculating the likelihood of this or that coincidence. The perceptual system does work as if it were generating hypotheses and the like, but the key phrase, of course, is "as if." Neural mechanisms somehow function in a way that leaves us, overall, with a process that seems quite logical, and seems to analyze and interpret the evidence, just as a scientist might. We do not know yet what those neural mechanisms are, but in the meantime, these "logical principles" can help us make sense of a great deal of evidence concerning how we do, and how we do not, interpret the visual forms we encounter.

## Object Recognition

In Chapter 2, we saw how the nervous system begins its analysis of the visual input with a large set of detectors operating in parallel, each detecting a specific attribute of an image. Next, these various attributes are somehow bound together, so that the perceiver knows that the green-ness she detected was a property of the horizontal line and not the vertical one, or that the motion she detected was a property of the vertical line and not the horizontal. The processes of perception then have to *organize* this information: Were the horizontal and vertical lines part of the same object, or parts of different objects? This is the step of parsing, in which the perceiver figures out which elements go with which. Also necessary is the step of figure/ground organization and an interpretation of both the figure's orientation and its configuration in depth.

With the form organized in this fashion, we are ready (at last) to take the next steps toward identifying what the form actually is—a truck, a tree, or a character in a video game. Let's turn, therefore, to these next steps. Our goal in this chapter is to convey an understanding of how we recognize the thousands of objects we encounter in our day-to-day world, but initially, it will be useful for us to focus more narrowly: We'll start with a scrutiny of how we recognize a specific sort of object: the letters and words that make up printed language. We present the study of print as a microcosm for object recognition in general. To be sure, some questions about object recognition cannot be studied via print. (For example, the study of print, which is only two-dimensional, doesn't allow us to examine the recognition of three-dimensional objects.) Nonetheless, many of the lessons learned in studying word recognition will apply to a broader range of cases—how we recognize cabbages and kings, or auditory patterns like major chords or sad melodies, or even abstract patterns like injustices or schizophrenics. Indeed, many of the lessons learned here will apply far beyond the study of object recognition, so that, for example, our discussion of memory in Chapter 8 will bring us back to several of the key ideas that will be introduced here in the discussion of print.

In addition, let's note that this strategy of "study the simple cases first, then build from there" is a common strategy in psychology, and a reasonably successful one as well. Later in the chapter, we'll consider how successful this strategy has been in the case of object recognition.

## RECOGNITION: SOME EARLY CONSIDERATIONS

You are plainly able to recognize a huge number of different patterns. In the domain of print alone, you are able to recognize tens of thousands of different words. Beyond print, you are also able to recognize objects (cows, trees, hats), actions (running, jumping, falling), situations (crises, comedies), and so on.

Not only do you recognize all these different things, you also recognize many variations of each. You recognize cats standing up and cats sitting down, cats running and cats asleep. And of course the same is true for your recognition of pigs, chairs, and any other object in your recognition repertoire.

You also recognize objects even when your information is partial. For example, you can still recognize a cat if only its head and one paw are visible behind a tree. You recognize a chair even when someone is sitting on it, despite the fact that this blocks much of the chair from view.

All of this is obviously true for print as well. You recognize the letter "A" whether it printed in large type, bold type, italic, etc. You also recognize lowercase A's. Further, you recognize handwritten A's, for which the variation from one to the next is huge.

To all of this, let's add a further complication: Your recognition of various objects is, in important ways, influenced by the *context* in which the objects are encountered. For example, a fire hydrant will be recognized more easily (more quickly, more accurately) in the context of a "street corner scene," compared to a fire hydrant presented with no context. Moreover, to obtain this effect, the objects must be shown in *appropriate* contexts, and in the correct position within the context. Thus, the context will not facilitate performance if the fire hydrant is shown on top of a mailbox (Biederman, Glass & Stacy, 1973; Boyce & Pollatsek, 1992; but see also Hollingworth & Henderson, 1998).

## Context Influences Perception

FIGURE 3.6

# TAE CAT

Pattern recognition is influenced by the fact that "THE" is a commonly observed sequence of letters; "TAE" is not. Likewise, "CAT" is often encountered; "CHT" is not. Given this knowledge, one is likely to read this sequence as "THE CAT," reading the middle symbol as an "H" in one case and as an "A" in the other. [After Selfridge, 1955 ©1955 IRE (now IEEE).]

Context can also have stronger effects—not just changing how easily something is recognized, but also changing what it is recognized *as*. Consider Figure 3.6 (after Selfridge, 1955). The middle character is the same in both words, but the character doesn't *look* the same. Instead, the character looks more like an "H" in the left word and more like an "A" in the right. Likewise, one unhesitatingly reads the left word as "THE" and not "TAE"; the right word is read as "CAT" and not "CHT."

Let's also remember that context can determine whether an object is recognized *at all*. This was evident, for example, in our earlier discussion of embedded figures. For a further illustration, consider Figure 3.2 (p. 57). Pattern A contains the numeral "4," but you probably didn't notice this until it was pointed out. Pattern B contains pattern C, but again, this isn't obvious until you search for the "hidden" form. In each case, one perceives the embedded figure only if one dissects the overall pattern into the appropriate pieces—that is, if one parses the form in just the right way. With other parsings, the embedded figure is effectively hidden from view.

How should we think about all this? What mechanisms underlie all of these effects? In the next sections, we will develop a proposal for such a mechanism.

## FEATURES

One plausible suggestion is that many objects are recognized by virtue of their *parts*. You recognize an elephant because you see the trunk, the thick legs, the large body. You know a lollipop is a lollipop because you can see the circle shape on top of the straight stick. But how do you recognize the parts themselves? How, for example, do you recognize the circle in the lollipop? Perhaps you do so by virtue of *its* parts—the constituent arcs, for example.

To put this more generally, recognition might begin with the identification of **features** in the input pattern—features such as vertical lines, curves, or diagonals. With these features appropriately catalogued, you can start assembling the larger units: If you detect a horizontal together with a vertical, you know you're looking at a right angle. If you've detected four right angles, you know you're looking at a square. And so on.

How are the features themselves recognized? One possibility is that each of us has in memory a repertoire of specific patterns, one for each feature. These memory patterns are then compared to the pattern before your eyes. If some part of this input matches one of the patterns in your repertoire, then you know that the relevant feature is present. "That bit matches my 'corner' pattern, so I know a corner is present. That bit matches my 'curve' pattern, so I know a curve is present."

Let's be clear, though, that the features that matter here are the features in the *perceptually organized input*, not the features in the "raw" stimulus information. Why do we need to make this distinction? In some situations, features are present in the stimulus but are absent from the organized perception. [Look again at Figure 3.2B (p. 57); if the form is parsed as two X's, then two of the angles needed for "building" the parallelogram (the angle at the lower right-hand corner of Figure 3.2C, and the one at the top left) are not present in the organized perception.] In this case, the features will not be detected, even though they are physically on the scene. In other situations, the pattern is reversed, with features present in the organized perception, but absent from the stimulus itself (see Figure 3.7). In this case, the features *are* detected, even though they are physically *not* on the scene.

Even with this caution in place, some advantages of a feature system are obvious immediately. First, features such as line segments and curves could serve as *general-purpose* building blocks. Not only would

these features serve as the basis for recognizing letters, they could also serve as the basis for recognizing other, more complex visual patterns (chairs, jackets, smiling faces), opening the possibility of a single pattern recognition system able to deal with patterns of many sorts.

Second, we have noted that we recognize many variations on the objects we encounter—cats in different positions, A's in different fonts or different handwritings. But although the various A's are different from each other in overall shape, they do have a great deal in common—two inwardly sloping lines and a horizontal crossbar. Focusing on features might allow us to concentrate on what is common to the various A's, and so might allow us to recognize A's despite their apparent diversity.

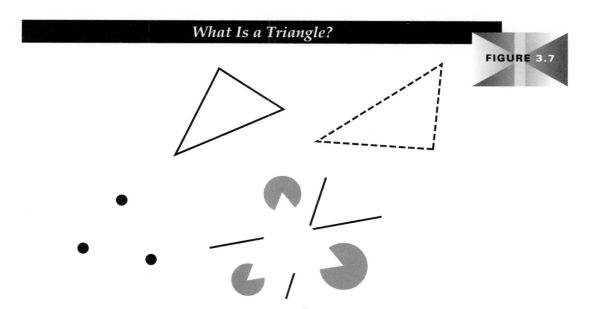

**What Is a Triangle?**

FIGURE 3.7

The features that we use in object recognition are not the features of the raw input. Instead, the features that we use are the ones in our organized perception of the input. This is evident in the fact that we recognize all of these forms as triangles—even though the essential features (three lines, three angles) are present in only one of them. The features are present, however, in our organized perception of the forms.

## VISUAL SEARCH

The considerations just sketched indicate that features might be useful as a base for recognition. But can we find more direct evidence for the existence of features? One line of evidence comes from **visual search** studies in which participants scan through a set of visual stimuli, searching for a particular target.

Some cases of visual search are easy; some are much more difficult. For example, it is generally easy to locate a target defined by a single feature—one red letter among a background of blue letters, or one round shape against a background of angular shapes. It is harder to search for a target defined via a *combination* of features—e.g., a red circle amid a backdrop of red squares and blue circles (Treisman, 1986; Treisman & Gormican, 1988; for earlier studies of visual search, see Neisser, 1964). Note, then, that there appears to be something primitive and basic about feature perception: Targets that can be distinguished by feature perception "pop out" from the background. Targets that cannot be distinguished in this fashion, i.e., targets that require some higher-order analysis, generally do not pop out.

Data also indicate striking **search asymmetries**. For example, see Figure 3.8: It is easy to find a tilted

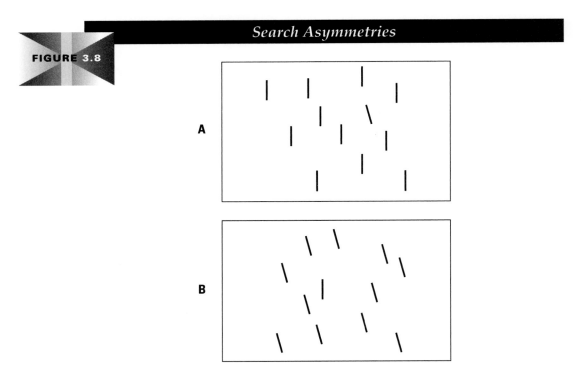

**FIGURE 3.8**

### *Search Asymmetries*

It is easy to find a tilted line against a background of vertical lines (A), but harder to do the reverse: to find a vertical against a background of tilted lines (B). This implies that "tilt" is a feature detected by the visual system and so, in searching for tilt, one is searching for a single feature. "Absence of tilt" seems *not* to be a feature detected by the visual system.

FIGURE 3.9

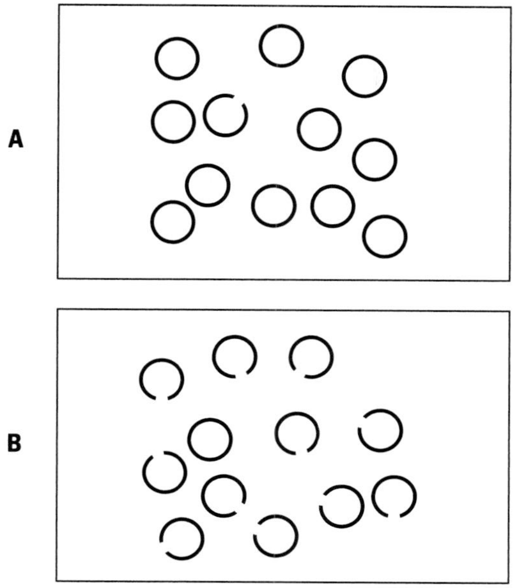

## Search Asymmetries

It is easy to find an incomplete circle against a background of complete circles (A), but harder to find a complete circle against a background of incomplete circles (B), even though the discrimination is the same in both cases. This implies that the visual system treats "gap" as a single feature, but not "absence of gap."

line against a background of vertical lines, but hard to do the reverse, to find a vertical line against a background of tilted lines. Likewise, it is easy to find an incomplete circle against a background of complete circles, but harder to find a complete circle against a background of incomplete circles (Figure 3.9). In some ways, these results seem peculiar, since the same discrimination is required (tilt vs. vertical, incomplete vs. complete) in both versions of the search. Researchers have interpreted these asymmetries, however, as implying that "gap" and "tilt" are features for the visual system. In searching for these, one is simply searching for a single feature, and as we've just seen, feature-based search is easy; targets defined in terms of a single feature pop out from their background. "Absence

of gap" or "absence of tilt" (vertical), however, are not features, making it more difficult to search for these (Treisman & Gormican, 1988; Treisman & Souther, 1985).

Note, then, that visual search data can be used to *identify* some of the specific features used by the visual system. That is, we could not tell from the outset whether "vertical" was a feature, or whether "tilt" was a feature, or whether *both* might be features. Search asymmetries can be used to explore these issues, since these data tell us that there is a priority to "tilt" that is not shared by "vertical." In this way, search data can literally tell us what is in the alphabet from which visual forms are assembled. More broadly, though, visual-search evidence indicates that patterns are easily distinguishable from each other if the patterns differ at the feature level. This is what one would expect if the process of pattern recognition began with features, and of course that is our main concern here.

## Word Recognition

Features play an important role in our perception, but how are the features assembled to allow the recognition of larger units—whole words, for example, or trees or Chihuahuas or fire hydrants? Before we tackle this question, let's fill in some more facts that we can use as a guide to our theory-building.

### THE LOGIC OF WORD-RECOGNITION STUDIES

Pattern recognition is, in general, pretty easy. It requires no great effort to see that a telephone is a telephone; you have no difficulties in identifying the letters on this page. In part, this simply reflects the degree to which the relevant skills are extremely well practiced. In addition, ordinary circumstances do little to challenge these recognition skills. Generally, the patterns you encounter are out in plain view, and you have plenty of time to inspect them. As a result, ordinary pattern recognition demands little of you and, consequently, may not tell us much about your abilities.

By analogy, think of a spelling test in which you are asked to spell words like "CAT" or "DOG." Surely you would do quite well on this test, but this wouldn't tell us how good a speller you are, since most people, good spellers or bad, would do well on this easy test. Nor would it tell us whether some words are more difficult to spell than others, since all words on the test are very easy. Performance in this test will be at **ceiling levels**, and so the test will be insensitive, unable to discriminate good spellers from poor ones or easy words from hard. To make the test more **sensitive**, it has to be more difficult, so that it will challenge your abilities in a more serious way.

By the same logic, if we want to uncover how pattern recognition works, we need a test that challenges the participants, to get performance away from ceiling levels. This is generally accomplished simply by presenting the words to participants very quickly, for fractions of a second. Older research did this by means of a **tachistoscope**—a device that allows presentation of stimuli for precisely controlled amounts of time, including very brief presentations. More modern research uses computers for this purpose, rather than tachistoscopes, but the brief presentations are still called "*tachistoscopic* presentations."

In an ordinary procedure, the participant is shown a series of stimulus words on a computer screen, each for some brief duration—perhaps 20 or 30 msec (milliseconds). Each word is followed by a **post-stimulus mask**—often just a random jumble of letters, such as "XJDKEL." This mask serves to disrupt any "sensory memory" that participants might have for the just-presented stimulus, allowing researchers to be certain that a stimulus presented for (say) 20 msec is visible for exactly 20 msec and no longer.

After a bit of practice, participants can recognize words presented for these very brief durations. Various factors, though, can increase or decrease the likelihood of recognizing a word; to study these factors, we need some means of measuring performance. One option is simply to ask how many participants recognize a particular word, in a particular setting. A different option is to ask, for each participant, how many words were recognized, and how many were not. Either of these methods will generate data assessed in terms of "percentage recognized." Alternatively, we can show a word briefly (say, for 10 msec). If the participant fails to recognize the word we reshow that word for a slightly longer exposure, perhaps 15 msec. If the participant still fails to recognize the word we reshow it, again for a slightly longer exposure. Eventually, we will show the word for enough time for the participant to recognize it; in this way, we can determine how long the exposure has to be for recognition to happen. This duration is referred to as the **recognition threshold**.

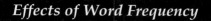

## Effects of Word Frequency

**FIGURE** 3.10

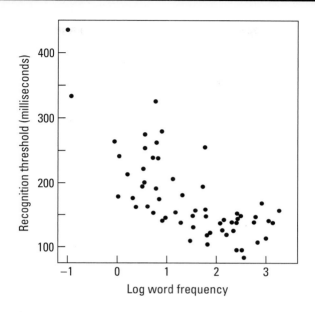

In a classic study, Howes and Solomon (1951) documented that participants easily recognize words that appear frequently in print; words that appear rarely are harder to recognize. Each dot in the figure represents the averaged data for one of their test words. "Recognition threshold" indicates the length of time for which a word had to be exposed in order for participants to identify it. Thresholds were much higher (more time needed) for rare words (low frequency).

## THE WORD-FREQUENCY EFFECT

One factor that distinguishes the easy-to-recognize words is simply their frequency in the language. This claim is based quite literally on counts of how often each word appears in newspapers, magazines, and books (Thorndike & Lorge, 1963; Kucera & Francis, 1967). These counts confirm that "smirk," "noodle," and "wart" are infrequent words, whereas "weather," "happy," and "marry" are frequent.

These counts turn out to be excellent predictors of tachistoscopic recognition. For example, Figure 3.10 shows the results of a classic study by Howes and

Solomon (1951). As you can see, there is an orderly relationship between threshold and frequency: The more frequent the word, the lower the threshold. Words that appear in print frequently are easy to recognize in tachistoscopic presentations; words that appear rarely are harder to recognize.

In a different experiment, Jacoby and Dallas (1981) showed their participants words that were either very frequent (appearing more than 50 times in every million printed words) or infrequent (occurring only 1 to 5 times per million words of print). In one of their studies, participants viewed these words for 35 msec, followed by a post-stimulus mask. On average, participants recognized 65% of the frequent words under these conditions, but only 33% of the infrequent words—a striking two-to-one advantage for frequent words.

## REPETITION PRIMING

Another factor that makes words easier to recognize is recency of view. If participants view a word and then, a little later, view it again, they will recognize the word much more readily the second time around. The first exposure primes the participant for the second exposure; more specifically, this is a case of **repetition priming**.

As an example, participants in one study read a list of words aloud. The participants were then shown a series of words in a tachistoscope. Some of the tachistoscopic words were from the earlier list, and so had been primed; others were not from the earlier list, and so were unprimed. For words that were high in frequency, 68% of the unprimed words were recognized, compared to 84% of the primed words. For words low in frequency, 37% of the unprimed words were recognized, compared to 73% of the primed words (Jacoby & Dallas, 1981, Exp. 3). These are large effects, with repetition priming doubling the rate of recognition for low-frequency words.

## THE WORD-SUPERIORITY EFFECT

Words frequently viewed are easier to perceive, as are words viewed recently. It also turns out that *words themselves* are easier to perceive, as compared to isolated letters. This finding is referred to as the **word-superiority effect**.

To demonstrate this effect, we first need to deal with the problem of guessing. Imagine a participant who wasn't able to recognize a target but knows that the target had a curve somewhere along its bottom edge. If the participant also knows that the target contained just a single letter, then he has a decent chance (one in seven) of guessing which letter was shown (since the only choices would be C, G, J, O, Q,

S, and U). But if the participant knew instead that the target was an entire word, then guessing is virtually impossible. (With a vocabulary of, say, 50,000 words, the participant has only a .002% chance of guessing correctly.) Therefore, guessing can provide some help for single letters but provides virtually no help for words, and this would create an unfair advantage for letters in an experiment.

To control for this, the word-superiority effect is usually demonstrated with a "two-alternative forced-choice" procedure. For example, in some trials, we might tachistoscopically present a single letter, let's say K, followed by a post-stimulus mask, and follow that with a question: "Was there an E or a K in the display?" In other trials, we present a word, let's say DARK, followed by a mask, followed by a question: "Was there an E or a K in the display?"

Notice that a participant has a 50-50 chance of guessing correctly in *either* of these situations, and so the contribution from guessing is now matched for the letters and the words. Moreover, note that, for the word stimuli, both of the letters we've asked about are plausible endings for the stimulus—either ending would create a common word (DARE or DARK). A participant who saw only part of the display (perhaps DAR), therefore, couldn't use his knowledge of the language to figure out what the display's final letter was. In order to choose between E and K, the participant really needs to have *seen* the relevant letter—and that, of course, is exactly what we want. The participants' responses will tell us how much they've been able to perceive in these brief exposures.

Many studies have used this procedure, and the result is clear: Recognizing words is easier than recognizing isolated letters. Or, to put this more precisely, participants are more accurate in identifying letters if those letters appear within a *word*, as opposed to appearing all by themselves (Reicher, 1969; Rumelhart & Siple, 1974; Wheeler, 1970).

In some ways, this is a peculiar result: In order to know what word you're looking at, you need to identify the word's letters. That's because the identify of a word is *determined* by the letters. (If the letters were different, then obviously the word would be different.) Cast in these terms, it seems that the step of identifying letters is *part of* the overall task of identifying a word, and thus common sense says that identifying letters should be easier than identifying words. Surely it's easier to do part of a job than it is to do the whole job! Yet the evidence says otherwise.

This effect obviously needs to be explained, and we'll say more about it later. For now, though, let's simply note that the word-superiority effect plainly provides another case in which identification of elements is influenced by context. In this case, the context actually seems to facilitate perception of an object's parts.

## DEGREES OF WELL-FORMEDNESS

Will any context produce the word-superiority effect? Imagine that we present a B within the context of "BWQX." Will this facilitate perception of the B, in comparison to a case in which the B is presented in isolation? Or is perception aided only by *familiar* contexts, or perhaps *meaningful* contexts?

It turns out that neither familiarity nor meaning is crucial for the word-superiority effect. For example, it is easier to recognize an E if it appears within the string "FIKE" than if it appears in isolation. But not all contexts provide an advantage: Recognition of the letter H is helped very little by contexts like "HGFD" or "HXXX."

Likewise, consider these two strings of letters: "JPSRW," and "GLAKE." Neither of these is a word, and neither is familiar, but one is easy to recognize when presented tachistoscopically; the other is not. Strings like JPSRW are difficult to recognize: With exposures of 20 or 30 msec, participants will identify one or two letters from a string like this, but no more. The non-word "GLAKE," however, is far easier to recognize when presented tachistoscopically, and will probably be read correctly with a 20 or 30 msec exposure.

The overall pattern of these data is straightforward: The word-superiority effect is obtained, and recognition is aided, if a letter appears within a context that is well formed according to the rules of the language. Moreover, this is a graded effect, not all-or-none: The more regular the context, the stronger the facilitation. For English speakers, the more a string resembles English, the easier it is to recognize. This is a well-documented pattern and has been known for a long time (e.g., Cattell, 1885).

But how should we assess "resemblance to English"? One way is via pronounceability (e.g., "GLAKE" is easy to say; "JPSRW" is not): In general, pronounceable strings are more easily recognized with tachistoscopic presentations than unpronounceable strings. Alternatively, one can assess "resemblance to English" in statistical terms. One can count up, in English, how often the letter P follows the letter J, how often the letter S follows the letter P, and so forth. In this way, one can ask which letter combinations are likely and which are rare. With this done, one can then evaluate any new string in terms of how likely its letter combinations are. Well-formedness measured in this way is also a good predictor of tachistoscopic performance (Gibson, Bishop, Schiff & Smith, 1964; Miller, Bruner & Postman, 1954).

## MAKING ERRORS

Which is more common in the English language, words beginning with "TO" or words beginning with "TH"? Are there more words in English ending with a T or more words ending with an L? Surely you don't know the answers to these questions—most of us have little (or no) explicit knowledge about the spelling patterns of our language. Nonetheless, our perception of words is unmistakably influenced by these spelling patterns. People have an easier time recognizing the more-probable sequences, a harder time with less-probable ones. The more-probable sequences have lower recognition thresholds, and they are also the sequences that produce the word-superiority effect.

The influence of spelling rules also emerges in another way—in the mistakes we make. With tachistoscopic exposures, word recognition is good, but not perfect, and the errors that occur are quite systematic: There is a strong tendency to misread less-common letter sequences as if they were more-common patterns; irregular patterns are misread as if they were regular patterns. Thus, for example, "TPUM" is likely to be misread as "TRUM" or even "DRUM." But the reverse errors are rare: "DRUM" is unlikely to be misread as "TRUM" or "TPUM."

These errors often involve the misreading of a feature or two (e.g., misperceiving the P as an R, or an O as a Q). But larger errors also occur (for example, someone shown the four letters "TRUM" might instead perceive "TRUMPET"). Both the large and the small errors show the pattern described: Misspelled words, partial words, or non-words are read in a way that brings them into line with normal spelling. In effect, people perceive the input as being more regular than it actually is, and so these errors are referred to as **over-regularization errors**. This suggests once again that our recognition is guided by (or, in this case, *mis*guided by) some knowledge of spelling patterns.

One more point about these errors should be emphasized. Participants in these procedures usually do not realize when they have made an error (e.g., Pills-bury, 1897). From their point of view, they are reporting what they see, and so, apparently, the misspelled or mangled letter sequences actually *look correct* to them. It seems, therefore, that people don't merely misidentify the stimuli; they *misperceive* them.

## Feature Nets and Word Recognition

How can we explain this pattern of evidence? Key elements of the explanation derive from a theory of pattern recognition first published more than 40 years ago (Selfridge, 1959).

### THE DESIGN OF A FEATURE NET

Imagine that you wanted to design a system that would recognize the words of printed English. How would you do it? (See Figure 3.11.) We can build here on some ideas already introduced. Let's imagine that

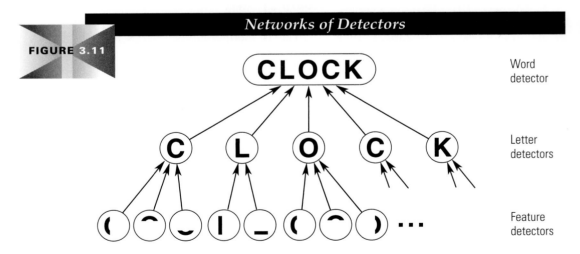

**FIGURE 3.11**

*Networks of Detectors*

Word detector

Letter detectors

Feature detectors

Word detectors might be triggered by letter detectors, so that the word detector would fire whenever the appropriate letters were presented. The letter detectors in turn might be triggered by feature detectors, so the letter detectors would fire whenever the features are on the scene.

one component of this system has the task of recognizing the word "CLOCK" whenever it is presented. This component is therefore the "CLOCK detector." How might the CLOCK detector work? Perhaps the CLOCK detector is "wired" to a C-detector, an L-detector, an O-detector, and so on. Whenever these letter detectors are all activated, this activates the word detector. But what activates the letter detectors? Perhaps the L-detector is "wired" to a horizontal-line detector, and also a vertical-line detector, and maybe also a corner detector, as shown in Figure 3.11. When all of these feature detectors are activated as a group, this activates the letter detector.

The idea here is that there is a network of detectors, organized in layers, with each subsequent layer concerned with more complex, larger-scale objects. The "bottom" layer is concerned with features, and that is why networks of this sort, drawing on features, are referred to as **feature nets**.

Some detectors are easier to activate than others— that is, some detectors require a very strong input to make them fire, whereas other detectors have a "hair trigger" and so will fire even with a weak input. How should we think about this "readiness" to fire? This section presents one way, designed to stay reasonably close to what we know about the functioning of neurons (Chapter 2).

At any point in time, each detector has a particular **activation level**, which reflects how activated that detector is at that moment. When a detector receives some input, this increases its activation level. A strong input will increase the activation level by a lot, as will a *series* of weaker inputs. In either case, the activation level eventually gets high enough to cause the detector to fire—that is, to send its signal to the other detectors to which it is connected. The detector's **response threshold** is the activation level at which this response occurs—that is, a detector fires when its activation level reaches the response threshold.

In addition, each detector has its own **baseline activation level**, or **resting level**. This is the detector's activation level prior to any inputs, its activation level when the detector is, so to speak, at rest. If a detector happens to have a high baseline level, then only a little input is needed to raise the acti-

vation level to threshold. This is why some detectors are relatively easy to activate. If another detector happens to have a low baseline level, then a strong input is needed to bring the detector to threshold; this detector will be relatively difficult to activate.

What determines a detector's baseline level? Detectors that have fired recently will have a higher baseline level. Detectors that have fired frequently in the past will gradually gain a higher and higher baseline level. Thus the baseline level is dependent on principles of *recency* and *frequency*.

We now can put this mechanism to work. Why are frequent words in the language easier to recognize with tachistoscopic exposures than rare words? Frequent words have, by definition, appeared often in the things you read. Therefore, the detectors needed for recognizing these words have been frequently used, and so they have relatively high levels of baseline activation. Thus, even a weak signal (e.g., a very brief presentation of the word) will bring these detectors to the response threshold, and so will be enough to make these detectors fire. Thus, the word will be recognized even with a weak or degraded input.

Repetition priming is explained in similar terms. Presenting a word once will cause the relevant detectors to fire. Once they have fired, baseline activation levels will be temporarily lifted, because of recency of use. Therefore only a weak signal will be needed to make the detectors fire again. As a result, the word will be more easily recognized the second time around.

## THE FEATURE NET AND WELL-FORMEDNESS

The net we've described so far, however, cannot explain all of the data. Consider the effects of well-formedness—for instance, the fact that people are quite efficient at reading strings like "PIRT" or "HICE," but are inefficient in reading strings like "ITPR" or "HCEI." None of these strings is a word, so word detectors don't come into play here. Hence, we cannot explain this observation—the efficiency of recognizing regular strings, the inefficiency of recognizing irregular strings—in terms of differential priming

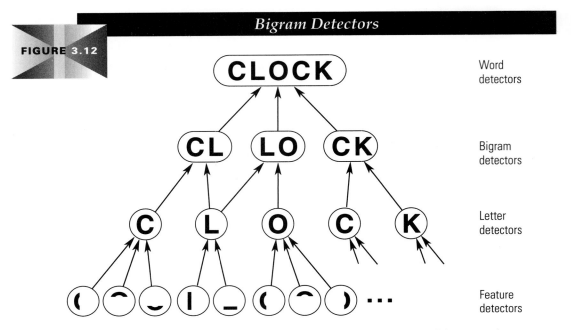

**Bigram Detectors**

FIGURE 3.12

It seems plausible that a layer of bigram detectors is interposed between letter detectors and word detectors.

in word detectors. We also can't explain this observation in terms of the priming of letter detectors, since, as it turns out, we have held constant the individual letters being used ("ITPR" is an anagram of "PIRT").

There are several ways we might accommodate these results: As one option, let's add another layer to the net, a layer filled with detectors for letter combinations. In Figure 3.12, we have added a layer of **bigram** detectors—detectors of letter *pairs*. These detectors, like all the rest, will each have a baseline activation level (their activation level when they're at rest), and also a moment-by-moment activation level, changing as new inputs arrive. As before, activation levels will be influenced by the frequency with which these detectors have fired in the past, and also the recency with which they have fired.

This turns out to be all the theory we need to explain the influence of well-formedness. Why are English-like non-words more easily recognized than strings *not* resembling English ("RSFK" or "IUBE")? Well-formed words involve familiar letter combina-

tions. You have never seen the sequence "HICE" before, but you have seen the letter pair "HI" (in HIT, HIGH, or HILL) and the pair "CE" (FACE, MACE, PACE). The detectors for these letter groups, therefore, have high baseline activations and don't need much additional input to reach their threshold. As a result, these well-used detectors will fire with only weak input. That will make the corresponding letter combinations easy to recognize, facilitating the recognition of strings like "HICE." None of this is true for "RSFK." None of these letter combinations is familiar, and so this string will receive no benefits from priming. A strong input will therefore be needed to bring the relevant detectors to threshold, and so the string will be recognized only with difficulty.

## RECOVERY FROM ERRORS AND BEING "ROBUST"

Human pattern recognition is remarkably robust. We can recognize patterns when the light levels are

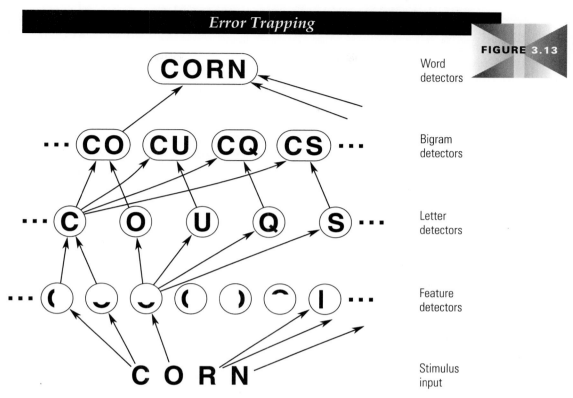

**Error Trapping**

FIGURE 3.13

Word detectors

Bigram detectors

Letter detectors

Feature detectors

Stimulus input

If CORN is presented briefly, not all of its features will be detected. Imagine, for example, that only the bottom curve of the O is detected, and not the O's top or sides. This will (weakly) activate the O-detector, but will also activate various other letters having a bottom curve, including U, Q, and S. This will, in turn, send weak activation to the appropriate bigram detectors. The CO-detector, however, is well primed, and so is likely to respond even though it is receiving only a weak input. The other bigram detectors (for CQ or CS) are less well primed, and so will not respond to this weak input. Therefore, CORN will be correctly perceived, despite the confusion at the letter level caused by the weak signal.

low. We can recognize patterns when we are tired. Even with tachistoscopic presentations, we recognize a great many stimuli. If a feature net serves as the basis for human pattern recognition, then the net needs to be similarly robust.

Imagine that we tachistoscopically present the word "CORN." With a brief presentation, the quantity of incoming information is small, and so the relevant detectors will fire only weakly. Figure 3.13

shows how this might play out: The fast presentation of the O wasn't enough to trigger all of the feature detectors appropriate for the O. As it turns out, only the "bottom-curve" detector is firing. This feature detector feeds into many letter detectors—for example, the O-detector, the U-detector, the Q-detector, and the S-detector. Thus, with only this single feature detector activated, each of these letter detectors will be weakly activated.

But look what happens at the next level. The CO, CU, CQ and CS bigram detectors will all receive a strong signal from the C-detector, and a weak signal about the second letter in the bigram. However, the CO-detector is well primed (because this is a frequent pattern), and so this detector has a frequency advantage. Consequently, a weak signal will be enough to fire this detector. The CU-detector is less primed (since this is a less-frequent pattern); the CQ- or CS-detectors, if these even exist, are not primed at all. The weak input will therefore not be enough to activate these detectors. Thus, at the letter level, there was confusion about the input letter's identity—several detectors were firing, and all were firing equally. At the bigram level, this confusion has been sorted out, and so an error has been avoided.

In this example, confusion at the letter level was straightened out at the bigram level. In the same way, uncertainty at the feature level can be sorted out at the letter level, and confusion at the bigram level can be straightened out at higher levels (e.g., the word detectors). Psychologists refer to this sort of process as **error trapping**—procedures that detect and correct errors before the errors cause further confusion.

### AMBIGUOUS INPUTS

The mechanism just described will also help in explaining some other evidence. Look again at Figure 3.6 (p. 62). The character in the middle of the left-hand string is the same as the character in the middle of the right-hand string. Yet the left-hand string is perceived as "THE," and the character as an H, and the right-hand string is perceived as "CAT," and the character as an A.

This observation is now easily explained. At the feature level, the ambiguous neither-A-nor-H has some features of an A and some features of an H. When the pattern is presented, the relevant feature detectors will fire. But not all of the A features will fire (since not all are present), and ditto for the H features. So the A-detector receives only partial input, and will fire only weakly. Likewise for the H-detector. At this level, therefore, there is uncertainty about what the incoming letter is.

The uncertainty is resolved at subsequent levels. The TH-detector is enormously well primed; so is the THE-detector. If there were a TAE-detector, it would be barely primed, since this is a string rarely encountered. Thus the THE- and TAE-detectors might be receiving comparable input, since both the A-detector and H-detector are (weakly) firing. But this weak input is sufficient for the well-primed THE-detector, and so it will be activated. In this way, the net will recognize the ambiguous pattern as "THE," not "TAE." Likewise for the ambiguous pattern on the right, perceived as "CAT," not "CHT."

A similar explanation will handle the word-superiority effect (see, for example, Rumelhart & Siple, 1974). To take a simple case, imagine that we present A in the context "AT." If the presentation is brief enough, participants may see very little of the A, perhaps just the horizontal cross-bar. This would not be enough to distinguish among A, F, or H, and so all these letter detectors would fire weakly. If this were all the information the participants had, they'd be stuck. But let us imagine that the participants did perceive the second letter in the display, the T. It seems likely that the AT bigram is far better primed than the FT or HT bigrams. (That is because you often encounter words like CAT or BOAT; words like SOFT or HEFT are less frequent in the English language.) Thus, the weak firing of the A-detector *would* be enough to fire the AT bigram detector, while the weak firing for the F and H might not trigger their bigram detectors. In this way, a "choice" would be made at the bigram level that the input was "AT" and not something else. Once this bigram has been detected, answering the question "Was there an A or an F in the display?" is easy. In this manner, the letter will be better detected in context than in isolation. This is not because context allows you to see more; instead, context allows you to make better use of what you see.

### RECOGNITION ERRORS

Note, though, that there is a downside to all this: Imagine that we present the string "CQRN" to participants. If the presentation is brief enough, participants will register only a subset of the string's

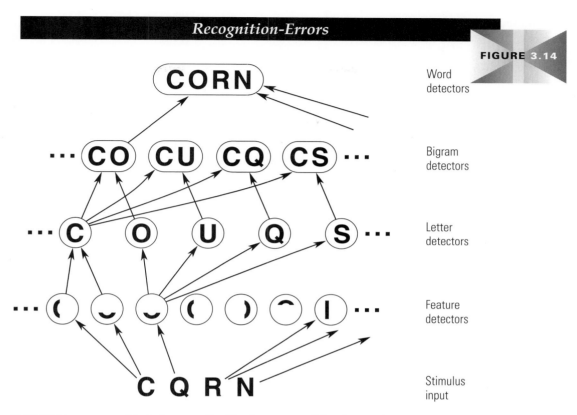

**Recognition-Errors**

FIGURE 3.14

Word detectors

Bigram detectors

Letter detectors

Feature detectors

Stimulus input

If CQRN is presented briefly, not all of its features will be detected. Perhaps only the bottom curve of the Q is detected, and this will (weakly) activate various other letters having a bottom curve, including O, U, and S. However, this is the same situation that would result from a brief presentation of CORN (as shown in Figure 3.13), and therefore, by the logic we have already discussed, this stimulus is likely to be *mis*perceived as CORN.

features. Let's imagine, in line with an earlier example, that they register only the bottom bit of the string's second letter. This detection of the bottom curve will weakly activate the Q-detector, and also the U-detector and the O-detector. The resulting pattern of network activation is shown in Figure 3.14, and you should notice that this figure is nearly identical to Figure 3.13.

We have already argued that the dynamic of network function in Figure 3.13 will lead to a response of "CORN." But, since the "grist" for the network is

the same in Figure 3.14, then this pattern, too, will lead to "CORN." Hence, in the first case, the functional dynamic built into the net aids performance; in the second case, the same dynamic causes us to misread the stimulus.

Let's make three points about this observation. First, we now have a straightforward account of over-regularization errors: Because of the pattern of priming, the network's responses will tend toward frequent words, and also toward words recently viewed. If the input was, in fact, a frequent word, then the bias built into the network facilitates perception. If the input was an infrequent word, or an irregular word, then the network's bias will lead to errors. Moreover, the network's mistakes will be systematic in their form: "CQRN" will be identified as "CORN," "TAE" as "THE," and so on.

Second, note that it's not a problem that our network is making errors; instead, it's an advantage. Humans make errors, so if our model is to provide a plausible account of human achievements, then it should make errors as well. Moreover, it should make errors as often as, and in the same settings as, humans do, and the particular errors made should match the errors that humans make.

Finally, note that these errors are usually unproblematic. Low-frequency words are likely to be misperceived but, by definition, low-frequency words aren't encountered that often. The network's bias facilitates perception of *frequent* words, and these (by definition) are the words you encounter most of the time. Hence, the network's bias aids recognition in the more frequent cases and hurts recognition only in the rare cases. Necessarily, then, the network's bias helps perception more often than it hurts.

**WHY AREN'T THE MISTAKES NOTICED?**

We mentioned earlier that research participants don't merely *misidentify* the input; they seem instead to *misperceive* it. When people in tachistoscopic procedures make errors, they often insist that they are reporting what they clearly saw. What produces this illusion?

Our answer to this question does little more than emphasize points we have already made: Consider the similarity between Figures 3.13 and 3.14. In Figure 3.13, the firing of the CO-detector is a legitimate detection. In Figure 3.14, the firing of this detector constitutes a false alarm, a detection even though there's no "CO" present. From the network's point of view, however, these cases are indistinguishable. Once the CO-detector fires, this will trigger subsequent detectors. The only information available to these subsequent detectors is the fact that the CO-detector is firing. There is no way for the subsequent detectors to

know *why* the detector is firing—whether in response to a genuine signal, or as a false alarm. Thus, the distinction between false alarm and genuine detection is soon lost.

Let's complicate things somewhat: Imagine that we again present the string "CQRN," as in Figure 3.14, but let's say that, this time, the participant detects a bit more information about the Q. Perhaps, for example, the participant also detects the Q's "tail." With this feature detected, we would expect a somewhat stronger response from the Q-detector. Therefore, in this scenario, the Q-detector will be firing at a moderate level, while the O-detector and the S-detectors, as before, are firing only weakly. None of this changes the fact that the CO-detector is well primed, while the CQ-detector is not. As a result, the outcome from this case may be the same as before: We've already said that a weak response from the O-detector may be enough to trigger the well-primed CO-detector. In contrast, even a moderate response from the Q-detector may not be enough to trigger the (unprimed) CQ-detector. Thus it is the CO-detector that fires, and we are right back in the situation of Figure 3.14. In this case, the Q was initially perceived *correctly* but, in the chain of subsequent events, this information is "lost."

There's no way for the network to record the fact that a detector has been "overruled," as the Q-detector was in the previous example. There is also, as we have seen, no way for the network to distinguish false alarms from detections. All of this guarantees that, for the network, mistakes will be indistinguishable from the "real thing." There will be no difference, as far as the net is concerned, between stimuli that actually occurred and stimuli that were merely inferred. In this particular domain, there is no clear distinction between reality and hallucination.

**PARALLEL PROCESSING AND DISTRIBUTED KNOWLEDGE**

We are almost ready to leave our discussion of the feature net. In closing, though, we need to work through two last points—first, the nature of the "knowledge" built into the network, and second, the broader question of *why* the network should function as it does.

We've seen many indications that, somehow, knowledge of spelling patterns is "built into" the network. For example, the network "knows" that CO is a common bigram in English, whereas CF is not. As a result, it's literally true that the system is better prepared for one of these patterns than for the other. One might say that the system "expects" one of these patterns (CO) to appear often, but has no such expectation for the other (CF). However, this "expectation" is an entirely passive one—built into the activation levels (and therefore the preparedness) of the net.

The sense in which the net "knows" these facts about spelling is worth emphasizing, since we will return to this idea in later chapters. This knowledge is not explicitly stored anywhere. Nowhere within the net is there a sentence like "CO is a common bigram in English; CF is not." Instead, this memory, if we even want to call it that, is manifest only in the fact that the CO-detector happens to be more primed than the CF-detector. The CO-detector doesn't "know" anything about this relation, nor does the CF-detector. Each simply does its job. In the course of doing their jobs, occasions will arise that involve a "competition" between these detectors. (We considered such situations in our discussion of error trapping, or ambiguous inputs.) In these cases, the better-primed detector will be more likely to respond to weak inputs and so will be more likely to influence subsequent events. That's how these "knowledge effects" arise.

In short, then, the knowledge that CO is a common bigram is manifest only by virtue of how the various elements of the net function relative to each other—which voices are influential, and which not—when all these detectors are doing their individual jobs. The knowledge is thus visible only if we take a "bird's-eye view" and consider how the entire system functions. The knowledge, therefore, is *not* **locally represented**, but is instead **distributed** across the pattern of network functioning.

The same can be said for all of the net's knowledge, and about the net's inferences. For example, if we present the stimulus "T-[smudge]-E," it is convenient to speak of the network "drawing the inference" that the input was THE, rather than, say, TAE. But of course, the net doesn't literally make an inference. Instead, the THE-detector is simply readier to fire than the TAE-detector and, once firing happens, something like an inference has taken place. There is no "inference-maker"—the inference is not a local process. The inference is only manifest, once again, in how various detectors work in conjunction with each other, and so the inference is a distributed process.

What is perhaps most remarkable about the feature net, then, lies in how much can be accomplished with simple, mechanical elements, correctly connected to one another. The net appears to make inferences and appears to "know" the rules of English spelling. But the actual mechanics of the net involve neither inferences nor knowledge (at least not in any conventional sense). Information about spelling patterns is, as we've said, distributed across the net, and so you or I could discern this information by taking the bird's-eye view, comparing the activation of one detector with the activation level of some other. But nothing in the net's functioning depends on a bird's-eye view. Instead, the activity of each detector is locally determined—influenced by just those detectors feeding into it. When all of these detectors work in conjunction with each other, the result is a process that acts as if it "knows the rules." But the rules themselves play no causal role in the network's moment-by-moment activities.

## EFFICIENCY VERSUS ACCURACY

The network we are describing has both advantages and disadvantages. On the positive side, the net is robust, able to deal with ambiguous inputs, and able to recover from its own errors. On the negative side, the net makes mistakes, misreading some inputs, misinterpreting some patterns. As we have seen, though, the mechanisms that produce the mistakes are exactly the same ones that produce the advantages; this was evident (for example) in Figures 3.13 and 3.14, in which the same pattern of activations helped us cope with a partial input in one case but led us to a mistake in another case.

Perhaps, therefore, we should view the errors as simply the price one pays in order to obtain the benefits associated with the net. But this invites a question: Do we really need to pay this price? Why couldn't evolution have provided a mechanism that was both robust *and* error-free? To tackle this question, we need to spell out some considerations about the network's *efficiency*.

Our world is in many ways a highly predictable place. When you look around a kitchen, it is extremely likely that you will find a stove and a refrigerator, far less likely that you will find a hippopotamus. When you attend a birthday party, it is likely that presents will be given and cake will be served, it is unlikely that wood will be chopped during the party, or floors will be scrubbed. Thus, it is redundant to say "I went to a birthday party, but we didn't scrub any floors," since the second claim is already implied by the first.

Our language itself is also quite redundant, so that many of the letters of a wrd are completely predictable from contxt; the same often true for words within a sentence. In fact, we can push this quite far: It's am-z-ng, f-r -x-mple, h-w m-ny l-tt-rs we c-n r-m-v- -nd st-ll h-v- a s-nt-nc- th-t's n-t d-ff-c-lt to r—d. Because of this redundancy, one does not need to scrutinize every letter on a page, or every word. Instead, one can selectively glance at the page and let the net "fill in" the rest.

Why should we exploit this redundancy? Why should we opt for efficiency? Are we simply an impatient species? We can think this through by considering the alternative to "being efficient." If, for example, we wished for perfect accuracy, then we would want to make no inferences (since these might be mistaken), and no assumptions (since these might be unwarranted). To achieve this, we would need to spell out *everything*. But what does this mean?

Think back to the "Betsy and Jacob" story, discussed in Chapter 1. This story leaves a great deal unsaid, relying on the fact that listeners (or readers) can fill in the missing information. The savings for the storyteller are enormous: The story can be told with a few short sentences, rather than extending for many pages. The savings for the listener are comparable: The story can be digested in a matter of seconds, rather than requiring hours of study. If, instead, we insisted on spelling out everything, this story would need to be intolerably long, and the telling of it impossibly slow. Moreover, the gains of spelling out everything would be tiny, since we'd be forced to include extraordinary quantities of information that, in truth, should be blindingly obvious (e.g., the fact that people need money to buy things). In short, spelling out everything would have an enormous cost and would gain us very, very little. If we insist on greater efficiency, then, we are not being impatient, we are simply being reasonable.

These claims are also true of word recognition and of reading in general. To maximize accuracy, we would, of course, want to scrutinize every character on the page. That way, if any character is missing or misprinted, we would be sure to detect it. But the cost associated with this strategy would be insufferable: Reading would be unspeakably slow. In contrast, one can make *inferences* about a page with remarkable speed, and this leads readers to adopt the obvious strategy: They read some of the letters and make inferences about the rest. This does risk error but, if the inferences are well guided, then the errors will be rare. Thus, the efficient reader is not being careless, or hasty, or lazy. Given the redundancy of text, and given the slowness of letter-by-letter reading, the inferential strategy is the only strategy that makes sense.

It's not surprising, therefore, that we do exploit the redundancy of text in our ordinary reading; this is reflected, for example, in studies of readers' eye movements. Those studies show that readers do not move their eyes across the page in a letter-by-letter fashion, so that each letter can be scrutinized in its turn. Instead, they look at a word, then skip many letters along, then look again, then skip again (Crowder & Wagner, 1992; Rayner, 1993, 1998). In this fashion, "reading" turns out to involve a mix of actually looking at the page, in order to gather input, and then a process of making inferences, in order to fill in the bits that *weren't* looked at.

Indeed, one of the major differences between fast and slow readers, or between adults and children, is that fast, skilled readers jump over *larger* sections of text with each eye movement, so that, in a sense, skilled readers are actually reading less, and inferring more, as they move down the page, in comparison to less-skilled readers. Put differently, the skill of reading does not involve "seeing more" on the page. Just the opposite: The skill involves seeing *less* but making more effective use of what one has seen. This same idea is at the core of "speed reading." A speed reader does not "see more in a single glance" (despite what the advertisements say). Instead, a speed reader learns to make maximum use of inference in order to minimize the reliance on actual look-at-the-page reading. That is why, for example, speed-reading courses often urge you to study a book's illustrations and its table of contents before starting to read; this "preview" provides a base for making inferences, helping you to make them swiftly and accurately.

Is speed reading a good thing? For some purposes, yes: In reading a newspaper, for example, many of the words and many of the ideas expressed can be inferred from context. To get the content as quickly as possible, therefore, speed reading can be helpful. In other settings, though, speed reading is a disaster. If you're trying to read material that is dense in information and rich with new ideas, a reliance on inference is a bad bet—your inferences will often be mistaken. Likewise, if you speed read Shakespeare, you will be able to infer the gist, but you won't be able to infer what phrasing Shakespeare used or what images he created. (To infer those things, you'd probably need to be as good a writer as Shakespeare was.) Therefore, if you speed read Shakespeare, you'll get the plot, but not the language itself—not much different from what you'd get from reading a comic-book version of Shakespeare rather than the original. For most of us, that utterly defeats the purpose of reading Shakespeare—even if speed reading did allow you to read the play in one-quarter the time.

## PROOFREADING

Think about the familiar task of proofreading to correct spelling or grammatical errors. This is a task in which you *do* want to read letter-by-letter, even if this is quite slow, in order to catch any errors. As it turns out, though, this is rather difficult to do, underscoring the important role of inference in reading.

It is obvious that proofreading is hard. Despite careful and repeated readings of your own paper, you fail to spot some of the errors; you overlook words that are misspelled or omitted, you fail to detect inappropriate substitutions (*from* when you meant to type *form*). Inevitably, though, some other reader (for example, your professor) does spot the errors and returns your paper covered with red ink.

We need no new theory to explain this, since we have already discussed how misperceptions can occur. Ironically, these misperceptions may be *more* likely in reading your own papers than in reading anything else. In reading something that you wrote yourself, you are particularly well primed for the words on the page. You know what you intended to write, and this knowledge will guide your inferences. In addition, odds are that you have read the page several times as you worked on successive drafts. With all of this priming, this is surely a case in which minimal input is needed to make the detectors fire. Hence, it is possible here for you to rely on maximal use of inference as you read down the page. And, like it or not, that is exactly what you do, reading efficiently but not spotting the errors. For these reasons, it is a useful strategy to have a friend proofread for you, since he or she will be less well primed for the words on the page and will therefore be less able to use the fully inferential strategy.

The difficulties of proofreading allow us to make one further point: It seems that you have little choice about adopting the efficient strategy of reading. In proofreading, you might prefer to read *less* efficiently in order to make no recognition errors: You want to find your typing mistakes. Nonetheless, the strategy of using inference is so well practiced, so automatic, that you use it even here. (For studies of proofreading, see Daneman & Stainton, 1991; Healy, Volbrecht & Nye, 1983; Healy, 1981.)

## Descendants of the Feature Net

As we mentioned early on, we have been focusing on one of the simpler and older versions of the feature net. This has allowed us to get a number of important themes into view—such as the trade-off between efficiency and accuracy, and the notion of distributed knowledge built into a network's functioning. However, it should be said that many variations on the feature-net idea are possible, each differing somewhat from the specific proposal we have discussed, and each with its own advantages and disadvantages. In this section, we consider two other, more recent, versions of the network idea.

## THE MCCLELLAND AND RUMELHART MODEL

An influential model of word recognition was proposed by McClelland and Rumelhart (1981); a portion of their model is illustrated in Figure 3.15. Once again, there is a feature base and a network of connections, as various detectors serve to influence one another. This net, like the one we have been discussing, is better able to identify well-formed strings than irregular strings; this net is also more efficient in identifying characters in context, as opposed to characters in isolation. However, several new features of this net make it possible to accomplish all this *without* bigram detectors.

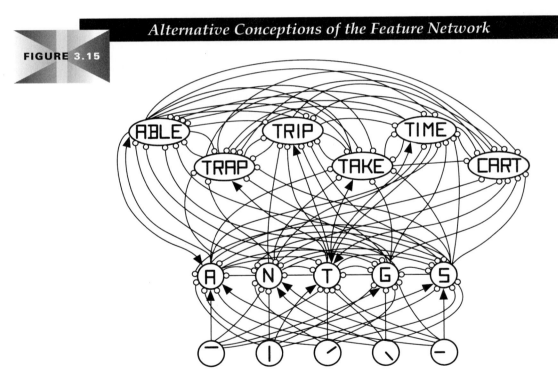

**FIGURE 3.15**

### *Alternative Conceptions of the Feature Network*

McClelland and Rumelhart (1981) offered a pattern-recognition model with no detectors for letter combinations. Instead, letter detectors directly activate word detectors. This model includes both excitatory connections (indicated by arrows) and inhibitory connections (indicated by connections with round heads). Connections *within* a specific level are also possible—so that, for example, activation of the TRIP detector will inhibit the detectors for TRAP, TAKE, or TIME.

In the network proposal we have considered so far, activation of one detector serves to activate other detectors; these **excitatory connections** are shown in Figure 3.15 with arrows, so that detection of a T serves to "excite" the TRIP-detector. In the McClelland and Rumelhart model, however, detectors can also *inhibit* each other, so that detection of a G, for example, inhibits the TRIP-detector. These **inhibitory connections** are shown in the figure with dots. In addition, this model allows for more complicated signaling than we have employed so far. In our discussion, we have assumed that lower-level detectors trigger upper-level detectors, but not the reverse. The flow of information, it seemed, was a one-way street. In the McClelland and Rumelhart model, though, higher-level detectors (word detectors) can influence the lower-level detectors, and detectors at any level can also influence the other detectors at the same level (e.g., letter detectors inhibit other letter detectors; word detectors inhibit other word detectors).

To see how this would work, let's say that the word "TRIP" is briefly shown, allowing a viewer to see enough features to identify, say, only the R, I, and P. Detectors for these letters will therefore fire, and this will in turn activate the detector for "TRIP." Activation of this word detector will cause two further effects. First, it will inhibit the firing of all the other word detectors (e.g., detectors for "ABLE," "TRAP," "TAKE," and so on). Second, activation of the TRIP-detector will excite the detectors for its component letters—i.e., detectors for T, R, I, and P. The R-, I-, and P-detectors, we've supposed, were already firing, so this extra activation "from above" has little impact. But the T-detector, we've supposed, was not firing before. The relevant features were on the scene, but in a degraded form, thanks to the brief presentation; this weak input was insufficient to trigger an unprimed detector. But the excitation from the word detector now primes the T-detector, making it more likely to fire, even with a weak input.

In essence, activation of the word detector for TRIP implied that this was a context in which a T was quite likely; hence the network "prepared itself" for a T by priming the appropriate detector. Once the network was suitably prepared, detection was facilitated. In this way, the detection of a letter sequence made the network more sensitive to elements likely to occur within that sequence. That is exactly what we need for the network to be responsive to the regularities of spelling patterns. And, of course, there is ample evidence that humans are sensitive to (and exploit) these regularities.

There are actually several reasons one might prefer this kind of net over the kind considered earlier. As one consideration, there is ample evidence that higher-level detectors *can* activate lower-level detectors, just as the McClelland and Rumelhart model proposes. We will return to these "top-down" effects in a few pages, and similar effects will be discussed in Chapter 4. Second, we can also find *biological* evidence for this sort of "two-way communication" in the nervous system: Neurons in the eyeballs send activation to the brain but also *receive* activation from the brain; neurons in the LGN send activation to the visual cortex but also receive activation from the cortex; and so on. These facts make it clear that visual processing is not a one-way process, with information flowing simply from the visual periphery toward the brain. Instead, signaling occurs in both an ascending (toward the brain) and a descending (away from the brain) direction, just as the McClelland and Rumelhart model claims.

## RECOGNITION BY COMPONENTS

We noted early on that our discussion would focus largely on the recognition of print. But what can we say about recognition of other things, including the recognition of three-dimensional objects? Can these also be recognized by a network?

In a series of studies, Biederman (1987, 1995; Biederman & Cooper, 1991) has presented a network theory of object recognition, dubbed the **recognition by components** (or RBC) model. The crucial innovation here is an intermediate level of detectors, sensitive to **geons**. Biederman's proposal is that geons (for "geometric ions") serve as the basic building blocks of all the objects we recognize; geons are, in essence, the "alphabet" from which all objects are constructed. Geons are simple shapes, such as cylinders, cones, and blocks (Figure 3.16A). And only a small set of these shapes is needed: According to Biederman, we need (at most) three dozen different geons to describe every object in the world, just as 26 letters are all that are needed to produce all the words of English. These geons can then be combined in various ways—in a "top-of" relation, or a "side-connected" relation, and so on, to create all the objects we perceive (see Figure 3.16B).

The RBC model, like the network we have been discussing, uses a hierarchy of detectors. The lowest-level detectors are feature detectors, which respond to edges, curves, vertices, and so on. These detectors in turn activate the geon detectors. Higher levels of detectors are then sensitive to combinations of

geons. More precisely, geons are assembled into more complex arrangements called "geon assemblies," and these in turn activate the "object model," a representation of the complete, recognized object.

The presence of the geon level within this hierarchy buys us several advantages. For one, we noted at the very start of this chapter that, quite obviously, we can recognize objects from many different angles. It is therefore an important attribute of geons that they can be identified from virtually any angle of view. Thus, no matter what your position, relative to a cat, you'll be able to identify its geons and thus identify the cat. Moreover, it seems that most objects can be recognized from just a few geons (in the appropriate configuration). As a consequence, geon-based models

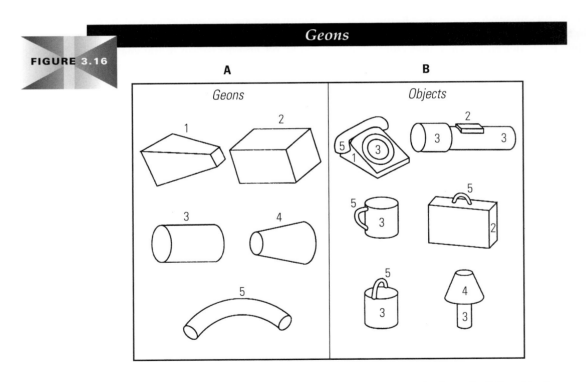

**Geons**

**A**      **B**

FIGURE 3.16

*Geons*      *Objects*

Biederman (1987, 1990) has proposed that geons serve as the basic building blocks of all the objects we recognize. In other words, we recognize objects by first recognizing their component geons. Panel A shows five different geons; Panel B shows how these geons can be assembled into objects. The numbers in Panel B identify the specific geons, so that a bucket contains Geon 5 "top-connected" to Geon 3.

## *Recognizing Degraded Pictures*

**FIGURE** 3.17

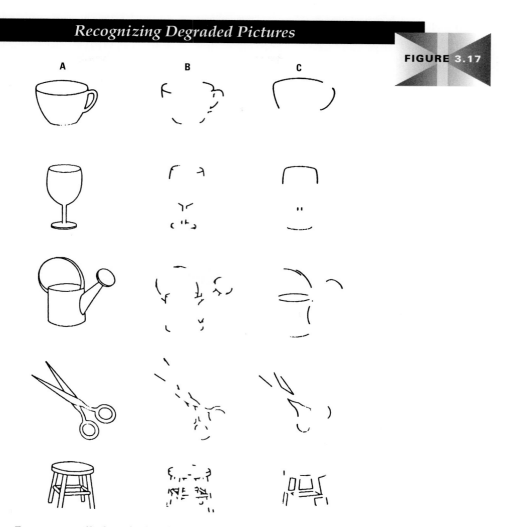

In Column B, one can still identify the objects' geons, and so the forms are easily recognized. In Column C, it is difficult to identify the geons, and correspondingly difficult to identify the objects. This adds strength to the claim that geon identification plays an important role in object recognition.

like RBC can recognize an object even if many of the object's geons are hidden from view. (For some discussion of whether this is truly an advantage, though, see Tarr & Bülthoff, 1998; Wallis & Bülthoff, 1999.)

In addition, several lines of evidence suggest that geons may in fact play a role in recognition. For ex-

ample, recognition of simple objects is relatively easy if the geons are easy to discern; recognition is much more difficult if the geons are hard to identify (e.g., Biederman, 1985). As an example, consider the objects shown in Figure 3.17. In columns B and C, about two-thirds of the contour has been deleted from each drawing. In column B, this deletion has been carefully done so that the geons can still be identified; as you can see, these objects can be recognized without much difficulty. In column C, however, the deletion has been done in a fashion that obscures geon identity; now object recognition is much more difficult. Thus, it really does seem that the geons capture something crucial for identification of these objects.

A different line of evidence draws on a procedure we have already discussed, namely, repetition priming. In this procedure, a stimulus is presented and then, some time later, the same stimulus is presented again. Thanks to repetition priming, the stimulus

will be easier to recognize the second time around. In general, repetition priming is maximal when the second stimulus is identical to the first (same size, same orientation, and so on). However, we can also observe repetition priming with non-identical stimuli. The trick, though, is that the two stimuli (the primer and the primed) must be related in the right way. More precisely, repetition priming is observed if the two stimuli employ the same geons.

To see how this works, note that the pictures in Figure 3.18 are in "complementary pairs"—if you superimpose picture A1 on picture A2, you'd get a complete drawing of a piano; superimposing B1 on

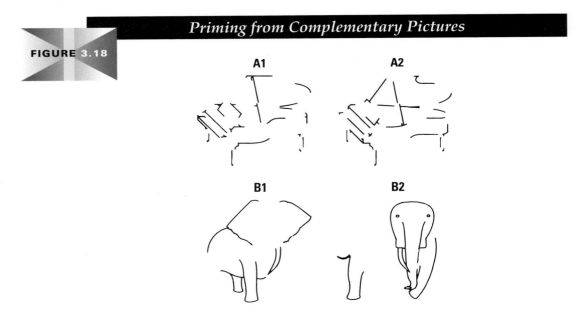

**FIGURE 3.18**

**Priming from Complementary Pictures**

Superimposing A1 and A2 would yield a complete drawing of a piano; superimposing B1 and B2 would yield a complete drawing of an elephant. But the drawings are fragmented in different ways: A1 and A2 depict different features, but the geons identifiable in A1 are the same as the geons shown in A2. Because of this "geon overlap," experience with A1 helps participants in later recognizing A2. For the elephant picture, the geons identifiable in B1 are different from those identifiable in B2. With no geon overlap, experience with B1 does *not* help in later recognizing B2.

B2 would yield a complete drawing of an elephant. But the two pairs are fragmented in different ways: A1 and A2 depict different features, but the geons included in A1 are the same as those shown in A2. That is because, for example, A1 might depict the left-hand side of the geon, while A2 depicts the right-hand side. In contrast, B1 and B2 do not share geons: If a geon is depicted in B1, it is not depicted in B2, and vice versa.

Biederman and Cooper (1991) used pictures like these in a repetition priming experiment. Participants were initially shown one partial picture (for example, A1 or B1), and then were subsequently shown that picture's complement (A2 or B2). The question was whether repetition priming would be observed—that is, whether A1 would prime A2, and whether B1 would prime B2. Biederman and Cooper hypothesized that priming takes place largely at the geon level. Since A1 and A2 depict the same geons, each should prime the other. On the other hand, B1 and B2 do not share geons, and so should not prime each other. The geon detectors needed for B1 are irrelevant to the perception of B2; thus, "warming up" these detectors (by presenting B1) should have no effect on the perception of B2. All of this fits with the data: Complementary pictures did prime each other if the complements shared geons; complementary pictures without shared geons did not prime each other. This indicates that priming in this procedure is indeed taking place at the level of geon detection and, for our purposes, confirms the central point: that geons do play a role in object identification.

The RBC model does an impressive job of object recognition—recognizing a wide range of objects, across a wide range of variations in size, position, and so on. Thus, this seems like a promising approach to object recognition and confirms the claim that a network of hierarchically arranged detectors plays an important part in object recognition. (For some concerns about the RBC model, see Ullman, 1989; Tarr & Bülthoff, 1998. For other current research, see Biederman, 1987; Biederman & Gerhardstein, 1993; Hummel & Biederman, 1992.)

## Different Objects, Different Recognition Systems?

The previous section shifted our focus away from print: A network can also be designed, it seems, to recognize three-dimensional objects. But how far can we travel on this path? Can other sorts of recognition—recognition of sounds, recognition of faces, recognition of smells—be approached in the same way?

These are, of course, questions to be settled by research, and in this section we will consider some of the relevant evidence. As we will see, many domains, rather distant from print, do show effects similar to the ones we have reviewed, suggesting that similar mechanisms are in play. Other domains, however, reveal a different dynamic, implying that, for these domains, we will need a different sort of theory.

### RECOGNITION ERRORS IN HEARING

Many of the principles surveyed so far do generalize to other domains. For example, it seems true in general that more frequently viewed (or more frequently heard) patterns are easier to recognize. Likewise, repetition priming can be demonstrated with many different kinds of stimuli. It is also true in general that regular or well-formed patterns are easier to recognize than ill-formed patterns. And, when recognition errors occur, they are, in general, in the direction of "regularizing" the input, just as in the case of print. All of this invites the conclusion that a uniform theoretical treatment will be possible across diverse domains.

As an illustration of the relevant research, consider studies of the so-called **restoration effect**. In these procedures, sounds are tape-recorded and then carefully modified. For example, the "s" sound in the word "legislature" might be removed, and replaced by a brief burst of noise. When people hear this degraded input, however, they do not detect the omission; instead, they report hearing the *com-*

*plete* word, "legislature," *accompanied by* a burst of noise. In effect, they supply the missing sound on their own. If they are asked exactly when the "accompanying" noise occurred (simultaneous with the first syllable? the second?), they often cannot tell (Repp, 1992; Samuel, 1987, 1991; for further discussion of the recognition of speech, see Chapter 10). Similar effects have been documented with musical stimuli. In this case, simple melodies or scales are recorded, and then single notes are replaced by bursts of noise. Once again, people report hearing the notes that are not there, and once again, they are inaccurate in judging when, within the sequence, the noise appeared (DeWitt & Samuel, 1990).

These restoration errors are plainly related to the errors we have described in print recognition—for example, proofreading errors. In both cases, the perceiver goes beyond the information actually provided, filling in the information that should be there. In the case of print, we attributed this to well-primed detectors. Thanks to priming, these detec-

tors will fire even in response to a weak input; that makes the network robust. Unfortunately, though, we can find circumstances in which the detectors fire in the *absence* of an input—producing what we called a false alarm response. Apparently, the same is true with auditory stimuli such as speech, or even with non-linguistic stimuli, such as musical phrases.

## FACES

However, at least one category of input does seem to require a different sort of recognition system: faces. Several pieces of evidence support the claim that face memory is served by specialized structures and mechanisms. One indication comes from individuals who have suffered brain damage leading to agnosia. It turns out that there are many subtypes of agnosia, one of which is called **prosopagnosia**. People with this disorder lose their ability to recognize faces, even though their other visual abilities seem

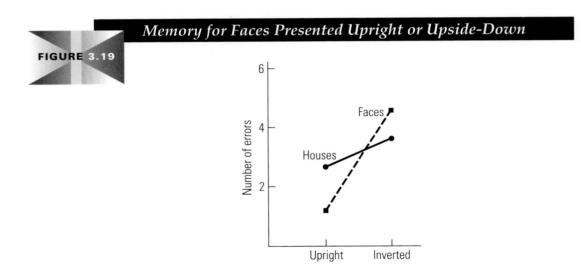

**FIGURE 3.19**

*Memory for Faces Presented Upright or Upside-Down*

People's memory for faces is quite good, compared with memory for other pictures (in this case, pictures of houses). However, research participants' performance is very much disrupted when the pictures of faces are inverted. Performance with houses is also worse with inverted pictures, but the effect of inversion is far smaller. (After Yin, 1969.)

## *Perception of Upside-Down Faces*

**FIGURE** 3.20

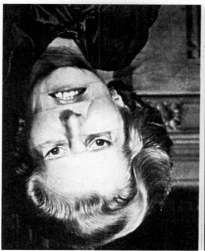 

The left-hand picture looks somewhat odd, but the two pictures still look relatively similar to each other. Now try turning the book upside-down (so that the faces are upright). In this position, the left-hand face (now on the right) looks ghoulish, and the two pictures look very different from each other. Perception of upside-down faces is apparently quite different from our perception of upright faces. (From Thompson, 1980.)

to be relatively intact. This seems to imply the existence of a special neural structure involved almost exclusively in the recognition and discrimination of faces (Alexander & Albert, 1983; Burton, Young, Bruce, Johnston & Ellis, 1991; Damasio, Damasio & Van Hoesen, 1982; Damasio, Tranel & Damasio, 1990; De Renzi, Faglioni, Grossi & Nichelli, 1991; Ellis, 1989; Hecaen, 1981; Sergent & Poncet, 1990; Tranel, Damasio & Damasio, 1988).

A second distinguishing principle of face recognition is its strong dependence on orientation. It is generally more difficult to recognize things if they are presented at a novel orientation (e.g., upside-down), but the effects of disorientation are particularly pronounced with faces. In one study, for example, four categories of stimuli were considered: right-side-up

faces, upside-down faces, right-side-up pictures of common objects other than faces, and upside-down pictures of common objects. As can be seen in Figure 3.19, performance suffered for all of the upside-down stimuli. However, this effect is much larger for faces than it is for other kinds of stimuli (Yin, 1969).

The same point can be made informally. Figure 3.20 shows two upside-down photographs of former British prime minister Margaret Thatcher (from Thompson, 1980). You can probably detect that something is odd about them, but now try turning the book upside-down, so that the faces are right-side-up. As you can see, the difference between these faces is immense, and yet this rather fiendish contrast is largely lost when the faces are upside-down. Once again, it seems that the perception of faces is strikingly different when we view the faces upside-down. (Also see Rhodes, Brake & Atkinson, 1993; Valentine, 1988.)

All of this seems to imply that face recognition is different from recognition of other sorts—served by its own neural "apparatus" and particularly dependent on orientation. But is it just faces that show these patterns? Consider first the evidence of prosopagnosia. Our understanding of this syndrome has grown as a greater number of cases have been examined. For example, there is a well-documented report of a prosopagnosic farmer who not only lost the ability to recognize faces, but also lost the ability to recognize his individual cows. Likewise, there is a case of a prosopagnosic bird-watcher who has, it seems, lost both the ability to discriminate faces and also the ability to discriminate warblers (Bornstein, 1963; Bornstein, Sroka & Munitz, 1969). Still another patient has lost the ability to tell cars apart; she is able to locate her car in a parking lot only by reading all the license plates until she finds her own (Damasio et al., 1982). Thus, prosopagnosia is not strictly a disorder of face recognition.

Likewise, it appears that other categories of stimuli, not just faces, show the "upside-down effect" we have already described. For example, similar data have been reported in a study of highly experienced judges from dog shows, people who know a particular breed extremely well. Diamond and Carey (1986) compared how well these judges recognized right-side-up and upside-down stimuli in each of two categories: faces and dogs in the familiar breed. Not surprisingly, performance was much worse with upside-down faces than with right-side-up faces, replicating the pattern of Figure 3.19. The critical result, though, is that performance suffered just as much with upside-down pictures of dogs.

This overall pattern of evidence has led some authors to suggest that humans have a specialized recognition system, not just for faces, but for recognizing specific individuals within any highly familiar category (cf. Diamond & Carey, 1986; for neuroimaging data confirming this proposal, see Gauthier, 2000). It is this system that is impaired in people with prosopagnosia, disrupting their recognition of faces,

but also disrupting the recognition of warblers for someone highly familiar with birds, the recognition of cows for someone highly familiar with the herd, and so on. Likewise, it is this same system that is unable to operate when stimuli are presented upside-down. Again, this compromises the recognition of faces, but it will also compromise other forms of recognition *provided* that the viewer is trying to distinguish individuals *and* is also highly familiar with the category (for example, the category of dogs, for an expert dog-judge).

A related proposal has been offered by Farah (1992, 1995), who proposes that humans have two distinct pattern-recognition systems. One system is specialized for the recognition of simple parts and the assembly of those parts into larger wholes. This is presumably the system we have been discussing throughout this chapter. A second system is specialized for the recognition of larger configurations. This system is less able to analyze patterns into their parts and less able to recognize these parts, but this system is more sensitive to larger-scale configurational properties. Presumably it is this system that is crucial for the recognition of faces and the other cases discussed in this section. In this view, prosopagnosia would involve damage to the second system but not the first. Farah notes, though, that other forms of brain damage have the opposite effect—for example, disrupting the ability to recognize words, with no damage to the ability to recognize faces. These cases would result from damage to the first, more analytic system, while the second, more configurational system is spared. (Also see Farah, Wilson, Drain & Tanaka, 1998.)

Further work is needed to refine these distinctions and to specify how the configurational system functions. Nonetheless, the available evidence does indicate the need for a distinction of some sort. The feature-net approach we have discussed in this chapter seems very powerful and applicable to a wide variety of patterns. Indeed, no one is arguing that we can do *without* the feature net. Quite the contrary: The feature net plays a critical role in the processes of pattern recognition. But the feature net can't do it all. Some patterns, including faces, seem to involve a different sort of pattern recognition. (For examples of other research on memory for faces, see Baddeley, 1982; Bower & Karlin, 1974; Burton et al., 1991; Etcoff & Magee, 1992; Hay, Young & Ellis, 1991; Young & Bruce, 1991. For an alternative theoretical treatment of face recognition, see Burton, Bruce & Hancock, 1999.)

## Top-down Influences on Object Recognition

The previous section had a two-part message: On the one side, we saw that the feature-net idea is applicable to a great many domains: Not only is it useful for the recognition of print, it is also applicable to the recognition of common objects, speech sounds and, it seems, musical phrases. At the same time, though, there are limits on what the feature net can do. More specifically, there are domains for which the feature net is not well suited. The suggestion, then, is that we need multiple recognition systems. The feature net will be one of those systems, used for a broad class of targets (print, three-dimensional objects, and perhaps music). A different system (about which we know relatively little) will be used for other sorts of targets (faces).

In the present section, we explore a different limit on the feature net. Our concern here is with targets for which the feature net *is* useful—print, common objects, and so on. Even in this domain, it turns out that the feature net must be supplemented with some further mechanisms. This doesn't undermine the importance of the feature-net idea—the net is plainly needed as part of our theoretical account. The key word, though, is *part*, since, as we'll see, we need to place the feature net within a larger theoretical frame.

### THE BENEFITS OF LARGER CONTEXTS

Let us begin with some evidence. We have already seen that letter recognition is improved by context, so that the letter V, for example, is easier to recognize in the context "VIMP" than it is if presented alone. It turns out that the same is true for *words*—these too are better recognized in context, in particular, in the context of a sentence.

In an early demonstration of this effect, research participants were asked to read a phrase and then were briefly shown a word that completed the phrase (Tulving & Gold, 1963). The length of the phrase was varied: In some trials, the test word was accompanied by no context, so that participants might read "[blank]," followed by the test word "airplane." In other trials, one context word was given so that, for example, participants might read "the . . . ," followed by "airplane." In still other trials, eight context words were given, so that the test word completed a nine-word sentence. Sometimes this context was appropriate for the test word, and sometimes the context was inappropriate. As an inappropriate context, participants might read "The governor planned soon to initiate the new . . . ," followed by the test word "birdhouse."

The results from this study are easy to describe: Word recognition was facilitated by context if the context was appropriate for that word. Larger contexts provided stronger effects, so that participants were better able to recognize the test stimuli after eight-word (appropriate) contexts than after four-word or two-word contexts. The size of context also mattered for the "inappropriate" condition—recognition was *worse* after an eight-word inappropriate context than after a four-word or two-word inappropriate context.

One might worry that participants are simply *guessing* the target word, based on the context, so that context is not really aiding perception of the word itself. We can measure this guessing effect by presenting the context *without* the target stimulus, and asking participants directly to guess that target's identity. In this condition, context does produce a benefit: People are better able to guess the target if given a larger (appropriate) context. But the benefits of context in this guessing condition are relatively small (Tulving, Mandler & Baumal, 1964). The real benefit of context comes by the facilitation of perception, not by the support of guessing; to obtain this benefit, one needs to have something to perceive. (See also Rueckl & Oden, 1986.)

These effects obviously resemble the word-superiority effect described earlier in this chapter. In both cases, a target in context is easier to recognize than a target in isolation. In both cases, the effect is obtained with well-formed contexts, but not with ill-formed or inappropriate contexts (Potter, Moryadas, Abrams & Noel, 1993; Simpson, Peterson, Castell & Burgess, 1989). Despite these parallels, however, we probably need rather different accounts of how word context benefits letter recognition, and of how sentence context benefits word recognition.

To explain how word context benefits letters, we relied on bigram detectors, all primed in the right ways, allowing people to make maximal use of the incoming information and, in particular, allowing easier identification of well-formed strings. Thus, the detector for "TH" is better primed than the detector for "HT," allowing easier recognition of "THE" than of "HTE." Now let's extend this same argument to sentences: We know, for example, that people can easily read "THE BOY RAN"; they have more trouble with the (ill-formed) sentence "BOY THE RAN." By analogy with word recognition, we could explain this by supposing that there is a detector for "THE BOY," and another detector for "BOY THE." The former detector would be well primed, since the relevant word combination is often encountered; the latter detector would not be well primed. Hence, the former detector would fire more easily and more quickly, even with a weak input. This would "explain" the easier perception of the grammatical sentence.

But is this plausible? This explanation presumes that there are detectors for the various word combinations ("bi-word" detectors), all primed in the right way. How many of these detectors would we need? Assuming a vocabulary of 50,000 words, the number of possible word pairs is huge (2.5 billion, to be exact), and so one might need billions of bi-word detectors. And that's just the beginning: As we've just seen, an eight-word context provides a greater recognition benefit than a four-word context. To account for this in terms of primed detectors, we would presumably need detectors sensitive to eight-word sequences. With a vocabulary of 50,000 words, the number of eight-word combinations is 39 trillion trillion trillion. For comparison, recall that the number of neurons on the brain has been estimated at about one trillion. Thus, the word combinations outnumber the neurons by a hundred billion trillion to one!

It is therefore absurd to claim we have detectors for each of these combinations. And with no detectors on the scene, we obviously can't appeal to detector *priming* in explaining the data.

So how *should* we explain the benefits of phrase context? Some would argue that we simply cannot explain these effects in network terms. Others, however, have argued that a different *style* of network modeling will explain the data. We'll return to this debate in Chapter 8, and we will return, more broadly, to patterns of linguistic knowledge in Chapter 10. For now, though, our point is modest: We cannot explain these data simply by enlarging the model we so far have in place. This model is enormously useful, but to explain how we recognize complex, larger-scale stimuli, we will need more than just a vast army of primed detectors.

## INTERACTIVE MODELS

The same broad conclusion can be reached in another way: So far, our focus has largely been on **data-driven**, or bottom-up processing. That is, we have discussed how the incoming information (the "data") triggers a response by feature detectors, which in turn triggers a response by letter detectors (or geon detectors), and so on. The data take the initiative; the data get things going. However, there is reason to believe that there is more to object recognition than this. Object recognition is also influenced by a broad pattern of knowledge and expectations. These influences are generally referred to as **concept-driven**, or top-down. Models that include both top-down and bottom-up components are described as **interactive models**.

We have already mentioned one interactive model: the McClelland and Rumelhart word-recognition model. (Recall that this model has activation flowing upward from lower-level units, like letter detectors, and downward from higher-level units, like word detectors.) But this model won't be enough to handle the full range of top-down effects. To see this, imagine that we tell research participants, "I am about to show you a word very briefly on a computer screen; the word is the name of something that you can eat." If we forced the participants to *guess* the word at this point, they would be unlikely to name the target word. But if we now tachistoscopically show the word "ARTICHOKE," we are likely to observe a large priming effect—that is, participants are more likely to recognize "ARTICHOKE" with this cue than they would have been without the cue.

Consider what this priming involves. First, the person needs to understand all of the words in the instruction. If she did not understand the word "eat" (if, for example, she mistakenly thought we had said, "something that you can *beat*"), we would not get the priming. Second, the person must understand the *syntax* of the instruction and, specifically, the relations among the words in the instruction. Again, if she mistakenly thought we said "something that *can eat you*," we would expect a very different sort of priming. Third, the person has to know some facts about the world—namely, the kinds of things that can be eaten; without this knowledge, we would expect no priming.

Priming of this sort is concept-driven, since it obviously depends on things the person knows. The same is true for the "sentence-based" priming discussed in the previous section. Both of these stand in contrast to the other sorts of priming we have discussed. With repetition priming, for example, what mattered was not someone's knowledge, but merely their "stimulus history," i.e., what stimuli the person had seen recently. The same was true for frequency-based priming. In an obvious way, therefore, these sorts of priming are data-driven, or perhaps we should say "stimulus-driven."

Concept-driven priming relies on knowledge that is *separate* from one's knowledge about letters, words, and letter combinations. This is why, for example, the McClelland and Rumelhart model, while interactive, is not "interactive *enough*"—that is, it

does not draw on a wide enough knowledge base to handle the effects we are now considering. Notice, though, where this conclusion brings us: The evidence suggests that we cannot view object recognition as a self-contained process. Instead, knowledge that is external to object recognition (e.g., knowledge about what is edible) is imported into and clearly influences the process. Put differently, the "ARTICHOKE" example, and all the studies described in the previous sections, do not depend on stimulus history, at least not in any straightforward way. Instead, what is crucial for priming is what a person knows coming into the experiment, and also how this knowledge is used.

We have, therefore, reached an important juncture. We have tried in this chapter to examine object recognition in isolation from other cognitive processes, considering how a separate "object-recognition module" might function, with the module then handing its "product" (the object it had recognized) on to subsequent processes. We have made good progress in this attempt and have described how a significant piece of object recognition might proceed. But in the end we have also run up against a problem, namely, concept-driven priming. This sort of priming depends on what is in memory, and on how that knowledge is accessed and used, and so we really cannot tackle concept-driven priming until we have said a great deal more about memory, knowledge, and thought. We therefore must leave object recognition for now in order to fill in some other pieces of the puzzle. We will have more to say about object recognition in later chapters, once we have some more theoretical machinery in place.

## Chapter Summary

1. Visual perception is a highly active process in which the perceiver goes "beyond the information given" in organizing and interpreting the visual input. This includes specifying a *figure/ground organization* for the input, *parsing* the figure into

its components, and specifying how the figure is organized in depth. To describe these processes, some investigators speak of the *"logic of perception,"* referring to the fact that perception, like a good scientist, arrives at an interpretation that fits with all the evidence, and without appeals to coincidence.

2. We easily recognize a wide range of objects in a wide range of circumstances. Our recognition is heavily influenced by context, which can determine how or whether we recognize an object. To study these achievements, investigators have often focused on the recognition of printed language, using this case as a microcosm within which to study how object recognition in general might proceed.

3. Many investigators have proposed that recognition begins with the identification of *features* in the (parsed, organized) input pattern. Some evidence for this claim comes from neuroscience studies of "feature detectors." Other evidence comes from *visual search*, which shows that targets are extremely easy to find if they are identified by a single feature.

4. To study word recognition, investigators often use *tachistoscopic* presentations. In these studies, words that appear frequently in the language are easier to identify, and so are words that have been recently viewed, an effect known as *repetition priming*. The data also show a pattern known as the *word-superiority effect*; this refers to the fact that words are more readily perceived than isolated letters. In addition, well-formed nonwords are more readily perceived than letter strings that do not conform to the rules of normal spelling. Another reliable pattern is that recognition errors, when they occur, are quite systematic, with the input typically perceived as being more regular than it actually is. These findings together indicate that recognition is shaped by learning, often relying on inference, and certainly influenced by the regularities that exist in our environment (e.g., the regularities of spelling patterns).

5. These results can be understood in terms of a network of detectors. Each detector collects input, and fires when the input reaches a threshold level. A network of these detectors can accomplish a great deal, for example, it can interpret ambiguous inputs, recover from its own errors, and make inferences about barely viewed stimuli. This provides a powerful demonstration of how complex intellectual achievements can sometimes be built up out of very simple components.

6. The feature net seems to "know" the rules of spelling and "expects" the input to conform to these rules. However, this knowledge is *distributed* across the entire network, and emerges only through the network's parallel processing. This set-up leads to enormous efficiency in our commerce with the world, because it allows us to recognize patterns and objects with relatively little input and under highly diverse circumstances. But these gains are purchased at the cost of occasional error. This trade-off may be necessary, though, if we are to cope with the informational complexity of our world.

7. A *feature net* can be implemented in different ways—with or without inhibitory connections, for example. With some adjustments (e.g., the addition of "*geon* detectors"), the net can also recognize three-dimensional objects, and, with other adjustments, may be able to recognize sounds. However, some stimuli—for example, faces—probably are not recognized through a feature net, but instead require a different sort of recognition system.

8. The feature net also needs to be supplemented to accommodate *top-down* influences on object recognition. These influences can be detected in the benefits of larger contexts in facilitating recognition, and also in forms of priming that are plainly *concept-driven*, rather than *data-driven*. These other forms of priming demand an interactive model, which merges *bottom-up* and top-down processes.

# *Paying Attention*

In discussing object recognition, we began with a situation simplified in many ways. The experiments we described all took place in a quiet setting, so that no noise distracted the research participants. The stimuli were presented briefly, but they were presented one at a time, in a known location, with nothing else on the computer screen. The participants therefore had no difficulty in locating the target information, nor did they have to decide which bits of the input were crucial for the task, and which irrelevant. The participants' task was difficult, since the stimuli were degraded, but they had exactly one task to do, so they could focus their full attention on this task.

One's ordinary commerce with the world takes place in a very different situation. Consider your circumstances right now. You are paying attention to this page, reading these words. However, think of the other inputs available to you, things you could pay attention to if you chose. You are concentrating on this line of print, but you can easily see that there are other lines of print on the page. You are paying attention to the meanings of these words, but you could choose instead to look at the shapes of the letters, or you could attend to the font in which the words are presented, rather than the words themselves. There are also many sounds in the room. Perhaps the radio is on, or perhaps you can hear someone at the next desk turning pages. There are also stimuli available to you from other modalities. You could, if you wished, pay attention to the weight of the book in your hands, or to the pressure of your chair against your body. Or, if you liked, you could pay attention to none of these things, and choose instead to think about what you did last weekend, or what you'll write in your term paper.

There are two crucial facts here, and explaining these facts will be the task of this chapter. First, you can choose to pay attention to any of the things just mentioned and, if you do, you will be virtually oblivious to the other things on the list. In fact, until you read the previous paragraph, you may not even have noticed these other stimuli. Second, there seems to be one thing you cannot easily do: pay attention to all of these things at once. If you start musing about your weekend, you are likely to lose track of what's on the page; if you start planning your paper, you won't finish the reading assignment. Of course, it is possible, in some circumstances, to divide your attention, to deal with two different inputs at once, or to perform two different tasks at once. You can, if you choose, hum a melody while reading these words. But where are the limits? When can you do two (or more) things at the same time, and when can't you? Can these limits be changed, so that, potentially, you could learn to do several things at once?

These questions set the agenda for the present chapter. We will start with **selective attention**—the processes through which you somehow select one input and "tune out" the rest. We will then turn to questions about **divided attention**, examining when (and if) you can do multiple tasks at once. Selective and divided attention are clearly linked to each other (since one has to select when one cannot divide!), but it will be useful to start by treating them separately.

## Selective Listening

Let's first look at some classic studies of attention. We will then turn to theoretical accounts that might help to explain these results.

### BASIC FINDINGS FROM SELECTIVE LISTENING

Many early studies of attention employed a task called **shadowing**. In this task, participants hear a tape-recording of someone speaking and must echo this speech back, word for word, while they are listening to it. Shadowing is initially difficult, but becomes easy with just a few minutes' practice. (You might try it, shadowing a voice on the radio or TV.)

In most experiments, the to-be-shadowed message, the **attended channel**, is presented through stereo headphones, so that participants hear the attended channel through, say, the right earphone. We play a different message—the unattended channel—in the left earphone, and participants are instructed simply to ignore this message. This overall setup is referred to as **dichotic listening**.

Under these circumstances, participants easily follow one message, and their shadowing performance is generally near perfect. At the same time, however, they hear remarkably little from the unattended channel. If we ask them, after a minute or so of shadowing, to report what the unattended message was about, they cannot (e.g., Cherry, 1953). They cannot even tell if the unattended channel contained a coherent message or just random words. In fact, in one study, participants shadowed coherent prose in the attended channel, while, in the unattended channel, they heard a text in Czech, read with English pronunciation. Thus, the individual sounds (the vowels, the consonants) resembled English, but the message itself was (for an English speaker) gibberish. After a minute of shadowing, only four of thirty participants detected the peculiar character of the unattended message (Treisman, 1964; for related findings with visual inputs, see Neisser & Becklen, 1975).

However, people are not *deaf* to the unattended channel: They easily and accurately report whether the unattended channel contained human speech, musical instruments, or silence. If the unattended channel contains human speech, they can report whether the speaker was male or female, had a high or low voice, and so on. We can also arrange to change the apparent location of the unattended channel from one ear to the other (simply by adjusting the controls on the stereo running the study). Participants easily note and can report the location of this voice. (For reviews of this early work, see Broadbent, 1958; Kahneman, 1973; Moray, 1969.)

## SOME UNATTENDED INPUTS ARE DETECTED

So far the pattern of evidence shows that *physical attributes* of the unattended channel are easily heard: Research participants can describe the type of sound, the loudness, the pitch, and the direction. But they seem oblivious to the *semantic* content of the unattended channel—they can't even tell if the unattended channel contained English prose or gibberish.

However, some results do not fit this pattern. Some bits of the unattended input do leak through and are noticed. In one study, people were asked to shadow one passage while ignoring a second passage. Embedded within the unattended channel, though, was a series of names, including the participant's own name. Overall, participants heard very little of the unattended message, in keeping with the other studies mentioned. Nonetheless, about a third of them did hear their own name (Moray, 1959). As we commonly say, the name seemed to "catch" their attention. Other contents will also catch your attention, if you are suitably primed for them: Mention of a movie you just saw, or of your favorite restaurant, will often be noticed in the unattended channel. Likewise, words with some personal importance will also be noticed (e.g., Corteen & Dunn, 1974; Corteen & Wood, 1972; for a recent review, see Wood & Cowan, 1995).

These results are often referred to under the banner of the cocktail party effect: There you are at a cocktail party, engaged in conversation. Many other conversations are taking place in the room but, somehow, you're able to "tune them out." You are aware that other people in the room are talking, but you don't have a clue what they're saying. All you "hear" is the single conversation you're attending, plus a "buzz" of background noise. But now imagine that someone a few steps away from you mentions your name, or mentions the name of a close friend of yours. Your attention is immediately caught by this, and you find yourself listening to that other conversation, and (momentarily) oblivious to the conversation you had been engaged in.

A similar point emerges from an early study by Anne Treisman (1964). In this experiment, the participants were bilingual, fully fluent in English and in French. For these people, the attended channel contained a message in one of these languages; the unattended channel contained the same message, but translated into the other language. Nonetheless, 50% of the participants still noticed the identity of these messages. Note that in this case the messages were "identical" in their semantic content, but not in their form, and not in their sounds. Thus, to notice the identity, the participants must have been sensitive to the *meaning* of both messages.

Overall, then, the pattern of results is uneven: On the one hand, many studies document how little we hear from the unattended channel. Other studies, though, show that, in some circumstances, we *do* understand the unattended message. (See also Hirst, 1986; Johnston & Dark, 1986.) Our theory will plainly need to explain both sets of results—the general insensitivity to the unattended channel and also the cases in which the unattended channel "leaks through."

## Perceiving and the Limits on Cognitive Capacity

How should we begin thinking about all of this? What steps do we take in order to hear the attended channel and *not* hear the unattended channel? One suggestion, pivotal for early theories of attention, was that we take steps to *block* processing of the unattended channel—we shut out the information we don't want. Put differently, we erect a **filter** that shields us from potential distractors. Desired information (the attended channel) is not filtered, and so goes on to receive further processing (e.g., Broadbent, 1958).

Current evidence suggests that we do have the capability of shutting out distractors in this way; we can, in fact, take action that specifically blocks the processing of unwanted inputs (for discussion, see Anderson & Spellman, 1995; Fox, 1994, 1995; Milliken & Tipper, 1998; Milliken, Joordens, Merikle & Seiffert, 1998; Reisberg, Baron & Kemler, 1980). But other evidence suggests that filtering is only a small part of the story. That's because not only do we *block* the processing of distractors, we are also able to *promote* the processing of desired stimuli.

## INATTENTIONAL BLINDNESS

Perceiving seems extraordinarily easy: You open your eyes and you see. You don't feel like you're expending any effort, and even when your resources are sharply limited (when you're extremely tired, for example), you're still able to perceive! As we saw in Chapter 3, however, perception involves a considerable amount of activity—as you parse and organize and interpret the incoming stimulus information. One might think that this activity *should* require some initiative, and some resources, from you. The evidence suggests that it does.

In one experiment, participants were told that they would see large "+" shapes on a computer screen, presented for 200 milliseconds, followed by a pattern mask. If the horizontal bar of the "+" was longer than the vertical, the participants were supposed to press one button; if the vertical was longer, then they had to press a different button. As a complication, participants weren't allowed to look directly at the "+." Instead, they "fixated" (pointed their eyes at) a mark in the center of the computer screen—a **fixation target**—and the "+" shapes were shown just off to one side.

For the first three trials of the procedure, events proceeded just as the participants expected, and the task was relatively easy. On trial number 3, for example, participants made the correct response 78% of the time. On trial number 4, though, things were slightly different: While the target "+" was on the screen, the fixation target disappeared and was replaced with one of three shapes—either a triangle, a rectangle, or a cross. Then the entire configuration (target "+" plus this new shape) was replaced by a pattern mask.

Immediately after the trial, participants were asked: Was there anything different on this trial? Was there anything present, or anything changed, that wasn't there on previous trials? Remarkably, 89% of the participants reported that there was no change; they had failed to see anything other than the (attended) "+." They were not expecting any shapes to appear; they were not in any way prepared for these shapes; and, as a consequence, they failed to see these shapes, even though they were staring straight at them! This

failure to see, caused by inattention, has been dubbed **inattentional blindness** (Mack & Rock, 1998).

Perhaps the 200 millisecond exposure was simply too brief. As a check on this, the investigators ran another procedure: Participants were given the same task of judging the "+," but they were also told, before the experiment began, that they should report any other stimuli that appeared on the screen. In essence, this warned participants that other stimuli *might* appear, and so participants were alert for these other stimuli. With this warning, the vast majority of the participants (33 out of 36) *did* detect the targets. Plainly, then, the targets were visible, if one was looking for them.

## CONSCIOUS PERCEPTION, UNCONSCIOUS PERCEPTION

Mack and Rock, the investigators who documented the inattentional blindness phenomenon, draw a strong claim from these data: *There is no perception,* they claim, *without attention.* But what exactly is meant by "perception"? To be more precise, Mack and Rock argue that there is no *conscious* perception without attention (Mack & Rock, 1998, p. 14).

To see why this refinement is needed, consider the following experiment (Moore & Egeth, 1997; for other data pertinent to this claim, see Mack & Rock, 1998). Participants were shown a series of images on a computer screen; each image contained two horizontal lines surrounded by a pattern of black and white dots (Figure 4.1A), and the participants' task was to decide which of the two lines was longer.

For the first three trials of this procedure, the background dots on the computer screen were arranged randomly. On trial number 4, with no warning to participants, the pattern of dots shown was like the one in Figure 4.1B, creating a stimulus configuration that reproduces a standard geometric illusion, the Müller-Lyer illusion. However, the participants, focusing their attention on the two horizontal lines, didn't perceive this pattern. When they were asked immediately after the trial whether they had noticed any pattern in the dots, none reported seeing the pattern. They were then told directly that there *had* been

**FIGURE 4.1**

## Unconscious Perception

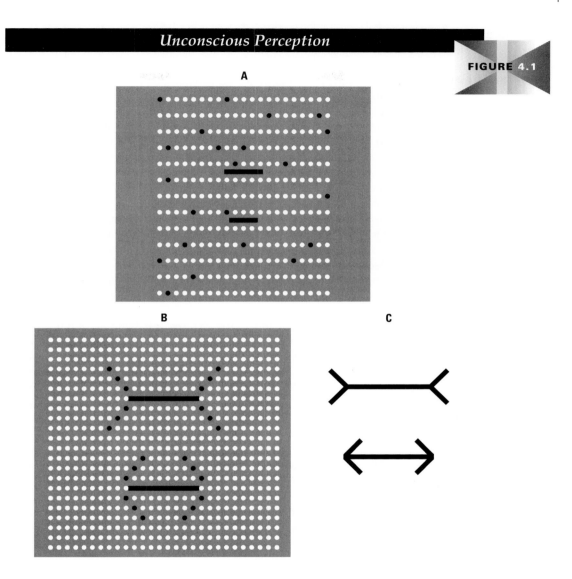

Participants were shown a series of images, each containing a pair of horizontal lines; their task was to decide which of the two lines was longer. For the first three trials, the background dots were arranged randomly (Panel A). For the fourth trial, the dots were arranged as shown in Panel B, roughly reproducing the configuration of the Müller-Lyer illusion; Panel C shows the standard form of this illusion. The participants in this study did not perceive the "fins" consciously, but they were nonetheless influenced by the fins—judging the top horizontal line in Panel B to be longer, fully in accord with the usual misperception of this illusion.

a pattern and were asked to choose it (out of four choices available); 90% selected one of the *incorrect* patterns. Plainly, then, this experiment reproduces the finding of inattentional blindness.

Nonetheless, the participants were influenced by the dot pattern. In the standard Müller-Lyer display, the "fins" make the top horizontal line in Figure 4.1C appear *longer* than the bottom horizontal line, even though both lines are exactly the same length. The dot pattern in the Moore and Egeth displays did the same, and 95% of the participants reported that the top line in Figure 4.1B was longer than the bottom one.

Notice, then, that the participants were completely unaware of the "fins," but they were still heavily influenced by them. No participant reported seeing the fins, but virtually all responded in the length judgment in a fashion consistent with the fins. The obvious conclusion, then, is that participants did perceive the fins in some way, but did not *consciously* perceive them. We will return to issues of consciousness and unconscious perception in Chapter 15, but for now, it seems attention may not be needed for *unconscious* perception.

### INATTENTIONAL BLINDNESS OR INATTENTIONAL AMNESIA?

There is, however, another way to think about these two studies. Perhaps the participants *were* able to see the unexpected stimuli, and perhaps they even *consciously* perceived these stimuli. Why, then, didn't they report these stimuli when asked about them a moment or two later? Because they forgot them. In this view, attention is not needed for perceiving. Instead, attention is needed for *memory*. In the absence of attention, this proposal suggests, there is incredibly rapid forgetting—so rapid, in fact, that the participants have no recollection of the stimulus at all, even if asked about the display just a few seconds after seeing it.

One way to examine this proposal is through **neuroimaging** data. In a study by Rees, Russell, Frith and Driver (1999), participants were shown a series of displays, each of which contained a string of letters superimposed on a picture. In one condition, the par-

ticipants were instructed to pay attention to the strings of letters and to ignore the pictures; in another condition, the instruction was the reverse: ignore the letters, attend to the pictures. While participants were engaged in these tasks, their brain activity was monitored, using the fMRI technique (see Chapter 2).

As a further manipulation in this study, some of the letter strings shown to the participants formed meaningful, familiar words; other letter strings consisted of random letters. When the participants were attending to the letters, the fMRI data showed, as one might expect, very different brain responses to the words and to the random letters, with different activation patterns observed in the temporal lobe, the parietal lobe, and the prefrontal cortex. However, when the participants were attending to the pictures (and thus not attending to the letters), the fMRI data showed *no difference at all* between trials in which a(n) (unattended) familiar word was shown and trials in which a(n) (unattended) random letter string was shown. Thus, in the absence of attention, the brain seems completely insensitive to the various properties that distinguish words from random strings.

This seems, then, like a case of genuine inattentional blindness, not inattentional amnesia. It's *not* the case that these research participants detected the difference between words and random strings and then forgot what they had seen. Instead, they were wholly blind to the difference between words and random strings. Of course, words are highly familiar and meaningful stimuli, and the participants were staring directly at the words. Even so, in the absence of attention, perception fails.

### CHANGE BLINDNESS

Similar conclusions emerge from studies of **change blindness**. This term refers to observers' remarkable *in*ability to detect changes in scenes they are looking at. In some experiments, for example, participants are shown pairs of pictures, separated by a brief blank interval (e.g., Rensink, O'Regan & Clark, 1997). The pictures in the pair are identical except for some single aspect—an "extra" engine shown on the airplane in one picture and not in the other; a man not wearing a hat in one picture, but wearing one in the other; and so on. Participants know from the start that their task is to detect these changes, but even with this clear understanding of the task, the task is quite difficult. If the change involves something central to the scene, observers may need as many as 8 or 9 alternations between the pictures before they detect the change. If the change involves some peripheral aspect of the scene, then as many as two dozen alternations may be required. (This effect of "centrality" is likely to be tied to the pattern of observers' eye movements—e.g., Henderson & Hollingworth, 1999.)

A related pattern emerges when participants watch movies. In one study, observers watched a movie of two women having a brief conversation. During the film, the camera first focused on one woman, then on the other, just as it would in an ordinary TV show or movie. Crucially, though, aspects of the scene changed every time the camera angle changed. When the camera was pointing at Woman A, you could plainly see the red plates on the table in between the women. When the camera was pointing at Woman B, just a fraction of a second later, the plates had miraculously turned white, but with the food just where it was a moment ago—on Woman B's plate. Then, when the camera angle shifted to focus on Woman A again, the food instantly changed position—off of B's plate and onto A's. And so on.

Most observers noticed none of these changes. In one experiment, for example, a film containing a total of nine changes was shown to ten participants. Only one participant claimed to notice the changes, and when pressed, this participant merely said there was a difference in "the way people were sitting." When allowed to watch the film again and told explicitly to look out for changes, observers noticed (on average) only two of the nine changes—still missing more than three-quarters of these seemingly large changes (Levin & Simons, 1997; Shore & Klein, 2000; Simons, 2000).

We all have the impression that our perception of the world is relatively complete, without large "gaps" in what we see. But the results we are considering imply that there *are* gaps. Conspicuous objects directly in front of our eyes are not seen unless we are expending some effort to see them. This is revealed in the fact that we have no recollection whatsoever of these objects just a moment later (in the inattentional blindness experiments) and the fact that we are unlikely to detect any change if the objects are altered or removed altogether (in the change blindness experiments).

In addition, these results underscore the *active* nature of perception. In Chapter 3, we argued that we are not "passive detectors" of the stimulus information. Instead, we parse, organize, analyze, and interpret what we see. And, apparently, these steps require some work. Having the stimulus in front of our eyes is not enough.

## SELECTIVE PRIMING

If perceiving requires "work," what is the nature of this work? If looking directly at something isn't by itself enough to allow conscious perception, then what else is needed? In addition, how can we tie all of this back to our discussion of selective listening, earlier in the chapter?

Here is a proposal: To perceive, we must spend some "mental resources" in order to prepare ourselves for the incoming stimulus information. We still need to say what these "mental resources" are, but even at this general level, we can begin to knit together the various results we have already encountered. In the inattentional blindness paradigm, we spend resources only on the attended target (in the experiments we described, the "+"). With no resources spent elsewhere, perception of other inputs (e.g., the unexpected form at the center of the screen) is grossly impaired. A similar explanation applies to the change blindness paradigm: In this case, one has no reason to devote resources to, say, the plates, and so, with no resources spent, the plates are not perceived (even though they are quite conspicuously in the scene).

What about selective listening? In this case, one does not *want* to hear the distractor. It is irrelevant to the main task (shadowing the attended channel), and so devoting resources to the distractor would be, at best, a waste of these resources. With no resources devoted, the distractor is not perceived—entirely in line with the results we reviewed earlier. In other words, if perceiving has a "cost" attached to it, then ignoring is easy: One simply chooses not to pay the cost.

What does one achieve with these resources? How are the resources "spent?" One possibility builds on mechanisms we have already described. In Chapter 3, we proposed that recognition depends (in part) on a network of detectors, and we argued that these detectors fire most readily, and most quickly, if they are suitably primed. Perhaps, therefore, we prepare ourselves for perceiving by taking steps to prime the relevant detectors, and it is this step of priming that requires resources.

This idea fits with many of the results we have already mentioned, including cases of "leakage" in selective attention. In general, you do not prepare yourself to perceive the unattended channel, and thus you don't perceive its contents. But what happens if the unattended channel happens to contain your name? The detectors for this stimulus are already primed, simply because this is a stimulus you have frequently encountered in the past. Thanks to this prior exposure, the activation level of these detectors is already high; you don't need to prime them further. So these detectors will fire even if your attention is elsewhere.

The same logic allows us to explain other results. For example, people have a relatively easy time in shadowing regular, predictable messages. It is more difficult to shadow less predictable messages— sequences of random words, or even text that you don't comprehend (e.g., Moray, 1959; also see Neisser & Becklen, 1975). This fits with the priming idea: With predictable messages, one can more easily anticipate what the upcoming signal will be, and therefore one can more readily prime just the right detectors. With unpredictable messages, you don't know what is coming, so you can't prepare, and attending is difficult.

Once again, though, all of this raises new questions. For example, common sense tells us there are limits on our ability to pay attention. If you try to read a book while listening to a complex lecture, you are likely to understand the book, or the lecture, but not both. When attending to one channel, we have seen, you hear rather little from the other channel.

What sets these limits? If we attend to stimuli by priming the relevant detectors, then why can't we prime two sets of detectors (one for each incoming message) at the same time?

## TWO TYPES OF PRIMING

We have already suggested that preparation for an input requires some mental resources, and perhaps these resources are in short supply. Thus, if you commit the resources needed to perceive a message, there might not be enough resources left over for the perception of a second message. As a different way of stating this, we could argue that the mind has a limited capacity for handling inputs or, for that matter, for dealing with any tasks. Perhaps the situations we have described (e.g., listening to two simultaneous messages, or reading and listening at the same time) exceed this capacity.

But what are these "resources?" Why is there a "limited capacity?" And, above all, can we get some direct evidence for these (allegedly) limited resources?

In a classic series of studies, Posner and Snyder (1975) gave people this simple task: A pair of letters was shown on a computer screen, and participants had to decide, as swiftly as they could, whether the letters were the same or different. So someone might see "A A" and answer "same," or might see "A B" and answer "different."

Before each pair, participants saw a warning signal. In the neutral condition, the warning signal was a plus sign ("+"). This notified participants that the stimuli were about to arrive but provided no other information. In a different condition, the warning signal was itself a letter and actually matched the stimuli to come. So someone might see the warning signal "C" followed by the pair "C C." In this case, the warning signal actually served to prime the participants for the stimuli. In a third condition, though, the warning signal was *misleading*. The warning signal was again a letter, but it was a letter different from the stimuli to come. Participants might see "C" followed by the pair "G G." Let's call these three conditions *neutral*, *primed*, and *misled*.

In each condition, Posner and Snyder recorded how swiftly people responded—that is, they measured response times, or RTs. By comparing RTs in the primed and neutral condition, we can ask what benefit there is from the prime. In particular, we would expect faster responses, and so shorter response times, in the primed condition. Likewise, by comparing RTs in the misled and neutral condition, we can ask what cost there is, if any, from being misled.

We need one further complication before we turn to the results: Posner and Snyder ran this procedure in two different versions. (The design is depicted in Figure 4.2.) In one version, the warning signal was an excellent predictor of the upcoming stimuli: For

## Design of Posner and Snyder's Experiment

**FIGURE 4.2**

| | Type of trial | Typical sequence | | Provides repetition priming? | Provides basis for expectation? |
| | | Warning signal | Test stimuli | | |
| --- | --- | --- | --- | --- | --- |
| **Low validity condition** | Neutral | + | AA | No | No |
| | Primed | G | GG | Yes | No |
| | Misled | H | GG | No | No |

| | Type of trial | Typical sequence | | Provides repetition priming? | Provides basis for expectation? |
| | | Warning signal | Test stimuli | | |
| --- | --- | --- | --- | --- | --- |
| **High validity condition** | Neutral | + | AA | No | No |
| | Primed | G | GG | Yes | Prime leads to correct expectation |
| | Misled | H | GG | No | Prime leads to incorrect expectation |

The sequence of events was the same in the high validity and low validity conditions. What distinguished the conditions was *how often* the various events occurred. In the low validity condition, "misled" trials occurred *four times as often* as "primed" trials (80% vs. 20%). Therefore, participants had reason *not* to trust the primes, and correspondingly had no reason to generate an expectation based on the prime. In the high validity condition, things were reversed: Now "primed" trials occurred four times as often as "misled" trials. Therefore, participants had good reason to trust the primes, and good reason to generate an expectation. For most of the trials, this expectation will be correct. Note, though, that if participants base their expectations on the prime, then they will generate the *wrong* expectation in the "misled" trials.

example, if the warning signal was an A, there was an 80% chance that the upcoming stimulus pair would contain A's. In Posner and Snyder's terms, the warning signal provided a "high validity" prime. In a different version of the procedure, the warning signal was a poor predictor of the upcoming stimuli: If the warning signal was an A, there was only a 20% chance that the upcoming pair would contain A's. This is the "low validity" condition.

Let's consider the low validity condition first, and let's focus on those rare occasions in which the prime *did* match the subsequent stimuli. That is, we are focusing on 20% of the trials, and ignoring the other 80%. In this condition, the participant can't use the prime as a basis for predicting the stimuli since, after all, the prime is a poor indicator of things to come. Therefore, the prime should *not* lead to any specific expectations. Nonetheless, we do expect faster RTs in the primed condition than in the neutral condition: Thanks to the prime, the relevant detectors have just fired, and so the detectors should still be warmed up. When the target stimuli arrive, therefore, the detectors should fire more readily, allowing a faster response. This is, in effect, a case of repetition priming, as described in Chapter 3.

The results bear this out. RTs were reliably faster in the primed condition than in the neutral condition; Figure 4.3 shows this as a 30 millisecond *difference* between the primed and neutral conditions. Apparently, the detectors can be primed by mere exposure to a stimulus. Or, to put it differently, priming is observed even in the absence of expectations. This priming seems truly stimulus-based.

What about the misled condition? With a low-validity prime, misleading participants had no effect: Performance in the misled condition was the *same* as performance in the neutral condition. Priming the "wrong" detector, it seems, takes nothing away from the other detectors—including the detectors actually needed for that trial. This fits with our discussion in Chapter 3: Each of the various detectors works independently of the others. Thus, if one detector is primed, this obviously influences the functioning of that specific detector, but this neither helps nor hinders the other detectors.

In sum, the low validity primes document two things: First, priming can be produced by stimulus repetition alone, even in the absence of expectations. Second, the detectors work independently of each other, so that priming one detector takes nothing away from the other detectors.

What about the high validity primes? In this case, people might see, for example, a "J" as the warning signal, and then the stimulus pair "J J." Presentation of the prime itself will fire the J-detectors, and so it should, once again, "warm up" these detectors, just as the low validity primes did. Thus, we expect a stimulus-driven benefit from the prime. However, the high validity primes may also have a further influence. High validity primes are excellent predictors of the stimulus to come. Participants are told this at the outset, and they have lots of opportunity to see that it is true. High validity primes will therefore produce a warm-up effect and also an expectation effect, whereas low validity primes only produced the warm-up. Consequently, we can explore the influence of expectations by comparing the impact of high and low validity primes.

As Figure 4.3 shows, high validity primes produced a *larger* benefit than low validity primes. The combination of warm-up and expectations produces a larger benefit than warm-up alone. From the participants' point of view, it pays to know what the upcoming stimulus might be.

The key finding, though, lies in the misled condition: With high validity primes, responses in the misled condition were slower than responses in the neutral condition. That is, misleading participants actually hurt performance. As a concrete example, F-detection was *slower* if G was primed, compared to F-detection when the prime was simply the neutral warning signal ("+").

## EXPLAINING THE COSTS AND BENEFITS

How should we think about all this? As we have already noted, there is nothing new for us in the data pattern from low validity primes. When the prime matches the subsequent stimuli, we observe a benefit

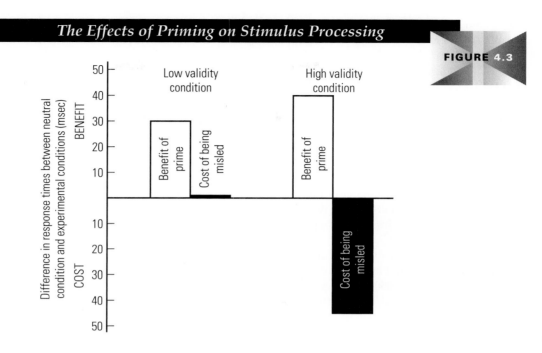

## The Effects of Priming on Stimulus Processing

FIGURE 4.3

As one way of assessing the Posner and Snyder (1975) results, we can subtract the response times for the neutral condition from those for the primed condition; in this way, we measure the benefits of priming. Likewise, we can subtract the response times for the neutral condition from those for the misled condition; in this way, we measure the *costs* of being misled. In these terms, the low validity condition shows a small benefit (from repetition priming) but zero cost from being misled. The high validity condition, in contrast, shows a larger benefit, but also a substantial cost. The results shown here reflect trials with a 300 msec interval between the warning signal and the test stimuli; the results were somewhat different at other intervals.

from "detector warm-up." However, warming up one detector takes nothing away from the other detectors. The detectors work independently of each other, and so there is no cost attached to warming up the "wrong" detector.

The high validity primes, though, do give us new information. First, note that the benefits of warm-up *plus* expectations are larger than the benefits from warm-up alone. Therefore, there is a form of priming that is different from (and larger than) repetition priming. It also turns out that this form of priming is somewhat slower: Priming based on warm-up can

be observed almost immediately; priming based on expectations takes time to develop. Concretely, expectation-based priming is only observed if there's a half-second or so in between the priming stimulus and the test stimulus (e.g., Neely, 1977).

These results—indicating the existence of two types of priming—strengthen the claims offered at the end of Chapter 3. There we distinguished between data-driven (or bottom-up) priming and concept-driven (or top-down) priming. This obviously parallels the distinction under scrutiny here, between stimulus-based and expectation-based primes. Data-driven priming, once again, is small in magnitude, depends only on stimulus presentation (not on expectations), and is relatively quick to appear. Concept-driven priming, in contrast, is larger, does depend on expectations, and is slower to appear.

Moreover, and crucial for our purposes here, consider the cost observed when a high validity prime turns out to be misleading. In this condition, it looks as if priming the "wrong" detector takes something away from the other detectors. Once people were misled, the other detectors ended up less primed, less well prepared, than they would have been with no prime at all. And, of course, in the misled condition, it is one of these less well prepared detectors that is needed.

What produces this pattern? As an analogy, think about being on a limited budget. Imagine, for example, that you have just $50 to spend on groceries. In that case, you can spend more on ice cream if you wish, but if you do, you'll have that much less to spend on other foods. Any increase in the "ice cream allotment" must be covered by a decrease somewhere else. This trade-off only arises, though, because of the limited budget. If you had unlimited funds, you could spend more on ice cream and still have enough money for everything else.

Expectation-based priming shows the same pattern. If the Q-detector is primed, this takes something away from the other detectors. Getting prepared for one target seems to make people less prepared for other targets. But we just said that this sort of pattern implies a limited "budget." If an unlimited supply of activation were available, one could prime the Q-detector and leave the other detectors just as they were. And that is the point: Expectation-based priming, by virtue of revealing costs when misled, reveals the presence of a limited-capacity system.

We can now put the pieces together: Ultimately, we need to explain the facts of selective attention, including the fact that, while listening to one message, one hears little content from other messages. To explain this, we have proposed that perceiving involves some work: One must *prepare* for upcoming stimuli, preparation that takes the form of priming the relevant processing path. This preparation, we

supposed, draws on some limited mental resources. That is why you can't listen to two complex messages at the same time: This would require more resources than you have. And now, finally, we are seeing evidence for those limited resources: The Posner and Snyder research (and many other results) reveals the workings of a limited-capacity system, just as our hypothesis demands.

## CHRONOMETRIC STUDIES AND SPATIAL ATTENTION

The Posner and Snyder study provides important data, but it also introduces an important method, useful for studying attention and many other topics. The study draws on a **chronometric** analysis. Chronometric studies (literally, "time-measuring") exploit the simple fact that mental tasks take time. Of course, mental tasks do proceed swiftly—we are talking about decisions and identifications that take, at most, a fraction of a second. But, with suitable devices, one can measure precisely how long these tasks take. Then, with the appropriate logic, one can use these chronometric results to figure out exactly what the task involves, exactly what factors influence performance, and so on.

Chronometric studies have been used to address a number of questions. For example, what is the nature of people's "expectations" in these studies? How precise, or how vague, are those expectations? To see the point, imagine that participants are told, "The next stimulus will be a T." In this case, they know exactly what to get ready for. But now imagine that participants are told, "The next stimulus will be a letter," or "Here comes the next stimulus." Will these cues allow people to prepare themselves?

In these latter cases, participants obviously can't prepare for the *content* of the upcoming message, because they have no basis for anticipating what that content will be. They can, however, prepare in a more general sense: They can prepare for a stimulus, for example, coming from a specific *position in space*, so that they will be ready for anything that appears in that location.

A number of studies have examined such "spatial anticipations." For example, Posner, Snyder, and Davidson (1980) required people to detect letter presentations—their task was to press a button as soon as a letter appeared. Participants kept their eyes pointed at a central fixation mark, and letters could appear either to the left or to the right of this mark.

For some trials, a neutral warning signal was presented, so that participants knew a trial was about to start, but had no information about stimulus location. For other trials, an *arrow* was used as the warning signal. Sometimes the arrow pointed left, sometimes right, and the arrow was generally an accurate predictor of the stimulus-to-come's location—if the arrow pointed right, the stimulus would be on the right side of the computer screen. (In the terms we used earlier, this is a high validity cue.) On 20% of the trials, however, the arrow *misled* participants about location. By comparing correctly cued trials with misleading trials, we can again ask about the benefits of anticipating a stimulus, and also the (potential) costs of having incorrect expectations.

The results show a familiar pattern (Posner et al., 1980, Experiment 2): With high validity priming, the data show a large *benefit* from cues that correctly signal where the upcoming target will appear. Concretely, with a neutral warning signal, people took 266 msec to detect the signal. With a correct prime, they were faster—249 msec. This isn't a huge difference, but keep the task in mind—all participants had to do was detect the input. Even with the simplest of tasks, therefore, it pays to be prepared.

The data also show a *cost* when the cue misled participants about the target's position. RTs in this condition averaged 297 msec, 31 msec (about 12%) slower than the neutral condition.

These results indicate that people can direct their attention to a position in space and, once this is done, they are more efficient in processing signals that appear in this position. Conversely, once people have focused their attention in this way, they are *less* efficient in processing signals that appear elsewhere. That is the cost of being misled—a cost, once again, that reveals some sort of limited-capacity system. It also should be said that these results involve move-

ments of *attention*, and not movements of the eyes. Participants were required, throughout these procedures, to keep their eyes in one position. In addition, we can rule out eye movements on grounds of speed. Eye movements are surprisingly slow, requiring 180 to 200 msec. Yet the benefits of primes can be detected within the first 150 msec after the warning signal is presented (e.g., Remington, 1980). Thus the benefits of attention occur prior to any eye movement and so cannot be a consequence of eye movements.[1]

Given results like these, some psychologists have likened visual attention to a "searchlight beam" that can "shine" anywhere in the visual field. The "beam" marks the region of space for which one is prepared, so that inputs within the beam are processed more efficiently and more swiftly. The beam can be wide or narrowly focused (Castiello & Umiltá, 1990; Eriksen & St. James, 1986; Eriksen & Yeh, 1985; Navon, 1977; Podgorny & Shepard, 1983; Shulman & Wilson, 1987), and can be moved about at will as one explores (attends to) one aspect of the visual field or another.

Let's note, though, that this searchlight metaphor must not be taken too literally. Imagine, for example, that you shine an actual searchlight on a donut. The light will illuminate the donut, but it will also shine through the donut's hole, illuminating a small bit of the plate on which the donut sits. If attention were truly like a searchlight, therefore, attention to the donut would entail attention to at least part of the plate. But this is generally not what the data show. Attention to an object (like a donut) seems usually to apply to the object itself, and not to other things that happen to be within a certain radius of the target. Be that as it may, the metaphor of attention as a searchlight beam does convey important properties about attention, so it still seems instructive to think of attention in these terms. (We will have more to say on

---

[1]Of course, eye movements do play an important role in our seeking out, and selecting, information from the world. (See, for example, Henderson, Weeks & Hollingworth, 1999.) Our point here, though, is that the selection via spatial anticipation is not reducible to an effect of eye movements; instead, it involves a separate mechanism.

this point in just a moment; for some of the research on this theme, see Baylis & Driver, 1993; Kahneman, Treisman & Gibbs, 1992; Egly, Driver & Rafal, 1994. For a broad assessment of the searchlight metaphor, see Cave & Bichot, 1999.)

## STUDYING THE NEURAL BASIS FOR VISUAL ATTENTION

We have been discussing attention in *functional* terms—asking what it is that attention accomplishes (preparing detectors and so on). But these functions are obviously made possible by brain activity, and we can gain further insights into attention by examining the relevant events in the nervous system. Useful information comes from many sources, including the neuroimaging techniques we introduced in Chapter 2 and also clinical data, focused on individuals whose brain damage seems specifically to produce problems in attending.

Brain-imaging data tell us that *multiple* areas of the brain are needed for attention, with each area doing a rather specific job. According to one proposal, three different brain areas control the searchlight beam— one area seems to *disengage* the beam from its current focus, one area controls the *movement* of the beam to its new target, and then a third area serves to *lock* the beam into its new focus (Allport, 1989; Posner, 1992; Posner & Petersen, 1990; Posner, Petersen, Fox & Raichle, 1988; for an alternative view of the brain systems supporting attention, see Cohen, Romero, Servan-Schreiber & Farah, 1994). Damage to each of these brain areas has correspondingly specific effects. For example, patients who have suffered lesions in the parietal cortex seem to lose the ability to disengage attention from its current focus. If their attention has just been drawn to one position, they respond very slowly to a stimulus presented at some other position, as if their attention, once "locked in" to a position, cannot be "unlocked" to move elsewhere.

This triple system of "disengage + move + lock in" is itself complex, but it is only part of the brain circuitry needed for attention. In addition, different brain regions constitute the **anterior attention system** (or AAS). This system seems to be the traffic director, coordinating various activities and keeping track of different inputs. Anatomically, this system is closely tied to brain regions associated with working memory (see Chapter 5). The AAS is also closely tied to brain regions involved in the initiation of action. PET scans reveal that the level of AAS activity increases as a task becomes more complex (e.g., Posner et al., 1988); it also seems that AAS involvement *decreases* as a task becomes better practiced.

Lesions in any of these areas can cause problems in attending. Some of the most extraordinary attention problems, however, occur in the **unilateral neglect syndrome.** Patients with this syndrome quite simply ignore all inputs coming from one side of the body. At its worst, the patient is unaware of the problem, and therefore makes no attempt to compensate (e.g., by just turning the head). A patient with neglect syndrome will eat food from only one side of the plate, will wash only half of his or her face, and will fail to locate sought-for objects if they are on the neglected side (Heilman, Watson & Valenstein, 1985; Sieroff, Pollatsek & Posner, 1988). In the laboratory, such patients will read only half of words shown to them (e.g., will read "PIGPEN" as *pen*, "PARTIES" as *ties*). If asked to cross out all the E's on a page, the patient will cross out the E's on only one side of the page. Unilateral neglect syndrome generally results from damage to the parietal cortex and provides confirmation of the claim that this area is crucial for the spatial "tuning" of attention.

The study of unilateral neglect syndrome can illuminate a number of issues, including one we raised earlier in this chapter. We have suggested that visual attention seems in some ways like a "searchlight," but how exactly does the "searchlight" operate? Does it "illuminate" a certain *area of space*, or does it instead highlight certain *objects*? On the face of things, the symptoms of neglect syndrome seem to support a space-based account: The afflicted patient seems insensitive to all objects within a spatially defined region. Other evidence, however, challenges this view. In one study, patients with unilateral neglect syndrome had to respond to targets that appeared within

## Space-Based or Object-Based Attention?

**FIGURE 4.4**

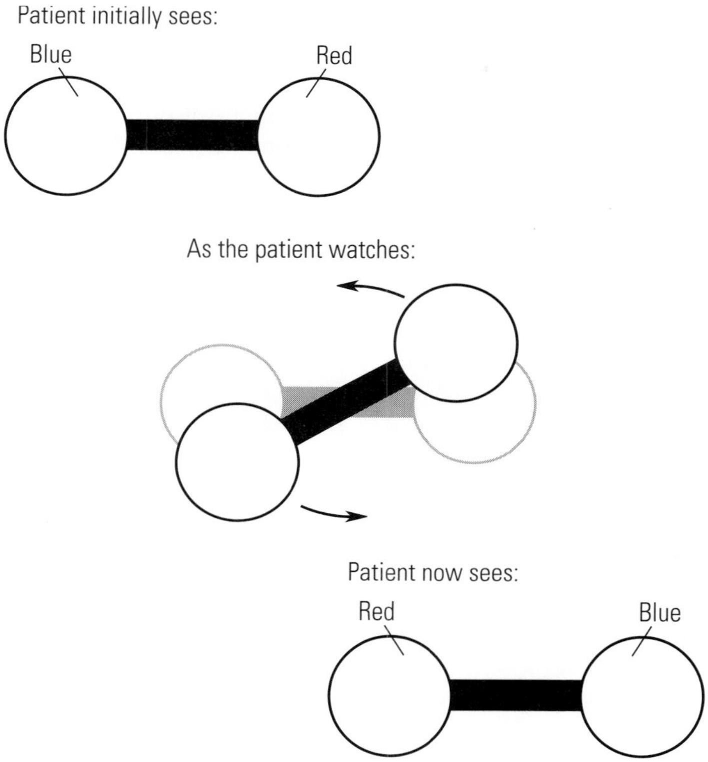

Patient initially sees:

Blue        Red

As the patient watches:

Patient now sees:

Red        Blue

Patients with unilateral neglect syndrome were much more sensitive to targets appearing within the red circle (on the right) and missed many of the targets appearing within the blue circle (on the left); this simply confirms their clinical diagnosis. Then, as the patients watched, the "barbell" frame rotated, so that now the red circle was on the left and the blue circle was on the right. After this rotation, participants were still more sensitive to targets in the red circle (now on the left), apparently focusing on this attended object even though it had moved into their "neglected" side.

a barbell-shaped frame (Figure 4.4). Not surprisingly, they were much more sensitive to the targets appearing within the red circle (on the right) and missed many of the targets appearing in the blue circle (on the left); this simply confirms the patients' diagnosis. What is crucial, though, is what happened next: While

the patient watched, the barbell frame was slowly spun around, so that the red circle, previously on the right, was now on the left, and the blue circle, previously on the left, was now on the right.

What should we expect in this situation? If the patients consistently neglect a region of space, they should now be more sensitive to the right-side blue circle. A different possibility is more complicated: Perhaps these patients have a powerful bias to attend to the right side, and so initially attend to the red circle. Once they have "locked in" to this circle, however, it is the *object*, and not the position in space, that defines their focus of attention. In this view, if the barbell form rotates, they will continue attending to the red circle (this is, after all, the "focus of their attention"), even though it now appears on their "neglected" side. This prediction turns out to be correct: When the barbell rotates, the patients' "focus of attention" seems to rotate with it (Behrmann & Tipper, 1999).

To describe these patients, therefore, we need (at least) a two-part account. First, the symptoms of neglect syndrome plainly reveal a spatially defined bias: These patients neglect *half of space*. Second, once attention is directed toward a target, it is the target itself that defines the focus of attention; if the target moves, the focus moves with it. In this way, the focus of attention is object-based, not space-based. (For more on these issues, and on neglect syndrome in general, see Bisiach, 1996; Duncan et al., 1999; Halligan & Marshall, 1994; Logie, 1995.)

### AN INTERIM SUMMARY

Let's take stock of where we are. We have suggested that two rather different mechanisms are involved in selective attention. One mechanism serves to *inhibit*, or block out, the processing of unwanted inputs; this is, in effect, a mechanism for "ignoring." A second mechanism *facilitates* the processing of desired inputs, by virtue of an anticipatory process that paves the way for these inputs. This is a mechanism for "paying attention."

We have also seen that mental tasks generally have a "cost" attached to them—that is, they require the commitment of mental resources, and so we pay attention by committing the resources needed to perceive. More precisely, we attend by preparing ourselves for the upcoming stimulus, by spending the resources needed to prime the relevant processing pathway. Mental resources are in limited supply, and this sets limits on our performance: We can do multiple tasks simultaneously *only if* the combined demand from these tasks is within our "budget." If we attempt to carry out multiple tasks and these require more resources than we have available, then performance will suffer.

The studies of dichotic listening, reviewed early in this chapter, easily fit with this conception. In these studies, the attended channel is fully understood because one is committing the resources to prime the relevant detectors. The unattended channel is not understood, largely because the detectors needed for this material are unprimed. And, in fact, the detectors *cannot* be primed, since the resources needed for this (i.e., for understanding two simultaneous messages) would exceed the resources available. Trying to follow two messages would "break the budget."

Consistent with all these claims, the chronometric studies tell us that even the simplest of signals are more efficiently processed when the perceiver is prepared for them. Part of this preparation is stimulus-driven and seems not to require any resources. But part of the preparation does reveal the operation of a limited-capacity system.

All of this is moving us toward a fairly involved conception, with multiple mechanisms, and with each mechanism having multiple components. Attention cannot be understood, therefore, as a single skill, or as a unitary faculty of the mind. Instead, what we call attention may instead be a family of effects, all of which together provide the function of selection—promoting the processing of inputs about which we desire to know more, while avoiding the processing of other inputs.

## Divided Attention

We are ready to shift the focus of our discussion, although, as we will soon see, many of the issues will remain the same. So far in this chapter, we have been concerned with *selective* attention. That is, we have emphasized situations in which there was a clear primary task and a clear primary input. If other tasks and other inputs were on the scene, they were mere distractors. Our focus, therefore, has been on how people manage to select just the desired information, while avoiding the distractors.

There are also circumstances, however, in which you *want* to do multiple things at once, in which you try to divide your attention among various tasks or various inputs. In some cases, you can do this, but your ability to perform concurrent tasks is clearly limited. Almost anyone can walk and chew gum simultaneously, but it is far harder to solve calculus problems while reading a history text. Most drivers can converse while navigating through traffic, but few people can write poetry while reading a novel. Therefore, we need to ask why some task combinations are difficult, while others are easy.

As a further question, we might wonder how rigid these limits on performance are. It would be rather useful if you *could* do calculus problems while reading a text; it would be terrific if you could complete your assignment for one course while also participating in another course. So the question is, Can you learn to do several things at once? Can you learn to divide attention more effectively? Or are there fixed and unchangeable boundaries on what humans can achieve?

Our initial answer to these questions is already in view. We have proposed that mental tasks require resources that are in short supply. This provides a straightforward account of divided attention: One can perform concurrent tasks only if the sum of the tasks' demands is within the "cognitive budget." To trace through one of our examples, solving calculus problems requires some mental resources, and so does reading a text. You have enough resources to do either one of these tasks by itself, but not enough for both; if you try to do both at the same time, you will fail.

But what are these hypothesized mental resources? Do all tasks, no matter what they involve, draw on the *same* mental resources? This is a hypothesis of **general resources**. Or are mental resources somehow special-

ized, so that the resources required by a task will depend on the exact nature of the task? This is a hypothesis of **task-specific resources**.

## TESTING CLAIMS ABOUT TASK SPECIFICITY

The hypotheses just sketched differ with regard to their predictions about when concurrent performance of tasks will be possible and, conversely, when task interference will be observed. Consider first the proposal that performance is limited by *general* resources. General resources, by definition, are relevant to all tasks, so all tasks, no matter what their nature, will compete for this limited pool of resources. Consequently, in asking whether concurrent performance of two tasks will be possible, we do not need to worry about the nature of the task. All we need to worry about is the resource demand—the cost—of the tasks. If the combined demand from the simultaneous tasks is greater than the available resources, then task interference will be observed.

Contrast this with the hypothesis that performance is limited by task-specific resources. These resources, by definition, are needed for some tasks but not others; the nature of the task determines *which* resources will be needed. Moreover, two tasks will interfere with each other only if they make conflicting demands on the *same set* of resources. To make this concrete, let us say that Task 1 requires some sort of spatial reasoning, and therefore draws on resources pertinent to this reasoning. Task 2, let us say, is a verbal task, and so draws on "verbal resources." In this case, combining Task 1 and Task 2 should be easy, since the tasks make non-overlapping resource demands. It won't even matter if Task 1 requires *all* the "spatial reasoning resources" or if Task 2 requires *all* the "verbal resources." Even in this case, concurrent performance will not "break the budget."

In short, if resources are task-general, then the possibility of divided attention should depend only on the resource demands of the individual tasks, and not on the nature of the tasks being combined. If, on the other hand, resources are task-specific, then the nature of the tasks is critical: Interference will be observed only to the extent that the tasks draw on overlapping sets of resources. If the tasks are sufficiently different, divided attention should be easy, since the tasks will require different sets of (task-specific) resources, and so will not compete with each other.

These predictions lend themselves easily to experimental test, and the results are clear: *Both* hypotheses capture an element of the truth. The nature of the tasks being combined does matter, consistent with the claim of task-specific resources, but interference can be observed even with extremely different tasks, consistent with the claim of task-general resources. Let us consider each of these claims in turn.

### EVIDENCE FOR TASK-SPECIFIC RESOURCES

Many studies show that divided attention is difficult with similar tasks, and much easier with dissimilar tasks (Hirst, 1986; Hirst & Kalmar, 1987). As an example, consider an early study by Allport, Antonis and Reynolds (1972). Participants heard a list of words, presented through headphones into one ear, and their task was simply to shadow these words. At the same time, they were also presented with a second list. No immediate response was required to this second list, but later on memory was tested for these items. In one condition, these memory items consisted of words presented into the other ear, so the participants were hearing (and shadowing) a list of words in one ear while simultaneously hearing the memory list in the other ear. In a second condition, the memory items were presented visually. That is, while the participants were shadowing one list of words, they were also seeing, on a screen before them, a different list of words. Finally, in a third condition the memory items consisted of pictures, also presented on a screen.

These three conditions have similar task requirements, namely shadowing one list while memorizing another. But the first condition (hear words + hear words) involves very similar tasks; the second condition (hear words + see words) involves less similar tasks; the third condition (hear words + see pic-

tures), even less similar tasks. If performance is limited by task-specific resources, then it seems most likely that the first pair of tasks will compete with each other for resources, and least likely that the last pair will. Thus, in terms of task-specific resources, we would expect most interference in the first condition, least in the third. And that is what the data show.

As a different example, consider a study by Brooks (1968). In one condition, people were asked to memorize a sentence, such as "A bird in the hand is not in the bush." Then they had to scan through this sentence and indicate whether each word was a noun or not (and so the correct answers are "no, yes, no, no, yes . . ."). In a different condition, the participants were shown a block letter like the one in Figure 4.5. Then the block letter was removed and, relying on their memory of it, participants had to scan around the outline of the letter and indicate whether each corner was at the extreme top or extreme bottom, or somewhere in between. (Thus, if "yes" indicates "extreme top or extreme bottom," the responses, starting at the asterisk, would be "yes, yes, no. . . .")

Half of the participants made their responses verbally, literally saying "yes" and "no." The remaining participants made their responses by pointing—toward a "Y" or toward an "N." It turns out that the *verbal* mode of responding was rather difficult with the sentence task, but relatively easy with the block-letter task. The pattern reversed for the *pointing* response: This was easy for the sentence task, but difficult with block letters.

What is going on here is a species of task interference. More precisely, we are seeing here interference between elements of a single task, namely, the making of a judgment and the production of a response. The verbal response is largely incompatible with the verbal judgment, but easily combined with the spatial judgment. The spatial response interferes with the spatial judgment, but not the verbal one. Clearly, the degree of interference depends, in an orderly fashion, on the nature of the tasks being performed. Verbal interferes with verbal; spatial interferes with spatial. But interference across these categories is minimal.

## Brooks' Block-Letter Task

**FIGURE 4.5**

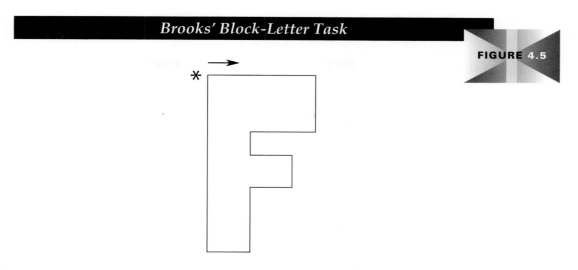

In this task, participants are asked to visualize a letter, like the F shown here. Starting at the top-left corner (marked with an asterisk), participants must scan around the outline of the letter and indicate whether each corner is at the extreme top or extreme bottom of the letter, or somewhere in between. The task is relatively easy if participants make their response verbally, but more difficult if they make their response spatially.

### EVIDENCE FOR TASK-GENERAL RESOURCES

Other results favor claims about task-general resources. Specifically, task interference can sometimes be observed even with extremely dissimilar tasks, suggesting that, even when tasks have little in common, they still compete for resources. Indeed, some of the evidence is provided by common sense: As we mentioned early on, it is easy for most of us to drive a car while holding a conversation; apparently these two tasks (driving + conversing) can be combined. But what happens if the driver must navigate through a complicated intersection, or do a high-speed merge into traffic? When these complexities enter the scene, concurrent performance seems to be impossible: If you are the driver, you may suddenly realize that you don't know what your friend has been saying for the last minute or so. If it is your turn to talk, there are suddenly long pauses in the conversation while you focus on the driving.

Presumably, routine driving through ordinary traffic makes light demands on mental resources, and so does "routine" conversation. The combined demands are therefore within your budget. But, if the complexity of either activity is increased, the resource requirements are correspondingly increased. Eventually, the combined demands will exceed the resources available, resulting in interference.

Of course, driving and talking are very different from each other—one is verbal, one is not. One requires visual inputs, the other doesn't. One requires a spoken output, the other does not. Therefore, it is highly unlikely that these tasks are competing for task-specific resources. Or, to put this differently, any resource that is required by both of these activities is plainly a resource applicable to highly diverse tasks—

that is, it must be task-general. And that brings us to the point: We can use this interference as an indication that task-general resources do, in fact, exist.

We should also mention one side-point: Is it possible to converse while driving a car? In some circumstances, it is not, and this may be one of the reasons why cell-phone use has been implicated in many automobile accidents (e.g., Lamble, Kauranen, Laakso & Summala, 1999). The phone conversation draws task-general mental resources away from the task of driving a car, putting the driver (and others) at risk.

## UNITARY RESOURCES, DIVISIBLE RESOURCES

Where does this leave us? Overall, it seems that it's easier to combine two tasks if the tasks are quite different from each other (reading while humming; listening to words while seeing pictures). This implies that performance is, in some cases, limited by task-specific resources. At the same time, though, we can observe interference even with highly dissimilar tasks (talking and driving). This implies the existence of task-general resources, in limited supply, that are competed for whenever the tasks get too complex. Apparently, then, there is more than one constraint on performance—task-specific constraints *and* task-general constraints—with the consequence that divided attention will be possible only if *all* the constraints are satisfied.

Let's acknowledge, though, that we have still said little about what exactly mental resources *are*. At the more task-specific end of things, the characterization of resources must be done task by task, as we ask what each mental task involves and what resources it requires. This means we cannot specify these resources until we have first analyzed the individual tasks. That enterprise is under way for many tasks, so that, just for some examples, we know a great deal about the processes involved in reading (e.g., Crowder & Wagner, 1992) or the processes involved in many motor activities (typing, walking, running, singing, and so on—Rosenbaum, 1991). In addition,

it seems likely that some resources will be general enough to apply to *many* tasks, but specific enough so that they don't apply to *all* tasks. A capacity for spatial working memory seems to be one plausible candidate; capacity for language processing seems to be another (e.g., Shah & Miyake, 1996).

But what about the task-general resources? What can we say in characterizing those? This issue is still being debated, and therefore, we cannot provide a definitive account. Nonetheless, let's look at how some of the argument has unfolded.

Some theories liken mental resources to an energy supply, or a bank account, drawn on by all tasks, and we have obviously used this analogy in much of our discussion. For example, Kahneman (1973) hypothesized that mental tasks require the expenditure of mental effort (also see Eysenck, 1982). The term *effort* was meant rather literally here, so that mental tasks require effort in about the same fashion that physical tasks do.

Other authors, however, have offered a different view, conceiving of these resources more as "mental tools," rather than as some sort of mental "energy supply." Thus, there is a task-general resource needed for *planning*, another needed for *response initiation*, and so on (Allport, 1989; Baddeley, 1986; Johnson-Laird, 1988; Norman & Shallice, 1986). Let's trace through the details of one of these proposals.

Pashler and Johnston (e.g., McCann & Johnston, 1992; Pashler & Johnston, 1989, Pashler, 1991, 1992) have proposed that a single mental mechanism is required for selecting and initiating responses, including both physical responses and mental ones (such as the beginning of a memory search, or the making of a decision). This "response selector" will be needed for a wide range of tasks, and so it is certainly a task-general resource. Crucially, though, this mechanism can initiate only one response at a time, and so it is not possible to divide this resource in any literal sense. If two concurrent tasks each require the response selector then one of them must wait its turn while the selector deals with the other task.

This clearly stands in contrast to notions like "mental effort," which imply that mental resources are *divisible*, so that you could devote 90% of your effort to a task, leaving 10% available for other chores, or you could devote 23%, leaving 77% available, or any other split you chose.

If one rejects this notion of divisible resources—if one, instead, conceives of resources as unitary—then what does this imply for divided attention. Again, let's focus on the response selector. Most tasks, of course, do not require a constant stream of new actions: You select and then initiate action, and then you spend some time *carrying out* that action. Only when the action is completed do you need to select the next step. It is this pattern that makes divided attention possible. If, for example, you are trying to divide your attention between Task A and Task B, you could first select and launch some action that is part of Task A. This will require the response selector, and so the selector won't be available for Task B. However, while you are carrying out the just-selected step for A, you no longer need the response selector for this task. Therefore, the response selector is momentarily free to select and launch a step for Task B. Then, while that step is being carried out, you can use the response selector to launch the next step of A. This kind of back-and-forth, turn-taking arrangement is referred to as **time-sharing**.

## EVIDENCE FOR THE RESPONSE SELECTOR

Many computer systems appear to do multiple tasks at once, but in fact, the computers are time-sharing: quickly switching from one task to another, and actually doing just one thing at a time. If you are working on such a system, the machine appears to be devoting all its resources to you, but that is only because you fail to notice the very brief delays as the machine hops from your task to some other task, and then back to you. You *would* detect the time-sharing if you were able to detect these very brief delays. And that is the point: One can detect time-sharing (as opposed to truly simultaneous processing) only by careful timing of the relevant activities.

Thus, to study time-sharing within human performance, we need a moment-by-moment analysis of how people allocate attention. To make this analysis possible, we often need to study rather simple tasks. For example, we can present two signals (call them S1 and S2) to participants, with each signal requiring its own response. Thus, S1 might be a number, "1" or "2", presented on a computer screen, with participants required to press, say, a red button if a "1" was shown, and a green button if a "2" was presented. Let's call this response R1. Likewise, S2 might be a letter, "A" or "B", and again participants must respond to indicate which was shown. This second response we will call R2—a button on the left for "A", one on the right for "B."

Each of these tasks—R1 in response to S1; R2 in response to S2—is, by itself, rather easy. But *combining* them is surprisingly difficult. We can, for example, present S1 and then, 150 msec later, while the participant is still "working on" S1, we present S2. This requires the participants, in effect, to deal with both stimuli at the same time.

In this setup, responses to the second stimulus will be quite slow. The time that elapses between S2 and R2 will be much longer than the time that elapses between S1 and R1, often by several hundred milliseconds. In percentage terms, participants are 30%–40% slower with the second signal than they are with the first. This delay is known as the **psychological refractory period** (PRP), and can be observed in a wide variety of procedures. (For reviews, see Pashler, 1991, 1992, 1994.)

How should we think about this result? An account in terms of *mental effort* would suggest that participants must commit a certain amount of effort to processing the first signal, with little effort left over for the second. As a result, the second signal will be processed less efficiently. An account in terms of the *response selector* in contrast, would propose that processing of the second signal is placed on hold until the selector has finished with the first signal. The delay, therefore, comes while the second signal waits its turn for processing.

These two hypotheses make different predictions about what will happen if we vary the procedure in certain ways. For example, what will happen if we make the signals difficult to perceive (perhaps dimmer or smaller)? What will happen if we make the selection of responses more complex—so that (for example) participants must press the left-most button if the middle light comes on, the right-most button if the left-most light comes on, and so on. According to the divisible effort hypothesis, either of these manipulations will increase the effort required for the task. This will simply widen the gap between "effort needed" and "effort available," and so will increase the size of the PRP.

The response-selector hypothesis makes different predictions and, in fact, makes rather fine-grained predictions: To choose the response for S1, one must first identify whether the stimulus is a "1" or a "2". Then, once the stimulus is identified, a response can be selected and initiated. At that point, the actual execution of the response begins. We can think of this as taking place in three steps: perceive, select a response, execute a response, as shown in Figure 4.6. What about S2? Let's hypothesize that the *perception* of S2 goes on in parallel with processing of S1, as shown in the figure. In other words, we are proposing that, for this task, perception is *not* where the bottleneck lies. Once S2 has been identified, though, we are ready for the next step—the selection and initiation of a response. This requires the selector, and our proposal is that the selector can't do two things at once. Therefore, what *can't* happen is shown in Figure 4.6A. In this scenario, the response selector is working on two things at the same time and that, according to our hypothesis, is impossible. Instead, what happens is shown in Figure 4.6B: Processing of S2 is put on hold until the response selector has finished with S1; only then is the selector available to deal with S2. In essence, then, we have four steps: perceive, wait for your turn, select a response, execute a response.

Let's now think through what will happen, according to this view, if we slow the perception of S1 (e.g., by using a dimmer signal). If this bit of perceiving is slowed, this will delay the start of *response selection* for S1. (This is shown in Figure 4.6C.) This will in turn delay the *completion* of response selection for S1. This will cause a delay in the *start* of response selection for S2, since S2's response selection can

begin only after S1's response selection is completed. Ultimately this will lead to a delay in R2. In short, then, slowing the *perception* of S1 will delay R2.

Things will go differently, though, if we slow down the perception of S2, rather than S1. Recall the sequence of events for S2: perceive, wait for the selector, select a response, and then execute the response. Thus, there is some "slack" in the sequence of events for this signal, thanks to the moment of waiting for the selector. Whether S2 is perceived slowly or perceived quickly, the response selector is only ready when it is done with S1. In effect, then, slowing down the perception of S2 is just a way of "killing time" while waiting for the selector. Therefore slowing down S2's perception will not delay the start of response initiation, and so will not delay R2. (This sequence is shown in Figure 4.6D.)

These and other specific predictions have all been confirmed in the laboratory, indicating that the response selector does indeed provide a bottleneck in the flow of mental events (McCann & Johnston, 1992; Pashler, 1991, 1992, 1995; Pashler & Johnston, 1989). Since the selector can only deal with one decision at a time, other decisions get stacked up, waiting for their turn at the selector. (For some complications, though, see De Jong, 1993; De Jong & Sweet, 1994; Pashler, 1994; Schumacher et al., 1999.)

## DIVIDED ATTENTION: AN INTERIM SUMMARY

Once again, it may be useful to take stock of where we are. Our consideration of selective attention drove us toward a several-part account, and the same seems to be true here. On the one side, *task-specific* interference can easily be demonstrated: Interference between tasks plainly depends on the nature of the tasks, and the interference is greatest when the tasks overlap in their processing demands. This fits with the claim of task-specific limited resources. At the same time, *task-general* interference can also be demonstrated. That is, concurrent tasks can interfere with each other even if there is no detectable overlap in the tasks' processing demands. Thus, we also need to include task-general resources in our account.

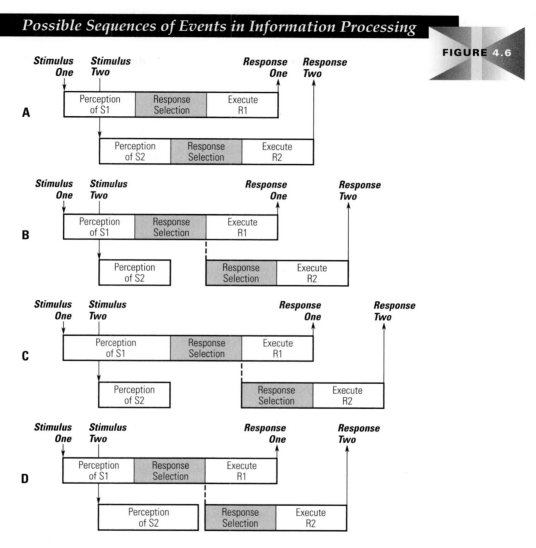

**Possible Sequences of Events in Information Processing**

FIGURE 4.6

According to Pashler (1991, 1992), Panel A shows what *can't* happen: Notice that, in this case, the selection of Response 2 *overlaps* with the selection of Response 1. This would require the response selector to do two things at once. What will happen instead is shown in Panel B: The selection of Response 2 must *wait* until the selection of Response 1 is completed, and this will cause a delay in the production of Response 2. Panel C shows what will happen if we slow the perception of S1 (for example, by using a dimmer signal). This leads to a delay in Response 2 (compare Panel C to Panel B). In contrast, Panel D shows what happens if we slow the perception of S2. This will *not* cause a delay in Response 2 (again, compare Panel D to Panel B).

Therefore, we need a complex account, but with a single unifying principle: Tasks will interfere with each other if they compete for resources. However, the nature of the "resource competition" will vary from case to case. If two tasks each require a complex series of responses, then the tasks will place heavy demands on the response selector. Since the response selector can only do one thing at a time, divided attention will be difficult. (Or, more precisely, divided attention will be possible only via time-sharing.) If, in contrast, one of the tasks requires few responses, or if the responses are easily predictable in advance, then there will be little competition for the response selector, but there may still be competition for some other resource.

We emphasize, though, how many questions are still to be asked, particularly about task-general resources. For example, we have discussed one such resource, the response selector, but what other task-general resources might there be? Duncan (1994) has argued for the existence of a different general resource, needed for *planning* and the *setting of goals* (also see Allport, 1989; Duncan et al., 1996; Just et al., 1996). We won't pursue this argument here, since our point in mentioning this claim is merely this: A planning resource would surely be applicable to a wide variety of tasks and would, in our terms, be a task-general resource. Moreover, this resource would be separate from the mechanism that actually launches activities—that is, it would be separate from the response selector. And, again, we would need to ask various questions about this resource— exactly which tasks need it, whether this resource is divisible or unitary, and so on. Thus, our catalogue of task-general resources is almost certainly not yet complete, and for each proposed resource, there are obvious questions to ask. (Also see Allport, Styles & Hsieh, 1994.)

## Practice

We have been discussing the possibility of doing "two tasks at the same time." But what exactly is a "task?" For example, we have talked about the case of driving while talking, and we described this as *two* simultaneous tasks. Is this realistic? After all, driving itself has several clearly distinguishable parts: You have to pay attention to the curve of the road in order to steer. You also have to pay attention to your speed, to the car in front of you, to the cars behind you, and to the oncoming traffic. Is it fair to call all of this "one task"? Or is driving all by itself an example of divided attention, an example of multiple simultaneous activities? Likewise, in talking, you must coordinate the movements of your teeth, tongue, and lips, the vibration of your vocal chords, and also the movement of air out of the lungs, not to mention the selection of what you are going to say, decisions about how you are going to phrase your thoughts, and so on.

As these examples suggest, virtually any complex task can be thought of as an assembly of specific sub-tasks. Indeed, when a complex task is first being mastered, it does feel like a problem in divided attention, and task interference can be observed: If the steering becomes complex, the novice driver may lose track of how fast he or she is going; if the novice is paying attention to the road, he or she may forget to shift gears. These components of driving seem truly separate for the novice, competing with each other for attention, and making concurrent performance difficult. Once the skill of driving is mastered, however, it seems to be run off as a single organized unit: A skilled driver handles all these components simultaneously, with no apparent interference among the subtasks.

All of this implies that problems of divided attention may crop up fairly often. In essence, every time you seek to master a new task, you are called on, at least initially, to divide your attention among the task's components. With practice, though, the task's demands change, and you are able to perform the various elements of the task as a single, integrated package. It would seem, then, that if we are to understand divided attention, we need to understand *practice*.

## PRACTICE IN VISUAL SEARCH

At a very general level, there is an obvious way for our theory to accommodate the effects of practice: Practice decreases the resource demand of a task. Various versions of this idea have been suggested (Kahneman, 1973; Norman & Bobrow, 1975), and the idea, general as it is, fits easily with the data. Early on, steering a car demands a lot of resources and so doesn't leave enough resources available for other activities (for example, shifting gears); hence, interference is observed. With practice, steering requires fewer resources, so more is left over. As a result, driving can now be combined with shifting.

However, this plainly leaves a great deal unsaid. We have, for example, discussed a diversity of mental resources, some task-general, some task-specific. Which of these are needed less, as practice proceeds?

Moreover, *why* does practice diminish a task's resource demand? Through what mechanism? Will any sort of practice diminish the resource demand? Or does the practice have to be of a special type? Let's start with these latter questions, and then build from there.

In an influential pair of papers, Schneider and Shiffrin proposed that practice diminishes resource demand only if it is practice of the right sort (Schneider & Shiffrin, 1977; Shiffrin & Schneider, 1977). In support of this claim, they reported data concerned with the effects of practice on a single task, visual search. Their research participants were shown a group of letters (see Figure 4.7); let's call these the "targets." They were then shown a different group of letters, and had to decide if any of the targets were present in this second group. The targets on a particular trial might be J and T, and now participants

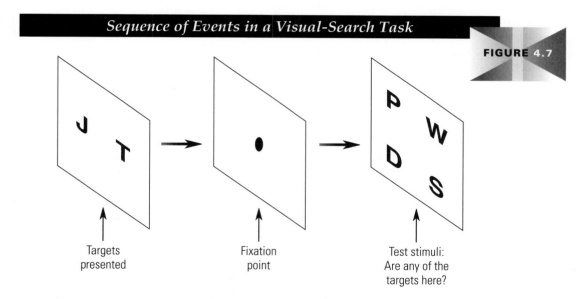

**Sequence of Events in a Visual-Search Task**

**FIGURE 4.7**

Targets presented

Fixation point

Test stimuli: Are any of the targets here?

Participants are first shown a group of "targets"; the number of targets varies from trial to trial. Then participants are shown a fixation point, to ensure that their eyes are pointed in the right direction. Finally, participants are shown a group of test letters, and they must respond "yes" if *any* of the targets are present in this group.

have to decide if any targets are present in the group "P W D S J F." The answer in this case would be "yes" because a J was present.

Participants were given much practice with the task, searching for a particular set of targets within a given field, and then searching for a new set of targets within a new field. Importantly, there was no consistency in which letters appeared as targets, and which appeared as distractors. To make this concrete, the targets for trial 28 might be S and H, and the participant might have to search among this set: "A M S." In this case, a "yes" response would be correct, since one of the targets is present. The targets for trial 29 might then be F and C, and the participant might have to search among this set: "P S R" (the response should be "no"). Notice that the appearance of the S in the first of these trials demanded a "yes" response, whereas the appearance of the S in the second of these trials does *not* demand a "yes" response. In other words, there is no consistent linkage between letters and responses, since the response appropriate for each letter will vary from trial to trial. Schneider and Shiffrin call this a **varied mapping** between inputs and responses.

In a different version of the procedure, the setup was different: Before starting the procedure, Schneider and Shiffrin selected a portion of the alphabet to be the "potential targets." For example, we might identify A, E, I, M, Q, U, and Y as the potential targets. Every trial of the procedure involves different targets, but the targets are always drawn from this group. In addition, these potential target letters never appear as the distractor letters. Thus, a Q may or may not appear in any individual trial but, if it appears, it will appear as a target. In other words, if a Q appears, it demands a "yes" response. On no trial is Q one of the distractors, and so a Q never demands a "no" response. The letter F cannot be a target, because it is not in the set of potential targets. Therefore a "yes" response is never appropriate for the letter F. Overall then, this condition provides a **consistent mapping** between inputs and responses.

Schneider and Shiffrin found that practice with consistent mapping had very different consequences from practice with varied mapping. To understand this, we need one more fact about the Schneider and Shiffrin procedure. In some trials, only one target was presented so that, for example, the participant searched the display for the letter A, and responded "yes" only if an A was present. On other trials, multiple targets were presented so that, for example, participants had to respond "yes" if an E or an X or a Z was in the display. How might this matter? As one possibility, participants might search the display for the E, and then for X, and then for the Z. This one-at-a-time process is called a serial search (since the individual searches are lined up in a series). With a serial search, it would take longer to search for two targets than for one, longer to search for three than for two, and so on.

As a different possibility, participants might be able to divide their attention and, in effect, do several searches at once—look for the E at the same time they are looking for the X at the same they are looking for the Z. With this parallel search, search time should not depend on the number of targets.

Schneider and Shiffrin's data indicate that participants trained with a *varied* mapping always used a serial search. Even after much practice with the overall task, they still searched for one target, then the next, then another. Consequently, search times were slower for two targets than for one, slower still for three targets. In the early trials, participants trained with a *consistent* mapping showed the same pattern. However, after some practice, they were able to do a parallel search (and so needed the same time to search for multiple targets as they did to search for single targets).

A parallel search is just like a divided-attention procedure: The research participants are searching for the Z at the same time that they are searching for the L; they are, in short, doing two things at once. Yet the results indicate no interference between these concurrent searches: Participants can do two simultaneous searches, or even three or four simultaneous searches, just as quickly, and just as efficiently, as they can do a single search. Apparently, then, the individual searches are not competing with each other for some limited resource; if they were, we would observe interference. And that is the point: Consistent-mapping practice makes possible "resource-free" searching.

Another aspect of the data is also quite striking: After giving people extensive practice in the consistent-mapping task, Schneider and Shiffrin *reversed* the categorization of targets and distractors. From this point forward, stimuli that had been in the set of possible targets were now *never* targets; stimuli that had never been targets now became the possible targets. This reversal was enormously difficult for the participants—their responses were now quite slow, they made many errors, and they reverted to a serial search, rather than a parallel one. In short, it appeared that the earlier consistent-mapping practice had created a new "reflex" for the participants: They had acquired immense skill in searching, but they had also, in a sense, lost control of their performance—they could not turn off their newly established skill, even when the procedure demanded it.

## AUTOMATICITY

According to some theoretical accounts, visual search has, for the consistent mapping participants, become automatic. Early discussions suggested that **automaticity** has several interesting features: Automatized skills require few resources, and so are unlikely to compete for resources with other tasks. Hence, it should be easy to divide attention between an automatized task and virtually any other task. Likewise, many authors suggested that automatized skills are largely independent of *intention*; they should, in essence, be out of control. (Indeed, some authors speak of automatized skills as we just did, as "mental reflexes.") Finally, in many cases, automatized activities should go forward independent of *awareness*. We

have said little about what awareness *is*, but at the least, one might expect that awareness will be intimately tied up with the control systems of attention (including the response selector). Since automatized activities are performed without these control systems, it seems likely that one can do automatized acts without thinking much about them—you can do them on "autopilot." (We return to this theme in Chapter 15.)

These claims certainly fit with the Shiffrin and Schneider data. We hasten to say, though, that these claims about automaticity need to be refined somewhat. For example, we have listed three traits of automatized behaviors—these behaviors are produced without intention, without awareness, and without requiring resources (and thus not disrupting, and not being disrupted by, other simultaneous activities). It turns out, however, that these traits need not cluster together—i.e., we can document cases of behaviors that are produced without intention, but that do require resources; behaviors that don't require resources, but do seem to be under the person's control, and so on. Therefore, we need a theory that accounts individually for these aspects of skilled behavior, rather than a theory that accounts for them as a group. (For discussion, see Bargh, 1989; Kahneman & Chajczyk, 1983; Logan, 1989; Paap & Ogden, 1981; Zbrodoff & Logan, 1986; for debate specifically focused on the Shiffrin and Schneider paradigm, see Cheng, 1985; Fisher, 1984; Logan & Stadler, 1991; Ryan, 1983; Schneider & Shiffrin, 1985; Shiffrin & Schneider, 1984; Strayer & Kramer, 1994a, 1994b.)

Even with these complexities acknowledged, certain features of automaticity remain quite striking—particularly the reflex-like quality of automatized behaviors. This quality was nicely demonstrated in a classic experiment conducted by Stroop (1935). Stroop showed participants a series of words and asked them to name aloud the color of the ink used for each word. The trick, though, was that the words themselves were color names. So people might see the word "BLUE" printed in green ink, and would have to say "green" out loud.

This task turns out to be enormously difficult. There is a strong tendency to read the printed word itself, rather than naming the ink color, and people make many mistakes in this task. What is going on here? Word recognition, especially for college-age adults, is enormously well practiced and, as a consequence, word recognition can proceed automatically. This is a condition, therefore, in which we expect great difficulties in *ignoring* a stimulus, great difficulties in *not* perceiving, and that is exactly what the **Stroop effect** shows. (For reviews of Stroop research, see MacLeod, 1991; Yee & Hunt, 1991; for a variant of Stroop interference, see Figure 4.8. Although the Stroop effect has been known for many years, there is still debate about its underlying mechanisms; for different perspectives than the one offered here, see Besner, Stoltz & Boutilier, 1997; Besner & Stolz, 1999; Durgin, 2000.)

## THE "REFLEX" QUALITY OF AUTOMATICITY

Why does practice produce this reflex quality? To address this, let's again focus on Schneider and Shiffrin's visual-search task. Think back to the variable-mapping condition, in which a stimulus can be a target in one trial, but a distractor in the next trial. This condition, by its design, requires participants to keep track, trial by trial, of the response appropriate for each stimulus. Hence, participants must, throughout the experiment, monitor what response is appropriate for an S on *this* trial; what response is appropriate for a T on *this* trial. This certainly implies that this condition will make heavy use of the response selector; it will also make heavy use of the planner. Moreover, this is a fixed feature of this condition; it is, after all, built into the definition of variable mapping, and so will not be changed by practice. Thus, whatever the level of prac-

**FIGURE 4.8**

## Stroop Interference

| How many items are in each row? | How about these rows? |
|---|---|
| # # | 4 4 |
| ? ? ? ? | 2 2 2 2 |
| & | 3 |
| & & | 3 3 |
| / / / / | 1 1 1 1 |
| # | 4 |
| ? ? | 2 2 |
| / / / | 1 1 1 |
| # # # | 4 4 4 |
| & & & & | 3 3 3 3 |
| ? | 2 |
| / / | 1 1 |

Stroop's original demonstration involved color naming, but many variations on this effect can be demonstrated. For example, scan down the left column, saying out loud how many items are in each row. Now do the same with the right column. Here the task is more difficult, because of the strong tendency to *read* the numerals, rather than *counting* them.

tice, this condition will continue to place a heavy demand on these resources.

Contrast this with consistent mapping. Here, each stimulus is reliably associated with a specific response. If an S requires a "no" response on one trial, it will require a "no" response on all trials. With practice, therefore, planning and response selection will become a matter of familiar routine: When you see the S, you don't have to ponder what the response should be; all you need to do is recall how you responded to a S the last time you saw one. And likewise for all the other stimuli so that, in this condition, the role of the planner and the response selector soon becomes trivial. Consequently, these resources will cease to be a bottleneck in the flow of events, allowing a move away from serial processing.

This reliance on routine can be enormously helpful: After some practice, participants in this procedure no longer need to make choices; they no longer need to weigh the factors favoring one response over another. Instead, all they have to do is ask, "What did I do the last time I was in this situation?" This "memory lookup" will usually be easier than working through the actual decision. Indeed, for more complicated tasks, a reliance on routine will allow someone to replace a whole *series* of decisions (one for each of the task's steps) with a *single* memory lookup. ("What was the *sequence* of decisions I made last time?") Presumably, the response selector will be needed to choose and launch this overall routine but, with that done, the person can simply run off the routine, with no further need for the selector.

Note, though, that there is a price paid for this efficiency: By relying on routine, you sacrifice flexibility. If you always repeat what you did the last time around, you lose the option of changing your response; indeed, you lose the option of choosing to do nothing this time. That is why diminished use of the planner and the response selector, and the increased use of routine, gives automatic actions their reflex character.

Let's be careful, though, about what is meant here by "reflex." In the account just sketched, a sequence of actions will run off automatically *once the routine has been launched*. Once you have decided to tie your shoes, you rely on the familiar routine of shoe-tying. Hence, you don't make decisions about the individual steps of this process and, correspondingly, you have little control over the details of this process. However, you did make the initial decision—to tie your shoes. Shoe-tying is automatic *once started*, but it is not a reflex in any literal sense. The same is true for Stroop interference: Once you have initiated the routine of uttering color names, you are vulnerable to this interference. But, of course, you don't say "red" aloud every time you encounter the letters "r-e-d." Color naming is only automatic once the overall sequence has been launched. Thus, current researchers speak of *contingent* automaticity, rather than automaticity in general, to emphasize the fact that automaticity is contingent on the person first being in the appropriate "response mode" (for discussion, see Bargh, 1989; Bargh & Chartrand, 1999; for evidence that we *can* sometimes control *some* automatized acts, see Logan, 1982).

## THE "LIMITS" OF DIVIDED ATTENTION

A key benefit of practice, therefore, is the establishment of a routine. With a routine in place, you no longer need to make decisions, step by step, about what to do next as you are performing the task. Instead, you can rely on the sequence of decisions you used last time around, with corresponding gains in speed, efficiency, and ease.

In addition, we may be able, in some circumstances, to obtain these advantages without practice. For example, even before people get any practice with a task, we might be able to explain the task to them in a way that makes clear the appropriate routine. If they can remember this procedure, they will be able to rely on it when they *first* try the task. In other words, they will draw immediately on the routine, even without the benefit of any practice. This sort of "automaticity without practice" has in fact been documented, at least for some tasks (Logan, 1989; Logan & Klapp, 1991).

What are the limits of all this? Are there things that cannot be reduced to a routine? Or, with practice, can you automatize any activity? Likewise, given the link between routine and divided attention, could you learn, with enough practice, to divide attention between *any* two tasks? Or are some task combinations simply impossible?

In an extraordinary series of experiments, people were trained to read and write simultaneously (Spelke, Hirst & Neisser, 1976; Hirst, Spelke, Reaves, Caharack & Neisser, 1980). To understand the task, imagine sitting in a lecture, taking careful notes, *and simultaneously* reading the assignment for your next class. What a time-saver that would be!

In the actual experiments, the participants were given stories to read and, while they were reading, they listened to the experimenters dictating lists of words. They were required to write down these dictated words, and were also tested on the reading material, later on, to ensure that they comprehended what they were reading.

Initially, to no one's surprise, this combination of tasks was very difficult—participants either read more slowly, or skipped lines, or missed some of the dictated words. After about six weeks of practice, however, they learned to combine the tasks, and could read while taking dictation just as well as they did when reading was their sole concern.

The comprehension tests confirm that participants did understand what they were reading. Were they also comprehending what they *heard*—that is, the dictated materials? To find out, Hirst et al. (1980) changed what was being dictated, so that the dictated material actually formed sentences, and the sentences formed miniature stories. For example, participants, while reading one story, might hear these three sentences: "The dancers performed. They were excellent. The director bowed." Later on, the participants were given 30 more sentences in a recognition test and had to judge which of these had been presented earlier. Some of the test sentences were identical to the sentences contained within the dictation; some of the test sentences were

different (e.g., "The dancers bowed"). Our main interest, though, is with a third category of test sentences. These sentences were *implied* by what was presented, but not literally said. A test sentence in this category might be, "Dancers were excellent."

If participants say "yes" to this last category, this is an interesting error, implying that they understood the gist of the story that was dictated to them. A "yes" response would indicate that they understood how the sentences were linked to each other. And, in fact, participants did say "yes" to this third category of "implied" sentences, suggesting that they did grasp the meaning of the dictated material—at the same time that they were reading other material, at their normal speed, and with their normal comprehension.

## THE IMPORTANCE OF "COMBINED" PRACTICE

The Spelke, Hirst, and Neisser experiments are for many people mind-boggling. At the least, one has to be impressed by what these participants could accomplish. Moreover, one has to wonder what else could be accomplished by sufficient practice. Where are the limits? What *can't* we do, given sufficient practice? These are important questions that need further examination.

In addition, the Spelke, Hirst, and Neisser data force us to enlarge our view of the relationship between practice and divided attention. After all, the participants in this study were well practiced in reading, with at least 15 years of experience prior to the experiment's start. Likewise, before the experiment began, the participants all had extensive practice in note-taking. Therefore, if practice is the key to divided attention, why couldn't these people combine these well-practiced activities on the very first day they were tested?

The obvious suggestion is that the participants didn't need more practice in reading or in note-taking. Instead, they needed practice in *combining* these two activities. They were already skilled enough in the individual tasks; what they needed to learn was the complex of reading-while-taking-dictation. (For fuller discussion of this point, see Allport, 1989.)

Why is "combined practice" so important? One possibility is that, in some cases, the limits to divided attention are not limits of resources. Instead, performance may be limited by problems in "bookkeeping," that is, the chore of keeping straight which task is which. Think about the game of rubbing your stomach with one hand while simultaneously tapping your head with the other hand. The difficulty of this task lies simply in keeping track of which hand is doing the rubbing, and which hand the tapping. This problem is technically known as **channel segregation**—it isn't easy to keep the "stomach-rubbing channel" separate from the "head-tapping channel." Said differently, one suffers from **crosstalk** between the two channels (Kinsbourne, 1981).

Channel segregation is probably relevant to several of the studies we have discussed. For example, consider the result reported by Allport et al. (1972): Their participants had little trouble memorizing a series of pictures while simultaneously shadowing a series of words; it was difficult, though, to memorize a series of words heard through one ear while shadowing different words heard through the other ear. In this latter condition, the simultaneous inputs are obviously quite similar to each other, and so easily confused with each other. For example, participants may know they have just heard the word "box" but may not be certain whether they heard it in the left ear or the right. As a result, they wouldn't know if this is a word to be shadowed or a word to be memorized. This sort of confusion is far less likely, though, with dissimilar tasks, like listening to words while viewing pictures. Now, if one hears the word "box," it could only have come from one source, making it easy to keep track of which input is which. With easy channel segregation, participants won't become confused, and successful divided attention is more likely.

To connect this back to practice effects, we merely need to argue that channel segregation is a skill that can be improved with practice. This suggests that we might think of divided attention itself as a practiceable skill: When one learns to sing while riding a bicycle, one is not merely learning to sing, and not merely learning to ride a bicycle. Instead, one is specifically learning how to divide attention between these activities, and this may in turn depend largely on learning how to keep these two activities segregated.

How plausible is this? Channel segregation obviously depends on being able to discriminate the channels: If you can't tell your left ear from your right, you will never be able to segregate a left-ear message from a right-ear message. It also seems clear that the ability to discriminate among categories improves with practice: The novice bird-watcher may think that all small birds look alike. With a little experience, however, the bird-watcher learns to distinguish the warblers from the wrens and, eventually, to distinguish among the different warblers. If segregation depends on discrimination, and if discrimination improves with practice, then the ability to segregate should improve with practice. This is, of course, exactly the argument we need in order to explain the Spelke, Hirst, and Neisser results in terms of channel segregation.

## DIVIDED ATTENTION: A REPRISE

Let us again summarize where we are: We have argued that there are multiple constraints, multiple limits, on divided attention. If two tasks make competing demands on task-specific resources, this will rule out concurrent performance of the tasks. If two tasks make competing demands on task-general resources (such as the response selector), this too will rule out concurrent performance. Finally, if two tasks cannot be segregated, this will also rule out concurrent performance, because of problems with crosstalk.

Do we really need *all* of these mechanisms? Or might a simpler theory of attention be possible? Some researchers have argued that considerations of channel segregation may be all we need to explain the limits of divided attention (Allport, 1989; Navon, 1984, 1985; Neisser, 1976), making any claims about "resources" superfluous. Despite these arguments, though, it does seem likely that we need a multipart theory of attention, with performance limited by different factors in different occasions. For example, difficulties in divided attention can be documented even when channel segregation is easy, but there is competition for resources (e.g., Holtzman et al., 1911; Pashler & O'Brien, 1993). Thus, it does seem that interference between concurrent activities can arise for several different reasons.

What, then, is "attention"? It would seem that attention isn't just a skill, or a mechanism, or a capacity. Instead, attention is an *achievement*—an achievement of performing multiple activities simultaneously, or an achievement of successfully avoiding distraction, when you wish to focus on a single task. And, as we have now seen, this achievement rests on an intricate base, so that many skills, mechanisms, and capacities contribute to our ability to attend.

Moreover, we have argued for an intimate connection between divided attention and skilled performance: That is, any complex task—whether it is playing tennis, or driving a car, or even ordinary talking—can be thought of as an assembly of subtasks, and these must be done simultaneously (and be coordinated with each other) to achieve task proficiency. The ability to divide attention among a task's components is therefore an essential ingredient in the development of skill. The achievement of paying attention is thus crucial in its own right, and is also a fundamental element of almost everything else we do.

## Chapter Summary

1. People are often quite oblivious to unattended inputs; they are unable to tell if an unattended auditory input is coherent prose or random words, and often fail altogether to detect unattended visual inputs, even though they are right in front of the viewer's eyes. However, some aspects of the unattended inputs are detected. For example, people can report on the pitch of the unattended sound and whether it contained human speech or some other sort of noise. Sometimes they can also detect stimuli that are especially meaningful; some people, for example, hear their own name if it is spoken on the unattended channel.

2. These results suggest that perception may require the commitment of *mental resources*, with some of these resources helping to prime the detectors needed for perception. This proposal is supported by studies showing that we do perceive more efficiently when we can anticipate the upcoming stimulus (and so can prime the relevant detectors). In many cases, this anticipation is *spatial*, if for example we know that a stimulus is about to arrive at a particular location. This priming, however, seems to draw on a *limited-capacity system*, and so priming one stimulus or one position "takes away" resources that might be spent on priming some other stimulus.

3. *Neuroimaging techniques* and clinical data indicate that many brain areas and many mechanisms are needed to make these perceptual anticipations possible. For example, different brain mechanisms are needed to "disengage" the *search-light beam* of attention from its current position, to move it to a new position, and then to lock the beam into the new position. Disruption to any of these mechanisms causes problems in attending, but the most striking problems are those evident in *unilateral neglect syndrome*, in which an individual attends only to one half of space.

4. Perceiving, it seems, requires the commitment of resources, and so do most other mental activities. This provides a ready account of *divided attention*: It is possible to perform two tasks simultaneously only if the two tasks do not in combination demand more resources than are available. Some of the relevant mental resources are *task-general*, and so called on by a wide variety of mental activities. These include the *response selector, mental effort*, and resources needed for planning. Other mental resources are *task-specific*, required only for tasks of a certain type.

5. Divided attention is clearly influenced by practice, and so it is often easier to divide attention between familiar tasks than it is between unfamiliar

tasks. However, the relationship between practice and attention depends on the nature of the task. If a task has a *consistent mapping* between inputs and responses, practice can lead to very fast responses, and the resource requirements of the task can decrease dramatically. If there is a *varied mapping* between inputs and responses, practice with these tasks has a much smaller effect.

6. In the extreme, practice may produce *automaticity*, in which a task seems to require virtually no mental resources but is also difficult to control. One proposal is that automaticity results from the fact that decisions are no longer needed for a well-practiced routine; instead, one can simply run off the entire routine, doing on this occasion just what one did on prior occasions.

7. In some circumstances, practice with an individual task is not enough. Instead, it is important to practice doing two tasks simultaneously. One benefit from this will be increased skill in *channel segregation*, which decreases *crosstalk* between the tasks.

8. Some investigators have questioned whether we need all of these different elements in our theory of attention—various task-general resources, various task-specific resources, skill in channel segregation, and also (in some circumstances) mechanisms that inhibit unwanted responses. However, evidence suggests that all of these elements do play a role, suggesting that "attention" is not a process or a particular mechanism. Instead, "attention" is the name of a complex achievement made possible by many different mechanisms.

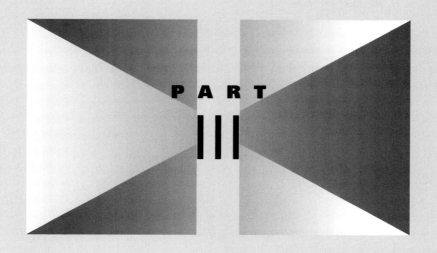

# Memory

In this section, we'll discuss how people learn new things and how they remember this information later on. We'll also consider some of the apparent failures of memory, including cases in which people "draw a blank" and can't remember anything at all, and also cases in which people *seem to* remember, but are actually far from the truth in their recollection. Throughout the section, we'll be concerned both with theoretical and practical questions—for example, questions about how students should study their class materials, and also questions about how much trust a jury can place in an eyewitness's recollection of a crime.

Two themes will be prominent throughout this section—the *active nature* of memory, and the crucial role for *memory connections*. As one example of the active nature of memory, our discussion of learning will lead us to recognize the importance of how the learner "engages" or thinks about the to-be-remembered material. As we'll see, passive exposure to information, with no intellectual engagement, leads to poor memory later on. In addition, we'll learn why some forms of engagement lead to good memory, and other forms do not.

The active nature of memory will also be visible in many other contexts, including our discussion of what it means to "remember." Here we'll see that remembering involves a lot of integration and interpretation. Indeed, in many cases what *seems* to be remembering is really after-the-fact reconstruction, and we'll need to consider how this reconstruction proceeds and what it implies for memory accuracy.

The second theme—the role of memory connections—will be equally prominent. In Chapter 5, we'll see that, at its essence, learning involves the creation of connections, and the more connections formed, the better the learning. In Chapter 6, we'll explore the idea that these connections are helpful because they serve as *retrieval paths* later on—a path, one hopes, that will lead you from your memory search's starting point to the information you're trying to remember. As we'll see, this idea of connections-as-retrieval-paths has powerful implications for when you will succeed in remembering, and when you will fail, and the chapter explores many of these implications. In particular, we'll consider why it is that you can often help someone to remember by reinstating the physical, emotional, and mental circumstances that were in place during learning; we'll also explore why excellent preparation for one type of test may be poor preparation for another type of test. We'll trace this idea through several contexts, but, crucially, we'll use this idea as a means of exploring the contrasts between conscious and unconscious remembering.

Chapter 7 explores a different ramification of the connections idea: Memory connections can actually be a source of memory errors. In learning, you create connections that knit together the new material with things you already know. These connections are helpful (because they serve as retrieval paths), but, even so, the more connections you create, the harder it will be to keep track of which elements are which—which were contained within the episode itself and which are connected to that episode only because you connected them during the learning process. We'll learn what this means for memory accuracy overall, and we'll also learn what one can do to minimize error and to improve the completeness and accuracy of human memory.

**CHAPTER 5**

# The Acquisition of Memories and the Working-Memory System

In Chapter 1, we argued that *memory* plays a pivotal role in our mental lives. Without memory, there would be no learning. Without memory, we would get no benefit from our prior experiences. And, of course, there are many questions to ask about memory: How does learning proceed? Are there more or less effective ways to learn? Why do we sometimes forget? And, finally, how much trust should we place in our memories—how accurate, and how complete, is our recollection of previous events? These questions will be our focus for the next three chapters.

There is an obvious way to organize our inquiry into memory. Before there can be a memory, some learning must occur—that is, new information must be acquired. Therefore, *acquisition* should be our first topic for discussion. Then, once information has been acquired, it must be held in memory until it is needed. We refer to this as the *storage* phase. Finally, we use the information that is in memory; we remember. Information is somehow found in the vast warehouse that is memory and brought into active use; this is called *retrieval*.

This organization probably strikes you as intuitively sensible; it fits, for example, with the way most "electronic memories" (e.g., computers) work. Information ("input") is provided to a computer (the acquisition phase). The information then resides in some dormant form, perhaps in the computer's memory, or perhaps on a magnetic disk (the storage phase). Finally, the information can be brought back from this dormant form, often via a search process that hunts through the memory or disk (the retrieval phase). Of course, there's nothing special about a computer here, since "low-tech" information storage works the same way.

Think about a file drawer: Information is acquired (i.e., filed), then rests in this or that folder, and then is retrieved.

This framework makes it sound like acquisition, storage, and retrieval are separate processes that happen in sequence. This in turn implies that these three elements of remembering can be discussed independently of each other. So we begin our inquiry by focusing on the acquisition of new memories, leaving discussion of storage and retrieval for later. As it turns out, though, we will soon find reasons for challenging this overall approach to memory. In discussing acquisition, for example, we might wish to ask: What is good learning? What guarantees that material is firmly recorded in memory? As we will see, the evidence indicates that what is good learning depends on how the memory is retrieved—good preparation for one kind of test can be poor preparation for a different kind of test. Claims about acquisition, therefore, must be interwoven with claims about retrieval. These interconnections between acquisition and retrieval will be the central theme of Chapter 6.

In the same way, we cannot separate claims about memory acquisition from claims about memory storage. To put it simply, how you learn and how well you learn depend heavily on what you already know. That needs to be explored and explained, and will provide a recurrent theme for both this chapter and Chapter 7.

With these caveats in mind, we will begin by describing the acquisition process. Our approach will be roughly historical: We will start with a simple model, emphasizing data collected largely in the 1970s. We will then use this as the framework for examining more recent research, adding refinements to the model as we proceed.

## The Route into Memory

Starting in the late 1950s, much theorizing in cognitive psychology was guided by a new way of thinking about mental events, a perspective known as **information processing**. This perspective borrowed heavily from developments in electronic information processing, including developments in computers (see Chapter 1). Leaving the details aside, the notion was that complex mental events such as learning, remembering, or deciding could be understood as being built up out of a large number of discrete steps. These steps occurred one-by-one, each with its own characteristics and its own job to do, and with each providing as its "output" the input to the next step in the sequence. Within this framework, theories could often be illustrated with charts such as the one in Figure 5.1. In this diagram, each enclosed shape represents a separate event or process, and the arrows represent the flow of information from one event to the next. The research goal was to make the charts more and more complete, by analyzing each box into still smaller boxes, continuing until the complex process under scrutiny could be described in terms of elementary information-processing components.

A great deal of information-processing theory focused on the processes through which information was detected, recognized, and entered into memory storage—that is, on the process of information *acquisition*. While there was disagreement about the details, there was reasonable consensus on the bold outline of events. An early version of this model was described by Waugh and Norman (1965); later refinements were added by Atkinson and Shiffrin (1968). The consensus model came to be known as the **modal model**, and it is on this model that we will focus.

## THE MODAL MODEL

According to the modal model, our information processing involves different kinds of memory, two of which are short-term memory and long-term memory. Short-term memory holds onto information currently "in use," much as your desk contains the papers or books with which you are currently working. Short-term memory is limited in how much it can hold but, most important, information in short-term memory is instantly and easily available to you.

## An Information-Processing View of Memory

**FIGURE 5.1**

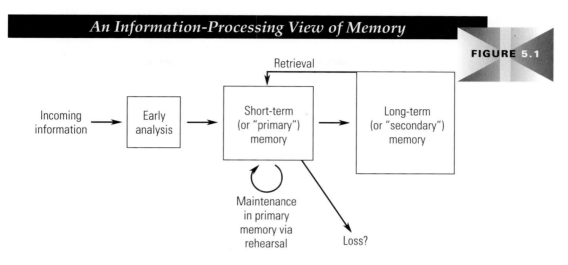

In this view, the boxes represent separate events, processes, or storage spaces; arrows represent the flow of information from one process to another.

We first mentioned short-term memory in Chapter 1, although there we used the more modern terminology, working memory, a term that emphasizes the function of this memory. As we noted in Chapter 1, virtually all mental tasks rely on working memory. To mention one of our earlier examples, as you read this sentence, your interpretation of the early words will depend on what comes later; therefore, you will need to store the early words for a second or two, until you have read the entire sentence. Those early words, presumably, would be stored in working memory. Cases like this make it clear why this memory is referred to as working memory—it is where you store information while you are working on it. (In Chapter 1, we also emphasized the fact that working memory has different components—we spoke of a *working-memory system*. We will return to this point later in the chapter.)

If working memory provides a mental "desk space," then long-term memory is the mental "reference library." Long-term memory (LTM) is a vast store and contains all of the information you remember—your memories of what you did yesterday, how you spent your childhood, a vast number of facts about your favorite topic, the names and faces of a hundred acquaintances, and so on.

Although there is a close association between working memory and the contents of your current thinking, there is no such association for long-term memory. At any point in time, much of the material in LTM lies dormant, neither influencing nor influenced by your current thoughts. Correspondingly, the process of retrieving information from LTM, and thus making the information available for use, is often effortful and slow.

### WORKING MEMORY AND LONG-TERM MEMORY: ONE MEMORY OR TWO?

Many pieces of evidence demand this distinction between working memory and LTM, but much of the evidence comes from a single task: Participants are read a series of words, like "bicycle, artichoke, radio, chair, palace." The length of the list can vary, and so can the rate at which the words are presented. Typical experiments, though, use lists of about 30 words, presented at a rate of about one word per second.

Immediately after the last word is read, participants are asked to repeat back as many words as they can. They are free to report the words in any order they choose, which is why this is referred to as a **free recall** procedure.

People usually remember 12 to 15 words in such a test, in a consistent pattern: They are extremely likely to remember the first few words on the list, something known as the **primacy effect**, and are also likely to remember the last five or six words on the list, a **recency effect**. Results of such a study are shown in Figure 5.2, with a U-shaped curve showing the relation between position within the series (or serial position) and likelihood of recall (Baddeley & Hitch, 1977; Deese & Kaufman, 1957; Glanzer & Cunitz, 1966; Murdock, 1962; Postman & Phillips, 1965).

This **serial position curve** is easily explained by the modal model. At any point in time, according to our model, working memory contains the material someone is "working on" at just that moment. So what are participants working on during the list presentation? Presumably, they are thinking about the words they are hearing, and so it is these words that are in working memory. Working memory, though, is limited in its size, capable of holding only five or six words. Therefore, as participants try to keep up with the list presentation, they will be placing the "just heard" words into working memory, and this will bump the previous words out of this memory. Consequently, as participants proceed through the list, their working memories will, at each moment, contain just the half-dozen words that arrived most recently.

On this account, the only words that don't get "bumped" out of working memory are the last few words on the list, since obviously no further input arrives to displace these words. Hence, when the

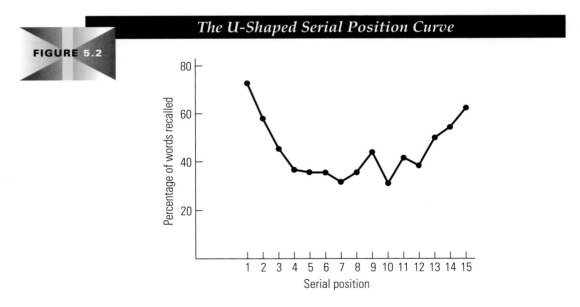

**FIGURE 5.2**

### The U-Shaped Serial Position Curve

Participants are read a list of words, and then, immediately after this presentation, they must recall as many of the words as they can. They are most likely to remember the first few words presented to them and the last few words. [After Glanzer & Cunitz, 1966.]

list presentation ends, these few words are still in working memory. Moreover, our hypothesis is that materials in working memory are readily available—easily and quickly retrieved. When the time comes for recall, we expect accurate and complete recall for these last few words. This is the source of the recency effect.

The primacy effect comes from a different source. According to the modal model, the transfer of material from working memory to LTM depends on processes that require time and attention, so let's examine how participants allocate their attention to the list items. As participants hear the list, they do their best to be good memorizers, and so, when they hear the first word, they repeat it over and over to themselves ("bicycle, bicycle, bicycle"), a process referred to as **memory rehearsal**. When the second word arrives, they rehearse it, too ("bicycle, artichoke, bicycle, artichoke"). Likewise for the third ("bicycle, artichoke, radio, bicycle, artichoke, radio . . ."), and so on through the list. Note, though, that the first few items on the list are *privileged*: For a brief moment, "bicycle" was the only word participants had to worry about, and so it had 100% of their attention lavished on it; no other word received this privilege. For a brief moment, "artichoke" had 50% of the participants' attention, more attention than any word except the first. When "radio" arrived, it had to compete with "bicycle" and "artichoke" for the participants' time, and so it received only 33% of their attention.

Words later in the list receive even less attention. Once six or seven words have been presented, the participants need to divide their attention among all of these, which means that each word receives only a small fraction of the participants' efforts. As a result, words later in the list literally get rehearsed fewer times than words early in the list, a fact we can confirm simply by asking participants to rehearse out loud (Rundus, 1971).

This easily provides an explanation of the primacy effect—that is, the observed memory advantage for the early list items. These early words didn't have to "share" attention with other words, and so more time and more rehearsal were devoted to these

early words than to any others. This means that the early words have a greater chance of being transferred into LTM—since, as we've already said, this transfer depends on processes requiring time and attention. And, of course, with a greater chance of being transferred into LTM, the list's early words also have a greater chance of being recalled after a delay, and that's what shows up in our data as the primacy effect.

This account of the serial-position curve leads to many further predictions. First, note that the model claims that the recency portion of the curve is coming from working memory, while the other items on the list are being recalled from LTM. Therefore, any manipulation of working memory should affect recall of the recency items, but not recall of the other items on the list. To see how this works, consider a modification of our procedure: In the standard procedure, we allow participants to recite what they remember immediately after the list's end. In place of this, we can delay recall by asking participants to perform some other task prior to the recall. For example, we can ask them, immediately after hearing the list, to count backward by three's, starting from 201. They do this for just 30 seconds, and then they try to recall the list.

This counting activity will itself draw on working memory (to keep track of where one is in the sequence), and so it will bump the recency items out of working memory. Therefore, this activity should eliminate the recency effect but have *no* effect on recall of items earlier on the list, since these items are being recalled from long-term memory, not working memory, and LTM is not dependent on current activity. Figure 5.3 shows that these predictions are correct: An activity interpolated between the list and recall essentially eliminates the recency effect, but has no influence elsewhere in the list (Baddeley & Hitch, 1977; Glanzer & Cunitz, 1966; Postman & Phillips, 1965; other influential data were reported early on by Brown, 1958; Peterson & Peterson, 1959). Note that merely delaying the recall (with no interpolated activity) has no impact. In this case, participants can continue, during the delay, to maintain the recency items—no new materials are coming in,

**FIGURE 5.3** *The Impact of Interpolated Activity on the Recency Effect*

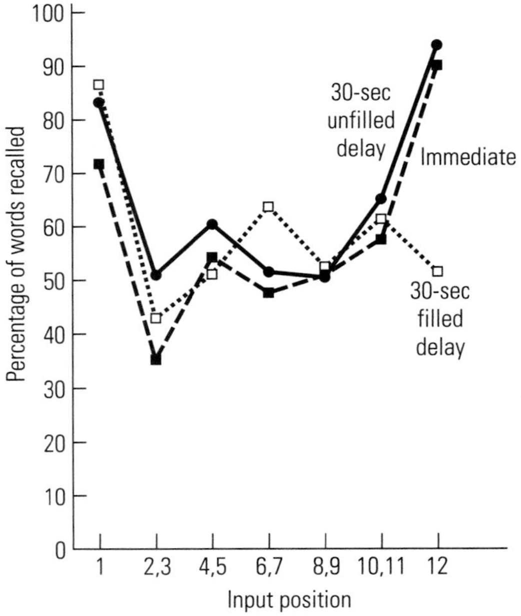

With immediate recall, or if recall is delayed by 30 seconds with no activity during this delay, a strong recency effect is detected. In contrast, if participants spend 30 seconds on some other activity, between hearing the list and the subsequent memory test, the recency effect is eliminated. This interpolated activity has no impact on the pre-recency portion of the curve.

and so nothing displaces these items from working memory.

The modal model also predicts that manipulations of long-term memory should affect all performance *except* for recency. For example, what happens if we slow down the presentation of the list? Now, participants will have more time to spend on *all* of the list items, increasing the likelihood of transfer into more permanent storage. This should improve recall for all items coming from LTM. Working memory, in contrast, is limited by its *size,* not by ease of entry or ease of access. Therefore, the slower list presentation should have no influence on working-memory performance. As predicted, Figure 5.4 shows that slowing

list presentation improves retention of all the pre-recency items, but does not improve the recency effect. Other variables that influence entry into long-term memory have comparable effects. Using more familiar or more common words, for example, would be expected to ease entry into long-term memory, and does improve pre-recency retention, but has no effect on recency (e.g., Sumby, 1963).

Over and over, therefore, the recency and pre-recency portions of the curve are open to separate sets of influences and obey different principles. This strongly indicates that these portions of the curve are the products of different mechanisms, just as the modal model proposes.

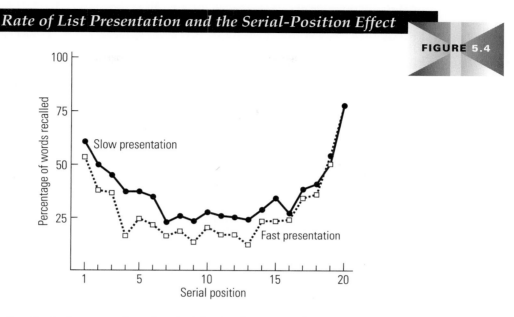

## Rate of List Presentation and the Serial-Position Effect

**FIGURE 5.4**

Presenting the to-be-remembered materials at a slower rate improves pre-recency performance, but has no effect on recency. The slow rate in this case was 9 seconds per item; the fast rate was 3 seconds per item.

## RECENCY REVISITED

For many years, the recency effect was considered the "signature" of working memory: If a recency effect appeared in the data, it was because the last-presented items were still in working memory, and because items in working memory were easily recalled. It turns out, however, that recency effects can also be created in other ways. This doesn't mean our account so far is wrong. Instead, it's simply the case that recency effects cannot be attributed to just one mechanism. Several different mechanisms can each produce a recency effect, and ironically, these various mechanisms may all be working in concert in the experiments just described.

For example, take a piece of paper and write down the names of as many U.S. presidents as you can. Or list every vacation you have ever taken. Tests like these yield a pattern of results quite similar to the serial-position data we have already described.

For example, Figure 5.5 shows data from a study in which people were asked to recall U.S. presidents (after Crowder, 1993). Notice that the curve looks much like the U-shaped curves we've been considering, with a clear primacy effect (that is, accurate memory for Washington, Adams, and Jefferson) and a clear recency effect (Carter, Reagan, Bush; these were the most recent presidents when the study was conducted). People were less likely to remember the presidents in the middle of the series, with the exception of highly memorable Abraham Lincoln.

Similar results have been obtained with a variety of other ordered material, for example rugby players recalling the teams they've played against that season; here, too, a recency effect was observed, with memory performance best for the most recent games (Baddeley, 1963; Baddeley & Hitch, 1977; Bjork & Whitten, 1974). In the same vein, research participants who had visited a laboratory many times were asked to recall where exactly they had parked on

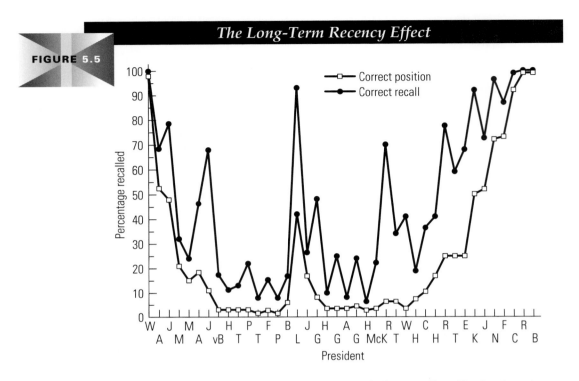

**The Long-Term Recency Effect**

FIGURE 5.5

Participants were asked to recall, in any order (a free-recall task), the American presidents. The results yield a roughly U-shaped curve, with best memory for Washington, Adams, and Jefferson (a "primacy" effect) and also for Ford, Carter, Reagan, and Bush (a "recency" effect in this 1993 study). The conspicuous exception to this pattern, though, comes from the presidents whose names are associated with the Civil War. [After Crowder, 1993.]

each occasion; again, a recency effect was observed in their recall (da Costa Pinto & Baddeley, 1991).

For convenience, let's generate some terminology: we will call the recency effect that results from list-learning experiments (i.e., the recency effect we had been discussing prior to this section) the "standard recency effect." In standard recency, one is recalling material learned just moments ago. For contrast, we will call these new effects, in which one is recalling material learned some time ago, **long-term recency effects**.

How should we think about long-term recency? Standard recency, we have proposed, comes from the

fact that the last few items heard are still "on your mind," are still in working memory, and the retrieval of items from working memory is easy. Moreover, the reason these items are in working memory is because you have just heard them and you haven't heard anything else since. Within this frame, consider what happens if you are asked, with no warning, to name the American presidents. Prior to the request, you were surely thinking about something *other than* presidents' names. Therefore, prior to the question, presidents' names were not in your working memory. Thus you have to dredge up the names from long-term memory, not from working memory, and so our account of standard recency *does not apply* to your recall. Obviously, then, we will need some different explanation for the long-term recency effect.

## RECENCY IS MULTIPLY-DETERMINED

Let's be clear, though, that what is at stake here is the status of the recency effect, and not the status of our overall model. This is because a variety of other evidence, some of which we will present later, also supports the model and, in particular, demands a distinction between working memory and long-term memory. (For some of the evidence, see Vallar & Shallice, 1990. For discussion of this issue, see Crowder, 1993, or Pashler & Carrier, 1996.) Thus, we need to continue thinking in terms of a two-memory system, with a long-term memory vast in size, which serves as the repository for all of our knowledge, and a working memory small in size, which holds only that information which is currently "active."

What does need to change, however, is our account of recency because, apparently, the recency effect is multiply determined—the product of several different mechanisms all working in parallel. One mechanism is the one we have already described—the easy retrieval of items still in working memory. What are the other mechanisms? We can only sketch an account here, since the proposal draws on themes not yet presented. In essence, though, the account rests on the simple claim that memory is, for several reasons, easier for *distinctive* items, items that are readily discriminated from the vast background of all the other information in long-term storage. There are many ways for an item to become distinctive—e.g., a word spelled in capital letters when all the other words to be remembered are lower-case; a frightening even when the other events to be recalled are emotionally neutral; a bizarre image when the other images to be recalled are mundane. One way to be distinctive, though, is via position—being the first in a series, or the last. And now we have (at least the bare bones of) our account: Items late in a to-be-remembered list are distinctive *because* they are late in the list; this distinctiveness makes the

items easier to recall. (For further discussion of these points, including why and how distinctiveness aids memory, see Chapters 6, 7, and 8.)

With this said, the position we are moving toward is that on the one side, evidence indicates (a) that we need to distinguish working memory from long-term memory, (b) that items just heard are likely to be still in working memory, and (c) that items in working memory are easily and accurately retrieved. This provides one source of recency effects. In addition, other evidence indicates (d) that distinctive items are easier to recall, and (e) that items at the end of a series are distinctive, by virtue of their position. This provides a second source of recency effects. Thus, at least two different mechanisms are simultaneously operative in creating the standard recency advantage. (For elaborations of this argument, including distinctiveness-based accounts of recency, see Baddeley & Hitch, 1993; Thapar & Greene, 1993. For further discussion of the claim that multiple mechanisms contribute to the standard recency effects, see Cowan, Wood & Borne, 1994. For evidence that some forms of brain damage eliminate one of these recency mechanisms, while leaving the other mechanisms intact, see Vallar, Papagno & Baddeley, 1991.)

## A Closer Look at Working Memory

There is still a great deal to be said about memory acquisition and, in particular, about how materials are "entered" into long-term memory. Before turning to these matters, though, we should pause to consider working memory more fully. This will allow us to fill in some details about this store and to say more about this memory's function.

### THE FUNCTION OF WORKING MEMORY

As we noted in Chapter 1, virtually all mental activities require the coordination of several pieces of information or several inputs. We often need to start by working on these ideas or inputs one at a time, and only then integrating them into a full package. We earlier mentioned the example of reading a sentence: One first must decipher the sentence's early words, then place these words on "hold" while working on the sentence's later words. Then, once these have been identified, one can integrate all the words to understand the full phrase. Likewise, consider a simple plan: One must first choose one's goal but then must put this choice on hold in order to concentrate on the early steps needed to reach this goal. Then, once these early steps are taken, one must think about the goal again, in order to select one's next steps.

These examples underscore the important interplay between thought and memory: In order to devote attention to one aspect of a problem, one must set other aspects to the side. But these other aspects, while set to the side, must remain easily available, so that they can be coordinated into a full package. (If, in thinking about a plan's early steps, you forgot the goal, then you wouldn't know what to do after the early steps.)

As we have already noted, the memory making this possible is working memory. When information is currently in use, or likely to be needed soon, it is stored in working memory. This clearly implies that working memory will be involved in a wide range of tasks, and this suggestion has been confirmed in many studies. Some of the studies exploit the fact that working memory's capacity varies somewhat from one individual to the next. One can therefore ask about this memory's function by asking what tasks are facilitated by a slightly larger working memory, and what tasks are compromised by a smaller memory. For example, research on reading reveals a crucial role for working memory, with strong correlations observed between working memory's capacity and various measures of reading comprehension and reading speed. That is, someone with a larger-capacity working memory is likely also to be a more efficient reader (Baddeley, Logie, Nimmo-Smith & Brereton, 1985; Daneman & Carpenter, 1980; Just & Carpenter, 1992). Similar results have been obtained with assessments of reasoning skills, with positive correlations reported between working-memory capacity and overall performance (Carpenter, Just & Shell, 1990; Kyllonen & Cristal, 1990).

## THE HOLDING CAPACITY OF WORKING MEMORY

The research just mentioned relies on measurements of working memory's holding capacity, but where do these estimates come from? We've already said that the capacity is relatively small and, indeed, one could argue that it *has to be* small: Given working memory's function, information in this store must be quickly and readily available. This by itself implies that working memory is limited in capacity. To make this clear, recall our analogy between working memory and your desk: If there is information you use all the time, it makes sense to keep that information on your desk, rather than in your file drawer or on your book shelf. That way, the information will be quickly available when you need it. But you will lose this advantage if there is too much on your desk—then it will take time and effort to sort through the desk's contents, to locate any particular bit of information. Thus, there is a trade-off between accessibility and amount stored; as one of these increases, the other decreases. To serve its function as an efficient workplace, then, working memory must be small.

But just how big is this memory? For many years, working memory's capacity was measured with a **digit-span task**. In this task, people are read a series of digits (e.g., "8, 3, 4") and must immediately repeat them back. If they do this successfully, they are given a slightly longer list (e.g., "9, 2, 4, 0"). If they can repeat this one without error, they're given a still longer list, and so on. This continues until the person starts to make errors—something that usually happens when the list contains more than seven or eight items.

Procedures such as this imply that working memory's capacity is around seven items or, more cautiously, at least five items, and probably not more than nine items. These estimates are often summarized by the statement that this memory holds "7 plus-or-minus 2" items (Chi, 1976; Dempster, 1981; Miller, 1956; Watkins, 1977).

However, these "measurements" of working memory may be misleading. We've said that working memory can hold 7 plus-or-minus 2 items, but what exactly is an "item"? Can we remember seven sentences as easily as seven words? Seven letters as easily as seven equations? In a classic paper, George Miller proposed that working memory holds 7 plus-or-minus 2 **chunks** (Miller, 1956). The term "chunk" is a deliberately unscientific-sounding term, in order to remind us that a chunk does not hold a fixed quantity of information. Instead, Miller proposed, working memory holds 7 plus-or-minus 2 packages, and what those packages contain is largely up to the individual person.

The effects of chunking are easily visible in a digit-span test, since performance in this task turns out to depend enormously on how the person thinks about or organizes the items. For example, someone might hear a list like "H, O, P, T, R, A, E, G," etc. If the person thinks of these as individual letters, then he or she will remember 7 of them, more or less. If the same person instead thinks of the list as composed of syllables, "ho, pit, rah, egg," then he or she will remember approximately 7 syllables, or 14 letters. If the person happens to form three-letter syllables, ("hop, tra, . . ."), he or she may remember close to 21 letters, and so on (Postman, 1975; Simon, 1974).

This chunking process, however, does have a cost attached. Working memory seems able to hold 7 plus-or-minus 2 digits or letters, but slightly fewer syllables, and slightly fewer words, and even fewer sentences. There are probably several reasons for this, but here is one: All we need to assume is that attention is required to "repackage" the materials (assembling the letters into syllables, or the syllables into words). With some amount of attention spent in this way, less attention is available for maintaining these items in working memory. Hence, the greater the amount of repackaging, the fewer the items that can be retained. (Simon, 1974, offers a slightly different explanation of this finding.)

Even with these costs of repackaging, though, we should not understate the flexibility of the chunking strategy, and consequently, the flexibility of what working memory can hold. Consider a remarkable individual studied by Chase and Ericsson (Chase & Ericsson, 1978, 1979, 1982; Ericsson, Chase & Faloon, 1980). This fellow happens to be a fan of track events and, when he hears numbers, he thinks of them as finishing times for races. "3, 4, 9, 2," for example, becomes "3 minutes and 49 point 2 seconds, near world-record mile time." In this fashion, four digits become one chunk of information. This person can then retain seven finishing times (seven chunks) in memory, and this can involve 20 or 30 digits! These chunks can then be grouped into large chunks, and these into even larger chunks. For example, finishing times for individual racers can be chunked together into heats within a track meet, so that, now, four or five finishing times (more than a dozen digits) become one chunk. With strategies like this and with a considerable amount of practice, this person has increased his apparent memory span from the "normal" seven digits to 79 digits!

However, let's be clear that what has changed through practice is merely this person's chunking strategy, not the size of working memory itself. This is evident in the fact that, when tested with sequences of letters, rather than numbers, this individual's memory span is a (perfectly normal) six consonants. Thus, the seven-chunk limit is still in place for this fellow, even though (with numbers) he is able to make extraordinary use of these seven "slots"!

## WHAT IS WORKING MEMORY?

Our discussion of chunking calls attention to a crucial issue—namely, how we should conceptualize working memory. The language of the modal model implies that working memory is something like a box in which information is stored or, continuing our earlier desk analogy, something like a location in which information can be displayed. On this view, learning would be a matter of transferring information from one position (working memory) to another (long-term memory), as though working memory were the "loading dock" just outside the large "memory warehouse." Likewise, memory *retrieval* would also be a matter of transfer—in this case, copying information from the long-term memory box into the working-memory box (out of the warehouse, back onto the dock).

However, contemporary authors regard this conception as far too static. As one concern, working memory might not be a "place" at all. Instead, working memory might refer to just those memories, *within* long-term storage, that are currently activated. By analogy, think of a huge choir, with most of the singers quiet, but with just a few singing out. Each member of the choir would represent a memory. The full set of singers would represent the broad contents of long-term memory. The group of singers currently active would then represent working memory. In this way, "working memory" wouldn't refer to those items in a specific *place*, it would instead refer to those items, within a broader set, which happen to be in a specific *state* (in our analogy: in the "state" of singing).

This conception is fully consistent with the data we have reviewed so far: The data indicate that working memory and long-term memory are qualitatively distinct from each other, with each following its own rules. That assertion would, of course, still be true within the active/dormant distinction just described.

The box conception of working memory may also be misleading in other ways: Our discussion of chunking indicates that some amount of "repackaging" is taking place on the memory "loading dock." Indeed, we'll consider cases later in this chapter in which the repackaging involves sophisticated analysis of the to-be-remembered materials and often involves the finding of *connections* between the incoming information and other information already in storage. Given these points, the notion of a loading platform may be simplistic, as is the notion of mechanical transfer between one position and another. If working memory is a place at all, it's not a mere box. It is instead more like the office of a busy librarian, who is energetically categorizing, cataloging, and cross-referencing new material.

Moreover, our discussion of chunking also mentioned the *cost* of chunking, as though attention was required to repackage the to-be-remembered items. With attention spent in this way, less is available for maintaining items within working memory, and so there is a decrease in the total number of items that

can be held. (As we said earlier, the greater the amount of repackaging, the fewer the items that can be retained.) Quite clearly, this implies that items in working memory don't just sit there; instead, they must be actively maintained, and this maintenance requires attention. This is just what one might expect if working memory were some sort of dynamic store, and *not* what you would expect if working memory were a passive "memory box."

## MEASURES OF "ACTIVE SPAN"

This emphasis on the active nature of working memory raises new questions about how we should *measure* working memory's capacity. We earlier noted that this capacity has traditionally been measured by a "span" test. However, this test places too much emphasis on the number of slots in working memory, and not enough emphasis on working memory's capacity to *do things* with these slots. This concern has led researchers to develop more dynamic measures of working memory—so-called measures of **active span**, designed to measure the efficiency of working memory when it is "working."

For example, research participants might be shown a series of items like the ones in Figure 5.6. For each, participants must first announce out loud whether the equation is true or false and then must read the associated word aloud. (For the first item in the figure, the participant would say: "True; dog.") After a series of such items, a cue appears, at which point the participants write down as many of the words as they can remember.

This task might seem peculiar, but look at what it involves: storing some materials (the words) for later use (in the recall test), while simultaneously working with other materials (the equations). These are exactly the operations crucial for working memory in its ordinary functioning in most real-world tasks. Therefore, performance in the active-span test is likely to reflect the efficiency with which working memory will operate in more natural settings.

The data confirm this prediction. Performance in the active-span task turns out to be well correlated

## *Dynamic Measures of Working Memory*

**FIGURE 5.6**

(7 x 7) + 1 = 50; dog
(10 / 2) + 6 = 10; gas
(4 x 2) + 1 = 9; nose
(3 / 1) + 1 = 5; beat
(5 / 5) + 1 = 2; tree

In recent years, researchers have argued for more dynamic measures of working memory—measures that reflect the *efficiency* of working memory and not just its "holding capacity." These dynamic measures use stimuli like the ones shown here.

with many other measures, including performance on the verbal SAT, tests of reasoning, reading comprehension, and more (Cantor & Engle, 1993; Carpenter, Just & Shell, 1990; Daneman & Carpenter, 1980; Howe, Rabinowitz & Powell, 1998; Just & Carpenter, 1992). Similar results have also been found with children, and so active-span measures are predictive of problem-solving performance in school-children (Passolunghi, Cornoldi & De Liberto, 1999; for more on the *development* of working memory across the years of childhood, see Jenkins, Myerson, Hale & Fry, 1999). These correlations are *not* usually observed with the more traditional (and more static) digit-span measure, confirming the advantage of the more dynamic measures. This, in turn, strengthens the overall claim that working memory is not a passive storage box but is instead a highly active information processor.

### THE WORKING-MEMORY SYSTEM

Working memory, it seems, deserves its name: It is indeed the workplace of cognition. But if working memory is to serve this function, then it must be capable of storing and working with all the diverse content that we can contemplate and attend—pictures and words and smells and abstract ideas, to name just a few. We need to reconcile this claim, however, with the fact that working memory shows a strong inclination toward a single kind of content: one drawing on a speech-like code.

For example, we mentioned in Chapter 1 that, when participants make mistakes on working-memory tasks, they often make "sound-alike" confusions and not "look-alike" confusions—remembering D instead of B, but not F in place of E (Baddeley, 1966; Coltheart, 1993; Conrad, 1964; Conrad & Hull, 1964; Sperling, 1960; Sperling & Speelman, 1970). This implies that memory, even for a visually presented list, draws on processes akin to those used in hearing speech, and is vulnerable to the same confusions as hearing.

Chapter 1 also mentioned a related observation, the so-called **word-length effect**. This effect is observed when memory-span is measured using lists of words. The measured span (whether 5 or 6 or 7) turns out to depend on how quickly the individual words can be pronounced (Baddeley, Thomson & Buchanan, 1975; Ellis & Henneley, 1980). And it is literally the pronunciation time that matters, not the length of the word in number of letters or number of syllables. For example, people can remember slightly more words with lists like "tip, pack, cat"; these happen to be words that can be pronounced very quickly, in comparison to lists like "fine, wish, lob," all of which take slightly longer to say. This is true even if the words are *seen* initially, indicating once more that *saying the words* (or subvocalizing them) has a key role in working memory. Again, this implies that working memory often relies on a speech-like mode of representation. (For other evidence on this point, see Baddeley, 1966; Baddeley & Dale, 1966; Dale & Baddeley, 1969.)

In Chapter 1, we also considered how these observations might be reconciled—namely, the proposal that working memory is not a single entity but is instead a *system* built out of several components (Baddeley, 1986, 1992; Baddeley & Hitch, 1974; Salame & Baddeley, 1982). At the center of the system is the **central executive**, a multi-purpose processor capable of running many different operations on many different types of material. The central executive is closely associated with the processes of attention: When one focuses attention on some task, this turns out to mean (among other things) that the central executive is engaged with that task.

If one has to work on some bit of information—analyze it, or transform it in some way—this requires the executive. But if one merely needs to "hold on" to some information, this can be done by one of working memory's low-level assistants. One of these assistants is the **visuospatial buffer**, used for storing "visual" materials, such as mental images (see Chapter 11). Another assistant is the **rehearsal loop**, crucial for subvocalized rehearsal.

Roughly speaking, the executive is where the "real work" happens in working memory; the assistants serve merely as internal scratch pads, storing information you will soon need but don't need right now. To see how this works, try reading the next few sentences while "holding onto" this list of numbers: "1, 4, 6, 4, 9." Got them? Now read on. You are probably repeating the numbers over and over to yourself, rehearsing them with your inner voice. But this turns out to require very little effort, so that you can continue reading while doing this rehearsal. And, of course, the moment you need to recall the numbers (what were they?), they are available to you. The claim, of course, is that the numbers were maintained by one of working memory's assistants—namely, the rehearsal loop. Because the loop provided this maintenance, the central executive

was free to continue reading. And that is the advantage of this system: with mere storage handled by the assistants, the executive is available for other, more demanding tasks.

## THE REHEARSAL LOOP

In Chapter 1, we argued that working memory's assistants themselves involve multiple components. To reiterate the claims made there, the rehearsal loop appears to comprise two parts, sometimes referred to as the inner ear and the inner voice (Baddeley, 1986). How do these components work? Let's continue the example used in the previous section—storing numbers while reading. In this situation, the executive first identifies what the numbers are, but then needs to shuffle the numbers off to storage, in order to free up capacity for reading. To do this, the executive uses the inner voice to pronounce the numbers. (In effect, you silently say the numbers to yourself.) This step of *covert speaking* draws on skills that are normally used for actual (overt) speech; these skills, of course, are immensely well practiced, so that minimal attention is required to direct this step. This is what allows the executive to launch the inner speech but then turn to other matters (namely, the reading).

This pronunciation by the inner voice creates a representation of the to-be-remembered numbers in the inner ear. In essence, an auditory image, representing your own pronunciation, is created. This image will gradually fade away, and when it does, the executive is again needed, to launch the next cycle. The executive "reads" the contents of the inner ear, initiates the next pronunciation by the inner voice, and then can go back to its other business.

Let's also note that the terms "inner ear" and "inner voice" are more than mere metaphors. Recent neuroimaging studies have shown that when people are engaged in working-memory rehearsal, there is considerable activity in two areas of the brain—areas ordinarily involved in the production of overt speech, and areas ordinarily involved in the processing of auditory signals. The first of these, presumably, is the neural basis for the inner voice, so that, in fact, the inner voice really does involve some of the mechanisms of actual speaking. The second of these areas is likely to be the neural basis for the inner ear, so that the inner ear really does use some of the brain mechanisms normally involved in audition (Awh et al., 1996; Smith, 2000).

All of this provides a ready account for why speech-like effects are observed in working memory. The central executive can deal with any sort of material—concrete or abstract, visual or verbal, but the rehearsal loop is specialized for dealing with *verbal* material. In a sense, then, the rehearsal loop is limited in its function, but the limit certainly isn't severe: After all, a vast number of things can be labeled with words, and so any of these can be maintained in working memory via the rehearsal loop. Moreover, the rehearsal loop is a highly efficient, well-practiced aid for the executive. It would be no surprise, therefore, if the executive relied on the loop in a wide range of tasks.

The use of the loop will, in turn, shape memory performance. Since, for example, the inner ear literally draws on mechanisms used for ordinary hearing, the traits of the inner ear will resemble those of actual audition. Consequently, inputs that can be confused with each other in normal hearing will also be confusable in the inner ear. This is why errors in short-term remembering reflect perceptual confusions. Likewise, the inner voice literally draws on mechanisms ordinarily used for speech. Therefore, words that can be said more quickly with overt speech can also be more readily pronounced by the inner voice. This provides our account of the word-length effect: The inner voice is more efficient in rehearsing quickly pronounceable words, and so, when the rehearsal loop is used, quickly pronounceable words are more easily remembered. (For reviews of this and other evidence supporting the proposal we are discussing, see Chapter 1; also see Baddeley, 1986; Richardson, 1984. For some concerns about these claims, however, see, for example, Jones & Macken, 1994; Nairne & Kelley, 1999; Neely & LeCompte, 1999.)

In addition, let's emphasize that the rehearsal loop we have described is only one of the assistants within the working-memory system. We have mentioned the visuospatial buffer, presumably used like a "sketch pad" to rehearse visual or spatial materials, much as the rehearsal loop is used to rehearse verbal materials (Baddeley, 1986, 1990; Smyth & Scholey, 1994). It also appears that the deaf use a *manual* rehearsal loop (Bellugi, Klima & Siple, 1975; Shand, 1982; Wilson & Emmorey, 1998), and there is evidence that the hearing population can be taught to use a (somewhat different) manual system to perform rehearsal (Reisberg, Rappaport & O'Shaughnessy, 1984). Clearly, then, the term "working-memory *system*" is appropriate here, with many components working together to serve working memory's overall functions.

## THE CENTRAL EXECUTIVE

We have now said a lot about the structure of the working memory system, and also a lot about one of working memory's assistants. But what about the main player within working memory—the central executive itself? Here our knowledge is less well advanced, presumably because the central executive, able to analyze information, interpret it, and transform it, is surely much more complex than the reasonably well understood assistants. Nonetheless, we can offer some ideas about what the central executive is, and how it functions.

One line of argument builds on the idea that the central executive is intimately connected with the processes of attention. In particular, Chapter 4 discussed a number of task-general mental resources—resources needed for a wide range of mental activities. Some of these resources do seem to involve "executive" functions, such as the selection and launching of responses (Pashler, 1991, 1992, 1994), or planning and the setting of goals (Duncan, 1994; Duncan et al., 1996; Just et al., 1996). It may turn out, therefore, that these task-general mental resources *are* the central executive, or more plausibly, that they are key elements within the executive. Put differently, the central executive is simply the name we give for the use of these cognitive components.

A second line of argument builds on evidence drawn from neuropsychology. We know from neuroimaging studies that many sites in the frontal cortex are particularly active when people are engaged in tasks that make heavy use of the central executive (Courtney et al., 1998; Goldman-Rakic, 1995). This leads us to ask what symptoms result if someone has suffered brain damage in these areas, and the answer is intriguing: Often people who have suffered frontal lobe damage can still lead relatively normal lives. In much of their day-to-day behavior, they show no obvious symptoms; they perform normally on conventional tests of intelligence.

Nonetheless, with appropriate tests, we can reveal the disruption that results from frontal lobe damage, especially if the damage is in the frontmost part of the frontal lobe, the prefrontal cortex. For example, one patient was asked to copy Figure 5.7A; the patient produced the drawing shown in Figure 5.7B. The copy preserves many features of the original, but close inspection makes it clear that the patient drew the copy with no particular plan in mind. The large rectangle that defines much of the shape was never drawn; the diagonal lines that organize the figure were drawn in a piecemeal fashion. Many details are correctly reproduced but were not drawn in any sort of order; instead, these details were added whenever they happened to catch the patient's attention (Kimberg, D'Esposito & Farah, 1998). Another patient, asked to copy the same figure, produced the drawing shown in Figure 5.7C. This patient started to draw the figure in a normal way, but then got swept up in her own artistic impulses, adding stars and a smiley face (Kimberg et al., 1998).

Yet another problem shown by patients with damage to the prefrontal cortex is **perseveration**. This pattern emerges in the patients' drawings and in many other tasks, and involves a strong tendency to produce the same response over and over, even when it's plain that the task requires a change in the response. For example, in one commonly used task, the patients are asked to sort a deck of cards into two piles. At the start of the task, the patients have to sort the cards according to *color*; later, they need to switch strategies and sort according to the *shapes* shown

on the cards. The patients have enormous difficulty in making this shift, and continue to sort by color (that is, they *persevere* in their original pattern) even though the experimenter tells them again and again that they are placing the cards onto the wrong piles (e.g., Goldman-Rakic, 1998).

These data make it clear that the prefrontal cortex does not have a single function. This area of the brain seems pivotal in allowing people to plan and organize their activities (that seems to be the difficulty with the patient who drew Figure 5.7B); it also seems crucial for the inhibition of impulses (lack of inhibition led to the drawing in Figure 5.7C). The prefrontal cortex also seems crucial for "turning off" responses once they have been launched (the problem in perseveration). All of these are likely to contribute to what we are here calling the central executive. However, there may not be one single executive, holding the reins for all our mental activities. Instead, there may be a "committee of executives" that serves to order, organize, and control our mental lives. (For further treatment of this complex topic, see Duncan, 1995; Kimberg et al., 1998; Shallice & Burgess, 1991.)

## THE DIFFERENCES BETWEEN WORKING MEMORY AND LONG-TERM MEMORY

Let's pause to take stock. Working memory is not a mere box or storage container. Instead, working memory may simply be the name we have given to an organized set of activities—the activities of the inner voice and inner ear, and, above all, the complex activities of the central executive. But how does all of this fit into the larger picture with which we began this chapter? In particular, where are we with regard to the modal model, introduced several sections ago?

As in the modal model, we are still conceiving of working memory as limited in its storage capacity but easily loaded and easily accessed. We're still thinking about long-term memory, in contrast, as vast in size, since this is the repository in which we carry around all of the things we know. It also seems not so easy to enter information into long-term memory: Items must be attended and contemplated

## Drawings by Patients with Prefrontal Brain Damage

**FIGURE 5.7**

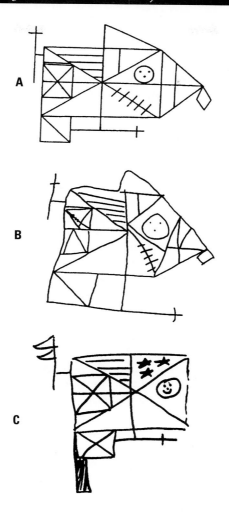

Two patients with damage to the prefrontal cortex were asked to copy the figure shown in A. The drawing shown in B, by one of the patients, is reasonably accurate, but was plainly drawn in a feature by feature fashion, with no overall plan in mind. The patient who drew C started out in a normal way, but then ended up following her own artistic impulses, rather than carrying out the task as she'd first intended.

for some time before they can be entered into long-term storage; this played a key role, earlier in the chapter, in our account of the primacy effect. Likewise, it is often difficult to locate information within this warehouse; memory retrieval can take some time and, for that matter, may sometimes fail altogether. (We will have more to say about cases of retrieval failure in Chapters 6 and 7.)

But this leaves a central question unanswered. Working memory is quite fragile, since each shift in attention brings new information into working memory, and the newly arriving materials will displace earlier items. Storage in working memory, therefore, is plainly temporary. How is it, then, that we manage to remember information we encountered an hour ago, or yesterday, or last year? This requires long-term memory, leading us to ask, how does information get established in long-term storage?

## Entering Long-Term Storage: The Role of the Intent to Learn

When you take your next exam, you will be drawing on information you studied the night before, and perhaps information you learned many days earlier. When you think back to your childhood, you're recalling events from even longer ago. This sort of remembering must draw on long-term storage, but how does this form of memory work? How does information enter long-term memory in the first place? We provided a number of suggestions about this issue in our discussion of primacy, but the time has come to to tackle this topic directly.

### TWO TYPES OF REHEARSAL

In our earlier discussion, we suggested that the more an item was rehearsed, the more likely it is to be remembered. But we have to complicate this claim in an important way, because a great deal depends on *how* an item is rehearsed.

As one option, people can engage in **maintenance rehearsal**, in which they simply focus on the to-be-remembered items themselves, with little thought about what the items mean, or how they are related to other bits of knowledge. This is a rote, mechanical process, recycling items in working memory simply by repeating them over and over. Evidence indicates that this form of rehearsal requires relatively little

effort, but is also quite limited in what it accomplishes. Specifically, maintenance rehearsal is effective in holding onto materials for a short time but if you want to recall the material later on, maintenance rehearsal is of little use.

Contrast this with relational, or **elaborative rehearsal**. Roughly speaking, this form of rehearsal involves thinking about what the to-be-remembered items mean, and how they are related to each other, or to other things in the surroundings, or to other things you already know. This form of rehearsal often requires more effort than mere maintenance, but also pays off in the long run, since items rehearsed in this fashion will be easier to recall later on.

The difference between these types of rehearsal is easy to demonstrate. Imagine that you want to telephone a friend, but don't know the number. You might call directory assistance, or look up the number in the telephone book. Once you've learned the number, you recite it over and over to yourself, while finding a quarter for the phone, and then dialing. But it turns out that the line is busy, so you wait a minute or so, and try again. You then discover that you don't have a clue what the number is, even though you knew it just moments earlier, even though you had the number in memory long enough to dial it the first time. The problem here lies in the fact that the number was rehearsed via mere maintenance. There was no reason to use the more effortful elaborative rehearsal, because you anticipated that you would only need to remember the number for a few seconds—long enough to dial it. But when that expectation turns out to be wrong, the limitations of maintenance rehearsal become clear.

A more formal demonstration of this effect was provided in a study by Craik and Watkins (1973). Participants were asked to listen to a series of word lists and to monitor each list for words beginning with the letter "B." At the end of each list, their task was to report the *most recent word* on the list that began with a "B". Thus, the participants might hear "basket, spoon, telephone, cub, lamp, fish, hair, plant, lake, book, chair, foot, baby, hill, tree"; for this list, they would report "baby." Then they would hear a new list, and again had to report the most recent "B word." Things proceeded in this fashion until the end of the session when, to the participants' surprise, they were asked to write down *all* of the "B words" they had heard, during the entire session. Up until that moment, they had no idea their memories were being tested, and no idea that they had reason to remember "B words" other than the most recent one.

Consider this task from the participants' point of view. While listening to the list, they are presumably keeping track of just one word—namely, the most recent "B word." To continue with the example from before, when they hear "basket," they should try to remember it, on the chance that the list will contain no other "B words"—in that case, "basket" would be the word to be reported. The moment they hear "book," they can cease thinking about "basket," since they now know that "basket" won't be the last "B word" on the list.

In this setup, participants are quite likely to rely on maintenance rehearsal. Bear in mind that this form of rehearsal is easier, and so participants will use it whenever they can "get away with it." And participants believe that they *can* get away with it in this task: They anticipate no memory test, so don't need to take steps to promote long-term retention. Moreover, during the list presentations they only need to keep track of one word at a time, and so nothing will interrupt their continued maintenance of this single item.

Let's now add one further complication. The stimuli in this experiment were actually devised with a scheme in mind. Sometimes the "B words" were positioned very closely together on the list (like "book" and "baby" in our example, with just two words in between). Other words (like "basket" in our example) were followed by several words not beginning with "B." How should this matter for memory? Words like "book" were presumably kept in working memory for only a short time, since this word was quickly followed by (and so displaced by) another "B word." Consequently, "book" was only rehearsed a few times. Words like "basket" were kept in working memory for a longer period, and so were rehearsed many times.

If participants are only doing maintenance rehearsal, then memory performance in this procedure should be very poor. In addition, it should not matter how much of this rehearsal participants did: If maintenance rehearsal is an ineffective preparation for the memory test, then it is irrelevant whether they did a lot, or a little, of this ineffective activity. Therefore, we should expect similar results if a "B word" was quickly followed by another (and so rehearsed only briefly) or if a "B word" was followed by another only after a long interval. All of this is exactly what the data show.

Another study makes the same point: There are certain objects, and certain scenes, that we encounter day after day after day. Each day, you pass the same houses on your way to school. Each day, you see the same forks in the cafeteria, the same furniture in your home. But the Craik and Watkins result implies that these countless exposures may not be enough to lay down useful memory traces. Instead, recallable memories will be created only if you do elaborative rehearsal, that is, only if you engage the materials in an active fashion. This implies that you may have poor memory for these items in your surroundings, despite the fact that you have seen these items literally tens of thousands of times.

In fact, evidence suggests that you do not remember the familiar objects in your world very well. For example, try drawing a picture of a Lincoln penny. Obviously, Lincoln's head is on the "heads" side, but what else is? Is Lincoln facing to the left, or to the right, on the penny? Most people do very poorly with these questions; indeed, they often don't have a clue which way Lincoln is facing (Nickerson & Adams, 1979). Even though you encounter the penny day after day after day, you seem unable to recall what it looks like. Mere exposure is plainly limited in its memory effects. (For similar results, see Bekerian & Baddeley, 1980; Rinck, 1999.)

It should be said, though, that maintenance rehearsal *does* have a lasting impact if memory is tested in just the right way. (For a review, see Wixted, 1991; we will return to this issue in Chapter 6.) However, this doesn't touch the point we are trying to make here: Quite plainly, maintenance rehearsal is distinct from elaborative rehearsal, and more important, maintenance rehearsal is a poor preparation for many forms of memory testing.

One final point should also be mentioned about maintenance rehearsal: We have spoken as if participants make a strategic choice between maintenance and elaborative rehearsal—as though they know about both forms of rehearsal, know the advantages and disadvantages of each, and so make a deliberate choice about which is appropriate for their present circumstances. All of this does seem true, but with an important proviso: Participants are generally aware of none of this. Their choice between rehearsal strategies is sensibly influenced by various factors in the task setting, implying that they are sensitive to the circumstances that permit maintenance, and the factors that demand elaboration (Watkins & Watkins, 1974; Wixted, 1991). But they make these decisions without realizing they are doing so. Apparently, the choice is sensibly tuned to the task setting, but also is quite automatic.

## INCIDENTAL LEARNING, INTENTIONAL LEARNING, AND DEPTH OF PROCESSING

What about elaborative, or relational, rehearsal? How does it function? We have also implied that people shift to this more effortful form of rehearsal when they anticipate an upcoming memory test—i.e., when they intend to memorize. But can we be more precise about what this intention to remember actually contributes?

The evidence suggests that the effects of the intention to memorize are actually *indirect*. That is, when people are trying to memorize, they approach the material in a certain way, and it is the approach, rather than the intent itself, that has consequences for memory. As an illustration, consider the following procedure. The experiment is a bit complicated, so we have illustrated the design in Figure 5.8. (Actually, this experiment represents a composite of many procedures, all of which converge on the same conclusion. An early procedure by Hyde & Jenkins, 1969,

is quite close to the one we're about to describe, but related data have been reported by Bobrow & Bower, 1969; Craik & Lockhart, 1972; Hyde & Jenkins, 1973; Jacoby, 1978; Lockhart, Craik & Jacoby, 1976; Parkin, 1984; Slamecka & Graf, 1978, and others.)

Some of the research participants are told that we are studying how quickly they can make judgments about letters. No indication is given that we are actually interested in memory. The participants are shown a series of word pairs on a computer screen. For each pair, they decide as quickly as possible whether the two words are typed in the same case (both capitalized or both not) or typed in different cases. Let's refer to this as **shallow processing**, since participants are engaging the information in a relatively superficial fashion. (Other examples of shallow processing would be a decision about whether the words are printed in red or in green, high or low on the screen, and so on.) At the end of this sequence, the participants are surprised to learn that their memories are being tested, and they are asked to write down as many of the words as they can remember. This is the top-left cell in the design shown in Figure 5.8. This sort of procedure assesses **incidental learning**, that is, learning in the absence of any intention to learn.

A second group of participants is given the same instructions, but with one change. Like the first group, these participants are told that we want them to make judgments about word pairs, specifically, whether the words in each pair are in the same case or in different cases. This group, however, is also told that their memories will be tested, so that when the memory test arrives, it comes as no surprise. These participants, therefore, have been led to do shallow processing, but they are doing this processing in the context of the intention to learn. This is the top-right cell in Figure 5.8, and examines intentional learning.

A third group of participants is brought into the lab, and they are told that we are studying how quickly people can make judgments about rhyme. If the two words shown on the computer screen rhyme, they press one button; if not, they press a different

## Studying the Effects of Intention and the Effects of Levels of Processing on Memory

**FIGURE 5.8**

| Type of processing | "Incidental learning" | "Intentional learning" |
|---|---|---|
| "Shallow" | Are these words in the same typeface? "HOUSE—trick" | Are these words in the same typeface? "HOUSE—trick" *and*, in addition, you'll have to remember these words later on! |
| "Medium" | Do these words rhyme? "BALL—TALL" | Do these words rhyme? "BALL—TALL" *and*, in addition, you'll have to remember these words later on! |
| "Deep" | Are these words synonyms? "CAR—AUTOMOBILE" | Are these words synonyms? "CAR—AUTOMOBILE" *and*, in addition, you'll have to remember these words later on! |

Illustrated here is a composite of many procedures examining how memory performance is shaped by the intention to memorize, and also by how one approaches the to-be-remembered material at the time of learning.

button. Again, a surprise memory test follows this presentation. These participants are doing what we might call **medium processing**.

A fourth group is given the same rhyme task, but is warned about the upcoming memory test. This group is doing medium processing *with* the intention to memorize the words they are viewing.

The fifth and sixth groups (the bottom row in Figure 5.8) are led to do **deep processing**—that is, to think about the meaning of the items. Participants in the fifth group are shown pairs of words on a computer screen, with the instruction that they should

press one button if the words on the screen are synonymous, another button if they are not. No warning is given about a memory test, and therefore, these participants presumably have no intention to memorize the words. Participants in the sixth group are given the same task but are warned about the memory test, so this group is doing deep processing *with* the intention to learn.

Let's frame the results in terms of Figure 5.8. When the time comes for recall, participants from the bottom left (deep processing with *no* intention to learn) perform quite well, whereas participants from the top left (shallow processing) do rather poorly. In other words, attention to meaning really pays off for recall, while attention to surface characteristics produces little memory benefit. Moderate levels of processing (attention to sound) produce a moderate level of recall performance.

What about the right column of the table? Here the result is quite straightforward: There is no difference between the left and right columns of the table. That is, the intention to learn seems to add nothing. For purposes of memorizing, there is *no difference* between shallow processing with the intention to learn, and shallow processing without this intention. Likewise, there is no difference between deep processing with the intention to learn, and deep processing without this intention.

### THE INTENTION TO LEARN

In the design just sketched, incidental learning and intentional learning yielded identical patterns, indicating little role for the intention to learn. But let's take a closer look at the importance of intentions, by considering one last group of participants: This group is told that they are about to be shown words on a computer screen, and they are asked to memorize these words. No further instructions are given, so they are free to approach this memorization in any way they choose. These participants are then shown a sequence just like the ones described in the previous section.

When people are instructed to memorize, each uses the strategy that he or she thinks best. And, in fact, different people have different beliefs about the "best way" to memorize. Some of us, for example, have discovered that thinking about meaning is an effective strategy and so, if asked to memorize, spontaneously draw on deep processing. Others seem to believe that the best way to memorize is by listening to the sound of the word over and over. These people will end up indistinguishable from the participants in the middle right of Figure 5.8, while people who spontaneously employ deep processing will end up equivalent to participants in the lower right.

Of course, the participants we were discussing before had been *instructed* to use a particular form of processing, while the people we are now considering have self-instructed. But, as it turns out, this difference between instruction and self-instruction is irrelevant to performance.

All of this leads to the expectation that results from this "just memorize" condition will be rather variable, depending on *how* participants self-instruct, i.e., on what strategy they choose. If they have figured out, on their own, that attention to meaning aids memory, then they perform quite well. More precisely, they perform as well as—but no better than—participants specifically told to do deep processing. If they select a less-than-optimal strategy, then they perform at a lower level. And, in fact, it turns out that people do often have peculiar beliefs about what "works" in placing material into memory; if they choose their memorizing strategy based on these (faulty) beliefs, their performance will be correspondingly poor. (For studies of people's spontaneous strategies, see Anderson & Bower, 1972; Brown, 1979; Hyde & Jenkins, 1969; Nelson, 1976; Postman, 1964.)

As an example, consider a case reported by John Anderson (1985, pp. 112–113), a researcher whose work we will discuss extensively in Chapter 8. Anderson reports that he himself served as a participant in a memory experiment during his sophomore year of college. He was determined to perform well and, therefore, applied his personal theory of memorizing: that the best strategy was to say the items out loud, over and over, preferably as loudly and as quickly as possible. Needless to say, this "loud and fast" theory stands in contrast to the true means of improving memory and, to Anderson's embarrassment, his performance was the worst in his class.

What, therefore, should we conclude about the role of intention in guiding the learning process? Clearly, intention does matter: Someone who has no intention to learn may end up doing maintenance processing, rather than elaborative processing, and this obviously will affect what is remembered. Likewise, someone who intends to learn will select the strategy he or she thinks best and, as we have seen, this choice of strategy will also affect the quality of memory. But these effects of intention are all *indirect*. The intention to learn leads people to approach the materials in a certain fashion, and it is the *approach*, not the intention, that matters for memory. If we can lead people to approach the materials in the same way without the intention, we get the same memory results.

## The Role of Meaning and Memory Connections

We've now seen that memory is strongly influenced by how someone engages the materials at the time of learning. But what does this "engagement" amount to? Attention to *meaning*, it seems, leads to good recall, but why is this? And what about other study techniques? Are there other, more effective ways to learn?

A great many studies have shown that attention to meaning does indeed promote subsequent recall (e.g., Elias & Perfetti, 1973; Jacoby & Craik, 1979; Till & Jenkins, 1973). Our understanding of what lies behind this effect, though, has evolved over the years (for an early view, see Craik & Lockhart, 1972; Lockhart et al., 1976; for more recent developments, see Baddeley, 1978; Craik & Tulving, 1975; Nelson, Walling & McEvoy, 1979; Postman, Thompkins & Gray, 1978). Several factors are relevant, but a pivotal one is that the benefits of deep processing may not lie in the learning process per se. Instead, deep processing may influence *subsequent* events. More precisely, attention to meaning may promote recall by virtue of facilitating *retrieval* of the memory, later on.

Consider what happens when a library acquires a new book. It would be no good at all if the book were merely tossed on a shelf somewhere. In that case, users of the library might never be able to locate the book when they wanted it. Indeed, unless the book was properly entered into the catalogue, users of the library might not even realize the book was in the building. Obviously, then, the library must place the book on the shelf and also arrange for appropriate cataloguing, so that the book can be located by users. And, of course, cataloguing doesn't in any sense influence the book's "arrival" into the library—the book isn't "more firmly" or "more strongly" in the library thanks to the cataloguing. Instead, cataloguing has its effects on events subsequent to the book's arrival—that is, it influences the subsequent retrieval of the book.

Likewise for the vast library that is our memory: The task of "learning" is not merely a matter of placing information into long-term memory. Learning also needs to establish some appropriate indexing; it must, in effect, pave a path to the newly acquired information, so that this information can be retrieved at some future point. In essence, then, one of the main chores of memory *acquisition* is to lay the groundwork for memory *retrieval*.

We now need to ask what it is that facilitates memory retrieval. There are, in fact, several ways to search through memory, but a great deal depends on memory *connections*. Connections allow one memory to trigger another, and then that to trigger another, so that, like a series of dominoes falling, one is "led" to the sought-for information. If remembering the experimenter's shirt reminds you of materials you learned during the experiment, this will help you to locate these materials in memory. In this case, there must have been some connection in your thoughts between the shirt and the target materials, and this is what triggered the reminding. Likewise, if remembering the third word on a list reminds you of the fourth and fifth, this too will improve memory performance, because of connections among the items.

This line of reasoning easily accounts for why attention to meaning promotes memory. Attention to meaning is likely to lead to understanding and, at least in part, understanding is a matter of "seeing connections." When you understand the meaning of a story, you understand how the pieces of the story fit together, you understand the resemblances between this story and other stories you've read, you know what the story's implications are. Each of these connections, each of these relationships, will serve as a potential reminder, and so will help you to remember the story later on. Likewise for attention to the meaning of a picture, or a sentence, or even a list of words.

These are broad claims and, in fact, it will take us several chapters to work through all the evidence for these claims. One bit of evidence, though, is immediately accessible: On the hypotheses just sketched, attention to meaning should not be the only way to improve memory. Other strategies should have similar effects, provided that these strategies help the memorizer to establish memory connections.

As an example, consider a study by Craik and Tulving (1975). Participants were shown a word, and then were shown a sentence with one word left out. Their task was to decide whether the word fit into the sentence. For example, they might see the word "chicken," then the sentence "She cooked the _____." The appropriate response would be "yes," since the word does fit in this sentence. After a series of these trials, there was a surprise memory test, with participants asked to remember all the words they had seen.

This experiment was arranged so that some of the sentences shown to participants were simple, while others were more elaborate. For example, "She cooked the _____" would be a simple sentence, while a more complex sentence might be "The great bird swooped down and carried off the struggling _____." The data showed that words were more likely to be remembered if they appeared with these rich, elaborate sentences.

To make their decisions about these sentences, the research participants obviously have to think about the *meaning* of the words in the sentences. It would seem, than, that participants must think about the meaning of every word presented to them, and if this were all that matters for memory, then all of the words should be remembered equally. But that's not what the data show. Instead, "deep and elaborate" processing led to better recall than deep processing alone.

These data fit well, though, with our claims about the importance of memory connections. Perhaps the "great bird swooped" sentence calls to mind a barnyard scene, with the hawk carrying a chicken away. Or perhaps it calls to mind the thought of predator-prey relationships. One way or another, the richness of this sentence offers the potential for many connec-

tions, as it calls other thoughts to mind, each of which provides a potential **retrieval path**. All of this seems less likely for the impoverished sentences. These will evoke fewer connections and will establish a narrower set of retrieval paths. Consequently, they'll be less likely to be recalled later on.

## Organizing and Memorizing

We have just suggested that memory connections are crucial for recall, since these connections provide a means of locating material within memory later on. Sometimes, these connections link the to-be-remembered material to other material already in memory. In other cases, these connections will link one aspect of the material to some other aspect. This will ensure that, if any *part* of the material is recalled, then all will be recalled.

How does one go about discovering (or creating) these connections? More than sixty years ago, a German psychologist, George Katona, argued that the key lies in *organization* (Katona, 1940). Katona's argument, in fact, was that the processes of organization and memorization are inseparable: We memorize well when we discover the order within the material. Said differently, if we find (or impose) an organization on the material, we will easily remember it. These suggestions are of course, fully compatible with the conception we are developing, since what organization provides is, once again, memory connections.

### MNEMONICS

For thousands of years, people have wished for "better" memories—they have wished to learn more quickly, and to remember more accurately. Motivated by these wishes, a number of techniques have been designed to "improve" memory, techniques known as **mnemonic strategies**. Some of these mnemonics are modern inventions, but most are very old, dating back to ancient Greece.

There are actually many different mnemonic strategies, but most of them involve a straightforward and familiar principle, namely, that organization helps. If an organization can be found within the materials, then locating this organization will lead to good memory. If an organization cannot be found, then often an "external" organization can be imposed on the material, with the same memory benefit.

Let us take a concrete case. You want to remember a list of largely unrelated items, perhaps the entries on your shopping list, or a list of questions you want to ask when you next see your adviser. You might try to remember this list using one of the so-called **peg-word systems**. Peg-word systems begin with a well-organized structure, such as this one:

One is a bun.

Two is a shoe.

Three is a tree.

Four is a door.

Five is a hive.

Six are sticks.

Seven is heaven.

Eight is a gate.

Nine is a line.

Ten is a hen.

Not great poetry, but highly memorable, since you already know the numbers, and the rhyme scheme makes the sentences easy to reconstruct. The rhymes provide ten "peg words"—"bun, shoe, tree," and so on—and, in memorizing something, you can "hang" the to-be-remembered materials on these "pegs." Let's imagine, therefore, that you are trying to memorize the list of topics you want to discuss with your adviser. If you want to discuss your unhappiness with your chemistry class, you might form an association between chemistry and the first peg, *bun*. You might, for example, form a mental image of a hamburger bun floating in an Erlenmeyer flask. If you also want to discuss possible graduate school plans, form an association between some aspect of those plans and the next peg, *shoe*—perhaps you might

think about how you plan to pay your way in graduate school by selling shoes. If you continue in this fashion, then, when the time comes to meet with your adviser, all you have to do is think through that silly rhyme again. When you think of "one is a bun," it is highly likely that the image of the flask (and therefore of chemistry lab) will come to mind.

Hundreds of variations on this strategy are possible, some taught in self-help courses (you've probably seen the ads—"How to Improve Your Memory!"), some presented by corporations as part of management training, and on and on. Some mnemonic strategies rely heavily on visualization (for example, we mentioned that you might form an image of the bun floating in the flask), others do not. (For further discussion of imagery and visualization, see Chapter 11.) But all employ the same basic scheme. To remember a list with no apparent organization, impose an organization on it, by employing a skeleton or scaffold that is itself tightly organized. The number-rhyme provides one such scaffold, but other scaffolds are easily located.

For example, the ancient Greeks used a system called the **method of loci** to remember speeches they were to give in the Forum. In this method, the memory pegs are not words, but places. To use this technique to memorize a speech, you might think about a walk you often take, and then associate the various topics within the speech with conspicuous locations along that walk. Thus, you might form an association between your first topic and your front door. (Imagine, for example, that you wanted to start your speech by talking about your childhood. You might, in that case, think about some favorite childhood toy dangling from the door knob.) Next, you might form some association between your second topic and the sidewalk just outside your house. When the time comes to remember, you would simply think about the familiar routine of locking your door, walking down the sidewalk, and so on, and, at each position along the route, the relevant association is available.

In later chapters, we will consider why these systems work. Our point for now is simply that these systems *do* work (Bower, 1970, 1972; Bower & Reitman, 1972; Christen & Bjork, 1976; Higbee, 1977; Roediger,

1980; Ross & Lawrence, 1968; Yates, 1966), not only helping you to remember individual items, but also helping you to remember those items in a specific sequence. All of this confirms our central claims: Organizing improves recall. Mnemonics work by imposing an organization on the to-be-remembered materials, by establishing connections between the material and some other easily remembered structure.

Mnemonic techniques fit well with the theoretical picture we are painting, but let's also note that mnemonic techniques have important *practical* uses. As we mentioned, the ancient Greeks developed these techniques to help them remember speeches. In the modern world, students often use mnemonics to help them in school settings. For example, many students use the *first-letter mnemonic* to turn lists of items into an integrated single unit. As one illustration, many students remember the "standard" colors of the rainbow by recalling the name "Roy G. Biv." These seven letters can help a student remember *r*ed, *o*range, *y*ellow, *g*reen, *b*lue, *i*ndigo, and *v*iolet. Likewise, many students use this sentence: "King Phillip crossed the ocean to find gold and silver," in order to remember the taxonomic categories: *k*ingdom, *p*hylum, *c*lass, *o*rder, *f*amily, *g*enus, and *s*pecies.

These techniques serve students well, underscoring the fact that mnemonics are indeed effective. The first-letter mnemonic imposes organization and unity on a list, and here as always, organization aids memory. But let's also note that there's a downside to using mnemonics in a classroom setting: In using a mnemonic, you typically focus on just one aspect of the to-be-remembered material—just the first letter of the to-be-remembered word, for example, or (returning to an earlier case) just some specific relationship between *bun* and *chemistry*. This guarantees that the focused-on link receives much attention, and so is well established in memory. But focusing in this way also means that you *won't* pay much attention to *other* aspects of the to-be-remembered material. In many settings, this means that you'll cut short your effort toward *understanding* this material, and likewise your effort toward finding multiple connections between the material and other things you know.

This implies that mnemonics will be most useful for memorizing material that has no organization of its own—for example, the list of taxonomic categories. But mnemonics are probably a *bad* choice for anyone seeking to memorize material that is meaningful. In this latter case, you would be better served by a memory strategy that leads you to seek out multiple connections, while studying, between the material you're trying to learn and things you already know. This effort toward multiple links will help you in two ways. First, it will obviously foster your understanding of the to-be-remembered material, and so will lead to better, richer, deeper learning. Second, the multiple links will also help you to retrieve this information later on: We've already suggested that memory connections serve as *retrieval paths*, and the more paths there are, the easier it will be to find the target material later. (If lots of highways lead to Chicago, then you can get to Chicago from almost anywhere. Memory works the same way, a point we'll return to in Chapter 6.)

In short, then, mnemonics do nothing to encourage understanding, and by leading you to focus on a small number of specific memory connections, mnemonics can actually *obstruct* progress toward understanding. This emphasis on just a few memory links also means that mnemonics create only a narrow set of retrieval paths, with the result that information memorized in this fashion can be retrieved later on only if approached from just the right direction. (Continuing our metaphor: If the only highway into Chicago comes in from the south, then it will be difficult to approach Chicago from the west.) For these reasons, mnemonic use is probably ill-advised for most classroom learning. Nonetheless, the fact remains that mnemonics *are* useful in some settings (what were those rainbow colors?), and this in turn confirms our initial point: Organization promotes memory.

## RECALL AND CLUSTERING

Mnemonic techniques can dramatically improve memory by imposing order on the to-be-remembered material. But you might object: These techniques are based on tricks and unusual strategies someone might employ, if he or she were especially motivated to remember. What do these have to do with "ordinary" remembering?

It is easy to show, however, that people spontaneously use organizing schemes to help them remember, without special instruction to do so, and without extraordinary motivation. A lot of the evidence comes from experiments similar to those discussed earlier in this chapter. Participants are given lists of 25 to 35 words to learn. They hear the words once, and repeat them back immediately. It turns out that participants' recall performance is considerably better if the words are not chosen at random, but fall into categories. People will perform quite well, for example, with this list: "Apple, plum, cherry, pear, shoe, pants, shirt, belt, sofa, chair."

For that matter, we don't have to present the list category by category. If we take the same items, and scramble the sequence, the availability of a categorization scheme still seems to help. In fact, if the items are scrambled together in presentation, they will be "unscrambled" when the participant reports them back. That is, we can present this list: "apple, shoe, sofa, plum, cherry, chair, belt." In the recall test, participants are likely to report back one category of items (perhaps the furniture), then pause, then report back one of the other categories, and so on. This highly reliable pattern is referred to as **clustering** in free recall. The recall is "free" since we have allowed the participants to report back the items in any sequence they choose. Nonetheless, the sequence they do choose consistently shows the pattern just described (Bousfield, 1953; Bower, Clark, Lesgold & Winzenz, 1969; Cofer, Bruce & Reicher, 1966).

You might still object that these are artificial materials, since they fall so neatly into categories. Perhaps this by itself is what triggers a clustering strategy. That objection also quickly falls, through experiments on subjective organization. There are actually several ways to run these experiments (Buschke, 1977; Tulving, 1962). In one, Tulving presented participants with a list to learn, as described already. In

this experiment, though, there were no obvious categories of material in the list; the list was instead randomly chosen, with no apparent structure or order. The participants were tested on this list three times. First, they were asked to report back the items immediately after the presentation, as is normal in these experiments. Some time later, they were tested a second time, and had to recall as much as they could about the list presented earlier. Then, after another delay, participants were tested a third time on this same list.

Tulving reasoned that the participants were probably spontaneously organizing the list of randomly chosen words. With no obvious order in the list, the organization participants would choose would be idiosyncratic, with each participant finding his or her own pattern. We could nonetheless find out how successful they had been in finding an organization by comparing the results of the first and second tests. We look at the sequence of report, and ask what items were reported close together, what items were not. If a participant has tightly organized the list, we might expect an absolutely identical order of report in the first two tests. If the participant has found no organization, there is no reason to expect the order-of-report on the second testing to match that of the first.

Tulving used a statistical assessment of match-between-the-orderings as a measurement of the degree of "subjective organization" that had been imposed on the list by the participant. If organization is critical for remembering, then we make the following prediction: The more agreement between the first order-of-report and the second—i.e., the greater the degree of inferred subjective organization—the better participants will do on the third, and final test. In short, the earlier stability of organization should pay off in better remembering. This is what the data show. With no coaching, with no special instructions, and with materials that are randomly chosen, the participants spontaneously rely on an organizational strategy, and the better they can organize, the better they can recall (cf. Bower et al., 1969; Mandler & Pearlstone, 1966).

## UNDERSTANDING AND MEMORIZING

So far, we have been focusing on memory for rather impoverished stimulus materials—for example, lists of randomly selected words. This allowed us to argue that recall is improved by organization even when there is nothing within the materials to encourage that organization. In our day-to-day lives, though, we typically want to remember more meaningful, and more complicated, material—we wish to remember the episodes of our lives, the details of rich scenes we have observed, the plots of movies we have seen, or the many-step arguments we have read in a book. Do the same principles apply to these cases?

The answer to this question is clearly "yes." Our memory for events, or pictures, or complex bodies of knowledge is enormously dependent on our being able to organize the to-be-remembered material. We remember best what we have organized best; we remember poorly when we can neither find nor create an organizing scheme. With these more complicated materials, though, our best bet for organization is not some arbitrary skeleton, like those used in peg-word systems. Instead, the optimal organization of these complex materials is generally dependent on *understanding*. That is, we remember best what we understand best.

There are many ways to show that this is true. For example, one can give people a sentence or paragraph to read, and test their comprehension by asking questions about the material, or asking them to paraphrase the material. Some time later, we can test their memory for this material. Moreover, we can use memory materials difficult enough so that understanding is not guaranteed and, in this way, we can look at different degrees of success in understanding, and ask how these influence memory.

The results are straightforward: If participants understand a sentence or a paragraph, they will better remember it. If their paraphrase was more accurate or more complete, so will be their report from memory, whether we give the memory test ten minutes later or ten days later. If they could accurately answer questions immediately after reading the material, they will probably be able to remember the material after a delay. (For reviews of the relevant research, see Baddeley, 1976; Bransford, 1979. For some complications, see Kintsch, 1994; we'll return to these complications in Chapters 6 and 7.)

As a different way of making this point, it is also possible to *manipulate* whether people will understand the material or not. For example, in an often-quoted experiment by Bransford and Johnson (1972), participants read this passage:

> The procedure is actually quite simple. First you arrange items into different groups. Of course one pile may be sufficient depending on how much there is to do. If you have to go somewhere else due to lack of facilities that is the next step; otherwise you are pretty well set. It is important not to overdo things. That is, it is better to do too few things at once than too many. In the short run, this may not seem important but complications can easily arise. A mistake can be expensive as well. At first, the whole procedure will seem complicated. Soon, however, it will become just another facet of life. It is difficult to foresee any end to the necessity for this task in the immediate future, but then, one never can tell. After the procedure is completed one arranges the materials into different groups again. Then they can be put into their appropriate places. Eventually they will be used once more and the whole cycle will then have to be repeated. However, that is part of life.

You are probably puzzled by this passage; so are most research participants. The story is easy to understand, though, if we give it a title: "Doing the Laundry." In the experiment, some participants were given the title before reading the passage; others were not. The first group easily understood the passage, and was able to remember it after a delay. The second group, reading the same words, was not confronting a meaningful passage, and did poorly on the memory test.

These effects, with a memory benefit when participants understand verbal materials, have been widely documented (Bransford & Franks, 1971; Sulin & Dooling, 1974). Similar effects can be documented with nonverbal materials. Consider, for example, the picture shown in Figure 5.9. This picture at first looks like a bunch of meaningless blotches; with some study, though, you may discover that a familiar object is depicted. Wiseman and Neisser (1974) tested people's memory for this picture. Consistent with what we have seen so far, their memory was good if they understood the picture, and bad otherwise. (Also see Bower, Karlin & Dueck, 1975; Mandler & Ritchey, 1977; Rubin & Kontis, 1983.)

### CHUNKING AND ENTRY INTO LONG-TERM MEMORY

One might still object to these examples, however, on the grounds that they involve a trick: In the "laundry" study, we are not really testing people's memory *for the passage*. All the participants need to remember is the passage's *title*. Given their prior knowledge about how one washes clothes, that would be enough to allow them to *reconstruct* the passage at the time of test. Likewise for pictorial materials: To do well on a memory test, participants don't need to remember the complex pattern of blotches in Figure 5.9. Instead, remembering a one-word summary (e.g., "dalmatian") might be enough. In either case, it is no surprise that understanding aids memory, because understanding might literally reduce the amount of information to be remembered—a title instead of a passage, a summary instead of a complicated pattern.

This suggestion, that understanding reduces the load on memory, turns out to be well founded. The only bit of confusion in the preceding paragraph lies in the idea that this is some sort of memory "trick." Instead, what is at stake here is an important principle of memory, a principle with wide application. As we have already noted, understanding a story de-

*Comprehension also Aids Memory for Pictures*

**FIGURE 5.9**

People who perceive this picture as a pattern of meaningless blotches are unlikely to remember the picture. People who perceive the "hidden" form do remember the picture. [After Wiseman & Neisser, 1974.]

pends in part on the discovery of various connections—among the various elements of the story, and between the story and other things you know. We have argued that one function of these connections is to render the story *findable* in memory later on. But an equally important function of the connections is to *unify* the elements of the story, so that we think of them, not as individual elements, but as constituents in an interconnected whole. It is then this "whole" that enters memory, rather than the separate items—one unit rather than many.

You should note that this suggestion parallels the earlier claims we made about "chunking." We noted that more information could be "packed" into working memory if the information was "chunked." Rather than trying to remember a list of letters, one could instead think of the list as containing three-letter syllables. By assembling the material into more complex packages, one reduces the total number of packages—one is thinking about seven syllables, rather than 21 letters. By integrating and unifying the materials, one ends up with less to remember. We earlier made these points with regard to short-term remembering, but all of this obviously resembles our current point with longer-term remembering: Understanding serves to integrate and unify materials, reducing the load on memory.

There are a great many illustrations of this point, but a classic example was devised by Katona, whose work we have already mentioned. Katona asked his research participants to learn the following string of digits:

$$1\ 4\ 9\ 1\ 6\ 2\ 5\ 3\ 6\ 4\ 9\ 6\ 4\ 8\ 1\ 1\ 0\ 0\ 1\ 2\ 1$$

The data follow a familiar pattern. People remember well the first two or three digits (a primacy effect) and the last few (recency), but cannot easily remember the full list. We then point out to the participants that the list follows a simple pattern. To help them see the pattern, we add some punctuation:

$$1, 4, 9, 16, 25, 36 \ldots$$

In this form, you probably recognize the series as being $1^2, 2^2, 3^2, 4^2, 5^2, 6^2, \ldots 11^2$. Once participants see this, the results are rather different. They can now remember the entire list perfectly and, in fact, can remember the list even if we extend it ( . . . 1 4 4 1 6 9).

When participants find the connections that unify this list, they turn the 21 separate digits into a single whole. In effect, they are translating the number series into a rule or a sentence ("The list consists of the squares of the integers from 1 to 11"), and the sentence is appreciably easier to remember than the original series was. In a sense, this "translation" from a number series to a sentence actually increases the sophistication and complexity of what is being remembered: Memorizing the original number series merely required that one recognize the various digits. In contrast, the summary sentence requires comprehension of English syntax, and of the mathematical terms "squares" and "integers." But this is not what is crucial for memory. The number of "memory packages" is more important than the internal complexity of these packages, and so there is considerable gain from translating 21 packages into one.

## The Study of "Memory Acquisition"

This chapter has ostensibly been about "memory acquisition." How do we acquire new memories? How is new information, new knowledge, established in long-term memory? Or, in more pragmatic terms, what is the best, most effective, most efficient way to learn?

### THE CONTRIBUTION OF THE MEMORIZER

In some ways, the answer to the questions just posed is straightforward: Over and over, we have seen that memory is facilitated by *organizing* and *understanding* the to-be-remembered materials. Hand in hand with this, it appears that memories are not established by sheer contact with the items you're hoping to remember. If people are merely exposed to the items, without giving those items any thought, then subsequent recall of those items will be poor.

Note how large a role is played by the memorizer. If we wish to predict whether this or that event will be recalled, it is not enough to know that someone was exposed to the event. Likewise, if we wish to predict memory performance, it is not enough to describe the memory "equipment" possessed by each of us—e.g., a working memory with various components, a long-term memory with a specific structure. Instead, if we wish to predict someone's recall performance, then we need to pay attention to what the person was *doing* at the time of learning. Did she elect to do mere maintenance rehearsal, or did she engage the material in some other way? If the latter, *how* did she think about the material? Did she pay attention to the appearance of the words or to their meaning? If the latter, was she able to grasp the meaning? Did she think about the words as isolated words or as constituents in a sentence or story? Did she think about the implications of the story and how the story fits with other beliefs? It is these considerations that are crucial for predicting the success of memory.

The contribution of the individual memorizer is also visible in another way: We have argued that learning depends on the person's making *connections*, but connections to what? If someone wants to connect the to-be-remembered material to other knowledge, to other memories, then the person needs to have that other knowledge, she needs to have other (potentially relevant) memories. Thus, what people contribute to learning also includes their own prior knowledge. If someone happens to enter the learning situation with a great deal of relevant knowledge, then he or she arrives with a considerable advantage—a rich framework onto which the new materials can be "hooked." If someone enters the learning situation with little relevant background, then there is no framework, nothing to connect to, and learning will be correspondingly more difficult. Thus, if we wish to predict the success of memorizing, we also need to consider what other knowledge the individual brings into the situation.

## THE LINKS AMONG ACQUISITION, RETRIEVAL, AND STORAGE

These points lead us to another theme of immense importance. Our emphasis in this chapter was on memory *acquisition*, but we have now seen several indications that claims about acquisition cannot be separated from claims about memory storage and memory retrieval. For example, why is recall improved by organization and understanding? We have suggested that organization provides *retrieval paths*, making the memories "findable" later on, when the time comes for memory retrieval. Therefore, our claims about acquisition rest on assumptions about memory retrieval and the utility of memory connections within retrieval.

Likewise, we have just noted that a person's ability to learn new material depends, in part, on having a framework of prior knowledge to which the new materials can be tied. In this way, claims about memory acquisition must be coordinated with claims about the nature of what is already in storage.

The same can be said about chunking, both in working memory and in long-term storage. In most cases, chunking depends on understanding, and understanding rests on things you already know. The number series, "1 4 9 16 . . ." can only be chunked as the squares of the digits if you already know what the squares of the digits are. The passage about laundry is understood only by virtue of your prior knowledge about how clothing gets washed. In both of these cases, therefore, chunking at the time of memory acquisition is completely tied up with knowledge you already have, and so again we see the interdependency of memory acquisition and knowledge already in storage.

We close this chapter, then, with a two-sided message. We have offered several claims about memory acquisition, and about how memories are established. In particular, we have offered claims about the importance of memory connections, organization, and understanding. At the same time, though, these claims cannot stand by themselves. At the level of theory, our account of acquisition has already made references to the role of prior knowledge and to the nature of memory retrieval. At the level of data, we will soon see that these interactions among acquisition, knowledge, and retrieval have important implications—for learning, for forgetting, and for memory accuracy. We turn next to some of those implications.

## Chapter Summary

1. It is convenient to think of memorizing as having separate stages: First, one acquires new information (*acquisition*). Next, the information remains in *storage* until it is needed. Finally, the information is *retrieved*. However, this separation among the stages may be misleading: For example, in order to memorize new information, one forms connections between this information and things one already knows. In this fashion, the acquisition stage is intertwined with the retrieval of information already in storage.

2. Information that is currently being considered is stored in *working memory*; information that is not currently active, but nonetheless in storage, is in *long-term memory*. Working memory is sometimes likened to the mental "desk-space," long-term memory to the mental "library." The distinction between these two forms of memory is often described in terms of the *modal model*, and has been examined in many studies of the *serial position curve*. The *primacy* portion of this curve reflects those items that have had extra opportunity to reach long-term memory; the *recency* portion of this curve reflects the accurate retrieval of items currently in working memory.

3. Working memory is more than a passive "storage container." Instead, this is where the mind's filing, cross-referencing, and active contemplation take place. This activity is carried out by working memory's *central executive*. For mere storage, the executive often relies on a small number of low-level assistants, including the *articulatory rehearsal loop* and the *visuospatial buffer*, which work as mental scratch-pads. The activity inherent in this overall system is reflected in the flexible way material can be *chunked* in working memory; the activity is also reflected in current measures of the *active memory span*.

4. We currently know more about working memory's assistants than we do about the central executive. However, the executive probably includes a set of different functions, all supported by tissue in the *frontal cortex*.

5. *Maintenance rehearsal* serves to keep information in working memory and requires little effort, but has little impact on subsequent recall. To maximize one's chances of recall, the more effortful *elaborative rehearsal* is needed, in which one seeks connections within the to-be-remembered material, or connections between the to-be-remembered material and things one already knows. Evidence suggests that people are somehow alert to the contrast between these two types of rehearsal and shift to the (easier) maintenance rehearsal if they anticipate no need for long-term retention.

6. In many cases, elaborative processing takes the form of attention to meaning. This attention to meaning is called *deep processing*, in contrast to attention to sounds or visual form; these are considered *shallow processing*. Many studies have shown that deep processing leads to good memory performance later on, even if the deep processing was done with no intention of memorizing the target material. In fact, the intention to learn has little effect on performance; what matters instead is how someone engages or thinks about the to-be-remembered material.

7. Deep processing has its beneficial effects by creating effective *retrieval paths* that can be used later on. Retrieval paths depend on connections linking one memory to another; each connection provides a path potentially leading to a target memory. *Mnemonic strategies* build on this same idea, and focus on the creation of specific memory connections, often tying the to-be-remembered material to a frame (a familiar location, or a strongly structured poem).

8. Perhaps the best way to form memory connections is to understand the to-be-remembered material. In understanding, one forms many connections within the to-be-remembered material, and also between this material and other knowledge. With all of these retrieval paths, it becomes easy to locate this material in memory. Consistent with these suggestions, studies have shown a close correspondence between the ability to understand some material and the ability to recall that material later on; this pattern has been demonstrated with stories, visual patterns, number series, and many other sorts of stimuli.

# Interconnections between Acquisition and Retrieval

Putting information into long-term memory helps us only if we can retrieve it later on. Otherwise, it would be like putting money into a savings account from which no withdrawals are possible, or like writing books that could never be read. And it is equally clear that there are different ways to retrieve information from memory. We can try to *recall* the information ("What was the name of your tenth-grade homeroom teacher?") or to *recognize* it ("Was the name perhaps 'Miller'?"). If we try to recall the information, a variety of cues may or may not be available (we might be told, as a hint, that the name began with an "M" or rhymed with "tiller").

In Chapter 5, we largely ignored these variations in retrieval. We talked as if material was well established in memory or was not, with no regard for how the material would be retrieved from memory. We spoke about certain principles as promoting memory, as though these claims held true independent of how the memory will be used.

There is every reason to believe, however, that we cannot ignore these variations in retrieval. Imagine that you knew that an upcoming German vocabulary test would be in multiple-choice format ("Which of the following is the German word for 'backpack'?"). Would you study differently from the way you would if the vocabulary test were fill-in ("What is the word for 'backpack'?")? Moreover, what would happen if you studied anticipating one sort of test, and you instead received a different sort of test? Would this affect your performance?

In a study by Barbara Tversky (1973), participants were asked to study a series of pictures for an upcoming test. Half were told that they would have to recall the names of the objects shown in the pictures. A **recall** test is defined as one in which the tester names a context ("the series of pictures you saw earlier"), and the participant must come up with the target materials. A recall procedure is similar to an essay test, or a fill-in-the-blank test. The remaining participants were told they would be given a **recognition** test. They were told that, after seeing the to-be-remembered pictures, they would be shown test pictures, some of which were from the earlier group, some of which were new. Their task would be to discriminate which of the test pictures they had seen before, and which they had not. This is similar to a multiple-choice or true-false test.

When the time came for the test, half of each group got what they expected, but half did not. Hence, we end up with four groups: people who expected recall and got it; ones who expected recognition and got it; some who expected recall but got recognition; and some who expected recognition but got recall. The results (Figure 6.1) show a clear interaction between type of preparation and type of test. That is, people who got the recall test did better if they had prepared for a recall test than if they had prepared for recognition (62% vs. 40%). People who got the recognition test did better if that was what they were expecting (87% vs. 67%).

Is it better, therefore, to prepare for the recognition test or to prepare for recall? Which of these produces "better learning"? Tversky's data indicate that these are the wrong questions to ask. In these results, which of the learning strategies is "better" depends on how memory is tested. We will not try to draw strong conclusions from this study by itself but, as we will see, this interdependency between learning and retrieval is indeed the pattern of things: Learning prepares us for using our memories in a particular way. Learning that is effective preparation for one test may be less effective with other tests.

## Retrieval Hints and Cues

Why should there be a connection between the particular form of learning and the particular form of memory retrieval? Imagine that you hear a history lecture, and think about it in the context of other lectures you have heard from that same professor. These thoughts will establish a memory connection between this lecture and others you have heard, and this connection can in turn serve as a retrieval path. If asked, later on, "What did Professor Jones say about such and such?" your retrieval path will lead you to the sought-after material.

But now imagine that we try to locate this same memory via a *different* retrieval path: "Does the current political situation remind you of anything you have learned recently?" Under these circumstances, what you need is some memory connection between "current political situation" and the target memory. That connection would lead you from your starting point to your goal. It is of little use, though, that you've established a connection between "Professor Jones" and the target memory, since that is not the connection you need. Therefore, for this memory search, your earlier learning may be irrelevant. By analogy, if you're trying to reach Chicago from the south, it doesn't matter that there's a good highway going into Chicago from the west. Likewise, if a memory search begins at a particular starting point, you need a path from that starting point to your target; it is irrelevant that paths from *other* starting points might eventually lead to your goal.

To put this broadly, establishing a particular retrieval path during learning may be of little use if you later on need some *other* path! As a result, your learning will serve you best if, at the time of retrieval, you approach the material in the same way (with the same focus, with the same connections) as you did at the time of learning. Then the connections you need will match the ones that are already available in memory.

Of course, during learning you often don't know how you'll be approaching the material later on. To continue our analogy, you may know that you'll soon want to reach Chicago, but you don't know

## Memory Performance with Two Different Types of Tests and Two Different Types of Expectations

FIGURE 6.1

**Test Used**

|  |  | Recall | Recognition |
|---|---|---|---|
| **Participants Expect** | Recall | 62% | 67% |
|  | Recognition | 40% | 87% |

Half of the people in this study were led to expect a recall test; half expected a recognition test. Half of each group got the test they expected; half did not. In the left-hand column of data, we see that people did better with a recall test if this is what they expected (62% vs. 40%). Likewise, in the right-hand column, people did better with a recognition test if this is what they had been led to expect (87% vs. 67%). [After B. Tversky, 1973.]

yet whether you'll be approaching the city from the north, the south, or the west. In this circumstance, your best bet might be to build multiple highways, so that you can reach your goal from any direction. Memory works the same way. If you initially thought about Professor Jones's lecture in conjunction with other lectures *and* in conjunction with political concerns *and* in conjunction with some other ideas, then each of these would establish a retrieval path, and so the memory could be retrieved from each of these perspectives. This multi-perspective approach, therefore, might provide something close to an "optimal learning strategy." But we usually don't adopt this multi-perspective approach. Hence, our memories are typically bound to the particular perspective we had in mind at the time of learning, and so the mem-

ory is most likely to be retrieved if that perspective is reinstated at the time of retrieval.

### STATE-DEPENDENT LEARNING

We'll be relying on these ideas throughout this chapter, so let's make certain the key points are clear: In Chapter 5, we argued that memory depends on *connections*, either connections within the to-be-remembered material, or connections between this material and other things you already know. We also suggested that these connections function by making memories "findable." In other words, these connections serve as *retrieval paths*, along which you can "travel" in order to reach information in long-term storage.

If a memory connection links, say, Memory A and Memory B, this will guide your thoughts toward B whenever you're thinking about A. But this same memory connection will have no impact if you happen *not* to be thinking about A. In order to use the path, you need first to be at the path's "starting point." Otherwise, the path (i.e., your previous learning) is of no use to you.

Is all of this right? Evidence to support this view comes from many sources. For example, consider a broad class of studies on **state-dependent learning** (Eich, 1980; Overton, 1985). In these studies, there are typically two different learning situations, and two different tests. One of the test formats is matched to one of the learning situations, and one to the other learning situation. Hence, we end up with what psychologists call a "2 × 2" design.

One such design is illustrated in Figure 6.2. Godden and Baddeley (1975) asked deep-sea divers to learn various materials. Some of the divers learned the material while sitting by the edge of the water, not wearing their diving masks. Others learned the material while approximately 20 feet underwater, hearing the material via a special communication set. Within each group, half of the divers were then tested while above water, and half were tested below.

Being underwater clearly changes one's perspective in many ways, and so we would expect the divers' thoughts while underwater to be rather different from those while on land. These thoughts, in turn, will influence what memory connections are formed during learning, and this will influence what retrieval paths are available later on. To put this concretely, imagine that a diver is thinking about the

**The Design of a State-Dependent Learning Experiment**

FIGURE 6.2

|  | **Test while** | |
|  | On land | Underwater |
| **On land** | Learning and test circumstances "match" | |
| **Underwater** | | Learning and test circumstances "match" |

**Learn while**

Half of the participants (deep-sea divers) learned the test material while underwater; half learned while sitting on land. Likewise, half were tested while underwater; half were tested on land. We expect a retrieval advantage if the learning and test circumstances "match." Hence, we expect better performance in the top-left and bottom-right cells.

sound of his breathing while underwater. This might lead the diver to form some memory connection between this thought about breathing and some of the to-be-remembered materials. If this diver is then back underwater at the time of the memory test, then the sound of underwater breathing is again heard, and this may lead the diver back into the same thoughts, which will then allow the diver to use the memory connection established earlier as a retrieval path. But if this diver is on land during the memory test, then the sound of breathing is absent, and so this retrieval path will have no influence.

With this logic in mind, we would expect the divers who learned material while underwater to re-member the material best if tested underwater—this will increase the chance that they're able to use the memory connections they established earlier. Likewise for the divers who learned on land; they should do best if tested on land. This pattern is exactly what the data show (Figure 6.3).

Related results have been obtained with odors present or absent during learning (Cann & Ross, 1989; Schab, 1990)—memory is best if the olfactory "environment" is the same during memory retrieval as it was during the initial learning. Similar data have been obtained in studies designed to mimic the real-life situation of a college student: The research participants read a two-page article on psychoimmunology, simi-

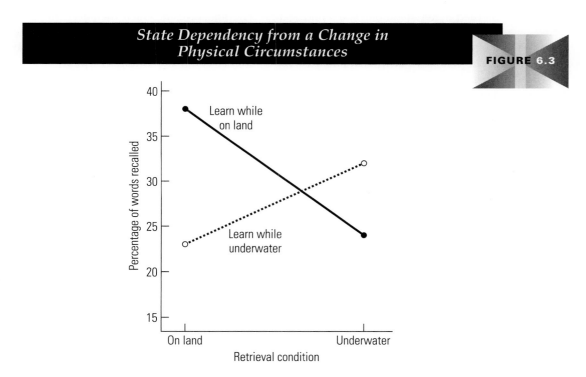

**State Dependency from a Change in Physical Circumstances**

FIGURE 6.3

Materials learned while on land are best recalled while on land. Materials learned while underwater are best recalled while underwater. The change in circumstances doesn't obliterate the benefits of learning (in all conditions, performance is considerably better than 0%); nonetheless, the differences between conditions are substantial.

lar to the sorts of readings they might encounter in their college courses. Half the participants read the article in a quiet setting; half read it in noisy circumstances. When given a short-answer test later on, those who read the article in quiet did best if tested in quiet—67% correct answers, compared to 54% correct if tested in a noisy environment. Those who read the article in a noisy environment did better if tested in a noisy environment—62% correct, compared to 46% (Grant et al., 1998; also see Balch, Bowman & Mohler, 1992; S. Smith, 1985).

Smith, Glenberg, and Bjork (1978) report the same pattern if learning and testing simply take place in different rooms—recall is best if done in the room in which the initial learning took place. Here, though, there is an interesting twist: In one procedure, the participants learned materials in one room and were tested in a different room. Just before testing, however, the participants were urged to think about the room in which they had learned—what it looked like, how it made them feel, and so on. When tested, these participants performed as well as those participants for whom there was no room change (S. Smith, 1979). What seems to matter, therefore, is not so much the physical context, but the psychological context, consistent with our account of this effect.

Similar studies have examined the memory effects of participants' moods. There are many ways to run such studies, including hypnotic procedures for placing people in a happy mood or a sad one, or procedures that involve the research participants reading a series of statements, designed to lift or depress their spirits. The design, though, is a by now familiar one: Participants learn the experimental materials either while happy or while sad; they are later tested either while happy or sad. And once again, memory is best if the mood state at test matches the mood state in learning (Bower, 1981).

This effect of mood on memory has a number of interesting implications. Among them, it serves to keep our moods stable: When we are happy, we are better able to think of experiences and events we learned about while happy, and this helps to keep us happy. Unfortunately, the same pattern holds when we are depressed. It is worth saying, though, that

unlike other state-dependency effects, these mood effects have proven somewhat unreliable. That is, several experiments have sought to reproduce the mood findings just described, but with no success. Other studies, however, have confirmed state-dependency effects with moods. It remains unclear why this particular variety of state dependency sometimes does appear in the results and sometimes does not. (For reviews, see Balch et al., 1999; Blaney, 1986; Brewin, Andrews & Gotlib, 1993; Eich, 1995; Kwiatkowski & Parkinson, 1994; Varner & Ellis, 1998.) One possibility, though, is quite interesting: People may, in many cases, use their memories to *influence* their moods—if you are feeling blue, you may seek out happy memories to cheer yourself up (Parrott & Sabini, 1990; Wegner, 1994). Therefore, this may be a circumstance in which memory influences mood at the same time that mood influences memory. No wonder, therefore, that mood and memory studies yield a complex pattern of results.

If we set aside the mood and memory data, however, the evidence is quite clear. Recall performance is best if people's state (internal or external) at the time of a test matches their state at the time of learning. This is because your state influences your mental perspective, and perspective influences both the retrieval paths that are established during learning and also, later on, the retrieval paths that are needed. If your perspective is the same at learning and retrieval, you'll be able to use the memory connections established earlier. If your perspective changes, these retrieval paths may not be useful for you.

## CHANGES IN ONE'S APPROACH TO THE MEMORY MATERIALS

Someone's state, we have argued, will influence how he or she approaches to-be-remembered materials, and this is what matters for memory. What happens if we manipulate someone's thinking more directly?

Fisher and Craik (1977) presented their participants with a series of word pairs. The participants were instructed to learn the *second* word in each pair, and to use the first word in each pair only "as an aid

| Percentage of Words Recalled on Testing after Prior Association with either Meaning or Sound | | | TABLE 6.1 |
|---|---|---|---|
| | **Type of hint** | | |
| | **Meaning** | **Sound** | **Both combined** |
| Type of processing at time of learning | | | |
| Meaning | 44% | 17% | 30.5% |
| Sound | 17% | 26% | 21.5% |

[After Fisher & Craik, 1977.]

to remembering the target words." For half of the pairs, the "context word" was semantically associated with the target word; for example, if participants were shown "cat," they were also shown the context word "dog." This should have encouraged them to think about the words' meanings. For the other pairs, the context word was one that rhymed with the target (e.g., if shown "cat," they were also shown the context word "hat"). This should have encouraged participants to think about the target word's sound.

When the time came for a test, participants were given either a hint concerning meaning ("Was there a word on the list associated with 'dog'"?) or a hint concerning sound ("Was there a word on the list associated with 'hat'"?). Table 6.1 shows the results. Note, first, the column all the way to the right (averaging together trials with meaning hints and trials with sound hints). Consistent with the data in Chapter 5, thinking about meaning generally leads to better memory, in this case with an impressive 30.5 to 21.5 advantage. That is, people who thought about meaning at the time of learning remembered about 50% more than people who thought about sound. But now look at the table's other two columns. If participants thought about meaning at the time of learning, they did considerably better in the test if the cues provided by the experimenter concerned meaning. Likewise for sound: If they thought about

sound at the time of learning, then they did better with a cue concerning the word's sound.

In fact, the table shows two separate influences on memory working at the same time: an advantage for thinking about meaning (overall, performance is better in the top row) and an advantage for "matched" learning and test conditions (overall, performance is best in the "main diagonal" of the table). In the table's top-left cell, these effects combine, and here performance is better than in any other condition. These effects clash in the column showing the results of the sound hint. The advantage from thinking about meaning favors the top cell in this column; the advantage from "matched" learning and test favors the bottom cell. As it turns out, the "match" effect wins over the levels-of-processing effect: "Deep but unmatched" (17%) is inferior to "not so deep, but matched" (26%). Thus, the advantage for deep processing is simply overturned in this situation.

## Encoding Specificity

We are starting to accumulate a broad set of cases in which memory performance depends on a "match" between someone's mental state at the time of learning, and his or her mental state at the time of retrieval. As a result, learning that is effective for one sort of test may be ineffective with some other test. Let's be clear, though, about what is going on in these experiments. People who are currently sad haven't, in any sense, lost their memories of happier days. The problem is that people in the "wrong state" have a hard time *locating* these memories. Once the person's state changes those memories will readily come to mind.

Moreover, we have emphasized that it is not just people's *physical state* that matters. What is crucial is their *thoughts* about the to-be-remembered items, and how they approach those items, both at the time of learning and at the time of retrieval. A further set of results will help to illustrate this point. We ask a group of people to memorize a list of words. Midway down the list is the word "jam" and, by manipulating the context, we arrange things so that participants understand this word as indicating the stuff one makes from berries or grapes. (This can be done in various ways; e.g., we can precede the word "jam" with a word like "jelly" or "fruit." In this situation, the context "primes" people to understand "jam" as we intend. We will discuss how this priming works in Chapter 8.) Some time later, we test memory by presenting various items and asking whether or not these appeared on the previous list. "Jam" is presented, but now we arrange context so that "jam" is understood as in "traffic jam." Under these circumstances, people typically will say that the word was not on the previous list, even though their memory for the list seems to be quite good. That is, people are quite likely to remember most of the other words on the list, even though they don't recall our test word.

This kind of demonstration is often referred to as **encoding specificity**, and has been reported in numerous forms by Endel Tulving (Tulving, 1983; also see Hunt & Ellis, 1974; Light & Carter-Sobell, 1970). The notion of encoding specificity, roughly, is that one learns more than just the word; one learns the word together with its context. In this case, the context would include what one thinks and understands about the word. As a result, when participants are later presented with the word in some *other* context, they ask themselves, "Does this match anything I learned previously?" and answer *correctly*, "no." And their answer is indeed correct. It is as if the par-

ticipants learned the word "other" and were later asked whether they had been shown the word "the." In fact, "the" does appear as part of "other" or, more precisely, the letters T H E do appear within the word "other." But it is the whole that people learn, not the parts. Therefore, if you've seen "other," it's entirely sensible to deny that you have seen "the" or, for that matter, "he" or "her," even though all these letter combinations are contained within "other."

Learning a list of words works in much the same way. The letters "J A M" were contained in what the research participants learned, just as "T H E" is contained in "other." In both cases, however, what was learned was the broader, integrated experience, the word as the perceiver organized it, the word as the perceiver understood it.

In fact, a great many results fit with these assertions. For example, we can show people the pattern in Figure 6.4, and arrange things so that they perceive the pattern as a vase on a black background. (As before, we can use a priming procedure, perhaps previously showing the participants pictures of other vases, or other white figures on black backgrounds.) A few minutes later, we show the picture again, but this time we prime participants so that they see two profiles, against a white background. We now ask them whether they have ever seen this figure before. This should be an extremely easy task since, after all, they have just seen this pattern. Nonetheless, people often assert that they have not seen the figure before (Kanizsa, 1979; Rock, 1983). Apparently, what matters for figure memory is, just as with words, the "stimulus as understood," not the geometrically defined picture itself. (We considered a number of related results in the early pages of Chapter 3, when we discussed the active interpretive nature of perception.)

Encoding specificity can be observed even with relatively subtle changes in meaning. Tulving and Thomson (1973; also Watkins & Tulving, 1975; Flexser & Tulving, 1978) showed participants a list of words, with each word accompanied by a context word "grasp-baby," for example—with "baby" being the to-be-remembered item. In the next step of the procedure, participants were shown a *new* list of words and asked to write down what these new words called to mind. Included in this new list was the word "infant" and, not surprisingly, many participants wrote down "baby" in response. Finally, participants were asked to look over their own responses, and to circle any of their responses that they recognized as having occurred in the previously seen input list. In many cases, the participants did not recognize "baby" as a list word. Simply by virtue of the change in context, memory seems to have been significantly disrupted. (For related results, see Bransford, Franks, Morris & Stein, 1979; Morris, Bransford & Franks, 1977; Tulving & Osler, 1968.)

Once again, we are led to some familiar themes. What happens during learning is the establishment of a memory that can be retrieved in a certain way, from a certain perspective. If the perspective changes—if, in particular, your understanding of the test item changes—then the original memory may not be retrieved. In light of this, it seems that we cannot speak of "good learning" (or "less good learning") *in general*. Instead, what counts as good learning depends on later events: Whether it is better to learn underwater or on land depends on where one will be tested.

Whether it is better to learn while listening to jazz or while sitting in a quiet room depends on the music background of the memory test. Even whether it is best to attend to meaning depends to some extent on whether meaning will be prominent when the time comes for memory retrieval.

## Different Forms of Memory Testing

In some of the studies described so far, memory has been tested via a *recall* test; other studies have used recognition. Recall and recognition testing differ in many ways, but they also have an important attribute in common: In a recall test, we ask people what words they can remember from a specific prior presentation. We are not interested, for example, in what words they encountered yesterday, or in the morning paper; we instead want them to recall the words from the list we gave them. Thus, we are asking them to do more than simply recall some words; we are, in fact,

### The Ambiguous "Vase/Profiles" Figure

**FIGURE 6.4**

This figure, which we first met in Chapter 3, can be perceived either as a white vase against a black background or as two black profiles against a white background.

asking them to recall an *episode* (namely, the episode in which the words were learned).

The same is true for a recognition test: In this procedure, participants are shown test words (for example), and must decide whether each had or had not appeared on a previously shown list. It will not be enough for the participants to decide which of the test words seem familiar, or which ones they have seen before. *All* of the test words are familiar (i.e., all are in the participants' vocabulary), and all of the test words have been encountered *somewhere* before. Therefore, the participants must do more than register the familiarity of the test items; they must in addition identify the context in which they last encountered the item; in essence, they must say, "The last time I met this word was on the previous list." Thus, once again, participants are required to remember an episode, and not just a list of words.

Against this backdrop, consider the following common experience: You are walking down the street, or perhaps you turn on the television, and you see a familiar face. Immediately, you know the face is familiar, but you are unable to say just *why* the face is familiar. Is it someone you saw in a movie last month? Is it the driver of the bus you often take? You are at a loss to answer these questions; all you know is that the face is familiar.

In cases like this, you cannot "place" the memory, you cannot identify the episode in which the face was last encountered. But, as we have just seen, it is precisely this identification of an episode that is required by recall and recognition measures. Thus, if we assess your memory via these measures, you are failing to remember. It is as if you said to the experimenter, "Yes, the test word is familiar to me, but I haven't a clue where I last saw it, and I haven't a clue whether it was on that list you showed me." If we require you to remember the connection between an item and the context of a previous encounter, then you have failed.

But this seems too harsh, since you clearly are remembering something. You know that the face is familiar; you probably also know that the face is usually encountered in a context sharply different from the current one. We therefore need to say something about this sort of memory and, in general, about the feeling of familiarity.

## REMEMBERING SOURCE VERSUS FAMILIARITY ALONE

*Familiarity* has been extensively investigated, with a great deal of the early work done by George Mandler (Mandler, 1980; Graf & Mandler, 1984; Mandler, Graf & Kraft, 1986). Mandler's proposal starts by formalizing the distinction introduced in the last section. That is, we need to distinguish **source memory** from familiarity. Source memory refers to the recollection of the *source* of one's current knowledge. That is, one remembers the episode in which the learning took place; one remembers the time and place in which a stimulus was encountered. Familiarity, in contrast, refers only to a feeling one has—a specific picture before your eyes "seems familiar" or a tune "sounds familiar."

Mandler proposed that source memory and familiarity derive from different memory processes, with each set of processes being fully independent of the other. That's what makes it possible for us to have familiarity without source memory—as in the example we just considered (you know a face is familiar, but can't figure out why). The reverse is also possible: source memory without any feelings of familiarity. We considered an illustration of this pattern in Chapter 2, when we considered Capgras Syndrome.

Source memory and familiarity influence us in different ways. To see this, consider the relation between recall and recognition testing. By definition, a recall test is one in which the questioner names a prior episode, and the participant must generate the items learned in this episode. The episode might be "the list presented earlier," in which you must generate the items on the list. Or the episode might be "the last big party you attended," with you being asked to generate what happened at the party, or who was there. In either case, your memory search begins with the episode, and moves from there to the associated items. Thus, by its very nature, a recall test requires memory for the initial episode; it requires source memory.

The situation is more complicated with recognition. Let's say that you are taking a recognition test. The fourth word on the test is "loon." You might say to yourself, "Yes, I remember seeing this word on the previous list. In fact, I'm certain that this word was on the list, because I remember the image that came to mind when I encountered this word." This line of reasoning draws on a memory for a particular episode, i.e., a source memory, and this would of course guide your response on the recognition test. But now let's say that the fifth word on the test is "butler." In response to this word, you might say to yourself, "I don't specifically remember seeing this word on the list, but this word feels extraordinarily familiar. If the word *wasn't* on the list, then it wouldn't seem so familiar. Therefore, it must have been on the list." In this case, there is no source memory. Instead, you are being guided by a sense of familiarity *plus* an inference about where that familiarity came from. And, thanks to the inference, you will probably respond "yes" on the recognition test.

In sum, recall tests provide a relatively "pure" assessment of source memory. But responses on a recognition test can be guided *either* by source memory or by the combination of familiarity and inference. If you remember the episode of seeing a word on the prior list, that can guide your response. If, on the other hand, a word seems extremely familiar, you are likely to *infer* that you saw it on the list, even if you cannot remember the actual encounter (Atkinson & Juola, 1974; Glucksberg & McCloskey, 1981; Jacoby & Brooks, 1984; Rajaram, 1993).

It also turns out that different kinds of learning set the basis for source memory and for familiarity. Thus, when people anticipate a memory test, they are likely to do what we earlier called "relational" or "elaborative" rehearsal. In this form of rehearsal, they pay attention to the meaning of the material; perhaps they also form images of the material. Crucially, this form of rehearsal is also likely to include attention to the *context* of the to-be-remembered material. For example, people are likely to think about how the various items they're trying to learn are related to each other, or how the items are related to other things they happen to be thinking about dur-

ing the learning episode. This will create a memory record that helps the person to remember the setting in which they encountered each one of the to-be-remembered items, and this will, of course, provide good preparation for any task that requires memory for this setting—that is, for source memory.

But if, on the other hand, people anticipate no memory test, then they will probably elect to do the (easier) "maintenance" or "item-specific" rehearsal. No connections to the context will be sought, nor will any be made. The context of the items will not be encoded, and so this form of rehearsal will be poor preparation for tasks requiring source memory (e.g., recall). However, maintenance rehearsal does have an effect: In doing this rote, non-associative rehearsal, people will be exposed to the material over and over. As a result, the material will become more and more familiar to them. Thus, maintenance rehearsal should benefit tasks that depend on familiarity.

## THE HYBRID NATURE OF RECOGNITION

A wide range of evidence fits with the conception we have just sketched. For example, we noted in Chapter 5 that someone's ability to recall an earlier-presented list is much improved if the list is organized; it turns out, however, that the effects of organization are far weaker with recognition testing (Mandler, 1981; also see Murname et al., 1999). This is sensible if we claim that recall depends on source memory, which in turn depends on memorial connections. In contrast, recognition can be based on familiarity, which does not depend on memory connections.

The results are different, though, if we delay testing. If people learn a list on one occasion, and are tested some weeks later, then organization has the same effect on recognition as it does on recall—that is, organization will then have a large benefit for both forms of testing. This can easily be explained if we make one further assumption: Recognition testing is more likely to be based on familiarity when the items are still "fresh" in one's mind. To see why, let's return to our earlier example, and imagine someone who has just encountered the word "butler" on a recognition test. The person might realize the word is familiar, but wonder why this is: "Perhaps it's familiar because I encountered it on the experimenter's list. Or perhaps it's familiar because I heard it in a conversation yesterday. . . ." With numerous sources possible for the familiarity, the person will be wary about attributing the familiarity to the earlier-presented list. The familiarity is clear, but the interpretation of the familiarity is uncertain. Under these circumstances, research participants might hesitate to offer a judgment based on familiarity alone; instead, they will respond only if they can locate a source memory. In this case, recognition should be influenced by memory connections, just as recall is, and this is precisely what the data show.

This perspective also leads to the claim that recognition will be more difficult with common words than with relatively rare words. Common words, by definition, are encountered in many contexts. If a common word seems familiar, therefore, research participants might be certain they have recently encountered it but uncertain *where* they encountered it. For obvious reasons, this ambiguity is less severe with uncommon words. Consistent with this, recognition testing does yield poorer results with familiar words than with unfamiliar ones (Glanzer & Adams, 1985).

Finally, pertinent evidence also comes from studies that manipulate how people *approach* the materials in their initial learning. We can, in particular, structure a task so that participants do *maintenance* rehearsal for some of the items, and *elaborative* rehearsal for other items. (There are several ways to arrange this. As an example, the Craik and Watkins, 1973, "B-word" experiment, described in Chapter 5, illustrates one way to lure people into maintenance rehearsal.) The hypothesis we are considering indicates that elaborative rehearsal, which promotes source memory, will serve as good preparation for either recall or recognition testing. Maintenance rehearsal, in contrast, is good preparation for recognition testing, but should be largely ineffective for recall. This also turns out to be correct (Bartz, 1976; Glenberg & Adams, 1978; Glenberg, Smith & Green, 1977; Woodward, Bjork & Jongeward, 1973).

## THE COMPLEXITY OF RECALL

These results fit well with the conception we are developing and also highlight the complex nature of recognition—sometimes based on familiarity, sometimes based on the recollection of a specific episode. Moreover, when recognition depends on familiarity, it does so in a complicated way: You notice that a test word seems familiar, and then you make an *inference* about the origins of this familiarity. If you decide the word is familiar because it appeared on the prior list, that will lead to one response; if you decide the word is familiar for some other reason, that will lead to the opposite response. Note, then, that the recognition response depends as much on the inference as it does on the familiarity itself.

What about recall? First, recall clearly depends on a memory search. In recognition testing, the experimenter provides the sought-after items. "Was this picture in the earlier series?" (or "this word?" or "this sentence?") In recall testing, the participant has to come up with the specific items on her own; the experimenter merely supplies the *category* of sought-after items ("a story you heard in childhood" or "the faces you saw at yesterday's meeting"). Coming up with these items will require *locating* them in memory, and that's where the memory search enters—a search beginning with the memory cue (the experimenter's question, perhaps) and ending with the sought-after memories. It is this search that is facilitated by memory connections, and that is why connections matter so much for recall.

However, the task of recalling items does not end once the sought-after items are brought to mind. The person then needs to ask, "*Why* did this item come to mind? Is it a memory, or just some chance association? If a memory, is it drawn from the right source? Did the word 'loon' come to mind because it was on the experimenter's list, or because I was reminded of loons by something on the experimenter's list?" These questions are, of course, parallel to those demanded by recognition testing. In recognition, a test item might seem familiar, and the research participants must decide why this is. In recall, a potential response comes to mind, and again participants must decide why this is. In both cases, an *attribution* step is required, and whether the participants will respond one way or another is determined by this attribution. Evidence suggests that this attribution step is far from trivial, and attribution errors can occur. (We will return to this issue, and, with it, the sources of memory errors, in Chapter 7. For a discussion of how memories are "attributed" to a particular source, see, for example, Johnson, Hashtroudi & Lindsay, 1993.)

In summary, then, recall and recognition are both surprisingly complex. Recall clearly depends on a memory search and is therefore influenced mightily by the presence or absence of relevant memory connections. Recognition turns out to be something of a hybrid and can be based either on source memory (in which case it is just like recall) or on familiarity. In any event, both recognition and recall require a step of inference, as one attributes familiarity (in the case of recognition) or the retrieval of a particular memory (in recall) to some specific source.

## Implicit Memory

We have emphasized that recognition, in many circumstances, relies on familiarity plus an inference. But what is this inference all about? And when someone attributes a "feeling of familiarity," deciding that the feeling comes from a particular source, what sort of "feeling" are we talking about?

### MEMORY WITHOUT AWARENESS

In a study by Jacoby (1983; also Jacoby & Dallas, 1981; Winnick & Daniel, 1970), participants were initially shown a series of words and then, later on, their memory for the words was tested. During the learning phase of the experiment, however, participants experienced the words in one of three ways. In the "no context" condition, they were shown each word without any context. For example, they saw "XXXX, DARK" on the computer screen, and their task was to read "dark" aloud. In the "context" con-

dition, participants saw each word along with its antonym. For example, they were shown "HOT, COLD" and had to read "cold" aloud. Finally, in the "generate" condition, participants saw the antonym only ("LOW, ???") and had to say out loud what the target word was.

In this experiment, the "generate" condition involves the most conceptual activity, since the participant must attend to the cue word's meaning and come up with the antonym. In contrast, the "no context" condition provides neither reason nor encouragement to think about the word's meaning; it seems likely that people in this condition will read the word without thinking much about it. The "context" condition will probably involve an intermediate level of activity, since this condition does draw attention to meaning (via the antonym), but does not require the participants to do anything with the antonym.

In Chapter 5, we argued that *attention to meaning* is often an effective way to memorize; mere exposure, in contrast, seems to provide little memory benefit. Based on this, we would expect the participants to remember words encountered in the "generate" condition, but probably not those encountered in the "no context" condition. That is what the data show: Half of the participants were tested via a conventional recognition procedure and, in this test, performance was best for words presented in the "generate" condition, worse if the words had appeared in the "context" condition, and worst of all in the "no context" condition (Figure 6.5).

So far, then, this looks just like studies we have already seen. The twist, though, comes from the other half of the participants, tested in a rather different fashion. They were seated in front of a tachistoscope and shown a series of briefly presented words. Their task was simply to say what the words were—that is, to read them out loud. Some of the words presented had also been presented during the learning phase, and some of the words were novel—i.e., had not been recently viewed.

As we saw in Chapter 3, word recognition can be difficult, especially if the presentations are quite brief. Crucially, though, repetition helps. For example, let's say that the tenth word presented to participants was "boat." If the fourteenth word in the series is also "boat," participants will recognize the word more easily the second time around. In Chapter 3, we referred to this as repetition priming. Of course, priming involves some sort of memory since, obviously, a previous event is influencing current performance. This is only possible if the person preserves some record, some memory, of that previous event. But what kind of memory is this? And what *creates* this memory? This brings us back to the Jacoby study.

Figure 6.5 shows the data. With tachistoscopic testing, performance was best if participants had encountered the words in the "no context" condition, worst if they had encountered the words in the "generate" condition. This is, of course, exactly the opposite of the results from the standard recognition test. In that condition, performance was, it seems, dependent on "conceptual work"—thinking about the meaning of the words. The more conceptual work participants had done, the better their recognition memory. In contrast, tachistoscopic performance seems dependent on *perceptual* "work," that is, on literally seeing the items. Participants obviously see the words in the "no context" condition, and this condition produces strong priming. They don't see the words in the "generate" condition, and this condition produces negligible priming. The "context" condition again takes an

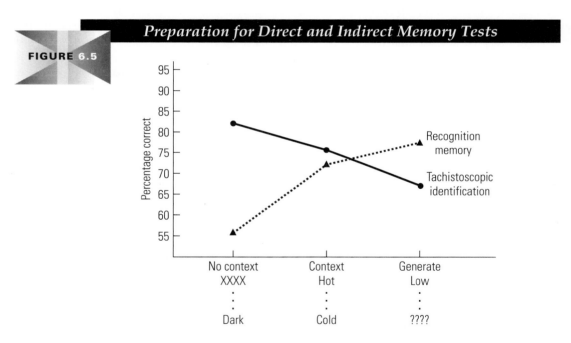

**FIGURE 6.5**

**Preparation for Direct and Indirect Memory Tests**

Participants in the "no context" condition saw words and read them aloud; those in the "generate" condition had to generate the words (antonyms) on their own (and did not see them). Participants in the "context" condition saw the words, but had a meaningful context (antonyms) and so only had to glance at the words in order to identify them. The "generate" condition was the best preparation for a direct test ("Are these the words you saw before?") but worst for an indirect test (tachistoscopic identification). [After Jacoby, 1983.]

intermediate position: Given the context, participants do not need to look at the word with any great care. Having seen "hot," a quick glance will confirm what the next word ("cold") must be. Hence, there will be some "perceptual contact" with the stimulus, but it will be slight. It makes sense, therefore, that this condition produces an intermediate level of priming.

At the very least, it appears that we are seeing two different types of memory here. One type seems relevant to the standard recognition test and is promoted by conceptual engagement with the materials. We reveal this type of memory if we test people *directly*, asking them explicitly what they remember. The other type of memory seems relevant to the tachistoscopic test and is promoted by perceptually working with the materials. To reveal this sort of memory, we must test participants *indirectly*, asking not what they remember, but how their current performance is influenced by recent events.

Similar results have been obtained with other tasks. For example, in a lexical-decision task, participants are shown strings of letters (STAR, LAMB, HIRL); the task is to indicate (by pressing one button or another) whether the string of letters is a word in English or not. Lexical decisions are appreciably quicker if the person has recently seen the test word; that is, lexical decision shows its own version of repetition priming. This priming is observed even when participants have no explicit memory for having encountered the stimulus words before (e.g., Oliphant, 1983).

How is this demonstrated? We can show participants a list of words, and then later test them in two different ways. The direct test uses a standard recognition procedure: "Which of these words were on the list I showed you earlier?" The indirect test is a lexical decision: "Which of these letter strings form real words?" In this setup, the two tests will often yield different results: At a sufficient delay, the direct-memory test is likely to show that the participants have *forgotten* most of the words presented earlier; according to the lexical-decision results, however, they still remember the words (that is, show a robust priming effect). Put differently, people demonstrate a clear influence by a past event even though they do not consciously remember that past event.

The same pattern has been observed with a task called **word-stem completion**. In this task, people are given the first few letters of a word and must produce a word with this beginning. For example they might be asked to name a word that begins "CLA." In some versions of this task, an obscure word is required to complete the word-stem. In this situation, people are more likely to come up with the word if they have encountered it recently—even if, when asked directly, they report no memory at all of that earlier encounter. In other versions of this task, more than one word provides a plausible ending to the stem (e.g., CLAM, CLASS, CLATTER), and the question of interest is *which* of these words the person produces. If one of these words has been seen recently, people are likely to produce it, rather than a legitimate alternative, as the completion to the word stem. Once again, though, this priming effect is observed even if participants, when tested directly, show no memory of having seen the word recently (e.g., Graf, Mandler & Haden, 1982).

Thus it seems that, in a range of settings, people are influenced by a previous encounter even if they have no conscious recollection of the encounter. (For reviews, see Richardson-Klavehn & Bjork, 1988; Schacter, 1987.) Results like these have led psychologists to distinguish two types of memories. **Explicit memories** are those revealed by *direct* memory testing and are typically accompanied by the conviction that one is remembering a specific prior episode. Recall is a direct memory test; so is the standard recognition test. **Implicit memories** are those revealed by *indirect* testing and are often manifested as *priming* effects. In this form of testing, one's current behavior or current judgments are demonstrably influenced by a prior event, but one may be quite unaware of this. Tachistoscopic recognition, lexical decision, word-stem completion, and many other tasks provide indirect means of assessing memory.

## THE BREADTH OF IMPLICIT MEMORY

The effects of implicit memory can also be demonstrated in many other circumstances. To describe the evidence, though, we first need to say more about how implicit memory *feels* from the rememberer's point of view. This will then lead us back into our discussion of familiarity and source memory.

Let us say that we show people a stimulus and then, some time later, show them the same stimulus again. Let us say further that we arrange things so that the participants have no explicit memory. (There are many ways to do this; we can, for example, simply allow some time to pass between the initial exposure and the subsequent test.) The evidence indicates that the participants' reaction to the stimulus, in the second encounter, will depend a great deal on the context. Thanks to the implicit memory, the stimulus is likely to feel in some ways "special." We have several expressions in English that seem to capture this specialness: We sometimes say that something "rings a bell," or that it "strikes a chord." But exactly what this means, and exactly how this feels, seems to depend on the circumstances.

Several experiments will help to illustrate this point. Jacoby, Kelley, Brown and Jasechko (1989) presented participants with a list of names to read out loud. The participants were told nothing about a memory test; they thought the experiment was concerned with how they pronounced the names. Some time later, though, the participants were given the second step of the procedure. They were shown a new list of names, and asked to rate each person named on this list according to how famous each was. The list included some real, very famous people, some real but not-so-famous people, and also some fictional names. Crucially, the fictional names were of two types: Some were names that had occurred on the prior list, and some were simply new names.

Let's focus on the names that were fictional but familiar—that is, names taken from the prior list. How the participants responded to these names depended on *how much time had elapsed* between presentation of the two lists. To understand this, imagine yourself in the role of a participant. If you see the "famous" list right after the "pronounce" list, you might decide "This name rings a bell, but that's because I just saw it on the previous list." In the terms we have been using, you have a feeling of familiarity

for the name, and you also remember the source of this familiarity. If, however, the two lists are presented 24 hours apart, things are different. At this delay, the familiarity still remains, but memory for the source of the familiarity has faded. In taking the test, therefore, you might say, "This name rings a bell, and I have no idea why. I guess this must be a famous person." And this is indeed the pattern of the data: When the two lists are presented one day apart, the participants rate the made-up names as being famous. Apparently, they correctly note that these names seem familiar, but then they misinterpret this feeling of familiarity. And, critically, this misinterpretation is only possible once memory for the actual source has become less prominent; in this particular procedure, this is accomplished by the 24-hour delay. Without the 24-hour delay, we get no effect. Hence, Jacoby et al. refer to their study as the "how to become famous overnight" experiment.

Let's be clear that, in this study, the participants were *correct* in noting that some of the names did "ring a bell," did have a certain feeling of familiarity. The participants' *mistake*, though, lies in how they interpreted this feeling, and in what conclusions they drew from it. In other words, they forgot the real source of the familiarity (appearance on a recently viewed list) and instead filled in a bogus source ("Maybe I saw this name in the newspaper?"). Of course, it's not hard to see why they made this particular misattribution. After all, the experiment was described to them as being about fame, and other names on the list were indeed those of famous people. From the participants' point of view, therefore, it is a reasonable inference under these circumstances that any name that "rings a bell" belongs to a famous person. With this acknowledged, though, the fact remains that participants' reaction to their implicit memory depended critically on how they *interpreted* that memory.

## IMPLICIT MEMORY AND THE "ILLUSION OF TRUTH"

A different example is somewhat frightening. Participants in one study heard a series of statements and had to judge how interesting each statement was

(Begg, Anas & Farinacci, 1992). As an example, one sentence was "The average person in Switzerland eats about 25 pounds of cheese each year." (This is false; the average is closer to 18 pounds.) Another was, "Henry Ford forgot to put a reverse gear in his first automobile." (This is true.) After hearing these sentences, the participants were presented with some more sentences, but now had to judge the *credibility* of these, rating them on a scale from "certainly true" to "certainly false." Needless to say, some of the sentences in this "truth test" were repeats from the earlier presentation; the question of course is how sentence credibility is influenced by sentence familiarity.

The result was a propagandist's dream: Sentences heard before were more likely to be accepted as true: Familiarity increased credibility (Begg, Armour & Kerr, 1985; Brown & Halliday, 1990; Hasher, Goldstein & Toppino, 1977). To make this worse, this effect emerged even when the participants were explicitly warned in advance not to believe the sentences in the first list. In one procedure, the participants were told that half of the statements had been made by men, and half by women. The women's statements, they were told, were always true; the men's always false. (Half the participants were told the reverse.) Then participants rated how interesting the sentences were, with each sentence attributed either to a man or a woman. "Frank Foster says that house mice can run an average of four miles per hour" or "Gail Logan says that crocodiles sleep with their eyes open." Finally, participants were presented with new sentences and had to judge their truth, including of course these assertions about mice and crocodiles and so forth.

Let's focus on the sentences initially identified as being false—in our example, Frank's claim about mice. If someone explicitly remembers this sentence ("Oh yes—Frank said such and such.") then he should judge the assertion to be *false* ("After all, the experimenter said that all the men's statements were lies."). But what about someone without this explicit memory? This person might still have an implicit memory ("Gee, that statement rings a bell."), and this might increase the credibility of the statement. ("I'm sure I've heard that somewhere before; I guess it must be true.") This is exactly the pattern of the

data: Statements plainly identified as false when they were first heard still created the so-called illusion of truth—that is, these statements were subsequently judged to be more credible than sentences never heard before.

The relevance of this to the political arena, or to advertising, should be clear. A newspaper headline inquires: "Is Mayor Wilson a crook?" Or perhaps the headline declares: "Known criminal claims Wilson is a crook!" In either case, the assertion that Wilson is a crook has now become familiar. The Begg et al. data indicate that this familiarity will, by itself, increase the likelihood that you'll later believe in Wilson's dishonesty. This will be true even if the paper merely raised the question; it will be true even if the allegation came from a disreputable source. Malicious innuendo does in fact work nasty effects (e.g., Wegner, Wenzlaff, Kerker & Beattie, 1981).

## ATTRIBUTING IMPLICIT MEMORY TO THE WRONG STIMULUS

In all these experiments, participants seem not to realize that they are being influenced by a specific prior experience. In the illusion-of-truth experiments, they are convinced that they are drawing on some sort of general knowledge, not on memory for specific episodes. From their perspective, they are relying on what they *know*, rather than on what they *remember*. (For discussion of when people say they "know" something, and when they say they "remember," see Gardiner & Java, 1991; LeCompte, 1995; Rajaram, 1993; see also Chapter 7.)

This observation is consistent with our earlier assertion that implicit memories often don't feel like memories. Instead, implicit memories leave you only with a vague sense that a stimulus is "special." Of course, you don't leave things in that vague state; instead, without even realizing that you're doing it, you try to attribute the sense of "specialness" to some source. This attribution step is far from foolproof. As the last few pages have made clear, it's easy to find cases in which the sense of specialness is attributed to the wrong source.

Indeed, in some cases, we are completely off in our attributions. In one experiment, participants were presented with bursts of noise and asked to judge how loud each noise was (Jacoby, Allan, Collins & Larwill, 1988). Embedded within each burst of noise, though, was a sentence. Some of the sentences were new to participants, but crucially, some of the sentences had been presented earlier. In this setup, therefore, we are asking about the participants' memory for the *sentences*.

In this study, memory appeared in an odd way: If a sentence was one of the familiar ones, participants had an easier time hearing it against the backdrop of noise. This is just another case of repetition priming, and so is consistent with results already described. But then the participants seemed to reason in this fashion: "Well, that sentence was easy to hear. I guess, therefore, the noise couldn't have been so loud." Likewise, for the *unfamiliar* sentences, they seemed to reason: "Gee, that noise must have been loud, since it really drowned out the sentence." As a result of these (completely unconscious) inferences, noise containing familiar sentences was (mis)perceived as being softer than it actually was; noise containing novel sentences was (mis)perceived as being loud.

In this experiment, therefore, the (objectively) familiar sentences do stand out from the rest and, presumably participants register the fact that these sentences are easier to discern against the background of noise than the (objectively) unfamiliar sentences. However, they seem to attribute none of this to the sentences themselves. Instead, they attribute the "specialness" to the noise, so that memory is here producing a "loudness illusion." It is the *sentences* that are familiar, but it is the *noise judgment* that is influenced. This makes plain the role of an attribution process and illustrates how far this process can go astray.

## ATTRIBUTING IMPLICIT MEMORY TO THE WRONG SOURCE

Many times, though, people *do* attribute the familiarity of a stimulus to a specific prior episode: They correctly realize that they have encountered the familiar stimulus once before, at a particular time and place. Even here, however, there is a possibility for error, namely, that the memory will be attributed to the *wrong* episode! This sort of error is referred to as **source confusion**.

Does this kind of confusion really occur? In a study by Brown, Deffenbacher and Sturgill (1977), research participants witnessed a staged event. Two or three days later, they were shown "mug shots" of individuals who supposedly had participated in the event. Of course, the people in the photos were different from the people who were actually on the scene. Finally, after four or five more days, the participants were shown a lineup of four persons, and asked to select the individuals seen in step one—namely, the original event. The data show massive source confusion, with 29% of the participants "indicting" individuals they had seen only in the mug shots. Apparently, they were correctly noting that these individuals seemed familiar, but they were confused about *why* they were familiar. They correctly realized, "I have seen this face before," but then they were mistaken about *where* they had seen it before—falsely believing they'd seen the face in the original "crime," when, in truth, they'd seen it only in the subsequent photograph.

Does this sort of confusion happen outside of the laboratory? It certainly does. One example comes from a court case in England in which a crime victim confidently identified a sailor as the person who had robbed him. The sailor, however, was able to prove that, at the time of the crime, he was many miles away. How did this mistaken identification arise? It turns out that the crime victim was a ticket agent in a train station, and the sailor had, on several prior occasions, purchased tickets at this station. Apparently, then, the ticket-seller correctly realized that the sailor's face was familiar but (unwittingly) drew the wrong conclusion about *why* the face was familiar (Ross, Ceci, Dunning & Toglia, 1994). Similar examples are easy to find. (Findings like these have interesting implications for how the police should run eyewitness identification procedures; for the Supreme Court's views on this point, see, for example, *Simmons et al. v. United States*, 1968; also Gorenstein & Ellsworth, 1980.)

## Theoretical Treatments of Implicit Memory

One unmistakable message coming from all of these studies is that we are often better at remembering *that* something is familiar than in remembering *why* it is familiar. This underscores the point made earlier that source memory is supported by different mechanisms than *familiarity*. This is why it's possible to have a sense of familiarity with no source memory ("I've seen her somewhere before, but I can't figure out where!"), and also why it's possible to be correct in judging familiarity but mistaken in judging source. (This was the case in many of the examples we have just considered.)

This separation between familiarity and source memory opens the door to many memory illusions. In some cases, we attribute our familiarity to the wrong episode (this was evident in the example of eyewitness misidentification). In other cases, we attribute our familiarity to general knowledge, rather than a specific episode (e.g., the "false fame" experiment, or the "illusion of truth"). And in some cases, we are influenced by the familiarity of a stimulus even if we don't realize that the stimulus is in fact familiar. This is the heart of many implicit memory effects, including the "illusion of loudness" we considered earlier. The same can be shown in studies of *aesthetic preferences*: Investigators have demonstrated a preference for familiar stimuli, even when participants don't have any idea at all that the stimuli are familiar (Anand & Sternthal, 1991; Peretz et al., 1998; Seamon et al., 1995; Zajonc, 1980).

These findings have important practical implications—we have already discussed, for example, the impact of innuendo and propaganda. They also raise profound theoretical questions. For example, consider what these results may be telling us about learning and memory in other species: When we speak of animals' learning or remembering the past, what we often mean is that the animals' current behavior reveals the influence of past experiences. In humans, this is close to what we are now calling implicit memory. It is conceivable, therefore, that explicit memory—being able to comment on the past or to describe a specific past event—is a uniquely human form of remembering or at least a form of remembering found only in complex organisms (primates and perhaps dolphins).

Likewise, as we have mentioned, participants in implicit-memory studies often have no idea they are displaying an influence of past exposures—to use Jacoby and Witherspoon's (1982) term, they are displaying "memory without awareness." Conversely, explicit memory might be defined as "memory with awareness" and may include the possibility of consciously "reliving" the prior event. This implies a connection between explicit memory and awareness of one's self, and awareness of the sources of one's thoughts and actions. This too may provide a signal that this is a very special form of memory, perhaps unique to humans. (For relevant discussion, see Fivush, 1988; Nelson, 1988; Oakley, 1983; Reber, 1992; Squire & Zola-Morgan, 1991.)

But what exactly is an implicit memory? What is the content of these memories? It is to these questions that we now turn.

### IMPLICIT MEMORY: A HYPOTHESIS

We have already noted (e.g., in Chapter 3) that perceptual processes are improved by practice. Having once perceived a stimulus, it will be easier to perceive that same stimulus in the future, because the relevant processes will now run more smoothly and efficiently. That is what repetition priming is all about.

Presumably, though, the same can be said for other bits of intellectual performance: Just as perceiving a word leads to fluency in perceiving, perhaps contemplating a word's meaning leads to fluency of a parallel sort. The next time one contemplated the same word's meaning, one might be a little quicker or more efficient.

We would expect these practice effects to be rather specific. Exercising your legs makes your legs stronger, not your arms. In the same way, practice at perceiving Gladys will help you when next you see Gladys; the practice will not improve your ability to perceive Sally or Lola. More generally, practice in perceiving a stimulus will improve your ability to perceive *that* stimulus; similarly, practice in thinking through a specific chain of associations will make it easier to retrace *those* mental steps, and not some others.

With this as backdrop, here is a hypothesis: Implicit memory is simply the name we give to these practice effects and to the resulting increase in **processing fluency**. For some tasks, this increase in processing fluency is by itself enough to influence performance. Consider, for example, implicit memory's effect on tachistoscopic identification or on lexical decisions. These tasks require little more than the identification of the presented stimuli, and so these tasks would benefit directly from anything that speeds up processing. Thus, the claim of implicit memory here simply summarizes the fact that, once a stimulus has been perceived, it will be easier to perceive the next time around.

To explain other implicit-memory effects, though, we need a further assumption, namely, that people are sensitive to the degree of processing fluency. That is, people know when they have perceived easily and when they have perceived only by expending more effort. They likewise know when a sequence of thoughts was particularly fluent and when the sequence was labored. Note that we are *not* claiming that people experience the fluency as fluency. When a stimulus is easy to perceive, people usually do not experience a feeling of "ease." Instead, they merely register a vague sense of specialness. They feel that the stimulus "rings a bell." No matter how it is described, though, our hypothesis is that the sense of specialness has a simple cause—namely, ease in processing, brought on by fluency, which in turn was created by practice.

We still need one more step in our hypothesis, but it is a step we have already introduced: When a stimulus feels special, people typically want to know *why*. Thus, the feeling of specialness (again produced by fluency) triggers an attribution process, as people seek to attribute the specialness to some source. What happens next, though, depends enormously on how the attribution goes. In some circumstances, the specialness will be (correctly) interpreted as "familiarity."

In other situations, people may attribute the fluency to other sources, often incorrectly. As we have seen, this can lead to a variety of consequences beyond the "sense of familiarity"—including the false-fame effect, the illusion of truth, and so on.

It also seems likely that we can detect *decreases* in perceptual fluency, as well as increases, and we considered an example of this back in Chapter 2. Imagine that someone you know well changes her hairstyle, or gets new eyeglasses. In such cases, you often have the uncomfortable feeling that something in your friend's appearance has changed, but you can't figure out what it is. In our terms, your friend's face was a stimulus that you had seen often, and therefore a stimulus you were fluent in perceiving. Once the stimulus is changed, however, your well-practiced steps of perceiving don't run as smoothly as they have in the past, and so the perception is less fluent than it had previously been. This lack of fluency is detected and produces the "something is new" feeling. But then the attribution step fails—you cannot identify what produced this feeling. This case provides the mirror image of the cases we have been considering, in which familiarity leads to an *increase* in fluency, so that something "rings a bell," but one cannot say why.

In summary, then, we should think of implicit memory as being more of a "skill" than a memory per se—a skill, as it turns out, in doing mental work (perceiving, or thinking about an idea, or whatever). This skill, and its concomitant fluency, will facilitate processing the next time the relevant mental steps are taken, and so the steps will go more easily and quickly the next time around. You will then detect the skill and seek to interpret it.

## ILLUSIONS OF FAMILIARITY

The study of implicit memory has sparked a complex theoretical debate, and so some amount of controversy is attached to almost any claim one might make about this sort of memory—including the hypothesis just sketched. Even so, let's pursue this hypothesis, and consider in particular what it implies for the often-experienced feeling of *familiarity*.

You encounter a stimulus, and perceive it, and perhaps think about the stimulus in a certain way. This experience will then help you the next time you meet the same stimulus: Thanks to the first encounter, you've already had some "practice" in perceiving and thinking about the stimulus, and as a result of this practice, your perception and thinking will be swifter and easier the second time around. This is what we're calling "processing fluency." You detect this fluency, and (perhaps guided by a source memory) you attribute the fluency to a prior exposure. This detection + attribution, though, is entirely unconscious; what you experience consciously (as a direct result of this detection + attribution) is simply a sense that the stimulus is "familiar." This chain of events is depicted in Figure 6.6.

The key idea, therefore, is that *fluency* is the direct trigger for the feeling that the stimulus is somehow "special," and this is what triggers the attribution of familiarity. Within this context, notice what will happen if we make a stimulus easy to perceive *without* a prior exposure. In this case, we will have externally produced a situation in which processing is fluent. By the logic of Figure 6.6, this may create an "illusion of familiarity."

In one study, participants were shown a rapidly presented series of seven words and then a test word. In half of the trials, the test word was identical to one of the just-presented seven words; in half of the trials, the test word was new. The task was to announce, in each trial, whether the test word was "old" (one of the previous seven) or "new" (Whittlesea, Jacoby & Girard, 1990).

This experiment also manipulated how easy the test word was to perceive. The test word in each trial, presented on a computer screen, was obscured

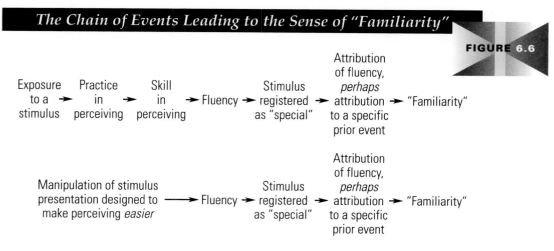

**The Chain of Events Leading to the Sense of "Familiarity"**

**FIGURE 6.6**

Practice in perceiving leads to fluency. Once the fluency is detected, the person may try to figure out what is *causing* this fluency. In many cases, the person is likely to attribute the fluency to some specific prior encounter and, if so, the stimulus will "feel familiar." The *bottom* line in the figure, however, indicates that fluency can be created in other ways: A stimulus may be fluently perceived because the stimulus is presented more clearly, or presented for a longer exposure. Once this fluency is detected, though, it can set off a series of steps identical to those in the top row. Hence, an "illusion of familiarity" can be created.

by a swarm of constantly moving dots, as though the word were viewed through a snow storm. In some trials, the swarm of dots was relatively dense, making the word difficult to perceive. In other trials, the test word was obscured by fewer dots and so was easier to perceive.

On some trials, therefore, the test word was easier to perceive because it was objectively familiar—presented just a moment ago, leading to an increase in perceptual fluency. (This is a chain of events similar to those shown in the top line of Figure 6.6.) We expect that participants will detect this increase in perceptual ease, and, as a consequence, they should regard the stimulus as familiar. In other trials, though, the test word was easier to perceive, not because it was familiar, but because it was, in fact, more clearly presented. (This is the situation shown in the second line of Figure 6.6.) Participants should again detect this increase in perceptual ease and, in this context, are likely to attribute the ease to familiarity. Thus, the more clearly presented stimuli should seem familiar, even when they are not.

Consistent with these claims, participants in this study were often fooled: Clarity of presentation created an illusion of familiarity. In a follow-up experiment, participants showed the reverse illusion: They were explicitly asked to judge whether a stimulus was clearly presented or not. The data show these judgments to be heavily influenced by familiarity: When a word was a repetition of an earlier-presented stimulus, it seemed clearer; when the word was novel, it seemed less clear.

In short, participants seem unable to distinguish perceptual ease created by familiarity from perceptual ease created by stimulus clarity. When asked to judge the former, they are inadvertently influenced by the latter; when asked to judge the latter, they are unwittingly influenced by the former. All of this is striking confirmation of the fluency notion and, in particular, of the claim that the feeling of familiarity derives in large measure from ease of processing. (For related results and some complications, see Goldinger, Kleider & Shelley, 1999; Johnston, Hawley & Elliott, 1991; Poldrack & Logan, 1997; Whittlesea & Leboe, 2000.)

## IMPLICIT MEMORIES ARE ACTIVITY-BASED

If this view of implicit memory is correct, then, in an important sense, this sort of memory is *activity-based*. In other words, an implicit memory isn't simply a record of a stimulus you have encountered, or an event you have experienced. Instead, the implicit memory preserves a record of what you *did* in response to the stimulus or in response to the event. More precisely, the implicit memory is nothing other than the residual *skill*, created by your prior activity. It is this skill, "practiced" during the initial exposure, that produces fluency on the subsequent exposures.

The nature of an implicit memory, therefore, will depend crucially on what you did, what activities you engaged in, during the initial learning. Thus, imagine that you look at the word "hot." This doesn't create a broad implicit memory of this word. Instead, what is created is an implicit memory of *perceiving* this stimulus. This memory, this newly created skill, will serve you well if, later on, you have occasion to perceive this same stimulus again. In that case, the fluency will pay off with greater ease in perceiving the second time around. But this skill won't help if, later on, you want to *think about* this same stimulus, or contemplate its meaning; that is a different sort of activity, requiring a different sort of skill.

Likewise, an experimenter tells you, "Think about the opposite of 'cold.'" You will obviously think about the word "hot," but again, this won't create a broad implicit memory for the word itself. Instead, it will create a memory of *thinking about* "hot," and this will lead to greater fluency the next time you think about this concept. You haven't, in this setup, practiced perceiving "hot," and so this exposure won't help you when next you try to perceive this word.

Confirmation of these claims can be seen in a study by Blaxton (1989; Roediger & Blaxton, 1987a, 1987b). In this study, two different implicit-memory tasks were used: word-fragment completion and a general knowledge test. As an example of the first task, participants might be asked, "What's the first word that comes to mind beginning with the letters 'COP'?" In this case, there is obviously a perceptual cue available, since the letters COP are there on the page for participants to look at. Therefore, if the participants are fluent in *perceiving* the word "copper," they will have an advantage in this task. They won't be helped in this task by fluency of other sorts, such as fluency in *thinking about* copper. That's not the fluency they need here.

In the general knowledge task, participants might be asked, "What metal makes up 10% of yellow gold?" For this task, there is no perceptual cue, and so fluency in *perceiving* the word "copper" should provide no advantage. Participants will be helped, though, if they've recently thought about the *meaning* of "copper." This experience would have promoted the sort of conceptual fluency that's relevant for this task.

Table 6.2 shows the data from this experiment, fully in line with this analysis. A recent experience of thinking about a word (in the "Generate" condition) produced *conceptual* fluency, and this was helpful for the general knowledge test, but not for word-fragment completion. A recent experience of perceiving a word (in the "No context" condition) produced *perceptual* fluency, and this was helpful for word-fragment completion but not for the general knowledge test. (For explanation of the "Generate," "Context," and "No context" conditions, see the discussion in this chapter of Figure 6.5.)

To put this bluntly, then, practice in perceiving creates fluency in perceiving, and this helps you when you perceive later on. Practice in thinking about meaning produces fluency in thinking about meaning. This will help you if, later on, meaning is what you need. In both cases, though, the message is the same: Implicit memories preserve a record of the activity you engaged in during your earlier encounter. The memory will be best revealed, therefore, if later on you "retrace your steps," performing again the same activity with the same input.

## THE SPECIFICITY OF IMPLICIT MEMORIES

This view also implies that implicit memories will be quite specific: As we said earlier, practice in perceiving Gladys will help you to recognize Gladys later on; it won't help you to recognize Lola. For that matter, practice in perceiving Gladys from the side will increase your skill in recognizing her from that angle; this may not help if, later on, you need to recognize her from another perspective.

Consistent with these ideas, implicit memories are indeed specific. For example, considerable priming is observed if participants are asked to complete word-fragments (What is this word: "_L_P_A_T"?) and are subsequently retested with the *same fragments*. However, virtually no priming is observed if participants initially see one fragment ("_L_P_A_T") and are then tested with a *different* fragment of the *same word* ("E_E_H_N_"). Why is this? The initial exposure provided skill in working with a particular fragment. To reveal that skill, therefore, we need to present again the same fragment.

| Summary of Blaxton's Results: Percentage of Words Correctly Identified on Test | | | |
|---|---|---|---|
| | **Study condition** | | |
| **Type of test** | **Generate** | **Context** | **No context** |
| General knowledge | 50 | 38 | 33 |
| Word-fragment completion | 46 | 62 | 75 |

TABLE 6.2

[After Blaxton, 1989.]

In the same fashion, consider the priming effect observed in lexical-decision tasks. In the standard version of this procedure, participants first see a list of words, and then they see the (visually presented) lexical-decision test items. In an alternate version of this procedure, participants first *hear* a tape-recorded list of words, and then *see* the test items. This shift in modality tremendously reduces the priming effect. Apparently, therefore, perceptual practice with an *auditory* presentation of a word doesn't help you if you later need perceptual skill with a *visual* presentation of the same word (Jacoby & Witherspoon, 1982; Kirsner, Milech & Standen, 1983; Roediger & Blaxton, 1987a).

Other implicit memory tasks involve different sorts of fluency and different forms of specificity. For example, we have discussed the "illusion of truth," in which prior exposure to a sentence increases subsequent ratings of how credible that sentence is. In the "illusion of truth" procedures, the stimuli are clearly presented and in view for a long time. In this situation, perceiving the stimuli should be extremely easy, so there's little use here for perceptual skill. As a consequence, there should be little benefit in this task from any increase in perceptual fluency. If, therefore, we interpret the "illusion of truth" in terms of fluency, it's probably not *perceptual* fluency that's critical. Instead, the key must be *conceptual* fluency—fluency in thinking about an idea's meaning or an idea's implications.

This implies that we *shouldn't*, in this situation, observe stimulus specificity. That form of specificity is crucial for the skill of perceiving, but that skill isn't useful in this task. Consistent with this idea, the "illusion of truth" effect is still observed even if the sentences are *heard* the first time around and then *seen* in the actual test (Begg, Anas & Farinacci, 1992). This effect is therefore largely independent of stimulus format. (For related data, see Brown, Neblett, Jones & Mitchell, 1991; Craik, Moscovitch & McDown, 1994; Srinivas, 1993; Weldon, 1993.)

It seems, then, that implicit memory effects sometimes *are* dependent on stimulus format and sometimes *are not*. Both of these findings, though, fit into the theoretical picture we are presenting: Implicit memory involves processing fluency, and fluency effects are quite specific. But the nature of the specificity depends on the type of fluency we're considering: Fluency in perceiving is fluency in dealing with a particular stimulus, and therefore the fluency is specific to that stimulus. Therefore, if a procedure depends on perceptual fluency, then the format of the stimulus will matter. More specifically, if the stimulus format is changed, then the implicit memory effects may be lost. In contrast, fluency in thinking about meaning is not dependent on the format of the stimulus, and so, if this is the fluency needed for a particular task, the results will be unchanged if the stimulus format is altered. (For further discussion of these points, see Jacoby, Levy & Steinbach, 1992; Weldon, 1993.)

## THE RELATION BETWEEN IMPLICIT AND EXPLICIT MEMORY

Overall, then, we seem well served by the idea that implicit memory is like a *skill*. This idea, and with it the (closely related) idea that implicit memory consists of an increase in processing fluency, has allowed us to make sense of a wide range of data. Nevertheless, this is a controversial domain, and many loose ends remain.

Part of the controversy hinges on how we should *define* explicit and implicit memory. For some researchers, the key distinction lies in the experience of remembering—whether one does or does not have the conscious conviction of remembering the past. This conviction is presumably absent in implicit memory, present in explicit (e.g., Graf & Komatsu, 1994). Others argue that the key difference between implicit and explicit remembering lies in whether one is *trying* to remember or not. Hence implicit memories represent "automatic" uses of memory, independent of intention; explicit memories represent "deliberate, intentional" memory retrieval (e.g., Graf & Schacter, 1985; Jacoby, 1991; Richardson-Klavehn, Lee, Joubran & Bjork, 1994).

Still other authors have suggested that we need to distinguish between **declarative memories** and **pro-**

**cedural memories**, rather than between explicit and implicit. Declarative memories are memories that a particular event took place; these are memories that, in most cases, can be described in terms of specific propositions. Procedural memories, in contrast, are memories for *how* to do something. Moreover, this claim continues, each of these classes has its own profile, its own set of characteristics. For instance, each of these classes is separately represented in the brain, so that some forms of brain damage will disrupt the declarative system but not the procedural, whereas other forms of brain damage will do the opposite. (We will return to these claims about brain damage in a moment. For discussion and extensions of this proposal, see Cooper & Schacter, 1992; Schacter, 1992; Tulving, Hayman & MacDonald, 1991.)

A related debate arises directly from the available data: In defining implicit memory, it would be helpful if we could say "implicit memory is a sort of memory having this characteristic and that characteristic, and these characteristics distinguish implicit memory from explicit memory." Unfortunately, though, the data are not so clear, because implicit memory seems to have somewhat different characteristics in different settings. For example, implicit memory in some studies seems to be established through mere exposure to a stimulus; attention to meaning (as in "deep" vs. "shallow" processing; see Chapter 5) has no effect. (For one example of this pattern, see the discussion of Figure 6.5.) In other studies, though, the depth of processing does matter, with larger implicit-memory effects observed after deep processing (e.g., Brown et al., 1994; Challis & Brodbeck, 1992; Hamann, 1990; Nelson, Schreiber & Holley, 1993; Srinivas & Roediger, 1990; Thapar & Greene, 1994).

In light of these data, several authors have suggested that we may need to make distinctions *within* the category of implicit memory. This is consistent with the approach we've taken in this chapter; we have several times distinguished between *perceptual* and *conceptual* implicit memories. (This distinction seemed useful, for example, in explaining why implicit memory is sometimes influenced by perceptual form, and sometimes not.) Many investigators

have offered versions of this perceptual-conceptual distinction (e.g., McDermott & Roediger, 1994; Mulligan, 1998; Roediger & Blaxton, 1987b; Reinitz & Demb, 1994; Schmitter-Edgecombe, 1999; Srinivas & Roediger, 1990), and the value of this distinction remains a point of active discussion.

## PROCESS PURITY

The debate over implicit memory has also raised another important point: In the laboratory, we rely on certain tasks to reveal the traits of implicit and explicit memory. Word-stem completion, for example, relies on implicit memory, and so by studying this task, we can learn about this sort of memory. Recall relies on explicit memory; by studying recall, then, we learn about this type of memory.

But how well founded are these claims? Imagine a participant trying to solve the word-stem "S T U ___". We intend this as an implicit memory task, but if this participant has an *explicit* memory of recently seeing the word "stupor," then she might offer this word as a response, rather than "stupid" or "stuck" or "stuff." In this case, an "implicit memory task" would be influenced by explicit memory.

The reverse is also possible: A participant might have enormous processing fluency in thinking about the word "warehouse," thanks to a specific prior exposure. This fluency might then influence the participant when he is taking a recall test. In this case, an "explicit memory task" would be influenced by implicit memory.

To put this more formally, it seems that our laboratory tasks may not be ***process pure***. Instead, more than one process may be contributing to performance in each task, and this clouds the interpretation of data from that task. For example, consider the fact that attention to meaning (deep processing) sometimes improves performance in word-stem completion, a task usually thought of as relying on implicit memory. Does this result tell us that deep processing contributes to implicit memory? It would if our tasks were process-pure (as in the top half of Figure 6.7). In that case, the traits visible in word-

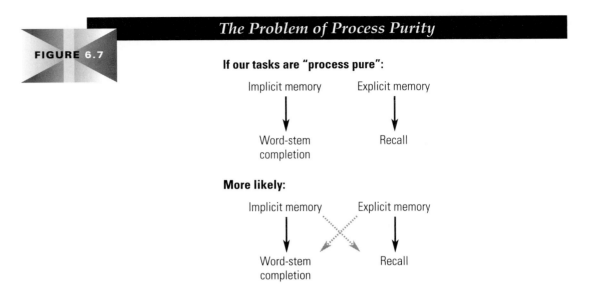

**FIGURE 6.7**

## The Problem of Process Purity

**If our tasks are "process pure":**

Implicit memory     Explicit memory

↓                   ↓

Word-stem           Recall
completion

**More likely:**

Implicit memory     Explicit memory

↓                   ↓

Word-stem           Recall
completion

If recall were influenced only by explicit memory, then any characteristics associated with recall could be attributed to the way that explicit memory operated, and likewise for word-stem completion and implicit memory. This situation, shown in the top panel, would be one in which our tasks are "process pure." More likely, though, is the situation shown in the bottom panel, with "process impure" tasks. In this case, recall is influenced both by explicit and implicit memory, and so there is no way to conclude whether characteristics associated with recall reflect the operation of explicit or implicit memory; the same is true for an implicit memory task like word-stem completion.

of the traits of implicit memory. According to this view, if deep processing matters for this task, then deep processing matters for implicit memory.

But, of course, there is another possibility, one that is much more plausible. Our tasks are likely *not* to be process pure (as in the bottom half of Figure 6.7). In this case, the traits visible in word-stem completion *might* reflect the traits of implicit memory (which certainly contributes to this task), but might also reflect the traits of explicit memory (which may, in some settings, also contribute to this task). According to this view, we cannot draw claims about *memory* by studying *tasks*, because we can't be sure about which memory is shaping the task.

This concern about process *im*purity seems undeniable—there simply is no reason to assume that our tasks are process pure. But what should we do about this? This, too, has been a topic of some debate. Larry Jacoby and his colleagues were the investigators who drew the field's attention to this concern about process purity, and they have proposed a particular way to analyze the data in order to derive process-pure measurements from process-*im*pure tasks (e.g., Jacoby, 1991; Jacoby & Kelley, 1992). Others have expressed reservations about this form of data analysis, in some cases arguing that the analysis works only under certain circumstances, and in other cases arguing for an altogether different mode of data analysis (see, e.g., Brainerd, Reyna & Mojardin, 1999; Curran & Hintzman, 1995; Graf & Komatsu, 1994; Hirshman, 1998; Jacoby, 1998; Joordens & Merikle, 1993; Richardson-Klavehn & Gardiner, 1998).

It is too soon to tell how this debate will be resolved. The concern about process purity must be taken seriously, and our standard measures of task performance are almost certainly *not* process pure. How (or whether) we can obtain process-pure measures is far less clear, and until this point is resolved, it may be difficult to gain a fully clear picture of what implicit memory is and how it operates.

## Amnesia

We have been caught up in controversy in the last few sections, so it may be helpful to take a step back, to emphasize what is uncontroversial. At the very least, it is clear that we are often influenced by the past without our being aware of that influence. We often respond differently to familiar stimuli, even if we have no subjective feeling of familiarity. Thus, our conscious recollection seriously underestimates what is in our memories. Moreover, it is clear that some attribution step plays a crucial role in determining *how* we are influenced by our own implicit memories, with that attribution step often going astray. And, above all, it seems certain that we have only begun to document the many unconscious influences of memory on what we do, what we say, and what we think.

In addition, it seems clear that there are at least two different kinds of memory—one typically conscious, deliberate, and concerned with conceptual knowledge; one typically unconscious, automatic, and concerned with procedures. As we have seen, there is disagreement about how exactly we should *define* these two types of memory, but there is no disagreement about the need for some distinction, some categorization scheme.

In fact, two further lines of evidence also speak to the need to distinguish these categories of memory. One, which we'll simply mention, involves the at-

tempt to "chart" memory performance across the life span. Many studies are pertinent to this point but, in general, the pattern is that *implicit* memory can be documented at all ages, from very early childhood to very old age. Indeed, what is remarkable is the *similarity* in implicit memory performance by people at very different ages. Performance on explicit memory tasks, on the other hand, is strongly age-dependent, with children and the aged both out-performed by those in their middle years (e.g., Graf & Masson, 1993; Newcombe, et al., 2000). These two different patterns add to the evidence that a distinction is needed here, with the memory systems distinguishable *developmentally* as well as *functionally*.

The distinction is also demanded by clinical evidence, in particular, evidence from cases of brain damage.

### ANTEROGRADE AMNESIA

A variety of injuries or illnesses can lead to a loss of memory, or **amnesia**. Some forms of amnesia are **retrograde**, meaning that they disrupt memory for things learned prior to the event that initiated the amnesia. Retrograde amnesia is often caused, for example, by blows to the head; often one is unable to recall events occurring just prior to the blow. Other forms of amnesia have the reverse effect, causing disruption of memory for experiences *after* the onset of amnesia; these are cases of **anterograde amnesia**. (We should note that many cases of amnesia have both retrograde and anterograde memory loss.) Here we will focus on anterograde amnesia; as we will see, this form of memory loss can tell us a great deal about the issues we have been discussing. (For more on retrograde amnesia, see Conway & Fthenaki, 1999; Kapur, 1999.)

We discussed a famous case of anterograde amnesia in Chapter 1—the patient H.M. (For a review of H.M.'s case, see Milner, 1966, 1970.) H.M. suffered from profound epilepsy, and a variety of attempts at curing him had all failed. As a last resort, doctors sought to contain H.M.'s disease by brain surgery, specifically by removing portions of the brain that seemed to be the source of the seizures. The surgery did improve the epilepsy but at an incredible cost: H.M. seems unable to learn anything new. He can function normally in some regards and can, for example, hold a coherent and consistent conversation. Within the conversation, H.M. may even talk about prior events in his life, since he seems fully able to recall events that took place prior to the surgery. However, he can't recall anything that has taken place subsequent to his surgery. The severity of the problem is visible in many ways, but the problem becomes instantly clear if a conversation with H.M. is interrupted for some reason: If you leave the room, for example, and come back three or four minutes later, H.M. seems to have totally forgotten the conversation. Thus, thoughts currently in mind can be kept there by H.M.; thoughts out of mind seem lost forever.

H.M.'s specific case is unique, but a similar amnesia can be found in patients who have been longtime alcoholics. The problem is not the alcohol itself; the problem instead is that alcoholics tend to have inadequate diets, getting most of their nutrition from whatever they are drinking. As it turns out, though, most alcoholic beverages are missing several key nutrients, including vitamin B1 (thiamine). As a result, longtime alcoholics are vulnerable to a number of problems caused by thiamine deficiency, including **Korsakoff's syndrome** (Rao, Larkin & Derr, 1986; Ritchie, 1985).

A Korsakoff's patient seems in many ways similar to H.M. There is no problem in remembering events that took place before the alcoholism's onset. Current topics can be maintained in mind as long as there is no interruption. New information, though, if displaced from mind, is seemingly lost forever. Korsakoff's patients who have been in the hospital for decades will casually mention that they arrived only a week ago; if asked the name of the current president or events in the news they unhesitatingly give answers appropriate for two or three decades back, whenever the disease began (Marslen-Wilson & Teuber, 1975; Seltzer & Benson, 1974).

## LEARNING FROM AMNESIA

These cases of amnesia can teach us a great deal about memory. For example, the study of amnesia can illuminate questions about the *biological basis* for memory. H.M. and Korsakoff's amnesics typically have brain damage that involves the hippocampus and its neighboring brain areas, clearly implying that these brain sites play a crucial role in memory. Let us be clear, though, that evidence does *not* imply that the hippocampus is the "seat" of memory in the brain. As one concern, notice that damage to the hippocampus does not disrupt already-established memories. (Remember that hippocampus damage is associated with anterograde amnesia, not retrograde.) Apparently, then, the hippocampus plays its main role in memory *acquisition*, not memory storage or retrieval. (For recent discussion of the hippocampus's role, and also the role played by other brain sites, see Aggleton & Shaw, 1996; Baddeley, 1999; Nadel & Jacobs, 1998; Reed & Squire, 1997; Squire & Zola-Morgan, 1991.)

The study of amnesia can also provide important lessons about the *function* of memory in our daily lives. As one perhaps surprising example, a researcher in one study sat with an amnesic patient as he ate a full lunch (Rozin et al., 1998). When the patient had finished the meal, they conversed for a few minutes, and then an attendant brought another full tray. "Oh, look! Your lunch is here." The amnesic had no recollection of the first lunch, and so unhesitatingly ate the second. This reveals both the completeness of the amnesia *and*, it seems, an important role for memory in determining how we regulate our own calorie intake. One might think we stop eating when we sense that our stomachs are full. This study, however, suggests a different mechanism: We stop eating in many situations simply because we remember the fact that we have just eaten!

As a different example, consider again the patient H.M. We mentioned that H.M. can function normally in some arenas: he can, for example, hold a reasonable conversation. But he is also limited in profound ways. To take just one case, if H.M. notices that his conversational partner is smiling, he often does not know *why*. Was there a funny joke in the conversation a moment ago? Or did someone say something embarrassing? Or is it a smile of sympathy, because someone said something sad? Because of this sort of ambiguity, H.M. lives with a constant sense of awkwardness: "Right now, I'm wondering, have I done or said anything amiss? You see, at this moment everything looks clear to me, but what happened just before? That's what worries me" (Hilts, 1995, pg. 138). Here, too, in everyday social interaction, memory plays a crucial role. (For further discussion of memory's role in our lives, see Chapters 1 and 7.)

Finally, the study of amnesia can also help us with a number of theoretical questions—including the question that was before us a few pages back: the contrast between implicit and explicit memory.

## ANOTHER LOOK AT AMNESIA: WHAT KIND OF MEMORY IS DISRUPTED?

For many years, cases of anterograde amnesia were taken as striking confirmation of the memory model we first met in Chapter 5. In those terms, the amnesics seem to have intact long-term memories; that is why they remember events from before the amnesia's start. They also seem to have intact working memories; that is how they remember events as they think about them. What seemed to be wrong, though, was that the path from working memory into long-term memory was disrupted, so no new information could enter permanent storage. Hence, if something was displaced from working memory, it vanished without a trace.

More recent findings, however, have led to significant refinements in this account of amnesia. As it turns out, though, some of the relevant evidence has been available for a long time: In 1911, Edouard Claparède (1911/1951) reported the following incident: He was introduced to a young woman suffering from Korsakoff's amnesia, and he reached out to shake the patient's hand. However, Claparède had secretly positioned a pin in his own hand so that, when they clasped hands, the patient received a

painful pin prick. (Respect for patient's rights would prevent any modern physician from doing this experiment, but ethical standards for physicians were rather different in 1911.) The next day, Claparède returned and reached to shake hands with the patient. Not surprisingly for a Korsakoff's amnesic, the patient initially gave no indication that she recognized Claparède or remembered anything about the prior encounter. Nevertheless, when the time came to clasp hands, the patient at the last moment abruptly withdrew her hand and would not shake hands with Claparède. Claparède asked her why this was and, after some confusion, the patient simply said vaguely that "sometimes pins are hidden in people's hands."

This patient seems to have no *explicit* memory of the prior encounter with Claparède. She does not mention the encounter in explaining her refusal to shake hands; if questioned closely about the prior encounter, she indicates no knowledge of it. Nonetheless, some sort of memory is retained. The patient knows something about the previous day's mishap but cannot report on the knowledge.

This peculiar kind of remembering can be demonstrated with Korsakoff's patients in many other ways. In one experiment, Korsakoff's patients were asked a series of trivia questions (Schacter, Tulving & Wang, 1981). For each question, possible answers were offered in a multiple-choice format, and the patient had to choose which was the right answer. If the patient did not know the answer, he or she was told it, and then (unbeknownst to the patient) the question was replaced in the stack. Sometime later, therefore, as the game continued, the question came up again, and this time the patient was quite likely to get it right. Apparently, the patient had "learned" the answer in the previous encounter and "remembered" the relevant information. Consistent with their diagnosis, though, the patients had no recollection of the learning—they were consistently unable to explain why their answers were correct. They did not say, "I know this bit of trivia because the same question came up just five minutes ago." Instead, they were likely to say things like "I read about it somewhere," or "My sister once told me about it."

A different experiment makes a similar point: In a procedure by Johnson, Kim and Risse (1985), Korsakoff's amnesics heard a series of brief melodies. Some time later, they were presented with a new series and told that some of the tunes in the second batch were repeats from the earlier presentation. The amnesics' assignment was to tell which were the repeats, and which they were hearing for the first time. As expected, the amnesics did poorly on this task; indeed, their memory responses were close to random. This is, of course, consistent with their clinical diagnosis. Remarkably, though, when asked which melodies they *preferred*, the amnesics uniformly preferred the familiar ones. The patients had no (explicit) memory for these tunes, but a memory did emerge with indirect testing—emerged, in this case, as a preference.

A great many results show this pattern, with amnesics showing profound memory loss on some measures but looking perfectly normal on other measures (Cohen & Squire, 1980; Graf & Schacter, 1985; Moscovitch, 1982; Schacter, 1996, Schacter & Tulving, 1982; Squire & McKee, 1993). Thus, on the one side, these patients seem completely incapable of recalling episodes or events. In the terms we have been using, these patients seem to have no *explicit* memory. At the same time, though, these patients do learn and do remember; they seem to have intact *implicit* memories. Indeed, in most tests of implicit memory, amnesic patients seem indistinguishable from ordinary individuals.

These results obviously add to the package of evidence we have been considering in the last several sections. As we've seen, many experiments indicate that explicit and implicit memory can be distinguished on *functional* grounds, with these two types of memory apparently created by different sorts of learning, and evoked by different sorts of test. The amnesia data indicate that these two types of memory can also be distinguished on *neurological* grounds—with specific forms of brain damage disrupting some sorts of memory but sparing others.

More broadly, the amnesia data also draw us back to the issues with which this chapter began. It is obvious that people with amnesia suffer from a terrible disruption in their lives; in crucial ways, their memories are horribly impaired. But, at the same time, it would be a mistake to claim that, across the board, amnesics have "no memory." Instead, their memories seem normal *on certain sorts of tests*. Likewise, it would be wrong to claim that, in general, amnesics are "bad learners." They can learn perfectly well, provided that the learning is set up to capitalize on their (intact) implicit memories, rather than relying on their (damaged) explicit memories.

All of this echoes themes that should by now be familiar: We cannot speak of learning and memory only in global terms; we cannot offer blanket claims about "good strategies" for learning, or "bad" ones, or sweeping generalizations about people who are "good" in memory or "weak." Instead, we need to cast our claims more specifically: A study technique that is perfectly fine, for example, as preparation for one sort of memory retrieval may be worthless as preparation for a different sort of retrieval. Someone who is quite weak in one sort of remembering may be quite strong in a different sort. These finer-grained claims are needed because, as we have seen over and over, learning and memory must be understood with reference to how that memory is later going to be retrieved and used. The study of memory acquisition cannot be separated from considerations of memory retrieval.

## Chapter Summary

1. In general, the chances of someone remembering an earlier event are greatest if the physical, mental, and emotional circumstances in place during memory retrieval match those in place during learning. This is reflected in the phenomenon of *state-dependent learning*, in which one is most likely to remember material learned while underwater if tested underwater, most likely to remember material learned while listening to music if again listening to music during the test, and so on.

2. In the same vein, if one focused on the meaning of some material while learning it, then hints concerned with meaning will be especially helpful

when the time comes to recall the material. If one focused on the sound of the material during learning, then hints concerned with sound will be most helpful at the time of recall.

3. A similar pattern is reflected in the phenomenon of *encoding specificity*. This term refers to the idea that one usually learns more than the specific to-be-remembered material itself; one also learns that material within its associated context. As a result, remembering is most likely if that context is recreated at the time of recall.

4. All these results arise from the fact that learning establishes connections among memories, and these connections serve as retrieval paths. Like any path, these lead from some starting point to some target. To use the path, therefore, one must return to the appropriate starting point. In the same way, if there is a connection between two memories, then activating the first memory is likely to call the second to mind. However, if the first memory is not activated, this connection, no matter how well established, will not help in locating the second memory, just as a large highway approaching St. Louis from the south will not be helpful if you are trying to reach St. Louis from the north.

5. In the same way, some learning strategies are effective as preparation for some sorts of memory test, but ineffective for other sorts of test. Some strategies, for example, are effective at establishing *source memory*, rather than *familiarity*; other strategies do the reverse. Source memory is essential for *recall; recognition* can often be achieved either through source memory or through familiarity.

6. Different forms of learning also play a role in producing *implicit* and *explicit memories*. Implicit memories are those that influence us even when we have no awareness that we are being influenced by a specific previous event. In many cases, implicit memory effects take the form of *priming*—e.g., in tachistoscopic recognition or word-stem completion. But implicit memories can also influence us in other ways, producing a number of memory-based illusions.

7. Implicit memory may be the consequence of *processing fluency*, produced by experience in a particular task with a particular stimulus. The fluency is sometimes detected and registered as a sense of "specialness" attached to a stimulus. Often, this specialness is then attributed to some cause, but this attribution can be inaccurate. Because the fluency is created by a particular task and stimulus, the fluency will have its effects only when the same task and stimulus are re-encountered.

8. Investigators disagree about the specifics of how implicit memory should be described, and this is in part a reflection of a mixed data pattern, with implicit memory showing slightly different characteristics in different experiments. However, this data pattern may reflect only the fact that our measures of implicit memory are not *process pure*.

9. Implicit memory is also important in understanding the pattern of symptoms in *anterograde amnesia*. Amnesic patients perform badly on tests requiring explicit memory and may not even recall events that happened just minutes earlier. However, they often perform at near-normal levels on tests involving implicit memory. This underscores the fact that we cannot speak in general about good and bad memories, good and poor learning. Instead, learning and memory must be matched to a particular task, and a particular form of test; learning and memory that are excellent for some tasks may be poor for others.

# Memory Errors, Memory Gaps

Where did you spend last summer? Have you ever been in a canoe? Where were you five minutes ago? These are, of course, extremely easy questions. The sought-after information is in your memory, and you effortlessly retrieve the information the moment you need it. And the same is true for countless other bits of information; these too are at your fingertips, swiftly and easily recalled whenever you wish.

Simple facts like these testify to the breadth, efficiency, and general success of human memory. Each of us carries a huge quantity of information in memory, and we can generally retrieve this information with ease. But we must also acknowledge the circumstances in which remembering is *less* successful. Sometimes, you try to remember an episode and you simply "draw a blank." Or you recall something, but with no conviction that you're correct: "I *think* her nickname was Dink, but I'm not sure."

Memory can also fail us in another way: Sometimes you recall a past episode, but then it turns out that your memory is *mistaken*. Perhaps details of the event were different from the way you recall them. Or perhaps your memory is altogether wrong, misrepresenting large elements of the original episode. In some cases, you even remember entire events that never happened at all!

In this chapter, we will consider all these examples of memory failure. We will consider how memory errors occur, and how often they occur. We will also discuss whether memory errors can be detected once they occur. Finally, we will also discuss some of the advantages associated with memory errors, and, with that, why a memory without these errors, and without any forgetting, might be worse than the (sometimes flawed) memories that we actually have. Let us start, though, with some examples.

## Memory Errors: Some Initial Examples

In 1992, an El Al cargo plane lost power in two of its engines just after taking off from Amsterdam's Schiphol Airport. The pilot attempted to return the plane to the airport but could not make it; a few minutes later, the plane crashed into an 11-story apartment building. The building collapsed and broke into flames; 43 people were killed, including the plane's entire crew.

Ten months later, researchers questioned 193 people about the crash, asking them in particular, "Did you see the television film of the moment the plane hit the apartment building?" More than half of the participants (107 of them) reported seeing the film, *even though there was no such film*. No camera had recorded the crash; no film (nor any re-enactment) was shown on television. The participants were remembering something that never took place (Crombag, Wagenaar & van Koppen, 1996).

In a follow-up study, the investigators surveyed another 93 people about the crash. These people were also asked whether they had seen the (nonexistent) TV film, and then they were asked some more detailed questions about what they had seen in the film: Was the plane burning when it crashed, or did it catch fire a moment later? Did it come down vertically, with no forward speed, or horizontally, moving at considerable speed?

Two-thirds of these participants remembered seeing the film, and most of them confidently answered questions about what they had seen. When asked about the plane's direction and speed of movement, for example, only 23% prudently said that they couldn't remember. The others gave various responses, based on their "memory" of the film; as it turns out, only 11% gave the correct answer.

This is not a case of one or two people making a mistake; a large majority of the people questioned seemed to have a detailed recollection of the nonexistent film. Also, let's emphasize that the El Al crash was an emotional, important, and much-discussed event for these Dutch participants; the researchers were not asking them to recall a minor occurrence.

Perhaps these errors emerged simply because the research participants were trying to remember something that had taken place almost a year earlier. Is memory more accurate with shorter retention intervals? In a study by Brewer and Treyens (1981), the participants were asked to wait briefly in the experimenter's office, prior to the procedure's start. After 35 seconds, participants were taken out of this office and told that there actually was no experimental procedure. Instead, the study was concerned with their memory for the room in which they had just been sitting.

The participants' recollection of the office was plainly influenced by their prior knowledge—in this case, their knowledge about what an academic office typically contains. For example, participants surely knew, in advance of the study, that academic offices usually contain a desk and a chair, and as it turns out, these pieces of furniture were present in this particular office. This agreement between prior knowledge and the specific experience led to accurate memory, and 29 of 30 participants correctly remembered that the office contained a desk and chair. For other aspects of the office, participants probably had no expectations one way or the other, and these aspects were much less well remembered. For example, only 8 of 30 participants remembered the bulletin board. Crucially, though, still other aspects of the office were quite different from what the participants might have expected. For example, participants would surely expect an academic office to contain shelves filled with books, yet in this particular office no books were in view. (Figure 7.1). Nonetheless, the participants' recall was in line with their expectations, and not with reality: Almost one-third of them (9 of 30) remembered seeing books in the office when, in fact, there were none.

## The Potential Sources of Memory Error

How could this be? How could so many Dutch participants be wrong in their recall of a significant emotional episode? How could intelligent, alert college students fail to notice that an office's book-

## The Office Used in the Brewer and Treyens Study

**FIGURE 7.1**

No books were in view in this office, but participants, biased by their expectations for what *should be* in a scholar's office, often remembered seeing books! [After Brewer & Treyens, 1981.]

shelves contained no books? How could they fail to remember what they had seen in an office just moments earlier? The explanation for these errors has several parts, and in this section, we will consider some of the potential sources of memory errors.

### INATTENTION

Let's begin with some points we first met in Chapter 4. Think back to our discussion of *change blindness*. There we saw that someone's perception of the world is actually filled with gaps—large objects go completely unnoticed, and prominent stimuli are not even registered. People have the *illusion* that their perception is complete and detailed, but this is indeed an illusion. We can show this by probing their perception—for example, by changing some element in the scene or removing some object, and seeing if people spot the change. This is, of course, the logic of the change blindness studies, and as we saw in Chapter 4, these large-scale changes often go entirely undetected.

It's remarkable, of course, that these gaps in perception generally do go unnoticed, so that we can maintain the illusion that our perception of the world is complete and detailed. But the explanation of this is straightforward. As we saw in Chapter 4, perceiving requires resources. When we pay attention to an input, therefore, we are spending the resources needed to perceive. When we *don't* pay attention to something, we're not spending those resources, and so our perception of that input is not developed. This is how the gaps occur—the gaps represent an absence of perception caused by an absence of attention (that is, an absence of resources).

Notice, then, that the gaps are always associated with stimuli we're *not* attending, because it is our inattention that *causes* the gaps. Cast in these terms, it's unsurprising that we don't notice the gaps: They are always located at sites we're not paying attention to.

Of course, if our initial perception of the world contains gaps, it seems inevitable that our memories will contain similar gaps. But we usually don't leave things in that state; instead, we do our best to *fill* these gaps as best we can. How does this happen? We draw on our prior knowledge about what is likely to have been in the situation, and what is typical for that sort of event. This process is known as **memory recon-struction**; we try to *reconstruct* what the past must have been based on the bits that we do remember and on our broader pattern of knowledge. Thus, for example, if you don't remember how you spent last Tuesday, you might nonetheless be able to reconstruct the day's activities based on your schematic knowledge about how, in general, your Tuesdays proceed. Likewise, if you didn't notice the office bookshelves, you might still infer that the shelves were filled with books, because usually they are. This is the likely source of the error in the Brewer and Treyens study.

It's important, though, that the Brewer and Treyens participants didn't "feel like" they were inferring the books. Instead, they vividly *recalled* seeing books. We will return to this peculiar fact later in the chapter, when we consider the possibility of detecting false memories when they occur. In the meantime, though, let's simply note that we have seen this pattern before: When we discussed proofreading in Chapter 3, we argued that people often cannot tell the difference between "letters seen" and "letters inferred." The same pattern, it seems, emerges with remembering: Here, too, it is difficult to distinguish "items recalled" from "items inferred," items genuinely remembered and items simply assumed.

## REMEMBERING WHAT WAS SAID VS. REMEMBERING GIST

The role of attention in governing what we remember is also evident in our memory for conversations we have participated in, or stories we have read. Generally, our attention during a conversation is on the *meanings* that are being expressed; we have little reason to care how the meaning was "packaged"— whether, for example, the speaker used an active sentence to express the idea or a passive one, whether she said, "The city is just north of the lake," or "The lake is just south of the city."

If we have no reason to attend to a sentence's exact phrasing, then we probably will not remember the phrasing—even if we are tested just minutes after hearing the sentence. This prediction has been confirmed in numerous studies. In these studies, participants hear a series of sentences, and then read three types of test sentences: Some of the test sentences are exact duplicates of the sentences presented earlier; some of the test sentences are legitimate paraphrases of the original sentences; and some of the test sentences differ in meaning from the original sentences. The pattern of results is then quite reliable: Participants reject the changed-meaning sentences, immediately realizing these are not the sentences heard earlier. But they are unable to distinguish between the exact repeats and the legitimate paraphrases. They remember the gist of what they heard, but do not remember how that gist was expressed. (For examples of this broad pattern, see Begg & Wickelgren, 1974; Bransford, Barclay & Franks, 1972; Bransford & Franks, 1971; Brewer, 1977; Paris & Lindauer, 1976; Sachs, 1967; Sulin & Dooling, 1974; Thorndyke, 1976.)

Occasionally, though, we *do* have reason to pay attention to a sentence's exact phrasing. For example, participants in one study were asked to read a series of sentences, some of which had complicated syntax, and some of which were simple. Participants had to pay close attention in order to understand the complicated sentences; as a result, they were able to remember these sentences in detail later on, including their word-by-word phrasing. In contrast, they couldn't remember the phrasing of the simple sentences; for these, they remembered only the gist (McDaniel, 1981).

In another study, the investigators began by tape-recording a discussion by a group of psychologists. (The psychologists knew they were being tape-recorded but did not know why.) A day later, the psychologists were given a recognition test for sentences uttered during this discussion; their task was to choose between sentences actually spoken and close paraphrases of these sentences (Keenan, MacWhinney & Mayhew, 1977).

All of the sentences from the discussion had been categorized in terms of their "interactional content"—i.e., whether the sentence had been phrased in a way that was itself important for the conversation. A "high interactional content" sentence is one in which the exact phrasing conveys information about the speaker's intentions or his or her relations to the listener. Such a sentence might be particularly rude, for example, or witty or elegant.

With the "low interactional content" sentences, participants could not distinguish sentences actually spoken from paraphrases—that is, they remembered only the gist, not how the sentence was worded. With the high interactional content sentences, participants did remember the exact phrasing, and they rejected the paraphrases as unfamiliar. Thus, they remembered the exact phrasing when the phrasing caught their attention, when the sentence was said in a noteworthy fashion.

Let us be clear, though, that the last two studies cited serve only to identify *exceptions* to a much broader pattern. That pattern, simply put, is that people generally do quite poorly in remembering the exact phrasing, the exact formulation, of sentences they have heard, even if they were the ones who spoke those sentences. This is, of course, consistent with the theme we are developing: We barely attend to many aspects of our world, and we do not remember what we do not attend.

## UNDERSTANDING HELPS AND HURTS MEMORY

So far, we have described memory errors that grow out of inattention—inattention to an office's bookshelves, or to a sentence's wording. But memory errors can also occur when we are paying close attention to the input. In one study, half the participants heard the following sentences:

"John was trying to fix the birdhouse. He was pounding the nail when his father came out to watch him and to help him do the work." Other participants heard these sentences: "John was trying to fix the birdhouse. He was looking for the nail when his father came out to watch him and to help him do the work." Some time later, participants were asked whether the following was among the sentences they had heard: "John was using the hammer to fix the birdhouse when his father came out to watch him and to help him do the work."

If the participants were in the first group ("pounding the nail"), they were likely to say (incorrectly, but often confidently) that they had heard this sentence earlier. If they were in the second group ("looking for the nail"), they were less likely to recall having heard the test sentence (Johnson, Bransford & Solomon, 1973). What is going on here? In the "pounding" case, the initial sentences had invited the participants to assume a hammer was part of the scene; after all, John had to be using something to "pound the nail." This (implied) hammer seems then to have become part of the remembered material. (See also Bower, Black & Turner, 1979.)

This is, in fact, a very common pattern. In Chapter 5, we argued that the process of *understanding* something—whether it's a sentence, or a story, or an event in your life—involves the discovery of links between this new experience and things you already know. You'll understand Peter's reaction yesterday only if you see the connection between his reaction and how he has behaved on other occasions. You'll understand Moe's laughter only if you see the connection between this and your more general knowledge about what it is that makes people laugh.

These various links are crucial for understanding, and they're no less important for memory: In Chapter 5, we argued that these links provide you with *retrieval paths*, so that later on you can use these connections to locate the new material in long-term storage. But, in addition, these same memory connections can be a source of memory error. When you interweave the new information with your prior knowledge, you create the potential for confusion, because you can easily lose track of which elements are which—that is, which of these linked elements were actually contained within the episode you are trying to recall, and which elements were supplied by *you*. And the denser the pattern of connections— the more links there are—the greater the chance for this sort of confusion.

To put this briefly, then, understanding (and the memory connections that come with it) can both help and hurt memory. Understanding promotes recall, thanks to the retrieval paths, but it also promotes errors, thanks to the fact that ideas linked to an episode in your understanding are likely to be (mis)remembered as part of that episode. A study by Owens, Bower, and Black (1979) puts these points nicely in view. Half of the participants in their experiment read the following passage.

> Nancy arrived at the cocktail party. She looked around the room to see who was there. She went to talk with her professor. She felt she had to talk to him but was a little nervous about just what to say. A group of people started to play charades. Nancy went over and had some refreshments. The hors d'oeuvres were good but she wasn't interested in talking to the rest of the people at the party. After a while she decided she'd had enough and left the party.

Other participants read the same passage, but with a prologue that set the stage:

> Nancy woke up feeling sick again and she wondered if she really were pregnant. How would she tell the professor she had been seeing? And the money was another problem.

All participants were then given a recall test, in which they were asked to remember the sentences as exactly as they could. As can be seen in Table 7.1, participants who had read the prologue recalled considerably more of the original story. This is consistent with claims made in Chapter 5: The prologue provided a meaningful context for the remainder of the story and this helped understanding. Understanding, in turn, promoted recall.

At the same time, the story's prologue also led participants to include many things in their recall that were not mentioned in the original episode. These are called **intrusion errors,** because they represent other knowledge "intruding" into the recall. In fact, participants who had seen the prologue made *four times* as many intrusion errors as did participants who did not see the prologue. For example, they might recall, "The professor had gotten Nancy pregnant." This is implied by the story, and so will probably be part of the participants' understanding of the story, and it is then this understanding (including the imported element) that is remembered.

## SCHEMATIC KNOWLEDGE

It is clear, then, that memory is shaped by the background knowledge that you bring to a situation. This background knowledge guides your understanding and so provides a source of intrusion errors. Background knowledge also provides the basis for reconstruction if there are any gaps in the memory record. But what exactly is this background knowledge? In many situations, it is your knowledge about what is *typically* included in a particular setting—what sorts of things you would normally find in a kitchen, for example, or what sorts of things you would see in a typical academic office. This background knowledge also contains information about how *events* usually unfold—what usually happens when you go to the dentist, what occurs when you go to a restaurant, and so on.

This **generic knowledge**—knowledge about how things unfold in general—is often referred to with the Greek word **schema** (plural, schemata). Schemata derive from the fact that there is considerable redundancy in our world: Rather predictably, one gets food, not gasoline, in a restaurant; rather predictably, academic offices contain many books, but no washing machine. Schemata summarize this redundancy. (Many psychologists use the term "script" to refer to our dynamic knowledge about events, and reserve the term "schema" for more static knowledge about places and things; in this book, we will use the term "schema" to refer to both sorts of knowledge. For

| *Number of Propositions Remembered by Participants* | Theme Condition | Neutral Condition | TABLE 7.1 |
|---|---|---|---|
| Studied propositions (those in story) | 29.2 | 20.2 | |
| Inferred propositions (those not in story) | 15.2 | 3.7 | |

*Note*: In the "Theme Condition," a brief prologue set the theme for the to-be-remembered passage.

[After Owens, Bower, & Black, 1979.]

more on schemata and scripts, see Abelson, 1981; Brewer, 1987; Friedman, 1979; Mandler, 1984; Rumelhart & Ortony, 1977; Schank, 1982; Schank & Abelson, 1977.)

Schemata guide us in many ways, starting with how we pay attention when we are in a scene. For example, it is your schematic knowledge that tells you that kitchens virtually always have stoves, and this is what leads you to pay little attention to the stove—after all, you have every reason to think the stove is present, so why seek out information to confirm what you already know? Instead, you'll attend to other, potentially more informative aspects of the kitchen, and as a result, you will remember little about the stove later on (e.g., Friedman, 1979). The same logic applies to the Brewer and Treyens study that we described earlier: Their participants had every reason to think that the office bookshelves would contain books, and so paying attention to the shelves, they expected, would merely confirm something that was already obvious. This is why they barely looked at the shelves, and simply assumed the shelves were filled with books.

In addition, schemata also guide our understanding. Indeed, one view of what we are doing when we understand something is that we are "fitting" the new information into a schema. Once this is done, our understanding consists of the new information *plus* this schematic context, and what is then remembered is the scene-as-understood, the episode and the schema. As we will see in a moment, this has important implications for how we remember and what we remember.

Schemata have still another role: We have already mentioned that a process of *reconstruction* allows us to fill any gaps in our recollection, and this process, too, is guided by schematic knowledge. Some of these gaps, we have seen, arise from inattention during an event; others arise through the gradual process of forgetting. (We will have more to say about forgetting later in this chapter.) In either case, we rely on our schemata to tell us what *probably* occurred in a situation, based on our understanding of what normally occurs in such situations.

How does all of this shape memory? First, a reliance on schemata virtually guarantees that memory will go beyond the information actually contained within an event, since memory will include both the particulars of the episode and also many elements provided by schematic understanding. Thus, if a story describes a visit to the dentist, but makes no mention of magazines in the waiting room, there is a good chance that you will remember the magazines anyhow, because they are part of your dentist's office schema. Likewise, if you hear about someone going to a restaurant, you are likely to recall that they ate food, whether you heard that information or not.

In addition, a reliance on schemata will produce an interesting bias in memory. Imagine, as an illustration, that you visit a farm. Some elements of your visit will be perfectly understandable, perhaps because they are just what you'd expect in a farm visit—seeing cows and a tractor, for example. These elements will fit easily with your farm schema, and so it will be easy to forge links between the schema and these specific experiences. These links, in turn, will make it easy to recall these experiences later on. And even if you cannot recall these experiences, they may still be supplied by schema-based reconstruction, which, after all, is quite likely to include these highly typical elements.

In contrast, some elements of your farm visit may be less understandable. Perhaps there was no barn, or perhaps the farmer was wearing shorts. These elements probably do not fit with your farm schema, and this makes it more difficult to link these elements to the schema. This will make it more difficult to remember these elements later. (Without links to the schema, you have no retrieval paths.) And, in this case, schema-based reconstruction will work against memory accuracy, since reconstruction will probably supply more typical elements—a farmer wearing overalls, perhaps, and a lovely red barn.

Overall, then, it seems that a reliance on schemata will make memory selective and biased, favoring what is typical or normal in a particular setting. As a result, you will remember the past as being more ordinary, more sensible, more in line with your expectations, than it actually was.[1]

---

[1]To be complete, we should add one last complication to this pattern: In some circumstances, a reliance on schemata can also lead you to remember highly *atypical* elements within a scene. For example, imagine that you are having dinner in a restaurant. You'll easily remember that there were menus, tables, and chairs, because these all fit with your restaurant schema. But now imagine that, during your dinner, a small pig wanders across the room. The pig's motion is likely to catch your eye, and then, once you realize it's a pig, you'll probably stare at this unexpected animal. But why exactly do you stare? Because of your schematic knowledge, which tells you that pigs are highly unlikely in this setting! Then, because of this close attention to the pig, you're quite likely to remember the pig later. Notice, therefore, that schemata favor memory for the ordinary features of a scene, because these features are easily linked to the schema, and likely to be reconstructed, even if forgotten. But schemata can also favor memory for the truly extraordinary, because of the ways that schemata can guide attention!

## EVIDENCE FOR SCHEMATIC KNOWLEDGE

The classic demonstration of schema effects in memory comes from research published many years ago—in 1932—in Frederick Bartlett's book *Remembering*. Bartlett presented his participants with stories taken from the folklore of Native Americans. When tested later, the participants did reasonably well in recalling the *gist* of the stories, but made many errors in recalling the particulars. Often, details of the original story were simply omitted from their recall; other details were either added to the original or changed. The pattern of errors, though, was quite systematic: The details omitted tended to be details that made little sense to Bartlett's British participants. Likewise, aspects of the story that were unfamiliar were changed into aspects that were more familiar; steps of the story that seemed inexplicable were supplemented to make the story seem more logical.

In Bartlett's study, the participants' memories seem to have "cleaned up" the story—making it more coherent, more sensible, than it actually was. This is exactly what we would expect if the memory errors derived from the participants' attempt to understand the story, and with that, their efforts toward fitting the story into a familiar schematic frame. Elements that fit with the frame remained in their memories; elements that did not fit dropped out of memory or were changed.

In the same spirit, think back to the two examples with which we began this chapter—the misremembered plane crash and the hallucinated books. In both cases, the memory error distorts reality by making the past seem more regular, more typical, than it really was. After all, most academic offices do have books in them, and so the office-as-remembered seems closer to the "average office" than the office as it was actually experienced. Likewise, the Dutch survey respondents probably hear about most major news events via a television broadcast, and this broadcast typically includes vivid video footage. So in this case, too, the past-as-remembered is assimilated into the pattern of the ordinary. The event-as-it-unfolded was unusual, but the event-as-remembered is quite typical of its kind. All of this is just as we would expect if remembering is guided by schemas, with those schemas representing the way things generally unfold.

Many other studies show the same pattern (Bower, Black & Turner, 1979; Bransford & Johnson, 1972, 1973; Graesser, Woll, Kowalski & Smith, 1980; Spiro, 1977). Over and over, material that fits with someone's understanding is likely to be remembered. Elements that were part of someone's understanding, but not part of an episode, are nonetheless recalled as part of the episode. Similarly, aspects of an event that are somewhat at odds with the participants' understanding are likely to be distorted, to bring them into alignment with the schemata. Bartlett's participants read a story with supernatural elements that made little sense to them; in their recollection, these elements were reshaped so that they did make sense. Over and over, the past is distorted in a fashion that makes it more understandable, more typical; this is essentially guaranteed by our reliance on schematic knowledge as an aid to memory.

## THE DEESE-ROEDIGER-MCDERMOTT PARADIGM

Our recall of the past, it seems, is shaped by what we understand. Elements that are part of our understanding are (falsely) remembered as being part of the original episode, producing a consistent pattern of intrusion errors. But is this pattern inevitable? Do intrusion errors show up, for example, if people are urged to be careful in their remembering? And do the errors show up only when people are remembering complex, multipart stories or scenes? Or do the errors emerge even with simple stimuli?

In a number of studies, participants have been presented with lists like the following: "Bed, Rest, Awake, Tired, Dream, Wake, Snooze, Blanket, Doze, Slumber, Snore, Nap, Peace, Yawn, Drowsy." Immediately after hearing these fifteen words, participants are asked to recall as many of the words as they can. Then, a few minutes later, they are given a longer list of words, and asked which of these had occurred on the original 15-word list.

As you may have noticed, all of the words in this list are words associated with the word "sleep," but "sleep," the "root" of the list, is not included. Nonetheless, the participants spontaneously "make the connection" between the list words and this associated word, and this leads to a memory error: When the time comes for recall, they are extremely likely to recall that they heard "sleep." In fact, they are just as likely to recall sleep as they are to recall the actual words on the list! This pattern also emerges in the recognition test: Participants are as likely to recognize "sleep" as being one of the list words as they are to recognize actually presented list words. When asked how confident they are in their memories, participants are just as confident in their (false) recognition of "sleep" as they are in their (correct) recognition of genuine list words (Roediger & McDermott, 1995, 2000; also see Brainerd & Reyna, 1998; Bruce & Winograd, 1998; Deese, 1959; McEvoy et al., 1999; Stadler, Roediger & McDermott, 1999).

This paradigm is referred to as the Deese-Roediger-McDermott (or DRM) procedure, in honor of the investigators who developed it. The procedure yields striking results—with a very simple task leading to large numbers of memory errors. The errors reliably emerge in both recall testing and recognition, and the errors are often expressed with high confidence. Perhaps most impressive, the errors are observed even if participants are put on their guard before the procedure begins. In one experiment, participants were warned that their task was "trickier than it seems at first." Next, everything about the procedure was put out in plain view. In particular, the participants were told explicitly that each memory list would revolve around a single theme, and warned, "Many people have a tendency on the memory test to recall words that fit with the theme even if those words actually weren't on the original list. Try not to do that; try to be careful, and recall only words you actually heard on the list." Even with this clear warning, participants still made the DRM errors—although they did make slightly fewer errors than participants who received no warning (Reisberg, 1999; also Gallo, Roberts & Seamon, 1997; McDermott & Roediger, 1998). Apparently, then, the mechanisms leading to these memory errors are quite automatic, and not mechanisms that the participants can somehow inhibit.

## THE CAUSES OF FORGETTING

A crucial factor in predicting memory accuracy is the **retention interval**—the amount of time that has elapsed between the initial learning and the subsequent retrieval. In general, memory for distant events tends to be less accurate—less complete and more prone to error—than memory for recent events. Common sense tells us this is true; is, in any case, a pattern easily documented in the laboratory, with many studies showing larger numbers of errors as the interval grows (e.g., Anderson & Pichert, 1978; Belli, Windschitl, McCarthy & Winfrey, 1992; Ceci & Bruck, 1993; Dooling & Christiaansen, 1977; Spiro, 1977). But why is this? Why does the passage of time influence memory?

One hypothesis is **decay**. With the passage of time, memories may fade or erode. Perhaps this is because the relevant brain cells die off. Or perhaps the connections among memories need to be constantly refreshed; if not, the connections may gradually weaken. In any event, it is largely the passage of time that triggers these events.

A different possibility is that new learning somehow works against, or interferes with, older learning. According to this **interference** account, less is remembered about older events because, as time passes, there is more and more opportunity for interference, more and more opportunity for new learning that can disrupt the old learning. For recent events, in contrast, there has been little opportunity for interference, and therefore little forgetting.

A third hypothesis blames **retrieval failure**. After all, the retrieval of information from memory is far from guaranteed, and we argued in Chapter 6 that retrieval is most likely if your perspective (mental, emotional, and physical) at the time of retrieval matches that in place at the time of learning. If we now assume that your perspective is likely to change more and more as time goes by, we can make a prediction about forgetting: The greater the retention interval, the greater the likelihood that your perspective has changed, and therefore the greater the likelihood of retrieval failure.

There is no doubt that retrieval failure does occur. In many circumstances, we are unable to remember some bit of information, but then, a while later, we *do* recall that information. Since the information eventually was retrieved, we know that the information was not "erased" from memory through decay or interference. Our initial failure to recall the information, therefore, must be counted as an example of retrieval failure. Chapter 6 described many experiments in which participants tested one way were able to remember an earlier event, whereas participants tested a different way were unable to remember the same event. This pattern is easily understood as a case of retrieval failure for the second group; the pattern is difficult to explain in terms of decay or interference.

But what about these other mechanisms? Do they contribute to forgetting? To find out if decay contributes, all we need to do is teach something to our research participants and then have them spend some time without learning anything new (so there is no interference) and without thinking any new thoughts (so that we minimize the chance of a change in perspective, and so minimize the chance of retrieval failure). If we observe forgetting after a time spent in this fashion, we know the forgetting is attributable to decay.

Of course, this experiment would be virtually impossible to implement (how could we prevent participants from thinking new thoughts?), but similar experiments have been carried out, mostly with other species. These procedures take advantage of the fact that many animals do spend long periods of time seemingly doing nothing or close to it. This allows us to test the decay claim.

Experiments with cockroaches, for example, exploit the fact that roaches, once they enter a warm, dark, dry place, will lie still for many minutes. We can therefore teach the cockroach a simple response, then provide a warm, dry place, and wait. If we wait a short time, then, on the decay hypothesis, little forgetting will take place. If we wait a longer interval,

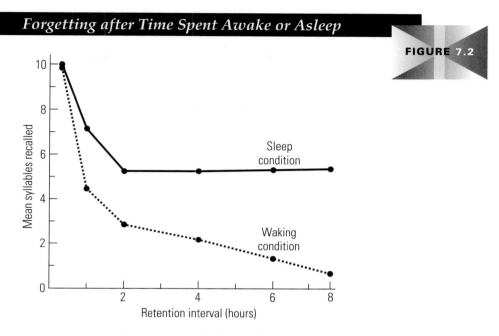

## Forgetting after Time Spent Awake or Asleep

FIGURE 7.2

Participants learned a series of nonsense syllables and were tested either after a period of time spent asleep or after a period of time spent awake. Forgetting was greater after time awake, presumably because during that time participants were thinking about and learning new things, leading to memory interference. [After Jenkins & Dallenbach, 1924.]

forgetting should be correspondingly greater. These predictions turn out to be wrong: In studies like these the passage of time is a poor predictor of forgetting (e.g., Minami & Dallenbach, 1946). Forgetting does occur, however, if we allow the cockroaches to crawl about in the interval between learning and test. In other words, the data favor an interference account, not decay.

We do not have exactly comparable data from humans, but we have something close: Many studies have looked at learning just before sleep in comparison with learning just before a day's activities. There is unquestionably mental activity during sleep, but there is surely less during sleep than during the day. Therefore, in this study we are comparing "less interference" with "more," rather than "no interference" with "interference."

In a study by Jenkins and Dallenbach (1924), two groups of participants learned lists of nonsense syllables, like "BIV" or "ZAR." The participants were then tested after retention intervals of one, two, four, or eight hours. Critically, some participants slept during the retention interval and some were awake. Figure 7.2 shows the data. In both conditions, performance dropped as the interval between learning and test increased. However, this drop was much more pronounced if participants were awake during the retention interval. That is, one hour with much interference produced more forgetting than one hour with minimal interference; likewise for two hours or four or eight. (See also Ekstrand, 1967, 1972; Hockey, Davies & Gray, 1972.) Thus, time seems not to be the crucial factor, and these data again favor an interference account.

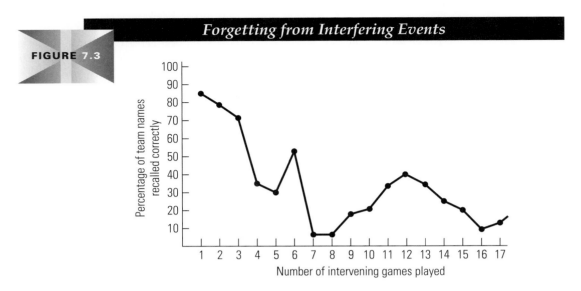

**Forgetting from Interfering Events**

FIGURE 7.3

Members of a rugby team were asked to recall the names of teams they had played against. Their performance was influenced by the number of games that intervened between the to-be-recalled game and the attempt to remember. This fits with an interference view of forgetting. [After Baddeley & Hitch, 1977.]

Baddeley and Hitch (1977) offer yet another way of getting at this question. They asked rugby players to recall the names of the teams they had played against over the course of a rugby season. Not all players made it to all games, because of illness, injuries, or schedule conflicts. This allows us to compare players for whom "two games back" means two weeks ago, to players for whom "two games back" means four weeks ago. Thus, we can look at the effects of retention interval (two weeks vs. four) with the number of intervening games held constant. Likewise, we can compare players for whom the game a month ago was "three games back" with players for whom a month means "one game back." Now we have the retention interval held constant, and we can look at the effects of intervening events. In this setting, Baddeley and Hitch report that the mere passage of time accounts for very little; what really matters is the number of intervening events (Figure 7.3).

None of these tests is perfect. One might worry about extrapolating from cockroach memory to that of other species; one might worry about what other things were going on in the lives of Baddeley and Hitch's rugby players. For example, a player for whom the previous game was long ago is obviously a player who missed many games. Why is this? Frequent illness? A schedule filled with other things? Could these influence the pattern of data? With these questions unanswered, we must be cautious in interpreting the Baddeley and Hitch data.

Nevertheless, there is a consistent message emerging from these studies: There is a strong relationship between forgetting and the arrival of new information and new events; this is consistent both with the claim of interference and with the claim of retrieval failure. However, there is relatively little evidence that unambiguously demonstrates decay (although, for some very promising evidence, see Altmann and Gray, 2002). In addition, later in this chapter we will consider some cases of excellent memory even with extremely long delays (even several decades), a result plainly contrary to decay claims. Our best summary of the data, therefore, seems to be that interference and retrieval failure play substantial roles; the role of decay is less well established.

## INTERFERENCE: BLURRING OF SIMILAR EPISODES

In the studies just described, newly arriving information seemed to disrupt memory for material learned earlier. This is consistent with the idea that some forgetting is caused by memory interference, but it also invites a new question: Why should memory interference occur? Why can't newly acquired information peacefully coexist with older memories?

In truth, interference can arise for many reasons (e.g., Anderson, Bjork & Bjork, 2000). Part of the explanation lies in a pattern called **source confusion**. We first met this term in Chapter 6; it refers to the fact that we are often able to remember things we have learned, or conversations we have heard, even though we are mistaken about *where* or *when* we learned the facts or heard the conversations. In such cases, we have a memory for a particular event or a particular stimulus, but we are confused about the *source* of that memory—where it was that we experienced that event, or when it was that we met that stimulus. This is obviously linked to another distinction we made in Chapter 6, when we argued that we sometimes (correctly) register that a stimulus is familiar, but cannot recall *why* that stimulus is familiar; this is referred to as *source amnesia*. (For data exploring the nature of source memory, source confusion, and source amnesia, see, for example, Bornstein & LeCompte, 1995; Dodson, Holland & Shimamura, 1998; Jurica & Shimamura, 1999; Marsh & Landau, 1995.)

Source confusion helps us understand why memory errors are less likely when people are remembering some unique event, as opposed to one episode within a series of similar episodes (e.g., Brewer, 1988). With unique events, source confusion is unlikely: If you've seen only one ballet in your life, there's no risk of confusion when you try to remember in which ballet you saw the dancing fireflies. But with multiple related events, episodes can easily start to "blur together" in memory, making it difficult for you to recall which elements occurred in which episode. Let's say that you remember a train ride with a truly comical conductor. Do you remember *which* train ride it was? You may not, simply because the many train rides in your experience have blurred together in memory. As a result, interference is observed, with new learning (many train rides) impeding memory for the specific event you're trying to recall.

A compelling example of this blurring together comes from the Watergate scandal that ended the Nixon presidency. As that scandal unfolded, it became clear that Nixon's advisers had committed a series of illegal acts. There was uncertainty, however, about Nixon's own role in the planning or the coverup of these crimes. In order to pursue this question, a Senate committee carefully interrogated John Dean, the former legal counsel to Nixon, about conversations that had taken place in the Oval Office prior to and after the illegal acts.

It later came to light that Nixon had tape-recorded all Oval Office conversations, and so we can check the accuracy of Dean's testimony against these tapes. This comparison reveals that Dean's testimony was quite accurate in its gist (consistent with the evidence we have already reviewed) but often wrong on the details. His errors were far from random, however. Instead, Dean often reported snippets of conversation as having taken place in one context when, in fact, they took place in a different context. In other words, the individual episodes were being blurred together. Neisser (1981) argues that this is extremely likely whenever one is remembering repeated and related episodes and proposes the term "repisodes" for our memories of these *re*peated *episodes*. Other evidence confirms this pattern (Jobe, Tourangeau & Smith, 1993; Reinitz, Lammers & Cochran, 1992; Roberts & Blades, 1998): Memory for detail is likely to suffer when episodes are similar, as details get exchanged from one episode to another.

A similar effect may underlie a different episode involving a U.S. president: Ronald Reagan spent the years of World War II in Hollywood, but during his presidential campaign, he vividly described his (non-existent) wartime actions in Europe, including his participation in the liberation of a Nazi concentration camp. It later came to light that many of the details of his recollection were identical to details of the 1944 movie *Wing and a Prayer*, inviting the suggestion that Reagan's mistaken recall may represent yet another case of source confusion—in this case a confusion about whether certain details were in memory because they had been experienced, or whether these details were in memory because they had been observed in a popular film (Sagan, 1996).[2]

## INTERFERENCE: THE EFFECT OF LEADING QUESTIONS

Imagine that you are a witness to a crime. Some time later, you read an account of this crime in the newspaper, and this account *differs* from your own recollection. Perhaps the newspaper's version includes details you didn't notice, or perhaps it contains elements flatly contradicting what you remember. How will this affect your memory? Will your recollection be influenced by this experience?

Many studies address these questions, with procedures modeled closely after the situation of the eyewitness. The research participants witness an event and are then exposed to some new information about the event. Sometimes this postevent information is presented as an alternative account of the event. (This would be similar to the example just described, in which a witness to a crime reads a newspaper report about the same crime.) In other procedures, the postevent information is delivered in a subtler fashion, via leading questions. For example, Loftus and Palmer (1974) showed participants a series of projected slides depicting an automobile collision. Some time later, some of the participants were asked, "How fast were the cars going when they hit each other?" Others were asked, "How fast were the cars going when they smashed into each other?" The difference between these questions ("hit" vs. "smashed") is

slight, but it is enough to bias someone's estimates of speed. Participants in the first group estimated the speed to have been 34 mph; participants in the second group estimated 41 mph. But what is critical comes next: One week later, the participants were asked whether they had seen any broken glass in the slides. Participants who had initially been asked the "hit" question tended to remember (correctly) that no glass was visible; only 14% said they had seen glass. Participants asked the "smashed" question, though, were reasonably likely to remember glass: 32% asserted that glass was visible. It seems, therefore, that the change of just one word within the initial question can have a large effect—in this case, more than doubling the likelihood of memory error.

Loftus has reported a number of variations on this experiment, offering many refinements and extensions of the basic finding (Loftus, 1975, 1979; Loftus, Miller & Burns, 1978). In one experiment, Loftus showed participants a slide sequence in which a car ran past a stop sign and then subsequently misled them by asking them about the car's speed when it passed a *yield* sign. When later asked about the scene, participants remembered quite clearly having seen the (fictitious) yield sign, choosing it when given the options of a stop sign, a yield sign, and a one-way sign. Loftus then told the participants directly that their response was incorrect and asked them to choose their answer from the remaining two. Now, participants were equally likely to choose the (correct) stop sign and the (out-of-nowhere) one-way sign. Even given this "second-guess" option, participants showed no sign of remembering the original event (although see also McCloskey & Zaragoza, 1985; Wright & McDaid, 1996).

Similar effects can be documented if the original event is viewed on a videotape, or even "live." Likewise, a wide range of memories can be changed in this fashion. Thus, with different versions of the misinformation procedure, psychologists have arranged things so that screwdrivers originally seen are remembered as hammers and blue sedans are remembered as brown pickup trucks. In still other studies, misinformation has been used, after the fact, to alter how people remember the age, body size, or

---

[2]President Reagan developed Alzheimer's disease after leaving the presidency; this memory slip, however, took place many years earlier, making it clear that the disease is not the cause of this memory error.

facial characteristics of actors within an event (Christiaansen, Sweeney & Ochalek, 1983; Loftus & Greene, 1980; for a broad review, see Ayers & Reder, 1998).

## ARE THERE LIMITS ON THE MISINFORMATION EFFECT?

Apparently, then, memories can be altered after the fact by suitable suggestions or questioning. This pattern is often referred to as the **misinformation effect**, since the participants' memory is plainly being influenced by *misinformation* they received after an episode was over. Let us note, though, that this effect is, in essence, just another example of source confusion: In the misinformation studies, the participants *correctly* recall that, at some point in their past, they heard about or were thinking about, say, a yield sign. Their error lies in their belief about the *source* of this memory: They believe the sign was contained in the original episode they witnessed, when in fact it was contained in the misinformation they acquired subsequently.

Said differently, the misinformation effect simply provides another illustration of *forgetting* created by *interference*. In this case, the interference is caused by the misinformation itself, and the forgetting we observe is not merely a *loss* of the earlier information, it is a *replacement* of the earlier information: "I saw a stop sign" is replaced by the newer idea "I saw a yield sign." Even so, the misinformation effect (made possible by source confusion) provides us with insights into the power of and the mechanisms behind memory interference.

What are the limits on this effect? We have mentioned studies in which postevent misinformation changes some details in the remembered episode—changes screwdrivers into hammers, and so on. Other evidence, though, suggests that this is just the tip of the iceberg. In one study, college students were told that the investigators were trying to learn how different people remember the same experience. The students were then given a list of events that they were told had been reported by their parents; the students were asked to recall these events as best as they could, so that the investigators could compare their recall with their parents' (Hyman, Husband & Billings, 1995).

Some of the events on the list had, in fact, been reported by the participants' parents. Other events were bogus—made up by the experimenters. (In fact, the experimenters checked with the parents to make certain that these bogus events really had not happened.) One of the bogus events was an overnight hospitalization for a high fever; in a related procedure, the bogus event was attending a wedding reception and accidentally spilling a punch bowl on the parents of the bride.

The college students were easily able to remember the genuine events—the ones actually reported by their parents. In an initial interview, more than 80% of these events were recalled; by a second interview, this number had climbed to almost 90%. In the first interview, none of the students recalled the bogus events, but repeated attempts at recall changed this pattern: By the third interview, 25% of the participants were able to remember the embarrassment of spilling the punch bowl, and many were able to supply the details of this (fictitious) episode. Other studies have yielded similar results, with participants led to recall details of particular birthday parties that, in truth, they never had (Hyman, Husband & Billings, 1995) or an incident of being lost in a shopping mall, even though this event never took place (Loftus, 1997; Loftus & Pickrell, 1995; also see Porter et al., 1999). The same result has also been documented with children, with repeated interviews leading children to recall (for example) episodes in which they got their finger caught in a mousetrap and had to be taken to the hospital—even though, of course, no such episode ever occurred (Ceci, Huffman, & Smith, 1994; for discussion of how this line of research is relevant to children's testimony in the courtroom, see Ceci & Bruck, 1995; Bruck & Ceci, 1999).

It is clear, then, that entire events can be planted in someone's memory, so that the person ends up recalling—confidently and in detail—an episode that never took place. Moreover, it seems relatively *easy* to plant these memories: Two or three brief interviews, with no particular pressure, no effort toward coercion, are all that is needed.

We still need to ask, though, whether there are limits on the false memories that can be planted. Or can any event at all be planted in someone's recollection? Investigators do not have clear answers to these questions. We know that it is more difficult to plant memories if the participants find the suggested event implausible: If the research participants are Jewish, for example, it is difficult to plant a memory of receiving Holy Communion; if the participants are Catholic, it is difficult to plant a memory of participating in a Shabbat celebration (Pezdek, Finger & Hodge, 1997; for similar results with children, showing more easily planted memories for plausible events, see Ornstein et al., 1998; Pezdek & Hodge, 1999). But this may be a flimsy shield against false recollection, since people's judgments of plausibility can easily change, and with them, the pattern of false memories that can be planted changes as well (Hyman, 2000).

We also know a number of factors that *increase* the likelihood of planting a false memory. The likelihood of false memory goes up, for example, if there are repeated suggestions that the (non-existent) event actually occurred (e.g., Bruck & Ceci, 1999; Zaragoza & Mitchell, 1996). These repetitions are even more effective if each suggestion of the false event is slightly different from the ones presented earlier (Mitchell & Zaragoza, 1996). False memories are also more easily planted if the target event supposedly happened long ago, rather than recently (e.g., Belli et al., 1992). The probability of a false memory is further increased if the research participants are urged to *imagine in detail* how the suggested event unfolded—an effect referred to as "imagination inflation" (Goff & Roediger, 1998; Garry & Polaschek, 2000; Hyman et al., 1998; although also see Paddock et al., 1998).

Finally, we also know that some individuals are more susceptible than others to false memories; individuals who are particularly susceptible seem to be people with vivid imaginations and people who often report *dissociative experiences,* such as the experience of finding yourself in a place but having no idea how you got there, or the experience of becoming so involved in a daydream that it feels like the daydream is really happening (Clancy et al.,

2000; Heaps & Nash, 1999; Hyman & Billings, 1998; Read & Winograd, 1998; Winograd, Peluso & Glover, 1998; for related data, see Bremner, Shobe & Kihlstrom, 2000). These dissociative experiences may indicate that someone is vulnerable to a "blurring together" of the external world and the world of imagination; if so, it would not be surprising that this person is less able to distinguish actually experienced events from merely suggested ones. As a result, such a person might be more susceptible to "memory implantation."

## Evaluating Human Memory

We seem to be moving toward a fairly grim portrait of human memory. As we have now seen, many factors can contribute to misremembering, and indeed, memory errors are easy to document. Some of these errors are small—for example, recalling that a hammer was actually mentioned when, in fact, it was merely implied. But other memory errors are much larger, including the false recall of entire events that never took place. Indeed, if there are limits on the size of memory errors, or limits on the *types* of errors that are possible, these limits have not yet been discovered.

This pattern of results is obviously troubling, since it raises the unsettling possibility that the objective past may be rather different from the past as we remember it. This in turn has implications for how we should think about the past, and for how much faith we should put in our own memories. These memory errors also have important pragmatic implications, for example, for the legal system: Eyewitness testimony is taken very seriously by the courts, but of course this testimony relies on what the witness remembers. It is no surprise, therefore, that much research on memory accuracy has been applied directly to the situation of the eyewitness; it is also no surprise that memory experts are sometimes called on to testify in court, with the goal of helping the jury understand that eyewitness evidence must be interpreted with caution.

But are things really this grim? Is human memory really that poor?

## ACCURATE MEMORIES

So far in this chapter, we have emphasized evidence that highlights the *inaccuracy* of memory, but this does not mean that memory errors happen all the time. In fact, the opposite is the truth: Our memories are, for the most part, enormously accurate. Errors certainly do occur, and sometimes those errors are large. In some circumstances (such as the various experiments we have described), the errors are quite common. But, even so, the fact remains that in our daily lives we usually *can* trust our memories. More often than not, our recollection is complete, detailed, long-lasting, and *correct*.

Many lines of evidence are pertinent to these claims. For example, Yuille and Cutshall (1986) interviewed 13 witnesses to an actual crime, four to five months after the event. The witnesses' memory for the crime was impressively accurate, despite this delay, and despite the fact that the investigators used stringent criteria in evaluating the witnesses' recall: Reported ages of the perpetrators, for example, had to be within 2 years to be counted as correct; reported weights within 5 pounds. No leeway was given for the estimation of the number of shots fired in the incident. Even with these strict rules, the witnesses were correct in 83% of the details reported about the action itself within the episode, 90% correct in their descriptions of objects on the scene. (Also see Fisher, Geiselman & Amador, 1989; Yuille & Kim, 1987.)

Similar levels of accuracy have been observed in many other studies. For example, Howes, Siegel, and Brown (1993) asked their adult participants to recall events from very early in childhood. When checked, most of these memories turned out to be reasonably accurate. Likewise, Brewin, Andrews, and Gotlib (1993) summarize a number of studies showing that our autobiographical recollection is correct most of the time.

Even when memory errors do occur, these errors are sometimes reversible: With appropriate cueing, or suitable instruction, participants can still retrieve a memory of the event as it actually unfolded. For example, several studies document participants' poor recall for stories they did not understand (Bartlett, 1932; Bransford & Johnson, 1972; Dooling & Lachman, 1971). It turns out, however, that participants do seem to remember these very same materials if memory is tested via a recognition procedure, instead of by recall (Alba, Alexander, Hasher & Caniglia, 1981). In this procedure, the original materials do seem to be preserved in memory, independent of their "fit" with the participants' understanding. (For a wide range of related data, see Alba & Hasher, 1983.)

Even with recall testing, some studies show that memory errors can be avoided, if participants are suitably instructed. For example, Hasher and Griffin (1978) presented their participants with a story about a man walking through the woods. Some of the participants read the story together with an appropriate title ("Going Hunting"), and then were given this same title at the time of the recall test. Hasher and Griffin expected that this would encourage participants to rely on the title itself in reconstructing the story. This, they predicted, would lead to many errors: Elements not consistent with the overall gist should drop out of the recollection; intrusion errors consistent with the gist should also be observed. The data confirm these predictions. When participants had reason to believe their understanding of the story's gist was correct, they relied on this gist and used it to reconstruct the story.

Other participants read the story with the same title, but then, at the time of the test, participants were told that an error had occurred and that they had inadvertently been given the wrong title for the story. They were given a new title ("An Escaped Convict") that was, in fact, also consistent with the story's contents. Hasher and Griffin reasoned that these participants, now convinced that their prior understanding of the story was incorrect, would try to set aside this understanding and to recall the exact story as it actually was presented. On this basis, Hasher and Griffin predicted that participants in this group would recall the story without interpretation and without intrusions. That is exactly what the results show.

It seems that, at least in some circumstances, people can control whether they will reconstruct a story based on remembered gist or try to reproduce it faithfully by digging through memory for the actual sentences. Participants did the former in the experiment's first condition, and so produced many errors and intrusions. But participants did the latter in the experiment's second condition and thus avoided these errors.

A different study makes roughly the same points: In an experiment by Anderson and Pichert (1978), participants read a story about two boys playing in a house. Half of the participants were told to read the story pretending that they were potential home-buyers; this should presumably draw their attention to the information within the story that might be relevant to a home-buyer, and this should in turn bias what they remember later on. The remaining participants were told to read the story pretending that they were potential burglars, thinking about robbing this house. Again, this should bias the participants' attention, and also their memories.

When the time came to recall the story, the pattern was as expected: Participants who had taken the "buyer" perspective recalled more of the information that would be useful to a home-buyer; participants who had taken the "burglar" perspective recalled more of the information pertinent to a burglar. The twist, though, comes in the next step of the procedure. After a brief delay, the participants were again asked to recall the story, but this time they were encouraged to change perspective—from that of a burglar to that of a buyer, or vice versa. With this change in perspective, participants were able to remember things they had earlier "forgotten" and, in particular, were able to remember things relevant to their new perspective. Once again, therefore, it seems that people do remember information that is external to their initial understanding, and that they can recover this information if their understanding changes.

We should note, though, that not all memory errors are "reversible" in this fashion. As we have seen, memory errors can occur for many different reasons, and as a result, some memory errors can be undone, whereas others cannot. If, for example, the errors arose at retrieval, then it is possible that a change in strategy, or a new hint, might lead participants back to the "original records" in memory,

thus reversing the error, or perhaps allowing participants to fill in something they had apparently "forgotten." This is presumably what happened in the Hasher and Griffin and Anderson and Pichert studies. Sometimes, though, errors arise at *encoding*—perhaps because the target information was never noticed in the first place, or because participants encoded only a biased version of the target information. In this case, the error will be irreversible. Even if participants are told that their initial impression of an event was mistaken, they cannot return to the "raw data" and reinterpret the event. This is because, in this scenario, there are no "raw data" in memory to be returned to.

## MEMORY CONFIDENCE

Overall, then, it seems that many memories are accurate, even if some are not. Some memory errors can be reversed, even if others cannot. Against this backdrop, then, all would be fine if we could tell which memories were the accurate ones. We could then rely on these and not trust the others. But the evidence on this point is disappointing: Most memory errors are undetectable.

Sometimes we are certain about the past ("I distinctly remember her yellow jacket") and sometimes we are not ("Gee, I think he was wearing blue, but I'm not sure"). Common sense tells us that memories of the first sort are likely to be correct, and we tend to trust confident recollection. Conversely, we put little faith in less-confident recollections, and we are not surprised if these turn out to be mistaken. This common sense then influences us in many ways. For example, courtroom juries place much more weight on testimony that is delivered confidently and tend to distrust testimony that is hesitant or hedged (Brigham & Wolfskiel, 1983; Cutler, Penrod & Dexter, 1990; Loftus, 1979; Wells, Lindsay & Ferguson, 1979; for some of the other factors that make a memory seem more or less credible, see Ross, Buehler & Karr, 1998). And it is not just juries who hold this view: Judges believe the same. According to the United States Supreme Court, jurors *should* consider witness confidence in evaluating a witness's testimony (*Neil v. Biggers*, 1972). Similarly, in the state of Oregon, for example, the "certainty expressed by a witness" is an important factor in deciding whether an eyewitness identification is deemed trustworthy (*State of Oregon v. Classen*, 1979); other states have similar rules.

This is a case, however, in which common sense, juries, and the courts are all mistaken. Many studies have systematically compared research participants' confidence when they are reporting a correct memory with their confidence when they are reporting a false memory. This research has employed many of the procedures we have discussed in this chapter—memory for sentences, the DRM technique, the misinformation paradigm—and also a number of studies designed to mimic the situation of an actual eyewitness to a crime. Across all of these procedures, the pattern is quite clear: There is little or no relationship between memory confidence and memory accuracy. Any attempt to categorize memories as "correct" or "incorrect" based on the rememberer's confidence, will be riddled with errors. (This fact has been demonstrated in many studies; see, among others, Busey et al., 2000; Chandler, 1994; Loftus, 1979; Bothwell, Deffenbacher & Brigham, 1987; Roediger & McDermott, 1995; Sporer, Penrod, Read & Cutler, 1995; Thompson & Mason, 1996; Wells, Luus & Windschitl, 1994.)

How could this be? How could we be so poor in evaluating our own memories? Several factors contribute to this weakness. In many cases, familiarity with the general themes being remembered may lead to the illusion that the details are remembered as well (Chandler, 1994). Our memory confidence is also influenced by how easily a memory comes to mind; as a result, practice in reporting a false memory will increase the confidence associated with that false memory (Shaw, 1995). In the same way, the exercise of imagining an event in detail will also increase our confidence that the event actually occurred, and that it unfolded just as we remember (Garry et al., 1996). External support also influences confidence: If an investigator confirms a witness's identification ("Good, you identified the actual sus-

pect!"), this will inflate the witness's recollection of how confident he or she was at the time of the identification and will also influence other judgments—such as the witness's recollection of how good his or her view of the perpetrator was at the time of the crime (Wells & Bradfield, 1999).

Of course, we should mention that the relationship between memory accuracy and memory confidence is not always zero; in some circumstances, there is a (weakly) positive relationship, with participants expressing slightly greater confidence in their correct memory judgments than in their incorrect ones (e.g., Sporer et al., 1995). Studies of eyewitnesses indicate, for example, that confidence expressed *after* a lineup selection ("Are you sure that was the thief?") is more closely associated with accuracy than confidence expressed prior to the lineup ("Are you sure that you'll recognize him?"; Cutler & Penrod, 1989). Likewise, an eyewitness's confidence is more closely associated with accuracy if the suspect happens to be distinctive in appearance (Brigham, 1990; for other, related studies, see Cutler & Penrod, 1989; Deffenbacher, 1980; Fleet, Brigham & Bothwell, 1987; Kassin, 1985). It should be emphasized, though, that even in circumstances favoring an accuracy-confidence correlation, this correlation is never a strong one. And, in fact, we can also identify domains in which there is a negative relationship between confidence and accuracy, with participants actually more confident in their wrong answers than in their right ones (e.g., Reisberg, Culver, Heuer & Fischman, 1986).

Overall, therefore, memory confidence is at best a very poor index of memory accuracy. Consistent with this fact, it is easy to identify circumstances in which people are absolutely certain that their memories are correct when in fact their memories contain large-scale errors (e.g., Neisser & Harsch, 1992). Obviously, then, this speaks against the possibility of *detecting* false memories when they occur.

## "REMEMBERING" VS. "KNOWING"

We cannot distinguish correct memories from false memories on the basis of *confidence*, but perhaps we can distinguish them in some other way. Investigators have asked whether false memories are perhaps less detailed than genuine memories, or perhaps *more* detailed. There is typically little difference. Investigators have also tried urging their participants to be extremely careful in these experiments, to respond "Yes, this is familiar" only if they are quite certain about their judgments. These warnings reduce the number of errors somewhat, suggesting that at least *some* errors are detectable and avoidable. Even with these warnings, however, many memory errors remain (e.g., Greene, Flynn & Loftus, 1982; Tousignant, Hall & Loftus, 1986).

Still other investigators have tried timing their participants' responses, on the idea that responses based on inference or assumption might involve a moment of hesitation and so should be somewhat slower than responses based on clear, detailed memories. Typically, though, there is no difference in speed of responding between correct and incorrect answers (Begg & Wickelgren, 1974; Bransford, Barclay & Franks, 1972; Bransford & Franks, 1971; Paris & Lindauer, 1976; etc.).

Nonetheless, investigators continue to hunt for measures that might allow us to distinguish accurate memories from inaccurate ones. For example, consider the way a memory "feels" from the point of view of the person doing the remembering (Rajaram, 1993; Tulving, 1985). Sometimes, the person feels like he actually "remembers" the past; perhaps he remembers where he was when an event occurred, or what he was doing at the time. "I remember that this word was on the list, because I remember that, when I saw the word, it reminded me of my math professor." Sometimes, though, our recollection does not contain these episodic details; in this case, we might speak of "knowing" something rather than "remembering" it. "This word seems very familiar, and so I know it was on the list, but I don't remember the experience of seeing it."

A great deal of recent research has explored this subjective difference and has asked why a memory sometimes arrives in your thoughts with the feeling of "remembering," and why it sometimes arrives with the feeling of "knowing" (e.g., Gardiner, 1988;

Hicks & Marsh, 1999; Jacoby et al., 1998). But will this distinction help us in detecting false memories? The evidence suggests that the feeling of "remembering" is, in fact, somewhat more likely with correct memories than it is with false memories (e.g., Conway et al., 1996; Lane & Zaragoza, 1995). Put differently, false memories often arrive with only a general sense of familiarity and no recollection of a particular episode. ("I'm sure there were books there, although, to tell you the truth, I don't remember anything about what they looked like.") But there are numerous exceptions to this pattern, and so in many cases fully correct memories arrive in your thoughts with only a feeling of "knowing," and fully false memories arrive with a detailed sense of "remembering." As a result, this subjective distinction between knowing and remembering, like the other efforts we have described, cannot serve as a reliable means of distinguishing correct memories from false ones (Holmes, Waters & Rajaram, 1998; Roediger & McDermott, 1995; for other research, pursuing still other leads in telling apart true memories from false ones, see Geiselman et al., 2000; Johnson, 1988; Johnson & Raye, 1981; Lamb, 1998; Leippe et al., 1992; Pickel, 1999).

## EXOTIC STRATEGIES FOR IMPROVING MEMORY

We are moving toward a mixed evaluation of human memory. On the positive side, people seem to remember accurately most of the time; correct memories are more common than incorrect ones. On the negative side, though, large-scale memory errors do occur, and it seems these errors are largely undetectable: Memories that contain errors, or memories that are wholly false, can be just as vivid, just as detailed, just as emotional, and recalled with just as much speed and confidence as memories that are completely accurate. These errors can occur when we are remembering actual events in our own lives (e.g., Neisser & Harsch, 1992); they can occur when we are trying to remember events important to us professionally (Vicente & Brewer, 1993); they can even occur in contexts in which the false memory leads us to confess to a crime we never committed (Kassin, 1997; Kassin & Kiechel, 1996; Ofshe, 1992).

Is there anything we can do to improve this situation? Can we somehow become better rememberers? As one option, a great deal has been asserted about the value of hypnosis in helping people to remember. Indeed, the suggestion is sometimes made that, under hypnosis, witnesses to an earlier event can remember everything about the event, including aspects they did not even notice (much less think about and interpret) at the time.

Many studies have examined these claims, and the evidence is clear: Hypnotized participants who are instructed to remember do their very best to comply, and this means that they will give a full and detailed reporting of the target event. However, it is not the case that the hypnotized participants remember more. Instead, they simply *say* more, in order to be cooperative. By saying more things, they will (just by chance) say some things that happen to be true. But most of the memory report by hypnotized people turns out not to be true and, worse, the hypnotized individuals cannot tell you which of the reported details are correct and which are made up or are guesses. In other words, hypnosis does not improve memory; it just changes the willingness to talk (Dinges, Whitehouse, Orne, Powell, Orne & Erdelyi, 1992; Dywan & Bowers, 1983; Hilgard, 1968; Smith, 1982; Spiegel, 1995).

In fact, there is reason to believe hypnosis may actually *compromise* memory accuracy rather than improve it. Bear in mind that someone hypnotized will be quite compliant, quite cooperative. Therefore, suggestions made to someone who is hypnotized will be taken very seriously. Now, combine this with our earlier comments about postevent misinformation: We know, in general, that this misinformation can shape the way earlier events are recalled. There is every reason to believe these effects will be even stronger if the misinformation is delivered under hypnosis.

Similar observations apply to various drugs alleged to improve memory—sodium amytal, for example. Many of these drugs work (in part) as sedatives, and this puts an individual in a less-guarded, less-cautious state of mind. This state of mind allows people to report more about the past—not because they remember more, but simply because, in this relaxed state, they are willing to *say* more. Likewise, this less-guarded state leaves an individual more vulnerable to the effects of leading or misleading questions, which of course can undermine memory accuracy. Plainly, then, these techniques are *not* the way to improve recollection.

A more exotic way to improve recall is suggested by reports of people whose brains have been directly stimulated, usually as part of brain surgery. Patients are typically awake during this surgery, and the surgeon uses their responses to brain stimulation as a way of locating certain structures and regions within the brain. Sometimes, though, when the brain is prodded or poked, the patient suddenly remembers scenes from long ago, often in clear and remarkable detail. Could this be the way to defeat forgetting and to recover one's "lost past"?

In fact, only a small number of patients report recollections in response to this stimulation of the brain. But the memories evoked in this fashion are extraordinary—clear, detailed, as though the patients were reliving the earlier experience. Unfortunately, though, we have no way of knowing whether these are really *memories*. These experiences might, for example, be hallucinations of some sort. Or these experiences might be very vivid reconstructions. Because this evidence comes from an extreme circumstance, it has been difficult to track down the historical facts to confirm (or disconfirm) these patients' recollections. Until this is done, we have no evidence that they are remembering, much less remembering accurately. Hence, we have no basis for claiming that this technique promotes memory retrieval. (See Sacks, 1985, for similar cases, also without documentation about whether the remembering is bona fide.)

## TECHNIQUES FOR MAXIMIZING RECALL

There are, however, some techniques that do promote the recovery of "lost" memories. The techniques are not exotic but simply capitalize on the fact that a great deal of forgetting involves retrieval failure. As a consequence, it is often possible for a "lost" memory to be recovered once the appropriate retrieval cues are on the scene.

How should one seek "appropriate cues"? One possibility is simply to try out a variety of *different* cues. In practice, this amounts to little more than trying to remember, with the efforts spread out over a period of time and a variety of circumstances. This does work, and less and less "forgetting" is observed as recall efforts continue. The technical term for this process is **hypermnesia**, sometimes referred to as "unforgetting."

Hypermnesia is alleged to occur as part of the process of psychotherapy, as the patient recalls more and more of the forgotten past. However, hypermnesia in this setting is hard to interpret, largely because we often have no way of checking whether the patient's reports are true. There is also some concern here about the possibility of memories being *suggested* by a therapist or mutually "constructed" by the therapist and client. Finally, memories "recovered" in therapy often involve events that should have been memorable in the first place—significant events in the patient's life or events for which many retrieval cues have long been available. The fact that these events *weren't* recalled prior to the therapy is often difficult to understand, and this adds to the suspicion that some of the memories recovered in therapy aren't memories at all. (We will return to these points later. For further discussion, see Erdelyi & Goldberg, 1979; Holmes, 1991; Loftus, 1993. For discussion of hypermnesia in forensic settings, see Turtle & Yuille, 1994.)

Nonetheless, it is clear that hypermnesia does exist, at least in some contexts. For example, participants in one study were asked to recall pictures that they had earlier seen (Erdelyi & Kleinbard, 1978). The participants then continued trying to recall the pictures over a period of several days. As can be seen in Figure 7.4, the participants' early recall indicated much forgetting. However, this forgetting steadily dissipated as participants continued their recall efforts. (See also Bahrick & Hall, 1993; Erdelyi & Becker, 1974; Erdelyi, Buschke & Finkelstein, 1977;

Erdelyi, Finkelstein, Herrell, Miller & Thomas, 1976; Roediger & Payne, 1982, 1985; Roediger & Thorpe, 1978; Roediger & Wheeler, 1993; Wheeler, 1995.)

Is there anything one can do to promote hypermnesia? A promising approach has been developed by Fisher, Geiselman, and their colleagues (Fisher, Geiselman & Amador, 1989; Fisher, Geiselman, Raymond & Jurkevich, 1987; Geiselman, 1984). Their so-called cognitive interview is often used in questioning eyewitnesses to crimes, in order to maximize what they recall. This technique employs several different strategies. For example, witnesses are encouraged to recount the event in more than one sequence (e.g., from first to last and from last to first) and from more than one perspective. Witnesses are also led to reconstruct the environmental and personal context of the witnessed event. In short, the technique tries to generate a large number, and a large variety, of retrieval cues, and this does seem to promote recall with adults and with children (Bekerian & Dennett, 1993; Geiselman & Padilla, 1988; Fisher & Geiselman, 1992; Fisher & McCauley, 1994; for some complexities, though, see Memon & Highan, 1999). Let's emphasize that there's no surprise in the fact that this interview technique works: As we've repeatedly noted, much forgetting involves retrieval failure, and retrieval failure is less likely when multiple retrieval cues are provided. Retrieval failure is also less likely when remembering happens in a context that reinstates the circumstances of the to-be-remembered event. We saw much evidence for these points in Chapter 6, and it's exactly these points that underlie the success of the cognitive interview.

## MEMORY: AN OVERALL ASSESSMENT

Where does all of this leave us? We obviously cannot take memory accuracy for granted, since we have seen over and over in this chapter that memory errors do happen. People sometimes confidently, sincerely, and vividly recall events that never took place. In other settings, they recall actual events, but in a fashion that is systematically different from the way the events really unfolded.

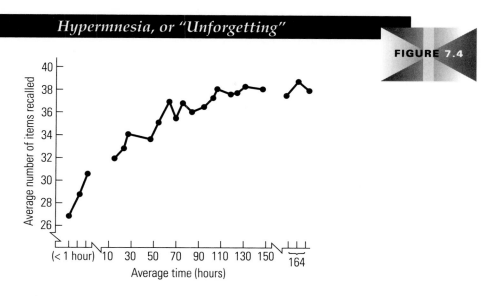

### Hypermnesia, or "Unforgetting"

**FIGURE 7.4**

Participants in this experiment continued, over the period of one week, to try remembering materials they had learned. As the figure shows, participants' efforts were rewarded: With more time and effort spent on trying to remember, participants actually remembered more and more. [After Erdelyi & Kleinbard, 1978.]

Most of these errors have been documented in the laboratory, but it is easy to identify the same sorts of errors in various real-world settings—including settings in which the stakes are extremely high. An obvious example is an eyewitness to a crime, and there is no question that eyewitness accounts are sometimes mistaken, a fact well documented by investigators (e.g., Ceci & Bruck, 1995; Loftus & Ketcham, 1991; Schacter, 1999; Wright & Davies, 1999; Wright & McDaid, 1996) and acknowledged by the U.S. Department of Justice (Connors, Lundregan, Miller & McEwan, 1996).

At the same time, though, there is also much to *praise* about human memory. We have mentioned a number of studies showing extraordinary accuracy in what people remember, even after long delays (Brewin et al., 1993; Howes et al., 1993; Yuille & Cutshall, 1986). We might also mention a number of *case studies* testifying to the power of human mem-

ory. The anthropologist Gregory Bateson (1958) has described masters of totemic knowledge in New Guinea who are able to recall the names of thousands of significant totems. The conductor Arturo Toscanini apparently had memorized the complete scores of a huge number of works of music and could remember details of each score with ease (Marek, 1975). And so on. (See Neisser, 1982, for other examples.)

And even when memory errors occur, they may have a positive side. As we have repeatedly noted, the quantity of information in long-term storage is vast, and this creates a problem: How are we to locate any specific memory within this huge repository? We have argued that search through memory is facilitated by memory *connections*, with each connection serving as a retrieval path. Thus, to make memories retrievable, we need the connections. Yet it is these same connections that lead to many memory errors: As we have discussed, the connections interweave our memories, and also interweave the records of specific episodes with more generic knowledge. This interweaving makes it difficult to discern which bits "belong with" which memories, and this is what produces many of our memory mistakes.

Viewed in this way, the memory errors may simply be the price we have to pay for effective memory retrieval: To avoid the errors, we would need to restrict the connections. If we did that, we would lose the ability to locate our own memories within long-term storage.

Other memory errors need to be understood in a different way. We have noted (e.g., in Chapter 3) that the information provided to us by the world is often ambiguous or incomplete. In addition, and perhaps more important, the world often presents us with far more information than we can use. This is illustrated in Figure 7.5. The cartoon is silly, but it makes a profound point: Our environments provide us with a vast number of things that we *might* notice. If we notice the wrong things, or if we try to notice everything, we will be overwhelmed by foolish irrel-

## The Importance of Schemata in Guiding Our Attention

**FIGURE 7.5**

Our world is rich with information, far more information than we could use. Worse, much of this information is not useful for many of our purposes. We therefore need some means of making intelligent selections from the overall information available to us. Guidance of this sort seems to be exactly what this corporate spy is missing.

evancies. We therefore need to make some intelligent choices so that we focus on useful information, not the trivia.

It is these undeniable facts that force us to rely on inference and assumption in our intellectual commerce with the world. In particular, we deal with the ambiguity in our world by relying on interpretations that have worked in the past. We cope with incomplete information by "plugging the gaps" with schematic knowledge. We choose what to pay attention to by, again, relying on our schematic knowledge, using this knowledge as a guide to what's important and what's not.

These are not matters of choice or convenience; they are matters of necessity if we are to escape the disaster depicted in Figure 7.5. And, usually, these strategies are successful, since the world is, after all, a reasonably regular place; it's this regularity that is summarized in our schematic knowledge.

However, even though the world is generally a uniform place, it isn't entirely so. Sometimes kitchens don't have stoves, and sometimes academic offices contain no books. Although our assumptions will often be correct, sometimes they are not, and this is another source of memory error: When we rely on background knowledge to supplement our perception, or to supplement what we recall, we risk inaccuracy. But we really have no option here: We need to make the assumptions in order to make possible our moment-by-moment interactions with the world. If this strategy sometimes leads to mistakes, that is just the price we must pay.

Finally, what about *forgetting*? Remarkably, this too may be a blessing in disguise, for sometimes it is to our advantage to remember less, and to forget more.

In an extraordinary short story titled "Funes the Memorious," Jorge Luis Borges describes a character named Funes, who has a perfect memory. Funes never forgets anything, but rather than being pleased or proud of this capacity, he is immensely distressed by his memorial prowess. "My memory, sir, is like a garbage heap," he complains. Funes's problem is that he is"almost incapable of ideas of a general, Platonic sort. Not only was it difficult for him to comprehend

that the generic symbol *dog* embraces so many unlike individuals of diverse size and form; it bothered him that the dog at 3:14 (seen from the side) should have the same name as the dog at 3:15 (seen from the front)" (Borges, 1964).

This story is a work of fiction, but Funes is remarkably similar to an actual person. Luria (1968) describes a case of a man, identified only as "S," who, like Funes, never forgets anything. S, just like Funes, is not well served by his extraordinary memory. In tests of intelligence, S does not do well; he is often distracted, it would seem, by the rich detail of his own recollections. Like Funes, S finds it difficult to think in abstract terms.

These remarkable cases imply a positive side to forgetting. To think abstractly, one must overlook many concrete details. To continue with Borges's example, individual dogs do differ in many ways, and if you're keenly alert to those differences, this will impede your thinking about dogs *in general*. Therefore, you need to gloss over the differences, gloss over the details, in order to think about the general category; forgetting helps to make this possible. This is presumably why S, the real character, complains about his "perfect" memory, just as Funes did. Apparently, a perfect memory, with no forgetting, is far from desirable. (For other discussion of the *advantages* of forgetting, see Garner et al., 1989; Johnson et al., 1993; Riccio, Rabinowitz & Axelrod, 1994.)

It seems, then, that our overall assessment of memory can be reasonably upbeat. We have, to be sure, discussed a wide range of memory errors—often in domains where we would prefer to avoid error. Worse, we have argued that the errors can be large, and that, once made, the errors seem to be largely undetectable, so that one never realizes the past is incorrectly recalled. But, despite all of this grim news, we have also emphasized that errors are the exception rather than the rule. In general, our memories preserve the past with impressive fidelity. In addition, we are now suggesting that, even in making errors, and even in forgetting, human memory functions in a fashion that serves us well.

## Autobiographical Memory

We have now considered many different types of memories—memories of word lists, memories of sentences and stories, memories for places and events. All of these count as **episodic memories**, since they provide a record of what happened in a particular time and place; they are different from generic memories, which contain our knowledge of how things work in general (i.e., our various memory schemata) and our knowledge of many facts (the fact that the sky is blue on a sunny day, or that $2+2=4$).

There is no question that episodic and generic memory are different from each other. Some forms of brain damage, for example, seem to disrupt episodic memory but not generic memory; other forms of brain damage do the reverse (e.g., Schacter, 1996; Tulving, 1993). This makes it clear that episodic and generic memory are served by different brain systems.

In addition, it may be useful to subdivide these categories of memory still further—so that we might, for example, need different theoretical accounts for different types of episodic memory. Remarkably, though, we have made considerable progress without these more fine-grained distinctions. The principles we have discussed—the sources of memory error, the difficulty of detecting memory error—seem to apply to *all* episodic memories, including memory for arbitrary word lists *and* memory for complex episodes. (For some debate on this issue, though, see Banaji & Crowder, 1989; Neisser, 1982.)

One type of episodic memory, however, may need special consideration: the **autobiographical memory** that each of us has, containing the full recollection of events in our lives. Autobiographical memory may be distinctive, first of all, because it obviously includes memories pertinent to our sense of self, our sense of who we are. How does this relevance to oneself guide remembering? Second, autobiographical memory contains our recollection of various formative events in our lives; these events are likely to have been emotional at the time they occurred. That invites us to consider a topic we have largely neglected so far—namely, the impact of emotion on memory. Finally, autobiographical memory also includes events from

very far back in our lives, memories of events that took place years, or perhaps decades, ago; how are memories recalled across these very long time spans? (For more on autobiographical memory, including how this memory is structured and organized, and what brain systems underlie autobiographical remembering, see Brown & Schopflocher, 1998; Burt et al., 1998; Conway & Pleydell-Pearce, 2000.)

### MEMORY AND THE SELF

Relevance to the self is a powerful force in shaping memory. As one consideration, information perceived to be relevant to the self is, in general, *better remembered*, a result referred to as the **self-reference effect** (Symons & Johnson, 1997). This effect emerges in many forms, including an advantage in remembering things you have said as opposed to things others have said, better memory for adjectives that apply to you relative to adjectives that do not, better memory for names of places you have visited relative to names of places you have never been, and so on.

Why should this be? Why should self-relevant material be better remembered? One possibility is attention: Each of us tends to take special interest in events that are related to our own lives, and so we are likely to attend to these events with special care. This may account for much of the self-reference effect. Schemata are another factor: Each of us knows an enormous amount about ourselves, and so we are likely to have a rich and detailed *self-schema*. This schema will serve as a powerful mnemonic device, organizing and interconnecting any self-relevant information.

A separate role for the self arises from our earlier argument that some "remembering" is, in fact, *reconstruction* based on current knowledge and current understanding. When, for example, you try to recall what you did last Tuesday, you're likely to rely on your understanding of how, in general, your Tuesdays unfold; that will guide your memory search and also help you to fill any gaps in your recollection. Similarly, when you're trying to recall how you acted, say, at last year's Christmas party, you will probably draw on your understanding of what things you're likely to have done at this party and what things you're likely not to have done. This will depend, in turn, on how you view yourself: If you think of yourself, say, as a quiet and polite person, you're unlikely to reconstruct a drunken dance on the table. If you think of yourself as a funny person, you're unlikely to reconstruct your sitting quietly in the corner.

Does our self-perception influence memory in this way? Consider the fact that many people believe that they have been reasonably consistent, reasonably stable, over their lifetimes. They believe, in other words, that they've always been pretty much the same as they are now. People with this belief do end up recalling their past in a biased fashion, one that maximizes the (apparent) stability of their lives. Specifically, their recall of their attitudes in the past, and the past status of their romantic relationships, and their health, all tend to be biased in a direction emphasizing the consistency in their lives. In contrast, people who have the opposite current view of themselves—namely, the belief that they have changed a lot over the years—show the opposite memory bias (e.g., Holmberg & Homes, 1994; Levine, 1997; Marcus, 1986; Ross, 1989). And if your views on this point change—if you decide you've been less consistent, for example, than you once thought—your memory changes accordingly (Conway & Ross, 1984).

It's also true that most of us would prefer to have a *positive* view of ourselves, including a positive view of how we have acted in the past. This, too, can shape memory, via several different mechanisms. One mechanism is *biased retrieval*, in which we spend effort to seek out memories that make us look good, and spend much less effort in the search for less-flattering episodes. In one study, for example, half of the participants were led to believe that being *introverted* is a particularly good quality, and the other half were led to the opposite view—that being *extroverted* is the more desirable trait. When asked about their past, each group searched through memory in a biased manner, selectively recalling events in the past in which they did, in fact, have the desired quality (Kunda, 1990).

As a different example, Bahrick, Hall and Berger (1996) asked college students to recall their high school grades as accurately as they could. The students were much more accurate in recalling their good grades than they were in recalling their poor ones—89% of the A's but only 29% of the D's were remembered correctly. Moreover, the errors were reasonably uniform in their content: When memory mistakes were made, it was because students remembered their grades as being better than they actually were. Close analysis of the data, however, suggested that this pattern is *not* the result of "motivated forgetting." Instead, the data suggest that students sometimes forget their grades for reasons having nothing to do with self-service. Once the grades were forgotten, though, *then* self-service could enter the scene, biasing the reconstruction of what the grades must have been. (For other mechanisms through which current motivations and current goals can color autobiographical recall, see Conway & Holmes, 1999; Conway & Pleydell-Pearce, 2000; Mather et al., 2000.)

## MEMORY AND EMOTION

Our clearest, most vivid memories tend to be memories for emotional events. It does not seem to matter whether the event was a happy one or a sad one, an event that made you angry or an event that made you afraid. Across all these categories, there is a strong positive relationship between memory vividness and emotion (Bohannon, 1988; Brown & Kulik, 1977; Christianson & Loftus, 1990; Pillemer, 1984; Reisberg, Heuer, McLean & O'Shaughnessy, 1988; Rubin & Kozin, 1984; White, 1989).

Several mechanisms shape how we remember emotional events. At a biological level, emotional events seem to trigger a response in the amygdala, and among other effects, this leads to an increase in blood levels of the hormone norepinephrine. This in turn leads to an increase in the level of glucose in the blood, which then promotes the process of **memory consolidation**—the process through which memories are biologically "cemented in place." (For research examining the various steps of this sequence, see Cahill et al., 1996; Gold, 1987; White, 1991; van Stegeren et al., 1998; for more on consolidation, see

Hasselmo, 1999; McGaugh, 2000.) All of this is then probably the reason the process of forgetting is relatively slow for emotional events. Eventually, emotional events are forgotten, but this forgetting seems to be slower than forgetting of emotionally neutral (but otherwise comparable) events (Bohannon, 1993; Burke, Heuer & Reisberg, 1992; Pillemer, 1984; Yuille & Tollestrup, 1992).

In addition, many authors have argued that arousal, including the arousal caused by emotion, leads to a "narrowing" of attention so that, in an emotional event, all of one's attention will be focused on just a few aspects of the scene (Easterbrook, 1959). These aspects therefore receive "concentrated" attention and will be firmly placed into memory. The rest of the event, however, will be excluded from this "narrowed" focus and so won't be remembered later on. As a result, people will have good memory for the emotional event's "center" but poor memory for the event's "periphery."

These claims are consistent with a pattern often observed in eyewitnesses to crimes—a pattern referred to as **weapon focus**. Witness will often "zoom in" on some critical detail (such as a weapon), to the exclusion of all else. As a result, the witness will remember the perpetrator's gun or knife with great clarity, but may remember little else about the crime—including such crucial details as what the perpetrator's face looked like!

Many studies have documented this sort of "memory narrowing," both in the laboratory and in the recollection of actual crimes (e.g., Burke et al., 1992; Christianson, 1992; Steblay, 1992). But this narrowing is not always observed (e.g., Libkuman et al., 1999), for reasons that are as yet unclear. One suggestion is that much depends on *why* someone is aroused—whether it is because the person has seen a particular stimulus that caused the arousal (a weapon, the sight of a bloody wound) or whether the person experienced some frightening thought, or perhaps empathy. At least some evidence suggests that memory narrowing is produced by only the first (stimulus-based) type of arousal (Laney, Campbell, Heuer & Reisberg, 2000), but other evidence on this point is needed.

## FLASHBULB MEMORIES

One group of emotional memories, however, seems to be in a category all its own. These are the so-called **flashbulb memories**—memories of extraordinary clarity, typically for highly emotional events, retained despite the passage of many years. When Brown and Kulik (1977) introduced the term "flashbulbs," they pointed as a paradigm case to the memories people have of first hearing the news of President Kennedy's assassination. Their participants, interviewed more than a decade after that event, remembered it "as though it were yesterday," recalling details of where they were at the time, what they were doing, and whom they were with. Many participants were able to recall the clothing worn by people around them, the exact words uttered, and the like. Memories of comparable clarity have also been reported for other, more recent, events, including the *Challenger* space shuttle disaster in 1986, the 1995 reading of the verdict in the O.J. Simpson trial, and the news of Princess Diana's death in 1997 (see, e.g., Pillemer, 1984; Rubin & Kozin, 1984; see also Weaver, 1993; Winograd & Neisser, 1993).

There are many questions to be asked about flashbulb memories. One crucial question concerns the *accuracy* of these memories. As we have seen repeatedly in this chapter, their accuracy cannot be taken for granted, no matter how vivid or compelling these memories seem to be. Indeed, some flashbulb memories do turn out to contain large-scale errors. For example, Neisser and Harsch (1992) interviewed college students one day after the space shuttle explosion, asking them how they first heard about the explosion, what they were doing at the time, and so on. They then re-interviewed these students three years later, asking the same questions about the shuttle explosion. The results show *remarkably little agreement* between the immediate and delayed reports, even with regard to major facts such as who delivered the news or where the person was when the news arrived. It appears, then, that the three-year reports are mostly false, although it should be said that the students were highly confident about the accuracy of this reports. (For similar data, see Christianson, 1989; Linton, 1975, pp. 386–387; Wagenaar & Groeneweg, 1990.)

There is no question, therefore, that people can make conspicuous errors in remembering emotional events. Let's emphasize, however, that people also retain a great deal about these events. For example, McCloskey, Wible and Cohen (1988) also examined students' recollection of the space shuttle disaster, assessing memory accuracy by comparing reports collected immediately after the event with reports collected nine months later. Like Neisser and Harsch, they observed many errors in the students' recall, but we can equally well focus on how much their participants *did* remember. Nine months after the disaster, 81% of the participants still remembered where they had been when they first learned about the explosion; 70% remembered who had told them the news.

What should we make of this? Why did the Neisser and Harsch participants remember so little, while the McCloskey et al. participants remembered a great deal? One predictor of memory accuracy seems to be the *consequentiality* of the flashbulb event. If the event matters directly for the participant's life, it seems, then the event will be well remembered. If the event is largely inconsequential for that person, then memory accuracy will be poor. Several results point toward this claim. For example, one study examined how accurately people remembered the 1989 San Francisco earthquake. For individuals who lived in Georgia, thousands of miles from the earthquake's epicenter, memory accuracy was quite low. For people who lived in Santa Clara (at the epicenter), the earthquake was remembered accurately and in detail (Neisser, Winograd & Weldon, 1991; Palmer, Schreiber & Fox, 1991). Similarly, another study examined people's memories for the abrupt and unexpected resignation of British prime minister Margaret Thatcher. People differed widely in the accuracy of their recall for this event, but this accuracy was closely linked to their assessments of how important the event was for them: If it was important for them, they remembered it, so that, again, consequentiality predicted accurate recollection (Conway, Anderson, Larsen, Donnelly, McDaniel, McClelland, Rawles & Logie, 1994).

In summary, some flashbulb memories do turn out to be marvelously accurate, whereas others turn out to be filled with error. From the point of view of the person doing the remembering, however, there is no difference between these accurate memories and the inaccurate ones—both are recalled with great detail, both are recalled with enormous confidence. In both cases, the memory can be intensely emotional. This obviously adds strength to our earlier claim that memory errors can occur even in the midst of our strongest, most confident recollection.

## TRAUMATIC MEMORIES

Flashbulb memories tend to be highly emotional—some people still cry when they think about Princess Diana's death, even though her death was several years ago; other people still grow angry (or, in some cases, relieved) when they think of O. J. Simpson's acquittal. But, sadly, we can easily find cases of much stronger emotion, evoked by much more consequential events. How are these events remembered? If someone has witnessed wartime atrocities, can we count on the accuracy of their testimony in a war crimes trial? If someone reports a sexual assault, can we count on the accuracy of her recall? And, for that matter, if someone suffers through the horrors of a sexual assault, will the painful memory eventually fade? Or will the memory remain as a horrific remnant of the experience?

We can certainly document cases in which horrible events are well remembered for many years, and indeed, victims of some atrocities seem plagued by a cruel enhancement of memory, leaving them with extra-vivid and long-lived recollections of the terrible event (Brewin, 1998; Golier et al., 1997; Harber & Pennebacker, 1992; Horowitz & Reidbord, 1992; Pope et al., 1998). But we can also find cases in which people who suffered through truly extreme events seem to have little or no recall of the horrors (Arrigo & Pezdek, 1997; Brown et al., 1998). We can even find cases in which people seem to remember a horrible event extremely well, but with many errors—often large-scale errors—contained within their recall (e.g., Gourevitch, 1999).

Why are some traumatic events remembered so well, and others lost altogether? The most promising hypothesis is that traumatic events are sometimes not remembered because the intense emotion of trauma disrupts the processes needed for memory consolidation. In this case, no memory is ever established; the seeds of memory, so to speak, are washed from the soil before they have a chance to take root. Moreover, it is likely that people differ in how they react to trauma (both psychologically and biologically), and this is why some traumatic memories are disrupted in this fashion, while others are not. (For discussion of what causes these differences among people, see Heim et al., 1997; McCranie et al., 1992; Bremner et al., 1993; Schacter, 1996; Yehuda, 1997.)

A different possibility is that there are different *species* of trauma, some of which are likely to be well remembered, and others not. For example, some investigators have proposed that isolated cases of trauma will be remembered, whereas repeated trauma will not (Terr, 1991, 1994); other investigators have suggested that trauma involving betrayal will be lost from memory, whereas other traumas will be remembered (Freyd, 1996, 1998). However, evidence currently speaks against both of these suggestions (Shobe & Kihlstrom, 1997), making the interrupted-consolidation hypothesis seem all the more plausible (although see also Nadel & Jacobs, 1998).

Finally, one last hypothesis is highly controversial: Several authors have argued that highly painful memories will be *repressed*. Repressed memories, it is claimed, will not be consciously available later on, but will still exist in a person's long-term storage. As a result, these memories may continue to influence a person in one form or another, and, in suitable circumstances, may be "recovered"—that is, made conscious once again.

Many memory researchers, are deeply skeptical of this claim, and find the evidence offered in support of the repression idea unpersuasive. One line of evidence rests on the subtle ways an unconscious memory can (allegedly) show itself—in someone's dreams or in their personal quirks and habits. This evidence can be taken seriously, however, only if one accepts a rather elaborate system (often based on the theories of Sigmund Freud) for how these "symbols" should be interpreted. That system of interpretation is itself controversial, with many scholars arguing that the system of interpretation is so loose, so flexible, that it is unusable. In short, almost anything can be interpreted in almost any way, leaving us with little confidence that any particular interpretation is "correct." As a result of all this, the system of interpretation—of dreams, of symptoms—cannot provide compelling evidence for repression; if repression exists, we need to document it in some other manner.

A different line of evidence comes from the "recovered memories" themselves. If an event is completely forgotten for years and years, and then is finally remembered, isn't this proof that memories can be "repressed" and then "recovered"? Unfortunately, it is no proof at all. Some "recovered memories" were probably remembered all along; the person simply refused to discuss them (presumably because the remembered events were quite painful). In this case, the "recovery" reflects the fact that the person is at last willing to discuss these memories out loud. Such a "recovery" may be extremely consequential—emotionally and perhaps legally—but it does not tell us anything about how memory works.

In other cases, memories lost and then found may reveal the effects of ordinary retrieval failure. This certainly is a mechanism that can hide memories from view for long periods of time, only to have the memories re-emerge once a suitable retrieval cue is available. In this case, too, the "recovery" is of enormous importance for the person finally remembering the long-lost episodes, but again, this merely confirms the role of an already-documented memory mechanism; there is no need here for any exotic theorizing about "repression."

Finally, and most troubling, we need to entertain the possibility that at least some of these "recovered memories" are, in fact, false memories. After all, we know that false memories occur, and that they are more likely when recovering the distant past than when trying to remember recent events. It is also worth mentioning that many recovered memories seem to emerge only with the assistance of a therapist who is genuinely convinced, for instance, that the client's psychological problems stem from childhood abuse. Even if the therapist scrupulously avoids leading questions, bias might still lead him or her to shape the client's memory in other ways—by giving signs of interest or concern if the client hits on the "right" line of exploration, by spending more time on topics related to the alleged memories, and so forth. In these ways, the climate within a therapeutic session could subtly guide the client toward finding exactly the "memories" the therapist expects to find.

These are, of course, difficult issues, especially when we bear in mind that recovered memories often involve horrible episodes, such as episodes of sexual abuse; if these memories are true, therefore, they are evidence for repugnant crimes. But here, as in all cases, the veracity of recollection cannot be taken for granted. This caveat is obviously important for anyone trying to think through whether "repression" exists or not, and it is far more important for anyone wrestling with this sort of traumatic recollection. (For broad discussion of this difficult issue, see Crews, 1996; Holmes, 1991; Kihlstrom, 1993, 1998; Loftus, 1993; Pendergast, 1995; Read, 1999; Schacter, 1996. As an illustration of how easily a false memory might emerge in therapy, see Mazzoni et al., 1999. For a sharply different view of these themes, see Bass & Davis, 1988; Freyd, 1996.)

## LONG, LONG-TERM REMEMBERING

Our discussion has already touched on the fact that people sometimes seek to recall events that happened long, long ago—perhaps several decades earlier. Of course, distant events are often difficult to remember, and some of our memories from long ago will certainly turn out to be mistaken. But, impressively, our memories from long ago can also turn out to be wonderfully accurate.

Bahrick, Bahrick and Wittlinger (1975) tracked down the graduates of a particular high school, people who had graduated last year, and the year before, and the year before that and, ultimately, people who had graduated fifty years before. All of these alumni were shown photographs from their own year's high school yearbook. For each photo, they were given a group of names and had to choose the name of the person shown in the picture. The data show remarkably little forgetting—performance was approximately 90% correct if tested three months after graduation, the same after seven years, and the same after 14 years. In some versions of the test, performance was still excellent after 34 years (Figure 7.6).

Recall performance in this study was slightly worse than recognition but was still impressive. When asked to come up with the names on their own, rather than choosing the correct name from a list, the participants were able to name 70% of the faces when tested three months after graduation, and 60% after nine months. Remarkably, they were still able to name 60% of their classmates after seven years.

As a different example, what about the material you are learning right now? You are presumably reading this textbook as part of a course on cognitive psychology. Five years from now, will you still remember things you have learned in this course? How about a decade from now? Conway, Cohen and Stanhope (1991) explored precisely these questions, testing students' retention of a cognitive psychology course taken years earlier. The results broadly echo the pattern we have already seen: Some forgetting of names and specific concepts was observed during the first three years after the course. After the third year, however, performance stabilized, so that students tested after ten years still remembered a fair amount and, indeed, remembered just as much as did students tested after three years. Memory for more general facts and memory for research methods showed even less forgetting.

Some loss of memories is observed in these studies, but what is remarkable is how much people do remember, and for how long. In study after study, there is an initial period of forgetting, generally for the first three or four years. After that, performance remains impressively consistent, despite the passage of several decades. In other words, if you learn the material well enough to retain it for three years, odds are that you will remember it for the rest of your life. Indeed, Bahrick (1984) has claimed that memories can achieve a state of **permastore** (for "permanent storage"),

## Memory over the Very Long Term

**FIGURE 7.6**

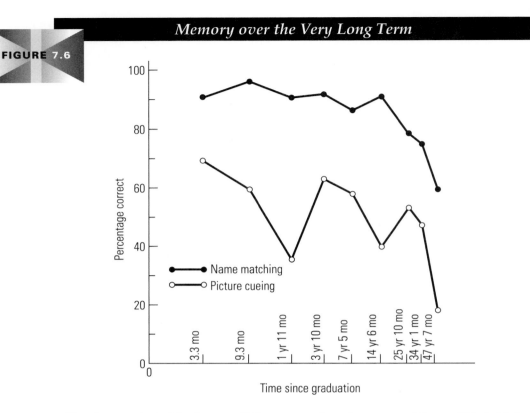

People were tested for how well they remembered names and faces of their high school classmates. In one version, the research participants were given a group of names and had to select which name belonged to the face shown. In this task ("name matching"), participants were 90% correct even 14 years after graduation. In a different version, participants were shown the pictures and had to come up with the names on their own ("picture cueing"). In this test, participants were still 60% accurate after 7 years. The data do show a dropoff after 47 years, but it is unclear whether this reflects an erosion of memory or a more general dropoff in performance caused by the normal process of aging. [After Bahrick, Bahrick & Wittlinger, 1975.]

although he argues that only some memories achieve this status. Permastore is more likely, for example, if the material is extremely well learned in the first place (Bahrick, 1984; Bahrick & Hall, 1991; Conway et al., 1991; Conway, Cohen & Stanhope, 1992). Permastore is also more likely if the person continues to learn new materials in that domain. Thus, students who take calculus courses in college are likely to remember their high school algebra even fifty years after high school (Bahrick & Hall, 1991). Some learning strategies also seem more likely to produce permastore (Bahrick, Bahrick, Bahrick & Bahrick, 1993).

Very-long-term retention is also helped by one further factor: rehearsal. For many years, Linton (1975,

1978, 1982, 1986; also Wagenaar, 1986) has kept careful notes on the events that fill each of her days, sort of like keeping a detailed diary. After certain intervals, she selects events from the diary and tests her own memory for what transpired; this memory can then be checked against the written record. Linton reports impressive memory accuracy for these mundane events—over 65% remembered after three years, roughly the same after four years. In addition, Linton often retests her memory for a given event. This way, we can ask about the effects of rehearsing these memories since, after all, the experience of testing memory constitutes a re-encounter with the original episode. (Thus, the first test provides a rehearsal that may then benefit the second test.) This rehearsal turns out to have enormous impact. For those events previously tested (rehearsed), forgetting after three years was cut in half, from 32% forgotten with no rehearsals, to 16% with one rehearsal (Figure 7.7).

This powerful effect of reminders can also be demonstrated outside of autobiographical recall. For example, Berger, Hall and Bahrick (1999) tested their participants' knowledge for various bits of information: "What is the last name of the singer who popularized a dance known as the Twist?" "What was the last name of the first person to set foot on the moon?" If the participant could not recall the answer, it was shown briefly on the screen—for just five seconds. This quick reminder, though, was extremely effective: Nine days later, there was a 64% chance that participants would recall this now-refreshed memory. The results were different, though, if participants were given a five-second exposure to some fact they had never met before. In that case, there was merely a 3% chance of recalling the fact nine days later. It seems, then, that five seconds is *not* enough time to learn something if you're starting from scratch, but it certainly is enough time to refresh an already-existing memory.

## HOW GENERAL ARE THE PRINCIPLES OF MEMORY?

As we have now seen, autobiographical memory is in some ways different from other sorts of remembering and is in some ways the same. Autobiograph-

ical memories can last for years and years, but so can memories that do not refer directly to one's own life. Autobiographical remembering is far more likely if the person occasionally revisits the target memories; these rehearsals dramatically reduce forgetting. But the same is true in nonautobiographical remembering. Indeed, the Berger et al. result just described has powerful implications for education in general: Occasional reminders of things once learned can have enormous effects!

Autobiographical memory is also open to error, just as other forms of remembering are. We saw this in cases of flashbulb memories that turn out to be false (e.g., Neisser & Harsch, 1992). We have also seen that misinformation and leading questions can plant false autobiographical memories—about birthday parties that never happened, and trips to the hospital that never took place.

These facts strengthen a claim that has been implicit in much of our discussion over the last three chapters: Certain principles do seem to apply to memory in general, quite independent of what it is that is being remembered. But of course this does not mean that all principles of memory apply to all types of remembering. As we saw in Chapter 6, for example, the rules that govern implicit memory may be different from those that govern explicit memory. And, as we have seen here, at least some of the factors important for autobiographical remembering (e.g., the role of self-flattery) may be irrelevant to other sorts of memory. Similarly, debate continues about whether memories for traumatic events are systematically different from other sorts of memory (Nadel & Jacobs, 1998; Shobe & Kihlstrom, 1997).

In the end, therefore, our overall theory of memory is likely to need more than one level of description. On the more specific side, we will need some principles that apply only to certain types of memory—principles, for example, specifically aimed at autobiographical remembering. (These principles would presumably include some discussion of the role of emotion, the self, and the motivations and goals of the person doing the remembering.) On the broader side, we must not lose track of how much we can explain in terms of principles cast more gener-

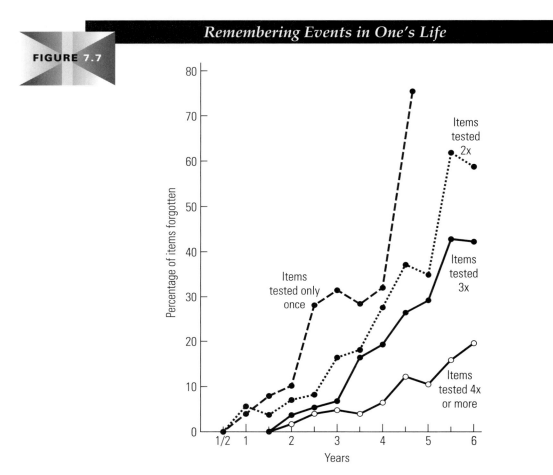

### Remembering Events in One's Life

FIGURE 7.7

Each day, the author of this study recorded what had happened during that day. At various later times she tested her memory for different events. Some events were tested only once; two-thirds of these were still remembered after 3 or 4 years. Other items were tested multiple times; each test served to remind the investigator of the event, and so "refreshed" the memory. Even a single "refresher" can markedly decrease forgetting. [After Linton, 1978.]

ally—cast, for example, in terms of the role of *memory connections*. As we have seen over the last three chapters, these more general principles have moved us forward considerably in our understanding of memory in many different domains and have allowed us to illuminate many aspects of learning, of memory retrieval, and of the sources of memory error.

## Chapter Summary

1. Our memories are usually accurate, but errors do occur and can be quite large. Some errors result from inattention during an event, which leads to gaps in the memory record. Other errors result from one's initial understanding of an episode. This un-

derstanding promotes accurate memory for some aspects of the episode, but can also lead to *intrusion errors*, since elements that were part of the understanding, but not part of the actual episode, are often recalled as being part of the episode.

2. *Retention interval* is an important variable in governing memory accuracy and completeness. As the interval grows, there is more opportunity for *retrieval failure*, and also more opportunity for *memory interference* to occur. However, the mere passage of time seems to do little to erode our memories, and so relatively little forgetting is directly attributable to *decay* of the original memories.

3. Memory interference can take many forms. In some cases, *generic knowledge* interferes with the recall of a specific episode. In other cases, related episodes are blurred together in memory, and this can produce *source confusion* with regard to which elements occurred in which episode. Interference can also be produced by *misinformation* received after an event—delivered either in leading questions, or in suggested descriptions for how the event took place. In either case, misinformation can change how we remember the people or the actions within an event, and in some cases can plant memories for entire events that never happened at all.

4. Most memory errors seem undetectable, because the false memory is recalled with just as much detail, emotion, and confidence, as a historically accurate memory. Some memory failures appear to be reversible, with warnings allowing people to increase both the completeness and the accuracy of their recall. Many errors, however, are not reversible, and remain even with strong and explicit warnings—either prior to the initial event itself, or at the time of recollection. Memory errors also cannot be defeated with exotic techniques such as hypnosis or "memory-improving" drugs. However, memory accuracy can be promoted by more mundane techniques, such as a reinstatement of the original context, as a way of promoting recall.

5. While memory errors are troubling, they may simply be the price we pay in order to obtain other advantages. For example, many errors result from the dense network of connections that link our various memories. These connections sometimes make it difficult to recall which elements occurred in which setting, but these same connections serve as retrieval paths, and, without the connections, we might have great difficulty in locating our memories in long-term storage. Even forgetting may have a positive side, by virtue of trimming details from memory in a fashion that may foster abstract thinking.

6. *Autobiographical memory* is influenced by the same principles as any other form of memory, but is also shaped by its own set of factors. For example, episodes connected to the self are, in general, better remembered, a pattern known as the *self-reference effect*. Autobiographical memories are also often emotional, and this has multiple effects on memory. Emotion seems to promote *memory consolidation*, but may also produce a pattern of *memory narrowing*.

7. Some events give rise to very clear, long-lasting memories called *flashbulb memories*. Despite their subjective clarity, these memories, like memories of any sort, can contain errors, and, in some cases, can be entirely inaccurate. Flashbulb memories are most likely to be accurate if the remembered events were perceived to be consequential at the time they occurred.

8. At the extreme of emotion, trauma has mixed effects on memory. Some traumatic events are not remembered, probably because of interrupted consolidation. Other traumatic events are remembered for a long time and in great detail. It is not obvious why the results are mixed in this way, but the pattern may be shaped by how the individual reacts to the traumatic event. There is also great controversy over *recovered memories*, but at least some of these memories are likely to be false memories of events that did not occur.

9. Some events can be recalled even after many years have passed. In some cases, this is because the knowledge was learned so well that it reached a state of *permastore*. In other cases, occasional rehearsals preserve a memory for a very long time.

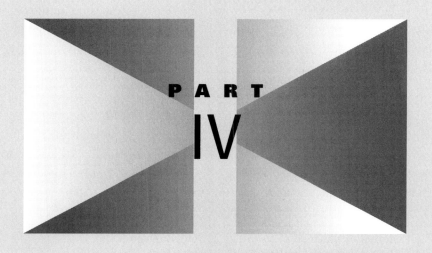

# PART IV

# Knowledge

In Sections 2 and 3, we saw case after case in which our interactions with the world are guided by *knowledge*. In perceiving, we make inferences guided by knowledge about the world's regular patterns. In attending, we anticipate inputs, guided by knowledge about what's likely to occur. In learning, we connect information to things that we already know. And so on. But what is knowledge? How is knowledge represented in the mind? How do we locate knowledge in memory when we need it? How can we manipulate or explore our knowledge, in order to make full use of it?

These questions will be at the heart of this section. In Chapter 8, we explore the proposal that knowledge is represented in the mind by means of a network of interconnected ideas. We'll discuss how this conception can explain the results surveyed in Chapters 5, 6, and 7, and, related, we'll use the network ideas to put some flesh on the ideas, so crucial for these earlier chapters, that learning consists of the creation of memory connections, and that these connections then serve as retrieval paths. In Chapter 8, we'll also return to an idea that was prominent in Chapter 3, namely, that complex processes can be built up from a network of simple elements relying on distributed representations and parallel processing. In the earlier chapter, we applied this idea to the recognition of objects; here we'll apply it to the learning and use of knowledge.

In Chapter 9, we'll take a closer look at the building blocks of our knowledge—our individual concepts. What is it we know when we know what a "dog" is, or when we know what "reading" is? We'll consider several different hypotheses about what this knowledge might be; in the end, we'll see that each of the hypotheses captures a part of the truth, and so we'll be driven toward a several-part theory, combining these various views. In the process, we'll also be driven toward an overall framework in which our knowledge about "dog," "reading," and the like turns out to depend in interesting ways on our knowledge about many other concepts. For example, one probably cannot know what a "dog" is without also understanding what an "animal" is, what a "living thing" is, and so on. As a result, connections among ideas will again enter our view—this time, connections that play a central role in representing our conceptual knowledge.

Chapters 10 and 11 then look at two special types of knowledge: our knowledge about language, and our knowledge about nonverbal representations, specifically visual images. In Chapter 10, we will see that our knowledge of language is highly creative, in the sense that we can produce new words and new sentences that no one has ever used before. But, at the same time, the creativity is somehow constrained, and there are some words and sentences that are considered unacceptable by virtually any speaker. In order to understand this pattern of "constrained creativity," we'll consider the possibility that language knowledge involves abstract rules that are, in some fashion, known and honored by every user of the language.

In Chapter 11, we'll discuss the fact that mental images seem to involve processes and representations that are qualitatively distinct from those involved in other forms of knowledge, but we will also consider some of the ways in which memory for visual appearances is governed by the *same* principles as other forms of knowledge. In pursuing these themes, the chapter surveys the rich pattern of data and theory that constitutes our current understanding of mental imagery; but at the same time, the chapter also has a broader agenda: it attempts to sketch what it means to ask in a serious way whether there are "different forms" of knowledge, or just one.

# Associative Theories of Long-Term Memory

Long-term memory is huge. It has to be, in order to contain all of the information we remember—memories for episodes and for mundane facts, phone numbers, lyrics for songs, the faces of a thousand different acquaintances, the layout of our hometown, the definitions of 50,000–60,000 different words, and on and on and on.

But how do we ever find anything in this huge storehouse? How do we manage to locate a particular bit of information among the millions and millions of other bits contained within this vast warehouse? We emphasized in Chapter 7 how "seamlessly" we integrate remembered information with current environmental input, so that we are often not aware that we have supplemented the actual input with information supplied from memory. Apparently, then, we don't merely succeed in retrieving information from memory; we succeed swiftly, effortlessly, and unwittingly.

We have also suggested that memory search is aided by *connections* between the to-be-learned materials and things one already knows, or connections between the material and aspects of the learning context. We have claimed that these connections provide *retrieval paths*, routes that one can take when searching for some particular memory. But what are these connections? Who or what does the "traveling" on these retrieval paths? We turn now to these questions, and more broadly to the questions of how all of our knowledge is stored in long-term memory, and how that information is located when needed.

235

## The Network Notion

Much of this chapter will be devoted to exploring a single idea: that memory connections provide much more than retrieved paths; instead the connections *are* our memories. For example, you know your mother's name; this fact is recorded in your memory. The proposal to be considered is that this memory is literally represented by a memory connection, in this case a connection between some memory content representing your mother and some memory content representing the sound pattern of her name. That connection isn't some appendage to the memory. Instead, the connection *is* the memory. Likewise for all the other facts you know (the opposite of "hot", how you spent last Thanksgiving, the color of rubies), so that all of knowledge is represented via a sprawling network of these connections, a vast set of **associations**.

The notion that memory contains a network of associations is hardly new. The idea has been discussed, both in philosophy and in psychology, for several centuries. Modern conceptions of the network, however, differ from their predecessors in important ways; we will discuss some of these differences as we proceed. Our initial focus, though, will not be on the modern conceptions *per se*. Instead, we will be concerned with broader themes: What motivates this approach to memory? Why should we think that memory has an "associative" base? Then, once we have discussed these issues, we will turn to some of the specific ways an associative theory might be implemented. We will first consider a form of theorizing patterned after the work of Collins and Loftus (1975) and Anderson (1976, 1980; Anderson & Bower, 1973). Later in the chapter, we will turn to the most recent version of associative theorizing, a sophisticated treatment known as "connectionism."

### HOW MIGHT THE NETWORK WORK?

The essence of a memory network is straightforward. First, we need some means of representing individual ideas; these representations will be the **nodes** within the net, just like the knots within a fisherman's net. (In fact, the word "node" is derived from the Latin word for knot, *nodus*.) These nodes are then tied to each other via connections that we will call associations or associative links. If you like, you can think of the nodes as being akin to cities on a map, and associations as being the highways that link the cities. Learning, within this metaphor, would be similar to building a highway between two cities, or perhaps improving an existing highway, so that it is more easily and quickly traveled.

In this view, what it means to "search" through memory is to begin at one node (one "city") and to travel via the connections until the target information is reached. Critically, not all associations are of equal strength. Some "cities" are linked by superhighways, others only by country roads. Other "cities" are not linked to each other at all, but you can get from one to the next by traveling via some intermediate cities. This will immediately provide part of our account for why some memories are easily called up, while others are not: For example, if asked, "When is your birthday?" you answer quickly and easily. Presumably, this is because there is a strong connection between the MY BIRTHDAY node and the node representing a specific date. This connection has been established by the fact that this date and the idea of birthdays have frequently been thought about in conjunction with each other, creating an easily traveled path from one to the other. (Throughout this chapter, we will use small capital letters when we are referring to a NODE in memory; we will use normal type when referring to the word or stimulus represented by that node.)

Even at this early stage of presentation, though, we reach a point in which modern versions of the network differ from older versions. According to philosophers like John Locke or George Berkeley, associations among ideas are largely "stamped in" by the environment. If you heard the word "birthday" and then heard a date, this would be enough to create a mental association. As we have seen in earlier chapters, however, this claim is not correct: Memory connections are not established in this passive manner. (See, for example, our discussion of maintenance rehearsal and elaborative rehearsal in Chapter 5.)

Modern network theories therefore require a more active role for the learner. Memory connections will be established only if the learner pays attention to the to-be-remembered items during the learning episode. Likewise, a great deal depends on *how* the learner engages the items. For example, if the learner chooses to think about the material in several different ways, this will create multiple connections, each of which can later be used as a retrieval path. The learner will also be helped if he or she thinks about the material in *distinctive* ways. For example, if you establish an association between "THE LIST I STUDIED EARLIER" and "SOME CAPITALIZED WORDS," this connection isn't very informative and probably won't help you later on to remember the to-be-remembered words. In contrast, an association between "THE LIST I STUDIED EARLIER" and, say, "THE OPPOSITE OF LOVE" *is* distinctive and will help you to remember.

## SPREADING ACTIVATION

Theorists speak of a node becoming **activated** when it has received a strong enough input signal, sort of like a lightbulb being turned on by incoming electricity. This implies that what travels through the associative links is akin to energy or fuel, and the associative links themselves can be thought of as "activation carriers"—hoses carrying the fuel or wires carrying electricity. Then, once a node has been activated, it can in turn activate other nodes: Energy will spread out from the just-activated node, via its associations, and this will activate nodes connected to the just-activated node.

To put all of this more precisely, the **activation level** of each node depends on how much activation that node has received and how recently the activation arrived. Eventually, though, the activation level will reach the node's **response threshold**, and this triggers several other events, including an *outward* spread of activation from that node. Activation of a node will also serve to summon attention to that node; this is what it means to "find" a node within the network.

Activation levels below the response threshold, so-called **subthreshold activation**, also have an important role to play: Activation is assumed to accumulate, so that two subthreshold inputs may add together, or **summate**, and bring the node to threshold. Likewise, if a node has been partially activated recently, it is, in effect, already "warmed up," so that even a weak input will be sufficient to bring the node to threshold.

These claims mesh well with points we raised in Chapter 2, when we considered how neurons communicate with each other. Neurons receive activation from other neurons; once a neuron reaches its threshold, it fires, and this sends activation to other neurons. All of this is precisely parallel to the suggestions we are offering here, and this invites the hope that our theorizing about the network will be easily translated into biological terms. If so, we can look forward to a point in which we will understand both how the memory network functions and how it is realized in the nervous system. In addition, the claims we are developing here also parallel those we offered in Chapter 3, when we described how a network of *detectors* might function in object recognition. Detectors receive their activation from other detectors; they can accumulate activation from different inputs; once activated to threshold levels, they fire. We will return to these parallels later in this chapter, when we will argue that the network of nodes in long-term memory *includes* the network of detectors we considered in Chapter 3.

Returning to long-term storage, however, the key idea is that activation travels from node to node via the associative links. As each node becomes activated, it serves as a source for further activation, spreading onward through the network. This process, known as **spreading activation**, allows us to deal with a key issue. How does one navigate through the maze of associations? If you start a search at one node, how do you decide where to go from there? Our initial proposal is that you do not "choose" at all. Instead, activation spreads out from its starting point in all directions simultaneously, flowing through whatever connections are in place. Think of fuel flowing through hoses: If two hoses radiate out from a starting point, the fuel does not "choose" the left hose or the right. If there are two hoses in place, the fuel will flow through both.

This is not to say, however, that all pathways are equally effective in carrying the activation, and in fact, we have already suggested that they're not. Some associative links, thanks to recent or frequent use, are particularly effective; others are less so. (To push the metaphor a bit further, some of the hoses are tiny and so can carry only a small amount of fuel; other hoses are much larger.) For that matter, perhaps some associations are "built in," that is, are innately strong. In any event, the stronger or better-established links will carry activation more efficiently and so will be more successful at activating subsequent nodes.

## Evidence Favoring the Network Approach

This sketch of the network leaves a great deal unspecified, but that is deliberate: Associative nets can be implemented in various ways, and we are not ready yet to talk about the details of particular implementation. We first need to ask whether we are even on the right track. Is this a sensible approach at all? What can be explained in these terms?

### HINTS

Why do hints help us to remember? Why is a free recall procedure ("What was on the list?") more difficult than cued recall ("Was there a word on the list that rhymed with *glove*?")?

Any effort at recall starts with some designation of what it is you are trying to recall: Who was at the party last week? What do you know about Shakespeare's sonnets? What is the capital of South Dakota? These designations then provide the starting point for your memory search: Mention of South Dakota will activate the nodes in memory that represent your knowledge about this state. Activation can then spread outward from these nodes,

eventually reaching nodes that represent the capital city's name.

It is possible, though, that there is only a weak connection between the SOUTH DAKOTA nodes and the nodes representing "Pierre." Perhaps you are not very familiar with South Dakota, or perhaps you haven't thought about this state, or its capital, for some time. In these cases, insufficient activation will flow into the PIERRE nodes, and so these nodes won't reach threshold and won't be "found."

Things will go differently if a hint is available. If you were told "South Dakota's capital is also a man's name," this will cause activation of the MAN'S NAME node, and so activation will spread out from this source at the same time that activation is spreading out from the SOUTH DAKOTA nodes. Therefore, the nodes for "Pierre" will now receive activation from two sources simultaneously, and this combined activation is much more likely to raise the target node to threshold levels (see Figure 8.1).

### STATE DEPENDENCY

State-dependent learning works in much the same way. As we saw in Chapter 6, memory is best if the state you're in during memory retrieval is the *same* as the state you were in during learning. If you were sad during learning, you'll have an easier time remembering what you learned if you're again sad during the memory test. If you were happy during learning, you'll do better if you are happy during the test.

Why should this be? One hypothesis holds that various emotional or mental states have a particular set of nodes connected to them. Perhaps there is literally a SAD node that is activated when you are sad; perhaps, instead, there is a set of thoughts that often occur when you are sad, and so the nodes representing these thoughts will be activated whenever you are in a sad state. In either case, if these nodes were active during learning, associations may have been formed between them and the nodes for the to-be-remembered material (cf. Gilligan & Bower, 1984; Bower, 1981).

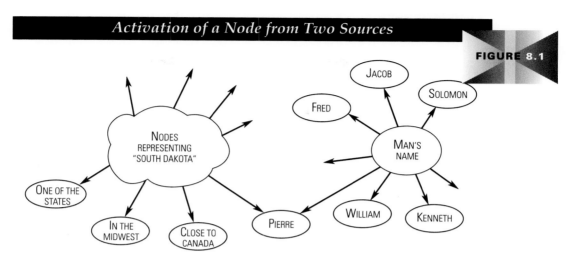

### Activation of a Node from Two Sources

**FIGURE 8.1**

A participant is asked, "What is the capital of South Dakota?" This activates the SOUTH DAKOTA nodes, and activation spreads outward from there to all of the associated nodes. However, it is possible that the memory connection between SOUTH DAKOTA and PIERRE is weak; in that case, PIERRE may not receive enough activation to reach threshold, and so the desired information will not be located. Things will go differently, though, if the participant is also given the hint, "The capital is a man's name." Now, the PIERRE node will receive activation from two sources—from the SOUTH DAKOTA nodes *and* from the MAN'S NAME nodes. With this "double input," it is more likely that the PIERRE node will reach threshold. This is why the hint ("man's name") makes the memory search easier.

At the time of test, these "state-marker" nodes would work the same way that hints do. Let us assume that you were sad during learning, and so memory connections have been established between the nodes affiliated with sadness and the nodes representing the to-be-remembered material. If you are once again sad at the time of the test, then the nodes affiliated with sadness will be activated. Activation will therefore spread out from these nodes, and thanks to the connections established during learning, some of this activation will reach the nodes for the target material. This will combine with the activation arriving at these nodes from other sources—for example, activation from nodes that were directly triggered by cues on the memory test. Thus the target nodes will be receiving a "double input"—they'll receive activation from the nodes representing the memory cues *and* from the nodes representing your (sad) state. This will make it more likely that these sought-after nodes will reach threshold levels (Figure 8.2), and this is what we observe as "state-dependent learning."

### MNEMONICS

In Chapter 5, we saw that mnemonic devices such as the method of loci clearly improve memory. These mnemonics take advantage of the fact that activation can spread more efficiently through well-established *indirect* connections than it can via more direct, but less well-established connections. Thus, it is often in

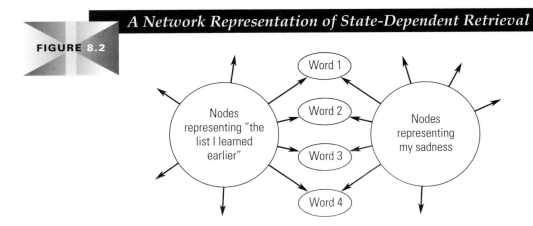

**FIGURE 8.2**

**A Network Representation of State-Dependent Retrieval**

A research participant learns a word list while in a specific context (a particular room, a particular time of day) and also while in a specific mood. Associations are therefore created between the nodes representing the list words and the nodes representing the context, *and also* between nodes representing the words and nodes representing the emotion. If the participant is in the same mood during the memory test, then the word nodes will be receiving activation from this mood source as well, making it more likely that the sought-after nodes will be activated. [Adapted from Bower, 1981.]

the memorizer's interest to let new connections be "parasitic" on old ones, linking materials together by hanging them onto an already well-connected frame. In the method of loci, for example, you exploit the fact that strong associations already exist in memory binding together your knowledge of a series of familiar sites. These strong, already-existing associations then provide the glue that holds the to-be-remembered items together. When the time comes to recall these items all you have to do is find any piece of the mnemonic. Once the first piece is found, the strong connections among the mnemonic's parts will guarantee that the rest of the mnemonic (and the material it is carrying) will be found as well (Figure 8.3).

In addition, we mentioned in Chapter 5 that someone using a mnemonic is likely, during learning, to focus on a rather small set of memory connections. This strategy guarantees that these few connections receive a lot of effort and a lot of thought, and this in turn will guarantee that these

connections end up relatively strong. This, too, will promote memory, because activation can easily flow through these well-established links.

Of course, we also mentioned in Chapter 5 the downside to this strategy: Mnemonics leave you with only a narrow set of retrieval paths. Suppose, for example, that during learning you focused on the link between "shoe" and "firewood" (see Figure 8.3). In this case, you'd be well prepared to answer this question: "What was the second word on the list you memorized?" This memory cue would activate the node for TWO; activation would flow from there to the node representing the peg word SHOE, and activation would flow from there to the sought-after list word, firewood. You'd have a harder time, though, with this question: "What was the next word on the list after 'firewood'?" That's because, during learning, you gave little thought to the relationship between "firewood" and "picture." As a result, you've established no memory link between these words. For this

## Connections among Nodes in a Mnemonic Strategy

FIGURE 8.3

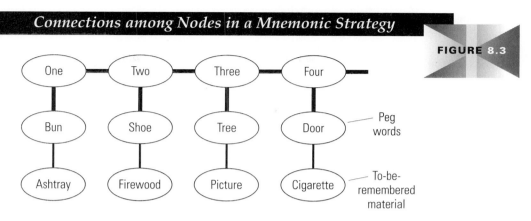

Someone memorizes a series of words ("ashtray," "firewood," "picture") using a mnemonic strategy. The mnemonic is based on the rhyme "one is a bun, two is a shoe, three is a tree, etc." The rhyme is easily learned, given the links already in place between ONE and TWO, TWO and THREE, and so on, and also the strong connections between the rhymes ("one" and "bun," "two" and "shoe," etc.). In learning the word list, the person makes connections between each word and its *peg*—for example, between "bun" (the peg) and "ashtray." (The person might think of a hamburger bun filled with ashes and cigarette butts.) With these connections, the person easily remembers which word was in each place on the list, or which was associated with "tree" and so on. He will perform less well if asked what word followed "picture" on the list, since there is no connection between picture and its successor ("cigarette").

question, therefore, you will need to think through, slowly and laboriously, the fact that "firewood" was associated with "shoe," which rhymes with "two," and so "firewood" must have been second on the list. Therefore, the next word must have been the third, and this will lead you to think of "three," and then "tree," and eventually "picture." You will reach the goal, but only after some effort.

This point echoes the warning we attached to mnemonic use in Chapter 5, and, of course, is fully consistent with the claims we made in Chapter 6: Learning creates memory connections, and those connections serve as retrieval paths. If the path you've created (e.g., a path from SHOE to FIREWOOD) happens to be the path you need later on, then your learning will serve you very well. But this same path will be far less useful if you later on need a *different* path (e.g.,

a path from FIREWOOD to PICTURE). That's one of the reasons mnemonic use is often a poor choice as a study technique: By virtue of creating only a small number of retrieval paths, mnemonics leave you with few options for locating the target materials in memory, with the result that retrieval of these materials can be very easy if you get just the right cue but much more difficult otherwise. This seems far from the fluid and flexible retrieval that students generally need.

## More Direct Tests of the Network Claims

It seems, therefore, that the network provides a natural way to bring together the evidence presented in the last few chapters. This by itself suggests that the network notion is a coherent and useful way to think about memory—a single framework into which we can bring many different findings. But in addition, the network approach makes its own predictions about memory, allowing a more direct test of the claim that memory does indeed have an associative base.

## SPREAD OF ACTIVATION AND PRIMING

A key idea of the associative network is that sub-threshold activation can "accumulate" if, for example, activation reaches a node from more than one source. This was, for example, the heart of our proposal for why hints work, and why state-dependent learning is observed. More direct evidence for this claim comes from several paradigms, one of which is the lexical-decision task.

In a lexical-decision experiment, participants are shown a series of letter sequences on a computer screen. Some of the sequences spell words; other sequences are **pseudowords**—that is, letter strings that look like words, but aren't (e.g., "blar" or "plome" or "tuke"). The participants' task is to hit a "yes" button if the sequence spells a word and a "no" button otherwise. Presumably, they perform this task by "looking up" these letter strings in their "mental dictionary," and they base their response on whether they find the string in the dictionary or not. We can therefore use the participants' speed of response in this task as an index of how quickly they can locate the word in their memories. (We have already encountered this task in Chapter 6.)

Meyer and Schvaneveldt (1971; Meyer, Schvaneveldt & Ruddy, 1974) presented their participants with pairs of letter strings; the participants had to decide whether each letter string was a word or not. Sometimes, both letter strings were words (nurse, butter); sometimes neither was a word (plame, reab); sometimes the first string was a word and the other not (wine, plame). If both strings were words, sometimes the words were related to each other (bread, butter) and sometimes they were not (table, music).

Consider a trial in which participants see a *related* pair, "bread, butter." They first respond "yes" to "bread." Presumably, they have located the BREAD node in memory, which is equivalent to saying that this node has been activated. This triggers a spread of activation outward from the BREAD node, bringing activation to other, nearby nodes. It seems likely that the association from "bread" to "butter" is a strong one and, therefore, once BREAD is activated, some activation should also spread to the BUTTER node.

The participant now turns his or her attention to the second word in the pair, "butter." To select a response, the participant must locate "butter" in memory. But of course the process of activating this node has already begun, thanks to the activation received from BREAD. This should accelerate the process of bringing this node to threshold, and so it will require less time to activate. Hence, we expect quicker responses to "butter" in this context, compared to a context in which "butter" was preceded by some unrelated word, or by a nonword.

As the table shows, this is exactly what occurs. Participants' lexical-decision responses are faster if the present stimulus word was preceded by a semantically related word. This sort of priming effect is easy to demonstrate and can actually be used as a way to "map" the network. That is, we can discover how closely associated two nodes are by assessing the degree to which activation of one primes the other. By repeating this for many pairs of nodes, we can begin to outline the patterns and organizations of memory. (For reviews, including some alternative conceptions of priming, see McKoon & Ratcliff, 1992; McNamara, 1992a, 1992b, 1994; Neely, 1991; for a somewhat different perspective, see Smith, Besner & Miyoshi, 1994.)

## SENTENCE VERIFICATION

When one searches through the network, activation spreads from node to node to node. Search through the network, therefore, is like travel, and so the further one must travel, the longer it should take to reach one's destination. In a classic experiment, Collins and Quillian (1969) tested this claim using a sentence verification task. The participants were shown sentences on a computer screen, such as "A robin is a bird" or "A robin is an animal," or "Cats have claws," or "Cats have hearts." Mixed together with these obviously true sentences was a variety of false sentences ("A cat is a bird"). Participants had to hit a "true" or "false" button as quickly as they could.

Collins and Quillian reasoned as follows: Participants perform this task by "traveling" through the network from the ROBIN node to the BIRD node. This travel allows the participant to confirm that there is, in fact, an associative path between these two nodes, and this tells the participant that the sentence about these two concepts is *true*. This "travel" will require little time, of course, if the two nodes are directly linked by an association, as ROBIN and BIRD probably are. In this case, participants should answer "true" rather quickly. The travel will require more time, however, if the two nodes are connected only indirectly (like ROBIN and ANIMAL), and so we should expect slower responses to sentences that require a "two-step" connection than to sentences that exploit a single connection.

In addition, Collins and Quillian noted that there is no point in storing in memory the fact that cats have hearts and the fact that dogs have hearts and the fact that squirrels have hearts. Instead, they proposed, it would be more efficient just to store the fact that these various creatures are animals, and then the separate fact that animals have hearts. Hence the property "has a heart" would be associated with the ANIMAL node rather than the nodes for each individual animal, and likewise for all the other properties of animals, as shown in Figure 8.4. According to this

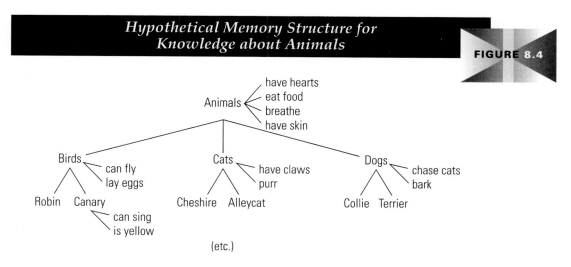

**Hypothetical Memory Structure for Knowledge about Animals**

FIGURE 8.4

Collins and Quillian proposed that memory has a hierarchical structure. This system avoids redundant storage of connections between CATS and HAVE HEARTS, and between DOGS and HAVE HEARTS, and so on for all the other animals. Instead, HAVE HEARTS is stored as a property of *all* animals. To confirm that cats have hearts, therefore, one must traverse two links: from CATS to ANIMALS, and from ANIMALS to HAVE HEARTS. This should take more time than it would to confirm that cats have claws and that cats purr, which require traversing only one link. [After Collins & Quillian, 1969.]

logic, we should expect relatively slow responses to sentences like "Cats have hearts," since, to choose a response, a participant must locate the linkage from CAT to ANIMAL and then a second linkage from ANIMAL to HEART. We would expect a quicker response to "Cats have claws," because here there would be a direct connection between CAT and the node representing this property: Although all cats have claws, other animals do not, and so this information could not be entered at the higher level.

As Figure 8.5 shows, these predictions are all borne out. Responses to sentences like "A canary is a canary" take approximately 1000 msec (one second). This is presumably the time it takes just to read the sentence and to move one's finger on the response button. Sentences like "A canary can sing" require an additional step of traversing one link in memory, and yield slower responses. Sentences like "A canary can fly" require the traversing of two links, from CANARY to BIRD and then from BIRD to CAN FLY, and are correspondingly slower.

The picture presented in the Collins and Quillian data is remarkably clear-cut: To predict response times, all we need to do is count the number of associative steps that must be traversed to support a response. In addition, the evidence seems to fit nicely with the claim that material is not stored redundantly in memory. Instead, information is stored as high as possible in the hierarchy, so that what we remember is properties of *classes* not properties of individuals.

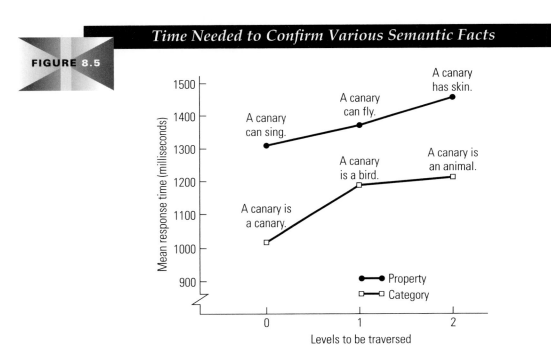

### Time Needed to Confirm Various Semantic Facts

**FIGURE 8.5**

Participants must answer "true" or "false" to sentences such as "A canary is a bird." The graph shows the relation between the type of sentence and how long it took participants to respond to each sentence (response time). Participants were fastest when no links in the network had to be traversed, slower when the necessary ideas were separated by one link, and slower still if the ideas were separated by two links. [After Collins & Quillian, 1969.]

However, these claims have not gone unchallenged (McCloskey & Glucksberg, 1978; Rips, Shoben & Smith, 1973; Smith, Rips & Shoben, 1974). Collins and Quillian are surely correct that response times are influenced by the number of associative steps traversed, but this turns out not to be the whole story. For example, participants are much quicker to assent to "A robin is a bird" than to "A peacock is a bird" (Rosch, 1973, 1975; Smith et al., 1974). If we were simply to count nodes, these are both one-step connections and so should yield similar response times. In general, though, the more "typical" the exemplar, the faster the response times, and so these **typicality effects** must be accommodated with this sort of "connection-counting" theory. (We will say a great deal more about typicality in Chapter 9.)

The evidence also suggests that the principle of nonredundancy envisioned by Collins and Quillian does not always hold. For example, from the standpoint of economy, the property of "having feathers" should be associated with the BIRD node rather than (redundantly) with the ROBIN node and the EAGLE node and so forth. Therefore responses will be relatively slow to sentences like, "Pigeons have feathers," since verifying this sentence requires a two-step connection, from PIGEON to BIRD and then from BIRD to HAS FEATHERS. However, participants respond very quickly to a sentence like "Peacocks have feathers." This is because, in observing peacocks or speaking of peacocks, one often thinks about their prominent tail feathers (cf. Conrad, 1972). Even though it is informationally redundant, a strong association between PEACOCK and FEATHERS is likely to be established.

Finally, there is also reason to be skeptical about the proposal that our knowledge, in general, can be represented via neat hierarchies like the one shown in Figure 8.4. This is because, to put it simply, most things can be classified in more than one way, yielding a complex pattern of multiple, overlapping hierarchies. For example, the concept PERSONAL COMPUTERS might be represented within the hierarchy of ELECTRONIC DEVICES, and so would be represented along with RADAR, CELL PHONES, and STEREO AMPLIFIERS. However, PERSONAL COMPUTERS can also be represented within the hierarchy of OFFICE EQUIPMENT, and so

would now be joined by STAPLERS, PENCILS, and FILE CABINETS. For that matter, PERSONAL COMPUTERS can also be represented within the hierarchy of MODERN INVENTIONS, with yet a different set of conceptual cousins. This complexity obviously speaks against a strict hierarchical organization such as the one depicted in Figure 8.4.

For these reasons, psychologists have moved away from the model proposed by Collins and Quillian. However, let's not lose sight of the contribution here: It does seem that, all other things being equal, we can predict memory access by counting the number of nodes participants must traverse in answering a question. This by itself strengthens the claim that associative links play an important role in memory representation. But we also cannot neglect the phrase "all other things being equal." Speed of memory access also depends on several other factors, including the efficiency of individual associations, the existence of special connections, and also something referred to as the "degree of fan."

## DEGREE OF FAN

Imagine a sentence verification task in which a participant confronts (on separate trials) the following two sentences: "A robin has wings," and "An aardvark has legs." The associations between ROBIN and its properties are likely to be stronger than those between AARDVARK and its properties, simply because participants in these experiments have probably encountered many more robins than aardvarks. In addition, though, there are probably many more associations radiating out from ROBIN than there are from AARDVARK. As illustrated in Figure 8.6, this implies that the ROBIN node will look like the hub of a many-spoked wheel, whereas the AARDVARK node will not. In the standard terminology, ROBIN has a "high degree of fan" (many things fanning out from it), AARDVARK has a low degree of fan.

The notion of "fan" has been extensively explored by Anderson and his associates (Anderson, 1974, 1976; Lewis & Anderson, 1976; also see Peterson & Potts, 1982; Thorndyke & Bower, 1974). Why should

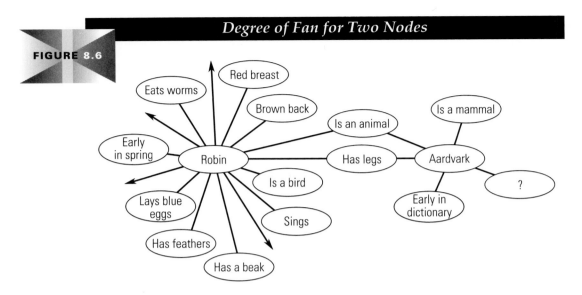

**FIGURE 8.6**

### Degree of Fan for Two Nodes

One knows many facts about robins, and so there are many linkages radiating out from the ROBIN node—a high degree of fan. In contrast, one knows relatively few facts about aardvarks, and so few linkages radiate out from the AARDVARK node—a low degree of fan.

degree of fan matter? Recall that, once a node is activated, the links radiating out from this node will all receive activation energy simultaneously—the links will be activated in parallel with each other, rather than in some serial order. In addition, it seems sensible to assume that the quantity of activation is limited. Therefore, the more the activation is divided, the less will go to each recipient. Activation spreading outward from AARDVARK will be divided only five ways, and so each link will receive 20% of the total. The activation spreading outward from ROBIN will be much more thinly divided, and so each link will receive a smaller share of the whole.

Does degree of fan matter for memory retrieval? This question is difficult to ask with "robin" and "aardvark," because these concepts differ both in degree of fan and in strength of association. Imagine that we asked participants to verify the sentences, "Aardvarks have legs," and "Robins have wings." The prediction is that the ROBIN node has a greater degree of fan, and this will slow down verification of the "robin" sentence. At the same time, the links radiating from ROBIN are likely to be more efficient, thanks to frequency of use, and this will speed up verification of the "robin" sentence. Hence, we have two effects on the scene, working in opposite directions, and potentially canceling each other out.

To ask whether degree of fan matters, we need to find a case in which two nodes differ *only* in degree of fan. One way to do this is to start so to speak, from scratch. For example, Anderson (1974) taught his research participants a set of sentences about people in locations. "The doctor is in the bank." "The fireman is in the park." "The lawyer is in the church." "The lawyer is in the park." And so on. In the full set of sentences, some of the actors (e.g., the doctor) appeared in only one location (the bank); others (the lawyer) appeared in two locations. Likewise, some locations (the church) contained only one person; other locations (the park) contained two. In this way, Anderson controlled the degree of fan from the nodes representing each of these terms—there was greater fan for PARK than for CHURCH, greater fan for LAWYER than for DOCTOR.

All of these were new facts for the participants, since Anderson had just made them up. Therefore, the strength of the association for these sentences started out at zero. Then, by controlling the learning process, Anderson controlled the growth of association strength and, in particular, made certain that association strength was the same for all of the sentences. In this way, Anderson ended up with a set of nodes that differed in degree of fan, but not in the strength of their connections to other nodes.

Once the participants had memorized these sentences, they were given a recognition test, in which they had to decide as quickly as possible whether each of the test sentences had been presented as part of the learning set. As Table 8.1 shows, speed of response was influenced by degree of fan: Response times were fastest when only one sentence mentioned a specific person or a specific place, response

times were slowest when multiple sentences named a specific person or place. This is exactly what we would expect if activation were a fixed quantity and so, the more ways divided, the less to each recipient. The less to each recipient, the longer it takes for the target node to be fully activated and so, finally, the longer for the response to be chosen. (For a somewhat different account of the fan effect, and also some complications, see Radvansky & Zacks, 1991; Radvansky, 1999; Anderson & Reder, 1992a, 1992b.)

## IS THERE A COST TO KNOWING "TOO MUCH"?

Note an odd consequence of the experiment just described, and of the notion of fan: In some circumstances, there may be a cost attached to knowing "too much." If you know just one fact about aardvarks, then this fact will be easily remembered whenever you think about aardvarks. That is because, with such a low degree of fan, all the activation from the AARDVARK node will spread down

### Influence of Degree of Fan on Decision Time

**TABLE 8.1**

| Number of sentences using a specific location | Number of sentences about a specific person | |
|---|---|---|
| | **1 sentence** | **2 sentences** |
| 1 sentence | 1.11 sec | 1.17 sec |
| 2 sentences | 1.17 sec | 1.22 sec |

*Note*: Participants were slower in recognizing sentences that involved nodes with a higher degree of fan and faster with sentences that involved a lower degree of fan. The sentences were of the form "The lawyer is in the park." Fan was manipulated by varying how many facts the participants knew about the lawyer (that is, whether the lawyer appeared in only one of the sentences that had been learned or in two), and also how many facts they knew about the park (that is, whether the park had been mentioned in one of the sentences or in two). The effect observed in this experiment is not large (for example, a 0.06-second difference in the left-hand column), but this is probably because we are considering only small differences in degree of fan (1 versus 2).

[After Anderson, 1974.]

this single association. However, as you learn more and more about aardvarks, the degree of fan is increasing, and so less and less activation will spread down any particular association. That very first fact you learned about aardvarks is still associated with the AARDVARK node, and so it will still receive some activation whenever you are thinking aardvark thoughts. But, because of the greater fan, it may not receive a large enough share of this activation to become activated itself.

In this way, new knowledge about a topic is *interfering* with older learning. More precisely, the new knowledge (and the corresponding increase in fan) is making it more difficult to access the older memory, so that in this case, the interference is actually leading to a form of retrieval failure.

Notice that this demands some revisions in the claims we offered about interference in Chapter 7. In Chapter 7, we suggested that interference can arise because the new and old memories get blurred together, or because the rememberer gets confused about which memory is which. But here we see another contributor to interference—with new learning literally competing with the old learning for activation energy. In addition, Chapter 7 presented retrieval failure and interference as separate mechanisms, each making its own contribution to forgetting. We now see, however, that these two mechanisms are sometimes overlapping. There are, to be sure, cases of interference that do not involve retrieval failure, and cases of retrieval failure that do not involve interference. But now before us is a case in which retrieval failure is actually caused by interference. (For more on forgetting within a network, see Anderson, Bjork & Bjork, 1994; 2000.)

Let's be very careful, though, not to overstate all these points. It is true that sometimes there is a cost to knowing too much, for the reasons just described. But, in many cases, things turn out quite differently, so that new learning actually *promotes* retrieval of previously learned facts. To see why, consider the three situations shown in Figure 8.7. Situation 1 shows a very early stage of learning, with the person knowing just a single fact (represented by node B) about a topic (node A). In this situation, there is just a

single association radiating out from node A, and so, whenever A is activated, all of its activation will be channeled to node B. Activation of node A, therefore, is almost certain to activate B.

At a later stage of learning (Situation 2), more has been learned about A, and so the degree of fan from node A has increased. Now node B receives only one-tenth of A's activation; as a consequence, thinking about A is *less* likely to remind you of B in Situation 2 than it was in Situation 1. This is the case of new learning leading to retrieval failure. Let's be clear, though, that this situation involves a case in which someone has learned a group of separate, individual facts, all about the same topic, but with the facts not connected to one another. In contrast, consider the learning you are doing right now, as you read this chapter. You are not (I hope) simply learning a list of individual facts, each associated with the concept "associative networks." Instead, you are learning a set of *interrelated* facts, so that you are acquiring a whole network of new connections, more closely modeled by Situation 3 than by Situation 2. In Situation 3, A's degree of fan has once again increased, relative to Situation 1, and so here too, B receives less input from A than it did initially. At the same time, however, B can now receive input from many other sources and, as a result, node B will be *easier* to activate in Situation 3 than in the other situations—receiving less input from A, but receiving more input overall. Hence, the fan effect gave an advantage to Situation 1, but Situation 3 has a greater advantage: the advantage created by the existence of multiple retrieval paths. It is in this fashion that, even with the fan effect, learning new facts can *aid* retrieval.

## Retrieving Information from a Network

So far, things look good for the network model. We have easily encompassed a large set of prior findings; likewise, many results confirm our claims about spreading activation and fan. In addition, the network idea offers us one further benefit: it holds

## Degree of Fan versus Number of Retrieval Paths

**FIGURE** 8.7

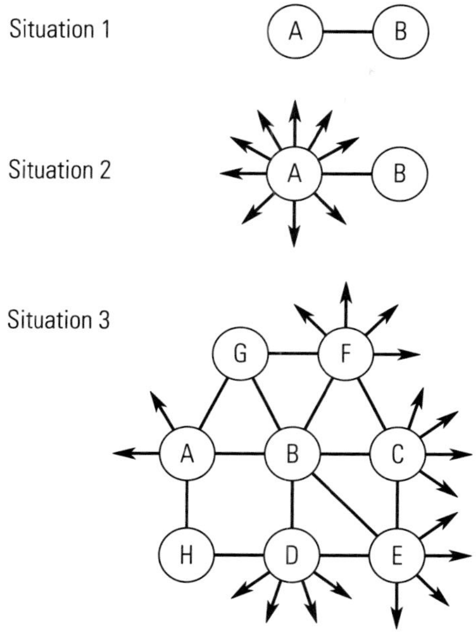

Situation 1

Situation 2

Situation 3

Early in learning (Situation 1), a person knows only a single fact about A, namely, that it is associated with B. Later in learning (Situation 2), the person may have learned more about A. Thanks to the increased fan, less of A's activation spreads to B. This makes it more difficult to activate Node B in Situation 2 than in Situation 1. As an alternative, the person may learn a rich network of interconnected facts (Situation 3). In this case, A's degree of fan is increasing, so that less of A's activation spreads to B. At the same time, B is receiving activation from many new sources. As a result, B will be *easier* to activate in this case than in Situation 1.

the promise of explaining how we search through memory so quickly and easily.

### SEARCHING THROUGH THE NETWORK VIA ASSOCIATIVE LINKS

Think about how an encyclopedia is organized. There is obviously a vast amount of information contained within the encyclopedia, neatly compartmentalized into individual entries. Therefore, if you

want to learn about *dogs*, you turn to the entry on that topic; if you want to learn about *glaciers*, you turn to that topic, and so on.

Imagine, though, that your dog is ill, and you are trying to figure out what the problem is. You read the entry about dogs, but you find nothing useful. It is possible that the information you need is present in the encyclopedia, but is contained within a different entry. Perhaps the entry on *veterinary medicine* talks about particular diseases, their symptoms and their cures. But you won't find this information as long as you are focusing on the "dog" entry. Indeed, perhaps the information you seek is quite close to the "dog" entry, in an entry 10 pages further along, or 12 pages back. (Perhaps your dog has an illness called "doffinitis." Given the encyclopedia's alphabetic organization, this [fictional] disease might be described in an entry just a few pages away from the "dog" entry.) Even in this case, though, you might not find the target information, since few of us adopt a strategy of "exploring the neighborhood" when looking for information in an encyclopedia.

Editors of encyclopedias, however, have anticipated these situations, and they have done something to help you out: At the end of many entries, you will find a series of "pointers," saying "For related information, see the entry on X or the entry on Y." If the right pointers are in place, you will be led to the entry containing the information you want. In some cases, you may need to repeat this process (perhaps the entry on "dogs" leads you to the entry on "veterinary medicine," and, from there, a new series of pointers leads you to the entry talking about "doffinitis"). Indeed, with enough of these pointers in place, one could imagine leading a reader to "doffinitis" from several different starting points. We've just described how a search might start with "dog" and get from there to your target. Likewise, the "disease" entry might have a pointer that leads you to the "medicine" entry, which has a pointer that leads to the "veterinary medicine" entry, which would lead you to the desired information. And so on.

This idea of pointers is also crucial for another information-storage system: the World Wide Web. To search the Web, one often begins with a search engine (Yahoo, Lycos, etc.), but in many cases, this does not bring you directly to the information you want. Nevertheless, you can often find the desired information by using the labeled *hyperlinks* that carry you from one site to the next. These links are the equivalent of pointers saying, "For more information, see..." One great advantage of the Web, though, is that you don't have to flip pages to find the related entries; instead, the entries are promptly displayed on your monitor the moment you request them. Even so, the idea is still the same, and so one

can imagine finding information on "doffinitis" by first locating a Web page on pets which contains links to pages on veterinary medicine, and so forth.

Of course, all depends on having the right pointers and, indeed, on having a lot of pointers—otherwise, bridges between related topics may be omitted. However, the system won't work if you have too many pointers. Imagine that, at the end of an encyclopedia entry, you find the message, "For related information, see all of the rest of this encyclopedia." This obviously would provide no guidance whatsoever. Similarly, imagine that you found a Web page that said, "For further information, you're on your own!" Or imagine a page that said, "For more information, check out these sites!" and then included 343,912 links to other pages. Neither of these would be helpful; the first provides too few links, and the second provides too many (and so you might need weeks to sift through the options to find the one that's useful). But presumably, an appropriate middle number of links can be found, so that we could end up with a Web page providing useful guidance to your further searching.

All of this is easily translated into network terms. Associative links can guide search through memory, just as the pointers guide search through an encyclopedia. To continue our example, let's imagine that, at some prior point, you have thought about the relationship between *disease* and *medicine*, and the relationship between *medicine* and *veterinary medicine*. Therefore, the corresponding nodes will be linked, and so activating the DISEASE node will cause activation to spread to the MEDICINE node. Activation of that node will in turn activate the VETERINARY MEDICINE node, and so on, leading eventually to the material you seek.

It is also important that spreading activation can proceed from more than one source simultaneously; we relied on this claim in our discussion of hints and state dependency. This is actually better than what you do with an encyclopedia or the World Wide Web. It is the equivalent of looking up one encyclopedia entry and finding its list of pointers, and then looking up a different entry, with its own list of pointers, and then, finally, asking which pointers appear on *both* lists. Obviously, this could narrow your search considerably, but with the encyclopedia or the Internet, it would be a cumbersome process. In the associative net that supports your memory, however, this process is achieved automatically: Activation will simply spread out from both of the entry points and, with no intervention and no guidance, will "converge" on the sought-after node.

## FINDING ENTRY NODES

Sometimes a memory search begins with an idea or some other memory. You are contemplating what a friend said to you last week, for instance, and you are reminded of related comments you've heard from other friends. Here, entry into the associative net is easy: Your recollection of last week's conversation is represented via some number of nodes, and these are activated when you think about the con-

versation. Activation can then spread out from these nodes, representing your initial idea, to other nodes, representing other, related thoughts.

What about memory searches triggered by a perceptual cue? For example, perhaps you smell an aroma and are reminded of your childhood. For cases like this, one option is simply to link the network directly to the mechanisms of perception, so that some nodes within the net are *input nodes*. In their functioning, these nodes will be like any others: They will receive activation via associative links; once triggered, they will send activation to other nodes. What is special about these input nodes is that they receive most of their input activation from appropriate detectors, with these in turn connected to the eyes, ears, and so on.

Consider, for example, the portion of the network shown in Figure 8.8. This bit of network includes ties between the node for APPLE and nodes corresponding to certain colors, and these color nodes are tied

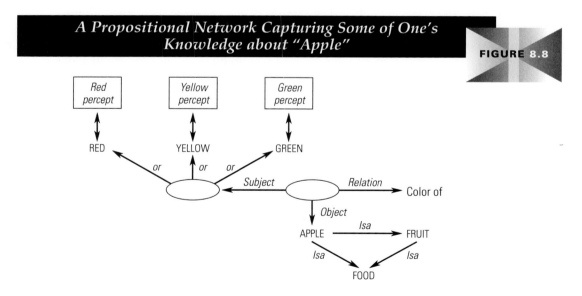

**A Propositional Network Capturing Some of One's Knowledge about "Apple"**

**FIGURE 8.8**

Some of the nodes in this bit of network are tied directly to the mechanisms of perception, so that the presence of a red stimulus, or a yellow one, or a green one will contribute activation to nodes within the network. In this way, perceptual processes can directly activate nodes. [After Anderson, 1980.]

in the appropriate way to the visual system. The presence of the specified colors, therefore, would lead to the activation of these nodes, which in turn would lead to the activation of the APPLE node. Needless to say, this leaves out a great deal, since apples are not merely a certain color, they are also a certain shape and size. However, these other attributes could be similarly tied, on the one side, to the APPLE node and, on the other side, to the mechanisms of vision.

In fact, we have already considered more complicated cases than this. In Chapter 3, we discussed how you recognize words. We suggested that detectors for words might be triggered by detectors for the appropriate letter combinations. These in turn would be triggered by letter detectors, which are themselves triggered by feature detectors. All we need to do now is notice that these various detectors are actually nodes within a network, functioning just like any other nodes—accumulating activation, eventually reaching threshold, and then sending activation to other nodes. And, since they are nodes, there is no problem with these perceptually driven "input nodes" (the detectors) sending their activation to the long-term memory nodes we are describing in this chapter.

However, we do need to be cautious here: We argued in Chapter 3 that this sort of "data-driven" network cannot, by itself, explain all of object recognition. By the same token it cannot provide our full account for how search within the memory network is initiated. As an example, notice that you would respond differently to these two memory questions: "Tell me what you ate for dinner yesterday" and "Tell me what ate you for dinner yesterday." You must have some means of discriminating between these two requests, but the process we have so far sketched, in terms of simple detectors, does not provide these means. (See Chapter 3 for further discussion of this point, and also Chapter 10.)

Obviously, then, we'll need more theory before we are through. Our point for the moment, though, is a modest one. How do we begin a search through memory? In most cases, it is a thought or idea that triggers a memory search and, for these, "entry"

into the system is easy. For perceptual cues, we can hope to initiate memory searches by allowing direct connections between the network and the mechanisms of perception. This will surely work for simple stimuli but, for more complex stimuli, we will need a more elaborate process, and we will say more about this later in this chapter. In either case, however, the key idea is that perceiving and identifying an input will involve, among other steps, the locating and activating of that input's node in the network. Perceiving itself will launch memory search.

## Unpacking the Nodes

We have so far spoken of nodes as representing "ideas" or "memories." But what does this mean? Could a node contain, for example, "my full memory of last semester's courses"? A node such as this would create two problems. First, this node would encompass a great deal of information. We would then need to figure out how one searches through the information *inside* of a node, in addition to the problem of how one finds nodes in the first place. Second, if we build a lot of information into a single node, we invite a worry about how one "interprets" or "reads" the information in a node. If each node contained a book-length description of an event or episode, we would need to incorporate into our theorizing some device capable of reading and interpreting this corpus of material. Conversely, the simpler we keep each node's informational content, the less we have to rely on some interpretive device.

These claims apply to any network model, to any model seeking to describe memory in terms of a pattern of associations. To say more than this, however, we need to start distinguishing among the various types of associative model, and in particular, we need to distinguish the most recent versions of associative theory from earlier versions. Let's start with the older perspective; we will consider the more recent innovations later on.

## DIFFERENT TYPES OF ASSOCIATIVE LINKS

One proposal is that nodes represent single concepts, and nothing more complicated than that. This is consistent with the examples we have used so far, in which nodes have stood for concepts such as *chair* or *doctor*. This still leaves many questions: *How* does a node represent a concept? Does the DOG node contain a brief definition of the concept "dog"? A small picture of a dog? Perhaps the node contains a list of the perceptual features that characterize dogs, so that you could use this list to help you in recognizing a dog the next time you encounter one. It turns out that none of these proposals is satisfactory, and we will need most of Chapter 9 to work through the problem of *how* concepts are represented in the mind.

In the meantime, we can use the network notion to help us with a related problem—namely, how we might represent more complex ideas, such as "George Washington was the first president," or "My favorite movie is *Casablanca*." For that matter, how do we represent an idea as complicated as "My understanding of Darwin's theory of evolution," or a memory as complicated as "How I spent last summer"?

Oddly enough, these complex ideas are represented with more network. As a first approximation, an associative link may exist between "George Washington" and "first president," and a set of links may tie together "movie" and "favorite" and *Casablanca*." But this is too simple. How, for example, would one represent the contrast between "Sam has a dog," and "Sam is a dog"? If all we have is an association between SAM and DOG, we won't be able to tell these two ideas apart. Early theorizing sought to deal with this problem by introducing different *types* of associative links, with some representing equivalence (or partial equivalence) relations and others representing possessive relations. These links were termed **"isa" links**, as in "Sam isa dog," and **"hasa" links**, as in "A bird hasa head," or "Sam hasa dog" (Norman, Rumelhart & Group, 1975).

## PROPOSITIONAL NETWORKS AND ACT

There are clear limits, however, on what we can accomplish with these labeled associations. The prob-

lem is that we are able to remember, and to think about, a wide range of relationships, not just equivalence and possession. We can, for example, consider the relationship "is the opposite of," or the relationship "is analogous to," and a thousand others as well. If each type of relationship is represented by a specific type of associative link, then we risk losing the simplicity that made the network idea so attractive in the first place. Worse, if we have too many types of links, we'll end up needing a "link reader" of some sort, and a reader is one of the things we were hoping to avoid.

Researchers have therefore sought other mechanisms through which network models might represent complex ideas. Their proposals differ in many ways, so once again we cannot talk about network models in general; we are forced instead to consider a specific model. Let's look at a model developed by John Anderson (1976, 1980, 1993; Anderson & Bower, 1973), bearing in mind that this is simply one way a network might be implemented; other implementations are possible.

Central to Anderson's conception is the idea of *propositions*; these are defined as the smallest unit of knowledge that can be either true or false. For example, "Children love candy" is a proposition but "Children" is not; "Susan likes blue cars" is a proposition but "blue cars" is not. Propositions are easily represented as sentences, but this is merely a convenience. In fact, the same proposition can be represented in a variety of different sentences: "Children love candy," "Candy is loved by children," and "Kinder lieben bonbons" all express the same proposition. For that matter, this same proposition can also be represented in various non-linguistic forms, including a structure of nodes and linkages, and that is exactly what Anderson's model does.

Anderson's theory is embodied in a computer program known as ACT (and, in later versions, as ACT-R—see Anderson, 1993, 1996). Within ACT, propositions are represented as shown in Figure 8.9. The ellipse identifies the proposition itself; associations connect the ellipse to the ideas that are the proposition's constituents. The associations are labeled, but only in general terms. That is, the as-

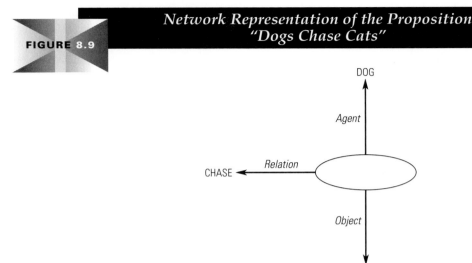

**FIGURE 8.9**

**Network Representation of the Proposition "Dogs Chase Cats"**

The ellipse denotes a proposition; the ellipse is, in essence, the "meeting point" for the various elements of the proposition. Three nodes are involved in this proposition: DOG, CAT, and the action CHASE. Arrows indicate associations among the nodes; labels on the arrows specify the nature of the association. [After Anderson, 1980.]

sociations are identified in terms of their syntactic role within the proposition. This allows us to distinguish the proposition "Dogs chase cats" from the proposition "Cats chase dogs."

This simple network can be expanded to represent more complex bits of knowledge. Figure 8.10 shows the proposition "Dogs chew bones" in the context of other propositions about dogs; the overall structure represents (part of) our knowledge about what a dog is and how it behaves, just as Figure 8.8 showed a portion of the network representing our knowledge about apples.

How does ACT represent more specific memories? Our examples so far have centered on *semantic* or *generic* knowledge rather than *episodic* knowledge. Likewise, we have provided no means for ACT to distinguish between knowledge about,

say, dogs in general (as in Figure 8.10) and knowledge about a specific dog, say, Leo's dog, Merlin.

To represent specific episodes, or a specific being, ACT makes a distinction between **type** nodes and **token** nodes. "Type" refers to a general category, and type nodes are embedded in propositions true for the entire category. A "token" is a specific instance of a category, and token nodes are therefore found in propositions concerned with specific events and individuals. Note that type and token nodes are typically connected to each other, as shown in Figure 8.11.

In addition, the ACT model distinguishes between timeless truths, like "Jacob feeds the pigeons," and more specific statements, like "Last spring, Jacob fed the pigeons in Trafalgar Square." ACT does this by incorporating time and location nodes

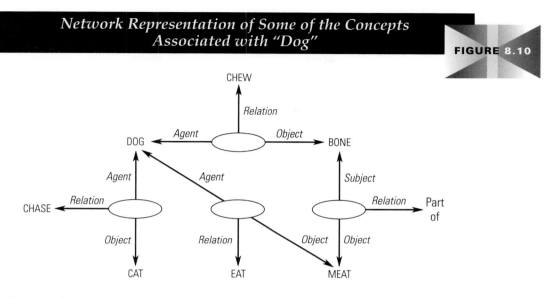

**Network Representation of Some of the Concepts Associated with "Dog"**

FIGURE 8.10

One's understanding of dogs—what dogs are, what they are likely to do—is represented by an interconnected network of propositions, with each proposition indicated by an ellipse. Thus, one's understanding involves the propositions "Dogs chase cats," "Dogs eat meat," "Dogs chew bones," and so on. A complete representation of knowledge about dogs would of course include a far greater number of propositions. [After Anderson, 1980.]

as part of propositions, and in this fashion can mark when and where the proposition was true. This allows ACT to represent facts about specific episodes (Figure 8.12).

The ACT model shares many claims with other network models: Nodes are connected by associative links. Some of these links are stronger than others, with the strength of the link depending on how frequently and recently the link has been used. Once a node is activated, the process of spreading activation causes the nearby nodes to become activated as well. ACT is distinctive, however, in its attempt to represent knowledge in terms of propositions, and the promise of this approach has attracted the support of many researchers in this area.

## Evaluating Network Models

Associative theories of memory have generated much excitement and much research and strike many as our best hypothesis about how knowledge is represented in the mind.

At the same time, these models have been controversial. In this section, we will review some of the concerns that have arisen about network models in an attempt to ask whether these models do represent the optimal way to theorize about memory.

### HOW TO TEST NETWORK MODELS?

The evidence we have considered confirms many of the network claims. Mechanisms such as spreading

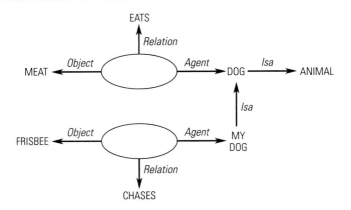

FIGURE 8.11

### Networks Contain Information about Categories and about Individuals

This fragment of a network contains a "type node," representing dogs in general, and a "token node," representing a specific dog (MY DOG). The type node is linked to propositions true for all dogs; the token node is linked to propositions true only for MY DOG. That is, all dogs eat meat. Not all dogs chase Frisbees, although "my dog" does. The type node and token node are linked to each other, indicating that "my dog" is a member of the category "dogs."

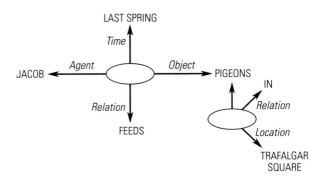

FIGURE 8.12

### Representing Episodes within a Propositional Network

In order to represent episodes, the propositional network includes time and location nodes. This fragment of a network represents two propositions—the proposition that Jacob last spring fed pigeons, and the proposition that the pigeons are in Trafalgar Square. Note that no time node is associated with the proposition about pigeons being in Trafalgar Square. Therefore, what is represented is that the feeding of the pigeons took place last spring, but the pigeons are generally in the square.

activation and subthreshold priming, for example, clearly do play a role in memory search. However, the data presented so far do not speak to a larger and more interesting issue. The network claim is not merely that these mechanisms are involved in memory search. The claim instead is that these mechanisms, by themselves, can provide our entire account of memory retrieval, that these mechanisms are enough "to get the job done."

Can the network deliver on this promise? Bear in mind just how vast our memories are. This leads one to ask, will spreading activation by itself support a search through a huge number of nodes, each with a very high degree of fan? Or will we need to add other mechanisms to support and perhaps guide the search?

Perhaps the best way to address these questions might be simply to give networks a serious try. If one has a theory of memory and memory organization, a powerful test of the theory would be to build a "working model," based on the theoretical claims, and to examine how well the model performed as an information storage and retrieval device. With these ideas in mind, many psychologists are seeking to construct such models, usually implemented as a computer system that functions according to the rules and procedures specified by the theory. (We mentioned earlier, for example, that Anderson's ACT model is embodied in such a system.) This allows us to see how well the computer does in "learning"— that is, in storing new information—and then in retrieving facts, based on some cue or hint. If the computer fails in these tasks, or does less well than humans do, we know that something is missing (or wrong) in the theory. What if the computer succeeds? This would indicate that the processes and strategies programmed into the computer are sufficient to accomplish the tasks of learning and remembering. This would not by itself show that humans use the same processes and strategies. It would, however, be a strong argument that the theory must be taken seriously as an account of human performance.

It would take us rather far afield to evaluate these modeling efforts in any detail. To make a long story short, though, it is not currently possible to point to an associative network that successfully simulates all of human memory. The available models work reasonably well, but all have various limitations and bugs and work only on a scale far more modest than "all of knowledge." How should we think about this? One possibility is that these limitations reflect deep inadequacies in the network approach. But it is also possible that the limitations merely reflect the early state of the models' evolution. With further work and refinements, perhaps these weaknesses will be overcome.

As one way of exploring these issues, let's look at some points that seem, at least initially, to pose problems for the network approach. We'll then consider ways that a network might handle these challenges.

## RETRIEVAL BLOCKS AND PARTIAL RETRIEVALS

One attractive feature of the associative net is that activation spreads out indiscriminately through all of the available connections. We need no means of "directing" the activation or supervising the search. Instead, one simply allows the activation to travel wherever the connections lead.

This approach keeps our theorizing simple, but do things always work in a fashion consistent with this "automatic" view? Try to think of the word that means a type of carving done on whale bone, often depicting whaling ships, or pictures of whales. Try to think of the name of the navigational device used by sailors to determine the positions of stars. Try to think of the name of the Russian sled drawn by three horses. Chances are that, in at least one of these cases, you found yourself in a frustrated state—certain you knew the word but unable to come up with it. The word was, as they say, right on the "tip of your tongue"; following this lead, psychologists refer to this as the **T.O.T. phenomenon**. People in the T.O.T. state often know correctly that the word is somewhere in their vocabulary, they often correctly remember what letter the word begins with, how many syllables it has, and approximately what it sounds like. Thus a person might remember "It's something like Sanskrit" in trying to remember "scrimshaw," or "something like secant" in trying to remember "sextant" (Brown, 1991;

Brown & McNeill, 1966; Harley & Bown, 1998; James, 1890; Read & Bruce, 1982; Reason & Lucas, 1984; Schwartz, 1999). Similar results have been obtained when people try to recall specific names: Who played the nervous man with the knife in the shower scene in Hitchcock's *Psycho*? What was the name of the Greek orator who taught himself to speak clearly by practicing speeches with pebbles in his mouth? With clues like these, research participants are often able to recall the number of syllables in the name and the name's initial letter, but not the name itself (Brennen, Baguley, Bright & Bruce, 1990; Yarmey, 1973). (The orator was Demosthenes, and Anthony Perkins was the nervous man with the knife. The Russian sled is a troika.)

On first inspection, these findings seem not to fit with the network view. It seems clear that a person in the T.O.T. state has reached the memory vicinity of the sought-after word. After all, the person is able to come up with the correct starting letter and the correct number of syllables. In addition, the nodes in this area of memory are presumably receiving a great deal of activation, given the time and effort one spends in trying to find the word. But this activation seems not to spread to the sought-after node, or if it does, the activation of this node is not being recognized or acknowledged. In short, you are in the right neighborhood; there is lots of activation on the scene, but the activation does not reach the target. All of this is peculiar if we conceive of spreading activation as a purely mechanical process whose success is guaranteed once one is in the correct memory vicinity.

### FINDING MORE DISTANT CONNECTIONS

A different concern is, in a sense, the mirror image of the points just raised. In the T.O.T. state, we fail to locate a target memory, despite our being in the right memory vicinity with plenty of activation. Here is the inverse case: How do we *succeed* in locating memories when there are no close connections between our starting point and our target?

The crux of the issue here is part psychology, part arithmetic. Consider first the range of jobs we want

associative links to do for us—they tie together episodic memories, they tie together generic memories, they tie together aspects of our concepts (e.g., the "possession of feathers" is presumably part of, or closely tied to, our concept of "bird," and the linkage between these is, once again, a memory association). Given all this, it becomes clear that the number of associative links radiating out from any individual concept—that is, the realistic degree of fan—will be very high indeed.

We have already said that only some of the links radiating out from a node will be efficient carries of activation—namely, those links that are used frequently or recently. But, realistically, what is the number of these likely to be? How many strong associations does one have, for example, to "water"? Is 100 a halfway plausible number? We suspect that this is a gross underestimate, but it will serve for the moment. Using this estimate, think about what happens when activation spreads outward from the WATER node. One hundred new nodes each receive some activation (Figure 8.13). If the sought-for information is directly associated with the WATER node, things will now go well: One only has to choose which among these hundred is the node one seeks.

But what if the sought-for node is *not* directly tied to WATER? What if it is tied by means of one intermediate step? We have already said that 100 nodes receive activation directly from WATER; now, activation spreads out from these. If each of these 100 is connected to 100 more nodes, we end up with activation reaching 10,000 nodes. And, of course, if the sought-for node is still one more step removed, we need to let activation spread once again, so that now activation reaches a million nodes ($100 \times 100 \times 100$).

It would seem, then, that we will create problems if we let the spreading activation spread too far. Even if the spread is only three or four steps, we will end up with far too many nodes activated, and so we will lose the selective guidance we hoped for in the first place. You were hunting for one memory, but you've activated a million memories instead!

Of course, we can avoid this danger if we place limits on how far the activation can spread, or equivalently, if we arrange things so that the spreading activation gets weaker and weaker as it moves outward from its source. In either of these cases, we will avoid the risk of activating too many nodes, but we also risk not finding the node we seek: If the activation peters out, for example, after a single link, then your memory search will never find information that is two links away from your starting point.

The same ideas can also be framed in terms of the degree of fan. If each node is connected to every other node (i.e., if there is a very high degree of fan),

we lose the selective guidance that the linkages were supposed to provide. A point in every direction is the same as no point at all (Nillson, 1971). If, on the other hand, we decrease the fan at each node, then it becomes likely that our entry and target nodes will be connected only indirectly. In this case, we are forced to rely on more steps from entry to target, inviting the multiplication of nodes: Each time we let the activation go another step, we multiply again the number of nodes reached. In this fashion, too high a degree of fan is problematic and so is

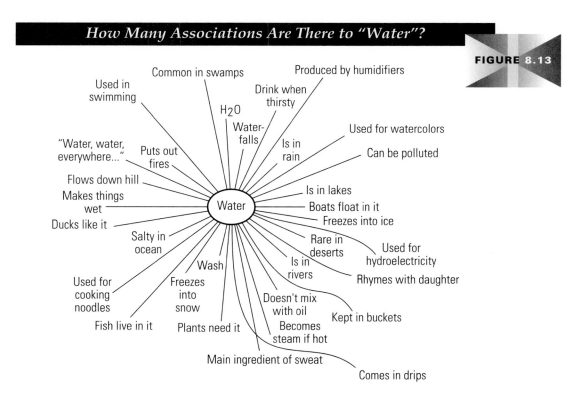

**How Many Associations Are There to "Water"?**

FIGURE 8.13

There is probably a huge number of linkages radiating out from each node; we have shown here only some of the ideas associated with the node for WATER. Each of these associations leads to some other node, and there are many linkages radiating out from those other nodes. If activation spreads out just one step, a large number of nodes will be activated. If activation spreads out two steps, how many nodes receive activation?

too low a degree of fan. Whether there is a middle value that escapes these concerns simply remains to be seen.

## WINNER TAKES ALL

There are several ways a network model might respond to these challenges. One option is to add a mechanism similar to one we met in Chapters 2 and 3, a mechanism through which nodes in the network *inhibit* each other.

How would this help? Whenever you search through memory, activation spreads outward from the nodes representing your search's starting point. In many cases, this will activate the nodes representing the information you seek, but it will also activate many other nodes—nodes associated with your search's starting point, but irrelevant to your current concerns. What you need, therefore, is some means of narrowing things down, of picking out just a *subset* of the now-activated nodes. In this way, you could focus on the nodes representing the desired information, and ignore the nodes representing irrelevancies.

One way to achieve this is by launching a process of *competition* among the nodes. More specifically, let's imagine a process in which each node sends out inhibition, rather than activation, to the nodes associated with it. Let's also imagine that the more active a node is, the more strongly it will inhibit its neighbors. To see what this will accomplish, imagine a strongly activated node—let's call it s—that happens to be linked to a weakly activated neighbor—call it w. The strongly activated node, s, will send out a strong inhibitory signal, largely "shutting down" its weaker neighbor, w. Initially, w will reciprocate, and will try to inhibit *its* neighbors (including s), but since it was only weakly activated to begin with, it will send out weak inhibition. The w node, therefore, will have only a minimal effect on s. And, in fact, the inhibition received *from* the s node will further weaken w—decrease its activation level. Then, with less activation, w will send out even less inhibition,

and so will have even less impact on s than it did at the start. This allows s to become still stronger, so that it sends more inhibition to w, which becomes still weaker.

Let us say that, initially, s had twice the activation that w did. In principle, this might mean that s would demand two-thirds of your attention, and w one third. Thanks to the inhibitory signals, though, s has grown stronger and w weaker; in fact, w might now have no activation—it might be back in its resting state. As a result, s can now demand *all* of your attention, and you won't be distracted by w. This is referred to as a winner-takes-all system, in which the stronger candidate (node s in this case) not only gets its initial share of the power, it gets all the power.[1]

A winner-takes-all system could help us with both of the network problems we described earlier. Concretely, let's say that you're in a chemistry exam and trying to remember some facts about water. Your thinking about water will activate the node for this concept, and this will send activation to many nodes that are entirely irrelevant for your current purposes—the nodes representing your memory of the vacation at the lake, or the nodes representing your annoyance at the rainy weather. These nodes will get shut down, however, thanks to the competition we have described: In this setting, it's likely that the node $H_2O$ will receive activation both from the WATER node and from the CHEMISTRY node; this will make the $H_2O$ node strong enough to win the winner-takes-all contest, shutting down the other distracting thoughts. If activation now spreads outward from the $H_2O$ node, you are likely to find the information you seek. And, crucially, with the RAINY WEATHER node now shut down, you won't activate *its* associated nodes, and so the distracting thoughts won't trigger other distract-

---

[1]The terminology here is borrowed from politics. In most parliamentary systems—the United Kingdom's, for example, or Germany's—each party gets a share of power corresponding to its share of votes. If the X party, therefore, gets 28% of the votes, then this party gets 28% of the seats in parliament. In contrast, the United States has a winner-takes-all system: If a presidential candidate gets 58% of the vote, she doesn't gets 58% of the presidency, she gets 100%.

ing thoughts. This will, of course, help keep your thinking on track. In this way, the winner-takes-all system will provide a *selective* mechanism that reduces distraction and helps you swiftly cull through the nodes activated in your search.

Sometimes, though, this mechanism will work against you. Imagine that you are trying to remember the name of the main character in the movie *The Matrix*. This thought activates nodes representing your recall of the movie, and activation spreads from there to the associated nodes. One of those nodes might be MORPHEUS, and this is close (Morpheus was in the movie) but not quite right (Morpheus wasn't the main character). But perhaps the MORPHEUS node becomes strongly activated. This launches the winner-takes-all process which *weakens* the other associated nodes. At this point, your early activation of MORPHEUS will actually work against your finding the information you seek. (Who was the main character, by the way?) Your best bet for finding the target information, therefore, may simply be to *give up on your search* for now. This will allow the MORPHEUS activation to decay, which will then weaken the inhibition now attached to this node's neighbors, which will then make it easier to activate these neighbors. In this fashion, the winner-takes-all system can actually produce a retrieval block, and can, in particular, produce the pattern we have labeled the T.O.T. state. (For more on competition among nodes, and how, in particular, this might apply to the T.O.T. phenomenon, see Anderson et al., 1994; Schwartz, 1999.)

## THE HOMUNCULUS

We mentioned earlier that a memory network needs the right number of connections. With too few, activation will not reach the desired target. With too many, activation will spread too far. In exactly the same fashion, the network needs the proper balance between activation and inhibition. If the inhibition is too weak, or starts too late, then too many memories will be activated, and we lose the advantages we hoped to gain from inhibition. But if the inhibition is too strong, or starts too early, then it may deactivate

nodes that represent the target information, and this will obviously defeat the memory search.

How does one find the appropriate balance? This is an issue for which computer modeling is particularly helpful: By trying out different configurations, one can ask how best to set up the network. Of course, it may also turn out that *no* configuration gets the job done. In that case, we'll need some other mechanism to guide search within the network, so this, too, is something we can hope to learn from modeling.

In the same spirit, note that we have described inhibition as dependent on a node's activation level: the greater the activation, the more inhibition the node will send out. As a result, the winner in the competition among nodes will reliably be the node that is the most strongly activated when the inhibition begins. Is this appropriate? Will this weed out just those nodes representing retrieval dead ends and leave the nodes that lead to the desired information? This is again an issue that can be pursued by modeling, but so far, there are no data that clearly settle these questions.

If the modeling is *not* successful, though, what then? The network as we have described it has the advantage of working in an extremely straightforward manner: There's no complex guidance system for the spread of activation; instead, activation simply flows wherever the connections lead. Inhibition likewise requires no guidance system but works in a fashion that seems automatic and mechanical. If these processes get the job done, then we end up with a model that is impressively simple (and, one might even say, *elegant*). But if these processes do not get the job done, perhaps we need some less mechanical, more *intelligent* means of searching through the network.

Consider an analogy. Imagine that you are looking at a recipe, and note that it calls for the spice *tamarind*. You immediately register the fact that this is not a spice you encounter often; perhaps you've never even heard of it. From this, you draw the sensible conclusion that it won't be productive to search for tamarind in your local supermarket. You know that the supermarket has a limited selection in many departments, and so it's likely to be comparably limited in its spices. So off you go to the gourmet store.

Notice that this involves several steps of reasoning, and these steps guide your search: There's no point in looking at the supermarket, even though this is where you buy most of your spices. There's also no point in looking in the yellow pages under "tamarind"; you know from the start that the yellow pages don't contain entries that are this specialized, so this, too, would probably be a dead end. But, crucially, you know that you're looking for a specialized cooking ingredient, and you know what sorts of shops carry those ingredients. That knowledge then tells you where to hunt for the tamarind.

Could there be a similar process in memory search—a process also guided by intelligence and reasoning? This would surely be helpful: This process could make smart choices about where to begin the search, and then it could guide the flow of activation so that the activation is channeled away from paths that are likely to be dead ends and toward the paths that seem more promising. This obviously would streamline memory search and make successful retrieval more likely.

Let's note the danger here, however. Memory search does seem intelligent; after all, memory is vast, and yet we usually find just the information we need, with no detectable effort or delay. In explaining this, it is tempting to say that there must be some processes in the mind that are themselves intelligent, strategic, and insightful in guiding our search. No wonder, then, that the search is so often successful. The problem, though, is that this appeal to "intelligent, strategic processes" really explains nothing. It is like saying we act intelligently because we are guided by an intelligent little "person in the head." This simply postpones an explanation, because the little person—or **homunculus**—would himself need to be explained. (We first met this term in Chapter 1, also in the context of discussing memory search.)

"Homunculus" explanations, in short, are not really explanations. Instead, they are IOUs, a promise of an explanation to come, since eventually, we'll need to explain how the homunculus himself functions. But

even so, sometimes we need homunculi in our theories, because sometimes a mental process *does* involve steps that are intelligent and insightful. In such cases, we must accept the IOU, that is, accept the burden of explaining, at some future point, how the homunculus might function.

Is memory search one of those cases? Is there an intelligent little executive in our heads who guides the search? If so, what procedures does he use in choosing a search's starting point? What rules does he rely on in choosing which nodes to pursue? These are unsettled issues, although, again, they are issues that can productively be addressed through the enterprise of modeling.

We leave this section, therefore, with a number of dangling questions. It is clear that we can productively think of memory as being a network of associations, with activation flowing from one node to another. This simple conception has allowed us to explain a wide range of data in this chapter; the conception also makes good biological sense (see Chapter 2). What is unclear, though, is whether this is all the theory we need. Will spreading activation plus some sort of node competition be enough to explain memory search and memory retrieval? Or will we need to supplement these mechanisms with some sort of "memory executive," guiding memory search? For these difficult questions, we do not yet have answers.

## The Newest Chapter: Connectionism

In the last 20 years or so, an important descendant of the network idea has appeared on the intellectual scene and has generated enormous excitement in psychology as well as in computer science and philosophy. This development seeks to address (among other things) exactly the worries we have just been considering. Rather than adding a more intelligent component to the network (i.e., a homunculus), this new approach goes in the opposite direction and tries to show just how much we can accomplish with network and more network.

## DISTRIBUTED PROCESSING, DISTRIBUTED REPRESENTATIONS

A small number of important innovations has spurred this new wave of theorizing, a wave referred to as connectionism, or parallel distributed processing (PDP). (For detailed descriptions of connectionist proposals, see Ackley, Hinton & Sejnowski, 1985; Hinton & Anderson, 1981; McClelland & Rumelhart, 1986; Rumelhart & McClelland, 1986b; Rumelhart, 1997; for somewhat broader perspectives, and excellent introductions to this domain, see Churchland, 1989; Flanagan, 1991; Haugeland, 1997.)

In the networks we have considered so far, what it means to "think about" or "remember" a particular idea is to activate the node for that idea. This assumes a system of **local representations**, with one idea per node, or one content per location. In a connectionist system, in contrast, there are only **distributed representations**, so that any particular idea is represented not by a single node, but by a pattern of activation across the network. To take a simple case, the concept *birthday* might be represented by a pattern in which nodes B, F, H, and R are firing, whereas the concept *computer* might be represented by a pattern in which nodes C, G, H, and S are firing. Note that node H is part of both these patterns and probably part of the pattern for many other concepts as well. Thus, we can't attach any meaning or interpretation to this node by itself; we can only learn what is being represented by looking at many other nodes simultaneously to find out what *pattern* of activation exists across the entire network. (For more on local and distributed representations, see Chapter 3.)

This reliance on distributed representation has important consequences for how a connectionist network functions. Imagine being asked what sort of computer you use. In order for you to respond, the idea *computer* needs to trigger the idea *Macintosh G3* (or *Dell* or *Compaq* or whatever it is you have). In a distributed network, this means that the many nodes representing *computer* have to manage collectively to activate the many nodes representing *G3*. To continue our simple illustration, node C has to trigger node L at the same time that node G triggers node A

and so on, leading ultimately to the activation of the L-A-J-T combination that, let's say, represents *G3*. In short, then, a network using distributed representations must employ processes that are similarly distributed, so that one widespread activation pattern can have broad enough effects to evoke a different (but equally widespread) pattern. In addition, the steps bringing this about must all occur simultaneously—in parallel—with each other, so that one entire representation can smoothly trigger the next. This is why connectionist models are said to involve **parallel distributed processing** (PDP).

These are in some ways radical ideas, and so it is worth spending a moment to think through what all of this involves. Think about a complicated spy novel, in which the Master Spy has a plan involving many operatives. Each operative receives her instructions, and this puts the plan into motion, piece by piece. Of course, for secrecy's sake, each operative is told only about her small part of the operation; each has no idea about how her actions fit into the overall scheme. That larger view, like the plan itself, is known only to the Master Spy.

And now chance enters: Immediately after instructing the last operative, the Master Spy dies of a heart attack. Even so, the plan can still go forward, since all of the operatives have their orders, and they need no further supervision. The plot will therefore run itself, even though the plot's designer (the Master Spy) is no longer on the scene.

In this situation, how should we think about the plan's status? As long as the Master Spy was alive, the overall plot was represented in her thoughts; there was, therefore, a local representation of the plan. After the Master Spy's death, however, there is no one place where the plan is represented in a unitary form. Nonetheless, the plan does continue to exist—in the collective actions of the full set of operatives. We would perceive the plan if only we could get a broad enough view, if only we could take a large step back, view all the operatives simultaneously, and understand how the actions of each fit into the whole. The plan still exists, therefore, in a distributed fashion and would be detected if we viewed the actions at the aggregate level, not at the level of the parts.

Moreover, notice that, if the Master Spy's plan is well devised, then it has to be *flexible*. Steps late in the plan may depend on how earlier steps have unfolded; at various points, adjustments may be needed because of new information coming in. But who is making these adjustments? The Master Spy is dead, and even before her death, there was no provision in the plan for the operatives to "check back" periodically with headquarters. So there is no way for any centralized authority to adjust the plan; all adjustments, therefore, must be made by the individual operatives themselves. But recall that each operative has no sense of how her actions fit into the overall scheme; indeed she doesn't even know there *is* an overall scheme. Hence, there is no way for an operative to make decisions about how well this or that action fits into the full pattern. If the operatives are making adjustments, these must be based entirely on each operative's understanding of just her part of the operation and based just on information locally available to her. Nonetheless, if we set this up right, these local adjustments, each based on local information, will as a package add up to a plan that is, overall, coherent, flexible, and sensibly responsive to large-scale changes.

It would, without question, require an extraordinary Master Spy to set up this kind of scheme. Things would be easier, of course, if we envisioned someone continuing to supervise the plan, so that this authority could coordinate the operations, making certain that the actions of one spy complement the actions of the others. But that would defeat the purpose, if we are after a *distributed* process. That is why, in our metaphor, we "killed off" the Master Spy as soon as the plan was set up. That way, we could be sure of no centralized, localized authority.

In fact, one could argue that our metaphor is limited in its value, because it is not distributed *enough*. The operatives are themselves individuals with knowledge and intelligence. Even if each is ignorant about the overall plan, each is able to contemplate ideas and meanings in her own actions and her own decision-making. Compared to the nodes within a connectionist network, this is far too much processing going on at the local level.

To make our metaphor more accurate, we would need to replace our crew of spies with something less sophisticated, less intelligent. In effect, the Master Spy would need to recruit a vast army of morons. This would require that the tasks assigned to each operative be extremely simple, so that the tasks would be within the morons' very limited competence. But that is precisely the proposal of connectionism. With enough morons connected together in the right ways, and with each doing the appropriate, very simple task, the aggregate activity of the network will reproduce the full intelligence of which the mind is capable.

How plausible is this? Is it possible that the complexity of our mental lives depends entirely on such simple components? It is important to bear in mind here how much depends on one's *point of view*. Think back to Chapter 3, where we discussed how a feature net could act as if it knew the rules of English spelling and could act as if it were making "inferences" to fill in missing information. This kind of description, in terms of "knowing rules" and "making inferences," describes what the feature net is doing *on aggregate*. On a more local level, though, the detectors within the net don't make inferences, and they don't know anything. The detectors simply have a certain firing threshold and fire whenever they receive the appropriate inputs. Thus, if one takes a close look at the mechanism, one finds interactions and processes that are extremely simple and driven entirely by local concerns. Things look much more sophisticated and intelligent, however, if we consider what an organism "equipped" with this mechanism will accomplish. Clearly, one's point of view is crucial: whether one is looking at the mechanism, which is quite simple, or at what the mechanism accomplishes, which is complex. Indeed, this is a consistent message of connectionism: Behaviors that look complicated from the outside can be produced by the combined actions of many very simple mechanisms.

In addition, consider the brain. Individual neurons within the brain are structurally and biochemically complicated, but their function is not: Inputs reach the neuron; activation accumulates; when the activation gets to a high enough level, the neuron fires. This is a relatively simple plan, and yet these simple units, when connected together in the right ways, are obviously capable of producing complicated and intelligent outcomes. This surely adds plausibility to the claim that simple units can be used to build complex processes.

## WHY BOTHER?

We have now highlighted some of the difficulties inherent in the connectionist approach. With no centralized authority, for example, it is clearly a challenge to make certain that local processes remain properly coordinated. But many investigators believe that these difficulties are a small price to pay for the *advantages* gained through connectionist modeling.

One advantage hinges on a point just made—a potential analogy between connectionist networks and the brain. Like the networks, the brain's functioning depends on the activities of many, many simple units, each accumulating activation and sending activation to its neighbors. We also know that many of the brain's parts are active at any particular point in time, strongly implying that the brain relies on parallel processing spread out over many neurons—just like a connectionist network. Finally, there is also reason to believe the brain relies on distributed processing and distributed representations.

For these reasons, advocates of the connectionist approach argue that their models make good biological sense and may provide insights into how the brain itself functions. Indeed, because of this analogy between the models and the brain, connectionist nets are often referred to as **neural nets**. Let's be careful, though, in understanding this label: These are not networks made up of neurons, but instead, networks hypothesized to function as we believe assemblies of neurons do.

In addition, many theorists have argued that humans routinely face tasks in which there are many clues and many requirements, but no formal rules or procedures available for how the tasks should be accomplished. Connectionist models seem particularly well suited for this sort of situation. First, these models have no need for formal rules or procedures. (Presumably, these rules would be followed by some centralized authority, and, of course, connectionist models have no such authority.) Second, sensitivity to multiple cues is a natural feature for a distributed process. To return to our spy metaphor, the overall progress of the Master Spy's plan will depend on the accumulation of each operative's actions, and each operative will be sensitive to just those cues that are in her view. In this way, many different cues will play a role in shaping the final outcome—just as we want, for many tasks.

To put this same point slightly differently, each operative in our spy scheme will face certain constraints—limits on her action and obstacles facing her part of the plan. The plan will go forward, therefore, only if each operative satisfies these constraints in order to do her part of the whole. As a result, the *overall* progress of the plan will involve the simultaneous satisfaction of multiple constraints, and that is exactly what we want. Think back to your hunt for tamarind. Here, too, there are multiple constraints: You know that you want a spice (so there's no point in looking in the hardware store); you know that the spice is uncommon (so there's no point in looking at your local supermarket); you know that your need is relatively specific (so there's no point in looking for tamarind in the yellow pages); and so on. The solution to this puzzle, therefore, must address all these constraints, and that is exactly what a distributed process is good at.

## LEARNING AS THE SETTING OF "CONNECTION WEIGHTS"

In various ways, then, connectionist models do seem promising, and this has spurred investigators to develop models of this type for many different psychological tasks. Only time will tell, though, exactly what these models can accomplish, and with that, whether this line of research will be as fruitful as many now believe.

In the meantime, though, there is one large issue still be addressed: The success of distributed processing obviously depends on having the appropriate connections in place, so that activation will spread to the desired target rather than in some other direction. But how are the connections set up in the first place? How, in a connectionist account, does *learning* take place?

Let us first be clear about what it means, in network terms, to "know something." In any associative network, connectionist or otherwise, knowledge is literally contained within the connections themselves. We already took a step in this direction when we discussed the "unpacking" of the nodes—that what it means to know "George Washington was a president" is to have a connection between a node for GEORGE WASHINGTON and a node for PRESIDENT. This is, of course, phrased in terms of *local* representations, with individual nodes having specific assigned referents. The basic idea, however, is the same in a distributed system. What it means to know this fact about Washington is to have a pattern of connections between the many nodes that together represent "Washington" and the many nodes that together represent "president." Once these connections are in place, activation of either of these patterns will lead to the activation of the other.

Notice, then, that knowledge refers to a *potential* rather than to a *state*. If you know that Washington was a president, then the connections are in place so that *if* the "Washington" pattern of activations happens to occur, this will lead to the "president" pattern of activations. And, of course, this state of "readiness" will remain even if you happen not to be thinking about Washington right now. Thus "thinking about" something, in network terms, corresponds to which nodes are active right now, with no comment about where that activation will spread next. "Knowing" something, in contrast, corresponds to how the activation will flow if there is activation on the scene.

This conception of "knowing" has obvious implications for the nature of "learning." The idea, in brief, is that learning must involve an adjustment in the connections among nodes, so that, after learning, activation flows in different ways than it did before. For example, let's say that you didn't know that George Washington was a president. This implies that activating your WASHINGTON node will not cause activation to flow toward the PRESIDENT node. (Or, in the language of distributed representations, activating the many nodes representing *Washington* will not cause activation of the many nodes representing *president*.) But now that you've learned this fact about Washington, activation will flow differently through your memory. Now, activating the WASHINGTON nodes *will* activate the PRESIDENT nodes. What's changed, therefore, is how the activation flows, and this requires an adjustment in connections.

In a connectionist network, however, this adjustment of the connections cannot be done via some central authority's intervention. That's because, in a connectionist network, there is no central authority. Instead, the adjustment must be governed entirely at the local level. In other words, the adjustment of **connection weights**—the strength of the individual connections—must be controlled entirely by mechanisms in the immediate neighborhood of each connection and influenced only by information about what's happening in that neighborhood.

Moreover, let's be clear that any bit of learning requires the adjustment of a great many connection weights: We need to adjust the connections, for example, so that the thousands of nodes representing *Washington* manage, together, to activate the thousands of nodes representing *president*. Thus learning, just like everything else in the connectionist scheme, must be a distributed process, involving thousands of microscopic changes, taking place all over the network, with no attempt at, and indeed, no mechanism for, any coordination of these adjustments.

This is, to be sure, an amazing proposal. In order to achieve learning in the entire network, the various adjustments in connection weights must, in some way, end up coordinated with each other. Otherwise, adjustments at one connection might cancel out adjustments made at another! Thus, if learning is to happen at all, we need to ensure that there is some coherence in the changes made across the network. And yet, as we have repeatedly said, there is no explicit mechanism in place to achieve this coordination. How, therefore, is learning possible? Here we arrive at one of the most important intellectual innovations driving connectionism forward. Connectionists have offered a number of powerful computing schemes, "learning algorithms," that seek to accomplish learning within this setup. The learning typically requires a large number of learning trials and some sort of feedback about the correctness or appropriateness of the response. But given this, connectionists have offered schemes, with names like the "delta rule" and "back propagation," that accomplish learning on the local level, without an executive, and that seem to make the entire system grow gradually and impressively smarter.

These learning algorithms cause connection weights to increase or decrease whenever specific, locally described configurations are present. As a simple example, we might set things up so that the connection weight between two nodes will increase whenever the two nodes are both activated or both not activated; the connection weight will decrease when either is activated but the other is not. With this rule in place, the connection weight will be determined by the correlation between the activation levels of the two nodes. If the correlation is strong, that is, if node A tends to be activated whenever node B is activated, the connection weight will often be incremented and will end up fairly strong. If the correlation is weak, that is, if A is often activated without B, or B without A, the connection weight will often be decremented and will end up weak.

As a different example, we can "teach" the network new information by allowing it to produce an output and then comparing this output to the desired output. (This is analogous to saying, "No, the answer isn't X; it is Y.") If the network has, in fact, produced the desired response, then there is no difference between its output and the one that we desired; hence, there is no error. If the network has gone wildly astray, there will be a large difference between the output produced and that desired. It is then possible to feed this information about error back into the network. Locally, each node will receive an **error signal**, a flow of activation *proportional* to the *magnitude* of error (i.e., proportional to the difference between output produced and output desired). Each node can then use the error signal to adjust its pattern of connection weights. If there is a weak error signal (i.e., if little or no error was made), then there is no reason to make adjustments. If there is a strong error signal, then a large adjustment in connection weights will be made. It is as if each node were saying, "I made an error, so my inputs must have led me astray. Therefore, let me ask *which* inputs favored this (incorrect) response and then adjust things, so that I will be less influenced by these inputs in the future. If the error was large, I'll make a big adjustment. For a small error, I'll make a small adjustment." If this process goes on at all of the nodes in the network and then is repeated over and over across a number of learning trials, then all of the connections leading to error will gradually be weakened. This will, of course, decrease the chance of error's happening again in the future, and this is obviously just what we want.

We have left the details of these learning algorithms to the side, both because they are mathematically complex and also because, when we talk about the state of the art, anything we say will be quickly out of date. We emphasize, though, that in all of these algorithms, the adjustment of connection weights depends entirely on local conditions. Moreover, let's bear in mind that individual nodes are extremely simple in their processing capacities. In making use of an error signal, for example, a node does nothing more than compare one activation level to another and make specific adjustments on this basis. The interesting question, therefore, lies in whether the accumulation of such simple mechanisms can be used as the basis for much more complex, much more sophisticated cognition. This question is at the heart of current controversy.

## POSSIBLE LIMITS ON CONNECTIONIST NETWORKS

Psychologists are clearly divided in their assessments of connectionist models—some view these models as an important step forward; others argue that the models are inadequate and that we should be pursuing other approaches. (For advocates of the connectionist approach, see Rumelhart & McClelland, 1986b; Churchland & Sejnowski, 1992; Christiansen & Chater, N., 1999; Rumelhart, 1997; McClelland & Seidenberg, 2000; for more critical views, see Fodor & Pylyshyn, 1988; Fodor, 1997; Holyoak, 1987; Lachter & Bever, 1988; Pinker & Prince, 1988; Pinker, 1999.)

What arguments might sway us for or against the connectionist approach? First, as we have already noted, many argue that connectionist models make biological sense—these models fit well, they claim, with what we know about the nervous system. Second, there seems little doubt that connectionist models do offer a powerful means of information storage. Third, we need to take these models seriously simply because of what they can accomplish. Connectionist models have so far learned to recognize patterns and can generalize what they have learned in appropriate ways. Connectionist models can, it is claimed, learn the rules of English grammar, can learn how to read, and can even learn how to play strategic games such as backgammon. (Many of these accomplishments are summarized in Rumelhart & McClelland, 1986b; McClelland, 1999.) All of this has led to considerable enthusiasm for connectionist approaches.

Others, however, have expressed considerable skepticism about these claims. There is, first of all, room for debate about the biological realism of connectionist models. Some aspects of these models (distributed processing, parallel activities) surely do make biological sense, but other aspects may not. (For example, it is not clear how some of the learning algorithms, particularly those involving "back propagation" of error signals, are to be translated into neural terms.) Second, some have argued that connectionist models can learn only when the programmers "stack the deck" in the right way. Since the models often learn by inspecting examples, it is possible to "help" the models enormously by providing just the right examples, in just the right sequence. Perhaps, then, connectionist models can't learn as we learn, or more precisely, perhaps they can learn what we learn only if we give them a great deal of help. (For concerns about the "psychological realism" of connectionist learning, see French, 1999; McCloskey & Cohen, 1989; Pinker & Prince, 1988; for an example of how this debate unfolds, see Marcus, 1995, 1996; Plunkett & Marchman, 1996; Pinker, 1999; Marcus et al., 1999; McClelland & Seidenberg, 2000.) Third, the existing connectionist models are fairly specific in their focus, modeling one or another well-defined task. But humans are capable of a huge variety of tasks, raising questions about how (or whether) connectionist models might rise from the miniature to the grand scale.

The state of the art, therefore, resembles what we saw with networks in general. There have been, to be sure, some remarkable successes for connectionist theory, with seemingly complex mental activities successfully modeled. However, the range of these successes is still limited, and questions have been raised about whether this learning matches the learning that humans do.

As a result of all this, controversy remains, and many in the field have adopted a wait-and-see attitude about what connectionist modeling will eventually accomplish. (For discussion, see Gluck & Rumelhart, 1990; Ramsey, Stich & Rumelhart, 1991.) Others are ready to predict that connectionism will meet only with limited success—providing an excellent account of some phenomena but unable to explain other phenomena (see, for example, Fodor & Pylyshyn, 1988). Still others have taken a different approach, proposing "hybrid" models that perform part of a task using more traditional approaches (e.g., approaches involving rules or set procedures) and part using connectionism (e.g., Holyoak & Thagard, 1989).

We leave this chapter, therefore, with some very obvious loose ends. There is no doubt that network theorizing can encompass an enormous range of memory data. Hand in hand with this, it is virtually certain that the "warehouse" of our long-term storage does indeed rely on some sort of network representation, with activation spreading from node to node, just as we have described in this chapter. What remains unsettled, though, is whether we will need other mechanisms, and more theory, beyond that provided by the network. Does the associative network serve merely as the "library" of long-term storage? Or does it also serve as the librarian, the indexer, the guy who retrieves books from the stacks, and the patron using the library? Said differently, does the network provide a theory of how knowledge is *represented* (with other mechanisms then needed to explain how the knowledge is *used*), or does the network provide a theory that explains *everything*?

We don't yet have answers to these questions, either for propositional networks (like Anderson's ACT model) or connectionist nets. Perhaps this is unsurprising, given the scale of the questions that are at stake here. In the meantime, though, we should surely take comfort from the fact that, unsolved mysteries or no, we have at least part of the puzzle under control. Our theorizing is allowing us to handle a lot of data and is leading us to new discoveries. This is, on anybody's account, a positive and promising sign.

## Chapter Summary

1. Many theorists have proposed that memory consists of a huge network of *nodes*, with each joined to others via *connections* or *associations*. An individual node becomes *activated* when it receives enough of an *input signal* to raise its *activation level* to its *response threshold*. Once activated, the node sends activation out through its connections to all the nodes connected to it.

2. The network approach easily accommodates many results. For example, hints are effective because the target node can receive activation from nodes identifying the previous encounter with the desired information while also receiving activation from nodes representing the hint. State dependent learning is explained in roughly the same fashion.

3. Many specific predictions of network theorizing have been directly confirmed. For example, activating one node does seem to prime nearby nodes through the process of *spreading activation*. Similarly, search through the network does seem to resemble travel in the sense that greater travel distances (more connections to be traversed) require more time.

4. If a node has a high degree of *fan*, it will be less effective in activating neighboring nodes, since each neighbor will receive only a small fraction of the activation energy radiating out from the initial node. This can in some circumstances impede memory search, creating a "cost of knowing too much." However, this cost is usually offset by the fact that, as knowledge grows, the target node is likely to receive input from many nodes, and not just one.

5. The quantity of knowledge in long-term storage can make it difficult to locate any particular bit of information when needed. However, search through memory can be guided by the structure of the network itself. Once in the vicinity of the target information, connections will guide activation toward the target. This requires having the right connections in place, and neither too many nor too few connections. However, many investigators believe that the right number of connections can be found so that search through the network may become a relatively mechanical affair. To launch the search, some nodes must be tied to the mechanisms of perception, and presentation of the appropriate stimulus will trigger these nodes.

6. To store all of knowledge, the network may need more than simple associations among ideas. One proposal is that the network stores *propositions*, with different nodes each playing the appropriate role within the proposition. In addition, a distinction between *type nodes* and *token nodes* may be needed for the network to store both generic knowledge and knowledge about individual objects and events.

7. To test network theories, investigators have often translated their theories into computer models. It is too soon to tell how successful these models will be, but the development of computer models has already spurred theoretical development. For example, any model based on a relatively mechanical process of spreading activation has difficulty explaining *retrieval blocks* or the *tip-of-the-tongue* phenomenon. However, an additional *winner-takes-all* mechanism may solve this problem.

8. Much recent effort has gone into the development of *connectionist* nets. These are distinctive

in relying entirely on *distributed processes* and *representations*. In these models, all learning consists of the setting (and adjusting) of *connection weights*. One attraction of this mode of theorizing is biological realism; another is the lack of any need for formal rules. Still another advantage is the fact that processing by a connectionist net is sensitive to many constraints simultaneously, just as the mind seems to be.

9. There continues to be controversy over what network models can accomplish. There is no doubt that associations and spreading activation do play a crucial role in long-term memory, but questions remain about whether these mechanisms are sufficient to explain memory storage and memory search, or whether, alternatively, some sort of "guide" or "executive" is needed to direct the operations of the network.

# Concepts and Generic Knowledge

In Chapter 7, we made a distinction between *episodic* memories and *generic* memories. Episodic memories record specific events—the party you went to last weekend, or the lecture you heard last Tuesday, or the adventure you had last summer. In each case, the memory records an *episode* tied to a particular time and place.

Generic memories, in contrast, are not tied to any particular episode; instead, these memories record *facts* and *beliefs*. These memories often contain knowledge of a commonplace sort, knowledge about low-level, unsophisticated facts: What is a dog? What is "jumping"? What appliances does one usually find in a kitchen? These cases seem neither glamorous nor complicated, but the *importance* of this knowledge within our mental lives is extraordinary. We saw in Chapters 5 and 7 that generic knowledge plays a huge role in our day-to-day commerce with the world. Indeed, we argued in Chapter 7 that, without a reliance on generic knowledge, our ordinary functioning would be much less efficient, much more difficult. Thus, although this knowledge seems commonplace, it is an ingredient without which cognition cannot proceed.

In this chapter, we will examine generic knowledge. What is this knowledge? How is it represented in the mind? Our initial focus will be on cases that seem relatively simple—the knowledge each of us has about concepts like "dog" or "chair" or "tree." As we will see, however, describing these concepts is more difficult than one might initially guess. In addition, it is clear that each of us understands a great *diversity* of concepts—not just concepts of things ("cat," "movie star," "sitting Supreme Court Justice"), but also concepts concerned with actions ("walking," "wanting," "waltzing"), events ("birthday party," "trips to the zoo," "taking an examination"), complex systems

**271**

("free-market capitalism," "automobile industry"), and so on. It is not obvious at the outset whether one theory, or one form of representation, will serve for this broad range of concepts. Nonetheless, we will proceed on the assumption that one theory will do the job; we will see how far we can get with this assumption. (For more on whether we'll need different theories for different types of concepts, see Medin et al., 2000.)

## Definitions: What Do We Know When We Know What a Dog Is?

We all know what a dog is. If someone sends us to the pet shop to buy a dog, we are sure to succeed. If someone tells us that a particular disease is common among dogs, we know that our pet terrier is at risk and so are the wolves in the zoo. Clearly, our store of knowledge about dogs will support these not-very-exciting achievements. But what is that knowledge?

One possibility is that we know something akin to a dictionary definition. That is, what we know is of this form: "A dog is a creature that is (a) mammalian, (b) has four legs, (c) barks, (d) wags its tail . . ." This definition would presumably serve us well. When asked whether a candidate creature is a dog, we could use our definition as a checklist, scrutinizing the candidate for the various defining features. When told that "A dog is an animal," we would know that we had not learned anything new, since this information is already contained, presumably, within our mental definition. If we were asked what dogs, cats, and horses have in common, we could scan our definition of each looking for common elements.

The difficulty with this proposal, however, comes when we try to spell out just how these terms are defined. The relevant argument here comes not from a psychologist, but from an important twentieth-century philosopher, Ludwig Wittgenstein. Wittgenstein (1953) noted that philosophers had been trying for thousands of years to define terms like "virtue" or "knowledge." There had been some success, inasmuch as various features had been identified as im-

portant aspects of these terms. However, even after thousands of years of careful thought, these terms were still without accepted, full definitions.

Perhaps this is unsurprising, since these are subtle, philosophically rich terms, embedded in a complex web of human activities and so naturally resistant to definition. However, Wittgenstein wondered if this really was the problem. He wondered whether we could find definitions even for simple, ordinary terms, for example, the word, "game."

What is a game? Consider, for example, the game of hide-and-seek. What makes hide-and-seek a game? Hide-and-seek (a) is an activity most often practiced by children, (b) is engaged in for fun, (c) has certain rules, (d) involves multiple people, (e) is in some ways competitive, (f) is played during periods of leisure. All these are plausible attributes of games, and so we seem well on our way to defining "game." But are these attributes really part of the definition of "game"? Consider (a) and (b): What about the Olympic games? The competitors in these games are not children, and runners in marathon races do not look like they are having a great deal of fun. Consider (d) and (e): What about card games played by one person? These are played alone, without competition. Consider (f): What about professional golfers?

For each clause of the definition, one can find an exception: an activity that we call a game but that does not have the relevant characteristic. And the same is true for most any concept: We might define "shoe" as an item of apparel made out of leather, designed to be worn on the foot. But what about wooden shoes? What about a shoe, designed by a master shoemaker, intended only for display and never for use? What about a shoe filled with cement, which therefore cannot be worn? Similarly, we might define "dog" in a way that includes four-leggedness, but what about a dog that has lost a limb in some accident? We might specify "communicates by barking" as part of the definition of dog, but what about the Egyptian basenji, which has no bark? Quite consistently, our most common terms, terms denoting concepts that we use easily and often, resist being defined. When we do come up with a definition, it is all too easy to find exceptions to it.

To put this more precisely, we cannot equate "knowing a term" or "knowing a concept" with "knowing a definition." To be sure, each of us can correctly define *some* of the terms we know (e.g., "triangle"), but it seems we are unable to define many other terms that we commonly use. Of course, many of these concepts can be defined by the relevant experts. A botanist, for example, might be able to define "elm tree" fully, with a definition that distinguishes between an elm and a beech. Similarly, a biologist might be able to define "dog" in terms of a particular genetic pattern. But these technical definitions are unknown to most of the people who know and use these concepts. If asked to define "dog," these concept-holders are unlikely to spell out the correct genetic pattern. Instead, they will list plausible dog features, but once again, we can easily find exceptions to their proposed definitions.

## FAMILY RESEMBLANCE

If asked to define commonplace terms, we do not name foolish or inappropriate features. If asked to define "dog," for example, we do not say, "A dog is a creature who lives in Brooklyn and has green hair." Instead, we name plausible "dog features." It might be that not all dogs have these features, but many dogs do.

Given all of this, perhaps what concept-holders have is not a firm, "works every time" definition but instead something less rigid. It looks like we cannot say, "A creature with features X, Y, and Z is a dog." But we can say, "A creature with these features is *probably* a dog, and a creature without these features *probably* isn't." This probabilistic phrasing preserves what is good within definitions—e.g., the fact that definitions do name sensible, relevant features. But this phrasing also allows some degree of uncertainty, some number of exceptions to the rule.

Wittgenstein's proposal was roughly along these lines. His notion was that members of a category have a **family resemblance** to each other. Consider the ways that members of a family resemble each other: Some features are common in the family (a

particular hair color, a particular shape of nose), but this does not mean that everyone in the family has these features. You might resemble your mother because you both have the same high cheekbones. You might resemble your sister because you both have the same eye shape and the same strong chin (neither of which your mother shares). You might resemble your brother because of yet some other features. In these ways, if we take members of the family two or even three at a time, we will find considerable feature overlap. However, if we consider *all* of the members of the family, we may find no features that they all share. Nevertheless, because of the feature overlap, family members do resemble each other.

Family resemblance will give us something like a probabilistic definition. A rigid "definition" of a family's appearance ("What it *means* to 'look like a Smith' is brown hair, green eyes . . .") that works every time won't be possible, since there may be no features shared by all family members. But there are characteristic features for each family, so that someone who has these features will *probably* be perceived as being a member of the family. Moreover, the more of these features someone has, the more likely we are to believe they are in the family. Family resemblance is a matter of degree, not all-or-none.

In the same fashion, there may be no definition of categories like "dog," because there may be no attributes that consistently distinguish dogs from non-dogs. More precisely, there may be no **necessary conditions** of being a dog—i.e., attributes you must have in order to be a dog.[1] Likewise, there may be no **sufficient conditions**—i.e., attributes that, if you have them, are sufficient to qualify you as a dog.

---

[1] As a subtle point, note that there are some necessary conditions for being a dog: For example, it is necessary that an entity be a physical object in order to be a dog. It is likewise necessary that an entity consist of more than one molecule in order to be a dog. But these conditions, while necessary for "dogdom," obviously won't distinguish dogs from cats or even fire hydrants. Hence, this condition is not distinctive for dogs and is therefore not necessary for being counted as a dog *as opposed to* being counted as a member of one of these other categories.

However, this does not mean that the category of "all dogs" is a random assembly. Instead, any two or three dogs we might consider are likely to have a great deal in common, just as you and your brother have a great deal in common, or your brother and your father. *What* they have in common may shift from case to case, just as the features you and your brother share may be different from the features shared by your brother and your father. Nonetheless there will be resemblance among the members of the category, even though we cannot specify anything that all members of the category have in common (Figure 9.1).

There are several ways we might translate all of this into a psychological theory, but the most influential translation was proposed by Eleanor Rosch, in the mid-1970s (Rosch, 1973, 1978; Rosch & Mervis, 1975; Rosch, Mervis, Gray, Johnson & Boyes-Braem, 1976), and it's to her model that we now turn.

## Prototypes and "Typicality" Effects

One way to think about definitions is that they set the "boundaries" for a category: If a test case has certain attributes, then it is "inside" the category. If the test case does not have the defining attributes, then it is "outside" the category. (For discussion of this "classical" view, see Smith, 1988; Margolis, 1994; Smith & Medin, 1981.)

**FIGURE 9.1**

### What Attributes Define a Chair?

*"Attention, everyone! I'd like to introduce the newest member of our family."*

Some chairs have four legs, some three, some none. Most chairs can be sat upon, but some are too small for sitting. It seems that chairs have a "family resemblance" to each other but not a definition.

**Prototype theory** begins with a different tactic: Perhaps the best way to identify a category, to characterize a concept, is to specify the "center" of the category rather than the "boundaries." Perhaps the concept of "dog," for example, is represented in the mind by some representation of the "ideal" dog, the *prototype* dog. In this view, all judgments about dogs are made with reference to this ideal. Categorization, for example, would involve some sort of comparison between a test case (the furry creature currently before your eyes) and the prototype. If there is no similarity between these, then the creature before you is probably not in the category; if there is considerable similarity, then you draw the opposite conclusion.

What is a prototype? For most purposes, we can think of a prototype as an "average" of the various category members one has encountered. The prototype will be of average color, age, size, and so forth. When averaging is not appropriate, the prototype's attributes will match the most frequent attributes in the category. The prototype for "family," for example, will be of average age, average education level, and average income, but will have one child, not (the average of) 1.19. In still other cases, a prototype may represent an "ideal" for the category rather than an average. (The prototype diet soft drink, for example, might have zero calories, yet taste great, even if no actual soft drinks reach this ideal.)

Likewise, it seems plausible that different people will have different prototypes. If a prototype reflects the ideal for a category, then people may disagree about what that ideal would involve. If a prototype reflects the average of the cases you have encountered, then an American's prototype for "house" might have one form, whereas for someone living in Japan, the prototype "house" might be rather different.

Thus we will need to allow some flexibility in how we characterize prototypes. (For some further complexities here, see Armstrong, Gleitman & Gleitman, 1983; Barsalou, 1987; Lynch, Coley & Medin, 2000; Neuman, 1977.) Nonetheless, in all these cases, the prototype will serve as the "anchor," the "benchmark," for our conceptual knowledge. When we reason about a concept, or use our conceptual knowledge, our reasoning is done with reference to the prototype.

## FUZZY BOUNDARIES AND GRADED MEMBERSHIP

Our hypothesis is that what it means to "know" a concept is simply to have some mental representation of the concept's prototype. How does this work? Consider the simple task of categorization: As we suggested before, one might categorize objects by comparing them to prototypes stored in memory. If, for example, the creature now before your eyes has many attributes in common with the dog prototype, it will easily and quickly be recognized as a dog. Dogs that have fewer attributes in common with the prototype will probably cause you uncertainty about their identity. Similarly, in deciding that a particular ceramic vessel is a cup and not a bowl, you might compare the vessel to both your cup prototype and your bowl prototype. By discovering that the vessel is more similar to one than to the other, you reach a decision.

This sounds plausible enough, but there is an odd implication here. Imagine a range of vessels, each one further and further removed from the cup prototype. The first might, for example, be the shape and size of a teacup, and white in color. The second might be the same shape and size, but shocking pink in color. The third might be shocking pink, and twice the size of a normal teacup; the next might be all these things, and also made of lead. According to a definition view (the "classical" view), our cup definition would tell us that some of these cases do count as cups and others do not. That is all. The category of cups has a boundary somewhere, and each test case is either on one side of the boundary or the other. Moreover, all of the cups inside the boundary are "equal citizens," each one fully and legitimately entitled to be called a cup. All of the non-cups are also "equal citizens," each one fully and equivalently not a cup. You are a cup, or you are not a cup. End of story.

The prototype view would allow us to say none of this. We could certainly say that some of the vessels under consideration are closer to the prototype than others, and that the ones closer to the prototype are more likely to be cups, the ones further from it are less likely. But at no point is there a boundary between "inside" the category and "outside." Instead, the category of cup has a **fuzzy boundary**, with no clear specification of membership and non-membership.

Hand in hand with this, not all cups are equal. Instead, some are "cup-ier" than others, namely the ones nearer the prototype. To put this more generally, prototype-based categories not only have fuzzy boundaries, they also have **graded membership**. Thus, some dogs are "better" dogs than others, according to how close they are to the prototype. The graded membership notion, therefore, is a striking and important implication of the prototype view.

### TESTING THE PROTOTYPE NOTION

Consider the sentence verification task, which we first met in Chapter 8. In this task, research participants are presented with a succession of sentences; their job is to indicate (by pressing the appropriate button) whether each sentence is true or false. The sentences are simple in form: "A sparrow is a bird. A chair is furniture. A collie is a cat." (The responses here would obviously be "true, true, false.")

The participants' speed in this task depends on several factors. As we have seen, response speed depends on the number of "steps" the participants must traverse to confirm the sentence (see Chapter 8). Participants also respond more quickly for true sentences than for false, and also more quickly for familiar categories. Most important for our purposes, though, the speed of response varies from item to item within a category. For example, response times are longer for sentences like "A penguin is a bird" than for "A robin is a bird"; longer for "An Afghan hound is a dog" than for "A German shepherd is a dog" (e.g., Smith, Rips & Shoben, 1974).

Why should this be? According to a prototype perspective, participants make these judgments by comparing the thing mentioned (penguin, for example) to their prototype for that category (their bird prototype). When there is much similarity between the test case and the prototype, participants can make their decisions quickly; judgments about items more distant from the prototype take more time. Given the results, it seems that penguins and Afghans are more distant from their respective prototypes than are robins and German shepherds.

There are several different ways to flesh out this proposal, and, in particular, different ways to unpack this idea of being "more distant" or "less distant" from the prototype. Let's hold these points to the side, though, because we first need to deal with a problem in the argument just offered: Why does "robin" yield fast responses, while "penguin" doesn't? Because robins are closer to the prototype than penguins. How do we know that robins are closer to the prototype? Because they yield faster responses. This is plainly circular: We are using proximity to the prototype as a basis for predicting fast responses, but we are then turning around and arguing the reverse: fast responses as a basis for claiming proximity to the prototype.

The escape from this circle is easy to find. What we cannot do is make "double use" of the same results: We can't use a set of data to determine which cases are close to the prototype, and which are distant, and then use those same data to support the prototype perspective. What we can do, however, is make predictions from one data set to a *different* data set. For example, we can use experiments like the sentence verification task to identify which category members seem to be close to the prototype. We can then use this information to predict the results of other studies. As one option, we can ask people to name as many birds as they can (cf. Mervis, Catlin & Rosch, 1976). According to a prototype view, they will do this production task by first locating their bird or dog prototype in memory and then asking themselves what resembles this prototype. In essence, they will start with the center of the category (the prototype) and work their way outward from there. Thus, birds close to the prototype should be mentioned first, birds further from the prototype later on. More concretely, the first birds to be mentioned in this task should be the birds that yielded fast response times in the verification task; the birds mentioned later in production should have yielded slower response times in verification. This is exactly what happens.

This sets the pattern of evidence for prototype theory: Over and over, in category after category, members of a category that are "privileged" on one task (e.g., yield the fastest response times) turn out also to be privileged on other tasks (e.g., are most likely to be mentioned). That is, various tasks **converge** in the sense that each task yields the same answer, i.e., indicates the same category members as special. (For some examples of these "privileged" category members, see Table 9.1.)

This notion of **converging evidence** provides two benefits. First, it allows us to escape the problem of circular arguments. Second, and perhaps more important, consider what it *means* to study concepts: Presumably, concepts constitute the knowledge we draw on for a variety of purposes—we use our "fish" concept to identify fish, to talk about fish, to draw inferences about fish. In other words, a variety of tasks are based on the same underlying conceptual knowledge. Thus, if we are trying to study the concept of "fish," we are less interested in how people do this or that particular task, and more interested in what these various tasks have in common; we are less interested in the processes or strategies involved in the task, and more interested in the knowledge that supports the task. Given this, the idea that we are getting data from a spectrum of

| Participants' Typicality Ratings for the Category "Fruit" and the Category "Bird"  TABLE 9.1 ||||
|---|---|---|---|
| **Fruit** | **Rating** | **Bird** | **Rating** |
| Apple | 6.25 | Robin | 6.89 |
| Peach | 5.81 | Bluebird | 6.42 |
| Pear | 5.25 | Seagull | 6.26 |
| Grape | 5.13 | Swallow | 6.16 |
| Strawberry | 5.00 | Falcon | 5.74 |
| Lemon | 4.86 | Mockingbird | 5.47 |
| Blueberry | 4.56 | Starling | 5.16 |
| Watermelon | 4.06 | Owl | 5.00 |
| Raisin | 3.75 | Vulture | 4.84 |
| Fig | 3.38 | Sandpiper | 4.47 |
| Coconut | 3.06 | Chicken | 3.95 |
| Pomegranate | 2.50 | Flamingo | 3.37 |
| Avocado | 2.38 | Albatross | 3.32 |
| Pumpkin | 2.31 | Penguin | 2.63 |
| Olive | 2.25 | Bat | 1.53 |

*Note*: Ratings were made on a 7-point scale, 7 corresponding to the highest typicality. [After Malt & Smith, 1984.]

tasks, and that these data are converging on the same answer, gives us reason to believe that we are not "merely" studying how people do a particular task. Instead, this gives us reason to believe that we are studying knowledge of a broadly useful, fundamental sort, exactly the kind of knowledge that we would expect concepts to provide.

## THE CONVERGING EVIDENCE FOR PROTOTYPES

We have mentioned two lines of experiments with converging data patterns, but there are many more. We list six of them here, to give you a sense of the evidence:

1. *Sentence verification.* As indicated, items close to the prototype are more quickly identified as category members. This presumably reflects the fact that category membership is determined by assessing the similarity to the prototype (Rosch, Simpson & Miller, 1976; although, for some complications in the sentence verification procedure, see Glass, Holyoak & Kiger, 1979; McCloskey & Glucksberg, 1979; Smith, 1978; Smith et al., 1974).

2. *Production.* As indicated, items close to the prototype are the earliest and the most likely to be mentioned in a production task. This presumably reflects the fact that the memory search supporting this task begins with the prototype and "works outward" (Barsalou, 1983, 1985; Barsalou & Sewell, 1985; Mervis et al., 1976).

3. *Picture identification.* This task is similar to the sentence verification task. Participants are told that they are about to see a picture that may or may not be a dog; they are asked to hit a "yes" or "no" button as quickly as they can. Pictures of dogs similar to the prototype (e.g., German shepherd or collie) are more quickly identified, pictures of dogs less similar to the prototype (for example, chihuahua or dachshund) are more slowly identified (Rosch, Mervis et al., 1976; Smith, Balzano & Walker, 1978).

4. *Explicit judgments of category membership.* Rosch (1975; also Malt & Smith, 1984) explicitly asked par-

ticipants to judge how typical various category members were for the category. In these **typicality** studies, the participants are given instructions like these: "We all know that some birds are 'birdier' than others; some dogs are 'doggier' than others, and so on. I'm going to present you with a list of birds or of dogs, and I want you to rate each one on the basis of how 'birdy' or 'doggy' it is." People are easily able to render these judgments, and quite consistently, they rate items as being very "birdy" or "doggy" when these instances are close to the prototype (as determined in the other tasks). They rate items as being less "birdy" or "doggy" when these are further from the prototype. This suggests that people perform this task by comparing the test item to the prototype.

5. *Induction.* An interesting result involves someone's willingness to extrapolate from current information. In one study, participants were told a new fact about robins and were willing to infer that the new fact would also be true for ducks; if they were told a new fact about ducks, however, they would not extrapolate to robins (Rips, 1975). Apparently, people will make inferences from the typical to the whole category but will not make inferences from the atypical to the category.

6. *Tasks asking people to "think about" categories.* The procedure here has three steps (after Rosch, 1977a). First, we ask participants to make up sentences about a category. If the category were "birds," they might make up such sentences as, "I saw two birds in a tree," or "I like to feed birds in the park." Next, the experimenters rewrite these sentences, substituting for the category name either the name of a prototypical member of the category (e.g., robin) or a not-so-prototypical member (e.g., penguin). In our example, we would get "I like to feed robins in the park," and "I like to feed penguins in the park." Finally, we take these new, edited sentences to a different group of participants and ask this group to rate how silly or implausible the sentences seem.

The hypothesis is that, when we ask people to think about a category, they are in fact thinking about the prototype for that category. Therefore, in making up their sentences, participants will come up with statements appropriate for the prototype. It follows from this that the sentence's sensibility will be pretty much unchanged if we substitute a prototypical category-member for the category name, since that will be close to what the participant had in mind in the first place. Substituting a non-prototypical member, on the other hand, may yield a peculiar, even ridiculous, proposition. This is fully in line with the data. When the new group of participants rates these sentences, they rate as quite ordinary the sentences into which we have placed a prototypical case ("I saw two robins in a tree") and reject as silly the sentences into which we have placed a non-prototypical case ("I saw two penguins in a tree").

## BASIC-LEVEL CATEGORIES

Much of the research just reviewed derives from Eleanor Rosch's theorizing about the nature and function of mental prototypes. We should mention, though, that Rosch's work also contains a further theme. As a way of introducing this point, consider the following task: I show you a picture of a chair, and I ask, "What is this?" What you are likely to say is that the picture shows a chair. You are far less likely to offer a more specific response ("It's a Windsor chair") or a more general response ("It's an item of furniture"), although these responses would also be correct. Likewise, how do people get to work? In responding, you are unlikely to say, "Some people drive Fords; some drive Chevies." Instead, your answer is likely to use more general terms, such as cars and trains and buses.

In keeping with these observations, Rosch has argued that there is a "natural" level of categorization, neither too specific nor too general, that we tend to use in our conversations and in our reasoning. She refers to this level as providing **basic-level categorization**. Basic-level categories are usually represented in our language via a single word, while more specific categories are identified only via a phrase. Thus, "chair" is a basic-level category and so is "apple." The subcategories of "armchair" or

"wooden chair" are not basic level; nor is "red apple" or "Golden Delicious apple." If asked to describe an object, we are likely spontaneously to use the basic-level term. If asked to explain what members of a category have in common with each other, we have an easy time with basic-level categories (what do all chairs have in common?) but some difficulty with more encompassing categories (what does all furniture have in common?).

There has been some debate about these claims. Do all categorization schemes have a basic level? How "stable" is the designation of the basic level? Do novices and experts agree, for example, in defining the basic level? (People in general might regard "plant" as basic level; a gardener might regard "annual" or "perennial" as basic levels; and a botanist might regard "monocots" and "dicots" as basic level.) Likewise, is the designation of basic level stable from one task to the next or from one context to the next? The evidence is mixed on these various questions.

Even with these complexities, basic-level categorization is important for a variety of purposes. For example, in studies of children who are learning how to talk, there are some indications that basic-level terms are acquired earlier than the more specific subcategories or the more general, more encompassing categories. Thus, basic-level categories do seem to reflect a natural way to categorize some of the objects in our world (Rosch, Mervis et al., 1976; for discussion and some complications, see Corter & Gluck, 1992; Jolicoeur et al., 1984; Morris & Murphy, 1990; Palmer et al., 1989; Tanaka & Taylor, 1991; Tversky & Hemenway, 1991).

## Exemplars

Let's return, though, to our main agenda. As we have seen, a broad spectrum of tasks reflects the "graded membership" of mental categories. Some members of the categories are "better" than others, and the "better" members are recognized more readily, mentioned more often, judged more typical, and so on. Thus, people give fast verifications for sentences like,

"An apple is a fruit" and slower responses to "An olive is a fruit." If asked to name fruits, people are likely to name apple fairly quickly; if they name olive at all, it will be much later. If asked to rate how "fruity" apples and olives are, they will give a higher rating for the former.

Likewise, it seems plain that typicality does guide many of our category judgments: In diagnosing diseases, for example, physicians often seem to function as if asking themselves: "How much does this case resemble a typical case of disease X? How closely does it resemble a typical case of disease Y?" The greater the resemblance to this or that diagnostic prototype, the more likely the diagnosis will be of that disease. (See, e.g., Klayman & Brown, 1993.)

All of this is obviously in accord with prototype theory: Our conceptual knowledge is represented via a prototype, and we categorize by making comparisons to that prototype. It turns out, though, that prototype theory isn't the only way one can think about these data. Another perspective is available, providing a different way to explain typicality effects and the graded membership of categories. In this section , we examine this alternate view.

### ANALOGIES FROM REMEMBERED EXEMPLARS

Imagine that we place a wooden object in front of you and ask, "Is this a chair?" According to the prototype view, you would answer this question by calling up your chair prototype from memory and then comparing the candidate to that prototype. If the resemblance is great, you announce, "Yes, this is a chair."

But you might make this decision in a different way: You might notice that this object is very similar to an object in your Uncle Jerry's living room, and you know that the object in Uncle Jerry's living room is a chair. After all, you've seen Uncle Jerry sitting in the thing, reading his newspaper. If Jerry's possession is a chair, and if the new object resembles Jerry's, then it is a safe bet that the new object is a chair, too.

The idea here is that, in some cases, categorization can draw on knowledge about specific category members rather than more general information about the overall category. In our example, the categorization is supported by memories of a *specific* chair, rather than remembered knowledge about chairs in general. This is referred to as an **exemplar-based approach**, with an exemplar defined as a specific remembered instance—in essence, an example.

This approach overlaps with the prototype view in several regards. According to each of these views, you categorize objects by comparing them to a mentally represented "standard." For prototype theory, this standard is the prototype; for exemplar theory, the standard is provided by whatever example of the category comes to mind. In either case, though, the process is then the same: You assess the similarity between a candidate object and this standard. If the resemblance is great, you judge the candidate as being within the relevant category; if the resemblance is minimal, you seek some alternative categorization.

It should be emphasized, though, that these two views diverge on some key points. For one, the prototype view implies that reasoning will always draw on the same standard, namely, the prototype itself. According to the exemplar view, however, this need not be true—it is quite possible that different examples will come to mind on different occasions, and this will influence your performance. An illustration will help show how this matters and will also show us how far an exemplar approach might be extended.

You are reading along, and encounter the novel word "tave." How should you pronounce this letter string? You might call to mind the rules of English spelling, which tell you that this pattern of consonant, vowel, consonant, "e" demands a long vowel. Therefore, the word is pronounced as though it rhymes with "save" or "cave."

Alternatively, you might look at the word "tave" and be reminded, not of a rule, but of other words, such as "save" or "cave." By analogy with these, you would pronounce "tave" with a long vowel. In this way, you would arrive at the same decision as you would have via the rule. But this process of find-an-instance, draw-an-analogy leaves open another possibility: "Tave" might also remind you of "have" and, in this case, the analogy would lead you to a short-vowel pronunciation. And, interestingly enough, college students, asked to pronounce this letter string, do on occasion come up with the short-vowel pronunciation, a peculiar finding if they are using the rule, but easily explained if they are using instances plus analogies (Baron, 1977).

Our confidence that this is what is going on is increased by the fact that we can prime our research participants in a simple way: The participants read down a list of words, some of which are real words, some of which are made up. Word number 23 on this list might be "have." Word number 26 is the test word, "tave." It turns out that this recent activation of "have" makes the short-vowel pronunciation of "tave" much more likely, just as we would expect on an instance-plus-analogy account: If the instance "have" is made more likely to come to mind, it is more likely that it (and not *save* or *cave* or *rave*) will be the basis for the analogy, and so, by manipulating memory availability of "have," we influence how the analogy will turn out.

We should emphasize, though, that a person's reliance on exemplars is typically unwitting. If we ask people directly why they pronounced the letter string as they did, they generally don't mention the earlier-presented word. But the data tell us that they are, in fact, being influenced by this earlier presentation. This obviously resembles the pattern we encountered again and again in Chapter 6. There we distinguished between "explicit" memories, of which the person is aware, and "implicit" memories, which influence us without any awareness. It seems likely that exemplars are remembered in the latter way—*implicitly*, with people plainly being influenced by remembered exemplars without realizing it. (For discussion, see Ashby & Waldron, 1999; Brooks, 1990; Knowlton & Squire, 1993. For a similar pattern, in which remembered instances influence *problem-solving*, see pp. 458–464.)

## EXPLAINING TYPICALITY DATA WITH AN EXEMPLAR MODEL

The proposal to be considered, then, is that judgments about concepts are often made via analogies based on specific remembered instances. Many authors have endorsed this proposal, albeit with some variations in the particulars of how these analogies are selected or created (Brooks, 1978, 1987; Estes, 1976, 1993; Hintzman, 1986; Medin, 1975, 1976; Medin & Schaffer, 1978; Nosofsky, 1986; Reed, 1972; Shin & Nosofsky, 1992).

Why should we take this proposal seriously? First, it seems undeniable that we do have knowledge about particular cases: Not only do we know about dogs, we also know about Fido and Spot and Rover. In some cases, this specific knowledge conflicts with our conceptual knowledge, and when this happens, the specific knowledge dominates. (For a discussion of this point, see, e.g., Brooks, 1990.) Thus we know that, in general, birds fly, but we overrule this knowledge when we are considering a specific bird that we know to be flightless.

In addition, it turns out that exemplar-based approaches can also explain the graded-membership pattern so often seen in concept tasks. For example, consider a task in which we show people a series of pictures and ask them to decide whether each picture shows a fruit or not. We already know that they will respond more quickly for typical fruits than for less typical fruits, and we have seen how this result is handled by a prototype account. How could an exemplar model explain this finding?

According to exemplar theory, people make their judgments in this task by comparing the pictures to specific memories of fruits—that is, to specific, mentally represented examples. But how exactly will this work? Let's imagine that you're looking at a picture of some object, and trying to decide whether it's a fruit or not. To make your decision, you'll try to think of a fruit exemplar that resembles the one in the picture; if you find a good "match," then you know the object in the picture *is* a fruit. No match? Then it's not a fruit.

If the picture shows, say, an apple, then your memory search will be extremely fast: Apples are common in your experience (often seen, often eaten, often mentioned), and so you've had many opportunities to establish apple memories. Moreover, these memories will be well primed, thanks to your frequent encounters with apples. As a result, you'll easily find a memory that matches the picture; you have many memories that will fill the bill, and these memories are already primed. But if the picture shows, say, a fig, or a carob, then your memory search will be more difficult: You probably don't have as many memories that will match these pictures, and these memories aren't well primed.

In this fashion, you'll respond quickly to the typical fruit and less quickly to the unusual fruit. But this isn't because of prototyping; it is instead because of the pattern of what's available in memory. A similar argument will handle the other tasks showing the graded membership pattern—for example, the *production* task. Let's say that you are asked to *name* as many fruits as you can. You'll quickly name apples and oranges, because these fruits are represented many times in your memory, thanks to the many encounters you've had with them. These memories are also well primed, for the same reason, making them easy to retrieve. Therefore apple memories and orange memories will easily come to mind. Fig and date memories, however, will have none of these advantages, and so will less readily come to mind. In this way, your production will favor the typical fruits.

## EXEMPLARS PRESERVE INFORMATION ABOUT VARIABILITY

As we have just seen, exemplar-based views can easily explain typicality effects, largely by appealing to a "typicality bias" in people's memories: Items that are frequent in the world will be frequently represented (and well primed) in memory, and so will readily come to mind. This is all we need to explain the graded-membership pattern—with no appeal whatsoever to mental prototypes.

It seems, therefore, that the graded membership pattern favors *neither* the prototype nor the exemplar theory; *both* theories are fully compatible with the evidence. Other results, however, do favor the exemplar view. For example, we have noted that a

prototype can be thought of as the *average* for a category, and as such, it provides a summary of what is typical or frequent for that category. But much information is lost in an average. For example, an average, by itself, doesn't tell you how *variable* a set is, and sometimes information about variability is rather useful (after Rips, 1989a; Rips & Collins, 1993). The average size of a pizza is twelve inches. The average size of a ruler is, of course, also twelve inches. Now let's imagine that I hand you a new object that is 19 inches across. Is it more likely that this new object is a pizza or a ruler? If you make this decision by comparing the test case to the averages, then you have no basis for a judgment—the test case departs from both averages by 7 inches. But of course you know that pizzas vary in size enormously, and so a pizza could easily be 19 inches across. Rulers do not vary, and so the test case is almost certainly not a ruler.

In this situation, your judgment is plainly influenced by knowledge about variability. This knowledge would not be reflected in a prototype (which is just like an average), but *could* be reflected via exemplars. If you remember both a 7-inch pizza and one that was 30 inches across, this tells you in an instant that a pizza can vary in its size (at least) from 7 to 30 inches. For that matter, if you reflect on the full set of pizzas you have seen, you can make a reasonable assessment of how variable the set has been.

In short, a set of exemplars preserves information about variability; a prototype does not. Since people do seem sensitive to variability information, this seems a strike against prototype theory and in favor of exemplars. (For further discussion of people's sensitivity to variability, see Fried & Holyoak, 1984; Nisbett, Krantz, Jepson & Kunda, 1983.)

## EXEMPLARS PRESERVE INFORMATION ABOUT CORRELATED FEATURES

Here is a different type of information that would be preserved in a set of exemplars but lost in a prototype: Consider two hypothetical softball teams. Both the Blue Team and the Red Team include some members who are tall, and some who are short, some who are thin and some who are fat (see Table 9.2.) In fact, the average height of a Blue Team member is the same as the average for the Red Team, and likewise for average weight. It turns out, though, that all of the Red Team members who are tall are also fat. All on this team who are short are also thin. In sum, there is a correlation between these two traits. No such correlation exists for the Blue Team.

Let us now imagine that a new team player, Alice, appears in the field, and she happens to be 6 feet, 2 inches tall, and is also quite slender. Is Alice a Blue Team member or a Red Team member? If we compare her to the prototype for each team, we have no basis for judgment since, you will recall, the averages for the two teams (and so the prototypes) were identical. We will do better, though, if we com-

pare Alice to specific team members. Alice resembles none of the Red Team players. Members of that team who happened to be 6 foot 2 were also quite fat; members of that team who were slender were also short. But Alice does resemble some of the Blue Team players. For Blue, there was no correlation between height and weight, and in fact, there happens to be a player (George) who is tall and slender (just like Alice). Hence, resemblance to exemplars provides a basis for categorization; resemblance to the prototype does not.

Are people sensitive to these patterns and, in particular, to correlations among features? In one study, participants learned about a fictitious disease, "burlosis," by examining a series of case studies (Medin, Altom, Edelson & Freko, 1982; also see Wattenmaker, 1991). In these case studies, there was a pattern of correlation among the symptoms: If a patient had discolored gums, he or she was certain to have nosebleeds,

## *Using Correlated Features in Categorization*

TABLE 9.2

| Blue team | | | Red team | | |
|---|---|---|---|---|---|
| **Name** | **Height** | **Weight** | **Name** | **Height** | **Weight** |
| George | 6'3" | 120 | Fred | 6'4" | 250 lb. |
| Tina | 4'1" | 240 | Sam | 4'1" | 110 lb. |
| Lee | 6'4" | 250 | Susan | 6'3" | 240 lb. |
| Alyson | 4'2" | 110 | Jane | 4'3" | 90 lb. |
| Tom | 4'3" | 160 | Chris | 6'2" | 240 lb. |
| Mary | 6'2" | 170 | Jeff | 4'2" | 120 lb. |
| **Average** | **5'2½"** | **175 lb.** | **Average** | **5'2½"** | **175 lb.** |

A new player, Alice, has arrived on the field. Alice is 6'2" tall, and quite slender. Is she more likely to be a Red Team member or a Blue Team member? Note that the two teams are, *on average*, the same height and the same weight. Therefore, if we try to categorize Alice by comparing her to these averages, then we have no basis for categorization. However, Alice does resemble some of the *individuals* on the Blue Team (e.g., George, who happens, like Alice, to be tall and thin). She resembles none of the individuals on the Red Team. (No Red Team members are both tall and thin.) Therefore, if we categorize by comparing Alice to the individuals, she is more likely to be on the Blue Team than on the Red.

and vice versa (see Table 9.3). Other symptoms, though, were uncorrelated: A patient with burlosis might have swollen eyelids and also nosebleeds, or one of these symptoms without the other, or neither.

Participants were subsequently asked to diagnose several test cases, some of which had symptoms in line with this correlated pattern, and some of which did not. For example, we might present the participants with two patients—Jack, who has swollen eyelids, discolored gums, and nosebleeds, and Jill, who has nosebleeds, swollen eyelids, and splotches on her ears, but normal gums. Which of these is more likely to have burlosis? Jack's symptoms are consistent with the correlation in the training cases, but Jill's are not. Therefore, even though these patients have the same number of burlosis symptoms, Jack is more likely to have the disease.

Participants in this study were clearly influenced by the correlation pattern. That is, they tended to choose the case that preserved the correlation among symptoms over the case that broke the correlation. This would be peculiar if they were basing their diagnosis on a burlosis prototype, since, as we have seen, the prototype will not preserve information about this correlation. The result is sensible, though, if participants are basing their diagnosis on exemplars: Jack resembles several individuals known to have burlosis, since his symptoms are in the same configuration as theirs. This is not true for Jill—none of the studied patients had her configuration of symptoms. Jack therefore resembles the exemplars more than Jill does. Thus, once again, the results favor the exemplar view. (For more or correlated features see Wattenmaker et al., 1995.)

## THE PLIABILITY OF MENTAL CATEGORIES

Here's a different line of evidence favoring the exemplar perspective: One might think that the concept of giraffe that I have today is the same as the concept I had yesterday (assuming that I haven't learned any new facts about giraffes). Likewise, the concept that I use in identifying giraffes is presumably the same concept I use when talking about giraffes or drawing inferences about them. There is every reason to believe, however, that our concepts are more pliable, more flexible, than these cases suggest. With just a few words of instruction, for example, people can be led to change their views about which cases are in a category and which are not, and also which cases are *typical* for a category and which are not. These facts are easily accommodated by the exemplar view but not by prototype theory.

To understand the relevant data, let's recall that *typicality* is heavily influenced by experience: For example, what counts as a "typical animal" will depend on the animals you have seen, and this will be different for a pet-store owner than it is for a zookeeper. Likewise, your idea of a "typical gift" will depend on the gifts you have given and received, and this will be different for, say, a college student than it would be for a professor.

What is striking, though, is that each of us can adopt the other's perspective, and our judgments of typicality can change accordingly. To demonstrate this, we repeat the standard typicality demonstrations (e.g., the sentence verification tasks mentioned earlier, or the explicit judgments of typicality), but this time we instruct participants to respond on these tasks from a particular point of view. When this is done, participants easily shift perspective and give rather different answers as their vantage point changes. For instance, participants instructed to take an "American point of view" rate robin and eagle as highly typical birds; the same participants taking a "Chinese point of view" rate robin and eagle much lower and rate swan and peacock as being more typical (Barsalou, 1988; Barsalou & Sewell, 1985).

How should we think about this result? One option is that people simply have many different prototypes—a prototype for "American bird" and one for "Chinese bird," a prototype for "student gift" and one for "faculty gift." According to this view, the procedure just described is simply urging the participants to move from one prototype to another as they do the various tasks.

However, some further evidence speaks against this proposal. So far, almost all of the categories we have considered involve the meanings of single

## Training and Test Cases for Diagnosis of "Burlosis"

**TABLE** 9.3

| | Symptoms | | | |
| --- | --- | --- | --- | --- |
| | Swollen eyelids (A) | Splotches on ears (B) | Discolored gums (C) | Nosebleed (D) |
| *Training cases*: All of these cases have burlosis. | | | | |
| R.C. | Yes | Yes | Yes | Yes |
| R.M. | Yes | Yes | Yes | Yes |
| J.J. | — | Yes | — | — |
| L.F. | Yes | Yes | Yes | Yes |
| A.M. | Yes | — | Yes | Yes |
| J.S. | Yes | Yes | — | — |
| S.T. | — | Yes | Yes | Yes |
| S.E. | Yes | — | — | — |
| E.M. | — | — | Yes | Yes |
| *Test cases*: Within each pair, which case is *more* likely to have burlosis? | | | | |
| Pair 1: A (Jack) | Yes | — | Yes | Yes |
| B (Jill) | Yes | Yes | — | Yes |
| Pair 2: X | — | — | — | Yes |
| Y | — | Yes | — | — |

*Note*: Participants learned about the disease "burlosis" by examining the nine case studies. Each of the symptoms occurs in 6 of 9 training cases; therefore, these symptoms are all indications of burlosis. The prototypical burlosis sufferer, therefore, would probably have all of these symptoms. In addition, discolored gums and nosebleeds are correlated symptoms: If a patient has one of these symptoms, he or she has both. In the test cases, which patient in each of the pairs is more likely to have burlosis? The number of symptoms is the same for both members of each pair; however, one patient in each pair has the symptoms in the correlated pattern and the other does not. Participants typically choose the patients with correlated symptoms, evidence of an exemplar approach.

[After Medin, Altom, Edelson & Freko, 1982.]

words (e.g., "bird" or "gift"). But Barsalou (1988) notes that there are also (in his terms) *goal-derived* categories and completely *ad hoc* categories. In the first of these, we might include "things to eat on a diet" or "things to carry out of your house in case of a fire"; in the latter group we might include "things that could fall on your head" or "things you might see while in Paris." Interestingly, these categories also turn out to have a graded membership: People identify some category members as being more typical than others; they more quickly recognize the typical ones in a sentence-verification task. If we interpret *graded membership* as indicating *reliance on a prototype*, then it seems that participants must have a prototype for these categories—a prototypical thing to see in Paris, a prototypical thing that could fall on your head, and so on.

Of course, we can proliferate categories like these endlessly: There is, for example, the category of "gifts to give one's former high-school friend who has just had her second baby," the category of "things you could do to entertain a four-year-old with the flu," and so on. We surely don't want to argue that people have a ready-made prototype for each of these; that would be tantamount to assuming an infinite stockpile of prototypes. If categories like these do have prototypes, then people must be making up the prototypes on the spot.

At the very least, all of this suggests that conceptual knowledge must include *more* than prototypes. People must also have some knowledge that allows them to "adjust" their prototypes and to create new prototypes whenever they are needed. We can therefore conclude that prototype theory is, at best, *incomplete* as an account of conceptual knowledge; "knowing a concept" must involve more than "having a prototype."

But we can also make a stronger argument. We have just suggested that people can create these ad hoc prototypes on the spot, whenever they need to perform this or that experimental task. So what stops us from arguing the same for *other* prototypes—for example, the "bird" prototype, or "dog" or "fruit"? Perhaps these, too, are created on the spot, as needed. That would certainly fit with the fact that people are easily able to "adjust" these prototypes to fit a new context or a new perspective. If this is right, however, then prototypes might not characterize our conceptual knowledge at all. Instead, prototypes might be a form of representation that can be *created from* our conceptual knowledge.

Things look much simpler, though, if we adopt an exemplar-based view. In this view, category judg-

ments depend on the specific exemplars that come to mind, and we have already noted that different exemplars may come to mind on different occasions. This is because the search for remembered exemplars, like any memory search, can be influenced by various forms of cueing or priming. Thus, the set of exemplars evoked by the cue "Chinese bird" may well be different from the set evoked by the cue "bird." With different exemplars coming to mind, different judgments will be rendered. Therefore, it is certainly no surprise that typicality judgments are influenced by context.

With this view there is also no problem with ad hoc categories. In making judgments about these categories, people are relying on specific remembered cases (or, perhaps, specific *imagined* cases). Since there is no reliance here on prototypes, there is no issue of creating ad hoc prototypes on the spot. Indeed, according to the exemplar-based view, there is no difference between how people judge familiar categories and how they judge ad hoc categories: In both cases, they draw on a remembered (or imagined) instance and base their judgment on that instance. It is sensible, in this account, that participants behave similarly with familiar and unfamiliar categories.

## EXEMPLAR USE AND CONCEPT LEARNING

A variety of results, then, indicate that we do rely on exemplars in making category judgments. Exemplar storage provides an easy way of talking about our knowledge of variability within a category, as well as our sensitivity to patterns of correlation among a category's features. Exemplar storage also provides an easy way of accounting for category pliability and ad hoc categories.

In addition, consider the acquisition of *new* concepts. Consider, for example, a child's first trip to the zoo, and thus the child's first sight of a camel. Immediately after this encounter, the child has knowledge about that specific camel but no information about the camel category. Concretely, the child has no way of knowing whether the camel just seen was typical or not, and no way of knowing which of the camel's features will be shared by others of the breed, and which will not be shared. At least for the moment, then, this remembered exemplar represents the full breadth of the child's camel knowledge. After the child has seen *several* camels, though, she can take the next step—"averaging" these together, potentially creating a camel prototype.

This example implies that novice category users are especially likely to rely on exemplars. Indeed, exemplars may be all they have, all they know about. More experienced category users, however, have the option of "pooling" the various examples they have encountered in order to create a prototype. Indeed, they may have no choice about this: If someone has seen many different camels, then they may have trouble in recalling which camel was which. In other words, the various camels they've encountered may "blur together" in memory, creating a single memory that essentially averages across the various exemplars, just as a prototype would. (See Chapter 7 for more on how "blurring" might take place.)

This implies that prototype use would be unlikely for novices (people who are just learning about a category) but more likely for experts. To test this claim, a number of studies have examined the course of category learning. These studies use novel (usually fictional) categories, to ensure that the participants are unfamiliar with the category at the experiment's start. The participants are then shown pictures of category members, so that they can begin learning about them: "This animal is called a 'lepton.' Here's a different lepton. This is not a lepton, and this isn't either." As this process unfolds, the participants are periodically tested: They are given cases without labels and asked, "Do you think this is a lepton or not?"

By choosing our cases with care, we can use these tests to find out what sort of representation the participants have in mind for the category of leptons. To make this concrete, let's suppose that most leptons have long necks—a long neck, therefore, is typical for the category. But not all leptons have long necks, and one or two of the leptons you've seen during training had relatively short necks. Now suppose that one of the test pictures shows a short-necked creature; is it a lepton? If you compare this picture to

the "lepton prototype," you'll say "no," since the test case does not resemble the average (long-necked) lepton. But if you compare this picture to particular leptons you've seen (that is, compare it to exemplars), then you may say "yes," because you've seen other leptons just like this one. In this way, your response will tell us whether you were relying on a prototype or on exemplars.

The pattern will reverse with a different type of test picture. This picture might show you the "ideal" lepton—one that has *all* of the features that are common in the species. We can arrange things in the experiment, though, so that this picture resembles *none* of the specific leptons you've seen so far. To continue the example, we have already said that having a long neck is common for this species, as is having a bushy tail and floppy ears. And, as part of your training, you've seen many long-necked leptons, and many bushy-tailed leptons, and many floppy-eared leptons. But you've never seen a lepton before that had all of these features together, and so the test case now before your eyes is the first time you've seen the category's ideal—the "perfect" lepton. If you compare *this* case to the lepton prototype, you'll surely say, "yes, it's a lepton." But if you compare the case to particular leptons you've seen (exemplars), then you may decide it's *not* a lepton. Again, your response will tell us what sort of representation was guiding your judgment.

Investigators have used this logic to ask what sort of representations participants have in mind at different stages of category learning. The results are consistent with a claim we have already made: Early in category learning, participants say "yes" to test pictures that resemble specific leptons they've already seen, even if the test pictures show creatures that aren't typical for the category. They're likely to say "no" to test pictures that *don't* resemble the creatures they've already seen, even if the pictures do show the category ideal. This strongly suggests a reliance on exemplars. As the training proceeds, however, this pattern reverses. Now it doesn't matter if the test picture resembles particular leptons you've already seen. You'll say "yes" to the picture if it resembles the category average, and "no" otherwise.

The obvious suggestion, then, is that a reliance on a prototype is gradually emerging as your experience with the category grows. (For discussion and relevant data, see Homa, Sterling & Trepel, 1981; Homa, Dunbar & Nohre, 1991.)

Notice, then, that we are on the verge of a great compromise: Which is the better theory, one based on prototypes or one based on exemplars? The answer may be that *both* theories capture an element of the truth, with people shifting from exemplar-based to prototype-based knowledge as they gather more and more familiarity with a concept or category.

We must, however, attach some words of caution to this claim. First, some evidence suggests that the pattern of category learning may depend on the particular category. Many categories do show the trajectory we have just described, with exemplars early and a prototype later. Other categories, however, may show a different pattern. If the category is quite large and its members highly diverse, people may be discouraged from relying on exemplars, since a useful set of exemplars would be difficult to remember. In this case, people may rely on a (rough) prototype early on, and turn to exemplars only when they have become quite familiar with the category (Smith & Minda, 1998). Even here, though, our "great compromise" remains in place, since in this case, too, participants would be relying on *both* prototypes *and* exemplars, so that our theory of concepts will still need to include both forms of representation.

Second, and consistent with the first point, even if we have a clear prototype for a category, this does not mean we cease relying on exemplars. Instead, the evidence suggests that, with familiar categories, we use *both* sorts of information. For example, Brooks, Norman, and Allen (1991; also Brooks, 1990) have studied how expert dermatologists achieve their diagnoses. These physicians have viewed an enormous number of patients, and so they certainly have a basis for deriving a prototype for each diagnostic category. In addition, dermatologists are explicitly trained in the use of rules and definitions in achieving their diagnosis. Therefore, this seems a group highly likely to rely on abstract information in their categorization and unlikely to rely on exemplars. Nonetheless, the dermatologists show clear evidence of relying on exemplars: A correct diagnosis is more likely if the physicians have recently seen a specific case that resembles the one currently under scrutiny. Apparently, this prior case is still "fresh" in the doctors' memories and so comes readily to mind. Therefore, this prior case serves as a likely basis for analogy (and so a likely basis for *diagnosis*) for the new case now in view. Even the experts, in other words, rely on exemplars.

## The Difficulties with Categorizing via Resemblance

Where are we so far? It seems clear that typicality plays a large role in our thinking about concepts and in our use of concepts. In many cases, this is probably due to our reliance on a prototype abstracted from our experiences with the category's members. In other cases, typicality arises from our use of specific exemplars, drawn from memory. Exemplar use is particularly likely, we have suggested, early in our learning about a category. Once we grow knowledgeable about a category, though, we have both exemplars and a prototype available to us, and we probably use both in an opportunistic fashion. In other words, if an object before your eyes happens to remind you of a specific prior experience, you can reason via an exemplar. If, instead, the object before you calls up some prototype knowledge, you will use that knowledge in your reasoning. In short, you will rely on whichever sort of information comes to mind more readily. (For a discussion of the principles governing how these different species of conceptual knowledge are triggered, see Whittlesea, Brooks & Westcott, 1994. For evidence that exemplar and prototype use are supported by different *neural systems*, see Marsolek, 1999.) In either case, though, the process will be substantially the same, with a judgment based simply on the *resemblance* between this conceptual information, supplied by memory, and the novel case currently before you.

All of this seems straightforward enough. However, there are some observations and some results

| Participants' Typicality Ratings For Well-Defined Categories | | | | TABLE 9.4 |
|---|---|---|---|---|
| **Even number** | | **Odd number** | | |
| **Stimulus** | **Typicality rating** | **Stimulus** | **Typicality rating** | |
| 4 | 5.9 | 3 | 5.4 | |
| 8 | 5.5 | 7 | 5.1 | |
| 10 | 5.3 | 23 | 4.6 | |
| 18 | 4.4 | 57 | 4.4 | |
| 34 | 3.6 | 501 | 3.5 | |
| 106 | 3.1 | 447 | 3.3 | |

Notes: Participants rated each item for how "good an example" it was for its category. Ratings were on a 0 to 7 scale, with 7 meaning the item is a "very good example." Participants rated some even numbers as being "better examples" of even numbers than others, although, mathematically, this is absurd: Either a number is even (divisible by 2 without a remainder) or it is not.

[After Armstrong, Gleitman, & Gleitman, 1983.]

that do not fit easily into this picture. The time has come to broaden our conception of concepts.

## ODD NUMBER, EVEN NUMBER

In the views we have been developing, judgments of typicality and judgments of category membership both derive from resemblance to an exemplar or to a prototype. If the resemblance is great, then a test case will be judged to be typical, and it will also be judged to be a category member. If the resemblance is small, then the test case will be judged atypical and probably not a category member. Thus, typicality and category membership should go hand in hand.

As we have seen, much evidence fits with this claim. It turns out, however, that we can also find situations in which there is *no relation* between typicality and category membership, and this is surely inconsistent with our claims so far. For example, Rips and Collins (1993) have shown that the factors that influence typicality judgments are often different from the factors that influence judgments of category membership. As a striking example of this pattern, consider a study by Armstrong, Gleitman and Gleitman (1983). These researchers asked their research participants to do several of the concept tasks we have been discussing—for example, sentence verification, or explicit judgments about whether individuals were typical or not for their category. The twist, though, is that Armstrong et al. used categories for which there clearly is a definition, for example, the category "odd number." As a participant, therefore, you might be told, "We all know that some numbers are odder than others. What I want you to do is to rate each of the numbers on this list for how good an example it is for the category 'odd'." Participants felt that this was a rather silly task but nevertheless, they were able to render these judgments and, interestingly, were just as consistent with each other using these stimuli as they were with categories like "dog" or "bird" or "fruit" (see Table 9.4).

The obvious response to this experiment is that participants knew the definition of odd number but were somehow "playing along" in response to the experimenters' peculiar request. Even with this point acknowledged, however, the fact still remains that participants' judgments about typicality were, in this case, "disconnected" from their judgments about category membership: They knew that all the test numbers were in the category of "odd number," but they still judged some to be more "typical" than others. Apparently, then, there is no necessary linkage between typicality and membership.

In addition, these results suggest limits on what we should conclude when we observe a typicality effect. In particular, the *presence* of a graded-membership pattern cannot imply the *absence* of other conceptual knowledge. In the Armstrong et al. study, we have both—graded membership *and* a definition. This is an important fact to remember when considering the many other results revealing the graded-membership pattern. These results *do* indicate that typicality is prominent in people's judgments about categories, but we shouldn't conclude from this that typicality is *all* that people know about the category.

At the same time, these results also convey a different message: The participants in this experiment were able to judge the typicality of odd numbers with ease and consistency, effortlessly overruling what they really knew about oddness. This is important, since it suggests that thinking in terms of typicality is quite "natural" for people, even when this thinking is not practiced and (in this case) not even legitimate. This "naturalness" needs to be explained, and we will return to this point later in the chapter.

## LEMONS AND COUNTERFEITS

Many results echo the messages just described: On the one side, people find it easy and "natural" to judge typicality. At the same time, though, they often find some basis for judging category membership that is independent of typicality—so that a test case can be a category member without being typical or can be typical without being a category member. This is obviously troublesome for any theory proposing that both these judgments derive from the same source.

For example, it is true that robins strike us as closer to the typical bird than penguins do. Nonetheless, most of us are quite certain that both robins and penguins are birds. Likewise, Moby Dick was definitely not a typical whale, but he certainly was a whale; Abraham Lincoln was not a typical American, but he was an American. These informal observations are easily confirmed in the laboratory. For example, participants judge whales to be more typical of the concept of "fish" than sea lampreys are, but these same participants respond (correctly) that sea lampreys *are* fish and whales are *not* (McCloskey & Glucksberg, 1978).

It seems, therefore, that category judgments are often *not* based on typicality. What *are* they based on? As a way of approaching the problem, let's think through some examples. Consider a lemon. Paint the lemon with red and white stripes. Is it still a lemon? Most people believe that it is. Now inject the lemon with sugar water, so that it has a sweet taste. Then run over the lemon with a truck, so that it is flat as a pancake. What have we got at this point? Do we have a striped, artificially sweet, flattened lemon? Or do we have a non-lemon? Most people still accept this poor, abused fruit as a lemon, but consider what this entails: We have taken steps to make this object more and more distant from the prototype and also very different from any specific lemon you have ever encountered (and thus very different from any remembered exemplars). But this seems not to shake our faith that the object remains a lemon. To be sure, we have a not-easily-recognized lemon, an exceptional lemon, but it is still a lemon. Apparently, one can be a lemon with virtually *no resemblance* to other lemons. (For discussion of a similar case, with category members transformed by exposure to toxic waste, see Rips, 1989a.)

Here is the opposite case. Consider a really perfect counterfeit $20 bill. This bill will be enormously similar to the prototype for a real $20 bill and also highly similar to any remembered exemplar of a $20 bill. Yet we still consider it to be counterfeit, not real. Apparently, resemblance to other cases is not enough to qualify this bill for membership in the category of real money. In fact, think about the *category* "perfect counterfeit." One can certainly imagine a prototype for this category, and of course, the prototype would have to be very similar to the prototype for the category of real money. But despite this resemblance, you have no trouble keeping the categories distinct from each other: You know many things that are true for one category but not for the other, and you clearly understand, despite the near-identical prototypes, that counterfeit money is not the same thing as real money. You might be *perceptually* confused between a real bill and a counterfeit (because they do look alike), but you are not confused about the concepts, and you certainly know when you are thinking about one and when you are thinking about the other.

These examples underscore the distinction between typicality and category membership. In the case of the lemon, we see category membership even though the test case bears no resemblance to the prototype and, indeed, no resemblance to any of the other members of the lemon category. Conversely, one can have close resemblance to category members and high typicality without category membership (the counterfeit bill). If we take these cases at face value, then category membership cannot rest on typicality.

But can we take these cases at face value? Perhaps these cases are too playful. Perhaps people think about mutilated lemons in some artificial way, differently from how they think about more conventional concepts. Similarly, perhaps the Armstrong, Gleitman and Gleitman participants realized they were doing something bizarre in judging the odd numbers and treated the task as a game, somehow different from their customary way of thinking about concepts. So again one might ask whether the data pattern would be different with more typical concepts, in more typical settings.

Relevant evidence for this point comes from work by Keil (1986). Keil was particularly interested in how children come to have concepts, and what children's concepts do or do not include. For our purposes, this is ideal, since it allows us to ask about concept holders who are relatively untutored and relatively naive. These preschool children have not yet learned technical definitions for their concepts, nor have they been trained to reflect on, or manipulate, their mental categories. Thus, we can use the data from children as a way of asking about concepts "uncontaminated" by education or training.

In one of Keil's studies, preschool children were asked what it is that makes something a "coffeepot" or a "raccoon," and so on. In one aspect of the procedure, the children were asked whether it would be possible to turn a toaster into a coffeepot. Children often acknowledged that this would be possible. One would have to widen the holes in the top of the toaster and fix things so that the water would not leak out of the bottom. One would need to design a place to put the coffee grounds, and so on. But the children saw no obstacles to these various manipulations, and they were quite certain that, with these adjustments in place, one would have created a bona fide coffeepot.

Things were quite different, though, when the children were asked a parallel question, namely, whether one could, with suitable adjustments, turn a skunk into a raccoon. The children understood that we could dye the skunk's fur, teach it to climb trees, and that we could teach it to behave in a raccoon-like fashion. Even with these provisions, though, the children steadfastly denied that we would have created a raccoon. A skunk who looks, sounds, and acts just like a raccoon might be a very peculiar skunk, but it is a skunk nonetheless. (For related data, see Gelman & Wellman, 1991; Keil, Smith, Simons, & Levin, 1998. Walker, 1993, offers an interesting extension of Keil's findings, including data on how people from other cultures make these judgments.)

What lies behind all these judgments? If people are asked why the abused lemon still counts as a lemon, they are likely to mention the fact that it grew on a lemon tree, is genetically a lemon, and so on. It is these "deep" features that matter and not the lemon's current properties. Likewise, counterfeit money is defined as such not because of its current attributes, but because of its history—real money was printed by the government, in special circumstances; counterfeit money was not. And so, too, for raccoons: In the child's view, being a raccoon is not merely a function of having the relevant features; there is something deeper to raccoonhood than that. What is this "something deeper"? In the eyes of the child, the key to being a raccoon involves (among other things) having a raccoon mommy and a raccoon daddy. Thus, a raccoon, just like lemons and counterfeit money, is defined in ways that refer to deep properties and not to mere appearances.

It appears, then, that some properties are essential for being a lemon or a raccoon, and if an object has these essential properties, it doesn't matter what the object looks like. Likewise, *without* these essential properties, an item is *not* in the category, no matter what its appearance. (This is the case of the counterfeit bill.) In addition, notice that these claims about an object's "essential properties" depend on a web of other beliefs—beliefs about cause and effect and about how things come to be as they are. For example, concern about a raccoon's parentage comes into play in your thinking about raccoons *only because* you have certain beliefs about how biological species are created, and about the role of inheritance in biological species. You do not worry about parentage when you are contemplating other categories, because you do not have the belief that inheritance matters for those categories. (In thinking through whether someone is really and truly a *doctor*, you are unlikely to worry about whether she has a doctor mommy and a doctor daddy. Perhaps she does, and perhaps she doesn't, but this is simply irrelevant for whether the person is or is not a doctor.)

Likewise, in judging the category of counterfeit bills, you consider "circumstances of printing" only because of your other beliefs—beliefs in this case about ownership, authenticity, and monetary systems. You wouldn't consider "circumstances of printing" if asked whether a copy of the Lord's Prayer is "counterfeit" or not (or authentic, or legitimate). Your beliefs tell you that the Lord's Prayer is the Lord's Prayer no matter where (or by whom) it's printed. What's crucial for the prayer is whether the words are the correct words, and so again, what's "essential" for the category depends on the category *and* depends on other beliefs you have about that category.

All of this is obviously driving a wedge between "typicality" and "category membership." Typicality matters a lot in many of our judgments; we saw that over and over in the earlier part of this chapter. But, even so, typicality is not crucial for category membership, nor is resemblance to other category members. What seems to matter instead is having the "essential" properties for that category: With those properties, a case can be in the category even if it's highly atypical; without those properties, the case is excluded from the category.

This invites several questions: How should we think about a category's "essential properties"? What are these "other beliefs" that seem to guide your thinking about what's essential for a particular category, and what's superfluous? And how does typicality (which, without question, *does* have a powerful influence in many settings) fit into this enlarged picture? We'll turn to these issue in a moment; first, though, we need to consider an objection that might be raised to the argument we've just presented.

## THE COMPLEXITY OF SIMILARITY

Both the prototype and exemplar views depend, at their base, on judgments of resemblance—resemblance to the prototype or to some remembered instance. And there is no doubt that resemblance does have a strong influence on category judgments; this is reflected in a great many experimental results. Yet, as we have now seen, an object can be in a category even with minimal resemblance to other category members; an object can be excluded from a category even with enormous resemblance to other category members. Therefore, we cannot base category membership on resemblance alone.

One might argue, however, that even though the abused lemon doesn't resemble the lemon prototype *perceptually*, it does resemble the lemon prototype in *the ways that matter.* For example, the abused lemon has a DNA pattern that resembles the DNA pattern of the prototype. Likewise, the abused lemon has seeds inside it that, if planted, would grow into lemon trees; this, too, is a property of the prototype. Therefore, if we could focus on these "essential" properties and ignore the "superficial" attributes, then we could preserve the claim that category membership depends on properties shared with the prototype or shared with exemplars. In this way, we could preserve the claim that category membership depends on resemblance.

The problem, though, lies in explaining what we mean by "resembling the prototype in the ways that matter." How do we decide which properties of the prototype are really important and which properties we can ignore as irrelevant? This seems once again to demand that our judgments are guided by some further knowledge and further beliefs—beliefs about what it is that really matters for that category (parentage for the category of "raccoon," training and certification [and not parentage] for the category of "doctor," and so on). In other words, we can use resemblance to the prototype, or resemblance to the exemplars, only if we guide our resemblance judgments with other knowledge.

We have made this argument by appealing to some peculiar cases—mutilated lemons and transformed skunks. Even with more conventional cases, though, it turns out that categorization via resemblance is a problematic idea because, when closely examined, *resemblance* is a problematic idea. For example, research participants judge *snake* and *raccoon* to be rather dissimilar from each other. However, if both are put in the context of "pet," then their perceived similarity increases appreciably (e.g., Barsalou, 1982). Both are perceived as atypical but possible pets and, in the process, their similarity to each other goes up. Likewise for *Italy* and *Switzerland*: These countries are judged to be rather different from each other, but their similarity goes up if we make it a three-way comparison, among, let's say, *Italy*, *Switzerland*, and *Brazil*. This third country calls attention to the attribute shared by the first two, "in Europe." This attribute initially contributed little to the perceived similarity between Italy and Switzerland, but given the appropriate context, it can play a large role (Tversky, 1977).

Apparently, then, we can't rely on similarity as a stable and solid base on which to build category judgments. Instead, similarity seems quite flexible, and certainly context-dependent. In the same vein, consider *plums* and *lawn mowers*. How similar are these to each other? Actually, these two have a great deal in common: Both weigh less than a ton, both are found on earth, both cannot hear well, both have an odor, both are used by people, both can be dropped, both cost less than a thousand dollars, and so on. (For discussion, see Goldstone, 1996; Goodman, 1972; Medin & Ortony, 1989; Medin, Goldstone & Gentner, 1993.) Of course, we ignore most of these shared features in judging these two entities, and so, as a result, we regard plums and lawn mowers as rather different from each other. But that brings us back to a familiar question: How do we decide which features to ignore when assessing similarity, and which features to consider? How do we decide which features are essential and which superficial, which attributes are important and which trivial?

We have already suggested an answer to these questions: A decision about which features are trivial and which are crucial depends, at least in part, on your *beliefs* about the concept in question. We know, for example, that what matters for being a lawn mower is suitability for getting a particular job done. Costing less than a thousand dollars is irrelevant to this function. (Imagine a lawn mower covered with diamonds; it would still be a lawn mower, wouldn't it?) Therefore, cost is an unimportant feature for lawn mowers.

Cost is a critical attribute, however, for other categories (consider the category "luxury item"). Similarly, we were unimpressed by the fact that plums and lawn mowers both weigh less than a ton: Weight is not critical for either of these categories. But weight is crucial in other settings (imagine a paperweight made out of gaseous helium). Apparently, then, the importance of an attribute—cost, or weight, or whatever—varies from category to category, and varies, in particular, according to your beliefs about what matters for that category.

To tie this back to issues of categorization, imagine that a furry creature stands before you, and you reason, "This creature reminds me of the animal I saw in the zoo yesterday. The sign at the zoo indicated that the animal was a gnu, so this must be one, too." This sounds like a simple case of categorization via exemplars. But of course, the creature before your eyes is not a "perfect match" for the gnu in the zoo, and so you might reason this way, "The gnu in the zoo was a different color, and slightly smaller. But I bet that does not matter. Despite the new hue, this is a gnu, too."

In this case, you have decided that color isn't a critical feature, and you categorize despite the contrast on this dimension. Things will go differently, though, in this case: "This stone in my hand reminds me of the ruby I saw yesterday. Therefore, I bet this is a ruby, too. Of course, the ruby I saw yesterday was red, and this stone is green, but . . ." You surely would *not* draw this analogy because, in this case, you know that it is wrong to ignore hue. Rubies are red. If a stone isn't red, it isn't a ruby. Color might not matter for gnus, but it does matter here, and our category judgments respect this fact.

Moreover, let's be clear that what's at stake here is a rather broad issue: So far, we have been focusing on the *categorization* of an object—the decision that an animal is, in fact, a gnu, or that a stone is indeed a ruby. But this step of categorizing is only a small part of how we use our conceptual knowledge. We also use our conceptual knowledge whenever we are *reasoning* about concepts and whenever we are *thinking about* the objects and events in the world around us (cf. Solomon et al., 1999). These other settings, as it turns out, involve complexities that are virtually identical to the ones we have been discussing. For example, if we encounter a single gnu, and discover it likes to eat oats, we are willing to extrapolate this property to other gnus. If we discover, in addition, that this particular gnu has a red-haired keeper, we are likely *not* to extrapolate this property. Here, too, we seem guided by other knowledge, other beliefs—in this case, beliefs about which features are directly derived from gnu-hood, and which features are likely to be accidental. And

this is knowledge, once again, not captured within prototypes or exemplars.

## Concept as "Implicit Theories"

Let's pause to take stock. Early in the chapter, we saw many results indicating that our use of concepts is often influenced by *typicality*. Typicality plays a role when we are categorizing objects we have just met; it also guides us when we are reasoning about our concepts. Our theory of concepts, therefore, needs to explain how these typicality effects emerge, and the best way to do this, we suggested, is by including prototypes or exemplars in our theory. Indeed, we saw indications (for example, in our discussion of category learning) that our theory must include *both* prototypes *and* exemplars.

At the same time, however, our theory of concepts also needs *more than* prototypes and exemplars. This is evident, for example, in the fact that some category judgments (counterfeit money, the mutilated lemon) are entirely independent of typicality. And even when typicality *does* play a role, this role seems to be shaped and guided by other knowledge, knowledge that tells us which attributes to pay attention to in judging resemblance to the prototype, and which to regard as trivial.

In fact, the influence of this other knowledge, reaching beyond prototypes or exemplars is ubiquitous. Is the object in front of you a desk? You decide that it is, despite its peculiar color, *because you believe* that color is not an important attribute for desks. If the first wolf you ever saw was limping, would you conclude that all wolves limp? Probably not, *because you believe* that most species have regular gaits, and that limps are usually the result of an injury. And so on.

All of this seems to be driving us toward a two-part theory of concepts: On the one side, there are prototypes and exemplars, often playing their role by means of a judgment of resemblance between the remembered case (the prototype or the exemplar) and the case you are now considering. On the other side, there are other beliefs, and other knowledge, guiding and supplementing your use of prototypes.

But how should we characterize these other beliefs? And within this broader context, what role is played by prototypes and exemplars?

## CATEGORIZATION HEURISTICS

One plausible hypothesis is that people rely on prototypes and exemplars whenever they need to make category decisions that are fast and efficient. Said differently, categorization via resemblance may count as a **heuristic**—a strategy that is reasonably efficient and works most of the time. Heuristics take their value from the fact that, if you want a strategy that always works and never leads you astray, you may need a strategy that is relatively laborious and slow. In order to be reasonably efficient, therefore, you may need a strategy that does, on occasion, permit some errors. (This trade-off between efficiency and accuracy should look familiar, since it was a prominent feature in Chapters 3 and 5. Indeed, this trade-off is an important feature of our mental lives, and will come up again in several other contexts.)

Why is categorization via resemblance efficient? In most cases, this resemblance (and typicality in general) is judged on the basis of relatively superficial features rather than on the basis of more abstract knowledge about a category. This emphasis on superficial characteristics is precisely what we want for a categorization heuristic: These traits can generally be judged swiftly, allowing comparisons that are quick and easy.

Like any heuristic, however, the use of typicality will occasionally lead to error: If you rely on the bird prototype to categorize flying creatures, you may misidentify a bat. That is the price one pays for heuristic use. If the heuristic is well chosen, though, these errors will be relatively rare, and on this point, too, a reliance on typicality seems sensible. Prototypes, by their very nature, represent the most common features of a category, and so prototypes will be representative of most category members. Thus, categorization via prototypes will usually be accurate—most members of the category *do* resemble the prototype, even though some members do not. The same considerations apply to a reliance on

exemplars: As we have seen, the exemplars coming to mind will usually be examples of *typical* category members and so, more often than not, will resemble the new category members you encounter.

This view of things, therefore, preserves a central insight of both the prototype and exemplar views: As we have seen we cannot equate "goodness of example" with "membership in a category." But even so, "membership" and "exemplariness" are clearly related to each other, and this is critical for the heuristic idea. Creatures closely resembling a robin are not guaranteed to be birds, but they are highly likely to be birds, and it is this which allows us to use typicality as a fast and efficient basis for judging category membership.

## MENTAL MODELS, IMPLICIT THEORIES

The previous section gives us a picture of what role prototypes and exemplars serve, and therefore why they are so important. Over and over, though, we have argued that there is more to category knowledge than this. What is the "more"?

We have already seen a broad set of hints about this issue: Someone's understanding of a concept seems to depend on a network of interwoven beliefs, and these beliefs, in turn, draw on a number of other concepts: To understand what counterfeit is, one needs to know what money is, and probably what a government is, and what crime is. To understand what a raccoon is, one needs to understand what parents are, and with that, one needs to know some facts about life cycles, and heredity, and the like.

Perhaps, therefore, we need a different approach. We have been trying, throughout this chapter, to characterize concepts one by one, as though each concept could be characterized independently of other concepts. We talked about the prototype for *bird*, for example, without any thought about how this prototype is related to the *animal* prototype or to the *egg* prototype. Perhaps, though, we need a more holistic approach, one in which we place more emphasis on the interrelationships among concepts. This would allow us to include in our accounts the wide network of beliefs in which concepts seem to be embedded.

Consider the concept "blood pressure." It would be surprising if this concept could be characterized in isolation from a set of other terms, terms such as "circulation" or "heart" or "arteries." To understand blood pressure, one must understand these other terms, and one needs a web of beliefs about how these various terms are interrelated (Banks, Thompson, Henry & Weissmann, 1986; Carey, 1985). This set of beliefs is surely less sophisticated, and probably less accurate, than a medically correct, scientific model of blood pressure. Nonetheless, our beliefs serve the same function as a scientific model: These beliefs unify our understanding of these various terms and provide a global cause-and-effect account that corresponds to our understanding of the processes involved.

There have been several proposals for how this web of beliefs should be characterized. Neisser (1987) has proposed that these beliefs can be thought of as an implicit "theory" about the relevant subject matter, a theory that the individual holds about how the various terms are interconnected. Lakoff (1987) has offered a related notion defined as an "idealized cognitive model." Several psychologists have explored the idea of a "mental model" (Gentner & Stevens, 1983), with this model embodying our set of beliefs about the terms in question. (Also see Johnson-Laird, 1987; Keil, 1989; Komatsu, 1992; Medin & Ortony, 1989; Rips & Collins, 1993; Wisniewski & Medin, 1994. For some of the philosophical roots of these arguments, see Kripke, 1972; Putnam, 1975.)

Implicit theories seem essential for describing complex concepts such as blood pressure. It may turn out, though, that we also need implicit theories to describe seemingly simpler concepts. Our discussion so far in this chapter has clearly pointed in this direction. As a different example, consider the concept "drunk" (after Medin & Ortony, 1989). Jumping into a pool with your clothes on is surely not a defining feature of being drunk; it is probably not even a typical feature. Still, this behavior is certainly indicative of being drunk, thanks to a variety of other causal beliefs we have about how drunks behave. In effect, each of us has a "theory" about drunkenness—what being drunk will

cause you to do, what it will cause you *not* to do—and we rely on this theory in identifying someone who is drunk and in reasoning about his or her behavior.

A different example is the term "bachelor." This noun is a particularly interesting example, since the term seems to be easily defined: A bachelor is an unmarried adult male. However, it turns out that here, too, we need some sort of implicit theory, since being a bachelor can, in fact, only be understood in the context of certain expectations about marriage and marriageable age (cf. Fillmore, 1982). The examples in Figure 9.2 will help make this clear. As you read these examples, your judgments about each case are guided by a rich understanding of who is eligible to marry and who is likely to marry. Thus, understanding even a term like "bachelor" may depend on a mental model, in this case a model that encompasses your understanding of matrimonial customs in our culture. (For related examples, see Lakoff, 1987; Neisser, 1987.)

## IMPLICIT THEORIES

But what exactly is an "implicit theory"? Consider the concept "airplane." Your knowledge of this concept probably includes a prototype for "airplane" and a set of remembered airplane exemplars. But you also have a set of beliefs about airplanes, many of which can be expressed as straightforward propositions: Airplanes have wings. Airplanes can fly. Airplanes are manufactured by people (and so they're not, for example, living organisms, nor are they naturally occurring in the way that rocks or mountains are).

These propositions, however, don't exhaust your full understanding of the "airplane" concept. Consider these questions: Could an airplane be made out of glass? Could one be made out of whipped cream? You surely said "no" to the whipped cream, but the decision is less clear for glass, and you may suspect that a glass airplane (with very thick glass, to be sure) might be possible.

What is the basis for these responses? Neither exemplars nor prototypes will help us here: Both a glass airplane *and* a whipped-cream airplane would be extremely different from any exemplar you've

## What Makes Someone a Bachelor?

**FIGURE 9.2**

**Various potential bachelors**

Alfred is an unmarried adult male, but he has been living with his girlfriend for the last 23 years. Their relationship is happy and stable. Is Alfred a bachelor?

Bernard is an unmarried adult male and does not have a partner. But Bernard is a monk, living in a monastery. Is Bernard a bachelor?

Charles is a married adult male, but he has not seen his wife for many years; Charles is earnestly dating, hoping to find a new partner. Is Charles a bachelor?

Donald is a married adult male, but he lives in a culture that encourages males to take two wives. Donald is earnestly dating, hoping to find a new partner. Is Donald a bachelor?

The term "bachelor" is often considered to have a firm definition: A bachelor is an unmarried adult male. However, this noun can be understood only in the context of certain expectations about marriage and marriageable age. As you read the examples shown here, think about what it is that guides your judgments. [After Fillmore, 1982.]

ever seen, and also extremely different from your prototype. Therefore, if "distance from exemplars" or "distance from prototype" is the key, then you should give the same response to "whipped cream" and "glass." But you don't.

What about your beliefs? Your set of beliefs about airplanes is likely to contain the proposition "Airplanes are often made out of metal," and perhaps also the proposition "Airplanes used to be made out of wood." But, again, neither of these beliefs will help us here: Neither proposition mentions "glass" or "whipped cream," and so neither can directly support a response to our test questions about whether we could build airplanes from these materials.

How, then, do you answer questions about glass or whipped-cream airplanes? The key lies in the fact that you have certain beliefs about airplanes, and you also have a rough understanding of *how these beliefs fit together* and what the beliefs imply. You know that airplanes are often made out of metal, and you know the *reason for this*: In order to fly, airplane wings must have a certain shape, and so they need to be made out of something that is rigid enough to

maintain that shape. Likewise, you know that airplanes in flight are exposed to strong winds, and this, too, requires that they be made out of something that is reasonably rigid, as well as something that cannot break easily. It's this understanding of *why airplanes are as they are* that allows you to infer that planes could not be made out of whipped cream (or paper or fish nets), but could perhaps be made out of glass (if the glass were thick enough to be rigid and also suitably resistant to breakage).

Here's another way to make (roughly) the same points: It is interesting that people will reliably say "no" if asked whether planes could be made of whipped cream, and it is also interesting that people can *explain* this response. Apparently, each of us has some understanding of how an airplane works, and we can use this understanding to guide our thinking about airplanes. This understanding probably is incomplete, and may not be completely accurate, but it summarizes our beliefs about *why* certain aspects of airplanes' structure and function are as they are, and it is this understanding that we are calling an "implicit theory" about airplanes.

We have traced through this example for airplanes, and indeed, for a silly question about airplanes made of whipped cream. But it is precisely the same kind of understanding that guides our thinking about bachelors and raccoons and counterfeits. To put things briefly, this understanding reflects our views about why the concept is as it is ("Airplanes are often made out of metal *because* . . ."). As we have seen, this allows us to use our conceptual knowledge in productive ways (e.g., it allows us to consider the novel idea of an airplane made out of glass), but the understanding also helps us in more mundane settings. For example, it's this same understanding that helps us to see what is important for the concept (it's essential that planes have wings, because wings are tied to the function of flying) and what is less important (it doesn't matter what color the airplane is, because this has nothing to do with flying). This in turn is what allows us to use other aspects of our conceptual knowledge—for example, the prototype and the exemplars—because it's this understanding that tells us what to pay attention to and what to ignore when comparing any particular case to these mental representations.

Where, then, does all of this leave us? One might think that there's nothing glorious or complicated about knowing what a dog is, or an airplane, or a lemon. Our use of these concepts is effortless and ubiquitous, and so is our use of the thousands of other concepts in our repertoire. As we have seen, however, human conceptual knowledge is impressively complex. At the very least, this knowledge contains several parts—a prototype for each concept, a set of remembered exemplars, a set of beliefs about the concept, and, as we have now discussed, an understanding of how these beliefs fit together. How we use these various elements probably depends on the context and on how exactly the concept is being used, and probably also on which concept is being contemplated. Even with these qualifications, however, the fact remains that even our simplest concepts require a multifaceted representation in our minds, and at least part of this representation (the "implicit theory") seems reasonably sophisticated. It is all this richness, presumably, that makes human conceptual knowledge extremely powerful and flexible, and also so easy to use.

## Chapter Summary

1. People cannot provide definitions for most of the concepts they use; this suggests that knowing a concept, and being able to use it competently, does not require knowing a definition. However, when trying to define a term, people mention properties that are indeed closely associated with the concept. One proposal, therefore, is that our knowledge specifies what is typical for each concept, rather than naming properties that are *necessary and sufficient* for the concept. Concepts based on *typicality* will have a *family resemblance structure*, with different category members sharing features, but with no features shared by the entire group.

2. Concepts may be represented in the mind via *prototypes*, with each prototype representing what is most typical for that category. This implies that categories will have *fuzzy boundaries* and *graded membership*, and many results are consistent with this prediction. The results *converge* in identifying some category members as "better" members of the category. This is reflected in *sentence verification tasks, production tasks, explicit judgments of typicality*, and so on.

3. In addition, *basic-level categories* seem to be the categories we learn earliest and use most often. Basic-level categories (like "chair") are more homogeneous than their superordinate categories ("furniture") and much broader than their subordinate categories ("arm chair"), and are also usually represented by a single word.

4. Typicality results can be also be explained with a model that relies on specific category *exemplars*, and with category judgments made by drawing analogies to these remembered exemplars. The exemplar model also has other advantages. It can explain our sensitivity to *category variability*, and also our sensitivity to patterns of *correlated features* within a category. This model can also explain the pliability of

categories, including our ability to view categories from a new perspective, and also our ability to create *ad hoc categories*.

5. One proposal is that conceptual knowledge includes both prototypes and exemplars. When first learning a category, one only knows a few exemplars, but then a prototype can be derived as experience with the category grows. This does not imply, however, that exemplar use falls away as category knowledge grows; instead, expert category users have exemplar knowledge and a category prototype.

6. Sometimes, categorization does not depend at all on whether the test case resembles a prototype or a category exemplar. This is evident with some abstract categories (odd number), and some weird cases (a mutilated lemon), but it is also evident with more mundane categories (raccoon). In these examples, categorization seems to depend on knowledge about a category's *essential properties*.

7. Knowledge about essential properties is not just a supplement to categorization via resemblance.

Instead, knowledge about essential properties may be a prerequisite for judgments of resemblance. With this knowledge, we are able to assess resemblance with regard to just those properties that truly matter for the category, and not be misled by irrelevant or accidental properties.

8. Which properties are essential for a category varies from one category to the next. The identification of these properties seems to depend on beliefs we have about the category, including casual beliefs that specify why the category features are as they are. These beliefs are referred to as *mental models* or *implicit theories*, and describe the category, not in isolation, but in relation to various other concepts.

9. Prototypes and exemplars may serve as *categorization heuristics*, allowing efficient and usually accurate judgments about category membership. These heuristics may not be adequate, though, for some of the ways we use our category knowledge; for these, our implicit theories about the concept play a pivotal role.

# CHAPTER 10

# *Language*

In chapters 8 and 9, we said a lot about generic and conceptual knowledge. One type of knowledge, though, seems worth singling out for special consideration—our knowledge of language.

Scholars have long been intrigued by language, and it's not hard to see why. Virtually every human being knows and uses a language; some of us know and use several languages. Indeed, to find a human *without* language, we need to seek out people in extraordinary circumstances—people who have suffered serious brain damage or people who have grown up completely isolated from other humans. In sharp contrast, no other species has and uses a language comparable to ours in complexity, sophistication, or communicative power (cf. Demers, 1989). In a real sense, then, knowing a language is a key part of being a human: a near-universal achievement in our species, yet unknown in its full-blown form in any other species.

Language seems no less central if we consider how language is used and what language makes possible. We use language to convey our ideas to each other, and our wishes, and our needs. Without language, our social interactions would be grossly impoverished, and cooperative endeavors would be a thousand times more difficult. Without language, the transmission of information, and the acquisition of knowledge, would be enormously impaired. (How much have you learned by listening to others or by reading?) Without language, there would be no science and no culture. Language is at the heart of, and essential for, a huge range of human activities and achievements. What is this tool, therefore, that is universal for our species, unique to our species, and crucial for much of what our species does?

## Phonology

The study of language is the subject matter for an important academic discipline, **linguistics**. At the boundary between linguistics and psychology stands a separate area of study, **psycholinguistics**, which is concerned with how linguistic knowledge is acquired, represented, and used by the human mind. In this chapter, we will provide a broad overview of psycholinguistic research, and we will begin with a consideration of the *sounds* of language—the domain of **phonology**.

It is convenient to think of language as having a hierarchical structure (Figure 10.1). At the top of the hierarchy, there are sentences—coherent sequences of words that express the intended meaning of a speaker. Sentences are composed of phrases, which are in turn composed of words. Words are com-posed of **morphemes**, the smallest language units that carry meaning. Meaning is largely carried by **content morphemes**, such as "umpire" or "talk" in Figure 10.1. However, **function morphemes** also add information crucial for interpretation, signaling the relations among words and also providing information about a word's grammatical role within a sentence. Examples of function morphemes in Figure 10.1 are the past-tense morpheme "ed" or the plural morpheme "s."

In spoken language, morphemes are conveyed by sounds called **phonemes**. Some phonemes are easily represented by letters of the alphabet, but others are not, and that is why the symbols look strange in the bottom row of Figure 10.1—the symbols correspond to the actual sounds produced, independent of how those sounds are expressed in our (or any) alphabet.

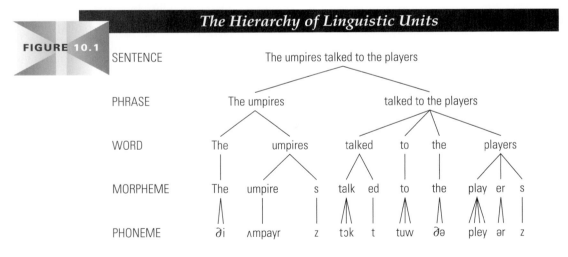

**FIGURE 10.1** — *The Hierarchy of Linguistic Units*

It is often useful to think of language as having a hierarchical structure. At the top of the hierarchy, there are sentences. These are composed of phrases, which are themselves composed of words. The words are composed of morphemes, the smallest language units that carry meaning. When the morphemes are pronounced, the units of sound are called phonemes. In describing phonemes, the symbols correspond to the actual sounds produced, independent of how these sounds are expressed in ordinary writing.

## *The Production of Speech*

**FIGURE** 10.2

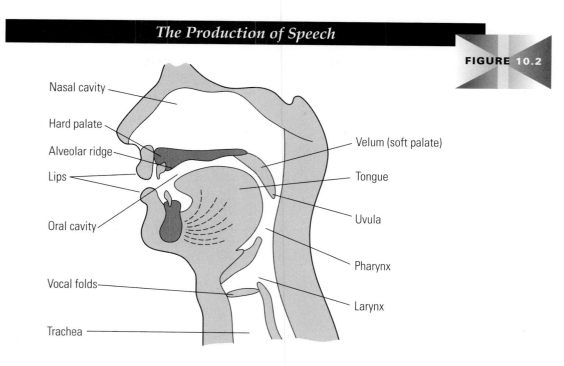

Nasal cavity

Hard palate

Alveolar ridge

Lips

Oral cavity

Vocal folds

Trachea

Velum (soft palate)

Tongue

Uvula

Pharynx

Larynx

In ordinary breathing, air flows out of the lungs, through the larynx, and up through the nose and mouth. To produce speech, this passageway must be constricted in a fashion that impedes or interrupts the airflow. For example, the uvula can be closed to block air from moving into the nasal cavity. Likewise, the tongue and lips control the movement of air through the oral cavity.

## THE PRODUCTION OF SPEECH

In ordinary breathing, air flows quietly out of the lungs, through the larynx, and up through the nose and mouth (Figure 10.2). However, noises are produced if this passageway is constricted in any fashion that impedes or interrupts the airflow. There are many forms that this constriction can take, allowing humans to produce a wide range of different sounds.

For example, within the larynx there are two flaps of muscular tissue called the "vocal folds." (These structures are also called the "vocal cords," although they are not cords at all.) The vocal folds can be rapidly opened and closed, producing a buzzing sort

of vibration known as **voicing**. You can feel this vibration by putting your palm on your throat while you produce a [z] sound. You will feel no vibration, though, if you hiss like a snake, producing a sustained [s] sound. The [z] sound is voiced, the [s] is not.

Sound can also be produced by narrowing the air passageway within the mouth itself. For example, hiss like a snake again, and pay attention to your tongue's position. To produce this sound, you have placed your tongue's tip near the roof of your mouth, just behind your teeth. The [s] sound is the sound of the air rushing through the narrow gap you have created.

If the gap is elsewhere, a different sound results. For example, to produce the "sh" sound (as in "shoot" or "shine"), the tongue is positioned so that it creates a narrow gap a bit further back in the mouth; air rushing through this gap causes the desired sound. Alternatively, the narrow gap can be more toward the front. Pronounce an [f] sound; in this case, the sound is produced by air rushing between your bottom lip and your top teeth.

Other sounds are produced by air moving through the nose rather than the mouth. Try humming an [m] sound while opening and closing your lips. This will cause some changes in the quality of the sound, but there is no interruption in the sound when your lips close. But now try humming an [m] sound and, while humming, pinch your nose shut. With air unable to move through your nose, the sound ceases.

All these aspects of speech production allow us to *categorize* the various speech sounds. Thus, linguists distinguish, first, between sounds that are *voiced*—produced with the vocal folds vibrating—and those that are not. The sounds of [v], [z], and [n] (to name a few) are voiced; [f], [s], [t], and [k] are unvoiced. (You can confirm this by running the hand-on-throat test while producing each of these sounds.) Second, sounds can be categorized according to *where* the airflow is restricted; this is referred to as **place of articulation**. Thus, you close your lips to produce "bilabial" sounds, like [p] or [b]; you place your top teeth close to your bottom lip to produce "labiodental" sounds, like [f] or [v]; and you place your tongue just behind your upper teeth to produce "alveolar" sounds, like [t] or [d].

Sounds can also be categorized according to *how* the airflow is restricted. This is referred to as **manner of production**. Thus, as we have seen, air is allowed to move through the nose for some speech sounds but not for others. Similarly, for some speech sounds, the flow of air is fully stopped for a moment—for example, [p], [b], and [t]. For other sounds, the air passage is restricted, but some air continues to flow (e.g., [f], [z], and [r]).

This categorization scheme allows us to describe any speech sound in terms of a few simple features. For example, the [p] sound is produced (1) without voicing, (2) with air moving through the mouth (not the nose), and with a full interruption to the flow of air, and (3) with a bilabial place of articulation. If any of these features changes—voicing, manner of production, or place of articulation—so does the sound's identity.

Put differently, these few features, in varying combinations, allow us to make all the sounds our language needs. In English, these features are combined and re-combined to produce 40 or so different phonemes. Other languages use as few as a dozen phonemes; still others, many more. (For example, there are 141 different phonemes in the language of Khoisan, spoken by the "Bushmen" of Africa; Halle, 1990.) In all cases, though, the phonemes are created by simple combinations of the features just described.

### THE COMPLEXITY OF SPEECH PERCEPTION

These features of speech production also correspond to what listeners *hear* when they are listening to speech. Phonemes that differ only in one production feature sound similar to each other, phonemes that differ in multiple features sound more distinct. This is reflected in the pattern of *errors* people make when they try to understand speech in a noisy environment. Their misperceptions are usually off by just one feature, so that [p] is confused with [b] (a difference only in voicing), [p] with [t] (a difference only in place of articulation), and so on (Miller & Nicely, 1955; Wang & Bilger, 1973).

This makes it seem like the perception of speech may be a straightforward matter: A small number of features is sufficient to characterize any particular speech sound. All the perceiver needs to do, therefore, is detect these features and, with this done, the speech sounds are identified.

As it turns out, though, speech perception is far more complicated than this. For one problem, consider Figure 10.3, which shows the moment-by-moment sound amplitudes produced by a speaker uttering a brief greeting. It is these amplitudes, in the form of air-

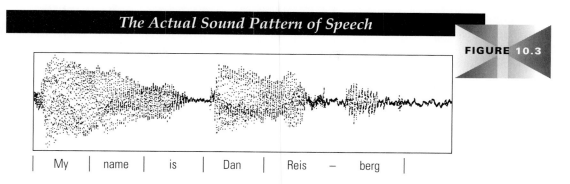

## The Actual Sound Pattern of Speech

**FIGURE** 10.3

| My | name | is | Dan | Reis | — | berg |

This figure shows the moment-by-moment sound amplitudes produced by a speaker uttering a greeting. Notice that there is no gap between the sounds carrying the word "my" and the sounds carrying "name." Nor is there a gap between the sounds carrying "name" and the sounds carrying "is." Therefore, the listener needs to figure out where one sound stops and the next begins, a process known as *segmentation*.

pressure changes, that reach the ear and so, in an important sense, the figure shows the pattern of input with which "real" speech perception begins.

Notice that, within this stream of speech, there are no markers to indicate where one phoneme ends and the next begins. Likewise, there are often no gaps, or signals of any sort, to indicate the boundaries between successive syllables or successive words. Therefore, as a first step *prior* to phoneme identification, you need to "slice" this stream into the appropriate segments—a step known as **speech segmentation**.

For many people, this pattern comes as a surprise. As perceivers of speech, we are usually convinced that there are pauses between words, marking the word boundaries. This turns out to be an illusion, and we are "hearing" pauses that, in truth, aren't there. The illusion is revealed when we physically measure the speech stream (as we did in order to create Figure 10.3) or when we listen to speech we can't understand—for example, speech in a foreign language. In this latter circumstance, we lack the skill needed to segment the stream, and so we are unable to "supply" the word boundaries. As a consequence, we hear what is really there—a continuous, uninterrupted flow of sound. That is why speech in a foreign language often sounds so fast.

Speech perception is further complicated by a phenomenon known as **coarticulation** (Liberman, 1970; also Daniloff & Hammarberg, 1973). This term refers to the fact that, in producing speech, one does not utter one phoneme at a time. Instead, the phonemes "overlap." While you are producing the [s] sound in "soup," for example, your mouth is getting ready to say the vowel. While uttering the vowel, you are already starting to move your tongue and lips and teeth into position for producing the [p].

This overlap in production allows speech to be faster and considerably more fluent. But this overlap also has important consequences for the sounds produced, and so the [s] produced while getting ready for one upcoming vowel is actually different from the [s] produced while getting ready for a different vowel. As a result, we can't point to a specific acoustical pattern and say, "This is the pattern of an [s] sound." Instead, the acoustical pattern is different in different contexts. Speech perception therefore has to "read past" these context differences in order to identify the phonemes produced.

Speech sounds also vary in other ways: For example, each of us has our own individual speech habits, and each of us has a slightly differently shaped mouth, and slightly differently shaped tongue. As a result, there is some variation from one speaker to the next in how each word is pronounced. However, this change in acoustical properties does not change the identities of the phonemes involved. Hence, this variation must be ignored in the process of identifying phonemes and in the process of recognizing speech.

## AIDS TO SPEECH PERCEPTION

These complications—the need for segmentation in a continuous speech stream, the variations caused by coarticulation, and the variations from speaker to speaker or from occasion to occasion—render speech perception surprisingly complex. As one measure of this complexity, note that speech recognition *by machine* is still relatively primitive. Speech recognition programs do exist but are quite limited. Some of these programs "understand" a wide range of speech but only from a single speaker. (That is, the programs have great difficulty with speaker-to-speaker variation.) Other programs can "understand" many different speakers but can handle only a limited vocabulary.

Obviously, though, humans manage quite well to perceive speech. How do we do it? Several mechanisms contribute. For one, we are generally able to supplement what we hear with expectations and knowledge, and this guides our interpretation of difficult-to-perceive speech. Note the similarity between this claim and our arguments about reading, in Chapter 3: There we noted that reading typically involves a considerable amount of inference, with "top-down" processes working to fill in information about letters you have barely glanced at. In the same fashion, top-down process in speech perception allow you to identify phonemes that are unclear in the sound stream.

In Chapter 3, we pointed to proofreading errors as one manifestation of this inferential process: In proofreading, one "sees" what one expects to see and therefore misses the misspelled word, or the misformed phrase. A parallel phenomenon is evident in speech perception, and this phenomenon was also discussed in Chapter 3: In the so-called restoration effect, people "hear" speech sounds that were not presented. This provides clear evidence for inference and extrapolation in speech perception.

In many cases, the inferences used to guide speech perception rely on knowledge external to language. For example, if you hear me say, "He put mustard on his [cough] dog," you easily infer what the missing word is, thanks to your knowledge of the popular foods of our culture. In other cases, though, the inferences are guided by redundancies inside of language—that is, the fact that many phonemes are predictable, given the surrounding phonemes and the vocabulary (and structure) of English.

We will provide some examples of these redundancies later on when we consider how phonemes are (and are not) combined. In the meantime, though, we can ask how much we are helped by these redundancies and by context overall. Pollack and Pickett (1964) tape-recorded a number of naturally occurring conversations. From these recordings, they spliced out individual words and presented these, now in isolation, to their research participants. Remarkably, the participants were unable to identify only half of these words. If restored to their context, though, these same stimuli were easy to identify.

Our chore of recognizing speech is also helped by the fact that the speech we encounter, from day to day, tends to be rather limited in its range. Each of us knows tens of thousands of different words, but most of these words are rarely used. In fact, it has been estimated that the 50 most commonly used words in English make up more than half of the words we actually utter. (After Miller, 1951. For discussion of other top-down effects in speech perception, see Cole & Jakimik, 1980; Garnes & Bond, 1976; Samuel, 1986.)

## CATEGORICAL PERCEPTION

Apparently, then, the incoming speech signal is predictable in important ways: A relatively small number of words, it seems, get used over and over. The structure of the language adds further predictability and so does the meaningful context. All of this can then be exploited by speech perception via inferential processes that supplement the information actually reaching the ear.

However, let's not put too much weight on these inferential processes. Humans are, in addition, exquisitely talented in deriving information from the speech signal. Indeed, there is every indication that we have evolved highly specialized mechanisms for this purpose and, more broadly, specialized mechanisms for the perception, acquisition, and use of language. (We will describe some of these specializations later in the chapter.)

The power of our speech recognition abilities is well revealed in the phenomenon of **categorical perception**. This refers to our tendency to hear speech sounds "merely" as members of a category—the category of [z] sounds or the category of [p] sounds. More precisely, we are quite adept at hearing differences *between* categories, but we are relatively *insensitive* to variations *within* the category. Thus, we easily hear the difference between a [p] and a [b], but we are rather inept in distinguishing one [p] from the next or one [z] from the next. Of course, this insensitivity is precisely what we want, since it allows us to separate the wheat from the chaff: We easily detect what category a sound belongs in, but we are virtually oblivious to the inconsequential (and potentially distracting) background variations.

Let's examine categorical perception in terms of an example. Consider the consonants [p] and [b]. Both of these are "bilabial" consonants (that is the "place of articulation"), and both are "stops" (that is the "manner of production"). In other words, both involve a complete interruption of the flow of air, caused by closing the lips. These consonants differ, though, in the feature of voicing—[b] is voiced, [p] is not. But let's be more precise about what that means: Place your hand flat on your throat, and pronounce

the word "pit." If you pay close attention, you will notice that the sound of the word begins slightly *before* you feel the vibration in your throat. In fact, there is (approximately) a 60 msec gap between the word's start (i.e., when you release your lips, which is when the air starts moving) and the onset of voicing. In other words, there is a 60 msec **voice-onset time**, or VOT.

Place your hand on your throat again, and now pronounce the word "bit." This time, you will detect no gap between the word's start and onset of voicing. For the phoneme [b], the VOT is essentially zero. (We note in passing that English uses only these two VOTs—one of 60 msec or so, and one of zero. Other languages use other VOTs. Many Asian languages, for example, use *negative* VOTs, so that the vocal folds start vibrating slightly *before* the air is released.)

What about "compromise" VOTs? With the aid of a computer, we can create synthetic speech with any specifications we like. Thus we can ask: How will (English-speaking) participants perceive a bilabial stop with a 30 msec voice-onset time? Acoustically, this stimulus is midway between an ordinary [b] and an ordinary [p]. Will people perceive it as midway between these syllables? Will they perceive it as a sort-of-p, sort-of-b? Or will they perhaps be uncertain about what the sound is? Likewise, how will people perceive a "compromise" between a [t] and [d]? (Again, these two consonants differ only in VOT.) Or between [f] and [v]?

To address these questions, let's consider a *series* of compromise sounds, created via synthetic speech. Thus, one of our stimuli might be a bilabial stop with a zero VOT. (This is an ordinary [b] sound.) Another stimulus might be a bilabial stop with a 10 msec VOT (this is a [b] with the voicing just slightly delayed). Another stimulus might have a 20 msec VOT; one might have a 30 msec VOT (that is our balanced compromise between [b] and [p]); and so on, up to a bilabial stop with a 60 msec VOT (that is, an ordinary [p]). We can now attach a vowel to each of these synthetic consonants and ask people to identify the resulting syllables. More precisely, we might add an "a" sound, and then ask them whether each stimulus is the syllable "ba" or the syllable "pa."

The top panel of Figure 10.4 shows the pattern we might expect. After all, our stimuli are gradually shading from a clear "ba" to a clear "pa." Therefore, as we move through the series, one might expect people to be less and less likely to identify each stimulus as a "ba," and correspondingly more and more likely to identify each as a "pa." In the terms we used in Chapter 9, this would be a "graded membership" pattern: Test cases close to the "ba prototype" should be reliably identified as "ba." As we move away from this prototype, though, cases should be harder and harder to categorize.

The graded membership pattern emerged again and again in Chapter 9, but it doesn't show up here. The actual data are shown in the bottom of Figure 10.4. As you can see, all of the sounds with short VOTs are perceived as "ba." Moreover, in terms of their categorizations, research participants seem indifferent to whether the syllable resembles the "ba prototype" (with a 0 msec VOT) or not (e.g., a 20 msec VOT). Likewise, all of the long-VOT sounds are perceived as "pa." And, again participants seem indifferent to the contrast between a prototypical "pa" (e.g., 60 msec VOT) or a lousy exemplar (40 msec VOT). We might mention that the steep cutoff, visible in Figure 10.4, occurs at slightly different points for different participants; nonetheless, every participant shows the pattern of a well-defined category boundary. (For the classic presentation of this pattern, see Liberman, Harris, Hoffman & Griffith, 1957; for reviews, see Handel, 1989; Yeni-Komshian, 1993. For studies of this pattern in children, see Werker & Desjardins, 1995.)

In a variation of this procedure, we can present these stimuli two by two. This time, the participants are asked whether the two stimuli they hear are the *same* or *different*. If the first stimulus in a pair has a VOT of 20 msec, then how different (in terms of VOT) does the second stimulus in the pair have to be in order for people reliably to hear the difference? Likewise, if the first stimulus in a pair has a 30 msec VOT, how different does the second have to be for people to hear the difference?

In this discrimination task, participants have great difficulty in hearing the difference between a stimu-

lus with a 10 msec VOT and one with a 30 msec VOT. To put it bluntly, all "ba's" sound alike. Likewise, people have difficulty in hearing the difference between a stimulus with a 40 msec VOT and one with a 60 msec VOT. Apparently, all "pa's" sound alike. But the problem is *not* that the participants are insensitive to these 20 msec differences. They do quite well, in fact, in hearing the difference between a 20 msec VOT and a 40 msec VOT. Discriminations *across the category boundary* are relatively easy.

The identification data (Figure 10.4) indicate that people are reasonably tolerant in their categorization: Stimuli at some distance from a "classic ba" are still counted as a "ba," and likewise for stimuli at some distance from a "classic pa." But this isn't because people hear the stimulus-to-stimulus variation but then elect to ignore it. Instead, people seem genuinely insensitive to differences within each category. Thus, in a real sense, they hear these sounds only as instances of their respective categories. What is perceived, in other words, is only the fact of a stimulus being in this or that category—hence the term "categorical perception."

## COMBINING PHONEMES

What about more complicated sounds? We have already noted that speech sounds have relatively few features, yet from these, English speakers fashion 40 different phonemes. Those 40 phonemes, in turn, can be combined and recombined to form tens of thousands of different morphemes, which can themselves be combined to create word after word after word.

These combinations don't happen, however, in a helter-skelter fashion. Instead, there is a pattern to the combinations—some combinations seem common, others are rare; others seem prohibited outright. For example, imagine an advertising executive trying to name a new breakfast cereal. One possibility is "Pritos." Another is "Glitos." But here is an option that seems a non-starter: "Tlitos." In English, words simply don't begin with the tl combination. This restriction isn't shared by all languages (there is, for example, a Northwest Indian language called

## Categorical Perception

**FIGURE** 10.4

**Hypothetical identification data**

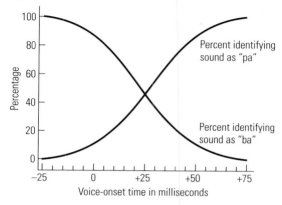

Percent identifying sound as "pa"

Percent identifying sound as "ba"

Voice-onset time in milliseconds

**Actual identification data**

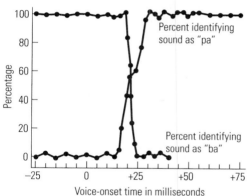

Percent identifying sound as "pa"

Percent identifying sound as "ba"

Voice-onset time in milliseconds

In ordinary speech, the syllable "ba" is pronounced with a zero voice onset time (VOT). That is, *voicing* begins at the same time as the air begins to flow. The syllable "pa" is pronounced with a 60 or 70 msec VOT—that is, voicing begins approximately 60 or 70 msec after the air begins to flow. With computer speech, we can produce a variety of compromises between these two sounds, and the top panel shows a plausible prediction about how these sounds will be perceived: As the sound becomes less and less like an ordinary "ba," people should be less and less likely to perceive it as a "ba." The bottom panel, however, shows the actual data: Research participants seem indifferent to small variations on the "ba" sound, and categorize a sound with a 10 or 15 msec VOT in exactly the same way that they categorize a sound with a 0 VOT. The categorizations also show an abrupt categorical "boundary" between "pa" and "ba," although there is no corresponding abrupt change in the stimuli themselves. (After Lisker & Abramson, 1970.)

"Tlingit"), but it is a restriction learned by, and honored by, all speakers of English.

Other principles govern the pattern of *change* that must occur when two morphemes are married together. For example, consider the "s" ending that marks the English plural—as in *books, cats, tapes,* and so on. In the cases just listed, the plural is pronounced as an [s]. In other contexts, though, the plural ending is pronounced differently. Say these words out loud: *bags, duds, pills.* If you listen carefully, you will realize that these words actually end with a [z] sound, not an [s]. The choice between these—a [z] pronunciation or an [s]—depends on how the base noun ends. If it ends with a *voiced* sound, then the [z] ending is used to make the plural. If the base noun ends with an *unvoiced* sound, then the plural is created with an [s].

It should be said that there is nothing inevitable about this pattern. The human voice can, for example, easily create the sound of "pills" with an [s] on the end, instead of a [z]. Nonetheless, it is the [z] pronunciation that we always use, suggesting that English speakers have internalized something equivalent to a "rule" for how this word (and every other plural) should be pronounced. These phonological rules thus provide part of the knowledge one must acquire if one is "to know English." (For a classic treatment of these issues, see Chomsky & Halle, 1968; for a more recent discussion, see Halle, 1990.)

## Words

The average American high-school graduate knows about 45,000 different words (cf. Miller, 1991). For college students, the estimates are larger—between 75,000 and 100,000 words in their speaking vocabulary (Oldfield, 1963). For each of these, the speaker must know the *meaning* that corresponds to the word's *sound*, and so, in general, our word knowledge allows us to tie together a phonological representation with a **semantic** representation—that is, a representation of the word's meaning.

There is an obvious connection between semantic knowledge and the conceptual knowledge we dis-cussed in Chapter 9. To be sure, some concepts are difficult to express in words; other concepts can be expressed only via many words. Nonetheless, many words do express single concepts, and more generally, one can only understand a word's meaning if one understands the relevant concepts. It is no surprise, therefore, that the issues discussed in Chapter 9 also emerge in discussions of word meaning. Thus, some have proposed that, to know a word, one must know the word's *definition*. Others have argued that, to know a word, one must know a *prototype* for the concept named by that word. These are, of course, exactly the hypotheses we examined in Chapter 9. (For more on what it means to know a word, see Miller, 1999.)

## SENSE AND REFERENCE

One further distinction, though, is worth making explicit: Words are generally used to name objects or events in the world around us. The word "page," for example, refers to the sort of thing you are looking at right now; the word "reading" refers to the activity you are now engaged in, and so on. What a word refers to is called the word's **referent**.

However, it is crucial not to confuse a word's referent with the word's meaning. There are several reasons for this. For one, a word's referent is often a matter of accident or coincidence. Thus, the referent of the phrase "president of the United States" changes at regular intervals, but the *meaning* of the phrase is surely more stable than that.

In addition, we can often find two phrases that refer to the same objects in the world but that mean different things. These cases of "same referent, different meaning" make it clear that there must be more to meaning than reference. We refer to this "more" as the **sense** of a word, distinct from its referent (cf. Frege, 1892).

For example, consider the phrase "creature with a heart" and also the phrase "creature with a kidney." As it turns out, these phrases refer to the same creatures: In the biology of our planet, all creatures that have hearts also have kidneys, and all creatures that have kidneys also have hearts. Thus, these two phrases have the same *referent*. Nonetheless, these two phrases mean different things. (For example, we could imagine a planet in which "creatures with kidneys" were distinct from the "creatures with hearts." This wouldn't be possible if the two phrases *meant* the same thing.)

The phrase "creature with a heart" allows us to pick out a set of creatures in the world, and this set constitutes the referent for this phrase. But this phrase also identifies these creatures *in a specific way*—by virtue of their having hearts. This means of identifying the creatures provides the *sense* of the term, and the sense matters in many contexts. For example, by virtue of having identified these creatures via their heart possession, we also know some other things about them (e.g., that they have blood of some sort). This implication might not be conveyed by some other sense, even if that sense picked out exactly the same creatures.

Notice the parallels between these points and issues that we raised in Chapter 9. Prototypes and exemplars, for example, provide a reasonable way to categorize many of the objects in the world around us: We can categorize, in effect, by comparing the objects (or events) we encounter to these mental representations. Thus, prototypes and exemplars provide one way to capture the *referent* of a term. However, we have just argued that there is more to meaning than this, and that is entirely consonant with the message of Chapter 9. There we argued that concepts must contain more than prototypes and exemplars, in order to guide our judgments and reasoning about concepts. In effect, then, the latter half of Chapter 9 provides one way we might think about a term's sense.

## BUILDING NEW WORDS

We have mentioned the average vocabulary size for a high-school student or a college student. But these counts are difficult to nail down, since one can easily create *new* words as needed. This happens, for example, whenever a new style of music or new style of clothing demands a correspondingly new descriptive vocabulary. Likewise for the world of computers—"e-commerce" is a recent arrival in the language, as is "geek." In many cases, these novel words are made up from scratch. More often, though, new words are "built" out of other morphemes. Thus, as Pinker (1994) points out, some foods are "unmicrowaveable"—a vocabulary item of recent vintage.

Scholars often speak of the **generativity** of language, to capture this idea that one can combine and recombine the units to create (or "generate") new linguistic entities. This generativity may, in fact, be limitless. For example, as children, many of us were told that "antidisestablishmentarianism" is the longest word in the English language. Notice, though, that most of this word's length comes from the concatenation of various morphemes—from establish to *dis*establish, from there to disestablish*ment*, from there to disestablish*ment**arian*, and so on.[1] The same thing happens routinely at more modest levels: Thus there are shakes and handshakes; grandmothers, great-grandmothers, and great-great-grandmothers; leftists, rightists, and centrists; street-sweepers and mine-sweepers. In each case, the language is effortlessly enhanced by the combination of existing elements.

This ability to combine and recombine morphemes provides an enormous advantage: You don't need to memorize, as separate vocabulary items, the word "hat" and its plural "hats," or "cow" and "cows." Instead, all you need is the base noun in each case, plus the plural morpheme, "s." With these ingredients, you can create the plural, when needed. You can then generalize this procedure for other nouns, including nouns you are meeting for the first time. (I have one "grattiff." If I get another, I'll have two . . . ?) Likewise, once you know the past tense morpheme "ed" you can create the past tense of most verbs.

---

[1] Antidisestablishmentarianism is in fact *not* the longest word in English. That's because we can always create an even longer word by adding another morpheme or two onto this base. For example, there are antidisestablishmentarianism*s*. And circumstances that lead to antidisestablishmentarianisms are, of course, *pre*antidisestablishmentarianisms. And so on.

This generativity therefore lightens the load of anyone seeking to learn the vocabulary of a language and also allows us to deal with novel cases as they arise. Imagine that you have just heard the word "hack" for the very first time. You know immediately that someone who likes to hack is a *hacker*, the activity is called *hacking*, and you understand someone who says "I've been *hacked*." Once again, though, these combinations are not done in a helter-skelter fashion. Instead, a number of rules govern the combinations of morphemes. For example, you are now reasonably familiar with the Reisberg writing style; we might call this style "Reisbergian." And perhaps there are many who write in this style; we might call them all "Reisbergians." So there is no problem in the sequence of "Reisberg" + "ian" + "s." But things can't go the other way around: What if there are many Reisbergs who write in this style? In that case, what would we call someone else who writes in the style of (many) Reisbergs? The word "Reisbergsian" sounds awkward, and terms like this one virtually never appear in spontaneous speech. Apparently, then, some principle prohibits the sequence composed of "base word" + "s" + "ian," and all speakers of English somehow know and honor this principle.

## PRESCRIPTIVE RULES, DESCRIPTIVE RULES

In what sense, though, are these combinations of morphemes "prohibited"? Prohibited by whom? Likewise, we earlier noted that there is a "rule" governing the construction of plurals, so that "bugs" is pronounced with a [z] sound, while "bucks" is pronounced with an [s]. What sort of rule is this?

Let's first be clear about what these rules and prohibitions are *not*. We were all taught, at some stage of our education, how to talk and write "properly." We were all taught never to say "ain't." Many of us were scolded for writing in the passive voice; others were reprimanded for splitting infinitives. Many of us were counseled to say "For whom are you looking?" rather than "Who are you looking for?"; "It is I!" rather than "It's me."

The rules at stake in these cases are called **prescriptive rules**, rules describing how language is "supposed" to be. Often these rules seek to preserve a pattern of usage or a pattern of speaking that was common in some prior period, for some prior generation. Often these rules are intended to mark the difference between social classes, so that "upper class" people speak in one way, whereas "lower class" people don't talk so good. Thus, if one wishes to avoid being stigmatized, or if one wishes for membership in the elite, one tries to use the rules and to speak "proper" English.

One might well be skeptical about these prescriptive rules. All languages change with the passage of time, and what is considered "proper usage" in one time period is likely to be different from what is proper a generation later. Hence, the prescriptive rules try, in a sense, to "stop the clock" on language change, and it is not obvious *why* the clock should be stopped: Do we have reason to believe that the English of 1928 is better than the English of 1992 or 2001? If not, then why should the English of 2001 conform to the pattern that was deemed acceptable in the earlier time?

The rules we are concerned with in this chapter, though, are rules of a different sort—not prescriptive rules but **descriptive**, i.e., characterizing the language as it is ordinarily used by fluent speakers and listeners. There are strong regularities in the way English is used, and the rules we are discussing describe these patterns. No value judgment is offered (nor should one be) about whether these patterns constitute "proper" or "good" English. These patterns simply describe how English *is* or, perhaps we should say, *what* English is.

Notice also how we go about discovering these regularities. In some cases, it is important to track what is said and what is not said in ordinary language usage. This type of study, however, provides evidence only of a limited sort. For one consideration, the *absence* of a word or construction from ordinary usage is difficult to interpret: If Leo never uses the word "boustrephedon," is this because he doesn't know the word or because he simply has no interest in talking about boustrephedon? If Miriam never uses the word "unmicrowaveable," is this because she regards the word as illegitimate or merely because she is in the habit of using some other term to convey this idea?

In addition, the pattern of spontaneous speech is filled with performance errors. Sometimes, you start a sentence with one idea in mind, but then change your idea as you are speaking. You might end up saying something like, "He went my father went yesterday," even though you realize, as you are uttering it, that the sentence contains an error. On other occasions, you slip in your production, and so end up saying something different from what you had intended. You might say, "They were I mean weren't fine," even though you notice (and regret) the slip the moment you produce it.

These speech errors are of considerable importance if we are studying the ways in which speech is actually produced. However, these slips are a nuisance if we are trying to study linguistic knowledge: In most cases, you would agree that you had, in fact, made an error. In many cases, you even know how to "repair" the error, in order to produce a "correct" sentence. Clearly, therefore, your original performance, with its errors, doesn't reflect the full extent of your linguistic knowledge.

Because of considerations like these, we sometimes need to examine language **competence** rather than language performance, with competence defined as the pattern of skills and knowledge that might be revealed under optimal circumstances (after Chomsky, 1957, 1965). One way to reveal this competence is via linguistic *judgments*: People are asked to reflect on one structure or another and to tell us whether they find the structure acceptable or not. Note that we are not asking people whether they find the structure to be clumsy, or pleasing to the ear, or useful. Instead, we are asking them whether the structure is something that one *could* say, if one wished. Thus, to use an earlier example, "Reisbergians" seems acceptable but "Reibergsian" does not. Likewise, "There's the big blue house" seems fine, but "There's house blue big the" does not. Or, to return to an earlier example, you might slip and say, "He went my father went yesterday," but you cer-

tainly know there is something wrong with this sequence. It's these "acceptability judgments" that reveal linguistic competence, and it's these judgments that, ultimately, our theory needs to explain.

It should be said that these judgments do involve a peculiar use of language: Normally, we use language to communicate about some (nonlinguistic) object or event; language is the medium of expression and not by itself the topic of discussion. In the judgments we are considering, though, language *is* the topic of scrutiny, and so, in our data collection, we are asking people to make a judgment *about* language rather than simply *using* language. Judgments like these are called **metalinguistic judgments**, and these in turn are members of a broader category: **metacognitive judgments**. Metacognitive judgments are in general defined as judgments in which one must stand back from a particular mental activity and comment on the activity, rather than participating in it.

## THE "PSYCHOLOGICAL REALITY" OF LINGUISTIC RULES

Metalinguistic judgments reveal a number of strong patterns: Certain combinations of phonemes are reliably regarded as acceptable, others are not. Likewise, certain combinations of morphemes are regarded as acceptable, others are not. In most cases, it is convenient to describe these patterns in terms of a rule: If a word's final phoneme is voiced, then the plural ending must be voiced as well (i.e., a [z] rather than an [s]). If a noun has an *irregular* plural, then it can be combined with other morphemes in the plural form. (Thus a beaver can leave "teethmarks," and a house can be "mice-infested.") If a noun has a *regular* plural, though, it is combined with other morphemes only in the *singular* form. (A house might be a "rat-infested," but not "rats-infested." A porcupine leaves "claw-marks," not "claws-marks.")

What is the nature of these rules? One possibility is that the rules are consciously known and deliberately followed, just as most people know the spelling rule "*i* before *e* except after *c*." (Never mind that this rule has many exceptions—like "either" or "neither." What matters is that people know the rule, can report the rule, and try explicitly to apply the rule.)

However, we can swiftly rule out this claim: Linguistic rules are surely not conscious. Indeed, before reading these paragraphs, you probably didn't realize there was a relation between regularity of plurals and how a word combines with other words. Nonetheless, you have followed this rule for most of your life—at least since you were three or four years old (Gordon, 1986).

A different possibility is that you know the rules *unconsciously* and apply them without realizing you are doing so. Evidence for this claim comes from studies of children learning language. For example, English-speaking children seem initially to learn the past tense in a word-by-word fashion, and so they memorize the fact that the past tense of "play" is "played," that the past tense of "climb" is "climbed," and so on. By age two or three, however, children realize that there is a pattern here, so that one doesn't have to memorize each word's past tense as a separate vocabulary item. Instead, they realize, you can produce the past tense by manipulating morphemes—that is, by adding the "ed" ending onto a word. Once children make this discovery, they are able to apply this principle to many new verbs, including verbs they have never encountered before. Thus, Berko (1958) showed children a picture and told them, "Here is a man who likes to rick. Yesterday, he did the same thing. Yesterday, he . . ." Prompted in this way, three-year-olds unhesitatingly supply the past tense: "ricked."

However, children seem to get carried away with this pattern and so, at this age, children's spontaneous speech contains many **over-regularization errors**: Children say things like, "Yesterday, we goed," or "Yesterday, I runned." The same thing happens with other morphemes, and so children of this age also over-generalize in their use of the plural ending: They say things like "I have two foots," or "I lost three tooths." They also over-generalize in their use of contractions, using, for example, the pattern of "You aren't" to produce "I amn't"—meaning, of course, "I am not."

Remarkably, these same children were *correctly* using the irregular forms (*feet, teeth, went, ran*) just a few months earlier, and so, to the casual viewer, it seems that the child's linguistic development is going *backward*—first using the correct forms, and then later using incorrect ones. Adding to the puzzle, it is clear that the child still remembers the irregular past tense; this is revealed in the fact that a child of this age will flip-flop between using the correct form and the incorrect one, using "went" in one sentence and "goed" in the very next sentence. Worse, the child will sometimes *combine* the correct and incorrect forms, and so one can hear children of this age voicing such peculiarities as "He wented." (For a review, see Marcus, Pinker, Ullman, Hollander, Rosen & Xu, 1992.)

This pattern makes it clear that language learning is not a matter of *imitation*, since these over-regularizations are never produced by adults. Nor is language acquisition a matter of explicit *instruction*, since no adult would encourage children to make these errors. Instead, in describing these data, it is tempting simply to say that children are inducing a rule about how the past tense is formed. Before they learn the rule, their use of the past tense is reliably correct, but it is limited to those cases they've memorized. Once they learn the rule, this limit vanishes, and now they can form the past tense even for unfamiliar verbs. At this point, however, the children are plainly confused about when to use the rule and when not, and this is the stage at which they produce over-regularization errors—in essence, they are *over-using* the rule. Later on, they straighten out which verbs are regular (and for these, they use the rule) and which are irregular; once this is done, children are able to use the past tense in a mature fashion.

According to this view, the rule governing the past tense is literally in place in the child's mind (although unconsciously), and is governing the child's linguistic productions. Likewise for the rules governing plurals and those governing contractions. Each of these rules is in some sense "known" to the child (although, again, not consciously), and is used in forming the relevant linguistic combinations.

It should be said, though, that there is considerable controversy attached to these claims. There is no doubt that children do produce over-regularization errors, and many authors interpret this as we just did—as evidence for language rules. Other authors, however, have argued that these errors could also emerge from a connectionist network, involving (as all connectionist networks do) nothing more than a number of simple associations. According to this view, our linguistic judgments are *well described* by rules, but this does not mean that we know the rules in any sense. (For glimpses of this debate, see Hajiwara et al., 1999; Marchman, Plunkett & Goodman, 1997; Marcus, 1995, 1996; MacWhinney & Leinbach, 1991; Pinker, 1991, 1999; Pinker & Prince, 1991; Plunkett & Marchman, 1996; Rohde & Plaut, 1999.)

The distinction at stake here is a subtle one: Everyone agrees that our linguistic judgments are readily described in terms of rules. What is at issue is the nature of the processes that lead to these judgments. Are the rules somehow built into these processes, in the same way that, say, the rules of arithmetic are literally built into most computer programs? Or do the processes involve some other mechanism that just happens to work in a fashion that produces this rule-described behavior? It is too soon to know how this issue will be resolved.

In the meantime, though, several points are certain: Our linguistic behavior is, on anyone's account, highly creative (in the sense that new forms can always be generated) but also highly constrained (in the sense that many of the possible combinations of units are deemed unacceptable by speakers and hearers of the language). These constraints fall into patterns that are well described by rules, and in large measure it is the business of linguistics to discover these rules. However, whether the rules are literally represented in the mind, and thus govern our linguistic practices, remains to be seen.

## Syntax

We have already mentioned that a few production features are all you need to create dozens of phonemes, and these phonemes then allow you to create tens of thousands of words. But now let's consider what you can do with those words: If you have 40,000 words in your vocabulary, or 60,000, or 80,000, how many *sentences* can you build from those words? How many sentences are you able to understand or to produce?

Sentences can range in length from the very brief ("Go!" or "I do.") to the absurdly long. (According to the Guinness *Book of World Records*, the longest sentence ever printed contains 1,300 words.) Most sentences, though, contain 20 words or fewer. With this "length limit," it has been estimated that there are 100,000,000,000,000,000,000 possible sentences in English (that's $10^{20}$; after Pinker, 1994). For comparison, this is 100 million times larger than the number of neurons in your brain.

Do we need obscure or complicated sentences to produce this absurdly large number? It turns out that we don't. Think of how many ways you can complete this sentence: "I can see the . . ." Or imagine endings to this sentence, "I detest Coco-Puffs because . . ." If you press ahead in this exercise, you will realize that even commonplace, easily generated sentences are vast in number.

Of course, some sequences of words *aren't* sentences: Thus, in English, one could say, "The boy hit the ball," but couldn't say "The boy hit ball the." Likewise, one could say, "The bird squashed the car," but couldn't say "The bird the car," or "The bird squashed the," or just "Squashed the car." These sequences are (more or less) interpretable, but virtually any speaker of the language would agree these sequences have something wrong in them. They are unacceptable; they are not sentences. Once again, therefore, it is tempting to appeal to *rules*—rules that permit endless numbers of word combinations, but which *prohibit* other combinations. These rules, governing the sequences and combinations of words in the formation of phrases and sentences, are called rules of **syntax**. Syntactic rules determine whether a sequence of words is **grammatical**—i.e., conforms to the patterns acceptable within the language.

One might think that grammatical acceptability is a matter of *meaning*: Sentences are meaningful, but non-sentences aren't. This suggestion, though, is plainly wrong. To see this, consider these two sentences (which are surely the two most widely quoted bits of gibberish ever composed):

'Twas brillig, and the slithey toves
did gyre and gimble in the wabe.
Colorless green ideas sleep furiously.

(The first of these is part of Lewis Carroll's famous poem "Jabberwocky"; the second was penned by the important linguist Noam Chomsky.) These sentences are, of course, without meaning—colorless things aren't green; ideas don't sleep; toves aren't slithey. Nonetheless, these sequences are sentences: Speakers of English, perhaps after a moment's reflection, do regard these sequences as grammatically acceptable in a way that "Furiously sleep ideas green colorless" is not. It seems, therefore, that we need principles of syntax that are largely independent of semantics and sensibility.

## PHRASE STRUCTURE

We have already noted that syntactic rules "prohibit" some sequences of words or, more precisely, the rules designate these sequences as "ungrammatical." In addition, the rules of syntax specify the "role" of each word within the sentence. To put it rather crudely, the rules specify which word within the sentence identifies the doer of the action, and which identifies the recipient of the action. This is one of the reasons grammar is important: If a sequence isn't grammatical, then often we can't decipher the role of each word or phrase, blocking interpretation of the sequence.

These roles are specified, in part, by the **phrase structure** of the sentence, a structure often illustrated via an (upside-down) tree, such as the one shown in Figure 10.5. If you read this structure from bottom to top, the structure specifies how the words in the sentence are grouped together: The first three words constitute one phrase—in particular, a "noun phrase." The last three words in the sentence form another

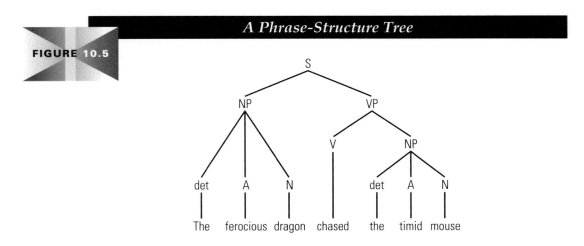

**FIGURE 10.5**

### A Phrase-Structure Tree

The syntax of a sentence is often depicted via a "tree" diagram. The diagram shows that the overall sentence itself (S) consists of a noun phrase (NP) followed by a verb phrase (VP). The noun phrase is composed of a determiner, followed by an adjective and a noun. The verb phrase is composed of a verb followed by a noun phrase.

## Syntactic Rewrite Rules

$$S \longrightarrow NP \quad VP$$
$$NP \longrightarrow (det) \quad A* \ N$$

$$VP \longrightarrow V \ (NP)$$
$$VP \longrightarrow V \ S$$
$$VP \longrightarrow V \ PP$$
$$VP \longrightarrow V \ AP$$
$$AP \longrightarrow A \ A$$

**FIGURE** 10.6

Most syntactic rules can be captured in terms of "rewrite rules." The top rule indicates that a sentence can consist of a noun phrase followed by a verb phrase. A verb phrase, however, can take several different forms—a verb by itself, or a verb followed by a noun phrase, or a verb followed by a prepositional phrase, and so on. Note that these rules are *recursive*: A sentence can contain a verb phrase, which can contain a sentence.

NP. This last NP joins with the word "chased" to constitute a larger phrase—a "verb phrase."

Of course, there are constraints on the pattern of branching in a phrase-structure tree, and these constraints are specified by phrase-structure rules. Thus, a *sentence* (S) always consists of a noun phrase (NP) followed by a verb phrase (VP). Therefore, every phrase-structure tree starts with the branching of NP + VP visible at the top of Figure 10.5. This rule is often written in this fashion:

$$S \rightarrow NP \quad VP$$

Expressed this way, the rule is referred to as a **rewrite rule**, such that whenever you find a sentence (S) in a tree structure, you can rewrite it as a noun phrase followed by a verb phrase. Equivalently: Whenever there is a sentence in a tree structure, it can "branch out" into a noun phrase plus a verb phrase.

Likewise, the rule

$$NP \rightarrow (det) \ A \quad * \quad N$$

means that whenever you find a noun phrase in a tree structure, you can rewrite it as a *determiner* (like "a" or "one" or "the"), followed by an *adjective* (A), followed by a *noun* (N). Notice that you need not have a determiner—there is none in this sentence: "Trees like sunlight." This is why the symbol "det" is in parentheses, connoting that this term is optional. Likewise, there can be any number of adjectives, including none; this is indicated by the asterisk. Other rewrite rules are listed in Figure 10.6.

These rewrite rules also have another interesting feature, called **recursion**. A rule system is recursive if a symbol can appear both on the left side of a definition (the part being defined) and on the right side (the part providing the definition). Thus, a sentence always includes a noun phrase and a verb phrase (remember: S → NP VP; here it is the S that is being defined). The verb phrase, in turn can be unpacked in several different ways, including

$$VP \rightarrow V \quad NP$$

or:

$$VP \rightarrow V \quad S$$

Notice that in this last rule, S appears *as part of the definition*. This allows us to create sentences like this one:

I believe she is the thief.

Here, there is a sentence ("She is the thief.") within the sentence. (The relevant phrase structure is shown in Figure 10.7; notice that we begin, as always, with an S node at the top, but then unpack the S node in a fashion that leads to another S node, in the middle of the tree.) We can then repeat this cycle, if we wish, with sentences including verb phrases including sentences including verb phrases including sentences, as in

I fear that you believe Sam told her I am the thief.

Recursion provides an easy way to accommodate this pattern. In addition, recursion is one of the features of language supporting vast generativity, since one can, quite literally, use recursion to create an infinite number of sentences.

## THE FUNCTION OF PHRASE STRUCTURE

Phrase-structure rules provide part of our account for why some sequences of words are rejected as ungrammatical. As we have noted, these rules specify what must be included within a sentence, and they often specify an *order* for the sentence. Sequences of words that break these rules, therefore, can't be sentences.

Phrase-structure rules also reflect the "natural" groupings of words within each sentence: Groups of words identified by the rules (e.g., the noun phrase,

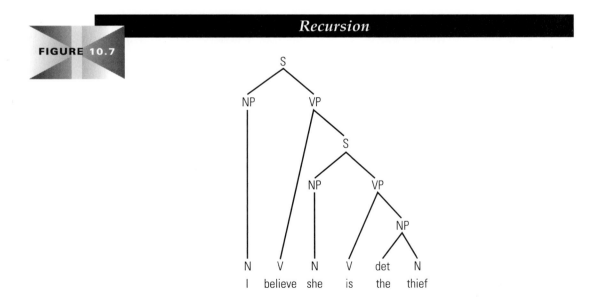

**FIGURE 10.7**

*Recursion*

Shown here is the phrase-structure tree for a sentence that makes use of recursion. Recursion refers to the possibility for an element to appear as part of its own definition. Thus, sentences are defined as including verb phrases, but verb phrases can include sentences, leading to the possibility of sentences within sentences.

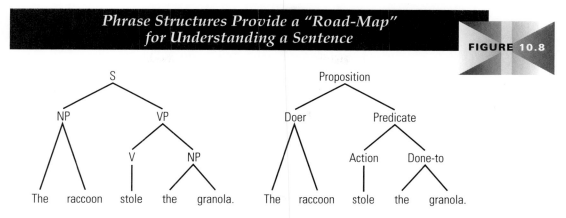

**Phrase Structures Provide a "Road-Map" for Understanding a Sentence**

**FIGURE 10.8**

Phrase structures specify the syntactic relationships among a sentence's parts, but these syntactic relationships often provide a guide for how the sentence should be understood.

the verb phrase, and so on) really do seem to "hang together." There are many ways to demonstrate this, including direct probes of people's intuitions about sentences. For example, where are the "natural" break points in this sentence: "The tall girl tackled the runner"? For most people, the sentence is sensibly split into "The tall girl" and "tackled the runner," and this is, of course, a split between the sentence's main noun phrase and its main verb phrase. If asked to split the sentence again, most people would divide it into "The tall girl," "tackled," and "the runner," fully in accord with the structure dictated by the phrase-structure rules.

In addition, notice that phrase-structure rules define the sequence of a noun phrase independently of where the noun phrase appears within a sentence. As a result, the rules define a noun phrase "module" that can be "plugged in" wherever a noun phrase is appropriate. This allows us to explain some important facts. For example, anyone who will reject this sentence as ill formed: "The ball big rolled away," is guaranteed to reject these as well: "He chased the ball big," and "The ant was squashed under the ball big." That is because all three sentences are prohibited by the same phrase-structure rule. Likewise, anyone who accepts this sentence as legitimate: "I kissed a

girl who is allergic to coconuts" is guaranteed also to accept these: "A girl who is allergic to coconuts was chased by a moose," and "He hid the flowers behind a girl who is allergic to coconuts." That is because one rule tells you that if a "module" can be plugged into one of the noun-phrase positions, then it can be plugged into any of the noun-phrase positions.

Phrase-structure rules also seem to guide our *interpretation* of a sentence: The rule S → NP VP divides a sentence into the "doer" (the NP) and some information about that doer (the VP)—in other words, the rule divides the sentence into the subject and the predicate. If the verb phrase is rewritten VP → V NP, then the initial verb indicates the action described by the sentence, and the NP specifies the recipient of that action. In these ways, the phrase structure of a sentence provides an initial "roadmap" useful in understanding the sentence, as shown in Figure 10.8.

Interestingly, sometimes more than one phrase structure, more than one roadmap, is compatible with a sentence. If the phrase structure guides interpretation then, in these cases, there should be more than one way to interpret the sentence. There should, in other words, be a **phrase-structure ambiguity**. (This is in contrast to other forms of ambiguity—e.g.,

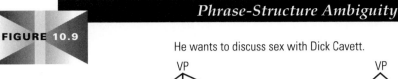

**FIGURE 10.9**

## Phrase-Structure Ambiguity

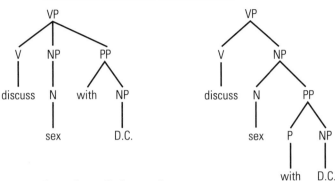

He wants to discuss sex with Dick Cavett.

I saw the gorilla in my pajamas.
The shooting of the hunters was terrible.
They are roasting chickens.
Visiting relatives can be awful.
Two computers were reported stolen by the TV announcer.

Often, the words of a sentence are compatible with more than one phrase structure; in this case, the sentence will be ambiguous. Thus, one can understand the first sentence as describing a *discussion* with Cavett, or as describing *sex* with Cavett; both analyses of the verb phrase are shown. Can you find both interpretations for the remaining sentences?

the ambiguity of an individual word, like "bank" or "ball" or "hood.") Some examples of phrase-structure ambiguity are shown in Figure 10.9 and, for the first of these, we have illustrated the two alternative phrase structures consistent with the sequence of words. Thus, ambiguity is predicted, on the basis of the phrase-structure rules, and the ambiguity is (often humorously) observed.

### MOVEMENT RULES

We have now seen several influences of phrase-structure rules. First, these rules play an important part in determining which sequences of words are

sentences and which are not. Second, these rules identify sections within a sentence that really do seem to provide natural groupings. Third, the rules also explain the pattern of "interconnections" among our linguistic judgments: If, for example, we find a noun phrase unacceptable in one sentence position, we find it unacceptable in *any* sentence position. This is because the sequence of words identified as a "noun phrase" really does function as an operative unit within our linguistic knowledge, just as the phrase-structure rules require. (And likewise for the other units identified by the rules.) Fourth, phrase-structure rules seem to guide interpretation of a sentence, and correspondingly, a sentence will be ambiguous if more than one phrase-structure analysis can be computed.

It turns out, though, that some aspects of syntax cannot be explained in terms of phrase-structure rules. Instead, we need a two-part system: Phrase-structure rules allow us to "grow" a sentence tree, but then a separate set of rules allows us to "reshape" the tree by exchanging the positions of some of the tree's branches. This "reshaping" allows us to express different attitudes about the sentence's content (for example, it allows us to express the content as a question, rather than an assertion); it also allows us to change the 'focus' of a sentence, in order to draw the listener's (or reader's) attention to some particular element in the proposition.

To put this more precisely, the phrase-structure rules allow us to generate an abstract representation of the sentence; this representation is called the sentence's underlying structure, or **d-structure**. Then a series of *movement rules* allow us to change the positions of various elements within the sentence, in order to create the sentence's surface structure, or **s-structure**.[2] It is the d-structure that provides the starting point for semantic analysis, since it is this structure that makes clear who did what to whom. It is the s-structure, though, that is expressed in speech. (This form of theorizing, and indeed, many of the ideas in this domain, were launched by Noam Chomsky about 40 years ago, and work in this area continues to be shaped by his theorizing. See, for example, Chomsky, 1957, 1965; for reviews of how the theory has evolved, see Cook, 1988; Riemsdijk & Williams, 1986.)

## TRACE THEORY

A sentence's underlying structure cannot be observed directly. Instead, this structure is *inferred* from various patterns in the surface structure. To see how this works, let's consider an example.

Linguists generally argue that questions are formed by moving an element out of a sentence's underlying

structure and replacing that element with the appropriate "wh-" word. For example, the question "What did he give?" is derived from an underlying structure that looks something like "He did give X." In the surface structure, "what" has replaced the "place holder" that used to reside in the position appropriate for the sentence's direct object. Similarly, the proposition "He will go to X" is the basis for "Where will he go?" In this case, "where" has replaced a place holder that used to reside in the position appropriate for the object of the preposition "to."

Figure 10.10 illustrates roughly how this swapping of elements takes place. What is shown on the left is a representation of the sentence's underlying structure, created in accordance with the phrase-structure rules. The movement rules then govern how these elements are shifted around to create the surface structure shown on the right.

This claim has a number of interesting consequences. For example, since we are moving elements from one position to another, there is no way an element could end up in both places at once. Hence, we will never end up with strings such as

What will she see an animal?

or

Who will he speak to some guy?

In these, an element has both moved out of its initial position and remained in its initial position. Since these strings are obviously ungrammatical, it is entirely appropriate that they can't be produced by our transformational scheme.

In addition, when an element vacates a position to move somewhere else, it doesn't depart cleanly. Instead, it leaves a **trace** behind—much as a burglar sometimes leaves footprints, indicating where he has been. The trace isn't expressed out loud, but it is evident in the speech pattern. As one way to demonstrate this, we can exploit the fact that speech is often filled with contractions. For example, these words.

I want to go to bed.

are usually pronounced as

---

[2]Older texts refer to the underlying structure as the "deep structure" and to the movement rules as "transformations."

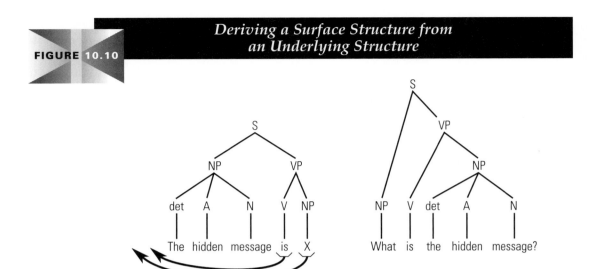

**FIGURE 10.10**

## Deriving a Surface Structure from an Underlying Structure

The panel on the right shows the phrase structure for the surface form of the question. This surface structure was derived, however, from the phrase structure shown on the left. The arrows indicate how the elements of this (underlying) d-structure have been moved around, in order to create the (surface) s-structure.

I wanna go to bed.

This contraction—from "want to" to "wanna"—is possible only if the word "want" appears in the sentence right alongside the word "to." You can't contract "want to" in this next sentence, because the two crucial words aren't adjacent:

I want Jacob to go to bed.

This sentence can't become "I wanna Jacob go to bed." The contraction, in other words, is blocked if anything appears between the "want" and the "to." With that said, we are ready for traces.

Consider the sentence

I want Sol to have the next turn.

From this, we can create the question

Who do you want to have the next turn?

Notice that in this question "want" and "to" *seem* adjacent to each other, and so contraction should be possible. But it isn't. If you read this question out loud, you are likely to pronounce "want" with a clear /t/ on the end. You won't pronounce it this way:

Who do you wanna have the next turn?

Why is this? In the base sentence, "Sol" appeared between "want" and "to." When this word was removed, to create the question, it left a trace behind. Therefore, in the question, "want" and "to" *aren't* adjacent, even though they seem to be. Instead, there is a trace in between them, and this blocks the contraction.

Traces can also be detected in a variety of other ways. For example, if we measure the electrical activity of the brain, moment by moment, we discover a shift in the electrical pattern the moment a listener reaches the trace—as if the listener were saying: "Aha—*here* is where the moved element belongs!" (For this and related evidence, see Chomsky, 1981; Kluender & Kutas, 1993; MacDonald, 1989; Nicol & Swinney, 1989.)

Traces thus allow us to document that elements in a sentence have been moved around, and more important, they show us where the elements have been moved from. This in turns establishes the point we are after: Questions are not formed simply by running through the appropriate phrase-structure rules. Instead, questions are formed by moving elements around in a tree structure—all in accord with the movement rules.

## LINGUISTIC UNIVERSALS

Let's pause to take stock. We have slowly climbed up the linguistic hierarchy—from subphonemic features (like voicing or place of articulation) to phonemes, from there to morphemes, then to words, and finally, to full sentences. At each step, we have seen how linguistic elements can be combined to create larger and more sophisticated linguistic units. In the process, we have seen how a relatively small number of elements can be used to create a vast (and, at some levels, infinite) number of combinations.

We have argued, though, that these combinations are rule-governed, with the rules visible in a number of ways. Thus, some combinations of elements are permitted by the rules; others are not. In addition, the rules often impose a *structure* on our linguistic products; this was evident, for example, in our discussion of phrase-structure rules. In still other cases, we detect the operation of the rules by virtue of the "traces" the rules' operation leaves behind. In one fashion or another, though, the rules do leave their mark, and in this way we can discover the rules.

It seems unquestionable that these rules capture some striking regularities—in the patterns of language we accept and the patterns we reject. Indeed, many of these regularities hold up even if we consider other languages, such as Japanese and Turkish, Mayan, Walbiri, and Kivunjo. To describe these other lan-

guages, we need to adjust the rules in small ways, by shifting a "parameter" or two. With that done, though, the rules do seem to hold. Thus, some have argued that these rules constitute **linguistic universals**—that is, they are applicable to every human language (after Chomsky, 1965, 1975, 1986; see also Comrie, 1981; Cook, 1988; Greenberg, Ferguson & Moravcsik, 1978; Hawkins, 1988).

The proposed universals are of various sorts. Some are framed in terms of probabilities. Thus, in all the world's languages, some sequences of words are quite common, while other sequences are quite rare. As an example, it is possible in English to put a sentence's object *before* the sentence's subject ("A bear he shot."), but this isn't the normal pattern for English—the normal pattern, instead, is subject then verb then object. And it is not only English that shows this pattern: The subject of a sentence tends to precede the object in roughly 98% of the world's languages. The sequence of subject before verb is preferred in roughly 80% of the world's languages. (Cf. Crystal, 1987.)

Most universals, though, concern linguistic features that seem to come and go together. Thus, for example, if a language's preferred word order is subject-object-verb, the language is likely to form its questions by adding some words at the *end* of the question. If, in contrast, a language's preferred sequence is subject-verb-object (as in English), then the language will place its question words at the *beginning* of the question (as in, *Where* did he . . . ? *When* did they . . . ?).

The existence of these linguistic universals opens an intriguing possibility: Consider the fact that every human child learns how to speak. Indeed, children acquire language rather rapidly. A two-year-old's linguistic skills are quite limited; a four-year-old, in contrast, speaks perfectly well. Hence, the learning process is somehow compressed into a period lasting just a couple of years. Moreover, what is learned seems quite complex—with rules governing the combinations of phonemes and different rules governing the combinations of morphemes, and phrase-structure rules and movement rules. Finally, bear in mind that we have already considered evidence that language is not learned via simple imitation or via instruction by the parents. (Many considerations rule out these possibilities, including the over-regularization errors we considered earlier in the chapter.) How, then, is language learning possible?

A number of scholars have argued that language learning is possible only because the child enters this process with an enormous head start: a biological heritage that (somehow) stipulates the broad outline of human language. In this view, the child might begin the process already knowing the universal rules of language. The process of language learning would therefore be a process of figuring out exactly how the rules are realized within the language community in which the child is raised. The child might actually begin with some complex "language machinery," so that the process of learning is a process of adjusting the "switches" on this machinery so that the child ends up speaking Portuguese instead of Urdu, or Swedish instead of Mandarin. This seems a plausible account of language learning, with the plausibility deriving from the fact that many of the rules we have discussed do seem, with the appropriate adjustments of parameters, universal. (For further discussion of these suggestions, see Bloom, 1994; Hyams, 1986.)

## Sentence Parsing

What about linguistic *performance*? So far we have focused on linguistic *judgments*, but how do we actually manage to comprehend the speech (or printed language) that we encounter?

As we have discussed, a sentence's phrase structure conveys crucial information about who did what to whom. Thus, once you know the phrase structure, you are well on your way to understanding the sentence. But how do you figure out the phrase structure in the first place? This would be an easy question if sentences were uniform in their structure: "The boy hit the ball. The girl chased the cat. The elephant trampled the geraniums." But, of course, sentences are vastly more variable than this,

and this makes the identification of a sentence's phrase structure appreciably more difficult.

How, therefore, do you **parse** a sentence—that is, figure out each word's syntactic role? One possibility is that you wait until the sentence's end, and only then go to work on figuring out the sentence's structure. With this strategy, your comprehension might be slowed a little (because of the wait for the sentence's termination), but you would avoid errors, since your interpretation could be guided by full information about the sentence's content.

A different possibility is that you parse the sentence as you are hearing it, trying to figure out the role of each word the moment you hear the word. This might be more efficient (since there's no waiting), but will sometimes lead to error, in ways that we will describe in a moment.

Evidence favors the latter view; this turns out, therefore, to be one more case in which humans favor a strategy that is efficient but occasionally misleading, in comparison to a strategy that is less efficient, but more accurate. (For other illustrations of this sort of trade-off, see Chapter 3, 7, 9, and 12.) One form of evidence comes from studies in which participants are shown sentences one word at a time. For example, they might see the word "The" on a computer screen then, a moment later, "Chinese," then "who," and so forth through the sentence. Crucially, though, we allow the participants to set the pace for the presentation, pressing a key as soon as they are ready for the next word. Figure 10.11 shows the pattern of their key presses: They look at "The" for 800 msec or so before requesting the next word; they look at "Chinese" for about a full second before requesting the next word, and so on.

Note that the pattern of "scallops" in these results corresponds reasonably well to the sentence's phrase structure: The moment the participants see "who," for example, they realize that they are beginning a relative clause, and race swiftly forward to see the other words in that clause. The moment they see "used," they know they are beginning a verb phrase, and move quickly on to pick up the other words in that phrase. Then, a bit later, the moment they see "kites," they realize they have completed the relative

**The Pace at Which Language Comprehension Proceeds**

**FIGURE** 10.11

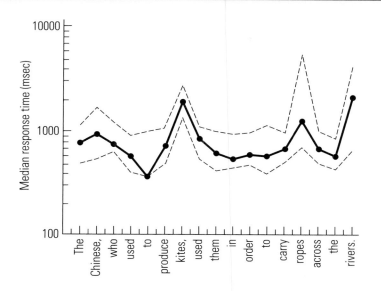

Participants were shown the sentence, "The Chinese, who used to produce kites . . . ," one word at a time. The pace of presentation, however, was controlled by the participants, with participants pressing a key, as they read, each time they felt ready for the next word. The key presses come quickly when participants are in the middle of the phrase; the key presses are slower at the phrase boundaries (e.g., just after the word "kites"). This probably reflects the fact that, at the phrase boundaries, participants are pausing to "assemble" the words they have heard so far, and request the next word only after they have finished this "assembly."

clause, and they pause at this point to compile and integrate what they have read so far (Stine, 1990; also Aaronson & Scarborough, 1977).

This strategy of "compile as you go" is also reflected in the pattern of *difficulties* people have in comprehending some sentences. We have already mentioned that sentences can sometimes be ambiguous. Several examples of ambiguity were provided in Figure 10.9, but let's note that even common sentences can be ambiguous if one is open-minded (or perverse) enough:

Mary had a little lamb. (But I was quite hungry, so I had the lamb and also a bowl of soup.)

Time flies like an arrow. (But fruit flies, in contrast, like a banana.)

*Temporary* ambiguity is also common *inside* a sentence. More precisely, the early part of a sentence is often open to multiple interpretations, but then the later part of the sentence clears things up:

The old man the ships.

In this sentence, one tends to read the initial phrase as a three-word noun phrase—"the old man." However, this interpretation leaves the sentence with no verb. A different interpretation is demanded by the rest of the sentence, with the subject of the sentence being "the old" and with "man" as the verb. Likewise:

> The secretary applauded for his efforts was soon promoted.

Here one tends to read "applauded" as the sentence's main verb but, of course, it isn't. Instead, this sentence is just a shorthand way of answering the question: "Which secretary was soon promoted?" (Answer: "The one who was applauded for his efforts.")

These last two examples are referred to as **garden-path sentences**: You are initially led to one interpretation (you are, as they say, "led down the garden path"), but this interpretation then turns out to be *wrong*. Hence, you need to reject your initial construal and seek an alternative. Here are two more examples:

> Fat people eat accumulates.

> Because he ran the second mile went quickly.

Garden-path sentences highlight the fact that the "compile as you go" strategy is indeed risky. Sometimes the information you need in order to clear up an ambiguity arrives only late in the sentence. To avoid an interpretive dead-end, therefore, you would be well advised to remain neutral about the sentence's interpretation until you've gathered enough information. But this is not what you do. Instead, you commit yourself fairly early to one interpretation and then try to "fit" subsequent words, as they arrive, into that interpretation. This strategy is probably an efficient one more often than not, but it does lead to the "double take" reaction when late-arriving information forces you to abandon your interpretive efforts so far. (For more on this interpret-as-you-go tendency see Just & Carpenter, 1987, 1992; Marslen-Wilson & Tyler, 1987; Morton, 1969, 1970; Sedivy et al., 1999.)

We can also use garden-path sentences as a research tool: What is it that leads us down the garden path? Why do we initially choose one interpretation, one parsing, rather than another? As we will see in a moment, garden-path sentences provide us with a useful means of addressing these questions.

## SYNTAX AS A GUIDE TO PARSING

People use a bundle of different strategies in parsing the sentences they encounter. For one, we tend to assume, in general, that we will be hearing or reading *active* sentences rather than *passive*, and so we tend to interpret a sentence's initial noun phrase as the "doer" of the action not the recipient. As it happens, English speakers do use the active form more often than the passive (Svartik, 1966), and so this assumption is correct more often than not. However, this assumption works against us whenever we do encounter a passive sentence and, as a result, active sentences are somewhat easier to understand than are passive sentences (e.g., Hornby, 1974; Slobin, 1966).

Let's pause briefly, though, to add a note of caution to this claim: Some style books offer a blanket injunction against passive sentences, arguing that the passive should always be avoided. This is bad advice. The assumption of active voice is only *one* of the factors that guides parsing. In some contexts, therefore, with other factors on the scene, passive sentences can be *easier* to understand, not harder. (For discussion, see Pinker, 1994.)

What are the other factors guiding parsing? It is not surprising that parsing is also influenced by the little function words that appear in a sentence and also by the various morphemes that signal syntactic role (cf. Bever, 1970). One quickly grasps the structure of "He gliply rivtched the flidget." That's because the "-ly" ending indicates that "glip" is an adverb; the "-ed" ending identifies "rivtch" as a verb; and "the" signals that "flidget" is a noun—all excellent cues to the sentence's structure.

In addition, parsing seems to be guided by a number of other strategies, including an assumption of so-called **minimal attachment**. Roughly, this means that the listener or reader proceeds through a sentence seeking the simplest possible phrase structure that will accommodate the words heard so far. Consider the earlier sentence, "The secretary applauded for his efforts was soon promoted." As you read "The secretary applauded," you had the option of interpreting this as a noun phrase plus the beginning of a separate clause modifying "secretary." This is, of course, the *correct* construal and is demanded by the way the sentence ends. However, the principle of minimal attachment led you to ignore this possibility, at least initially, and to proceed instead with a simpler interpretation—of a noun phrase + verb, with no idea of a separate embedded clause.

The "secretary" sentence also capitalizes on some other factors. The embedded clause is in the passive voice (the secretary was applauded by someone else); your tendency to assume active voice, therefore, worked against the correct interpretation of this sentence. Likewise, this sentence deliberately omits the helpful function words. Notice that we *didn't* say, "The secretary *who was* applauded . . ."

With all these factors stacked against you, no wonder you were led to the incorrect construal. Indeed, with all these factors in place, garden-path sentences can sometimes be enormously difficult to comprehend. For example, spend a moment puzzling over this (fully grammatical) sequence:

The horse raced past the barn fell.

(If you get stuck with this sentence, try adding commas after "horse" and after "barn.")

## SEMANTICS AS A GUIDE TO PARSING

The "secretary" sentence was also complicated by one further factor: The sentence said, "The secretary applauded for *his* efforts . . ." Many people assume, in reading this sentence, that the secretary is a woman, hence "his" must refer to someone else. The suggestion, therefore, is that parsing is also guided by *semantic* factors, and not just syntax, and this turns out to be correct.

For example, we have already noted that, in general, it is easier to understand active sentences than it is to understand the corresponding passive sentence. However, this is only true if the sentence is "reversible," such as "The dog chased the cat." This

sentence is considered reversible because the opposite sentence ("The cat chased the dog") also makes sense. This is in contrast to sentences such as "The elephant squashed the peanut." This sentence isn't reversible: Elephants can certainly squash peanuts, but peanuts can't squash elephants. In this case, therefore, you don't need the syntax to figure out who was the squasher and who was the squashed. And, indeed, for sentences like this, there is no processing advantage for the active form, relative to the passive (Slobin, 1966).

In addition, listeners and readers also seem sensitive to certain statistical properties in the language. If a word has several meanings, you tend to assume its most frequent meaning whenever you encounter the word. You therefore tend to assume that "train" means the thing on tracks rather than the activity one engages in to teach tricks to a dog. Likewise, you tend to assume that "tree" refers to a type of plant, rather than an activity (as in "The hounds want to tree the raccoon"). Similarly, we tend to assume that adjectives, when they occur, will be followed by nouns. This isn't an obligatory pattern, but it is certainly a frequent pattern, and so the assumption seems safe.

Once again, we can see these factors in action in some of the garden-path sentences: The assumption of adjective-noun gets us in trouble when we encounter "Fat people eat accumulates." Likewise, our reliance on frequent meanings is part of our problem in understanding sentences like "The old man ships," or "The new train quickly, but the old train more slowly."

## THE EXTRALINGUISTIC CONTEXT

It's rare that we encounter a single, isolated sentence. Instead, sentences are uttered in some context, and the context can provide important aids for sentence parsing and sentence understanding. Thus, the garden-path problem is much less likely to occur in the following setting:

Luke: Which horse fell?

Emma: The horse raced past the barn fell.

The **extralinguistic context** (factors outside of the language itself) is also important. To see how, consider the following sentence:

Put the apple on the towel into the box.

For many people, this sentence causes a temporary false interpretation. Early on, it seems to be an instruction to put an apple onto a towel; this understanding must be abandoned, though, when the words "into the box" arrive. Now listeners realize that the box is the apple's destination; "on the towel" is simply a specification of which apple is to be moved. (Which apple should be put into the box? The one that is on the towel.) In short, this is another example of a garden-path sentence—initially inviting one analysis, but eventually demanding another.

This confusion would be avoided, however, if this sentence were uttered in the appropriate setting. Imagine that two apples are in view, one on a towel, and one not (Figure 10.12). In this context, a listener would immediately see the possibility for confusion (which apple is being referred to?) and so would expect the speaker to specify which apple is to be moved. (After all, the speaker can also see the possibility for confusion and presumably wishes to be clear.) When the phrase "on the towel" is uttered, then, the listener immediately and quite naturally understands it (correctly) as the needed specification. Hence, there is no confusion and no garden path.

Of course, there are also *linguistically* unambiguous ways to express this message, such as "Put the apple that is on the towel into the box." But this example illustrates the fact that sometimes *extralinguistic factors* can be as useful as clear syntax (Eberhard et al., 1995; Tanenhaus & Spivey-Knowlton, 1996).

**FIGURE 10.12**

*The Extra Linguistic Context*

*"Put the apple on the towel into the box."* Without the setting shown here, this sentence causes momentary confusion as the listener comes across "on the towel" before grasping the greater context of "into the box." But when simultaneously presented with this picture, the listener finds "on the towel" useful in clearing up the ambiguity of "the apple."

## INTERACTIONS BETWEEN SYNTAX AND SEMANTICS

We have now seen that many different factors contribute to parsing. But how do all these factors combine? One possibility is that all of your knowledge is simultaneously brought to bear on a sentence. This would be a powerful procedure, since you would have a variety of resources to draw on as you parsed any bit of language. Semantic considerations would guide syntactic analyses, and syntactic considerations would guide semantic analyses. This position is referred to as an **interactionist** view (cf. Tyler & Marslen-Wilson, 1977).

A different possibility is that one uses different sources of information at different points in parsing a sentence. One might first attempt to analyze the sentence's syntax, uninfluenced by semantic considerations. With that done, one then brings semantic knowledge to bear. In this **modular** scheme, each individual stage seems less powerful, but stages might end up more streamlined, with less information to juggle, and so the stages might function more swiftly (cf. Fodor, 1983, 1985; Garfield, 1987).

The choice between these two approaches has been a matter of considerable debate, and much of the research has, again, relied on garden-path sentences. Consider this example:

> The defendant examined by the lawyer turned out
> to be unreliable.

In reading this sentence, people initially interpret "examined" as a verb in the active voice, with the defendant doing the examining. When they reach the word "by," though, they realize their error, and recompute. (This is evident either in their reading speed or in their eye movements.)

But now consider this sentence:

> The evidence examined by the lawyer turned out to
> be unreliable.

The syntax of this sentence is identical to that of the "defendant" sentence. But now common sense tells us that "examined" can't be in the active voice, since "evidence" isn't capable of examining anything. And,

in fact, common sense prevents the garden-path misreading from occurring: People march smoothly past the word "by," apparently having assumed from the start that "examined" was a past participle, not an active verb. Thus, it seems that moment-by-moment, word-by-word, parsing *is* influenced by semantics. (Cf. Tanenhaus, Spivey-Knowlton, Eberhard & Sedivy, 1995; Pickering & Traxler, 1999. But also see MacDonald et al., 1994; McElree & Griffith, 1995; Mecklinger, Schriefers, Steinhauer, & Fridererici, 1995; Trueswell, Tanenhaus & Kello, 1995. For neuropsychological data bearing on these issues, see Breedin & Saffran, 1999.)

This suggests that the interactionist perspective provides a better fit with the facts, since the syntactic analysis of a sentence does seem to be guided by semantic considerations. The picture may be different, though, if we consider the process of *word identification*. According to the interactionist view, the process of interpreting the individual words in a sentence should be interwoven with the process of integrating the various words to form coherent phrases. According to a modular view, however, these two processes—identifying individual words and then integrating them—should be separate and independent. It turns out that the modular view is closer to the truth.

For example, the word "bug" can mean a sort of insect, or it can mean a hidden microphone. Only one of these meanings is plausible, though, in this context:

> Rumor had it that, for years, the government
> building had been plagued with problems. The man
> was not surprised when he found several spiders,
> roaches, and other bugs in the corner of his room.

Do listeners use this context, as they go, to identify the meaning of "bug"? Or are they initially neutral, or uncertain, about what this word means? The first outcome would be consistent with the interactionist perspective; the second outcome would favor a modular view.

Swinney (1979) probed these issues with a lexical-decision task. (We first encountered this task in Chapter 8.) Research participants heard tape-recorded sentences like the "Rumor had it . . ." sequence just quoted. Right after the word "bugs," though, a computer flashed a string of letters on a screen, and participants had to report, as quickly as they could, whether the string was a legitimate word or not. In some trials, the string "ant" was presented, and participants' responses to this string were quite fast. Apparently, then, the sentences they were hearing had served to *prime* the idea of bug-as-type-of-insect, and this priming had spread to the word "ant." But priming was also observed for the word "spy," and so responses to this word were reliably faster than responses to an independent control word (such as "sew"). It would seem, therefore, that the presentation of "bug" had also activated the idea of bug-as-hidden-microphone, despite the fact that this interpretation of bug is ruled out by the context.

Things were different if the lexical-decision task was delayed slightly. Thus, for example, participants might again hear the "Rumor had it . . ." sequence, but this time the test word was presented right after participants heard "corner"—i.e., a few syllables *after* "bugs." In this condition, priming *was* observed for "ant" (as before) but was *not* observed for "spy."

What is happening here? When the word "bugs" is heard, it seems to call to mind *both* the (appropriate) idea of bug-as-type-of-insect *and* the (inappropriate) idea of bug-as-hidden-microphone. Hence, the initial activation is insensitive to the context, and so we are here seeing evidence for a modular process, with the processes of word identification *not* influenced by participants' understanding of the surrounding words. A moment later, though, participants have had a chance to "digest" the surrounding context and to integrate this context with their "bug" thoughts. The inappropriate idea, bug-as-hidden-microphone, is somehow "turned off," and so it ceases the priming of the related idea, "spy." In effect, the word-identification process is initially quite "open-minded" but, a moment later, it makes its selection and "shuts down" all ideas but one. (For related data, see Beeman & Chiarello, 1998; Onifer & Swinney, 1981; Seidenberg, Tanenhaus, Leiman & Bienkowski, 1982; Simpson, 1984. For discussion of related phenomena, see May, Kane & Hasher, 1995. For some *contrary* data, however, see

Vu, Kellas, Metcalf & Herman, 2000, and the various papers summarized by Vu et al.)

## THE USE OF LANGUAGE: WHAT IS LEFT UNSAID

Earlier in this chapter, we argued that a rich set of rules is needed to explain why some sound combinations, some words, and some sentences seem acceptable to speakers of a language, while others do not. These rules must be acquired by anyone who wishes to learn a language; indeed, these rules are a part of what it means "to know a language."

As we have now seen, we need a further set of principles to account for how the language is perceived and understood—either by the listener or by the reader. Several different syntactic principles seem relevant, as do several different semantic principles. These factors then interact in an intricate fashion—with some bits of semantic knowledge penetrating into syntactic processing, but with other aspects of processing proceeding in a modular fashion.

Note, though, that this brief overview surely *understates* the complexity of sentence parsing. For one thing, we have said nothing about how one deals with *pronouns*, as in

Fred went swimming; Sam played tennis; later he napped.

Who napped? Here, a principle of "recency" seems crucial, and most people believe that it is Sam who napped. In other cases, though, other principles come into play:

Susan waved at Maria, but then she insulted her.

Who insulted whom? Here it is grammatical role that seems to matter, so that "she," the subject of the second phrase, seems to refer to "Susan," the subject of the first phrase. In short, then, we will need still other principles to deal with pronouns. (For a fuller treatment of pronouns, see Gordon & Scearce, 1995; Just & Carpenter, 1987.)

We have also not mentioned a further source of information useful in parsing: the rise and fall of speech intonation and the pattern of pauses. These rhythm and pitch cues are together called **prosody** and play an important role in speech perception. Prosody can reveal the mood of a speaker; it can also direct the listener's attention by, in effect, specifying the focus or theme of a sentence (Jackendoff, 1972). Prosody can also render unambiguous a sentence that would otherwise be entirely confusing (Beach, 1991). (Thus, garden-path sentences and ambiguous sentences are much more effective in print, where prosody provides no information.)

Finally, we have not even touched on several related puzzles. For one, how is language *produced*? How does one turn ideas, intentions, and queries into actual sentences? How does one turn the sentences into sequences of sounds? These are important issues, but for brevity's sake, we have held them to the side here. (For a tutorial review of these issues, see Dell et al., 1997; Fromkin, 1993.)

Likewise, what happens *after* one has parsed and understood an individual sentence? How is the sentence integrated with earlier sentences or subsequent sentences? Here, too, more theory is needed to explain the inferences we routinely make in ordinary conversation. If you are asked, "Do you know the time?" you understand this as a request that you *tell* the time—despite the fact that the question, understood literally, is a yes/no question about the extent of your temporal knowledge. In the same vein, consider this bit of conversation (after Pinker, 1994):

Woman: "I'm leaving you."

Man: "Who is he?"

We easily provide the soap-opera script that lies behind this exchange, but we do so by drawing on a rich set of further knowledge, including knowledge of **pragmatics** (that is, knowledge of how language is ordinarily used) and, in this case, also knowledge about the vicissitudes of romance. (For discussion, see Austin, 1962; Ervin-Tripp, 1993; Graesser et al., 1997; Grice, 1975; Hilton, 1995; Kumon-Nakamura, Glucksberg & Brown, 1995; Sperber & Wilson, 1986.)

If you are intrigued by the topic of language, then these topics—pronouns, prosody, production, and pragmatics—certainly warrant further exploration.

For our purposes, though, this fast mention of these topics merely serves to lend emphasis to a central message of this chapter: Each of us uses language all the time—to learn, to gossip, to instruct, to persuade, to express affection. We use this tool as easily as we breathe; we spend more effort in choosing our clothes in the morning than we do in choosing the words we will utter. But these observations must not hide the fact that language is a remarkably complicated tool, and we are all exquisitely skilled in its use.

## The Biology of Language

How is all of this possible? How is it that ordinary human beings—indeed, ordinary two-and-a-half-year-olds—manage the extraordinary task of mastering and fluently using language? We have already suggested part of the answer: Humans are equipped with extremely sophisticated neural machinery, specialized for learning, and then using, language. Let's take a quick look at this machinery.

### APHASIAS

Much of what we know about the neural basis for language comes from the study of brain damage. As we have seen in other chapters, brain damage can cause a variety of effects, depending on where and how widespread the damage is. For a number of brain sites, though, damage causes disruption of language—a disruption known as **aphasia**.

Aphasias take many different forms and are often quite specialized, with the specific symptoms observed largely dependent on the locus of the brain damage. It should be said, however, that this correspondence between brain location and type of aphasia is somewhat rough, since two patients with similar brain damage will sometimes show very different forms of aphasia. This probably reflects the fact that the hunk of brain tissue supporting any particular function is anatomically quite small; moreover, the bits of brain tissue needed for a function may be anatomically interlaced with brain tissue involved in some other function. Therefore, if the zone of damage extends just a few neurons further on one patient than it does on another, this may have a large impact on the pattern of damage observed. This is why it is often difficult to discern a precise relation between site of damage and nature of symptoms.

Nonetheless, the study of aphasias has allowed us to locate many brain regions crucially involved in the production and comprehension of language. For example, damage to the left frontal lobe of the brain (see Figure 10.13) produces a pattern known as **Broca's aphasia**, in which patients show relatively good language *comprehension* but disrupted *production*. Moreover, the speech they produce is "agrammatic": They produce strings of nouns and (to a lesser extent) verbs, but with none of the function words ("of," "to," "by"), and with no inflections (e.g., no marking of plural, no marking of verb tense).

In contrast, damage in another area produces **Wernicke's aphasia**. Patients with this disorder seem largely unable to *comprehend* speech, but the speech that they produce sounds effortless and fluent, with the function words and the appropriate suffixes all correctly in place. As it turns out, though, their speech makes no sense. Here is a quotation from a patient with Wernicke's aphasia (after Gardner, 1974):

> Oh sure, go ahead, any old think you want. If I could I would. Oh I'm taking the word the wrong way to say, all of the barbers here whenever they stop you it's going around and around, if you know what I mean, that is tying and tying for repucer, repuceration, well, we were trying the best that we could while another time it was with the beds over there the same thing . . .

Still other aphasics show a pattern called **echolalia**: They turn into virtual echo-boxes, able to repeat back anything they hear. However, these patients show no sign of understanding the speech they are echoing, nor do they produce speech on their own. Other patients show yet another pattern, with brain damage causing disruption to their "mental dictionary." These patients suffer from **anomia** and lose the ability to *name* various objects. Anomias can

be extraordinarily specific: Some patients can use concrete nouns but not abstract nouns; some can name animate objects but not inanimate ones; some patients lose the ability to name colors. Still other patients show a pattern called "pure word deafness." These patients can speak, write, and read normally, and they can hear perfectly well, but they can't make any sense out of the language they hear. (For descriptions of the various aphasias, see Caplan, 1987, 1992; Dingwall, 1993; Gabrieli, 1998; Hillis & Caramazza, 1991.)

The specificity of these disorders seems to imply that separate "processing units" are responsible for this or that particular chore, within the larger scheme of producing and understanding language. By close examination of these patients, researchers hope that they will be able to characterize each "processing unit" and then, eventually, understand how the units work together for intact language use.

Our prospects for reaching this goal have been substantially enhanced in recent years through new evidence provided by neuroimaging data. As we described in Chapter 2, neuroimaging allows us to examine the functioning of normal (undamaged) brains, and in fact, PET and fMRI techniques strongly confirm the claims derived from the study of aphasia. For example, we have noted that damage to Wernicke's area produces an inability to comprehend speech. Consistent with this, we find strong activation in the Wernicke's area in people (without brain damage) who have been asked to make simple judgments about words (e.g., Peterson, Fox, Posner, Mintern & Raichle, 1989; Peterson, Fox, Snyder & Raichle, 1990). Similarly, we have noted that the speech of Broca's aphasics is highly agrammatic. This lines up nicely with the finding that Broca's area, in an intact brain, is particularly activated by tasks that require grammatical processing—e.g., telling a story or understanding complicated sentences (e.g., Caplan, 1992). In short, then, we have ample evidence that specific sections of the brain are, indeed, specialized for one or another aspect of language use. This is clearly the message of the aphasia evidence; it is plainly reflected in studies recording the activity of intact, healthy brains.

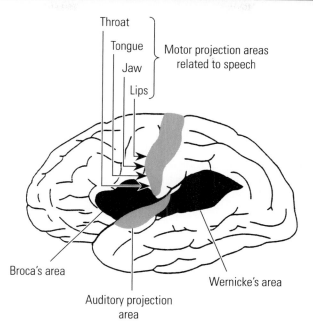

**Brain Areas Crucial for the Perception and Production of Language**

FIGURE 10.13

Throat
Tongue
Jaw
Lips

Motor projection areas related to speech

Broca's area

Auditory projection area

Wernicke's area

Many different brain regions are involved in the ordinary understanding or production of language. Many of these regions, however, are positioned close together; for most individuals, these regions are in the left cerebral hemisphere (as shown here). Broca's area is heavily involved in language production; Wernicke's area plays a crucial role in language comprehension.

## CONSIDERATIONS FROM LANGUAGE LEARNING

Further evidence for the biological roots of language come from studies of *language learning*. As we have mentioned, virtually all humans learn language, and they learn it very quickly: By the age of 3 or 4, virtually every child is reasonably competent in communicating her wishes and desires, and for that matter, in communicating fairly sophisticated beliefs.

It is also noteworthy that language learning proceeds in a (roughly) normal way in an astonishingly wide range of environments. Children who talk a lot with adults learn language, and so do children who

talk very little with adults. Children who are blind learn language, and so do children who are deaf. In some cases, deaf children learn sign language from their caretakers and peers. In other cases, this is not an option (for example, because the children's caretakers don't know how to use sign language). Even in these cases, though, language emerges: The children *invent* their own gestural language, and the language they invent shows many parallels to ordinary language. Their invented language has many of the formal structures routinely seen in the world's existing languages, and the pattern of "emergence" for these invented languages follows the same sequence as that observed in ordinary language learning (Feldman et al., 1978; Goldin-Meadow & Feldman, 1977; Senghas et al., 1997).

These (and other) observations make it clear that language is not "learned" in any simple way. Earlier in the chapter, we noted that language learning contains elements that cannot be explained as mere imitation and elements that cannot be explained in terms of explicit instruction to the child. The facts we have now considered lead us to a stronger claim: In a sense, language is not learned at all. Instead, language may be invented by the child, and so is truly a product of the human mind.

All of this suggests that language really is rooted in the biology of the human brain—and so learning to talk is as natural (and as inevitable) as learning to walk or to run. Further confirmation for this claim comes from evidence that underscores the *specialization* of brain areas responsible for language learning. Specifically, individuals with an apparently inherited syndrome known as *specific language impairment* are generally slow to learn language, and throughout their lives, they have difficulty in understanding and producing many sentences. Yet these individuals seem normal on most other measures, including measurements of intelligence (Tallal, Ross & Curtiss, 1989; Pinker, 1994). Apparently, then, their deficit lies in brain areas specifically responsible for learning language; this deficit does not cause problems in other arenas. We can also find cases with the reverse pattern—severe disruption of all mental capacities *except* language. Individuals with Williams Syndrome, for example, are severely mentally retarded (with IQ scores 40 points below the population average) but are still capable of fluent and articulate language (Bellugi et al., 1991; Pinker, 1995). Thus damage to brain regions specialized for language learning causes severe disruption of language; damage elsewhere in the brain can sometimes have little or no impact on language.

We can close this section, therefore, by circling back to a theme that was prominent at the chapter's start. We argued early on that language is something central to our species, and crucial for many of the activities our species engages in. As we have now seen, it is likewise clear that specializations for language are very much evident in the biology of our species, making it certain that, in an important sense, we are indeed linguistic creatures.

## LANGUAGE AND THOUGHT

One last topic will bring our consideration of psycholinguistics to a close. We have argued that the nature of language learning and, perhaps, the nature of language itself are both shaped by the biology of the human brain. In a sense, language takes the form it does because our brains are structured in a certain way. But what about the reverse: Is it possible that the language we speak shapes the way we think?

One frequently mentioned example concerns the number of terms for *snow* in Eskimo languages such as Aleut. This number is sometimes claimed to be as large as three hundred, with different terms for naming types of snow such as *powder, slush, ice,* and so on. The claim is then made that speakers of such languages are influenced by this extravagance of vocabulary and so end up able to make much finer distinctions among snow types than speakers of other languages.

But this example is flawed in several ways. The initial claim about vocabulary size is actually false; English turns out to have more snow-related terms than Aleut does (Pinker, 1995). Even if it were true that Aleut had more words for snow, would this explain why Aleut speakers are more sensitive to snow distinctions (if they are) than, say, English-speaking residents of Florida? A plausible alternative is that the Eskimos' day-to-day activities create a functional *need* for these discriminations, and this leads both to the larger vocabulary *and* to the greater skill in picking out different types of snow. According to this view, language does not shape perception. Instead, language *and* perception are both shaped by environment and culture.

Can we perhaps find better, more persuasive evidence for the claim that language influences thought? Some of the early evidence was offered by the anthropologist Benjamin Whorf, who was a strong proponent of the view that language categories force us into certain modes of thought (Whorf, 1956). The "results" Whorf offered, however, were quite weak. He tried to show, for example, that Hopi speakers think about time differently from English speakers, but his only evidence came from the ways that the Hopi *expressed themselves* when talking about different kinds of events. But this evidence is without value: Perhaps the Hopi think in just the same ways that English speakers do but express these thoughts differently because their language differs from English. In this case, the evidence indicates only that the way one expresses oneself is influenced by one's language—a conclusion that seems both unsurprising and not very interesting.

Still other investigators have asked whether our perception of color is shaped by the color vocabulary available in our language, and whether our perception of spatial position is influenced by the ways position is described in our language. The data do show some effects—for example, colors that are easier to name are easier to remember. But this is probably because participants are remembering the name, and not the color itself; there is no evidence that color vocabulary influences color perception (Brown & Lenneberg, 1954; Berlin & Key, 1969; Rosch, 1977b; Heider, 1972). Likewise, there is no persuasive evidence to show that the ways we *describe* space influence the ways we *perceive* or *think about* space (Landau & Munnich, 1998).

Overall, then, the evidence speaks against Whorf's claim that language deeply influences how we think, or what we *can* think. Nonetheless, Whorf's claim has a strong intuitive appeal for many people, and it seems worthwhile to ask why this is. Perhaps the intuition derives from the fact that language *does* guide our thoughts in some ways. For example, if a speaker says, "I saw a dog," this will of course lead the listener to a different idea than if the speaker had said, "I saw a cat." Or, as a more ambitious example, let's note that linguistic descriptions often provide a convenient way of coding, or chunking, information, with important consequences for memory (the process of chunking was discussed in Chapter 5). The way information is framed in language can also influ-

ence our decisions, so that a patient is more likely to choose a medical treatment if told that the treatment has a 50 percent chance of success than if told it has a 50 percent chance of failure (Chapter 13).

These various cases remind us that, in important ways, language does influence thought—by drawing attention to some points and away from others, by highlighting certain themes, by framing issues in a certain way. The mechanisms that underlie these effects are quite straightforward, but the effects are large, and language's influence on us is correspondingly large. Even so, let's emphasize that this influence is a far cry from the claims offered by Whorf a half-century ago. Whorf's argument was that language shapes what we *can* think, so that there are literally some ideas, for example, that a native Hopi speaker can contemplate but that a native French speaker cannot. There is no compelling evidence in favor of this stronger claim.

Throughout this chapter, we have emphasized how central language is in a range of human activities, and in a way, this forces us to *endorse* (one construal of) Whorf's claims: Language does influence us. Without language, we would be very different— as individuals, as a culture, as a species—than we are. But (and contrary to Whorf's claim) the *differences* from one language to the next seem not to lead to corresponding differences in thought. Perhaps this shouldn't be a surprise: We have emphasized the biological roots of language, with the structure of language and the nature of language *learning* very much influenced by the pattern of human biology. This biology is shared by all in our species, and so, as a result, the 4,000 or so languages used on this planet actually have an enormous amount in common. If language influences thought, therefore, it is likely to influence all people in the same way.

## Chapter Summary

1. All speech is built up from a few dozen *phonemes*; which phonemes are used varies from language to language. Phonemes in turn are built up from a small number of production features, includ-

ing *voicing, place of articulation*, and *manner of production*. Phonemes can be combined to form more complex sounds, but combinations are constrained by a number of rules.

2. Speech perception is more than a matter of detecting the relevant features in the input soundstream. The perceiver needs to deal with speaker to speaker variation in how sounds are produced; he also needs to *segment* the stream of speech, and cope with *coarticulation*. The process of speech perception is helped enormously by context, but we also have the impressive skill of *categorical perception*, which makes us keenly sensitive to differences between categories of speech sounds but insensitive to distinctions within each category.

3. People know many thousands of words, and, for each, they know the sound of the word, its syntactic role, and its *semantic* representation. This semantic knowledge includes knowledge about the word's *referent* and also the word's *sense*. Our understanding of words is also *generative*, allowing us to create limitless numbers of new words. Some new words are wholly made up ("geek"), but, more often, new words are created by combining morphemes. These combinations of morphemes, like the combinations of phonemes, are governed by rules. The rules are *descriptive*, not *prescriptive*, and are often best revealed by studies of *metalinguistic judgments* that display someone's *linguistic competence*, rather than by studies of their *linguistic performance*.

4. The *psychological reality* of language rules is suggested by many facts, including *over-regularization errors*. There is controversy over whether some representation of the rules is literally encoded in the mind, but there is no doubt that language use is highly creative but also highly constrained in a fashion that seems well described by rules.

5. The rules of *syntax* govern whether a sequence of words is grammatical. One set of rules is the *phrase-structure rules*, which can be understood as specifying how a sentence structure is created, or as specifying how an already existing sentence should be parsed. The word groups identified by phrase structure rules do correspond to natural groupings of words, and the phrase structure rules also guide interpretation. Phrase structure rules also specify groups of words that can be moved around as "modules"; this helps explain some of the interconnections among our linguistic judgments.

6. Phrase-structure rules generate a sentence's *underlying structure*, but then *movement rules* or *transformations* shift the elements around to create the sentence's *surface structure*. When an element is moved, it seems to leave a *trace* behind, and the trace can be detected in various ways, including the fact that the trace blocks some contractions.

7. To understand a sentence, a listener or reader needs to *parse* the sentence, determining each word's syntactic role. Evidence suggests that people parse the sentence as they see or hear each word, and this sometimes leads them into parsing errors that must be repaired later; this is revealed by *garden-path sentences*. Parsing is guided by syntax, semantics, and the *extralinguistic context*. These factors may interact so that all sources of guidance for parsing are used simultaneously.

8. The biological roots of language are revealed in many ways. The study of aphasias and neuroimaging data make it clear that some areas of the brain are specialized for learning and using language. The rapid learning of language, in a fashion dependent on neither imitation nor explicit instruction, also speaks to the biological basis for language; this rapid learning is certainly helped by the existence of *linguistic universals*, structural properties shared by all languages.

9. There has been considerable discussion about the ways in which thought might be shaped by the language one speaks. Language certainly guides and influences our thoughts, and the way a thought is formulated into words can have an effect on how fluently our thinking proceeds. However, no compelling evidence supports the stronger claim that the language we speak shapes what we can think.

# Visual Knowledge

In Chapter 10, we focused entirely on knowledge about language. In Chapters 8 and 9, we weren't focusing on language, but as it turns out, we were largely concerned with knowledge we might call "verbal"—knowledge that can be expressed in words. This knowledge probably *isn't* represented in the mind via words; we argued, in fact, for a different, more abstract mental code. Nonetheless, the knowledge we were describing could be readily translated into mental propositions with a "subject-predicate" format.

What about knowledge of other sorts? You know what ammonia smells like, as well as apple pie and strawberries. Knowledge of this sort is not readily verbalizable and is not in any obvious way translatable into propositions. How is this "smell knowledge" represented in the mind? Likewise, you remember the sound of a guitar or a fire-engine's siren; you know what Judy's voice sounds like, and you can recall how it contrasts with Barbara's. What can we say about this auditory knowledge? You also have visual memories, and memories for pains and for tastes. In each case, how is this nonverbal knowledge encoded in memory?

Psychologists have examined many of these types of knowledge—memory for odors (Algom & Cain, 1991; Gilbert et al., 1998; Lyman & McDaniel, 1990; Reed, 2000; Schab, 1990, 1991), for familiar voices (Van Lancker, Kreiman & Wickens, 1985; Van Lancker, Kreiman & Emmorey, 1985; Nairn & Pusen, 1984), for movements (Engelkamp, Zimmer, Mohr & Sellen, 1994), and for pain (Algom & Lubel, 1994; Eich, Reeves, Jaeger & Graff-Radford, 1985; Kahneman, Fredrickson, Schreiber & Redelmeier, 1993; Kent, 1985; Linton & Melin, 1982; Rachman & Eyrl, 1989), to name just a few.

In this chapter, we will explore this nonverbal knowledge, with our main emphasis on visual knowledge. We will ask how this knowledge is recorded in memory, and also how this knowledge is used. Several factors motivate this focus on visual knowledge, but the main consideration is straightforward: Far more is known about visual knowledge than about knowledge in any other modality. As we proceed, though, you should try to read this chapter on two different levels. At a concrete level, we will be surveying what is known about visual knowledge and visual imagery. At the same time, we will also be pursuing a broader agenda, as we seek to illustrate more generally how one can do research on nonverbal knowledge and what questions need to be asked about such knowledge.

## Visual Imagery

How many windows are there in your house or your apartment? Who has bushier eyebrows, Sylvester Stallone or Bill Clinton? For most people, questions like these seem to elicit "mental pictures." You know what Clinton and Stallone look like, and you call a "picture" of each before your "mind's eye" in order to make the comparison. Likewise, you call to mind a "map" of your apartment, and count the windows by inspecting this "map." Many people even trace the "map" in the air, by moving their finger around, following the imagined map's contours.

Various practical problems also seem to evoke images. There you are in the store, trying on a new sweater. Will the sweater look good with your blue pants? To decide, you will probably try to visualize the blue of the pants, thus using your "mind's eye" to ask how they will look with the sweater. Equivalently, there you are in the hardware store, hoping to fix your leaky faucet. Is this washer the right size? You will probably try to visualize what the old washer looked like, comparing it to the one in your hand. Or, as a different example, "Where did I leave my keys? Did I leave them on my desk?" I may try to decide by visualizing what my desk looked like when I left my office—were the keys in view?

These examples illustrate the common, everyday use of visual images—as a basis for making decisions, as an aid to remembering. But what are these images? Surely there is no tiny eye somewhere deep in your brain; thus the phrase "mind's eye" cannot be taken literally. Likewise, mental "pictures" cannot be actual pictures—with no eye deep inside the brain, who or what would inspect such pictures?

## INTROSPECTIONS ABOUT IMAGES

Mental images have been described and discussed for thousands of years. However, it is only within the last century or so that psychologists have begun to gather systematic data about imagery. Among the earliest researchers was Francis Galton, who asked various people to describe their images and to rate them for vividness (Galton, 1883). In essence, Galton asked his research participants to introspect, and to report on their own mental contents. The self-report data he obtained fit well with common sense: The participants reported that they could "inspect" their images much as they would inspect a picture. In their images, scenes were represented as if viewed from a certain position and a certain distance. They also reported that they could "read off" from the image details of color and of texture. All of this implies a mode of representation that is in many ways picture-like and is of course quite consistent with our informal manner of describing mental images as "pictures in the head," to be inspected with the "mind's eye."

There was also another side of Galton's data: Galton's participants differed widely from each other. Many described images of photographic clarity, rich in detail, almost as if they were *seeing* the imaged scene, rather than visualizing it. Other participants, however, reported very sketchy images, or no images at all. They were certainly able to think about the scenes or objects Galton named for them, but in no sense were they "seeing" these scenes. Their self-reports rarely included mention of color or size or viewing perspective; indeed, their reports were largely devoid of visual qualities.

These observations are in themselves interesting—do individuals really differ in the nature of their mental imagery? If so, what consequences does this have? Are there tasks that the "visualizers" can do better than the "non-visualizers" (or vice versa)? If so, this could provide crucial information about how visual imagery is used, and what it is good for.

Before we can answer these questions, though, we must address a methodological question raised by Galton's data, a question that we have met before: Can we take these self-reports at face value? Perhaps all of Galton's participants had the same imagery skill, but some were cautious in how they chose to describe their imagery, whereas others were more extravagant. In this way, Galton's data might reveal differences in how people *talk* about their imagery, rather than differences in the imagery *per se*. (For further discussion of this issue, see Chapters 1 and 15.)

These concerns highlight the difficulties inherent in self-report data. These data, by their nature, are always filtered through a person's verbal habits. What is revealed in the data, therefore, is not *imagery*. Instead, what is revealed is "imagery as the person elects to describe it." And there is always a danger that these descriptions will be misleading in some way, or incomplete, or perhaps just imprecise. What seems required is a more *objective* means of assessing imagery, one that does not rely on the subjectivity inherent in self-reports. With this more objective approach, we could assess the differences, from one individual to the next, evident in Galton's data. Indeed, with this more objective approach, we could hope to find out exactly what images *are*.

## CHRONOMETRIC STUDIES OF IMAGERY

One useful strategy would be to ask research participants to *do* something with their images—to read information off of them, or to manipulate them in some way—allowing us to measure how well they do. This more objective approach has characterized the last thirty years of imagery research, with much of this research drawing on a straightforward claim: Mental processes are relatively quick, but they do take some measurable amount of time. Even the simplest of decisions requires a quarter of a second or so (250 msec), and more complex decisions take correspondingly longer. This opens up an interesting research strategy for us: We can ask what factors slow down a task or speed it up; likewise, we can ask which variations of a task require slightly more time, and which require slightly less. We can then use this information to develop a theory about the mental processes and representations needed for task performance.

We can use this technique, for example, to ask what information is available in a mental image. What can people "read" from their images easily, and what can they read only with difficulty? These questions can provide important clues about the nature of imagery representation, but to understand the data, we need a bit of background: Think about how pictures themselves are different from verbal descriptions. Concretely, consider what would happen if you were asked to write a paragraph describing a cat. It seems likely that you would mention the distinctive features of cats—their claws, their whiskers, and so on. You probably would not include the fact that cats have heads, since this is too obvious to be worth mentioning. Now consider, in contrast, what would happen if we asked you to draw a sketch of a cat. In this format, the cat's head would be prominent, for the simple reason that the head is relatively large and up front. The claws and whiskers might be less salient, because these features are small, and so would not take up much space in the drawing.

The point here is that the pattern of what information is included, and what information is prominent, depends on the mode of presentation. For a *description* of a cat, size or position won't matter for prominence, but these factors will matter for a *depiction* of a cat. Conversely, distinctiveness and strength of association will heavily influence what is mentioned in a description; these factors matter less for a depiction.

Against this backdrop, let's now ask what information is available in a visual image. Is it the pictorially prominent features, which would imply a depictive mode of representation, or verbally prominent ones,

FIGURE 11.1

## Map of a Fictional Island Used in Image-Scanning Experiments

Participants in the study first memorized this map, including the various landmarks (the hut, the well, the patch of grass, and so on). They then formed a mental image of this map for the scanning procedure. [After Kosslyn, 1983.]

implying a descriptive mode? Self-reports about imagery surely indicate a picture-like representation; is this confirmed by the data?

In a study by Kosslyn (1976), participants were asked to form a series of mental images, and to answer yes/no questions about each. For example, they were asked to form a mental image of a cat, and then asked: Does the cat have a head? Does the cat have claws? Participants responded to these questions quickly but, strikingly, responses to the head question were quicker than those to the claws question. This suggests that information quickly available in the image follows the rules for pictures, not paragraphs. In contrast, a different group of participants was asked merely to think about cats (with no mention of imagery). These participants, asked the same questions, gave quicker responses to claws

than to head, the *reverse* pattern of before. Thus, it seems that people have the option of thinking about cats via imagery, and also the option of thinking about cats without imagery; as the mode of representation changes, so does the pattern of information availability.

Here is a different experiment, making a related point (Kosslyn, Ball & Reiser, 1978). Participants were asked to memorize the fictional map shown in Figure 11.1 and, in particular, to memorize the locations of the various landmarks: the well, the straw hut, and so on. The experimenters made sure participants had the map memorized by asking them to draw a replica of the map from memory; once they could do this, the main experiment began. Participants were asked to form an image of the island, and to point their "mind's eye" at a specific landmark, let

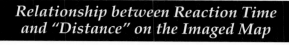

**Relationship between Reaction Time and "Distance" on the Imaged Map**

FIGURE 11.2

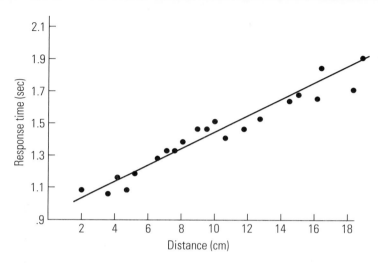

Participants had to "scan" from one point on their mental image to another point; they pressed a button to indicate when their "mind's eye" had arrived at its destination. Response times in this task were closely related to the "distance" participants had to scan across on the image, implying that mental images are similar to actual pictures in how they represent positions and distance. [After Kosslyn, 1983.]

us say the well. Another landmark was then mentioned, perhaps the straw hut, and participants were asked to imagine a black speck moving in a straight line from the first landmark to the second. When the speck "reached" the target, participants pressed a button, stopping a clock. This provides a measure of how long it takes to scan from the well to the hut. The same was done for the well and the palm tree, the hut and the rock, and so on, so that we end up with "scanning times" for each of the various pairs of landmarks.

Figure 11.2 shows the results. The data clearly suggest that participants scan across their image at a constant rate, so that doubling the scanning "distance" doubles the time required, tripling the distance triples the time required. This in turn implies that the image somehow preserves the various distance relationships that were present in the original map: Points that

were close together on the map are somehow close together in the image; points that were farther apart on the map are farther apart in the image. Thus, in a very real sense, the image preserves the spatial layout of the original map. The image *depicts* the map, rather than describing it.

Similar results are obtained if participants are given a task that requires them to "zoom in" on their images (for example, a task that requires them to inspect the image for some small detail), or a task that requires them to "zoom out" (e.g., a task that requires a more global judgment). In these studies, response times are directly proportional to the amount of "zoom" required, suggesting once again that travel in the imaged world resembles travel in the actual world, at least with regard to timing. Participants in one study were asked to imagine a mouse standing next to an elephant, and were then asked to confirm, by inspecting their image, that the mouse has whiskers. This task yields relatively slow response times, since participants need some time to zoom in, in order to "see" the whiskers. Response times are faster if participants are initially asked to imagine the mouse standing next to a paper clip. For this image, participants start with a "close-up" view and so, in this setup, no zooming is needed.

## PHYSICAL DISTANCE, FUNCTIONAL DISTANCE

The data pattern in these experiments is just what we would expect if participants were literally zooming in on, or scanning across, actual pictures. If the participants were scanning across an actual map, for example, using some sort of pointer that moved at a constant rate, then it follows from simple algebra that scanning times would be directly proportional to scanning distance. However, we don't need to interpret these imagery data as implying that images are literally laid out the way pictures or maps are. Instead, what the scanning data are telling us is simply that points close together on the map are *functionally* close together on the image. This does not require that these points be *physically* close together on the image (and similarly for the "zooming" data).

To understand this distinction between physical and functional proximity, consider Figure 11.3. Imagine that the list shown in the figure is recorded in some computer's memory. Imagine further that the process of scanning down the list is extremely fast—so fast, in fact, that even a brief scan will move you *five* positions down the list: If you launch a scan, you will move five positions before you have a chance to stop. Consequently, there is no way you can move *fewer than* five positions in any one scan. Now let's think about a specific scan: If you read the list's first entry (A) and then do the briefest possible scan, the next entry you encounter will be F. If you scan again, the next entry you encounter will be C (thanks to the loop-back feature we've included in the list). Therefore, A and F are *physically separated*, but *functionally close*. Physically, they are five steps

apart, but functionally, they are merely one scanning step apart. A and B, in contrast, are physically close, but functionally distant (five scanning steps apart).

Of course, functional proximity depends both on physical locations and also on how one "travels" or scans through physical locations. A and F are close together only by virtue of this five-step scan. With different travel modes, different sets of points would be functionally close. For example, if the briefest possible scan carried you only *three* steps, then A and D would be just one step apart; A and F would, with this scan, be *seven* scans apart, instead of one.

Returning to the image-scanning data, we know that participants can scan quickly from the imaged hut to the imaged well. But this does not mean that some brain activity, corresponding to the imaged hut, is physically side by side with brain activity corresponding to the imaged well. In our computer-list example, someone could scan quickly from A to F, even though these were physically separated in the computer's memory. The same may be true for the imagined hut and well: We know that these two are functionally close—this is just another way of saying that each is quickly reached starting from the other. But this does not mean that they are physically close. Perhaps they are, and perhaps they are not. The scanning data don't tell us that.

Let's be clear, then, that the chronometric studies of imagery don't tell us how images are physically manifested in the brain. In terms of their *physical* layout, we simply don't know if images are picture-like or not. But what the scanning data do tell us is of enormous importance. Images preserve distance relationships, so that *functional proximity* in the image directly reflects *physical proximity* in the imaged scene. As a direct consequence of this, the image also preserves information about shapes and sizes within the imaged scene, and also many of the spatial relations present in the scene (relations such as one point being *between* two other points, or *aligned with* other points, and so on). It is in this fashion that images preserve the geometry of the depicted scene, and indeed, it is in this way that images *depict* spatial layout.

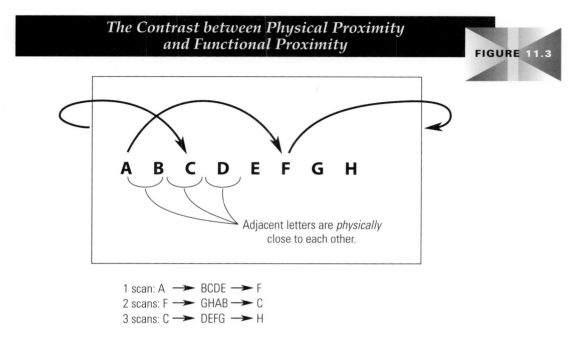

**The Contrast between Physical Proximity and Functional Proximity**

FIGURE 11.3

A B C D E F G H

Adjacent letters are *physically* close to each other.

1 scan: A → BCDE → F
2 scans: F → GHAB → C
3 scans: C → DEFG → H

Physical proximity depends on where items are located in space. Hence, A and B are physically close, so are B and C. *Functional* proximity, in contrast, depends on how one "travels" from one item to the next. For example, assume a scanning process that always moves five steps. With this scanning process, A and F are just one "scanning step" apart, and so they are *functionally* quite close together, even though they are *physically* distant from each other. A and C are two "scanning steps" apart (thanks to the "loop-back" feature we have built into the scan). A and B are actually five scanning steps apart—hence, physically close, but functionally far from each other.

## MENTAL ROTATION

So far, we have seen impressive correspondence between the time needed to travel within a mental image and the time needed to move relative to an actual picture—in both cases, greater "distances" require greater "travel time." Other results make a similar point with regard to the *transformation* of mental images.

Consider the display shown in Figure 11.4A. In a series of experiments by Shepard, Cooper, and Metzler, participants were asked to decide whether displays like this one showed two different shapes, or just one shape viewed from two different perspectives. In other words, is it possible to "rotate" the form shown on the left in Figure 11.4A so that it will end up looking just like the form on the right? What about the two shapes shown in Figure 11.4B, or the two in 11.4C?

To perform this task, participants seem first to imagine one of the forms rotating into "alignment" with the other. Then, once the forms are oriented in

### Stimuli for a Mental Rotation Experiment

**FIGURE** 11.4

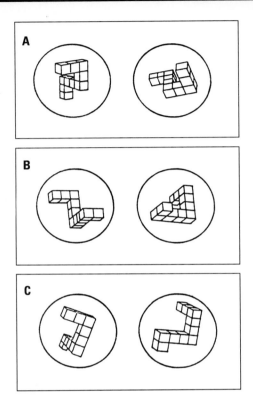

Participants had to judge whether the two stimuli shown in panel A are the same as each other, but viewed from different perspectives; likewise for the pairs shown in B and C. Participants seem to make these judgments by imagining one of the forms rotating until its position matches that of the other form. [After Shepard & Metzler, 1971.]

the same way, participants can make their judgment. This step of imagined rotation takes some time, and in fact, the amount of time it takes depends on how much rotation is needed. Figure 11.5 shows the data pattern, with response times clearly influenced by how far apart the two forms were in their initial orientations. Thus, once again, imagined "movement" resembles actual movement—the farther a form has

to be rotated, the longer it takes (Cooper & Shepard, 1973; Shepard & Metzler, 1971).

The mental-rotation task can be used to answer a number of questions about imagery. For example, notice that the two forms in Figure 11.4A are identical except for a *"picture-plane"* rotation. In other words, if you were to cut out the left-hand drawing, and spin it around (while leaving it flat on the table),

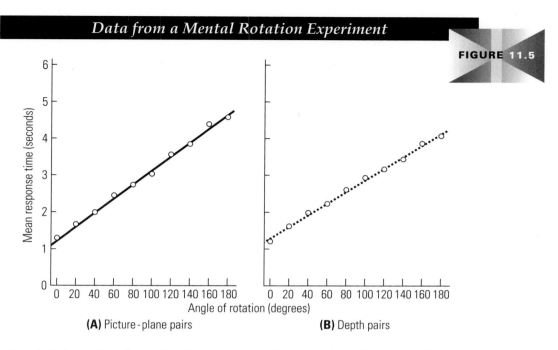

## Data from a Mental Rotation Experiment

**FIGURE 11.5**

**(A)** Picture-plane pairs

**(B)** Depth pairs

Panel A shows data from stimulus pairs requiring mental rotation in two dimensions—such that the imaged forms stay "within" the imagined picture-plane. Panel B shows data from pairs requiring an imagined rotation in depth. The data are obviously similar, indicating that participants can imagine three-dimensional rotations as easily, and as swiftly, as they can imagine two-dimensional rotations. In both cases, the greater the degree of rotation required, the longer the response times. [After Shepard & Metzler, 1971.]

you could align it with the drawing on the right. The relevant rotation, therefore, is a rotation that leaves the pictures within the two-dimensional plane in which they are drawn. In contrast, the two forms shown in Figure 11.4B are identical except for a rotation *in depth*. No matter how you spin the *picture* on the left, it will not line up with the picture on the right. You can align these forms, but to do so you need to spin them around a vertical axis, in essence lifting them off the page.

People have no trouble with depth rotation. They make very few errors (with accuracy levels around 95%), and the data resemble those obtained with picture-plane rotation. Figure 11.5A shows data from

picture-plane rotation; Figure 11.5B shows data from pairs requiring depth rotation. In both cases, there is a clear relation between angle of rotation and response times, and the speed of rotation seems similar for both. Apparently, then, participants can represent three-dimensional forms in their images, and they can imagine these forms moving in depth. In some circumstances, therefore, visual images are not mental pictures—they are more like mental sculptures. (For a review, see Shepard & Cooper, 1982. For data on image *scanning* in three dimensions, see Pinker & Finke, 1980; Pinker, 1980.)

We should mention in passing that there has been some controversy about the exact relationship between response time and degree of rotation. In Figure 11.5, this relationship is linear, with the implication that participants imagine these forms rotating at a constant velocity (around 60 msec for every degree of rotation). Other studies have suggested that, in some circumstances, the speed of mental rotation is *not* constant, particularly if participants are imagining familiar forms rotating, rather than the made-up forms illustrated in Figure 11.4. (See, for example, Bauer & Jolicoeur, 1996.)

However, let's not allow this complication to distract us from the main finding: Across procedures, response times reliably increase as the angle of rotation increases. Thus, in mental rotation, just as in mental scanning, "distance" relations are functionally preserved so that, in all cases, the further the imagined "travel," the longer it takes.

## INTERACTIONS BETWEEN IMAGERY AND PERCEPTION

We have now observed a number of correspondences between visual images and actual visual stimuli, and this leads to a question: If images are so much like pictures, then are the processes used to inspect images similar to those used to inspect stimuli? To put it more broadly, what is the relation between imaging and perceiving?

In a study by Segal and Fusella (1970, 1971), participants were asked to detect very faint signals—either dim visual stimuli or soft tones. On each trial, the participants' task was merely to indicate whether a signal had been presented or not. Participants did this in either of two conditions: either while forming a visual image before their "mind's eye," or while forming an auditory image before their "mind's ear." Thus we have a 2 × 2 design—two types of signals to be detected, and two types of imagery.

Let's hypothesize that there is some overlap between imaging and perceiving—that is, there are some mental structures, or mental processes, used by both activities. Therefore, if these processes or structures are occupied with imaging, they are not available for perceiving, and vice versa, and so we should expect competition if participants try to do both activities at once. That is exactly what Segal and Fusella observed: Their results, shown in Figure 11.6, indicate that forming a visual image interferes with seeing, and that forming an auditory image interferes with hearing (see also Farah & Smith, 1983).

Notice, though, that the Segal and Fusella participants were trying to visualize one thing while perceiving something altogether different. What happens if participants are trying to image a stimulus *related to* the one they are trying to perceive? Can visualizing a stimulus "pave the way" for perception? Farah (1985) had participants visualize a form (either an "H" or a "T"). A moment later, either an "H" or a "T" was actually presented, although at a very low contrast, making the letter difficult to perceive. Perception was facilitated if participants had just been visualizing the target form, and again, the effect was quite specific—visualizing an "H" made it easier to perceive an "H," visualizing a "T" made it easier to perceive a "T." This provides further confirmation of the claim that visualizing and perceiving draw on similar mechanisms, so that one of these activities can serve to prime the other. (For further discussions, see Farah, 1989; Heil, Rösler & Henninghausen, 1993; also see McDermott & Roediger, 1994.)

Similar conclusions can be drawn from biological evidence. For example, we know a great deal about the specific brain structures required for vision; it turns out that many of the same structures are crucial for imagery. This can be documented in several ways, including the neuroimaging techniques described in Chapter 2 that map the moment-by-moment pattern of activity in the brain. These techniques can tell us which brain regions are heavily activated during a particular task and which are not. Thus, we know that when participants are visualizing, activity levels are high in various parts of the occipital cortex—the brain area central for visual perception (Behrmann, 2000; Farah, 1988; Isha & Sagi, 1995; Kosslyn, 1994; Miyashita, 1995; Thompson & Kosslyn, 2000).

Likewise, consider studies of brain damage, usually damage resulting from stroke. We mentioned in Chapters 1, 2, and 3 that this damage can, in some cases, disrupt someone's ability to perceive; in Chapter 4, we saw that other forms of brain damage can

## Can One Visualize and See at the Same Time?

FIGURE 11.6

| | Percentage detections | | | Percentage false alarms | |
|---|---|---|---|---|---|
| | Visual signal | Auditory signal | | Visual signal | Auditory signal |
| While visualizing | 61% | 67% | While visualizing | 7.8% | 3.7% |
| While maintaining an auditory image | 63% | 61% | While maintaining an auditory image | 3.6% | 6.7% |

Participants were less successful in detecting a weak visual signal if they were simultaneously maintaining a visual image than if they were maintaining an auditory image. (The effect is small, but highly reliable.) The reverse is true with weak auditory signals: Participants were less successful in this detection if maintaining an auditory image than if visualizing. In addition, visual images often led to "false alarms" for participants for trying to detect visual signals; auditory images led to false alarms for auditory signals. [After Segal & Fusella, 1970.]

disrupt the ability to pay attention to visual inputs. It turns out that these same forms of brain damage disrupt the ability to image, so that patients often have "parallel" gaps in their perception and their imagery: Patients who, because of a stroke, lose the ability to perceive color often seem to lose the ability to imagine scenes in color; patients who lose the ability to perceive fine detail seem also to lose the ability to visualize fine detail, and so on (Farah, 1988; Farah, Soso & Dasheiff, 1992; Kosslyn, 1994; for some contrasting data, however, see Behrmann, 2000; Behrmann, Moscovitch & Winocur, 1994; Goldenberg et al., 1995; Jankowiak et al., 1992).

In one striking case, a patient had suffered a stroke and, as a result, had developed the "neglect syndrome" we described in Chapter 4: If this patient was shown a picture, he seemed to see only the right side of it; if asked to read a word, he only read the right half. The same pattern of neglect was evident in the patient's imagery: In one test, the patient was urged to visualize a familiar plaza in his city, and to list the buildings "in view" in the image. If the pa-

tient imagined himself standing at the southern edge of the plaza, he listed all the buildings on the plaza's west side, but none on the east. If the patient imagined himself standing on the northern edge of the plaza, he listed all the sights on the plaza's east side, but none on the west. In both cases, therefore, he "neglected" the right half of the imaged scene, just as he did with perceived scenes (Bisiach & Luzzatti, 1978; Bisiach, Luzzatti & Perani, 1979).

Still further evidence on this issue comes from a technique called **transcranial magnetic stimulation** (TMS). This technique creates a series of strong magnetic pulses at a specific location on the scalp; this causes a (temporary!) disruption in the small brain region directly underneath this scalp area. In this fashion, it is possible to disrupt Area V1 temporarily in an otherwise normal brain; Area V1, you will recall, is the brain area where axons from the visual system first reach the cortex (see Chapter 2). Not surprisingly, using TMS in this way causes problems in vision, but it also causes parallel problems in visual imagery, providing powerful argument that Area V1 is crucial *both* for the processing of visual information *and* for the creation and maintenance of visual images (Kosslyn et al., 1999).

## "SENSORY" EFFECTS IN IMAGERY

Clearly, the neural "machinery" needed for imagery overlaps with that needed for perception. If the machinery is occupied with one of these functions, it is not available for the other. If the machinery is disrupted (permanently, as by a stroke, or temporarily, as by TMS), then both activities are compromised. If we scrutinize activation patterns, we find that, to a large extent, the same brain structures are involved in visualizing and in vision. All of this indicates an intimate relationship between imagery and perception.

Against this backdrop, we would expect imagery and perception to share many traits, and research indicates that this is the case. For example, consider **visual acuity**, that is, the ability to see fine detail. In vision, acuity is much greater at the center of the visual field than it is in the visual periphery. Can we find a comparable pattern in imagery? Is it easier to discern detail at the image's center than at its periphery?

There are many ways to measure acuity, one of which is an assessment of "two-point acuity." In this test, observers are shown two dots. If the dots are 5 mm apart, can the observer see that there are two separate dots, or do the dots seem to "fuse" into one? How about a 4 mm separation? By determining the point at which the dots seem to fuse together, we can assess someone's ability to discern the small gap that actually separates the dots.

In vision, two-point acuity is greatest when people are looking directly at the dots; under these circumstances, even minuscule gaps can be detected. However, if we position the dots 10 degrees away from someone's line of vision, acuity is far worse. What about imagery? In one study, participants were first shown two dots of the appropriate size. The dots were then removed, but participants were asked to imagine that the dots were still present. The partici-

pants then moved their eyes away from the imaged dots' position, and as they looked further and further away, they had to judge whether they could still "see" that the dots were separate. In this way, "two-point acuity" was measured with imaginary stimuli (Finke & Kosslyn, 1980).

The data show a remarkable correspondence between participants' performance with actually perceived dots and their performance with imagined dots. In both cases, acuity fell off abruptly if the dots were not in the center of vision, and indeed, the pattern of fall-off was virtually the same in perception and in imagery. Moreover, in vision, acuity falls off more rapidly if participants look *above* or *below* the two dots, rather than to the left or right. This pattern was also observed in the imagery condition. Thus, qualitatively and quantitatively, the imagery data match the perceptual data. (For a variety of related data, see Finke, 1989. We should note, though, that there has been some controversy about these data; for alternative views, see Harris, 1982; Intons-Peterson & White, 1981; Kolers, 1983; Kunen & May, 1981.)

## SPATIAL IMAGES AND VISUAL IMAGES

We are building an impressive case, therefore, for a close relationship between imagery and perception. Indeed, the evidence implies that we can truly speak of imagery as being *visual* imagery, drawing on the same mechanisms, and having the same traits, as actual vision. Other results, however, add some complications.

A number of studies have examined imagery in people blind since birth (Carpenter & Eisenberg, 1978; Kerr, 1983; Marmor & Zabeck, 1976; also see Jonides, Kahn & Rozin, 1975; Paivio & Okovita, 1971; Zimler & Keenan, 1983). In tests involving mental rotation, or image scanning, these individuals yield data quite similar to those obtained with *sighted* research participants—with response times proportionate to the "distance" traveled, and so on.

It seems unlikely that blind people are using *visual* imagery to perform these tasks. Therefore, they must have some *other* means of thinking about spatial layout and spatial relations. This "spatial imagery" might be represented in the mind in terms of a series of imagined movements, so that it is "body imagery" or "motion imagery" rather than visual imagery. (Reisberg & Logie, 1993, provide a discussion of motion-based imagery; also Engelkamp, 1986, 1991; Logie et al., 1999; Saltz & Donnenwerth-Nolan, 1981.) Alternatively, perhaps spatial imagery is not tied to any sensory modality, but is part of our broader cognition about spatial arrangements and layout.

One way or another, though, it seems we do need to distinguish between visual imagery and spatial imagery, and moreover, it seems likely that sighted people have access to *both* of these types of imagery. As further evidence for this distinction, consider the interference observed between imagery and vision. We have already noted that many studies have documented this interference: It is difficult to image one stimulus while looking at another. (In addition to the studies already mentioned, pertinent data are reported by Johnson, 1982; Logie, 1986; Matthews, 1983.) Other studies, though, have not shown this pattern. For example, Baddeley and Lieberman (1980) asked their participants to imagine a 4 × 4 matrix; within this matrix, the second square in the second row was designated as the starting square. The participants then heard a series of sentences telling them how to "fill" this imagined matrix: "In the starting square, place a '1'; in the next square to the right, put a '2'; in the next square up, put a '3'," and so on. Then, after a short delay, the participants had to report back the "contents" of the matrix.

It seems likely that this task requires imagery, but what sort of imagery is relevant? In one condition, participants tried to remember these matrices while simultaneously doing a visual interference task: As they were hearing the sentences, they were shown a series of lights, some of which were bright and others dim; their task was to press a key whenever they saw a bright stimulus. In a second condition participants had to remember the matrices while simultaneously doing a spatial interference task: They were required to move their hands in a particular spatial pattern, but they were blindfolded, so that they could not rely on vision in guiding their motions.

In this study, no interference was observed when participants were asked to memorize the matrices while simultaneously doing the visual task. It would appear, therefore, that memorizing the matrices does *not* depend on "visual skills," and so it doesn't matter if these skills are otherwise occupied. Interference was observed, though, when the matrix task was combined with spatial interference—these two tasks, it seems, do overlap in their processing demands, and so cannot be done simultaneously. Apparently, then, memorizing this matrix depends on some sort of spatial skills, and correspondingly, it seems that the imagery relevant to this task is spatial, not visual, in nature. (For related evidence, see Logie & Marchetti, 1991; Morris, 1987; Quinn, 1988; Quinn & Ralston, 1986; Smyth & Pendleton, 1989. For more on how visual imagery and imagery for movement might *interact*, see Kosslyn, 1994; Logie, 1995; Wexler et al., 1998.)

In short, some imagery tasks are disrupted by simultaneous visual activity; we used this as an argument that these tasks draw on visual imagery. Other imagery tasks are not disrupted by simultaneous visual activity but are disrupted by simultaneous spatial activity, with the implication that these tasks draw on spatial imagery, not visual. Apparently, we do need to distinguish different types of imagery, and it appears that both forms of imagery are available to most people.

The same claims are reflected in neuropsychological data. Consider the case of L.H., a brain-damaged individual studied by Farah, Hammond, Levine, and Calvanio (1988). L.H.'s brain damage was the result of an automobile accident, but he recovered remarkably well. Even after his recovery, however, he continued to have trouble with a variety of visual tasks: In one test, the experimenter named a number of common objects (e.g., "football"), and L.H. had to report the color of each (for the football, "brown"). Control participants got 19 of 20 items correct; L.H. got only 10 correct. In another test, the experimenter named an animal (e.g., "kangaroo"), and L.H. had to indicate whether the animal had a long tail or short, relative to its body size. Again, control participants got 19 of 20 items correct on this test; L.H. got only 13 correct.

In contrast, L.H. does well in spatial tasks, including several of the tasks we have already described—image scanning, mental rotation, and the like. Indeed, on the Baddeley and Lieberman matrix task (described a few paragraphs back), L.H. was correct on 18 of 20 items, virtually identical to the performance of control participants.

Thus, L.H. does poorly on tasks requiring judgments about visual appearance, or memory for visual appearance. He does quite well on tasks requiring spatial manipulations, or memory for spatial positions. To make sense of L.H.'s profile, therefore, it seems once again crucial to distinguish between visual tasks and spatial ones and, correspondingly, between visual imagery and spatial imagery.

## INDIVIDUAL DIFFERENCES

It seems, therefore, that at least two forms of imagery are available to most of us—visual imagery, relying on mechanisms usually involved in seeing, and spatial imagery, perhaps represented in the mind via imagery for movements, or perhaps represented in some abstract, "non-sensory" format.

Some tasks will surely require visual imagery rather than spatial. (Consider, for example, the tasks that L.H. could *not* do.) Other tasks may require spatial imagery rather than visual. In addition, still other tasks can go either way—that is, they can be supported by imagery of either type. In this last sort of task, which form of imagery we use will depend on our preferences, aspects of the instructions, and (probably) a variety of other factors. The choice between these forms of imagery may also be influenced by each individual's ability levels. In essence, some people may be poor visualizers but good "spatializers"; these people would surely rely on spatial imagery, not visual, in most tasks. And, of course, for other people, this pattern would be reversed.

We need to be careful, though, in describing these individual differences. The evidence suggests that it is too crude to speak of "good imagers" or "bad imagers" in general. Instead, some individuals seem quite adept at scanning their images, and so they do well on imagery tasks that involve a lot of scanning. These same individuals might be less talented, say, in elaborating their images, and so they will do less well on tasks that require elaboration. Other people have a different profile: They might be good at elaboration, but poor at *finding* things in their images, and so they will do well if an imagery task requires a lot of elaboration, and they will do poorly if the task requires a lot of finding. (For discussion, see Kosslyn, Brunn, Cave & Wallach, 1985.)

Thus our analysis of imagery skill must be fairly fine-grained: Imagery tasks turn out to depend on a number of "subskills," and each of us seems to have our own profile of strengths and weaknesses across these various subskills. Rather than speaking of "good" and "bad" imagers, therefore, we need to be more specific in describing which *aspects* of imagery a person can or cannot do well.

This still leaves us with a question about one rather striking way in which individuals seem to differ in their imagery, namely, *image vividness*. Recall Galton's data, mentioned early on in this chapter. Some of Galton's participants described their imagery as rich and vivid—in short, very much like "seeing." Others described their imagery as being relatively sparse, and not at all like vision. What should we make of these reports?

On the face of things, Galton's data suggest that people differ markedly in their *conscious experience* of imaging. People with vivid imagery report that their images truly are picture-like—usually in color, quite detailed, and with all of the depicted objects "viewed" from a particular distance and a particular viewing angle. People without vivid imagery, on the other hand, will say none of these things. Their images, they report, are not at all picture-like. It's meaningless to ask them, therefore, whether an image is in color or in black and white; their image simply isn't the sort of thing that *could be* in color or in black and white. Likewise, it's meaningless to ask whether their image is viewed from a particular perspective; their image is abstract in a way that makes this question incoherent. In no sense, then, do these "non-imagers" feel like they are "seeing" with the "mind's eye." From their perspective, these figures of speech are (at best) loosely metaphorical. This stands in clear contrast to the reports offered by vivid imagers; for them, mental seeing really does seem like actual seeing.

Roughly 10% of the population will, in this fashion, "declare themselves entirely deficient in the power of seeing mental pictures" (after Galton, 1883). As William James put it, they "have no visual images at all worthy of the name" (James, 1890). But what should we make of this? Is it truly the case that the various members of our species differ in whether or not they are capable of experiencing visual images?

To explore this issue, one research strategy would be this: Based on these self-reports about imagery vividness, we could categorize people as "vivid imagers," "sparse imagers," and so on. We could then test these people on tasks like image scanning or mental rotation. The obvious prediction would be that people with vivid imagery will do well in these tasks, while those with sparse imagery will do poorly. If this prediction worked out, we would have confirmation of the self-report data, and indeed, we would have indication that individuals truly differ in how they consciously experience images.

A number of studies have tested these predictions, and the results are surprising: In a great many studies, there has been no relation between the vividness of someone's imagery—assessed via self-report—and performance on these imagery tasks. (For reviews, see Ernest, 1977; Katz, 1983; Marks, 1983; Reisberg, Culver, Heuer & Fischman, 1986; Richardson, 1980.) There is no difference, for example, between vivid imagers and sparse imagers in how they do mental rotation, how quickly or accurately they scan across their images, or how effective their images are in supporting memory. Indeed, individuals who insist they have *no* imagery do as well as everyone else on these tasks; individuals who insist they have clear and detailed imagery show no corresponding performance advantage.

Given this pattern, we might choose to disbelieve the self-reports of imagery vividness. As we mentioned earlier in the chapter, perhaps individuals all have the same imagery experience, but simply choose to describe their experience in different ways. In this case, the vividness reports reflect different styles of talking about imagery, not differences in imagery. (These are precisely the concerns that made us wary of introspective data from the start.)

However, we would urge a different view of the evidence, guided by the distinction between visual and spatial imagery: When people describe their images as "vivid," they are, in general, describing the *visual* richness of their imagery. Indeed, many questionnaires, seeking to measure the imagery experience, explicitly ask participants how much their image experience is "like seeing." In contrast, many imagery tasks require *spatial* judgments (e.g., judgments about relative distance or position) or spatial manipulations (scanning, rotation, folding). The obvious proposal, therefore, is that the self-reports assess visual imagery, while these laboratory tests require spatial imagery. No wonder, then, that there is little relation between the self-reports and the laboratory data—they are measuring different things.

If this view is correct, then vividness reports—a measure of *visual* imagery—should be related to performance on tasks that require visual imagery. For example, consider the two-point acuity experiment already described. This experiment seems to require little in the way of spatial judgments; instead, this test requires someone to imagine exactly what something would *look like*. Therefore, this test seems likely to draw on visual, not spatial, imagery. And, consistent with our prediction, it turns out that performance in this test *is* related to imagery self-report: People who describe their imagery as vivid yield data in this experiment in close correspondence to the perceptual data; people with less-vivid imagery do not show this correspondence (Finke & Kosslyn, 1980). This experiment (and many others—e.g., Heuer, Fischman & Reisberg, 1986; Reisberg & Leak, 1987) lends credibility to our claim: When people report on their conscious imagery experience, they are primarily reporting on the *visual* richness of that experience. These reports are not related to how well they do on *spatial* tasks. However, these reports do seem related to how well they do on *visual* tasks. (For a broad review, see McKelvie, 1995.)

Other data point in roughly the same direction. For example, people with vivid imagery (according to their self-report) show markedly increased blood flow in the occipital cortex whenever they are asked to form visual images; people without vivid imagery (according to their self-report) generally do not show this pattern (e.g., Behrmann, 2000). This fits well with the conception we are developing: When people say they have "vivid imagery," they are reporting that their imagery (subjectively) resembles actual vision. It is sensible, therefore, that these reports would be associated with increased activity levels in areas of the brain crucial for vision. Correspondingly, if people report impoverished imagery, they are reporting that their imagery (subjectively) does *not* resemble vision, and in this case, it is sensible that their reports are associated with little or no activity increase in the visual areas of the brain.

Perhaps, therefore, we can take imagery self-reports at face value—as a reflection of the visual quality, the visual richness, of someone's imagery experience. If so, this carries the fascinating implication that people may in fact *differ* in the nature of their conscious experience, with at least some experiences (namely, vivid visual images) available to most, but not all, members of our species. This invites many questions: How do these differences in experience influence us? What can people "with imagery" do that people "without imagery" cannot? These points are not yet clear, although they are obviously a target for further research.

## IMAGES ARE NOT PICTURES

Let's pause to take stock. We began this section by offering an informal comparison between imagery and "mental pictures." That comparison is hardly new—it is embedded in the way most of us talk about our imagery. Yet we have seen a number of cases in which this comparison may be misleading. First, the data tell us that images functionally preserve the layout of the imaged scene, but this does not mean that images physically preserve this layout. Thus, the image might *function* like a picture, but this is different from saying the image *is* (or *is like*) a picture. Second, we have seen that mental images can depict a scene in three dimensions, not just two; this also places limits on the image-picture comparison. Third, we have now seen grounds for distinguishing between visual images, which might be more picture-like, and spatial images, which may be movement-based or perhaps more abstract. Visual images are likely to draw on processes overlapping with those used in ordinary vision, but this is probably not the case for spatial images. Again, this implies that the idea of the "mind's eye" inspecting a "mental picture" often will be inappropriate.

Another line of research indicates a further way in which images and pictures differ. To understand this research, let's return to some issues we first raised in Chapter 3, and to an example we first met in that chapter. The top of Figure 11.7 shows a figure known as the *Necker cube*. The drawing of this cube—the stimulus itself—is ambiguous: It can be understood as a depiction of the (solid) cube shown as cube A in the drawing, or it can be understood as a depiction of the cube shown as cube B. The *picture* of the Necker cube, therefore, is neutral with regard to interpretation, and so is fully compatible with either interpretation. Our *perception* of the cube, however, is not neutral, is not indeterminate with regard to depth. Instead, we perceive the cube either as similar to cube A in the picture or as similar to cube B. Our perception, in other words, "goes beyond the information given" by specifying a configuration in depth, a specification that, in this case, "supplements" an ambiguous drawing in order to create an unambiguous perception.

As we discussed in Chapter 3, the configuration in depth is just one of the ways that perception goes beyond the information given in a stimulus. Our perception of a stimulus (including our perception of a *picture*) also specifies a figure/ground organization, the form's orientation (e.g., identifying the form's "top"), and so on. These specifications serve to organize the form, and have an enormous impact on the *subjective appearance* of the form, and with

## The Necker Cube

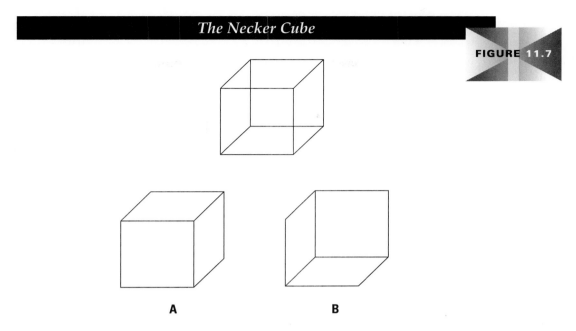

**FIGURE** 11.7

**A**          **B**

This cube can be perceived as if viewed from above (in which case it is a transparent version of cube A) or as if viewed from below (i.e., a transparent version of cube B).

that, what the form is seen to resemble, and what the form will evoke in memory. (For more on these points, see Chapter 3.)

In this fashion, our percepts—our mental representations of the stimuli we are perceiving—are different from pictures: Our percepts are organized and unambiguous in a fashion that pictures are not. Yet, at the same time, percepts and pictures are also alike in important ways. Crucially, both are *depictions*, representing in a direct fashion key aspects of the three-dimensional layout of the world. Percepts, in other words, are not "descriptions" of a stimulus; instead, percepts show directly *what a stimulus looks like*, and in this regard, percepts are just like pictures.

It will be useful to have some terminology here. Let's refer to pictures as *neutral depictions*—showing what something looks like, but in a fashion that is neutral with regard to the various specifications we

have mentioned. Let's refer to percepts as *organized depictions*—again showing what something looks like, but in a fashion that specifies how the form is organized. Finally, let's refer to the various specifications, organizing the form, as a *perceptual reference frame*, and so the difference between a neutral depiction and an organized one is that the latter is understood within a perceptual reference frame, but the former is not. (The "reference frame" terminology is adopted from Peterson et al., 1992.)

We're now ready (at last) to ask about mental images. Are they neutral depictions, the way pictures are, and so open to many different interpretations? Or are they organized depictions, the way percepts seem to be, and so, in a sense, "already interpreted," already organized? One line of evidence comes from studies of ambiguous figures: In a study by Chambers and Reisberg (1985), participants were briefly shown a drawing of an ambiguous figure (such as the Necker

**FIGURE 11.8**

## The Duck/Rabbit

This figure can be perceived either as a duck or as a rabbit. With the picture in view, people readily find both interpretations of the figure. However, if people are *imaging* the figure, they have great difficulty finding a different interpretation. That is, people imaging the "duck" have great difficulty in discovering the "rabbit"; people imaging the "rabbit" have great difficulty in discovering the "duck."

cube, or the duck/rabbit—Figure 11.8). The participants were then asked to form a mental image based on that drawing. All of the participants had previously been trained so that they understood what was meant by an ambiguous figure and had successfully reinterpreted a series of practice figures. They were then asked if they could reinterpret their image, just as they had reinterpreted the practice figures.

The results are easily summarized: Across several experiments, not one of the participants succeeded in reinterpreting his or her images: They reliably failed to find the duck in a "rabbit image" or the rabbit in a "duck image." Is it possible that they did not understand their task, or perhaps did not remember the figure? To rule out these possibilities, participants were given a blank piece of paper, immediately after their failure at reinterpreting their images, and asked to draw the figure, based on their image. Now, looking at their own drawings, all of the participants were able to reinterpret the configuration in the appropriate way. Thus, we have 100% failure in reinterpreting these forms with images, and 100% success, a moment later, with the drawings. This

result is obviously problematic for the claim that images are neutral depictions, subject to reinterpretation. Instead, this result seems strong confirmation of the claim that images are inherently organized, just as percepts are, and so entirely unambiguous.

### LEARNING FROM IMAGES

In some ways, the results just cited are puzzling. It seems clear from common experience that mental images often surprise us, or remind us of something. We routinely consult our images in solving problems or in making decisions. Indeed, the history of science is filled with examples of discoveries apparently inspired by an image (see, for example, Miller, 1986). Many laboratory studies have also shown that people can invent new forms, or new devices, by inspecting and manipulating their images (Anderson & Helstrup, 1993; Finke, 1990; Finke & Slayton, 1988; Pinker & Finke, 1980; also see Chapter 14). Yet, in the Chambers and Reisberg study, participants universally failed to make a discovery from imagery—even though they easily made the comparable discovery from a picture. How should we reconcile all these findings? Why are discoveries from imagery sometimes possible and sometimes not?

We have just suggested that images (like percepts) are organized depictions, and not (like pictures) neutral depictions. In other words, images exist only within the context of a perceptual reference frame, and perhaps this reference frame sets "boundaries" on image-based discovery. More specifically, let's distinguish two types of discovery that one might make about an imaged form. Some discoveries about this form will be compatible with the reference frame that the imager initially had in mind when first forming the image. Other discoveries about this form, however, will not be compatible with this initial reference frame, and so will require a *change* in the image's reference frame.

With this distinction made, the hypothesis to be considered is this: Image-based discovery will be easy if the discovery does not require a reference-frame change; these discoveries will be relatively frequent, with no need for special hints or instructions. In contrast, image-based discovery will be difficult if the discovery does require a reference-frame change; these discoveries will be rare and will benefit enormously from hints. (An early version of this hypothesis was offered by Reisberg & Chambers, 1991; refinements and extensions have been offered by Peterson, Kihlstron, Rose & Glisky 1992; Verstijnen, Hennessey et al., 1998; Verstijnen, van Leeuwen et al., 1998.)

To make this concrete, let's say that someone initially perceives Figure 11.8 as a rabbit, but then discovers that the form can also be seen as a child with her hair tied in pigtails. This discovery requires no change in the person's understanding of the figure's basic shape, including where its top is, where its front is, and so on. This discovery, in other words, requires no change in the figure's reference frame and so should, according to our hypothesis, be a discovery that happens easily and often. And, in fact, it does (Peterson et al., 1992).

In contrast, let's say that someone initially perceives Figure 11.8 as a rabbit, but then manages to discover that the form can also be seen as a duck.

This *does* involve a change in the person's organization of the form, including where the form's front is, and also the relationships among the form's parts. This discovery, therefore, does require a reference-frame change, does require the person to jettison one organization of the form and replace it with another. According to our hypothesis, this sort of discovery should be rare and dependent on hints, and in fact, it is (Chambers & Reisberg, 1985; Peterson et al., 1992).

Further evidence comes from a study by Reisberg and Chambers (1991), in which participants were asked to memorize a series of "nonsense shapes." The tenth shape in the series, presented with no special notice, was the one depicted in Figure 11.9. Participants had five seconds in which to memorize this shape, and then the picture was removed. Participants were next asked to form an image of the shape, and then to imagine the shape rotated 90° clockwise. At this point the participants were told that the shape "resembles a familiar geographic form" and were asked to identify that form.

It seems likely that participants understood the side topmost in the original drawing as being the shape's top. This understanding probably did not change when the participants imagined the rotation. In other words, when participants imagined the rotation, they rotated both the form *and* its reference frame. As a consequence, the participants were, in this experiment, imaging the "right geometry" for Texas, but with the "wrong understanding," that is, specifying the wrong top. Therefore, discovering Texas in this image requires a reference-frame change—a shift in how the form is understood. As a result, we should predict that participants will *not* make this discovery. This is correct: Exactly zero participants were able to discover Texas in their image.

In a subsequent experiment, participants were led through the same procedure, but this time they were explicitly instructed in how to *change* their understanding of the imaged form. That is, they were told directly to think of the form's left edge as being the "top." With this instruction, many participants were able to discover Texas in the image. Apparently, then, the obstacle to discovery is indeed how participants understand the image. When this under-

FIGURE 11.9 **Limitations on Learning from Imagery**

Participants imaged this form, thinking of it merely as an abstract shape. When asked to imagine the form rotated by 90 degrees, they failed to discover the familiar shape of Texas. Their understanding of the imaged form (and, in particular, their understanding of the form's "top") prevented them from recognizing the Lone Star state. When participants were explicitly instructed to change this understanding, many were able to discover Texas.

standing changes, there is a corresponding change in performance.

These results obviously fit with the claim that images are inherently understood in a certain way—a way that specifies, for example, which side of the form is the *top*, which side is the *front*, and so forth. This understanding then sets "boundaries" on what can be discovered about the image, so that (as we've seen) discoveries compatible with the imager's understanding of the form flow easily from the image, while discoveries incompatible with the understanding are rare.

Of course, imagers do have the option of *changing* how they understand the form. For example, we have just discussed a case in which participants, with explicit instruction, changed their assignment of the image's "top." And, once these changes occur, they have powerful effects: When the imager's understanding of the form changes, a range of new discoveries, compatible with the new understanding, becomes available. Evidence suggests, however, that these changes in reference frame are surprisingly

difficult and often dependent on specific instructions, or specific training examples. Therefore, one's *initial* understanding of the form has a strong effect on what can be discovered from an image. (For further discussion, see Chapter 14; also Reisberg, 1996.)

## IMAGES AND PICTURES: AN INTERIM SUMMARY

Images, both visual and spatial, provide a distinctive means of representing the world, so that imagining a robot (for example) is quite different from thinking about the word "robot" or describing a robot to yourself, or merely contemplating the idea "robot." As one distinctive attribute, images seem functionally to preserve the spatial layout of the imaged scene: Aspects of the scene that are, in fact, close together are functionally close together in the image. Aspects of the scene that are large will, functionally, occupy a large portion of the image. And so on.

In these regards, then, images (both visual and spatial) are indeed picture-like. At the same time, though, we have also highlighted ways in which images are *not* picture-like and, correspondingly, regards in which the processes of imagery are distinct from those of perception. A picture of the Necker cube (Figure 11.7) is neutral with regard to depth; an image of the Necker cube, in contrast, seems to specify an arrangement in depth, seems to specify whether it is cube A or cube B that is being thought about. In this sense, then, the image contains *more information* than the corresponding picture.

As one last example, consider these two pictures: One picture shows three rows of dots, with four dots in each row. The second picture shows four columns of dots, with three dots in each column. Needless to say, these two pictures would be identical. The corresponding images, though, turn out not to be identical. Research participants take longer, for example, to generate the second image, presumably because it contains a larger number of "units"—four columns, rather than three rows (cf. Kosslyn, 1983). So here, too, we have an example of an image more specific than a picture: A picture of the dots would contain no indication of whether we are looking at three rows of dots, or four columns. A mental image, though, does specify this information.

Where does all this leave us? Images are plainly different from pictures in important ways. However, this cannot distract us from how much images *do* have in common with pictures and, likewise, of the considerable overlap between imagery and perception. In short, images share *some* properties with pictures, and so images are, in many ways, picture-like. Nonetheless, images are not pictures. (For more on the differences between images and pictures, see Arnheim, 1969; Chambers & Reisberg, 1992; Dennett, 1981; James, 1890; Titchener, 1926.)

## Long-Term Visual Memory

So far, our discussion has focused on "active" images, images currently being contemplated, images presumably held in working memory. What about visual information in long-term memory? For exam-

ple, if you wish to form an image of an elephant, you need to draw on your knowledge of what an elephant looks like. What is this knowledge, and how is it represented in long-term storage? Likewise, if you recognize a picture as familiar, this is probably because you've detected a "match" between it and some memory of an earlier-viewed picture. What is the nature of this memory?

### IMAGE INFORMATION IN LONG-TERM MEMORY

In Chapter 8, we suggested that your concept of *birthday* (for example) is represented by some number of nodes in long-term memory. When you think about birthdays, those nodes are activated, and conversely, when those nodes are activated, you are thinking about birthdays. Perhaps we can adapt this proposal to account for long-term storage of visual information (and likewise information for the other sensory modalities).

One possibility is that nodes in long-term memory can represent entire, relatively complete *pictures*. Thus, to think about a mental image of an elephant, you would activate the ELEPHANT PICTURE nodes; to scrutinize an image of your father's face, you would activate the FATHER'S FACE nodes; and so on.

However, evidence speaks against this idea. Research by Kosslyn (1980, 1983) suggests instead that mental images are stored in memory in a piecemeal fashion. To form an image, therefore, one first activates the nodes specifying the "image frame," which depicts the form's global shape. Then elaborations can be added to this frame, as the imager wishes, to create a full and detailed image.

Many results support this claim. For one, we know that images containing more parts take longer to create, just as we would expect if images are formed on a piece-by-piece basis. Second, we know that images containing more *detail* take longer to create, in accord with our hypothesis. Third, we also know that imagers have some degree of control over how complete and detailed their images will be, so that (depending on the task, the imagers' preferences, and so on) images can be quite sketchy or can be quite elaborate (Reisberg, 1994). This is easily explained if imagers first create an image frame and only then add as much detail as they want.

This process of image construction depends on information in **image files** in long-term memory. Each file contains the information you need in order to create a mental image—information about how to create the image frame, and then information about how to elaborate the frame in this way or that, if desired. But what form does this information take? One proposal is that the image files contain *descriptive* information, so that, in essence, an image file can be thought of as a set of instructions, or even a "recipe," for creating an image. By analogy, someone could instruct you in how to create a picture by uttering the appropriate sentences: "In the top left, place a circle. Underneath it, draw a line, angling down. . . ." Such instructions would allow you to create a picture, but there is nothing pictorial about the instructions themselves—the instructions are sentences, not pictures. In the same way, the instructions within an image file allow you to create a representation that, as we have already seen, is picture-like in important ways. However, this information in long-term memory may not be at all picture-like.

The distinction between an active image and an image file is important for several reasons. For one, we have argued that the active image represents information in a distinctive way, compared to other forms of representation, and is operated on with special processes (such as "scan," "rotate," or "zoom"), processes that are irrelevant to other forms of thought. At the same time, though, image *files* may have no special status within long-term memory. These files can be encoded as propositions, and thus stored within the network in the same fashion as other materials. Thus, we do want to distinguish imagery from other forms of thought, but this may have no consequences at all for our theorizing about long-term memory.

The distinction between active images and image files also matters for imagery function. Bear in mind that the image file will often contain more information than is represented in the currently active image. This "extra" information is not available to someone scanning or inspecting the image—he or she is inspecting the active image, not the image file. As a result, we can find seemingly paradoxical cases in which people know quite well what something looks like but fail to "see" this information in their image. But there is no paradox here; instead, this simply describes a case in which some information, perhaps information crucial for a task, is recorded in the image file but not represented in the currently active image. (For relevant data, see Chambers & Reisberg, 1992; for other evidence illuminating the contrast between active images and image files, see Hitch, Brandimonte & Walker, 1995.)

## VERBAL CODING OF VISUAL MATERIALS

In long-term memory, we have suggested, images are represented in some non-image format, specifying a "recipe" for the image. In other cases, though, long-term memory will contain something even simpler—a verbal label.

For example, consider memory for color. It is appreciably easier to remember a color if one has a label for it, so that individuals with large "color vocabularies" have better color memories. This leads to striking contrasts if we gather data in different cultures, capitalizing on the fact that some languages have many words for describing and categorizing colors, whereas other languages have only a few. It turns out that this linguistic variation has no impact on how people *perceive* color, but does play an important role in memory—color memory is superior in those cultures with a greater number of color terms (Brown & Lenneberg, 1954; Rosch, 1977b). This is because, in many cases, people are remembering a verbal description for the stimulus colors, rather than the colors themselves. (See also the discussion of color vocabulary and memory in Chapter 10.)

A related point was made by Carmichael, Hogan and Walters (1932). Their research participants were shown pictures like those in Figure 11.10. Half of the participants were shown the top form and told, "This is a picture of eyeglasses." The other half were told, "This is a picture of a barbell." The participants were later required to reproduce, as carefully as they could, the pictures they had seen. Those who had understood the picture as spectacles produced drawings that resembled spectacles; those who understood the picture as weights distorted their drawings appropriately. This is again what one would expect if the participants had memorized the description, rather than the picture itself, and were recreating the picture based on this description.

It seems, then, that in some cases visual information may be stored in memory, not via imagery, but as a description of the previously viewed object. Moreover, this is a *helpful* strategy: Memory is im-

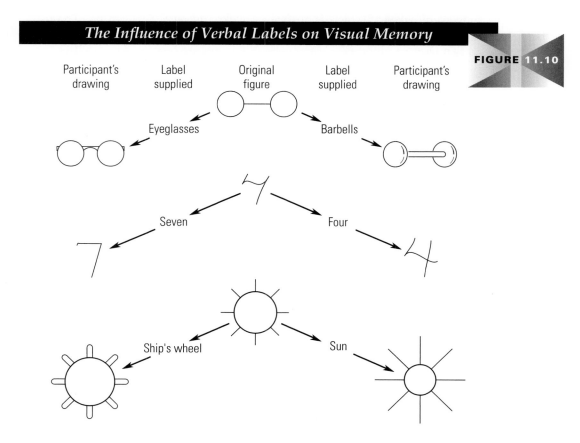

## The Influence of Verbal Labels on Visual Memory

FIGURE 11.10

Participant's drawing — Label supplied — Original figure — Label supplied — Participant's drawing

Eyeglasses

Barbells

Seven

Four

Ship's wheel

Sun

Participants were shown the figures in the middle column. If the top figure was presented with the label "eyeglasses," participants were later likely to reproduce the figure as shown on the left. If the figure was presented with the label "barbells," they were likely to reproduce it as shown on the right. (And so on for the other figures.) One interpretation of these data is that participants were remembering the *verbal label* and not the drawing itself and then, at the time of test, reconstructed what the drawing must have been based on the remembered label.

proved when an appropriate label, or appropriate description, is available. (This is certainly true in the color-memory studies.) However, this strategy can backfire: People may end up recalling a picture in a fashion that is distorted by their understanding of it, or perhaps selective in ways that their description was selective. This obviously resembles the schema effects described in Chapter 7.

A similar message emerges from tasks that require participants to reason about *spatial position*. In one study, participants were asked, "Which is further north, Seattle or Montreal? Which is further west, Reno, Nevada, or San Diego, California?" Many participants responded that Montreal is further north, and that San Diego is further west, but both of these responses are *wrong*. Montreal, for example, is at roughly the same latitude as Portland, Oregon, a city almost 200 miles *south* of Seattle (Stevens & Coupe, 1978).

What is going on here? Participants seem to be reasoning this way: Montreal is in Canada; Seattle is in the United States. Canada is north of the United States. Therefore, Montreal must be further north than Seattle. This kind of reasoning is sensible, since it will often bring you to the correct answer. (That's because most parts of Canada are, in fact, further north than most parts of the United States, and likewise most parts of California are further west than most parts of Nevada.) Even so, this reasoning will sometimes lead to error, and it does so in both the questions at stake here.

What is important, though, is not the participants' knowledge about the longitude and latitude of these particular cities. What is important is that the sort of reasoning revealed in these studies hinges on *propositional knowledge,* and not any sort of mental images or maps. *Some* of our spatial knowledge surely does rely on mental representations that are truly map-like (cf. Jonides & Baum, 1978). But some relies on some sort of symbolic code, and that is the point: At least some of the visual (or spatial) information in long-term memory is encoded in propositional (or maybe even verbal) form. (For more on reasoning about geography, see Friedman & Brown, 2000.)

## IMAGERY HELPS MEMORY

We have so far been concerned with *how* visual information is represented in long-term memory. However, no matter how images are stored, it is also clear that images *influence* long-term memory in important ways. More precisely, there are numerous ways in which imagery can improve memory. For example, materials that evoke imagery are considerably easier to remember than materials that do not evoke imagery. This can be demonstrated in many ways, including this two-step procedure: First, participants are presented with a list of nouns and asked to rate each noun, on a 1-to-7 scale, for how readily it evokes an image (Paivio, 1969; Paivio, Yuille & Madigan, 1968). Examples of words receiving high ratings are "church," with an average rating of 6.63, or "elephant," rated at 6.83. Words receiving lower ratings included "context" (2.13) and "virtue" (3.33).

As a second step, we ask whether these imagery ratings, generated by one group of participants, can be used to predict memory performance with a new group of participants. The new participants are asked to memorize lists of words, using the words for which we have imagery ratings. The data indicate that participants learn high-imagery words more readily than low-imagery words (Paivio, 1969). If asked to learn word pairs, participants perform best if both words in the pair are high-imagery words, perform worst if both are low-imagery words, and perform at intermediate levels if one word in the pair is a high-imagery word and the other is not (Paivio, Smythe & Yuille, 1968; but also see Marschark & Hunt, 1989).

In the same fashion, memory can be enormously aided by the use of imagery mnemonics. In one study, some participants were asked to learn pairs of words by rehearsing each pair silently. Other participants were instructed to make up a sentence for each pair of words, linking the words in some sensible way. Finally, other participants were told to form a mental image for each pair of words, with the image combining the words in some interaction. The results showed poorest recall performance by the rehearsal group, and intermediate performance by the group

## *The Effects of Bizarreness on Memory*

**FIGURE 11.11**

Noninteracting, nonbizarre

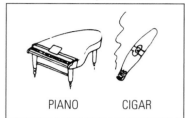

PIANO    CIGAR

Noninteracting, bizarre

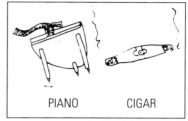

PIANO    CIGAR

Interacting, nonbizarre

PIANO    CIGAR

Interacting, bizarre

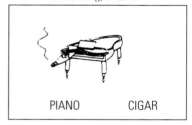

PIANO    CIGAR

People were required to memorize word pairs (for example, the pair PIANO and CIGAR). The pairs were accompanied by drawings that were either non-bizarre (left column) or bizarre (right column), and that involved the two items either not interacting in any way (top row) or interacting (bottom row). Memory was improved if the two items were shown as interacting; bizarreness had no effect. [After Wollen, Weber & Lowry, 1972.]

that generated the sentences. Both of these groups, though, did appreciably less well than the imagery group (Bower & Winzenz, 1970; for discussion of other mnemonic techniques, see Chapter 5).

We might mention that imagery instructions have comparable effects with people who have been blind from birth. They benefit from instructions to remember words by forming images, just as sighted participants do (Jonides et al., 1975). Likewise, the memory advantage for easily imaged words can also be observed with blind research participants (Paivio & Okovita, 1971; Zimler & Keenan, 1983). Apparently, then, spatial images can improve memory just as much as visual images. (For further discussion of

whether mnemonic images need be "visual," see Keenan, 1983; Keenan & Moore, 1979; Kerr & Neisser, 1983; Luria, 1968; Neisser & Kerr, 1973.)

We should also mention one side issue: In using imagery mnemonics, participants are generally encouraged to make their images as elaborate or as bizarre as they like, and in fact, the suggestion is often made that bizarre images are more readily remembered. However, the evidence for this claim is mixed. For example, participants in one study learned word pairs, with each pair illustrated by a line drawing. Four kinds of drawings were used, as shown in Figure 11.11. The drawings depicted the objects either interacting in some way or separate, and in either a bizarre or a non-bizarre fashion. The results show no memory impact of bizarreness. Memory was considerably improved, however, when the objects were shown in some interaction than when the objects were shown separately (Wollen, Weber & Lowry, 1972).

It is surely no surprise that memory is aided by interacting images. As we saw in Chapter 5, memory is improved in general if one can find ways to organize the material; interacting images provide one means of achieving this organization. But what about bizarreness? The study just described shows no memory advantage for bizarre images, but other studies do show an advantage, with people more likely to remember bizarre images than common ones. Einstein and McDaniel have argued that this effect will be observed only if the bizarre images are mixed together with more common images. If participants see only a succession of bizarre images, then they cease thinking of the images as bizarre. In the context of more ordinary images, though, the bizarreness is noticed and contemplated, leading to a memory improvement. (For reviews, see Einstein, McDaniel & Lackey, 1989; McDaniel & Einstein, 1986, 1990; for related data, see Hunt & Elliot, 1980. For a different perspective on these points, see Hirshman, Whelley & Palij, 1989; Kroll, Schepeler & Angin, 1986; Riefer & Rouder, 1993.)

## DUAL CODING

Setting aside the issue of "bizarreness," the message of the preceding section is clear: Imagery improves memory. Materials that can be imaged are more easily remembered. Instructions to use imagery during memorization improve memory performance. Why is this? What memory aid does imagery provide?

One proposal is that imageable materials, such as high-imagery words, will be doubly represented in memory: The word itself will be remembered, and so will the corresponding picture. This pattern is referred to as **dual coding**, and the advantage of this should be obvious: When the time comes to retrieve these memories, either record, the verbal or the image, will provide the information you seek. This gives you a "double chance" of locating the information you need, thereby easing the process of memory search. Imagery mnemonics work the same way, by encouraging people to lay down two different memory records—a propositional record of the material, plus an image—rather than one.

In addition, Paivio (1971) has argued that these two memories—one verbal in character, one an image—will differ from each other in important ways. For example, *access* to the verbal memory will be easiest if one starts with a word, as in, "Do you know the word *squirrel*?" Access to the remembered image, in contrast, will be easiest if one begins with a picture, "Do you recognize this pictured creature?" Moreover, Paivio argues, some types of information—for example, semantic associations—are more easily stored via verbal memories. Other types of information, such as information about size or shape, are more readily accessed from the remembered images. (Also see Paivio & Csapo, 1969; Yuille, 1983.)

Putting these suggestions together, we are led to a series of predictions, many of which have been tested by Paivio and his collaborators. In one study, participants were shown pairs of items and had to indicate whether there was a close association between the items in each pair (te Linde, 1983). If shown the pair "mouse-cheese," they should press the "yes" button; if shown the pair "car-tomato," they should press the "no" button. This task is hypothesized to draw heavily on the system of verbal memories, because it is here that abstract, semantic information is stored.

In another condition, the participants had to make a different judgment—they had to indicate whether the two items in the pair were of similar size. They would respond "yes" to "thimble-acorn," and "no" to "key-dress." This judgment should draw on the system of remembered *images*, because this is where spatial information (including information about size) is represented.

For both of these tasks, some of the stimuli were presented in verbal form. Participants might see the word "mouse" and the word "cheese," and then have to render the requested judgment. Other stimuli were presented pictorially—e.g., a picture of a mouse and a picture of cheese. The pictures were scaled so that all were of uniform size. That way, participants making the size judgments could not respond based on the pictures themselves; instead, they had to draw on memory to recall the actual size of the depicted object.

We therefore have a 2 × 2 design, with two different judgments and two different types of stimulus information (see Figure 11.12). What should we expect here? The size task draws on remembered images, and these are more quickly accessed with picture stimuli than with words. Therefore, for this task, we expect to see a picture advantage—faster responses to pictorial stimuli than to verbal stimuli. Things should reverse with the other task: Judgments about association depend on verbal memories, and these are more

quickly accessed with word stimuli. For this task, we expect to see a disadvantage for pictures, with faster responses to the verbal stimuli.

Before we turn to the data, though, we need to add a complication. There is reason to believe that simple pictures are, overall, recognized more quickly than words, perhaps because pictures are more distinctive from each other than words are (Friedman & Bourne, 1976). This effect will, therefore, be superimposed on the effect we are after.

Let's think through what this means for our predictions: With questions about size, participants should be quicker with pictures for two reasons: Pictures are quicker overall, and pictures are also just the right input with which to access size information. In answering questions about semantic associations, pictures have the advantage of being quickly recognized in general, but they also have the dis-

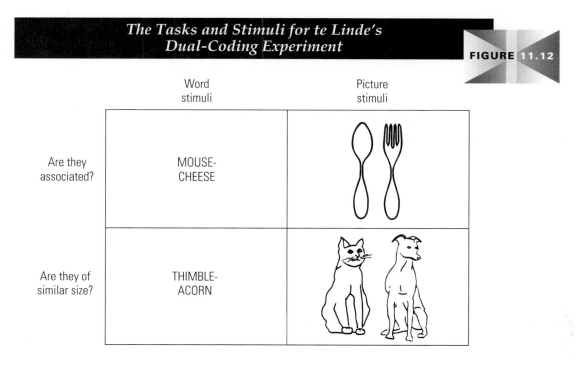

**The Tasks and Stimuli for te Linde's Dual-Coding Experiment**

FIGURE 11.12

|  | Word stimuli | Picture stimuli |
|---|---|---|
| Are they associated? | MOUSE-CHEESE | |
| Are they of similar size? | THIMBLE-ACORN | |

Participants were asked either a question about association or a question about size. Half of the questions were presented in word form and half in pictorial form.

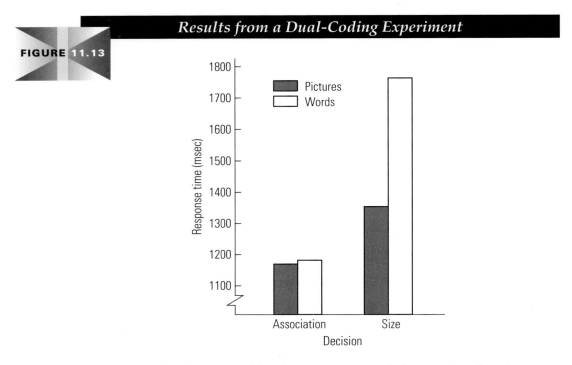

**Results from a Dual-Coding Experiment**

FIGURE 11.13

Size questions are answered by drawing on nonverbal memories; therefore, responses should be faster with picture stimuli (that is, short response times with picture stimuli, long response times with word stimuli). This prediction is confirmed. With questions about association, the information is coming from verbal memories, and so we expect faster responses with word stimuli. However, this effect is offset by the general advantage of picture stimuli over word stimuli. These two effects "cancel" each other, leaving us with no difference between picture and word stimuli for the association decision.[After te Linde, 1983.]

advantage of being an inappropriate input for accessing the desired information. These two effects should cancel each other, yielding no difference between pictures and words with the association questions.

As can be seen in Figure 11.13, the results fit with these predictions. For the size questions, response times were shortest when test items were presented as pictures. Responses were much slower if test items were presented as words. The association questions, however, yield a rather different pattern. These questions should be answered with information based on

verbal memories, and these memories are best accessed with words. This effect is masked, however, by the overall quickness of pictures. With this task, therefore, we observe no difference between picture and word stimuli.

## MEMORY FOR PICTURES

These data indicate that we do need to distinguish between visual memories and other, more symbolic memories, with these categories differing from each other both in their content and in their functioning. But how should we think about this? Paivio (1971) has proposed that there are two separate and distinct memory systems, one containing verbal memories, the other containing images. However, many psychologists would argue instead that there is just a single, vast, long-term memory, capable of holding diverse contents. Within this single memory, each type of content would have its own traits, its own pattern of functioning—consistent with the data just reviewed. Nonetheless, there would still be one unified memory system, with images and verbal memories fully and intimately interwoven. (For discussion of this point, see Heil, Rösler & Hennighausen, 1994.)

To put this differently, images and verbal memories are distinct from each other in important ways—including how they are accessed, and also the types of information they contain. At the same time, these two types of memory also have a great deal in common, reflecting the fact that both types of memory reside within a single memory system. Thus, many of the claims we made in Chapters 5, 6, and 7 apply with equal force to visual memories and verbal memories: Recall of both memory types, for example, is dependent on memory connections; schema effects can be observed with both types of memory; encoding specificity is observed in both domains, and so on.

As an illustration of this broad point, consider memory for *pictures*. In many ways, the principles governing "picture memory" are the same as the principles governing memory for other materials. For example, recall our discussion of "schema effects," in Chapter 7. There we argued that participants' memories are clearly influenced by generic knowledge, knowledge about how events unfold in general. In support of this claim, Chapter 7 relied largely on evidence for verbal memories, such as memory for sentences and stories. Similar effects, though, can easily be demonstrated with pictures.

In one study, Friedman (1979) showed participants pictures of scenes such as a typical kitchen or a typical barnyard. In addition, the pictures also contained some unexpected objects. The kitchen picture, for ex-

ample, included a stove and a toaster, but also included items less often found in a kitchen, such as a fireplace. Participants were later given a recognition test, in which they had to discriminate between pictures they had actually seen and altered versions of these pictures, in which something had been changed.

In some of the test pictures, one of the *familiar* objects in the scene had been changed. For example, participants might be shown a test picture in which a different kind of stove appeared in the place of the original stove, or one in which the toaster on the counter was replaced by a radio. Participants rarely noticed these changes, and so they tended (incorrectly) to respond "old" in these cases. This is sensible on schema grounds: Both the original and altered pictures were fully consistent with the kitchen schema, and so both would be compatible with a schema-based memory.

On the other hand, participants almost always noticed changes to the *unexpected* objects in the scene. If the originally viewed kitchen had a fireplace and the test picture did not, participants consistently detected this alteration. Again, this is predictable on schema grounds: The fireplace did not fit with the kitchen schema and so was likely to be specifically noted in memory. In fact, Friedman recorded participants' eye movements during the original presentations of the pictures. Her data showed that participants tended to look twice as long at the unexpected objects as they did at the expected ones—clearly these objects did catch the participants' attention. (For more on schema guidance of eye movements, see Henderson et al., 1999.)

In essence, then, what Friedman's participants seemed to remember was that they had seen something we might label "kitchen plus a fireplace," a description that both identifies the relevant schema and also notes what was special about this particular instance of the schema. If recognition memory is tested with a kitchen without a fireplace, participants spot this discrepancy easily, since this picture does not fit with the remembered description. If tested with a kitchen plus or minus a toaster, this still fits with the "kitchen plus a fireplace" description, and so the alternation is likely not to be noticed.

(See also Pezdek, Whetstone, Reynolds, Askari & Dougherty, 1989.)[1]

A different line of evidence also shows schema effects in picture memory: Recall our claim that, in understanding a story, people place the story within a schematic frame. As we have seen, this can often lead to intrusion errors, as people import their own expectations and understanding into the story, and so end up remembering the story as including more than it actually did.

A similar phenomenon can be demonstrated with picture memory: Intraub and her collaborators have documented a consistent pattern of *boundary extension* in picture memory (Intraub & Richardson, 1989; Intraub, Bender & Mangels, 1992; Intraub & Bodamer, 1993; Intraub et al., 1998). That is, people remember a picture as including more than it actually did, in effect "pushing out" the boundaries of the remembered depiction. For example, participants shown the top panel in Figure 11.14 were later asked to sketch what they had seen. Two of the participants' drawings are shown in the bottom of Figure 11.14, and the boundary extension is clear—participants remember the scene as less of a close-up view than it actually was and, correspondingly, they remember the scene as containing more of the backdrop than it actually did. This effect is observed whether participants initially see a few pictures or many, whether they are tested immediately or after a delay, and even when

participants are explicitly warned about boundary extension and urged to avoid this effect.

Intraub has argued that this boundary extension arises from the way in which people perceived these pictures in the first place. In essence, people understand a picture by means of a perceptual schema (e.g., Hochberg, 1978, 1986). This schema places the picture in a larger context, informing the perceiver about the real-world scene only partially revealed by the picture. This leads to a series of expectations about what people would see if they could somehow look beyond the photograph's edges. All of this influences memory, as the memory interweaves what people *saw* with what they *expected*, or what they knew they might see if they explored further. In important ways, this resembles the intrusion errors, produced by knowledge schemata, observed with verbal memory.

Overall, then, it does look like picture memory follows the same rules, and is influenced by the same factors, as memory for verbal materials. Schema effects, for example, can be found in both domains, with people showing better memory for the schema itself than for details of the particular stimulus. Intrusion errors can be documented in both domains. Similarly, participants show *primacy* and *recency* effects when they learn a series of pictures (Tabachnick & Brotsky, 1976), just as they do when they learn a series of words (Chapter 5). Phenomena such as spread of activation and priming can be demonstrated with nonverbal materials (Kroll & Potter, 1984), just as they can be demonstrated with verbal materials (Chapter 8). In short, picture memory is distinct from other sorts of memory, but there is also enough communality to sustain our suggestion of a single memory system, with diverse contents but with a uniform set of operating principles.

## MEMORY FOR FACES

What about memory for *faces*? What is the relation between face memory and the other categories of memories we have considered? As we saw in Chapter 3, face recognition does seem to involve special-

---

[1]Note the complex interplay here among schematic knowledge, memory, and typicality: If some object within a scene is highly typical (a stove, for example, in a kitchen), then you'll have no reason to look at it and so won't remember much about it later on. Nonetheless, your schema will tell you that this typical element was present, and in this fashion, you're likely to remember that a stove was included in the scene, even though you remember no particulars about the specific stove that was in view. If, in contrast, an element within the scene is *slightly* unusual (a radio on the counter), then it may or may not catch your attention. If it doesn't, then you'll have no basis for remembering it later on. Finally, if an object within the scene is quite unusual (that is, not congruent with your schematic knowledge), then it's likely to catch your attention and so likely to be remembered. Thus you will remember the kitchen's fireplace. For more on schema effects, see Chapter 7.

## *Boundary Extension in Picture Memory*

**FIGURE** 11.14

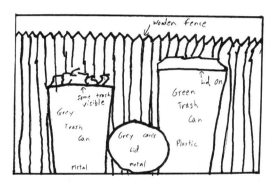

Participants were initially shown the photograph at the top of this figure. The two panels below show drawings of the scene, drawn from memory by two different participants. The participants clearly recalled the scene as a "wide-angle" shot, revealing more of the background than it actually did. [After Intraub & Richardson, 1989.]

ized brain areas. This is indicated, for example, by the existence of prosopagnosia, a syndrome in which the ability to recognize familiar faces is disrupted, even though other aspects of recognition seem undisturbed. Moreover, it seems sensible that we might have specialized memories for faces. After all, our ancestors' survival, millions of years ago, may well have depended on the successful recognition of friends, foes, and family. This may have created evolutionary pressure for especially accurate face memory, which

may, in turn, have demanded neural mechanisms specialized for this purpose.

Consistent with these comments about evolution, evidence indicates that memory for faces is quite good, with accuracy at high levels even after long retention intervals (Bahrick, Bahrick & Wittlinger, 1975; Bruck, Cavanagh & Ceci, 1991). Nonetheless, memory for faces is far from perfect, and large-scale errors have been documented (e.g., Baddeley, 1982; Wright & McDaid, 1996). A number of factors can erode the accuracy of face memory, including such unsurprising factors as poor lighting or brief exposure during the initial encounter. It is also well documented that individuals are better in remembering faces from their own race than those of other races (Brigham, 1986; Deffenbacher & Loftus, 1982; Shapiro & Penrod, 1986).

As we described in Chapter 3, it seems certain that faces are remembered as complex configurations, and not feature by feature (Bruce, Doyle, Dench & Burton, 1991; Farah, Tanaka & Drain, 1995; Rhodes, Brake & Atkinson, 1993). Beyond this, however, it appears that face memory follows many of the same principles as other categories of memory. For example, a number of studies have alleged that "deep processing" of faces (e.g., thinking about the personality of the person, rather than about the size or shape of specific features) leads to better face memory. However, there is reason to believe this effect is best explained in terms of the number and variety of features attended to while doing deep processing (Bloom & Mudd, 1991; Reinitz, Morrissey & Demb, 1994; Shapiro & Penrod, 1986; Sporer, 1991). Thus, just like other categories of memory, face memory is best if, when the face is being observed, one pays attention to many and diverse aspects of the stimulus. Likewise, rehearsal of a face (via visualization) seems to improve memory, just as with other forms of memory (Sporer, 1988).

Similarly, people often seem able to recognize a face as *familiar* without being able to identify *why* the face is familiar. As a result, they will sometimes *misattribute* a face's familiarity—that is, identify a person as having been encountered in one circumstance when, in fact, the person was encountered in a rather different setting (Brigham & Cairns, 1988; Brown, Deffenbacher & Sturgill, 1977; for some contrary data, see Read, Tollestrup, Hammersley & McFadzen, 1990). This is the same separation between familiarity and source memory that we discussed with other categories of memory in Chapter 6.

Once again, therefore, we find a familiar pattern: There are some attributes unique to face memory (e.g., the sensitivity to facial *configurations*) but, at the same time, there are numerous parallels between memory for faces and memory for verbal materials. These parallels allow us to leave intact our claim that we don't need to subdivide long-term memory. Instead, there is but a single long-term memory. The contents are diverse, so that the attributes of one sort of content (e.g., memory for faces) will be somewhat different from the attributes of other contents. Nonetheless, all of long-term memory's contents will be subject to the same broad rules.

Finally, we should mention one other line of research concerning face memory—a line of research with important consequences. Eyewitnesses to crimes are often called on to identify or to describe the crimes' perpetrators, and this has made face memory an important topic for eyewitness research. Eyewitness memory for faces is often assessed via a "lineup," in which the witness must select, from a group of people, the person observed during the original crime, and numerous studies have examined the factors that influence lineup identifications. As examples, it appears that identification is equally accurate from a live or from a videotaped lineup (e.g., Cutler, Fisher & Chicvara, 1989); the likelihood of correctly identifying a culprit is also surprisingly unaffected by clothing or disguise (Lindsay, Wallbridge & Drennan, 1987). However, an *innocent* suspect is more likely to be misidentified as the culprit if he or she is wearing clothes similar to those remembered for the suspect.

Nonetheless *errors* in lineup identifications are frighteningly easy to document (Connors et al., 1996; Wright & McDaid, 1996; Wright & Davies, 1999). Crucial for lineup accuracy is the appearance of the other individuals in the lineup. Likelihood of accurate identification is maximized when the others resemble the suspect in relevant ways—including age, race, height, and weight. In addition, if the eyewitness has verbalized other features of the culprit (e.g., that he was attractive, or looked fierce), the others must be matched on these features as well. Indeed, it seems more important that the others resemble the witnesses' *description* of the culprit, rather than resembling the suspect (Brigham, Ready & Spier, 1990; Deffenbacher, 1988; Loftus & Kallman, 1979; Luus & Wells, 1991; Nosworthy & Lindsay, 1990).

Lineup identifications are also heavily influenced by instructions to the eyewitness (Malpass & Devine, 1981; Warnick & Sanders, 1980; but see also Kohnken & Maass, 1988), and by whether the members of the lineup are viewed one at a time, rather than simultaneously—in general, it seems that sequential presentation leads to better accuracy than does simultaneous (Cutler & Penrod, 1988; Lindsay & Wells, 1985; Lindsay, Lea & Fulford, 1991; Lindsay, Lea, Nosworthy, Fulford, Hector, LeVan & Seabrook, 1991). Accuracy can also be improved by allowing witnesses to hear the suspects' voices and to view the suspects in their customary posture and gait and in three-quarter profile (Bruce, Valentine & Baddeley, 1987; Cutler & Penrod, 1988; Logie, Baddeley & Woodhead, 1987; Wogalter & Laughery, 1987).

## The Diversity of Knowledge

Several themes have appeared again and again in this chapter. It is plain that we have diverse types of memories and knowledge in diverse domains. It is equally clear that our theories must acknowledge and accommodate this diversity. To describe face memory, for example, we need to consider configural properties that may well be specific to faces. Similarly, to describe images, we need to consider processes of "scanning" and "image rotation," processes that seem irrelevant to other kinds of representation. Likewise, images seem able to support a number of discoveries and creations not accessible from other routes, and this too needs to be accommodated by our theories.

At the same time, however, we have also seen important communalities across these domains, particularly with regard to long-term remembering. Across domains, rehearsal promotes memory. Across domains, schema effects are observed, in which memories for specific cases become entangled with more generic knowledge. Across domains, priming effects are observed, and so on. Consistent with these observations, we have seen no reason to set aside the claim that there is a single long-term memory, with a set of rules consistently applicable to all its diverse contents.

We offer all these claims with some reservation, though—especially our claims about the singularity of long-term memory. In this chapter, we have focused entirely on visual memories, and one might well ask whether similar conclusions would emerge with other categories of knowledge. For example, can memories for tastes or smells be encoded propositionally? Do these memories benefit from rehearsal, show schema effects, and the like? Little research speaks to these questions.

There is no question, however, that imagery in other modalities, and memories in other modalities, do exist. For example, think about your favorite song, performed by your favorite artist. Can you "hear" the song playing in your head? Evidence suggests that this "mental playback" is likely to be in exactly the same key, and at exactly the same tempo, as the original performance (Levitin, 1993; Levitin & Cook, 1996; also Halpern, 1989). Apparently, we have auditory memories, and in some cases, these memories are impressively accurate. (For related data, showing the accuracy of our memory and imagery for *timbre*, see Reisberg, 2000.)

Researchers have begun to explore auditory imagery and auditory memory, just as they have visual imagery and memory, and in important ways, the results for the two sensory modalities are quite similar. Auditory images seem to be (functionally) extended in time, just as visual images are (functionally) extended in space, and so it takes more time to "scan" an auditory image if the scanning "distance" is longer (as we saw in our discussion of Figure 11.1; see also Halpern, 1988, 1991). Just as in vision, auditory images seem to rely on many of the same mechanisms as actual hearing (Farah, 1988; Zatorre & Halpern, 1993; Zatorre et al., 1996). Auditory images seem resistant to reinterpretation, just as, say, the visual image of the duck-rabbit is (see Figure 11.8; also, Reisberg et al., 1989; Reisberg, 1994). Turning to auditory *memory*, evidence provided by an *ear*witness follows many of the same principles as evidence provided by an *eye*witness (Cook & Wilding, 1997a, 1997b; Olsson et al., 1998). And so on.

At the same time, there are also some differences between visual and auditory memory, and between visual and auditory imagery. In the auditory domain, for example, people have the option of "supplementing" their images by (silently) talking to themselves. This use of the "inner voice" seems to employ many of the brain mechanisms ordinarily used for overt speech and also seems to create a representation in the "inner ear"—mechanisms ordinarily used for actual hearing. We first met the "inner voice" and the "inner ear" when we described their role in *working-memory rehearsal* (Chapters 1 and 5), and it turns out that the same mechanisms contribute to auditory imagery: When participants are prevented from using the inner-voice + inner-ear partnership, performance suffers in many auditory imagery tasks (Reisberg, 1994; Smith et al., 1996; for more on auditory imagery, see Reisberg, 1992).

Our point here, however, is not to survey auditory imagery or auditory memory in detail. Instead, we mention these other domains simply to make the point that many aspects of visual imagery will find parallels in other domains, while other aspects may not. Moreover, these quick comments have suggested some of the questions we might want to ask as we explore new sensory domains. Indeed, as we said at the very start, our agenda in this chapter has been both methodological and substantive. We have tried to show by example what it means to explore the idea that a certain content is distinctive in working memory, and also what it would mean to propose a separate system within long-term memory. We have also seen how things stand on these issues with regard to *visual* materials; the field awaits further data before these issues can be resolved for other modalities.

## Chapter Summary

1. People differ enormously in how they describe their imagery experience, particularly the vividness of that experience. However, these self-reports are difficult to interpret, and this has led investigators to seek more objective means of studying mental imagery.

2. *Chronometric studies* indicate that the pattern of what information is more available and what is less available in an image closely matches the pattern of what is available in an actual picture. Likewise, the time needed to scan across an image, or to zoom in on an image to examine detail, or to imagine the image rotating, all correspond closely to the times needed for these operations with actual pictures.

3. In many settings, visual imagery seems to involve mechanisms that overlap with those used for visual perception. This is reflected in the fact that imaging one thing can make it difficult to perceive something else, or that imaging the appropriate target can prime a subsequent perception. Visual images also show sensory effects similar to those observed in vision. Further evidence comes from neuroimaging and studies of brain damage; this evidence confirms the considerable overlap between the biological basis for imagery and that for perception.

4. Not all imagery, however, is visual in nature. In some cases, imagery is disrupted by simultaneous spatial activities, and not by visual activity. This suggests that we may need to distinguish between visual and spatial imagery. This proposal is confirmed by studies of individuals with brain damage, some of whom seem to lose the capacity for visual imagery but retain their capacity for spatial imagery. This proposal may also help us understand the pattern of individual differences in imagery ability, with some individuals particularly skilled in visual imagery, and some in spatial.

5. Even when imagery is visual in nature, mental images are picture-like, and not pictures. Unlike pictures, mental images seem to be accompanied by a *perceptual reference frame*, which guides the interpretation of the image, and also influences what can be discovered about the image. Discoveries flow easily from an image if the discoveries are compatible with the imaged geometry and its reference frame; discoveries are much more difficult if the sought-after form is compatible with the imaged geometry but not the reference frame.

6. To create a mental image, one draws on information stored in an *image-file* in long-term

memory. These image-files can be thought of as recipes for the construction of a mental image, usually by first constructing a *frame* and then by elaborating the frame as needed. In addition, at least some information about visual appearance or spatial arrangement is stored in long-term memory in terms of verbal labels or conceptual frameworks. For example, information about the locations of cities may be stored in terms of propositions ("Montreal is in Canada; Canada is north of the United States") rather than being stored in some sort of mental map.

7. Imagery helps people to remember, and so word lists are more readily recalled if the words are easily imaged; similarly, instructions to form images help people to memorize. These benefits may be the result of *dual coding*: storing information in both a verbal format and in a format that encodes appearances; this doubles the chances of recalling the material later on. When trying to remember combinations of ideas, it is best to imagine the to-be-remembered objects interacting in some way. There has been some dispute over whether bizarre images are more easily remembered than ordinary images, and evidence suggests that bizarre images will have an advantage only if the other images to be remembered are not bizarre.

8. Memory for pictures can be accurate, but it follows most of the same rules as any other form of memory—for example, it is influenced by schematic knowledge. Memory for faces is probably served by special brain mechanisms, but, here too, memory is influenced by the same set of broad principles. For example, deep processing improves memory for faces, and familiarity for faces is distinct from source memory, so that in some cases the familiarity for faces is misattributed to the wrong source.

9. It is unclear what other categories of memory there may be. In each case, other kinds of memory are likely to have some properties that are distinctive and also many properties that are shared with memories of other sorts.

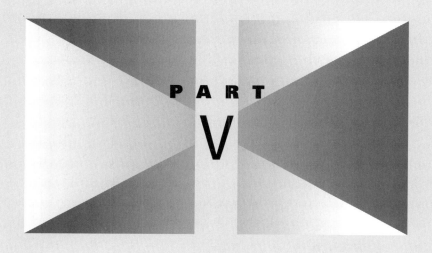

# Thinking

Throughout our lives, we draw conclusions based on things we have observed or heard about. We make inferences, deriving new ideas from our current beliefs. We solve problems, figuring out ways to reach our goals. And we make decisions, choosing paths of action that (we hope) will lead us toward those goals.

In this section, we will consider all of these achievements. As we proceed, we'll compare the ways people *do* think with the ways that various scholars have suggested we *should think*. In this comparison, we'll find (not surprisingly) that human reasoning and judgment are often excellent, but, even so, we will encounter numerous examples in this section of bad judgment, improper reasoning, and highly inefficient problem-solving.

How should we understand these intellectual shortcomings? One suggestion will be a recurrent theme in this section, and, indeed, it has been a recurrent theme throughout the book: In case after case, we have seen that humans rely on cognitive shortcuts—strategies that are reasonably efficient, but which risk error. These shortcuts played an important role in Chapter 3, when we discussed object recognition, in Chapter 7, when we discussed memory errors, and in Chapter 9, when we discussed categorization heuristics. Similar shortcuts will emerge again in this section, and, as we'll see, they play an important part in governing and guiding human thought.

Another factor will also be evident several times in this section: Humans do make many errors in their judgment and reasoning, but this is not because we don't know how to think well. In fact, we think quite well *if* the circumstances or the problem manages to "trigger" the appropriate knowledge. In many settings, for example, people are far too quick to draw conclusions from a tiny sample of evidence (this is one of the errors people routinely make), but, if the problem has the right "cues" built into it, this tendency reverses, and people become quite cautious about small sets of observations. Findings like this will drive us toward a multi-layered conception of thinking, since we will need to describe how people think when their better-quality strategies are triggered, and also how they think when the strategies are not triggered. Hand and hand with this, we will need to say more about what these triggers *are*, and what exactly the factors are that can turn poor reasoning into excellent reasoning.

These considerations also point the way toward another important theme in this section: If good quality reasoning and judgment can be "triggered" by suitable cues, are there things we can do to make this "triggering" more likely, so that people will judge and reason more effectively in their day-to-day lives? More generally, is there anything we can do to improve the quality of human thinking? These educational questions will emerge several times in our discussion; as we will see, the data point toward rather optimistic answers!

Finally, throughout this book, we have encountered theories and results that bear on questions about *consciousness*. How much of our mental lives is conscious? Are there benefits associated with conscious thought, as opposed to unconscious thought? We will tackle these (and other) questions in Chapter 15, but, in doing so, we'll be considering relatively little *new* material. Instead, Chapter 15 addresses these issues by pulling together a number of points we have made in earlier chapters; in this way, Chapter 15 provides something of a review for the text at the same time that it tackles a series of enormously important theoretical questions.

# Judgment: Drawing Conclusions from Evidence

So far, we have said a great deal about the *acquisition* and *retention* of knowledge but little about what people *do* with their knowledge once they've acquired it. It is to this broad concern that we now turn. We begin with a discussion of *judgment*—processes through which we think about evidence, draw conclusions, and make inferences.

The study of judgment takes part of its importance from the fact that the knowledge we need in our day-to-day lives is typically not supplied by the world in neat, ready-to-use packages. When we act on the basis of what we know, it is generally not because we have memorized a single relevant fact, nor is it because we have received some specific instruction about what to do in that situation. Instead, our actions are typically based on knowledge that we have, in effect, created ourselves—by drawing inferences from things we have seen, or by extrapolating from what we have experienced.

Imagine that you wish to cheer up your friend Fred. Chances are that Fred has never said to you, "Flowers are a good way to cheer me up." Therefore, you will need to figure out what will do the trick, based on things you have seen Fred do or heard him say. A more consequential case may have you asking, Should you vote for candidate X or candidate Y in the upcoming election? In this case, you *have* received instructions—you have seen X on television saying "Vote for me!" and likewise for Y. You will probably ignore these instructions, though, in making your decision. Instead, you will try to recall what you have read about X and Y, and you will make inferences from this information about how each is likely to behave in the future.

In other situations, we use our judgment simply because we want to figure things out, because we want to understand the pattern of our experiences. "Why was I in such a bad mood today?" "Does she really like me?" "What will the consequences of the election be?" In these cases, too, we build on what we already know, as we seek to draw some conclusion from the information available to us.

In this chapter, we will examine how these judgments are made. What strategies do we rely on in evaluating evidence? What factors influence us? Our focus will be on cases involving **induction**—a process in which one begins with specific facts or observations and then draws some general conclusion from them. In Chapter 13, we will consider the related topic of deduction, in which one usually begins with a general statement and tries to figure out what specific claims follow from it. For example, you might know, in general, that people with allergies often suffer during the spring. What conclusions can you (deductively) draw from this concerning Alicia, who has allergies?

Induction and deduction are key elements of our intellectual life, and they are ubiquitous in human reasoning. But induction and deduction also play a role in more formal settings, and in those settings, induction and deduction proceed according to clear rules. The rules of deduction have been specified in detail by logicians; these rules tell us rather precisely which deductive conclusions are valid—that is, warranted by the available information—and which are invalid. Likewise, scientists and statisticians have formalized many rules of induction. In scientific discourse, one cannot offer any conclusion one chooses. Instead, certain statistical and methodological principles govern how evidence is to be summarized and interpreted. Thus, one's inductive inferences are valid only if they are made in accordance with these principles.

According to many scholars, logic specifies the *correct* way to reason deductively, and so logic provides a *normative* account of deduction, as opposed to a *descriptive* account. **Normative** accounts tell us how things *ought to* go; **descriptive** accounts tell us merely

how things are. In the same way, statistics and scientific methodology provide normative rules for inductive reasoning, telling us how this form of reasoning *ought* to proceed.

Of course, most people have never studied logic or statistics, and this invites us to ask how their reasoning compares with the normative procedures: In our informal, day-to-day judgment, do we think sensibly and draw the "correct" conclusions? Or is our thinking foolish, and are our conclusions unjustified? These questions will be very much in view as we consider research in this domain.

## Availability

Judgments usually don't depend on single facts or single observations. Instead, judgments depend on *patterns* of observations. Hence, as a first step in making a judgment, we typically seek some means of summarizing the evidence, in order to discern the pattern. This summary often takes the form of a **frequency estimate**, as we ask about the various events in our lives: How often has this event occurred?

Frequency estimates are crucial in many domains, including any case in which you are trying to figure out some cause-and-effect relation. You are in a particularly good mood, for example, and you wonder why. Could it be the sunny weather? One way to check on this is by asking how often in the past you've been in a good mood on sunny days. If good moods occur on 80% of the sunny days, and on only 40% of the rainy days, then this is an indication that the weather does matter for you. Clearly, though, this conclusion hinges on frequency estimates, on *how often* good moods have been observed in this setting or in that one.

Frequency judgments are also needed when you are looking for *predictors* or *diagnostic tools*. Your friend just recommended a new movie; should you take his recommendation? Again, a frequency judgment is pertinent. (How often has he recommended movies that turned out to be terrific, and how often has he recommended films that were real losers?)

Country X has just threatened to attack a neighboring country; should we take the threat seriously? Here, one might consult historical patterns, asking how often such threats have been indicators of violence to come, and how often not.

It seems, then, that frequency estimates are at the root of a wide range of inductive judgments. How do we make this first step in inductive reasoning?

## THE AVAILABILITY HEURISTIC

Daniel Kahneman and Amos Tversky—two enormously important researchers in this area—have proposed that people use a simple strategy in making frequency judgments: They scan quickly through memory, seeking relevant cases. If cases come easily to mind, people conclude that there must be a lot of cases in that category, and so they give a high frequency estimate. If cases come to mind slowly, or only with effort, people draw the opposite conclusion: This must be a rare category.

The idea, therefore, is that people use *availability* as a means of judging *frequency*, and often this strategy will lead to the right answer. Which is a more common pet among college students—dogs or cats? You'll probably answer this question by thinking about the specific dog-owners and cat-owners in your acquaintance. If you easily think of eight dog-owners but recall only two or three cat-owners, you'll surely conclude that dogs are the more common pet. And the odds are good that your estimate will be correct.

But it is easy to find cases in which this strategy will lead to error. For example, Tversky and Kahneman asked participants this question: Are there more words in the dictionary beginning with the letter "r" (rose, rock, rabbit) or more words with an "r" in the third position (tarp, bare, throw)? Most participants asserted that there are more words beginning with "r" (Tversky & Kahneman, 1973, 1974), but the reverse is true, by a margin of two to one.

Why do people get this wrong, and by so much? The answer lies in availability. If you search your memory for words starting with "r," many will

come to mind. (Try it: how many "r" words can you name in ten seconds?) But if you search your memory for words with an "r" in the third position, fewer will emerge. (Again, try this for ten seconds.) This difference, favoring the words beginning with "r," arises simply because your memory is organized roughly like a dictionary is, with the words sharing a starting sound all grouped together. As a consequence, it's easy to search memory using "starting letter" as your cue; a search based on "r in third position" is much more difficult. In this way, the *organization of memory* creates a bias in what's easily available, and this bias in availability leads directly to an error in frequency judgment.

Of course, there is a way to get the "r-word" question right: One could, if one chose, count through the pages of a dictionary, determining how many words there are with each spelling pattern. But this would be very time-consuming and surely more trouble than the question deserves. It's sensible, therefore, that you choose the more efficient strategy, even though, in this case, your strategy leads to the wrong judgment.

Note the trade-off here: On the one side is a cumbersome strategy (search the dictionary) that is guaranteed to yield the correct answer. On the other side is a far more efficient strategy (rely on availability) that often works, even though, it does lead to error in this case. This trade-off has, of course, appeared in our discussion several times already, and in Chapter 9, this sort-of trade-off led us to introduce the notion of a **heuristic**—a strategy that risks some error in order to gain efficiency. Tversky and Kahneman (1973, 1974) speak, in fact, of the **availability heuristic** as a means of judging frequency.

## THE WIDE RANGE OF AVAILABILITY EFFECTS

Use of the availability heuristic seems quite sensible in the "r-word" task. After all, the task isn't very interesting, and participants probably don't want to spend much effort or time in choosing their response. But evidence suggests that people use this shortcut strategy in a wide range of other cases, including cases in which they're making judgments of some importance. Indeed, this suggestion will be a consistent theme in this chapter: A surprisingly small number of simple strategies seem to support many of the judgments we make in our day-to-day lives.

For example, consider the fact that people regularly overestimate the frequency of events that are, in actuality, quite rare (Attneave, 1953; Lichtenstein, Slovic, Fischhoff, Layman & Combs, 1978). This probably plays a part in people's willingness to buy lottery tickets—they overestimate the likelihood of winning! Sadly, it also can play a role in more important domains. For example, there is evidence that physicians may, in many circumstances, overestimate the likelihood of a rare disease and, in the process, fail to pursue other, perhaps more appropriate, courses of treatment. (For a clear example of this, see Elstein, Holzman, Ravitch, Metheny, Holmes, Hoppe, Rothert & Rovner, 1986.)

What causes this pattern? Events that are unusual or peculiar are, by their nature, likely to catch your attention. You will therefore notice these events and think about them, ensuring that these events are well recorded in memory. This will, in turn, make these events easily available to you. As a consequence, if you rely on the availability heuristic, you will overestimate the frequency of these unusual events and, correspondingly, will overestimate the likelihood of similar events happening in the future.

Related effects are easily demonstrated in the laboratory. For example, Tversky and Kahneman presented participants with a list of names; these participants were later asked to judge whether the list contained more names of men, or more names of women. For some participants, the men on the list were quite famous (e.g., Richard Nixon) while the women on the list were less famous (e.g., Lana Turner). These participants recalled the list as containing more men's names than women's. For other participants, it was the women on the list who were quite famous (e.g., Elizabeth Taylor). These participants recalled the list as containing more women's names than men's.

In this procedure, the famous names are more likely to catch participants' attention, and so are more likely to be remembered. Thus, when participants think back over the list, the famous names are more available, and this biases their assessments of the list's membership. Once again, availability governs frequency estimates. (For other examples of availability effects, including effects in the social sphere, see Ross & Sicoly, 1979; Taylor, 1982; Taylor, Fiske, Etcoff & Ruderman, 1978.)

## OTHER SOURCES OF AVAILABILITY BIAS

Where are we so far? A wide range of conclusions, inferences, and extrapolations turn out to depend on frequency estimates, and these estimates, in turn, often depend on availability. The pattern of availability then seems to depend, in large measure, on memory. As a result, virtually any factor that influences memory will, sooner or later, influence the pattern of our conclusions and the quality of our judgments. For example, availability is influenced by memory's organization, since this organization makes some memories more retrievable than others. (This was crucial for the "r-word" task.) Availability is likewise influenced by what we notice and what we pay attention to. (This was central for some of the examples in the previous section.) Availability is also influenced by recency, and thus we are likely to overestimate the frequency of events recently encountered. (For relevant data, see Johnson & Tversky, 1983.)

In fact, we can put this more broadly: In making inferences or in drawing conclusions, the information we need is often supplied to us by memory. When you decide how to vote, you draw on memories of the candidates' positions and past deeds. If you are wondering why your friend is in a foul mood, you will try to recall events or conversations that might have led to the mood. In this way, failures of memory take on new importance. If memory is selective, or inaccurate, this will play a crucial role in shaping the progress of thought.

Factors external to memory can also bias availability. For example, imagine that you have been asked to advise the government on next year's budget. In particular, you are trying to decide how much money to spend on various research projects, all aimed at saving lives. It seems sensible that you would choose to spend your resources on the more frequent causes of death, rather than investigating rare problems, and that leads to our questions: Should we spend more on preventing death from motor vehicle accidents or death from stomach cancer? Which is more common? Should we spend more on preventing homicides, or diabetes? People reliably assert that motor vehicle accidents and homicide are the more frequent in each pair, although the opposite is true both times, as shown in Table 12.1 (Combs & Slovic, 1979; Slovic, Fischhoff & Lichtenstein, 1982). Why is this?

In estimating the likelihood of these events, people are heavily influenced by the pattern of media coverage. Homicide makes the front page, while diabetes does not, and this is reflected in participants'

estimates of frequency. Indeed, their estimates, for each of the causes of death, correspond rather closely to frequency of report in the media, rather than to actual frequency of occurrence. Thus, once again, we find an influence of availability. Just as some information is less available to us via the selectivity of memory, some information is less available via the selectivity of the media. And it is the available data that people use, making the media bias as important as the memory bias.

In the same vein, it is noteworthy that media critics have expressed considerable concern over how often African Americans are portrayed as criminals on television. Given the data we have just described, it is plausible that this pattern of media misrepresentation may well influence national estimates of who is committing crimes, a prospect with obvious political and social ramifications.

| *Availability Bias in Estimates of Frequency of Death from Various Causes* | | **TABLE 12.1** |
|---|---|---|
| **Most overestimated** | **Most underestimated** | |
| All accidents | Smallpox vaccination | |
| Motor vehicle accidents | Diabetes | |
| Pregnancy, childbirth, and abortion | Stomach cancer | |
| Tornadoes | Lightning | |
| Flood | Stroke | |
| Botulism | Tuberculosis | |
| All cancer | Asthma | |
| Fire and flames | Emphysema | |
| Venomous bite or sting | | |
| Homicide | | |

*Note*: People estimated how many deaths are caused by each of these factors. Their judgments were clearly influenced by how often each factor is reported in the media: Stomach cancer is usually not reported; homicide and death from fires are often reported.

[From Slovic, Fischhoff & Lichtenstein, 1982.]

## ANCHORING

In some ways, these availability effects should not be surprising. After all, it is no shock that we are more influenced by the facts we remember, rather than by the facts we fail to remember. Likewise, it is hardly news that some facts catch our attention, while other facts do not. And, of course, we are influenced by the pattern of how things are reported in the media.

What seems more surprising, though, is our apparent inability to overcome these effects, even when we are alerted to them. For example, you surely knew that homicide is generally considered newsworthy, while death from diabetes is not. You might, therefore, adjust for this media bias in making your estimates—increasing your estimate of diabetes deaths, since you know these are underreported. However, it seems that people do *not* make these adjustments, do *not* compensate for availability bias, even when the bias is out in plain view.

A tendency known as **anchoring** is relevant here: This term refers to the fact that, once an answer to a question is on the scene, people seem to use this answer as a reference point and select their own judgments only by making adjustments to this "anchor." Strikingly, they show this tendency even when the initial answer—the anchor—is obviously not worth trusting.

Participants in one study were asked to estimate the proportion of African nations in the United Nations. (The correct answer was 35%.) Participants first watched while the experimenter spun a wheel marked with numbers from 1 to 100. As far as the participants knew, this wheel was just a "random-number generator" but, in truth, the wheel was rigged, so that for half of the participants it stopped at "10," and for half it stopped at "65." Participants were asked whether the actual percentage was above or below this "estimate" obtained from the wheel, and then they were asked to give their own estimate. Participants who saw the wheel stop at 10 offered, on average, an estimate of 25%. Those who saw the wheel stop at 65 offered, on average, an estimate of 45%. Even in this case, participants are apparently taking the wheel's "selection" as a reference point, and making their own estimate with reference to this anchor (Tversky & Kahneman, 1974).

Likewise, it is no accident that fund-raisers often ask you how much you wish to contribute: "$100? $50? $30? $10?" Note that they don't phrase the question this way: "$10? $30? $50? $100?" It seems likely that the fund-raisers are capitalizing on your tendency to treat the first-viewed numbers as anchors and to set your contribution relative to this anchor. (See Loftus & Zanni, 1975, for many related cases.)

Anchoring effects are important for several reasons, but for our purposes, they indicate that, once an error is made, it may be difficult for people to set the error aside and start again. Thus, if someone's initial estimates are biased by media reporting, or by the selectivity of memory, we can't remove these effects by reminding the person about media bias or memory selection. In both cases, the initial response, even though clearly in error, will serve as an anchor for subsequent judgments. Once an initial estimate is made, its effect seems long-lived. (For related claims, see Wilson & Brekke, 1994.)

## JUDGMENTS OF QUANTITY

We have catalogued several factors influencing information availability, and as we have seen, these factors have a direct impact on our judgments. All of this serves to confirm the claim that is central here: Judgments often rely on the availability heuristic, and this is why judgments are so strongly influenced by how easily the relevant examples come to mind.

Similar heuristics allow us to make a number of related judgments, such as judgments of *quantity*. Imagine that you are working on a paper for your English course; have you offered enough arguments to make your claims persuasive? Or imagine an attorney trying to persuade a jury; at what point has enough evidence been presented to "make the case"? These judgments, like frequency judgments, are often made via heuristics.

As an illustration, Josephs, Giesler, and Silvera (1994) asked their participants to write an essay on the topic, "Why it is better to buy American cars than Japanese cars." Participants were given no instructions about how *long* the essay should be but were told to continue working until they felt they had written an essay "that, if submitted for a grade, would earn an A." Half the participants wrote their essays in a single-spaced format, with a small type-font; the other participants wrote their essays in a double-spaced format, with a much larger font. Those in the former group ended up writing essays, on average, 25% longer than participants in the latter group. Apparently, the participants all judged the adequacy and the completeness of their essay in a fairly crude fashion, and so thought the essay "finished" when it had the appropriate number of pages.

We don't want to suggest that all judgments are made in such a crude way, and surely we can find circumstances in which people use more precise, more systematic strategies for estimating quantity. For example, people are sometimes alert to the fact that they don't know very much about a category, and this dissuades them from relying on the availability heuristic. How many sumo wrestlers are there in your state? If you relied on availability in answering this question, you might answer "zero" (assuming that none of your friends are sumo wrestlers). But in this situation you are probably alert to your own lack of expertise, and so you will seek some other basis for making this judgment (Schwarz, 1998; for other research examining *when* people rely on other grounds for judging frequency, see Brown & Siegler, 1993; Bruce, Hockley & Craik, 1991; Sedlemeier et al., 1998; Watkins & LeCompte, 1991).

Nonetheless, the fact remains that we often do rely on these shortcuts in judging quantity or frequency, and we emphasize that this is, in many cases, a sensible strategy—efficient and generally leading to a reasonable estimate. As we have seen, however, it is easy to find cases in which these heuristics lead us astray—to estimates far from the truth. Given the impact of anchoring, these errors, once they occur, may have an enduring influence on our judgments.

## Representativeness

So far, we have considered the strategies people use when trying to summarize and assess the information to which they've been exposed. But, of course, people often want to do more than this. They want to extrapolate from this information, and so they draw inferences and make predictions, all based on the experiences they have already encountered. How do people go about these steps?

Once again, evidence points to the prominent use of a heuristic strategy, a strategy closely related to one we first met in Chapter 9. In that context, we saw that people often categorize by use of prototypes. This strategy exploits the fact that, while "being typical" for a category is different from "being *in*" the category, these qualities do overlap: Something that resembles a "typical bird" is likely to be a bird when closely inspected. This allows us to use typicality as an efficient, and usually successful, categorization strategy.

It turns out that this categorization strategy is just a special case of a broader heuristic, namely the **representativeness heuristic**. This heuristic involves making the assumption that each member of a category is "representative" of the category—that is, has all of the traits that we associate with that category. Thus, if someone is a lawyer, we give in to the stereotype and expect her to have the traits we associate with lawyers. Conversely, if someone looks like (our idea of) a typical lawyer, we conclude she is a lawyer. (This is the strategy we met in Chapter 9.) This assumption also leaves us quite willing to draw conclusions from a relatively small sample: If each member of a group is representative of the group, then it's fair to draw conclusions about the whole after one or two observations, and thus we agree to statements such as "If you've seen one lawyer, you've seen 'em all."

To put this differently, the representativeness heuristic amounts to an assumption of *homogeneity* in the categories we are reasoning about and a willingness to reason according to similarity. This emphasis on similarity is then easily extended, and so we develop a reasoning guideline that can be summarized by the phrase "like goes with like" (Gilovich, 1991; Gilovich & Savitsky, 1996). This leads us to expect that effects will resemble causes (and so eating fish will make you a better swimmer, a belief endorsed by many people; Nemeroff & Rozin, 1994), and momentous events (like an assassination) must have equally momentous triggers (perhaps a large-scale conspiracy). By the same token, we also "are more inclined to see jagged handwriting as a sign of a tense rather than a relaxed personality" (Gilovich, 1991, p. 18).

Of course, these reasoning patterns will often lead us to the correct conclusions, since many categories we encounter *are* homogeneous. If after one or two nights at a Howard Johnson's, you conclude that all hotel rooms have Bibles in them, your conclusion is warranted. If you conclude that Irv probably is comfortable with math, because he is, after all, an engineer, this conclusion, too, is probably correct—engineers are likely to be reasonably homogeneous in this particular dimension. But as with all heuristics, it is easy to find cases in which this sort of reasoning can lead to error.

## REASONING FROM THE POPULATION TO AN INSTANCE

Imagine tossing a coin over and over; let's say that the coin has landed heads up six times in a row. Many people (and many gamblers) believe that, in this situation, the coin is more likely to come up tails than heads on the next toss. But this conclusion is wrong; and this belief is commonly referred to as the "gamblers fallacy." The "logic" leading to this fallacy seems to be that, if the coin is fair, then a series of tosses should contain equal numbers of heads and tails. If no tails have appeared for a while, then some are "overdue" to bring about this balance.

But how could this be? The coin has no "memory," so it has no way of knowing how long it has been since the last tails. More generally, there simply is no mechanism through which the history of the previous tosses could influence the current one. Therefore, the likelihood of a tail on toss #7 is 50-50 (i.e., .50), just as it was on the first toss, and as it is on every toss.

Where, then, does our (mistaken) belief come from? The explanation lies in our assumption of category homogeneity. We know that, over the long haul, a fair coin will produce equal numbers of heads and tails. Thus, the category of "all tosses" has this property. Our assumption of homogeneity, though, leads us to expect that any "representative" of the category will also have this property—that is, any sequence of tosses will also show the 50-50 split. But this isn't true: Some sequences of tosses are 75% heads, some are 5% heads, some are 100% heads. It is only when we combine all these sequences that the 50-50 split emerges.

A different way to say this appeals to the notion of sample size. If we examine a large number of cases, we will find patterns close to those in the population at large. This is what statisticians refer to as the "law of large numbers." There is, however, no "law of small numbers": There is no tendency for small samples to approximate the pattern of the population. Indeed, small samples can often stray rather far from the population values. But people seem not to appreciate this and act as though they expect small samples to show the pattern of the whole.

Here is a related example, from a study by Kahneman and Tversky (1972). Participants were given the following problem:

In a small town nearby, there are two hospitals. Hospital A has an average of 45 births per day; Hospital B is smaller, and has an average of 15 births per day. As we all know, overall the number of males born is 50%. Each hospital recorded the number of days in which, on that day, at least 60% of the babies born were male. Which hospital recorded more such days, (a) Hospital A, (b) Hospital B, (c) both equal?

The majority of the participants chose response "both equal," but this answer is statistically unwarranted. All of the births in the country add up to a 50-50 split between male and female babies. The larger the sample one examines, the more likely one is to approximate this ideal. Conversely, the *smaller* the sample one examines, the more likely one is to stray from this ideal. Days with 60% male births, straying from the ideal, are therefore more likely in the smaller hospital, Hospital B.

If you don't see this, consider a more extreme case. Hospital C has 1,000 births per day; Hospital D has exactly one birth per day. Which hospital records more days with "at least 90% male births"? This value will be observed in Hospital D rather often since, on many days, all the babies born (one out of one) will be male. This value is surely less likely, though, in Hospital C: 900 male births, with just 100 female, would be a remarkable event indeed. In this case, it seems clear that the smaller hospital can more easily stray far from the 50-50 split.

In the hospital problem, just like in the gambler's fallacy, participants seem not to take sample size into account. They seem to think a particular pattern is just as likely with a small sample as with a large sample, although this is plainly not true. This belief, however, is just what one would expect if people were making the assumption that each instance of a category—or, in this case, each subset of a larger set—should show the properties associated with the entire set.

## REASONING FROM A SINGLE CASE TO THE ENTIRE POPULATION

In the cases just described, people seem to expect that each individual in a category will have the properties of the category overall. The reverse error can also be demonstrated: People expect the overall category to have the properties of the individuals, and so they are quite willing to extrapolate from a few instances to the entire set. In fact, evidence suggests that they generalize in this fashion even when they are explicitly told that the instance is *not* representative of the larger group.

Hamill, Wilson, and Nisbett (1980) showed their participants a videotaped interview in which a person identified as a prison guard discussed his job. In one condition, the guard was compassionate and kind, and expressed great concern for rehabilitation. In the other condition, the guard expressed contempt for the prison inmates, and he scoffed at the idea of rehabilitation. Before seeing either of these videotapes, some participants were told that this guard was quite typical of those at the prison; other participants were told that he was quite atypical, chosen for the interview precisely because of his extreme views. Still other participants were given no information about whether the interviewed guard was typical or not.

Participants were later questioned about their views of the criminal justice system, and the data show that they were clearly influenced by the interview they had seen: Those who had seen the humane guard indicated that they believed prison guards to be decent people in general; those who had seen the inhumane guard reported more negative views of guards. What is remarkable, though, is that participants seemed largely to ignore the information about whether the interviewed guard was typical or not. Those who were explicitly told the guard was *atypical* were influenced by the interview just as much, and in the same way, as those who were told that the guard was typical.

These data, and other laboratory findings (e.g., Hamill et al., 1980), make it clear that people are quite willing to draw conclusions from a single case, even when they have been explicitly warned that the case is not representative. This is exactly what we would expect if they are using the representativeness heuristic. If one makes the assumption that categories are homogeneous, then it is reasonable to extrapolate from one observation to the entire category, and that seems sadly close to what these participants are doing.

Similar data are easily observed outside of the laboratory. Consider what Nisbett and Ross (1980) have referred to as "man who" arguments. You are shopping for a new car. You have read various consumer magazines and decided, based on their reports of test data and repair records, that you will buy a Smacko brand car. You report this to your father, who is aghast. "Smacko?! You must be crazy. Why, I know a man who bought a Smacko, and the transmission fell out two weeks after he got it. Then the alternator went. Then the brakes. How could you possibly buy a Smacko?"

What should you make of this argument? The consumer magazines tested many cars, and reported that 20% of all Smackos break down. In your father's "data," 100% of the Smackos (one out of one) break down. Should this "sample of one" outweigh the much larger sample tested by the magazine? Your father presumably believes he is offering a persuasive argument, but what is the basis for this? The only basis we can see is the presumption that the category will resemble the instance; only if that were true would reasoning from a single instance be appropriate.

If you listen to conversations around you, you will regularly hear "man who" (or "woman who") arguments. "What do you mean cigarette smoking causes cancer?! I have an aunt who smoked for 50 years, and she runs in marathons!" Often, these arguments seem persuasive. But these arguments have force only by virtue of the representativeness heuristic—our assumption that categories are homogeneous, and therefore our peculiar willingness to take a small sample of data as seriously as a larger sample.

## Support Theory

Strategies like availability and representativeness influence us in many ways, and in many settings. Often these strategies lead to sensible judgments, but sometimes they lead us to foolishness. And sometimes these strategies leave us open to influence by factors that really should be irrelevant to our judgments— including the exact way that a situation or event is described.

Right now, you're working your way through a textbook chapter. How likely is it that you'll be finished in an hour? How likely is it that you'll be finished in sixty minutes? Surely your answers to these questions should be the same, since "one hour" means the same thing as "sixty minutes." The idea, then, is that your assessment of the hypothesis, "I'll be finished in X amount of time," should be independent of the phrasing, and independent of how the event is described.

A great deal of evidence, however, suggests that different descriptions of the same event can give rise to very different judgments. Tversky and Koehler (1994) developed a mathematical model of this effect, but the basic idea of their "support theory" is straightforward: People make judgments about a claim by asking themselves how much support they perceive for the claim; how much support they perceive, in turn, depends on how the claim is phrased, and in particular, on how *explicit* the description is.

To see how this works, consider a study by Johnson et al. (1993). They asked some of their participants how much they would be willing to pay for an insurance policy that covered "hospitalization for any reason." Other participants were asked how much they would be willing to pay for a policy that covered "hospitalization for any disease or accident." Participants in the second group were willing to pay a substantially higher price, presumably because the explicit mention of "disease or accident" had increased the perceived chances of hospitalization, and so the attractiveness of the insurance.

Similarly, Tversky and Kahneman (1983) asked one group of participants how likely they thought it was that "sometime in the next year, a massive flood in North America would drown more than 1,000 people." A different group of participants were asked how likely they thought it was that "sometime in the next year, there would be an earthquake in California causing a massive flood in which more than 1,000 people would drown." Of course, the second event is simply a more specific version of the first event, and so, if the second event occurs, then the first event has also occurred. Therefore, the second event cannot be more likely than the first event. Even so, participants regarded the second (more specific) event as substantially more likely. Why? Because the second event is described in a fuller, more explicit fashion, and this makes it easier for the participants to imagine how the event might actually happen. In essence, this makes the event more *available* for the participants, with clear implications for their judgment. (For more on how *imagining*, or even just thinking about an event, can increase estimates of probability, see Garry et al.,

1996. For more on how we are influenced by changes in description, see Chapters 10 and 13.)

## Detecting Covariation

We seem to be moving toward an unsettling indictment of human judgment. People place too much faith in the easily available evidence, even when they know the evidence to be biased. People "anchor" their judgments, even when they know the anchor to be arbitrary. People take small samples of evidence too seriously and treat evidence as though it were representative, even if told explicitly that it is not. And all of this leaves us open to a host of further effects, including the effect of small changes in phrasing.

Is this grim picture correct? Is human judgment as poor as the evidence so far suggests? We will have more to say about this before we are through. First, though, we need to add some further "charges" to the indictment.

Many of the judgments we informally make hinge on questions about **covariation**. This term has a technical meaning, but for our purposes, we can define it this way: X and Y "covary" if X tends to be on the scene whenever Y is, and if X tends to be absent whenever Y is absent. X might also covary with the *absence* of Y—X is present when Y is absent and absent when Y is present.

For example, exercise and stamina covary—people who do the first tend to have a lot of the second. Owning audio CDs and going to concerts also covary, although less strongly than exercise and stamina. (Some people own many CDs but rarely go to concerts.) Note then that covariation is a matter of degree— covariation can be strong or weak. Covariation can also be either negative or positive. Exercise and stamina, for example, covary positively (as exercise increases, so does stamina). Exercise and body fat, in contrast, covary negatively (as exercise increases, body fat *de*creases).

Why is covariation important? Covariation is what we look at in assessing the quality of a diagnostic technique. Can we diagnose schizophrenia on the basis of some blood test? We can find out by asking whether schizophrenic symptoms covary with some blood value. Covariation is also what we look at to test a hypothesis about cause and effect. Does education lead to a higher-paying job? If so, then degree of education and salary should covary. Likewise, does taking aspirin prevent heart attacks? If so, then aspirin use and heart attacks should covary negatively, with the presence of one being associated with the absence of the other.

In these ways, assessing covariation is of crucial importance for scientific data analysis, and it is no less important in day-to-day reasoning. Do my colleagues at work act in a friendlier fashion when I am formal, or when I'm casual? Can you study more effectively if you have a period of physical exercise early in the day? These are, once again, questions about covariation, and they are the sorts of questions we frequently ask. So how well do we do when we think about covariation?

### "ILLUSIONS" OF COVARIATION

Psychologists have developed a wide variety of tests designed to measure personality characteristics or behavioral inclinations. One well-known example is the Rorschach test, in which participants are shown ink blots and asked to describe them. These descriptions are then examined, looking for certain patterns. A mention of humans in motion is said to indicate imagination and a rich inner life; responses that describe the white spaces around the ink blot are taken as indications of rebelliousness.

Is this valid? Do specific responses, or signs, as they are called, really covary with certain personality traits? And how astutely do psychologists detect this covariation? To attack these questions, Chapman and Chapman (1971) created a number of Rorschach protocols, that is, written transcripts of a person's responses. The protocols were actually fictional, made up for this study, but were designed to resemble real Rorschach responses. The Chapmans also made up fictional descriptions of the people who had supposedly offered these responses: One protocol was attributed to someone who "believes other people are plotting against him." Another protocol was attributed to someone who "has sexual feelings toward other men."

The Chapmans *randomly* paired the protocols and the personality descriptions—one protocol and one description, the next protocol and a different description. These randomly assembled protocol-profile pairs were then shown to a group of undergraduates, students who had no prior experience with the Rorschach test and who did not know the theory behind the test. These students were asked to examine the pairs, and asked to determine what signs covaried with what traits. In particular, the students were asked which signs covaried with homosexuality.

Before pressing on, we should mention the fact that the Chapmans' research was done more than three decades ago, in a period of time when many psychologists viewed homosexuality as a "disorder" to be diagnosed. Psychologists have long since abandoned this view, and so we discuss the Chapmans' research because it is a classic study of covariation, and not because it tells us anything about homosexuality.

Returning to the study itself, we know that, thanks to the random pairing, there was no covariation in this set of "data" between protocols and descriptions, between signs and personality traits. Nonetheless, the students reported seeing a pattern of covariation. Certain signs, they reported, seemed consistently good indicators that the respondent was a homosexual. For example, they reported that homosexual respondents were particularly likely to perceive buttocks in the ink blots. Therefore, mention of buttocks was a reasonable indicator, they claimed, of homosexuality.

We emphasize that there was no pattern in these made-up data, and therefore the covariation the students are perceiving is illusory—"observed" in the data even though it is plainly not there. And, oddly enough, the covariation "perceived" by these students was identical to that alleged at the time by professional clinicians. Clinicians, based on extensive experience with patients, were convinced that certain signs *were* valid indicators of homosexuality, and the signs they mentioned were, remarkably, exactly the ones nominated by the participants in the

Chapman and Chapman study. The clinicians, like the Chapmans' participants, reported that use of the "buttocks" response does covary with sexual orientation, with homosexuals much more likely to use this response.

Is this just a coincidence—that the pattern "observed" by the undergraduates, in bogus data, matches the pattern reported by professionals, based on "real" data? Further evidence suggests it is not at all a coincidence: A number of researchers have examined the actual Rorschach responses from homosexuals and heterosexuals and asked statistically whether "buttocks" responses are more likely from one group than the other. As it turns out, the two groups do not differ at all in the likelihood of this response—that is, there is no covariation between sexual orientation and use of the "buttocks" response. Therefore, this is not a valid indicator. Nonetheless, a wide range of clinicians, the Chapmans found, continued to insist that this response was indicative of homosexuality.

Notice where this leaves us: In the Chapmans' laboratory studies, we know there was no pattern of covariation in the Rorschach data; nonetheless, participants perceived a pattern—perceived, specifically, covariation between sexual orientation and a particular response. Likewise, in *authentic* Rorschach data, professional clinicians saw the same pattern, the same covariation. When the data are carefully tabulated, though, there is no such covariation. The clinicians, just like the undergraduates, were seeing something that wasn't there; the professionals, with years of experience and training, were vulnerable to the same **illusory covariations** as the laboratory participants. (For related evidence, see Arkes & Harkness, 1983; Schustack & Sternberg, 1981; Shaklee & Mims, 1982; Smedslund, 1963.)

## THEORY-DRIVEN AND DATA-DRIVEN DETECTION OF COVARIATION

Each of us seeks to learn from our experiences—both the experiences of daily life, and also experiences in our professional domains. Indeed, in our professional worlds we can accumulate great quantities of experience—a physician has seen many cases of the flu; a salesperson has seen many customers; a teacher, many students. Therefore, each of us has had enormous opportunity to accumulate "professional wisdom" within our area of special expertise.

The clear message of the Chapmans' data, though, is that we might be wary of this "professional wisdom." Their data remind us that professional training does not make you immune to illusions, that professionals, just like everyone else, are fully capable of "projecting" their beliefs onto the evidence and perceiving patterns that aren't there. Thus, if one starts with the intuition that there is some association between homosexuality and rear ends, then one will "detect" a pattern, "confirming" this intuition, in the data.

Given all this, perhaps we should be cautious when a police officer assures us that crimes are more frequent under a full moon, or when a hairstylist tells us that a certain shampoo cures split ends. In each of these cases, a professional is making a claim about covariation, and we all tend to trust such claims, as they are based on so much firsthand experience. Nonetheless, we might want to ask how these conclusions were drawn. Was the evidence systematically recorded and rigorously reviewed? Or are these claims simply derived in an informal way, based on the professional's "global impression" of the facts? If the latter, one might argue that these claims can't be taken seriously, since they could turn out merely to be further examples of illusory covariation. (For other evidence echoing this concern about "professional wisdom," see the studies reviewed by Shanteau, 1992.)

For that matter, if experts show these effects, what about the rest of us? Does each of us project our own biases onto the data, seeing only the pattern of covariation we expect to see? We are not surprised if such errors happen to someone very dogmatic, e.g., to the sexist who believes all women are moody (that is, expects to see, and "sees," covariation between gender and moodiness), or to the racist who believes all blacks are lazy (again, a covariation claim). Someone dogmatic would surely distort the

evidence in order to "support" these ugly beliefs. But, alas, it's not just the dogmatic who show this pattern: We discover the same patterns of prejudice in ourselves.

In a study by Jennings, Amabile, and Ross (1982), college students were asked to make covariation judgments in two types of situations: situations in which they had no prior expectations or biases, and situations in which they did. For example, in the "prior belief" (or "theory-based") case, the participants were asked to estimate how strong the covariation is between (a) children's dishonesty as measured by false report of athletic performance, and (b) children's dishonesty as measured by amount of cheating in solving a puzzle. If a child is dishonest according to one of these indices, is he or she also dishonest according to the other? Or, as a different example, participants estimated the covariation between (a) how highly a student rated U.S. presidents' performance in the last decade, and (b) how highly the student rated business leaders' performance in the last decade. If you think highly of our presidents, do you also think highly of the business community?

The participants presumably made these judgments by reflecting on their prior experience and their intuitions; no new data were presented in the experimental procedure. Participants expressed these judgments by selecting a number between 0 and 100, where 0 indicated that the two traits were unrelated, did not covary, and 100 indicated that the traits covaried perfectly. Participants could also use negative values (to −100) to indicate the belief that the two traits covary, but with the presence of one indicating the absence of the other.

The participants were also asked to make a comparable judgment in a "no prior belief" (or "data-based") case, that is, with variables they had never met or considered before. For example, they were presented with ten pictures, each showing a man holding a walking stick. The heights of the men varied in the pictures, as did the length of the walking stick, and participants had to judge whether these two variables covaried, again choosing a value between −100 and +100.

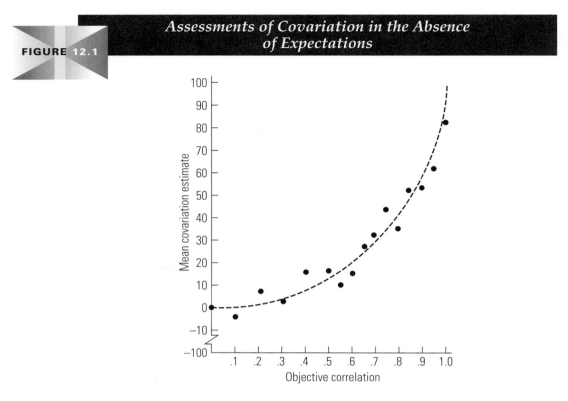

**FIGURE 12.1**

*Assessments of Covariation in the Absence of Expectations*

When participants enter a situation with no expectations about the data, their estimates of covariation are quite orderly: The estimates grow stronger and stronger as the actual (objective) correlation grows stronger and stronger. In addition, participants give low estimates unless the actual correlation is very strong. [After Jennings, Amabile & Ross, 1982.]

Figure 12.1 shows the results from the data-based cases, i.e., the cases in which participants had no prior beliefs. Here, their estimates of covariation were reasonably regular: the stronger the covariation, the stronger the estimate. Their judgments also tended to be rather conservative: Estimates exceeded +30 only when the objective correlation was very strong. Figure 12.2 shows a very different picture for the theory-based cases. The participants tended to be far more extravagant in these estimates,

with estimates of +60 and +80. They were also far less regular in the theory-based cases, with only a weak relation between the magnitude of the estimated covariation and the magnitude of the actual covariation. For example, the "children's dishonesty" pair, mentioned earlier, is shown as the black square in the figure. In this case, the objective correlation, statistically measured, is fairly small. That is, children who are dishonest in one context are often honest in other contexts. Participants estimated

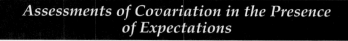

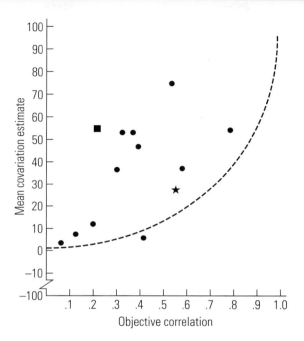

When participants enter a situation with expectations about the data, their estimates of covariation are often inaccurate. In this instance, participants were asked to assess the covariation in 16 cases. The square and the star indicate the two cases discussed in the text. Participants often estimated the covariation as strong even when it was quite weak, or as being weak even when it was strong. The systematic pattern observed in Figure 12.1 is clearly absent here. (For purposes of comparison, this figure includes the curve describing the data from Figure 12.1.) [After Jennings, Amabile & Ross, 1982.]

this covariation to be quite large, though, with an average estimate of +60. For the "presidents and business leaders" case (the black star in the figure), the objective correlation is much stronger than in the "dishonesty" pair, but participants estimated it to be much weaker.

At the very least, then, participants are performing differently in the theory-based and data-based judgments. The former judgments are often extravagant; the latter tend to be conservative. The data-based judgments track the objective facts fairly well; the theory-based judgments do not. Given these results, it is difficult to avoid the conclusion that theory biased what the participants "saw" in the data, and led them to see much stronger (or weaker) covariation than was there. (Other relevant data are reviewed by Allan, 1993; Alloy & Tabachnik, 1984; Baron, 1988.)

## ILLUSORY COVARIATION: ANOTHER AVAILABILITY EFFECT?

Why do beliefs and expectations mislead participants in judgments of covariation? One possibility is that participants are being dogmatic, and so it is a case of "I've already made up my mind; don't distract me with the facts." This is surely true in some occasions, but unpromising as a general explanation: In the experiments we have considered, participants seem to be taking their task seriously—carefully examining the Rorschach responses, for example, and giving every indication that they are weighing the evidence as well as they can. Hence, it seems unlikely that participants are simply ignoring the facts in these experiments.

A different possibility is that people don't know how to compute covariation, so they end up using an estimation strategy that bears little resemblance to the correct formula. If this were the problem, however, then performance in judging covariation should be uniformly poor—if people don't know how to compute covariation, then they'll never get it right! But this is not what the evidence shows. Instead, as we have seen, people do quite well in judging covariation in data-driven cases, when they don't have a prior theory. Plainly, therefore, people *do* have the means of computing covariation, at least in some circumstances.

Why, then, do people go astray in the theory-based cases? Here is one promising proposal (cf. Baron, 1988; Evans, 1989; Gilovich, 1991; Jennings, Amabile & Ross, 1982). In making most of their judgments, people usually don't survey *all* of the evidence. Instead, they consider only a *selected subset* of the evidence. This would be fine if the subset were selected in some fair manner, but often it's not. That's because, if someone has expectations from the start about what patterns they'll see in the evidence, this can lead to a *bias* in which bits of evidence they'll consider and which bits they'll ignore. This

almost guarantees a biased conclusion: Even if the judgment process were 100% fair, a biased input will probably lead to a biased output.

Support for these claims comes from many sources. The fact that people often use the availability heuristic, for example, makes it clear that we are willing to draw conclusions based on only a small set of observations (namely, those observations that are readily available). Likewise, the power of "man who" arguments also indicates our willingness to draw claims from a narrow slice of evidence. For that matter, consider the fact that working memory is limited in size (Chapter 5); this, too, may place limits on many judgment strategies and may, in particular, place limits on how much information someone can contemplate at any particular moment in time.

All of this forces us to ask, therefore, *which* observations people are likely to consider when they are assessing covariation. Will it be a random set? A representative sample? Or perhaps a biased sample? Many factors are pertinent here, but one important contributor is known as **confirmation bias** (Nisbett & Ross, 1980; Tweney, Doherty & Mynatt, 1981). This term actually encompasses several different mechanisms, but what these mechanisms have in common is that, collectively, they make us more alert and more responsive to evidence that *confirms* our beliefs in comparison to evidence that might challenge our beliefs.

We will have more to say about confirmation bias in Chapter 13, and there we will consider some of the data documenting the breadth and the power of this bias. For now, though, let's think through how confirmation bias applies to the assessment of covariation. Let us say, for sake of discussion, that you have the belief that big dogs tend to be vicious. As a result of this belief, whenever you are thinking about dogs, or looking at dogs, confirmation bias will lead you to notice the big dogs that are, in fact, vicious, and the little dogs that are friendly. Your memory schemata will also help you to remember episodes that fit with this belief and will work against your remembering counter-examples. (Recall that one effect of memory schemata is to "regularize" our past experiences, bringing our recollections into line with our schema-based expectations—see Chapter 7.)

Thanks to these various mechanisms, a biased sample of dogs is available to you—both in the dogs you perceive (because of a bias in attention) and also in the dogs you remember (because of the bias in attention *and* the effects of memory schemata). Therefore, if you are asked to estimate covariation between dog size and temperament, you will probably overestimate the covariation. This isn't because you are ignoring the facts, nor is it because you're incompetent in thinking about covariation. The problem instead lies in your "data," and if the data are biased, so will be your judgment.

How often does this sort of error happen? How many of our covariation estimates are in error? No one really knows, but it seems worth some concern. We have mentioned sexist hypotheses that depend on "observed covariation" for their support, and racist hypotheses in the same boat. Many medical hypotheses also hinge on covariation. Thus, the stakes are often quite high in judgments involving covariation. If misjudging covariation merely meant buying the wrong shampoo or developing an odd (but benign) superstition, then we might not worry about these errors. But the cost of these errors is potentially far greater than this.

## Base Rates

A further line of evidence is also relevant here and highlights a type of information we often overlook in our assessment of covariation. As a way of entering these issues, consider the following problem (after Kahneman & Tversky, 1973; Nisbett & Ross, 1980):

> I have a friend who is a professor. He likes to write poetry, is rather shy, and is small in stature. Which of the following is his field: (a) Chinese studies or (b) psychology?

This is once again a question about covariation; in this case, we are asking whether certain traits (writing poetry, being shy) covary with profession. In re-

sponse to this question, most people conclude that the friend is in Chinese studies. Presumably, this judgment is based on something like the representativeness heuristic: The example describes someone close to many people's stereotype of a Chinese scholar, and so they draw the appropriate conclusion.

However, this judgment overlooks an important bit of information. As you can probably guess, the number of psychologists in this country is much greater than the number of scholars in Chinese studies. To see how this matters, let us assume, just for sake of argument, that virtually all Chinese scholars—let's say, 90%—fit the stereotype. Let us assume further that only 5% of the psychologists fit the stereotype. In this case, "fitting the stereotype" would be high-quality **diagnostic information**—information that does indeed indicate that you are in one category rather than another.

But now we need to factor in how many psychologists there are and how many Chinese scholars. Remember that there are relatively few Chinese scholars in this country; even if 90% of these fit the description, this is still 90% of a small number. In contrast, merely 5% of the psychologists fit the description, but this will be 5% of a much larger number. To make this concrete, let's say there are 10,000 Chinese scholars in this country, and 200,000 psychologists. In this case, 9,000 Chinese scholars fit the description (90% of 10,000), but 10,000 psychologists do as well (5% of 200,000). Therefore, even though the *proportion* of Chinese scholars fitting the description is larger than the *proportion* of psychologists (90% vs. 5%), the *number* of psychologists who fit the description is greater than the *number* of Chinese scholars fitting the description. As a result, chances are that the friend is a psychologist, since the description is compatible with more psychologists than Chinese scholars.

To put this more generally, you need two types of information in order to make judgments like this one: both the diagnostic information and also the **base rate**—the overall likelihood that a particular case will be in this category or that one, independent of the diagnostic information. Often, the base rate is expressed as a probability or as a proportion, and so, in our example, the base rate for "being a Chinese scholar," rather than a psychologist, is roughly .05. (That's the proportion of Chinese scholars within the entire group of people we're considering.) Base rate information is always important, and in some cases, it can offset the diagnostic information. In our example, the diagnostic information by itself favored the conclusion of "Chinese studies," but the diagnostic information in conjunction with the base rate pointed toward the opposite conclusion.

Base rates are essential to a wide range of judgments. For example, imagine that we are testing a new drug and discover that 70% of the patients who take this drug recover. Does that mean the drug is effective? The answer depends on the base rate: In general, how many patients recover? If the answer is 70%, then the drug is having no effect whatsoever. Likewise, do good-luck charms help? Let's say that you wear your lucky socks whenever your favorite team plays, and the team has won 85% of their games. We again need to ask about base rates: How many games has your team won over the last few years? Perhaps they have won 90% overall, but only 85% when you are wearing your lucky socks; in that case, your socks are actually a jinx.

## BASE RATES AND DIAGNOSTIC INFORMATION

A number of studies have examined how people employ base rates. For example, Kahneman and Tversky (1973) asked their participants this question: If someone is chosen at random from a group of 70 lawyers and 30 engineers, what is his profession likely to be? Quite obviously, chances are that the person is a lawyer. To be precise, there is a 70% chance that the individual selected will be a lawyer, and participants seemed to understand this perfectly well: When asked the *probability* that this randomly chosen individual would be a lawyer, they respond .70. Thus, in this setting, participants made full and accurate use of the base-rate information.

Other participants were asked a different question. They were told that a "panel of psychologists" had interviewed and administered personality tests to a group of engineers and lawyers. No base rates were provided. Instead, participants were given "thumbnail descriptions" of these individuals, allegedly based on the "personality tests." They were asked to use this information to judge whether that individual was more likely to be an engineer or a lawyer.

The "thumbnail descriptions" provided to the participants were carefully designed, so that some evoked the participants' engineer stereotype, while others evoked a lawyer stereotype. For example, a description favoring the engineer stereotype described a man whose hobbies include home carpentry, sailing, and mathematical puzzles and who has no interest in political or social issues. Thus, from the participants' point of view, the "thumbnail descriptions" provided reasonably clear indications of the individuals' professions.

In this setup, participants are being given diagnostic information but, as we noted, no information about base rates. They were easily able to use this information, and thus their judgments sensibly reflected the content of the thumbnail sketches.

In short, therefore, the participants are responsive to base rates if this is the only information they have, indicating that they do know that base rates are relevant to this judgment. Likewise, they make appropriate use of the diagnostic information, if this is all they have. But now let's ask: What happens if we provide participants with both sorts of information—the base rates *and* the diagnostic information?

Participants in a third group were again provided with the thumbnail descriptions, but they were told, in addition, that the individuals being described had been selected, at random, from a group of 30 engineers and 70 lawyers. We have just seen evidence that participants understand the value of *both* pieces of information—the thumbnail sketch and the overall composition of the group. Therefore, we should expect the participants, when given both, to consider both, and to *combine* these two sources of information as best they can. Thus, if the base rate and the diagnostic information both favor the lawyer response, participants should offer this response with some confidence. If the base rate indicates one

## Does the Base Rate Apply to Me?

**FIGURE** 12.3

Suppose that you are at a concert in a nearby town. When the concert ends, you discover that there is snow and ice on the ground. Nonetheless, you decide to drive home.

On average, 50% of college students who drive home during such weather will be in a car accident.

What is your chance of being in a car accident that day? _____%

Suppose that you are at a concert in a nearby town. When the concert ends, you discover that there is snow and ice on the ground. Nonetheless, you decide to drive home.

The chance of a college student being in a car accident during such weather is 55% for bad drivers and 45% for good drivers.

What is your chance of being in a car accident that day? _____%

response, and the diagnostic information the other response, then participants should temper their estimates accordingly.

However, this is not what the participants do. When they are provided with base rates and diagnostic information, they neglect the first and base their responses entirely on the second. Thus, in the lawyer/engineer problem, participants' responses were completely determined by the degree of resemblance between the individual described and their stereotype of a lawyer or an engineer. Indeed, they responded the same way if the base rates were as already described (70 lawyers, 30 engineers) or if the base rates were *reversed* (30 lawyers, 70 engineers). This reversal had no impact on their judgments, confirming that they were ignoring the base rates.

### HOW WIDESPREAD IS BASE RATE NEGLECT?

It is easy to demonstrate that, in many circumstances, people do underutilize base rate information. However, this pattern of *base rate neglect* is not observed in all circumstances. Individual participants differ from each other in how alert they are to

base rates, and so some people reliably do better on problems like the one we've just described, and some people reliably do worse (Stanovich & West, 1998). Whether base rate neglect is observed also depends on how exactly a problem is phrased, with some phrasings apparently drawing attention away from the base rates, and some phrasings doing the opposite (we will return to this point later in the chapter; relevant data have been reported by Anderson, 1996; Gigerenzer & Hoffrage, 1995; Kahneman & Tversky, 1982a; Lovett & Schunn, 1999; Tversky & Kahneman, 1982).

In still other circumstances, people seem to understand the general idea that base rates are important but are convinced that the particular base rate information supplied with a problem is not the right base rate to use! For example, consider the problem shown in the top of Figure 12.3. A participant reading this problem might choose to ignore the 50% base rate, because of reasoning along these lines: "I know I'm a better-than-average driver, so the '50%' estimate doesn't apply to me." In contrast, consider the problem shown in the bottom of Figure 12.3. In this case, *separate* base rates are given for good and bad drivers, and so it's less likely that the participant will decide, "This doesn't apply to me."

**FIGURE 12.4**

## Mammogram Accuracy Expressed as a Percent

### Mammogram Indicates

|  | Cancer | No cancer | Total |
|---|---|---|---|
| Cancer present | 85% | 15% | 100% |
| Cancer absent | 10% | 90% | 100% |

Diagnostic mammography is reasonably accurate. The correct detection rate is close to 85%, the "false alarm" rate is only 10%. (These numbers are approximate, and intended only for purposes of illustration.) [After Eddy, 1982.]

Consistent with this proposal, participants are much more likely to consider the base rates if they are given in the more specific form (e.g., separate base rates for good and bad drivers, as in the bottom of the figure) than if they are given in the more general form (Chandler et al., 1999). This result probably reflects the fact that most people think they're "better than average" on many dimensions, and so they're convinced that statistics describing the "average person" don't apply to them! (For more on this "I'm better than average" effect, see Chapter 13.)

Even with these points acknowledged, though, the fact remains that base rate neglect *is* often observed, even in circumstances involving enormously consequential judgments, and even when the person making the judgment is an "expert" in the relevant field. To see how this plays out, imagine reading about Julia, age 42, who is worried about breast cancer. We might start by asking: How common is breast cancer for women of Julia's age, with her family history, her dietary pattern, and so on? Let us assume that, for this group, the statistics show an overall 1% likelihood of cancer. This is the base rate, the probability we estimate prior to any diagnostic testing. And it should be reassuring to Julia: There is a 99% chance that she is cancer-free.

Is the base rate relevant here? If the base rate were higher (30%), then we would expect Julia to be that much more anxious. If the base rate were lower (.000001%), then the odds are heavily in Julia's favor, and her anxiety should diminish. Without question,

therefore, it seems reasonable to consider the base rates, in considering Julia's case.

Of course, we can also gather more information, since reasonably accurate procedures are available for detecting breast cancer. Let's say that mammograms are approximately 85% accurate. This is the likelihood of a positive test if cancer is on the scene. If there is no cancer, let's say that there is a 90% chance the test will correctly come back negative; that is, the possibility of a false positive is just 10%. (After Eddy, 1982.)

What should Julia conclude, therefore, if her mammogram comes back indicating that cancer is present? She might well schedule surgery as quickly as possible: We have just said that the diagnostic tests are quite reliable. However, we have also agreed that the base rate is relevant to Julia's case. Therefore, the base rate needs somehow to be integrated with the diagnostic information.

How should this information be combined? As a way of thinking this through, let's start with the information in Figure 12.4. We have laid out the diagnostic "credentials" of the mammogram, with 85% of all cancer cases correctly diagnosed, and 15% misdiagnosed. Of all the non-cancer cases, 90% will be correctly diagnosed; 10% will be misdiagnosed.

But now let us place *number* of occurrences in the table, rather than percentages. The correct numbers are shown in Figure 12.5. To understand this table, bear in mind that the base rate shows a 1% likelihood of cancer for the patient group we are consid-

## Mammogram Accuracy Expressed as Number of Cases

FIGURE 12.5

### Mammogram Indicates

|  | Cancer | No cancer | Total |
|---|---|---|---|
| Cancer present | 850 | 150 | 1,000 |
| Cancer absent | 9,900 | 89,100 | 99,000 |

This table combines the percentage information (from Figure 12.4) with the *base rates* for cancer. The base rates are reflected in the rightmost column: With a(n) (estimated) base rate of 1%, there are 99,000 cases with *no* cancer for every 1,000 cases with cancer. Of these 99,000 cases, 10% will be misdiagnosed (see Figure 12.4). Hence, 9,900 of the women without cancer will be misdiagnosed; for the remaining 89,100, the mammogram will correctly indicate no cancer. Of the 1,000 cases with cancer, 15% will be misdiagnosed (again, see Figure 12.4). Hence, 150 women with cancer will be misdiagnosed; for the remaining 850, the mammogram will correctly indicate the presence of cancer. What then should we conclude if a mammogram indicates cancer? This places us in the left-hand column of the table; in this column, 850 women have cancer, out of a total of 10,750 (850 + 9,900). Therefore, with a base rate of 1%, a positive mammogram indicates an 8% chance of cancer (850/10,750). [After Eddy, 1982.]

ering. This means there are 99 patients in the bottom row of the table (cancer absent) for every one in the top row (cancer present). To keep our arithmetic straightforward, let us imagine that there are 99,000 patients in the bottom row (without cancer) and 1,000 in the top row (with cancer).

Of the 1,000 patients with cancer, we know that 85% (850 cases) will be correctly diagnosed by the mammogram. Of the 99,000 patients not having cancer, the mammogram will be correct for 90% of them, or a total of 89,100 patients. The mammogram will be incorrect, though, for 10%, a total of 9,900 patients.

We are now in a position to ask what it means if Julia's mammogram indicates cancer. In Figure 12.5, a positive mammogram result places us in the left-hand column ("Mammogram indicates cancer"). But note that, within this column, the "cancer absent" cases far outnumber the "cancer present" cases, by a margin of 9,900 to 850, or more than 10 to 1. In short, with this patient group, a mammogram indicating cancer is *wrong* more than ten times as often as it is right. This is not because the mammogram is a poor

test. Just the opposite: We have already commented that mammograms are, overall, very accurate as diagnostic tools. A mammogram's being correct is, *proportionally*, much more likely than a mammogram's being incorrect. But, given the base rate, there are more opportunities for the less-likely event to occur, with the result evident in the table.

Thus, the likelihood of Julia having cancer, given a positive test, and given the numbers quoted, is about 8%. For most women, this risk is serious enough to warrant further action—for example, other tests. Nonetheless, this probability is much lower than one might have guessed, based simply on the mammogram's accuracy. One's response and, indeed, one's anxiety level, might be rather different, based on the diagnostic information *plus* the base rate, than it would have been on the basis of the diagnostic information alone.

Our discussion of this case has so far been statistical, not psychological: All we have done is to show how important it is, in understanding this diagnostic information, to take base rates into account. If one looks only at the mammogram's reliability as a test, one might conclude that a positive test on a mammogram is a sure sign of cancer. If one looks at both the mammogram and the base rate, one draws a different conclusion. What we need to ask now, though, is whether medical professionals are sensitive to these issues. We have already seen that laboratory participants do poorly on base rate problems, but one might hope that doctors, trained in the use of diagnostic information, might do better. In fact, this is not the case. Evidence suggests that doctors, just like the rest of us, do not take base rate information into account when evaluating evidence (Dawes, 1988; Eddy, 1982; Klayman & Brown, 1993; although also see Weber, Böckenholt, Hilton & Wallace, 1993). Doctors (and other professionals) show the same patterns of reasoning that we have already observed in laboratory participants—with errors, in this case, that can lead to serious misassessments of a patient's status.

## Assessing the Damage

So far, we seem to be painting a grim portrait of human judgment. We have discussed several sources of error, and we have suggested that these errors are rather widespread. The studies we have cited have mostly been run on university campuses, including some of the world's most prestigious educational institutions. Thus, the participants are, presumably, talented and intelligent. The errors occur nonetheless. (For reviews, see Arkes, 1991; Einhorn & Hogarth, 1981; Gilovich, 1991; Kahneman, Slovic & Tversky, 1982; Nisbett & Ross, 1980.)

Even experts make these errors. We have discussed poor diagnostic reasoning in physicians and illusory correlations in experienced therapists. Likewise, if we add just a little subtlety to our problems, analogous errors can be observed even among those with considerable training in statistics and methodology (Kahneman & Tversky, 1982a; Tversky & Kahneman, 1971, 1983; also see Mahoney & DeMonbreun, 1978; Shanteau, 1992). In some cases, the experts do avoid error, but only if the problems fit precisely into their areas of expertise. If we ask these

same experts to make relatively unpracticed judgments, the errors appear in full force (e.g., Smith & Kida, 1991).

Finally, we make these errors even when the stakes are high. In a number of studies participants have been offered cash bonuses if they perform accurately; these incentives have little impact on performance (Arkes, 1991; Gilovich, 1991). More strongly, we have discussed errors in the context of cancer diagnosis; surely the stakes here are high indeed, yet the errors occur nonetheless.

## OPTIMIZING VS. SATISFICING

One might draw rather cynical conclusions from all these findings: Human reasoning is fundamentally flawed; errors are appallingly common. No wonder, then, that racism and warfare are so widespread. No wonder that people are so ready to believe in telepathy, astrology, and a variety of bogus cures (cf. Gilovich, 1991). However, this view of things leaves many questions unanswered. If our reasoning is so poor, then how is it possible that we have survived at all? Indeed, the history of humanity is filled with a huge number of egregious deeds, but our history is also filled with great intellectual accomplishments and enormous technological progress. How was all of this achieved, given our flawed reasoning skills?

Perhaps there is nothing wrong with human reasoning. Perhaps instead there is something wrong with the research we have presented. As we have already mentioned, however, the participants in these studies were well motivated and, one would think, adequately skilled; the problems themselves are generally straightforward. Some scholars have expressed concern about the instructions in these studies (perhaps the instructions are obscure or misleading), but it seems unlikely that this could explain the full pattern of evidence. (For discussion, see Kahneman & Tversky, 1982a; Schwartz, Strack, Hilton & Naderer, 1991; Wolford, Taylor & Beck, 1990.)

A more promising way to think about all of this is contained within an idea we mentioned earlier in the chapter—*heuristics*. Heuristics, you will recall, are strategies that are efficient and that work most of the time. This definition implies that heuristics always involve a trade-off: Heuristics do allow errors to occur (because they only work "most" of the time), but in return, heuristics allow us to live our lives at a sane and reasonable pace. Some other strategy might avoid the errors but might require so much time and effort that each judgment we encounter, and each decision we make, would become intolerably demanding. As a result, we could end up frozen in thought, unable to move forward in any way.

With this context, perhaps we should cease lamenting the judgment errors that humans make. These errors may simply be the price we pay in order to purchase a reasonable degree of efficiency in our lives. Alas, sometimes the errors we make are consequential (as in erroneous medical diagnoses), but even so, in light of the *advantages* associated with heuristics—namely, the efficiency—it might be madness *not* to use these strategies, even if they do, on occasion, lead us astray.

The classic statement of this view comes from Simon (1957). In many cases, Simon argues, it is foolish to seek an *optimal* decision, or an *optimal* choice, since this may require more time, and more effort, than the decision is actually worth. If you are shopping for a car, you could test-drive every model on the market, and this would guarantee that you would find the *best* car on the market. But this would require an enormous amount of your time. Therefore, Simon argues, we compromise in a sensible way: Rather than searching for the optimal choice, we instead search only for a choice that is *good enough* to satisfy us, and then we cut short our search. In Simon's terms, it's more sensible to **satisfice** than to optimize—seeking a satisfactory outcome rather than seeking the best possible outcome.

It is easy to see how this applies to human reasoning. We could seek judgment strategies that would yield error-free performance. However, "optimizing" in this fashion would require more resources than we have. We therefore elect to "satisfice"—relying on judgment strategies that are *good enough*: accurate more often than not, and above all, efficient. In this view, therefore, there may be nothing wrong

with human reasoning. Yes, we do make errors, but these are the exception and not the rule. Moreover, the errors need to be balanced against the enormous savings—in time, in effort—afforded by our use of heuristics. (For discussion, see Einhorn & Hogarth, 1981; Nisbett & Ross, 1980; von Winterfeldt & Edwards, 1986.)

## SUCCESSFUL STATISTICAL REASONING

With all this said, we still need to bear in mind, that people don't *always* make judgment errors. We mentioned earlier that people are sometimes sensitive to base rate information, and that not all judgments of frequency depend on availability. Likewise, we have seen that people are able to judge covariation accurately in at least some settings.

Similar points can be made about *sample size*. As we have seen, people are, in many cases, equally willing to draw conclusions from a small sample of evidence as from a large one; this was visible, for example, in our discussion of "man who" arguments and this tendency is also reflected in the "Hospital A or B problem" discussed earlier. This seems to suggest that people don't understand the fact that small samples are, in general, less reliable than larger samples.

Yet other observations make it clear that people *do* understand the importance of sample size. As one illustration, imagine the following dialogue:

Alan: "I've got a great system for choosing lottery numbers! I chose a number yesterday, and I won!"

Amy: "Come on—that doesn't mean your system's great; maybe you just got lucky."

In this setting, Amy's response sounds perfectly fine—we all know that lucky accidents do happen, and so Alan's boast does sound unjustified. But now consider this bit of dialogue:

Lila: "I've got a great system for choosing lottery numbers! I've tried it eleven times and I won every time!"

Henry: "Come on—that doesn't mean your system's great; maybe you just got lucky each time."

This time, Henry's response sounds odd, and Lila's boast does seem sensible. Yes, lucky accidents do happen, but they don't keep happening over and over. If something does happen over and over, therefore, it's probably not an accident.

These are very easy points to grasp, and virtually anyone can see that Amy's comment is sensible whereas Henry's is not. And it's precisely this ease of understanding that's important here, because it reveals a comprehension of some crucial facts about sample size. Specifically, you understand these bits of dialogue only because you already know that it's dangerous to draw conclusions from a small sample of evidence. This is why you side with Amy, not Alan. Hand in hand with this, you side with Lila because you understand that it's legitimate to draw conclusions from a larger sample; you know that a pattern in a larger set is less likely to be the result of accident.

Experimental data also make it clear that, *in some circumstances*, people are alert to the size of the data set they are considering. For example, Nisbett, Krantz, Jepson, and Kunda (1983) asked participants in one study to imagine that they had encountered a new bird, the shreeble. The one shreeble observed so far was blue, and with this basis, participants were asked how likely they thought it was that *all* shreebles were blue. Participants were also asked to imagine that they had encountered a new element, floridium. Only one sample of floridium had been examined, and when heated, it burned with a blue flame. Given this evidence, the participants were asked how likely they thought it was that all floridium, when heated, burns with a blue flame. Finally, in still other trials, participants were told about a previously unknown tribe living on a Pacific island. One member of the tribe has been observed and was obese. With this information, the participants were asked how likely they thought it was that *all* members of this tribe were obese.

For floridium, participants were quite willing to believe that a single instance allows generalization to the whole set, and so they asserted that all floridium would burn blue when heated. They were less willing to extrapolate from a single case when thinking about shreebles, and even less willing when thinking about obese islanders. For these categories, the participants were willing to draw conclusions only after they were told about several observations (several shreebles or several tribespeople) in addition to the initial case.

Quite obviously, then, people sometimes are influenced by sample size. More broadly, we cannot claim that human judgment is consistently poor. In many cases, our judgments are quite accurate and guided by the appropriate considerations (sample size, base rates, and so on).

All of this invites a crucial question: Why is it that judgment is sometimes accurate, and sometimes not? What are the factors that control the quality of our judgment? Two different hypotheses are prominent in the literature—one emphasizing the role of the "data format" in evoking good reasoning, and the other emphasizing the "triggers" needed to evoke good-quality statistical reasoning.

## THE IMPORTANCE OF DATA FORMAT

In recent years, a number of scholars have argued that we can gain considerable insight into psychological questions by considering these questions from an *evolutionary perspective*. The way humans think, these scholars argue, and many of our behavior patterns, are shaped in important ways by the biology of the brain; the brain, in turn, has been powerfully shaped by the forces of natural selection. For this reason, they argue, it will often be helpful, in understanding a psychological process, to consider the circumstances under which the process evolved (e.g., Brase, Cosmides & Tooby, 1998; Cosmides & Tooby, 1996; Cummins & Allen, 1998; Gigerenzer & Hoffrage, 1995).

How does this perspective apply to human judgment? One line of argument focuses on the role of *frequency*. It seems likely that our ancient ancestors did need to keep track of frequencies (How many antelope are at the watering hole? How many days will I need for this hunting trip?), and so our cognitive capacities evolved in a fashion that left us reasonably competent in thinking about frequencies. In contrast, our ancient ancestors did not need to think about probabilities (When I hunt, there's a .15 chance that I'll return empty-handed). Indeed, the whole idea of "probabilities" is a modern invention, dating back only two centuries or so. Our cognitive capacities have therefore not had anywhere close to the time needed to evolve in a way that would support thinking about probabilities.

According to this view, our minds are well prepared for thinking about frequencies, and so we will reason well when thinking in these terms. If the same problems are cast in terms of probabilities (".8" instead of "8 out of 10," ".01" instead of "1 in a hundred"), however, this is the wrong data format for our minds, and so performance will suffer.

Consistent with this view, judgments are improved if people are given frequency information rather than probabilities. For example, in problems involving base rates, people are much more likely to use the base rate information if it is phrased in terms of frequencies ("10 out of every 1,000 cases") rather than as a probability or percentage ("1%"). Likewise, people are appreciably more accurate in using diagnostic information cast as a frequency ("8 correct out of 10") than they are in using the same information cast as a probability or percentage ("80%"; Gigerenzer & Hoffrage, 1995; also Brase, Cosmides & Tooby, 1998; Cosmides & Tooby, 1996).

Let's note, however, that casting information in terms of frequencies improves performance but still leaves many errors in place; this suggests that this factor cannot provide the entire account of judgment competence. In addition, it is worth mentioning that there has been some controversy over whether the evolutionary perspective is the best way to think about these data (Lewis & Keren, 1999; Mellers & McGraw, 1999; but then see Gigerenzer & Hoffrage, 1999; also Kahneman & Tversky, 1996; but then see Gigerenzer, 1996; also Mellers, Hertwig & Kahneman, 2000).

With these points acknowledged, we must not lose track of a central finding: Participants' performance in dealing with judgment problems is certainly influenced by the data format and, in particular, is improved if the data are cast in terms of frequencies (although, we emphasize, errors still occur, even with frequencies). This influence of frequencies may be for evolutionary reasons; it may be for some other reason. In any case, this result helps us to understand why human judgment about evidence is sometimes so poor, and sometimes entirely accurate.

## TRIGGERING STATISTICAL KNOWLEDGE

Nisbett and his associates have offered a different (but related) view of these issues (e.g., Nisbett et al., 1983). Their argument starts with the suggestion that people *do* understand the principles that should guide their judgment—they do know, for example, that base rates are relevant to many judgments, and that a conclusion based on a large sample of evidence is more likely to be correct than a conclusion based on a tiny sample. In other words, people do, in their view, have sensible intuitions about these statistical issues. The problem, though, is that people often fail to *apply* these intuitions when they are making judgments. That is why people end up relying on their "backup" strategies, such as availability or representativeness—strategies that are efficient, but risky.

In support of this position, it is easy to demonstrate that, in many settings, people do have reasonable ideas about statistics and about the interpretation of evidence. Our earlier (fictional) dialogs between Alan and Amy, Lila and Henry were intended to illustrate this point. Nisbett et al. offer their own example. They invite us to imagine hearing this comment: "I can't understand it. I have nine grandchildren, and all of them are boys." This sounds like a sensible statement; something does seem odd in this case if 100% of the children, nine out of nine, are of the same gender. But now imagine this comment: "I can't understand it. I have three grandchildren, and all of them are boys."

This statement sounds peculiar. With this small sample (three children), we easily believe that 100% of the cases (three out of three) could be of the same gender, just by accident—a clear reflection of a sensible understanding of sample size.

If we have these good "statistical intuitions," why is our judgment so often poor? Nisbett et al. argue that, in many settings, we fail to realize that our statistical knowledge is relevant; in other settings, we don't know how to apply this knowledge. In either case, we end up under-using our statistical knowledge. Nisbett et al. have proposed three factors that, in their view, are critical in triggering the use of this knowledge. With these factors on the scene, a person's (informal, intuitive) understanding of statistics is likely to be called into play, and so his or her judgments will be sophisticated and accurate. When these factors are absent, though, people don't call up their statistical knowledge and, instead, rely on much cruder judgment strategies (such as representativeness).

What are these triggering factors? First, statistical strategies are likely to be applied if the role of *chance*, or of accident, is prominent in the problem under scrutiny. Consistent with this claim, manipulations that highlight the role of chance do increase the likelihood of a person's reasoning in a statistically appropriate manner. For an example, Gigerenzer, Hell, and Blank (1988) presented participants with an urn containing 100 pieces of paper. Thirty of the pieces of paper, the participants were told, contained descriptions of engineers; 70 contained descriptions of lawyers. The participants themselves were then required to draw the "thumbnail descriptions" out of the urn, and to render a judgment about the likelihood that the individual selected was a lawyer. This manipulation emphasized for participants the role of chance in the selection of these descriptions and, accordingly, much improved the quality of their judgment—that is, it diminished their neglect of base rates. (For related data, see Baratgin & Noveck, 2000; Gigerenzer, 1991; Tversky & Kahneman, 1982.)

As a second "trigger," people seem more likely to use their statistical knowledge if the problem highlights the role of *sampling*, so that people can easily understand an experience as a sample of data drawn from a larger set of potential observations. This is particularly useful if the "data" arrive in a format that supports ready comparisons from one sample to the next.

Consider a study by Kunda and Nisbett (1986). Participants were asked to judge covariation with two different types of cases: Some of the judgments were made about events that were easily coded in terms of single, repeatable observations— for example, athletic performance. These events are easily quantified, in terms of points per game and the like. Other judgments were made about less easily coded events. For example, participants made judgments about things like friendliness and honesty. "Such events are manifestly difficult to code reliably. . . . Should friendliness be measured in smiles per minute, 'good vibrations' per encounter, or what?" (Holland, Holyoak, Nisbett & Thagard 1986, p. 212).

Kunda and Nisbett predicted that participants would be more accurate in assessing covariation with the codable data, like athletic performance— these are data that should trigger the use of statistical knowledge. Participants should be less accurate with cases that are difficult to code, like social behaviors. The data clearly support this prediction.

Finally, as a third trigger, the use of statistical knowledge is also influenced by certain *background beliefs*, perhaps beliefs built into our cultural knowledge. For example, each of us has beliefs about the role of luck in certain achievements, and this will shape whether we think about these achievements with reference to luck, and therefore with reference to chance, and therefore with reference to statistical principles. Likewise, each of us has beliefs about the homogeneity or heterogeneity of certain sets, and this too will influence our thinking about these sets. (For related discussion, see Bar-Hillel, 1982; Tversky & Kahneman, 1982, 1983; Kahneman & Tversky, 1982c; Wilson & Brekke, 1994.) This factor, presumably, is what lies behind the shreebles vs. floridium vs. tribe members study described earlier. Our cultural knowledge tells us that minerals don't vary much, and that is why a small sample of floridium is taken as adequate for drawing conclusions. Our cultural knowledge is different for human tribes, and so here we demand a larger sample.

## TRAINING PARTICIPANTS TO USE STATISTICS

The triggering of statistical knowledge is far from trivial. The use of mental shortcuts (like availability or representativeness) seems a well-entrenched habit and so will often continue even in situations emphasizing the role of chance, or situations with "codable" data. These situations do make it more likely that people will consider sample size, sample bias, and base rates, but even in these settings, someone's sensitivity to these statistical factors is far from guaranteed. That's why it has been so easy, throughout this chapter, to catalogue cases of poor-quality, unwarranted reasoning.

Is there anything we can do to change this situation, to make it more likely that people will reason in a statistically sensible fashion? One might expect that *training* of the appropriate sort might be helpful, and several studies confirm this optimistic prediction. For example, Fong, Krantz, and Nisbett (1986) provided participants with just a half-hour of training, focusing on the importance of sample size. The participants were taught (or perhaps we should say, "reminded") that accidents do indeed happen, but that accidents don't keep on happening, over and over. Therefore, a small sample of data might be the result of some accident, but a large sample probably isn't. Consequently, large samples are more reliable, more trustworthy, than small samples.

Some of the participants in this study were taught about these issues in a fairly abstract way—the principles were illustrated by drawing samples of red or blue gumballs out of a jar. Other participants were given examples during the training, showing them how considerations of sample size applied to real-world cases (e.g., a public opinion poll). Both forms

of training were remarkably effective: After training, the participants (adults and high-school students) were appreciably more likely to apply considerations of sample size to test cases, and their application of this principle tended to be reasonable and appropriate. (See also Fong & Nisbett, 1991.)

If a half-hour's training in statistics improves participants' judgment, what about an entire course in statistics? Fong et al. conducted a telephone survey of "opinions about sports," calling students who were taking an undergraduate course in statistics. Half of the students were contacted during the first week of the semester; half were contacted during the last week. Note, though, that there was no indication to the students that the telephone interview was connected to their course; as far as the students knew, they had been selected entirely at random.

The students in this study were asked several questions to increase the likelihood that they would indeed think they were simply being interviewed about sports, and to ensure that they didn't perceive the relation between the interview and their statistics course. Then they were asked the question quoted in Figure 12.6. The results clearly showed that their reasoning about this question was influenced by their training: For those contacted early in the term, only 16% gave statistical answers. For those contacted later, the number of statistical answers more than doubled (to 37%). The quality of the answers also increased, with students more likely to articulate the relevant principles correctly at the end of the semester than at the beginning.

Let's note, though, that the effects of statistical training were modest in size. It is true that the training doubled the likelihood of statistically warranted answers, but it is also true that, even after a statistics course, only 37% of the students gave such an answer; almost two-thirds of the students, in other words, did not. This echoes our earlier remarks about the "triggers" for statistical reasoning: The triggers make this reasoning *more likely*, but the triggers leave many of the errors untouched. Likewise, training in statistics improves the quality of one's reasoning, but again, many of the errors remain in place.

FIGURE 12.6

## Sample Problem Used to Test Statistical Reasoning

### The problem:

"In general, the major league baseball player who wins Rookie of the Year does not perform as well in his second year. This is clear in major league baseball in the past 10 years. In the American League, eight Rookies of the Year have done worse in their second year; only two have done better. In the National League, the Rookie of the Year has done worse the second year 9 times out of 10. Why do you suppose the Rookie of the Year tends not to do as well his second year?"

### Non-statistical answer:

When a player does well in his first year, he receives an enormous amount of media attention. This puts great pressure on the player, and most players have a difficult time continuing to do well amidst all that pressure.

### Statistical answer:

All of the players in the Major Leagues are talented—otherwise they wouldn't have made it into the Major Leagues! To stand out from the pack, then, you need more than talent—you need talent *and* some degree of luck—good health during the season, no distraction from personal problems, a lucky selection of pitchers, and so on. The Rookie of the Year, therefore, is probably someone who's talented *and* lucky during his first year. Therefore, the first year performance probably *overestimates* the player's true talent. And, of course, the problem with luck is that it's unreliable and may not continue into a second year.

The "non-statistical answer" offered here is plausible, and may be true. The statistical answer, however, is better than "merely plausible," it is virtually certain to be true! It is surely the case that any performance, athletic or otherwise, depends both on talent and on some number of chance factors. It is also extremely likely that the Rookie of the Year has benefited from some degree of luck: Chance factors will favor some players and will work against others. If chance works against you, you are unlikely to emerge as Rookie of the Year. Therefore, the Rookie of the Year is someone who is benefiting from some degree of luck. And, of course, lucky breaks—like any other sort of accident—don't keep happening over and over. Therefore, as the "sample size" grows (two years of observation versus just the rookie year), factors like luck will play a smaller role. Hence, the Rookie of the Year won't continue to benefit from good luck, and so his performance will decline.

Even with this caution, however, these are rather cheerful data: Students' reasoning about evidence, it seems, can be improved, and the improvement applies to problems in new domains and in new contexts. Training in statistics, it seems, can have widespread benefits.

## Example of a Problem Used by Lehman and Nisbett

**FIGURE 12.7**

A recent study sought to determine whether *noise* harms plants. In the study, two identical coleus plants were transplanted from the same greenhouse and grown under identical conditions, except that the first plant was exposed to loud noise—approximately the same as a person would hear while standing on a busy subway platform—while the other plant grew in quiet conditions. After 1½ weeks of continuous exposure, only the sound-treated plant wilted.

**Response indicating sensitivity to statistical factors:**
With only two plants in the study, there is a possibility that the sound-treated plant was just weaker to begin with. This sort of chance difference between the two conditions would be less likely if a larger number of plants were included in the study. That way, it would be quite improbable that *all* of the sound-treated plants, just by luck, were weaker to begin with than the plants growing in quiet.

College seniors were more likely to give statistical responses to this problem, in comparison with first-year students.

### OTHER FORMS OF TRAINING

What about other forms of training? For example, think about students who major in psychology, or who go to graduate school in psychology. These students are likely to take many courses that include discussion of methodological and statistical issues. Does this training carry over into other domains? If so, then one might expect that majoring in psychology will broadly improve one's reasoning.

Consistent with this suggestion, Lehman, Lempert, and Nisbett (1988) showed that graduate training in psychology does improve one's ability to reason about evidence, including evidence having little to do with psychology. Similar results have been observed as a function of undergraduate training (Lehman & Nisbett, 1990). Students were tested during their first term at the university, and then retested in the middle of their senior year. The question of interest lies in the *change* in scores for these students: How much have they learned from their four years of undergraduate study? What problems can they solve at the end of their college career that they couldn't solve when they were fresh out of high school?

Test problems in this study included problems in scientific domains (see Figure 12.7), and also problems in everyday life (Figure 12.6). As Figure 12.8 shows, a college education did indeed help students in solving these problems—in all of the groups, the seniors significantly outperformed the first-year students (i.e., all improvement scores were positive). This improvement was considerably larger, though, for students who had majored in social science or psychology. These are disciplines that emphasize problems of sampling and statistical variation. Apparently, this training pays off, not only helping these students to do work in their specific major, but also helping them to solve problems with content some distance away from their academic studies.

In looking at Figure 12.8, though, one might ask why social science training seemed superior to training in natural science. Let's be clear, first of all, that

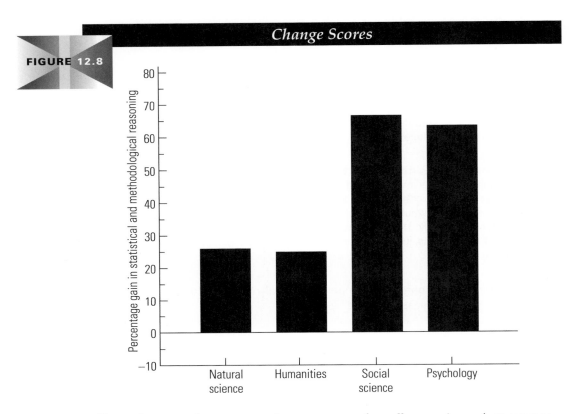

Shown here are change scores (average scores for college seniors *minus* average scores for first-year students) in statistical and methodological reasoning. All change scores are positive (seniors outperformed first-year students), but the change is particularly large for psychology and social science majors. Somewhat surprisingly, training in the natural sciences has only a modest impact on these tests—no larger than the impact from training in the humanities.

the data showed *no differences* among these groups in their first-term scores; apparently, the groups were well matched at the start. Therefore, it is the *change scores* that need to be explained. Let's also emphasize that the natural science students did improve (a gain of about 25%), but they clearly gained less than the psychologists and social scientists, and the natural science students showed no advantage relative to the humanities students. Why is this? Students in natural science obviously do a great deal

of quantitative work, but they also have the good fortune to work with homogeneous populations: One carbon atom behaves rather similarly to every other carbon atom; the properties of one electron are similar to the properties of all other electrons. Hence, issues of variability and sampling loom less large in these domains. As a consequence, students in the natural sciences receive less training in issues of sampling and the like. The implications of this are clear in Figure 12.8.

Let's also acknowledge that the pattern of Figure 12.8 would be rather different if we looked at improvement in other domains—for example, improvement in generating literary criticism, or improvement in thinking through the steps of a chemical reaction. In these domains, we obviously wouldn't expect an advantage for psychology or social science students. But there is a good reason for focusing on statistical problems such as those sketched in Figures 12.6 and 12.7. These are problems that correspond reasonably well to the sorts of judgments we all need to make every day of our lives—whether we're thinking about some facts we heard on the news, some observations we heard from a friend, or some facts we've seen for ourselves. If training in social science or psychology helps with judgments like these, then this training is truly providing a very useful skill. (For related data, see Schunn & Anderson, 1999.)

## THINKING ABOUT EVIDENCE: SOME CONCLUSIONS

How, then, should we think about the results described throughout this chapter? As we have seen, it is easy to document judgment errors in bright, motivated undergraduates or in highly trained professionals. These errors are made even when the consequences are extreme—e.g., errors in diagnosing a serious medical problem. At the same time, the fact remains that the intellectual accomplishments of our species—in science, in technology, in social matters—are huge. Apparently, our reasoning errors can't be too damaging.

How should we reconcile these observations? For a start, it is important to realize that the accomplishments of our species often derive from collective enterprises. Therefore, even if 90% of the participants make an error, the remaining 10% may detect the error and bring it to the attention of the group. (For a less sanguine view of group problem-solving, see Janis, 1972; also Schulz-Hardt, Frey, Lüthgens & Moscovici, 2000.) In addition, many intellectual achievements are rooted in domains that employ formal, explicitly defined means of data collection and data analysis, domains that should therefore be immune to the effects of informal reasoning described in this chapter.

In addition, we have now catalogued several factors that reliably improve the quality of our judgment—factors that seem to trigger our statistical knowledge, and certain forms of training that make these errors less likely. This training probably helps us by making the statistical principles more prominent in memory and, therefore, easier to trigger. The training also helps us to see how our statistical intuitions apply to a range of new cases. Thus, with training, one realizes that an interview can be thought of as a small sample of data, and perhaps should be trusted less than some other source of information based on a larger sample of evidence. Likewise, one can think of an athlete's rookie year in these terms, or a dancer's audition. Once the situation is coded in this fashion, the application of statistical rules is much more straightforward and much more likely.

Moreover, we have emphasized the fact that there is a *reason* for our making mistakes: The world around us offers a wealth of information; still more information is provided by our memories. In addition, there is a wide range of options available to us, in considering what to do with this corpus of information. It is this great wealth—of information, of options—that forces us to be selective in our information processing: We cannot consider every fact or pursue every path. Pressure toward efficiency is created and, correspondingly, a demand that we "satisfice" rather than optimize. If we make errors in reasoning, therefore, this may simply be the price we pay for efficiency.

Even with all these points made, though, the fact remains that errors in judgment are ubiquitous and often troubling. We close the chapter, then, with a forward-looking note: We have seen that training can help in reducing the frequency of error, and we have seen indications that it is sometimes possible to be *both* efficient and accurate. In some situations, we do realize how to apply our statistical knowledge, and how to adjust for sample size or sample bias. All of this implies that judgment, as one might expect, is a skill, a skill that we all have to some extent, and a skill that can be improved by suitable training and practice. Errors in drawing conclusions, and in making inferences, are remarkably widespread, but the path is open to reducing these errors and to improving the quality of human judgment.

## Chapter Summary

1. In *induction*, one begins with specific observations and draws some general conclusion from them; in *deduction*, one starts with a general claim and asks what follows from this claim. Induction often begins with a *frequency estimate*, serving as an initial description of the data. In many cases, people make frequency estimates by using the *availability heuristic*, in which they judge an observation to be frequent if they can easily think of many examples of that observation. The more available an observation is, the greater the frequency is judged to be.

2. Judgments via availability are often accurate, but do risk error. This is because many factors can influence availability, including the pattern of what is or is not easily retrievable from memory, bias in what we notice in our experiences, and also bias in what the media report. Even if people detect these biases, they often fail to adjust for them, because of *anchoring*.

3. People also rely on the *representativeness heuristic* when they extrapolate from observations they have made. This heuristic rests on the assumption that categories are relatively homogeneous, so that any case drawn from the category will be representative of the entire group. Because of this assumption, people expect a relatively small sample of evidence to have all the properties that are associated with the entire category; one example of this is the *gambler's fallacy*. Similarly, people seem insensitive to the importance of *sample size*, and so believe that a small sample of observations is just as informative as a large sample. In the extreme, people are willing to draw conclusions from just a single observation, as in *"person who"* arguments.

4. People's evaluation of a claim can be strongly influenced by how the claim is phrased, largely because a more explicit formulation of the claim makes it easier to recall or imagine support for the claim. This increases the availability of evidence for the claim, and so makes the claim seem more credible.

5. People are also likely to make errors in judging *covariation*. In particular, their beliefs and expectations sometimes lead them to perceive *illusory covariations*. These errors have been demonstrated not just in novices working with unfamiliar materials but also with experts dealing with the sorts of highly familiar materials they encounter in their professional work.

6. People are accurate in assessing covariation if they have no prior beliefs or expectations about the data. This suggests that people do understand the concept of covariation, and understand (roughly) how to assess covariation. When people have prior beliefs, though, their judgments of covariation are sometimes extreme and often erratic. This may be attributable to the fact that *confirmation bias* causes people to notice and remember a biased sample of the evidence, which leads to bad covariation judgments.

7. People also seem insensitive to *base rates* and, again, this can be demonstrated both in novices evaluating unfamiliar materials and in experts making judgments in their professional domains. *Base rate neglect* is not always observed, however. This neglect is less likely, for example, if the base rates are phrased in a way that makes it clear they are relevant to the particular person making the judgment.

8. Some have argued that judgment errors are simply the price we pay for heuristic use. We *satisfice* in making our judgments, rather than optimizing, and this may be an appropriate choice if we are to live our lives at a reasonable pace. In addition, it is important that people do reason correctly in some settings, so that they are, for example, sometimes quite sensitive to sample size. There has been dispute, however, about what the factors are that govern when we make judgments that are sensible, and when we make judgments that are error-filled. One

proposal is that much depends on the format of the information we are given: We judge well, it is claimed, when information is cast in terms of frequencies; we judge more poorly when information is cast in terms of percentages or probabilities. A different proposal is that we judge well whenever key factors are present triggering our statistical intuitions. These factors include a salient role for chance, or a presentation of the problem that highlights the role of sampling.

9. Judgment errors can be reduced through suitable training. Courses in statistics seem to be beneficial, and also training of the appropriate sort within the graduate or undergraduate curriculum.

# Reasoning: Thinking through the Implications of What You Know

In Chapter 12, we discussed how humans make judgments about evidence. Sometimes, the evidence is provided to us directly through the senses—something that we see, or something we hear about. Sometimes, the evidence is supplied by memory, as we think back to observations we've made in the past. In either case, though, each bit of evidence is usually concerned with a particular event or a particular observation, and so our focus in Chapter 12 was on how humans draw general conclusions from these specific cases.

This type of reasoning—from specific bits of evidence to more general conclusions—is called induction. In induction, we confront a sample of evidence and seek to extrapolate from this sample. That is why considerations of sample size and sample bias played such a large role in our discussion.

Obviously, though, not all thinking is inductive in character. Perhaps we have already concluded that Thai food is often spicy, or that relationships based only on physical attraction rarely last. We might then want to ask: What follows from this? What implications do these claims have for our other beliefs or actions? These questions rely on **deduction**—a process through which we start with general claims or general assertions and ask what follows from these premises.

Among its other roles, deduction allows us to make predictions about upcoming events: If you are meeting a particular six-year-old for the first time, you can anticipate many of her characteristics, based on your knowledge of six-year-olds in general. These anticipations rely on *deductions* from your general knowledge.

**411**

Likewise, if you are going for a job interview, you can predict many of the questions you'll be asked, and again these predictions are deduced from your general knowledge.

Predictions like these are obviously useful in our day-to-day lives, and this is one of the reasons deduction is so important. But in addition, the ability to deduce predictions from our beliefs also provides a way of keeping our beliefs in touch with reality: If our predictions turn out to be *wrong*, this tells us that something is awry in our beliefs. Conversely, if a set of beliefs leads to *correct* predictions, this obviously lends support to those beliefs.

Does our reasoning respect these principles? If you encounter evidence confirming your beliefs, does this strengthen your convictions? If evidence challenging your beliefs should come your way, do you adjust? And what if you realize, from the start, that you are uncertain about a belief? Perhaps you have drawn a tentative conclusion, and want to check on the conclusion before taking action. What evidence do you seek to verify or disprove your view? Our discussion of reasoning will begin with these crucial questions.

## Confirmation and Disconfirmation

How should one go about testing a belief? What evidence might strengthen the belief? What would undermine it? These normative questions—about how one *ought* to reason—have been discussed at length by philosophers of science. Their main concern has been with how scientists should proceed in testing their theories. Nonetheless, we can draw broad lessons from their work in asking how *anyone* should proceed in evaluating his or her beliefs. What sorts of evidence should be gathered? How should the evidence be used?

One important point emerging from this discussion concerns the ambiguity of *confirming* evidence and, correspondingly, the great value of *disconfirm-*ing evidence. To see this, consider a concrete case. You believe that Natasha likes you, because you've noticed that she always smiles at you when you meet. In fact, you can think of dozens of occasions in which she's smiled at you, and so it seems that you have ample confirmation for your view that, yes, Natasha really does like you.

Unfortunately, though, all of these confirmations are ambiguous. It may be true that Natasha smiles at you because she likes you. But perhaps Natasha is just friendly in general and smiles at everybody. Or perhaps she is quite unfriendly, and smiles only to be polite. Collecting more confirmations won't remove this ambiguity. If you continue to encounter Natasha, over and over, and she continues to smile, this is consistent with your initial belief, but it is also consistent with these other possibilities.

Similar examples are easy to find. The rooster is said to believe that his crowing each morning brings the sun into the sky. Plenty of evidence confirms his belief: Day after day he has crowed, and each time the sun has risen. Despite these confirmations, though, we believe the rooster's hypothesis to be false. Apparently, confirmations—no matter how numerous—cannot show a belief to be true.

Disconfirmations, on the other hand, can be enormously informative. Thus it might be useful for the rooster to ask, "What if I'm wrong? How else might I think about the evidence?" This might lead the rooster to the obvious experiment—to let one morning pass *without* crowing. The sun's arrival on that morning would surely tell the rooster a great deal.

### CONFIRMATION BIAS

It is for these reasons that disconfirmation, rather than confirmation, plays such an important role in science. Indeed, the philosopher Karl Popper (e.g., 1959) argued that the search for disconfirming evidence is the earmark of science: Unless one seeks out this evidence, potentially challenging one's views, one is not doing science at all. Other scholars have expressed reservations about Popper's claim (e.g., Friedrich, 1993; Klayman & Ha, 1987; Lakatos, 1970; Tweney,

Doherty & Mynatt, 1981; Tweney, 1998) but, on anyone's account, it is clear that evidence that might disconfirm a belief is generally useful and often worth seeking. Likewise, consideration of *alternative hypotheses* is usually helpful: In asking, "Is there another way to explain the facts?" one will often discover that the evidence is indeed ambiguous.

However, despite the usefulness of disconfirmation, and the utility of considering alternatives, people generally do neither. Instead, people display a strong tendency to seek out *confirming* evidence and to rely on that evidence in drawing their conclusions. We first met this pattern, usually called **confirmation bias**, in Chapter 12. This bias emerges in numerous forms: First, when people are assessing a belief or a hypothesis, they are far more likely to seek evidence that confirms the hypothesis than evidence that might disconfirm it. Second, when disconfirming evidence is made available to them, people often fail to use it, in adjusting their beliefs. Third, people often seem to *forget* disconfirming cases and show a memory bias toward cases consistent with their beliefs. Finally, people regularly fail to consider alternative hypotheses that might explain the available data just as well as their current hypothesis. (An enormous amount of evidence is consistent with these claims. For reviews, see Evans, 1982; Gilovich, 1991; Higgins & Bargh, 1987; Rothbart, Evans & Fulero, 1979; Schulz-Hardt, Frey, Lüthgens, & Moscovici, 2000; Stangor & McMillan, 1992; Tweney et al., 1981.)

In a classic demonstration of confirmation bias, Wason (1966, 1968) presented research participants with a series of numbers, such as "2, 4, 6." The participants were told that this trio of numbers conformed to a specific rule, and their task was to figure out what the rule was. Participants were allowed to propose their own trios of numbers ("Does 8, 10, 12 follow the rule?"), and in each case, the experimenter responded appropriately ("Yes, it does follow the rule" or "No, it doesn't"). Then, once participants were satisfied they had discovered the rule, they announced their "discovery."

The rule was, in fact, quite simple: The three numbers had to be in ascending order. Thus "1, 3, 5" follows the rule; so does "18, 19, 236." The trio, "6, 4, 2"

does not follow the rule, nor does "10, 10, 10." Despite this simplicity, though, participants had considerable difficulty in discovering the rule, often requiring many minutes. This was in part due to the kinds of information they requested, as they sought to evaluate candidate rules: To an overwhelming extent, they sought to confirm the rules they had proposed; requests for disconfirmation were relatively rare. Attempts to test alternate hypotheses were also rare. (For related data, see Mynatt, Doherty & Tweney, 1977, 1978; Shaklee & Fischhoff, 1982; Snyder & Swann, 1978. For similar results with trained scientists, see Mitroff, 1981, or Mahoney & DeMonbreun, 1978. For a review of this domain, see Baron, 1988.)

In short, the participants fail to reason in the fashion "recommended" by philosophers of science—that is, they fail to seek out disconfirming evidence. As one consequence of this, they are less effective in their reasoning: In the Wason task, the number rule was discovered more quickly by the occasional participants who *did* seek disconfirmation, in comparison to the (more typical) participants who displayed confirmation bias. Thus, confirmation bias is plainly on the scene and interferes with performance.

## BELIEF PERSEVERANCE

A different manifestation of confirmation bias is more troubling: Even when disconfirming evidence is out in plain view, people seem not to use it. Tweney et al. (1981) review a variety of studies making this point, but the most striking studies are those concerned with a phenomenon called *belief perseverance*.

Participants in one study were asked to read a series of suicide notes; their task was to figure out which notes were authentic, collected by the police, and which were fake, written by other students as an exercise. As participants offered their judgments, they were provided with feedback about how well they were doing—that is, how accurate they were in detecting the authentic notes. The trick, though, was that the feedback was predetermined and had nothing to do with the participants' actual judgments.

Some participants were told that they were well above average in this task (again, independent of their judgments); other participants were told the opposite—that they were much below average (Ross, Lepper & Hubbard, 1975; also Ross & Anderson, 1982).

Later on, participants were debriefed. They were told that the feedback they had received was utterly bogus and had nothing to do with their performance. Indeed, they were shown the experimenter's instruction sheet, which had assigned them in advance to the "success" or "failure" group. They were then asked a variety of further questions, including questions for which they had to assess their own "social sensitivity." Specifically, they were asked to rate their actual ability, as they perceived it, in tasks like the suicide-note task.

Let's emphasize that participants were making these judgments about themselves *after* they had been told the truth about the feedback. That is, they had been told clearly and explicitly that the feedback was randomly determined and had no credibility whatsoever. Nonetheless, participants were clearly influenced by the feedback: Those who had received the "above average" feedback continued to think of their social sensitivity as being above average, and likewise their ability to judge suicide notes. Those who had received the "below average" feedback showed the opposite pattern. The participants, in other words, persevered in their beliefs even when the basis for the belief had been completely discredited. (For reviews of similar results, see Baron, 1988, especially Chapter 5; Nisbett & Ross, 1980.)

How does all of this connect to confirmation bias? As we have already mentioned, one form of this bias is a tendency to underutilize information that challenges your beliefs, and that pattern is certainly evident here: Because of the (bogus) feedback, the participants in this study had been led to a certain belief about themselves and then, once that belief was in place, a powerful challenge to the belief (namely, the discrediting of the feedback) was largely ignored.

In addition, we need to ask why the participants continued to believe in, and be influenced by, information that had been thoroughly discredited. Here, too, confirmation bias is pertinent. Let's say that we tell you that you are particularly bad at the suicide-note task. Initially, this information seems fully credible—it came, after all, from a scientist looking at the pattern of your responses. This might lead you to wonder whether, perhaps, you are in general a less discerning person than you previously thought. To check on this possibility you might search through your memory, looking for evidence that might help you evaluate this suggestion.

What sort of evidence will you seek in memory? Given the broader pattern of confirmation bias, chances are good that you will specifically seek other facts or other prior episodes that might *confirm* your lack of social perception. Therefore, you will soon have *two* sources of evidence for your social insensitivity: the (bogus) feedback provided by us, and the supporting information you came up with yourself, thanks to your selective memory search. Thus, even if we discredit the information we provided, you will still have the information *you* provided and, on this basis, you might maintain your belief. (For discussion, see Nisbett & Ross, 1980; also Johnson & Seifert, 1994).

Of course, in this experiment, participants could be led either to an enhanced estimate of their own social sensitivity, or to a diminished estimate, depending on which false information they were given in the first place. Presumably, this is because the range of episodes in participants' memories is rather wide—in some previous episodes, they have been sensitive, and in some, they haven't been. Therefore, if they search through their memories seeking to confirm the hypothesis that they have been sensitive in the past, they will find confirming evidence. If, on the other hand, they search through memory seeking to confirm the opposite hypothesis, this too will be possible. In short, they can confirm *either* hypothesis, via a suitably selective memory search. Indeed, we could probably lead them to a wide range of different conclusions, simply by leading them to launch one type of memory search or another. This highlights the dangers built into a selective search of the evidence and, more broadly, the danger associated with confirmation bias.

## Examples of Categorical Syllogisms

**FIGURE 13.1**

All M's are B.
All D's are M's.
  Therefore all D's are B.

All X's are Y.
Some A's are X's.
  Therefore some A's are Y.

Some A's are not B's.
All A's are G's.
  Therefore some G's are not B's.

All of the syllogisms shown here are valid—that is, if the two premises are true, then the conclusion must be true.

## Logic

We seem to be moving toward a picture of human reasoning that is as unflattering as the portrait we considered in Chapter 12: If people encounter evidence that contradicts or undermines one of their views, they maintain the view anyhow. Likewise, in *evaluating* their beliefs, people generally seek out only confirming evidence, not disconfirming evidence, and when the confirming evidence arrives, they fail to notice that some other belief, or some other hypothesis, might fit with the facts just as well as their own beliefs do. They fail to realize, in other words, that the evidence is *consistent* with their beliefs, but doesn't *favor* their beliefs (since the evidence is also consistent with other views).

In short, people in these experiments seem to be reasoning in a fashion that is not logical. Indeed, that invites a question: How well do participants do if we explicitly invite them to think things through logically? Is thought logical?

### REASONING ABOUT SYLLOGISMS

The relationship between *thought* and *logic* has been discussed by philosophers for thousands of years.

Indeed, in developing systems of logic, mathematicians and philosophers have often asserted that they were doing nothing more than formalizing the rules of everyday thought, the rules we all use in our thinking and reasoning (Boole, 1854; Mill, 1874). According to this view, there is no question about whether humans are "logical" or not. By definition, we are, since logic (allegedly) does nothing more than describe us and our rules of thought. If we make reasoning errors, therefore, it cannot be because we are illogical; instead the errors come from some other source—carelessness, or an initial misreading of the problem, or some such. (For one version of this argument, see Henle, 1962, 1978.)

It turns out, however, that errors in logical reasoning are ubiquitous. If we are careless, or misread problems, we do so with great frequency. Much of the research relevant to this claim comes from studies employing **categorical syllogisms**. These begin with two assertions—the problem's *premises*—each containing a statement about a category. These statements usually involve quantifiers, such as "some," "all," or "none." A premise might state, "All men are mortal," or "Some houses are not wooden."

The syllogism can then be completed by specifying what conclusion follows from these premises. Examples of categorical syllogisms are shown in Figure 13.1. These are all valid syllogisms—that is, the conclusion does follow from the premises in each case. Here is an example of an invalid syllogism:

> All P's are M.
> All S's are M.
>    Therefore, all S's are P's.

To see that this is invalid, try translating it into concrete terms, such as "All professional plumbers are mortal," and "All sadists are mortal." Both of these are surely true, but it doesn't follow from this that "All sadists are professional plumbers." This *might* be true (although it seems extraordinarily unlikely), but there is surely no way in which this conclusion is demanded by these premises.

As you can see, syllogisms can involve concrete statements (such as "All men are mortal") or abstract statements ("All are B"). The logic of a syllogism, however, depends only on its form: No matter how we fill in, "All A are B," the logical status of this statement remains the same. (Indeed, this dependence only on the *form* of a statement is the basis for the term *formal* logic.)

Research participants asked to reason about syllogisms do remarkably poorly. Chapman and Chapman (1959) gave their participants a number of syllogisms, including the one just discussed, with premises of "All P are M," and "All S are M." The vast majority of participants, 81%, endorsed the *invalid* conclusion, "All S are P." Another 10% endorsed other invalid conclusions; only 9% got this problem right. Other studies, with other problems, yield similar data—with error rates regularly as high as 70–90%. (Gilhooly, 1988, provides a review.) participants' performance is somewhat better when the syllogisms are spelled out in concrete terms, but here, too, performance remains relatively low (Wilkins, 1928).

Participants also show a pattern dubbed **belief bias**: If a syllogism's conclusion happens to be something people believe true anyhow, they are more likely to judge the conclusion as following logically from the premises. Conversely, if the conclusion happens to be something they believe false, they are likely to reject the conclusion as invalid. (For reviews, see Evans, Over & Manktelow, 1993; Newstead, Pol-

lard, Evans & Allen, 1992; Oakhill & Garnham, 1993; Revlin, Leirer, Yopp & Yopp, 1980.)

In displaying belief bias, participants are endorsing claims they believe to be true, based on the totality of their knowledge, and rejecting claims they believe to be false. Note, though, that this is *not* what these logic problems require: Logic is instead concerned with more "local" issues of reasoning—specifically, whether a particular conclusion is warranted by a particular set of premises. Thus, when people show the belief-bias pattern, they are failing to distinguish between good arguments (those that are logical and persuasive) and bad ones: They are willing to endorse a bad argument, if it happens to lead to conclusions they already believe true, and they are willing to reject a good argument, if it leads to conclusions already believed false.

## ATMOSPHERE ERRORS AND CONVERSION

A misunderstanding of logic is also suggested by the so-called **atmosphere pattern**, first described by Woodworth and Sells (1935). The claim, in essence, is that the premises of a logic problem create a certain "atmosphere" in which some conclusions seem more appropriate, and some less. For example, premises involving the word "all" create an "atmosphere" in which conclusions about "all" seem appropriate; premises containing the word "some" make conclusions containing "some" seem appropriate. Thus, if one sees a premise such as "All A are B," and another premise such as "All D are B," one is "primed" to accept a conclusion that contains the word "all." None of this is logically sensible, but many of the logic errors we observe fall into this pattern, suggesting that participants' reasoning is somehow influenced by these atmosphere effects. You might, for example, look back at the syllogism concerned with sadists and professional plumbers; the errors in this case plainly do conform with the atmosphere pattern.

There has been considerable argument over what processes or strategies lie behind the atmosphere pattern. Moreover, while many of the errors made by research participants do fall into this pattern, some do not. As a result, it may be best to think of the atmosphere pattern as providing a reasonable—albeit crude—summary of the data and, as such, it implies that participants approach these logic problems in a superficial manner and with minimal understanding. (For discussion, see Begg & Denny, 1969; Gilhooly, 1988; Johnson-Laird, 1983. For discussion of "matching" errors similar to the atmosphere errors, see Gilhooly, Logie, Wetherick & Wynn, 1993; Wetherick, 1989.)

Another pattern is also prominent in people's errors: People often interpret "All A are B" as though it were identical to "All B are A." (Of course this isn't warranted: "All trees are plants" isn't the same as "All plants are trees.") Likewise, people treat these as equivalent: "Some F are not G" and "Some G are not F." These errors are referred to as **conversion errors**, since people are "converting" these statements from one form into another.

So where does all of this leave us? Errors in logical reasoning are extremely common, and the errors don't look at all like the product of carelessness. Instead, there is a systematic pattern to the errors—a pattern captured in the phenomena of belief bias, atmosphere errors, and conversion errors. This pattern indicates that our reasoning *is* guided by certain principles, but the principles are *not* the rules of logic! Put differently, it appears that scholars have simply been mistaken when they have argued that systems of formal logic describe the actual rules of thought.

## REASONING ABOUT CONDITIONAL STATEMENTS

Similar conclusions derive from research on a different aspect of logic, namely, reasoning about **conditional statements**. These are statements of the familiar "If X, then Y" format, with the first statement providing a "condition" under which the second statement is guaranteed to be true.

Just as with syllogisms, people make enormous numbers of errors when asked to reason about conditional statements. Once again, errors are more common if people are asked to reason about abstract problems ("If P, then Q"), in comparison to performance with concrete problems ("If John plays baseball, then he is tense"). Errors are also more common if the logic problems involve negatives ("If John does not play baseball, then he won't be late"). Moreover, and again just like syllogisms, belief bias can be demonstrated: people will endorse a conclusion if they happen to believe it true, even if the conclusion doesn't follow from the stated premises. Conversely, people will reject a conclusion if they happen to believe it false, even if the conclusion is logically demanded by the premises. (For broad reviews in this domain, see Evans, 1982; Evans, Newstead, & Byrne, 1993; Rips, 1990; Wason & Johnson-Laird, 1972.)

In reasoning about conditionals, people also make many conversion errors. In fact, these conversions are encouraged by our ordinary conversational habits, since many terms have a different meaning in day-to-day conversation than they do within logic. For example, in logic the statement "A *or* B" means that either A is true, or B is true, or perhaps both are true. In ordinary conversation, though, we use "or" somewhat differently, usually ruling out this third possibility (namely, that *both* A and B are true). To see this, imagine that a child rings your doorbell and announces, "Trick or treat!" You are likely to understand this as an "exclusive" use of the word "or"—that is, you don't expect that both clauses will turn out to be true. (That is, the truth of either clause *excludes* the truth of the other.) You would feel betrayed if you provided the treat, but got the trick nonetheless.

Similarly, logicians interpret "If P then Q" this way: If P is true, then Q is guaranteed to be true. If P is *false*, then Q may turn out to be true anyhow. Again, this is different from common usage: I might tell you, "If you touch my computer, I'll punish you." You therefore prudently leave my computer alone. If I punish you anyhow, surely you would feel this unjust. To put this in technical terms, we routinely interpret conditionals as if they were **biconditionals**, which are statements of the form, "If X, *and only if* X, then Y." In that case, if X isn't true, then Y won't be, either. To continue our example, a biconditional would imply that, if you didn't touch my computer, then you won't be punished—

**FIGURE 13.2** — The "Four-Card Task"

Each card has a letter on one side and a number on the other side. Which cards must be turned over to check this rule? *If a card has a vowel on one side, it must have an even number on the other side.*

"Punish if touch, and *only if* touch." (For further discussion of these conversions, see Evans, 1982; Staudenmayer, 1975; Staudenmayer & Bourne, 1978; Wason & Johnson-Laird, 1972.)

Given these comments, one might argue that research participants' "errors" in logic may not be errors at all. The participants understand these logic problems in their own terms, and in particular, they understand them in a fashion consonant with the ordinary usage of words like "or" and "if." Perhaps the participants then reason sensibly about the premises *interpreted in this fashion*. In this case, they might not offer the same responses as a logician, but that is not because their reasoning is bad. Instead, they are simply understanding the terms differently than a logician would. Thus, we don't have illogical participants; instead, we simply have two different "dialects" in play—one the dialect of ordinary English, and one the dialect of logic. Each dialect is legitimate, each leads to its own interpretation of the problems, and each, therefore, leads to its own set of responses.

A number of psychologists have endorsed claims along these lines, arguing that people do reason well, but with a vocabulary somewhat different from that of standard logic. Once the participants' performance is understood, therefore, from the participants' own perspective, the performance does not look so dismal. Indeed, we might even push this one step further:

Perhaps participants also have their own set of logical *rules*—rules that are sensible and coherent but that are different from those used by the logicians. In effect, the participants have their own "natural logic," a system somewhat different from logic as the logicians define it, but defensible nonetheless. (For discussion of this view, see Braine, 1978; Braine, Reiser & Rumain, 1984; Braine & O'Brien, 1991; Braine et al., 1995; Rips, 1983; Henle, 1962.)

This view has much to recommend it, but let's hold it to the side for now. There is another line of results we need to consider before we can start assembling the pieces into an overall account.

### THE FOUR-CARD TASK

In the **four-card task** (sometimes called the selection task), research participants are shown four playing cards, as in Figure 13.2 (after Wason, 1966, 1968). The participants are told that each card has a number on one side and a letter on the other. Their task is to evaluate this rule: "If a card has a vowel on one side, it must have an even number on the other side." Which cards must be turned over to put this rule to the test?

Many people assert that the "A" card must be turned over, checking for an even number. Others assert that the "6" card must be turned over, checking for a vowel. Still others assert that both of these must be turned over. In Wason's research, 46% of the participants turned over the "A" and the "6." Thirty-three percent turned over just the "A." The correct answer, however, was obtained by only 4% of the participants—turning over the "A" and the "7." In brief, then, performance is atrocious in this problem, with 96% of the participants giving wrong answers.

Why is "A and 7" the right answer? If we turn over the "A" card, and find an even number, that's consistent with the rule. But if we turn it over and find an odd number, that's inconsistent. Therefore, by turning over the "A," we'll discover if this card is consistent with the rule or not. In other words, there's something to be learned by turning over this card. What about the "J"? The rule makes no claims about what is on the flip side of a consonant card, so no matter what we find on the other side, it satisfies the rule. Therefore, there's nothing to be learned by turning over this card; we already know (without flipping the card over) that it's consistent with the rule. How about the "6"? If we find a vowel on the reverse side of this card, this would fit with the rule. If we find a consonant on the reverse, this also fits, since again, the rule makes no claims about what is on the reverse of a consonant card. Therefore, we'll learn nothing by turning over the "6"—no matter what we find, it satisfies the rule. Finally, if we turn over the "7" and a consonant is on the other side, this would fit with the rule. If there's a vowel on the other side, this wouldn't fit. Therefore, we do want to turn over this card—there is a chance that we might find something informative.

Why do people make so many errors in this task? Several hypotheses have been offered. As one possibility, participants might be converting the proposed rule and then reasoning about this (converted) rule. They might, in particular, be interpreting this rule as a biconditional, rather than a conditional. Thus, they would be trying to test the rule, "If a vowel on one side, *and only if* a vowel on one side, then an even number on the other side." If this were the participants' understanding, though, then they should turn over *all* the cards to test the rule. However, this pat-

tern—turning over all the cards—is shown by relatively few participants (generally less than 20%), and so this seems a poor account of their performance.

A different possibility is that the participants understand some logical rules, but not other rules, including a rule needed for this task. For example most people do understand the logical rule called *modus ponens*, which justifies the conclusion in this case:

> If P then Q.
> P is true.
>   Therefore, Q must be true.

People generally reason well with problems resting on *modus ponens*, such as "If Herbert waves at me, I'll be happy. Herbert did wave at me. What follows from this?"

People have difficulty, though, with the rule of *modus tollens*, which justifies the conclusion in this case:

> If P then Q.
> Q is false.
>   Therefore, P must also be false.

In very simple cases, people do understand this rule: "If Herbert waves at me, I'll be happy. I'm not happy. Therefore, it must be the case that Herbert didn't wave at me—if he had, I'd be happy." If we add any complexity at all, though, people are easily confused by problems resting on *modus tollens*, often rejecting conclusions if they are based on this rule (Braine & O'Brien, 1991; Evans, 1982; Rips, 1983, 1990; Taplin & Staudenmayer, 1973).

Could this be the problem in the four-card task? Because of their understanding of *modus ponens*, participants would realize that they need to turn over the card with a vowel on it (that is, the "A"). That is because *modus ponens* tells them that a conclusion can be drawn from the combination of the rule ("if a vowel, then an even number") and the presence of a vowel. If participants also fail to understand *modus tollens*, then they will fail to realize that they should turn over cards with odd numbers (the "7"). This is because they won't see that a conclusion can be drawn from the combination of the rule ("if a vowel, then an even number") and the presence of a "not-even" number.

Therefore, a participant who understands *modus ponens* but not *modus tollens* will turn over the "A" card, but not the "7." This describes 33% of the participants, so perhaps we are on the right track in understanding participants' performance. But we have not explained why even more participants (46%) chose the "A" and also the "6." Thus, a failure to understand *modus tollens* seems relevant here, but cannot provide our full account.

## THE EFFECTS OF PROBLEM CONTENT

Poor performance in the four-card task has been widely replicated. However, some studies, using variations on this problem, have found much better performance. For example, Johnson-Laird, Legrenzi and Legrenzi (1972) showed British participants the figure illustrated in Figure 13.3, and asked them to test this rule: "If a letter is sealed, then it has a 50-lire stamp on it." The participants did reasonably well in this version of the test, although, in its form, this test is identical to the original four-card problem.

Other studies, also using concrete materials, have likewise observed high levels of performance. For example, Griggs and Cox (1982) asked their participants to test this rule: "If a person is drinking beer, then the person must be over 19 years of age." As in the other studies the participants were shown four cards and asked which cards they would need to turn over to test the rule. In this version, participants did quite well: 73% (correctly) selected the card labeled "drinking a beer," and also the card labeled "16 years of age." They did not select "drinking a Coke" or "22 years of age." Griggs and Cox also tested their participants with the "standard" version of the test (if vowel, then even number), and none of their participants got this problem right. (For discussion, see Cheng & Holyoak, 1985; Evans, 1982; Evans, Newstead et al., 1993; Griggs, 1983; Legrenzi, Girotto & Johnson-Laird, 1993; Wason, 1983.)

Could it simply be the *concreteness* of these examples that improves performance? Other results

argue against this suggestion: As just noted, the "envelope" problem produced good performance with British participants. However, when the same problem was given to American participants, poor performance was observed (Griggs & Cox, 1982; Johnson-Laird et al., 1972).

Perhaps the problems must be concrete and also *familiar*. The British participants who did well with the envelope problem were familiar with a similar postal regulation that used to be in force in England. (The rule required slightly higher postage for sealed letters than for unsealed letters.) The American participants, in contrast, have had no experience with such a rule, and their performance was correspondingly poor. In addition, it turns out that younger citizens in Britain are not familiar with this postal rule (which has not been enforced for many years). It is therefore interesting that younger British participants do poorly with the envelope problem (and so look just like Americans in this regard). It is only older British participants, familiar with the rule, who do well. (This latter result, reported by Golding, is summarized by Cheng & Holyoak, 1985.)

We'll have more to say about this point in just a moment, but in the meantime, note where all these data are pushing us: We began, many pages back, with the hypothesis that *logic* describes the rules of thought. According to this view, thinking proceeds on a rather abstract level since, after all, logic depends only on the form or syntax of the assertions being considered, and not at all on their content. *Modus ponens*, for example, applies to any assertion of the form "If P, then Q," and also "P." It does not matter for *modus ponens* what P is or what Q is. That's why *modus ponens* applies to this case:

> If you sleep, you dream.
> You sleep.
> > Therefore you dream.

It also applies to this case:

> If Fred eats, then Carla is happy.
> Fred eats.
> > Therefore Carla is happy.

## An Easier Version of the Four-Card Problem

FIGURE 13.3

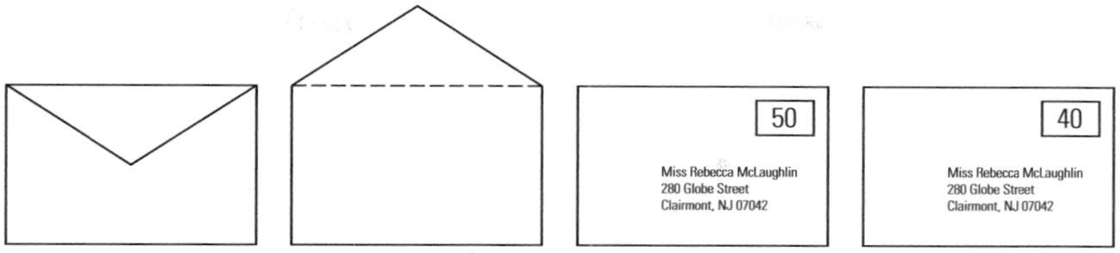

Which envelopes would you need to turn over to find out if this rule is true? *If a letter is sealed, then it has a 50-lire stamp on it.* Older British participants have an easier time with this problem than with the standard four-card problem (see Figure 13.2), even though the two problems are identical in form. [After Wason & Johnson-Laird, 1972.]

It also applies to this case:

> If Machamp does a seismic toss, then Bellsprout does a vine whip.
> Machamp does a seismic toss.
>     Therefore, Bellsprout does a vine whip.

These three cases obviously differ in their content, but they all have the same form, and it's only the form that matters for logic.

If our thought followed the rules of logic, then the same should be true for thought: It should be the *form* of the argument that matters, quite independent of the *content*. But, as we have seen, this is not the pattern of the data. When people show the pattern of *belief bias*, for example, they are clearly being influenced by the content of what they're reasoning about, and not just the logical form. And certainly in the four-card problem, the content matters a lot. The logical form of the original problem (cast in terms of vowels and even numbers) is identical to the form of the "letters and stamps" version and the "over 19 and drinking beer" version. Even so, the data are very different for these other versions, and so, quite plainly, the content of these problems does matter for performance. This seems highly problematic for the claim that logic (or any other formal system) reflects the way people typically think. Instead, the evidence is driving us toward the view that thought *is* influenced by the content, the meaning, and the pragmatics of the material we are contemplating.

## DETECTING CHEATERS

But *how* does the content influence us? More specifically, why are some versions of the four-card problem difficult, and others easy? Different investigators have offered different views of this issue, and the data do not yet allow a clear choice among these views; indeed, in the end, we may need to seek some combination of these different views in order to encompass the full data pattern.

What are our options? One proposal comes from the *evolutionary perspective* on psychology, a perspective we first met in Chapter 12. According to this perspective, many questions in psychology are better understood if we think about how the relevant skills, or relevant processes, have been shaped by evolutionary pressures over the last million years or so. To apply this to the broad topic of *reasoning*, several investigators have argued this way: Our ancient ancestors didn't have to reason about whether or not all A's are B's, nor did they have to reason about vowels and even numbers. Instead, our ancestors had to worry about issues like *social interactions*, including issues of betrayal and cheating: "I asked you to do something. Have you done it, or have you betrayed me?" "None of our clan is supposed to eat more than one share of meat; is Joe perhaps cheating and eating too much?"

If our ancestors needed to reason about these issues, then any individuals who were particularly skilled in this reasoning might have had a survival advantage, and so, little by little, those who were skillful would become more numerous, and those without the skill would die off. In the end, only those skillful at social reasoning would be left. And, of course, we are the biological heirs of these survivors, and so we inherited their skills.

According to this proposal, therefore, people in the modern world will reason well about a logical rule whenever they understand that rule as involving *cheating* or *betrayal*, or the like (Cosmides, 1989; Cummins & Allen, 1998; Gigerenzer & Hug, 1992). In this case, the skills that people have (thanks to their biology) will be well matched to the reasoning problem, and this will lead to good performance.

This claim is certainly consistent with the data we have seen so far: The "drinking beer and over 19" problem, for example, involves the detection of "cheaters" and yields good performance. The "envelope and stamp" problem can also be understood in this way *if* someone understands this as a rule involving "permission," and not as an arbitrary association. (This may be why familiarity with this rule is important—familiarity allows participants to see this as a case requiring permission, and so a case that potentially involves cheaters.) Good performance is also observed with other problems that can be understood as "detecting cheaters"—even if the problems involve unfamiliar situations or principles (Cosmides, 1989; Gigerenzer & Hug, 1992; but also see Liberman & Klar, 1996).

## PRAGMATIC REASONING SCHEMATA

Other investigators, however, have offered different hypotheses about the four-card problem. Cheng and Holyoak, for example, have offered a hypothesis cast in terms of **pragmatic reasoning schemata**. These schemata are defined in terms of *pragmatic goals*, and summarize that which is redundant or typical in achieving these goals. (Notice, then, that reasoning schemata are in this regard just like any other schemata: Schemata in general are derived from experience and summarize that which is redundant or predictable in our world—see Chapter 7.) Thus, for example, we have a *cause-and-effect* schema, which summarizes our experiences with cause-and-effect relations, and which we use in reasoning about causal relations. We also have an *obligation* schema, which we use in reasoning about social relations of the appropriate sort; we also have a *permission* schema, and so on.

These schemata embody rules that are quite similar to the rules of logic and so these schemata can be used to guide reasoning. For example, the permission schema includes rules like "If one wishes to take a certain action, then one must have permission," and "If one has permission to take a certain action, then one may take the action." We use these rules whenever we are trying to think about a situation requiring permission. Let's emphasize, though, that these rules support reasoning *about permission*; they are not general, abstract, if-then rules. In this way, reasoning schemata are more concrete than logical rules (Cheng & Holyoak, 1985; Cheng, Holyoak, Nisbett & Oliver, 1986; Nisbett, 1993).

How does all of this apply to the four-card problem? The original version of this problem contained no practical or meaningful relations; the rule of "if a vowel, then an even number" is completely arbitrary. The problem is therefore unlikely to evoke a reasoning schema, and this leaves participants at a loss: With their primary reasoning strategy not called into play, it is no wonder that they do poorly on this task.

According to this view, we should be able to improve performance on the four-card task by altering the problem so that it *will* trigger a pragmatic reasoning schema. Then people will be able to employ their usual means of reasoning and should perform quite well. To this end, participants in one experi-

## The Role of a "Rationale" in the Four-Card Problem

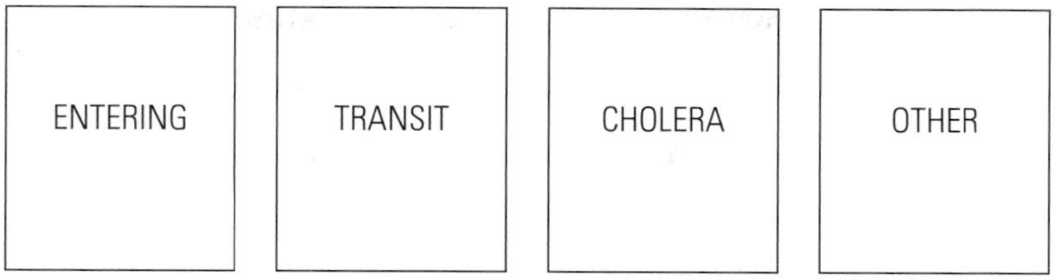

**FIGURE** 13.4

| ENTERING | TRANSIT | CHOLERA | OTHER |
|:---:|:---:|:---:|:---:|

Participants were asked which cards they would need to turn over to find out if this rule is true: *If the form says ENTERING on one side, then the other side includes cholera among the list of diseases.* Participants perform well on this problem if they are provided with a rationale; otherwise they perform poorly.

ment were given several variations of the basic problem (one example is illustrated in Figure 13.4). Their task was to decide which cards to turn over to test the rule "If the form says ENTERING on one side, then the other side includes cholera among the list of diseases."

For half of the participants, this problem was given with no further rationale. The prediction here is that no schema will be evoked and performance should be poor. The other participants, however, were given a rationale, designed to trigger the permission schema. These participants were told that the cards listed diseases against which airline passengers had been inoculated. In addition, they were told that cholera inoculation was required of all passengers seeking to enter the country. These participants were then given the same rule as stated above, but now the rule can be understood in permission terms, something like "If a passenger wishes to enter the country, he or she must first receive a cholera inoculation." Thus, with the rationale in view, the problem should trigger a schema, and participants should perform well.

Participants were also given the "envelope" version of the problem, with the rule of "If an envelope is sealed, then it must have the higher value stamp." Half of the participants were given no rationale; half were told that first-class mail was always sealed,

and that the post office charged a higher rate for first-class mail.

As can be seen in Figure 13.5, participants did rather well with the rationale versions of these problems, averaging about 90% correct. Without rationale, they did quite poorly (about 60%). The figure shows one exception to this pattern: Participants in Hong Kong did well with the envelope problem, even when no rationale was provided by the experimenters. This result is not difficult to understand: Residents of Hong Kong were familiar with an actual postal rule similar to the one described within the experiment. These participants therefore had no trouble coming up with the rationale on their own, since the problem involved a familiar case.

In terms of their form, all of the problems used in this study are identical, all involving simple inferences about an "if-then" rule. Therefore, if participants were reasoning about these problems by use of logic, then we should have observed equivalent performance in all conditions. This clearly is not the pattern we observe in the figure.

If familiarity is the key, then we should have observed low levels of performance with all versions of the problem except the Hong Kong-envelope condition. This condition presented a familiar problem to participants; all other conditions presented novel problems. But, once again, this is not the pattern we

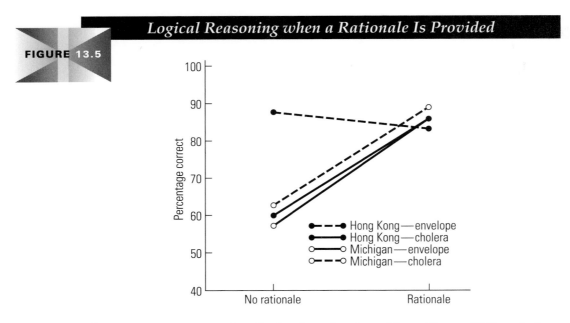

**FIGURE 13.5**

**Logical Reasoning when a Rationale Is Provided**

Participants were tested with the "envelope" problem (Figure 13.3) and the "cholera" problem (Figure 13.4). When a rationale was provided, participants performed well with both problems. When no rationale was provided, only the Hong Kong participants working on the envelope problem did well. These participants, familiar with the envelope rule, could provide a rationale for themselves. [After Cheng & Holyoak, 1985.]

observe. Performance is good in the Hong Kong–envelope condition, but it is equally good in several other conditions. This speaks against interpretation of these data emphasizing familiarity.

Finally, if participants were reasoning by using pragmatic schemata, then we expect good performance when the schemata are called into play and poor performance otherwise. In this case, we predict high performance either with a familiar case, *or* with a case accompanied by a rationale triggering a specific schema. This is, of course, exactly what the data show.

Moreover, even with *abstract* problems, performance is improved the moment a reasoning schema is triggered. Participants in one study were told, "Suppose you are an authority checking whether or not people are obeying certain regulations. The regu-

lations all have the general form, "If one is to take Action A, then one must first satisfy Precondition P" (Cheng & Holyoak, 1985). Participants were then given four cards, labeled as shown in Figure 13.6. In this task, 61% of the participants solved the problem correctly, compared to 19% correct in a control group, given the standard (vowel–even number) problem. This makes it clear that concreteness is not crucial for correct reasoning—here participants are doing reasonably well with an abstract problem.

## NECESSITY AND SUFFICIENCY

Yet another account of the four-card problem hinges on how people think about "if-then" sentences. For

## Reasoning in the Abstract with a Rationale

FIGURE 13.6

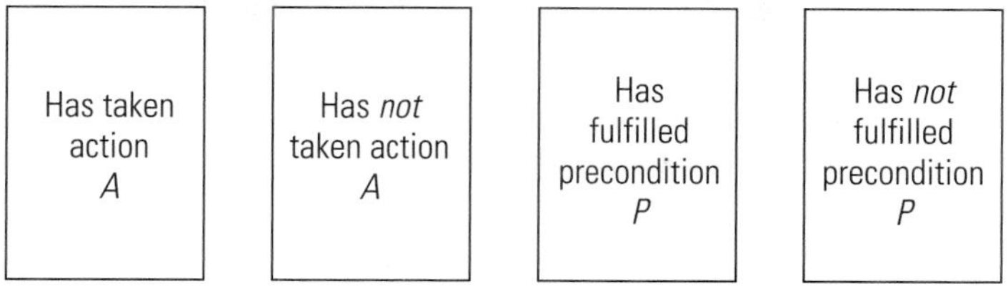

| | | | |
|---|---|---|---|
| Has taken action *A* | Has *not* taken action *A* | Has fulfilled precondition *P* | Has *not* fulfilled precondition *P* |

Which cards would you turn over to test this rule? *If one is to take Action A, then one must satisfy Precondition P.* This rule is relatively abstract, but does trigger the reasoning schema for permission. With the schema triggered, participants perform well with this problem.

example, consider this case (after Ahn & Graham, 1999): "If an applicant has more than 3 years of experience, he may get the job." In this case, the experience is *necessary* for getting the job (if you don't have the experience, you won't get the job), but is not *sufficient* (even if you do have the experience, it's possible that you won't get the job). The situation is different in this case: "If a person drinks beer, the person must be over 21 years old." In this case, the "if" clause is *not* necessary for the "then" clause: It's possible to be over 21 even if you're not drinking beer! But now the "if" clause *is* sufficient for the "then" clause (if you're drinking beer, then it must be the case that you're over 21).

It seems likely that people draw different conclusions when thinking about "necessary conditions" than they do when thinking about "sufficient conditions," and this may be why the content of the four-card problem is so important: Some problems (like the "over 21" version, or problems involving permission) invite an interpretation that involves *sufficiency*, and this triggers a pattern of reasoning that's similar to the way logicians define "if-then" relationships. No wonder, then, that these problems lead to a high proportion of "correct" answers (answers in line with those endorsed by logicians). Other problems invite different interpretations, and so trigger different patterns of reasoning. And still other problems (like the

original "vowel and even number" version) are ambiguous with regard to interpretation, and so different participants interpret the problem in different ways, yielding a somewhat chaotic pattern of results. (For further discussion and supporting data, see Ahn & Graham, 1999. For related proposals, see Oaksford & Chater, 1995; Polk & Newell, 1995; Sperber et al., 1995; Thompson & Mann, 1995.)

Where does all of this leave us? There is no question that the content of the four-card problem does matter. Some versions of the problem produce miserable levels of performance; some versions yield excellent performance. Is this because of a biologically rooted skill of thinking about "cheating," or a skill, gained from experience, of reasoning about pragmatically defined goals? Or is it a reflection of the way that the problem's content leads us to interpret the "if-then" relationship? It is difficult to say, and part of the reason is that these conceptions overlap in important ways. Cases that involve "cheater detection," for example, usually involve some sort of "permission," and so the evolutionary account and the pragmatic reasoning account often make the same predictions about which versions of the problem will be easy, and which hard. Likewise, cases that involve "permission" usually invite an interpretation in terms of "sufficient but not necessary conditions" and so the two perspectives also often lead to similar predictions. It is not surprising, therefore, that researchers have so far found it difficult to devise tests that will allow us to choose one of these theoretical accounts over the others. In the meantime, though, one thing is clear: A purely formal account of our reasoning, one that emphasizes only the logical form of the problems we face, and not the content of those problems, does not mesh with the way humans reason.

## TRAINING STUDIES

Although there is disagreement about the exact *source* of errors in the four-card problem, there is agreement on one crucial point: The poor performance originally observed with this problem is not an accurate reflection of human reasoning in general. Humans *can* reason well *if* the problem somehow triggers the appropriate skills. This obviously resembles a claim we made in Chapter 12 and leads us to ask the same question here that we asked in the earlier chapter: Is it possible to train people so that good-quality reasoning is more easily triggered? The answer is "yes."

Let's note at the start, though, that people's reasoning about everyday problems seems *not* to be improved by courses in formal logic. As one example of the data, Morris and Nisbett (1993) tested people using a number of variants of the four-card task. Their research participants were graduate students in philosophy—some in their first year in the program, and some in their third year. The graduate training included several courses in logic and so, if these courses helped, we would expect the third-year students to outperform the first-year students. This was not the case: Both groups performed poorly. When the content of the problems was unfamiliar, for example, first-year students got 33% correct; third-year students got 32% correct.

Similar results have been obtained when people are trained in logic within the context of the experimental procedure: This training has little impact on performance in the four-card task (Cheng et al., 1986). Likewise, an undergraduate course in logic seems not to improve performance on this task: Cheng et al. (1986) tested students both in the first week of a logic course, and again in the final week of the semester. While these students obviously learned a great deal during the term, this knowledge did not carry over into the four-card task, and performance was basically the same at the end of the course as it was initially.

However, a rather different result is obtained if research participants are trained to use reasoning schemata, rather than formal rules. Cheng et al. (1986) gave their participants a two-page booklet detailing the nature of obligations and the procedures necessary for checking to see if a violation of the obligation had occurred. Participants were also given an example of an obligation statement, framed in if-then terms. This training, brief as it was, had a dramatic impact on performance. These participants were 92% correct with test problems designed to trigger the obligation schema (e.g., a problem involving the rule "If a steel support is intended for the roof, then it must be rust-proof"). Participants who received *no* training were only 64% correct. For more abstract problems (such as the "If vowel, then even number" problem), participants trained in the nature of obligation got 55% right, compared to 27% for the control group.

In short, performance is little influenced by training in logic: There is little impact from a brief logic course within the experiment, or a full undergraduate course in logic, or even years of graduate training. In marked contrast, just a few minutes' training in the use of reasoning schemata *does* improve performance, even with arbitrary problems.

## DEDUCTIVE LOGIC: AN INTERIM SUMMARY

Before pressing on, let's summarize where we are. As a start, common sense tells us that some people, in some circumstances, can use the rules of logic. Logic teachers, for example, can obviously use these rules. Even those untutored in logic can use "natural logic." Natural logic comes into play, for example, if I tell you "If G is true, then H is true. G happens to be true." With no difficulty, people draw the conclusion that H, too, is true. This problem, abstract and unfamiliar, relies on our intuitive understanding of *modus ponens*, and we use this understanding to draw the correct conclusion.

In other circumstances, though, we seem to rely on other reasoning strategies. As we have seen, there is debate over what those other strategies are, and also what it is that triggers their use. Perhaps these "other strategies" are evolutionarily prepared reasoning skills that we use whenever we are thinking about cheaters, betrayal, or the like. Perhaps, instead, the "other strategies" are pragmatic reasoning schemata, used whenever a problem can be understood in terms of pragmatic goals. In either case, two things are clear: First, these other reasoning strategies are tied to a particular content but also general enough so that they can sometimes be applied to unfamiliar cases. Second, these reasoning strategies are sophisticated enough that they often yield conclusions identical to those endorsed by logical rules.

Thus, our account of human reasoning will need at least two layers: Humans are capable in some circumstances of truly abstract reasoning (consider again the fact that people easily understand the entirely abstract rule of *modus ponens*). In addition, we've seen evidence that humans also rely in many settings on a separate set of more concrete reasoning strategies, strategies somehow tied to a particular content, and triggered only when that content is in view.

But this isn't all. Our account of reasoning also needs a third layer, describing the way people reason when these relatively sophisticated reasoning strategies are *not* triggered. For example, the atmosphere hypothesis can be thought of as describing the inferences you will try if you don't know how else to proceed. Likewise, if you can't figure out a problem, you might try to help yourself by "smuggling in" other knowledge, external to the problem. In this case, you will show the pattern that we earlier called belief bias. This inclusion of other knowledge isn't warranted according to logic, but it may be your best bet, if you don't have some other plan available.

Overall, then, the suggestion is that the rules of logic, some sort of content-specific reasoning strategies, and various heuristics may all co-exist in our mental repertoire, and each will surface in appropri-

ate circumstances. Some of these approaches to reasoning are more likely to yield the correct conclusion than others, and it is striking how often we rely on approaches that can lead to error. But this simply reflects the fact that the more "sophisticated" strategies come into play only when appropriately triggered—by cues in the problem setting or by virtue of relevant training.

Note the parallels between all of this and the pattern we saw in Chapter 12: When you are trying to make a judgment about evidence, there are several paths you might follow. If you have been trained in statistics and methodology, you may elect to translate the problem into these terms, and thus reason it through. This is likely to require some time and effort, but it is also likely to yield the right answer. As a second option, you may elect to think about the problem using statistical heuristics—heuristics, we suggested, that capture the gist of important statistical principles. Use of these heuristics, it seems, is more likely if you have been trained to use them, and more likely if the problem contains features that trigger these heuristics—for example, if the problem highlights the role of *chance* in determining an outcome. If all else fails, though, you will rely on a different set of heuristics, such as availability and representativeness. These may produce error, but they probably work more often than not, and at least they are efficient.

Clearly, this resembles the pattern described in the present chapter. We should emphasize, however, an interesting contrast between the data in this chapter and those in Chapter 12: In Chapter 12, we saw that a single undergraduate course in statistics has a large benefit for everyday reasoning; in this chapter, we have seen that a course in logic does not have this benefit. In Chapter 12, we saw that even brief instruction in statistics can improve reasoning; in this chapter, we've failed to find a parallel benefit from brief instruction in logic. What produces this contrast?

One possibility is that statistics courses are able to build on intuitions we already have and to remind us of beliefs we already hold. There is, for example, a reasonable correspondence between our intuitive understanding of chance events and the statistician's "law of large numbers," and statistics courses can exploit this correspondence in conveying the law. One might argue that the same is not true for logic courses—apparently, there are important divergences between formal logic, as it is generally taught, and the natural logic that each of us already holds. For example, *modus tollens* is routinely included in logic courses, but seems foreign to our intuitions.

A related possibility is that statistics courses are, by their nature, often concerned with pragmatic examples; statistics textbooks are filled with problems asking you to apply statistical concepts to real-world cases. The study of formal logic, on the other hand, is more self-contained; logic texts rarely require you to translate commonsense problems into logical terms. This probably contributes to the fact that statistics courses do have an impact on everyday reasoning, but logic courses do not. (For broader discussion of this contrast between statistics and logic training, see Nisbett, 1993.)

## Mental Models

An important message in the previous section was that different reasoning strategies may exist side-by-side in the mind and are called into play in different situations. If we sometimes reason poorly, this is largely because we are using inappropriate strategies. If we can change the reasoner's strategies (by means of instruction) or change the situation (so that different strategies are triggered), reasoning can be much improved.

It is against this backdrop that we consider one further reasoning strategy that people use, a strategy that, once again, is more concrete than reasoning via formal rules, yet more abstract than reasoning about specific cases. It is a strategy of creating, and then reasoning about, mental models. (Let's note from the start that there is some risk of confusion here, since we used the term "mental model" differently in Chapter 9. Unfortunately, though, it just is the case that researchers interested in concepts use this term in one fashion, while researchers interested in

logic use the term differently. It will be best, therefore, if you hold the following sections separate from the themes we discussed in Chapter 9.)

Let us return for the moment to categorical syllogisms, like this one:

All of the artists are beekeepers.
Some of the beekeepers are chemists.

What follows from these premises? One way to think about this problem is by imagining a room full of people. Some of the people in the room are artists (perhaps you imagine them as wearing sweatshirts with a big "A" on the front). Others in the room are not artists (they have no sweatshirts). Perhaps you then imagine all of the artists as having a bee perched on their heads, and perhaps you also imagine some non-artists as having bees on their heads, as well. (After all, the premise said that all artists are beekeepers, but it *didn't* say that all beekeepers are artists.) Continuing in this fashion, you will end up imagining a little world, or a mental model, in which all of the premises are fulfilled. You can then inspect this model in order to ask what else is true about it: Once the premises are fulfilled, what other claims are entailed? Does it follow, for example, that some artists are chemists? (As it turns out, this *doesn't* follow from these premises, and so would be an invalid conclusion. You might confirm this by constructing a suitable mental model—"staffing" the imagined room as needed.) Other premises can also be represented in this fashion. For example, if the premise were "No artists are beekeepers," you could imagine a room divided by a barrier, with the artists on one side, and the beekeepers on the other.

Johnson-Laird and his colleagues have argued that mental models are widely used in reasoning. Broadly put, the idea is that one first constructs a mental model of a problem (or perhaps multiple models). Next, one scrutinizes the model, seeking to discover what conclusions follow from the modeled premises. Finally, one can check on these conclusions by trying to discover counterexamples—models that are compatible with the premises, but not with the proposed conclusion. If no counterexamples are found, then one concludes that the conclusion is valid (Johnson-

## Mental Models of a Premise

**FIGURE** 13.7

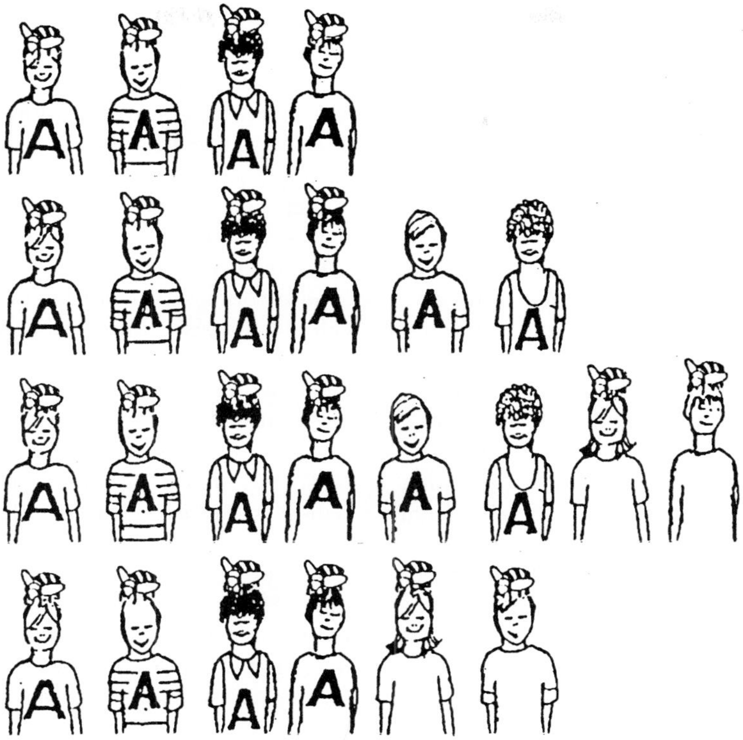

Many premises can be modeled in more than one way. For example, the figure shows several possible models for the premise "Some of the artists are beekeepers." In other words, each row within the figure depicts a situation in which this premise is true. Artists are shown with A's on their shirts; non-artists don't have A's. Beekeepers are shown with bees on their heads; non-beekeepers are bare-headed.

Laird, 1983, 1990; Johnson-Laird & Byrne, 1989, 1991; Johnson-Laird & Steedman, 1978; for related views, see Gentner & Stevens, 1983; Guyote & Sternberg, 1981; Kahneman & Tversky, 1982b).

Participants in reasoning studies sometimes, on their own, mention the use of such models. One participant commented, "I thought of all the little artists in the room and imagined that they all had beekeeper's hats on." As more formal evidence, though, the mental-model approach leads to a number of predictions about reasoning performance, and many of these predictions have been confirmed. For example, some premises can be modeled in more than one way (see Figure 13.7). In these cases, people trying to reason about these premises will have to examine multiple models, or else keep track of mental models with "optional" parts. One would expect this to make a problem more difficult, and this is indeed the case: The greater the number of models needed in reasoning through the problem, the more likely errors are to occur (Johnson-Laird, Byrne & Tabossi, 1989; Johnson-Laird & Steedman, 1978).

Researchers have also suggested a role for mental models in other forms of reasoning, including reasoning about conditional problems (Evans, 1993; Johnson-Laird, Byrne & Schaeken, 1992; Legrenzi et al., 1993). For example, imagine that we tell you, "If it is sunny, the boys play baseball." You might then construct a mental model of this conditional—perhaps by contemplating a sunny day, with the boys out on the field. Imagine that we now add, "Today, it is sunny." This is obviously consistent with the model you've constructed, implying that is okay to draw conclusions from this model. Therefore, you correctly conclude, "Today, the boys play baseball."

Evidence suggests that people do sometimes reason about conditionals in this fashion. Hence, mental models take their place as part of the repertoire of human reasoning strategies. This obviously invites future researchers to explore more fully the pattern of triggers that lead us on one occasion to use one strategy, and on another occasion some other strategy. (For further discussion of mental models, see Evans, 1993; Ford, 1995; Goldvarg & Johnson-Laird, 2000; Johnson-Laird et al., 1992; Johnson-Laird & Savery, 1999; Johnson-Laird et al., 1999; Rips, 1986, 1989b.)

## Decision-Making

We turn now to one last category of reasoning—reasoning about *choices*. How do we choose what courses to take next semester or what movie to see on Saturday? How do we choose which candidate to support in an election? How do we choose an apartment or a job? Choices like these fill our lives. Often, little is at stake in these decisions, but in other cases a decision can have enormous consequences—e.g., when a cancer patient must decide between surgery and radiation (or no treatment at all), or when a government must decide how to treat a hostile neighbor. How do we make these decisions?

## UTILITY THEORY

There is an obvious and seemingly simple way one might make decisions: Each of us has his or her own values—things we like, things we prize and, for that matter, things we hope to avoid. Likewise, each of us has a series of goals—things we hope to accomplish or things we hope to see—including both near-term goals (what we hope to accomplish soon) and longer-term goals. The obvious suggestion, then, is that we use these values and goals in making decisions: In choosing courses for next semester, you will choose courses that are interesting (something you value) and also courses that help fill the requirements for your major (one of your goals). In choosing a medical treatment, you will hope to avoid pain, and you will also hope to retain all of your physical capacities as long as possible.

To put this a bit more formally, each decision will have certain costs attached to it (that is, consequences that will carry us further from our goals) and also certain benefits (consequences moving us toward our goals, and providing us with things we value). In deciding, we weigh the costs against the benefits and seek a path that will minimize the former and maximize the latter. When we have several options open to us, we will presumably choose the one that provides the most favorable balance of benefits and costs.

This weighing of benefits against costs allows us to accommodate the fact that many decisions pose trade-offs of one sort or another. Should you go to Miami for your vacation this year, or to Tucson? The weather is better in Tucson, but the flight to Miami is less expensive. Hence, you have got to trade off the more desirable weather against the more attractive plane fare. Likewise, should you drive a less comfortable car, if it happens to pollute less? Here, the trade-off is between your comfort and protection of the environment.

Notice that these trade-offs involve factors that are, to say the least, highly disparate—comfort versus pollution, the pleasure made possible by good weather versus the $50 you might save in airfare. Can you really translate your pleasure into dollar amounts? Is your pleasure worth more than, or less than, $50? Likewise, how do you compare a 10% reduction in comfort with a .0001% reduction in pollution levels? In these examples (and, indeed, in most decisions), comparing these factors seems like the proverbial comparison of apples and oranges—the values at stake seem incommensurable.

Somehow, though, we do make these comparisons. We have to, if we are going to make these choices. Presumably, we compare them in a rather subjective way, by asking how important each factor is *to us*. This is often expressed as the **subjective utility** of each factor, meaning, quite simply, the value of that factor for us. These utilities can then be summed (e.g., the utility of a pleasant vacation minus the "disutility" of spending more on airfare) to evaluate the overall utility for each outcome. These summed utilities for the various options can then be compared to each other, with the goal of selecting the option with the greatest overall utility.

In most decisions, though, there is also a degree of uncertainty or risk. Is Professor X an interesting instructor? Four of your friends have said she is, but two have said she is not. How should you factor these "mixed reviews" into your decision? Should you go to Miami for your vacation? At this time of year, let's say there is a 20% chance of rain. Do you want to take that chance?

One way to think about these risks follows a model formalized by von Neumann and Morgenstern (1947). Within their model, one calculates the **expected utility** or expected value of each option, using this simple equation:

Expected utility = (probability of a particular outcome) × (utility of the outcome).

Thus, imagine that I offer to sell you a lottery ticket. The ticket costs $5 but gives you a one-in-a-hundred chance of winning $200. In this case, the expected value of the ticket is (.01 × $200), or $2. At a cost of $5, then, I'm selling the ticket for far more than it is worth.

With more complicated decisions, you will calculate the expected value of each factor and then add these up to compute the *overall* expected value asso-ciated with a particular choice. Let's say that you are choosing courses for next year. Course 1 looks interesting, but also has a heavy workload. To evaluate this course, you will first need to estimate the subjective utility of taking an interesting course and also the *disutility* of being burdened by a heavy workload. Next, you will have to factor in the uncertainties. Perhaps there is a 70% chance that the course will be interesting, but a 90% chance that it will have a heavy workload. In this case, the overall utility for this course will be (.70 × the utility of an interesting course) *minus* (.90 × the disutility of a heavy workload). You could then make similar calculations for the other courses available to you and choose the one with the greatest expected value.

All of this points the way toward a theory of choice: The claim is that, in making choices, we seek to maximize utility—that is, to gain as much as we can of those things we value, and to avoid those things we don't like. We do this by consistently selecting the option with the greatest *expected utility*, calculated as described. (For discussion, see von Neumann & Morgenstern, 1947; also Baron, 1988; Savage, 1954.)

Before continuing, though, let's be clear that the term "utilities" is used here in a very broad sense, referring to whatever it is that is important to you. Hence, there is no connection between, say, seeking to maximize utilities and being *greedy* or *materialistic*. If you happen to value money, then the attempt to maximize utilities will turn out to be an attempt to gather wealth. But if you happen to value leisure, or happiness in those around you, or a reduction of world hunger, then these will be the utilities you seek to maximize. Thus, there is no stigma attached to the notion of utility maximization, and it surely seems sensible to make decisions that move you, as efficiently as possible, toward your goals.

## FRAMING OF OUTCOMES

There is no doubt that many of our choices and decisions do follow the principle of utility maximization. Which would you rather have—$90 or $100? Which

**FIGURE 13.8**

## The Asian Disease Problem

### Positive Frame

Imagine that the United States is preparing for the outbreak of an unusual Asian disease, which is expected to kill 600 people. Two alternative programs to combat the disease have been proposed. Assume that the exact scientific estimates of the consequences of the programs are as follows:

If Program A is adopted, 200 people will be saved.

If Program B is adopted, there is a ⅓ probability that 600 people will be saved, and a ⅔ probability that no people will be saved.

### Negative Frame

Imagine that the United States is preparing for the outbreak of an unusual Asian disease, which is expected to kill 600 people. Two alternative programs to combat the disease have been proposed. Assume that the exact scientific estimates of the consequences of the programs are as follows:

If Program A is adopted, 400 people will die.

If Program B is adopted, there is a ⅓ probability that nobody will die, and ⅔ probability that 600 people will die.

There is clearly no "right answer" to the question posed here—one could defend selecting the "risky" choice (Program B) or the less-rewarding, but less-risky choice (Program A). Nonetheless, people do have strong preferences between these two programs, and the preferences depend heavily on how the problem is framed! In the positive frame (shown at the top), the clear majority of people lean toward Program A, with 72% choosing it over Program B. In the negative frame (shown at the bottom), the preference pattern reverses, and 78% choose Program B over Program A. Let's be clear that this shift in framing changes nothing of importance wthin the decision: 400 people dead, out of 600, is identical to 200 saved, out of 600. Even so, this utterly inconsequential shift in framing has a huge effect, turning a landslide victory for one option (with one frame) into a landslide victory for the opposite option (with the other frame).

gamble would you prefer, a 1% chance of winning a prize, or a 5% chance of winning the same prize? In each case, we are (rather obviously) sensitive to both the value of the "payoff" associated with a decision (i.e., its utility) and also to the probability of a payoff.

However, an enormous number of studies show that, in many circumstances, we are *not* utility maximizers and, more broadly, that we are profoundly influenced by factors having little to do with utilities. In the process, we regularly make choices that are flatly inconsistent with other choices we have made. We will first review a number of these cases, and then we'll turn to how a theory of choice might accommodate them.

Consider the question posed in the top half of Figure 13.8. Research participants show a clear preference between these options, and 72% choose program A (Tversky & Kahneman, 1987). Now consider the question posed in the bottom of Figure 13.8. This problem is the same as the one in the top of the figure—200 people saved out of 600 is identical to 400 people dead out of 600. Therefore, the utilities involved in this problem have not changed one whit. Nonetheless, this change in how the problem is phrased—that is, the **frame** of the decision—has a strong impact on participants' choices. In the lives "saved" frame, they favor program A by almost a 3-to-1 margin. In the "will die" frame, this pattern of preferences *reverses*, and 78% opt for Program B.

It should be emphasized that there is nothing wrong with participants' individual choices. In either version of the Asian disease problem, there is no "right answer," and one can persuasively defend either the decision to avoid risk, by selecting Program A, or the decision to take the chance, by selecting Program B. The problem, though, lies in the *contradiction* created by choosing Program A in one context and Program B in the other context. Indeed, if a single participant is given both frames, on slightly different occasions, the participant is quite likely to contradict himself. For that matter, if a propagandist wanted to manipulate voters' evaluations of these programs, framing provides an effective way to do this.

Framing effects of this sort are easy to demonstrate. Figure 13.9 shows another example, in which people are asked to choose between two different medical treatments. When participants were given the "survival frame," only 18% chose radiation over surgery. When participants were given the "mortality frame," this number more than doubled—with 44% now favoring radiation (Tversky & Kahneman, 1987).

## Framing Effects in Medical Decision-Making

**FIGURE 13.9**

### Survival Frame

**Surgery**: Of 100 people having surgery, 90 live through the post-operative period, 68 are alive at the end of the first year, and 34 are alive at the end of five years.

**Radiation**: Of 100 people having radiation therapy, all live through the treatment, 77 are alive at the end of one year, and 22 are alive at the end of five years.

### Mortality Frame

**Surgery**: Of 100 people having surgery, 10 die during surgery, 32 die by the end of the first year, and 66 die by the end of five years.

**Radiation**: Of 100 people having radiation therapy, none die during the treatment, 23 die by the end of one year, and 78 die by the end of five years.

The options shown in the "survival" frame are identical to the options shown in the mortality frame. The only difference between the frames is in how the options are described. With the survival frame, only 18% of the participants choose radiation over surgery. With the mortality frame, this number more than doubles, with 44% now choosing radiation.

As one final example, consider the two problems shown in Figure 13.10. When participants are given the first problem, almost three-quarters of them (72%) choose the first option—the sure gain of $100. Participants contemplating the second problem generally choose the second option, with only 36% selecting the sure loss of $100 (Tversky & Kahneman, 1987). Note, though, that the problems are once again identical. Both pose the question of whether you would rather end up with a certain $400, or with an even chance between $300 and $500. Despite this equivalence, participants treat these problems very differently, preferring the sure thing in one case, and the gamble in the other.

Across these (and many other) examples, there is a consistent pattern to framing effects. If the frame casts a choice in terms of *losses*, decision-makers tend to be **risk seeking**—that is, they are quite willing to gamble, presumably in hopes of avoiding or reducing the loss. To see this in action, look back at Figure 13.8. When the Asian disease problem is cast in terms of lives lost, this leads to risk-seeking choices: People choose the *gamble* that's inherent in Program B, apparently attracted by the (thin) possibility that, with this program, they may avoid the loss. Likewise, Problem 2 in Figure 13.10 casts your options in terms of financial losses, and this, too, triggers risk-seeking: Here people reliably choose the 50-50 gamble over the sure loss.

The pattern of preferences reverses, though, if the frame casts the exact same choice in terms of *gains*. When contemplating gains, decision-makers tend to be **risk averse**, not risk seeking. In other words, they are not willing to gamble, choosing instead to hold tight to what they already have. Thus, the top of Figure 13.8 casts the Asian disease problem in terms of gains (the number of people saved), and this leads people to prefer the risk-free choice (Program A) over

**FIGURE 13.10**

## *Framing Effects in Monetary Choices*

### Problem 1

Assume yourself richer by $300 than you are today. You have to choose between

    a sure gain of $100

    50% chance to gain $200 and 50% chance to gain nothing.

### Problem 2

Assume yourself richer by $500 than you are today. You have to choose between

    a sure loss of $100

    50% chance to lose nothing and 50% chance to lose $200.

These two problems are identical. In both cases, the first option leaves you with $400, while the second option leaves you with an even chance between $300 and $500. Despite this identity, people prefer the first option in Problem 1 (72% select this option), and the second option in Problem 2 (64% select this option). Once again, by changing the frames, we reverse the pattern of preferences.

## *The Influence of How a Question Is Framed*

**FIGURE** 13.11

Imagine that you serve on the jury of an only-child sole-custody case following a relatively messy divorce. The facts of the case are complicated by ambiguous economic, social, and emotional considerations, and you decide to base your decision entirely on the following few observations. To which parent would you award sole custody of the child?

Parent A    average income
average health
average working hours
reasonable rapport with the child
relatively stable social life

Parent B    above-average income
very close relationship with the child
extremely active social life
lots of work-related travel
minor health problems

When asked the question shown here, 64% of the participants decided to award custody to Parent B. Other participants, however, were asked a different question: "To which parent would you *deny* sole custody?" Asked this question, 55% of the participants chose to deny custody to B (and so, by default, to award custody to A). Thus, with the "award" question, a majority votes for granting custody to B; with the "deny" question, a majority votes for granting custody to A.

the gamble offered by Program B. (And likewise for Problem 1 in Figure 13.10.)

This pattern is powerful and easy to demonstrate: People are reliably risk seeking when contemplating losses, and reliably risk averse when contemplating gains. And we should emphasize that there is nothing wrong with either of these strategies by itself: If someone prefers to be risk seeking, this is fine; if someone prefers to be risk averse, this is okay, too. The problem arises, though, when people flip-flop between these strategies, depending on how the problem is framed. The flip-flopping, as we have seen, leaves people wide open to manipulation, to inconsistency, and to self-contradiction. (For more on the contrast between how people react to losses and how they react to gains, see pp. 437–38.)

## FRAMING OF QUESTIONS AND EVIDENCE

So far we have shown that people are influenced by how a problem's outcomes are framed. Related effects can be demonstrated by changing how the question itself is framed. For example, imagine that you serve on a jury in a relatively messy divorce case; the parents are battling over who will get custody of their only child. The two parents have the attributes listed in Figure 13.11. To which parent will you award sole custody of the child?

Research participants asked this question tend to favor Parent B, by a 64% to 36% margin. After all, this parent does have a close relationship with the child, and has a good income. Note, though, that we have asked to which parent you will *award* custody.

Things are different if we ask participants to which parent they would *deny* custody. This is, in obvious ways, the same question—if you are awarding custody to one parent, you are simultaneously denying it to the other parent. But, in this case, 55% of the participants choose to *deny* custody to Parent B (and so, by default, end up awarding custody to A). Thus, the decision is simply reversed: With the "award" question, the majority of participants awards custody to B. With the "deny" question, the majority denies custody to B, and so gives custody to A.

This effect has been observed in a number of contexts, including problems involving monetary gambles, problems involving which courses a student will take, and most troubling, problems involving decisions about political candidates (Shafir, 1993; also Downs & Shafir, 1999). As a related effect, people rate a basketball player more highly if the player has made 75% of his free throws, compared to their ratings of a player who has missed 25% of his free throws. They are more likely to endorse a medical treatment with a "50% success rate" than they are to endorse one with a "50% failure rate." And so on (Levin & Gaeth, 1988; Levin, Schnittjer & Thee, 1988; also see Dunning & Parpal, 1989).

None of this makes any sense from the perspective of utility theory, since these differences in framing have no impact on the expected utilities of the options. Yet these differences in framing can dramatically change peoples' choices and, in many cases, can actually reverse their pattern of preferences. (For further, related evidence, see Mellers, Chang, Birnbaum & Ordóñez, 1992; Schneider, 1992; Schwarz, 1999; Wedell & Bockenholt, 1990.)

## THE INSTABILITY OF VALUES

In short, then, utility theory often does a poor job of describing human decision-making. We are reliably influenced by factors having nothing to do with utility, and these factors can lead us to reverse our preferences and even to contradict ourselves. (For broad discussion of these data, from the perspective of utility theory, see Allais, 1953; Arkes & Blumer, 1985; Hos-

kin, 1983; Kahneman & Tversky, 1979; Lichtenstein & Slovic, 1971; Tversky & Kahneman, 1987.)

Other results are also problematic for utility theory. Recall that this theory rests on the idea that decision-makers somehow calculate and compare utilities, choosing the option, in the end, with the greatest expected value. But how exactly does this work? Imagine that your employer asks you to give up your vacation, and to spend those days working instead, for a $500 bonus. According to utility theory, you would evaluate this proposal by figuring out the value of your vacation, and in particular, figuring out whether the vacation is worth more or less than $500.

In the best of circumstances, these comparisons can be very difficult. As a significant complication, though, this sort of comparison often requires that you be able to predict the future, and this, obviously, is an uncertain enterprise. How good will you feel at the end of your vacation? Will you have shed some of the tension that created the need for the vacation in the first place? These things are very hard to know in advance, and obviously make it difficult to calculate the utility of the vacation. Or, as a different example, imagine that you are looking for a new apartment. You find one, but you don't like the fact that it faces a noisy street. Will you just grow used to the noise so that it ceases to bother you? If so, then you should take the apartment. Or will the noise grow more and more obnoxious to you as the weeks go by? Evidence suggests that we are rather *inept* in making this sort of prediction, and this will clearly erode our ability to assess utilities—in this case, the utility of a quiet apartment (Kahneman & Snell, 1992; Loewenstein & Schkade, 1999; Schkade & Kahneman, 1998; Wilson et al., 2000).

There is also reason to believe that our values may *fluctuate* from one occasion to another, and this certainly will undermine utility calculations. For example, how valuable would it be for you to lose weight? It is possible that the value you place on losing weight may be relatively small right now but might be larger after the weight loss is actually done: Only then would you realize how much better you felt, and how much more you were able to do. Likewise, how much inconvenience would you tolerate in order to reduce air pollution? This, too, might vary, according to the context: When you have just come back from a camping trip, for example, you might be particularly sensitive to the value of clean air.

In fact, think about how we might try to *assess* your values. To figure out how much you value clean air, we could ask you a series of questions such as, "Which do you think is more valuable, clean air or $100?" Or we could cast this in more concrete terms: "A plan has been proposed through which each citizen in the United States would contribute $100 to pay for new equipment that we are certain would help clean the air. Do you think this is a good idea?"

Questions like these would, presumably, provide us with information about your (relative) values for $100 and clean air, and, with similar questions, we could determine which is more important to you, clean air or crime prevention, crime prevention or more funding for schools, and so on. Notice, though, that these questions bear a strong resemblance to the questions posed in Figures 13.8, 13.9, 13.10, and so on. As we have seen, your responses to these questions flip-flop back and forth, depending on how the outcomes are framed, or how the question is phrased. If we use these questions as a way of assessing your values, it would seem that your values themselves flip-flop from one occasion to the next, one question to the next.

In other words, these imagined choices seem to provide a direct and sensible way of assessing your values. But, interpreted in this fashion, these questions reveal enormous *instability* in your values, with your preferences changing from question to question, occasion to occasion. Note where this leaves us: According to utility theory, we evaluate an action by asking: Does the action bring you the things you value? This requires us, in turn, to ask: What is it that you value? This question may not be answerable, though, if your values fluctuate from one moment to the next, depending on exactly what question you have just been asked. No wonder, then, that the predictions of utility theory are often at odds with the actual decisions that we make. (For reviews of research on values, see Fischhoff, 1991; Guagnano, Dietz & Stern, 1994; Kahneman, Ritov, Jacowitz & Grant, 1993;

Kahneman, Fredrickson, Schreiber & Redelmeier, 1993; Payne, Bettman & Johnson, 1992; Slovic, 1990, 1995; Stevenson, 1993. This research also has a rich set of implications for questions about what makes each of us *happy*. For a sophisticated treatment of this issue, see Kahneman, Diener & Schwarz, 1999.)

## LOSS AVERSION

Similar comments apply to a phenomenon known as **loss aversion**—a tendency to be far more sensitive to losses than to gains. We have already referred to the research indicating an asymmetry between how we perceive gains and losses, and loss aversion certainly fits into this larger pattern. As it turns out, though, loss aversion is often in conflict with the maximization of utility.

Imagine that we toss a coin. If it comes up heads, you win $10; if it comes up tails, you have to pay $10. Most people refuse this gamble. The risk of *losing* $10 is apparently more compelling than the attraction of *gaining* $10—again, we are more sensitive to losses than we are to (comparable) gains. Even though this is, economically, a fair bet, it is not fair from most people's point of view. Indeed, people still refuse to bet on a coin toss if we make the game more attractive: If the coin comes up heads, you gain $20; tails, you pay $10 (Kahneman & Tversky, 1984). Even with a "double payoff," people are more repelled by the (potential) loss than they are attracted by the (potential) gain.

Loss aversion is also evident when we are invited to give up something we already own. For example, participants in one experiment were each given a coffee mug and asked at what price they would be willing to sell this new possession. Other participants were given the opportunity to buy the same mug, and asked at what price they would make the purchase. On average, the "sellers" set a price for the mug of $7.12; the "buyers," a price of $2.87 (Kahneman, Knetsch & Thaler, 1991). Owning something, it seems, endows it with special worth.

Now let's combine this pattern with our earlier discussion of framing effects: By manipulating the frame, we can describe problems relative to the best-possible outcome, so that all other options would be perceived as losses, relative to this ideal. In this setting, loss aversion comes into play, so people are willing to take substantial risks in hopes of *avoiding* the loss. This is consistent with the data: As we mentioned earlier, people are consistently risk seeking when outcomes are framed negatively.

Conversely, we can change the frame so that we describe problems relative to the worst-possible outcome, so that all other options would be perceived as gains, relative to this worst-case scenario. In this case, we would expect people to seize whatever gain they can, and then take no chances with it—that is, they will avoid any risk of losing what they have gained. Again, this is consistent with the data: When outcomes are framed positively, people are markedly risk averse.

Likewise, we can influence what counts as a loss, and what counts as a gain, by manipulating your *basis for comparison*. Imagine that you are looking for a new job (Kahneman et al., 1991). Let's say that you are unhappy about the fact that your current job is located so far from your apartment, requiring an 80-minute commute each way. But you do like the fact that your job involves a lot of pleasant social interaction with your co-workers. Now, consider the two jobs described in Figure 13.12. Job A would provide a large reduction in your commuting time, but also a large loss in the social contact you will enjoy. Job B provides a much smaller reduction in your commuting time, but also a smaller loss in social contact. If you focus on the advantages of each, therefore, Job A wins (with a much-reduced commute). If you focus on the disadvantages, Job A *loses* (with much-reduced social interaction). In this situation, a clear majority of research participants (67%) choose Job B: Thanks to loss aversion, they are much more impressed by A's disadvantages than by its advantages.

For contrast, imagine that your present job involves only a ten-minute commute, but leaves you isolated from your co-workers for long periods of time. In this case, a move to Job A would provide a small improvement in social contact, at the cost of a slightly lengthened commute. Job B provides a large improvement in social contact, but at the cost of a much longer commute. Thus, if you focus on gains, Job B is the winner. If you focus on losses, you should go with Job A. In this setting, people are again guided by loss aversion: The disadvantage of B outweighs its advantage, and most (70%) choose Job A.

Obviously, then, what counts as an advantage or a disadvantage in these decisions depends on your current state and your current focus. By changing your focus, or by changing your starting point, we can reverse the decision. In the study just quoted, a change in starting point turns a 67–33 advantage for B into a 70–30 advantage for A—quite literally flipping things around.

We should also mention one further phenomenon, closely related to loss aversion: Imagine that you have invested some time or effort in a project, or imagine that you have taken a gamble and *lost*. In these circumstances, people seem extraordinarily sensitive to the fact that they have given up something they used to own and, as a result, they will often take extravagant steps to ensure that their investment, or their loss, "was not in vain." People do this even when their best strategy would be to *abandon* the now-lost resources and move on. This pattern is referred to as the **sunk-cost effect** and is illustrated by the example shown in Figure 13.13. In this case, the $100 deposit is the "sunk cost"—a cost that has already occurred and is now irreversible. In the example, your best bet would be to abandon this sunk cost and not continue on the journey. However, that is not what people do; instead, they end up "throwing good money after bad"—that is, they end up investing even more resources, as though this would somehow "redeem" the sunk cost. This pattern is consistent with other evidence showing our keen sensitivity to losses, but this pattern is, once again, not consistent with utility theory. (For discussion of the sunk cost effect, see Arkes & Blumer, 1985; Arkes & Ayton, 1999; Dawes, 1988; Thaler, 1980.)

## MAXIMIZING UTILITY VERSUS SEEING REASONS

Over and over, we have seen evidence of decisions not in accord with utility theory. And perhaps this evi-

## What Counts as a Gain Depends on Your "Reference Point"

**FIGURE 13.12**

### Version 1

You have decided to leave your current job, because it is located so far from your apartment, requiring an *80-minute* commute each way. But you do like the fact that your job involves much pleasant social interaction with your co-workers.

Your search for a *new* job has given you two options, and now you must choose between them. Which job would you prefer?

| Job A | Limited contact with others | Commuting time = 20 minutes |
| Job B | Moderately sociable | Commuting time = 60 minutes |

### Version 2

You have decided to leave your current job. The job involves only a ten-minute commute, which you rather like. But your job leaves you isolated from your co-workers for long periods of time.

Your search for a *new* job has given you two options, and now you must choose between them. Which job would you prefer?

| Job A | Limited contact with others | Commuting time = 20 minutes |
| Job B | Moderately sociable | Commuting time = 60 minutes |

In the first problem shown here, Job A provides a large reduction in your commuting time, but at the price of a large loss in social contact. Job B provides a much smaller reduction in your commute, but also a smaller loss in social contact. Therefore, if you focus on the gains (the shorter commute), Job A is preferable. If you focus on the losses (diminished social contact), Job B is preferable. In this setting, participants are more alert to the losses, and so most (67%) choose Job B. In the second setting, the job possibilities are the same; all that is changed is the description of your *current* job. Compared to this "reference point," Job A provides a small improvement in your social contact, but a slightly longer commute. Job B provides a large improvement in social contact, but a much longer commute. Now, in terms of gains (in social contact), Job B is preferable; if you focus on the losses (the longer commute), Job A is better. Once again, participants are more alert to the losses, and so, in this setting, most (70%) choose Job A.

dence isn't so surprising: Utility theory requires that we are able to judge risks and that we be able to assess our own values. Evidence suggests, though, that people are quite incompetent in judging risks and that our values and utilities change, from context to context.

The instability in people's values can be demonstrated in many ways but was certainly evident in our discussion of loss aversion. As we saw in case after case, changes in context, perspective, or frame had a substantial effect on research participants'

FIGURE 13.13

### The Sunk-Cost Effect

Some weeks ago, you saw an ad in the newspaper for a reduced-rate weekend at a nearby resort. Attracted by the ad, you sent a $100 non-refundable deposit to the resort.

The weekend has now arrived, and you and a companion have driven halfway to the resort. Unfortunately, though, both you and your companion are feeling slightly ill, and your assessment of the situation is that you would probably have a more pleasurable weekend at home, rather than at the resort.

You decide to press on, however. After all, you have already sent in the deposit, and you can't get it back. You have also already driven halfway to the resort. If you turn around at this point, your deposit will be lost—wasted!—and your driving will have been for nothing.

Is this sensible? Should you drive on, or should you turn back?

In the problem shown here, many people believe you *should* drive on, in order to avoid wasting the $100 deposit. However, this makes little sense. You have already spent the $100, whether you go to the resort or whether you go home. No matter what you do, you won't get the $100 back. Therefore, continuing to drive toward the resort won't "redeem" the $100. Thus, in deciding to drive on, you are being influenced by a "sunk cost," a cost that, in this case, leads you to spend the weekend at a place you would rather not be. [After Dawes, 1988.]

choices: Options and commodities preferred in one setting were rejected in another setting; objects given a low value in one context were given a much higher value in another context. With flexibility like this, it becomes difficult to argue that people have stable preferences and values, and without stable preferences, the calculation and comparison of utilities may be impossible.

In response to all this, a number of alternative theories have been proposed. (For examples, see Bell, 1982; Fishburn, 1982; Kahneman & Tversky, 1979; Loomes, 1987.) Many of these theories preserve the spirit of utility theory, arguing that, with some repairs or adjustments, utility theory, in modified form, *can* handle the data. Other theories, though, have taken a rather different approach.

For example, a number of authors have argued that, in making decisions, the maximization of utility is not our goal. Instead, our goal is to make decisions that we think are reasonable or justified. Thus, you will choose X rather than Y only if you find some persuasive argument justifying this choice. Your choice, in other words, will not rest on some calculation of risks and payoffs; instead, your choice will depend on your finding *reasons* for selecting one option rather than another (Shafir, Simonson & Tversky, 1993; Slovic, 1975).

On this view, our decision-making will be heavily influenced by any factor that helps make an argument seem more compelling or more persuasive. As an illustration, we have already seen that *confirmation bias* plays a large role when we are evaluating an argument and so, in the account just sketched, confirmation bias may be pertinent to decision-making. (Of course, confirmation bias is irrelevant for utility calculations.) To see this in action, let's reconsider a problem already discussed: the divorce/custody problem shown in Figure 13.11. You will recall that half the people presented with this problem were asked to which parent they would *award* custody. These people, influenced by confirmation bias, therefore ask themselves, "What would *justify* giving custody to one parent or another?" This draws their attention to one subset of the parental attributes—e.g., Parent B's close relationship with the child, and this in turn leads them to favor awarding custody to B.

The other half of the participants were asked to which parent they would *deny* custody and, with confirmation bias in place, this leads them to ask: "What would justify denying custody to one parent or another?" This question draws attention to a different subset of attributes—e.g., B's travel schedule or health problems. Thus, these participants easily find a basis for denying custody to B. (For related discussion, see Legrenzi et al., 1993.)

Here is another illustration of how decision-making is governed by "perceived justification." Tversky and Shafir (1992b) presented their participants with the problem posed in Figure 13.14. In the first version of the problem, participants are asked to imagine that they have just *passed* an important exam; in this situation, participants generally elect to buy the vacation package (54% buy), presumably as a celebration for their good exam performance. In the second version, participants imagine that they have *failed* the exam. These participants, too, elect to buy the package (57% buy), this time, one assumes, as a "consolation" for their failure. In the third version of the problem, however, participants imagine that they don't yet know if they have passed the exam or not. In this condition of uncertainty, most choose *not* to buy the package (only 32% buy).

What is going on here? If you pass the exam, you buy. If you fail, you buy. Hence, it doesn't matter if you pass or fail. Nonetheless, if you *don't know yet* whether you have passed or failed, you don't buy. Participants are deterred by their ignorance about the exam's outcome, even though the outcome is irrelevant to their decision. None of this makes sense if our decisions depend on utilities. But it does make sense if our decisions depend on *reasons* and *justifications*. It is the exam's outcome that gives you a compelling reason for buying the package. Possible outcomes, or

hypothetical outcomes, aren't compelling enough. Therefore, until you know the exam's outcome, you don't have a firm reason to buy the package, and so you don't buy.

In the same way, Tversky and Shafir (1992a) note that physicians often request medical tests that are, in fact, irrelevant to their choice of treatment—no matter how the test turns out, the treatment will be the same. Thus, in ordering the tests, the physicians are acting exactly like the research participants just described. (Cf. Baron, 1988.)

## THE PROCESS OF DECISION-MAKING

This emphasis on the justification of a decision may demand a new style of research. So far in this chapter, we have been focusing largely on the *outcomes* of decisions—"Do participants choose Option A, or Option B?"—rather than on the *process* of decision-making. Hand in hand with this, we have been assuming that the decision-makers themselves are focusing primarily on the outcomes of their decisions—"Which of these outcomes do I desire? Which is better for me, this trade-off or that one?"

This focus on outcomes was entirely appropriate for utility theory: That's because, according to this theory, our choices depend totally on our assessments of our options—the expected value of this choice, in comparison to the expected value of that choice. But if decision-making is determined by a search for *justifications*, then we need to focus less on the outcomes of a decision, and more on the process: What principles guide people as they search for a justification for this or that choice? What makes a potential justification seem persuasive or not? These questions have been largely neglected in our discussion so far, but loom larger as we step away from utility theory and toward a theory that emphasizes the role for justifications and reasons in decision-making (Connolly & Koput, 1996; Hsee, 1999; Medin & Bazerman, 1999; Messick, 2000).

So what are the principles governing the decision-making process? As one principle, people seem to keep their various goals separate from each other, as

FIGURE 13.14

## The Role of "Justification" in Decision-Making

### Version 1: Passed

Imagine that you have just taken a tough qualifying examination. It is the end of the fall quarter, you feel tired and run-down, and you find out that you passed the exam. You now have an opportunity to buy a very attractive 5-day Christmas vacation package in Hawaii at an exceptionally low price. The special offer expires tomorrow. Would you
  a. buy the vacation package?
  b. not buy the vacation package?
  c. pay a $5 non-refundable fee in order to retain the rights to buy the package at the same exceptional price the day after tomorrow?

### Version 2: Failed

Imagine that you have just taken a tough qualifying examination. It is the end of the fall quarter, you feel tired and run-down, and you find out that you failed the exam. You will have to take it again in a couple of months—after the Christmas holiday. You now have an opportunity to buy a very attractive 5-day Christmas vacation package in Hawaii at an exceptionally low price. The special offer expires tomorrow. Would you
  a. buy the vacation package?
  b. not buy the vacation package?
  c. pay a $5 non-refundable fee in order to retain the rights to buy the package at the same exceptional price the day after tomorrow?

### Version 3: Don't know yet if passed or failed

Imagine that you have just taken a tough qualifying examination. It is the end of the fall quarter, you feel tired and run-down, and you are not sure whether you passed the exam. In case you failed, you will have to take the exam again in a couple of months—after the Christmas holiday. You now have an opportunity to buy a very attractive 5-day Christmas vacation package in Hawaii at an exceptionally low price. The special offer expires tomorrow. Would you
  a. buy the vacation package?
  b. not buy the vacation package?
  c. pay a $5 non-refundable fee in order to retain the rights to buy the package at the same exceptional price the day after tomorrow, after you find out whether or not you passed the exam?

In Version 1 of this problem, 54% of the participants decide to buy the vacation package—presumably as a celebration for their having passed the exam. In Version 2, 57% choose to buy—presumably as consolation for having failed. Apparently, then, participants will buy the package whether they pass or whether they fail. Therefore, information about passing or failing isn't relevant to the decision. Nonetheless, when participants don't have this (irrelevant) information, as in Version 3, they behave rather differently: Here, only 32% buy the package.

## The Role of Separate Accounts in Decision-Making

**FIGURE 13.15**

Imagine that two students are visiting a gambling casino. In front of the casino, Student A finds $25 cash and puts the money in his wallet. Student A and Student B each pay the $25 entrance fee and enter the casino. Inside the casino, Student B finds $25 cash and puts the money into his wallet. Both students have not yet decided whether to gamble.

The students are then given an opportunity to place a $25 bet that has a 50% chance of winning $25 and a 50% chance of losing $25. Which student is more likely to place the bet? Or are they both equally likely?

if they were keeping separate "accounts" in which they recorded the gains and losses associated with each goal. As an example, consider the problem shown in Figure 13.15. Roughly three-quarters of the participants shown this problem said Student B was more likely to place the bet, presumably because Student A has already "assigned" the $25 he found to the "entry-fee" account and so no longer has any "windfall" money to spend. Student B is still holding his "windfall" and feels free to gamble with this money (Brendl, Markman & Higgins, 1998).

In addition, the process of justifying a decision is also influenced in obvious ways by *emotional factors*. As one example, should someone trade in his bicycle for a newer, shinier, version of the same bicycle? Most people say "yes." Should someone trade in his wedding ring for a newer, shinier, version of the same ring? Most people say "no," because the emotional meaning associated with a wedding ring makes this decision much more weighty than the bicycle decision (Medin, Schwartz, Blok & Birnbaum, 1999).

Evidence also suggests an important role in decision-making for the complex emotion of *regret*. More specifically, people seem powerfully motivated to avoid regret, and so one of the strong forces in guiding a decision is to choose a course of action that minimizes the chances for regret later on. Indeed, the avoidance of regret may be one of the reasons we are so strongly motivated to make decisions that we're sure we can *justify* later on—this may be our best defense against subsequent regret. (For more on the

avoidance of regret, see Kahneman & Miller, 1986; Kahneman & Tversky, 1982b; Medvec, Madey & Gilovich, 1995; Gilovich & Medvec, 1995; Gilovich et al., 1998.)

It's also important that many decisions involve, or have an impact on, other people, and in these cases, the decision-making process is influenced by the social relationships that are in place and by the decision-maker's sense of *fairness*. Do people try to be fair in their decisions? In many cases, yes. In one study, participants were given the following instructions: "Here is $10. The money is for you *and* the person in the next room, but it's entirely up to you how the money is divided. You can keep all; you can give all away; or you can divide it however you choose. The trick, though, is that the person in the next room must accept your proposed division. If the other person *refuses* your division, then no one gets any money."

In this setting, you could decide to be selfish— offering just $1 to the person in the next room, and keeping the other $9 for yourself. And, if this is your offer, then the other person should accept the deal: If he accepts it, he gets $1; if he refuses, he gets nothing. A dollar isn't much, but it's surely better than nothing, and so, in this setup, it's plainly in his interest to accept this (imbalanced) offer.

Of course, this selfish division of the money might make the other person angry, but the procedure insulates you from this anger: The other person doesn't know who you are, and you don't know who he is. The experimenter has also guaranteed that you're not going to meet this other person. Therefore, there will be no cost and no consequence for being selfish.

Despite all of this, a sense of fairness prevails in this experiment, and a clear majority of the participants divide the money in an equitable 50-50 split (Guth, Schmittberger & Schwarze, 1982; Bazerman, 1998). Small changes in the procedure, however, can change this outcome. If, for example, participants are encouraged to think of the procedure in terms of specific gains and losses, rather than as a sort of social dilemma, then participants are much less likely to "play fair," and more likely to make extreme offers (Larrick & Blount, 1997).

All of this clearly demands a broadening of our perspective in the study of decision-making. (For a compelling presentation of this point, see Medin & Bazerman, 1999.) To understand how people make decisions, and to predict their actual decisions, we need to understand how the decision is presented (the frame) and also how the decision is understood by the decision-maker: Does she think of the decision as involving "gains and losses," or "a social dilemma"? Does she understand the situation as one emphasizing profit, or one emphasizing fairness? Considerations like these have been absent from our utility-based theorizing so far, but plainly have an impact on decision-making, and need to be understood.

In addition, we obviously need to know more about the intellectual processes through which someone becomes convinced that a decision is (or is not) "adequately justified." We mentioned earlier that considerations of confirmation bias are likely to be relevant here, but other aspects of reasoning will also play a role. In the end, our theory of decision-making may need to rest on a theory about the nature of *argument* and *persuasion*, because, in the end, it appears that many of our choices hinge on our persuading ourselves that we know what the "right thing to do" is. (For more on this last point, see Brenner et al., 1999; Shafir et al., 1993; Wedell, 1991, 1993.)

## A NORMATIVE THEORY OF DECISION-MAKING

According to utility theory (and its variants), decision-making is, in essence, a matter of quantification and calculation, leading to a selection of the option that maximizes utility. As we have seen, though, this may be the wrong approach in describing most decisions. Instead, decision-making may be more a matter of argument and justification: We make the decisions that we can best explain and defend to ourselves and to others. We choose the options that will leave us, in the end, content that we have made a rational choice.

This is an account of how people *do* make decisions, but still leaves open the question of how people *should* make decisions. One might argue, for example, that utility theory does a poor job of describing our actual decision-making but nonetheless may be the way we *ought* to make decisions—it should, in other words, be our *normative theory* of decision-making even if it fails as our *descriptive theory*. What would justify this position? As we mentioned early on, decisions based on utility calculations will, in the end, maximize our chances of gaining the things we value and of reaching our goals (e.g., Baron, 1988, 1998; Larrick, Nisbett & Morgan, 1993). And, as we have seen, decisions that are *not* rooted in utility calculations can lead to a variety of problems: Such decisions can lead to self-contradictions and can also leave decision-makers vulnerable to external manipulation, as we shift from one decision frame to another. To put this point rather baldly, do you really want to make decisions in a fashion that flip-flops back and forth, depending on whether the question as posed mentions "awarding custody" or "denying custody"? If not, then maybe utility theory (which avoids these flip-flops) is the way to go.

These considerations seem to imply that utility theory *is* the proper way to make decisions, but let's be clear that other normative theories can also be defended. For example, it is obvious that we all wish to reach our goals and gain the things we value. But we also have other needs—for example, people generally don't want to feel foolish or capricious; instead, we all want to feel like our lives make some sense and have some integrity. Therefore, it is important to feel that the choices we have made have been reasonable choices and that, if these choices were ever challenged, we could explain and defend our selections.

From this perspective, if a decision brings us utility but leaves us feeling insecure or uncomfortable, then it is a bad decision, and one ought to avoid making such a decision. Notice the "ought": This is an assertion about how decisions *should* be made; it is, in other words, a normative assertion, and so we are moving toward a normative theory in which considerations of utility are not our only concern.

Moreover, some would argue that there are decisions that *shouldn't* be reduced to questions of utility. For example, consider choices involving morality—choices about theft or homicide or choices about respecting other people's rights. Should one calculate the utility of "doing the moral thing"? If so, then perhaps there is some other utility (for example, a large-enough bribe) that would outweigh the demands of morality. For many people, this seems an inappropriate way to talk about moral values, but it is the *right* way to talk about moral decisions if utility theory is our normative theory.

Moral values can be treated differently, however, within a theory of decision-making resting on *justification*. From this perspective, one shouldn't ask the "economic" question, "What *gain* would justify an immoral act?" Instead, one should ask the question, "What argument, or principle, would justify such an act?" Thus, in this view, there may be no payoff, no matter how large, to justify immorality. Instead, the only justification for an immoral action would be something like an even stronger, more compelling, moral claim.

This seems an attractive position, but let's emphasize that utility theory also has much to recommend it. We are certainly not going to settle here the choice between these two normative views—one based on utilities, one based on justification. We do hope, though, that these comments have made it clear that the choice between these views is not straightforward; intriguing arguments can be presented on either side of the debate.

There is, in any case, ample evidence that we don't make decisions in accord with utility theory. Instead, it does seem that our decisions are guided by principles of justification—we make decisions that seem sensible and defensible to us. Over the last few paragraphs, though, we have tried to indicate that how these decisions should be evaluated, from the standpoint of a normative theory, is still a matter open to discussion.

## Chapter Summary

1. Reasoning often shows a pattern of *confirmation bias*: People tend to seek evidence that might confirm their beliefs rather than evidence that might challenge their beliefs. When evidence challenging a belief is in view, it tends to be underused, and in many cases not remembered. One manifestation of confirmation bias is *belief perseverance*, a pattern in which people continue to believe a claim even after the basis for the claim has been discredited. This is probably because people engage in a biased memory search, seeking to confirm the claim. The evidence provided by this search then remains even when the original basis for the claim is removed.

2. People's performance with logic problems such as *categorical syllogisms* or problems involving *conditional statements* is often quite poor. The errors are not the product of carelessness; instead, many errors are due either to *belief bias* or to *conversion* of the problems (e.g., converting conditionals into biconditionals). Performance is also poor in the *four-card task*. Some of the errors in this task might be due to conversion, and some to a misunderstanding of *modus tollens*, but these considerations still leave many of the errors unexplained.

3. People perform quite well, however, with some variations of the four-card problem. This makes it clear that reasoning is not guided by *formal rules*, but is instead influenced by problem content. One proposal is that this effect should be understood in evolutionary terms, with people skilled at

reasoning about issues of cheating or betrayal; this is a type of reasoning, it is claimed, for which we are biologically well prepared. A different proposal is that our reasoning relies on *pragmatic reasoning schemata*; these summarize our experience in reasoning about situations involving permission, obligation, and so on. Reasoning performance will be good, therefore, if one of these schemata is triggered. Yet another proposal is that the content of a problem influences how we interpret the "if . . . then" relationship, with important consequences in how we reason about that relationship.

4. Training in formal logic has little impact on people's reasoning; this adds to the evidence that people normally do not use formal rules in their thinking. However, other forms of training do improve reasoning, including training that reminds people how to use pragmatic reasoning schemata.

5. Apparently, theories of reasoning need multiple layers. People can be trained to reason according to the rules of formal logic. In addition, people without training do have reasonably sophisticated reasoning skills, but these skills play a role only if they are triggered by the problem's content. People also have less sophisticated strategies that they employ when their reasoning skills are not triggered. Finally, people can also reason using *mental models*, in which they construct an imagined model of a situation, and then inspect this model to evaluate possible conclusions.

6. According to *utility theory*, people make decisions by calculating the *expected utility* or expected value of each of their options. Decisions made in this way will always maximize the decision-makers' chances of achieving the things they value, but, even so, much evidence suggests that decisions are *not* made in this way. Instead, decisions are often influenced by factors that have nothing to do with utilities—for example, how the question is *framed* or how the possible outcomes are described. If the outcomes are described as potential gains, decision-makers tend to be *risk averse*; if they are described as potential losses, decision-makers tend to be *risk seeking*.

7. Framing effects also raise questions about the stability of our values. One demonstration of instability involves *loss aversion*, in which someone's evaluation of an outcome is much more negative if the outcome is described as a loss than it is if the same outcome is described as a gain.

8. Some investigators have proposed that our goal in making decisions is not to maximize utility, but, instead, to make decisions that we think are reasonable or justified. Therefore, we are influenced by any factor that makes an argument in favor of an option seem more compelling. This suggests that we may need more research on the *process* of decision-making rather than focusing just on the utilities of the outcomes.

9. Decision-making guided by perceived justification may lead to self-contradiction, and may leave us open to external manipulation (because of frame effects). But this approach to decision-making may be appropriate nonetheless, and discussion about the *normative* theory of decision-making (how we should make decisions) is ongoing.

# Solving Problems

In Chapter 12, we considered the processes through which people form new beliefs, based on information they have encountered. In Chapter 13, we then examined how people reason about these beliefs—what implications they draw, and how they adjust their beliefs (or fail to), as new evidence comes in. That chapter also carried us one further step: People often use their beliefs as a basis for choosing among options or for selecting a course of action. Chapter 13 was concerned with how we take these steps and, thus, with how we make decisions.

Once we have formed a belief, though, drawn out its implications, and chosen a course of action, what happens next? In some cases, this is a straightforward matter. If you decide to buy one jacket, rather than another, your next steps will be easy: You go to the store and get the jacket. In many other cases, though, what you select is a *goal*, and that still leaves the question of how you will reach that goal. This is the domain of problem-solving, the process through which you figure out how to reach your goals, starting from your current state.

We solve problems all the time. "I want to reach the store, but Sol borrowed my car. How should I get there?" "I really want Amy to notice me; how should I arrange it?" "I'm trying to prove this theorem; how can I do it, based on these premises?" Some of the problems we face are trivial, but some have enormous consequences. Some problems are well defined, so that it is clear from the start what you need to accomplish, and what your options are. Other problems, though, are more diffuse. For example, what is the best way to educate the children of our country? In this case, there is obviously room for debate about how we should define our goal or what the options are in reaching the goal.

In this chapter, we will examine how people solve problems, both the trivial and the consequential, the well defined and the diffuse. We will begin by considering strategies relevant to problems of all sorts. We will then turn to more specialized strategies, applicable only to some sorts of problems.

## General Problem-Solving Methods

It is obvious that some problems require special expertise: If you are trying to achieve some bit of genetic engineering, you need the relevant training in biology and biochemistry. If you are trying to repair a computer, you need knowledge of electronics. Some problems, though, draw on more general skills and strategies that are available to all of us. What are these strategies?

### PROBLEM-SOLVING AS SEARCH

Many authors have found it useful to compare problem-solving to a process of search, as though you were navigating through a maze, seeking a path toward your goal. Some paths will (eventually) lead to the goal, but others will lead to dead ends or to the wrong goal. Some paths will be open, allowing you to pass, and others will be blocked. Some paths will be relatively direct; others will be long and circuitous. In all cases, though, your job is to select the right path, allowing you to get from your starting point to your target.

This idea of "problem solving as search" was central to the thinking of Newell and Simon (1972). They describe problem-solving as starting with an **initial state**, which includes the knowledge and resources you have at the outset, and working toward a **goal state**. The problem-solver has a set of **operators**, that is, tools or actions that can change her current state, and it is with these operators that the problem-solver seeks to move from the initial state to the goal state. In addition, there is likely to be a set of **path constraints**, ruling out some options or some solutions. These constraints might take the form of resource limitations (limited time or money) or other limits (ethical limits on what you can do).

Given one's initial state, the operators, and the path constraints, there is a limited number of intermediate states that one can reach, en route to the goal. For example, consider the "Hobbits and Orcs" problem, described in Figure 14.1. Figure 14.2 shows the states one can reach, early on, in solving this problem. Notice that these states can be depicted as a "tree," with each step leading to more and more

**FIGURE 14.1**

## The Hobbits and Orcs Problem

Five Orcs and five Hobbits are on the east bank of the Muddy River. They need to cross to the west bank and have located a boat. In each crossing, at least one creature must be in the boat, but no more than three creatures will fit in the boat.

And, of course, if the Orcs ever outnumber the Hobbits, on either side of the river, they will eat the Hobbits! Therefore, in designing the crossing, we must make certain that the Hobbits are never outnumbered, either on the east bank of the river, or on the west.

How can the creatures get across, without any Hobbits being eaten?

This problem has been used in many studies of problem-solving strategies. Can you solve it?

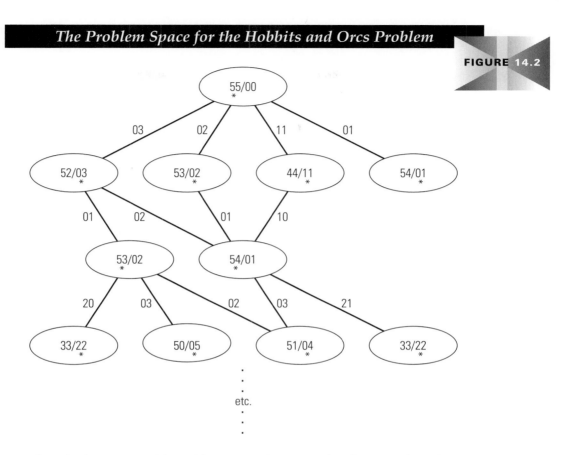

**The Problem Space for the Hobbits and Orcs Problem**

**FIGURE 14.2**

Each circle shows a possible problem state. The state 54/01, for example, indicates that five Hobbits and 4 Orcs are on the east bank; there are no Hobbits, but one Orc, on the west bank. The star shows the position of the boat. The numbers alongside of each line indicate the number of creatures in the boat during each river crossing. The move 02, for example, transports no Hobbits, but two Orcs. The problem states shown here are all the *legal* states. (Other states, and other moves, would result in some of the Hobbits getting eaten.) Thus, there are four "legal" moves one can make, starting from the initial state. From these, there are four possible moves one can make, but these lead to just two problem states (53/02, and 54/01). From these two states, there are four new states that can be reached, and so on. We have here illustrated the first three moves that can be made, in solving this problem; the shortest path to the problem's solution involves eleven moves.

branches. All of these branches together form the **problem space**, that is, the set of all states that can be reached in solving this problem. In these terms, what one is seeking, in solving a problem, is quite literally a path through this space, leading, step-by-step, from the initial state to the goal.

One option in solving a problem would be to trace through the entire problem space, exploring each branch in turn. This would guarantee that you would eventually find the solution (if the problem is solvable at all). However, for most of the problems we face, this sort of "brute force" approach would be hopeless. Consider, for example, the game of chess: Your goal is to win the game, so how should you proceed? Let's say that you move first. In opening the game, you have exactly 20 moves available to you. For each of these, your opponent has 20 possible responses. Therefore, for the first "cycle" of play, there are 400 possibilities (20 × 20) for how things might go. If you are going to choose the best move, you need to inspect all 400 of these possibilities.

Your best move, however, probably depends on what you are planning to do next—it depends on what defense you are looking to establish or what attack you are planning to launch. Therefore, in evaluating your options, you will probably want to ask, "Will this lead me where I want to go?" and that requires some looking ahead. Before you select your move, therefore, you might want to think through three or four cycles of play, and not just one.

There are 400 possibilities for how the first cycle can unfold, but there are more options for subsequent cycles, as the pieces get spread out, leaving more room to move. Let's estimate, therefore, that there are 40 different moves you might make next and, for each of these, 40 possible responses from your opponent. Thus, for two cycles of play, there are 640,000 (400 × 40 × 40) possible outcomes. If, at that point, there are again 40 options open to you, and 40 possible responses for each, three cycles of play leave us with 1,024,000,000 different options; four cycles of play, 16,384,000,000,000 options. If you are truly seeking the best possible move, maybe you will want to consider all sixteen trillion of these, to find the best one. (For further discussion, see Gilhooly, 1988; Newell & Simon, 1972.)

This proliferation of moves obviously rules out the strategy of "check every option." If you needed one second to evaluate each sequence, you would still need 455 million hours to evaluate the full set of possibilities for four cycles of play. And, of course, there

is nothing special about chess. Let's say that you are having dinner with Percy, and you want him to think you are witty. Your problem is to find things to say that will achieve this goal. How many possibilities are there for sentences you might utter? How many possible rejoinders are available to Percy? How many responses could you then make? Again, the number is vast. If you consider them all, searching for the best choice, you will impress Percy with your long pauses, but not with your wit.

It would be helpful if you could somehow "narrow" your search, so that you consider only a *subset* of your options, rather than searching the entire problem space. Of course, this would involve an element of risk: If you only consider *some* options, you take the risk of overlooking the *best* option. However, you may have no choice about this, since the alternative—the strategy of considering *every* option—would be absurd for most problems.

In essence, then, what you need is a problem-solving *heuristic*. Heuristics, you will recall, are strategies that are reasonably efficient, but at the cost of tolerating occasional errors. In the domain of problem-solving, a heuristic is a strategy that guides you through the problem space—narrowing your search appreciably, but (one hopes) in a fashion that still leads you to the problem's solution. What problem-solving heuristics do we employ?

## GENERAL PROBLEM-SOLVING HEURISTICS

Several problem-solving heuristics are revealed if we simply ask people to think out loud while working on a problem. By inspecting these running commentaries, or "problem-solving protocols," we can locate strategies that are deliberately and wittingly in use. Other heuristics have been discovered in a different fashion: A number of researchers have tried to program computers to solve problems, including the Hobbits and Orcs problem in Figure 14.1, or the so-called Tower of Hanoi (Figure 14.3). We will have more to say about these computer models later on, but for now, notice that these models provide a means of discovering and then evaluating problem-

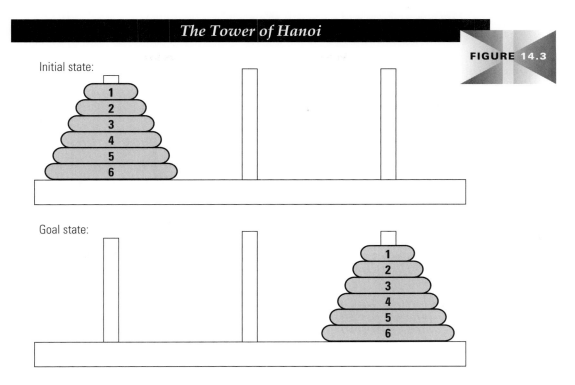

**The Tower of Hanoi**

FIGURE 14.3

Initial state:

Goal state:

The rings on the left pole need to be moved so that they end up on the right pole, as shown. The rings must be moved one at a time, and with each move, a ring can be placed only on a *larger* ring. Thus, Ring 1 can be placed on top of Ring 2, but Ring 2 can never be placed on Ring 1. Can you solve this?

solving strategies: By programming a computer to use this or that strategy, we can literally ask how well problem-solving would proceed with that strategy in place.

One often-used heuristic is the so-called hill-climbing strategy. To understand the term, imagine that you are hiking through the woods and trying to figure out which trail leads to the mountaintop. You obviously need to climb *uphill* to reach the top so, whenever you come to a fork in the trail, you select the path that is going uphill. The hill-climbing strategy works the same way: At each point, you simply choose the option that moves you in the direction of your goal.

This strategy is helpful for some problems: Imagine that there is a bad smell in your house, and you are trying to figure out where it's coming from. You might stand at the doorway between the kitchen and the dining room, and then figure out in which direction the smell is stronger. If it is stronger in the kitchen, then that is the direction to explore. If the smell gets stronger as you approach the sink, then explore that area. By always moving in the direction of the stronger smell, you will eventually discover the smell's source.

This strategy, however, is of limited use, largely because many problems require that you start by moving *away* from your goal; only then, from this

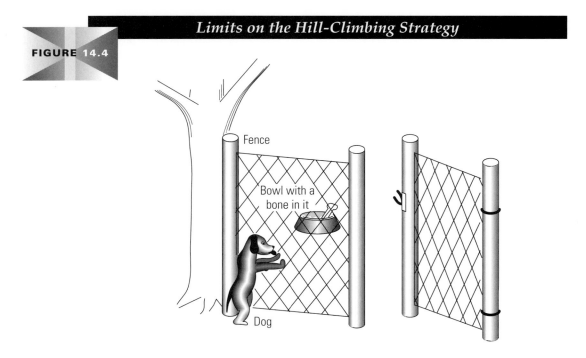

**FIGURE 14.4**

## Limits on the Hill-Climbing Strategy

Fence

Bowl with a bone in it

Dog

According to the hill-climbing strategy, the dog should, at each step, choose a path that moves it closer and closer to the goal. However, this strategy will *fail* here, since the dog needs first to move *away* from the bone in order to reach the bone.

new position, can the problem be solved. We have illustrated this in Figure 14.4, and other examples are easy to find. For instance, if you want Mingus to notice you more, it might help if you went away for a while; that way, he will be more likely to notice you when you come back. This ploy would never be discovered, though, if you relied on the hill-climbing strategy.

Despite these limitations, people do often rely on a hill-climbing strategy. As a result, they have difficulties whenever a problem requires them to move "backward in order to go forward"—that is, whenever the problem requires them to move (briefly) away from their goal in order (ultimately) to reach the goal. For example, solving the Hobbits and Orcs problem (Figure 14.1) requires, at various points, that one

carry creatures from the east bank *back* to the west— i.e., from the goal state back to the initial state. These points of "backward movement" turn out to be very difficult for people. Often, at these points, people become convinced they are on the wrong track, and they seek some other solution to the problem: "This must be the wrong strategy; I'm going the wrong way." (See, for example, Jeffries, Polson, Razran & Atwood, 1977; Thomas, 1974.)

Fortunately, though, people also have other, more sophisticated, heuristics available to them. For example, people often rely on a strategy called means-end analysis. To use this strategy, one starts by comparing the current state and the goal state. One then asks, "What means do I have available to get from here to there?" To see how this plays out, consider

## The Water Lilies Problem

**FIGURE** 14.5

Water lilies are growing on Blue Lake. The water lilies grow rapidly, so that the amount of water surface covered by lilies *doubles* every 24 hours.

On the first day of summer, there was just one water lily. On the 90th day of the summer, the lake was entirely covered. On what day was the lake *half covered*?

Working backward from the goal is useful in solving this problem. Can you solve it?

this commonsense example, offered by Newell and Simon (1972):

> I want to take my son to nursery school. What's the difference between what I have and what I want? One of distance. What changes distance? My automobile. My automobile won't work. What is needed to make it work? A new battery. What has new batteries? An auto repair shop. I want the repair shop to put in a new battery; but the shop doesn't know I need one. What is the difficulty? One of communication. What allows communication? A telephone . . .

A means-end analysis will generally lead you to break up a problem into smaller "sub-problems." By solving these, one at a time, the larger problem gets dealt with. In fact, some have suggested that this identification of sub-problems is itself a powerful problem-solving heuristic: By breaking a problem into smaller pieces, we make the initial problem easier to solve.

A related idea is that one can often solve a problem by focusing on the goal, rather than on one's current state, and then working backward from the goal. This strategy is quite useful, for example, for the "water lilies" problem, described in Figure 14.5. In problems like this one, you are once again using means-end analysis, but now in reverse—asking how the goal state can be made more similar to the current state.

A variety of evidence suggests that means-end analysis and working backward are commonly used strategies. For example, both strategies appear frequently in people's problem-solving protocols. And this turns out to be sensible, because these two strategies are often effective and are applicable to a large number of problems.

## MENTAL MODELS AND MENTAL IMAGES

In many cases, it also helps to translate a problem into concrete terms, perhaps relying on a mental image or a mental model. This will often make the elements of the problem easier to remember (see Chapter 11) and also easier to think about (see Chapter 13). Images and mental models are useful for a wide variety of problems but, not surprisingly, they are particularly helpful if the problem hinges on spatial arrangements: In this case, you can use your "mind's eye" to envision how the elements will look, once in their appropriate positions, and you can also visualize how the elements might look if rearranged.

A number of studies have examined the role of imagery in problem-solving (e.g., Cooper, 1990; Palmer, 1977; Shepard & Feng, 1972). Perhaps the most interesting studies, though, are those concerned with the role of imagery in *invention*. For example, participants in one procedure were asked to imagine how a half sphere, a wire, and a rectangular block might be combined to create something that "might have practical value" (Finke, 1990, 1993;

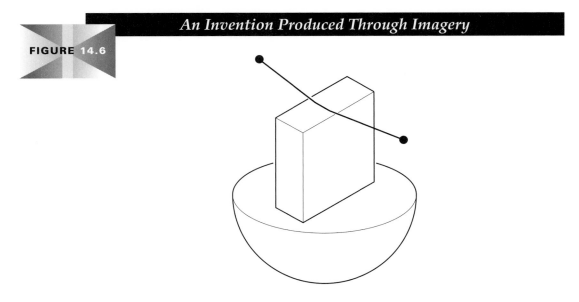

FIGURE 14.6

### An Invention Produced Through Imagery

A research participant was told to make something useful by combining, in imagination, a *half sphere*, some *wire*, and a *rectangular block*. The participant invented this "hip exerciser." To use the exerciser, one stands on the flat side of the half sphere, and holds onto the wires. By shifting weight from side to side, one can exercise one's hips.

Finke & Slayton, 1988). One participant's invention is shown in Figure 14.6. To use this "hip exerciser," you stand on the flat side of the hemisphere, and shift your weight from side to side while holding onto the post. (For related discussion, see Kaufmann, 1990; Koestler, 1964; McKim, 1980. For discussion of imagery's role in scientific discoveries, see Miller, 1986; Reed, 1993; Shepard, 1988.)

## PICTURES AND DIAGRAMS

Consider the "bookworm" problem, described in Figure 14.7. Most people try an algebraic solution to this problem (width of each volume, multiplied by the number of volumes, divided by the worm's eating rate), and end up with the wrong answer. People

generally get this problem right, though, if they start by *drawing a diagram* (like the one in Figure 14.8).

In this problem and in many others, diagrams help us by bringing spatial positions and relationships into clear view. The bookworm problem, for example, is easily solved as soon as you discern the actual positions of the worm's "starting point" and "end point." Moreover, it's plausible that you could figure out where these positions are *either* by inspecting a picture *or* by inspecting a mental image of the problem's layout, and, indeed, for many purposes, pictures and images may be interchangeable. Consistent with this idea, several studies have found no difference between problem-solving via picture and problem-solving via imagery (Anderson, 1993; Anderson & Helstrup, 1993; Reed, 1993).

For other purposes, though, there are important differences between mental images and pictures, with some problems more readily solved via imagery, and other problems showing the reverse. For example, mental images have the advantage of being more easily modified than diagrams: If one wishes to make a form larger, or a different shape, this is easy in imagination—one can, after all, imagine anything one wishes. Likewise, one can easily imagine *moving* patterns; it is much harder to depict motion with a diagram. Therefore, if a problem solution depends on motion, then the problem may be more easily solved with imagery than with a picture.

At the same time, however, it takes some effort to create and maintain a mental image (see Chapter 11); this can divert attention away from the problem under scrutiny, and so this provides an advantage for problem-solving via *pictures*. Likewise, elaborate or detailed forms are difficult to image clearly. If a problem depends on such forms, then, problem-solving via image will be difficult.

In addition, Chapter 11 presented evidence indicating that, in important ways, mental images are different from pictures. Specifically, we suggested that mental images are always created with a particular understanding in mind for how the imaged form is organized, and we referred to this understanding as a *perceptual reference frame*. Moreover, we argued that this reference frame sets "boundaries" on what can be discovered within the image: Image-based discoveries will be relatively common and relatively easy *if* the discoveries are compatible both with the imaged geometry and *also* with the image's reference frame. Image-based discoveries are far less likely if the discovery is not compatible with the reference frame, or, equivalently, if the discovery requires a change in the image's reference frame. (For evidence supporting these claims, see Chapter 11.)

None of this applies to discoveries about pictures. When a picture is perceived by someone, it is perceived within a particular reference frame, but crucially, the picture itself has no reference frame. That is why pictures are *ambiguous*, open to multiple interpretations, and, for problem-solving, this is actually an advantage: Since the picture is fully compatible with many different interpretations, there's no obstacle to imposing a *new* interpretation on the picture, and that's usually what one wants to do in making some discovery about the picture.

For this reason, it's often useful for a problem-solver to draw a picture, based on an image of the problem's setting or form. In many cases, this "external representation" will allow discoveries that weren't possible from the original image—even though the two representations, the drawing and the image, supposedly depict the same thing. This advantage of "externalizing" is easily demonstrated in the laboratory, both with visual images and with auditory ones

### The Bookworm Problem

FIGURE 14.7

Solomon is proud of his 26-volume encyclopedia, placed neatly, with the volumes in alphabetical order, on his bookshelf. Solomon doesn't realize, though, that there's a bookworm sitting on the front cover of the "A" volume. The bookworm begins chewing his way through the pages, on the shortest possible path toward the back cover of the "Z" volume.

Each volume is 3 inches thick (including pages and covers), so that the entire set of volumes requires 78 inches of bookshelf. The bookworm chews through the pages + covers at a steady rate of 3/4 of an inch per month. How long will it take before the bookworm reaches the backcover of "Z" volume?

People who try an algebraic solution to this problem often end up with the wrong answer.

(see Chapter 11; also Reisberg, 2000). This advantage can also be demonstrated in real-world settings—for example, in architects who gain by sketching out their designs, rather than trying to work out the design entirely "in their heads" (Verstijnen, Hennessey, et al., 1998; for more on the role of pictures and other external aids in support of problem-solving, see Cary & Carlson, 1999; Chen, 1995; Novick et al., 1999; Ormerod & Chronicle, 1999).

### COMPUTER MODELS OF PROBLEM-SOLVING

We have now catalogued several of the problem-solving strategies that people have available to them.

However, this catalogue still leaves a great deal unspecified. For example, imagine that you are using a means-end analysis and discover that your current state differs from the goal state in three different ways. Does it matter which of these differences you attack first? If so, what should the sequence be?

To answer questions like these, researchers are working on the development of more specific, more precise theories of problem-solving, theories that pull together all of the pieces we have considered so far. Often, these theories are realized in the form of computer programs. The basic idea is that, if the program fails to solve a problem that people can solve, we know that the theory embodied in the program is inadequate. Likewise, if the computer

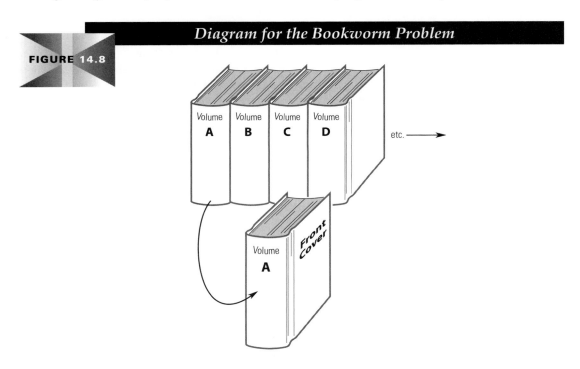

**FIGURE 14.8**

### Diagram for the Bookworm Problem

When the bookworm problem is illustrated, as shown here, people more easily solve it. Notice that a worm, starting on the *front* cover of the A volume, would not have to chew through volume A's pages in moving toward the Z volume. Likewise, at the *end* of the worm's travel, he would reach the *back* cover of the Z volume *before* penetrating into the Z volume!

program quickly solves problems that are difficult for humans, then again we know we are on the wrong track. In these ways, both the successes and the failures of the program provide a powerful means for assessing our theories.

Just as important, the mere step of translating a theory into a program is often quite useful. Computers do precisely what they are told. If they are not told what to do, they make no progress. Likewise, one can't give the computer vague instructions such as, "Oh, you know what I mean, so just do it." Instead, instructions to the computer must be clear, unambiguous, and complete. Therefore, if your theory is to be embodied in these instructions, then your theory, too, must be fully spelled out, with all the gaps filled. Getting the theory to this state is certain to be valuable and so, even if the program is never run, this exercise will improve the quality of our theorizing.

Many computer models of problem-solving are being developed, each seeking to realize a particular researcher's conception. The "classic" model, though, is that created by Newell and Simon (1972). Their model is designed to solve a wide range of problems, and thus its name: General Problem Solver, or "GPS" for short. GPS is intended not merely to solve problems, but to solve them in the same way humans do. Development of this model was heavily influenced by consideration of problem-solving protocols, and by consideration of the specific profile of human problem-solving—i.e., which problems we solve easily and which we don't.

GPS relies heavily on heuristics and, in particular, means-end analysis. Thus, the program compares the current state to the goal state, to detect the differences. GPS then considers the set of operators it has available, to determine which would reduce (or eliminate) these differences. The operators are applied, and then the cycle is repeated: Given the progress just made, what differences remain between current state and goal state? Which operators will reduce this difference?

GPS's operators generally involve actions, so that an operator might move some object to a new position, or might change an object from one specific form into another. More recent models, however, have considered other means of describing the operators. For example, many models rely on **production systems**, where each production involves (a) a goal, (b) some conditions that must be met before the action can be taken, and (c) a specific action (Anderson, 1993; Brown & Van Lehn, 1980; Holland, Holyoak, Nisbett & Thagard, 1986; Newell, 1973). A production might say, "IF the goal is to light the fire, and IF the fuel is ready, THEN strike the match." Or, as a more general production, "IF the goal is to transform the current state into the goal state, and IF D is the largest difference between these two states, THEN set as subgoals (1) to eliminate the difference D, and (2) to convert the resulting state into the goal state" (after Anderson, 1990).

With operators like these, computer models are able to solve an impressive range of problems. GPS, for example, is able to solve the Tower of Hanoi problem (Figure 14.3) and "transport" problems (like the Hobbits and Orcs of Figure 14.1); it is also able to prove logic theorems and to solve a variety of trigonometry problems. Moreover, GPS's performance in these problems seems well matched to that of humans: GPS takes longer with more difficult problems and makes errors roughly in the same ways that humans do. We can also compare GPS's step-by-step progress with people's problem-solving protocols. The correspondence between these is reasonably good, suggesting that GPS follows the same path in solving the problem that humans do. (For reviews, see Gardner, 1985; Kotovsky, Hayes & Simon, 1985; Simon, 1975.)

We can also assess these computer models in one other way: As people work on a problem, sometimes they work quickly, and sometimes they pause to consider their next move. Why is this? One possibility is that people move most slowly when they are contemplating a "stack" of subgoals: "What I next want to do is X. I can't do X, though, since I first need to do Y. And I can't do Y, because I first need to do Z. . . ." Consistent with this suggestion, Anderson (1993) reports a strong correlation between the number of subgoals active at any particular moment (determined via the computer model) and the actual speed with which people proceed (determined by assessing actual performance).

Finally, we should also note that computer models of problem-solving can be *useful* in important ways: Imagine that the computer has trouble with a particular problem and always gets bogged down at a certain point in trying to solve the problem. We obviously can look "inside" the computer in ways that we can't look inside a human, and so we can figure out exactly what is causing the hang-up. If it then turns out that humans have trouble with the same problem, we can use the computer model to figure out the source of the humans' difficulty.

In this fashion, computer models can be used to design educational programs: The computer model can tell us a great deal about the sources of a student's errors, and then we can use this information to fine-tune the instruction given to that student. The computer can also be used to model an expert's performance, allowing us to define exactly what skills should be taught, en route to expertise. Anderson (1993) describes one such endeavor, designed to improve instruction in mathematics; other similar projects are under way (e.g., Polson & Richardson, 1988; Reed & Bolstad, 1991).

## Relying on Past Knowledge

Our discussion so far has focused on strategies that apply to problem-solving in general, problem-solving of all sorts. This emphasis has highlighted a number of principles that do indeed seem to be general principles—for example, the role of heuristics or the widespread use of means-end analysis. Likewise, this emphasis has led researchers to computer models that

---

**FIGURE 14.9**

### Analogies Are a Useful Way to Convey New Information

**Literal Version:**

Collapsing stars spin faster and faster as they fold in on themselves and their size decreases. This phenomenon of spinning faster as the star's size shrinks occurs because of a principle called "conservation of angular momentum."

**Analogy Version:**

Collapsing stars spin faster as their size shrinks. Stars are thus like ice skaters, who pirouette faster as they pull in their arms. Both stars and skaters operate by a principle called "conservation of angular momentum."

**Question:**

What would happen if a star "expanded" instead of collapsing?
    a. Its rate of rotation would increase.
    b. Its rate of rotation would decrease.
    c. Its orbital speed would increase.
    d. Its orbital speed would decrease.

Participants were presented with new materials either in a "literal version" or in an "analogy version." Later, participants were asked questions about these materials. Those instructed via analogy reliably did better. [After Donnelly & McDaniel, 1993.]

**The Tumor Problem**

**FIGURE** 14.10

Suppose you are a doctor faced with a patient who has a malignant tumor in his stomach. To operate on the patient is impossible, but unless the tumor is destroyed, the patient will die. A kind of ray, at a sufficiently high intensity, can destroy the tumor. Unfortunately, at this intensity the healthy tissue that the rays pass through on the way to the tumor will also be destroyed. At lower intensities the rays are harmless to healthy tissue, but will not affect the tumor. How can the rays be used to destroy the tumor without injuring the healthy tissue?

The tumor problem, designed by Duncker (1945), has been studied extensively. Can you solve it? One solution is to aim *multiple* low-intensity rays at the tumor, each from a different angle. The rays will "meet" at the site of the tumor and so, at just that location, will "sum" to full strength.

are in many ways impressive. As a matter of technology, these models can solve an interesting range of problems. As a boon to education, these models can be used to design curricula, and then to guide instruction step-by-step as a student progresses. Finally, these models also point us toward explanations for a number of phenomena, providing insights, for example, into why some problems are harder than others and why problem-solving sometimes proceeds slowly, sometimes quickly.

It turns out that problem-solving also draws on particular and specialized knowledge, in addition to the flexible, widely applicable heuristics we have considered so far. To the extent that this is true, we need to turn away from models of problem-solving in general, and ask instead how problem-solving unfolds in more specialized domains.

## PROBLEM-SOLVING VIA ANALOGY

Often, in solving a problem, we are reminded of some other problem we have already solved, and this will tell us, by analogy, how to solve the problem now before us. Of course, this is possible only if we have the relevant prior experience, providing a base from which we can draw analogies. Obviously, therefore,

analogy use depends on specialized knowledge—that is, knowledge relevant to the problem now at hand.

Many authors have argued that the ability to draw analogies is a central intellectual tool. Certainly, within the history of science, analogies have often played an important role—with scientists furthering their understanding of the heart by comparing it to a pump, extending their knowledge of gases by comparing the molecules to billiard balls, and so on (cf. Gentner & Jeziorski, 1989). It is no wonder that analogies appear prominently in the SAT's and on many versions of the IQ test (see Holyoak, 1984; Spearman, 1923).

Likewise, many writers have recommended the use of analogies as a *teaching* tool. Thus, the atom is described to students as (very roughly) resembling the solar system, memory is compared to a library, and the like. In fact, evidence suggests that analogies do make for effective instruction. For example, Donnelly and McDaniel (1993) presented some of their participants with literal accounts of new scientific materials; other participants were given analogies of these same materials (Figure 14.9). When all the participants were later asked to make inferences about these new ideas, those instructed via analogy did better.

In addition, analogies plainly do help in solving problems. For example, the "tumor" problem (Figure 14.10) is quite difficult, but people generally

**FIGURE** 14.11

## The General and Fortress Problem

A small country was ruled from a strong fortress by a dictator. The fortress was situated in the middle of the country, surrounded by farms and villages. Many roads led to the fortress through the countryside. A rebel general vowed to capture the fortress. The general knew that an attack by his entire army would capture the fortress. He gathered his army at the head of one of the roads, ready to launch a full-scale direct attack. However, the general then learned that the dictator had planted mines on each of the roads. The mines were set so that small bodies of men could pass over them safely, since the dictator needed to move his own troops and workers to and from the fortress. However, any large force would detonate the mines. Not only would this blow up the road, but it would also destroy many neighboring villages. It seemed impossible to capture the fortress. However, the general devised a simple plan. He divided his army into small groups and dispatched each group to the head of a different road. When all was ready, he gave the signal and each group marched down a different road. Each group continued down its road to the fortress, so that the entire army arrived together at the fortress at the same time. In this way, the general captured the fortress and overthrew the dictator.

This problem is analogous in its structure to the tumor problem (Figure 14.10). If people read this problem, and then try the tumor problem, they are far more likely to solve the latter. [After Gick & Holyoak, 1980.]

solve it if they are able to use an analogy: Gick and Holyoak (1980) first had their participants read about a related situation (Figure 14.11), and then presented them with the tumor problem. When participants were encouraged to use this hint, 75% were able to solve the tumor problem. For participants not given the hint, only 10% solved the tumor problem.

### DIFFICULTIES IN FINDING AN APPROPRIATE ANALOGY

However, despite the clear benefit of using analogies, people routinely fail to use them. For example, Gick and Holyoak had another group of participants read the "General and Fortress" story, but no further hints were given. In particular, these participants were not told that this story was relevant to the tumor problem. Only 30% solved the tumor problem—far fewer than the 75% explicitly told that the "fortress" story was relevant to their task.

Similarly, Reed (1977; Reed, Ernst & Banerji, 1974) first had participants solve the "jealous-husbands" problem, shown in Figure 14.12; the participants were then asked to solve the Hobbits and Orcs problem (Figure 14.1). When the close relationship between these two problems was pointed out to the participants, they were considerably faster in solving the second problem. However, if this relationship was not explicitly pointed out, they showed no benefit at all from this "training." (See also Hayes & Simon, 1977; Ross, 1984, 1987, 1989; Weisberg, DiCamillo & Phillips, 1978.)

Apparently, then, people do use analogies if suitably instructed, but *spontaneous, uninstructed* use of analogies seems to be quite rare. Why is this? Part of the answer lies in how people search through their memories when seeking an analogy. In solving a problem about tumors, people seem to ask themselves, "What else do I know about tumors?" This will help them remember other situations in which they thought about, or learned about, tumors but, of course, this memory search *won't* lead them to the "General and Fortress" problem. This (potential) analogue will therefore lie dormant in memory and provide no help. Likewise, hobbit problems remind people of other hobbit problems, even though problems on other topics might point the way to a solution.

Consistent with this perspective, people solving hobbit problems *will* spontaneously use analogies if the previously studied problems also involved hobbits. In this case, the (rather obvious) relation between the current problem and the prior problems guarantees that the former will call the latter to mind. People are less likely to draw analogies if they have previously solved problems involving actors of a different sort. (For relevant evidence, see Bassok, Wu & Olseth, 1995; Bassok, 1996; Cummins, 1992; Holyoak & Koh, 1987; Novick, 1988; Ross, 1984, 1987; Spencer & Weisberg, 1986; Wharton, Holyoak, Downing & Lange, 1994.)

Similarities between the current problem and the previously studied case also help people in another way: In order to create, or even to understand, an analogy, people need to get beyond the superficial features of the problem and have to think instead about the principles governing the problem. Put differently, people can use analogies only if they figure out how to **map** the prior case onto the problem now being solved, only if they realize, for example, that converging groups of soldiers correspond to converging beams, and that a fortress-to-be-captured corresponds to a tumor-to-be-destroyed. This mapping process is often complicated and, in any case, requires insight into both the current problem and also the analogous case being drawn from memory. (For discussion of how this process of mapping unfolds, see Gentner, 1983, 1989; Holyoak, 1984; Holyoak & Thagard, 1989; VanLehn, 1998; Markman, 1997.) Failures to figure out this mapping are common, and these failures are another reason why people regularly fail to find, and fail to use, analogies.

However, mapping one problem onto another is certainly easier if the two problems are similar in their particulars: If you have recently solved one Hobbits and Orcs problem, it is easy to apply this experience to a new Hobbits and Orcs problem—what you earlier learned about hobbits can be mapped onto the new hobbits, what you earlier discovered about boats is immediately applicable to the boat in the current problem. If, instead, you have recently solved the jealous-husbands problem, then the prin-

---

## The Jealous Husbands Problem

**FIGURE** 14.12

Three jealous husbands and their wives, who have to cross a river, find a boat. However, the boat is so small that it can hold no more than two persons. Find the simplest schedule of crossings that will permit all six persons to cross the river so that no woman is left in the company of any other woman's husband unless her own husband is present. It is assumed that all passengers on the boat debark before the next trip and that at least one person has to be in the boat for each crossing.

If the experimenter points out the relationship between the jealous husbands problem and the Hobbits and Orcs problem (Figure 14.1), then participants benefit from first solving the jealous husbands problem. If this relationship is not pointed out to subjects, however, they show no benefit from this "training." [After Reed, Ernst, & Banerji, 1974.]

ciples learned in this experience might be applicable to the new problem, but only via a step of translation (hobbits become husbands; "cannot outnumber" is replaced with "cannot be left alone with"). This, by itself, makes use of the analogy more difficult, and provides a further reason for why analogy use is facilitated by similarity between the target problem and the analogous problem drawn from memory. (For discussion of still other factors impeding or facilitating the use of analogies, see Bassok, Wu & Olseth, 1995; Blanchette & Dunbar, 2000; Gick & Holyoak, 1980; Novick & Holyoak, 1991; Needham & Begg, 1991.)

## STRATEGIES TO MAKE ANALOGY USE MORE LIKELY

Overall, then, it seems that analogies can be extremely useful in solving problems, but, even so, people often fail to use analogies. Part of the difficulty lies in *finding* a proper analogy; part lies in *mapping* one problem onto another. In either case, though, people underuse analogies in their problem-solving and in this fashion, become less effective problem-solvers than we might wish.

Is there anything we can do about this? Is there any way to *promote* analogy use, and thus to improve problem-solving? Let's start with the memory search. When considering the tumor problem (for example), people seem to ask themselves, "What else do I know about tumors?" Surely there is nothing inevitable about this, and presumably people could, with suitable instruction, learn to ask themselves a different question, along the lines of, "How can I bring forces to bear on a specific target without losing or misusing the forces while they're on their way to the target?" With this question, people might well be reminded of a suitable analogue, even if the analogue differed from the current problem in a dozen superficial ways.

Similarly, let's be clear that analogies usually depend on a problem's "deep structure"—the pattern of causal relationships within the problem, and how the problem's parts are interrelated. The problem's "surface structure"—how the causal relationships

are manifested—is largely irrelevant. Perhaps we can promote analogy use, therefore, by urging people to pay attention to the deep structure from the very start, rather than attending to the problem's superficial content. In this way, a proper orientation, when working on a problem, might help both in the locating of analogues and also the mapping of one problem onto another.

Several studies have confirmed these optimistic predictions. For example, we have already seen that people are unlikely, on their own, to notice the analogy between the "General and Fortress" problem (for which they know the solution) and the "tumor" problem (which they are currently trying to solve). In a related procedure, though, people were initially given *two* analogous stories, prior to the test problem, rather than just one (Gick & Holyoak, 1983). These participants were much more likely to draw analogies from these stories in solving the tumor problem, compared to participants who had read only one (potential) analogue.

Why are two analogues better than one? The two analogues both involved the same principles (one was the "General and Fortress" problem, the other problem involved the use of many small hoses to put out a large fire). This may have been enough to call the participants' attention to these principles (e.g., the use of converging forces). This would, in turn, highlight the underlying structure of the stories, paving the way for the analogy.

A similar point emerges from an experiment by Cummins (1992). She presented her participants with a series of algebra word problems. One group of participants was asked to analyze these training problems, one by one; these participants tended to categorize the problems in terms of superficial features, and were unlikely, later on, to apply these analogies to new problems. Participants in a second group were explicitly asked to *compare* the training problems to each other. These participants tended to describe and categorize the problems in terms of their structures—in other words, they paid attention to the problems' underlying dynamic. These participants were much more likely to use these problems as a basis for analogies when later solving new problems. (For related evidence, see Catrambone & Holyoak, 1989; Catrambone, 1998; Lee & Hutchison, 1998; Loewenstein, Thompson & Gentner, 1999.)

Likewise, Needham and Begg (1991) presented their participants with a series of training problems. Some participants were told that they would need to recall these problems later on and were encouraged to work hard at remembering them. Other participants were encouraged to take a "problem-oriented" attitude during this training: They were encouraged to work at *understanding* each solution, so that they would be able to explain it later on.

When the time came for the test problems, participants in the second group were much more likely to transfer what they had earlier learned. As a result, those who had taken the "problem-oriented" approach were able to solve 90% of the test problems; subjects who had taken the "memory-oriented" approach solved only 69%. Interestingly, it didn't matter whether the training examples were presented as unsolved problems (so that the participants had actually worked on solving them) or as stories that included the solution. It also didn't matter whether participants had successfully solved the training problems or tried and failed to solve these problems. That is, what mattered *wasn't* a history of solving the problems. Instead, what mattered was a history of *thinking* about the problems in a certain way.

For purposes of problem-solving, therefore, there is a "preferred" way to learn. In essence, you want to attend to the *structure* of a problem rather than to its surface; this increases the likelihood of finding analogies later on, and thus the likelihood of benefiting from analogies later on. Comparing problems to each other, seeking parallels and points of similarity, seems to bring this about. As we have seen, a similar effect is observed if you simply spend time thinking about a problem's solution and, in particular, thinking about *why* the solution gets the job done. People are also helped by getting the *right* training problems, problems that call attention to the problems' underlying structure (Catrambone, 1994; Gick & Holyoak, 1983). Thus, there seem to be many ways to promote analogy use, ways that provide people both with the relevant analogues

and with the "sagacity to apply the knowledge to a new problem" (Needham & Begg, 1991; after James, 1890).

## EXPERT PROBLEM-SOLVERS

Our discussion so far has obvious implications for education. Let's say that we want students to be better problem-solvers; how should we proceed? First, we could teach our students some of the heuristics that appear useful for problem-solving in general. Second, analogies are plainly helpful in problem-solving, and so we could provide students with experience in the relevant domains, so that they would have a basis from which to draw analogies. Third, we now see that this training may have little effect unless we take steps to ensure students will use this knowledge when it is needed. To this end, we need to encourage students to approach the training problems in an appropriate way, to make certain the training problems will be retrievable from memory later on, and also to provide a basis for seeing the mapping between the training and test problems.

These training steps are designed to produce better problem-solving; in the extreme, these steps might even produce expert problem-solving. But can we really characterize *expertise* in the terms used so far? We have claimed an advantage, for example, in thinking about problems in terms of their deep struture; is this the way experts think about problems? We have likewise claimed that analogies often help problem-solving; is analogy use common among experts?

As we have seen, novices tend to think about problems in terms of their *surface structure*. As a result, novices often find analogues in memory only if those analogues have a surface structure that's similar to the problem now being solved. However, this is *not* the pattern with experts. Even with only moderate levels of expertise, people seem to think about problems in terms of their deep structure and type of solution, rather than in terms of superficial features (Hinsley, Hayes & Simon, 1977; Reeves & Weisberg, 1994). For example, college students, moderately well-versed in algebra, tend to categorize word problems in a fashion that's guided by the *type* of problem, rather than the problem's details. Thus, any problem involving an object moving against some force is categorized as a "river-current problem," whether the problem involves a boat sailing upstream, a fish swimming against the tide, or an airplane flying into the wind. Apparently, then, it's only the novices who attend exclusively to a problem's superficial features.

Likewise, Chi, Feltovich and Glaser (1981) asked their research participants to categorize simple physics problems. Novices tended to place together all the problems involving inclined planes, all the problems involving springs, and so on, in each case focusing on the surface form of the problem, independent of what physical principles were needed to solve the problem. In contrast, the experts in their study (Ph.D. students in physics) ignored the details of the problems and, instead, sorted according to the physical principles relevant to the problem's solution. (Also see Adelson, 1981; Chase & Simon, 1973; Chi, Glaser & Farr, 1988; Cummins, 1992; Hardiman, Dufresne & Mestre, 1989; Schoenfeld & Herrmann, 1982.)

Of course, we have already said that attention to a problem's structure promotes analogy use. Therefore, if experts are more attentive to this structure, then experts should be more likely to use analogies. Several studies indicate that this is correct. For example, Novick and Holyoak (1991) examined their participants' skill in using mathematical analogies (an example is shown in Figure 14.13). They first provided the participants with a training problem; the participants then tried to solve several analogous problems.

Novick and Holyoak assessed "math expertise" by looking at the participants' SAT scores, and they found a positive relation between these scores and the ability to form mathematical analogies. There was no relation between analogy use and verbal SAT's, or between analogy use and what they called "general analogy skill." What seems to matter in drawing analogies, therefore, is not some sort of generalized skill. Instead, analogy use depends specifically on expertise within the relevant domain. (For related results, see Clement, 1982; Novick, 1988.)

## CHUNKING AND SUBGOALS

Experts' sensitivity to a problem's deep structure is also evident in a series of classic studies of chess experts (De Groot, 1965, 1966; also Chase & Simon, 1973). These studies indicate that these experts are particularly skilled in organizing a chess game—in seeing the structure of the game, understanding its parts, and perceiving how these parts are related to each other. This is revealed in how chess masters remember board positions: In one procedure, chess masters were able to remember the positions of twenty pieces, after viewing the board for just five seconds. Moreover, there was a clear pattern to the experts' recollection: In recalling the layout of the board, the experts would place four or five pieces in their proper positions, then pause, then another group, then pause, and so on. In each case, the group of pieces was one that made "tactical sense," e.g., the pieces involved in a "forked" attack, a chain of mutually defending pieces, and the like.

This memory pattern suggests that the masters had memorized the board in terms of *groups* of pieces, rather than individual pieces, with these groups characterized according to their function within the game. Consistent with this suggestion, the masters showed no memory advantage if asked to memorize random configurations of chess pieces. In this case, there were no sensible groupings, and so the masters were unable to organize (and thus memorize) the board. (For more on this phenomenon, and chess expertise in general, see Gobet & Simon, 1996a, 1996b; but then also see Lassiter, 2000; Gobet & Simon, 2000.)

All of this should sound familiar to you. In Chapter 5, we discussed the fact that memory is generally improved if one can organize the to-be-remembered materials. More specifically, it often helps to repackage the materials into a small number of memory "chunks," allowing more effective use of working memory's limited capacity. Given this backdrop, it should be no surprise that chess experts, with their ability to organize a board and to perceive the large-level units, have superior memories for chess posi-

## Using Analogies to Solve Mathematical Problems

FIGURE 14.13

### The Garden Problem

Mr. and Mrs. Renshaw were planning how to arrange vegetable plants in their new garden. They agreed on the total number of plants to buy, but not on how many of each kind to get. Mr. Renshaw wanted to have a few kinds of vegetables and ten of each kind. Mrs. Renshaw wanted more different kinds of vegetables, so she suggested having only four of each kind. Mr. Renshaw didn't like that because if some of the plants died, there wouldn't be very many left of each kind. So they agreed to have five of each vegetable. But then their daughter pointed out that there was room in the garden for two more plants, although then there wouldn't be the same number of each kind of vegetable. To remedy this, she suggested buying six of each vegetable. Everyone was satisfied with this plan. Given this information, what is the fewest number of vegetable plants the Renshaws could have in their garden?

### Solution for Garden Problem

Since at the beginning Mr. and Mrs. Renshaw agree on the total number of plants to buy, 10, 4, and 5 must all go evenly into that number, whatever it is. Thus the first thing to do is to find the smallest number that is evenly divisible by those 3 numbers, which is 20. So the original number of vegetable plants the Renshaws were thinking of buying could be any multiple of 20 (that is, 20 or 40 or 60 or 80 etc.). But then they decide to buy 2 additional plants that they hadn't been planning to buy originally, so the total number of plants they actually end up buying must be 2 more than the multiples of 20 listed above (that is, 22 or 42 or 62 or 82 etc.). This means that 10, 4, and 5 will now no longer go evenly into the total number of plants. Finally, the problem states that they agree to buy 6 of each vegetable, so the total number of plants must be evenly divisible by 6. The smallest total number of plants that is evenly divisible by 6 is 42, so that's the answer.

### The Seashell Problem

Samantha's mother asked her how many sea shells she has in her collection. Samantha said she wasn't sure, but it was a lot—somewhere between 80 and 550. And she could count them by sevens without having any left over. However, if she counted them by threes, there was one shell left over. Things were even worse if she counted the shells by fives, by sixes, by nines, or by tens—there were always four shells left over. Samantha's mother promptly told her how many sea shells she had in her collection. What number did Samantha's mother come up with?

Participants first solved the "garden" problem, and then were tested with similar problems—such as the "seashell" problem shown in the figure. Participants with greater math expertise (measured via SAT scores) were more likely to rely on analogies in solving these problems, and so were more likely to apply what they had learned in the training problems to the subsequent test problems. [After Novick & Holyoak, 1991.]

tions. Indeed, similar memory advantages have been reported in other domains—e.g., masters in the game of Gō memorizing board positions (Reitman, 1976) or experts in electronics memorizing circuit diagrams (Egan & Schwartz, 1979).

This memory advantage will, by itself, aid problem-solving. If you are trying to remember the locations of 20 pieces, this will demand virtually all of your mental resources, with little left over for other chores—e.g., choosing your next move. If these 20 locations can be chunked as four tactical units, the burden on working memory is reduced, freeing capacity for the task at hand.

The perception of a problem's higher-order units also helps in another way: This perception is likely to draw attention to these units and to how they are related to each other. This allows the expert problem-solver to focus on the overall structure of the problem, rather than getting bogged down in the details. Thus, problem-solution can proceed at the level of "I'm being attacked, and I need to move away," without worrying about whether the attack comes from a bishop or a rook, from an opponent close by or one far away.

In addition, the perception of a problem's parts often leads directly to the identification of sub-problems and, with it, to the creation of "subgoals." Having perceived an opponent's "knight fork," for example, one realizes the need to defend against this attack. Having realized how few pieces defend a rook, one sets the subgoal of shoring up those defenses. In this fashion, breaking a problem into "chunks" can sometimes allow the expert to deal with the problem "one (large) piece at a time," rather than all at once.

Consistent with all these suggestions, De Groot's data show that the chess experts often didn't consider that many options in selecting their next move. That is because their perception of the game's organization allowed them to focus on just those options that were particularly promising in that situation. Indeed, the evidence suggests that the experts often considered fewer options in selecting their next move than less talented players.

## THE NATURE OF EXPERTISE

We have now suggested that experts may have several advantages in comparison to novices. But what exactly is "expertise" in a problem area? And what does it take to become an "expert"? It seems clear that experts know more about their domains of expertise than novices, and in fact, Hayes (1985) estimates that it takes at least ten years to become an expert in a domain, presumably because it takes that long to accumulate the relevant experience. (Also see Holding, 1985.) This is consistent with a claim we made in Chapter 9: There we argued that expert dermatologists routinely draw on remembered exemplars in reaching their diagnoses; part of their expertise, therefore, lies in having a large set of exemplars on which they can draw. (For further discussion of medical expertise, see Lesgold, Rubinson, Feltovich, Glaser, Klopfer & Wang, 1988; Brooks et al., 2000.)

Experts also have different *types* of knowledge than novices do. We have just suggested, for example, that chess masters are particularly conversant with higher-order patterns on the chess board, patterns often involving six or seven different pieces. Indeed, the expert may know a huge number of these patterns; it has been estimated that a chess master has roughly 50,000 different chess patterns in memory, compared to the 1,000 patterns known to someone who is merely a "good" player (Chase & Simon, 1973; also Bédard & Chi, 1992). Similar claims have been made for experts in a variety of other domains, including experts in the games of Gō, bridge, and poker (Gilhooly, 1988).

There are also indications that experts organize their knowledge more effectively than novices. In particular, studies indicate that experts' knowledge is heavily "cross-referenced," so that each bit of information has associations to many other bits (e.g., Bédard & Chi, 1992; Eylon & Reif, 1984; Heller & Reif, 1984). As a result, not only do experts know more, but they have faster, more effective access to what they know.

As an example of how this all plays out, consider the strategies chosen by experts when they are solving a problem. Both experts and novices make heavy use of means-end analysis, a strategy we discussed earlier in this chapter. However, in trying to reach their ends, novices often find it useful to work backward from the goal—to seek operators that will gradually make the goal state more and more similar to their current state. In contrast, experts are less likely to use this working-backward strategy (Bédard & Chi, 1992; Gick, 1986; Larkin, McDermott, Simon & Simon, 1980; Sweller, Mawer & Ward, 1983); instead, they work forward, from the initial state toward the goal.

One might think that the experts are using a risky strategy: If you start at the initial state and work forward, it is possible that the path you have selected might not lead where you want to go. However, this risk is relatively small for experts: Since they quickly recognize what type of problem they are working on, they realize what type of solution will be appropriate. Therefore, they are essentially guaranteed, as they work forward from their initial state, that they are moving in the right general direction.

Notice, then, that we are suggesting that experts work forward on a problem only because they recognize the type of problem and know how to tackle it. If this is right, then even experts will resort to the working-backward strategy with *unfamiliar* problems, problems that they cannot categorize. This is correct: When experts don't recognize a problem, they work backward from the goal to their current state, exactly as a novice would (Bhaskar & Simon, 1977; Gick, 1986). Thus, the expert's strategy choice is, in the end, dependent on the expert's knowledge base.

Finally, one other advantage for the experts should also be mentioned: In addition to their advantages in knowledge, experts are also, rather obviously, well practiced in working in their domain, well practiced in solving problems. As we discussed in Chapter 4, this allows the expert to "automatize" many tasks. Similarly, the expert has established certain routines for dealing with commonplace tasks or, as some would say, has "proceduralized" these tasks. In many cases, therefore, an expert will realize that a problem is functionally identical to problems met earlier and so will give the problem no further thought, relying instead on the well-rehearsed routine. (For discussion, see Anderson, 1982, 1983, 1987.)

## LIMITS OF EXPERTISE

There are important limits, however, on the function of (and advantages of) expertise. We have already suggested that a large part of an expert's advantage derives from his or her knowledge base: The expert knows more, and knows more higher-order patterns, than the novice does. However, if this knowledge can't be applied to a problem, then much of the expert's advantage will disappear. We've already seen some evidence for this claim: Experts generally work forward toward their goal in solving a problem, rather than working backward toward their current state. This contrast between experts and novices disappears, however, if experts fail to recognize a problem, and so fail to apply their base of knowledge.

Similarly, experts show no advantage in solving problems outside their domain. Thus, expert surgeons and psychiatrists show no special skill in solving cardiology problems (Patel, Evans & Groen, 1989). Likewise, in solving political problems, expert chemists do no better than novice political scientists. Both groups, however, are (by far) outperformed by expert political scientists (Voss, Blais, Means, Greene & Ahwesh, 1989; Voss & Post, 1988).

Finally, we should also note that, in some circumstances, expertise may actually convey disadvatages. Imagine that you want to solve a problem, but also want to remember the problem, later on. If you were an expert in that domain, you would pay little attention to the problem's details, and instead focus on the problem's gist or structure. This would help you in solving the problem, and also in remembering the gist. However, this emphasis on gist will probably undermine your memory for the problem's detail. Consistent with this suggestion, several studies indicate that experts are less able to remember problems' details and also commit many intrusion errors, as they import their own knowledge into the problem as remembered (Arkes & Freedman, 1984; also Adelson, 1984; Bédard & Chi, 1992).

Similarly, automaticity and a reliance on routine obviously help the expert in many settings but can also create problems of their own. For example, it's sometimes difficult for an expert to judge how easy or how difficult a problem would be in the *absence* of automaticity. As a result, experts are often quite inept in predicting which problems will be easy for a novice, and which ones will be hard (Hinds, 1999).

In the same way, an automatized routine can often be "run off" without much thought, and usually this is helpful. In some settings, though, this same reliance on automaticity can be problematic. For example, a reliance on routine can lead an expert to "compartmentalize" his or her knowledge, with *this* knowledge relevant to *that* routine, and then *this* knowledge relevant to some other routine. This can work against a full integration of the expert's knowledge and, in some cases, can undermine performance (Lewandowsky & Kirsner, 2000).

## Defining the Problem

As we have seen, one of the features of expertise lies in how experts *define* a problem. Novices seem to define problems in terms of their superficial features, and this guides how the novices think about the problem and how they try to solve it. Experts, in contrast, seem to define problems in terms of their deep structure or underlying dynamic. As a result, the experts are more likely to realize what other problems are analogous to the current problem and are more likely to benefit from analogies.

Notice, therefore, that there are better and worse ways to define a problem—ways that will lead to a solution, and ways that will obstruct it. But what does it mean to "define" a problem? And what determines how we define the problems we encounter? We turn next to these crucial questions.

## III-DEFINED AND WELL-DEFINED PROBLEMS

For many problems, the initial state, goal state, and operators are clearly defined from the start. In the Hobbit and Orcs problem, you know exactly where all the creatures stand at the beginning of the problem. You know exactly where you want the creatures to be at the problem's end. And you know exactly what operators you have available.

Many problems—including those we encounter in our day-to-day lives—are rather different. We all hope for peace in the world, but what exactly will this goal look like? There will be no fighting, of course, but what other traits will the goal have? Will the nations currently on the map still be in place? How will disputes be settled? How will resources be allocated? It is also unclear what the operators should be for reaching this goal. Should we try making diplomatic adjustments? Or would economic measures be more effective—perhaps some pattern of commerce through which nations become more dependent on each other?

Problems like this one are said to be ill-defined, with no clear statement at the outset of how the goal should be characterized or what steps one might try in reaching that goal. Many problems are ill-defined—"having a good time while on vacation," "saving money for college," "choosing a good paper topic" (Halpern, 1984; Kahney, 1986; Reitman, 1964; Schraw et al., 1995; Simon, 1973).

Problem-solvers have several options available when they confront ill-defined problems. An obvious option is one we have already met: Establish sub-goals. For many ill-defined problems, there may be well-defined sub-problems, and by solving each of these, one can move toward solving the overall problem. A different strategy is to add some structure to the problem—by adding extra constraints or extra assumptions. In this way, you might gradually render the problem well defined, instead of ill-defined—with a narrower set of options perhaps, but with a clearly specified goal state and, eventually, with a manageable set of operators to try.

This adding of structure to an ill-defined problem turns out to be one more way in which expert and novice problem-solvers differ: Before they even start working on a problem, experts spend time defining the problem and elaborating its problem states, far more time than novices spend (Voss et al., 1989; Voss & Post, 1988; Getzels & Csikszentmihalyi, 1976).

### FUNCTIONAL FIXEDNESS

Even for well-defined problems, there is often more than one way to understand the problem and

more than one way to structure the problem. We have already met an example of this, in the contrast between superficial and deeper-level descriptions of a problem. But other examples are easy to find.

Consider the "mutilated checkerboard" problem, described in Figure 14.14. The most obvious treatment of this problem represents it in terms of spatial positions. It doesn't matter how large the board is (as

## The Mutilated Checkerboard Problem

FIGURE 14.14

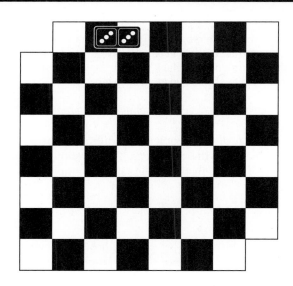

A checkerboard contains 8 rows and 8 columns, or 64 squares in all. You are given 32 dominoes, and asked to place the dominoes on the checkerboard so that each domino covers two squares. With 64 squares and 32 dominoes, there are actually many arrangements of dominoes that will cover the board.

We now take out a knife, and cut away the top-left and bottom-right squares on the checkerboard. We also remove one of the dominoes. Therefore, you now have 31 dominoes with which to cover the remaining 62 squares on the checkerboard. Is there an arrangement of the 31 dominoes that will cover the 62 squares? Each domino, as before, must cover two adjacent squares on the checkerboard.

Solving this problem usually requires a change in problem representation. Can you solve it?

## Solution to the Mutilated Checkerboard Problem

**FIGURE 14.15**

The squares on a checkerboard obviously have an alternating color scheme, and so the squares might be white-black-white-black (or any other alternating scheme). Therefore, if a domino covers two adjacent squares, it will necessarily cover one white square and one black. Said differently, we need one white square and one black square for each domino and so, more broadly, we need equal numbers of white squares and black squares—one of each for each domino.

On a "normal" checkerboard, that is easy—there are 32 white squares and 32 black, and so there are enough of each for the 32 dominoes.

Notice, though, that the top-left and bottom-right squares on a checkerboard *are the same color*. Therefore, if we cut away these squares, we no longer have equal numbers of white squares and black—we are left with 32 white squares, and 30 black. Therefore, we can't provide one square of each color for each domino. For the first 30 dominoes, we are fine—for each of these, we have one white square and one black. But, for the thirty-first domino, we are left with two more white squares, in need of cover.

Therefore, the mutilated checkerboard *cannot be covered* by the 31 dominoes!

The initial representation of this problem typically emphasizes spatial positions and various arrangements of the dominoes. The solution shown here, however, largely ignores these factors. Instead, the solution emphasizes the *color* of the checkerboard's squares.

long as the dominoes are sized accordingly), nor does it matter what colors the board is decorated in, nor how much the board weighs. The operators to consider also involve spatial positions—locating each domino here or there, en route to a solution.

But a rather different representation is possible, one that largely ignores spatial position, and instead focuses on the color of the squares. In this representation, different operators are relevant, different aspects of the problem are highlighted, and different aspects ignored. And it is this representation that leads speedily to the problem's solution. (See Figure 14.15.) Indeed, this particular problem is rarely solved if represented in spatial terms; the same problem is readily solved if represented with an emphasis on which colors get covered. Obviously,

then, how a problem gets represented is of considerable importance—with one representation making the problem difficult, while another representation speeds you toward the problem's solution.

As a different example, consider the "candle" problem presented in Figure 14.16. To solve this problem, you need to cease thinking of the box as a "container." You need instead to think of it as a potential platform, and so solving the problem depends heavily on how the box is represented.

As a way of emphasizing this point, we can compare two groups of research participants: One group is given the "equipment" shown in Figure 14.16—some matches, a box of tacks, and a candle. This configuration (implicitly) underscores the box's conventional function—namely, as a container. As a result, this configuration increases **functional fixedness**—that is, the tendency to be rigid in how one thinks about an object's function. With this fixedness in place, the problem is rarely solved.

Other participants are given the same tools, but configured differently. They are given some matches, a pile of tacks, the box (now empty), and a candle. In this setting, the participants are less likely to think of the box as a container and, as a result, they are more likely to solve the problem (Duncker, 1945; also Adamson, 1952; Glucksberg & Danks, 1968; Weisberg & Suls, 1973).

Functional fixedness is also evident in studies of the "two-string" problem (Figure 14.17). Few participants solve this problem, presumably because they are thinking of the pliers as a tool for grabbing and hold-

ing. To solve the problem, the pliers need to play a much simpler role, serving only as a *weight*, and participants will realize this only if they ignore the pliers' customary function. And, once again, we can make this problem even more difficult if we take steps to emphasize the pliers' standard function—if, for example, we use the pliers to pull a tack out of the table-top, while instructing the participant in the overall task. Under these circumstances, fixedness is maximal, and virtually no participants solve the problem.

### *"EINSTELLUNG"*

People also display other forms of rigidity in problem-solving, and this rigidity in general is referred to as *Einstellung*, the German word for "attitude."

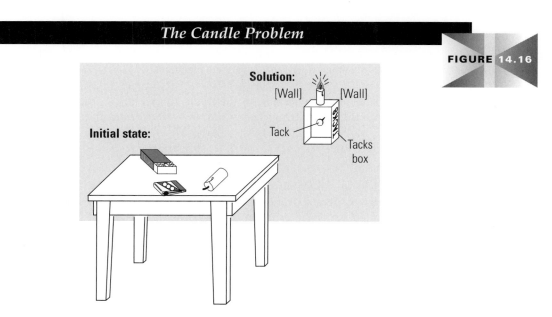

### The Candle Problem

**FIGURE 14.16**

**Initial state:**

**Solution:**
[Wall]   [Wall]
Tack
Tacks box

You are given the objects shown—a candle, a book of matches, and a box of tacks. Your task is to find a way to attach the candle to the wall of the room, at eye level, so that it will burn properly and illuminate the room.

What makes this problem difficult is the tendency to think of the box of tacks *as a box*—i.e., as a container. The problem is readily solved, though, once you think of the box as a potential platform.

FIGURE 14.17

### The Two-String Problem

You enter a room in which two strings are hanging from the ceiling. Your task is to tie the two strings together. Unfortunately, though, the strings are positioned far enough apart so that you can't grab one string and hold onto it while reaching for the other. How can you tie them together?

To solve the problem, you should tie the pliers to one string, then push them gently *away* from the other string. Then grab the *second* string, and wait until the pliers, as a pendulum, swing back to you. [After Maier, 1931.]

Functional fixedness provides one example of an *Einstellung* effect, but the classic demonstration of this effect employs the so-called water-jar problem. You are initially given three jars: A, which holds 18 ounces; B, which holds 43 ounces; and C, which holds 10 ounces. You have access to an unlimited supply of water. You also have a large, uncalibrated bucket. Your task is to pour exactly 5 ounces of water into the bucket. How would you do it?

The solution is to fill jar B (43 ounces), then to pour water from jar B into jar A (which holds 18). Twenty-five ounces remain in B. From this, fill jar C (which holds 10 ounces); 15 ounces now remain in B. Dump jar C, then fill it again from B. Now, 5 ounces remain in jar B, so you are done.

Once participants have solved this, we give them a new problem. Jar A now holds 9 ounces, B holds 42, and C holds 6. The goal is to end up with 21 ounces. We then give subjects a third problem: Jar A holds 21; B holds 127; C holds 3; you are seeking 100 ounces.

The series of problems is carefully designed, such that all can be solved in the same way: One starts by filling the largest jar (B), pouring from it once into the middle-sized jar (A), then pouring from it twice into the smallest jar (C), leaving the desired amount.

After solving four problems of this form, participants are given one more problem: Jar A holds 18 ounces; Jar B holds 48 ounces; Jar C holds 4 ounces; the goal is 22 ounces. Participants solve this problem the same way they have solved the previous problems. They fail to see that a different, more direct route to the goal is possible—by filling A, filling C, and then combining these (18 + 4). Their prior success in using the same procedure over and over renders them blind to this alternative.

More troubling, consider what happens if participants are given the "training" problems, all solved via the same path, and then are given this problem: Jar A holds 28 ounces; B holds 76; C holds 3. The goal is 25 ounces. The participants attack this problem by using their tried-and-true method: B minus A minus C twice. But this time the method fails (yielding 42 ounces, instead of the desired 25). When participants realize this, they are often stymied—their well-practiced routine won't work here, and they fail to see the much simpler path that would work (28 minus 3 equals 25). Remarkably, 64% of the participants fail to solve this problem, thanks to their history of using a now inapplicable strategy (Luchins, 1942; Luchins & Luchins, 1950, 1959).

In a sense, the participants are doing something sensible here: Once you discover a strategy that "gets the job done," you might as well use the strategy. Correspondingly, once you discover a strategy that works, there is little reason to continue hunting for other, alternative strategies. It is a little unsettling, though, that this mechanization of problem-solving prevents people from discovering other, simpler strategies. Worse, this mechanization actually interferes with problem-solving: Once they have learned one strategy for solving water-jar problems, people seem less able to discover new strategies. When a new problem arrives that is *not* solvable with the prior formula, performance suffers.

### PROBLEM-SOLVING SET

In the water-jar experiments, people develop a strategy within the experiment itself and then continue applying that strategy in a rigid, mechanical fashion. In other cases, though, people seem to approach a problem *from the start* with certain assumptions—about how the problem should be handled and what sorts of strategy are likely to be productive. These starting assumptions are referred to as a **problem-solving set**. Often, this "set" is quite helpful and gets someone started on the right path toward solving the problem. If the set turns out to be inappropriate, though, problem-solving suffers.

For example, consider Figure 14.18. In tackling this problem, people seem to assume that the lines they

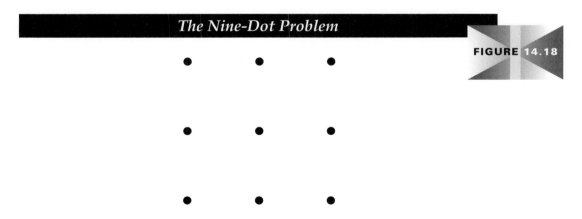

## The Nine-Dot Problem

FIGURE 14.18

Draw four straight lines, passing through all nine of these dots, without lifting your pencil from the page.

draw must remain within the "square" formed by the nine dots. This assumption isn't stated anywhere in the problem; instead, it is supplied by the problem-solver. As it turns out, though, this assumption is *wrong*: To solve this problem, your lines must go *outside* this square (Figure 14.19). It is not surprising, then, that people find this problem quite hard.

Problem-solving sets are often characterized as bad things, blocking the solution of a problem. Indeed, in the nine-dot problem, people do seem misled by their initial set. Likewise, functional fixedness can also be counted as a species of problem-solving set and, as we have seen, fixedness often impedes problem solution. These points must be balanced, though, with an equal emphasis on the *benefits* of a problem-solving set. In confronting an ill-defined problem, you often need to add some structure. If you add an appropriate structure, this will help problem-solving enormously. "Adding structure" is, of course, equivalent to approaching the problem with a particular set.

Even with well-defined problems, the number of options you might consider as you work your way toward a solution is often quite large. In the terms used earlier, a problem-solving space can be enormous, involving many thousands of options. A problem-solving set, therefore, serves to narrow your options, which, in turn, eases your search for a solution. For example, in solving the "candle problem" (Figure 14.16), you didn't waste any time wondering whether Martians might be summoned to hold the candle in place. You also didn't waste time trying to think of ways to melt the thumbtacks, in order to transform them into a candelabra. These are obviously silly options, so you brushed past them. But what identifies them as silly? It is your problem-solving set, which tells you, among other things, what options are plausible, which are physically possible, and the like.

In sum, there are benefits and costs to a problem-solving set. A set can blind you to important options,

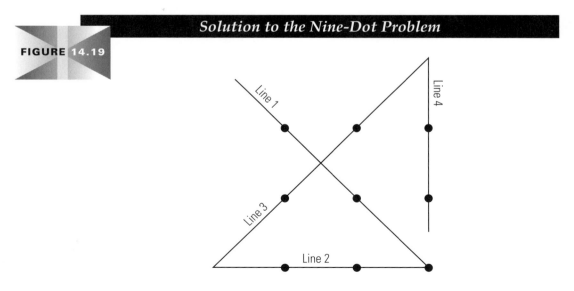

**FIGURE 14.19**

### Solution to the Nine-Dot Problem

In solving the nine-dot problem, people seem to assume that their dots must remain inside the "square" formed by the dots. However, the solution requires lines outside of this square.

and thus can, in some cases, be an enormous obstacle to problem solution. But a set also blinds you to a wide range of futile or impractical options, and this is a good thing: It allows you to focus, much more productively, on options likely to work out. Therefore, the key is not to approach a problem without a set. Instead, all depends on finding the right set.

## Creativity

Our argument so far can be easily summarized: For ill-defined problems, one often needs to make assumptions and to add constraints; otherwise, there are too many options to think through. Even for well-defined problems, there are often many ways to represent the problem, with some representations leading swiftly to a solution, while others render the problem quite difficult. Moreover, if one selects the wrong representation, it is often hard to "shift gears," thanks to phenomena like fixedness or *Einstellung*. In short, then, it seems that approaching a problem with the *right* set—the right assumptions, the right representation—helps us in important ways. But how does one find an appropriate problem-solving set? How does one figure out how to approach a problem?

### BRAINSTORMING

We have already noted that a problem's *solution* can, in many cases, be suggested by an analogy to a previously solved problem. In the same fashion, a *set* can also be suggested by analogy: If the current problem reminds you of a previously solved case, you are likely to adopt the same set that worked previously: You will make the same assumptions, you will try the same operations, as you did on the prior occasion. What if no analogy comes to mind? In this case, you will be forced to use some less insightful, more laborious strategy—perhaps trial and error, or hill-climbing, or working backward from the problem's solution.

What if you are already working on the problem and making no headway? Given our discussion so far, it seems plausible that you are being stymied by an inappropriate set. To help yourself along, therefore, you could try "relaxing" this set—you could try to be as open-minded as possible about how the problem might be approached. This will often help, for reasons that are quite straightforward: If you try being more open-minded, you might, by luck, stumble across a more productive approach to the problem. Likewise, if you continue rummaging through memory, seeking some alternative approach, you might well come across a useful analogue that you hadn't spotted before.

The suggestion, then, is that "relaxing" your set and "letting the ideas flow" can lead you to more ideas, and more options to be considered. This will, in turn, often suggest a new approach. Some authors, however, have suggested a more ambitious conception of what happens when you "let the ideas flow." In particular, some have argued that the ideas produced under these free-flowing circumstances will be *better* ideas, more creative ideas, than those produced with more deliberate, careful cogitation.

Relevant evidence comes from studies of **brainstorming**. This is a technique, pioneered by Osborn (1957), in which one really does try to "let the ideas flow." In brainstorming sessions, one tries to generate as many ideas and as many new approaches as possible. Criticism of these ideas is deliberately put on hold, to make sure the ideas are generated in a free, uninhibited fashion. Later, one can separate the wheat from the chaff.

A number of researchers have examined the output of "brainstorming sessions" and, while some of the evidence is encouraging, most is not. The uninhibited atmosphere of brainstorming does indeed increase the number of ideas generated, and often that is just what one needs. For these purposes, then, brainstorming is a good strategy. However, there is no evidence that brainstorming increases the *quality* of ideas being produced. (For reviews, see Baron, 1988; Gilhooly, 1988; Weisberg, 1986; for a more positive assessment of brainstorming, though, see Flower, 1980; Stein, 1975.)

A similar point emerges from a study by Weisberg and Alba (1981). They asked their participants to solve several problems, including the one in Figure 14.18. To help the participants along, Weisberg and Alba provided a hint: They told participants directly that the solution required lines outside of the square.

One might think that this hint will "free up" the participants' thinking, so that new ideas (including the solution) can flow forth. However, even with the hint, 80% of the participants still failed to solve the problem in the time allowed. It should be said that the hint did help, since, without it, *no* participants solved the problem. Nonetheless, the benefit of the hint was clearly modest, suggesting, once again, that "letting the ideas flow" provides no special path to problem solution. (Also see Dominowski, 1981; Weisberg & Alba, 1982; for an extraordinary extension of this finding with the nine-dot problem, see Chronicle, 2000.)

## MEASURES OF CREATIVITY

Brainstorming seems not to unleash a flood of creative ideas. Instead, brainstorming seems to involve memory search, the use of analogies, and perhaps the use of a greater range of heuristics. This helps, but there is nothing mysterious about it.

Surely, though, there is more to problem-solving than this. What about cases of *insight*, or cases in which one suddenly finds a new and creative way to approach a problem? These don't seem like cases of searching through memory for an analogy or cases based on heuristic use. What, then, can we say about these cases?

To tackle these questions, we first need to be more specific about what insight and creativity are. Psychologists generally define a creative discovery as one that is novel and also valuable or useful. Let's be clear, though, that this definition is still in need of explication: How do we decide, for example, if a discovery or a work of art is "valuable"? In the world of music, for instance, many new pieces have been reviled when they first premiered; years later, though, these pieces have been reevaluated and judged to be masterpieces. In these cases, we would first judge the piece of music not to be valuable and, therefore, the

composition of this music not to be creative. Later on, both of these decisions would be reversed. (For discussion, see Baron, 1988; Boden, 1991; Gilhooly, 1988; Hennessey & Amabile, 1988; Murray, 1959; Perkins, 1981; Stein, 1956.)

Even with these concerns, this rough definition of creativity has allowed research to proceed. Indeed, psychologists have sought not only to define creativity, but to *measure* it. For example, Guilford (1967, 1979) argued that the heart of creativity lies in discovering new, unanticipated approaches to a problem. Therefore, he sought directly to measure someone's effectiveness in this sort of "divergent thinking"— i.e., her ability to take an idea in a new, unprecedented direction. In his test of creativity, therefore, one is asked to think of new uses for a familiar object. How many different uses can you think of for a brick? (See Figure 14.20 for some suggestions.)

A different approach was suggested by Mednick (1962; Mednick & Mednick, 1967), who proposed that creativity often depends on finding new *connections* among ideas. His measure of creativity is designed to evaluate how readily a person finds these connections. The Remote Associates Test (or RAT) provides trios of words; your task is to find some fourth word that "belongs" with each of the three. A test item might be "snow, down, out." A good solution would be "fall" (as in "snowfall, downfall, and fallout"). Other test items are shown in Figure 14.21.

Both of these measures have received some validation. For example, individuals judged to be creative by their coworkers score somewhat higher on tests of divergent thinking (Guilford, 1967). Likewise, graduate students who score highly on the RAT are more likely to be judged creative by their advisers (Mednick & Mednick, 1967). These correlations are weak, however, so neither of these tests seems that effective at predicting creativity. Nonetheless, the correlations do suggest that these tests tap into at least some aspect of creativity. (For discussion, see Andrews, 1975; Nickerson, Perkins & Smith, 1985; Wallach, 1976. Sternberg & Lubart, 1992, offer a somewhat different approach to the study of individual differences in creativity.)

## Creativity as "Divergent Thinking"

**FIGURE** 14.20

Tests of divergent thinking require you to think of new uses for simple objects, or new ways to think about familiar ideas.

How many different uses can you think of for a *brick*?

As a paperweight.
As the shadow-caster in a sun dial (if positioned appropriately).
As a means of writing messages on a sidewalk.
As a step-ladder (if you want to grab something just slightly out of reach).
As a nut-cracker.
As a pendulum useful for solving the two-string problem.

Choose five names, at random, from the telephone directory.

In how many different ways could these names be classified?

According to the number of syllables.
According to whether there is an even or odd number of vowels.
According to whether their third letter is in the last third of the alphabet.
According to whether they rhyme with things that are edible.

Guilford argued that creativity lies in the ability to take an idea in a new, unprecedented direction. Among its other items, his *test* of creativity asks people to think of new uses for a familiar object. Some possible responses are listed here.

## CASE STUDIES OF CREATIVITY

A large part of what we know about creativity comes from case studies of enormously creative individuals, with the evidence often coming from reports from the individuals themselves. The poet Samuel Taylor Coleridge, for example, described in some detail how his poems came to be; the mathematician Poincaré wrote about how he discovered the proofs to certain theorems; Tchaikovsky wrote about his experiences in composing music; Crick and Watson have written a great deal about how they discovered the structure of DNA. (Many of these accounts are in Baron, 1988; Gilhooly, 1988; Weisberg, 1986.)

We need to be cautious, though, in interpreting these case studies. For one concern, these reports were often recorded years after the creative event, raising questions about whether the event was remembered correctly. (See, for example, Schunn &

Dunbar, 1996.) In addition, one might worry about some degree of self-service, as these creative individuals may well have sought to portray themselves (and their discoveries) in the most favorable light. Finally, it seems likely that creative discoveries often rely on nonverbal thoughts, and this raises questions about whether the discoveries can be adequately represented via verbal reports—even if the reporter is sincere and remembering accurately. (For further discussion of the limits of self-report, see Chapters 1 and 11; also Schooler, Ohlsson & Brooks, 1993.)

Even with these cautions in view, several researchers have argued that there is a systematic pattern to these self-reports. The classic formulation of this pattern comes from Wallas (1926), who argued that creative thought proceeds through four stages. In the first stage, **preparation**, the problem-solver gathers information about the problem. This stage is typically characterized by periods of effortful,

**FIGURE 14.21**

### Creativity as the Ability to Find New Connections

For each trio of words, think of a fourth word that is related to each of the first three. For example, for the trio "snow, down, out," the answer would be "fall" (snowfall; downfall; fallout).

| | | | |
|---|---|---|---|
| 1. | off | top | tail |
| 2. | ache | sweet | burn |
| 3. | dark | shot | sun |
| 4. | arm | coal | peach |
| 5. | tug | gravy | show |

Mednick argued that creativity lies in the ability to find new connections among ideas. This ability is measured in the Remote Associates Test, for which some sample items are shown here. The solutions are (1) spin (spin-off, top-spin, tail-spin); (2) heart; (3) glasses; (4) pit; (5) boat.

often frustrating, work on the problem, generally with little progress. In the second stage, **incubation**, the problem-solver sets the problem to the side and seems not to be working on it. Wallas argued, though, that the problem-solver was continuing to work on the problem during this stage, albeit unconsciously. Thus, the problem solution is continuing to develop, unseen, just as the baby bird develops, unseen, inside the egg. This period of incubation leads to the third stage, **illumination**, in which some key insight or new idea emerges, paving the way for the fourth stage, **verification**, in which one confirms that the new idea really does lead to a problem solution and works out the details.

This view of creativity has been endorsed by some authors but has been roundly criticized by others. For example, Patrick (1935, 1937) asked research participants to think aloud as they worked on a piece of poetry; her data largely conform with the four-stage view. (Also see Ghiselin, 1952; Harding, 1940.) In contrast, Weisberg (1986) argues that the data, including the historical accounts, do *not* fit with Wallas's formulation. Many of these accounts, he argues, do not include all four stages. In other cases, the four stages do occur, but in a complex, back-and-forth sequence. In still other cases, Weisberg suggests, the self-reports fit with Wallas's view, but there is reason to believe the self-reports are false. It is therefore of no interest that these *fictions* happen to conform to Wallas's scheme. (For further skepticism about Wallas's claims, see Baron, 1988; Weber & Dixon, 1989.)

### THE "MOMENT OF ILLUMINATION"

It seems clear, then, that the case studies of creativity are at best ambiguous, and this has led researchers to seek more persuasive evidence concerning creativity. Can we, for example, study creativity in a well-documented, well-controlled laboratory setting?

Consider Wallas's third stage, illumination. It typically signals a new *approach* to a problem, rather than a *solution* and so, at the moment of illumination, the problem is not yet solved and there is still work to be done. Nonetheless, illumination generally arrives with the conviction that—at last—you are on the right track. Is this correct? Even before solving a problem, can you detect when you are nearing the solution?

Metcalfe (1986; Metcalfe & Weibe, 1987) gave her participants a series of "insight problems," like those shown in Figure 14.22. As participants worked on each problem, they rated their progress, using a judgment of "warmth." ("I'm getting warmer . . . I'm getting warmer. . . .") These ratings did capture the "moment of insight": Initially, the participants didn't have a clue how to proceed and gave "warmth ratings" of "1" or "2." Then, rather abruptly, they saw how to solve the problem and, at that instant, their "warmth ratings" shot up to the top of the scale.

To understand this pattern, though, we need to look separately at those participants who subsequently announced the *correct* solution to the problem, and those who announced an *incorrect* solution.

As you can see in Figure 14.23, the pattern is the same for these two groups. Thus, some participants announce that they are getting "hot," and moments later solve the problem. Other participants make the same announcement, and moments later slam into a dead end. Indeed, if there is any difference at all between these two groups, it appears that the participants who are on the *wrong* track are more confident in their progress than those who are on the right track.

These data suggest that there's nothing magical about the "moment of illumination," nothing special about the "Aha!" experience. Sometimes we say "Aha!" when we finally perceive the right path. Just as often, though, and just as fervently, we say "Aha!" when we discover an apparently promising dead end. (For more on insight, illumination, and how one overcomes a problem-solving impasse, see Knoblich et al., 1999; Sternberg & Davidson, 1995.)

## Studies of "Insight Problems"

**FIGURE 14.22**

### Problem 1

A stranger approached a museum curator and offered him an ancient bronze coin. The coin had an authentic appearance and was marked with the date 544 B.C. The curator had happily made acquisitions from suspicious sources before, but this time he promptly called the police and had the stranger arrested. Why?

### Problem 2

A landscape gardener is given instructions to plant four special trees so that each one is exactly the same distance from each of the others. How could the trees be arranged?

As participants worked on these problems, they were asked to judge their progress, using an assessment of "warmth" ("I'm getting warmer . . . I'm getting warmer . . . I'm getting hot!"). For the first problem, notice that no one in the year 544 B.C. realized that it was 544 B.C.—that is, no one could have known that Christ would be born exactly 544 years later. For the second problem, the gardener needs to plant one of the trees at the top of a hill, and then plant the other three at the base of the hill, with the three together forming an equilateral triangle, and with the four forming a triangle-based pyramid (i.e., a tetrahedron).

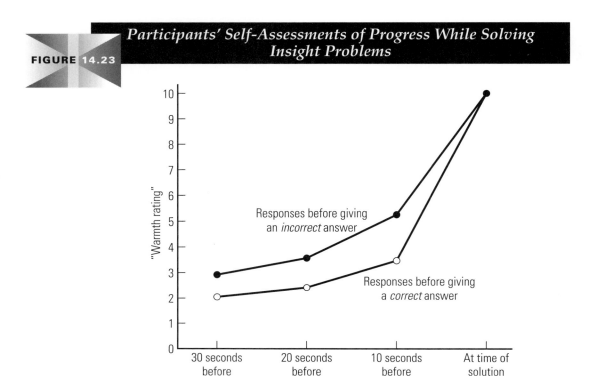

**FIGURE 14.23**

*Participants' Self-Assessments of Progress While Solving Insight Problems*

Initially, participants had little idea about how to proceed with these problems, and gave very low "warmth" ratings. Then, abruptly, they saw how to solve the problem and, at that moment, their "warmth ratings" shot up to the top of the scale. Importantly, though, the same pattern was observed for participants who then announced a *correct* solution to the problem *and* for those who then announced an *incorrect* solution. Thus, it seems that participants really *can't tell* when they are on the verge of correctly solving a problem. Sometimes, they shout "Aha!" only to slam into a dead end a moment later.

### INCUBATION

What about Wallas's second stage, the stage of "incubation?" In this stage, you will recall, problem-solvers seem to set the problem aside, but (allegedly) they continue to work on it unconsciously and, as a result, make considerable progress.

Many people find this an appealing idea, since most of us have had an experience along these lines: You are working on a problem, but getting nowhere.

After a while, you give up and turn your thoughts to other matters. Some time later, though, you try the problem again and are able to solve it. Or perhaps, later on, you are thinking about something altogether different, when the solution suddenly "pops" into your thoughts.

Many examples of this pattern have been recorded, with a number of authors pointing out that great scientific discoveries have often been made in this manner (e.g., Kohler, 1969). As a more modest example, consider the tip-of-the-tongue (T.O.T.) phenomenon, which we described in Chapter 8. In this phenomenon, you are struggling to think of a specific word, but can't. Often, your best strategy is to give up and try again later. When you do, there is a reasonable likelihood that the word will come to you.

Let's be careful, though, how we interpret these observations. After you "give up" on finding the word, are you unconsciously continuing to search for it? If so, then your subsequent discovery is presumably the fruit of this unconscious work. But here is a different way to think about the facts: Notice that, when you return to a problem, you are, quite simply, devoting more time to it: First you worked on the problem for five minutes, then you set the problem aside for an hour, and then you worked on the problem for another five minutes, and solved it. Did your hour's break help you? Perhaps the problem simply required ten minutes of work. In that case, you would have solved it in the second try, with or without the break.

This hypothesis is easy to test: We can allow one group of participants to work on a problem for ten minutes. A second group is allowed to work on the same problem for five minutes, then they are interrupted and forced to work on something else for a while. Then, this second group is allowed to return to the initial problem, for another five minutes. Thus, in the end, both groups have worked on the problem for ten minutes. If time away from the problem allows incubation, then participants in the second group should benefit from the interruption, and should be more likely to solve the problem than those given no time away (and hence no opportunity for incubation).

Many studies designed in this way have been carried out, and the results are at best mixed. A few studies have shown improved problem-solving after an interruption, consistent with the incubation claim. A large number of studies, however, have shown no such advantage. (See, among others, Dominowski & Jenrick, 1972; Dorfman et al., 1996; Fulgosi & Guilford, 1968; Gilhooly, 1999; Goldman, Wolters & Winograd, 1992; Murray & Denny, 1969; Olton, 1979; Olton & Johnson, 1976; Peterson, 1974.) As a consequence, many researchers are skeptical about the claim that incubation fosters problem solution.

Let's focus, though, on just those studies that do show a benefit of time away from the problem, that *do* show that an interruption promotes problem-solving. How should we interpret these findings? Wallas's explanation, of course, is that the interruption allows unconscious problem-solving activity. Others, however, offer more prosaic hypotheses. In some studies, the interruption may simply provide an opportunity for problem-solvers to gather new information. Perhaps, during the time away from the problem, they stumble across some clue in the environment, or in their own memories, that will help them when they return to the problem. In this case, time away will aid problem solution, but not because of any unconscious work on the problem.

In other cases, the interruption may simply allow problem solvers a "fresh start" on a problem. Their early efforts with a problem may have been tiring, or frustrating, and the interruption may provide an opportunity for this frustration or fatigue to dissipate. Likewise, their early efforts with a problem may have been dominated by a particular approach, a particular set. If they put the problem aside for a while, it is possible for them to forget these earlier tactics, and this will then free them to explore other, more productive, avenues.

In fact, there is some evidence for this "forgetting" account of incubation. Smith and Blankenship (1989, 1991) gave their participants puzzles to solve like those shown in Figure 14.24. To make these problems even more difficult, clues were given but, for many of the problems, the clues were designed to be misleading. Control participants had a minute to work on each puzzle; other participants worked on each puzzle for 30 seconds, then were interrupted, and later returned to the puzzle for an additional 30 seconds.

This interruption did improve performance, so that problem solution was more likely for the "incubation" group. Crucially, though, Smith and Blankenship also tested participants' memory for the misleading clues, and found that the incubation participants were less likely to remember the clues. Smith and Blankenship argue that this forgetting is what created the "incubation" advantage: After the interruption, participants were no longer misled by the bad clues, and their per-

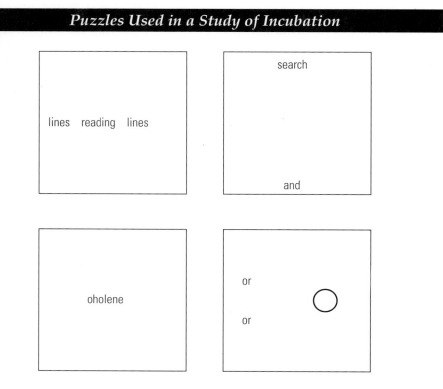

**Puzzles Used in a Study of Incubation**

FIGURE 14.24

Participants had to figure out what familiar phrase was represented by each picture. For example, the first picture represents the phrase "reading between the lines"; the second represents the phrase "search high and low"; the third represents "a hole in one"; the fourth represents "double or nothing." For some stimuli, these pictures were accompanied by helpful clues (for example, the last picture might be accompanied by the word "nothing"). For other stimuli, the clues were *misleading* (e.g., the third picture might be accompanied by the clue "chemical"). Time away from these puzzles, however, allowed participants to *forget* the misleading cues, and as a result, they were no longer misled by the clues, and were more likely to solve the puzzles. [After Smith & Blankenship, 1989, 1991.]

formance improved accordingly. (Also see Anderson, 1981; Smith & Vela, 1991. For more on why "time-off" can aid memory search, see Chapter 8.)

Let's emphasize, though, that it is *not* the problem itself that participants forget; instead, they forget their own *strategies*, and their unproductive lines of attack on the problem. Indeed, evidence suggests we are quite likely to remember problems we have not yet solved—more likely, in fact, than we are to remember problems we *have* solved. (For classic data, see Zeigarnik, 1927; for more recent findings, see Patalano & Seifert, 1994.) This memory pattern may actually contribute to the romance that surrounds incubation: We are particularly likely to recall unsolved problems, and therefore we are likely to return regularly to these problems, trying them again and again. As a consequence, we are likely, sooner or later, to discover the solution. But this doesn't speak to the utility of incubation. Instead, it testifies to the value of repeated efforts, and repeated tries, in tackling any difficult task.

## THE NATURE OF CREATIVITY

One stands in awe of creative geniuses like DaVinci, Einstein, or Mozart. So remarkable are their accomplishments, so different from what you and I produce, that it is natural to assume their thought processes are no less distinctive. You and I, equipped with heuristics and analogies, have troubles enough with Hobbits and Orcs. It seems unlikely, therefore, that these same intellectual tools could have led to the creativity obvious in great works of art, great innovations of science, or great inventions. The presumption, then, is that this creativity must arise from some other source—some different form of thinking, some other approach to problem-solving.

Of course, we have not studied DaVinci or Mozart in the laboratory, nor have we asked our research participants to create great art or great inventions. Nonetheless, one might hope that the laboratory data would provide some hint of this "special" form of thinking, this "other" approach to problem-solving. What the data show, though, is much more mundane. On the positive side, we have seen that brainstorming—a technique alleged to promote creative thinking—does lead to new ideas. There is little evidence, though, that brainstorming leads to *better* or more *creative* ideas, compared to other, more careful, forms of thought.

Likewise, it is clear that people do sometimes experience a sense of "illumination" when working on a problem, as though they have suddenly achieved some deep insight into the problem. When we closely examine it, though, we find that there is nothing magical about this "moment of illumination." This experience seems to occur when someone discovers a new line of attack on the problem. In essence, the person realizes that he now has new things to try, new approaches to explore. However, with this expe-

rience comes no guarantee of subsequent success. In many cases, people stumble onto a new approach and shout "Aha!" only to discover that the new approach leads them no closer to their goal.

Similarly, the topic of incubation has fascinated many authors, and much has been written about the role of incubation within the creative process. However, the evidence for incubation is uneven: It is unclear whether time off from a problem provides any consistent benefit, in contrast to continued effort on the same problem. Even when an "incubation" effect is observed, the mechanisms behind the effect are unclear. There is no persuasive evidence for an unconscious process of problem-solving. Instead, incubation seems best explained in terms of dissipation of fatigue, opportunity for discovering new clues, forgetting of previous false starts, and the like.

Finally, we have seen that participants in the laboratory do, sometimes, produce ideas that seem genuinely creative—consider the hip exerciser, in Figure 14.7. However, there is every reason to believe that these creative ideas are the product of processes similar to the ones already discussed—heuristics, analogies, and the like. (For discussion, see Finke, 1990; Finke, Ward & Smith, 1992.) For that matter, there is some indication that creativity *outside* of the lab can also be understood in these terms. (Cf. Gruber, 1989; McGuire, 1989; Simonton, 1989; Weber, 1993; Weisberg, 1986.)

Given all these results, is it possible that there is nothing "special" about the mental processes underlying creativity? To be sure, the creative *product* is extraordinary, but could it be that this product is the result of the same processes, the same forms of thinking, as more "ordinary" thought? Several authors have endorsed this idea, arguing that we need no special mental mechanisms to explain creativity. (See, for example, Goldenberg et al., 1999; Langley & Jones, 1988; Perkins, 1981; Sternberg, 1988; Weisberg, 1986, 1988.) The "ingredients" of creativity, in other words, are available to all of us—or, perhaps, *would* be available, if we simply acquired expertise in the relevant domain.

What, then, is so special about Newton, or Picasso, or Bach? The possibility before us is that these individuals did *not* rely on some special intellectual tools or some extraordinary thought processes in attaining their towering greatness. Instead, perhaps these individuals used the same tools, and the same processes, as every other human. What distinguished these extraordinary individuals, then, was that they had *all* of the right tools, and *all* of the right ingredients, and it was this convergence of ordinary elements that allowed their extraordinary achievements.

In other words, great scientists, artists, and inventors may rely on the same strategies as anyone else. What makes these people great, though, is that they have the heuristics, and the expertise, and just the right training and the right opportunities, and plenty of motivation, and, importantly, a personality of just the right sort. Very few people have *all* these ingredients, and it is the convergence of these elements that may, perhaps, be the recipe for achieving monumental creativity.

Is this the final word on creativity? Probably not. It does look like there is less to incubation, illumination, and brainstorming than first meets the eye. Nonetheless, a number of concerns remain. For one, it is certainly possible that we have not yet figured out how to study creativity in the laboratory. Perhaps something in the studies we have reviewed discourages creativity. In that case, creativity, no matter what its nature, might not appear in the data. Likewise, perhaps we haven't been studying the right people. Yes, creative inventions have been produced in the lab but, as we acknowledged, Darwin has not participated in our laboratory studies, nor has Beethoven or Georgia O'Keeffe. If we have uncovered no extraordinary "creative process," perhaps that is because we have not yet studied "true creativity" in the laboratory.

Yet another concern lies in what still remains *unsaid* about creativity. We have suggested that creative problem solutions (just like problem solutions in general) rely on memory search, as we seek out related problems or relevant principles. But how exactly does this memory search proceed? Is it possible that this memory search involves a different dynamic for creative discoveries? These are important questions; until they are adequately addressed, we must remain open-minded about what creativity involves and

what creativity is. For the moment, creativity appears to involve no special or magical processes. Quite plainly, though, the final word on creativity has not yet been written. (For further discussion of these themes, see Baer, 1993; Baron, 1988; Boden, 1991, 1994; Gruber, 1981; Holyoak & Thagard, 1989; Koestler, 1964; Langley & Jones, 1988; Langley, Simon, Bradshaw & Zytkow, 1987; Simonton, 1988; Sternberg & Lubart, 1992, 1996; Mednick, 1962.)

## Chapter Summary

1. Problem-solving is often likened to a process of search, in which one seeks a path leading from a starting point to the goal. In many problems, though, there are far too many paths to allow a search of each, and this is why *problem-solving heuristics* are crucial. Heuristics applicable to a wide range of problems include *hill climbing, means-end analysis,* and *working backward* from the goal.

2. Problem-solving is also often aided by mental models, visual images, or diagrams. For some purposes, these work equally well, but each has its own advantages. Visual images are easily adjusted if one wishes to change the size or position of some element. Diagrams, in contrast, have the advantage of standing independent of our interpretation of them, and this can facilitate reinterpretation.

3. An important way to develop theories of problem-solving is by translating the theory into a computer model. These models have been reasonably successful in solving a range of problems, and have also provided practical advantages—allowing investigators, for example, to discover the obstacles to problem-solving in a fashion that can then guide instruction.

4. *Analogies* to earlier-solved problems are often helpful, but, nonetheless, analogies seem to be underused by many problem-solvers. Analogy use is most likely if the problem now underway is similar in superficial ways to the (potential) analogue; these similarities help remind the problem-solver of the analogue, and also help him map the analogue onto the current problem. Analogy use can be promoted,

however, by suitable instruction. For example, people are more likely to find analogues (and so more likely to solve problems) if they focus on a problem's *deep structure*, rather than its surface characteristics.

5.  Experts in a domain generally pay more attention to a problem's underlying structure, rather than its surface form, and this helps the experts find and use analogues. Focusing on the problem's underlying structure also helps the experts to break the problem into *sub-problems*. There are, however, also disadvantages associated with expertise: For example, experts' reliance on routine can lead to a compartmentalization of their knowledge.

6.  The likelihood of solving a problem is enormously influenced by *problem-solving set*—how someone perceives or defines the problem. The problem definition can include unnoticed assumptions about the form the solution must take, assumptions about the use or function of elements contained within the problem, and also assumptions about what types of procedure one should try in solving the problem. These various forms of problem-solving set are usually helpful, because they guide the problem-solver away from pointless lines of attack on the problem. But problem-solving set can also be an obstacle to problem-solving—if, for example, the solution requires a change in the set.

7.  Investigators interested in creativity have often relied on detailed case studies of famous creative individuals. These case studies are said to reflect four stages of problem-solving: *preparation, incubation, illumination,* and *verification.* However, the case-study evidence is in some ways problematic. One concern is that self-reports about creativity may be inaccurate.

8.  Careful studies of creativity have provided little evidence to suggest that creativity involves special or exotic processes. For example, *brainstorming* is often mentioned as a technique for promoting uninhibited *divergent thinking,* but studies indicate that brainstorming increases only the quantity of ideas produced, not the quality. Similarly, *incubation* is often mentioned as a form of unconscious problem-solving, but studies indicate that the benefits of incubation, when they occur, can be understood in simpler terms—recovery from fatigue, or the forgetting of unfruitful earlier approaches. In the same way, the moment of *illumination* seems to indicate only that the problem-solver has located a new approach to a problem; in many cases, this new approach ends up leading to a dead end.

9.  In light of these data, many authors have suggested that creativity may simply be the extraordinary product that results from an assembly of ordinary elements—elements that include cognitive processes (memory search through spreading activation, heuristics, etc.), and also emotional and personality characteristics that foster the processes and circumstances needed for creativity.

# Conscious Thought, Unconscious Thought

It was only a bit more than a century ago that the field of psychology emerged as a separate discipline, distinct from philosophy or biology. And in those early years of our field, the topic of *consciousness* was a central concern: In Wilhelm Wundt's laboratory in Germany, researchers sought to understand the "elements" of consciousness. William James, in America, sought to understand the "stream of consciousness."

However, in its eagerness to be objective and scientific, the young field of psychology soon rejected this focus on consciousness, arguing that this research was both subjective and unscientific. By the early twentieth century, the topic of consciousness was largely gone from psychological research, and little was written on the topic for the next half-century. As we have seen in the previous chapters, though, psychologists have now realized that we *can* do scientific research on this topic, and so the field is, once again, ready to explore the issue of consciousness.

There is certainly much about consciousness that we still do not understand. What exactly is consciousness? How is it possible for a biological mechanism, namely the human brain, to be conscious at all? How is it possible for this mass of living tissue to be aware of itself, to be able to reflect on its own state and its own situation, to be able to feel such things as pain and love and gladness and remorse? Are other organisms conscious? Could machines (perhaps complex computers) be conscious? These questions remain the subject of debate, and generally speaking, philosophers have more to say about them than psychologists do. (For a survey of these philosophical discussions, see Churchland, 1988; Dennett, 1992; Flanagan, 1991. For other perspectives, see Crick, 1994;

Greenwald, 1992; Jackendoff, 1987; Kihlstrom, 1987; Marcel & Bisiach, 1988; Nelson, 1996; Reber, 1993.)

Psychological research has, however, illuminated several important issues about consciousness, and these will be our focus in this final chapter. Ironically, much of our progress has come not from examining consciousness directly, but by studying what happens in the *absence* of conscious awareness. This strategy has allowed us to detail what sorts of things can be done *without* consciousness, and this in turn has allowed us to refine our understanding of when consciousness is needed and, correspondingly, just what it is that consciousness contributes to our mental functioning. This understanding of what consciousness is *for* can then illuminate questions about what consciousness *is*.

As it turns out, much of the information we need for this discussion is already out in view—presented and discussed in previous chapters. Therefore, in this final chapter, we will draw repeatedly on topics covered earlier in this book. By weaving these strands together, we will see that we already have a great deal to say about the topic of consciousness.

## The Cognitive Unconscious

Throughout this book, we have seen that our intellectual life requires an elaborate "support structure." Thinking, remembering, and categorizing (to name just a few of our intellectual achievements) all feel like they're quick and effortless activities, but as we have seen, these activities depend on a great deal of work taking place "behind the scenes," and, in a sense, the describing of this "behind the scenes" action has been one of the main concerns of this book.

Psychologists refer to this "behind the scenes" activity as the **cognitive unconscious**—activity of which we are completely unaware but that makes possible our ordinary interactions with the world. Let's begin by cataloguing some of the things that go on in the cognitive unconscious.

## UNCONSCIOUS PROCESSES, CONSCIOUS PRODUCTS

Many investigators have found it useful to distinguish between the *processes* involved in our mental lives and the *products* that result from these processes. This distinction isn't clear-cut but nevertheless does provide us with a useful rule of thumb concerning what we are conscious of, and what we're not. In general, the proposal is that we are not conscious of our mental processes and are aware only of the products that emerge from those processes. (For discussion of the process/product distinction, see Miller, 1962; Neisser, 1967; Nisbett & Wilson, 1977; Smith & Miller, 1978; White, 1988.)

Consider these mundane bits of memory retrieval: What is your mother's first name? What is your father's first name? Odds are that the answers just "popped into" your mind. You presumably had no awareness of searching through memory, of "traveling" from node to node within a network. You surely had no awareness of activation spreading out from the node for MOTHER'S NAME, activation that then facilitated the retrieval of your father's name. Yet, as we saw in Chapter 8, there is reason to believe that all of these processes were relevant to this bit of memory retrieval. The processes were hidden from your view; all that you were aware of was the product—in this case, the two sought-after names.

Unconscious processes are also crucial in other domains. For example, in Chapter 3, we mentioned that our recognition of words is often guided by *inferences*, and that we are, in general, unaware of these inferences. This was pivotal in our discussion of proofreading; there we argued that we are systematically unable to distinguish letters we have *read* from letters we have *inferred*. That is why misspelled words often look correct, even when you are staring right at them. Thus, we are aware of the product (our perceptual apparatus reports that the word was "CAKE"), but not the process (we can't tell if the word was actually perceived or merely inferred).

Similar themes emerged in Chapter 7, when we discussed the seamless manner in which our experiences are fused together with our prior knowledge. As we saw in that chapter, our understanding of an event, as the event is unfolding, is often shaped by assumptions or inferences guided by schematic knowledge. Likewise, when we are trying to remember some previous event or scene, we are likely to rely on unnoticed schema-based inferences to fill any gaps in our recollection, and so, by using our general understanding of how events unfold, we are able to *reconstruct* that which we cannot recall.

As we have discussed, this use of schematic knowledge provides important advantages, because it allows us to grasp a huge range of inputs with extraordinary efficiency. This same process, however, can also lead to problems—for example, these "seamless" combinations can lead to memory errors. One way or another, though, this combination of "old" knowledge and "new" experience is done entirely without our awareness. This is evident, for example, in the fact that we are generally unable to distinguish elements we have remembered (i.e., drawn from memory) from elements we have reconstructed. This provides another case, therefore, in which we are conscious of the product (the event as experienced, the event as remembered) but not the process (perception *versus* inference; recall *versus* reconstruction).

## THE INFLUENCE OF UNCONSCIOUS ATTRIBUTIONS

The role of the cognitive unconscious is also evident in studies of *implicit memory* (Chapter 6). In these studies, participants are plainly being influenced by events they cannot consciously recall. Moreover, this influence often seems to require several steps of reasoning: "That name surely 'rings a bell,' but I'm not sure why. But the experimenter is asking me about famous names, and there are other famous names on this list in front of me. I guess, therefore, that this one must also be the name of some famous person." This inference surely sounds like something that we want to count as "thinking," but it is thinking, the evidence suggests, of which we are entirely unaware. (For powerful evidence that participants are indeed *unaware* of these effects, see, for example, Jacoby & Whitehouse, 1989.)

A similar pattern is evident in cases involving *source confusion* (Chapter 6). In these cases, someone seems to reason this way: "That face looks familiar to me, and the police think it's likely that this is the person who robbed me. I guess, therefore, that the face is familiar *because* I saw this person at the robbery." But, of course, it's not this reasoning that the person is aware of. Instead, the person simply (and sometimes *falsely*) "remembers" seeing the person at the robbery, and so can end up, in some circumstances, an unwitting victim of his own mistaken inference.

These examples suggest that our unconscious thinking can be rather sophisticated, with many layers of inference and reasoning. This is particularly likely when the unconscious thinking involves a *causal attribution*—that is, reasoning about the *cause* to which we should *attribute* some fact. ("The name rings a bell *because* it belongs to someone familiar." "The face looks familiar *because* I saw that person at the robbery.")

As another example, consider an early experiment by Nisbett and Schachter (1966). Their participants were asked to endure a series of electric shocks, with each shock slightly more severe than the one before. The question of interest was how far into the series the participants would go. What was the maximum shock they would voluntarily accept?

Before beginning the series of shocks, some of the participants were given a pill that, they were told, would diminish the pain, but that would also have several side effects: The pill would cause their hands to shake, would cause butterflies in the stomach, irregular breathing, and the like. Of course, none of this was true. The pill was a placebo and had no analgesic properties, nor did it produce any of these side effects. Yet this inert pill was remarkably effective: Participants given the pill and told about its side effects were willing to accept four times as much amperage as control participants.

Why was the placebo so effective? Nisbett and Schachter proposed that their *control* participants noticed that their hands were shaking, that their stomachs were upset, and so on. (These are standard reactions to electric shock.) The participants then used these self-observations as evidence in judging that they were quite uncomfortable in the experiment. It is as if participants said to themselves: "Oh look, I'm trembling! I guess I must be scared. Therefore, these shocks must really be bothering me." This led them to terminate the shock series relatively early. Placebo participants, in contrast, attributed these same physical symptoms *to the pill.* "Oh look, I'm trembling! That's just what the experimenter said the pill would do. I guess I can stop worrying, therefore, about the trembling. Let me look for some other indication of whether the shock is bothering me." As a consequence, these participants were less influenced by their own physical symptoms—they discounted the symptoms, attributing them to the pill, not to the shock. In effect, these participants overruled the evidence of their own anxiety and so misread their own internal state. (For related studies, see Nisbett & Wilson, 1977.)

Of course, participants' reasoning about the pill was entirely unconscious. It seems plain that they *were* thinking about the pill, since participants who received the pill (plus the instructions about the side effects) behaved in a fashion dramatically different from other participants. Nonetheless, when participants were specifically asked *why* they had accepted so much shock, they rarely mentioned the pill. When asked directly, "While you were taking the shock, did you think about the pill at all?" they responded with answers like, "No, I was too worried about the shock to think of anything else." Thus, once again we have a factor demonstrably influencing participants but entirely absent from their introspections.

More important, this study serves to illustrate the complexity of the processes underlying our conscious thoughts. The participants in this experiment seem to be reasoning about themselves in an intellectually sophisticated manner: They are observing "symptoms," generating hypotheses about those symptoms, drawing conclusions from this, and so on. Of course, in this case, the participants reached erroneous conclusions, because they had been misled about the pill by the experimenter. But that takes nothing away from what they are doing intellectually—and unconsciously.

## UNCONSCIOUS GUIDES TO OUR CONSCIOUS THINKING

So far, then, we have argued for a distinction between the *processes* involved in thought and the *products* that result from these processes. We need to acknowledge that there is room for debate about how exactly this distinction should be drawn, but as we've said, the distinction does support a useful rule of thumb about what we're aware of in our mental lives and what we're not. Thus, we arrive at a conclusion, but the steps leading to the conclusion are likely to be hidden from view. We reach a decision, but again, we are unable to introspect about the processes leading to that decision.

Sometimes, though, the processes of thought do seem to be conscious. Sometimes, you reason carefully and deliberately, weighing each step, scrutinizing each bit of logic. This surely sounds like a case in which your thoughts *are* conscious. Even here, though, an elaborate unconscious support structure is needed—a support structure that exists at the "fringe" or the "horizon" of your conscious thoughts (cf. Husserl, 1931; James, 1890).

To make this point clear, let's look a bit more closely at how this "careful, deliberate" thought proceeds: Often, when thinking in this manner, we try to put our thoughts into words. Perhaps we hold a silent debate with ourselves, formulating clear, verbal arguments for or against some position. Perhaps we even "think out loud" as we navigate our way through a difficult problem. What should we make of this inner narration, this internal monologue?

Consider how you would think about these two arguments:

The toy was in the carton.
The carton was in the closet
  Therefore, the toy was in the closet.

The pain was in his foot.
His foot was in his shoe.
  Therefore, the pain was in his shoe.

The first of these arguments seems acceptable, but not the second. Yet, in their wording, the arguments are obviously similar. If you were guided only by the wording, you would treat both arguments in the same way. But of course, you don't. Apparently, your thinking goes "beyond" the wording in important ways.

In this example, the arguments are out on the page for you to persue. The issue would be the same, though, if you were articulating these words as a verbalization of your own thoughts. In either case, there seems to be more to the argument, and more to the thought, than is directly expressed in the words themselves.

Related examples are easy to find. Thus, when you think, "I saw the sage," you are not puzzled about whether you saw an herb or a wise fellow. Likewise, if you were to think, "I saw the man with the binoculars," you might not even detect the ambiguity. In either case, your thought is embedded in a context of understanding that resolves the ambiguity, a context that tells you, in effect, how the thought is to be understood. The context isn't expressed in the words themselves, but is needed to avoid confusion, ambiguity, or slips. Notice, then, that even with explicit, clearly articulated, verbally expressed thoughts, thinking requires an unspoken, unnoticed support structure—a support structure that, in this case, specifies how the thought is to be interpreted.

Roughly the same claims can be made about nonverbal thought, such as cases in which you think carefully and deliberately about a mental image. Here, too, an unnoticed, unspoken support structure is on the scene, guiding how the image is to be understood. In Chapter 11, we referred to this support structure as a "perceptual reference frame," and there we argued that this frame renders a mental image unambiguous: A *picture* of a black disk on a white field is ambiguous—the same picture could also represent a white field with a circular hole in it, through which you see the darkness beyond. But your image of this scene is unambiguous—specifying what is figure, what is ground, what is close and what is far. (Also see Chapters 3 and 14.) This context of understanding isn't depicted in the image itself but seems, nonetheless, to be a crucial part of your thinking about the image. (For discussion, see Casey, 1976; Fodor, 1975.)

In fact, this point can be extended to many other domains: In our discussion of decision-making, we emphasized the role played by how a decision is framed (Chapter 13; also see Bassok, Wu & Olseth, 1995). In our discussion of problem-solving, we emphasized the role of set (Chapter 14). These again provide instances in which our thinking is done within a context, within a framework, which colors our thoughts and which plays a large role in determining the outcome of our thoughts—e.g., how a decision will be made or whether a problem will be solved.

We need to be clear, though, that one is usually not aware of this context of understanding—in decision-making, in imagery, or in verbally expressed thoughts. Our awareness, instead, is filled with the specific content of the thought—our ideas about the sage, our hypotheses about how the problem should be solved. The context of understanding certainly shapes this awareness, but is not itself part of the awareness—much as we see *through* our glasses, while we (typically) don't see our glasses. So here, too, unnoticed mental processes are guiding our thinking and shaping the sequence of our thoughts.

## AUTOMATIC ACTIONS

Yet another category of unconscious thought grows out of our discussion of automaticity (in Chapter 4) and also our discussion of routinizing problem solutions (Chapter 14). We will return to automaticity later in this chapter, when we offer some conjectures about what consciousness is *for*. For immediate purposes, though, note that automatization substantially broadens the range of activities performed without conscious supervision.

To put this in concrete terms, we noted in Chapter 4 that practice in a task has many consequences. Among them, practice allows us to perform the task without close monitoring and, in the end, without being aware of the task at all. We mentioned an extreme case in Chapter 4—the study by Spelke, Hirst and Neisser (1976) in which participants learned to read a book while simultaneously taking dictation. Participants were able to achieve this remarkable feat after many weeks of practice, but it's important to mention that the participants themselves did not realize what they had accomplished: When asked whether they could remember the material dictated to them, participants claimed they could not. When actually tested for their memory for this material, participants insisted they were guessing. But, in fact, the test indicated that participants had reasonably complete memory for the dictated material. Indeed, the evidence indicates that they had understood the dictated material's meaning and had integrated different sentences to form a coherent tale. Thus, the participants seem to have comprehended the dictated material without being aware of it, without consciousness.

### BLIND-SIGHT AND AMNESIA

We are accumulating an impressive catalogue of what can be done *without* consciousness. Further evidence comes from patients who have suffered one or another form of brain damage. Consider, for example, the cases of memory pathology that we described in Chapter 6. Patients suffering from Korsakoff's amnesia often have no conscious awareness of events they have witnessed or things they have done. If asked directly about these events, the patients will insist that they have no recollection. If asked to perform tasks that require recollection, the patients will fail. Yet the patients do remember these events in some sense— they are influenced, in their present beliefs and behaviors, by the specific content of the prior episodes. Apparently, amnesics can remember and can be influenced by their memories, with no conscious awareness that they are recalling the past. This is a pattern that Jacoby and Witherspoon (1982) dubbed "memory without awareness."

A similar pattern is evident in the phenomenon of "blind-sight." This is a pattern observed in patients who have experienced damage to the striate cortex. As a result of this brain damage, these patients are, for all practical purposes, blind: If asked to move around a room, they will bump into objects. They do not react to flashes of bright light, and so on. However, in one

experiment, visual stimuli were presented to these patients, and they were forced to *guess* whether the stimuli were (for example) X's or O's, or circles or squares. Quite reliably, these patients "guessed" correctly (Marcel, 1988; Weiskrantz, 1986, 1997). Similarly, if the patients were forced to guess where various objects were placed and to reach toward those objects, they tended to reach in the right direction with the appropriate hand position (given the shape and size of the target object). The patients did this, all the while asserting that the task was silly, that they could not see the targets, and insisting that they were reaching out at random. There is no indication that these patients are lying about their blindness. Instead, it seems that these patients can, in a sense, "see," but they are not aware of seeing.

### THE LIMITS OF INTROSPECTION

In the very first chapter of this book, we discussed some of the limits on *introspection* as a research tool. One concern lies in the *sincerity* of introspective self-report: In some circumstances, the nature of our thought is too personal to express, or perhaps embarrassing, or perhaps not well matched to our self-image. In any of these cases, we might be tempted to "clean up" our introspection before giving it a voice, and this obviously compromises introspection as a source of data.

In addition, self-report data are generally based on memory, and this invites questions about the accuracy of this memory. If the introspection is concerned with a distant event, then we might worry about schema effects or intrusion errors (see Chapter 7). Even if the introspection concerns a recent event, accurate memory is not guaranteed. This sort of recollection draws on working memory, and as we saw in Chapter 5, working memory is quite fragile. The contents of this memory can be displaced by any newly arriving thought, and this will undermine someone's ability to introspect about these displaced and therefore forgotten ideas.

In other cases, our thoughts are *nonverbal* in content (Chapter 11), and so, if asked to report on our thoughts, we must first "translate" them into words. This introduces a further risk, since our verbal descriptions might not capture the essence of our experience, and so the "translation" may give a distorted impression of our mental contents (for more on this issue, see Chapters 1 and 11).

These problems cut deeply into the value of introspection as a source for scientific evidence. But far worse problems for introspection are posed by our discussion so far in this chapter. Introspection assumes self-awareness, assumes that our mental states are "visible" to us, so that they can be introspected. But, as we've now seen, a great deal of our mental activity goes on *outside* of awareness, and so is, by its very nature, "invisible" to introspection. It seems, therefore, that introspection *must fail* as a basis for psychology, or for that matter, as a basis for self-knowledge.

Is this correct? Surely, there are cases in which we feel that we *can* offer a self-report on our mental processes. We are convinced that we remember the processes well and have no trouble expressing them in words. We feel no embarrassment about the events, so there is no concern about our "polishing" the report in any way. Can't we take introspection seriously in these cases?

A number of authors have suggested that introspection is problematic even in these "optimal" circumstances. Even at its best, they claim, introspection will often fail to reflect the content of our thoughts. In support of this view, Nisbett and Wilson (1977) reviewed a number of studies examining the accuracy of introspectively based self-report. In each of the studies they considered, some factor was manipulated and shown to influence the research participants' behavior. However, when the participants were asked *why* they had acted as they did, they steadfastly denied that this crucial factor played any role at all. Instead, they offered their own accounts about why they acted as they had—accounts that omitted the factor we know to be crucial. In short, then, it seems that the participants were simply *mistaken* about why they acted as they did. (For more recent surveys of evidence pertinent to these ideas, see Greenwald & Banaji, 1995; Uleman & Bargh, 1989; Bargh & Chartrand, 1999.)

As an example, participants in one study were presented with four pairs of nylon stockings, laid side-by-side on a table (Nisbett & Wilson, 1977). The participants were asked to evaluate the stockings and were asked, in particular, which was of the best quality. (In fact, the stockings were identical to each other, but the participants didn't know this.) Then, after participants had announced their choice, they were asked *why* they had chosen as they did.

The data revealed a pronounced effect of *position*: Participants showed a clear preference for the rightmost pair of stockings; indeed, this pair was preferred over the leftmost pair by almost four to one. When asked about the reasons for their choice, however, zero participants (out of 52) mentioned that they had been influenced by position. Participants were then asked directly whether the stockings' positions had influenced their choice; virtually all denied such an influence.

Similarly, participants in another study read a brief excerpt from the novel *Rabbit Run*. They were then asked to describe what emotional impact the excerpt had had on them and were also asked *why* the excerpt had the impact it did: Which sentences or which images, within the excerpt, led to the emotional "kick"? The participants were impressively unanimous in their judgments, with 86% pointing to a particular passage (describing the messiness of a baby's crib) as playing an important role in creating the emotional tone of the overall passage. However, it appears that the participants' judgments were simply wrong. Another group of participants read the same excerpt, but minus the passage about the crib. These participants reacted to the overall excerpt in exactly the same way as did the earlier group. Apparently, the passage about the crib was not crucial at all (Nisbett & Wilson, 1977).

Surely it is no surprise that we are often influenced by unnoticed factors. Likewise, it seems unsurprising that we often have little idea of *why* we acted as we did. ("Gee, I don't know . . . it just seemed like the right thing to do.") What is striking about these cases, though, is that the participants *think* they know why they acted as they did, but they are wrong. Their self-reports are offered with full confidence and in many cases, the participants report that they carefully and deliberately thought about their actions, and so the various causes and influences were, it seems, out in plain view. Nonetheless from our perspective as researchers, we can see that these introspective reports are mistaken—omitting factors we know to be crucial, highlighting factors we know to be largely irrelevant.

Perhaps we shouldn't be surprised by these results. After all, we have already argued that the *processes* of thought are often unconscious, and if so, then these research participants have no "special window" through which they can peer to discover why they acted as they did. What happens, therefore, when participants try to introspect? Chances are that they ask themselves, "Why did I act that way? Well, let me think about why, *in general*, people would act in a certain way in this situation. Then let me build, from that general knowledge, a plausible after-the-fact *inference* about why I acted as I did." In terms we used in Chapter 7, the participants are engaging in a schema-based reconstruction—building on generic knowledge to reconstruct what must have occurred in a particular episode.

Let's emphasize, though, that the research participants don't realize that this is what they are doing. Instead, they are convinced they are simply remembering their own mental processes—and remembering easily, since the target events took place just moments earlier. Hence these reconstructions *feel like* introspections.

Note the irony here. Because the processes of thought are unconscious, people are genuinely ignorant about why they acted as they did. Nonetheless they try to introspect. But introspection is just like any other mental activity, and so here, too, people are conscious of the product and not the process. Hence they are aware of the conclusion ("I acted as I did *because* . . .") but not aware of the process that led them to the conclusion. Hence they continue to believe (falsely) that the conclusion rests on an introspection rather than an inference. Hand-in-hand with this, they continue to believe confidently that they know themselves, even though, in truth, their self-perception is (in these cases at least) focusing on

entirely the wrong factors. (For more on this account of "introspection," see Sabini & Silver, 1981; Smith & Miller, 1978; White, 1988.)

## PROBLEMS CAUSED BY INTROSPECTION

Introspection is not faring well in our discussion. In Chapter 1, we considered a handful of arguments against introspection, and we have now added a number of other concerns: Much of our mental activity goes on outside of awareness, and so, by definition, isn't introspectable. And even when we're sure we *can* introspect, there is some danger that the introspection will be false, and indeed, some danger that the "introspection" isn't really an introspection at all.

In addition, at least some data suggest that introspection can even be *disruptive* of mental events—not just mischaracterizing thought, but also changing and undermining thought's progress. Why should this be? One possibility is that the attempt at introspection can lead someone to focus on just those aspects of thought that are easily verbalized. This may lead someone to give these aspects more attention than they deserve—both in the report and, crucially, in subsequent thinking. As a result, the requirement of self-report may redirect the sequence of thought, sometimes in ways that are counterproductive.

As an example, Schooler, Ohlsson, and Brooks (1993) asked their participants to solve a series of "insight problems" like the ones shown in Figure 14.23. After working on each problem for two minutes, participants were interrupted. Half of the participants were then asked to describe their thoughts about the problem, and the strategies they were using. The remaining participants spent the interruption time working on an unrelated activity (a crossword puzzle).

The results showed significant *disruption* from the self-report: Participants who had verbalized their thoughts were able to solve 36% of the problems; those who had not been asked to introspect solved 46%. Apparently, introspection can in some circumstances disrupt thought. (For related data, see

Fallshore & Schooler, 1995; Schooler & Engstler-Schooler, 1990; Wilson & Schooler, 1991. Also see Crutcher, 1994; Payne, 1994; Wilson, 1994. For evidence, though, that it sometimes helps to "think out loud," see Berardi-Coletta, Buyer, Dominowski & Rellinger, 1995.)

## THE COGNITIVE UNCONSCIOUS AND THE FREUDIAN UNCONSCIOUS

Let's pause to take stock. Our discussion so far in this chapter has clear methodological implications, and also theoretical implications. On the methodological side, we have obviously doubled and redoubled our concerns about introspection as a research tool. Introspections can be incomplete. Introspections can be false. Introspections can be disruptive. As it turns out, though, this does not mean that introspections have no value. You might have noticed, for example, that we did rely on introspective data in Chapter 14, since some of the evidence for heuristic use in problem-solving comes from "problem-solving protocols"—moment-by-moment narrations, by the problem-solvers themselves, of what they are thinking as they work on a problem. Thus, we can make use of *some* introspections, provided that these introspective data are handled with caution and, crucially, checked against other measures. (For advocates of this position, see Davison, Navarre & Vogel, 1995; Ericsson & Simon, 1980; Hayes, 1989; Stone, 2000.)

On the theoretical side, we have assembled a large catalogue of operations, and inferences, and achievements, all of which seem to go on within what we've called the cognitive unconscious. Before pressing ahead, though, we should probably say a few words more about what these "unconscious" steps are all about, and how the cognitive unconscious differs from other ideas about the unconscious mind popular in our culture.

Many people's understanding of the unconscious has been shaped by the ideas of Sigmund Freud. For Freud, the unconscious mind was a separate and largely autonomous player in the drama of mental life. The unconscious had its own wishes and goals, different from the wishes and goals of the conscious mind, and this set up a continuing struggle between the two, as each seeks control over our thoughts and actions. This struggle becomes all the more urgent when we realize that the unconscious mind includes a number of thoughts and memories that are highly threatening to the conscious mind, and so the conscious mind must work constantly to keep these thoughts out of awareness. Moreover, the unconscious mind is governed, Freud claimed, largely by instincts and a constant quest for pleasure; the conscious mind, he suggested, is governed largely by considerations of pragmatic reality. This contrast adds further fuel to the perpetual struggle between these two entities.

The unconscious described in this chapter, though, is entirely different. The cognitive unconscious is not in any way an "adversary" to the conscious mind, nor does it have wishes and goals at odds with those of the conscious mind. Instead, the cognitive unconscious functions as a sophisticated support service, working in harmony with our conscious thoughts and, indeed, making possible our conscious thoughts.

In addition, there is no indication that ideas are "confined" to the cognitive unconscious because of anxiety or pain. Quite simply, psychic distress is irrelevant to the procedures we have discussed. The cognitive unconscious is not, therefore, the place we hide our forbidden wishes. Indeed, there is remarkably little evidence that such a place exists. In other words, there is little evidence for the unconscious mind as Freud described it. Instead, the cognitive unconscious simply provides the machinery, the inner workings, of our ordinary intellectual functioning. The cognitive unconscious is rich and complex, and influences us in often surprising ways. But it is enormously different from the unconscious that Freud described.

With these points made, though, we should also acknowledge some of Freud's genuine contributions. For example, we have just argued that Freud's conception of the unconscious was inaccurate, but even so, Freud did play a major role in persuading the world that the unconscious mind—whatever its nature—did need to be explored and understood. Prior to Freud, many intellectuals believed that our thoughts, emotions, and actions were primarily shaped by some sort of rational thinking in the conscious mind, and Freud was surely correct in arguing against this conception.

Likewise, throughout his career, Freud generated both a body of theory and a large number of observations about human behavior. We have expressed skepticism about the theory, but we should nevertheless try to preserve Freud's observations and seek some other explanation for them. For example, Freud described a pattern that he called the *repetition compulsion*—a tendency to treat situations as if they were echoes of some previous setting and to act now as one did then. Freud explained this pattern in terms of repressed memories and wishes, but it seems more likely that we can understand this as another case of schema use (Chapter 7), in which you comprehend the current situation (or, perhaps, distort the current situation) by relying on some schematic frame drawn from previous experience. In this way, we can preserve the observation offered by Freud but provide a more promising explanation cast in cognitive terms. Other examples, translating Freudian phenomena into cognitive terms, are easily found. (For discussion, see Erdelyi, 1974, 1985; Erdelyi & Goldberg, 1979; Kihlstrom, 1999.)

## The Disadvantages of Unconscious Processing

Where, then, does all of this leave us? Clearly, a huge range of activities, including rather complex activities, can be accomplished unconsciously. So why do we need consciousness at all? What function is served by consciousness? Conversely, what things *can't* we do unconsciously?

### THE INFLEXIBILITY OF ROUTINE

Let's start with a simple case: When you first learned how to tie your shoes, you had to pay close attention

to what you were doing, and you were surely aware of your individual actions: First, you focused on crossing the laces. Then, with that done, you focused on putting the end of the right-hand lace through the loop. And so on. With practice, though, you became less and less aware of these steps, and indeed, if you were asked, right now, to list the steps of shoe-tying (as if instructing a child), you would probably *fail* to provide an adequate account. In a real sense, then, you have learned how to perform this task "without thinking about it." You have learned how to tie your shoes, in other words, in a fashion that depends on processes that are outside of your awareness.

What makes this possible, of course, is a reliance on *routine*. You can tie your shoes without thinking about it because you've performed this action thousands of times, and so, by now, you have stored in memory a complete, integrated procedure for shoe-tying. The individual steps are contained within this procedure, but you have no reason to think about the steps one-by-one. Instead, to tie your shoes, all you need to do is launch the overall routine. With that done, no further decisions are required; you simply repeat the familiar steps.

This reliance on routine has many advantages. For one, it allows mental tasks to run much more quickly, and we have seen many indications that speed is a desirable feature in our intellectual functioning. (This is, of course, one of the reasons we so often draw on "mental shortcuts" of one sort or another—see Chapters 9, 12, 13, and 14.) In addition, the routine seems to allow a "withdrawal" of attention from the task, and this allows you to devote your attention instead to other, more pressing, matters—including, in many cases, other aspects of your overall task. As an illustration, think back to our discussion of expertise, in Chapter 14. Experts, well practiced in their domain, no longer need to attend to the low-level details of task performance. This allows them to attend to higher-order factors, including the overall organization of the task. As a result, they are more sensitive to these organizational factors, better able to plan, and so on.

However, these advantages of routinization are purchased at a price: Reliance on routine sacrifices flexibility. As long as one is attending to the individual steps in a task, one has the option of substituting one step, or one sequence, for another. But if the steps are run off as a routinized sequence, this control is gone. One can elect to run off the entire sequence or not, but one cannot fine-tune the steps.

There are, in fact, a number of ways to demonstrate the inflexibility of routine. For example, the inferences used to fill gaps in memory generally serve us well—these inferences are likely to be correct more often than not and so genuinely supplement what we remember. However, as we have seen, these memory influences can on occasion lead us astray (Chapter 7). Knowing this, though, is no protection at all: Just as one cannot choose to avoid a perceptual illusion, one cannot choose to avoid memory error. The process of making inferences is automatic and effortless, but it is also irresistible. In the same fashion, the automatization of word recognition allows much quicker reading (Chapter 3) but also leaves us vulnerable to the Stroop effect (Chapter 4). Again, knowing about this effect is no protection—the processes are not open to control.

As yet another example, consider recent demonstrations of "implicit stereotyping" (Banaji & Bhaskar, 2000; Banaji & Hardin, 1996; Banaji & Greenwald, 1994; also Bargh & Chartrand, 1999). This term refers to the fact that many people have a number of automatic responses—often evaluative responses—to the names of an ethnic group. In most cases, these automatic responses are entirely unconscious but have an important influence, nonetheless, on subsequent judgments and decisions. What is important here is that these "implicit stereotypes" can be demonstrated even in people who want to be egalitarian and prejudice-free in their views. This desire, however, has little force: Implicit stereotyping, just like other forms of automatic processing, is not something one can control.

## WHY IS ROUTINE INFLEXIBLE?

One limit of unconscious processing, therefore, is in its *inflexibility*: Our unconscious steps seem to be automatic and uncontrollable; we can't "turn off" or "adjust" these steps even when we want to. And it's no accident that unconscious steps have this rigidity: Think back to the example of shoe-tying. Perhaps you are conscious of launching the entire routine (you decide to tie your shoes) but then, with that done, you have no need to supervise the individual steps of the procedure; instead, you're almost certain to attend to *something else* while the procedure is being run off. Indeed, you probably couldn't attend to the individual steps if you wanted to: Thanks to the enormous amount of practice you've had in shoe-tying, the individual steps run off at a high speed, with no detectable pauses between one step and the next.

Moreover, when you're tying your shoes, there are no decisions to be made, and, as a result, there's no need to check on the specific consequences of each step to figure out what's appropriate for the next move. There's also no need to monitor each step to figure out *when* to launch the next step; the timing, too, is built into the routine.

Now let's put these pieces together: You're not attending to the individual steps. You probably couldn't attend to the individual steps if you tried. You're making no individual decisions about what to do at this point or that within the routine. And you're probably not aware of the consequences or outcome from each step within the routine, and so you couldn't use the outcome as guidance for the next step even if you wanted to. These features of routine are crucial in allowing the routine to be fast, efficient, and not in need of our attention. These features, in other words, are what allows the routine to be run off unconsciously (freeing us to deal with other matters). But it is these same features that make the routine inflexible. The inflexibility, in other words, is an inevitable consequence of the fact that the routine has become unconscious.

## THE COST OF IGNORANCE

We have now identified one *dis*advantage associated with unconscious processing, and with that, we have identified one function that can be served by consciousness. Before we pursue this point, however, let's consider another (related) disadvantage of unconscious processing.

Earlier in this chapter, we argued that people are usually unaware of the *processes* involved in their thoughts; instead, they are aware only of the *products* that result from those processes. Oddly enough, this is often a good thing. To see the point, consider this analogy: When you are using your computer, do you need to know *how* it functions when it is (say) displaying a Web page on the screen? Probably not. Probably, you just want to see the Web page itself—that is, you want to see the product that results from the computer's (unseen, not understood) processing. In fact, it might actually be a nuisance to know too much about the computer's processing. As one worry, you might be *distracted* if you were burdened by the details of how the computer hunted through the Internet to locate the Web page, and how the computer retrieved the page's contents from the host site, and how the computer decoded these contents to produce the display you see on your screen. In addition, the displaying of all these details might slow down your computer by a lot. Better, then, to skip these details and simply go to the bit you really want: the Web page, complete with its text, graphics, sound, and whatever else it contains.

The logic is the same for mental processes: When you're in the midst of a conversation, you need, again and again, to search through memory to find suitable words for expressing your intended meanings. In this setting, you'd be distracted and slowed if you had to think through the mechanics of this memory search. Better, then, to keep those mechanics hidden from view. What you want to have in your awareness is the *words* resulting from the search, and not the search itself.

Cast in these terms, the "invisibility" of our mental processes is often an advantage, but like most advantages, it comes at a price: Sometimes it's desirable to know how we reached a particular conclusion or arrived at a particular decision, and in these cases, our ignorance can be a problem. In reading this page, for example, you have no reason to care which words you actually *saw* and which words you

merely *inferred*. That's because most of your inferences will be correct, and what you care about, presumably, is what the words on the page were, and not how you came to know about them. But imagine that you were proofreading the page. In that situation, you *would* care whether a word was truly seen or merely inferred, and in that situation, your ignorance about your own mental processes would be problematic. Similarly, imagine that you were an eyewitness to a crime. In that circumstance, you would certainly want to know which remembered details were actually memories and which were reconstructions or inferences supplied by you. But, of course, this is a distinction people seem unable to make, in large part because they are ignorant about their own mental processes.

## The Function of Consciousness

So far in this chapter, we've done two things: First, we've described the enormous amount of activity that goes on in the *cognitive unconscious*, and with that, we've documented just how much can be accomplished without conscious monitoring or supervision. Second, we have suggested that this unconscious processing carries both advantages and disadvantages: Routine is efficient and requires few mental resources, but is also inflexible. Similarly, our lack of awareness for our own mental processes probably buys us some speed and certainly spares us distraction, but it also leaves us *ignorant* about our mental processes in a fashion that can sometimes be disruptive.

All of this implies an obvious role for consciousness: In some circumstances, we gain mightily from the advantages associated with unconscious processing, and so we tolerate the disadvantages. But in other circumstances, the costs of unconscious processing outweigh the benefits; in these settings, we need to set aside the speed and flexibility associated with unconscious thinking and rely on conscious processes.

## THE CONTROL OF CONSCIOUSNESS

In many circumstances, of course, we cannot choose whether a process will be conscious or not. Some stimuli, for example, seize our awareness despite our best efforts at ignoring them; conversely, some processes go unnoticed no matter how hard we try to detect them. These facts are in some ways a reflection of our biology; they are in some ways a reflection of well-entrenched habits. One way or the other, though, in many settings we have no choice but to accept the pattern of advantages and disadvantages associated with conscious (or unconscious) mental events.

In other cases, though, we do have some degree of choice, with the choice implemented by how we elect to focus our attention. As an example, imagine a piano teacher telling his student, "Pay attention to what you're doing!" Presumably, this advice will emerge because the student has chosen to attend only casually to a somewhat-familiar action, and as a result, becomes the victim of habit—playing the piece mindlessly, and falling into the ruts defined by the routine. The piano teacher's advice, however, is designed to redirect the student's attention, moving him toward less of a reliance on routine, and correspondingly, more of an emphasis on conscious monitoring and supervision of the performance. (For more on "mindless" and "mindful" actions, see Langer, 1989.)

A different example is suggested by Jacoby, Kelley, Brown, and Jasechko (1989). They invite us to consider a case in which you have offered a suggestion to a friend, perhaps about how to write a paper, or how to deal with a troubling situation. Your friend rejects the idea, but then, sometime later, your friend reintroduces this same idea as if it were an insight that she just had. In this case, the unconscious retrieval of the earlier conversation serves as the source for your friend's "insight," but in the absence of any conscious recollection of the prior conversation, your friend claims the idea as her own.

This sort of inadvertent plagiarism might happen often if we simply relied on primed pathways and established channels in evaluating ideas or in choosing courses of action. Jacoby et al. suggest, however, that such plagiarism (and a variety of related problems) is generally blocked by the fact that we have the option, in thinking about the past, of conscious recollection. In other words, we don't choose our actions merely by relying on what's habitual, customary, or familiar. Instead, we *reflect* on our thoughts and also on the *sources* of these thoughts. This allows us to fine-tune our actions to the situation, and in particular, to avoid the sort of plagiarism just described. (Related examples are discussed by Baddeley & Wilson, 1994.)

These examples rest on the fact that we *are* conscious of much in our mental lives and can to some extent choose what we're conscious of. This allows us to control and regulate many of our mental processes, and in particular, to make sure that our actions are appropriate to the situation.

## CONSCIOUSNESS AS "JUSTIFICATION" FOR ACTION

The suggestion, therefore, is that consciousness does serve an important function: It allows us (in some settings) to monitor and reflect on our mental processes, and to adjust them as needed. This gives up the speed and ease of unconscious processing but buys us flexibility and control.

The ability to reflect on and assess our own mental states may also have another (related) function. As a way into this point, consider the blind-sight patients. We have so far emphasized the fact that these patients are sensitive to some visual information, and this tells us something important: Apparently, some aspects of vision can go forward with no conscious awareness, and with no conscious supervision. But it's also striking that these patients do insist that they are blind, and their behaviors are consistent with this self-assessment: They are fearful of walking across a room (lest they bump into something), they fail to react to many stimuli, and so on. How is this possible? Why don't these patients realize what they see? Why can't these patients take action (e.g., navigate across a room) based on what they see?

Roughly the same questions can be asked about amnesics. We have emphasized how much amnesics do remember, when properly tested. We drew from this the claim that memory encoding and memory retrieval seem not to depend on consciousness—this is the pattern of "memory without awareness." But note that we still need to explain the fact of amnesia itself: It is of course striking that the amnesic insists that he or she doesn't remember the prior event. How is it possible to retrieve a memory without becoming aware of the memory? Why don't (objectively) familiar events *seem* familiar?

Similar points can be made about neurologically intact subjects. For example, participants in one study were shown a list of words and then, later on, were tested in either of two ways (Graf, Mandler & Haden, 1982). Some were explicitly asked to recall the earlier list, and were given word stems as cues: "What word on the prior list began 'CLE'?" Other participants were tested indirectly: "Tell me the first word that comes to mind beginning 'CLE'."

The results show rather poor memory in the explicit test, but much better performance in the implicit test. This echoes many findings we have reviewed: We often have *implicit* memories for episodes we have *explicitly* forgotten. But note that there is something peculiar in this result: Participants could, in principle, proceed this way: "I don't recall any words from the list beginning 'CLE.' Perhaps I'll just *guess*. Let's see: What words come to mind that begin 'CLE'?" In this way, participants could use their implicit memory to *supplement* what they remember explicitly. If they did this, then the performance difference between the two conditions would be erased—performance on the explicit test would be just as good as performance on the implicit test. Given the results, though, participants are obviously not using this strategy. For some reason, participants in this situation seem unable to use their implicit memories to guide explicit responding.

What is going on in these cases? Why are we sometimes willing to rely on implicit memories in offering a response, and sometimes not? Why are blind-sight patients unable to *use* what they apparently can see? The answer, broadly, seems to be this: In many situations, we need to take action based on remembered or perceived information. In some cases, the action is overt (walking across the room, or making a verbal response); other times, the action is mental (reaching a decision, or drawing a conclusion). In either case, though, it seems *not enough* merely to have access to the relevant information. In addition, we also seem to need some justification, some reason, to take the relevant information seriously.

By analogy, imagine that you are trying to remember some prior event, and some misty thoughts about that event come to mind. You vaguely recall that friends were present on the target occasion; you have a dim idea that food was served. You might refuse to give these thoughts a voice, though, because you are not convinced that these thoughts are memories. (Perhaps they are chance associations or dreams you once had.) You will report your memory only if you're satisfied that you are, in fact, *remembering*. In other words, you need more than the remembered information; you also need some reason to believe that the remembered information is credible.

Against this backdrop, the suggestion is that the justification for action is generally provided by the conscious presentation of information. In other words, it is the nature and quality of our conscious experience that persuades us to take information seriously (or not to). When this experience is rich and detailed, this convinces us that the presented information is more than a passing fantasy, more than a chance association. When the conscious presentation is impoverished, though, as it seems to be in blind sight, or in amnesia, we fail to take seriously the information provided to us by our own eyes, or our own memory, and so we are paralyzed into inactivity.

This claim must be offered tentatively, since we are here reaching well beyond the evidence. Moreover, we have said little about what exactly it is, within the conscious experience, that makes information persuasive or compelling. Nonetheless, the unwillingness of blind-sight patients to acknowledge what they see, and the inability of amnesics to act on the basis of what they (implicitly) remember, does need explanation. Likewise, while it is clear that many judgments are routinely influenced by implicit memory, other judgments seem not to be, and this too needs to be explained. Our comments in this section provide at least one way to approach these issues. (For further discussion, see Johnson, Hashtroudi & Lindsay, 1993; Marcel, 1988; Reisberg & Heuer, 1989.)

## Consciousness: What Is Left Unsaid

Many of our remarks in this chapter have been speculative, and future research may force us to refine our conception of what consciousness is, and what consciousness is for. Likewise, it seems certain that consciousness has other functions in addition to the ones just discussed. For example, several authors have argued that consciousness plays a crucial role for each of us in forming our sense of who we are; this sense of self then plays an important part in guiding our thoughts and actions (e.g., Greenwald & Pratkanis, 1984). Here, too, further research is sure to illuminate these claims.

Perhaps most important, we should emphasize how much is still left unsaid. We have suggested that we must distinguish two broad categories of thought—one that is highly efficient but inflexible; and one that is maximally flexible but much slower. We have not explained, however, why this second category of thought needs to be conscious. Could there be a category of thought that is slow, deliberate, flexible, but unconscious?

In describing consciousness, philosophers speak of **qualia**—the "raw feels" of sensory experience. When you see a red apple, for example, you gain the information that a red apple is before you, but the red also *looks* a certain way to you, has a certain appearance that you are aware of. Likewise, when you feel pain, you *know* you are feeling pain, but you also have a specific sensory experience—the pain feels a certain way. These sensory experiences provide the basic "stuff" of which our awareness, our subjective states, is built. In these terms, we can refine our question: Could there be a category of thought that

is slow, deliberate, flexible, but *without qualia*? With such a category of thought, you would be sensitive to the relevant information—you would know that a red apple was present, you would know that there was pain—but you would not have the subjective experience. It would be like knowing that *someone else* was seeing red or feeling pain. In this case, you might know what this other person knows, but you wouldn't be experiencing what he or she is experiencing.

Does deliberate thought, reflective thought, require *qualia*? We have no ready answer for this; the data we have described do not bear directly on this question. (For further discussion of this issue, see Flanagan, 1991.) We close this chapter, therefore, as we began it—by emphasizing that psychologists can provide only a small piece of the puzzle of consciousness. There is no question, though, that the discussion will be informed by the data we have reviewed in this chapter—e.g., data about unconscious attributions, or blind sight, or implicit memory. This by itself—the mere fact that research can address these issues—is a source of considerable satisfaction for psychologists.

## Chapter Summary

1. An enormous amount of cognitive processing happens "behind the scenes," in the *cognitive unconscious*. In many cases, we are conscious only of the *products* that result from our mental *processes*; the processes themselves are unconscious. This is reflected in the fact that we are not conscious of searching through memory; we are aware only of the results produced by that search. Similarly, we cannot tell when we have truly perceived a word and when we have merely inferred the word's presence.

2. Unconscious processing can be rather sophisticated. For example, implicit memory influences us without our being aware that we are remembering at all; however, this influence is often mediated by a complex process through which we attribute a feel-

ing of familiarity to a particular cause. Unconscious attributions can also shape how we interpret and react to our own bodily states.

3. Even when our thinking is conscious, we are still influenced by unconscious guides that shape and direct our thought. This is evident in the effects of framing in decision-making and the effects of perceptual reference frames in perception and imagery.

4. The automaticity produced by practice can lead to yet another category of unconscious thought. With sufficient practice, we become largely unaware of the steps involved in an action, and may not even be aware of the outcomes of that action. Still further evidence for unconscious achievements comes from the study of *blind-sight* and *amnesia*; in both cases, patients seem to have knowledge (gained from perception or from memory) but no conscious awareness of that knowledge.

5. The breadth of the cognitive unconscious makes it clear that there are strong limits on what we can learn from introspection. Even when it appears that we *can* introspect, evidence suggests that our introspection sometimes does not reflect the content of our thoughts.

6. Unlike the Freudian unconscious, the cognitive unconscious is not in any way an "adversary" to the conscious mind, nor does it have wishes and goals at odds with those of the conscious mind. In addition, there is no indication that ideas are "confined" to the cognitive unconscious because the ideas are somehow painful or anxiety provoking.

7. The cognitive unconscious allows enormous efficiency, but at the cost of flexibility or control. Likewise, the cognitive unconscious keeps us from being distracted by the details of our mental processes, but in some cases there is a cost to our ignorance about how our mental processes unfolded, and how we arrived at a particular memory or particular perception. These trade-offs point the way toward the function of consciousness: Conscious thinking is less efficient but more controllable, and also better-informed by information about process.

8. In many settings, we have some degree of choice about whether a process will be conscious or not, with the choice implemented by how we elect to focus our attention. With attention appropriately focused, we are able to monitor and reflect on our mental processes, and to adjust them to some extent.

9. Consciousness may also serve to give us a sense that we have adequate justification for taking an action. This may be why amnesic patients seem unable to take action based on what they (unconsciously) recall and why blind-sight patients seem unable to respond to what they (unconsciously) see.

# Glossary

**activated node**   A *node* for which the current *activation level* has reached or passed that node's *response threshold*. An activated node will often trigger a response or summon attention, and can, in addition, serve as a source of activation for other nodes.

**activation level**   A measure of the current activation state for a *node* or *detector*. Activation level is increased if the node or detector receives the appropriate input from its associated nodes or detectors; activation level will be high if input has been received frequently or recently.

**active span**   A recently devised task for measuring working memory's capacity. In this task, participants are asked to remember items while simultaneously engaged in another activity. For example, participants might be asked to remember words while simultaneously judging sentences to be true or false.

**acuity**   The ability to discern fine detail.

**agnosia**   A disturbance in a person's ability to identify familiar objects.

**all-or-none law**   The principle that states that a neuron or detector either fires completely or does not fire at all; no intermediate responses are possible.

**ambiguous figure**   A drawing that can be readily perceived in more than one way.

**amnesia**   A broad inability to remember events within a certain category, due in many cases to brain damage.

**amygdala**   An almond-shaped structure in the limbic system that plays a central role in emotion and in the evaluation of stimuli.

**anarthria**   A disorder involving an inability to control the muscles needed for ordinary speech; hence, anarthric individuals cannot speak, although other aspects of language functioning are unimpaired.

**anchoring**   A tendency to use an initial answer to a question as an "anchor," so that subsequent answers to the question are selected by making (often inadequate) adjustments from this "reference point."

**anomia**   A disruption of language abilities, usually resulting from specific brain damage, in which the individual loses the ability to name objects, including highly familiar objects.

**anterior attention system**   A set of brain locations, identified largely through *neuro-imaging techniques*, hypothesized as the brain's "traffic director" coordinating various ongoing activities, and keeping track of different inputs.

**anterograde amnesia**   An inability to remember experiences that occurred *after* the event that triggered the memory disruption. Often contrasted with *retrograde amnesia*.

**aphasia**   A disruption to language capacities, often caused by brain damage.

**apraxia**   A disturbance in the initiation or organization of voluntary action.

**area V1**   The site on the *occipital lobe* where axons from the *lateral geniculate nucleus* first reach the cerebral cortex.

**articulatory rehearsal loop**   One of the low-level assistants, hypothesized as part of the *working memory system*. This loop draws on subvocalized speech, which serves to create a record in the *phonological buffer*. Materials in this buffer then fade, but can be refreshed by another cycle of covert speech, with this cycle initiated by working memory's *central executive*.

**association cortex**   The traditional name for the portion of the human cortex outside of the primary motor and sensory projection areas.

**associations**   Functional connections hypothesized as linking *nodes* within a mental network, or *detectors* within a detector network; these associations are often hypothesized as the "carriers" of activation, from one node or detector to the next.

**atmosphere pattern**   A tendency to endorse a conclusion in a logic problem if that conclusion is consistent with the "atmosphere" of the premises. Thus, two premises containing the word "not" make it more likely that participants will endorse a conclusion containing the word "not"; premises containing "all" make it more likely that they will endorse a conclusion containing "all."

**attended channel**   In *selective-attention* experiments, research participants are exposed to simultaneous inputs, and instructed to ignore all of these except one. The attended channel is the input participants are instructed to attend.

**autobiographical memory**   The aspect of memory that records the episodes and events in a person's life.

**automaticity**   A state achieved by some tasks and some forms of processing, in which the task can be performed with little or no attention. Automatized actions can, in many cases, be combined with other activities without interference. Automatized actions are also often difficult to control, leading many to refer to them as "mental reflexes."

**availability heuristic**   A strategy used to judge the frequency of a certain type of object, or the likelihood of a certain type of event. This strategy begins by assessing

**A1**

the ease with which examples of the object or event come to mind; this "availability" of examples is then used as an index of frequency or likelihood.

**axon**   The part of a neuron that transmits a signal to another location.

**base rate**   Information about the broad likelihood of a particular type of event (also referred to as "prior probability"). Base-rate information is distinguished from *diagnostic information.*

**baseline activation (or resting) level**   A *detector* or *node*'s activation level prior to the arrival of any inputs.

**basic-level category**   A level of categorization hypothesized as the "natural" and most informative level, neither too specific nor too general. It is proposed that we tend to use basic-level terms (such as "chair," rather than the more general "furniture" or the more specific "armchair") in our ordinary conversation and in our reasoning.

**behaviorist theory**   Broad principles concerned with how behavior changes in response to different configurations of stimuli (including stimuli often called "rewards" and "punishments"). In its early days, behaviorist theory sought to avoid *mentalistic* terms.

**belief bias**   A tendency, within logical reasoning, to endorse a conclusion if the conclusion happens to be something one believes is true anyhow. In displaying this tendency, people seem to ignore both the premises of the logical argument, and logic itself, and rely instead on their broader pattern of beliefs about what is true and what is not.

**biconditionals**   Logical statements of the form, "If X, and only if X , then Y." Such a statement is equivalent to asserting that *both* "X implies Y" *and* "Y implies X."

**bigram**   A pair of letters. For example, the word "FLAT" contains the bigrams "FL," "LA" and "AT."

**binding problem**   The problem of reuniting the various elements of a scene, given the fact that these elements are initially dealt with by different systems in the brain.

**brainstorming**   A technique sometimes used for problem-solving in which one tries to relax all constraints and to "let the ideas flow." In brainstorming sessions, one tries to generate as many ideas, and as many new approaches, as possible.

**Broca's aphasia**   A form of *aphasia* caused by damage to specific sites within the left frontal lobe of the brain. Patients suffering from this aphasia show relatively good language comprehension but disrupted production. Moreover, the speech they produce is "agrammatic."

**Capgras Syndrome**   A rare disorder, resulting from specific forms of brain damage, in which the afflicted person recognizes the people in his or her world, but denies that they are who they appear to be. Instead, the person insists, these familiar individuals are well-disguised impostors.

**categorical perception**   The tendency to hear speech sounds "merely" as members of a category—the category of "z" sounds, or the category of "p" sounds, and so on. As a consequence, one tends to hear sounds *within* the category as being rather similar to each other; sounds from different categories, however, are perceived as quite different.

**categorical syllogism**   A logical argument containing two premises and a conclusion, and concerned with the properties of, and relations between, categories. An example is "All trees are plants. All plants require nourishment. Therefore all trees require nourishment." This is a valid syllogism, since the truth of the premises guarantees the truth of the conclusion.

**cell body**   The area of the cell containing the nucleus and the metabolic machinery that sustains the cell.

**center-surround cells**   Neurons in the visual system with a "donut-shaped" *receptive field;* stimulation in the *center* of the receptive field has one effect on the cell, whereas stimulation in the surrounding ring has the opposite effect.

**central executive**   The hypothesized director of the *working-memory system.* This is the component of the system needed for any interpretation or analysis; in contrast, mere storage of materials can be provided by working memory's assistants, which works under the control of the central executive.

**cerebellum**   The largest area of the hindbrain, crucial for the coordination of bodily movements and balance.

**cerebral hemisphere**   One of the two hemispherical structures—one on the left side of the brain, one on the right—that comprises the major part of the forebrain in mammals.

**change blindness**   A pattern in which perceivers either do not see, or take a long time to see, large-scale changes in a visual stimulus. This pattern reveals how little we perceive, even from stimuli in plain view, if we are not specifically attending to the target information.

**channel segregation**   In performing simultaneous tasks, one needs to keep track of which task elements belong with which task. The task of keeping these elements separate, so that elements from one task do not intrude into the other task, is called channel segregation.

**childhood amnesia**   The difficulty, experienced by most adults, in remembering events that took place before one's third or fourth birthday.

**chronometric studies**   Literally "time-measurement" studies; generally, studies that measure the amount of time a task takes, often used as a means of examining the task's components, or used as a means of examining which *brain* events are simultaneous with specific *mental* events.

**chunk**   The hypothetical storage unit in working memory; it is estimated that working memory can hold $7 \pm 2$ chunks. An unspecified quantity of information can be contained within each chunk, since the content of each chunk depends on how the memorizer has organized the to-be-remembered materials.

**clustering**   A pattern often observed in free recall tasks in which participants will recall the earlier-learned materials category by category, independent of the sequence in which these materials were initially presented.

**coarticulation**   A trait of speech production in which the way a sound is produced is altered slightly by the immediately previous and the next sounds. Because of this "overlap" in speech production, the acoustic properties of each speech sound vary, according to the context in which that sound appears.

**cognitive economy**   The need to manage one's mental resources, including time, effort, and specific processing tools. Performance will suffer if one seeks to perform tasks (or combinations of tasks) that demand more resources than are available, and this leads people to use a variety of cognitive "short-cuts."

**cognitive neuroscience**   The study of the biological basis for cognitive functioning.

**cognitive unconscious**   The broad set of mental activities of which we are completely unaware that makes possible our ordinary thinking, remembering, reasoning, and so on.

**commissure**   One of the thick bundles of fibers via which information is sent back and forth between the two *cerebral hemispheres*.

**competence**   The pattern of skills and knowledge that might be revealed under optimal circumstances. Competence is generally distinguished from "performance," which refers to the pattern of skills and knowledge revealed under ordinary circumstances.

**complex cell**   A neuron within the visual system that fires maximally in response to lines or angles of a specific orientation; however, position of the line within the field of view is not critical.

**computerized axial tomography (CT scanning)**   A *neuroimaging* technique that uses X-rays to construct a precise three-dimensional image of the brain's anatomy.

**concept-driven processing**   A type of processing in which the sequence of mental events is influenced by a broad pattern of knowledge and expectations (sometimes referred to as "top-down" processing).

**concurrent-articulation task**   A task, used in many studies of working memory, in which participants are required to repeat a phrase or word over and over out loud. Concurrent articulation can be used to block use of *subvocalization*, and therefore can be used to study the function of subvocalization.

**conditional statements**   These are statements of the format "If X then Y," with the first statement (the "if" clause) providing a "condition" under which the second statement (the "then" clause) is guaranteed to be true.

**cones**   Photoreceptors that are able to discriminate hues, and which have high acuity; cones are concentrated in the retina's fovea and become less frequent in the visual periphery.

**confabulation**   A sincerely offered, often detailed, but utterly false recollection.

**confirmation bias**   A family of effects in which people seem more sensitive to evidence *confirming* their beliefs than they are to evidence *challenging* their beliefs. Thus, if people are given a choice about what sort of information they would like in order to evaluate their beliefs, they request information that is likely to confirm their beliefs. Likewise, if they are presented with both confirming and disconfirming evidence, they are more likely to pay attention to, to be influenced by, and to remember the confirming evidence, rather than the disconfirming.

**connection weight**   The strength of a connection between two *nodes* in a network. The greater the connection weight, the more efficiently activation will flow from one node to the other.

**consistent mapping**   An experimental procedure in which the response required to each stimulus is held constant across a block of trials. Thus, if a button-press is the appropriate response for, say, a "T" viewed on the first trial, then this button-press will be the appropriate response whenever a "T" appears. Often contrasted with *varied mapping*.

**consolidation**   The process through which memories are biologically "cemented in place." According to some investigators, consolidation takes place during the hours after a new bit of information has been learned.

**content morphemes**   *Morphemes* that carry meaning; generally contrasted with *function morphemes* (like the plural morpheme "s" or past-tense morpheme "ed"), which signal the relations among words.

**contralateral control**   A pattern in which the left half of the brain controls the right half of the body, and the right half of the brain controls the left half of the body.

**converging evidence**   A pattern of evidence in which various procedures, or various results, all point toward the same conclusion.

**conversion errors**   An error in which people convert statements from one form into another, for example, treating "All A are B" as though it is identical to "All B are A," or treating "If A then B" as though it were "If B then A."

**convolutions**   The wrinkles visible in the *cortex* that allow the enormous surface area of the human cortex to be stuffed into the relatively small volume of the skull.

**cornea** The transparent tissue at the front of each eye that plays an important role in focusing the incoming light.

**corpus callosum** The largest of the *commissures* linking the left and right cerebral hemispheres.

**cortex** The outermost surface of the brain.

**crosstalk** A pattern of errors in which elements of one task intrude into a second simultaneous task.

**data-driven processing** A type of processing in which the sequence of mental events is largely determined by the pattern of incoming information (sometimes referred to as "bottom-up" processing).

**decay theory of forgetting** The hypothesis that with the passage of time, memories may fade or erode.

**declarative memories** Memories, including both *episodic* and *generic knowledge*, that can be described as "remembering *that*" such and such is true. Often contrasted with *procedural memories*, which are remembering *how* to do something.

**deduction** A process through which we start with claims, or general assertions, and ask what follows from these premises.

**deep processing** A mode of thinking about material in which one pays attention to the meaning and implications of the material; deep processing typically leads to excellent memory retention.

**default values** Values we fill in unless we have some reason or information to the contrary.

**dendrites** The part of the *neuron* that usually detects the incoming signal.

**descriptive accounts** An account of how things actually are; often contrasted with *normative* or *prescriptive* accounts, which describe how things *ought* to be.

**detectors** A *node* within a processing network that fires primarily in response to a specific target contained within the incoming perceptual information.

**diagnostic information** Information about an individual case, which indicates whether the case belongs in one category or another; often contrasted with *base-rate* information, which is information about the overall category (primarily: how common that category is), rather than information about the individual case.

**dichotic listening** A task in which participants hear two simultaneous verbal messages, one presented via headphones to the left ear, while a second is presented to the right ear. In typical experiments, participants are asked to pay attention to one of these inputs (the *attended channel*) and urged to ignore the other.

**digit-span task** A task often used for measuring working-memory's storage capacity. Participants are read a series of digits (e.g., "8 3 4") and must immediately repeat them back. If they do this successfully, they are given a slightly longer list (e.g., "9 2 4 0"), and so forth. The length of the longest list a person can remember in this fashion is that person's digit span.

**direct memory testing** A form of memory testing in which people are asked explicitly to remember some previous event. *Recall* and standard *recognition* testing are both forms of direct testing.

**distributed representation** A mode of representing ideas or contents in which there is no one *node* representing the content, and no one place at which the content is stored. Instead, the content is represented via a pattern of simultaneous activity across many nodes. Those same nodes will also participate in other patterns, and so those same nodes will also be part of other distributed representations. Often contrasted with *local representation*.

**divided attention** The skill of performing multiple tasks simultaneously.

**dual-coding theory** A theory that imaginable materials, such as high-imagery words, will be doubly represented in memory: the word itself will be remembered, and so will the corresponding mental image.

**echolalia** A disorder in which patients turn into virtual echo-boxes, repeating back anything they hear. However, these patients show no sign of understanding the speech they are echoing, nor do they produce speech on their own.

**edge enhancement** A process created by lateral inhibition in which the neurons in the visual system give exaggerated responses to edges of surfaces.

*Einstellung* The phenomenon in problem-solving in which people develop a certain attitude or perspective on a problem, and then approach all subsequent problems with the same rigid attitude.

**elaborative rehearsal** A way of engaging to-be-remembered materials, such that one pays attention to what the materials mean and how they are related to each other or to other things in the surroundings, or to other things one already knows. Often contrasted with *maintenance rehearsal*.

**embedded figure** A pattern that is contained within a larger, more elaborate pattern, even though it is sometimes not perceived.

**encoding specificity** The tendency, when memorizing, to place in memory *both* the to-be-learned materials *and also* some amount of the context of those materials. As a result, these materials will be recognized as familiar, later on, only if the materials appear again in a similar context.

**episodic knowledge** Knowledge about specific episodes in one's life; often contrasted with *generic knowledge*.

**error signal** A flow of activation proportional to the magnitude of error (i.e., proportional to the difference between output-produced and output-desired).

**error trapping**  Procedures that detect and correct errors before the errors cause further confusion.

**evolutionary psychology**  A theoretical perspective that suggests that many psychological questions are best understood by considering how the relevant processes evolved in response to natural selection.

**excitatory connection**  Links from one *node*, or one *detector*, to another, such that activation of one node activates the other. Often contrasted with *inhibitory connections*.

**exemplar-based reasoning**  Reasoning that draws on knowledge about specific category members, rather than drawing on more general information about the overall category.

**expected utility**  An estimate of the value of a particular course of action, calculated as the *utility* of the likely outcome of that action, multiplied by the probability of reaching that outcome. (Also referred to as "expected value.")

**explicit memories**  Memories revealed by *direct memory testing*, and typically accompanied by the conviction that one is remembering a specific prior episode. Often contrasted with *implicit memories*.

**extra-linguistic context**  The social and physical setting in which a sentence is encountered; usually, cues within this setting guide the interpretation of the sentence.

**false alarm**  A detection even though the specified target is actually absent.

**family resemblance**  The notion that members of a category (all dogs, or all games) resemble each other. In general, family resemblance relies on some number of *features* shared by any group of category members, even though these features may not be shared by *all* members of the category. Therefore, the basis for family resemblance may shift from one subset of the category to another.

**feature**  One of the small set of elements out of which more complicated patterns are composed. Features can be identified in many ways and are, for example, reflected in the *search asymmetries* evident in many *visual search* tasks.

**figure/ground organization**  The processing step in which the perceiver determines which aspects of the stimulus belong to the central object or *figure*, and which aspects belong to the background.

**filter**  A hypothetical mechanism that would block potential distractors from further processing.

**fixation target**  A visual mark (such as a dot or a plus sign) that one points one's eyes at (or "fixates"). Fixation targets are used to help people control their eye position.

**flashbulb memories**  Memories of extraordinary clarity, typically for highly emotional events, retained despite the passage of many years.

**forebrain**  One of the three main structures of the brain; the forebrain plays a crucial role in supporting intellectual functioning.

**formal system**  A set of rules or processes in which everything depends on the *form* of the materials being considered; there is no influence from the *content* of the material. For example, arithmetic is a formal system: Any equation of the form "$2x + 2x = 4x$" will always be true; it does not matter what $x$ represents—i.e., what the content of the equation is. Logic is another example of a formal system.

**four-card task**  A task used in many studies of deductive reasoning. In this task, participants are shown four playing cards and are told that each card has a number on one side, and a letter on the other. Their task is to evaluate this rule: If a card has a vowel on one side, it must have an even number on the other side. (Also known as the "selection task.")

**fovea**  The center of the *retina*; when one "looks at" an object, one is lining up that object with the fovea.

**frame**  Aspects of how a decision is phrased, which are, in fact, irrelevant to the decision, but which influence people's choices nonetheless.

**frequency estimate**  People's assessment of how often they have encountered examples of a particular category and how likely they believe they are to encounter new examples of that category.

**frontal lobes**  The lobe in each *cerebral hemisphere* that includes the *prefrontal area* and the motor projection area.

**function morphemes**  *Morphemes* that signal the relations among words within a sentence, such as the morpheme "s" indicating a plural, or the morpheme "ed" indicating past tense. Often contrasted with *content morphemes*.

**functional fixedness**  A tendency to be rigid in how one thinks about an object's function. This generally involves a strong tendency to think of an object only in terms of its *typical* function.

**functional magnetic resonance imaging (fMRI)**  A neuroimaging technique that uses magnetic fields to construct a detailed three-dimensional representation of the activity levels in different areas of the brain at a particular moment in time.

**fuzzy boundary**  A distinction between categories that identifies each instance only as "more" or "less likely" to be in a category, rather than specifying whether each instance is or is not included in the category.

**garden-path sentences**  Sentences that initially lead the reader to one understanding of how the sentence's words are related, but that then require a change in this understanding in order to comprehend the sentence. Examples are "The old man ships," or "The horse raced past the barn fell."

**generic knowledge**   Knowledge of a general sort, as opposed to knowledge about specific episodes. Often contrasted with *episodic knowledge*.

**general resources**   Mental resources that are relevant to virtually all cognitive tasks, so that virtually all tasks, no matter what their nature, will compete for this limited pool. Often contrasted with *task-specific resources*.

**generativity**   The idea that one can combine and recombine basic units to create (or "generate") new and more complex entities. Linguistic rules, for example, are generative, and so govern how a limited number of words can be combined and recombined to produce a vast number of sentences.

**Gestalt psychologists**   A group of scholars who emphasized the importance of organizational factors in our mental lives. The organization, they argued, was a property of the whole configuration, and not contained within the configuration's features or parts.

**goal state**   The state one is working toward in trying to solve a problem. Often contrasted with *initial state*.

**geon**   One of the basic shapes proposed as the "building blocks" of all complex three-dimensional forms. Geons take the form of cylinders, cones, blocks, and the like, and are combined to form "geon assemblies." These are then combined to produce entire objects.

**graded membership**   The idea that some members of a category are "better" members, and therefore are "more firmly" in the category than other members.

**grammatical**   Conforming to the rules that govern the sequence of words acceptable within the language.

**"hasa" links**   Associative links representing possessive relations, such as "Sam *hasa* dog." Often contrasted with *"isa" links*.

**heuristics**   Strategies that are reasonably efficient, and work most of the time. In using a heuristic, one is in effect choosing to accept some risk of error in order to gain efficiency.

**hindbrain**   One of the three main structures of the brain; the hindbrain sits atop of the spinal cord, and includes several structures crucial for controlling key life functions.

**hippocampus**   A structure in the *temporal lobe* that is involved in long-term and spatial memory.

**homunculus**   The classic "little man in the head" used (wrongfully) in explaining the intelligence of behavior. Appeals to the homunculus amount to claiming that intelligent processes are produced by some mental processes that are themselves intelligent—providing, in essence, no real explanation.

**hypermnesia**   A process through which earlier-forgotten memories are now remembered. Sometimes referred to as "unforgetting," hypermnesia often results merely from continued efforts at remembering, with these efforts spread out over a period of time and a variety of circumstances.

**hypothalamus**   A small structure at the base of the *forebrain* that plays a vital role in the control of motivated behaviors such as eating, drinking, and sexual activity.

**illumination**   The third in a series of stages often hypothesized as crucial for creativity. Illumination refers to the stage in which some new key insight or new idea suddenly comes to mind.

**illusory covariation**   A pattern that people "perceive" in data, leading them to believe that the presence of one factor allows them to predict the presence of another factor. However, this perception occurs even in the absence of any genuine relationship between these two factors. As an example, people perceive that a child's willingness to cheat in an academic setting is an indicator that the child will also be willing to cheat in athletic contests. However, this perception is incorrect, and so the covariation that people perceive is "illusory."

**image**   A mental representation *depicting* an object or event, rather than *describing* the object or event. Generally, images have a strong subjective resemblance to perceptual experiences, and so visual images are described as being similar to actual pictures.

**image files**   Visual information stored in long-term memory, specifying what a particular object or shape looks like. Information within the image file can then be used as a "recipe" or set of instructions for how to construct an active image of this object or shape.

**implicit memories**   Memories revealed by *indirect memory testing* usually manifest as *priming effects* in which current performance is guided or facilitated by previous experiences. Implicit memories are often accompanied by no conscious realization that one is, in fact, being influenced by specific past experiences. Often contrasted with *explicit memories*.

**inattentional blindness**   A pattern in which perceivers seem literally not to see visual stimuli right in front of their eyes; this pattern is caused by the participants' attending to some other stimulus and not expecting the target to appear.

**incidental learning**   Learning that takes place in the absence of any intention to learn, and, correspondingly, in the absence of any expectation of a subsequent memory test.

**incubation**   The second in a series of stages often hypothesized as crucial for creativity. Incubation refers to (hypothesized) events that occur when one puts a problem being worked on *out of* one's conscious thoughts, but continues nonetheless to work on the problem unconsciously. Many current psychologists are skeptical about this process, and propose alternative accounts for data ostensibly documenting incubation.

**indirect memory testing**   A form of memory testing in which research participants are not told that their memories are being tested. Instead, they are tested in a fashion in which previous experiences can influence current behavior. Examples of indirect tests include *word-stem completion, lexical decision*, and tachistoscopic recognition.

**induction**   A pattern of reasoning in which one seeks to draw general claims from specific bits of evidence. Often contrasted with *deduction*.

**information processing**   A particular approach to theorizing in which complex mental events, such as learning, remembering, and deciding, are understood as being built up out of a large number of discrete steps. These steps occur one-by-one, with each providing as its "output" the input to the next step in the sequence.

**inhibitory connections**   Links from one *node*, or one *detector*, to another, such that activation of one node decreases the *activation level* of the other. Often contrasted with *excitatory connections*.

**initial state**   The state one begins in, in working toward the solution of a problem. In other words, problem solution can be understood as the attempt to move, with various operations, from the initial state to the *goal state*.

**insight problems**   Problems in which one's initial approach to the problem is likely to be unproductive, and for which a more appropriate approach often arrives quite abruptly.

**interactive models**   Models of cognitive processing that rely on an ongoing interplay between *data-driven* and *concept-driven processing*.

**interference theory of forgetting**   The hypothesis that materials are lost from memory because of *interference* from other materials also in memory. If the interference is caused by materials learned prior to the learning episode, this is called *proactive interference*; if the interference is caused by materials learned after the learning episode, this is called *retroactive interference*.

**introspection**   The process through which one "looks within," to observe and record the contents of one's own mental life.

**intrusion errors**   Memory errors in which one recalls elements not part of the original episode one is trying to remember.

**"isa" links**   Associative links representing equivalence (or partial equivalence) relations, such as "Sam *is a* dog." Often contrasted with *"hasa" links*.

**Korsakoff's syndrome**   A clinical syndrome characterized primarily by dense *anterograde amnesia*. Korsakoff's syndrome is caused by damage to specific brain regions, and is often precipitated by a form of malnutrition common among long-term alcoholics.

**lateral geniculate nucleus (LGN)**   An important way-station in the thalamus that is the first destination for visual information sent from the eyeball to the brain.

**lateral inhibition**   A pattern in which cells, when stimulated, inhibit the activity of neighboring cells. In the visual system, lateral inhibition in the optic nerve creates *edge enhancement*.

**lens**   The transparent tissue located near the front of each eye that plays an important role in focusing the incoming light. Muscles control the degree of curvature of the lens, allowing the eye to form a sharp image on the *retina*.

**lesion**   A specific area of tissue damage.

**letter span**   A traditional measure of working-memory's capacity, obtained by determining how many letters someone can repeat back, without error, moments after hearing them. (Similar to a *digit-span*.)

**lexical-decision task**   A test in which participants are shown strings of letters and must indicate, as quickly as possible, whether the string of letters is a word in English or not. It is supposed that people perform this task by "looking up" these strings in their "mental dictionary."

**limbic system**   A set of brain structures including the amygdala, hippocampus, mammillary bodies, and parts of the thalamus. It is believed to be involved in the control of emotional behavior and motivation, and also plays a key role in learning and memory.

**linguistic universals**   Rules that appear to apply to every human language.

**linguistics**   The academic study of language.

**local representation**   Representations of information that are encoded in some small number of identifiable *nodes*. Representations of this sort are sometimes spoken of as "one-idea-per-node," or "one-content-per-location." Often contrasted with *distributed representations*.

**localization of function**   The research endeavor of determining what specific job is performed by a particular region of the brain.

**long-term recency**   A *recency effect* observed in circumstances in which all the materials being recalled are drawn from long-term memory. Traditional accounts attribute the recency effect to the ease of retrieval from *working memory*, and so these accounts cannot explain long-term recency.

**loss aversion**   A tendency to be far more sensitive to losses than to gains, often accompanied by a willingness to take chances in hopes of avoiding losses.

**magnetic resonance imaging (MRI)**   A *neuroimaging* technique that uses magnetic fields (created by radio waves) to construct a detailed three-dimensional representation of brain tissue. Like CT scans, MRI scans reveal the brain's anatomy, but they are much more precise than CT scans.

**maintenance rehearsal**   A rote, mechanical process, in which items are continually cycled through *working memory*, merely by repeating them over and over. Also called "item-specific rehearsal," and often contrasted with *elaborative rehearsal*.

**mammillary bodies**   Structures within the *limbic system* that play a crucial role in long-term memory.

**manner of production**   In producing speech-sounds, the speaker momentarily obstructs the flow of air out of the lungs. This obstruction can take several forms. For example, the airflow can be fully stopped for a moment, as it is in the /t/ or /b/ sound, or the air can continue to flow, as it does in the pronunciation of /f/ or /v/. These differences in how the airflow is restricted are referred to as the manner of production for that speech sound.

**mapping**   The assignment of individual responses to individual stimuli. Some mappings are easy to learn, whereas others are more difficult (e.g., press a high button in response to a stimulus at the bottom of the computer screen; press a low button in response to a stimulus at the top of the screen).

**memory reconstruction**   A process in which one uses generic information in order to figure out how a past event is likely to have unfolded, or what a once-viewed scene is likely to have included.

**memory rehearsal**   Any mental activity that has the effect of maintaining information in working memory. Two types of rehearsal are often distinguished: *maintenance* (or item-specific) *rehearsal*, and *elaborative rehearsal*.

**mental model**   An internal representation in which an abstract description is translated into a relatively concrete representation, with that representation serving to illustrate how that abstract state of affairs might be realized.

**mentalism**   The view that human actions must be understood with theories that refer to unseen mental entities, such as beliefs, expectations, plans, and strategies.

**metacognitive judgments**   Judgments in which one must stand back from a particular mental activity, and comment on the activity, rather than participating in it.

**metalinguistic judgments**   A particular type of *metacognitive judgment*, in which one must stand back from one's ordinary language use, and comment on language or linguistic processes.

**method of loci**   A *mnemonic strategy* in which the to-be-remembered materials are each associated with a particular location. When the time comes to remember, one imagines that one is "returning" to these remembered locations, and "finds" at each spot the target materials.

**midbrain**   One of the three main structures of the brain; the midbrain plays an important role in coordinating movements, and also contains structures that serve as "relay" stations for information arriving from the sensory organs.

**minimal attachment**   A *heuristic* used in sentence perception. In using this heuristic, the listener or reader proceeds through the sentence seeking the simplest possible phrase structure that will accommodate the words heard so far.

**misinformation effect**   An effect in which research participants' reports about an earlier event are influenced by misinformation they received after experiencing the event. In the extreme, misinformation can be used to create false memories concerning an entire event that, in truth, never occurred.

**mnemonic strategies**   Techniques designed to improve memory accuracy, and to make learning easier; in general, these strategies seek in one fashion or another to help memory by imposing an organization on the to-be-learned materials.

**modal model**   This nickname refers to a specific conception of the "architecture" of memory. In this model, working memory serves both as the storage site for material now being contemplated, and also the "loading platform" for long-term memory. Information can reach working memory through the processes of perception, or it can be drawn from long-term memory. Once in working memory, material can be further processed, or can simply be "recycled" for subsequent use.

**modularity**   The claim that different aspects of processing work independently of each other, so that information available to one processing module may have no influence on the function of some other module.

*modus ponens*   A logical rule that stipulates that, from these two premises, "If p then q," and "p is true," one can draw the conclusion: "Therefore, q is true."

*modus tollens*   A logical rule that stipulates that, from these two premises, "If p then q," and "q is false," one can draw the conclusion: "Therefore, p is false."

**morphemes**   The smallest language units that carry meaning. Psycholinguists distinguish *content morphemes* (the primary carriers of meaning) from *function morphemes* (which specify the relations among words).

**necessary conditions**   Conditions that *must* be fulfilled in order for a certain consequence to occur. However, these conditions may not guarantee that the consequence will occur, since it may be true that other conditions must also be met. Often contrasted with *sufficient conditions*.

**Necker cube**   One of the classic *ambiguous figures*; the figure is a two-dimensional drawing that can be perceived either as a cube viewed from above or as a cube viewed from below.

**neural net model**   An alternative term for connectionist models, reflecting the hypothesized parallels between this sort of computer model and the functioning of the nervous system.

**neuroimaging**   A technique that allows investigators to take precise three-dimensional "pictures" of the living brain. Some techniques yield information about anatomy—which structures are where; other techniques yield information about function—which areas of the brain are particularly active, and which areas are less so, at any moment in time.

**neurons**   Individual cells within the nervous system.

**neuropsychology**   The branch of psychology concerned with the relation between various forms of brain dysfunction and various aspects of mental functioning. Neuropsychologists study, for example, *amnesia, agnosia,* and *aphasia.*

**neurotransmitter**   One of the chemicals released by neurons in order to stimulate the adjacent neuron. See *synapse.*

**nodes**   Individual units within an associative network. In a scheme employing *local representations, nodes* represent single ideas or concepts. In a scheme employing *distributed representations,* ideas or contents are represented by a pattern of activation across a wide number of nodes; the same nodes may also participate in other patterns and therefore in other representations.

**normative accounts**   Accounts of how an event or a process *should* or *ought* to unfold. Also referred to as *prescriptive* accounts.

**occipital lobes**   The rearmost lobe in each *cerebral hemisphere,* which includes the primary visual projection area.

**operators**   The tools or actions that one can use, in problem-solving, to move from the problem's *initial state* to the *goal state.*

**optic nerve**   The bundle of nerve fibers, formed from the retina's ganglion cells, that carries information from the eyeball to the brain.

**over-regularization errors**   Errors in which one perceives or remembers a word or event as being closer to the "norm" than it really is. For example, misspelled words are read as though they were spelled correctly; atypical events are misremembered in a fashion that brings them closer to more typical events; words with an irregular past tense (such as "ran") are replaced with a regular past tense ("runned").

**parallel processing**   A system in which many steps are going on at the same time; usually contrasted with *serial processing.*

**parietal lobes**   The lobe in each *cerebral hemisphere* that lies between the *occipital* and *frontal* lobes, and includes the primary sensory projection area, and also circuits crucial for the control of attention.

**parsing**   The process through which one divides an input into its appropriate elements—for example, divides the stream of incoming speech into its constituent words.

**path constraints**   Limits that rule out some operations in problem solving. These might take the form of resource limitations (limited time to spend on the problem, or limited money), or limits of other sorts (perhaps ethical limits on what one can do).

**pattern recognition**   The process of identifying or categorizing the objects in one's environment.

**peg-word systems**   A type of *mnemonic strategy* using words or locations as "pegs" on which one "hangs" the to-be-remembered materials.

**perseveration**   A pattern of responding in which one produces the same response over and over, even though one knows that the task requires a change in response; this pattern is often observed in patients with brain damage in the frontal lobe.

**phonemes**   The basic categories of sound used to convey language. For example, the words "peg" and "beg" differ in their initial phoneme—/p/ in one case, /b/ in the other.

**phonological buffer**   A passive storage device that serves as part of the *articulatory rehearsal loop.* The phonological buffer serves as part of the mechanisms ordinarily needed for hearing. In rehearsal, however, the buffer is loaded by means of *subvocalization.* Materials within the buffer then fade, but can be refreshed by new covert speech, under the control of the *central executive.*

**phonology**   The study of the sounds that are used to convey language.

**photoreceptors**   The cells on the *retina* that respond directly to the incoming light; photoreceptors are of two kinds: *rods* and *cones.*

**phrase-structure ambiguity**   Ambiguity in how a sentence should be interpreted, resulting from the fact that more than one phrase structure is compatible with the sentence. An example of such ambiguity is "I saw the bird with my binoculars."

**phrase-structure rules**   Constraints governing the pattern of branching in a phrase-structure tree. Equivalently, these are rules governing what the constituents must be for any syntactic element of a sentence.

**place of articulation**   In producing speech sounds, the speaker momentarily obstructs the flow of air out of the lungs. This obstruction can occur at several different positions, depending on the position of the tongue, teeth, and lips. The position at which this obstruction occurs is called the place of articulation. For example, the "place" for the /b/ sound is the lips; the "place" for the /d/ sounds is created by the tongue briefly touching the roof of the mouth.

**positron emission tomography (PET scanning)** A neuroimaging technique that determines how much glucose (the brain's fuel) is being used by specific areas of the brain at a particular moment in time.

**post-stimulus mask** A pattern displayed after a visual stimulus has been shown, designed to block sensory memory for that just-presented stimulus.

**postsynaptic membrane** The cell membrane of the neuron "receiving" information across the *synapse*.

**pragmatic reasoning schema** A collection of rules, derived from ordinary practical experience, that defines what inferences are appropriate in a specific situation. These reasoning schemata are usually defined in terms of a goal or theme, and so one schema defines the rules appropriate for reasoning about situations involving "permission," whereas a different schema defines the rules appropriate for thinking about situations involving cause-and-effect relations.

**pragmatic rules** Rules governing how language is ordinarily used, and also governing how this language will be interpreted. As an example, "Do you know the time?" is literally a question about one's knowledge, but this question is interpreted as a request that one *tell* what time it is.

**prefrontal cortex** The front-most part of the frontal lobe, crucial for planning and the organization of behavior.

**preparation** The first in a series of stages often hypothesized as crucial for creativity. Preparation refers to the stage in which one commences effortful work on the problem, often with little progress.

**prescriptive rules** Rules describing how things are *supposed* to be. Often called *normative rules*, and contrasted with *descriptive rules*.

**presynaptic membrane** The cell membrane of the neuron "sending" information across the *synapse*.

**primacy effect** An often-observed advantage in remembering the early-presented materials within a sequence of materials. This advantage is generally attributed to the fact that one can focus attention on these items, because, at the beginning of a sequence, one is obviously not trying to divide attention between these items and other items in the series.

**primary motor projection areas** The strip of tissue, located at the rear of the *frontal lobe,* that is the departure point for nerve cells that send their signals to lower portions of the brain and spinal cord, which ultimately result in muscle movement.

**primary sensory projection areas** The main points of arrival in the cortex for information arriving from the eyes, ears, and other sense organs.

**priming effect** An improvement in processing created by an earlier experience of working on the same task with the same stimulus materials. Many tasks show priming effects, including *lexical decision, word-fragment completion,* and tachistoscopic recognition.

**proactive interference** Interference observed when earlier-learned materials disrupt memory for later-learned materials. Often contrasted with *retroactive interference.*

**problem space** The set of all states that can be reached in solving a problem, as one moves, by means of the problem's *operators*, from the problem's *initial state* toward the problem's *goal state*.

**procedural memories** Memories for how to do something, not easily described in propositions. Often contrasted with *declarative memories*.

**processing fluency** An improvement in the speed or ease of processing, which results from prior practice in using those same processing steps.

**process purity** The claim that laboratory tasks rely only on a single mental process. If tasks are "process pure" in this way, then we can interpret the properties of task performance as revealing the properties of the underlying process. However, if tasks are not process pure, we cannot interpret performance as revealing the properties of a specific process.

**production systems** A system for representing actions. Each "production" within this system involves (a) a goal, (b) some conditions that must be met before the action can be taken, and (c) a specific action to be taken, when the conditions have been met.

**prosody** The pattern of pauses and pitch changes that characterize speech production. Prosody can be used to emphasize elements of a spoken sentence, to highlight the sentence's intended structure, or to signal the difference between a question and an assertion.

**prosopagnosia** A syndrome in which patients lose their ability to recognize faces and to make other fine-grained discriminations within a highly-familiar category, even though their other visual abilities seem relatively intact.

**prototype theory** The claim that mental categories are represented by means of a single "best example," or prototype, identifying the "center" of the category. In this view, decisions about category membership, and inferences about the category, are made with reference to this best example, often an "average" of the examples of that category that one has actually encountered.

**pseudowords** Letter strings designed to resemble actual words, even though they are not. Examples include "blar," "plome," or "tuke."

**psycholinguistics** The study of how linguistic knowledge is acquired, represented, and used by the human mind.

**qualia** The subjective qualities that provide the "raw feel" of sensory experience.

**recall**   The task of memory retrieval in which the rememberer must come up with the desired materials, sometimes in response to a cue that names the context in which these materials were earlier encountered ("Name the pictures you saw earlier."), sometimes in response to a question that requires the sought-after information ("Name a fruit," or "What is the state capital of California?"). Often contrasted with *recognition*.

**receptive field**   The portion of the visual field to which a cell within the visual system responds. Thus, if the appropriately shaped stimulus appears in the appropriate position, the cell's firing rate will change. The cell's firing rate will not change if the stimulus is of the wrong form or is in the wrong position.

**recency effect**   The tendency to remember materials that occur late in a series. In "standard" recency, the late-occurring items are probably being retrieved from working memory; in *long-term recency*, the late-occurring items are drawn from long-term memory, and probably gain their memory advantage from distinctiveness.

**recognition**   The task of memory retrieval in which the to-be-remembered items are presented and the person must decide whether or not the item was encountered in some earlier circumstance. Thus, for example, one might be asked, "Have you ever seen this person before?" or "Is this the poster you saw in the office yesterday?" Often contrasted with *recall*.

**recognition by components model**   A model (often referred to by its initials: RBC) of object recognition. In this model, a crucial role is played by *geons*, the (hypothesized) basic building blocks out of which all the objects we recognize are constructed.

**recognition threshold**   The briefest exposure duration for a stimulus that still allows accurate recognition of that stimulus. For words, the recognition threshold typically lies between 10 and 40 msec. Words shown for longer durations are usually easily perceived; words shown for briefer durations are typically difficult to perceive.

**reconstruction**   A process in which one draws on broad patterns of knowledge in order to figure out how a prior event actually unfolded. In some circumstances, we rely on reconstruction to fill gaps in what we recall; in other circumstances, we rely on reconstruction because it requires less effort than actual recall.

**recursion**   A property of rule systems that allows a symbol to appear both on the left-side of a definition (the part being defined) and on the right-side (the part providing the definition). Recursive rules within syntax, for example, allow sentences to include another sentence, as one of its constituents, as in the example: "Solomon says that Jacob is talented."

**referent**   That object or event in the world that a word or phrase refers to. For example, the word "apple" refers

to a particular type of fruit that grows on trees; "Daniel Reisberg" refers to the man who wrote this text.

**rehearsal loop**   See *articulatory rehearsal loop*.

**representativeness heuristic**   A strategy often used in making judgments about categories. This strategy is broadly equivalent to making the assumption that, in general, the instances of a category will resemble the prototype for that category, and, likewise, that the prototype resembles each instance.

**repression**   A (hypothesized) process through which anxiety-provoking thoughts are denied access to the conscious mind. Most researchers are skeptical about the existence of repression, although many clinical psychologists insist that the process is well documented.

**response selector**   A (hypothesized) mental resource needed for the selection and initiation of a wide range of responses, including overt responses (e.g., moving in a particular way) and covert responses (e.g., initiating a memory search).

**response threshold**   The quantity of information, or quantity of activation, needed in order to trigger a response.

**restoration effect**   A perceptual illusion in hearing, in which one "hears" sounds that are actually missing from the stimulus presented.

**retentionserval**   The amount of time that passes between the initial learning of some material and the subsequent memory retrieval of that material.

**retina**   The light-sensitive tissue that lines the back of the eyeball.

**retrieval failure**   A mechanism that probably contributes to a great deal of forgetting. Retrieval failure occurs when a memory is, in fact, in long-term storage, but one is unable to locate that memory when trying to retrieve it.

**retrieval path**   A connection (or series of connections) that can lead to a sought-after memory in long-term storage.

**retroactive interference**   Interference observed when memory for earlier-observed materials is disrupted by later-learned materials. Often contrasted with *proactive interference*.

**retrograde amnesia**   An inability to remember experiences that occurred *before* the event that triggered the memory disruption. Often contrasted with *anterograde amnesia*.

**rewrite rule**   One of the rules governing the possible forms that a sentence's phrase structure can take. Rewrite rules specify how each constituent within a phrase structure can be expanded (or "rewritten"). Thus, the rule "S → NP VP" indicates that a sentence can be expanded into a noun phrase followed by a verb phrase; the rule "NP → det N" indicates that a noun phrase can be expanded into a determiner followed by a noun.

**risk aversion**   A tendency toward avoiding risk. People tend to be risk averse when contemplating gains, choosing instead to hold tight to what they already have. Often contrasted with *risk seeking*.

**risk seeking**   A tendency toward seeking out risk. People tend to be risk seeking when contemplating losses, as they are willing to gamble in hopes of avoiding (or diminishing) their losses.

**rods**   *Photoreceptors* that are sensitive to very low light levels, but which are unable to discriminate hues, and which have relatively poor acuity.

**satisficing**   A decision-making procedure in which one seeks a satisfactory outcome, rather than searching more ambitiously for the *optimal* outcome. In satisficing, one seeks a choice that is "good enough," even if other (not yet detected) choices might be even better.

**schema (plural: schemata)**   A pattern of knowledge describing what is typical or frequent in a particular situation. Thus a "kitchen schema" would stipulate that a stove and refrigerator are likely to be present, whereas a coffeemaker may be or may not be present, and a piano is likely not to be present.

**search asymmetry**   A data pattern sometimes observed in *visual-search* tasks, and often used as a basis for identifying the basic features used by the visual system. As an example, it is relatively easy to locate a tilted line against a background of verticals, but difficult to find a vertical line against a background of tilted lines. This implies that "tilt" may be a basic feature for the visual system, whereas "vertical" is not.

**selective attention**   The skill through which one pays attention to one input or one task, while ignoring other stimuli that are also on the scene.

**self-reference effect**   The tendency to have better memory for information relevant to one's self than for other sorts of material.

**semantics**   The study of how a word's meaning is represented in the mind.

**sense**   The meaning of a word is determined both by the word's *referent* and also by how the word identifies that referent. Thus the "Morning Star" and the "Evening Star" both refer to the same object (the planet Venus) but they identify that object in different ways. This means of identifying the referent is called the word's (or phrase's) sense.

**serial position curve**   A data pattern summarizing the relationship between some performance measure (often, likelihood of *recall*) and the order in which the test materials were presented. In memory studies, the serial position curve tends to be U-shaped, with people best able to recall the first-presented items (the *primacy effect*) and also the last-presented items (the *recency effect*).

**serial processing**   A system in which only one step happens at a time (and so the steps go on in a series). Usually contrasted with *parallel processing*.

**set**   The assumptions one brings to a task concerning how the task should be approached, and also what sorts of strategies are likely to be productive in performing the task.

**shadowing**   A task in which research participants are required to repeat back a verbal input, word for word, as they hear it.

**shallow processing**   A mode of thinking about material in which one pays attention only to appearances and other superficial aspects of the material; shallow processing typically leads to poor memory retention.

**simple cell**   A neuron within the visual system that fires maximally to lines or angles of a specific orientation and at a specific position within the visual field.

**single-cell recording**   A technique for recording the moment-by-moment *activation level* of an individual neuron, within a healthy, normally functioning brain.

**source confusion**   A memory error in which one misremembers where a bit of information was learned, or where a particular stimulus was last encountered.

**source memory**   A form of memory that allows one to recollect the episode in which learning took place, or the time and place in which a particular stimulus was encountered.

**speech segmentation**   The process through which a stream of speech is "sliced" into its constituent words and, within words, into the constituent *phonemes*.

**spreading activation**   A process through which activation travels from one *node* to another, via associative links. As each node becomes activated, it serves as a source for further activation, spreading onward through the network.

**Stroop effect**   A classic demonstration of *automaticity*, in which people are asked to name the color of ink used to print a word, and the word itself is a color name. For example, research participants might see the word "yellow" printed in blue ink, and are required to say "blue." Considerable interference is observed in this task, with participants apparently unable to ignore the word's content, even though it is irrelevant to their task.

**subthreshold activation**   Activation levels below *response threshold*. Subthreshold activation, by definition, will not trigger a response; nonetheless, this activation is important because it can accumulate, leading eventually to an activation level that exceeds the response threshold.

**subvocalization**   Covert speech, in which one goes through the motions of speaking, or perhaps forms a detailed motor plan for speech movements, but without making any sound.

**sufficient conditions**   Conditions that, if satisfied, guarantee that a certain consequence will occur. However, these conditions may not be necessary for that consequence (since the same consequence might occur for some other reasons). Often contrasted with *necessary conditions*.

**summation**   The addition of two or more separate inputs so that the effect of these combined inputs is greater than the effect caused by any one of the inputs.

**sunk-cost effect**   A tendency toward taking extravagant steps to ensure that a previous expense was not "in vain." The previous expense is the "sunk cost," that is, a commitment already made. Often, it is more sensible to abandon this commitment, rather than expending further resources to justify the commitment. However, this abandonment is precisely what people tend not to do.

**support theory**   An account of how people evaluate assertions they encounter; according to this theory, people ask themselves how much support they perceive for the claim; their perception, in turn, often depends on how the claim is phrased.

**surface structure**   The representation of a sentence that is actually expressed in speech. In some treatments, this structure is referred to as the "s-structure" and is often contrasted with the *underlying structure* (or d-structure, with the "d" an abbreviation for deep).

**synapse**   The area that includes the *presynaptic membrane* of one neuron, the *postsynaptic membrane* of another neuron, and the tiny gap between them. The presynaptic membrane releases a small amount of *neurotransmitter* that drifts across the gap and stimulates the postsynaptic membrane.

**syntax**   Rules governing the sequences and combinations of words in the formation of phrases and sentences.

**tachistoscope**   A device that allows presentation of stimuli for precisely controlled amounts of time, including very brief presentations.

**task-specific resources**   Mental resources needed for some tasks but not others; thus the nature of each task determines which resources will be needed. Often contrasted with *general resources*.

**temporal lobes**   The lobe of the cortex lying inward and down from the temples. The temporal lobe in each cerebral hemisphere includes the primary auditory projection area, Wernicke's area, and, subcortically, the *amygdala* and *hippocampus*.

**thalamus**   A part of the lower portion of the forebrain that serves as a major relay and integration center for sensory information.

**threshold**   The activity level at which a cell or detector "fires" or responds.

**time-sharing**   A process through which one rapidly switches attention from one task to another, creating the appearance of doing two things at the same time.

**token**   A specific example or instance of a category, and therefore used in propositions concerned with specific events and individuals. Often contrasted with *type*.

**T.O.T. phenomenon**   An often-observed effect in which people are unable to remember a particular word, even though they are certain the word (typically identified via its definition) is in their vocabulary. People in this state often can remember the starting letter for the word and its number of syllables, and insist the word is "on the tip of their tongue" (hence the T.O.T label).

**trace**   The hypothesized remnant left when a word has been shifted from one position to another in a sentence's *underlying structure*. Although unexpressed, the trace can be detected in various ways.

**transcendental inference**   A step in reasoning in which one uses observed circumstances to figure out what causes brought about these circumstances, or what preconditions made these circumstances possible.

**transcranial magnetic stimulation (TMS)**   A technique in which a series of strong magnetic pulses at a specific location on the scalp cause temporary disruption in the brain region directly underneath this scalp area.

**transfer-appropriate processing**   Processing of a stimulus that prepares the person for an upcoming test. To judge processing as "transfer-appropriate," one must consider both the initial processing, which promotes a set of skills, and the subsequent processing, to which those skills may be applied (or "transferred").

**type**   A broad category; often contrasted with *token*, a term denoting an individual within the category.

**typicality effects**   Any of a number of experimental effects in which "typical" category members have an advantage, relative to atypical category members. Thus people are quicker to verify "A robin is a bird," than they are to verify "A heron is a bird." Likewise, they are more likely to name "robin" if asked to name a bird than they are to name "heron."

**underlying structure**   An abstract representation of the sentence to-be-expressed, sometimes called "deep structure" (or d-structure) and often contrasted with *surface structure*.

**unilateral neglect syndrome**   A pattern of symptoms in which patients ignore all inputs coming from one side of space. Thus, patients with this syndrome put only one of their arms into their jackets, eat food from only one half of their plates, read only one half of words (and so read "output" as "put"), and so on.

**utility theory**   A view proposing that humans make decisions in a fashion that maximizes "utility." Utility is defined as the subjective value associated with a particular circumstance.

**varied mapping**   An experimental procedure in which the response required for each stimulus varies from one trial to another. Thus, if an "X" is a target on one trial (and so demands a "yes" response), "X" might be a distractor on the next trial (and so demand a "no" response). Often contrasted with *consistent mapping*.

**visual acuity**   A measure of one's ability to see fine detail.

**visual cortex**   The portion of the brain primarily responsible for vision.

**visual periphery**   The area of the *retina* more distant from the *fovea*.

**visual search**   An experimental task in which people must scan through a set of visual stimuli, searching for a particular target.

**visuospatial buffer**   One of the low-level assistants used as part of the *working-memory system*. This buffer plays an important role in storing visual or spatial representations, including visual images.

**voicing**   One of the properties that distinguishes different categories of speech sounds. A sound is considered "voiced" if the vocal folds are vibrating while the sound is produced. If the vocal folds start vibrating sometime after the sound begins (that is, with a long *voice-onset time*), the sound is considered "unvoiced."

**voice-onset time (VOT)**   The time period that elapses between the start of a speech sound and the onset of *voicing*. VOT is the main feature distinguishing "voiced" consonants (such as /b/, with a near-zero VOT) and "unvoiced" consonants (such as /p/, with a VOT of approximately 60 msec).

**weapon-focus effect**   A pattern, often alleged for witnesses to violent crimes, in which one pays close attention to some crucial detail (such as the weapon, within a crime scene) to the exclusion of much else.

**Wernicke's aphasia**   A language disorder in which patients seem largely unable to comprehend speech, even though the speech that they produce sounds effortless and fluent, with the function words and the appropriate suffixes correctly in place. Typically, though, the speech produced by these patients makes no sense.

**"what" system**   The system of visual circuits and pathways leading from the visual cortex to the temporal lobe and especially involved in object identification.

**"where" system**   The system of visual circuits and pathways leading from the visual cortex to the parietal lobe, and especially involved in the spatial localization of objects and in the coordination of movements.

**winner-takes-all**   A process in which a stronger node inhibits weaker ones, so that the stronger node comes more and more to dominate the weaker nodes.

**word-fragment completion**   A task in which research participants are given fragments of a word (e.g., "A-S-S-I-") and must figure out what the full word is ("assassin"). This task is often used to study *implicit memory*.

**word-length effect**   A phenomenon observed in tests of working memory, such that memory is poorer for words that take a longer time to pronounce. This effect is attributed to the fact that these words take longer to subvocalize, and are therefore more difficult to rehearse efficiently.

**word-stem completion**   A task in which people are given the beginning of a word (e.g., "TOM . . .") and must provide a word that starts with the letters provided. In some versions of the task, only one solution is possible, and so performance is measured by counting the number of words completed. In other versions of the task, several solutions are possible for each stem, and performance is assessed by determining which of the responses fulfill some other criterion.

**word-superiority effect**   The data pattern in which research participants are more accurate and more efficient in recognizing words (and word-like letter strings) than they are in recognizing individual letters.

**working-memory system**   A system of mental resources used for holding information in an easily accessible form. The *central executive* is at the heart of this system, and the *executive* then relies on a number of low-level assistants, including the *visuospatial buffer* and the *articulatory rehearsal loop*.

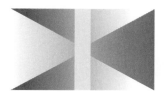

# References

Aaronson, D., & Scarborough, H. (1977). Performance theories for sentence coding: Some quantitative models. *Journal of Verbal Learning and Verbal Behavior, 16,* 277–304.

Abelson, R. P. (1981). Psychological status of the script concept. *American Psychologist, 36,* 715–729.

Ackley, D. H., Hinton, G. E., & Sejnowski, T. J. (1985). A learning algorithm for Boltzmann machines. *Cognitive Science, 9,* 147–169.

Adamson, R. (1952). Functional fixedness as related to problem solving: A repetition of three experiments. *Journal of Experimental Psychology, 44,* 288–291.

Adelson, B. (1981). Problem solving and the development of abstract categories in programming languages. *Memory & Cognition, 9,* 422–433.

Adelson, B. (1984). When novices surpass experts: The difficulty of the task may increase with expertise. *Journal of Experimental Psychology: Learning, Memory and Cognition, 10,* 483–495.

Aggleton, J. P., & Shaw, C. (1996). Amnesia and recognition memory: A re-analysis of psychometric data. *Neuropsychologia, 34*(1), 51–62.

Ahn, W.-K., & Graham, L. M. (1999). The impact of necessity and sufficiency in the Wason four-card task. *Psychological Science, 10,* 237–242.

Alba, J. W., Alexander, S. G., Hasher, L., & Caniglia, K. (1981). The role of context in the encoding of information. *Journal of Experimental Psychology: Human Learning and Memory, 7,* 283–292.

Alba, J. W., & Hasher, L. (1983). Is memory schematic? *Psychological Bulletin, 93,* 203–231.

Alexander, M. P., & Albert, M. L. (1983). The anatomical basis of visual agnosia. In A. Kertesz (Ed.), *Localization in neuropsychology.* New York: Academic Press.

Algom, D., & Cain, W. (1991). Remembered odors and mental mixtures: Tapping reservoirs of olfactory knowledge. *Journal of Experimental Psychology: Human Perception and Performance, 17,* 1104–1119.

Algom, D., & Lubel, S. (1994). Psychophysics in the field: Perception and memory for labor pain. *Memory & Cognition, 55,* 133–141.

Allais, M. (1953). Le comportement de l'homme rationnel devant le risque: Critique des postulats et axiomes de l'Ecole americaine. *Econometrica, 21,* 503–546.

Allan, L. (1993). Human contingency judgments: Rule based or associative. *Psychological Bulletin, 114,* 435–448.

Alloy, L. B., & Tabachnik, N. (1984). Assessment of covariation by humans and animals: The joint influence of prior expectations and current situational information. *Psychological Review, 91,* 112–149.

Allport, A. (1989). Visual attention. In M. Posner (Ed.), *Foundations of cognitive science* (pp. 631–682). Cambridge, MA: MIT Press.

Allport, A., Styles, E., & Hsieh, S. (1994). Shifting intentional set: Exploring the dynamic control of tasks. In C. Umiltà & M. Moscovitch (Eds.), *Attention and performance XV.* Cambridge, MA: MIT Press.

Allport, D., Antonis, B., & Reynolds, P. (1972). On the division of attention: A disproof of the single channel hypothesis. *Quarterly Journal of Experimental Psychology, 24,* 225–235.

Altmann, E. M., & Gray, W. D. (2002). Forgetting to remember: The functional relationship of decay and interference. *Psychological Science, 13,* 27–33.

Anand, P., & Sternthal, B. (1991). Perceptual fluency and affect without recognition. *Memory & Cognition, 19,* 293–300.

Anderson, J. R. (1974). Verbatim and propositional representation of sentences in immediate and long-term memory. *Journal of Verbal Learning and Verbal Behavior, 13,* 149–162.

Anderson, J. R. (1976). *Language, memory, and thought.* Hillsdale, NJ: Lawrence Erlbaum.

Anderson, J. R. (1980). *Cognitive psychology and its implications.* San Francisco: Freeman.

Anderson, J. R. (Ed.). (1981). *Cognitive skills and their acquisition.* Hillsdale, NJ: Lawrence Erlbaum.

Anderson, J. R. (1982). Acquisition of cognitive skill. *Psychological Review, 89,* 369–406.

Anderson, J. R. (1983). *The architecture of cognition.* Cambridge, MA: Harvard University Press.

Anderson, J. R. (1985). *Cognitive psychology.* New York: W. H. Freeman & Co.

Anderson, J. R. (1987). Skill acquisition: Compilation of weak-method problem solutions. *Psychological Review, 94,* 192–210.

Anderson, J. R. (1990). *The adaptive character of thought.* Hillsdale, NJ: Lawrence Erlbaum.

Anderson, J. R. (1993). Problem solving and learning. *American Psychologist, 48,* 35–44.

Anderson, J. R., & Bower, G. H. (1972). Recognition and retrieval processes in free recall. *Psychological Review, 79,* 97–123.

Anderson, J. R., & Bower, G. H. (1973). *Human associative memory.* Washington, DC: Winston & Sons.

Anderson, J. R. (1996). ACT: A simple theory of complex cognition. *American Psychologist*, 51, 355–365.

Anderson, J. R., & Reder, L. M. (1999a). The fan effect: New results and new theories. *Journal of Experimental Psychology: General*, 128, 186–197.

Anderson, J. R., & Reder, L. M. (1999b). Process, not representation: Reply to Radvansky (1999). *Journal of Experimental Psychology: General, 128*, 207–210.

Anderson, M. C., Bjork, R., & Bjork, E. (1994). Remembering can cause forgetting: Retrieval dynamics in long-term memory. *Journal of Experimental Psychology: Learning, Memory and Cognition, 20*, 1063–1087.

Anderson, M. C., Bjork, R. A., & Bjork, E. L. (2000). Retrieval-induced forgetting. Evidence for a recall-specific mechanism. *Psychonomics Bulletin & Review*, in press.

Anderson, M. C., & Spellman, B. (1995). On the status of inhibitory mechanisms in cognition: Memory retrieval as a model case. *Psychological Review*, 102, 68–100.

Anderson, R., & Helstrup, T. (1993). Visual discovery in mind and on paper. *Memory & Cognition*, 21, 283–293.

Anderson, R. C., & Pichert, J. (1978). Recall of previously unrecallable information following a shift in perspective. *Journal of Verbal Learning and Verbal Behavior, 17*, 1–12.

Andrews, F. (1975). Social and psychological factors which influence the creative process. In I. A. Taylor & J. W. Getzels (Eds.), *Perspectives in creativity*. Chicago: Aldine.

Arkes, H. (1991). Costs and benefits of judgment errors: Implications for debiasing. *Psychological Bulletin*, 110, 486–498.

Arkes, H., & Ayton, P. (1999). The sunk cost and Concorde effects: Are humans less rational than lower animals? *Psychological Bulletin*, 125, 591–600.

Arkes, H., & Blumer, C. (1985). The psychology of sunk cost. *Organizational Behavior and Human Decision Processes*, 35, 124–140.

Arkes, H., & Freedman, M. (1984). A demonstration of the costs and benefits of expertise in recognition memory. *Memory & Cognition*, 12, 84–89.

Arkes, H., & Harkness, A. (1983). Estimates of contingency between two dichotomous variables. *Journal of Experimental Psychology: General, 112*, 117–135.

Armstrong, S. L., Gleitman, L. R., & Gleitman, H. (1983). What some concepts might not be. *Cognition, 13*, 263–308.

Arnheim, R. (1969). *Visual thinking*. Berkeley: University of California Press.

Arrigo, J. M., & Pezdek, K. (1997). Lessons from the study of psychogenic amnesia. *Current Directions in Psychological Science, 6*, 148–152.

Ashby, F. G., & Waldron, E. M. (1999). On the nature of implicit categorization. *Psychonomics Bulletin & Review, 6*, 363–378.

Atkinson, R. C., & Juola, J. F. (1974). Search and decision processes in recognition memory. In D. H. Krantz, R. C. Atkinson, & P. Suppes (Eds.), *Contemporary developments in mathematical psychology*. San Francisco: Freeman.

Atkinson, R. C., & Shiffrin, R. M. (1968). Human memory: A proposed system and its control processes. In K. W. S. Spence, & J. T. Spence (Eds.), *The psychology of learning and motivation* (pp. 89–105). New York: Academic Press.

Attneave, F. (1953). Psychological probability as a function of experienced frequency. *Journal of Experimental Psychology, 46*, 81–86.

Austin, J. (1962). *How to do things with words*. Cambridge, MA: Harvard University Press.

Awh, E., Jonides, J., Smith, E. E., Schubacher, E. H., Koeppe, R. A., & Katz, S. (1996). Dissociation of storage and rehearsal in verbal working memory: Evidence from Positron Emission Tomography. *Psychological Science, 7*, 25–31.

Ayers, M. S., & Reder, L. M. (1998). A theoretical review of the misinformation effect: Predictions from an activation-based model. *Psychonomics Bulletin & Review, 5*, 1–21.

Baddeley, A. D. (1963). A Zeigarnik-like effect in the recall of anagram solutions. *Quarterly Journal of Experimental Psychology, 15*, 63–64.

Baddeley, A. D. (1966). Short-term memory for word sequences as a function of acoustic, semantic and formal similarity. *Quarterly Journal of Experimental Psychology, 18*, 362–365.

Baddeley, A. D. (1976). *The psychology of memory*. New York: Basic Books.

Baddeley, A. D. (1978). The trouble with "levels": A reexamination of Craik and Lockhart's framework for memory research. *Psychological Review, 85*, 139–152.

Baddeley, A. D. (1982). *Your memory: A user's guide*. New York: Macmillan.

Baddeley, A. D. (1986). *Working memory*. Oxford: Clarendon Press.

Baddeley, A. D. (1990). *Human memory: Theory and practice*. Needham Heights, MA: Allyn & Bacon.

Baddeley, A. D. (1992). Is working memory working? The fifteenth Bartlett lecture. *Quarterly Journal of Experimental Psychology, 44A*, 1–31.

Baddeley, A. D. (1999). *Essentials of human memory*. Hove, England: Psychology Press/Taylor & Francis (UK).

Baddeley, A. D., & Dale, H. C. A. (1966). The effect of semantic similarity on retroactive interference in long- and short-term memory. *Journal of Verbal Learning and Verbal Behavior, 5*, 417–420.

Baddeley, A. D., Gathercole, S., & Papagno, C. (1998). The phonological loop as a language learning device. *Psychological Review, 105*, 158–173.

Baddeley, A. D., & Hitch, G. (1974). Working memory. In G. Bower (Ed.), *Recent advances in learning and motivation*. New York: Academic Press.

Baddeley, A. D., & Hitch, G. (1977). Recency re-examined. In S. Dornic (Ed.), *Attention and performance VI* (pp. 646–667). Hillsdale, NJ: Lawrence Erlbaum.

Baddeley, A. D., & Hitch, G. (1993). The recency effect: Implicit learning with explicit retrieval? *Memory & Cognition, 21*, 146–155.

Baddeley, A. D., & Lieberman, K. (1980). Spatial working memory. In R. Nickerson (Ed.), *Attention and performance VIII* (pp. 521–539). Hillsdale, NJ: Lawrence Erlbaum.

Baddeley, A. D., Logie, R. H., Nimmo-Smith, I., & Brereton, J. (1985). Components of fluent reading. *Journal of Memory and Language, 24*, 119–131.

Baddeley, A. D., Thomson, N., & Buchanan, M. (1975). Word length and the structure of short-term memory. *Journal of Verbal Learning and Verbal Behavior, 14*, 575–589.

Baddeley, A. D., & Wilson, B. (1994). When implicit learning fails: Amnesia and the problem of error elimination. *Neuropsychologia, 32*, 53–68.

Baer, J. (1993). *Creativity and divergent thinking: A task-specific approach.* Hillsdale, NJ: Lawrence Erlbaum.

Bahrick, H. (1984). Semantic memory content in permastore: 50 years of memory for Spanish learned in school. *Journal of Experimental Psychology: General, 113*, 1–29.

Bahrick, H., Bahrick, L., Bahrick, A., & Bahrick, P. (1993). Maintenance of foreign language vocabulary and the spacing effect. *Psychological Science, 4*, 316–321.

Bahrick, H., Bahrick, P. O., & Wittlinger, R. P. (1975). Fifty years of memory for names and faces: A cross-sectional approach. *Journal of Experimental Psychology: General, 104*, 54–75.

Bahrick, H., & Hall, L. (1991). Lifetime maintenance of high school mathematics content. *Journal of Experimental Psychology: General, 120*, 20–33.

Bahrick, H., & Hall, L. (1993). Long intervals between tests can yield hypermnesia: Comments on Wheeler and Roediger. *Psychological Science, 4*, 206–208.

Bahrick, H., Hall, L. K., & Berger, S. A. (1996). Accuracy and distortion in memory for high school grades. *Psychological Science, 7*, 265–271.

Balch, W., Bowman , K., & Mohler, L. (1992). Music-dependent memory in immediate and delayed word recall. *Memory & Cognition, 20*, 21–28.

Balch, W., Myers, D. M., & Papotto, C. (1999). Dimensions of mood in mood-dependent memory. *Journal of Experimental Psychology: Learning, Memory and Cognition, 25*, 70–83.

Banaji, M., & Greenwald, A. G. (1994). Implicit stereotyping and prejudice. In M. P. Zanna & J. M. Olson (Eds.), *The psychology of prejudice: The Ontario symposium* (Vol. 7. Ontario symposium on personality and social psychology, pp. 55–76). Hillsdale, NJ: Lawrence Erlbaum.

Banaji, M. R., & Bhaskar, R. (2000). Implicit stereotypes and memory: The bounded rationality of social beliefs. In D. L. Schacter & E. Scarry (Eds.), *Memory, brain, and belief.* Cambridge, MA: Harvard University Press.

Banaji, M. R., & Crowder, R. G. (1989). The bankruptcy of everyday memory. *American Psychologist, 44*, 1185–1193.

Banaji, M. R., & Hardin, C. D. (1996). Automatic stereotyping. *Psychological Science, 7*(3), 136–141.

Banks, W. P., Thompson, S., Henry, G., & Weissmann, T. (1986). Mental models of physiological function in health and illness. Presentation at the 27th annual meeting of the Psychonomic Society, November 1986, New Orleans.

Bar-Hillel, M. (1982). Studies of representativeness. In D. Kahneman, P. Slovic, & A. Tversky (Eds.), *Judgment under uncertainty: Heuristics and biases.* New York: Cambridge University Press.

Baratgin, J., & Noveck, I. A. (2000). Not only base rates are neglected in the engineer-lawyer problem: An investigation of reasoners' underutilization of complementarity. *Memory & Cognition, 28*, 79–91.

Bargh, J. A. (1989). Conditional automaticity: Varieties of automatic influence in social perception and cognition. In J. Uleman & J. Bargh (Eds.), *Unintended thought.* New York: Guilford Press.

Bargh, J. A., & Chartrand, T. L. (1999). The unbearable automaticity of being. *American Psychologist, 54*, 462–479.

Baron, J. (1977). Mechanisms for pronouncing printed words: Use and acquisition. In S. J. Samuels (Ed.), *Basic processes in reading: Perception and comprehension.* Hillsdale, NJ: Lawrence Erlbaum.

Baron, J. (1988). *Thinking and reasoning.* Cambridge: Cambridge University Press.

Baron, J. (1998). *Judgment misguided: Intuition and error in public decision making.* New York: Oxford University Press.

Barsalou, L. (1982). Context-independent and context-dependent information in concepts. *Memory & Cognition, 10*, 82–93.

Barsalou, L. (1983). Ad hoc categories. *Memory & Cognition, 11*, 211–227.

Barsalou, L. (1985). Ideals, central tendency, and frequency of instantiation. *Journal of Experimental Psychology: Learning, Memory and Cognition, 11*, 629–654.

Barsalou, L. (1987). The instability of graded structure: Implications for the nature of concepts. In U. Neisser (Ed.), *Concepts and conceptual development.* Cambridge: Cambridge University Press.

Barsalou, L. (1988). The content and organization of autobiographical memories. In U. Neisser & E. Winograd (Eds.), *Remembering reconsidered*. Cambridge: Cambridge University Press.

Barsalou, L., & Sewell, D. R. (1985). Contrasting the representation of scripts and categories. *Journal of Memory and Language, 24*, 646–665.

Bartlett, F. C. (1932). *Remembering: A study in experimental and social psychology*. Cambridge: Cambridge University Press.

Bartz, W. H. (1976). Rehearsal and retrieval processes in recall and recognition. *Bulletin of the Psychonomic Society, 8*, 258.

Bass, E., & Davis, L. (1988). *The courage to heal: A guide for women survivors of child sexual abuse*. New York: Perennial Library/Harper & Row.

Bassok, M. (1996). Using content to interpret structure: Effects on analogical transfer. *Current Directions in Psychological Science, 5*, 54–57.

Bassok, M., Wu, L.-L., & Olseth, K. (1995). Judging a book by its cover: Interpretive effects of content on problem-solving transfer. *Memory & Cognition, 23*, 354–367.

Bateson, G. (1958). *Naven*. Stanford, CA: Stanford University Press.

Bauer, B., & Jolicoeur, P. (1996). Stimulus dimensionality effects in mental rotation. *Journal of Experimental Psychology: Human Perception and Performance, 22*, 82–94.

Baylis, G. C., & Driver, J. (1993). Visual attention and objects: Evidence for hierarchical coding of location. *Journal of Experimental Psychology: Human Perception & Performance, 19*, 451–470.

Bazerman, M. H. (1998). *Judgment in managerial decision making* (4th ed.). New York: Wiley.

Beach, C. M. (1991). The interpretation of prosodic patterns at points of syntactic structural ambiguity: Evidence for cue trading relations. *Journal of Memory and Language, 30*, 644–663.

Bédard, J., & Chi, M. (1992). Expertise. *Current Directions in Psychological Science, 1*, 135–139.

Beeman, M. J., & Chiarello, C. (1998). Complementary right- and left-hemisphere language comprehension. *Current Directions in Psychological Science, 7*, 2–8.

Begg, I., Anas, A., & Farinacci, S. (1992). Dissociation of processes in belief: Source recollection, statement familiarity, and the illusion of truth. *Journal of Experimental Psychology: General, 121*, 446–458.

Begg, I., Armour, V., & Kerr, T. (1985). On believing what we remember. *Canadian Journal of Behavioral Science, 17*, 199–214.

Begg, I., & Denny, J. (1969). Empirical reconciliation of atmosphere and conversion interpretations of syllogistic reasoning errors. *Journal of Experimental Psychology, 81*, 351–354.

Begg, I., & Wickelgren, W. A. (1974). Retention functions for syntactic and lexical vs. semantic information in sentence recognition memory. *Memory & Cognition, 2*, 353–359.

Behrmann, M. (2000). The mind's eye mapped onto the brain's matter. *Current Directions in Psychological Science, 9*, 50–54.

Behrmann, M., Moscovitch, M., & Winocur, G. (1994). Intact visual imagery and impaired visual perception in a patient with visual agnosia. *Journal of Experimental Psychology: Human Perception and Performance, 20*, 1068–1087.

Behrmann, M., & Tipper, S. (1999). Attention accesses multiple reference frames: Evidence from visual neglect. *Journal of Experimental Psychology: Human Perception and Performance, 25*, 83–101.

Bekerian, D. A., & Baddeley, A. D. (1980). Saturation advertising and the repetition effect. *Journal of Verbal Learning & Verbal Behavior, 19*, 17–25.

Bekerian, D. A., & Dennett, J. L. (1993). The cognitive interview technique: Reviving the issues. *Applied Cognitive Psychology, 7*, 275–298.

Bell, D. (1982). Regret in decision making under uncertainty. *Operations Research, 30*, 961–981.

Belli, R., Windschitl, P., McCarthy, T., & Winfrey, S. (1992). Detecting memory impairment with a modified test procedure: Manipulating retention interval with centrally presented event items. *Journal of Experimental Psychology: Learning, Memory and Cognition, 18*, 356–367.

Bellugi, U., Bihrle, A., & Corina, D. (1991). Linguistic and spatial development: Dissociations between cognitive domains. In N. A. Krasnegor & D. M. Rumbaugh (Eds.), *Biological and behavioral determinants of language development*. Hillsdale, NJ: Lawrence Erlbaum.

Bellugi, U., Klima, E. S., & Siple, P. (1975). Remembering in signs. *Cognition, 3*, 93–125.

Berardi-Coletta, B., Buyer, L., Dominowski, R., & Rellinger, E. (1995). Metacognition and problem-solving: A process-oriented approach. *Journal of Experimental Psychology: Learning, Memory and Cognition, 21*, 205–223.

Berger, S. A., Hall, L. K., & Bahrick, H. P. (1999). Stabilizing access to marginal and submarginal knowledge. *Journal of Experimental Psychology: Applied, 5*, 438–447.

Berko, J. (1958). The child's learning of English morphology. *Word, 14*, 150–177.

Berlin, B., & Key, P. (1969). *Basic color terms: Their universality and evolution*. Berkeley and Los Angeles: University of California Press.

Besner, D., & Stolz, J. A. (1999). What kind of attention modulates the Stroop effect? *Psychonomics Bulletin & Review, 6*, 99–104.

Besner, D., Stoltz, J. A., & Boutilier, C. (1997). The Stroop effect and the myth of automaticity. *Psychonomics Bulletin and Review, 4*, 221–225.

Bever, T. (1970). The cognitive basis for linguistic structures. In J. R. Hayes (Ed.), *Cognition and the development of language* (pp. 279–362). New York: Wiley.

Bhaskar, R., & Simon, H. (1977). Problem solving in semantically rich domains: An example from engineering thermodynamics. *Cognitive Science, 1*, 193–215.

Biederman, I. (1985). Human vision understanding: Recent research and a theory. *Computer Vision, Graphics, and Image Processing, 32*, 29–73.

Biederman, I. (1987). Recognition by components: A theory of human image understanding. *Psychological Review, 94*, 115–147.

Biederman, I. (1990). Higher-level vision. In D. Osherson, S. Kosslyn, & J. Hollerbach (Eds.), *Visual cognition and action*. Cambridge, MA: MIT Press.

Biederman, I. (1995). Visual object recognition. In S. M. Kosslyn & D. N. Osherson (Eds.), *Visual cognition: An invitation to cognitive science* (Vol. 2). Cambridge, MA: MIT Press.

Biederman, I., & Cooper, E. (1991). Priming contour-deleted images: Evidence for intermediate representations in visual object recognition. *Cognitive Psychology, 23*, 393–419.

Biederman, I., & Gerhardstein, P. (1993). Recognizing depth-rotated objects: Evidence and conditions for three-dimensional viewpoint invariance. *Journal of Experimental Psychology: Human Perception and Performance, 19*, 1162–1182.

Biederman, I., Glass, A. L., & Stacy, E. W. (1973). Searching for objects in real world scenes. *Journal of Experimental Psychology, 97*, 22–27.

Bisiach, E. (1996). Unilateral neglect and the structure of space representation. *Current Directions in Psychological Science, 5*, 62–65.

Bisiach, E., & Luzzatti, C. (1978). Unilateral neglect of representational space. *Cortex, 14*, 129–133.

Bisiach, E., Luzzatti, C., & Perani, D. (1979). Unilateral neglect, representational schema, and consciousness. *Brain, 102*, 609–618.

Bjork, R. A., & Whitten, W. B. (1974). Recency-sensitive retrieval processes. *Cognitive Psychology, 6*, 173–189.

Blanchette, I., & Dunbar, K. (2000). How analogies are generated: The roles of structural and superficial similarity. *Memory & Cognition, 28*, 108–124.

Blaney, P. H. (1986). Affect and memory: A review. *Psychological Bulletin, 99*, 229–246.

Blaxton, T. A. (1989). Investigating dissociations among memory measures: Support for a transfer-appropriate processing framework. *Journal of Experimental Psychology: Learning, Memory and Cognition, 15*, 657–688.

Bloom, L., & Mudd, S. (1991). Depth of processing approach to face recognition: A test of two theories. *Journal of Experimental Psychology: Learning, Memory and Cognition, 17*, 556–565.

Bloom, P. (Ed.). (1994). *Language acquisition*. Cambridge, MA: MIT Press.

Blount, G. (1986). Dangerousness of patients with Capgras Syndrome. *Nebraska Medical Journal, 71*, 207.

Bobrow, S., & Bower, G. H. (1969). Comprehension and recall of sentences. *Journal of Experimental Psychology, 80*, 455–461.

Boden, M. (1991). *The creative mind: Myths and mechanisms*. New York: Basic.

Boden, M. (Ed.). (1994). *Dimensions of creativity*. Cambridge, MA: Bradford Books.

Bohannon, J. N. (1988). Flashbulb memories of the space shuttle disaster: A tale of two theories. *Cognition, 29*, 179–196.

Bohannon, J. N. (1993). Affect and accuracy in recall: Studies of "flashbulb" memories. In E. Winograd & U. Neisser (Eds.), *Affect and accuracy in recall: Studies of "flashbulb" memories*. New York: Cambridge University Press.

Boole, G. (1854). *An investigation of the laws of thought, on which are founded the mathematical theories of logic and probabilities*. London: Walton G. Maberly.

Borges, J. L. (1964). *Labyrinths*. New York: New Directions Publishing Co.

Bornstein, B. (1963). Prosopagnosia. In L. Halpern (Ed.), *Problems of dynamic neurology*. Jerusalem: Hadassah Medical Organization.

Bornstein, B., & LeCompte, D. (1995). A comparison of item and source forgetting. *Psychonomic Bulletin & Review, 2*, 254–259.

Bornstein, B., Sroka, H., & Munitz, H. (1969). Prosopagnosia with animal face agnosia. *Cortex, 5*, 164–169.

Bothwell, R. K., Deffenbacher, K. A., & Brigham, J. C. (1987). Correlation of eyewitness accuracy and confidence: Optimality hypothesis revisited. *Journal of Applied Psychology, 72*, 691–695.

Bousfield, W. A. (1953). The occurrence of clustering in the recall of randomly arranged associates. *Journal of General Psychology, 49*, 229–240.

Bower, G. H. (1970). Analysis of a mnemonic device. *American Scientist, 58*, 496–510.

Bower, G. H. (1972). Mental imagery and associative learning. In L. W. Gregg (Ed.), *Cognition in learning and memory*. New York: Wiley.

Bower, G. H. (1981). Mood and memory. *American Psychologist, 36*, 129–148.

Bower, G. H., Black, J. B., & Turner, T. J. (1979). Scripts in memory for text. *Cognitive Psychology, 11*, 177–220.

Bower, G. H., Clark, M. C., Lesgold, A. M., & Winenz, D. (1969). Hierarchical retrieval schemes in recall of categorized word lists. *Journal of Verbal Learning and Verbal Behavior, 8*, 323–343.

Bower, G. H., & Karlin, M. B. (1974). Depth of processing pictures of faces and recognition memory. *Journal of Experimental Psychology, 103*, 751–757.

Bower, G. H., Karlin, M. B., & Dueck, A. (1975). Comprehension and memory for pictures. *Memory & Cognition, 3,* 216–220.

Bower, G. H., & Reitman, J. S. (1972). Mnemonic elaboration in multilist learning. *Journal of Verbal Learning and Verbal Behavior, 11,* 478–485.

Bower, G. H., & Winzenz, D. (1970). Comparison of associative learning strategies. *Psychonomic Science, 20,* 119–120.

Boyce, S., & Pollatsek, A. (1992). Identification of objects in scenes: The role of scene background in object naming. *Journal of Experimental Psychology: Learning, Memory and Cognition, 18,* 531–543.

Braine, M. (1978). On the relation between the natural logic of reasoning and standard logic. *Psychological Review, 85,* 1–21.

Braine, M., & O'Brien, D. (1991). A theory of *if*: A lexical entry, reasoning program, and pragmatic principles. *Psychological Review, 98,* 182–203.

Braine, M., O'Brien, D., Noveck, I., Samuels, M., Lea, R. B., Fisch, S. M., & Yang, Y. (1995). Predicting intermediate and multiple conclusions in propositional logic inference. *Journal of Experimental Psychology: General, 124,* 263–292.

Braine, M., Reiser, B. J., & Rumain, B. (1984). Some empirical justification for a theory of natural propositional logic. In G. H. Bower (Ed.), *The psychology of learning and motivation.* New York: Academic Press.

Brainerd, C. J., & Reyna, V. F. (1998). When things that were never experienced are easier to "remember" than things that were. *Psychological Science, 9,* 484–490.

Brainerd, C. J., Reyna, V. F., & Mojardin, A. H. (1999). Conjoint recognition. *Psychological Review, 106,* 160–179.

Bransford, J. (1979). *Human cognition: Learning, understanding and remembering.* Belmont, CA: Wadsworth.

Bransford, J., Barclay, J. R., & Franks, J. J. (1972). Sentence memory: A constructive versus interpretive approach. *Cognitive Psychology, 3,* 193–209.

Bransford, J., & Franks, J. J. (1971). The abstraction of linguistic ideas. *Cognitive Psychology, 2,* 331–350.

Bransford, J., Franks, J. J., Morris, C. D., & Stein, B. S. (1979). Some general constraints on learning and memory research. In L. S. Cermak & F. I. M. Craik (Eds.), *Levels of processing in human memory.* Hillsdale, NJ: Lawrence Erlbaum.

Bransford, J., & Johnson, M. K. (1972). Contextual prerequisites for understanding: some investigations of comprehension and recall. *Journal of Verbal Learning and Verbal Behavior, 11,* 717–726.

Bransford, J., & Johnson, M. K. (1973). Considerations of some problems of comprehension. In W. G. Chase (Ed.), *Visual information processing.* New York: Academic Press.

Brase, G. L., Cosmides, L., & Tooby, J. (1998). Individuation, counting and statistical inference: The role of frequency and whole-object representations in judgment under uncertainty. *Journal of Experimental Psychology: General, 127,* 3–21.

Breedin, S. D., & Saffran, E. M. (1999). Sentence processing in the face of semantic loss: A case study. *Journal of Experimental Psychology: General, 128,* 547–562.

Bremner, J. D., Shobe, K., & Kihlstrom, J. F. (2000). False memories in women with self-reported childhood sexual abuse: An empirical study. *Psychological Science, 11,* 333–337.

Bremner, J. D., Southwick, S. M., Johnson, D. R., Yehuda, R. et al. (1993). Childhood physical abuse and combat-related posttraumatic stress disorder in Vietnam veterans. *American Journal of Psychiatry, 150,* 235–239.

Brendl, C. M., Markman, A. B., & Higgins, E. T. (1998). Mental accounting as self-regulation: Representativeness to goal-derived categories. *Zeitschrift Fuer Sozialpsychologie, 29*(2), 89–104.

Brennen, T., Baguley, T., Bright, J., & Bruce, V. (1990). Resolving semantically induced tip-of-the-tongue states for proper nouns. *Memory & Cognition, 18,* 339–347.

Brenner, L., Rottenstreich, Y., & Sood, S. (1999). Comparison, grouping, and preference. *Psychological Science, 10,* 225–229.

Brewer, W. (1977). Memory for the pragmatic implications of sentences. *Memory & Cognition, 5,* 673–678.

Brewer, W. (1987). Schemas vs. mental models in human memory. In P. Morris (Ed.), *Modeling cognition* (pp. 187–197). New York: Wiley.

Brewer, W. (1988). Memory for randomly sampled autobiographical events. In U. Neisser & E. W. Winograd (Eds.), *Remembering reconsidered.* Cambridge: Cambridge University Press.

Brewer, W., & Treyens, J. C. (1981). Role of schemata in memory for places. *Cognitive Psychology, 13,* 207–230.

Brewin, C. R. (1998). Intrusive autobiographical memories in depression and post-traumatic stress disorder. *Applied Cognitive Psychology, 12,* 359–370.

Brewin, C. R., Andrews, B., & Gotlib, I. (1993). Psychopathology and early experience: A reappraisal of retrospective reports. *Psychological Bulletin, 113,* 82–98.

Brigham, J. (1986). The influence of race on face recognition. In H. D. Ellis, M. A. Jeeves, F. Newcombe, & A. Young (Eds.), *Aspects of face processing* (pp. 170–177). Dordrecht, Netherlands: Martinus Nijhoff.

Brigham, J. (1990). Target person distinctiveness and attractiveness as moderator variables in the confidence-accuracy relationship in eyewitness identifications. *Basic and Applied Social Psychology, 11,* 101–115.

Brigham, J., & Cairns, D. L. (1988). The effect of mugshot inspections on eyewitness identification accuracy. *Journal of Applied Social Psychology, 18,* 1394–1410.

Brigham, J., Ready, D., & Spier, S. (1990). Standards for evaluating the fairness of photograph lineups. *Basic and Applied Social Psychology, 11*, 149–163.

Brigham, J., & Wolfskiel, M. P. (1983). Opinions of attorneys and law enforcement personnel on the accuracy of eyewitness identification. *Law and Human Behavior, 7*, 337–349.

Broadbent, D. E. (1958). *Perception and communication.* London: Pergamon.

Brooks, L. (1968). Spatial and verbal components of the act of recall. *Canadian Journal of Psychology, 22*, 349–368.

Brooks, L. (1978). Non-analytic concept formation and memory for instances. In E. Rosch & B. Lloyd (Eds.), *Cognition and categorization.* Hillsdale, NJ: Lawrence Erlbaum.

Brooks, L. (1987). Decentralized control of categorization: The role of prior processing episodes. In U. Neisser (Ed.), *Concepts and conceptual development.* Cambridge: Cambridge University Press.

Brooks, L. (1990). Concept formation and particularizing learning. In P. Hanson (Ed.), *Information, language and cognition.* Vancouver, BC: University of British Columbia Press.

Brooks, L., LeBlanc, V. R., & Norman, G. R. (2000). On the difficulty of noticing obvious features in patient appearance. *Psychological Science, 11*, 112–117.

Brooks, L., Norman, G., & Allen, S. (1991). Role of specific similarity in a medical diagnostic task. *Journal of Experimental Psychology: General, 120*, 278–287.

Brown, A. (1991). A review of the tip-of-the-tongue experience. *Psychological Bulletin, 109*, 204–223.

Brown, A., Neblett, D., Jones, T., & Mitchell, D. (1991). Transfer of processing in repetition priming: Some inappropriate findings. *Journal of Experimental Psychology: Learning, Memory and Cognition, 17*, 514–525.

Brown, A. L. (1979). Theories of memory and the problems of development: Activity, growth, and knowledge. In L. S. Cermak & F. I. M. Craik (Eds.), *Levels of processing in human memory.* Hillsdale, NJ: Lawrence Erlbaum.

Brown, A. S., & Halliday, H. E. (1990). Multiple-choice tests: Pondering incorrect alternatives can be hazardous to your knowledge. Paper presented at the meeting of the Psychonomics Society, November 1990, New Orleans.

Brown, D., Scheflin, A. W., & Hammond, D. C. (1998). *Memory, trauma treatment, and the law.* New York: Norton.

Brown, E., Deffenbacher, K., & Sturgill, W. (1977). Memory for faces and the circumstances of encounter. *Journal of Applied Psychology, 62*, 311–318.

Brown, J. (1958). Some tests of the decay theory of immediate memory. *Quarterly Journal of Experimental Psychology, 10*, 12–21.

Brown, J. S., & Van Lehn, K. (1980). Repair theory: A generative theory of bugs in procedural skills. *Cognitive Science, 4*, 379–426.

Brown, N., & Siegler, R. (1993). Metrics and mappings: A framework for understanding real-world quantitative estimation. *Psychological Review, 100*, 511–534.

Brown, N. R., & Schopflocher, D. (1998). Event cueing, event clusters, and the temporal distribution of autobiographical memories. *Applied Cognitive Psychology, 12*, 297–304.

Brown, R., & Kulik, J. (1977). Flashbulb memories. *Cognition, 5*, 73–99.

Brown, R., & Lenneberg, E. H. (1954). A study in language and cognition. *Journal of Abnormal and Social Psychology, 49*, 454–462.

Brown, R., & McNeill, D. (1966). The "tip of the tongue" phenomenon. *Journal of Verbal Learning and Verbal Behavior, 5*, 325–337.

Bruce, D., Hockley, W., & Craik, F. (1991). Availability and category-frequency estimation. *Memory & Cognition, 19*, 301–312.

Bruce, D., & Winograd, E. (1998). Remembering Deese's 1959 articles: The Zeitgeist, the sociology of sciences, and false memories. *Psychonomic Bulletin & Review, 5*, 615–624.

Bruce, V., Doyle, T., Dench, N., & Burton, M. (1991). Remembering facial configurations. *Cognition, 38*, 109–144.

Bruce, V., Valentine, T., & Baddeley, A. D. (1987). The basis of the 3/4 view advantage in face recognition. *Applied Cognitive Psychology, 1*, 109–120.

Bruck, M., Cavanagh, P., & Ceci, S. (1991). Fortysomething: Recognizing faces at one's 25th reunion. *Memory & Cognition, 19*, 221–228.

Bruck, M., & Ceci, S. J. (1999). The suggestibility of children's memory. *Annual Review of Psychology, 50*, 419–440.

Bruner, J. S. (1973). *Beyond the information given.* New York: Norton.

Bruner, J. S., Goodnow, J., & Austin, G. (1956). *A study of thinking.* New York: Wiley.

Burke, A., Heuer, F., & Reisberg, D. (1992). Remembering emotional events. *Memory & Cognition, 20*, 277–290.

Burt, C. D. B., Watt, S. C., Mitchell, D. A., & Conway, M. A. (1998). Retrieving the sequence of autobiographical event components. *Applied Cognitive Psychology, 12*, 321–338.

Burton, A. M., Bruce, V., & Hancock, P. J. B. (1999). From pixels to people: A model of familiar face recognition. *Cognitive Science, 23*, 1–31.

Burton, A. M., Young, A., Bruce, V., Johnston, R., & Ellis, A. (1991). Understanding covert recognition. *Cognition, 39*, 129–166.

Buschke, H. (1977). Two-dimensional recall: Immediate identification of clusters in episodic and semantic memory. *Journal of Verbal Learning and Verbal Behavior, 16,* 201–215.

Busey, T. A., Tunnicliff, J., Loftus, G. R., & Loftus, E. F. (2000). Accounts of the confidence-accuracy relation in recognition memory. *Memory & Cognition, 7,* 26–48.

Cahill, L., Babinsky, R., Markowitsch, H. J., & McGaugh, J. L. (1996). The amygdala and emotional memory. *Nature, 377,* 295–296.

Cann, A., & Ross, D. (1989). Olfactory stimuli as context cues in human memory. *American Journal of Psychology, 2,* 91–102.

Cantor, J., & Engle, R. (1993). Working-memory capacity as long-term memory activation: An individual-differences approach. *Journal of Experimental Psychology: Learning, Memory and Cognition, 19,* 1101–1114.

Capgras, J., & Reboul-Lachaux, J. (1923). L'illusion des "sosies" dans un delire systematise chronique. *Bulletine de Societe Clinique de Medicine Mentale, 11,* 6–16.

Caplan, D. (1987). *Neurolinguistics and linguistic aphasiology.* New York: Cambridge University Press.

Caplan, D. (1992). *Language: Structure, processing and disorders.* Cambridge, MA: MIT Press.

Carey, S. (1985). *Conceptual change in childhood.* Cambridge, MA: Bradford/MIT Press.

Carmichael, L. C., Hogan, H. P., & Walters, A. A. (1932). An experimental study of the effect of language on the reproduction of visually perceived form. *Journal of Experimental Psychology, 15,* 73–86.

Carpenter, P., & Eisenberg, P. (1978). Mental rotation and the frame of reference in blind and sighted individuals. *Perception & Psychophysics, 23,* 117–124.

Carpenter, P., Just, M., & Shell, P. (1990). What one intelligence test measures: A theoretical account of the processing in the Raven Progressive Matrices Test. *Psychological Review, 97,* 404–431.

Cary, M., & Carlson, R. A. (1999). External support and the development of problem-solving routines. *Journal of Experimental Psychology: Learning, Memory and Cognition, 25,* 1053–1070.

Casey, E. (1976). *Imagining: A phenomenological study.* Bloomington: Indiana University Press.

Castiello, U., & Umiltá, C. (1990). Size of the attentional focus and efficiency of processing. *Acta Psychologica, 73,* 195–209.

Catrambone, R. (1994). Improving examples to improve transfer to novel problems. *Memory & Cognition, 22,* 606–615.

Catrambone, R. (1998). The subgoal learning model: Creating better examples so that students can solve novel problems. *Journal of Experimental Psychology: General, 127,* 355–376.

Catrambone, R., & Holyoak, K. J. (1989). Overcoming contextual limitations on problem-solving transfer. *Journal of Experimental Psychology: Learning, Memory and Cognition, 15,* 1147–1156.

Cattell, J. M. (1885). Uberdi Aeit der Erkennung and Benennung von Schriftzeichen, Bildern and Farben. *Philos, 2,* 635–650.

Cave, K. R., & Bichot, N. P. (1999). Visuospatial attention: Beyond a spotlight model. *Psychonomics Bulletin and Review, 6,* 204–223.

Ceci, S., & Bruck, M. (1993). Suggestibility of the child witness: A historical review and synthesis. *Psychological Bulletin, 113,* 403–439.

Ceci, S., & Bruck, M. (1995). *Jeopardy in the courtroom: A scientific analysis of children's testimony.* Washington, DC: American Psychological Association.

Ceci, S., Huffman, M., & Smith, E. (1994). Repeatedly thinking about a non-event: Source misattributions among preschoolers. *Consciousness and Cognition, 3,* 388–407.

Challis, B., & Brodbeck, D. (1992). Level of processing affects priming in word fragment completion. *Journal of Experimental Psychology: Learning, Memory and Cognition, 18,* 595–607.

Chambers, D., & Reisberg, D. (1985). Can mental images be ambiguous? *Journal of Experimental Psychology: Human Perception and Performance, 11,* 317–328.

Chambers, D., & Reisberg, D. (1992). What an image depicts depends on what an image means. *Cognitive Psychology, 24,* 145–174.

Chandler, C. (1994). Studying related pictures can reduce accuracy, but increase confidence, in a modified recognition test. *Memory & Cognition, 22,* 273–280.

Chandler, C., Greening, L., Robinson, L. J., & Stoppelbein, L. (1999). It can't happen to me . . . Or can it? Conditional base rates affect subjective probability judgments. *Journal of Experimental Psychology: Applied, 5,* 361–378.

Chapman, J., & Chapman, L. J. (1959). Atmosphere effect re-examined. *Journal of Experimental Psychology, 58,* 220–226.

Chapman, L. J., & Chapman, J. (1971). Test results are what you think they are. *Psychology Today,* November, 18–22, 106–110.

Charniak, E. (1972). *Toward a model of children's story comprehension.* Unpublished doctoral dissertation, M.I.T.

Chase, W., & Ericsson, K. A. (1978). Acquisition of a mnemonic system for digit span. Paper presented at the annual meeting of the Psychonomic Society, San Antonio, Texas.

Chase, W., & Ericsson, K. A. (1979). A mnemonic system for digit span: One year later. Paper presented at the annual meeting of the Psychonomic Society, Phoenix, Arizona.

Chase, W., & Ericsson, K. A. (1982). Skill and working memory. In G. H. Bower (Ed.), *The psychology of learning and motivation.* New York: Academic Press.

Chase, W., & Simon, H. (1973). Perception in chess. *Cognitive Psychology, 4,* 55–81.

Chen, Z. (1995). Analogical transfer: From schematic pictures to problem solving. *Memory & Cognition, 23,* 255–269.

Cheng, P. (1985). Restructuring versus automaticity: Alternative accounts of skill acquisition. *Psychological Review, 92,* 414–423.

Cheng, P., & Holyoak, K. J. (1985). Pragmatic reasoning schemas. *Cognitive Psychology, 17,* 391–416.

Cheng, P., Holyoak, K. J., Nisbett, R. E., & Oliver, L. M. (1986). Pragmatic versus syntactic approaches to training deductive reasoning. *Cognitive Psychology, 18,* 293–328.

Cherry, E. C. (1953). Some experiments on the recognition of speech with one and with two ears. *Journal of the Acoustical Society of America, 25,* 975–979.

Chi, M. (1976). Short-term memory limitations in children: Capacity or processing deficits? *Memory & Cognition, 4,* 559–572.

Chi, M., Feltovich, P., & Glaser, R. (1981). Categorization and representation of physics problems by experts and novices. *Cognitive Science, 5,* 121–152.

Chi, M., Glaser, R., & Farr, M. (Eds.). (1988). *The nature of expertise.* Hillsdale, NJ: Lawrence Erlbaum.

Chomsky, N. (1957). *Syntactic structures.* The Hague: Mouton.

Chomsky, N. (1965). *Aspects of a theory of syntax.* Cambridge, MA: MIT Press.

Chomsky, N. (1975). *Reflections on language.* London: Temple-Smith.

Chomsky, N. (1981). *Lectures on government and binding.* Dordrech, Netherlands: Foris.

Chomsky, N. (1986). *Knowledge of language: Its nature, origin and use.* New York: Praeger.

Chomsky, N., & Halle, M. (1968). *The sound pattern of English.* New York: Harper & Row.

Christen, F., & Bjork, R. A. (1976). On updating the loci in the method of loci. Paper presented at the meeting of the Psychonomic Society, November 1976, St. Louis.

Christensen-Szalanski, J., Beck, D., Christensen-Szalanski, C., & Koepsell, T. (1983). The effect of journal coverage on physicians' perception of risk. *Journal of Applied Psychology, 68,* 278–284.

Christiaansen, R., Sweeney, J., & Ochalek, K. (1983). Influencing eyewitness descriptions. *Law and Human Behavior, 7,* 59–65.

Christiansen, M. H., & Chater, N. (1999). Toward a connectionist model of recursion in human linguistic performance. *Cognitive Science, 23*(2), 157–205.

Christianson, S.-Å. (1989). Flashbulb memories: Special, but not so special. *Memory & Cognition, 17,* 435–443.

Christianson, S.-Å. (1992). Emotional stress and eyewitness memory: A critical review. *Psychological Bulletin, 112,* 284–309.

Christianson, S.-Å., & Loftus, E. F. (1990). Some characteristics of people's traumatic memories. *Bulletin of the Psychonomic Society, 28,* 195–198.

Christianson, S.-Å., & Loftus, E. F. (1991). Remembering emotional events: The fate of detailed information. *Cognition & Emotion, 5,* 693–701.

Chronicle, E. P., MacGregor, J. N., & Ormerod, T. C. (in press). When insight just won't come: The failure of visual cues in the nine-dot problem. *Quarterly Journal of Experimental Psychology.*

Churchland, P. (1988). *Matter and consciousness.* Cambridge, MA: MIT Press.

Churchland, P. (1989). *A neurocomputational perspective: The nature of mind and the structure of science.* Cambridge, MA: MIT Press.

Churchland, P., & Sejnowski, T. J. (1992). *The computational brain.* Cambridge, MA: MIT Press.

Clancy, S. A., Schacter, D. L., McNally, R. J., & Pitmann, R. K. (2000). False recognition in women reporting recovered memories of sexual abuse. *Psychological Science, 11,* 26–31.

Claparède, E. (1911/1951). Reconnaissance et moiité. In D. Rapaport (Ed.), *Organization and pathology of thought.* New York: Columbia University Press.

Clement, J. (1982). Analogical reasoning patterns in expert problem solving. Paper presented at the 4th Annual Conference of the Cognitive Science Society, August 1982, Ann Arbor.

Cobb, S. (1941). *Foundations of neuropsychiatry.* Baltimore: Williams & Wilkins.

Cofer, C. N., Bruce, D. R., & Reicher, G. M. (1966). Clustering in free recall as a function of certain methodological variations. *Journal of Experimental Psychology, 71,* 858–866.

Cohen, J. D., Romero, R. D., Servan-Schreiber, D., & Farah, M. J. (1994). Mechanisms of spatial attention. *Journal of Cognitive Neuroscience, 6,* 377–387.

Cohen, N. J., & Squire, L. R. (1980). Preserved learning and retention of pattern analyzing skill in amnesics: Dissociation of knowing how and knowing that. *Science, 210,* 207–210.

Cole, R. A., & Jakimik, J. (1980). A model of speech perception. In R. A. Cole (Ed.), *Perception and the production of fluent speech* (pp. 133–163). Hillsdale, NJ: Lawrence Erlbaum.

Collins, A. M., & Loftus, E. F. (1975). A spreading activation theory of semantic processing. *Psychological Review, 82,* 407–428.

Collins, A. M., & Quillian, M. R. (1969). Retrieval time from semantic memory. *Journal of Verbal Learning and Verbal Behavior, 8,* 240–247.

Coltheart, V. (1993). Effects of phonological similarity and concurrent irrelevant articulation on short-term-memory recall of repeated and novel word lists. *Memory & Cognition, 21*, 539–545.

Combs, B., & Slovic, P. (1979). Causes of death: Biased newspaper coverage and biased judgments. *Journalism Quarterly, 56*, 837–843, 849.

Comrie, B. (1981). *Language universals and linguistic typology.* Chicago: University of Chicago Press.

Connolly, T., & Koput, K. (1996). Naturalistic decision making and the new organizational context. In Z. Shapira (Ed.), *Organizational decision making.* Cambridge: Cambridge University Press.

Connors, E., Lundregan, T., Miller, N., & McEwan, T. (1996). *Convicted by juries, exonerated by science: Case studies in the use of DNA evidence to establish innocence after trial.* Alexandria, VA: National Institute of Justice.

Conrad, C. (1972). Cognitive economy in semantic memory. *Journal of Experimental Psychology, 92*, 149–154.

Conrad, R. (1964). Acoustic confusion in immediate memory. *British Journal of Psychology, 55*, 75–84.

Conrad, R., & Hull, A. J. (1964). Information, acoustic confusion and memory span. *British Journal of Psychology, 55*, 429–432.

Conway, M., Anderson, S., Larsen, S., Donnelly, C., McDaniel, M., McClelland, A. G. R., Rawles, R., & Logie, R. (1994). The formation of flashbulb memories. *Memory & Cognition, 22*, 326–343.

Conway, M., Cohen, G., & Stanhope, N. (1991). On the very long-term retention of knowledge acquired through formal education: Twelve years of cognitive psychology. *Journal of Experimental Psychology: General, 120*, 395–409.

Conway, M., Cohen, G., & Stanhope, N. (1992). Why is it that university grades do not predict very long term retention? *Journal of Experimental Psychology: General, 121*, 382–384.

Conway, M., Collins, A. F., Gathercole, S., & Anderson, S. J. (1996). Recollections of true and false autobiographical memories. *Journal of Experimental Psychology: General, 125*, 69–98.

Conway, M., & Fthenaki, K. (1999). Disruption and loss of autobiographical memory. In L. S. Cermak (Ed.), *Handbook of neuropsychology: Memory.* Amsterdam: Elsevier.

Conway, M., & Holmes, A. (1999). Psychosocial stages and the availability of autobiographical memories, under review.

Conway, M., & Pleydell-Pearce, C. W. (2000). The construction of autobiographical memories in the self-memory system. *Psychological Review, 107*, 261–288.

Conway, M., & Ross, M. (1984). Getting what you want by revising what you had. *Journal of Personality and Social Psychology, 39*, 406–415.

Cook, S., & Wilding, J. (1997). Earwitness testimony: Never mind the variety, hear the length. *Applied Cognitive Psychology, 11*, 95–112.

Cook, S., & Wilding, J. (1997). Earwitness testimony 2: Voices, faces and context. *Applied Cognitive Psychology, 11*, 527–542.

Cook, V. J. (1988). *Chomsky's universal grammar: An introduction.* Cambridge, MA: Basil Blackwell.

Cooper, L. (1990). Mental representation of three-dimensional objects in visual problem solving and recognition. *Journal of Experimental Psychology: Learning, Memory and Cognition, 16*, 1097–1106.

Cooper, L., & Schacter, D. (1992). Dissociations between structural and episodic representations of visual objects. *Current Directions in Psychological Science, 1*, 141–145.

Cooper, L., & Shepard, R. N. (1973). Chronometric studies of the rotation of mental images. In W. G. Chase (Ed.), *Visual information processing.* New York: Academic Press.

Corteen, R. S., & Dunn, D. (1974). Shock-associated words in a nonattended message: A test for momentary awareness. *Journal of Experimental Psychology, 102*, 1143–1144.

Corteen, R. S., & Wood, B. (1972). Autonomic responses to shock-associated words in an unattended channel. *Journal of Experimental Psychology, 94*, 308–313.

Corter, J., & Gluck, M. (1992). Explaining basic categories: Feature predictability and information. *Psychological Bulletin, 111*, 291–303.

Cosmides, L. (1989). The logic of social exchange: Has natural selection shaped how humans reason? Studies with the Wason selection task. *Cognition, 31*, 187–276.

Cosmides, L., & Tooby, J. (1996). Are humans good intuitive statisticians after all? Rethinking some conclusions from the literature on judgment. *Cognition, 58*, 1–73.

Courtney, S. M., Petit, L., Ma Maisog, J., Ungerleider, L., & Haxby, J. (1998). An area specialized for spatial working memory in human frontal cortex. *Science, 279*, 1347–1351.

Cowan, N., Wood, N., & Borne, D. (1994). Reconfirmation of the short-term storage concept. *Psychological Science, 5*, 103–107.

Craik, F. I. M., & Lockhart, R. S. (1972). Levels of processing: A framework for memory research. *Journal of Verbal Learning and Verbal Behavior, 11*, 671–684.

Craik, F. I. M., Moscovitch, M., & McDown, J. (1994). Contributions of surface and conceptual information to performance on implicit and explicit memory tasks. *Journal of Experimental Psychology: Learning, Memory and Cognition, 20*, 864–875.

Craik, F. I. M., & Tulving, E. (1975). Depth of processing and the retention of words in episodic memory. *Journal of Experimental Psychology: General, 104*, 269–294.

Craik, F. I. M., & Watkins, M. J. (1973). The role of rehearsal in short-term memory. *Journal of Verbal Learning and Verbal Behavior, 12*, 599–607.

Crews, F. (1996). The verdict on Freud. *Psychological Science, 7*, 63–68.

Crick, F. (1994). *The astonishing hypothesis: The scientific search for the soul.* New York: Charles Scribners' Sons.

Crombag, H. F. M., Wagenaar, W. A., & van Koppen, P. J. (1996). Crashing memories and the problem of 'source monitoring.' *Applied Cognitive Psychology, 10*, 95–104.

Crowder, R. (1993). Short-term memory: Where do we stand? *Memory & Cognition, 21*, 142–145.

Crowder, R., & Wagner, R. (1992). *The psychology of reading* (2nd ed.). New York: Oxford University Press.

Crutcher, R. (1994). Telling what we know: The use of verbal report methodologies in psychological research. *Psychological Science, 5*, 241–244.

Crystal, D. (1987). *The Cambridge encyclopedia of language.* Cambridge, MA: Cambridge University Press.

Cummins, D. (1992). Role of analogical reasoning in induction of problem categories. *Journal of Experimental Psychology: Learning, Memory and Cognition, 18*, 1103–1124.

Cummins, D., & Allen, C. (Eds.). (1998). *The evolution of mind.* New York: Oxford University Press.

Curran, T., & Hintzman, D. L. (1995). Violations of the independence assumption in process dissociation. *Journal of Experimental Psychology: Learning, Memory, & Cognition, 21*(3), 531–547.

Cutler, B. L., Fisher, R. P., & Chicvara, C. L. (1989). Eyewitness identification from live versus videotaped lineups. *Forensic Reports, 2*, 93–106.

Cutler, B. L., & Penrod, S. D. (1988). Improving the reliability of eyewitness identification: Lineup construction and presentation. *Journal of Applied Psychology, 73*, 281–290.

Cutler, B. L., & Penrod, S. D. (1989). Forensically relevant moderators of the relation between eyewitness identification accuracy and confidence. *Journal of Applied Psychology, 74*, 650–652.

Cutler, B. L., Penrod, S. D., & Stuve, T. E. (1988). Juror decision making in eyewitness identification cases. *Law and Human Behavior, 12*, 41–55.

Cutler, B. L., Penrod, S. D., & Dexter, H. R. (1990). Juror sensitivity to eyewitness identification evidence. *Law and Human Behavior, 14*, 185–191.

da Costa Pinto, A., & Baddeley, A. D. (1991). Where did you park your car? Analysis of naturalistic long-term recency effect. *European Journal of Cognitive Psychology, 3*, 297–313.

Dale, H. C. A., & Baddeley, A. D. (1969). Acoustic similarity in long-term paired-associate learning. *Psychonomic Science, 16*, 209–211.

Damasio, A., Damasio, H., & Van Hoesen, G. W. (1982). Prosopagnosia: Anatomic basis and behavioral mechanisms. *Neurology, 32*, 331–341.

Damasio, A. R., Tranel, D., & Damasio, H. (1989). Disorders of visual recognition. In H. Goodglass & A. R. Damasio (Eds.), *Handbook of neuropsychology* (Vol. 2). New York: Elsevier.

Damasio, A. R., Tranel, D., & Damasio, H. (1990). Face agnosia and the neural substrates of memory. *Annual Review of Neuroscience, 13*, 89–109.

Daneman, M., & Carpenter, P. (1980). Individual differences in working memory and reading. *Journal of Verbal Learning and Verbal Behavior, 19*, 450–466.

Daneman, M., & Stainton, M. (1991). Phonological coding in silent reading. *Journal of Experimental Psychology: Learning, Memory and Cognition, 17*, 618–632.

Daniloff, R., & Hammarberg, R. (1973). On defining coarticulation. *Journal of Phonetics, 1*, 185–194.

Davison, G., Navarre, S., & Vogel, R. (1995). The articulated thoughts in simulated situations paradigm: A think-aloud approach to cognitive assessment. *Current Directions in Psychological Science, 4*, 29–33.

Dawes, R. M. (1988). *Rational choice in an uncertain world.* San Diego: Harcourt Brace Jovanovich.

De Groot, A. (1965). *Thought and choice in chess.* The Hague: Mouton.

De Groot, A. (1966). Perception and memory versus thought: Some old ideas and recent findings. In B. Kleinmuntz (Ed.), *Problem solving.* New York: Wiley.

De Haan, E. E., Bauer, R. M., & Greve, K. W. (1992). Behavioral and physiological evidence for covert recognition in a prosopagnosic patient. *Cortex, 28*, 77–95.

De Jong, R. (1993). Multiple bottlenecks in overlapping task performance. *Journal of Experimental Psychology: Human Perception and Performance, 19*, 965–980.

De Jong, R., & Sweet, J. (1994). Preparatory strategies in overlapping-task performance. *Memory & Cognition, 55*, 142–151.

Deese, J. (1959). On the prediction of occurrence of particular verbal intrusions in immediate recall. *Journal of Experimental Psychology, 58*, 17-22.

Deese, J., & Kaufman, R. A. (1957). Serial effects in recall of unorganized and sequentially organized verbal material. *Journal of Experimental Psychology, 54*, 180–187.

Deffenbacher, K. (1980). Eyewitness accuracy and confidence: Can we infer anything about their relationship. *Law and Human Behavior, 4*, 243–260.

Deffenbacher, K. (1988). Eyewitness research: The next ten years. In M. Gruneberg, P. Morris, & R. Sykes (Eds.), *Practical aspects of memory: Current research and issues* (pp. 20–26). New York: Wiley.

Deffenbacher, K., & Loftus, E. F. (1982). Do jurors share a common understanding concerning eyewitness behavior? *Law and Human Behavior, 6,* 15–30.

Dell, G. S., Burger, L. K., & Svec, W. R. (1997). Language production and serial order: A function analysis and a model. *Psychological Review, 104,* 123–147.

Demers, R. (1989). Linguistics and animal communication. In F. Newmeyer (Ed.), *Linguistics: The Cambridge Survey. III. Language: Psychological and biological aspects.* Cambridge, MA: Cambridge University Press.

Dempster, F. N. (1981). Memory span: Sources of individual and developmental differences. *Psychological Bulletin, 89,* 63–100.

Dennett, D. (1981). The nature of images and the introspective trap. In N. Block (Ed.), *Imagery* (pp. 51–61). Cambridge, MA: MIT Press.

Dennett, D. (1992). *Consciousness explained.* Boston: Little, Brown.

De Renzi, E., Faglioni, P., Grossi, D., & Nichelli, P. (1991). Apperceptive and associative forms of prosopagnosia. *Cortex, 27,* 213–221.

DeWitt, L., & Samuel, A. (1990) The role of knowledge-based expectations in music perception: Evidence from musical restoration. *Journal of Experimental Psychology: General, 119,* 123–144.

Diamond, R., & Carey, S. (1986). Why faces are and are not special: An effect of expertise. *Journal of Experimental Psychology: General, 115,* 107–117.

Dinges, D., Whitehouse, W., Orne, E., Powell, J., Orne, M., & Erdelyi, M. (1992). Evaluation of hypnotic memory enhancement (hypermnesia and reminiscence) using multitrial forced recall. *Journal of Experimental Psychology: Learning, Memory and Cognition, 18,* 1139–1147.

Dingwall, W. O. (1993). The biological bases of human communicative behavior. In J. Berko Gleason & N. Bernstein Ratner (Eds.), *Psycholinguistics.* New York: Harcourt Brace Jovanovich.

Dodson, C. S., Holland, P. W., & Shimamura, A. P. (1998). On the recollection of specific- and partial-source information. *Journal of Experimental Psychology: Learning, Memory and Cognition, 24,* 1121–1136.

Dominowski, R. (1981). Comment on "An examination of the alleged role of 'fixation' in the solution of several insight problems" by Weisberg and Alba. *Journal of Experimental Psychology: General, 110,* 193–198.

Dominowski, R., & Jenrick, R. (1972). Effects of hints and interpolated activity on solution of an insight problem. *Psychonomic Science, 26,* 335–338.

Donnelly, C., & McDaniel, M. A. (1993). Use of analogy in learning scientific concepts. *Journal of Experimental Psychology: Learning, Memory and Cognition, 19,* 975–986.

Dooling, D. J., & Christiaansen, R. E. (1977). Episodic and semantic aspects of memory for prose. *Journal of Experimental Psychology: Human Learning and Memory, 3,* 428–436.

Dooling, D. J., & Lachman, R. (1971). Effects of comprehension on retention of prose. *Journal of Experimental Psychology, 88,* 216–222.

Dorfman, J., Shames, V. A., & Kihlstrom, J. F. (1996). Intuition, incubation, and insight: Implicit cognition in problem solving. In G. D. M. Underwood (Ed.), *Implicit cognition.* Oxford: Oxford University Press.

Downs, J., & Shafir, E. (1999). Why some are perceived as more confident and more insecure, more reckless and more cautious, more trusting and more suspicious, than others: Enriched and impoverished options in social judgment. *Psychonomics Bulletin & Review, 6,* 598–610.

Duncan, J. (1994). Attention, intelligence, and the frontal lobes. In M. Gazzaniga (Ed.), *The cognitive neurosciences.* Cambridge, MA: MIT Press.

Duncan, J. (1995). Attention, intelligence, and the frontal lobes. In M. S. Gazzaniga (Ed.), *The cognitive neurosciences.* Cambridge, MA: MIT Press.

Duncan, J., Bundesen, C., Olson, A., Hymphreys, G., Chavda, S., & Shibuya, H. (1999). Systematic analysis of deficits in visual attention. *Journal of Experimental Psychology: General, 128,* 450–478.

Duncan, J., Emslie, H., Williams, P., Johnson, R., & Freer, C. (1996). Intelligence and the frontal lobe: The organization of goal-directed behavior. *Cognitive Psychology, 30,* 257–303.

Duncker, K. (1945). On problem-solving. *Psychological Monographs, 58,* No. 270 (entire).

Dunning, D., & Parpal, M. (1989). Mental addition versus subtraction in counterfactual reasoning. *Journal of Personality and Social Psychology, 57,* 5–15.

Durgin, F. H. (2000). The reverse Stroop effect. *Psychonomics Bulletin & Review, 7,* 121–125.

Dywan, J., & Bowers, K. (1983). The use of hypnosis to enhance recall. *Science, 222,* 184–185.

Easterbrook, J. A. (1959). The effect of emotion on cue utilization and the organization of behavior. *Psychological Review, 66,* 183–201.

Eberhard, K. M., Spivey-Knowlton, M. J., Sedivy, J. C., & Tanenhaus, M. K. (1995). Eye movements as a window into real-time spoken language comprehension in natural contexts. *Journal of Psycholinguistic Research, 24,* 409–436.

Eddy, D. M. (1982). Probabilistic reasoning in clinical medicine: Problems and opportunities. In D. Kahneman, P. Slovic, & A. Tversky (Eds.), *Judgment under uncertainty: Heuristics and biases.* Cambridge: Cambridge University Press.

Edelstyn, N. M. J., & Oyebode, F. (1999). A review of the phenomenology and cognitive neuropsychological origins of the Capgras Syndrome. *International Journal of Geriatric Psychiatry, 14,* 48–59.

Egan, D., & Schwartz, B. (1979). Chunking in the recall of symbolic drawings. *Memory & Cognition, 7,* 149–158.

Egly, R., Driver, J., & Rafal, R. D. (1994). Shifting visual attention between objects and locations: Evidence from normal and parietal lesion subjects. *Journal of Experimental Psychology: General, 123,* 161–177.

Eich, E. (1995). Mood as a mediator of place dependent memory. *Journal of Experimental Psychology: General, 124,* 293–308.

Eich, E., Reeves, J., Jaeger, B., & Graff-Radford, S. (1985). Memory for pain: Relation between past and present pain intensity. *Pain, 23,* 375–380.

Eich, J. E. (1980). The cue-dependent nature of state dependent retrieval. *Memory & Cognition, 8,* 157–173.

Einhorn, H., & Hogarth, R. (1981). Behavioral decision theory: Processes of judgment and choice. *Annual Review of Psychology, 32,* 53–88.

Einstein, G. O., McDaniel, M. A., & Lackey, S. (1989). Bizarre imagery, interference, and distinctiveness. *Journal of Experimental Psychology: Learning, Memory, and Cognition, 15,* 137–146.

Ekstrand, B. R. (1967). Effect of sleep on memory. *Journal of Experimental Psychology, 75,* 64–72.

Ekstrand, B. R. (1972). To sleep, perchance to dream (about why we forget). In C. P. Duncan, L. Sechrest & A. W. Melton (Eds.), *Human memory: Festschrift for Benton J. Underwood* (pp. 59–82). New York: Appleton-Century-Crofts.

Elias, C. S., & Perfetti, C. A. (1973). Encoding task and recognition memory: The importance of semantic encoding. *Journal of Experimental Psychology, 99,* 151–156.

Ellis, D., & Young, A. (1990). Accounting for delusional misidentifications. *British Journal of Psychiatry, 157,* 239–248.

Ellis, H. (1989). Past and recent studies of prosopagnosia. In J. Crawford & D. Parker (Eds.), *Developments in clinical and experimental neuropsychology* (pp. 151–166). New York: Plenum.

Ellis, N., & Henneley, R. A. (1980). A bilingual word-length effect: Implications for intelligence testing and the relative ease of mental calculation in Welsh and English. *British Journal of Psychology, 71,* 43–52.

Elstein, A., Holzman, G., Ravitch, M., Metheny, W., Holmes, M., Hoppe, R., Rothert, M., & Rovner, D. (1986). Comparison of physicians' decisions regarding estrogen replacement therapy for menopausal women and decisions derived from a decision analytic model. *American Journal of Medicine, 80,* 246–258.

Engelkamp, J. (1986). Motor programs as part of the meaning of verbal items. In I. Kurcz, E. Shugar, & J. H. Danks (Eds.), *Knowledge and language.* Amsterdam: North-Holland.

Engelkamp, J. (1991). Imagery and enactment in paired-associate learning. In R. H. Logie & M. Denis (Eds.), *Mental images in human cognition* (pp. 119–128). Amsterdam: Elsevier.

Engelkamp, J., Zimmer, H., Mohr, G., & Sellen, O. (1994). Memory of self-performed tasks: Self-performing during recognition. *Memory & Cognition, 22,* 34–39.

Erdelyi, M. (1974). A new look at the New Look: Perceptual defense and vigilance. *Psychological Review, 81,* 1–25.

Erdelyi, M. (1985). *Psychoanalysis.* New York: W. H. Freeman & Co.

Erdelyi, M., & Becker, J. (1974). Hypermnesia for pictures: Incremental memory for pictures but not words in multiple recall trials. *Cognitive Psychology, 6,* 159–171.

Erdelyi, M., Buschke, H., & Finkelstein, S. (1977). Hypermnesia for Socratic stimuli: The growth of recall for an internally generated memory list abstracted from a series of riddles. *Memory & Cognition, 5,* 283–286.

Erdelyi, M., Finkelstein, S., Herrell, N., Miller, B., & Thomas, J. (1976). Coding modality vs. input modality in hypermnesia: Is a rose a rose a rose? *Cognition, 4,* 311–319.

Erdelyi, M., & Goldberg, B. (1979). Let's not sweep repression under the rug: Toward a cognitive psychology of repression. In J. F. Kihlstrom & F. J. Evans (Eds.), *Functional disorders of memory.* Hillsdale, NJ: Lawrence Erlbaum.

Erdelyi, M., & Kleinbard, J. (1978). Has Ebbinghaus decayed with time?: The growth of recall (hypermnesia) over days. *Journal of Experimental Psychology: Human Learning and Memory, 4,* 275–289.

Ericsson, K., Chase, W. G., & Faloon, S. (1980). Acquisition of a memory skill. *Science, 208,* 1181–1182.

Ericsson, K., & Simon, H. (1980). Verbal reports as data. *Psychological Review, 87,* 215–251.

Eriksen, C., & St. James, J. (1986). Visual attention within and around the field of focal attention. A zoom lens model. *Perception & Psychophysics, 40,* 225–240.

Eriksen, C., & Yeh, Y. (1985). Allocation of attention in the visual field. *Journal of Experimental Psychology: Human Perception and Performance, 11,* 583–597.

Ernest, C. (1977). Imagery ability and cognition: A critical review. *Journal of Mental Imagery, 2,* 181–216.

Ervin-Tripp, S. (1993). Conversational discourse. In J. B. Gleason & N. B. Ratner (Eds.), *Psycholinguistics.* New York: Harcourt Brace Jovanovich.

Estes, W. (1976). Structural aspects of associative models for memory. In C. N. Cofer (Ed.), *The structure of human memory.* San Francisco: Freeman.

Estes, W. (1993). Concepts, categories and psychological science. *Psychological Science, 4,* 143–153.

Etcoff, N., & Magee, J. (1992). Categorical perception of facial expressions. *Cognition, 44,* 227–240.

Evans, J. S. B. T. (1982). *The psychology of deductive reasoning.* London: Routledge & Kegan Paul.

Evans, J. S. B. T. (1989). *Bias in human reasoning*. Hillsdale, NJ: Lawrence Erlbaum.

Evans, J. S. B. T. (1993). The mental model theory of conditional reasoning: Critical appraisal and revision. *Cognition, 48*, 1–20.

Evans, J. S. B. T., Newstead, S. E., & Byrne, R. M. J. (1993). *Human reasoning: The psychology of deduction*. London: Lawrence Erlbaum.

Evans, J. S. B. T., Over, D., & Manktelow, K. (1993). Reasoning, decision making and rationality. *Cognition, 49*, 165–187.

Eylon, B., & Reif, F. (1984). Effects of knowledge organization on task performance. *Cognition and Instruction, 1*, 5–44.

Eysenck, M. W. (1982). *Attention and arousal: Cognition and performance*. Berlin: Springer Verlag.

Fallshore, M., & Schooler, J. (1995). Verbal vulnerability of perceptual expertise. *Journal of Experimental Psychology: Learning, Memory and Cognition, 21*, 1608–1623.

Farah, M. J. (1985). Psychophysical evidence for a shared representational medium for mental images and percepts. *Journal of Experimental Psychology: General, 114*, 91–103.

Farah, M. J. (1988). Is visual imagery really visual? Overlooked evidence from neuropsychology. *Psychological Review, 95*, 307–317.

Farah, M. J. (1989). Mechanisms of imagery-perception interaction. *Journal of Experimental Psychology: Human Perception and Performance, 15*, 203–211.

Farah, M. J. (1990). *Visual agnosia: Disorders of object recognition and what they tell us about normal vision*. Cambridge, MA: MIT Press.

Farah, M. J. (1992). Is an object an object an object? Cognitive and neuropsychological investigations of domain specificity in visual object recognition. *Current Directions in Psychological Science, 1*, 164–169.

Farah, M. J. (1995). Dissociable systems for visual recognition: A cognitive neuropsychology approach. In S. M. Kosslyn & D. N. Osherson (Eds.), *Visual cognition: An invitation to cognitive science* (Vol. 2). Cambridge, MA: MIT Press.

Farah, M. J., Hammond, K. M., Levine, D. N., & Calvanio, R. (1988). Visual and spatial mental imagery: Dissociable systems of representation. *Cognitive Psychology, 20*, 439–462.

Farah, M. J., & Smith, A. (1983). Perceptual interference and facilitation with auditory imagery. *Perception & Psychophysics, 33*, 475–478.

Farah, M. J., Soso, M., & Dasheiff, R. (1992). Visual angle of the mind's eye before and after unilateral occipital lobectomy. *Journal of Experimental Psychology: Human Perception and Performance, 18*, 241–246.

Farah, M. J., Tanaka, J., & Drain, H. M. (1995). What causes the face inversion effect? *Journal of Experimental Psychology: Human Perception and Performance, 21*, 628–634.

Farah, M. J., Wilson, K. D., Drain, M., & Tanaka, J. (1998). What is "special" about face perception? *Psychological Review, 105*, 482–498.

Feldman, H., Goldin-Meadow, S., & Gleitman, L. R. (1978). Beyond Herodotus: The creation of language by linguistically deprived deaf children. In A. Lock (Ed.), *Action, gesture, and symbol: The emergence of language*. London: Academic Press.

Fillmore, C. (1982). Towards a descriptive framework for spatial deixis. In R. J. Jarvella & W. Klein (Eds.), *Speech, place and action: Studies in deixis and related topics*. Chichester, England: Wiley.

Finke, R. (1989). *Principles of mental imagery*. Cambridge, MA: MIT Press.

Finke, R. (1990). *Creative imagery: Discoveries and inventions in visualization*. Hillsdale, NJ: Lawrence Erlbaum.

Finke, R. (1993). Mental imagery and creative discovery. In B. Roskos-Ewoldsen, M. J. Intons-Peterson, & R. Anderson (Eds.), *Imagery, creativity, and discovery* (pp. 255–285). New York: North-Holland.

Finke, R., & Kosslyn, S. M. (1980). Mental imagery acuity in the peripheral visual field. *Journal of Experimental Psychology: Human Perception and Performance, 6*, 126–139.

Finke, R., & Slayton, K. (1988). Explorations of creative visual synthesis in mental imagery. *Memory & Cognition, 16*, 252–257.

Finke, R., Ward, T., & Smith, S. (1992). *Creative cognition: Theory, research and applications*. Cambridge, MA: MIT Press.

Fischhoff, B. (1977). Perceived informativeness of facts. *Journal of Experimental Psychology: Human Perception and Performance, 3*, 349–358.

Fischhoff, B. (1991). Value elicitation: Is there anything in there? *American Psychologist, 46*, 835–847.

Fishburn, P. (1982). Nontransitive measurable utility. *Journal of Mathematical Psychology, 26*, 31–67.

Fisher, D. L. (1984). Central capacity limits in consistent mapping, visual search tasks: Four channels or more? *Cognitive Psychology, 16*, 449–484.

Fisher, R., & Craik, F. I. M. (1977). The interaction between encoding and retrieval operations in cued recall. *Journal of Experimental Psychology: Human Learning and Memory, 3*, 701–711.

Fisher, R., & Geiselman, R. (1992). *Memory-enhancing techniques for investigative interviewing: The cognitive interview*. Springfield, IL: Charles C. Thomas.

Fisher, R., Geiselman, R., & Amador, M. (1989). Field tests of the cognitive interview: Enhancing the recollection of actual victims and witnesses of crime. *Journal of Applied Psychology, 74*, 722–727.

Fisher, R., Geiselman, R., Raymond, D. S., & Jurkevich, L. M. (1987). Enhancing enhanced eyewitness memory: Refining the cognitive interview. *Journal of Police Science and Administration, 15,* 291–297.

Fisher, R., & McCauley, M. (1994). Improving eyewitness memory with the cognitive interview. In D. Ross, J. Read, & M. Toglia (Eds.), *Eyewitness memory: Current trends and development.* New York: SpringerVerlag.

Fivush, R. (1988). The functions of event memory: Some comments on Nelson and Barsalou. In U. Neisser & E. Winograd (Eds.), *Remembering reconsidered.* Cambridge: Cambridge University Press.

Flanagan, O. (1991). *The science of the mind* (2nd ed.). Cambridge, MA: MIT Press.

Fleet, M. L., Brigham, J. C., & Bothwell, R. K. (1987). The confidence-accuracy relationship: The effects of confidence assessment and choosing. *Journal of Applied Social Psychology, 17,* 171–187.

Flexser, A. J., & Tulving, E. (1978). Retrieval independence in recognition and recall. *Psychological Review, 85,* 153–172.

Flower, L. (1980). *Problem solving strategies for writing.* New York: Harcourt, Brace, Jovanovich.

Fodor, J. (1975). *The language of thought.* New York: Thomas Y. Crowell.

Fodor, J. (1981). Imagistic representation. In N. Block (Ed.), *Imagery* (pp. 63–86). Cambridge, MA: MIT Press.

Fodor, J. (1983). *The modularity of mind.* Cambridge, MA: MIT Press.

Fodor, J. (1985). Précis and multiple book review of "The modularity of mind." *Behavioral and Brain Sciences, 8,* 1–42.

Fodor, J. (1997). Connectionism and the problem of systematicity (continued): Why Smolensky's solution still doesn't work. *Cognition, 62,* 109–119.

Fodor, J., & Pylyshyn, Z. W. (1988). Connectionism and cognitive architecture: A critical analysis. *Cognition, 28,* 3–71.

Fong, G., Krantz, D., & Nisbett, R. (1986). The effects of statistical training on thinking about everyday problems. *Cognitive Psychology, 18,* 253–292.

Fong, G., & Nisbett, R. (1991). Immediate and delayed transfer of training effects in statistical reasoning. *Journal of Experimental Psychology: General, 120,* 34–45.

Ford, M. (1995). Two modes of mental representation and problem solution in syllogistic reasoning. *Cognition, 54,* 1–71.

Ford, M., Bresnan, J., & Kaplan, R. (1982). A competence-based theory of syntactic closure. In J. Bresnan (Ed.), *The mental representation of grammatical relations.* Cambridge, MA: MIT Press.

Fox, E. (1994). Interference and negative priming from ignored distractors: The role of selection difficulty. *Perception & Psychophysics, 56,* 565–574.

Fox, E. (1995). Negative priming from ignored distractors in visual selection: A review. *Psychonomic Bulletin & Review, 2,* 145–173.

Frege, G. (1892/1952). On sense and reference. In P. Geach & M. Black (Eds.), *Philosophical writings of Gottlob Frege.* Oxford: Oxford University Press.

French, R. M. (1999). Catastrophic forgetting in connectionist networks. *Trends in Cognitive Science, 3,* 128–135.

Freyd, J. J. (1996). *Betrayal trauma: The logic of forgetting childhood abuse.* Cambridge, MA: Harvard University Press.

Freyd, J. J. (1998). Science in the memory debate. *Ethics & Behavior, 8*(2), 101–113.

Fried, L. S., & Holyoak, K. J. (1984). Induction of category distributions: A framework for classification learning. *Journal of Experimental Psychology: Learning, Memory and Cognition, 10,* 234–257.

Friedman, A. (1979). Framing pictures: The role of knowledge in automatized encoding and memory for gist. *Journal of Experimental Psychology: General, 108,* 316–355.

Friedman, A., & Bourne, L. E., Jr. (1976). Encoding the levels of information in pictures and words. *Journal of Experimental Psychology: General, 105,* 169–190.

Friedman, A., & Brown, N. (2000). Reasoning about geography. *Journal of Experimental Psychology: General, 129,* 193–219.

Friedrich, J. (1993). Primary error detection and minimization (PEDMIN) strategies in social cognition: A reinterpretation of confirmation bias phenomena. *Psychological Review, 100,* 298–319.

Fromkin, V. (1993). Speech production. In J. B. Gleason & N. B. Ratner (Eds.), *Psycholinguistics.* New York: Harcourt Brace Jovanovich.

Fulgosi, A., & Guilford, J. (1968). Short term incubation in divergent production. *American Journal of Psychology, 81,* 241–246.

Gabrieli, J. D. E. (1998). Cognitive neuroscience of human memory. *Annual Review of Psychology, 49,* 87–115.

Gallo, D. A., Roberts, M. J., & Seamon, J. G. (1997). Remembering words not presented in lists: Can we avoid creating false memories? *Psychonomics Bulletin & Review, 4,* 271–276.

Galton, F. (1883). *Inquiries into human faculty.* London: Dent.

Gardiner, J., & Java, R. (1991). Forgetting in recognition memory with and without recollective experience. *Memory & Cognition, 19,* 617–623.

Gardiner, J. M. (1988). Functional aspects of recollective experience. *Memory & Cognition, 16*(4), 309–313.

Gardner, H. (1974). *The shattered mind.* New York: Vintage.

Gardner, H. (1985). *The mind's new science: A history of the cognitive revolution.* New York: Basic Books.

Garfield, J. (Ed.). (1987). *Modularity in knowledge representation and natural-language understanding.* Cambridge, MA: MIT Press.

Garner, R., Gillingham, M. G., & White, C. S. (1989). Effects of "seductive details" on macroprocessing and microprocessing in adults and children. *Cognition and Instruction, 6,* 41–57.

Garnes, S., & Bond, Z. (1976). The relationship between semantic expectation and acoustic information. In W. Dressler & O. Pfeiffer (Eds.), *Proceedings of the Third International Phonology Meeting.* Innsbruck: Phonologische Tagung.

Garry, M., Manning, C. G., Loftus, E. F., & Sherman, S. J. (1996). Imagination inflation: Imagining a childhood event inflates confidence that it occurred. *Psychonomics Bulletin & Review, 3,* 208–214.

Garry, M., & Polaschek, D. L. L. (2000). Imagination and memory. *Current Directions in Psychological Science, 9,* 6–10.

Gathercole, S. E., Service, E., Hitch, G., Adams, A.-M., & Martin, A. J. (1999). Phonological short-term memory and vocabulary development: Further evidence on the nature of the relationship. *Applied Cognitive Psychology, 13,* 65–77.

Gathercole, S., & Baddeley, A. D. (1989). Evaluation of the role of phonological STM in the development of vocabulary in children: A longitudinal study. *Journal of Memory and Language, 28,* 200–213.

Gathercole, S., & Baddeley, A. D. (1990). The role of phonological memory in vocabulary acquisition: A study of young children learning arbitrary names of toys. *British Journal of Psychology, 81,* 439–454.

Gauthier, I. (2000). Expertise for cars and birds recruits brain areas involved in face recognition. *Nature Neuroscience, 3,* 191–197.

Gazzaniga, M. S., Ivry, R. B., & Mangun, G. R. (1998). *Cognitive neuroscience: The biology of the mind.* New York: W. W. Norton.

Geiselman, R. E. (1984). Enhancement of eyewitness memory: An empirical evaluation of the cognitive interview. *Journal of Police Science and Administration, 12,* 74–80.

Geiselman, R. E., & Padilla, J. (1988). Cognitive interviewing with child witnesses. *Journal of Police Science & Administration, 16,* 236–242.

Geiselman, R. E., Schroppel, T., Tubridy, A., Konishi, T., & Rodriguez, V. (2000). Objectivity bias in eyewitness performance. *Applied Cognitive Psychology, 14,* 323–332.

Gelman, S., & Wellman, H. (1991). Insides and essences: Early understandings of the non-obvious. *Cognition, 38,* 213–244.

Gentner, D., & Jeziorski, M. (1989). Historical shifts in the use of analogy in science. In B. Gholson, W. Shadish, R. Neimeyer, & A. Houts (Eds.), *Psychology of science:*

*Contributions to metascience.* Cambridge: Cambridge University Press.

Gentner, D., & Stevens, A. L. (1983). *Mental models.* Hillsdale, NJ: Lawrence Erlbaum.

Gentner, D. (1983). Structure mapping: A theoretical framework for analogy. *Cognitive Science, 7,* 155–170.

Gentner, D. (1989). The mechanisms of analogical learning. In S. Vosniadou & A. Ortony (Eds.), *Similarity, analogy, and thought* (pp. 199–241). Cambridge: Cambridge University Press.

Getzels, J., & Csikszentmihalyi, M. (1976). *The creative vision: A longitudinal study of problem finding in art.* New York: Wiley.

Ghiselin, B. (1952). *The creative process.* New York: New American Library.

Gibson, E., Bishop, C., Schiff, W., & Smith, J. (1964). Comparison of meaningfulness and pronounceability as grouping principles in the perception and retention of verbal material. *Journal of Experimental Psychology, 67,* 173–182.

Gick, M. (1986). Problem-solving strategies. *Educational Psychologist, 21,* 99–120.

Gick, M., & Holyoak, K. J. (1980). Analogical problem solving. *Cognitive Psychology, 12,* 306–355.

Gick, M., & Holyoak, K. J. (1983). Schema induction and analogical transfer. *Cognitive Psychology, 15,* 1–38.

Gigerenzer, G. (1991). From tools to theories: A heuristic of discovery in cognitive psychology. *Psychological Review, 98,* 254–267.

Gigerenzer, G. (1996). On narrow norms and vague heuristics: A reply to Kahneman and Tversky. *Psychological Review, 103,* 592–596.

Gigerenzer, G., Hell, W., & Blank, H. (1988). Presentation and content: The use of base rates as a continuous variable. *Journal of Experimental Psychology: Human Perception and Performance, 14,* 513–525.

Gigerenzer, G., & Hoffrage, U. (1995). How to improve Bayesian reasoning without instruction: Frequency formats. *Psychological Review, 102,* 684–704.

Gigerenzer, G., & Hoffrage, U. (1999). Overcoming difficulties in Bayesian reasoning: A reply to Lewis and Keren (1999) and Mellers and McGraw (1999). *Psychological Review, 106,* 425–430.

Gigerenzer, G., & Hug, K. (1992). Domain-specific reasoning: Social contracts, cheating and perspective change. *Cognition, 43,* 127–172.

Gilbert, A. N., Crouch, M., & Kemp, S. (1998). Olfactory and visual mental imagery. *Journal of Mental Imagery, 22,* 137–146.

Gilhooly, K. J. (1988). *Thinking: Direct, undirected and creative* (2nd ed.). New York: Academic Press.

Gilhooly, K. J. (1999). Creative thinking: Myths and misconceptions. In S. Della Sala (Ed.), *Mind myths:*

*Exploring popular assumptions about the mind and brain.* New York: Wiley.

Gilhooly, K. J., Logie, R. H., Wetherick, N., & Wynn, V. (1993). Working memory and strategies in syllogistic-reasoning tasks. *Memory & Cognition, 21,* 115–124.

Gilligan, S. G., & Bower, G. H. (1984). Cognitive consequences of emotional arousal. In C. E. Izard, J. Kagan, & R. B. Zajonc (Eds.), *Emotions, cognitions, and behavior.* Cambridge: Cambridge University Press.

Gilovich, T. (1991). *How we know what isn't so.* New York: Free Press.

Gilovich, T., & Medvec, V. H. (1995). The experience of regret: What, when and why. *Psychological Review, 102,* 379–395.

Gilovich, T., Medvec, V. H., & Kahneman, D. (1998). Varieties of regret: A debate and partial resolution. *Psychological Review, 105,* 602–605.

Gilovich, T., & Saviutsky, K. (1996). Like goes with like: The role of representativeness in erroneous and pseudoscientific beliefs. *Skeptical Inquirer, 20,* 34–40.

Ginosar, Z., & Trope, Y. (1980). The effects of base rates and individuating information on judgments about another person. *Journal of Experimental Social Psychology, 16,* 228–242.

Glanzer, M., & Adams, J. (1985). The mirror effect in recognition memory. *Memory & Cognition, 13,* 8–20.

Glanzer, M., & Cunitz, A. R. (1966). Two storage mechanisms in free recall. *Journal of Verbal Learning and Verbal Behavior, 5,* 351–360.

Glass, A. L., Holyoak, K. J., & Kiger, J. I. (1979). Role of antonymy relations in semantic judgments. *Journal of Experimental Psychology: Human Learning and Memory, 5,* 598–606.

Gleitman, H., Fridlund, A. J., & Reisberg, D. (1999). *Psychology* (5th ed.). New York: W. W. Norton.

Glenberg, A., & Adams, F. (1978). Type I rehearsal and recognition. *Journal of Verbal Learning and Verbal Behavior, 17,* 455–463.

Glenberg, A., Smith, S. M., & Green, C. (1977). Type I rehearsal: Maintenance and more. *Journal of Verbal Learning and Verbal Behavior, 16,* 339–352.

Glisky, E., Schacter, D., & Tulving, E. (1986). Computer learning by memory impaired patients: Acquisition and retention of complex knowledge. *Neuropsychologia, 24,* 313–328.

Glisky, E. L., Polster, M. R., & Routhuieaux, B. C. (1995). Double dissociation between item and source memory. *Neuropsychology, 9,* 229–235.

Gluck, M., & Rumelhart, D. (1990). *Neuroscience and connectionist theory.* Hillsdale, NJ: Lawrence Erlbaum.

Glucksberg, S., & Danks, J. (1968). Effects of discriminative labels and of nonsense labels upon availability of novel function. *Journal of Verbal Learning and Verbal Behavior, 7,* 72–76.

Glucksberg, S., & McCloskey, M. (1981). Decisions about ignorance: Knowing that you don't know. *Journal of Experimental Psychology: Learning, Memory and Cognition, 7,* 311–325.

Gobet, F., & Simon, H. A. (1996). Recall of random and distorted chess positions: Implications for the theory of expertise. *Memory & Cognition, 24,* 493–503.

Gobet, F., & Simon, H. A. (1996). The roles of recognition processes and look-ahead search in time-constrained expert problem solving: Evidence from Grand-master-level chess. *Psychological Science, 7,* 52–55.

Gobet, F., & Simon, H. A. (2000). Reply to Lassiter. *Psychological Science, 11,* 174–175.

Godden, D. R., & Baddeley, A. D. (1975). Context-dependent memory in two natural environments: On land and underwater. *British Journal of Psychology, 66,* 325–332.

Goff, L. M., & Roediger III, H. L. (1998). Imagination inflation for action events: Repeated imaginings lead to illusory recollections. *Memory & Cognition, 26,* 20–33.

Gold, P. (1987). Sweet memories. *American Scientist, 75,* 151–155.

Gold, P. (1995). Modulation of emotional and non-emotional memories: Same pharmacological systems, different neuroanatomical systems. In J. McGaugh & N. Weinberger (Eds.), *Brain and memory.* New York: Oxford University Press.

Goldenberg, G., Muellbacher, W., & Nowak, A. (1995). Imagery without perception—A case study of anosognosia for cortical blindness. *Neuropsychologia, 33,* 1373–1382.

Goldenberg, J., Mazursky, D., & Solomon, S. (1999). Creative sparks. *Science, 285,* 1495–1496.

Goldinger, S. D., Kleider, H. M., & Shelley, E. (1999). The marriage of perception and memory: Creating two-way illusions with words and voices. *Memory & Cognition, 27,* 328–338.

Goldin-Meadow, S., & Feldman, H. (1977). The development of language-like communication without a language model. *Science, 197,* 401–403.

Goldman, P., Wolters, N., & Winograd, E. (1992). A demonstration of incubation in anagram problem solving. *Bulletin of the Psychonomic Society, 30,* 36–38.

Goldman-Rakic, P. S. (1995). Architecture of the prefrontal cortex and the central executive. In J. Grafman & K. J. Holyoak (Eds.), *Structure and functions of the human prefrontal cortex. Annals of the New York Academy of Sciences.* New York: New York Academy of Sciences.

Goldman-Rakic, P. S. (1998). The prefrontal landscape: Implications of functional architecture for understanding human mentation and the central executive. In A. C. Roberts & T. W. Robbins (Eds.), *The prefrontal cortex: Executive and cognitive functions.* New York: Oxford University Press.

Goldstone, R. (1994). Similarity, interactive activation, and mapping. *Journal of Experimental Psychology: Learning, Memory and Cognition, 20,* 3–28.

Goldstone, R. (1996). Alignment-based nonmonotonicities in similarity. *Journal of Experimental Psychology: Learning, Memory and Cognition, 22,* 988–1001.

Goldstone, R., & Medin, D. (1994). Time course of comparison. *Journal of Experimental Psychology: Learning, Memory and Cognition, 20,* 29–50.

Goldvarg, Y., & Johnson-Laird, P. N. (2000). Illusions in modal reasoning. *Memory & Cognition, 28,* 282–294.

Golier, J. A., Yehuda, R., & Southwick, S. (1997). Memory and posttraumatic stress disorder. In P. S. Appelbaum, L. A. Uyehara, & M. R. Elin (Eds.), *Trauma and memory: Clinical and legal controversies.* New York: Oxford University Press.

Goodale, M. A. (1995). The cortical organization of visual perception and visuomotor control. In S. M. Kosslyn & D. Osherson (Eds.), *Visual cognition: An invitation to cognitive science* (2nd ed.). Cambridge, MA: MIT Press.

Goodman, N. (1972). Seven strictures on similarity. In N. Goodman (Ed.), *Problems and projects* (pp. 437–446). New York: Bobbs-Merrill.

Gordon, P. (1986). Level-ordering in lexical development. *Cognition, 21,* 73–93.

Gordon, P., & Scearce, K. (1995). Pronominalization and discourse coherence: Discourse structure and pronoun interpretation. *Memory & Cognition, 23,* 313–323.

Gorenstein, G., & Ellsworth, P. (1980). Effect of choosing an incorrect photograph on later identification by an eyewitness. *Journal of Applied Psychology, 65,* 616–622.

Gourevitch, P. (1999, June 14). The memory thief. *The New Yorker.*

Graesser, A. C., Millis, K. K., & Zwaan, R. A. (1997). Discourse comprehension. *Annual Review of Psychology, 48,* 163–189.

Graesser, A. C., Woll, S. B., Kowalski, D. J., & Smith, D. A. (1980). Memory for typical and atypical actions in scripted activities. *Journal of Experimental Psychology: Human Learning and Memory, 6,* 503-515.

Graf, P., & Komatsu, S. (1994). Process dissociation procedure: Handle with caution! *European Journal of Cognitive Psychology, 6,* 113–129.

Graf, P., & Mandler, G. (1984). Activation makes words more accessible, but not necessarily more retrievable. *Journal of Verbal Learning and Verbal Behavior, 23,* 553–568.

Graf, P., Mandler, G., & Haden, P. E. (1982). Simulating amnesic symptoms in normals. *Science, 218,* 1243–1244.

Graf, P., & Masson, M. (Eds.). (1993). *Implicit memory: New directions in cognition, development and neuropsychology.* Hillsdale, NJ: Lawrence Erlbaum.

Graf, P., & Schacter, D. L. (1985). Implicit and explicit memory for new associations in normal and amnesic subjects. *Journal of Experimental Psychology: Learning, Memory and Cognition, 11,* 501–18.

Grant, H. M., Bredahl, L. C., Clay, J., Ferrie, J., Groves, J. E., McDorman, T. A., & Dark, V. J. (1998). Context-dependent memory for meaningful material: Information for students. *Applied Cognitive Psychology, 12,* 617–623.

Greenberg, J., Ferguson, C., & Moravcsik, E. (Eds.). (1978). *Universals of human language.* Stanford, CA: Stanford University Press.

Greene, E., Flynn, M., & Loftus, E. F. (1982). Inducing resistance of misleading information. *Journal of Verbal Learning and Verbal Behavior, 21,* 207–219.

Greenwald, A. (1992). New Look 3—Unconscious cognition reclaimed. *American Psychologist, 47,* 766–790.

Greenwald, A., & Banaji, M. (1995). Implicit social cognition: Attitudes, self-esteem and stereotypes. *Psychological Review, 102,* 4–27.

Greenwald, A., & Pratkanis, A. (1984). The self. In R. S. Wyer & T. K. Srull (Eds.), *Handbook of social cognition* (pp. 129–178). Hillsdale, NJ: Lawrence Erlbaum.

Grice, H. P. (1975). Logic and conversation. In P. Cole & J. L. Morgan (Eds.), *Syntax and semantics 3: Speech acts.* New York: Academic Press.

Griggs, R., & Cox, J. R. (1982). The elusive thematic-materials effect in Wason's selection task. *British Journal of Psychology, 73,* 407–420.

Gruber, H. E. (1981). *Darwin on man: A psychological study of scientific creativity* (2nd ed.). University of Chicago Press.

Gruber, H. E. (1989). Networks of enterprise in creative scientific work. In B. Gholson, W. Shadish, R. Neimeyer, & A. Houts (Eds.), *Psychology of science: Contributions to metascience.* Cambridge: Cambridge University Press.

Guagnano, G., Dietz, T., & Stern, P. (1994). Willingness to pay for public goods: A test of the contribution model. *Psychological Science, 5,* 411–415.

Guilford, J. (1967). *The nature of human intelligence.* New York: Scribner.

Guilford, J. (1979). Some incubated thoughts on incubation. *Journal of Creative Behavior, 13,* 1–8.

Guth, W., Schmittberger, R., & Schwarze, B. (1982). An experimental analysis of ultimatum bargaining. *Journal of Economic Behavior & Organizations, 3,* 367–388.

Guyote, M., & Sternberg, R. J. (1981). A transitive-chain theory of syllogistic reasoning. *Cognitive Psychology, 13,* 461–525.

Hajiwara, H., et al. (1999). Neurolinguistic evidence for rule-based nominal suffixation. *Language, 75,* 739–763.

Halle, M. (1990). Phonology. In D. Osherson & H. Lasnik (Eds.), *Language: An invitation to cognitive science.* Cambridge, MA: MIT Press.

Halpern, A. R. (1988). Mental scanning in auditory imagery for songs. *Journal of Experimental Psychology: Learning, Memory and Cognition, 14,* 434–443.

Halpern, A. R. (1989). Memory for the absolute pitch of familiar songs. *Memory & Cognition, 17,* 572–581.

Halpern, A. R. (1991). Musical aspects of auditory imagery. In Reisberg, D. (Ed.), *Auditory imagery.* Hillsdale, NJ: Lawrence Erlbaum.

Halpern, D. (1984). *Thought and knowledge: An introduction to critical thinking.* Hillsdale, NJ: Lawrence Erlbaum.

Hamann, S. (1990). Level-of-processing effects in conceptually driven implicit tasks. *Journal of Experimental Psychology: Learning, Memory and Cognition, 16,* 970–977.

Hamill, R., Wilson, T. D., & Nisbett, R. E. (1980). Insensitivity to sample bias: Generalizing from atypical cases. *Journal of Personality and Social Psychology, 39,* 578–589.

Handel, S. (1989). *Listening: An introduction to the perception of auditory events.* Cambridge, MA: MIT Press.

Harber, K. D., & Pennebaker, J. W. (1992). Overcoming traumatic memories. In S.-A. Christianson (Ed.), *The handbook of emotion and memory: Research and theory.* Hillsdale, NJ: Lawrence Erlbaum.

Hardiman, P., Dufresne, R., & Mestre, J. (1989). The relation between problem categorization and problem solving among experts and novices. *Memory & Cognition, 17,* 627–638.

Hardin, C., & Banaji, M. (1993). The influence of language on thought. *Social Cognition, 11,* 277–308.

Harding, R. (1940). *An anatomy of inspiration.* London: Cass.

Harley, T. A., & Bown, H. E. (1998). What causes a tip-of-the-tongue state? Evidence for lexical neighbourhood effects in speech production. *British Journal of Psychology, 89,* 151–174.

Harris, J. (1982). The VVIQ and imagery-produced McCollough effects: An alternative analysis. *Perception & Psychophysics, 32,* 290–292.

Harwood, D. G., Barker, W. W., Ownby, R. L., & Duara, R. (1999). Prevalence and correlates of Capgras syndrome in Alzheimer's disease. *International Journal of Geriatric Psychiatry, 14,* 415–420.

Hasher, L., Goldstein, D., & Toppino, T. (1977). Frequency and the conference of referential validity. *Journal of Verbal Learning and Verbal Behavior, 16,* 107–112.

Hasher, L., & Griffin, M. (1978). Reconstructive and reproductive processes in memory. *Journal of Experimental Psychology: Human Learning and Memory, 4,* 318–330.

Hasselmo, M. E. (1999). Neuromodulation: Acetylcholine and memory consolidation. *Trends in Cognitive Science, 6,* 351–359.

Haugeland, J. (Ed.). (1997). *Mind design 2: Philosophy, psychology, artificial intelligence* (2nd ed.). Cambridge, MA: MIT Press.

Hawkins, J. (Ed.). (1988). *Explaining language universals.* London: Basil Blackwell.

Hay, D., Young, A., & Ellis, A. (1991). Routes through the face recognition system. *Quarterly Journal of Experimental Psychology: Human Experimental Psychology, 43A,* 761–791.

Hayes, J. (1985). Three problems in teaching general skills. In S. Chipman, J. Segal, & R. Glaser (Eds.), *Thinking and learning skills* (pp. 391–406). Hillsdale, NJ: Lawrence Erlbaum.

Hayes, J. (1989). *The complete problem solver* (2nd ed.). Hillsdale, NJ: Lawrence Erlbaum.

Hayes, J., & Simon, H. (1977). Psychological differences among problem solving isomorphs. In N. Castellan, D. Pisoni, & G. Potts (Eds.), *Cognitive theory* (pp. 21–42). Hillsdale, NJ: Lawrence Erlbaum.

Healy, A. F. (1981). The effects of visual similarity on proofreading for misspellings. *Memory & Cognition, 9,* 453–460.

Healy, A. F., Volbrecht, V. J., & Nye, T. R. (1983). The effects of perceptual condition on proofreading for misspellings. *Memory & Cognition, 11,* 528–538.

Heaps, C., & Nash, M. (1999). Individual differences in imagination influation. *Psychonomic Bulletin & Review, 6,* 313–318.

Hecaen, H. (1981). The neuropsychology of face recognition. In G. Davies, H. Ellis, & J. Shephard (Eds.), *Perceiving and remembering faces.* New York: Academic Press.

Heider, E. R. (1972). Universals in color naming and memory. *Journal of Experimental Psychology, 93,* 10–20.

Heil, M., Rösler, F., & Hennighausen, E. (1993). Imagery-perception interaction depends on the shape of the image: A reply to Farah. *Journal of Experimental Psychology: Human Perception and Performance, 19,* 1313–1319.

Heil, M., Rösler, F., & Hennighausen, E. (1994). Dynamics of activation in long-term memory: The retrieval of verbal, pictorial, spatial and color information. *Journal of Experimental Psychology: Learning, Memory and Cognition, 20,* 169–184.

Heilman, K., Watson, R., & Valenstein, E. (1985). Neglect and related disorders. In K. Heilman & E. Valenstein (Eds.), *Clinical neuropsychology* (pp. 243–293). New York: Oxford University Press.

Heim, C., Owens, M., Polotsky, P., & Nemeroff, C. (1997). Endocrine factors in the pathophysiology of mental disorders. *Psychopharmacology Bulletin, 33,* 185–192.

Heller, J., & Reif, F. (1984). Prescribing effective human problem-solving processes: Problem description in physics. *Cognition and Instruction, 1,* 177–216.

Henderson, J. M., & Hollingworth, A. (1999). The role of fixation position in detecting scene changes across saccades. *Psychological Science, 10,* 438–443.

Henderson, J. M., Weeks, Jr., P. A., & Hollingworth. A. (1999). The effects of semantic consistency on eye movements during complex scene viewing. *Journal of Experimental Psychology: Human Perception and Performance, 25,* 210–228.

Henderson, J. M., Weeks, Jr., P., & Hollingworth, A. (1999). The effects of semantic consistency on eye movements during complex scene viewing. *Journal of Experimental Psychology: Human Perception and Performance, 25,* 210–228.

Henle, M. (1962). On the relation between logic and thinking. *Psychological Review, 69,* 366–378.

Henle, M. (1978). Foreword. In R. Revlin & R. Mayer (Eds.), *Human reasoning* (pp. xiii-xviii). New York: Wiley.

Hennessey, B., & Amabile, T. (1988). The conditions of creativity. In R. J. Sternberg (Ed.), *The nature of creativity* (pp. 11–35). Cambridge: Cambridge University Press.

Heuer, F., Fischman, D., & Reisberg, D. (1986). Why does vivid imagery hurt colour memory? *Canadian Journal of Psychology, 40,* 161–175.

Heuer, F., & Reisberg, D. (1990). Vivid memories of emotional events: The accuracy of remembered minutiae. *Memory & Cognition, 18,* 496–506.

Heuer, F., & Reisberg, D. (1992). Emotion, arousal and memory for detail. In S.-Å. Christianson (Ed.), *Handbook of emotion and memory* (pp. 151–180). Hillsdale, NJ: Lawrence Erlbaum.

Hicks, J. L., & Marsh, R. L. (1999). Remember-Know judgments can depend on how memory is tested. *Psychonomics Bulletin & Review, 6,* 117–122.

Higbee, K. L. (1977). *Your memory: How it works and how to improve it.* Englewood Cliffs, NJ: Prentice-Hall.

Higgins, E. T., & Bargh, J. A. (1987). Social cognition and social perception. *Annual Review of Psychology, 38,* 1–95.

Hilgard, E. R. (1968). *The experience of hypnosis.* New York: Harcourt Brace Jovanovich.

Hillis, A., & Caramazza, A. (1991). Category-specific naming and comprehension impairment: A double dissociation. *Brain, 114,* 2081–2094.

Hilton, D. (1995). The social context of reasoning: Conversational inference and rational judgment. *Psychological Bulletin, 118,* 248–271.

Hilts, P. J. (1995). *Memory's ghost: The strange tale of Mr. M and the nature of memory.* New York: Simon & Schuster.

Hinds, P. J. (1999). The curse of expertise: The effects of expertise and debiasing methods on the predictions of novice performance. *Journal of Experimental Psychology: Applied, 5,* 205–221.

Hinsley, D., Hayes, J., & Simon, H. (1977). From words to equations: Meaning and representation in algebra word problems. In P. Carpenter & M. Just (Eds.), *Cognitive processes in comprehension.* Hillsdale, NJ: Lawrence Erlbaum.

Hinton, G., & Anderson, J. R. (1981). *Parallel models of associative memory.* Hillsdale, NJ: Lawrence Erlbaum.

Hintzman, D. L. (1986). "Schema abstraction" in a multiple-trace memory model. *Psychological Review, 93,* 411–428.

Hirshman, E. (1998). On the logic of testing the independence assumption in the process-dissociation procedure. *Memory & Cognition, 26,* 857–859.

Hirshman, E., Whelley, M., & Palij, M. (1989). An investigation of paradoxical memory effects. *Journal of Memory and Language, 28,* 594–609.

Hirst, W. (1986). The psychology of attention. In J. E. LeDoux & W. Hirst (Eds.), *Mind and brain* (pp. 105–141). Cambridge: Cambridge University Press.

Hirst, W., & Kalmar, D. (1987). Characterizing attentional resources. *Journal of Experimental Psychology: General, 116,* 68–81.

Hirst, W., Spelke, E., Reaves, C., Caharack, G., & Neisser, U. (1980). Dividing attention without alternation or automaticity. *Journal of Experimental Psychology: General, 109,* 98–117.

Hitch, G., Brandimonte, M., & Walker, P. (1995). Two types of representation in visual memory: Evidence from the effects of stimulus contrast on image combination. *Memory & Cognition, 23,* 147–154.

Hochberg, J. (1978). *Perception* (2nd ed.). Englewood Cliffs, NJ: Prentice-Hall.

Hochberg, J. (1986). Representation of motion and space in video and cinematic displays. In K. J. Boff, L. Kaufman, & J. P. Thomas (Eds.), *Handbook of perception and human performance* (pp. 22:1–22:64). New York: Wiley.

Hockey, G. R., Davies, S., & Gray, M. M. (1972). Forgetting as a function of sleep at different times of day. *Quarterly Journal of Experimental Psychology, 24,* 386–393.

Hoffman, D. D. (2000). *Visual intelligence: How we create what we see.* New York: W. W. Norton.

Holding, D. (1985). *The psychology of chess.* Hillsdale, NJ: Lawrence Erlbaum.

Holland, J. H., Holyoak, K. F., Nisbett, R. E., & Thagard, P. R. (1986). *Induction.* Cambridge, MA: MIT Press.

Hollingworth, A., & Henderson, J. M. (1998). Does consistent scene context facilitate object perception? *Journal of Experimental Psychology, General, 127,* 398–415.

Holmberg, D., & Homes, J. G. (1994). Reconstruction of relationship memories: A mental models approach. In N. Schwarz & S. Sudman (Eds.), *Autobiographical memory and the validity of retrospective reports.* New York: Springer-Verlag.

Holmes, D. (1991). The evidence for repression: An examination of sixty years of research. In J. L. Singer (Ed.), *Repression and dissociation: Implications for personality theory, psychopathology and health* (pp. 85–102). Chicago: University of Chicago Press.

Holmes, J. B., Waters, H. S., & Rajaram, S. (1998). The phenomenology of false memories: Episodic content and confidence. *Journal of Experimental Psychology: Learning, Memory and Cognition, 24*, 1026–1040.

Holyoak, K. J. (1984). Analogical thinking and human intelligence. In R. J. Sternberg (Ed.), *Advances in the psychology of human intelligence*. Hillsdale, NJ: Lawrence Erlbaum.

Holyoak, K. J. (1987). Review of parallel distributed processing. *Science, 236*, 992.

Holyoak, K. J., & Koh, H. (1987). Surface and structural similarity in analogical transfer. *Memory & Cognition, 15*, 332–340.

Holyoak, K. J., & Thagard, P. (1989). Analogical mapping by constraint satisfaction. *Cognitive Science, 13*, 295–355.

Homa, D., Dunbar, S., & Nohre, L. (1991). Instance frequency, categorization, and the modulating effect of experience. *Journal of Experimental Psychology: Learning, Memory and Cognition, 17*, 444–458.

Homa, D., Sterling, S., & Trepel, L. (1981). Limitation of exemplar-based generalization and the abstraction of categorical information. *Journal of Experimental Psychology: Human Learning and Memory, 7*, 418–439.

Hornby, P. (1974). Surface structure and presupposition. *Journal of Verbal Learning and Verbal Behavior, 13*, 530–538.

Horowitz, M. J., & Reidbord, S. P. (1992). Memory, emotion, and response to trauma. In S.-A. Christianson (Ed.), *The handbook of emotion and memory: Research and theory* (pp. 343–357). Hillsdale, NJ: Lawrence Erlbaum.

Hoskin, R. (1983). Opportunity cost and behavior. *Journal of Accounting Research, 21*, 78–95.

Howe, M. L., Rabinowitz, F. M., & Powell, T. L. (1998). Individual differences in working memory and reasoning-remembering relationships in solving class-inclusion problems. *Memory & Cognition, 26*, 1089–1101.

Howes, D., & Solomon, R. (1951). Visual duration thresholds as a function of word probability. *Journal of Experimental Psychology, 41*, 401–410.

Howes, M., Siegel, M., & Brown, F. (1993). Early childhood memories: Accuracy and affect. *Cognition, 47*, 95–119.

Hsee, C. K. (1999). Value seeking and prediction-decision inconsistency: Why don't people take what they predict they'll like the most? *Psychonomics Bulletin & Review, 6*, 555–561.

Hubel, D., & Wiesel, T. (1959). Receptive fields of single neurones in the cat's visual cortex. *Journal of Physiology, 148*, 574–591.

Hubel, D., & Wiesel, T. (1968). Receptive fields and functional architecture of monkey striate cortex. *Journal of Physiology, 195*, 215–243.

Hummel, J., & Biederman, I. (1992). Dynamic binding in a neural network for shape recognition. *Psychological Review, 99*, 480–517.

Hunt, R., & Elliott, J. (1980). The role of nonsemantic information in memory: Orthographic distinctiveness effects on retention. *Journal of Experimental Psychology: General, 109*, 49–74.

Hunt, R., & Ellis, H. D. (1974). Recognition memory and degree of semantic contextual change. *Journal of Experimental Psychology, 103*, 1153–1159.

Husserl, E. (1931). *Ideas*. New York: Collier.

Hyams, N. (1986). *Language acquisition and the theory of parameters*. Dordrecht, Holland: Reidel.

Hyde, T. S., & Jenkins, J. J. (1969). Differential effects of incidental tasks on the organization of recall of a list of highly associated words. *Journal of Experimental Psychology, 82*, 472–481.

Hyde, T. S., & Jenkins, J. J. (1973). Recall for words as a function of semantic, graphic, and syntactic orienting tasks. *Journal of Verbal Learning and Verbal Behavior, 12*, 471–480.

Hyman, I. E., Jr. (2000). Creating false autobiographical memories: Why people believe their memory errors. In E. Winograd, R. Fivush, & W. Hirst (Eds.), *Ecological approaches to cognition: Essays in honor of Ulric Neisser*. Hillsdale, NJ: Lawrence Erlbaum.

Hyman, I. E., Jr., & Billings, F. J. (1998). Individual differences and the creation of false childhood memories. *Memory, 6*(1), 1–20.

Hyman, I. E., Jr., Gilstrap, L. L., Decker, K., & Wilkinson, C. (1998). Manipulating Remember and Know judgments of autobiographical memories: An investigation of false memory creation. *Applied Cognitive Psychology, 12*, 371–386.

Hyman, I. E., Jr., Husband, T., & Billings, F. (1995). False memories of childhood experiences. *Applied Cognitive Psychology, 9*, 181–198.

Intons-Peterson, M., & White, A. (1981). Experimenter naiveté and imaginal judgments. *Journal of Experimental Psychology: Human Perception and Performance, 7*, 833–843.

Intraub, H., Bender, R. S., & Mangels, J. A. (1992). Looking at pictures but remembering scenes. *Journal of Experimental Psychology: Learning, Memory and Cognition, 18*, 180-191.

Intraub, H., & Bodamer, J. (1993). Boundary extension: Fundamental aspect of pictorial representation or encoding artifact? *Journal of Experimental Psychology: Learning, Memory and Cognition, 19*, 1387–1397.

Intraub, H., & Richardson, M. (1989). Wide-angle memories of close-up scenes. *Journal of Experimental Psychology: Learning, Memory and Cognition, 15*, 179–187.

Intraub, H., Gottesman, C. V., & Bills, A. J. (1998). Effects of perceiving and imagining scenes on memory for pictures. *Journal of Experimental Psychology: Learning, Memory and Cognition, 24*, 1–16.

Isha, A., & Sagi, D. (1995). Common mechanisms of visual imagery and perception. *Science, 268,* 1772–1774.

Jackendoff, R. (1972). *Semantic interpretation in generative grammar.* Cambridge, MA: MIT Press.

Jackendoff, R. (1987). *Consciousness and the computational mind.* Cambridge, MA: MIT Press.

Jacoby, L. L. (1978). On interpreting the effects of repetition: Solving a problem versus remembering a solution. *Journal of Verbal Learning and Verbal Behavior, 17,* 649–667.

Jacoby, L. L. (1983). Remembering the data: Analyzing interactive processes in reading. *Journal of Verbal Learning and Verbal Behavior, 22,* 485–508.

Jacoby, L. L. (1991). A process dissociation framework: Separating automatic from intentional uses of memory. *Journal of Memory and Language, 30,* 513–541.

Jacoby, L. L. (1998). Invariance in automatic influences of memory: Toward a user's guide for the process-dissociation procedure. *Journal of Experimental Psychology: Learning, Memory and Cognition, 24,* 3–26.

Jacoby, L. L., Allan, L., Collins, J., & Larwill, L. (1988). Memory influences subjective experience: Noise judgments. *Journal of Experimental Psychology: Learning, Memory and Cognition, 14,* 240–247.

Jacoby, L. L., & Brooks, L. R. (1984). Nonanalytic cognition: Memory, perception and concept learning. In G. H. Bower (Ed.), *The psychology of learning and motivation: Advances in research and theory.* New York: Academic Press.

Jacoby, L. L., & Craik, F. I. M. (1979). Effects of elaboration of processing at encoding and retrieval: Trace distinctiveness and recovery of initial context. In L. S. Cermak & F. I. M. Craik (Eds.), *Levels of processing in human memory.* Hillsdale, NJ: Lawrence Erlbaum.

Jacoby, L. L., & Dallas, M. (1981). On the relationship between autobiographical memory and perceptual learning. *Journal of Experimental Psychology: General, 3,* 306–340.

Jacoby, L. L., & Hollingshead, A. (1990). Reading student essays may be hazardous to your spelling: Effects of reading incorrectly and correctly spelled words. *Canadian Journal of Psychology, 44,* 345–258.

Jacoby, L. L., Jones, T. C., & Dolan, P. O. (1998). Two effects of repetition: Support for a dual process model of know judgments and exclusion errors. *Psychonomics Bulletin & Review, 5,* 705–509.

Jacoby, L. L., & Kelley, C. (1992). A process-dissociation framework for investigating unconscious influences: Freudian slips, projective tests, subliminal perception, and signal detection theory. *Current Directions in Psychological Science, 1,* 174–179.

Jacoby, L. L., Kelley, C. M., Brown, J., & Jasechko, J. (1989). Becoming famous overnight: Limits on the ability to avoid unconscious influences of the past. *Journal of Personality and Social Psychology, 56,* 326–338.

Jacoby, L. L., Levy, B. A., & Steinbach, K. (1992). Episodic transfer and automaticity: Integration of data-driven and conceptually-driven processing in rereading. *Journal of Experimental Psychology: Learning, Memory and Cognition, 18,* 15–24.

Jacoby, L. L., Toth, J., & Yonelinas, A. (1993). Separating conscious and unconscious influences of memory: Measuring recollection. *Journal of Experimental Psychology: General, 122,* 139–154.

Jacoby, L. L., & Whitehouse, K. (1989). An illusion of memory: False recognition influenced by unconscious perception. *Journal of Experimental Psychology: General, 118,* 126–135.

Jacoby, L. L., & Witherspoon, D. (1982). Remembering without awareness. *Canadian Journal of Psychology, 36,* 300–324.

James, W. (1890). *The principles of psychology,* vol. II. New York: Dover Publications.

Janis, I. (1972). *Victims of groupthink.* Boston: Houghton Mifflin.

Jankowiak, J., Kinsbourne, M., Shalev, R. S., & Bachman, D. L. (1992). Preserved visual imagery and categorization in a case of associative visual agnosia. *Journal of Cognitive Neuroscience, 4,* 119–131.

Jeffries, R., Polson, P., Razran, L., & Atwood, M. (1977). A process model for missionaries-cannibals and other river-crossing problems. *Cognitive Psychology, 9,* 412–440.

Jenkins, J. G., & Dallenbach, K. M. (1924). Oblivescence during sleep and waking. *American Journal of Psychology, 35,* 605–612.

Jenkins, L., Myerson, J., Hale, S., & Fry, A. F. (1999). Individual and developmental differences in working memory across the life span. *Psychonomic Bulletin & Review, 6,* 28–40.

Jennings, D. L., Amabile, T. M., & Ross, L. (1982). Informal covariation assessment: Data-based versus theory-based judgments. In D. Kahneman, P. Slovic, & A. Tversky (Eds.), *Judgments under uncertainty: Heuristics and biases.* Cambridge: Cambridge University Press.

Jobe, J., Tourangeau, R., & Smith, A. (1993). Contributions of survey research to the understanding of memory. *Applied Cognitive Psychology, 7,* 567–584.

Johnson, E., & Tversky, A. (1983). Affect, generalization, and the perception of risk. *Journal of Personality and Social Psychology,* 20–31.

Johnson, E. J., Hershey, J., Meszaros, J., & Kunreuther, H. (1993). Framing, probability distortions, and insurance decisions. *Journal of Risk and Uncertainty, 7,* 35–51.

Johnson, H., & Seifert, C. (1994). Sources of the continued influence effect: When misinformation affects later inferences. *Journal of Experimental Psychology: Learning, Memory and Cognition, 20,* 1420–1436.

Johnson, M. K., Bransford, J. D., & Solomon, S. (1973). Memory for tacit implication of sentences. *Journal of Experimental Psychology, 98,* 203–205.

Johnson, M. K. (1988). Reality monitoring: An experimental phenomenological approach. *Journal of Experimental Psychology: General, 117,* 390–394.

Johnson, M. K., Hashtroudi, S., & Lindsay, S. (1993). Source monitoring. *Psychological Bulletin, 114,* 3–28.

Johnson, M. K., & Raye, C. L. (1981). Reality monitoring. *Psychological Review, 88,* 67–85.

Johnson, M. K., Hashtroudi, S., & Lindsay, S. (1993). Source monitoring. *Psychological Bulletin, 114,* 3–28.

Johnson, M. K., Kim, J. K., & Risse, G. (1985). Do alcoholic Korsakoff's syndrome patients acquire affective reactions? *Journal of Experimental Psychology: Learning, Memory and Cognition, 11,* 27–36.

Johnson, P. (1982). The functional equivalence of imagery and movement. *Quarterly Journal of Experimental Psychology, 34A,* 349–365.

Johnson-Laird, P. N. (1983). *Mental models.* Cambridge, MA: Harvard University Press.

Johnson-Laird, P. N. (1987). The mental representation of the meaning of words. *Cognition, 25,* 189–211.

Johnson-Laird, P. N. (1988). A computational analysis of consciousness. In A. Marcel & E. Bisiach (Eds.), *Consciousness in contemporary science.* Oxford: Oxford University Press.

Johnson-Laird, P. N. (1990). Mental models. In M. Posner (Ed.), *Foundations of cognitive science* (pp. 469–500). Cambridge, MA: Bradford Press.

Johnson-Laird, P. N., & Byrne, R. (1989). Only reasoning. *Journal of Memory and Language, 28,* 313–330.

Johnson-Laird, P. N., & Byrne, R. (1991). *Deduction.* Hillsdale, NJ: Lawrence Erlbaum.

Johnson-Laird, P. N., Byrne, R. M. J., & Schaeken, W. (1992). Propositional reasoning by model. *Psychological Review, 99,* 418–439.

Johnson-Laird, P. N., Byrne, R., & Tabossi, P. (1989). Reasoning by model: The case of multiple quantification. *Psychological Review, 96,* 658–673.

Johnson-Laird, P. N., Legrenzi, P., Girotto, V., Legrenzi, M. S., & Caverni, J.-P. (1999). Naive probability: A mental model theory of extensional reasoning. *Psychological Review, 106,* 62–88.

Johnson-Laird, P. N., Legrenzi, P., & Legrenzi, M. S. (1972). Reasoning and a sense of reality. *British Journal of Psychology, 63,* 395–400.

Johnson-Laird, P. N., & Savary, F. (1999). Illusory inferences: A novel class of erroneous deductions. *Cognition, 71,* 191–229.

Johnson-Laird, P. N., & Steedman, M. (1978). The psychology of syllogisms. *Cognitive Psychology, 10,* 64–99.

Johnston, W. A., & Dark, V. J. (1986). Selective attention. *Annual Review of Psychology, 37,* 43–75.

Johnston, W., Hawley, K., & Elliott, J. (1991). Contribution of perceptual fluency to recognition judgments. *Journal of Experimental Psychology: Learning, Memory and Cognition, 17,* 210–223.

Jolicoeur, P., Gluck, M. A., & Kosslyn, S. M. (1984). Pictures and names: Making the connection. *Cognitive Psychology, 16,* 243–275.

Jones, D., & Macken, W. (1994). Phonological similarity in the irrelevant speech effect: Within- or between-stream similarity. *Journal of Experimental Psychology: Learning, Memory and Cognition, 19,* 369–381.

Jonides, J., & Baum, D. R. (1978). *Cognitive maps as revealed by distance estimates.* Paper presented at the annual meeting of the Psychonomics Society, Washington, D.C.

Jonides, J., Kahn, R., & Rozin, P. (1975). Imagery instructions improve memory in blind subjects. *Bulletin of the Psychonomic Society, 5,* 424–426.

Josephs, R., Giesler, R. B., & Silvera, D. (1994). Judgment by quantity. *Journal of Experimental Psychology: General, 123,* 21–32.

Jurica, P. J., & Shimamura, A. P. (1999). Monitoring item and source information: Evidence for a negative generation effect in source memory. *Memory & Cognition, 27,* 648–657.

Just, M., & Carpenter, P. (1987). *The psychology of reading and language comprehension.* Boston: Allyn & Bacon.

Just, M., & Carpenter, P. (1992). A capacity theory of comprehension: Individual differences in working memory. *Psychological Review, 99,* 122–149.

Just, M., Carpenter, P. A., & Hemphill, D. D. (1996). Constraints on processing capacity: Architectural or implementational? In D. Steier & T. Mitchell (Eds.), *Mind matters: A tribute to Allen Newell.* Mahwah, NJ: Lawrence Erlbaum.

Kahneman, D. (1973). *Attention and effort.* Englewood Cliffs, NJ: Prentice-Hall.

Kahneman, D., & Chajczyk, D. (1983). Tests of the automaticity of reading: Dilution of Stroop effects by color-irrelevant stimuli. *Journal of Experimental Psychology: Human Perception and Performance, 9,* 497–509.

Kahneman, D., Diener, E., & Schwarz, N. (Eds.). (1999). *Well-being: The foundations of hedonic psychology.* New York: Russell Sage Foundation.

Kahneman, D., Fredrickson, B., Schreiber, C., & Redelmeier, D. (1993). When more pain is preferred to less: Adding a better end. *Psychological Science, 4,* 401–405.

Kahneman, D., Knetsch, J., & Thaler, R. (1991). The endowment effect, loss aversion, and status quo bias. *Journal of Economic Perspectives, 5,* 193–206.

Kahneman, D., & Miller, D. (1986). Norm theory: Comparing reality to its alternatives. *Psychological Review, 93,* 136–153.

Kahneman, D., Ritov, I., Jacowitz, K., & Grant, P. (1993). Stated willingness to pay for public goods. *Psychological Science, 4*, 310–315.

Kahneman, D., Slovic, P., & Tversky, A. (Eds.). (1982). *Judgment under uncertainty: Heuristics and biases.* New York: Cambridge University Press.

Kahneman, D., & Snell, J. (1992). Predicting a changing taste: Do people know what they will like. *Journal of Behavioral Decision Making, 5*, 187–200.

Kahneman, D., Treisman, A., & Gibbs, B. (1992). The reviewing of object files: Object-specific integration of information. *Cognitive Psychology, 24*, 175–219.

Kahneman, D., & Tversky, A. (1972). Subjective probability: A judgment of representativeness. *Cognitive Psychology, 3*, 430–454.

Kahneman, D., & Tversky, A. (1973). On the psychology of prediction. *Psychological Review, 80*, 237–251.

Kahneman, D., & Tversky, A. (1979). Prospect theory: An analysis of decision under risk. *Econometrica, 47*, 263–291.

Kahneman, D., & Tversky, A. (1982a). On the study of statistical intuitions. *Cognition, 11*, 237–251.

Kahneman, D., & Tversky, A. (1982b). The simulation heuristic. In D. Kahneman, P. Slovic, & A. Tversky (Eds.), *Judgment under uncertainty: Heuristics and biases* (pp. 201–208). New York: Cambridge University Press.

Kahneman, D., & Tversky, A. (1982c). Variants of uncertainty. *Cognition, 11*, 143–158.

Kahneman, D., & Tversky, A. (1984). Choices, values and frames. *American Psychologist, 39*, 341–350.

Kahneman, D., & Tversky, A. (1996). On the reality of cognitive illusions. *Psychological Review, 103*, 582–591.

Kahney, H. (1986). *Problem solving: A cognitive approach.* Milton Keynes, England: Open University Press.

Kanizsa, G. (1979). *Organization in vision.* New York: Praeger.

Kapur, N. (1999). Syndromes of retrograde amnesia. *Psychological Bulletin, 125*, 800–825.

Kassin, S. M. (1985). Eyewitness identification: Retrospective self-awareness and the accuracy-confidence correlation. *Journal of Personality and Social Psychology, 49*, 878–893.

Kassin, S. M. (1997). The psychology of confession evidence. *American Psychologist, 52*, 221–233.

Kassin, S. M., & Kiechel, K. L. (1996). The social psychology of false confessions: Compliance, internalization and confabulation. *Psychological Science, 7*, 125–128.

Katona, G. (1940). *Organizing and memorizing.* New York: Columbia University Press.

Katz, A. (1983). What does it mean to be a high imager? In J. Yuille (Ed.), *Imagery, memory and cognition.* Hillsdale, NJ: Lawrence Erlbaum.

Katz, B. (1952). The nerve impulse. *Scientific American, 18*, 55-64.

Kaufmann, G. (1990). Imagery effects on problem solving. In P. Hampson, D. Marks, & J.T. E. Richardson (Eds.), *Imagery: Current developments* (pp. 169–196). London: Routledge.

Keenan, J. M. (1983). Qualifications and clarifications of images of concealed objects: A reply to Kerr and Neisser. *Journal of Experimental Psychology: Learning, Memory and Cognition, 9*, 222–230.

Keenan, J. M., MacWhinney, B., & Mayhew, D. (1977). Pragmatics in memory: A study of natural conversation. *Journal of Verbal Learning and Verbal Behavior, 16*, 549–560.

Keenan, J. M., & Moore, R. E. (1979). Memory for images of concealed objects: A reexamination of Neisser and Kerr. *Journal of Experimental Psychology: Human Learning and Memory, 5*, 374–385.

Keil, F. C. (1986). The acquisition of natural-kind and artifact terms. In W. Demopoulos & A. Marras (Eds.), *Language, learning, and concept acquisition.* Norwood, NJ: Ablex.

Keil, F. C. (1989). *Concepts, kinds, and cognitive development.* Cambridge, MA: MIT Press.

Keil, F. C., Smith, W. C., Simons, D. J., & Levin, D. T. (1998). Two dogmas of conceptual empiricism: Implications for hybrid models of the structure of knowledge. *Cognition, 65*, 103–135.

Kent, G. (1985). Memory of dental pain. *Pain, 21*, 187–194.

Kerr, N. H. (1983). The role of vision in "visual imagery" experiments: Evidence from the congenitally blind. *Journal of Experimental Psychology: General, 112*, 265–277.

Kerr, N. H., & Neisser, U. (1983). Mental images of concealed objects: New evidence. *Journal of Experimental Psychology: Learning, Memory and Cognition, 9*, 212–221.

Kihlstrom, J. F. (1987). The cognitive unconscious. *Science, 237*, 1445–1452.

Kihlstrom, J. F. (1993). The psychological unconscious and the self. In Ciba Foundation (Ed.), *Experimental and theoretical studies of consciousness. Ciba Foundation Symposium, 174.* Chichester, England: Wiley.

Kihlstrom, J. F. (1998). Exhumed memory. In S. J. Lynn & K. M. McConkey (Eds.), *Truth in memory.* New York: Guilford.

Kihlstrom, J. F. (1999). The psychological unconscious. In L. A. Pervin & O. P. John (Eds.), *Handbook of personality: Theory and research* (2nd ed.). New York: Guilford.

Kimberg, D. Y., D'Esposito, M., & Farah, M. J. (1998). Cognitive functions in the prefrontal cortex in working memory and executive control. *Current Directions in Psychological Science, 6*, 185–192.

Kinsbourne, M. (1981). Single channel theory. In D. Holding (Ed.), *Human skills* (pp. 375–381). Chichester, England: Wiley.

Kintsch, W. (1994). Text comprehension, memory, and learning. *American Psychologist, 49,* 294–303.

Kirsner, K., Milech, D., & Standen, P. (1983). Common and modality-specific processes in the mental lexicon. *Memory & Cognition, 11,* 621–630.

Klayman, J., & Brown, K. (1993). Debias the environment instead of the judge: An alternative approach to reducing error in diagnostic (and other) judgment. *Cognition, 49,* 97–122.

Klayman, J., & Ha, Y. (1987). Confirmation, disconfirmation, and information in hypothesis-testing. *Psychological Review, 94,* 211–228.

Kluender, R., & Kutas, R. (1993). Bridging the gap: Evidence from ERPs on the processing of unbounded dependencies. *Journal of Cognitive Neuroscience, 5,* 196–214.

Knoblich, G., Ohlsson, S., Haider, H., & Rhenius, D. (1999). Constraint relaxation and chunk decomposition in insight problem solving. *Journal of Experimental Psychology: Learning, Memory and Cognition, 25,* 1534–1556.

Knowlton, B., & Squire, L. (1993). The learning of categories: Parallel brain systems for item memory and category knowledge. *Science, 262,* 1747–1749.

Koestler, A. (1964). *The act of creation.* London: Hutchinson.

Kohler, W. (1969). *The task of Gestalt psychology.* Princeton, NJ: Princeton University Press.

Kohnken, G., & Maass, A. (1988). Eyewitness testimony: False alarms on biased instructions? *Journal of Applied Psychology, 73,* 363–370.

Kolers, P. (1983). Perception and representation. *Annual Review of Psychology, 34,* 129–166.

Komatsu, L. (1992). Recent views of conceptual structure. *Psychological Bulletin, 112,* 500–526.

Koriat, A., Lichtenstein, S., & Fischhoff, B. (1980). Reasons for confidence. *Journal of Experimental Psychology: Human Learning and Memory, 6,* 107–118.

Kosslyn, S. M. (1976). Can imagery be distinguished from other forms of internal representation? Evidence from studies of information retrieval times. *Memory & Cognition, 4,* 291–297.

Kosslyn, S. M. (1980). *Image and mind.* Cambridge, MA: Harvard University Press.

Kosslyn, S. M. (1983). *Ghosts in the mind's machine.* New York: W. W. Norton.

Kosslyn, S. M. (1994). *Image and brain: The resolution of the imagery debate.* Cambridge, MA: MIT Press.

Kosslyn, S. M., Ball, T. M., & Reiser, B. J. (1978). Visual images preserve metric spatial information: Evidence from studies of image scanning. *Journal of Experimental Psychology: Human Perception and Performance, 4,* 1–20.

Kosslyn, S. M., Brunn, J., Cave, K., & Wallach, R. (1985). Individual differences in mental imagery ability: A computational analysis. *Cognition, 18,* 195–243.

Kosslyn, S. M., Pascual-Leone, A., Felician, O., Camposano, S., Keenan, J. P., Thompson, W. L., Ganis, G., Sukel, K. E., & Alpert, N. M. (1999). The role of area 17 in visual imagery: Convergent evidence from PET and rTMS. *Science, 284,* 167–170.

Kotovsky, K., Hayes, J., & Simon, H. (1985). Why are some problems hard? Evidence from Tower of Hanoi. *Cognitive Psychology, 17,* 248–294.

Kripke, S. (1972). Naming and necessity. In D. Davidson & G. Harman (Eds.), *Semantics of natural language.* Dordrecht: D. Reidel.

Kroll, J. F., & Potter, M. C. (1984). Recognizing words, pictures, and concepts: A comparison of lexical, object, and reality decisions. *Journal of Verbal Learning and Verbal Behavior, 23,* 39–66.

Kroll, N. E., Schepeler, E. M., & Angin, K. T. (1986). Bizarre imagery: The misremembered mnemonic. *Journal of Experimental Psychology: Learning, Memory and Cognition, 12,* 42–54.

Kucera, H., & Francis, W. N. (1967). *Computational analysis of present-day American English.* Providence, RI: Brown University Press.

Kumon-Nakamura, S., Glucksberg, S., & Brown, M. (1995). How about another piece of pie: The allusional pretense theory of discourse irony. *Journal of Experimental Psychology: General, 124,* 3–21.

Kunda, Z. (1990). The case for motivated reasoning. *Psychological Bulletin, 108,* 480–498.

Kunda, Z., & Nisbett, R. E. (1986). The psychometrics of everyday life. *Cognitive Psychology, 18,* 195–224.

Kunen, S., & May, J. (1981). Imagery-induced McCollough effects: Real or imagined. *Perception & Psychophysics, 30,* 99–100.

Kwiatkowski, S., & Parkinson, S. (1994). Depression, elaboration, and mood congruence: Differences between natural and induced mood. *Memory & Cognition, 22,* 225–233.

Kyllonen, P. C., & Cristal, R. E. (1990). Reasoning ability is (little more than) working-memory capacity? *Intelligence, 14,* 389–433.

Lachter, J., & Bever, T. G. (1988). The relation between linguistic structure and associative theories of language learning—a critique of some connectionist learning models. *Cognition, 28,* 195–247.

Lakatos, I. (1970). Falsification and the methodology of scientific research programmes. In I. Lakatos & A. Musgrave (Eds.), *Criticism and the growth of scientific knowledge* (pp. 91–196). New York: Cambridge University Press.

Lakoff, G. (1987). Cognitive models and prototype theory. In U. Neisser (Ed.), *Concepts and conceptual development*. Cambridge: Cambridge University Press.

Lamb, M. E. (1998). Assessments of children's credibility in forensic contexts. *Current Directions in Psychological Science, 7*, 43–46.

Lamble, D., Kauranen, T., Laakso, M., & Summala, H. (1999). Cognitive load and detection thresholds in car following situations: Safety implications for using mobile (cellular) telephones while driving. *Accident Analysis & Prevention, 31*, 617–623.

Landau, B., & Munnich, E. (1998). The representation of space and spatial language: Challenges for cognitive science. In P. Oliver & K.-P. Gapp (Eds.), *Representation and processing of spatial expressions*. Mahwah, NJ: Lawrence Erlbaum.

Lane, S., & Zaragoza, M. (1995). The recollective experience of cross-modality confusion errors. *Memory & Cognition, 23*, 607–610.

Laney, C., Campbell, H., Heuer, F., & Reisberg, D. (2000). Visually-induced and thematically-induced arousal. Manuscript under review.

Langer, E. (1989). *Mindfulness*. Reading, MA: Addison-Wesley Publishing Co.

Langley, P., & Jones, R. (1988). A computational model of scientific insight. In R. J. Sternberg (Ed.), *The nature of creativity* (pp. 177–201). Cambridge: Cambridge University Press.

Langley, P., Simon, H., Bradshaw, G., & Zytkow, J. (1987). *Scientific discovery: Computational explorations of the creative process*. Cambridge, MA: MIT Press.

Larkin, J., McDermott, J., Simon, D., & Simon, H. (1980). Expert and novice performance in solving physics problems. *Science, 208*, 1335–1342.

Larrick, R., Nisbett, R., & Morgan, J. (1993). Who uses the normative rules of choice? In R. Nisbett (Ed.), *Rules for reasoning* (pp. 277–294). Hillsdale, NJ: Lawrence Erlbaum.

Larrick, R. P., & Blount, S. (1997). The claiming effect: Why players are more generous in social dilemmas than in ultimatum games. *Journal of Personality & Social Psychology, 72*(4), 810–825.

Lassiter, G. D. (2000). The relative contributions of recognition and search-evaluation processes in high-level chess performance: Comment on Gobet and Simon. *Psychological Science, 11*, 172–174.

LeCompte, D. (1995). Recollective experience in the revelation effect: Separating the contributions of recollection and familiarity. *Memory & Cognition, 23*, 324–334.

Lee, A. Y., & Hutchison, L. (1998). Improving learning from examples through reflection. *Journal of Experimental Psychology: Applied, 4*, 187–210.

Legrenzi, P., Girotto, V., & Johnson-Laird, P. (1993). Focussing in reasoning and decision making. *Cognition, 49*, 37–66.

Lehman, D. R., Lempert, R. O., & Nisbett, R. E. (1988). The effects of graduate training on reasoning: Formal discipline and thinking about everyday-life events. *American Psychologist, 43*, 431–442.

Lehman, D. R., & Nisbett, R. (1990). A longitudinal study of the effects of undergraduate education on reasoning. *Developmental Psychology, 26*, 952–960.

Leippe, M. R., Manion, A. P., & Romanczyk, A. (1992). Eyewitness persuasion: How and how well do fact finders judge the accuracy of adults' and children's memory reports? *Journal of Personality and Social Psychology, 63*, 181–197.

Lesgold, A., Rubinson, H., Feltovich, P., Glaser, R., Klopfer, D., & Wang, Y. (1988). Expertise in a complex skill: Diagnosing x-ray pictures. In M. Chi, R. Glaser, & M. Farr (Eds.), *The nature of expertise*. Hillsdale, NJ: Lawrence Erlbaum.

Levin, D. T., & Simons, D. J. (1997). Failure to detect changes to attended objects in motion pictures. *Psychonomics Bulletin & Review, 4*, 501–506.

Levin, I., & Gaeth, G. (1988). How consumers are affected by the framing of attribute information before and after consuming the product. *Journal of Consumer Research, 15*, 374–378.

Levin, I., Schnittjer, S., & Thee, S. (1988). Information framing effects in social and personal decisions. *Journal of Experimental Social Psychology, 24*, 520–529.

Levine, L. J. (1997). Reconstructing memory for emotions. *Journal of Experimental Psychology: General, 126*, 165–177.

Levitin, D. J. (1993). Absolute representation in auditory memory: Evidence from the production of learned melodies. *Perception & Psychophysics, 56*, 414–423.

Levitin, D. J., & Cook, P. R. (1996). Memory for musical tempo: Additional evidence that auditory memory is absolute. *Perception & Psychophysics, 58*, 927–935.

Lewandowsky, S., & Kirsner, K. (2000). Knowledge partitioning: Context-dependent use of expertise. *Memory & Cognition, 28*, 295–305.

Lewis, C. H., & Anderson, J. R. (1976). Interference with real world knowledge. *Cognitive Psychology, 7*, 311–335.

Lewis, C., & Keren, G. (1999). On the difficulties underlying Bayesian reasoning: A comment on Gigerenzer and Hoffrage. *Psychological Review, 106*, 411–416.

Liberman, A. (1970). The grammars of speech and language. *Cognitive Psychology, 1*, 301–323.

Liberman, A., Harris, K., Hoffman, H., & Griffith, B. (1957). The discrimination of speech sounds within and across phoneme boundaries. *Journal of Experimental Psychology, 54*, 358–368.

Liberman, N., & Klar, Y. (1996). Hypothesis testing in Wason's selection task: Social exchange cheating detection or task understanding. *Cognition, 58*, 127–156.

Libkuman, T. M., Nichols-Whitenead, P., Griffith, J., & Thomas, R. (1999). Source of arousal and memory for detail. *Memory & Cognition, 27*, 166–190.

Lichtenstein, S., & Slovic, P. (1971). Reversals of preference between bids and choices in gambling decisions. *Journal of Experimental Psychology, 89*, 46–55.

Lichtenstein, S., Slovic, P., Fischhoff, B., Layman, M., & Combs, B. (1978). Judged frequency of lethal events. *Journal of Experimental Psychology: Human Learning and Memory, 4*, 551–578.

Light, L. L., & Carter-Sobell, L. (1970). Effects of changed semantic context on recognition memory. *Journal of Verbal Learning and Verbal Behavior, 9*, 1–11.

Lindsay, D. S. (1993). Eyewitness suggestibility. *Current Directions in Psychological Science, 2*, 86–89.

Lindsay, R. C., Lea, J. A., & Fulford, J. A. (1991). Sequential lineup presentation: Technique matters. *Journal of Applied Psychology, 76*, 741–745.

Lindsay, R. C., Lea, J. A., Nosworthy, G., Fulford, J., Hector, J., LeVan, V., & Seabrook, C. (1991). Biased lineups: Sequential presentation reduces the problem. *Journal of Applied Psychology, 76*, 796–802.

Lindsay, R. C., Wallbridge, H., & Drennan, D. (1987). Do the clothes make the man? An exploration of the effect of lineup attire on eyewitness identification accuracy. *Canadian Journal of Behavioural Science, 19*, 463–478.

Lindsay, R. C., & Wells, G. L. (1985). Improving eyewitness identifications from lineups: Simultaneous versus sequential lineup presentation. *Journal of Applied Psychology, 70*, 556–564.

Linton, M. (1975). Memory for real-world events. In D. A. Norman & D. E. Rumelhart (Eds.), *Explorations in cognition* (pp. 376–404). San Francisco: Freeman.

Linton, M. (1978). Real world memory after six years: An in vivo study of very long term memory. In M. M. Gruneberg, P. E. Morris, & R. N. Sykes (Eds.), *Practical aspects of memory* (pp. 69–76). London: Academic Press.

Linton, M. (1982). Transformations of memory in everyday life. In U. Neisser (Ed.), *Memory observed: Remembering in natural contexts* (pp. 77–92). San Francisco: Freeman.

Linton, M. (1986). Ways of searching and the contents of memory. In D. C. Rubin (Ed.), *Autobiographical memory*. Cambridge: Cambridge University Press.

Linton, S. J., & Melin, L. (1982). The accuracy of remembering chronic pain. *Pain, 13*, 281–285.

Lisker, L., & Abramson, A. (1970). *The voicing dimension: Some experiments in comparative phonetics*. Paper presented at the Proceedings of the Sixth International Congress of Phonetic Sciences, Prague.

Lockhart, R. S. (1989). The role of theory in understanding implicit memory. In S. Lewandowsky, J. C. Dunn, & K. Kirsner (Eds.), *Implicit memory: Theoretical issues*. Hillsdale, NJ: Lawrence Erlbaum.

Lockhart, R. S., Craik, F. I. M., & Jacoby, L. (1976). Depth of processing, recall, and recognition. In J. Brown (Ed.), *Recall and recognition*. New York: Wiley.

Loewenstein, G., & Schkade, D. (1999). Wouldn't it be nice? Predicting future feelings. In D. Kahneman, E. Diener, & N. Schwarz (Eds.), *Well-being: The foundations of hedonic psychology*. New York: Russell Sage Foundation.

Loewenstein, J., Thompson, L., & Gentner, D. (1999). Analogical encoding facilitates knowledge transfer in negotiation. *Psychonomics Bulletin & Review, 6*, 586–597.

Loewenstein, R. (1993). Psychogenic amnesia and psychogenic fugue: A comprehensive review. In D. Spiegel (Ed.), *Dissociative disorder: A clinical review*. Lutherville, MD: Sidran Press

Loftus, E. F. (1975). Leading questions and the eyewitness report. *Cognitive Psychology, 7*, 560–572.

Loftus, E. F. (1979). *Eyewitness testimony*. Cambridge, MA: Harvard University Press.

Loftus, E. F. (1992). When a lie becomes memory's truth: Memory distortion after exposure to misinformation. *Current Directions in Psychological Science, 1*, 121–123.

Loftus, E. F. (1993). Desperately seeking memories of the first few years of childhood: The reality of early memories. *Journal of Experimental Psychology: General, 122*, 274–277.

Loftus, E. F. (1997). Memory for a past that never was. *Current Directions in Psychological Science, 6*, 60–64.

Loftus, E. F., & Greene, E. (1980). Warning: Even memory for faces may be contagious. *Law and Human Behavior, 4*, 323–334.

Loftus, E. F., & Ketcham, K. (1991). *Witness for the defense: The accused, the eyewitness, and the expert who puts memory on trial*. New York: St. Martin's Press.

Loftus, E. F., Miller, D. G., & Burns, H. J. (1978). Semantic integration of verbal information into a visual memory. *Journal of Experimental Psychology: Human Learning and Memory, 4*, 19–31.

Loftus, E. F., & Palmer, J. C. (1974). Reconstruction of automobile destruction: An example of the interaction between language and memory. *Journal of Verbal Learning and Verbal Behavior, 13*, 585–589.

Loftus, E. F., & Pickrell, J. E. (1995). The formation of false memories. *Psychiatric Annals, 25*, 720–725.

Loftus, E. F., & Zanni, G. (1975). Eyewitness testimony: The influence of the wording of a question. *Bulletin of the Psychonomic Society, 5*, 86–88.

Loftus, G., & Kallman, H. (1979). Encoding and use of detail information in picture recognition. *Journal of Experimental Psychology: Human Learning and Memory, 5*, 197–211.

Logan, G. (1989). Automaticity and cognitive control. In J. Uleman & J. Bargh (Eds.), *Unintended thought*. New York: Guilford.

Logan, G., & Klapp, S. (1991). Automatizing alphabet arithmetic: I. Is extended practice necessary to produce automaticity? *Journal of Experimental Psychology: Learning, Memory and Cognition, 17,* 179–195.

Logan, G., & Stadler, M. (1991). Mechanisms of performance improvement in consistent mapping search: Automaticity or strategy shift? *Journal of Experimental Psychology: Learning, Memory and Cognition, 17,* 478–496.

Logan, G. D. (1982). On the ability to inhibit complex movements: A stop-signal study of typewriting. *Journal of Experimental Psychology: Human Perception and Performance, 8,* 778–792.

Logie, R. H. (1986) Visuo-spatial processing in working memory. *Quarterly Journal of Experimental Psychology, 38A,* 229–247.

Logie, R. H., Baddeley, A. D., & Woodhead, M. (1987). Face recognition, pose and ecological validity. *Applied Cognitive Psychology, 1,* 53–69.

Logie, R. H., & Marchetti, C. (1991). Visuo-spatial working memory: Visual, spatial or central executive. In R. H. Logie & M. Denis (Eds.), *Mental images in human cognition* (pp. 105–115). Amsterdam: Elsevier.

Logie, R. H. (1995). *Visuo-spatial working memory.* Hillsdale, NJ: Lawrence Erlbaum.

Logie, R. H., Engelkamp, J., Dehn, D., & Rudkin, S. (1999). Actions, mental actions, and working memory. In M. Denis, C. Cornoldi, J. Engelkamp, M. De Vega, & R. H. Logie (Eds.), *Imagery, language, and the representation of space.* Hove, England: The Psychology Press.

Loomes, G. (1987). Testing for regret and disappointment in choice under uncertainty. *Economic Journal, 97,* 118–129.

Lord, A. B. (1960). *The singer of tales.* Cambridge, MA: Harvard University Press.

Lord, C. G., Lepper, M. R., & Preston, E. (1984). Considering the opposite: A corrective strategy for social judgment. *Journal of Personality and Social Psychology, 47,* 1231–1243.

Lovett, M. C., & Schunn, C. D. (1999). Task representations, strategy variability, and base-rate neglect. *Journal of Experimental Psychology: General, 128,* 107–130.

Luchins, A. (1942). Mechanization in problem solving: The effect of Einstellung. *Psychological Monographs, 54*(1), (entire).

Luchins, A., & Luchins, E. (1950). New experimental attempts at preventing mechanization in problem solving. *Journal of General Psychology, 42,* 279–297.

Luchins, A., & Luchins, E. (1959). *Rigidity of behavior: A variational approach to the effects of Einstellung.* Eugene: University of Oregon Books.

Luria, A. R. (1968). *The mind of a mnemonist.* Chicago: Henry Regnery Co.

Luus, C. E., & Wells, G. L. (1991). Eyewitness identification and the selection of distracters for lineups. *Law and Human Behavior, 15,* 43–57.

Lyman, B., & McDaniel, M. (1990). Memory for odors and odor names: Modalities of elaboration and imagery. *Journal of Experimental Psychology: Learning, Memory and Cognition, 16,* 656–664.

Lynch, E. B., Coley, J. D., & Medin, D. L. (2000). Tall is typical: Central tendency, ideal dimensions, and graded category structure among tree experts and novices. *Memory & Cognition, 28,* 41–50.

MacDonald, M., Pearlmutter, N., & Seidenberg, M. (1994). Lexical nature of syntactic ambiguity resolution. *Psychological Review, 101,* 676–703.

MacDonald, M. C. (1989). Priming effects from gaps to antecedents. *Language and Cognitive Processes, 4,* 1–72.

Mack, A., & Rock, I. (1998). *Inattentional blindness.* Cambridge, MA: MIT Press.

MacLeod, C. (1991). Half a century of research on the Stroop effect: An integrative review. *Psychological Bulletin, 109,* 163–203.

MacWhinney, B., & Leinbach, J. (1991). Implementations are not conceptualizations: Revising the verb learning model. *Cognition, 29,* 121–157.

Mahoney, M., & DeMonbreun, B. (1978). Problem-solving bias in scientists. *Cognitive Therapy and Research, 1,* 229–238.

Maier, N. R. F. (1931). Reasoning in humans: II. The solution of a problem and its appearance in consciousness. *Journal of Comparative Psychology, 12,* 181–194.

Malpass, R. S., & Devine, P. G. (1981). Eyewitness identification: Lineup instructions and the absence of the offender. *Journal of Applied Psychology, 66,* 483–489.

Malt, B. C., & Smith, E. E. (1984). Correlated properties in natural categories. *Journal of Verbal Learning and Verbal Behavior, 23,* 250–269.

Mandler, G. (1980). Recognizing: The judgment of previous occurrence. *Psychological Review, 87,* 252–271.

Mandler, G. (1981). The recognition of previous encounters. *American Scientist, 69,* 211–218.

Mandler, G., Graf, P., & Kraft, D. (1986). Activation and elaboration effects in recognition and word priming. *Quarterly Journal of Experimental Psychology, 38,* 645–662.

Mandler, G., & Pearlstone, Z. (1966). Free and constrained concept learning and subsequent recall. *Journal of Verbal Learning and Verbal Behavior, 5,* 126–131.

Mandler, J. M. (1984). *Stories, scripts, and scenes: Aspects of schema theory.* Hillsdale, NJ: Lawrence Erlbaum.

Mandler, J. M., & Ritchey, G. H. (1977). Long-term memory for pictures. *Journal of Experimental Psychology: Human Learning and Memory, 3,* 386–396.

Marcel, A. (1988). Phenomenal experience and functionalism. In A. Marcel & E. Bisiach (Eds.), *Consciousness in contemporary science.* Oxford: Oxford University Press.

Marcel, A., & Bisiach, E. (Eds.). (1988). *Consciousness in contemporary science*. New York: Oxford University Press.

Marchman, V. A., Plunkett, K., & Goodman, J. (1997). Overregularization in English plural and past tense inflectional morphology: A response to Marcus (1995). *Journal of Child Language, 24*, 767–779.

Marcus, G. B. (1986). Stability and change in political attitudes: Observe, recall, and "explain." *Political Behavior, 8*, 21–44.

Marcus, G. F. (1995). The acquisition of the English past tense in children and multilayered connectionist networks. *Cognition, 56*, 271–279.

Marcus, G. F. (1996). Why do children say "breaked"? *Current Directions in Psychological Science, 5*, 81–85.

Marcus, G. F., Pinker, S., Ullman, M., Hollander, M., Rosen, T., & Xu, F. (1992). Overregularization in language acquisition. *Monographs of the Society for Research in Child Development, 57*, entire issue.

Marcus, G. F., Vijayan, S., Rao, S. B., & Vishton, P. M. (1999). Rule learning by seven-month-old infants. *Science, 283*(5398), 77–80.

Marek, G. R. (1975). *Toscanini*. London: Vision Press.

Margolis, E. (1994). A reassessment of the shift from the classical theory of concepts to prototype theory. *Cognition, 51*, 73–89.

Markman, A. B. (1997). Constraints on analogical inference. *Cognitive Science, 21*, 373–418.

Marks, D. (1983). Mental imagery and consciousness: A theoretical review. In A. Sheikh (Ed.), *Imagery: Current theory, research and application*. New York: Wiley.

Marmor, G. S., & Zabeck, L. A. (1976). Mental rotation by the blind: Does mental rotation depend on visual imagery? *Journal of Experimental Psychology: Human Perception and Performance, 2*, 515–521.

Marschark, M., & Hunt, R. R. (1989). A reexamination of the role of imagery in learning and memory. *Journal of Experimental Psychology: Learning, Memory and Cognition, 15*, 710–720.

Marsh, R., & Landau, J. (1995). Item availability in cryptonmnesia: Assessing its role in two paradigms of unconscious plagiarism. *Journal of Experimental Psychology: Learning, Memory and Cognition, 21*, 1568–1582.

Marslen-Wilson, W. D., & Teuber, H. L. (1975). Memory for remote events in anterograde amnesia: Recognition of public figures from news photographs. *Neuropsychologia, 13*, 353–364.

Marslen-Wilson, W. D., & Tyler, L. (1987). Against modularity. In J. L. Garfield (Ed.), *Modularity in knowledge representation and natural-language understanding*. Cambridge, MA: MIT Press.

Marsolek, C. J. (1999). Dissociable neural subsystems underlie abstract and specific object recognition. *Psychological Science, 10*, 111–117.

Mather, M., Shafir, E., & Johnson, M. K. (2000). Misremembrance of options past: Source monitoring and choice. *Psychological Science, 11*, 132–138.

Matthews, W. A. (1983). The effects of concurrent secondary tasks on the use of imagery in a free recall task. *Acta Psychologica, 53*, 231–241.

May, C., Kane, M., & Hasher, L. (1995). Determinants of negative priming. *Psychological Bulletin, 118*, 35–54.

Mazzoni, G. A. L., Loftus, E. F., Seitz, A., & Lynn, S. J. (1999). Changing beliefs and memories through dream interpretation. *Applied Cognitive Psychology, 13*, 125–144.

McCann, R., & Johnston, J. (1992). Locus of the single-channel bottleneck in dual-task interference. *Journal of Experimental Psychology: Human Perception and Performance, 18*, 471–484.

McClelland, J. L. (1999). Connectionist cognitive modeling. In R. A. Wilson & F. C. Keil (Eds.), *The MIT encyclopedia of the cognitive sciences*. Cambridge, MA: MIT Press.

McClelland, J. L., & Rumelhart, D. E. (1981). An interactive model of context effects in letter perception. Part 1. An account of basic findings. *Psychological Review, 88*, 375–407.

McClelland, J. L., & Rumelhart, D. E. (Eds.). (1986). *Parallel distributed processing, vol. 2*. Cambridge, MA: MIT Press.

McClelland, J. L., & Seidenberg, M. S. (2000). Why do kids say goed and brang? *Science, 287*, 47–48.

McCloskey, M., & Cohen, N. J. (1989). Catastrophic interference in connectionist networks: The sequential learning problem. In G. H. Bower (Ed.), *The psychology of learning and motivation: vol. 23*. New York: Academic Press.

McCloskey, M., & Glucksberg, S. (1978). Natural categories. Well-defined or fuzzy sets? *Memory & Cognition, 6*, 462–472.

McCloskey, M., & Glucksberg, S. (1979). Decision processes in verifying category membership statements: Implications for models of semantic memory. *Cognitive Psychology, 11*, 1–37.

McCloskey, M., Wible, C. G., & Cohen, N. J. (1988). Is there a special flashbulb-memory mechanism? *Journal of Experimental Psychology: General, 117*, 171–181.

McCloskey, M., & Zaragoza, Z. (1985). Misleading postevent information and memory for events: Arguments and evidence against memory impairment hypotheses. *Journal of Experimental Psychology: General, 114*, 3–18.

McCranie, E. W., Hyer, L. A., Boudewyns, P. A., & Woods, M. G. (1992). Negative parenting behavior, combat exposure, and PTSD symptom severity: Test of a person-event interaction model. *Journal of Nervous & Mental Disease, 180*(7), 431–438.

McDaniel, M. (1981). Syntactic complexity and elaborative processing. *Memory & Cognition, 9*, 487–495.

McDaniel, M., & Einstein, G. (1986). Bizarre imagery as an effective mnemonic aid: The importance of distinctiveness. *Journal of Experimental Psychology: Learning, Memory and Cognition, 12,* 54–65.

McDaniel, M., & Einstein, G. (1990). Bizarre imagery: Mnemonic benefits and theoretical implications. In R. Logie & M. Denis (Eds.), *Mental images in human cognition* (pp. 183–192). New York: North Holland.

McDermott, K., & Roediger, H. (1994). Effects of imagery on perceptual implicit memory tests. *Journal of Experimental Psychology: Learning, Memory and Cognition, 20,* 1379–1390.

McDermott, K. B., & Roediger, H. L. (1998). False recognition of associates can be resistant to an explicit warning to subjects and an immediate recognition probe. *Journal of Memory & Language, 39,* 508–520.

McElree, B., & Griffith, T. (1995). Syntactic and thematic processing in sentence comprehension: Evidence for a temporal dissociation. *Journal of Experimental Psychology: Learning, Memory and Cognition, 21,* 134–157.

McEvoy, C. L., Nelson, D., & Komatsu, T. (1999). What is the connection between true and false memories? The differential role of interitem associations in recall and recognition. *Journal of Experimental Psychology: Learning, Memory and Cognition, 25,* 1177–1194.

McGaugh, J. L. (2000). Memory—a century of consolidation. *Science, 287,* 248–251.

McGuire, W. (1989). A perspectivist approach to the strategic planning of programmatic scientific research. In B. Gholson, W. Shadish, & R. Neimeyer (Eds.), *Psychology of science: Contributions to metascience.* Cambridge: Cambridge University Press.

McKelvie, S. (1995). The VVIQ as a psychometric test of individual differences in visual imagery vividness: A critical quantitative review and plea for direction. *Journal of Mental Imagery,* 1–106.

McKenzie, C. R. M. (1998). Taking into account the strength of an alternative hypothesis. *Journal of Experimental Psychology: Learning, Memory and Cognition, 24,* 771–792.

McKim, R. (1980). *Experiences in visual thinking.* Belmont, CA: Wadsworth.

McKoon, G., & Ratcliff, R. (1992). Spreading activation versus compound cue accounts of priming: Mediated priming revisited. *Journal of Experimental Psychology: Learning, Memory and Cognition, 18,* 1155–1172.

McNamara, T. (1992a). Priming and constraints it places on theories of memory and retrieval. *Psychological Review, 99,* 650–662.

McNamara, T. (1992b). Theories of priming: I. Associative distance and lag. *Journal of Experimental Psychology: Learning, Memory and Cognition, 18,* 1173–1190.

McNamara, T. (1994). Theories of priming: II. Types of primes. *Journal of Experimental Psychology: Learning, Memory and Cognition, 20,* 507–520.

Meadows, J. C. (1974). Disturbed perception of colours associated with localized cerebral lesions. *Brain, 97,* 615–632.

Mecklinger, A., Schriefers, K., Steinhauer, K., & Fridererici, A. (1995). Processing relative clauses varying on syntactic and semantic dimensions: An analysis of event-related potentials. *Memory & Cognition, 23,* 477–494.

Medin, D. L. (1975). A theory of context in discrimination learning. In G. H. Bower (Ed.), *The psychology of learning and motivation.* New York: Academic Press.

Medin, D. L. (1976). Theories of discrimination learning and learning set. In W. K. Estes (Ed.), *Handbook of learning and cognitive processes.* Hillsdale, NJ: Lawrence Erlbaum.

Medin, D. L., Altom, M. W., Edelson, S. M., & Freko, D. (1982). Correlated symptoms and simulated medical classification. *Journal of Experimental Psychology: Learning, Memory, and Cognition, 8,* 37–50.

Medin, D. L., & Bazerman, M. H. (1999). Broadening behavioral decision research: Multiple levels of cognitive processing. *Psychonomics Bulletin & Review, 6,* 533–546.

Medin, D. L., Goldstone, R., & Gentner, D. (1993). Respects for similarity. *Psychological Review, 100,* 254–278.

Medin, D. L., Lynch, E. B., & Solomon, K. O. (2000). Are there kinds of concepts? *Annual Review of Psychology, 50,* 121–148.

Medin, D. L., & Ortony, A. (1989). Psychological essentialism. In S. Vosniadou & A. Ortony (Eds.), *Similarity and analogical reasoning* (pp. 179–195). New York: Cambridge University Press.

Medin, D. L., & Schaffer, M. (1978). Context theory of classification learning. *Psychological Review,* 207–238.

Medin, D. L., Schwartz, H., Blok, S. V., & Birnbaum, L. A. (1999). The semantic side of decision making. *Psychonomics Bulletin & Review, 6,* 562–569.

Mednick, S. (1962). The associative basis of the creative process. *Psychological Review, 69,* 220–232.

Mednick, S., & Mednick, M. (1967). *Examiner's manual, Remote Associates Test.* Boston: Houghton Mifflin.

Medvec, V. H., Madey, S. F., & Gilovich, T. (1995). When less is more: Counterfactual thinking and satisfaction among Olympic medalists. *Journal of Personality & Social Psychology, 60,* 603–610.

Mellers, B., Chang, S.-J., Birnbaum, M., & Ordóñez, L. (1992). Preferences, prices, and ratings in risky decision making. *Journal of Experimental Psychology: Human Perception and Performance, 18,* 347–361.

Mellers, B., Hertwig, R., & Kahneman, D. (2000). Do frequency representations eliminate conjunction effects? An exercise in adversarial collaboration. *Psychological Science,* in press.

Mellers, B. A., & McGraw, A. P. (1999). How to improve Bayesian reasoning: Comment on Gigerenzer and Hoffrage. *Psychological Review, 106,* 417–424.

Memon, A., & Higham, P. A. (1999). A review of the cognitive interview. *Psychology, Crime & Law* (5), 177–196.

Mervis, C. B., Catlin, J., & Rosch, E. (1976). Relationships among goodness-of-example, category norms and word frequency. *Bulletin of the Psychonomic Society, 7,* 268–284.

Messick, D. M. (2000). Alternative logics for decision making in social settings. *Journal of Economic Behavior & Organizations,* in press.

Metcalfe, J. (1986). Premonitions of insight predict impending error. *Journal of Experimental Psychology: Learning, Memory and Cognition, 12,* 623–634.

Metcalfe, J., & Weibe, D. (1987). Intuition in insight and noninsight problem solving. *Memory & Cognition, 15,* 238–246.

Meyer, D. E., & Schvaneveldt, R. W. (1971). Facilitation in recognizing pairs of words: Evidence of a dependence between retrieval operations. *Journal of Experimental Psychology, 90,* 227–234.

Meyer, D. E., Schvaneveldt, R. W., & Ruddy, M. G. (1974). Functions of graphemic and phonemic codes in visual word recognition. *Memory & Cognition, 2,* 309–321.

Mill, J. S. (1874). *A system of logic* (8th ed.). New York: Harper.

Miller, A. (1986). *Imagery in scientific thought.* Cambridge, MA: MIT Press.

Miller, G. A. (1951). *Language and communication.* New York: McGraw-Hill.

Miller, G. A. (1956). The magical number seven plus or minus two: Some limits on our capacity for processing information. *Psychological Review, 63,* 81–97.

Miller, G. A. (1962). *Psychology: The science of mental life.* New York: Harper & Row.

Miller, G. A. (1991). *The science of words.* New York: Freeman.

Miller, G. A. (1999). On knowing a word. *Annual Review of Psychology, 50,* 1–19.

Miller, G. A., Bruner, J. S., & Postman, L. (1954). Familiarity of letter sequences and tachistoscopic identification. *Journal of General Psychology, 50,* 129–139.

Miller, G. A., Galanter, E., & Pribram, K. (1960). *Plans and the structure of behavior.* New York: Holt, Rinehart and Winston.

Miller, G. A., & Nicely, P. (1955). An analysis of perceptual confusions among some English consonants. *Journal of the Acoustical Society of America, 27,* 338–352.

Milliken, B., Joordens, S., Merikle, P., & Seiffert, A. (1998). Selective attention: A reevaluation of the implications of negative priming. *Psychological Review, 105,* 203–229.

Milliken, B., & Tipper, S. (1998). Attention and inhibition. In H. Pashler (Ed.), *Attention.* Hove, U.K.: Psychology Press.

Milner, B. (1966). Amnesia following operation on the temporal lobes. In C. W. M. Whitty & O. L. Zangwill (Eds.), *Amnesia.* London: Butterworths.

Milner, B. (1970). Memory and the medial temporal regions of the brain. In K. H. Pribram & D. E. Broadbent (Eds.), *Biology of memory.* New York: Academic Press.

Minami, H., & Dallenbach, K. M. (1946). The effect of activity upon learning and retention in the cockroach. *American Journal of Psychology, 59,* 1–58.

Mitchell, K. J., & Zaragoza, M. S. (1996). Repeated exposure to suggestion and false memory: The role of contextual variability. *Journal of Memory & Language, 35*(2), 246–260.

Mitroff, I. (1981). Scientists and confirmation bias. In R. Tweney, M. Doherty, & C. Mynatt (Eds.), *On scientific thinking* (pp. 170–175). New York: Columbia University Press.

Miyashita, Y. (1995). How the brain creates imagery: Projection to primary visual cortex. *Science, 268,* 1719–1720.

Moore, C. M., & Egeth, H. (1997). Perception without attention: Evidence of grouping under conditions of inattention. *Journal of Experimental Psychology: Human Perception and Performance, 23,* 339–352.

Moray, N. (1959). Attention in dichotic listening: Affective cues and the influence of instructions. *Quarterly Journal of Experimental Psychology, 11,* 56–60.

Moray, N. (1969). *Attention: Selective processes in vision and hearing.* London: Hutchingson Educational Ltd.

Morris, C. D., Bransford, J. D., & Franks, J. J. (1977). Levels of processing versus transfer appropriate processing. *Journal of Verbal Learning and Verbal Behavior, 16,* 519–533.

Morris, M., & Murphy, G. (1990). Converging operations on a basic level in event taxonomies. *Memory & Cognition, 18,* 407–418.

Morris, M., & Nisbett, R. (1993). Tools of the trade: Deductive schemas taught in psychology and philosophy. In R. Nisbett (Ed.), *Rules for reasoning.* Hillsdale, NJ: Lawrence Erlbaum.

Morris, N. (1987). Exploring the visuo-spatial scratch pad. *Quarterly Journal of Experimental Psychology, 39A,* 409–430.

Morton, J. (1969). Interaction of information in word recognition. *Psychological Review, 76,* 165–178.

Morton, J. (1970). A functional model of human memory. In D. Norman (Ed.), *Models of human memory.* New York: Academic Press.

Moscovitch, M. (1982). Multiple dissociations of function in amnesia. In L. S. Cermak (Ed.), *Human memory and amnesia.* Hillsdale, NJ: Lawrence Erlbaum.

Moscovitch, M. (1994). Memory and working-with-memory: Evaluation of a component process model and comparisons with other models. In D. L. Schacter & E. Tulving (Eds.), *Memory systems 1994.* Cambridge, MA: MIT Press.

Moscovitch, M. (1995). Confabulation. In D. L. Schacter, J. T. Coyle, G. D. Fischbach, M.-M. Mesulam, & L. E. Sullivan (Eds.), *Memory distortions: How minds, brains and societies reconstruct the past.* Cambridge, MA: Harvard University Press.

Mulligan, N. W. (1998). The role of attention during encoding in implicit and explicit memory. *Journal of Experimental Psychology: Learning, Memory and Cognition, 24,* 27–47.

Murdock, B. B., Jr. (1962). The serial position effect of free recall. *Journal of Experimental Psychology, 64,* 482–488.

Murname, K., Phelps, M. P., & Malmberg, K. (1999). Context-dependent recognition memory: The ICE theory. *Journal of Experimental Psychology: General, 128,* 403–415.]

Murray, H. (1959). Vicissitudes of creativity. In H. Anderson (Ed.), *Creativity and its cultivation.* New York: Harper & Row.

Murray, H., & Denny, J. (1969). Interaction of ability level and interpolated activity (opportunity for incubation) in human problem solving. *Psychological Reports, 24,* 271–276.

Mynatt, C., Doherty, M., & Tweney, R. (1977). Confirmation bias in a simulated research environment: An experimental study of scientific inference. *Quarterly Journal of Experimental Psychology, 29,* 85–95.

Mynatt, C., Doherty, M., & Tweney, R. (1978). Consequences of confirmation and disconfirmation in a simulated research environment. *Quarterly Journal of Experimental Psychology, 30,* 395–406.

Nadel, L., & Jacobs, W. J. (1998). Traumatic memory is special. *Current Directions in Psychological Science, 7*(5), 154–157.

Nairn, J., & Pusen, C. (1984). Serial recall of imagined voices. *Journal of Verbal Learning and Verbal Behavior, 23,* 331–342.

Nairne, J. S., & Kelley, M. R. (1999). Reversing the phonological similarity effect. *Memory & Cognition, 27,* 45–53.

Navon, D. (1977). Forest before trees: The precedence of global features in visual perception. *Cognitive Psychology, 9,* 343–383.

Navon, D. (1984). Resources—A theoretical soup stone? *Psychological Review, 91,* 216–234.

Navon, D. (1985). Attention division or attention sharing? In M. I. Posner & O. S. Marin (Eds.), *Attention and performance XI.* Hillsdale, NJ: Lawrence Erlbaum.

Needham, D., & Begg, I. (1991). Problem-oriented training promotes spontaneous analogical transfer: Memory-oriented training promotes memory for training. *Memory & Cognition, 19,* 543–557.

Neely, C. B., & LeCompte, D. C. (1999). The importance of semantic similarity to the irrelevant speech effect. *Memory & Cognition, 27,* 37–44.

Neely, J. H. (1977). Semantic priming and retrieval from lexical memory: Role of inhibitionless spreading activation and limited capacity attention. *Journal of Experimental Psychology: General, 106,* 226–254.

Neely, J. H. (1991). Semantic priming effects in visual word recognition: A selective review of current findings and theories. In D. Besner & G. Humphreys (Eds.), *Basic processes in reading: Visual word recognition* (pp. 264–336). Hillsdale, NJ: Lawrence Erlbaum.

Neisser, U. (1964). Visual search. *Scientific American, 210,* 94–102.

Neisser, U. (1967). *Cognitive psychology.* New York: Appleton-Century-Crofts.

Neisser, U. (1976). *Cognition and reality.* New York: W. H. Freeman.

Neisser, U. (1981). John Dean's memory: A case study. *Cognition, 9,* 1–22.

Neisser, U. (1982). *Memory observed.* San Francisco: W. H. Freeman & Co.

Neisser, U. (1987). From direct perception to conceptual structure. In U. Neisser (Ed.), *Concepts and conceptual development.* Cambridge: Cambridge University Press.

Neisser, U., & Becklen, R. (1975). Selective looking: Attending to visually significant events. *Cognitive Psychology, 7,* 480–494.

Neisser, U., & Harsch, N. (1992). Phantom flashbulbs: False recollections of hearing the news about *Challenger.* In E. Winograd & U. Neisser (Eds.), *Affect and accuracy in recall: Studies of "flashbulb" memories* (pp. 9–31). Cambridge: Cambridge University Press.

Neisser, U., & Kerr, N. H. (1973). Spatial and mnemonic properties of visual images. *Cognitive Psychology, 5,* 138–150.

Neisser, U., Winograd, E., & Weldon, M. S. (1991). Remembering the earthquake: "What I experienced" vs. "How I heard the news." Paper presented at the meeting of the Psychonomic Society, San Francisco, November 24, 1991.

Nelson, K. (1988). The ontogeny of memory for real events. In U. Neisser & E. Winograd (Eds.), *Remembering reconsidered: Ecological and traditional approaches to the study of memory.* Cambridge: Cambridge University Press.

Nelson, D., Schreiber, T., & Holley, P. (1993). The retrieval of controlled and automatic aspects of meaning on direct and indirect tests. *Memory & Cognition, 20,* 671–684.

Nelson, R. L., Walling, J. R., & McEvoy, C. L. (1979). Doubts about depth. *Journal of Experimental Psychology: Human Learning and Memory, 5,* 24–44.

Nelson, T. O. (1976). Reinforcement and human memory. In W. K. Estes (Ed.), *Handbook of learning and cognitive processes, vol. 3*. Hillsdale, NJ: Lawrence Erlbaum.

Nelson, T. O. (1996). Consciousness and metacognition. *American Psychologist, 51*, 102–116.

Nemeroff, C., & Rozin, P. (1994). The contagion concept in adult thinking in the United States: Transmission of germs and of interpersonal influence. *Ethos, 22*, 158–186.

Neuman, P. G. (1977). Visual prototype information with discontinuous representation of dimensions of variability. *Memory & Cognition, 5*, 187–197.

Newcombe, F., Ratcliff, G., & Damasio, H. (1987). Dissociable visual and spatial impairments following right posterior cerebral lesions: Clinical, neuropsychological and anatomical evidence. *Neuropsychologia, 25(1B)*, 149–161.

Newcombe, N. S., Drummey, A. B., Fox, N. A., Lie, E., & Ottinger-Alberts, W. (2000). Remembering early childhood: How much, how, and why (or why not). *Current Directions in Psychological Science, 9*, 55–58.

Newell, A. (1973). Production systems: Model of control structures. In W. Chase (Ed.), *Visual information processing*. New York: Academic Press.

Newell, A., & Simon, H. (1972). *Human problem solving*. Englewood Cliffs, NJ: Prentice-Hall.

Newstead, S., Pollard, P., Evans, J., & Allen, J. (1992). The source of belief bias effects in syllogistic reasoning. *Cognition, 45*, 257–284.

Nickerson, R. S., & Adams, M. J. (1979). Long-term memory for a common object. *Cognitive Psychology, 11*, 287–307.

Nickerson, R. S., Perkins, D., & Smith, E. (1985). *The teaching of thinking*. Hillsdale, NJ: Lawrence Erlbaum.

Nicol, J., & Swinney, D. (1989). The role of structure in coreference assignment during sentence comprehension. *Journal of Psycholinguistic Research, 18*, 5–19.

Nilsson, H. (1971). *The point* [film]. Directed by Fred Wolf. Produced by Murikami-Wolf-Swenson.

Nisbett, R. (Ed.). (1993). *Rules for reasoning*. Hillsdale, NJ: Lawrence Erlbaum.

Nisbett, R., Krantz, D. H., Jepson, C., & Kunda, Z. (1983). The use of statistical heuristics in everyday inductive reasoning. *Psychological Review, 90*, 339–363.

Nisbett, R., & Ross, L. (1980). *Human inference: Strategies and shortcomings of social judgment*. Englewood Cliffs, NJ: Prentice-Hall.

Nisbett, R., & Schachter, S. (1966). Cognitive manipulation of pain. *Journal of Experimental Social Psychology, 2*, 277–236.

Nisbett, R., & Wilson, T. (1977). Telling more than we can know: Verbal reports on mental processes. *Psychological Review, 84*, 231–259.

Norman, D., & Bobrow, D. (1975). On data-limited and resource-limited processes. *Cognitive Psychology, 7*, 44–64.

Norman, D., Rumelhart, D. E., & Group, T. L. R. (1975). *Explorations in cognition*. San Francisco: Freeman.

Norman, D., & Shallice, T. (1986). Attention to action: Willed and automatic control of behavior. In R. Davidson, G. Schwartz, & D. Shapiro (Eds.), *Consciousness and self-regulation*. New York: Plenum Press.

Nosofsky, R. (1986). Attention, similarity, and the identification-categorization relationship. *Journal of Experimental Psychology: General, 115*, 39–57.

Nosworthy, G. J., & Lindsay, R. C. (1990). Does nominal lineup size matter? *Journal of Applied Psychology, 75*, 358–361.

Novick, L. (1988). Analogical transfer, problem similarity and expertise. *Journal of Experimental Psychology: Learning, Memory and Cognition, 14*, 510–520.

Novick, L., & Holyoak, K. (1991). Mathematical problem solving by analogy. *Journal of Experimental Psychology: Learning, Memory and Cognition, 17*, 398–415.

Novick, L. R., Hurley, S. M., & Francis, M. (1999). Evidence for abstract, schematic knowledge of three spatial diagram representations. *Memory & Cognition, 27*, 288–308.

Oakhill, J., & Garnham, A. (1993). On theories of belief bias in syllogistic reasoning. *Cognition, 46*, 87–92.

Oakley, D. A. (1983). The varieties of memory: A phylogenetic approach. In A. R. Mayes (Ed.), *Memory in humans and animals*. Wokingham, UK: Van Nostrand Reinhold.

Oaksford, M., & Chater, N. (1995). Information gain explains relevance which explains the selection task. *Cognition, 57*, 97–108.

O'Connor, M., Walbridge, M., Sandson, T., & Alexander, M. (1996). A neuropsychological analysis of Capgras syndrome. *Neuropsychiatry, Neuropsychology, and Behavioral Neurology, 9*, 265–271.

Ofshe, R. (1992). Inadvertent hypnosis during interrogation: False confession due to dissociative state; mis-identified multiple personality and the Satanic Cult Hypothesis. *International Journal of Clinical and Experimental Hypnosis, 40*, 125–136.

Oldfield, R. (1963). Individual vocabulary and semantic currency: A preliminary study. *British Journal of Social and Clinical Psychology, 2*, 122–130.

Oliphant, G. W. (1983). Repetition and recency effects in word recognition. *Australian Journal of Psychology, 35*, 393–403.

Olsson, N., Juslin, P., & Winman, A. (1998). Realism of confidence in earwitness versus eyewitness identification. *Journal of Experimental Psychology: Applied, 4*, 101–118.

Olton, R. (1979). Experimental studies of incubation: Searching for the elusive. *Journal of Creative Behavior, 13*, 9–22.

Olton, R., & Johnson, D. (1976). Mechanisms of incubation in creative problem solving. *American Journal of Psychology, 7*, entire.

Onifer, W., & Swinney, D. (1981). Accessing lexical ambiguities during sentence comprehension: Effects of frequency-of-meaning and contextual bias. *Memory & Cognition, 9*, 225–236.

Ormerod, T. C., & Chronicle, E. P. (1999). Global perceptual processing in problem solving: The case of the traveling salesperson. *Perception & Psychophysics, 61*, 1227–1238.

Ornstein, P. A., Merritt, K. A., Baker-Ward, L., Furtado, E., Gordon, B. N., & Principe, G. (1998). Children's knowledge, expectation, and long-term retention. *Applied Cognitive Psychology, 12*, 387–406.

Osborn, A. (1957). *Applied imagination.* New York: Charles Scribner's Sons.

Overton, D. (1985). Contextual stimulus effects of drugs and internal states. In P. D. Balsam & A. Tomie (Eds.), *Context and learning.* Hillsdale, NJ: Lawrence Erlbaum.

Owens, J., Bower, G. H., & Black, J. B. (1979). The "soap opera" effect in story recall. *Memory & Cognition, 7*, 185–191.

Paap, K., & Ogden, W. (1981). Letter encoding is an obligatory but capacity-demanding operation. *Journal of Experimental Psychology: Human Perception and Performance, 7*, 518–528.

Paddock, J. R., Joseph, A. L., Chan, F. M., Terranova, S., Manning, C., & Loftus, E. F. (1998). When guided visualization procedures may backfire: Imagination inflation and predicting individual differences in suggestibility. *Applied Cognitive Psychology, 12*, S63–76.

Paivio, A. (1969). Mental imagery in associative learning and memory. *Psychological Review, 76*, 241–263.

Paivio, A. (1971). *Imagery and verbal processes.* New York: Holt, Rinehart & Winston.

Paivio, A., & Csapo, K. (1969). Concrete image and verbal memory codes. *Journal of Experimental Psychology, 80*, 279–285.

Paivio, A., & Okovita, H. W. (1971). Word imagery modalities and associative learning in blind and sighted subjects. *Journal of Verbal Learning and Verbal Behavior, 10*, 506–510.

Paivio, A., Smythe, P. C., & Yuille, J. C. (1968). Imagery versus meaningfulness of nouns in paired-associate learning. *Canadian Journal of Psychology, 22*, 427–441.

Paivio, A., Yuille, J. C., & Madigan, S. (1968). Concreteness, imagery, and meaningfulness values for 925 nouns. *Journal of Experimental Psychology Monograph, 78* (1, Pt. 2).

Palmer, C. F., Jones, R. K., Hennessy, B. L., Unze, M. G., & Pick, A. D. (1989). How is a trumpet known? The "basic object level" concept and perceptions of musical instruments. *American Journal of Psychology, 102*, 17–37.

Palmer, S. (1977). Hierarchical structure in perceptual representation. *Cognitive Psychology, 9*, 441–474.

Palmer, S. (1999). *Vision science: Photons to phenomenology.* Cambridge, MA: MIT Press.

Palmer, S., Schreiber, C., & Fox, C. (1991). Remembering the earthquake: "Flashbulb" memory for experienced vs. reported events. Paper presented at the meeting of the Psychonomic Society, November 1991, San Francisco.

Paris, S. C., & Lindauer, B. K. (1976). The role of inference in children's comprehension and memory for sentences. *Cognitive Psychology, 8*, 217–227.

Parkin, A. J. (1984). Levels of processing, context, and facilitation of pronunciation. *Acta Psychologia, 55*, 19–29.

Parrott, W. G., & Sabini, J. (1990). Mood and memory under natural conditions: Evidence for mood incongruent recall. *Journal of Personality and Social Psychology, 59*, 321–336.

Pashler, H. (1991). Dual-task interference and elementary mental mechanisms. In D. E. Meyer & S. Kornblum (Eds.), *Attention and performance XIV.* Hillsdale, NJ: Lawrence Erlbaum.

Pashler, H. (1992). Attentional limitations in doing two tasks at the same time. *Current Directions in Psychological Science, 1*, 44–47.

Pashler, H. (1994). Graded capacity-sharing in dual-task interference. *Journal of Experimental Psychology: Human Perception and Performance, 20*, 330–342.

Pashler, H. (1995). Structures, processes and the flow of information. In E. Bjork & R. Bjork (Eds.), *Handbook of perception and cognition* (Vol. 10: Memory).

Pashler, H., & Carrier, M. (1996). Structures, processes, and the flow of information. In E. L. Bjork & R. A. Bjork (Eds.), *Memory. Handbook of perception and cognition* (2nd ed.). San Diego: Academic Press.

Pashler, H., & Johnston, J. (1989). Interference between temporally overlapping tasks: Chronometric evidence for central postponement with or without response grouping. *Quarterly Journal of Experimental Psychology, 41A*, 19–45.

Pashler, H., & O'Brien, S. (1993). Dual-task interference and the cerebral hemispheres. *Journal of Experimental Psychology: HumanPerception and Performance, 19*: 315–330.

Passolunghi, M. C., Cornoldi, C., & De Liberto, S. (1999). Working memory and intrusions of irrelevant information in a group of specific poor problem solvers. *Memory & Cognition, 27*, 779–790.

Patalano, A., & Seifert, C. (1994). Memory for impasses during problem solving. *Memory & Cognition, 22*, 234–242.

Patel, V., Evans, D., & Groen, G. (1989). Biomedical knowledge and clinical reasoning. In D. Evans & V. Patel (Eds.), *Cognitive science in medicine: Biomedical modeling.* Cambridge, MA: MIT Press.

Patrick, C. (1935). Creative thought in poets. *Archives of Psychology, 26,* 73.

Patrick, C. (1937). Creative thought in artists. *Journal of Psychology, 4,* 35–73.

Payne, J. (1994). Thinking aloud: Insights into information processing. *Psychological Science, 5,* 241–248.

Payne, J., Bettman, J., & Johnson, E. (1992). Behavioral decision research: A constructive process perspective. *Annual Review of Psychology, 43,* 87–131.

Pendergast, M. (1995). *Victims of memory.* New York: Upper Access.

Penfield, W., & Roberts, L. (1959). *Speech and brain mechanisms.* Princeton, NJ: Princeton University Press.

Peretz, I., Gaudreau, D., & Bonnel, A.-M. (1998). Exposure effects on music preference and recognition. *Memory & Cognition, 26,* 884–902.

Perfect, T., & Hanley, J. (1992). The tip-of-the-tongue phenomenon: Do experimenter-presented interlopers have any effect. *Cognition, 45,* 55–75.

Perkins, D. (1981). *The mind's best work.* Cambridge, MA: Harvard University Press.

Peterson, C. (1974). Incubation effects in anagram solution. *Bulletin of the Psychonomic Society, 3,* 29–30.

Peterson, L. R., & Peterson, M. J. (1959). Short-term retention of individual verbal items. *Journal of Experimental Psychology, 58,* 193–198.

Peterson, L. R., & Potts, G. R. (1982). Global and specific components of information integration. *Journal of Verbal Learning and Verbal Behavior, 21,* 403–420.

Peterson, M., Kihlstrom, J. F., Rose, P., & Glisky, M. (1992). Mental images can be ambiguous: Reconstruals and reference-frame reversals. *Memory & Cognition, 20,* 107–123.

Peterson, S., Fox, P., Posner, M., Mintern, M., & Raichle, M. (1989). Positron emission tomographic studies of the processing of single words. *Journal of Cognitive Neuroscience, 1,* 153–170.

Peterson, S., Fox, P., Snyder, A., & Raichle, M. (1990). Activation of extrastriate and frontal cortical areas by visual words and word-like stimuli. *Science, 249,* 1041–1044.

Pezdek, K., Finger, K., & Hodge, D. (1997). Planting false childhood memories: The role of event plausibility. *Psychological Science, 8,* 437–441.

Pezdek, K., & Hodge, D. (1999). Planting false childhood memories in children: The role of event plausibility. *Child Development, 70(4),* 887–895.

Pezdek, K., Whetstone, T., Reynolds, K., Askari, N., & Dougherty, T. (1989). Memory for real-world scenes: The role of consistency with schema expectation. *Journal of Experimental Psychology: Learning, Memory, and Cognition, 15,* 587–595.

Pickel, K. L. (1999). Distinguishing eyewitness descriptions of perceived objects from descriptions of imagined objects. *Applied Cognitive Psychology, 13,* 399–413.

Pickering, M. J., & Traxler, M. J. (1999). Plausibility and recovery from garden paths: An eye-tracking study. *Journal of Experimental Psychology: Learning, Memory and Cognition, 24,* 940–961.

Pillemer, D. B. (1984). Flashbulb memories of the assassination attempt on President Reagan. *Cognition, 16,* 63–80.

Pillsbury, W. B. (1897). A study in apperception. *American Journal of Psychology, 8,* 315–393.

Pinker, S. (1980). Mental imagery and the third dimension. *Journal of Experimental Psychology: General, 109,* 354–371.

Pinker, S. (1991). Rules of language. *Science, 253,* 530–535.

Pinker, S. (1994). *The language instinct.* New York: Penguin Press.

Pinker, S. (1995). Language acquisition. In L. R. Gleitman & M. Liberman (Eds.), *Language: An invitation to cognitive science* (Vol. 1; 2nd ed.). Cambridge, MA: MIT Press.

Pinker, S. (1999). *Words and rules: The ingredients of language.* New York: Basic Books.

Pinker, S., & Finke, R. (1980). Emergent two-dimensional patterns in images in depth. *Journal of Experimental Psychology: Human Perception and Performance, 6,* 244–264.

Pinker, S., & Prince, A. (1988). On language and connectionism: Analysis of a parallel distributed processing model of language acquisition. *Cognition, 28,* 73–193.

Pinker, S., & Prince, A. (1991). Regular and irregular morphology and the psychological status of rules of grammar. *Berkley Linguistic Society, 17,* 230–251.

Plunkett, K., & Marchman, V. A. (1996). Learning from a connectionist model of the acquisition of the English past tense. *Cognition, 61,* 299–308.

Podgorny, P., & Shepard, R. (1983). Distribution of visual attention over space. *Journal of Experimental Psychology: Human Perception and Performance, 9,* 380–393.

Poldrack, R. A., & Logan, G. D. (1997). Fluency and response in recognition judgments. *Memory & Cognition, 25,* 1–10.

Polk, T., & Newell, A. (1995). Deduction as verbal reasoning. *Psychological Review, 102,* 533–566.

Pollack, I., & Pickett, J. (1964). Intelligibility of excerpts from fluent speech: Auditory versus structural context. *Journal of Verbal Learning and Verbal Behavior, 3,* 79–84.

Polson, M., & Richardson, J. (Eds.). (1988). *Handbook of intelligent training systems.* Hillsdale, NJ: Lawrence Erlbaum.

Pope, H. G., Hudson, J. I., Bodkin, J. A., & Oliva, P. (1998). Questionable validity of 'dissociative amnesia' in trauma victims. *British Journal of Psychiatry, 172,* 210–215.

Popper, K. (1959). *The logic of scientific discovery.* New York: Basic Books.

Porter, S., Yuille, J. C., & Lehman, D. R. (1999). The nature of real, implanted, and fabricated memories for emotional childhood events: Implications for the false memory debate. *Law and Human Behavior, 23,* 517–538.

Posner, M. (1992). Attention as a cognitive and neural system. *Current Directions in Psychological Science, 1,* 11–14.

Posner, M., & Petersen, S. (1990). The attention system of the human brain. *Annual Review of Neuroscience, 13,* 25–42.

Posner, M., Petersen, S., Fox, P., & Raichle, M. (1988). Localization of cognitive operations in the human brain. *Science, 240,* 1627–1631.

Posner, M., & Snyder, C. (1974). Attention and cognitive control. In R. L. Solso (Ed.), *Information processing and cognition: The Loyola symposium.* Hillsdale, NJ: Lawrence Erlbaum.

Posner, M., & Snyder, C. (1975). Facilitation and inhibition in the processing of signals. In P. Rabbitt & S. Dornic (Eds.), *Attention and performance V.* New York: Academic Press.

Posner, M., Snyder, C., & Davidson, B. (1980). Attention and the detection of signals. *Journal of Experimental Psychology: General, 109,* 160–174.

Postman, L. (1964). Short-term memory and incidental learning. In A. W. Melton (Ed.), *Categories of human learning.* New York: Academic Press.

Postman, L. (1975). Verbal learning and memory. *Annual Review of Psychology, 26,* 291–335.

Postman, L., & Phillips, L. W. (1965). Short-term temporal changes in free recall. *Quarterly Journal of Experimental Psychology, 17,* 132–138.

Postman, L., Thompkins, B. A., & Gray, W. D. (1978). The interpretation of encoding effects in retention. *Journal of Verbal Learning and Verbal Behavior, 17,* 681–705.

Potter, M., Moryadas, A., Abrams, I., & Noel, A. (1993). Word perception and misperception in context. *Journal of Experimental Psychology: Learning, Memory and Cognition, 19,* 3–22.

Putnam, H. (1975). The meaning of "meaning." In K. Gunderson (Ed.), *Language, mind, and knowledge.* Minneapolis: University of Minnesota Press.

Pylyshyn, Z. W. (1984). *Computation and cognition.* Cambridge, MA: MIT Press.

Quinn, G. (1988). Interference effects in the visuo-spatial sketchpad. In M. Denis, J. Engelkamp, & J. T. E. Richardson (Eds.), *Cognitive and neuropsychological approaches to mental imagery* (pp. 181–189). Dordrecht: Martinus Nijhoff.

Quinn, G. (1991). Encoding and maintenance of information in visual working memory. In R. H. Logie & M. Denis (Eds.), *Mental images in human cognition* (pp. 105–115). Amsterdam: Elsevier.

Quinn, G., & Ralston, G. E. (1986). Movement and attention in visual working memory. *Quarterly Journal of Experimental Psychology, 38A,* 689–703.

Rachman, S., & Eyrl, K. (1989). Predicting and remembering recurrent pain. *Behavior Research and Therapy, 27,* 621–635.

Radvansky, G. A. (1999). The fan effect: A tale of two theories. *Journal of Experimental Psychology: General, 128,* 198–206.

Radvansky, G. A., & Zacks, R. T. (1991). Mental models and the fan effect. *Journal of Experimental Psychology: Learning, Memory and Cognition, 17,* 940–953.

Rajaram, S. (1993). Remembering and knowing: Two means of access to the personal past. *Memory & Cognition, 21,* 89–102.

Ramachandran, V. S., & Blakeslee, S. (1998). *Phantoms in the brain.* New York: William Morrow.

Ramsey, W., Stich, S., & Rumelhart, D. (1991). *Philosophy and connectionist theory.* Hillsdale, NJ: Lawrence Erlbaum.

Rao, G. A., Larkin, E. C., & Derr, R. F. (1986). Biologic effects of chronic ethanol consumption related to a deficient intake of carbohydrates. *Alcohol and Alcoholism, 21,* 369–373.

Rasmussen, T., and Milner, B. (1977). The role of early left brain injury in determining lateralization of cerebral speech functions. *Annals of the New York Academy of Sciences, 299,* 355-369.

Rayner, K. (1993). Eye movements in reading: Recent developments. *Current Directions in Psychological Science, 2,* 81–85.

Rayner, K. (1998). Eye movements in reading and information processing: 20 years of research. *Psychological Bulletin, 124,* 372–422.

Read, J. D. (1999). The recovered/false memory debate: Three steps forward, two steps back? *Expert Evidence, 7,* 1–24.

Read, J. D., & Bruce, D. (1982). Longitudinal tracking of difficult memory retrievals. *Cognitive Psychology, 14,* 280–300.

Read, J. D., Tollestrup, P., Hammersley, R., & McFadzen, E. (1990). The unconscious transference effect: Are innocent bystanders ever misidentified? *Applied Cognitive Psychology, 4,* 3–31.

Read, J. D., & Winograd, E. (Eds.). (1998). *Individual differences and memory distortion.* New York: Wiley.

Reason, J. T., & Lucas, D. (1984). Using cognitive diaries to investigate naturally occurring memory blocks. In J. E. Harris & P. E. Morris (Eds.), *Everyday memory actions and absent-mindedness.* London: Academic Press.

Reber, A. (1992). An evolutionary context for the cognitive unconscious. *Philosophical Psychology, 5,* 33–52.

Reber, A. (1993). *Implicit learning and tacit knowledge: An essay on the cognitive unconscious.* New York: Oxford University Press.

Reed, J. M., & Squire, L. R. (1997). Impaired recognition memory in patients with lesions limited to the hippocampal formation. *Behavioral Neuroscience, 111*(4), 667–675.

Reed, P. (2000). Serial position effects in recognition memory for odors. *Journal of Experimental Psychology: Learning, Memory and Cognition, 26*, 411–422.

Reed, S. (1972). Pattern recognition and categorization. *Cognitive Psychology, 3*, 383–407.

Reed, S. (1977). Facilitation of problem solving. In J. N. Castellan, D. Pisoni, & G. R. Potts (Eds.), *Cognitive theory* (pp. 3–20). Hillsdale, NJ: Lawrence Erlbaum.

Reed, S. (1988). *Cognition: Theory and applications.* Pacific Grove, CA: Brooks/Cole.

Reed, S. (1993). Imagery and discovery. In B. Roskos-Ewoldsen, M. J. Intons-Peterson, & R. Anderson (Eds.), *Imagery, creativity, and discovery: A cognitive perspective* (pp. 287–312). New York: North-Holland.

Reed, S., & Bolstad, C. (1991). Use of examples and procedures in problem solving. *Journal of Experimental Psychology: Learning, Memory and Cognition, 17*, 753–766.

Reed, S., Dempster, A., & Ettinger, M. (1985). Usefulness of analogous solutions for solving algebra word problems. *Journal of Experimental Psychology: Learning, Memory and Cognition, 11*, 106–125.

Reed, S., Ernst, G., & Banerji, R. (1974). The role of analogy in transfer between similar problem states. *Cognitive Psychology, 6*, 436–450.

Rees, G., Russell, C., Frith, C. D., & Driver, J. (1999). Inattentional blindness versus inattentional amnesia for fixated but ignored words. *Science, 286*, 2504–2507.

Reeves, L., & Weisberg, R. (1994). The role of content and abstract information in analogical transfer. *Psychological Bulletin, 115*, 381–400.

Reich, S. S., & Ruth, P. (1982). Wason's selection task: Verification, falsification and matching. *British Journal of Psychology, 73*, 395–405.

Reicher, G. M. (1969). Perceptual recognition as a function of meaningfulness of stimulus material. *Journal of Experimental Psychology, 81*, 275–280.

Reinitz, M. T., & Demb, J. (1994). Implicit and explicit memory for compound words. *Memory & Cognition, 22*, 687–694.

Reinitz, M. T., Lammers, W., & Cochran, B. (1992). Memory-conjunction errors: Miscombination of stored stimulus features can produce illusions of memory. *Memory & Cognition, 20*, 1–11.

Reinitz, M. T., Morrissey, J., & Demb, J. (1994). Role of attention in face encoding. *Journal of Experimental Psychology: Learning, Memory and Cognition, 20*, 161–168.

Reisberg, D. (Ed.). (1992). *Auditory imagery.* Hillsdale, NJ: Lawrence Erlbaum.

Reisberg, D. (1996). The non-ambiguity of mental images. In C. Cornold, R. H. Logie, M. Brandimonte, G. Kaufmann & D. Reisberg (Eds.), *Stretching the imagination: Representation and transformation in mental imagery.* New York: Oxford University Press.

Reisberg, D. (1999). The (non) effect of warnings on DRM errors. Unpublished class project in Psychology 121, Reed College.

Reisberg, D. (2000). The detachment gain: The advantage of thinking out loud. In B. Landau, J. Sabini, E. Newport, & J. Jonides (Eds.), *Perception, cognition and language: Essays in honor of Henry and Lila Gleitman.* Cambridge, MA: MIT Press.

Reisberg, D., Baron, J., & Kemler, D. (1980). Overcoming Stroop interference: The effects of practice on distractor potency. *Journal of Experimental Psychology: Human Perception and Performance, 6*, 140–150.

Reisberg, D., & Chambers, D. (1991). Neither pictures nor propositions: What can we learn from a mental image? *Canadian Journal of Psychology, 45*, 288–302.

Reisberg, D., Culver, C., Heuer, F., & Fischman, D. (1986). Visual memory: When imagery vividness makes a difference. *Journal of Mental Imagery, 10*, 51–74.

Reisberg, D., & Heuer, F. (1989) The consequences of vivid imagery: An empirical handle on the function of phenomenal states? Paper presented at the meetings of the Society for Philosophy and Psychology, Tucson, Arizona, April 1989.

Reisberg, D., Heuer, F., McLean, J., & O'Shaughnessy, M. (1988). The quantity, not the quality, of affect predicts memory vividness. *Bulletin of the Psychonomic Society, 26*, 100–103.

Reisberg, D., & Leak, S. (1987). Visual imagery and memory for appearance: Does Clark Gable or George C. Scott have bushier eyebrows? *Canadian Journal of Psychology, 41*, 521–526.

Reisberg, D., & Logie, R. H. (1993). The in's and out's of working memory: Escaping the boundaries on imagery function. In B. Roskos-Ewoldsen, M. Intons-Peterson, & R. Anderson (Eds.), *Imagery, creativity and discovery: A cognitive approach* (pp. 39–76). Amsterdam: Elsevier.

Reisberg, D., Rappaport, I., & O'Shaughnessy, M. (1984). The limits of working memory: The digit digit-span. *Journal of Experimental Psychology: Learning, Memory and Cognition, 10*, 203–221.

Reisberg, D., Smith, J. D., Baxter, D. A., & Sonenshine, M. (1989). "Enacted" auditory images are ambiguous; "Pure" auditory images are not. *Quarterly Journal of Experimental Psychology, 41A*, 619–641.

Reitman, J. (1976). Skilled perception in Go: Deducing memory structures from inter-response times. *Cognitive Psychology, 8*, 336–356.

Reitman, W. (1964). Heuristic decision procedures, open constraints, and the structure of ill-defined problems. In M. Shelley & G. Bryan (Eds.), *Human judgments and optimality*. New York: Wiley.

Remington, R. (1980). Attention and saccadic eye movements. *Journal of Experimental Psychology: Human Perception and Performance, 6*, 726–744.

Rensink, R. A., O'Regan, J. K., & Clark, J. J. (1997). To see or not to see: The need for attention to perceive changes in scenes. *Psychological Science, 8*, 368–373.

Repp, B. (1992). Perceptual restoration of a "missing" speech sound: Auditory induction or illusion? *Perception & Psychophysics, 51*, 14–32.

Revlin, R., Leirer, V., Yopp, H., & Yopp, R. (1980). The belief bias effect in formal reasoning: The influence of knowledge on logic. *Memory & Cognition, 8*, 584–592.

Reyna, V., & Kiernan, B. (1994). Development of gist versus verbatim memory in sentence recognition: Effects of lexical familiarity, semantic content, encoding instructions, and retention interval. *Developmental Psychobiology, 30*, 178–191.

Rhodes, G., Brake, S., & Atkinson, A. (1993). What's lost in inverted faces? *Cognition, 47*, 25–57.

Riccio, D., Rabinowitz, V., & Axelrod, S. (1994). Memory: When less is more. *American Psychologist, 49*, 917–926.

Richardson, J. (1980). *Mental imagery and human memory*. New York: St. Martin's.

Richardson, J. (1984). Developing the theory of working memory. *Memory & Cognition, 12*, 71–83.

Richardson-Klavehn, A., & Bjork, R. A. (1988). Measures of memory. *Annual Review of Psychology, 39*, 475–543.

Richardson-Klavehn, A., & Gardiner, J. M. (1998). Depth-of-processing effects on priming in stem completion: Tests of the voluntary-contamination, conceptual-processing, and lexical-processing hypotheses. *Journal of Experimental Psychology: Learning, Memory and Cognition, 24*, 593–609.

Richardson-Klavehn, A., Lee, M., Joubran, R., & Bjork, R. (1994). Intention and awareness in perceptual identification priming. *Memory & Cognition, 22*, 293–312.

Riefer, D., & Rouder, J. (1993). A multinomial modeling analysis of the mnemonic benefits of bizarre imagery. *Memory & Cognition, 20*, 601–611.

Riemsdijk, H. V., & Williams, E. (1986). *Introduction to the theory of grammar*. Cambridge, MA: MIT Press.

Rinck, M. (1999). Memory for everyday objects: Where are the digits on numerical keypads? *Applied Cognitive Psychology, 13*, 329–350.

Rips, L. (1975). Inductive judgements about natural categories. *Journal of Verbal Learning and Verbal Behavior, 14*, 665–681.

Rips, L. (1983). Cognitive processes in propositional reasoning. *Psychological Review, 90*, 38–71.

Rips, L. (1986). Mental muddles. In M. Brand & R. Harnish (Eds.), *The representation of knowledge and belief* (pp. 258–286). Tucson: University of Arizona Press.

Rips, L. (1989a). Similarity, typicality, and categorization. In S. Vosniadou & A. Ortony (Eds.), *Similarity and analogical reasoning* (pp. 21–59). Cambridge: Cambridge University Press.

Rips, L. (1989b). The psychology of knights and knaves. *Cognition, 31*, 85–116.

Rips, L. (1990). Reasoning. *Annual Review of Psychology, 41*, 321–353.

Rips, L., & Collins, A. (1993). Categories and resemblance. *Journal of Experimental Psychology: General, 122*, 468–489.

Rips, L., Shoben, E. J., & Smith, E. E. (1973). Semantic distance and the verification of semantic relations. *Journal of Verbal Learning and Verbal Behavior, 12*, 1–20.

Ritchie, J. M. (1985). The aliphatic alcohols. In A. G. Gilman, L. S. Goodman, T. W. Rall, & F. Murad (Eds.), *The pharmacological basis of therapeutics* (pp. 372–386). New York: Macmillan.

Roberts, K. P., & Blades, M. (1998). The effects of interacting in repeated events on children's eyewitness memory and source monitoring. *Applied Cognitive Psychology, 12*, 489–504.

Rock, I. (1983). *The logic of perception*. Cambridge, MA: MIT Press.

Roediger, H. L. (1980). The effectiveness of four mnemonics in ordering recall. *Journal of Experimental Psychology: Human Learning and Memory, 6*, 558–567.

Roediger, H. L., & Blaxton, T. A. (1987a). Effects of varying modality, surface features, and retention interval on word fragment completion. *Memory & Cognition, 15*, 379–388.

Roediger, H. L., & Blaxton, T. A. (1987b). Retrieval modes produce dissociations in memory for surface information. In D. S. Gorfein (Ed.), *Memory and cognitive processes: The Ebbinghaus centennial conference* (pp. 349–379). Hillsdale, NJ: Lawrence Erlbaum.

Roediger, H. L., & McDermott, K. (1995). Creating false memories: Remembering words not presented in lists. *Journal of Experimental Psychology: Learning, Memory and Cognition, 21*, 803–814.

Roediger, H. L., & McDermott, K. (2000). Tricks of memory. *Current Directions in Psychological Science, 9*, 123–127.

Roediger, H. L., & Payne, D. G. (1985). Recall criterion does not affect recall level or hypermnesia: A puzzle for generate/recognize theories. *Memory & Cognition, 13*, 1–7.

Roediger, H. L., & Payne, D. P. (1982). Hypermnesia: The role of repeated testing. *Journal of Experimental Psychology: Learning, Memory and Cognition, 8*, 66–72.

Roediger, H. L., & Thorpe, L. A. (1978). The role of recall of time in producing hypermnesia. *Memory & Cognition, 6*, 296–305.

Roediger, H. L., & Wheeler, M. (1993). Hypermnesia in episodic and semantic memory: Response to Bahrick and Hall. *Psychological Science, 4*, 207–208.

Rohde, D. L. T., & Plaut, D. C. (1999). Simple recurrent networks can distinguish nonoccurring from ungrammatical sentences given appropriate task structure. Reply to Marcus. *Cognition, 73*, 297–300.

Rosch, E. (1973). On the internal structure of perceptual and semantic categories. In T. E. Moore (Ed.), *Cognitive development and the acquisition of language.* New York: Academic Press.

Rosch, E. (1975). Cognitive representations of semantic categories. *Journal of Experimental Psychology: General, 104*, 192–233.

Rosch, E. (1977a). Human categorization. In N. Warren (Ed.), *Advances in cross-cultural psychology.* London: Academic Press.

Rosch, E. (1977b). Linguistic relativity. In P. Johnson-Laird & P. Wason (Eds.), *Thinking: Readings in cognitive science* (pp. 501–519). New York: Cambridge University Press.

Rosch, E. (1978). Principles of categorization. In E. Rosch & B. B. Lloyd (Eds.), *Cognition and categorization* (pp. 27–48). Hillsdale, NJ: Lawrence Erlbaum.

Rosch, E., & Mervis, C. B. (1975). Family resemblances. Studies in the internal structure of categories. *Cognitive Psychology, 7*, 573–605.

Rosch, E., Mervis, C. B., Gray, W., Johnson, D., & Boyes-Braem, P. (1976). Basic objects in natural categories. *Cognitive Psychology, 3*, 382–439.

Rosch, E., Simpson, C., & Miller, R. S. (1976). Structural bases of typicality effects. *Journal of Experimental Psychology: Human Perception and Performance, 2*, 491–502.

Rosenbaum, D. (1991). *Human motor control.* San Diego, CA: Academic Press.

Ross, B. (1984). Remindings and their effects in learning a cognitive skill. *Cognitive Psychology, 16*, 371–416.

Ross, B. (1987). This is like that: The use of earlier problems and the separation and similarity effects. *Journal of Experimental Psychology: Learning, Memory and Cognition, 13*, 629–639.

Ross, B. (1989). Distinguishing types of superficial similarities: Different effects on the access and use of earlier problems. *Journal of Experimental Psychology: Learning, Memory and Cognition, 15*, 456–468.

Ross, D. F., Ceci, S. J., Dunning, D., & Toglia, M. P. (1994). Unconscious transference and lineup identification: Toward a memory blending approach. In D. F. Ross & J. D. Read (Eds.), *Adult eyewitness testimony: Current trends and developments.* New York: Cambridge University Press.

Ross, J., & Lawrence, K. A. (1968). Some observations on memory artifice. *Psychonomic Science, 13*, 107–108.

Ross, L., & Anderson, C. (1982). Shortcomings in the attribution process: On the origins and maintenance of erroneous social assessments. In D. Kahneman, P. Slovic, & A. Tversky (Eds.), *Judgment under uncertainty: Heuristics and biases.* New York: Cambridge University Press.

Ross, L., Lepper, M., & Hubbard, M. (1975). Perseverance in self perception and social perception: Biased attributional processes in the debriefing paradigm. *Journal of Personality and Social Psychology, 32*, 880–892.

Ross, M., & Buehler, E. (1994). Creative remembering. In U. Neisser & R. Fivush (Eds.), *The remembered self.* New York: Cambridge University Press.

Ross, M., Buehler, R., & Karr, J. W. (1998). Assessing the accuracy of conflicting autobiographical memories. *Memory & Cognition, 26*, 1233–1244.

Ross, M., & Sicoly, F. (1979). Egocentric biases in availability and attribution. *Journal of Personality and Social Psychology, 37*, 322–336.

Rothbart, M., Evans, M., & Fulero, S. (1979). Recall for confirming events: Memory processes and the maintenance of social stereotypes. *Journal of Experimental Social Psychology, 15*, 343–355.

Rozin, P., Dow, S., Moscovitch, M., & Rajaram, S. (1998). What causes humans to begin and end a meal? A role for memory for what has been eaten, as evidenced by a study of multiple meal eating in amnesic patients. *Psychological Science, 9*, 392–396.

Rubin, D. C., & Kontis, T. S. (1983). A schema for common cents. *Memory & Cognition, 11*, 335–341.

Rubin, D. C., & Kozin, M. (1984). Vivid memories. *Cognition, 16*, 81–95.

Rueckl, J. G., & Oden, G. C. (1986). The integration of contextual and featural information during word identification. *Journal of Memory and Language, 25*, 445–460.

Rumelhart, D. E. (1997). The architecture of mind: A connectionist approach. In J. Haugeland (Ed.), *Mind design 2: Philosophy, psychology, artificial intelligence* (2nd rev. & enlarged ed.). Cambridge, MA: MIT Press.

Rumelhart, D. E., & McClelland, J. L. (Eds.). (1986). *Parallel distributed processing, vol. 1.* Cambridge, MA: MIT Press.

Rumelhart, D. E., & Ortony, A. (1977). The representation of knowledge in memory. In R. C. Anderson, R. J. Spiro, & W. E. Montague (Eds.), *Schooling and the acquisition of knowledge.* Hillsdale, NJ: Lawrence Erlbaum.

Rumelhart, D. E., & Siple, P. (1974). Process of recognizing tachistoscopically presented words. *Psychological Review, 81*, 99–118.

Rundus, D. (1971). Analysis of rehearsal processes in free recall. *Journal of Experimental Psychology, 89*, 63–77.

Ryan, C. (1983). Reassessing the automaticity-control distinction: Item recognition as a paradigm case. *Psychological Review, 90,* 171–178.

Sabini, J., & Silver, M. (1981). Introspection and causal accounts. *Journal of Personality and Social Psychology, 40,* 171–179.

Sachs, J. D. S. (1967). Recognition memory for syntactic and semantic aspects of connected discourse. *Perception & Psychophysics, 2,* 437–442.

Sacks, O. (1985). *The man who mistook his wife for a hat and other clinical tales.* New York: Harper & Row.

Sagan, C. (1996). *The demon-haunted world: Science as a candle in the dark.* London: Headline.

Salame, P., & Baddeley, A. D. (1982). Disruption of short-term memory by unattended speech: Implications for the structure of working memory. *Journal of Verbal Learning and Verbal Behavior, 21,* 150–164.

Saltz, E., & Donnenwerth-Nolan, S. (1981). Does motoric imagery facilitate memory for sentences? A selective interference test. *Journal of Verbal Learning and Verbal Behavior, 20,* 322–332.

Samuel, A. G. (1986). The role of the lexicon in speech perception. In E. C. Schwab & H. C. Nusbaum (Eds.), *Pattern recognition by humans and machines* (pp. 89–111). Orlando, FL: Academic Press.

Samuel, A. G. (1987). Lexical uniqueness effects on phonemic restoration. *Journal of Memory and Language, 26,* 36–56.

Samuel, A. G. (1991). A further examination of attentional effects in the phonemic restoration illusion. *Quarterly Journal of Experimental Psychology: Human Experimental Psychology 43,* 679–699.

Sanitioso, R., Kunda, Z., & Fong, G. (1990). Motivated recruitment of autobiographical memories. *Journal of Personality and Social Psychology, 59,* 229–241.

Savage, J. (1954). *The foundation of statistics.* New York: Wiley.

Schab, F. (1990). Odors and the remembrance of things past. *Journal of Experimental Psychology: Learning, Memory and Cognition, 16,* 648–655.

Schab, F. (1991). Odor memory: Taking stock. *Psychological Bulletin, 109,* 242–251.

Schacter, D. (1987). Implicit memory: History and current status. *Journal of Experimental Psychology: Learning, Memory and Cognition, 13,* 501–518.

Schacter, D. (1992). Understanding implicit memory: A cognitive neuroscience approach. *American Psychologist, 47,* 559–569.

Schacter, D. (1996). *Searching for memory: The brain, the mind and the past.* New York: Basic Books.

Schacter, D. (1999). The seven sins of memory. *American Psychologist, 54,* 182–203.

Schacter, D., & Tulving, E. (1982). Amnesia and memory research. In L. S. Cermak (Ed.), *Human memory and amnesia.* Hillsdale, NJ: Lawrence Erlbaum.

Schacter, D., Tulving, E., & Wang, P. (1981). Source amnesia: New methods and illustrative data. Paper presented at the meeting of the International Neuropsychological Society, Atlanta.

Schank, R. C. (1982). *Dynamic memory: A theory of reminding and learning in computers and people.* New York: Cambridge University Press.

Schank, R. C., & Abelson, R. (1977). *Scripts, plans, goals, and understanding.* Hillsdale, NJ: Lawrence Erlbaum.

Schkade, D. A., & Kahneman, D. (1998). Does living in California make people happy? A focusing illusion in judgments of life satisfaction. *Psychological Science, 9,* 340–346.

Schmitter-Edgecombe, M. (1999). Effects of divided attention on perceptual and conceptual memory tests: An analysis using a process-dissociation approach. *Memory & Cognition, 27,* 512–525.

Schneider, S. (1992). Framing and conflict: Aspiration level contingency, the status quo, and current theories of risky choice. *Journal of Experimental Psychology: Learning, Memory and Cognition, 18,* 1040–1057.

Schneider, W., & Shiffrin, R. M. (1977). Controlled and automatic human information processing: I. Detection, search, and attention. *Psychological Review, 84,* 1–66.

Schneider, W., & Shiffrin, R. M. (1985). Categorization (restructuring) and automatization: Two separable factors. *Psychological Review, 92,* 424–428.

Schoenfeld, A., & Herrmann, D. (1982). Problem perception and knowledge structure in expert and novice mathematical problem solvers. *Journal of Experimental Psychology: Learning, Memory and Cognition, 5,* 484–494.

Schooler, J., & Engstler-Schooler, T. (1990). Verbal overshadowing of visual memories: Some things are better left unsaid. *Cognitive Psychology, 22,* 36–71.

Schooler, J., Ohlsson, S., & Brooks, K. (1993). Thoughts beyond words: When language overshadows insight. *Journal of Experimental Psychology: General, 122,* 166–183.

Schraw, G., Dunkle, M., & Bendixen, L. (1995). Cognitive processes in well-defined and ill-defined problem solving. *Applied Cognitive Psychology, 9,* 523–538.

Schulz-Hardt, S., Frey, D., Lüthgens, C., & Moscovici, S. (2000). Biased information search in group decision making. *Journal of Personality and Social Psychology, 78,* 655–669.

Schumacher, E. H., Lauber, E. J., Glass, J. M., Zurbriggen, E. L., Gmeindl, L., Kieras, D. E., & Meyer, D. E. (1999). Concurrent response-selection process in dual-task performance: Evidence for adaptive executive control of task scheduling. *Journal of Experimental Psychology: Human Perception and Performance, 25,* 791–814.

Schunn, C. D., & Anderson, J. R. (1999). The generality/specificity of expertise in scientific reasoning. *Cognitive Science, 23,* 337–370.

Schunn, C. D., & Dunbar, K. (1996). Priming, analogy and awareness in complex reasoning. *Memory & Cognition, 24,* 271–284.

Schustack, M., & Sternberg, R. (1981). Evaluation of evidence in causal inference. *Journal of Experimental Psychology: General, 110,* 101–120.

Schwartz, B. (1982). Reinforcement-induced behavioral stereotypy: How not to teach people to discover rules. *Journal of Experimental Psychology: General, 111,* 23–59.

Schwartz, B., & Robbins, S. (1995). *Psychology of learning and behavior,* 4th ed. New York: W. W. Norton.

Schwartz, B. L. (1999). Sparkling at the end of the tongue: The etiology of tip-of-the-tongue phenomenology. *Psychonomics Bulletin & Review, 5,* 379–393.

Schwartz, N., Strack, F., Hilton, D., & Naderer, G. (1991). Base rates, representativeness and the logic of conversation: The contextual relevance of "irrelevant" information. *Social Cognition, 9,* 67–84.

Schwarz, N. (1998). Accessible content and accessibility experiences: The interplay of declarative and experiential information in judgments. *Personality and Social Psychology Review, 2,* 87–99.

Schwarz, N. (1999). Self-reports: How the questions shape the answers. *American Psychologist, 54,* 93–105.

Seamon, J., Williams, P., Crowley, M., Kim, I., Langer, S., Orne, P., & Wishengrad, D. (1995). The mere exposure effect is based on implicit memory: Effects of stimulus type, encoding conditions, and number of exposures on recognition and affect judgments. *Journal of Experimental Psychology: Learning, Memory and Cognition, 21,* 711–721.

Sedivy, J. C., Tanenhaus, M. K., Chambers, C. G., & Carlson, G. N. (1999). Achieving incremental semantic interpretation through contextual representation. *Cognition, 71,* 109–147.

Sedlemeier, P., Hertwig, R., & Gigerenzer, G. (1998). Are judgments of the positional frequencies of letters systematically biased due to availability? *Journal of Experimental Psychology: Learning, Memory and Cognition, 24,* 754–770.

Segal, S., & Fusella, V. (1970). Influence of imaged pictures and sounds in detection of visual and auditory signals. *Journal of Experimental Psychology, 83,* 458–474.

Segal, S., & Fusella, V. (1971). Effect of images in six sense modalities on detection of visual signal from noise. *Psychonomic Science, 24,* 55–56.

Seidenberg, M., Tanenhaus, M., Leiman, M., & Bienkowski, M. (1982). Automatic access of the meanings of words in context: Some limitations of knowledge-based processing. *Cognition, 7,* 177–215.

Selfridge, O. (1955). Pattern recognition and modern computers. Proceedings of the Western Joint Computer Conference, Los Angeles, CA.

Selfridge, O. (1959). Pandemonium: A paradigm for learning. In *The mechanisation of thought processes.* London: H. M. Stationery Office.

Seltzer, B., & Benson, D. F. (1974). The temporal pattern of retrograde amnesia in Korsakoff's Disease. *Neurology, 24,* 527–530.

Senghas, A., Coppola, M., Newport, E. L., & Supalla, A. (1997). *Argument structure in Nicaraguan Sign Language: The emergence of grammatical devices.* Proceedings of the Boston University Conference on Language Development, 21. Boston: Cascadilla Press.

Sereno, A. B., & Maunsell, J. H. R. (1998). Shape selectivity in primate lateral intraparietal cortex. *Nature, 395,* 500–503.

Sergent, J., & Poncet, M. (1990). From covert to overt recognition of faces in a prosopagnosic patient. *Brain, 113,* 989–1004.

Shafir, E. (1993). Choosing versus rejecting: Why some options are both better and worse than others. *Memory & Cognition, 21,* 546–556.

Shafir, E., Simonson, I., & Tversky, A. (1993). Reason-based choice. *Cognition, 49,* 11–36.

Shah, P., & Miyake, A. (1996). The separability of working memory resources for spatial thinking and language processing: An individual differences approach. *Journal of Experimental Psychology: General, 125,* 4–27.

Shaklee, H., & Fischoff, B. (1982). Strategies of information search in causal analysis. *Memory & Cognition, 10,* 520–530.

Shaklee, H., & Mims, M. (1982). Sources of error in judging event covariations. *Journal of Experimental Psychology: Learning, Memory and Cognition, 8,* 208–224.

Shallice, T., & Burgess, P. (1991). Higher-order cognitive impairments and frontal lobe lesions in man. In H. S. Levin & H. M. Eisenberg (Eds.), *Frontal lobe function and dysfunction.* New York: Oxford University Press.

Shand, M. (1982). Sign-based short-term coding of American Sign Language signs and printed English words by congenitally deaf signers. *Cognitive Psychology, 14,* 1–12.

Shanteau, J. (1992). The psychology of experts: An alternative view. In G. Wright & F. Bolger (Eds.), *Expertise and decision support* (pp. 11–23). New York: Plenum Press.

Shapiro, P. N., & Penrod, S. (1986). Meta-analysis of facial identification studies. *Psychological Bulletin, 100,* 139–156.

Shaw, J. (1995). Postevent questioning can lead to increased eyewitness confidence. *Psychonomics poster.*

Shepard, R. N. (1988). The imagination of the scientist. In K. Egan & D. Nadaner (Eds.), *Imagination and education* (pp. 153–185). New York: Teachers College Press.

Shepard, R. N., & Cooper, L. A. (1982). *Mental images and their transformations.* Cambridge, MA: MIT Press.

Shepard, R. N., & Feng, C. (1972). A chronometric study of mental paper folding. *Cognitive Psychology, 3*, 228–243.

Shepard, R. N., & Metzler, J. (1971). Mental rotation of three-dimensional objects. *Science, 171*, 701–703.

Shiffrin, R. M., & Schneider, W. (1977). Controlled and automatic human information processing: II. Perceptual learning, automatic attending and a general theory. *Psychological Review, 84*, 127–190.

Shiffrin, R. M., & Schneider, W. (1984). Automatic and controlled processes revisited. *Psychological Review, 91*, 269–276.

Shin, H., & Nosofsky, R. (1992). Similarity-scaling studies of dot-pattern classification and recognition. *Journal of Experimental Psychology: General, 121*, 278–304.

Shobe, K. K., & Kihlstrom, J. F. (1997). Is traumatic memory special? *Current Directions in Psychological Science, 6*, 70–74.

Shore, D. I., & Klein, R. M. (2000). The effects of scene inversion on change blindness. *Journal of General Psychology, 127*, 27–43.

Shulman, G., & Wilson, J. (1987). Spatial frequency and selective attention to local and global structure. *Perception, 16*, 89–101.

Siegler, R. S. (2000). Unconscious insights. *Current Directions in Psychological Science, 9*, 79–83.

Sieroff, E., Pollatsek, A., & Posner, M. (1988). Recognition of visual letter strings following damage to the posterior visual spatial attention system. *Cognitive Neuropsychology, 5*, 427–449.

Silbersweig, D. A., Stern, E., Frith, C., Cahill, C., Holmes, A., Grootoonk, S., Seaward, S., McKenna, P., Chua, S. E., Schnorr, L., Jones, T., & Frackowiak, R. S. (1995). A functional neuroanatomy of hallucinations in schizophrenia. *Nature, 378*, 176–179.

Simon, H. (1957). *Models of man*. New York: Wiley.

Simon, H. (1973). The structure of ill-defined problems. *Artificial Intelligence, 4*, 181–201.

Simon, H. (1974). How big is a chunk? *Science, 183*, 482–488.

Simon, H. (1975). The functional equivalence of problem solving skills. *Cognitive Psychology, 7*, 268–288.

Simons, D. J. (2000). Attentional capture and inattentional blindness. *Trends in Cognitive Science, 4*, 147–155.

Simonton, D. (1988). Creativity, leadership, and chance. In R. J. Sternberg (Ed.), *The nature of creativity*. New York: Cambridge University Press.

Simonton, D. (1989). Chance-configuration theory of scientific creativity. In B. Gholson, W. Shadish, R. Neimeyer, & A. Houts (Eds.), *Psychology of science: Contributions to metascience*. Cambridge: Cambridge University Press.

Simpson, G. B. (1984). Lexical ambiguity and its role in models of word recognition. *Psychological Bulletin, 96*, 316–340.

Simpson, G. B., Peterson, R. R., Castell, M. A., & Burgess, C. (1989). Lexical and sentence context effects in word recognition. *Journal of Experimental Psychology: Learning, Memory and Cognition, 15*, 88–97.

Slamecka, N. J., & Graf, P. (1978). The generation effect: Delineation of a phenomenon. *Journal of Experimental Psychology: Human Learning and Memory, 4*, 592–604.

Slobin, D. (1966). Grammatical transformations and sentence comprehension in childhood and adulthood. *Journal of Verbal Learning and Verbal Behavior, 5*, 219–227.

Slovic, P. (1975). Choice between equally valued alternatives. *Journal of Experimental Psychology: Human Perception and Performance, 1*, 280–287.

Slovic, P. (1990). Choice. In D. Osherson & E. Smith (Eds.), *An invitation to cognitive science: Thinking* (pp. 89–116). Cambridge, MA: MIT Press.

Slovic, P. (1995). The construction of preference. *American Psychologist, 50*, 364–371.

Slovic, P., & Fischhoff, B. (1977). On the psychology of experimental surprises. *Journal of Experimental Psychology: Human Perception and Performance, 3*, 544–551.

Slovic, P., Fischhoff, B., & Lichtenstein, S. (1982). Facts versus fears: Understanding perceived risk. In D. Kahneman, P. Slovic, & A. Tversky (Eds.), *Judgment under uncertainty: Heuristics and biases*. Cambridge: Cambridge University Press.

Smedslund, J. (1963). The concept of correlation in adults. *Scandinavian Journal of Psychology, 4*, 165–173.

Smith, E., & Miller, F. (1978). Limits on perception of cognitive processes: A reply to Nisbett & Wilson. *Psychological Review, 85*, 355–362.

Smith, E. E. (1978). Theories of semantic memory. In W. K. Estes (Ed.), *Handbook of learning and cognitive processes*. Potomac, MD: Lawrence Erlbaum.

Smith, E. E. (1988). Concepts and thought. In R. J. Sternberg & E. E. Smith (Eds.), *The psychology of human thought*. Cambridge: Cambridge University Press.

Smith, E. E. (2000). Neural bases of human working memory. *Current Directions in Psychological Science, 9*, 45–49.

Smith, E. E., Balzano, G. J., & Walker, J. H. (1978). Nominal, perceptual, and semantic codes in picture categorization. In J. W. Cotton & R. L. Klatzky (Eds.), *Semantic factors in cognition*. Hillsdale, NJ: Lawrence Erlbaum.

Smith, E. E., & Medin, D. L. (1981). *Categories and concepts*. Cambridge, MA: Harvard University Press.

Smith, E. E., Rips, L. J., & Shoben, E. J. (1974). Structure and process in semantic memory: A featural model for semantic decisions. *Psychological Review, 81*, 214–241.

Smith, J., & Kida, T. (1991). Heuristics and biases: Expertise and task realism in auditing. *Psychological Bulletin, 109*, 472–489.

Smith, J. D., & Minda, J. P. (1998). Prototypes in the mist: The early epochs of category learning. *Journal of Experimental Psychology: Learning, Memory and Cognition, 24,* 1411–1436.

Smith, J. D., Wilson, M., & Reisberg, D. (1996). The role of subvocalization in auditory imagery. *Neuropsychologia, 33,* 1433–1454.

Smith, M. (1982). Hypnotic memory enhancement of witnesses: Does it work? Paper presented at the meeting of the Psychonomic Society, Minneapolis.

Smith, M., Besner, D., & Miyoshi, H. (1994). New limits to automaticity: Context modulates semantic priming. *Journal of Experimental Psychology: Learning, Memory and Cognition, 20,* 104–115.

Smith, S. (1979). Remembering in and out of context. *Journal of Experimental Psychology: Human Learning and Memory, 5,* 460–471.

Smith, S. (1985). Background music and context-dependent memory. *American Journal of Psychology, 6,* 591–603.

Smith, S. M., & Blankenship, S. (1991). Incubation and the persistence of fixation in problem solving. *American Journal of Psychology, 104,* 61–87.

Smith, S. M., & Blankenship, S. E. (1989). Incubation effects. *Bulletin of the Psychonomic Society, 27,* 311–314.

Smith, S. M., Glenberg, A., & Bjork, R. A. (1978). Environmental context and human memory. *Memory & Cognition, 6,* 342–353.

Smith, S. M., & Vela, E. (1991). Incubated reminiscence effects. *Memory & Cognition, 19,* 168–176.

Smyth, M., & Scholey, K. (1994). Interference in immediate spatial memory. *Memory & Cognition, 22,* 1–13.

Smyth, M. M., & Pendleton, L. R. (1989). Working memory for movements. *Quarterly Journal of Experimental Psychology, 41A,* 235–250.

Snyder, M., & Swann, W. (1978). Behavioral confirmation in social interaction: From social perception to social reality. *Journal of Experimental Social Psychology, 14,* 148–162.

Solomon, K. O., Medin, D. L., & Lynch, E. (1999). Concepts do more than categorize. *Trends in Cognitive Science, 3,* 99–105.

Spearman, C. (1923). *The nature of "intelligence" and the principles of cognition.* London: Macmillan.

Spelke, E., Hirst, W., & Neisser, U. (1976). Skills of divided attention. *Cognition, 4,* 215–230.

Spencer, R., & Weisberg, R. (1986). Is analogy sufficient to facilitate transfer during problem solving? *Memory & Cognition, 14,* 442–449.

Sperber, D., Cara, F., & Girotto, V. (1995). Relevance theory explains the selection task. *Cognition, 57,* 31–95.

Sperber, D., & Wilson, D. (1986). *Relevance: Communication and cognition.* Cambridge, MA: Harvard University Press.

Sperling, G. (1960). The information available in brief visual presentations. *Psychological Monographs, 74,* entire issue.

Sperling, G., & Speelman, R. G. (1970). Acoustic similarity and auditory short-term memory: Experiments and a model. In D. A. Norman (Ed.), *Models of human memory* (pp. 152–202). New York: Academic Press.

Spiegel, D. (1995). Hypnosis and suggestion. In D. L. Schacter, J. T. Coyle, G. D. Fischbach, M.-M. Mesulam, & L. E. Sullivan (Eds.), *Memory distortion: How minds, brains and societies reconstruct the past.* Cambridge, MA: Harvard University Press.

Spiro, R. J. (1977). Remembering information from text: The "state of schema" approach. In R. C. Anderson, R. J. Spiro, & W. E. Montague (Eds.), *Schooling and the acquisition of knowledge.* Hillsdale, NJ: Lawrence Erlbaum.

Sporer, S. (1988). Long-term improvement of facial recognition through visual rehearsal. In M. Gruneberg, P. Morris, & R. Sykes (Eds.), *Practical aspects of memory: Current research and issues* (pp. 182–188). New York: Wiley.

Sporer, S. (1991). Deep-deeper-deepest? Encoding strategies and the recognition of human faces. *Journal of Experimental Psychology: Learning, Memory and Cognition, 17,* 323–333.

Sporer, S., Penrod, S., Read, D., & Cutler, B. (1995). Choosing, confidence, and accuracy: A meta-analysis of the confidence-accuracy relation in eyewitness identification studies. *Psychological Bulletin, 118,* 315–327.

Squire, L., & McKee, R. (1993). Declarative and nondeclarative memory in opposition: When prior events influence amnesic patients more than normal subjects. *Memory & Cognition, 21,* 424–430.

Squire, L., & Zola-Morgan, S. (1991). The medial temporal lobe memory system. *Science, 253,* 1380–1386.

Srinivas, K. (1993). Perceptual specificity in nonverbal priming. *Journal of Experimental Psychology: Learning, Memory and Cognition, 19,* 582–602.

Srinivas, K., & Roediger, H. L. (1990). Classifying implicit memory tests: Category association and anagram solution. *Journal of Memory and Language, 29,* 389–412.

Stadler, M. A., Roediger, H. L., & McDermott, K. B. (1999). Norms for word lists that create false memories. *Memory & Cognition, 27,* 494–500.

Stangor, C., & McMillan, D. (1992). Memory for expectancy-congruent and expectancy-incongruent information: A review of the social and social developmental literatures. *Psychological Bulletin, 111,* 42–61.

Stanovich, K. E., & West, R. F. (1998). Who uses base rates and P(D|~H)? An analysis of individual differences, *Memory & Cognition, 26,* 161–179.

*State of Oregon v. Classen,* 285 Or 221 (1979).

Staudenmayer, H. (1975). Understanding conditional reasoning with meaningful propositions. In R. J. Falmagne (Ed.), *Reasoning: Representation and process in children and adults.* Hillsdale, NJ: Lawrence Erlbaum.

Staudenmayer, H., & Bourne, L. (1978). The nature of denied propositions in the conditional reasoning task: Interpretation and learning. In R. Revlin & R. Mayer (Eds.), *Human reasoning*. New York: Wiley.

Steblay, N. J. (1992). A meta-analytic review of the weapon focus effect. *Law and Human Behavior, 16*, 413–424.

Stein, M. (1956). A transactional approach to creativity. In C. W. Taylor (Ed.), *The 1955 University of Utah research conference on the identification of creative scientific talent*. Salt Lake City: University of Utah Press.

Stein, M. (1975). *Stimulating creativity*. New York: Academic Press.

Sternberg, R. J. (1988). A three-facet model of creativity. In R. J. Sternberg (Ed.), *The nature of creativity* (pp. 125–147). Cambridge: Cambridge University Press.

Sternberg, R. J., & Davidson, J. E. (Eds.). (1995). *The nature of insight*. Cambridge, MA: MIT Press.

Sternberg, R. J., & Lubart, T. (1992). Buy low and sell high: An investment approach to creativity. *Current Directions in Psychological Science, 1*, 1–5.

Sternberg, R. J., & Lubart, T. I. (1996). Investing in creativity. *American Psychologist, 51*, 677–688.

Stevens, A., & Coupe, P. (1978). Distortions in judged spatial relations. *Cognitive Psychology, 10*, 422–437.

Stevenson, M. (1993). Decision making with long-term consequences: Temporal discounting for single and multiple outcomes in the future. *Journal of Experimental Psychology: General, 122*, 3–22.

Stine, E. A. L. (1990). On-line processing of written text by younger and older adults. *Psychology and Aging, 5*, 68–78.

Stone, A. A. (2000). *The science of self-report: Implications for research and practice*. Mahwah, NJ: Lawrence Erlbaum.

Strayer, D., & Kramer, A. (1994a). Strategies and automaticity: II. Dynamic aspects of strategy adjustment. *Journal of Experimental Psychology: Learning, Memory and Cognition, 20*, 342–365.

Strayer, D., & Kramer, A. (1994b). Strategies and automaticity: I. Basic findings and conceptual framework. *Journal of Experimental Psychology: Learning, Memory and Cognition, 20*, 318–341.

Stroop, J. R. (1935). Studies of interference in serial verbal reaction. *Journal of Experimental Psychology, 18*, 643–662.

Sulin, R. A., & Dooling, D. J. (1974). Intrusion of a thematic idea in retention of prose. *Journal of Experimental Psychology, 103*, 255–262.

Sumby, W. H. (1963). Word frequency and serial position effects. *Journal of Verbal Learning and Verbal Behavior, 1*, 443–450.

Svartik, J. (1966). *On voice in the English verb*. The Hague: Mouton.

Sweller, J., Mawer, R., & Ward, M. (1983). Development of expertise in mathematical problem solving. *Journal of Experimental Psychology: General, 112*, 639–661.

Swinney, D. (1979). Lexical access during sentence comprehension: (Re)consideration of context effects. *Journal of Verbal Learning and Verbal Behavior, 5*, 219–227.

Symons, C. S., & Johnson, B. T. (1997). The self-reference effect in memory: A meta-analysis. *Psychological Bulletin, 121*, 371–394.

Tabachnick, B., & Brotsky, S. (1976). Free recall and complexity of pictorial stimuli. *Memory & Cognition, 4*, 466–470.

Tallal, P., Ross, R., & Curtiss, S. (1989). Familial aggregation in specific language impairment. *Journal of Speech & Hearing Disorders, 54*, 167–173.

Tanaka, J. W., & Taylor, M. (1991). Object categories and expertise: Is the basic level in the eye of the beholder? *Cognitive Psychology, 23*, 457–482.

Tanenhaus, M., Spivey-Knowlton, M., Eberhard, K., & Sedivy, J. (1995). Integration of visual and linguistic information in spoken language comprehension. *Science, 268*, 1632–1634.

Tanenhaus, M. K., & Spivey-Knowlton, M. J. (1996). Eye-tracking. *Language & Cognitive Processes, 11*, 583–588.

Taplin, J., & Staudenmayer, H. (1973). Interpretation of abstract conditional sentences in deductive reasoning. *Journal of Verbal Learning and Verbal Behavior, 12*, 530–542.

Tarr, M., & Bülthoff, H. (1998). Image-based object recognition in man, monkey and machine. *Cognition, 67*, 1–208.

Taylor, S. E. (1982). The availability bias in social perception and interaction. In D. Kahneman, P. Slovic, & A. Tversky (Eds.), *Judgments under uncertainty: Heuristics and biases*. Cambridge: Cambridge University Press.

Taylor, S. E., Fiske, S. T., Etcoff, N., & Ruderman, A. (1978). The categorical and contextual bases of person memory and stereotyping. *Journal of Personality and Social Psychology, 36*, 778–793.

Teasdale, J., Proctor, L., Lloyd, C., & Baddeley, A. (1993). Working-memory and stimulus-independent thought: Effects of memory load and presentation rate. *European Journal of Cognitive Psychology, 5*, 417–433.

te Linde, J. (1983). Pictures and words in semantic decisions. In J. C. Yuille (Ed.), *Imagery, memory, and cognition*. Hillsdale, NJ: Lawrence Erlbaum.

Terr, L. C. (1991). Acute responses to external events and posttraumatic stress disorders. In M. Lewis (Ed.), *Child and adolescent psychiatry: A comprehensive textbook*. Baltimore, MD: Williams & Wilkins.

Terr, L. C. (1994). *Unchained memories: The stories of traumatic memories, lost and found*. New York: Basic Books.

Thaler, R. (1980). Toward a positive theory of consumer choice. *Journal of Economic Behavior and Organization, 1*, 39–60.

Thapar, A., & Greene, R. (1993). Evidence against a short-term store account of long-term recency effects. *Memory & Cognition, 21,* 329–337.

Thapar, A., & Greene, R. (1994). Effects of level of processing on implicit and explicit tasks. *Journal of Experimental Psychology: Learning, Memory and Cognition, 20,* 671–679.

Thomas, J. (1974). An analysis of behavior in the Hobbits-Orcs problem. *Cognitive Psychology, 6,* 257–269.

Thompson, P. (1980). Margaret Thatcher: A new illusion. *Perception, 9,* 483–484.

Thompson, V. (1994). Interpretational factors in conditional reasoning. *Memory & Cognition, 22,* 742–758.

Thompson, V., & Mann, J. (1995). Perceived necessity explains the dissociation between logic and meaning: The case of "only if." *Journal of Experimental Psychology: Learning, Memory and Cognition, 21,* 1554–1567.

Thompson, W. B., & Mason, S. E. (1996). Instability of individual differences in the association between confidence judgments and memory performance. *Memory & Cognition, 24,* 226–234.

Thompson, W. L., & Kosslyn, S. M. (2000). Neural systems activated during visual mental imagery: A review and meta-analyses. In J. Mazziotta & A. Toga (Eds.), *Brain mapping II: The applications.* New York: Academic Press.

Thorndike, E., & Lorge, I. (1963). *The Thorndike/Lorge teacher's word book of 30,000 words.* New York: Columbia University Press.

Thorndyke, P. W. (1976). The role of inferences in discourse comprehension. *Journal of Verbal Learning and Verbal Behavior, 15,* 437–446.

Thorndyke, P. W., & Bower, G. H. (1974). Storage and retrieval processes in sentence memory. *Cognitive Psychology, 5,* 515–543.

Till, R. E., & Jenkins, J. J. (1973). The effects of cued orienting tasks on the free recall of words. *Journal of Verbal Learning and Verbal Behavior, 12,* 489–498.

Titchener, E. B. (1926). *Lectures on the experimental psychology of the thought-process.* New York: Macmillan

Tousignant, J., Hall, D., & Loftus, E. (1986). Discrepancy detection and vulnerability to misleading postevent information. *Memory & Cognition, 14,* 329–338.

Tranel, D., Damasio, A., & Damasio, H. (1988). Intact recognition of facial expression, gender, and age in patients with impaired recognition of face identity. *Neurology, 38,* 690–696.

Treisman, A. (1964). Verbal cues, language, and meaning in selective attention. *American Journal of Psychology, 77,* 206–219.

Treisman, A. (1986). Features and objects in visual processing. *Scientific American, 255,* 114B-125.

Treisman, A., & Gormican, S. (1988). Feature analysis in early vision: Evidence from search asymmetries. *Psychological Review, 95,* 15–48.

Treisman, A., & Souther, J. (1985). Search asymmetry: A diagnostic for preattentive processing of separable features. *Journal of Experimental Psychology: General, 114,* 285–310.

Trueswell, J., Tanenhaus, M., & Kello, C. (1995). Verb-specific constraints in sentence processing: Separating effects of lexical preference from garden paths. *Journal of Experimental Psychology: Learning, Memory and Cognition, 19,* 528–553.

Tulving, E. (1962). Subjective organization in free recall of "unrelated" words. *Psychological Review, 69,* 344–354.

Tulving, E. (1983). *Elements of episodic memory.* Oxford: Oxford University Press.

Tulving, E. (1985). Memory and consciousness. *Canadian Psychologist, 26,* 1–12.

Tulving, E. (1986). What kind of a hypothesis is the distinction between episodic and semantic memory? *Journal of Experimental Psychology: Learning, Memory and Cognition, 12,* 307–311.

Tulving, E. (1989). Remembering and knowing the past. *American Scientist, 77,* 361–367.

Tulving, E. (1993). What is episodic memory? *Current Directions in Psychological Science, 2,* 67–70.

Tulving, E., & Gold, C. (1963). Stimulus information and contextual information as determinants of tachistoscopic recognition of words. *Journal of Experimental Psychology, 92,* 319–327.

Tulving, E., Hayman, C., & Macdonald, C. (1991). Long-lasting perceptual priming and semantic learning in amnesia: A case experiment. *Journal of Experimental Psychology: Learning, Memory and Cognition, 17,* 595–617.

Tulving, E., Mandler, G., & Baumal, R. (1964). Interaction of two sources of information in tachistoscopic word recognition. *Canadian Journal of Psychology, 18,* 62–71.

Tulving, E., & Osler, S. (1968). Effectiveness of retrieval cues in memory for words. *Journal of Experimental Psychology, 77,* 593–601.

Tulving, E., & Thomson, D. (1973). Encoding specificity and retrieval processes in episodic memory. *Psychological Review, 80,* 352–373.

Turtle, J., & Yuille, J. (1994). Lost but not forgotten details: Repeated eyewitness recall leads to reminiscence but not hypermnesia. *Journal of Applied Psychology, 79,* 260–271.

Tversky, A. (1977). Features of similarity. *Psychological Review, 84,* 327–352.

Tversky, A., & Kahneman, A. (1987). Rational choice and the framing of decisions. In R. Hogarth & M. Reder (Eds.), *Rational choice: The contrast between economics and psychology.* Chicago: University of Chicago Press.

Tversky, A., & Kahneman, D. (1971). Belief in the law of small numbers. *Psychological Bulletin, 76,* 105–110.

Tversky, A., & Kahneman, D. (1973). Availability: A heuristic for judging frequency and probability. *Cognitive Psychology, 5*, 207–232.

Tversky, A., & Kahneman, D. (1974). Judgments under uncertainty: Heuristics and biases. *Science, 185*, 1124–1131.

Tversky, A., & Kahneman, D. (1982). Evidential impact of base rates. In D. Kahneman, P. Slovic, & A. Tversky (Eds.), *Judgment under uncertainty: Heuristics and biases.* New York: Cambridge University Press.

Tversky, A., & Kahneman, D. (1983). Extensional versus intuitive reasoning: The conjunction fallacy in probability judgment. *Psychological Review, 90*, 293–315.

Tversky, A., & Koehler, D. J. (1994). Support theory: A nonextensional representation of subjective probability. *Psychological Review, 101*, 547–567.

Tversky, A., & Shafir, E. (1992a). Choice under conflict: The dynamics of deferred decision. *Psychological Science, 3*, 358–361.

Tversky, A., & Shafir, E. (1992b). The disjunction effect in choice under uncertainty. *Psychological Science, 3*, 305–309.

Tversky, B. (1973). Encoding processes in recognition and recall. *Cognitive Psychology, 5*, 275–287.

Tversky, B., & Hemenway, K. (1991). Parts and the basic level in natural categories and artificial stimuli: Comments on Murphy (1991). *Memory & Cognition, 19*, 439–442.

Tweney, R. D. (1998). Toward a cognitive psychology of science: Research and its implications. *Current Directions in Psychological Science, 7*, 150–154.

Tweney, R. D., Doherty, M. E., & Mynatt, C. R. (1981). *On scientific thinking.* New York: Columbia University Press.

Tyler, L., & Marslen-Wilsen, W. (1977). The on-line effects of semantic context on syntactic processing. *Journal of Verbal Learning and Verbal Behavior, 16*, 683–692.

Uleman, J., & Bargh, J. (Eds). (1989). *Unintended thought.* New York: Guilford.

Ullman, S. (1989). Aligning pictorial descriptions: An approach to object recognition. *Cognition, 32*, 193–254.

Ungerleider, L. G., & Haxby, J. V. (1994). "What" and "where" in the human brain. *Current Opinions in Neurobiology, 4*, 157–165.

Ungerleider, L. G., & Mishkin, M. (1982). Two cortical visual systems. In D. J. Ingle, M. A. Goodale, & R. J. W. Mansfield (Eds.), *Analysis of visual behavior.* Cambridge, MA: MIT Press.

Valentine, T. (1988). Upside-down faces: A review of the effects of inversion upon face recognition. *British Journal of Psychology, 79*, 471–491.

Vallar, G., Papagno, C., & Baddeley, A. D. (1991). Long-term recency effects and phonological short-term memory: A neuropsychological case study. *Cortex, 27*, 323–326.

Vallar, G., & Shallice, T. (Eds.). (1990). *Neuropsychological impairments of short-term memory.* Cambridge: Cambridge University Press.

Van Essen, D. C., & De Yoe, E. A. (1995). Concurrent processing in the primate visual cortex. In M. S. Gazzaniga (Ed.), *The cognitive neurosciences.* Cambridge, MA: MIT Press.

Van Lancker, D., Kreiman, J., & Emmorey, K. (1985). Familiar voice recognition: Patterns and parameters: I. Recognition of backward voices. *Journal of Phonetics, 13*, 19–38.

Van Lancker, D., Kreiman, J., & Wickens, T. (1985). Familiar voice recognition: Patterns and parameters: II. Recognition of rate altered voices. *Journal of Phonetics, 13*, 39–52.

VanLehn, K. (1998). Analogy events: How examples are used during problem solving. *Cognitive Science, 22*, 347–388.

van Stegeren, A. H., Everaerd, W., Cahill, L., McGaugh, J. L., & Gorren, L. J. G. (1998). Memory for emotional events: Differential effects of centrally versus peripherally acting beta-blocking agents. *Psychopharmacology, 138*, 305–310.

Varner, L. J., & Ellis, H. C. (1998). Cognitive activity and physiological arousal processes that mediate mood-congruent memory. *Memory & Cognition, 26*, 939–950.

Verstijnen, I. M., Hennessey, J. M., van Leeuwen, C., Hame, R., & Goldschmidt, G. (1998). Sketching and creative discovery. *Design Studies, 19*, 519–546.

Verstijnen, I. M., van Leeuwen, C., Goldschmidt, G., Hamel, R., & Hennessey, J. M. (1998). Creative discovery in imagery and perception: Combining is relatively easy, restructuring takes a sketch. *Acta Psychologica, 99*, 177–200.

Vicente, K., & Brewer, W. (1993). Reconstructive remembering of the scientific literature. *Cognition, 46*, 101–128.

von Neumann, J., & Morgenstern, O. (1947). *Theory of games and economic behavior.* Princeton, NJ: Princeton University Press.

von Winterfeldt, D., & Edwards, W. (1986). *Decision analysis and behavioral research.* New York: Cambridge University Press.

Voss, J., Blais, J., Means, M., Greene, T., & Ahwesh, E. (1989). Informal reasoning and subject matter knowledge in the solving of economics problems by naive and novice individuals. In L. Resnick (Ed.), *Knowing, learning and instruction: Essays in honor of Robert Glaser.* Hillsdale, NJ: Lawrence Erlbaum.

Voss, J., & Post, T. (1988). On the solving of ill-structured problems. In M. Chi, R. Glaser, & M. Farr (Eds.), *The nature of expertise.* Hillsdale, NJ: Lawrence Erlbaum.

Vu, H., Kellas, G., Metcalf, K., & Herman, R. (2000). The influence of global discourse on lexical ambiguity resolution. *Memory & Cognition, 28*, 236–252.

Wagenaar, W. A. (1986). My memory: A study of autobiographical memory over six years. *Cognitive Psychology, 18,* 225–252.

Wagenaar, W. A., & Groeneweg, J. (1990). The memory of concentration camp survivors. *Applied Cognitive Psychology, 4,* 77–88.

Walker, S. (1993). Supernatural beliefs, natural kinds, and conceptual structure. *Memory & Cognition, 20,* 655–662.

Wallach, M. (1976). Tests tell us little about talent. *American Scientist, 64,* 57–63.

Wallas, G. (1926). *The art of thought.* New York: Harcourt, Brace.

Wallis, G., & Bülthoff, H. (1999). Learning to recognize objects. *Trends in Cognitive Sciences, 3,* 22–31.

Wang, M., & Bilger, R. (1973). Consonant confusion in noise: A study of perceptual features. *Journal of the Acoustical Society of America, 54,* 1248–1266.

Warnick, D. H., & Sanders, G. S. (1980). Why do eyewitnesses make so many mistakes? *Journal of Applied Social Psychology, 10,* 362–366.

Wason, P. (1966). Reasoning. In B. Foss (Ed.), *New horizons in psychology.* Middlesex, England: Penguin.

Wason, P. (1968). Reasoning about a rule. *Quarterly Journal of Experimental Psychology, 20,* 273–281.

Wason, P. (1983). Realism and rationality in the selection task. In J. S. B. Evans (Ed.), *Thinking and reasoning: Psychological approaches.* London: Routledge & Kegan Paul.

Wason, P., & Johnson-Laird, P. (1972). *Psychology of reasoning: Structure and content.* Cambridge, MA: Harvard University Press.

Watkins, M. J. (1977). The intricacy of memory span. *Memory & Cognition, 5,* 529–534.

Watkins, M. J., & LeCompte, D. (1991). Inadequacy of recall as a basis for frequency knowledge. *Journal of Experimental Psychology: Learning, Memory and Cognition, 17,* 1161–1176.

Watkins, M. J., & Tulving, E. (1975). Episodic memory: When recognition fails. *Journal of Experimental Psychology: General, 104,* 5–29.

Watkins, M. J., & Watkins, O. C. (1974). Processing of recency items for free recall. *Journal of Experimental Psychology, 102,* 488–493.

Wattenmaker, W. (1991). Learning modes, feature correlations, and memory-based categorization. *Journal of Experimental Psychology: Learning, Memory and Cognition, 17,* 908–923.

Wattenmaker, W., McQuaaid, H., & Schwertz, S. (1995). Analogical versus rule-based classification. *Memory & Cognition, 23,* 495–509.

Waugh, N. C., & Norman, D. A. (1965). Primary memory. *Psychological Review, 72,* 89–104.

Weaver, C. (1993). Do you need a "flash" to form a flashbulb memory? *Journal of Experimental Psychology: General, 122,* 39–46.

Weber, E., Böckenholt, U., Hilton, D., & Wallace, B. (1993). Determinants of diagnostic hypothesis generation: Effects of information, base rates and experience. *Journal of Experimental Psychology: Learning, Memory and Cognition, 19,* 1151–1164.

Weber, R. J. (1993). *Forks, phonographs, and hot air balloons: A field guide to inventive thinking.* New York: Oxford University Press.

Weber, R., & Dixon, S. (1989). Invention and gain analysis. *Cognitive Psychology, 21,* 283–302.

Wedell, D. (1991). Distinguishing among models of contextually induced preference reversals. *Journal of Experimental Psychology: Learning, Memory and Cognition, 17,* 767–778.

Wedell, D. (1993). Effects of different types of decoys on choice. Paper presented at the meeting of the Psychonomic Society, Washington, DC.

Wedell, D., & Bockenholt, U. (1990). Moderation of preference reversals in the long run. *Journal of Experimental Psychology: Human Perception and Performance, 16,* 429–438.

Wegner, D. (1994). Ironic processes of mental control. *Psychological Review, 101,* 34–52.

Wegner, D., Wenzlaff, R., Kerker, R., & Beattie, A. (1981). Incrimination through innuendo: Can media questions become public answers? *Journal of Personality and Social Psychology, 40,* 822–832.

Weisberg, R. (1969). Sentence processing assessed through intrasentence word associations. *Journal of Experimental Psychology, 82,* 332–338.

Weisberg, R. (1986). *Creativity: Genius and other myths.* New York: W. H. Freeman.

Weisberg, R. (1988). Problem solving and creativity. In R. J. Sternberg (Ed.), *The nature of creativity* (pp. 148–176). Cambridge: Cambridge University Press.

Weisberg, R., & Alba, J. (1981). An examination of the alleged role of "fixation" in the solution of several "insight" problems. *Journal of Experimental Psychology: General, 110,* 169–192.

Weisberg, R., & Alba, J. (1982). Problem solving is not like perception: More on Gestalt theory. *Journal of Experimental Psychology: General, 111,* 326–330.

Weisberg, R., & Suls, J. (1973). An information processing model of Duncker's candle problem. *Cognitive Psychology, 4,* 255–276.

Weisberg, R., DiCamillo, M., & Phillips, D. (1978). Transferring old associations to new problems: A nonautomatic process. *Journal of Verbal Learning and Verbal Behavior, 17,* 219–228.

Weiskrantz, L. (1986). *Blindsight: A case study and implications.* New York: Oxford University Press.

Weiskrantz, L. (1997). *Consciousness lost and found.* New York: Oxford University Press.

Weldon, M. (1993). The time course of perceptual and conceptual contributions to word fragment completion priming. *Journal of Experimental Psychology: Learning, Memory and Cognition, 19,* 1010–1023.

Wells, G. L., & Bradfield, A. L. (1999). Distortions in eyewitnesses' recollections: Can the postidentification-feedback effect be moderated? *Psychological Science, 10,* 138–144.

Wells, G. L., Lindsay, R. C. L., & Ferguson, T. J. (1979). Accuracy, confidence, and juror perceptions in eyewitness identification. *Journal of Applied Psychology, 64,* 440–448.

Wells, G. L., Luus, C. A. E., & Windschitl, P. (1994). Maximizing the utility of eyewitness identification evidence. *Current Directions in Psychological Science, 3,* 194–197.

Werker, J., & Desjardins, R. (1995). Listening to speech in the first year of life: Experiential effects on phoneme perception. *Current Directions in Psychological Science, 4,* 76–80.

Wetherick, N. (1989). Psychology and syllogistic reasoning. *Philosophical Psychology, 2,* 111–124.

Wexler, M., Kosslyn, S. M., & Berthoz, A. (1998). Motor processes in mental rotation. *Cognition, 68,* 77–94.

Wharton, C., Holyoak, K., Downing, P., & Lange, T. (1994). Below the surface: Analogical similarity and retrieval competition in reminding. *Cognitive Psychology, 26,* 64–101.

Wheeler, D. (1970). Processes in word recognition. *Cognitive Psychology, 1,* 59–85.

Wheeler, M. (1995). Improvement in recall over time without repeated testing: Spontaneous recovery revisited. *Journal of Experimental Psychology: Learning, Memory and Cognition, 21,* 173–184.

White, N. M. (1991). Peripheral and central memory-enhancing actions of glucose. In R. C. A. Frederickson, J. L. McGaugh, & D. L. Felten (Eds.), *Peripheral signaling of the brain: Neural, immune and cognitive function.* Toronto: Hogrefe and Huber.

White, P. (1988). Knowing more than we can tell: "Introspective access" and causal report accuracy 10 years later. *British Journal of Psychology, 79,* 13–45.

White, R. T. (1989). Recall of autobiographical events. *Applied Cognitive Psychology, 3,* 127–136.

Whittlesea, B., Brooks, L., & Westcott, C. (1994). After the learning is over: Factors controlling the selective application of general and particular knowledge. *Journal of Experimental Psychology: Learning, Memory and Cognition, 20,* 259–274.

Whittlesea, B., Jacoby, L., & Girard, K. (1990). Illusions of immediate memory: Evidence of an attributional basis for feelings of familiarity and perceptual quality. *Journal of Memory and Language, 29,* 716–732.

Whittlesea, B. W. A., & Leboe, J. (2000). The heuristic basis of remembering and classification: Fluency, generation and resemblance. *Journal of Experimental Psychology: General, 129,* 84–106.

Whorf, B. L. (1956). *Language, thought, and reality.* Cambridge: Technology Press.

Wilkins, M. (1928). The effect of changed material on ability to do formal syllogistic reasoning. *Archives of Psychology, 16,* 83.

Wilson, M., & Emmorey, K. (1998). A "word length effect" for sign language: Further evidence for the role of language in structuring working memory. *Memory & Cognition, 26,* 584–590.

Wilson, T. (1994). The proper protocol: Validity and completeness of verbal reports. *Psychological Science, 5,* 249–252.

Wilson, T., & Brekke, N. (1994). Mental contamination and mental correction: Unwanted influences on judgments and evaluations. *Psychological Bulletin, 116,* 117–142.

Wilson, T., & Schooler, J. (1991). Thinking too much: Introspection can reduce the quality of preferences and decisions. *Journal of Personality and Social Psychology, 60,* 181–192.

Wilson, T. D., Wheatley, T., Meyers, J. M., Gilbert, D., & Axsom, D. (2000). Focalism: A source of durability bias in affective forecasting. *Journal of Personality and Social Psychology, 78,* 821–836.

Winnick, W., & Daniel, S. (1970). Two kinds of response priming in tachistoscopic recognition. *Journal of Experimental Psychology, 84,* 74–81.

Winograd, E., & Neisser, U. (Eds.). (1993). *Affect and accuracy in recall: Studies of "flashbulb" memories.* New York: Cambridge University Press.

Winograd, E., Peluso, J. P., & Glover, T. A. (1998). Individual differences in susceptibility to memory illusions. *Applied Cognitive Psychology, 12,* S5–S28.

Wiseman, S., & Neisser, U. (1974). Perceptual organization as a determinant of visual recognition memory. *American Journal of Psychology, 87,* 675–681.

Wisniewski, E., & Medin, D. (1994). On the interaction of theory and data in concept learning. *Cognitive Science, 18,* 221–282.

Wittgenstein, L. (1953). *Philosophical investigations* (G. E. M. Anscombe, Trans.). Oxford: Blackwell.

Wixted, J. (1991). Conditions and consequences of maintenance rehearsal. *Journal of Experimental Psychology: Learning, Memory and Cognition, 17,* 963–973.

Wogalter, M., & Laughery, K. (1987). Face recognition: Effects of study to test maintenance and change of photographic mode and pose. *Applied Cognitive Psychology, 1,* 241–253.

Wolford, G., Taylor, H., & Beck, J. (1990). The conjunction fallacy? *Memory & Cognition, 18,* 47–53.

Wollen, K. A., Weber, A., & Lowry, D. (1972). Bizarreness versus interaction of mental images as determinants of learning. *Cognitive Psychology, 3,* 518–523.

Wood, N., & Cowan, N. (1995). The cocktail party phenomenon revisited: How frequent are attention shifts to one's name in an irrelevant auditory channel? *Journal of Experimental Psychology: Learning, Memory and Cognition, 21,* 255–260.

Woodward, A. E., Bjork, R. A., & Jongeward, R.H., Jr. (1973). Recall and recognition as a function of primary rehearsal. *Journal of Verbal Learning and Verbal Behavior, 12,* 608–617.

Woodworth, R., & Sells, S. (1935). An atmosphere effect in formal syllogistic reasoning. *Journal of Experimental Psychology, 18,* 451–460.

Wright, D. B., & Davies, G. M. (1999). Eyewitness testimony. In F. T. Davies, R. S. Nickerson, R. W. Schwaneveldt, S. T. Dumais, D. S. Lindsay, & M. T. H. Chi (Eds.), *Handbook of applied cognition.* New York: Wiley.

Wright, D. B., & McDaid, A. T. (1996). Comparing system and estimator variables using data from real line-ups. *Applied Cognitive Psychology, 10,* 75–84.

Yarmey, A. (1973). I recognize your face but I can't remember your name: Further evidence on the tip-of-the-tongue phenomenon. *Memory & Cognition, 1,* 287–290.

Yates, F. A. (1966). *The art of memory.* London: Routledge and Kegan Paul.

Yee, P., & Hunt, E. (1991). Individual differences in Stroop dilution: Tests of the attention-capture hypothesis. *Journal of Experimental Psychology: Human Perception and Performance, 17,* 715–725.

Yehuda, R. (1997). Sensitization of the hypothalamic-pituitary-adrenal axis in posttraumatic stress disorder. In R. Yehuda & A. C. McFarlane (Eds.), *Psychobiology of posttraumatic stress disorder. Annals of the New York Academy of Sciences* (Vol. 821). New York Academy of Sciences.

Yeni-Komshian, G. (1993). Speech perception. In J. B. Gleason & N. B. Ratner (Eds.), *Psycholinguistics* (pp. 90–133). New York: Harcourt Brace Jovanovich.

Yin, R. (1969). Looking at upside-down faces. *Journal of Experimental Psychology, 81,* 141–145.

Young, A., & Bruce, V. (1991). Perceptual categories and the computation of "grandmother." *European Journal of Cognitive Psychology, 3,* 5–49.

Yuille, J. (Ed.). (1983). *Imagery, memory, and cognition.* Hillsdale, NJ: Lawrence Erlbaum.

Yuille, J., & Cutshall, J. L. (1986). A case study of eyewitness memory of a crime. *Journal of Applied Psychology, 71,* 291–301.

Yuille, J., & Kim, C. (1987). A field study of the forensic use of hypnosis. *Canadian Journal of Behavioral Sciences Review, 19,* 418–429.

Yuille, J., & Tollestrup, P. (1992). A model of the diverse effects of emotion on eyewitness memory. In S.-Å. Christianson (Ed.). *The handbook of emotion and memory: Research and theory* (pp. 201–215). Hillsdale, NJ: Lawrence Erlbaum.

Zajonc, R. B. (1980). Feeling and thinking. *American Psychologist, 35,* 151–175.

Zaragoza, M. S., & Mitchell, K. J. (1996). Repeated exposure to suggestion and the creation of false memories. *Psychological Science, 7(5),* 294–300.

Zatorre, R. J., & Halpern, A. R. (1993). Effect of unilateral temporal-lobe excision on perception and imagery of songs. *Neuropsychologia, 31,* 221–232.

Zatorre, R. J., Halpern, A. R., Perry, D. W., Meyer, E., & Evans, A. C. (1996). Hearing in the mind's ear: A PET investigation of musical imagery and perception. *Journal of Cognitive Neuroscience, 8,* 29–46.

Zbrodoff, N., & Logan, G. (1986). On the autonomy of mental processes: A case study of arithmetic. *Journal of Experimental Psychology: General, 115,* 118–130.

Zeigarnik, B. (1927). Das Behalten erledigter und unerledigter Handlungen. *Psychologische Forschungen, 9,* 1–85.

Zihl, J., Von Cramon, D., & Mai, N. (1983). Selective disturbance of movement vision after bilateral brain damage. *Brain, 106,* 313–340.

Zimler, J., & Keenan, J. M. (1983). Imagery in the congenitally blind: How visual are visual images? *Journal of Experimental Psychology: Learning, Memory and Cognition, 9,* 269–282.

# *Credits*

**Figure 2.5:** Penfield, W., & Rasmussen, T., *The Cerebral Cortex of Man*. Copyright © by Prentice Hall, Inc., Upper Saddle River, NJ.
**Figure 2.6:** "Primary sensory projection areas of the human cortex." In S. Cobb, *Foundations of Neuropsychiatry* 2E. Copyright © 1941 by Lippincott Williams & Wilkins.
**Figure 2.10:** Figure 5.24 from *Psychology*, Fifth Edition, by H. Gleitman, A. J. Fridlund, & D. Reisberg. Copyright © 1999, 1995, 1991, 1986, 1981 by W. W. Norton & Company, Inc. Used by permission of W. W. Norton & Company, Inc.
**Figure 2.11:** Figure 2.27A from *Psychology*, Fifth Edition, by H. Gleitman, A. J. Fridlund, & D. Reisberg. Copyright © 1999, 1995, 1991, 1986, 1981 by W. W. Norton & Company, Inc. Used by permission of W. W. Norton & Company, Inc.
**Figure 2.13:** Copyright © by John L. Howard. Reprinted by permission.
**Figure 3.2:** Figure 6.46 from *Psychology*, Fifth Edition, by H. Gleitman, A. J. Fridlund, & D. Reisberg. Copyright © 1999, 1995, 1991, 1986, 1981 by W. W. Norton & Company, Inc. Used by permission of W. W. Norton & Company, Inc.
**Figure 3.5:** Figure 6.27, from *Psychology*, Fifth Edition, by H. Gleitman, A. J. Fridlund, & D. Reisberg. Copyright © 1999, 1995, 1991, 1986, 1981 by W. W. Norton & Company, Inc. Used by permission of W. W. Norton & Company, Inc.
**Figure 3.15:** McClelland, J. L., & Rumelhart, D. E., "An interactive model of context effect in letter perception." *Psychological Review*, 88, 375–407. Copyright © 1981 by the American Psychological Association. Reprinted with permission.
**Figure 3.17:** "Human vision understanding: Recent research and a theory" by I. Biederman. In *Computer Vision, Graphics, and Image Processing*, 32, 29–73. Copyright © 1985 by Academic Press, reproduced by permission of the publishers.
**Figure 3.18:** "Priming Contour-Deleted Images" by I. Biederman & E. E. Cooper. In *Cognitive Psychology*, 23, 393–419. Copyright © 1991 by Academic Press, reproduced by permission of the publisher.
**Figure 5.9:** Wixeman, S., & Neisser, U., "Perceptual organization as a determinant of visual recognition." *American Journal of Psychology*, 87, 675–81. Copyright © 1974 by the Board of Trustees of the University of Illinois. Used with the permission of the University of Illinois Press.
**Figure 7.1:** Photograph from "Role of schemata in memory for places," by W. F. Brewer & J. C. Treyens. *Cognitive Psychology*, 13, 207–230.
**Figure 11.1:** Copyright © by Stephen M. Kosslyn. Reprinted by permission.
**Figure 11.4:** Shepard, R. N., & Metzler, J., "Mental rotation of three dimensional objects." *Science*, 171, 701–3. Copyright © 1971 by the American Association for the Advancement of Science. Reprinted by permission..
**Figure 11.12:** Te Linde, R. W. In J. C. Yuille (ed.), *Image, Memory, & Cognition*. Copyright © 1983 by Lawrence Erlbaum Associates, Inc. Reprinted by permission.
**Figure 11.14:** Intraub, H., & Richardson, M., "Boundary extension in picture memory." *Journal of Experimental Psychology*, 15, 179–87. Reprinted by permission.
**Figure 12.1:** Jennings, D. L., Amabile, T. M., & Ross, L., "Informational covariation assessment: Data-based versus theory-based judgments." In Kahneman, D., Slovic, P., & Tversky, A. (eds.), *Judgment under Uncertainty: Heuristics and Biases*. Reprinted with the permission of Cambridge University Press.
**Figure 12.2:** Jennings, D. L., Amabile, T. M., & Ross, L., "Informational covariation assessment: Data-based versus theory-based judgments." In Kahneman, D., Slovic, P., & Tversky, A. (eds.), *Judgment under Uncertainty: Heuristics and Biases*. Reprinted with the permission of Cambridge University Press.
**Figure 12.4:** Eddy, D. M., "Probabilistic reasoning in clinical medicine." In Kahneman, D., Slovic, P., & Tversky, A. (eds.), *Judgment under Uncertainty: Heuristics and Biases*. Reprinted with the permission of Cambridge University Press.
**Figure 12.5:** Eddy, D. M., "Probabilistic reasoning in clinical medicine." In Kahneman, D., Slovic, P., & Tversky, A. (eds.), *Judgment under Uncertainty: Heuristics and Biases*. Reprinted with the permission of Cambridge University Press.
**Figure 12.6:** Fong, G. T., Krantz, D. H., & Nisbett, R. E., "The effects of statistical training on thinking about everyday problems." In *Cognitive Psychology*, 18, 253–92. Copyright © 1986 by Academic Press, reprinted by permission of the publisher.
**Figure 12.8:** Lehman, D., & Nisbett, R. E., "A longitudinal study of the effects of undergraduate education on reasoning." *Developmental Psychology*, 26, 952–60. Copyright © 1990 by the American Psychological Association. Reprinted with permission.
**Figure 13.3:** Wason, P., & Johnson-Laird, P. "An easier version of the four card problem." In *The Psychology of Reasoning: Structure and Content*. Copyright © 1972 by B. T. Batsford, Ltd.
**Figure 13.5:** "Pragmatic reasoning schemas" by P. W. Cheng & K. J. Holyoak. *Cognitive Psychology*, 17, 391–416. Copyright © 1985 by Academic Press, reproduced by permission of the publisher.
**Figure 13.6:** "Pragmatic reasoning schemas" by P. W. Cheng & K. J. Holyoak. *Cognitive Psychology*, 17, 391–416. Copyright © 1985 by Academic Press, reproduced by permission of the publisher.
**Figure 13.8:** Tversky, A., & Kahneman, D., "Rational choice and the framing of decisions." *Journal of Business*, 59:4, pt. 2. Copyright © 1986 by the University of Chicago Press. Used by permission.
**Figure 13.9:** Tversky, A., & Kahneman, D., "Rational choice and the framing of decisions." *Journal of Business*, 59:4, pt. 2. Copyright © 1986 by the University of Chicago Press. Used by permission.
**Figure 13.10:** Tversky, A., & Kahneman, D., "Rational choice and the framing of decisions." *Journal of Business*, 59:4, pt. 2. Copyright © 1986 by the University of Chicago Press. Used by permission.
**Figure 14.18:** Maier, N. R. F., " Reasoning in humans II: The solution of a problem and its appearance in consciousness." *Journal of Comparative Psychology*, 12, 181–94. Copyright © by Lippincott Williams & Wilkins.
**Figure 14.24:** "Premonitions of insight predict impending error," by J. Metcalfe. In *Journal of Experimental Social Psychology*, 12, 623–34. Copyright © 1986 by Academic Press, reproduced by permission of the publisher.
**Figure 14.25:** Smith, S. M., & Blankenship, S. E., "Incubation effects." *Bulletin of the Psychonomic Society*, 27, 311–14. Copyright © 1989 by Psychonomic Society Publications. Reprinted by permission.
**Table 12.1:** Slovic, P., Fischoff, B., & Lichtenstein, S., "Facts versus fears: Understanding perceived risk." In Kahneman, D., Slovic, P., & Tversky, A. (eds.), *Judgment under Uncertainty: Heuristics and Biases*. Reprinted with the permission of Cambridge University Press.

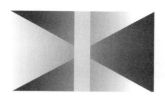

# Author Index

# Subject Index